SCHOOL AND SOCIETY

EDITED BY J. McKEEN CATTELL

WITH WHICH IS COMBINED THE

EDUCATIONAL REVIEW

EDITED BY WILLIAM McANDREW

Volume 35 | Saturday, January 2, 1932 | Number 888

COLLEGE PRESIDENTS: WHENCE THEY COME, WHITHER DO THEY GO, WHAT DO THEY DO?

By Dr. CHARLES FRANKLIN THWING

PRESIDENT EMERITUS OF WESTERN RESERVE UNIVERSITY

Not far from one hundred college presidents go out of office each year, and an equal number come in. The average length of the term is about five years. Of course there are long terms of twenty years, like that of Hibben, who is soon to retire, of Miss Pendleton at Wellesley, and like that of Lowell of Harvard who became president in 1909, following Eliot's term of twoscore years. But these lengths are the exceptions. The days and the years of a college president may or may not be full of trouble, but at any rate they are few. The question emerges, whence come these presidents, and whither on their retirement do they go? To this double question I wish to give answer.

College presidents have come, and still continue to come, from no less than four large groups. Historically, the office is recruited largely from the ministry. Such an origin is natural. For the first American colleges were founded as theological training schools. Harvard was known in its first years, as were the newer colleges in our Western states, as a school of the prophets. An argument used for the foundation of William and Mary in 1693 was that, without a divinity school, the souls of the colonists would perish. The ministers of Connecticut, at the beginning of the eighteenth century, wanted a school of a more orthodox type than was represented in Harvard. Yale was therefore founded. In the westward migration of more than two hundred years the religious and ecclesiastical forces have established hundreds of colleges. These colleges have in most instances embodied the spirit and the purpose of the earliest foundations on the Atlantic coast board. It was, therefore, and still is natural that the chief officer of these colleges should be a clergyman.

But, apart from the westward movement of population, the colleges of New England in the centuries following the foundation of her two oldest institutions, still embodying the religious motives, have usually and normally elected clergymen as their presidents. The presidents of Bowdoin, of Bates, of Colby, of Dartmouth, of Amherst, of Brown, of Trinity, have usually been drawn from the ministry. Of course there are exceptions, outstanding exceptions, but the tide and the trend are evident.

There is a further reason for such a method of selection. The minister may not be primarily a scholar, but he is at least scholarly. His sympathy with the members of his faculty, therefore, represents understanding and affection. Furthermore, as a minister, he holds important public positions as a leader, as a guide for the concerns, duties and rights of the people. His is the place of a prophet in both the narrow and the broad sense of interpretation. He is a shepherd of the people. Such a training and experience help to create in him a sense of leadership for a college or a university.

In a still further respect the clergyman is fitted to be a president. As a pastor one of his most constructive services lies in being a guide and friend and counsellor to the youth of his parish. One of the most beautiful services he can give to the young men and women of his college is of a like type. He is to help to create wisdom, to give council and friendship to every student.

Illustrations abound. Faunce went from a great ministry in a Fifth Avenue church of New York to an even greater ministry as the president of the historic Brown University. As he was resigning the pastorate he wrote to me saying that he found the great tides of influence were not flowing to or from the church. Burton went from an outstanding pastorate in the Church of the Pilgrims, Brooklyn, and from a theological chair at Yale, to the presidency of Smith College, as also, be it added, he went from the presidency of Smith to the University of Minnesota and thence to the presidency of the University of Michigan. Gunsaulus was minister of a Chicago church when he became president of Armour Institute, and he continued in both offices for twenty-six years. Bradley went to Grinnell College, Iowa, from a pastorate, and be it also said he came from the presidency to a pastorate in Cleveland. Barrows filled several pulpits before beginning his brilliant and brief term at Oberlin, which ended with his lamented death. Richmond moved to Schenectady and to its Union University from a church in its neighboring Albany. Moody went to Middlebury (Congregational) College, Vermont, from a Presbyterian ministry in New York. Hyde accepted the presidency of Bowdoin while serving in his pastorate in Paterson, New Jersey. Greatly lengthened might be the list. But already the names illustrate with impressiveness the historic fact of the ministry giving presidents to the colleges.

A second source of supply, and one more popular than the ministry, is the professorship. In fact, about one third of all the presidencies are drafted from the teaching staff. The president may be drafted from the staff of his own college or of another, though more and most often the transfer occurs within the same academic walls. The use of such a field of selection is most fitting. For the electing board of trustees knows the character and aptitudes of those who are considered for the higher office, as also they are cognizant of the limitations of their associates of the teaching staff. They consider the election of such candidates with comparative knowledge. The professor, too, accepts with a proper knowledge of the significance of his election. He knows the students, he knows his fellow teachers, he knows the problems which, as president, he will be obliged to consider and to help to solve. A cause which not infrequently acts to prevent a board of trustees from electing a member of the associated faculty lies in the fact that certain members might feel that an unjust discrimination had been made in an election. Other members of the staff may be regarded by some as more deserving than the one who has been elected. But such judgments and such feelings are usually transient and superficial.

In illustration it is easy to say that four great presidents have in the not remote past been chosen from the teaching staff of

four great universities. I refer to Harvard in its choice of Lowell, to Yale in its choice of Hadley, to Princeton in its choice of Hibben, and to Columbia in its choice of Butler. In the University of Pennsylvania, Pepper and Smith were made provosts from professorships. Garfield of Williams, Pease of Amherst, Howe of Case, Seelye of Amherst, and Seelye of Smith represent similar choices, although they, excepting two, were selected from other than the faculties of the colleges which they were asked to serve as presidents. Bartlett and Tucker of Dartmouth, Wheeler of California, Wilkins and King of Oberlin, Adams of Cornell, David Starr Jordan, first president of Stanford, also are examples of the lifting (or depressing) of the teacher into the administrator.

A third source of supply is found in the deanship. This source of supply is less affluent than the two already named, the ministry and the professoriate. For the deanship in the American college is a new office, borrowed from the church. But this office does really represent just as natural a source as either the ministry or the professorship. For a deanship is in many colleges a virtual vice-presidency. The dean takes over many of the duties formerly belonging to the president, especially those relating to students. Therefore he specially knows those whom he is called to serve. He also is friendly with all his fellow teachers. In such a knowledge and friendship the risk of an unfitting choice is reduced to the lowest terms.

Several illustrations spring to the memory. Ferry went from a deanship at Williams to the presidency of Hamilton. Butler went from a deanship and professorship to the presidency of Columbia. Judson was fitted by his deanship as well as professorship for his presidency of Chicago. Schurman likewise went from a deanship to the presidency of Cornell, Sills from a Bowdoin deanship to a Bowdoin presidency, Schneider from a scientific deanship at Cincinnati to the presidency, Hutchins from the deanship of the law school of the University of Michigan to its presidency, and also a younger Hutchins from a law deanship at Yale to the presidency of the University of Chicago. Miss Pendleton was a great dean before entering her greater presidency at Wellesley. Success in a deanship does not always insure success in a presidency. But experience usually justifies the succession.

A field quite unlike those already named is the presidency itself. Scores of presidents already in service have been asked to transfer their service. This method gives a yet more complete assurance of satisfaction and contentment to those concerned. Yet the history of second presidencies contains examples which do not repeat the history or the happiness of the first. But the annals are usually of contentment and of progress.

Did not Thompson repeat and enlarge his first presidency at Miami by his many years at Ohio State? Did not the elder Angell's record at the University of Vermont make yet more commanding his long-continued headship of the University of Michigan? Did not Little come from the presidency of the University of Maine likewise to the same office in the University of Michigan? Did not Alderman's two terms at North Carolina and Tulane prepare him for his yet greater work in the University of Virginia? Thomas Hill came from the presidency of Antioch to his term of six years as president of Harvard. Gilman came from California to his work as founder and president of Johns Hopkins, McVey from South Dakota to Kentucky, KleinSmid from the University of Arizona to the University of Southern California, as Marvin also came from Arizona to the presidency of George Washington University in Washington, Hunt from Dennison to Bucknell, Bowman from Iowa to Pittsburgh, Swain from Indiana to Swarthmore, Flint from Cornell of Iowa to Syracuse, Dabney from the University of Tennessee to Cincinnati, and Chase from the University of North Carolina to the University of Illinois. It is a long and worthy record of presidencies leading to presidencies.

But in addition to these chief sources of supply, presidencies, deanships, professorships, the ministry, there are several other sources which, though making small offerings, are to be noted. Among them are editorships, secretaryships, diplomacy, public school superintendencies, general executive work and research laboratories.

Among editors who have become presidents are to be named Glenn Frank, who graduated from the *Century Magazine* to the presidency of the University of Wisconsin, and Hamilton Holt, who, after a long editorship of the *Independent*, became the progressive president of Rollins College in Florida. Secretaryships and also executive work as heads of societies and of organizations of many types, lead to presidencies. Hopkins of Dartmouth was the secretary of the beloved Tucker, Wickenden, of Case School of Applied Science, was the secretary and executive manager of Engineering societies. Chandler of William and Mary came from a superintendency of schools in Richmond to its most historic college, Hunter from a superintendency to the headship of the University of Denver, and Tigert from the national commissionership of education to the presidency of the University of Florida. Moore, as director of the University of California at Los Angeles, went from the headship of the Los Angeles public schools. Diplomacy has given a president to the George Washington University in Collier, who graduated from his presidency to the ambassadorship in Chile. Edward Everett, it may be noted, having retired from the English Mission accepted the presidency of Harvard for a period which proved to be brief and troublesome. Executive work has contributed Morgan to the leadership of historic Antioch, and Charles C. Harrison to his effective Provostship of the University of Pennsylvania. Research laboratories also represent presidential contributions, for Little came from a laboratory to the presidency of the University of Maine, and finally went from the presidency of the University of Michigan, which he accepted while still a Maine president, likewise to a research laboratory.

Whether inheritance of natural ability and endowment on the one side or education and training on the other makes the richer contribution toward one's vocation is a question of constant discussion. To this discussion no precise answer can be given. It is likewise equally uncertain whether college presidents are born or made or are both born and made, or, as the pessimist might add, neither born nor made. The probability is that their fitness is both innate and acquired. Certain presidents who are well born for the office have also to be made or made over, and certain men are chosen to the office and are educated for it, who give evidence in their administration that they were not fitted by either birth or training for administration. Each factor is to offer its own happy contribution to one of the happiest of all callings.

And yet to say that a college presidency is one of the happiest of all callings would by many be regarded as a deceptive euphemism. For it is to be confessed that too many presidents do find the calling not at all happy. The causes which contribute to the unhappiness and consequent brevity of the term are both many and diverse. The strains of the office are heavy. Its demands are many, rigorous, exhaustive. Certain men can not long bear them by reason of physical or mental incapacity. Conflicts, too, with the board of trustees or regents are not uncommon, especially in the state universities. Such conflicts go back many a year. One recalls that in the seventh decade of the last century the able, singular, rather cantankerous Tappan was suddenly removed by the official board from the presidency of the University of Michigan. From the same office, sixty years after, another president was likewise removed. Another president of a chief university found his office declared vacant. The reason as stated by the member of the board was that the president expected the board or members of the board to do his work. In another state university political reasons caused the governor to remove the president. In private colleges ill health, the desire to return to teaching whence one came, the desire to enter political life, as in the case of Woodrow Wilson and Senator Fess, the desire for leisure and for freedom are frequent causes of resignation. The resignation from one presidency to accept an election to another is also not infrequent. I recall one commanding president who in about a score of years served three colleges, and retired from the last in order to enter business. Moreover, though the number is not great, yet certain presidencies come to their end through death.

And what is to be said of college presidents respecting their life and work subsequent to their retirement from the great office? The answer involves many elements.

Of course the interval between the academic retirement and the final end may be numbered by days or by decades. If one retire, as every one ought, before he becomes old and feeble—as Bryce once wrote Henry White that he wished to retire from his ambassadorship—he may have a long interval of happiness and of further service. Eliot retired from his presidency of forty years at the age of seventy-five, and lived almost a score of fruitful years. Hadley, retiring at the age of sixty-five, dying in 1930, had nine years of happy usefulness. Clark Seelye of Smith retired in 1910 at the age of seventy-three, living fourteen years after his retirement. The period of rest given to Barnard of Columbia, retiring at the age of seventy-nine was brief, of only a year. Taylor of Vassar, resigning at the age of sixty-five, died at sixty-seven. McCosh of Princeton lived six years after his resignation, dying at the age of eighty-three. Francis L. Patton, resigning the Princeton presidency at the age of seventy, still lives in Bermuda, happy, in reminiscence, an interpreter of the present and a prophet of the world's future. Hibben retires after twenty years of noble academic progress and peace.

It is becoming the custom to give to the retiring president the title of *emeritus*. This title means, essentially, that one has done his job well, and that the proper official body desires to recognize the value of his doing it well. It is, like a degree, an honorable title, carrying usually no specific duty or responsibility. It always seems to me to represent in an academic condition what the name of grandfather represents in the domestic, love given and love accepted without duties either assigned or formally accepted. The giving of such title by his trustees to a president is a gracious act for which he is lastingly grateful.

As a rule college presidents resign of their own wish. Few are those who are either directly or indirectly removed. The president should be the first to know and to appreciate the fact that his retirement is wise. He should appreciate the approach of the ending of his usefulness. Either changes in the college, or changes in the constituency which the college serves as from a rural to an urban one, or changes in the emphases which the college represents as from a liberal to a professional type, or changes in the available endowment either through a large increase or through a slight decrease, or changes in the religious element from a denominational form to a liberal one, any one of these changes may make a change in the nature of the office of the president desirable or even necessary. In him also changes quite as fundamental may occur with the lengthening of the years. Believing, as I do, in the long term, I yet also believe that not a few college presidents, like Judge Gary of the Steel Corporation, hold the office too long. The length, therefore, should begin at the beginning and not at the close of the term! It may be added that to undergraduates the president usually seems much older than perhaps he really is. This fact is as true in the college as it is with pastors in the church and with fathers in the family. At the time of retirement, moreover, pensions of the individual college or of the Carnegie Foundation may be available. From his own salary the president has usually been able to make only small savings. Even his small savings he may not have invested wisely. But be it said, and gratefully, that colleges, whose presidents have served long and well, recognize their services by the continuance of stipends which may represent no small share of the ordinary presidential income.

It is fitting to add that, unless there be reason to the contrary, as there frequently is, the place of the residence after retirement may well be the community in which the president has lived and worked. For, if the silent influence of presence and of character has any value at all for the community, that value is the richest where the president is known, recognized, appreciated, far beyond his merits! To the community, to the college, and to his successor his presence should be a beneficence, his speech a benediction, and his service a real communal value. President Hayes once said to me, apropos of a remark which I ventured to make, that he wanted to do that which ought to be done and which nobody else would do. Such a spirit may well inspire every retired college president.

There are several such fields of service. I wish to comment on three or four to which a president out of office may fittingly devote himself.

The first form which I name is service for the people through organizations and societies both formal and informal. Not a few notable examples are evident of great service given by great presidents. Most impressive illustration is found in Eliot of Harvard. For the worth of Eliot's services to the community, abundant and diverse, was hardly less rich and was certainly more diverse after his retirement than for the forty years in which he served as president. In this period of seventeen years he was a genuine shepherd of the people. Many were the institutions and movements with which he was associated, and with a few of them intimately. Among the institutions four were preeminent: "the General Education Board, the International Health Board, the Rockefeller Foundation, and the Carnegie Endowment for International Peace."[1] His biographer, Henry James, also says, "There lies before me a list of the Leagues, Associations, and temporary or more or less permanent Committees to which he lent his name during the last six and a half years of his life, and it consists of more than 200 items. Between 1910 and 1918 the number of those to which he gave support in some fashion was doubtless no less. Every one of them involved him in correspondence; to some he contributed addresses or printable statements. If any one had asked why he consented to disperse his energies so widely and encouraged such multifarious drafts upon his good will, he would have answered that it was a solid satisfaction to be able to aid so many excellent causes."[2] Not alone to

[1] "Charles W. Eliot," by Henry James, Vol. II, p. 185.

[2] *Ibid.*, p. 189.

executive service was his interest confined. James also writes: "In relation to the current of public affairs, it would be fair to say that Eliot occupied, during the last years of his life, a position like that of a respected publicist writing for a fortnightly or monthly review."[3] Of course such service, so constant, so diverse, so formative, was unique, as was the character of the man who gave it. But in kind it is the type which is open to every college president according to his ability and opportunity.

A similar service was also given by Witherspoon of Princeton. But the example of Witherspoon is not apt. For this president gave great service while still in office. Indeed it would be hard to discriminate between the worth of the contributions which Witherspoon made to the new nation in manifold relations during the whole period intervening between the Declaration of Independence and the adoption of the Constitution and the worth of his service as president of the new college. Both services went on together from his acceptance of the Princeton office in 1768 to his death in 1794.

A second field and work of influence for the retired president is found in the ministry. Two examples immediately emerge. The first and more recent, although less conspicuous, is that of Thomas Hill, president of Harvard College. Hill came to the presidency of Harvard from the Antioch presidency, in 1862. Contemporary with his earlier presidency he was minister of a church in Cincinnati. Three years after retiring from the Harvard presidency in 1868, he became the minister of an historic parish in Portland, Maine, a ministry of great worth to the church, to the whole state of Maine, and also to the Unitarian faith.

A yet more outstanding instance of a president returning to the ministry is that of Wayland, the great president of Brown University from 1827 to 1855. His administration was indeed constructive. For a decade following his resignation he served in and through the ministry. He became the pastor of the great Baptist church in Providence. Of his ministry Dean Murray of Princeton says, "His temporary pastorate of the First Baptist Church was an episode in his great career. Episode though it be, yet no measure of the man can be taken which does not take it into deep consideration. That after thirty years of academic labor abundant in educational schemes, writing text-books, managing students, he could take up and carry on such a pastorate is a marvel. This brief ministry of Dr. Wayland in the First Baptist Church has about it something apostolic. The true succession is there. Rightly it has been said that its triumph was owing in great part to the power of the *spiritual* man, owing also to the intense and absolute concentration of effort upon his work."[4] He interpreted his functions in the broadest and most human spirit. His last years were the years of the Civil War. Murray says, "the four years' terrible struggle—it was the absorbing thing with him. It stirred his religious being to its depths, it enlisted his intellectual nature in thought upon the issues involved. From beginning to end of the long strife, he had never faltered. In its darkest day his confidence in God kept him serene."[5]

A third field to which the president out of office gives himself relates to teaching. Not a few presidents, having completed their executive tasks, return to the earlier happiness of teaching. In fact having gone from a professorship to a presidency, they have later found that the professorship is more commanding. Illustrations are found in personalities and conditions as

[3] *Ibid.*, p. 192.

[4] "Francis Wayland," by James O. Murray, p. 134.

[5] *Ibid.*, p. 150.

unlike those of Samuel Harris of Bowdoin, of Barrows of California, as of Mark Hopkins of Williams.

It is worthy of note that in diplomacy are found instances which, even if few, are noteworthy of the service of the college president. The instances to which I refer relate to only four presidents, and are concerned largely with one university. The examples are of Andrew Dickson White and Jacob Gould Schurman of Cornell, Angell of Michigan and David Jayne Hill. Both White and Schurman were our representatives in Germany. Previous to his service in Germany, White had also served in Russia, and Schurman as our representative in Greece and Montenegro, and in China. Angell gave fruitful service both to America and to the world in China and in Turkey. Angell was by nature and by experience possessed of the great qualities of a great diplomat. David Jayne Hill is the only American who has at once been the president of two universities—Bucknell and Rochester—and envoy or ambassador at three states—Switzerland, the Netherlands and Germany. In passing, it may be added that Eliot was asked at least once by President Wilson to be our ambassador in London, as he had also years before been asked by President Taft.

Perhaps the twofold reason that diplomatic posts do not command acceptance of college presidents may be found in these two facts: first, that college presidents both in and after service are usually poor in purse. The salaries, too, attached to diplomatic posts are small in relation to the necessary or fitting expense of the positions. The president is, therefore, unable to represent his government as he desires to represent it and as it ought to be represented.

A further service which the president may render is not so much service as services, and not so much services as understandings, appreciations and sympathy. He is to be the most appreciative friend of his successor: sympathetic in the trials of the office, and the first and heartiest to bear congratulations for his successes and his triumphs. His leisure he is to seek to make remunerative to the university. He may no longer supervise the building of the walls of the academic Zion, but he may watch the progress of the building with a keen sparkle in his eye and with joy in his soul. If reading, writing, speaking were his avocations in his term of active service, he may now make them his vocation. Perhaps, too, the new vocation may have a wider and richer influence than his earlier vocation. His new life of leisure may prove to be an opportunity for both receiving and giving the best of life. In illustration I think of Woods of Bowdoin, of the great-hearted Northrop of Minnesota, of White of Cornell, of the beloved Tucker of Dartmouth, of the brothers Seelye of Amherst and of Smith, of Taylor of Vassar, of Wheeler of California. The list is indeed longer than Homer's catalogue of ships. But each name bears a loving and beloved personality.

EDUCATIONAL EVENTS

THE AMERICAN SCHOOLS OF MUSIC AND FINE ARTS IN FONTAINE-BLEAU

THE American Schools of Music and Fine Arts situated in the historic chateau of Fontainebleau, have received, according to a statement to *The New York Times* made by Mr. Walter Damrosch, president of the combined schools, as a gift from the town of Fontainebleau, near Paris, the free use for ninety-nine years of a tract of land in the center of the town, for the erection of a dormitory. The property, comprising several acres, is part of an extensive estate situated about two blocks from the chateau and nearly opposite the school restaurant.

Mr. Damrosch states that: "This gesture of friendship and good-will on the part of the French people most closely associated with our students came at a crucial point, and is therefore even more gratefully received. It became evident last year that there was considerable objection in certain governmental departments to the fact that sixty-five of the students were being allowed to live in the wing of the chateau which is set aside for the American schools. There were political reasons for these objections, and there was also the very good reason of the fire hazard involved. Both the American and French committees were puzzled how to solve the problem at minimum expense."

The French government manifested its interest in the American schools by contributing 600,000 francs toward the new dormitory building. Amounts of equal size are to be raised by subscription by the French and American committees of the schools themselves.

The new dormitory has been designed by Jacques Carlu, French architect and director of the School of Fine Arts. In addition to living quarters for seventy students, it will contain a library and assembly and recreation rooms. Until the building is completed the directors of the schools have been assured by the French government that students will be allowed to remain in the chateau.

The American Schools of Music and Fine Arts, housed in the Belle Cheminee wing of the palace which served as a country seat for the kings of France and for Napoleon, developed after the war as an overture of friendship on the part of the French government toward the United States. Many of the rooms now used as classrooms have historical importance, among them the theater, now used by the class in opera, which was built for the amusement of Napoleon III and his court. Although the school is for American students only, the administration in France and the faculty are French.

THE NORTHUMBERLAND WELFARE EDUCATIONAL INSTITUTE

THE new Welfare Educational Institute at Ashington, Northumberland County, England, was opened in the latter part of November at a ceremony presided over by Lord Noel-Buxton, chairman of the Central Committee of the Miners' Welfare Fund. This institute, the main object of which is to decrease the death and accident rates in mining, is the first of what it is hoped will be a series in the mining districts of Northumberland and Durham Counties. The new building has been erected at a cost of £11,000, approximately $53,460, and is the outcome of a scheme begun several years ago by the Ashington Coal Company and the Northumberland Education Committee for the education of young miners, with a view to producing from among the workmen a suitable type of official for the company.

The school, started in 1922 in Priestman Hall, Ashington, has so far provided higher education in mining, mechanical engineering and electrical engineering, for two hundred and sixty young men who, during an attendance of two days a week for three years, have received full pay as though following their normal employment at the pit. Opportunities to attend are offered to all miners between the ages of 16 and 18 and at present nearly one hundred students are in training. All fees for day classes are paid by the Ashington Coal Company, while the cost of evening classes is borne by the Northumberland Education Committee. The school is also prepared to extend further educational advantages to promising students as is instanced by the fact that at present two young men are taking a degree course in mining at Armstrong College, Newcastle-on-Tyne, and are in receipt of a weekly wage from the Colliery Company during the period of their studies. The general manager of the company, stated in regard to the school, when proposing a vote of thanks to Lord Noel-Buxton, that "There are jobs awaiting every lad who takes advantage of the facilities provided."

In the new building, which is so constructed that the maximum of natural light is obtained in all rooms, are two laboratories, each containing the most up-to-date equipment, a library, dark room, four class rooms, a lecture room and staff and principal's room.

It is understood that the coal fields in Scotland and Wales are rather more fully developed in the matter of mining education than Northumberland and Durham, but the Education Committees of these two counties now see prospects of realizing a long-cherished ambition in the establishment of four similar educational institutions in Northumberland and six in Durham.

EMPLOYMENT OF CHILDREN IN LONDON

AT a recent meeting of the Education Committee of the London County Council, according to the *Times Educational Supplement,* the Accommodation and Attendance Subcommittee stated that the International Labor Conference, at its meeting in 1932, proposed to discuss the question of framing an International Convention to regulate the admission of children to employment in non-industrial occupations. The Home Secretary consequently has asked to be furnished with certain statistical information and general observations. On November 1 there were 979 boys and 11 girls from 12 to 13 years of age authorized to be employed, and 2,469 boys and 22 girls from 13 to 14 years of age. Of these 2,327 were engaged in delivering newspapers.

Complaints of injury to health or to education in respect of employed children had been very rare, and it might be generally assumed that the restricted amount of employment permitted in London had no adverse effects and that, moreover, there would not appear to be any obvious need in present circumstances for raising the existing age of prohibition. Under the council's by-laws, the employment of children on a Sunday was restricted practically to light household work, and no child might work before 8 A. M. or after 10 A. M.

Practically no advantage was taken of that very limited permission for Sunday work, and no difficulty would arise if Sunday employment were prohibited entirely. The restrictions applying to public holidays were the same as those in force during school holidays. There would no doubt be considerable opposition to the entire prohibition of employment on public holidays so far as the delivery of newspapers was concerned.

The provisions of the Education Act and of the Council's by-laws governing employment of children were enforced by the school attendance officers. Those officers, in carrying out their main duty of enforcing school attendance, were required to visit the homes of absentee children and when passing through the streets for that purpose kept observation in order to detect infringements of the employment provisions. Further, special patrols were undertaken by school attendance officers after normal working hours and also on Saturday afternoons and evenings and on Sundays with the same object in view. Employers who were detected illegally employing children were, in the first instance, served with a warning notice and furnished with a copy of the council's by-laws; legal proceedings were resorted to when the circumstances justified such a course.

The general effect of the council's by-laws governing the employment of children was reflected in the decreasing number of infringements. For the year ended March, 1931, the number discovered was 4,372, as compared with 7,938 in the year 1922–23, during which the present by-laws were introduced.

REPORT OF THE NATIONAL CHILD LABOR COMMITTEE

THE annual report given out by Mr. Courtenay Dinwiddie, general secretary of the National Child Labor Committee, points out that since the committee began its work twenty-seven years ago, there has been a reduction of at least one million in the number of children under 16 years of age currently employed in the United States. In the opinion of the committee of children and young people under 18 years of age now at work or looking for work in competition with adults, a million or more should be in school. The major task of the National Child Labor Committee will be to keep these children in school and out of competition for employment until their training is completed.

The report states that the employment of boys under 14 and except in rare instances under 16 years of age, has been eliminated in certain occupations unfit for children, for instance, in the coal breakers, where the air is thick with coal dust, and in the fierce heat of the glass works "glory hole," and that the labor of children 12 and 13 years of age in southern cotton mills has been outlawed. On the other hand, there is still a large amount of industrial work under conditions that are strainful and injurious, involving thousands of children approximately two years older than was the case a generation ago. There remain also the scattered reaches of child labor, more difficult to control, but affecting many thousands of children, some of them extremely young.

Stories could be multiplied of very young migrants working 9 to 11 hours a day or deprived of from two to five months of schooling yearly, and of street vendors working through meal hours far into the night, beginning in the small hours of the morning, or exposed to serious moral as well as physical risks. Tenement home work also is described as a hotbed for the illegal employment of children. Canneries, it is stated, are exempt from the child labor law in several states; and except in half a dozen states there has been no effectual legislation directly restricting the employment of children in agriculture when schools are not in session. Yet there are more children under 14 years of age employed in agriculture than in all other occupations put together. The report stresses especially the need for improving standards of administration of child labor legislation.

An account is given of the progress made in extending educational advantages during the past twenty-five years. The percentage of children from 5 to 17 years of age, inclusive, who were not attending any school according to the Biennial Survey of Education, issued by the U. S. Office of Education, was reduced from 29.6 in 1905 to 18.5 in 1928. Nevertheless the 1930 census shows 3,326,152 children of 7 to 17 years, inclusive, to be out of school.

During the year the committee responded to requests covering all phases of child labor from every state in the Union and took an especially active part in legislative programs for child protection in eleven states. It participated in the preparation of reports on child labor for the White House Conference on Child Health and Protection. Among special investigations conducted by the committee, was a study of the operation of the child labor and school attendance laws in three cities of Ohio, in connection with a survey undertaken by the Bureau of Educational Research of the Ohio State University, as a result of which there is already in progress a movement to work out better plans for improving attendance and adjustment between child and school. The National Child Labor Committee is giving cooperation for the improvement of conditions relating to street trades in several states. An investigation now in progress deals with the compensation and rehabilitation of minors suffering permanent industrial injuries.

DECREASE IN NUMBER OF CHILDREN

THE number of preschool children in this country actually is decreasing, according to Mr. Emery M. Foster, chief statistician of the U. S. Office of Education.

Although there were 17,000,000 more people in the United States in 1930 than in 1920 there was a decrease of 128,840 children under five years of age. The year by year increase in first year enrolments which has been a fact to be faced in school administration has been passed and we have reached an era of actually decreasing numbers.

This decrease is not large enough, numerically, to make an appreciable difference in elementary school enrolments during the next five years, but indicates that unless the trend stops, first-grade enrolments may show appreciable decreases within the next 10 years.

Forty years ago America's population of children under five years of age was 7,634,693. Ten years later the 1900 Census showed a jump of this age group to 9,170,628. Another increase was noted in the 1910 Census, when 10,631,364 boys and girls five years old or younger were registered in the United States. Ten years ago another sharp rise in this age group was noted, from 10,631,364 to 11,573,230. This, apparently, was the peak, for in the last decade, for the first time in our history, a decrease was registered in the number of children five years of age or younger. The drop was from 11,573,230 to 11,444,390, or a difference of 128,840 fewer children in 1930 than in 1920 (five years old or younger). The general population over the same 10-year period increased more than 17 million.

Those under five years of age in 1930 were only 9.3 per cent. of the total population, while in 1920 the number of children in this age group represented 10.9 per cent. of the population.

SALARIES AT WESLEYAN UNIVERSITY

A NEW system of increased professorial salaries which follows, in its fundamental principles, a plan laid down a hundred years ago by Wilbur Fisk, the first president of Wesleyan University, has been announced by the trustees. Establishment of the new system has been made possible by the expected receipt by the college, during the year 1932, of the income of approximately half a million dollars. It is possible that the amount available in succeeding years will be greater.

This money comes to the college from Mrs. Charles L. Denison, of Saddle River, New Jersey, whose husband was a trustee for three years prior to his death. In his will, Mr. Denison left the college half his estate, subject to Mrs. Denison's use during her life; it is estimated that the ultimate gift will be considerably over a million dollars, the largest bequest in the history of the university. To inaugurate the plan in which Mr. Denison took much interest, Mrs. Denison is assigning to Wesleyan part of the income.

The first phase of the new plan is the recognition of a normal professorial salary, which shall apply to the professors on the faculty, numbering approximately thirty. Beyond that, all salary increases will be voted by the trustees, on a term basis—usually three years—the choice of men to receive the additional award being based on superiority in teaching, influence on undergraduates, eminence as scholars, intellectual growth and service to the college and the community. The awards are made payable in two semi-annual instalments; they do not apply during sabbatical leave.

The action taken by the board early in October will result in additional compensation to six professors on the basis of $2,500 extra for a calendar year, and to eight professors on the basis of $1,250 extra. If funds are available in the future the plan will be continued, and if they are increased it is possible that a larger number of men will be included.

DEDICATION OF THE STATE TEACHERS COLLEGE AT BUFFALO

THE dedication of the new building of the State Teachers College at Buffalo, New York, took place on December 17. At this time the college was inspected by the New York State Board of Regents and formally dedicated in a ceremony in which faculty, representatives of the State Education Department, and civic and educational institutions of the city took part. The Honorable Charles E. Roesch, mayor of Buffalo, brought greetings from the city, and Dr. Harry W. Rockwell, president of the college, spoke on "Our New College." Regent John Lord O'Brian, assistant attorney general of the United States, gave an address on "The State's Responsibility for Training Teachers." The dedicatory address was delivered by Dr. Frank Pierrepont Graves, president of the University of the State of New York and commissioner of education.

The new institution consists of four buildings devoted to instructional purposes grouped about a quadrangle, and a president's residence erected on a twenty-acre campus in the Delaware Park section of Buffalo. In the immediate vicinity are the Albright Art Gallery, the Buffalo Historical Museum, the new Rumsey Art School and the McKinley Vocational High School.

The buildings were erected by the City of Buffalo at a cost of approximately $1,850,000. The city received in return the former State Teachers College building, valued at about $700,000, and a tract of land, about 70 acres in area, which it expects to develop for educational or recreational purposes.

The cornerstone of the main college building housing administrative offices and recitation rooms was laid on October 9, 1929, and the new buildings were occupied on January 12, 1931.

The State Board of Regents held their December meeting at the college during the forenoon of December 17 and then participated in the activities of the day consisting of a luncheon, a formal inspection of the building, a dinner given by Mr. Edward H. Butler, publisher of the Buffalo *Evening News*, and president of the Local Board of Managers, and finally the formal dedicatory exercises.

EDUCATIONAL NOTES AND NEWS

DR. MARY EMMA WOOLLEY, president of Mount Holyoke College, South Hadley, Massachusetts, has been appointed by President Hoover a member of the American delegation to the General Disarmament Conference of the League of Nations, which will convene in Geneva on February 2.

PRESIDENT ROBERT MAYNARD HUTCHINS, of the University of Chicago, and Mrs. Hutchins were the guests of honor at a reception tendered by the faculty of Purdue University on December 7. In the afternoon President Hutchins addressed the Purdue students on the new educational plan of the University of Chicago.

AT a dinner given by members of the department of history of the University of California, the Italian Consul-General, L. Manzini, of San Francisco, made the announcement that Professor Herbert E. Bolton, chairman of the department of history, had been awarded the title of Knight Commander of the Crown of Italy, for his work on the achievements of an early Italian missionary, in Spanish-America, Father Eusebio Kino.

PROFESSOR HOWARD E. JENSEN has taken up his work as professor of sociology in Duke University.

DR. BERNARD FAY, professor of literature at the University of Clermont-Ferrand, has been appointed the first professor of American civilization at the Collège de France.

LORD MIDDLETON was installed as president of Hull University College, England, on December 9.

THE council of Mansfield College, Oxford, has appointed the Reverend Nathaniel Micklem, Yates professor of New Testament literature and exegesis and vice-principal of the college, to succeed as principal Dr. W. B. Selbie, who retires on account of ill health at the close of the academic year.

MR. H. H. HARDY, of Cheltenham College, England, has been appointed head master of Shrewsbury School in succession to Canon H. A. P. Sawyer, who is retiring. Mr. Hardy, who has been head master of Cheltenham since 1919, will take up his new work next September.

THE Council of the College Hall, London, has elected Sir Alexander Gibb, G.B.E., C.B., to the chairmanship of the hall, in succession to the late Sir Gregory Foster, who had held the office for over twenty years.

MR. WILLIAM SLOANE COFFIN, director of the firm of W. and J. Sloane, has been elected president of the Metropolitan Museum of Art, New York City, to succeed Robert W. de Forest, who died last May. Mr. Coffin has been a trustee of the museum since 1924. Mr. Myron C. Taylor, chairman of the finance committee of the United States Steel Corporation, has become first vice-president.

MR. CARL L. CANNON, chief of the acquisition and book order divisions of the New York Public Library, has been appointed head of the accessions division of the Yale Library. The appointment becomes effective on February 15.

MR. HOWARD S. GALT, ED.D. (Harvard, '27), has been elected chairman of the committee for the graduate division of Yenching University, Peiping, China. He has been chairman of the department of education at that institution for many years. The Harvard Yenching Institute, organized to promote Sinological studies in the Orient and Occident, has its most direct connection with Yenching University through the Graduate Division, in which the advanced students are registered.

PROFESSOR LETA S. HOLLINGWORTH, of Teachers College, Columbia University, recently conferred in Harrisburg, Pennsylvania, with superintendents and teachers from Altoona, Elkins Park and Wayne, where special projects are being initiated to take care of the education of exceptionally capable children. The conference was held under the auspices of the Pennsylvania Survey, which is being conducted jointly by the Carnegie Foundation for the Advancement of Teaching and the presidents of Pennsylvania colleges.

PRESIDENT LIVINGSTON FARRAND, of Cornell University, and Mrs. Farrand have embarked for a trip abroad. They will visit Gibraltar and several other places in Spain and other European countries. Dr. Farrand expects to return to Ithaca on February 1.

DR. VIRGINIA C. GILDERSLEEVE, dean of Barnard College, sailed for Europe on December 26.

PROFESSOR N. L. ENGELHARDT, of Teachers College, Columbia University, is on sabbatical leave for the first half of 1932. He is spending this period in visiting the schools of Central Europe.

DR. HARRY A. CARPENTER, specialist in science, Rochester public schools, New York, has returned from a six months' trip through various sections of the United States and Alaska, during which he made a study of the teaching of science in the public schools.

Mr. Ben M. Cherrington, professor of international relations and executive secretary of the Foundation for the Advancement of the Social Sciences of the University of Denver, has been sent to Europe by the university to study the international situation at first hand. After a brief visit to Moscow and other capitals he will attend the opening of the disarmament conference at Geneva. On his return early in March he will lecture in the East.

Shunzo Nakata, supervisor of social education of the Department of Education of Japan, and curator of the Tokyo Science Museum, is visiting the United States.

Professor R. B. Brode, of the department of physics of the University of California, will lecture at the Massachusetts Institute of Technology during the coming semester.

The sum of $2,500 which the Rosenwald Fund has placed at the disposal of the American National Committee of the International Union for the Scientific Investigation of Population Problems has been applied to two fellowships, one of $1,800 for one year awarded to Dr. E. E. Lewis, of Howard University, who is carrying on an investigation on "The Economic Aspects of the Shifts in Negro Population," and one of $800 for one year awarded to Miss Betty Freeman, of the Johns Hopkins University, who is investigating "The Relation between Fertility in Women and Longevity." A grant of $500 has also been made to Miss Mary Dublin out of the general fund of the committee, to meet expenses in the conduct of her investigation at the London School of Economics into "The Influence of the Declining Birth Rate on the Mortality from Puerperal Causes."

Dr. James Quinter Holsopple, chief psychologist of the Mental Hygiene Bureau of the New Jersey State Department of Institutions and Agencies and consulting psychologist of the Rutgers Psychological and Mental Hygiene Clinic, has been appointed lecturer in psychology on the faculty of arts and sciences of Rutgers University. He will give a series of lectures on mental hygiene and abnormal psychology.

Dr. Alvin Johnson will conduct at the New School for Social Research, New York, of which he is the director, twelve sessions under the title of the "Unpublished Review" on Mondays at six beginning January 11. The course will be organized under the form of the editorial office of a review in which weekly dinner conferences will be devoted to a discussion of current issues in politics, economics, literature and the arts.

The Carnegie Corporation of New York, through the American Association for Adult Education, has made a grant of $6,000 with which an experiment in adult education as a community activity will be made at Radburn, N. J., established in 1929. It has a population of about 1,200, consisting for the most part of the families of young professional and business men. Courses scheduled and the instructors are: International Affairs, Dr. Clyde Eagleton, lecturer for the International Relations Club; Contemporary Poetry and Drama, Dr. Charles H. Whitman, of Rutgers University; Handicrafts, Olsen Bowers, of the Henry Street Settlement; Home Decoration, Mrs. Ruth Tregenza, of Columbia University; Child Study, Mrs. Aletha M. Coffman and Mrs. Lillian Cushman Brown; Music Appreciation, Kenneth F. Damon, of Columbia University; Languages (German and French), Mrs. Annie H. Zachmann and Mrs. Patricia B. Russell.

Dr. Randall J. Condon, superintendent of schools of Cincinnati from 1913 to 1929, died on December 25, at the age of sixty-nine years. Dr. Condon was president of the Department of Superintendence of the National Education Association in 1926. Before going to Cincinnati he had been successively superintendent of schools at Everett, Massachusetts; Helena, Montana, and Providence, Rhode Island.

Dr. Melvil Dewey died on December 26. He celebrated his eightieth birthday on December 10. Dr. Dewey was the founder of the American Library Association, the Metric Bureau and the Spelling Reform Association, and is widely known as the inventor of the decimal classification system used in libraries. He had been librarian and professor of library economy at Columbia University, director of the New York State Library and the Home Educational Department; founder and director of the State

Library School and state director of libraries and a member of the Board of Regents of the University of the State of New York.

DR. JOHN D. WILLARD, a member of the faculty of Teachers College, Columbia University, died on December 22 at the age of forty-six years. Dr. Willard was appointed professor of education on the Schiff Foundation at Teachers College last July and divided his time between teaching and research as a member of the staff of the American Association for Adult Education.

HERMAN J. MAGEE, head of the teacher training division of the New York State Education Department, died on December 26, at the age of thirty-seven years.

THE Modern Language Association of America will hold its forty-eighth meeting on December 28, 29 and 30, at the University of Wisconsin.

THE International Federation of University Women will hold a conference in Edinburgh from July 28 to August 4, 1932.

THE Omaha Council of Social Agencies through its committee on recreation has recently closed a community-wide Recreation Institute. This was conducted by Mr. J. K. Batchelor, field representative of the National Recreation Association. The chairman of the committee is Dr. T. Earl Sullenger, professor of sociology in the Municipal University of Omaha. The committee was not content with conducting merely a successful institute, but organized a team of volunteer leaders who took the course to conduct free recreational programs in various sections of the city, throughout the winter months. Public buildings are being utilized for this enterprise. This program is in cooperation with the city-wide endeavor to raise the morale of the financially depressed during this economic crisis.

A NEW teaching museum has been opened at Rutgers University by the department of zoology of the New Jersey College for Women, a unit of the university. It occupies the Yardley Memorial Room in the zoology building, named in honor of Mrs. Margaret Tufts Yardley, first president of the New Jersey State Federation of Women's Clubs, under whose direction the money for the building was raised and given to the college. The museum is open to the public and contains about half the teaching exhibits of the department of zoology, including 225 mounted birds (New Jersey), 90 bird skins (native and exotic), skeletons of vertebrates, preserved materials, anatomical models and common invertebrates and smaller vertebrates of the state.

THE *Journal* of the American Medical Association reports that a comprehensive study of the strain on eyesight in school activities is being undertaken as a joint project of various departments of Columbia University and the National Society for the Prevention of Blindness. No time limit has been set for the completion of the work, nor is the scope of the problem being limited to fit a given group of workers, the report states. The plan is to carry the investigations over as long a period of time and into as many fields as is necessary. A study of the eyestrain of the school children from the ages of 5 to 10 years is now being carried on as the first step in the proposed work. The program of research will include the vision of the child, the lighting conditions under which he works, the materials he uses and the length of time he uses them. The announcement reports that plans have been completed for this research after a year of planning by Teachers College of Columbia University, staff members of the department of ophthalmology in the medical school, authorities in related fields within the university, and staff members of the National Society for the Prevention of Blindness.

IN an appeal from Wicomico County the Maryland State Board of Education on December 21 decided that a woman teacher in the public schools in Maryland could not be dismissed from her position because she married. The decision is said to be the first the board has handed down on the question, although women teachers who marry have frequently been replaced by unmarried applicants. In making known its ruling the state board also declared a clause in a teachers' contract reading, "If a female teacher marries in any school year she will be expected to resign at the close of the school year," was in plain conflict with the state school law. The state law, the decision says, provides no grounds for discrimination on account of sex, nor does it differentiate between married and single teachers.

A dispatch to *The New York Times* states that Dr. Luther B. Bewley, director of education in the Philippine Islands, has submitted a confidential memorandum to Representative Gregorio Anonas, chairman of the house committee on public instruction, taking sharp issue with Vice-Governor George F. Butte, who recently suggested the use of native dialects as a medium for instruction in the public schools. Mr. Bewley held the proposal to be highly impractical in light of the difficulty in obtaining teachers and textbooks and arranging for student transfers. The report was obtained by a reporter for the *Philippine Herald* and published, apparently annoying official and educational circles considerably. There is believed to be little likelihood of any dialect proposal passing the legislature anyway, except possibly a bill authorizing the director of the National Library to study the entire dialect question and make a formal report.

The French Government, through its embassy at Washington, has given Harvard University 50,000 francs, to be used "in strengthening the friendship between this country and France by spreading the knowledge of the French language." The interest of that sum will be used to provide every two years a scholarship for some student in the French department at Harvard who is working for the degree of Ph.D., but who can not complete his thesis without study in French libraries or archives. The announcement of the gift was made by Mr. J. C. J. Flamand, honorary French consul at Boston. The French department at Harvard suggests that the scholarship bear the name of the "Traveling Scholarship of the French Government."

DISCUSSION

SCIENTIFIC EDUCATION AND SOCIAL IDEALS

Sociologists are saying that, in large part, the solution of our present pressing problems lies in improved education. As early as 1915, the year after the outbreak of the world war, Randolph Bourne closed an article in the *New Republic* with the following sentence: "Quixotic as the enterprise may seem, it is the formation of opinion and not dusty scholarship and solemn cant that will enlist the good will and best endeavors of those who aim to think worthily." Two years later Bertrand Russell in his book entitled "Political Ideals" stated his conviction that education may be so shaped as to strengthen the "creative impulses" and diminish the "possessive instincts." Still more recently Everett Dean Martin, writing about the meaning of a liberal education, maintains that "the mind which has not disciplined itself 'swallows things whole.'" Wesley C. Mitchell, professor of economics at Columbia University, addressing mechanical engineers in February, 1931, says that "getting us to change our habits for something better will involve re-education. . . . Why not mix all the intelligence we can muster into this process of making over our habits, as we put intelligence into the continual rebuilding of our industrial plants?" Lastly, Sir J. Arthur Thomson points out in an article on "The New World of Science" that "for centuries there has been experimenting with education, but the new outlook is psychology for education or education as applied psychology."[1]

In the opinion of these leaders of thought, then, education should include training in discrimination, self-discipline and creative work. It is significant that each of them stresses the importance of activity rather than of passive learning. The method indicated is adaptation of means to ends at least as thorough and intelligent as that practiced by industrial engineers. In the educational field this means applied psychology.

For the teacher in daily contact with honest, eager, restless and inquisitive as well as deceitful, dull, lazy and apathetic boys and girls these generalities, while interesting and informing, are not enough. He or she will want to know just how psychology may be applied in the classroom or laboratory to stimulate and strengthen impulses and habits that are to remake society, in exactly what ways present practice is faulty and capable of improvement. Fortunately, since the

[1] "Essays in Contemporary Civilization." Edited by C. W. Thomas, Macmillan Company, 1931.

beginning of the century the pioneer work of Binet-Simon has been followed by that of Terman, Thorndike and other psychologists, and, owing to their labors, a considerable body of well-substantiated information exists as to mental development. Unfortunately, its practical application is not yet universal or even widespread.

If, as psychological studies show, mental development involves a gradual increase in number and variety of associations, in ability to control and coordinate visual images and to deal with abstract ideas, curricula and teaching methods should conform to these realities. The implication is that courses should begin with what is simple, concrete, practical and closely related to daily experience and introduce step by step what is more complex, abstract and less frequently experienced. In this way, if children are required to progress by their own efforts rather than by "spoon feeding," they may be led to form opinions of their own and to acquire habits of self-reliance.

Science, because of its subject-matter and method, is well suited to develop the habit of recognizing realities and of carefully considering their wider meaning. John Dewey, indeed, goes so far as to say that "the future of our civilization depends on the widening spread and deepening hold of the scientific habit of mind." How is science taught in our schools? Are we "putting all the intelligence we can muster" into this process as we put it into the rebuilding of our industrial plants?

In building factories certain very definite standards and specifications are used. Without them industrial efficiency would be impossible. In building scholastic courses such standards and specifications as exist relate chiefly to the number of hours spent and ground covered, *i.e.*, to the amount of information presumably acquired. This is especially true of college entrance requirements. In most schools, also, a definite sequence for courses in science is laid down, *viz.*, (1) general science, (2) biology, (3) chemistry, (4) physics. The question arises whether or not criteria such as these conduce to the greatest efficiency in preparing future citizens for civilized living. Certainly not, if efficiency consists not so much in instilling information as in training powers of mind, not so much in definite sequence of subject-matter as in proceeding from the simple, concrete and familiar to the complex, abstract and unknown.

In the seventh grade of a certain school, children, eleven to twelve years of age, are taught science as history, *i.e.*, "the history of the world, its geology and physical geography, the development of man and his evolution into the man of to-day." In the eighth grade they study science as mathematics, *i.e.*, mathematics as related "to earth history in simplified explanation of how astronomers know how far away is the moon, the sun and anything else that may happen to come to hand at the time." It is not until they enter the ninth grade that experiments and the solution of problems are prominent.

In another school astronomy is included in the introductory course. The children study the solar system, constellations, the physical condition of the sun and of Saturn's moons, the cause of eclipses, the direction in which planets travel and even the planetesimal hypothesis and the number of stars in the galaxy. A study of the earth follows in which such topics as diastrophism, volcanism, erosion and the cause of the equinoxes are included. Mendelism and the laws of heredity are considered in still another ninth-grade course, as well as the chemical constitution of protoplasm and the structure of cells.

While in all these courses there are also simple and practical experiments, it is apparent that no criterion of suitability to the child's psychology and stage of mental development has been consistently applied. For a course in science designed to cultivate powers of observation, comparison and reasoning, the subject-matter should be such that accuracy of observation can be easily verified. It must be sufficiently concrete so that *bona fide* conclusions can be drawn by the child himself. If it be too complex the child's powers of visualization and of mental manipulation will be unable satisfactorily to deal with it. For the purpose in view it is far better to spend time in getting the children to do their own thinking rather than in accumulating information, however interesting and important, that they can later acquire by reading.

It is open to question whether the history of the world, its geology and physical geography, the development of man and his evolution into the man of to-day is material suitable for the development of independent habits of thought in eleven to twelve year old children. It would seem almost inevitable that such a course, interesting though it might be in the hands of an enthusiastic teacher, should develop the listening and absorbing habit rather than that of reasoning from verified observation.

Somewhat similar objections apply to the study of the stars and the solar system by beginners. It is true that a limited number of observations may be made on the sun, moon and stars. They are not comparable, however, in regard to number and ease of verification, with the observations and comparisons that can be made on plants and animals, nor is it possible with such subject-matter to cultivate the experimental attitude, as is so easily possible with such simple apparatus as test-tubes, flasks, tuning-forks, etc., in the laboratory.

Under present economic conditions large numbers of children who formerly entered business offices and factories at the ages of fourteen to sixteen now remain in the public schools. Consequently it comes about that the percentage of pupils with intelligence quotients below 100 is increased. In other words, the ratio of concrete-minded to abstract-minded is greater. A considerable number reach the age of fifteen to seventeen while retaining the mentality of twelve to fourteen. If, for the future good of society, children are to be trained to form their own opinions and to discriminate between what they know and what they do not know, the material with which they deal must be within their comprehension. The concrete-minded can not be expected to form worth-while opinions about abstract matters. Even in the case of those with intelligence quotients above 100, forcing upon them, prematurely, ideas beyond their grasp, results in the habit of "swallowing whole" the opinions of others.

One of the chief difficulties in the way of retaining mental balance is the multiplicity of facts and ideas that are brought to the attention by modern improved methods of communication. Both adults and children are likely to suffer mental confusion and uncertainty from this superabundance. It becomes an important duty of the teacher to select from the welter of facts and ideas those most suitable to the pupils' stage of development and most readily utilizable for present and future living. If the habit of independent thinking is cultivated and the desire to acquire and use knowledge stimulated, young people, on leaving school and college, are better equipped to seek and to find what they need than if crammed with miscellaneous information. Might there not be a real advantage in reducing and simplifying courses of study while at the same time insisting on independent mental effort on the part of each pupil?

A tendency towards standardization in the United States strikes intelligent foreign observers. Bernard Fay, for example, in a recent article in *Harper's Magazine*, accuses Americans of encouraging "a strict intellectual conformity, at least in the masses." No doubt a certain amount of standardization is inevitable and even desirable. Efficiency requires it. Perhaps in the United States, however, there is too little realization of the difference between the kind of standardization needed for industrial and economic efficiency and that required in education. Teaching is after all a subtler, a more delicate matter than making shoes or filing bills. It is a profession and an art. Therefore factory methods will not suffice. Teachers, if they be real teachers and not merely laborers for hire, are personally interested in the success of their pupils and ought to be allowed to adapt the materials of instruction to individual differences. This is one of the strongest arguments against a too inflexible and overcrowded course of study.

Physicians test pulse, blood pressure, muscular balance and keenness of vision. Educational tests, also, should be functional in nature. It is not so important to discover the quantity of information that has been memorized as the extent to which power has been developed. The difficult task lying immediately ahead of educators is the creation of tests of this kind in sufficient variety so that all kinds of ability may be discovered and trained. Grading of tests according to difficulty is also important for determining the extent to which the kinds of ability possessed by different individuals may be trained. Some promising beginnings have been made in this field but much remains to be done.

The concrete-minded need to be differentiated from the abstract-minded because, while unable to cope with ideas remote from present reality, they are sometimes surprisingly ingenious in dealing with practical matters. Such individuals will pass extremely well tests for mechanical ingenuity. The powers that the study of science is well fitted to train, in concrete-minded and abstract-minded alike, such as keenness and accuracy of observation, readiness to perceive resemblances and differences and rigor in drawing conclusions, have considerable social value and are in need of testing and training.

Psychology as applied to education, then, consists in differentiating abilities and in setting up reasonable and flexible standards for the development of these abilities. With the gradual perfection of such standards, with the reduction, simplification and rationalization of courses and with the encouragement of initiative and insight on the part of teachers it may be hoped that education in science will contribute a fuller share than at present to the realization of social ideals.

M. LOUISE NICHOLS

SOUTH PHILADELPHIA
HIGH SCHOOL FOR GIRLS

WHAT PRICE THE PH. D.?

WHAT is the value of the doctor's degree as a requirement for appointment of college instructors if the doctor exhibits the literacy indicated by the following quotation from a letter recently received from a biologist who received his doctor's degree from one of the more important institutions? "I have been unable to get a position for next year. I thought I had a permanent job last year but some one did me dirty somewhere. A man in the office was jealous of Ph.D.s and I did not get much chance to explain to Catholics, it seems. I did good teaching. I need work bad this year and nothing is in sight. . . . I can teach parasitology and most anything desired. . . . I would like an instructorship. Someone that knows one is a great help to get a position. . . . People do not want one in other fields after being so long elsewhere. . . . I am generally truthful, as you know."

It is deplorable enough that a student with such poor command of English should be allowed to graduate with a bachelor's degree, but to admit such a one to "the rights, privileges, and immunities" of the doctorate would seem to render the higher degree paltry, to say the least.

B. W. KUNKEL, Ph.D. (alas)

LAFAYETTE COLLEGE

SPECIAL CORRESPONDENCE

THE PROGRESS OF ADULT EDUCATION IN CZECHOSLOVAKIA

THE importance of education has been always well understood by the Czechs. The regeneration of the Czech national life was made mostly possible because the leaders depended in their efforts on adult education. The faith in education, rooted in the glorious traditions of John Amos Comenius, was the backbone of strength during the dark days of national oppression.

Before the revolution of 1918 this work was purely nationalistically-defensive. The masses were instructed culturally in order not to drown in the inundation of foreign cultures; one of its aspects was also the social strengthening of the workers against the foreign capital. A large number of private educational bodies and societies arose, which also became part and parcel of the tradition of the national life.

The formation of the Czechoslovak Republic in 1918 brought changes in the ideals and tendencies of the adult education. The national ideal—the Czechoslovak state—was achieved; from the social view-point, the democratic form of the new state was created. Because these new conditions changed fundamentally the relations of the nation to the state, it was necessary to change the relations of adult education and the new state. While formerly the national efforts were negative, as far as the Austro-Hungarian monarchy was concerned, now the educational tendencies had to become positive and creative.

The influence of Masaryk's teachings has been most thorough. In summary, the president of the republic had for years insisted that the salvation of democracy can come only from education. The new state could stay democratic only if its citizens would be aware of their civic duties and obligations and responsible for the collective management of the state affairs. Adult education was to become the spiritual foundation of the new republican state.

As the democratic state is vitally interested in

education, it has the responsibility of the educational system. Hence adult education stopped being only the object-matter of interest of private institutions and merged into the state interests. The Czechoslovak Revolutionary Assembly passed a law on February 7, 1919, which provided for the organization of popular courses in civics; this was followed on July 22, 1919, by a law dealing with the establishment of public libraries. These two laws formed the foundation of a movement which placed Czechoslovakia in the forefront as regards adult education. The like of these two acts does not exist in any of the other central European states.

The progress during the past eleven years seems to have justified all expectations, though a great many difficulties had to be surmounted. Most of them have been due to the comparative backwardness of Slovakia and Carpathian Russia. Both these territories were neglected by their former masters. The evidence of it is noticeable to-day from the statistics on the illiteracy. In Czechoslovakia as a whole there are only 7.4 per cent. of illiterates. But the figures differ when we consider individual districts. In Bohemia there are only 2.4 per cent. illiterates; in Moravia and Silesia 3.3 per cent., but in Slovakia the proportion reaches 15 per cent. and in Carpathian Russia 50.1 per cent.

The whole system is under a special department of the ministry of education. In each court-district a district educational committee, and in every community a local education committee is appointed. These local committees number 10,893, with 555 district educational boards, including those for the minorities. Of this number, in 1930, 8,279 were Czechoslovakian, 2,246 German, 280 Ruthenian, 59 Polish and 29 Hungarian. The committees organize educational programs, lectures, courses, supervise the programs in the local moving-picture theaters, collect cultural statistics, and perform similar educational tasks, in addition to helping to organize the public libraries in their communities. In 1927, 126,150 educational undertakings were arranged, at which 42,492 lectures were attended by 3,837,939 persons.[1] There were 22,993 undertakings connected with amateur theatricals, 10,500 cinema performances, 7,148 puppet shows, 6,373 artistic socials, 10,903 debates of young people and 3,712 entertainments.[2] The figures would be even higher if the activities of the university extensions and cultural and gymnastic societies would be included, as well as the activities of the political parties, which in particular organize their cultural centers.

Direct contacts between the educational bodies and local educational committees are arranged by means of periodic educational conferences. Another step was taken in this direction in 1925, when a grant from President Masaryk helped to establish the Masaryk Institute for the Adult Education in Prague, which considers the problems theoretically, distributes books for community libraries, conducts model training schools for workers, conducts correspondence courses, advises on lectures, prepares educational films, etc. Another important work is done by the visual instruction division of the ministry of education, which is continuously adding to its collection a series of lectures with slides, which are loaned all over the republic. Projection machines and wireless sets are also loaned. Recently quite an ambitious program has been undertaken in regard to broadcasting. Though the radios are by no means so popular in Czechoslovakia as in this country (due to the high prices of the radios and the state license), the ministry provides regular educational programs on certain hours of the week. The State Publishing Office publishes a series "Občanská Knihovna" ("Civic Library") and "Knihy pro kazdého" (Books for Everybody). These books are either given away or sold for an insignificant sum. From the same source and private sources come a number of periodicals.

Special courses are given for the educational workers, and especially the functionaries of the educational committees, which last eleven days on the average. Schools for grown-ups have increased in numbers from three to forty-five. From the beginning special attention has been given to the teaching of illiterates in Slovakia and Carpathian Russia. The law of July 13,

[1] *The Central European Observer*, Nov. 14, 1930, p. 442.

[2] In comparison with the figures for 1923 the progress was enormous. In 1923 there were 4,390 educational committees, 51,947 educational undertakings.

1922, provides for the compulsory participation of public-school teachers in the adult education endeavors. In the communities under 2,000 they have to assume the duty of the public librarian.

The movement involves considerable expense. While the state assumes the major portion of the burden, the various local bodies contribute toward the general upkeep. The total amount expended by the state and local authorities during 1919–1927 for educational and library purposes was 115,685,220 Czechoslovak crowns.

A part of the educational burden is taken up by the army. The origins of this phase date back to the prison camps of Russia, where the Czechoslovak soldiers, later legionnaires, formed educational circles. Now illiterates among the recruits must attend classes in which they are taught reading, writing and elementary arithmetic. Since 1919, more than 50,000 soldiers have been taught the elements of learning. Of interest is the fact that the majority of Czech illiterates comes from Prague and the other large towns, while the German illiterates emanate from the rural districts.

The second cultural law, the Public Community Libraries Act of 1919, provides that every community must establish and maintain a public library. Where there is a larger proportion of minorities, they have their own special library. In 1927 from 12,840 communities, which are located in Bohemia, Moravia and Silesia, 11,633 had their own libraries, with 5,002,840 volumes; there were 12,752 readers who borrowed 13,380,121 books. The law has been applied in Slovakia only since 1924; and in 1927 there were already 3,451 communities, *viz.*, 92 per cent., with their own libraries, with 399,938 volumes, 160,310 readers and 983,022 borrowed volumes.[3] The figures for Carpathian Russia are not complete; so far it has been learned that there are 271 libraries with 42,106 books, 7,264 readers and 77,450 borrowed books. The state gave subsidy to 175 libraries with 24,389 volumes.

The general average is about as follows: in Bohemia, Moravia and Silesia there is an average of one library to 865 inhabitants, and to every 100 inhabitants an average of 48 volumes. Of the entire population there are 7.4 per cent. readers; to every reader is loaned an average of 18 books.

[3] Statní Úřad Statistický (State Statistical Institute), "Statistický Přehled Republiky Československé" ("The Statistical Outline of the Czechoslovak Republic"), Prague, 1930.

The libraries are under the control of district committees. The majority of the librarians are teachers, who are appointed in smaller towns, having from 2,000 to 10,000 inhabitants. This teacher has had a special training in a three-week librarian course. In smaller communities the librarians hear occasional lectures. In addition, special library courses are given in all state teachers colleges. Towns of over 10,000 inhabitants appoint special librarians with the graduation certificate from a secondary school and with a one-year special training in the State Librarian School in Prague or in Ústí nad Labem. The state supervises community libraries by four librarian supervisors. The ministry of education as a rule supports the libraries with good books and not with money.

This brief outline makes it evident that Czechoslovakia is one of the most progressive states as far as the system of adult education is concerned.

JOSEPH S. ROUCEK
CENTENARY JUNIOR COLLEGE,
HACKETTSTOWN, N. J.

FRESHMAN WEEK AT THE UNIVERSITY OF ILLINOIS

The first attempt to organize a Freshman Week at the University of Illinois was made in the fall of 1931. A faculty committee, after a study of the program in other universities and of the local situation, recommended a modification of the system as employed at the Ohio State University. The special feature of this program is that the incoming freshmen are assigned by the registrar to groups of thirty according to college, curriculum and, as far as practicable, to sex. Each group is provided with a faculty and a student adviser. The groups attend all larger gatherings as units.

The objectives aimed at were (1) to absorb the new students into the academic life of the university with speed and efficiency; (2) to inculcate an esprit de corps for the several units of which the university is composed; and (3) to afford as many personal contacts between the freshmen and the upperclassmen and faculty as possible.

The complicating factors of the local situation were (1) the large size of the freshman class, about twenty-five hundred; (2) the large number of curricula available, forty-one; (2) the time limits, one week between the first meetings of the faculties and the beginning of instruction; (4) the fact that registration must be accomplished during this period for both freshmen and upperclassmen, and (5) the fact that fraternity and sorority pledging is also carried on at this time.

The program as actually carried out may be summarized as follows. Approximately one hundred and twenty groups were formed and assigned faculty and student advisers interested in the particular curriculum concerned. Each group was assigned a classroom for headquarters during the period and a messenger service maintained contact between the different groups and the appropriate administrative headquarters.

The program commenced with a general meeting Wednesday evening at which the president addressed the freshmen and introduced the deans and the heads of the student union and woman's league. Thursday morning the groups met with their advisers to plan the program of studies for the first semester, while all departments conducting freshman courses kept office hours for advice on special subjects. That afternoon all athletic facilities of the university were thrown open for recreation. In the evening "mixers" were held by the several colleges in order that the freshmen might meet the faculty informally. This feature of the program was quite successful except in the largest group—the general curriculum of the Liberal Arts College—where a dance was substituted for the mixer. It has been suggested that next year departmental mixers might be tried for that unit.

Friday morning half of the groups completed their registration, while the other groups made a tour of the campus. That afternoon the program was reversed. In the evening an entertainment featuring extra-curricular activities was given by student organizations.

Saturday morning was devoted to completing individual registrations and personal interviews when desired. That afternoon the recreational facilities of the university were again thrown open and in the evening a stag party for men and a lantern festival for women were available to those not occupied with fraternity and sorority entertainments.

Monday and Tuesday saw the machinery for registering upperclassmen in full activity. But as the freshman registration had been completed these days were used for talks by the deans of men and women followed by group discussions and for psychological tests.

Monday evening the Y. M. C. A. and Y. W. C. A. combined to offer an entertainment followed by dancing, while the program closed on Tuesday afternoon with a concert by the university band. Wednesday morning instruction commenced in all departments.

It may be noted that the program included no lectures on "How to Study," "The Use of the Library," etc. It was the belief of the faculty committee that the ends of the program might easily be defeated by a surfeit of advice.

So far as time was concerned, it may be noted that the freshmen were called to the campus Wednesday evening instead of Friday morning as heretofore. Further programs may succeed in shortening the period.

But taking into consideration the difficulties attending the inauguration of a new undertaking, it may be said that the program worked well and will be continued with minor modifications next year.

WALDO SHUMWAY
UNIVERSITY OF ILLINOIS

QUOTATIONS

A SPECIAL COURSE FOR CRITIC TEACHERS

IN my report for the academic year 1928–1929, I discussed the educational innovation of a special program for critic teachers in normal schools, detailing the plan of informal study, concentration upon professional problems, and rich field experience in such centers as Harrisonburg and East Radford, Virginia; Buffalo, New York; Trenton, New Jersey; and Danbury, Connecticut. This offering has been highly successful and we feel that the training of prospective critic teachers is now being better carried on than ever before. But we feel that we have made only a small start. We must make better provision for the professors and administrative officers of the normal schools.

This provision, we believe, can not be made without far better facilities for practice, demonstration, and observation. Just as, at one time, when we were training elementary school teachers, there were established first the Horace Mann School and then the Speyer School, so now when we are training normal school and teachers' college professors, we are in need of a normal school or a teachers' college for observation, demonstration and practice. It is our plan, beginning in 1932, or as soon thereafter as seems wise, to organize such an institution completely under our control, in the hope that we can properly combine subject-matter with method, and relate theory to practice. In the practice normal school or teachers' college and in Teachers College itself, upon a different level, we can attack the same problems. It will be interesting to see how it all develops.

This Demonstration Teachers' College is to be located for the present within our own walls. We plan to hold classes at odd hours, so that the students may be accommodated within our already overcrowded classrooms, libraries and laboratories, and so that our students may observe. Tuition charges, entrance requirements and other regulations will be not inferior to those of other colleges of the university. The limit has been set at 360 students, allowing for three sections of thirty members for each of the four college years.

Those in charge of this experiment intend to "break a new way in teacher training." Their endeavor will be to "discover and develop new methods in the field of teacher education." They plan to avoid duplication of present procedures. Offering three separate curricula, for nursery school, for elementary school, and for high school teachers, they plan to substitute comprehensive examinations for the point and credit system and individual adjustment for the academic lock-step. . . .

It is planned that each student do part of his work abroad. It is not commonly realized that American students at no increase in expense can have the benefit of foreign study; and so intimate are the contacts of Teachers College with education in Germany, England, and France that arrangements of this kind can easily be made. It is the intention also to make the most of the rich facilities offered by New York City. . . .

It is also planned that each prospective teacher, during summer vacation periods or during a semester's absence, shall participate both in some form of industry and in some form of social work. Those responsible for the new college believe that effective appreciation and understanding of the new social order depend in part upon active participation in some form of industry; and that the teacher, who in essence is a social worker devoted to the relief of poverty and idleness, to the prevention of crime, to the development of effective citizenship, can carry on his task better when he has come into "close contact with the activities of society that have to do with the education of boys and girls outside of school, whether these activities be of a corrective or a preventive nature."

To those who have devoted their lives to the training of teachers, this educational experiment will come with something of a thrill. Here is a company of scholars who, throwing tradition to the winds, would build the best system of teacher training that they know. They introduce a new college. They scrap the system of points and credits. They devise a plan of entrance requirements of their own. By individual adjustment, group conferences and directed readings they supplement formal instruction. They utilize an occasional semester's break and the summer's vacation to give foreign travel and study and participation in industry and social life. They break up old subject matter divisions. They introduce new bases of integration.

It is an ambitious experiment. If practices approximate plans, a new standard will be set for teacher training. Success will depend upon the degree to which the old problems are settled, whether subject-matter can be combined with method, whether theory can be related to practice, whether by facing the education of teachers directly, a broad and cultural, as well as professional, end may be attained. It will mean the development of a new type of higher education. It is to be hoped that neither academic tradition nor pedagogical prejudice nor fear of the unbeaten path nor terror of accrediting agencies nor administrative timidity will stay these messengers from the swift completion of their appointed course.—*William F. Russell, in the Report of the Dean of Teachers College, Columbia University.*

SOCIETIES AND MEETINGS

THE DEPARTMENT OF SUPERINTENDENCE OF THE NATIONAL EDUCATION ASSOCIATION

THE sixty-second annual meeting of the Department of Superintendence will be held at Washington, D. C., from February 20 to 25, 1932, under the presidency of Dr. Edwin C. Broome, superintendent of the Philadelphia schools. The general sessions are to be in Constitution Hall, the new building of the Daughters of the American Revolution.

The entire Washington Auditorium at Nineteenth Street and New York Avenue, N.W., will be used for convention headquarters, registration, exhibits and convention service.

The preliminary program follows:

CONVENTION THEME—*"Education, Our Guide and Our Safeguard, and One of the Chief Sources of Our Spiritual Life, Our Cultural Growth and Our Material Power."*

SATURDAY, FEBRUARY 20, 4:00 P. M.

Review of convention exhibits by the president and other officers of the Department of Superintendence and the N. E. A.

SUNDAY, FEBRUARY 21, 2:00 P. M.

Patriotic Pilgrimages:

Washington Monument, leader, Edwin C. Broome, superintendent of schools, Philadelphia.

Tomb of the Unknown Soldier, leader, Norman R. Crozier, superintendent of schools, Dallas.

Lincoln Memorial, leader, George C. Bush, superintendent of schools, South Pasadena.

Old Christ Church, Alexandria, leader, Herbert S. Weet, superintendent of schools, Rochester.

SUNDAY, FEBRUARY 21, 4:00 P. M.
VESPER SERVICE

Presiding—Dr. Edwin C. Broome, superintendent of schools, Philadelphia, president of the Department of Superintendence.

Address—Rufus B. von KleinSmid, president, University of Southern California.

MONDAY, FEBRUARY 22, 8:45 A. M.

Presentation of the Yearbook on Character Education.

Speakers: Dr. A. L. Threlkeld, superintendent of schools, Denver, *chairman*, Commission on Character Education; Professor Frank N. Freeman, School of Education, University of Chicago; Mrs. Margaret Alltucker-Norton, associate director, Research Division, National Education Association; Charles B. Glenn, superintendent of schools, Birmingham, Alabama.

Patriotic Ceremony at 10:15 o'clock, the hour of George Washington's birth.

Education, the Nation's Safeguard—Dr. Charles H. Judd, director, School of Education, University of Chicago.

MONDAY AFTERNOON, FEBRUARY 22

Pilgrimage to Mount Vernon.

MONDAY, FEBRUARY 22, 8:00 P. M.

Convocation of George Washington University—presiding, Cloyd Heck Marvin, president.

The National Commission on the Enrichment of Adult Life—James A. Moyer, State Department of Education, Boston, *chairman.* School Building Planning and Construction—presiding, P. C. Packer, dean, College of Education, University of Iowa. Allied Departments and Organizations.

TUESDAY, FEBRUARY 23, 8:45 A. M.
The Present Crisis and Public Education

Presiding, Norman R. Crozier, superintendent of schools, Dallas.

The Crisis Defined—President Edwin C. Broome. What the Public is Getting and May Expect from Adequate Expenditures for Education—George D. Strayer, professor of educational administration, Teachers College, Columbia University. How Shall the Crisis Be Met?—David E. Weglein, superintendent of schools, Baltimore, *chairman*, Committee on School Costs. Improved Methods of Financing Education—Russell Dearmont, Missouri State Senator, Cape Girardeau. Report of the Committee on Financing Educational Research. Nomination of Officers.

TUESDAY, FEBRUARY 23, 2:00 P. M.

Administrative groups arranged according to size

of city. Allied departments and organizations.

TUESDAY, FEBRUARY 23, 8:00 P. M.
American Education—Past, Present and Future

From Past to Present—Dr. Albert B. Meredith, School of Education, New York University. American Education To-day—Dr. Frank P. Graves, State Commissioner of Education, Albany, N. Y. Future Needs and Prospects—Dr. Henry Suzzallo, director, Carnegie Foundation for the Advancement of Teaching, New York City.

WEDNESDAY, FEBRUARY 24, 8:45 A. M.
Education as a Source of our Spiritual Life and Cultural Growth

Intangible Values—Florence Hale, president of the National Education Association, Augusta, Maine. Art in Education—Lorado Taft, sculptor, Chicago. Music in Education—Walter Damrosch, music director, New York City. Literature in Education—John H. Finley, *The New York Times.*

Business Session.

Reports of Committees: Lay Relations, Dr. Charles S. Meek, superintendent of schools, Toledo, *chairman.* Audit, Louis Nusbaum, associate superintendent of schools, Philadelphia, *chairman.*

Election of Officers.

Ballot Box open 11:00 A. M. to 6:00 P. M.

WEDNESDAY, FEBRUARY 24, 2:00 P. M.

Discussion groups arranged according to subjects. Allied departments and organizations.

WEDNESDAY, FEBRUARY 24, 8:00 P. M.
Education for a Changing Social, Economic and Political World

Education for a Changing Social World—Dr. E. A. Ross, professor of sociology, University of Wisconsin, Madison. Education for a Changing Economic World—Stuart Chase, Labor Bureau, New York City. Education for a Changing Political World—Speaker to be announced.

THURSDAY, FEBRUARY 25, 8:45 A. M.

Education as a National Enterprise—Ray Lyman Wilbur, secretary, Department of the Interior.

Business Session.

Report of Committee on Resolutions: Paul C. Stetson, superintendent of schools, Indianapolis, *chairman.*

THURSDAY, FEBRUARY 25, 2:00 P. M.
Promoting the Physical and Mental Health of School Children

Presiding, Willis A. Sutton, superintendent of schools, Atlanta.

Promoting the Physical and Mental Health of School Children—Through Physical Preparation of the Pre-school Child; through Approved Courses of Study; through Properly Directed Medical Inspection and Follow-up Work; through Well Organized Recreational Programs.

Introduction of Newly Elected Officers.

THURSDAY, FEBRUARY 25, 8:00 P. M.

Historical Pageant, under the auspices of the George Washington Bicentennial Commission, in honor of the Department of Superintendence—Percy Jewett Burrell, *director.*

EDUCATIONAL RESEARCH AND STATISTICS

OCCUPATIONS OF PARENTS OF COLLEGE STUDENTS

A DISTRIBUTION of occupations of parents of students enrolled at the Pennsylvania State College was printed in SCHOOL AND SOCIETY for June 4, 1927. The concluding paragraph stated that "the changes (in the occupations represented) show a marked increase in the attendance of students whose parents have occupations in the 'ordinary' walks of life."

The distribution for the current year shows a further development in this same general direction. When the first distribution was published in SCHOOL AND SOCIETY in 1914, the groupings were made under eight general classes. The distributions have been continued under these same headings and for four representative years are as follows:

Percentage

Group	1914–15	1924–25	1926–27	1931–32
Industrial	18.04	20.22	20.40	19.37
Artisan	17.76	18.21	19.08	18.56
Mercantile	21.50	16.63	18.61	15.14
Professional	11.49	11.06	11.42	11.57
Agricultural	17.10	15.80	13.82	10.39
Clerical	5.28	7.24	5.87	6.97
Official	3.02	2.98	3.14	3.98
Miscellaneous	5.77	7.85	7.63	14.00

The most pronounced changes occur in the mercantile, agricultural and miscellaneous groups, the first two showing a marked decrease, and the third a pronounced increase. The numbers, however, from the two groups showing a relative percentage decrease show an actual increase, for in 1914 there were 434 and 345 in the mercantile and agricultural group, respectively, whereas, in 1931, there are 654 and 449.

The large increase in the miscellaneous group is due almost entirely to the increase in the number of insurance agents included in this group. Included under the heading "miscellaneous" there are, in addition, real estate agents, brokers, undertakers, editors, Y. M. C. A. secretaries, etc., and of these, the insurance agents, 86 in number, are more than twice as many as the next larger occupation within the group.

The twelve leading occupations for two representative years are:

1914–15	Rank in 1931–32	1931–32
1 Farmers	3	Superintendents
2 Storekeepers	2	Storekeepers
3 Superintendents	1	Farmers
4 R. R. employees	4	R. R. employees
5 Manufacturers	14	Laborers
6 Salesmen	6	Salesmen
7 Physicians	15	Teachers
8 Contractors	9	Miners
9 Carpenters	16	Contractors
10 Lawyers	19	Engineers
11 Ministers	21	Clerks
12 Clerks	11	Insurance Agents

Some representative occupational groups whose sons and daughters have relegated the sons and daughters of physicians, lawyers and ministers to their present low ranking, in addition to those listed in the leading twelve for this year, are: bank employees, real estate agents, machinists and bookkeepers.

From the above it is quite evident that the sons and daughters of those who have occupations in the more ordinary walks of life are attending the Pennsylvania State College in larger numbers.

It is interesting to note that during this period, in spite of this source change, the percentage of students from the upper divisions of the secondary school graduating classes has been regularly increasing. Two representative distributions for entering class are given to substantiate this statement.

September, 1924		September, 1931	
Rank	Per cent.	Rank	Per cent.
First-third	39.3	First-fifth	41.1
		Second-fifth	36.5
Second-third	39.6	Third-fifth	11.5
		Fourth-fifth	7.2
Third-third	15.4	Fifth-fifth	2.6
Not ranked	5.5	Not ranked	1.1

It is to be regretted that the rankings are not given in the same fractional parts, but it is easily noted that whereas those admitted from the upper third of the secondary school graduating class in 1924 made up only 39.3 per cent. of the entering class, those admitted from the upper two fifths of the class in September, 1931, form more than three quarters of the entering class, and the difference in size of the two groups (the first-third and the first-two-fifths) is only one fifteenth of the class or 6.66 per cent.

W. S. HOFFMAN

PENNSYLVANIA STATE COLLEGE

NEW BOOKS IN EDUCATION

CLOUD, ROY W. *On the Trails of Yesterday.* Pp. xiv + 219. Illustrated. Harr Wagner. $1.25.

EVANS, BESSIE and MAY G. *American Indian Dance Steps.* Pp. xix + 104. 8 plates and 12 figures. Barnes. $7.50.

Fifteenth Annual Report of the Federal Board for Vocational Education: 1931. Pp. xi + 129. United States Government Printing Office.

GARRISON, ELISHA E. *The Riddle of Economics.* Pp. xi + 329. Macmillan. $2.50.

HENMON, V. A. C. and F. O. HOLT. *A Report on the Administration of Scholastic Aptitude Tests to 34,000 High School Seniors in Wisconsin in 1929 and 1930.* Pp. 104. University of Wisconsin. (Bureau of Guidance and Records.)

Institute for Education by Radio: Second Yearbook, Education on the Air. Edited by J. H. MacLatchy. Pp. viii + 301. Ohio State University. $3.00.

MCLAUGHLIN, SISTER MARY AQUINAS. *The Genesis and Constancy of Ascendance and Submission as Personality Traits.* Pp. 95. University of Iowa. $1.00.

MORRISON, J. CAYCE and ARTHUR E. LAYMAN. *Character Building in New York Public Schools.* Pp. 96. University of the State of New York Press.

EDUCATIONAL REVIEW

Edited by WILLIAM McANDREW

EDITORIAL COMMENT

EDUCATIONAL DISTURBERS

To him who in the love of teaching holds communion with the men who speak their mind there comes a various language—changeable. Commencement talks and words at institutes trip gladly with a ritual of praise. Grant but the times be prosperous, the world will let the teacher go her quiet way unseen. Whenever bid, the crowds will come to see the boys and girls perform their plays, or hear them valedictorize the world. But when depression weighs upon the land, when government has robbed the people's store, when crime is worse than otherwheres on earth, lo, comes the voice of doubting and of blame: "What are you doing for the nation's weal? Why rank our virtues meanly in the world? Where are the patriots of worth your folk assured us would be fashioned in your schools? What will you *do,* or will you play the part like one who wraps the drapery of his couch about him and lies down to pleasant dreams?"

In other words, dearly beloved, to abandon blank verse for bleak prose, the discontent with the school program is louder than you ever knew it all these fifty years.

ALIBI

In Pennsylvania I heard a sit-down, around-the-table debate in which a newspaper editor was telling a bevy of schoolmasters that their claim to public support on the ground that they are training citizens is the worst kind of bluff. "Our paper," he said, "has exposed a dozen cases of political robbery of tax money and not one of your schools took time enough out of the hours given to ancient life to discuss any of these cases. Your Horace Mann promised if the people would tax themselves for schools that taxes in the gross would come down because of less crime, fewer courts, unneeded jails. Your schools cost us more than ever. We have more crime per capita and it costs us more than is the case in any country in the world."

One after another the schoolmasters retorted that schools do not teach crime; newspapers do, books do, movies do. The street and the home are to blame.

This sort of thing went on for some time until a participant said, "Here's Henry Schlessenger taking it all in and not saying a word. What do you think, Henry?"

"What strikes me as odd," said Schlessenger, who is an engineer of the highway department, "is that nobody says what he's going to do about it."

IT WAS SO IN 1775

This reminds me of a conversation in New York. A group of contented high-school principals was showing how impossible it is to find time for civics teaching. Not a one tackled the question as to whether any high-school subject is so valuable or necessary as citizenship. Finally the advocate who had been presenting a plea for more of it said: "Strange how history repeats itself. You are exactly what the safest and most respectable Americans of 1775 were, Tories."

TORYISM

That's what the most of my educational friends are. For instance, there is that group of University of Chicago professors who issue the *Elementary School Journal* and *The School Review.* You couldn't find an editorial board anywhere with more persistent determination to help education along, or with more reliable knowledge of what educational measures have, by tested experiment, proven the most successful. You could not discover editors less hampered by fear of alienating advertisers or of antagonizing the singularly meddlesome politicians who run Chicago. Gratitude, respect, admiration and affection are mine for the makers of these two University of Chicago magazines. The cause of my tears is this:

The Michigan legislature of 1931 passed a law requiring not less than one semester, five lessons a week, in civics, stressing the rights and responsibilities of citizens, no diploma to issue to any student failing to satisfy this requirement. All the normal schools and colleges shall give a course of four term hours in political science, stressing the rights and responsibilities of citizenship.

Recommendation of a student for graduation who has not successfully pursued this work shall be deemed a misdemeanor.

Now come the University of Chicago editors calling this act a fundamental error. "Through much painstaking experimentation the science of education has developed a respectable body of factual evidence with respect to the proper content of the curriculum. If the state legislatures ignore the findings of science the result will be nothing short of disastrous."

The trouble with this is that the respectable body of factual experience developed by the science of education has so ignored the rights and responsibilities of citizenship that the schools have not produced a citizenry that protects its rights or performs its duties. So widespread is that opinion that three days' work in a village library enabled an old man—me—not trained in researching, to spot over two hundred respectable citizens who charge the schools with neglect of their civic duty.

If it isn't the legislature's part to require the teaching of civics so much as set down in the Michigan's law, and to specify what it is to be taught for, whose duty is it?

The schoolmasters'?

Is it the duty of the painstaking and careful experimenters in the science of education?

If so, why, by the faith of our fathers, have they been so leisurely about doing it?

Where is the schoolmasters' association or society of experimenters that has pledged its members, on pain of being deemed guilty of misdemeanor, to give as much time to civic teaching as the Michigan law-makers demand and for the same purpose?

Oh, come, whose schools are they? Experimenters'? I am sure the owner of the car knows less about driving than we chauffeurs do, but if he insists that we shall not carry any Darwinism in his car and must take in more and better civic teaching we may properly address ourselves to persuading him. But generalities about what painstaking experimenters have done will not get us anywhere.

THE BEST OF THE NEW BOOKS

MAY I now invite you to attend my monthly praise service on the blessings of new books? Yes, I know, Mr. Monroe would like less applause for authors and more telling of what's wrong.

Tut! tut! Remember, I taste twice as many dishes as I put upon your table: Here are the ones I think will make your living less forlorn.

A CASE EXACTLY IN POINT

AT least from Xenophon's time onward the big teachers of boys have put acquaintance with heroes high in the list of influences to be sought in education. Both the ancient Greek and the modern Russian personal patterns for schoolboys seem less remote from the life desired than are the usual selections in American reading books. I can remember only a spirit of distant worship engendered in my school days by the presentation of Washington, Franklin, Patrick Henry and the other heroes, including the then very recent Lincoln. They were so great, their stage was so high, that we ordinaries could only sit and with awe applaud. Their lives had the myth and distance of Jack the Giant Killer and the Prince Who was Afraid of Nothing.

Maybe this is what Professor Kilpatrick means by saying our schools are sold out to the past.

Once I commended to you, as a snappy story of what American daring can still do, William Dudley Foulke's "Roosevelt and the Spoilsmen," at another time his "Lucius Swift." These are true stories of Americans fighting a political evil which still threatens and against which school is obligated to breed up warriors.

I now have another volume[1] to add to your school library of current heroism. It is a forthright, gripping story of an ordinary Chicago shopkeeper put upon a committee to try to clean up a patch of political banditry in his own district and so utilizing the honest majority as to win. Eighty-five per cent. of the people, George Cole was told, are honest and decent. Mark Twain had estimated their strength in the United States at 55 per cent.

[1] Hoyt King, "Citizen Cole of Chicago." Horder's, Inc., 231 So. Jefferson St., Chicago. 158 pp. $1.50.

"How did you happen to get out and fight for them?" asked Hoyt King, who writes the book.

"I owe a debt to the community," Cole answered. "But I was not actively appreciative. I was indifferent and civically lazy."

This was in 1894. Then, as now, there was on one side an intrenched camp of experienced and able political freebooters supported by financial, social and even moral interests and relying on the indifference, laziness and blindness of the people. Then, on the other side, was a man without prestige, experience or adaptability.

With vividness and humor Secretary King relates Cole's organization of citizens leagues; his fight with Yerkes, the traction magnate; his battles with the bandit aldermen; his breaking the backbone of the gang; his jailing of election crooks; his overturn of the legislature; his citation as the state's greatest public servant. Neither in Cole nor in Hoyt King's biography of him is there anything of the "big injun me." Scores of good Chicagoans are given credit in the story. One thing about the struggles would have pained Mr. Jefferson. In the various committees and workers named, not a school man or woman appears, notwithstanding that to purify politics was a prominent promise of the proponents of public schools when the campaigns for promoting them by public taxation were going on.

King has told his tale with a level head and an abstention from the panegyrics. If you don't say it is a quickening book I shall be disappointed in my estimate of your patriotism. It should be made a text in the social studies in the high schools of Chicago, New York, Detroit, and all cities of over 20,000. If you haven't the nerve to use it so, sneak it into the school library and recommend it to likely boys and girls. For you know beyond any chance of contradiction that the training of George Coles is what your schools are mainly for. "Leadership, leadership," orates the high-school defender. Good! Here's the kind of leader the country is languishing for, and the earth over him has barely settled. If out of its thousands each school trained only one George Cole there would be such a civic clean-up as America never saw. Dr. Kilpatrick, Dr. Snedden, Dr. Russell, Dr. Judd, William Allen White, Professor Gosnel, Bushnell Hart, Herman Hagedorn, Ruth Bryan Owen, Richard Welling, and I don't know how many others have said you can do it if you turn your hand to it.

WHAT CIVICS IS AND IS BECOMING

IF there are any more Merriam boys, their brothers have left them a wide field between extremes. John Merriam has specialized on paleontological life; Charles, on man in his latest development as a political animal. Both have filled Lowell's requirement for a scholar: cooperation in the present work of the world. In taking up Charles Edward Merriam's book on citizenship[2] you read with the confidence of a young physician consulting the work of a famous teacher who has continued in active medical practice. That Merriam, a professor of political science, is a practitioner of it, walking unafraid into the continuous epidemic of Chicago's civic septicity, serving in its notorious board of aldermen, guarding its expenditures, accepting Mayor Dever's urge to be his Colonel House, enduring jibes, sneers, and worse, serving the nation on special commissions in war and peace, giving the young men and women in his classes the straight truth on what they must do—that he has pursued and published a dozen major studies of present needs, that he is a live member of the leading associations devoted to the social studies, make the appearance of a book by him an event. This is the ninth in a series of studies in the making of citizens, edited by him and published by his University of Chicago.

Here he compares eight national systems of civic education: England's, France's, Germany's, Italy's, Soviet Russia's, Austria's, Switzerland's and our own. What is civic loyalty? What are the means used by these nations to train it? Of course the schools are considered an indispensable nursery of it. In one generation the entire population of an average state goes through them. These youths receive the impress society chooses to stamp. Of all civic agencies the school is the most systematic and highly organized. It is the most consciously contrived

[2] C. E. Merriam, "The Making of Citizens," University of Chicago Press. 371 pp. $3.00.

means of influencing directly the next generation.

England's schools disclose little conscious attempt to engender national sentiment. But since the advance of Soviet propaganda the British schools show the beginnings of a systematic attempt at a direct inculcation of the dominant principles of economics and politics. Always have the English schools taught social distinctions and values. Traditional government is by the "gentleman." What his characteristics are, how they are to be interpreted, are taught. The cult and the rules for him are in the schools.

The newer régimes in Europe show a vigorous use of the educational system for civic training. France, also, is exceptionally active in it. Germany, France, Switzerland and the United States represent types of civic education in which deliberate planning is emphasized.

Professor Merriam's survey shows that regional political feeling is growing weaker under the influence of modern communication. Local sentiment within a country is weakening before the larger idea of national unity. Russia has no regionalism of a pronounced type. The mere existence of a League of Nations minimizes separation. The solidarity of workers is increasing, knowledge in the field of political behavior may fundamentally change society, for such knowledge is growing with notable rapidity.

Old Civic Standbys

Tradition and symbolism have long been the principal staples of civic education, with music, literature, folk-lore and myth woven on a weft of custom, force and fear, safe from challenge by the existing political authority. Armies and navies continue to impress, but the determination of policy by the military class is on the wane.

In the main, patriotic organizations retain the older appeal to tradition rather than interest in reorganization to meet life under its new conditions.

Hero worship shows little sign of decline. Lenin, Mussolini, Gandhi, wield vast influence. Communism, Fascism and Democracy are the leading world-types of theory.

Thus far schools have retained the literal transmission of traditions in inelastic form rather than encouraging a forward look at civic needs. Allegiance to Russia and the Soviet system looms large in Russia; allegiance to America and the American system of government, in the United States. Doctrines are presented as finalities without critical examination or without intimations of needed improvement. In science and industry tradition has been abandoned; in civic education, retained. Our book heroes made no mistakes; their lives were never gray, their policies were always wholly right. There is lacking a keen and critical analysis of the traits and attitudes of the desired citizen. See Snedden, "Civic Education," for reprobation of current high-school teaching. The scientific task of discovering a central core of traits, dispositions, tendencies desirable in citizens is easy. In the near future incisive analyses of the objectives of civic education will be made, including political behavior. There will be more effective teaching. There will be struggles and controversies emerging with a more intelligent solution of the problem. There will be a different type of civic education from any that has appeared. Read Merriam's analysis of this teaching problem. Note the unusual quantity of demand for political instruction appearing in SCHOOL AND SOCIETY under the caption "A Breviary for these Times." What to do and how to do it are getting into more books and articles than ever in your life before.

A LEVEL-HEADED WOMAN

MRS. MCFEE, of Iowa and Arkansas, teacher, mother, housewife, domestic-science authority, text-book writer, engaging popularizer of science, industry and history, will get your applause for her handsome book on civics.[3] Instead of the dry skeleton frame of government here is a live, breathing, acting reality, a creature doing great things, up to tricks, rising to performance of grandeur, committing appalling stupidities, lunging forward, missing opportunities, winning superb victories and commanding thrilling interest. Whether picturing Washington city, taking you through Congress, outlining the constitution, visiting

[3] Inez N. McFee, "How Our Government is Run," Thomas Y. Crowell Company, New York. 336 pp. $2.50.

the federal departments, seeing the President or talking with the politicians, Mrs. McFee is not permitting you a dull moment. She has a continuous and varied charm and a canny sense of what Americans want to know about themselves and their public servants.

Professor Merriam's "Making of Citizens" deplores the smugness of civic teaching which turns out citizens fed with a static idea of our perfect democracy. Narrator McFee has none of it. America treated L'Enfant, planner of the capital city, with shabby injustice. Taxpayers in the District of Columbia are in the condition that brought on the Revolution. The keeping of national officials out of office four months after each election, while those repudiated by the voters hang on as if they represented popular opinion, is too stupid for words. All students of government agree that there are twice too many congressmen. The House of Representatives is the most expensive law-making mill in the world. If we had a direct accounting of the use made of our tax money we wouldn't be robbed of so much. Log-rolling in legislatures is acceptance of bribes and betrayal of trust.

Because you don't vote at the primaries bosses gain sweeping majorities. Lack of a merit civil-service system gives the boss the power to hold the city in his hand. A large number of candidates purchase offices. We have had situations in which boodlers nearly bought the presidency. Elections are stampeded by supplanting judgment by the psychology of coming sure victory. A national nominating convention is the most wasteful institution on earth. Big business has controlled the government and can again do so unless the citizens are vigilant and courageous. Party allegiance can easily do damage to the nation. I pick these samples from three hundred pages of text which are mostly devoted to representations of the sound fundamentals of the American plan and theory. I do it to show Citizen McFee's sane realization that a study leading to the preservation and strengthening of a hale democracy can not be an ostrich view when our imperfections are serious. The abundant spirit of this book is that we made a glorious start and have come far, but the revolution is not over. A government of the people must not be of people asleep or lazy or indifferent to the dangers within the nation.

This book abounds with stirring tales, incidents and songs. It's chapter on the flag is full of new and spirited matter. Attention to every part of our territory, use of fascinating bits of biography, flashes of humor, bracing of general statements by specific instance, make the work a model for text-book writers in these days of demand for "the objective manner."

POLITICAL RELIGION

STARTLINGLY fitting into this present comes Professor Cofer's[4] tracing of the growth of Carlyle's political religion from cautious feeling a way in "Sartor Resartus" to out-and-out jeremiad in "Chartism."

"In the long run," warns the "deadly in earnest" prophet in Craigenputtoch, "every government is the exact symbol of its people. Like people, like government."

"We shall again have a society with some heroism in it, noble industrialism and government by the wisest."

"God knows the task will be hard. No noble task was ever easy. For what purpose, if not for tasks like this, were lives given to men? Our world can not live as it is."

Professor Cofer has dug out of letters and pamphlets appertaining to Claude de St. Simon, soldier under Washington, French patriot, world philosopher and philanthropist, clues which, linked together, establish Carlyle's curiosity, interest and sympathy in the Frenchman's theories and ultimate conversion to them.

DEMOCRATIC PRACTICE

BARNES AND COMPANY'S Extra-Curricular Library now has ten handy volumes, with a promise of twelve more. Principals Jerry Vineyard and Charles Poole write the latest one.[5] It is a collection of experiences to aid sponsors who have or contemplate pupil apprenticeship in the American duty of self-government. Both authors have reported before on their studies

[4] David Brooks Cofer, "Saint-Simonism in the Radicalism of Thomas Carlyle." English Publishing Company, College Station, Texas. 65 pp. $1.00.

[5] Jerry J. Vineyard, Charles Poole, "Student Participation in School Government." A. S. Barnes and Company, New York. 104 pp. $1.00.

of democracy practice in schools east and west. They are not propagandists for any particular system. They hold that the meaning and philosophy of democracy can be made clear by precept and practice. To neglect adequate provision for cooperative government is to miss a main aim of the American program of education. No school is a good school which is not organized for a better community government and citizenship.

The trials and failures of student government are discussed. Its introduction as an aid to discipline and order is not so much urged as formerly. Instead, it is recognized as a practice-training for our democracy, as arithmetic is a means for forming certain business habits. It takes more skill and care to run a participating school than to manage one on the boss plan.

The authors are so patriotically desirous of seeing the principle universally put to work in school.

A BOOK BY OUR OWN

Many a kind-hearted philosopher has lamented his tendency to lose through a repetition of benefits the warmth of his gratitude, the parent of all virtues. Quintus Curtius, looking over a list of benefactors whose kindnesses to him he had recorded day by day, was amazed at his omission of members of his own household. Something of this remorse smites me as I look over the latest volume of proceedings[6] of the National Education Association.

For sixty-nine years these substantial books have been given to the members and counted by libraries, at home and abroad, indispensable treasuries of educational current history. Eighteen years ago the books changed from somber black to their present more attractive brown binding. My set has forty-three issues, shelved so near the door that, in case of fire, they stand a good chance of salvage. Only six short steps, and an outstretched hand suffices to call, from beyond the tomb, thinkers in my business whom I used to worship from the back seats of convention halls. Again Horace Scudder tells me that good literature is a living radiance and must not be cut to death by the surgery of the English teacher. William T. Harris argues once more why the young girl may be permitted to read the newspapers. Zalmon Richards shows us we don't know how to teach reading. John W. Cook defends moral training. Louis Soldan, Aaron Goye and Jim Greenwood fight like gentlemen. Albert Marble appears once more the best-dressed man on the platform, with speech and argument in keeping. Columbus Stevenson sees communism an approaching menace. Again I meet the few brilliant minds that withstood the succession of "abhorrent novelties" that now are "eternal verities" of later volumes. I view again the valiant and failing battles for the metric system or simple spelling or against the lecture monstrosity of college teaching, or tests and measurements, or the intrenched absurdity of the common high-school studies. For the discouragement that must come to superintendents an excellent antidote is an hour in the public library varied by reading first in the volume for 1881, and then in this newest and freshest output of fifty years later.

The editors have developed a considerate regard for the reader. The table of contents is a classification by groups. The index is an alphabetical finder, according to subject and speaker, so well cross-referenced that "Winship" is indicated as touching on "music" and "music" is treated by "Winship." In your preparation for your next appearance before the Parent-Teacher Association I know of no approach to ideas, no stimulus to thinking, more speedy than a study of the excellent indexes of the last five or six volumes. When Dr. Bagley was, just now, reporting upon the problem of affording work for old teachers needing help, I wished it might be possible to set large numbers of them preparing a complete subject-author index of the entire set of proceedings, to be printed in one book and expanded each year. This would make a superb encyclopedia of education, a "Tips for Teacher Talks."

In fine, brethren, let us thank and praise these of our own household who, year by year, present these volumes so well arranged as to be of instant use, so well typed as to gladden the

[6] Joy Elmer Morgan, Ernest R. Bryan, J. W. Crabtree and staff, editors, "Sixty-ninth Proceedings of Meetings of the National Education Association." Washington, D. C. 1,200 pp. $3.00.

eye, so strongly bound as to keep trim these forty years, and so rich in content as to win the verdict of an attendant of the British Museum that they make the most valuable educational library in the world. Mr. Morgan tells me the price of each preceding volume, so far as they are available, is $3.00.

PUPILS WHO PERPLEX

THE National Mental Hygiene Committee sends us two new helpers,[7] "Behavior Problems" gives aid to the teacher for guiding the nervous child, the truant, the bad boy and the retarded. "Mental Hygiene in the Classroom" considers the troublesomes, the failers, the tardy, the truants, the show-offs, the timid, the cheaters, the babyish, sex problems and other perplexities involving home and school.

The committee gives away for a two-cent stamp a classified "Suggestions for Reading in Mental Hygiene."

HALF OF THE SICK ARE CHILDREN

IMPROVEMENT of school-health service has come mostly from comparison of experiences. Of course, the big health congress, the third White House Conference,[8] hearing experts and researchers from city and country, brings much that is new and strengthening to this line of the school superintendent's service. Half of our diseases occur in children. From 50 per cent. to 75 per cent. of crippled children owe their plight to communicable disease. The book reviews and describes the best practices of control.

NEW HEALTH HINTS

BASIC principles for health teaching was the theme of the sixth American Health-Education Conference. The addresses and discussions[9] are given in a handsome volume efficiently indexed. It goes into modern methods of teaching and applies them to health instruction, sets up and defines objectives, treats of lunchroom service, cleanliness, home cooperation, epidemics, water supply, extra-curriculars, milk, teacher training, inspection, school nurses, rest periods, researches, outcomes, organization, administration and progress. The inclusion of all the discussions, objections, agreements and remarks makes lively reading. The experience and reputation of the participants give the findings high value.

STIMULANT

I LOVE Bertrand Russell, his style is so warm, and if I am careful he'll do me no harm. Samples from "The Scientific Outlook":[10]

When the man in the street has begun to believe thoroughly in science the man in the laboratory has begun to lose his faith.

And now the sun is nothing but waves of probability.

Physics, which is fundamental science, is undermining the whole structure of applied reason and presenting a world of fantastic dreams.

Professors are usually temperamentally timid.

To lose faith in knowledge is to lose faith in the best of man's capacities.

The number of people who own cars is greatly in excess of the number who had enough to eat one hundred and fifty years ago.

That God made the world is no reason why we should not make it over.

All history shows that great power is intoxicating. The modern holders of power are not aware of what they could do. When this knowledge dawns upon them a new era in human tyranny is to be expected.

Psychology, as pursued everywhere in the past (and still, at Oxford), was incapable of giving control over mental processes and never aimed at this result.

Children in school are taught to believe what they are told and are punished if they express disbelief.

The total abolition of poverty is at the present moment technically possible. Known meth-

[7] Committee, "Behavior Problems of School Children." 22 pp. 15 cents, $7.50 per hundred. Newark Bd. of Ed. Dept. of Child Guidance, "Mental Hygiene in the Classroom." 46 pp., 15 cents, $7.50 per hundred. National Committee for Mental Hygiene, 450 7th Ave., New York.

[8] White House Conference, "Communicable Disease Control." The Century Company, New York. 288 pp. $2.25.

[9] Various authors, "Principles and Practices in Health Education." American Child-Health Association, 450 7th Ave., New York. 485 pp. $1.50.

[10] Bertrand Russell, "The Scientific Outlook." W. W. Norton and Company, New York. 277 pp. $3.00.

ods of production, if wisely organized, could keep the whole population of the globe in tolerable comfort.

Revolutionist Russell scintillates through 277 pages of comment on the characteristics of the scientific method in biology, physiology, psychology, society, government, education and reproduction.

Reading him is no chore.

WORLD'S CULTURE IN ONE VOLUME

With an alphabetical index of 16,000 topics from "Abelard" to "Zyrians" the Putnams' "Outline of Modern Knowledge"[11] is a one-volume encyclopedia of a thousand pages so composed as to invite continuous reading, so arranged as to facilitate immediate consultation. It starts with a philosophic and scientific retroprospect. Its chapters are upon "The Idea of God," "The Universe," "Astronomy," "The Nature of Mathematics," "Biology and Human Progress," "Sex," "Psychology," "Psychoanalysis," "Morals," "Culture," "The Human Race," "Archeology," "Contemporary Philosophy," "Economics," "Finance," "Industrial Organizations," "Politics," "International Relations," "History as a Science," "Modern Geography," "Literary Criticism," "Architecture," "Music."

Samples: Cultural progress of any nation is increased by friendly contact with other peoples. This does not destroy nationalism, it strengthens and improves it.

Men cry out that democracy has failed. So has monarchy. People say education has not succeeded. Neither has ignorance. History shows how far we have come, but we are still coming.

Poetry is experience in utmost intensity.

The modernists among American architects have the seeds and potentiality for endless development.

Never has music had so wide an audience as it has to-day.

Industrial expansion, the rise of men of undeveloped spirituality, but of commanding wealth and position, produced vulgarity greater than under the Roman Empire. It created a demand for art accepted in proportion to its lack of charm.

England doesn't understand plastic art.

As the writer of each chapter is a university professor devoted to research and teaching a specialty, you may count on authoritative statement and consideration for the learner.

TEACHER COLLEGES' LIBRARY STANDARDS[12]

The title of this book describes it. When you report on the number of volumes only 15 per cent. of duplicates shall be recorded. One hundred and fifty periodicals should be subscribed for, appropriate to academic needs. A training-school library should be separate from the general collection. The librarians should be considered members of the faculty. These requisites and many others are demonstrated in this book.

RURAL READING PROBLEMS

It is Lucile Fargo[13] who can vitalize library service into a snappy story. She embodies all the essentials of the rural reading problem in a short and spicy adventure of two county superintendents.

INTERLUDE TO REST YOUR MIND

There are several more books that you should know. I am loath to overstrain you. Rest here a minute.

A Chicago rogue, dismissed from his teaching position, enlisted in a hold-up syndicate. On account of his good voice he was appointed to give the commands to the victims. In his first exploit, helping to raid a north-side restaurant, he did the trick this way: "Class, all who are prepared with pocketbooks raise hands."

"SO WE ARE PROOVED BY OUR SPEECHES"

"The play's the thing," exclaims Hamlet. I imagine Mrs. Owen[14] saying, "No, the audience is." The whole of her sprightly book is an enlargement of the hypothesis that you, on the platform, are not setting out to show your learning, skill or talent. Neither conceit nor fawning, but straight, neighborly equality and friendly

[11] William Rose and twenty-two collaborators, ''An Outline of Modern Knowledge.'' G. P. Putnam's Sons, New York. 1,103 pp. $5.25.

[12] Committee, ''Library Standards in Teachers Colleges and Normal Schools.'' American Library Association, Chicago. 15 pp. 15 cents.

[13] Lucile C. Fargo, ''The Superintendent Makes a Discovery.'' American Library Association, Chicago. 32 pp. 10 for $1.00; 500 for $30.00.

[14] Ruth Bryan Owen, ''Elements of Public Speaking.'' Horace Liveright, New York. 200 pp. $2.00.

interest is the atmosphere of the successful speech—and of successful teaching too. "They are my friends. I love them," says of her audiences Schumann-Heink, the most beloved of prima donnas. "What is the key to platform magnetism" asks Mrs. Owen. It is in the old lyric epic:

> ''Why does the lamb love Mary so?''
> The eager children cry.
> ''Why, Mary loves the lamb, you know.''
> The teacher doth reply.

Springing out of and contributory to this sympathy and respect, Psychologist Owen develops in convincing detail the matter of preparation, dress, attitude, gesture, voice, personality and adaptation, illuminating her points by hundreds of examples of speakers ancient and modern. She stresses essentials by "class suggestions." She concludes the discourse with a collection of "important trifles" so apt but so often neglected that they are worth pasting in your hat.

At our National Education Associations you have been refreshed and edified by Ruth Owen's addresses so as to count her the born orator, inimitable. Wm. Lyon Phelps is reminded by her of the happy one in St. Matthew's gospel who was intrusted with five talents. Along came Ruth, inheriting from father and mother fluency and ease, a generous and winning personality, intense interest in political and social questions, amazing physical and mental vitality and a shrewd common sense. She has by ambition and perseverance doubled her inheritance. So says the gallant Yale professor. Your memory of her is of an American beauty, irresistibly gracious and interested.

If you could look like that you could make a speech without half trying. The book antidotes this idea. It cites abundant examples of eminent speakers whom nature had blessed with few promises. What they, what she, had to do is told so convincingly that, as you read, you begin to see yourself cutting out hindrances and acquiring ways of performing those duties of yours which depend upon your bringing companies of people to your point of view.

THE GRAMMAR BEAUTIFUL

To write a truly beautiful grammar flavored with enthusiasm calls for unusual talent, doesn't it? Two professors of the University of Maryland have done this.[15] This is the sentiment in which it is written. "Words and clauses we have tossed about for years. There are hidden glories in them to which our ears have been deaf and our eyes blind. Lo, he that seeketh findeth: and to him that knocketh it shall be opened."

Very handsomely printed, here is a book so carefully indexed it is facile for reference. But it has the remarkable quality of being good to read.

TRAVELING WITH THOMPSON

To carry you through Alaska, the Hawaiian Islands, the Philippines, Samoa and Guam, informing you how you happen to own these countries, what they are worth and how their peoples live, Earle Thompson, New Jersey schoolmaster, comes forward with a well-illustrated book,[16] designed as a geographical reader. He is an entertaining tourist. He sees the picturesque. He puts what we Americans ought to know so that we find we are glad to know it.

GANDHI SAYS HELL WILL BE TO PAY

MR. BRAILSFORD[17] gathers by a tour through India, economic, social and political conclusions. He relates why its people follow Gandhi, how the village defies the empire, notes social changes, personal forces, the reason for poverty and the political outlook. It costs the labor of one man forty days to get the wheat from one acre. He would gain nothing but unproductive leisure if he were given modern machines. But caste in all the strictness of its bondage could not survive the promiscuity of modern industrialism. In principle the battle of equality has been won. Yet the religious taboo on the taking of life, the unchecked ravages of monkeys, the maintenance of aged and defective cattle, the plague of rats, cost more than the military defense of the country. Part of the curse of their subjection is that the natives, once they set their minds toward freedom, ascribe every ill to the foreigners among them and either ignore

[15] Homer C. House, Susan Emolyn Harman, ''Descriptive English Grammar.'' Prentice-Hall, Inc., New York. 366 pp. $1.85.

[16] J. Earle Thompson, ''Our Pacific Posessions.'' Charles Scribner's Sons, New York. 264 pp. 90 cents.

[17] H. N. Brailsford, ''Rebel India.'' The New Republic, New York. 262 pp. $1.00.

the effect of their own institutions or even idealize them, because they are their own. To transform the inherited mind, the nation must be free and self-governing. No radical movement for the overthrow of these customs can gather momentum under the present system of government.

This Englishman's comments upon the brutality and stupidity of his country's rule of an alien people set you wondering at the unproductiveness of lessons in history. What did the thirteen colonies teach England of liberty that she used in Ireland or elsewhere? Or how sure are we of applying the lesson to our alien possessions?

ADMIRED EDUCATION

From Lord Macaulay to Dr. Cubberley, the knowing ones who have testified to the excellence of Scottish education have stimulated a healthy curiosity to know wherein its merit lies. The University of London issues an admirably told story of the school development of one Scottish shire, in many respects typical of the entire country.[18] As early as 1494, a law required those who were "of substance" to put their eldest sons to school, there to abide until "competently founded." How the Scottish parent was given to looking for education for immediate ends, how commercial studies were demanded in some towns and the classics in others, where families of wealth were many, how handwriting was everywhere prized, how modern languages encroached to the dismay of the masters, how unfit persons addled education with their "adventure" schools, how industrial schools long ago were started in old buildings, as was the usage in America until a few years ago, how the infant school sprung up and flourished and how the compulsory education of all children between the ages of five and thirteen became the law—these developments and many others, quaint or unexceptional, are told in this readable and entertaining history.

JUST IN TIME

Determination of salaries, remarks Professor Elsbree, in beginning his new book[19] is the plague of school boards and superintendent. Schedules won't stay put. They are a bone of perpetual contention, a potent preventive of the best teaching service.

You can't read very far into the Elsbree essay without finding that he has gone deeply into his subject and knows how to meet the proposals of the business man, the political economist, the equal-pay enthusiast and other types of arguers whose schemes have reduced the percentage of men teachers and put premiums upon early professional sleep after getting into the pedagogical lodging house.

Three conspicuous situations depress teachers' wages: oversupply, lack of strong professional spirit, overfeminization. Professor Elsbree's discussion of costs of living, basic standards, supply and demand, loss of men, influence of marriage, single-salary schedules, other types, increments, rating the teachers, are flavored by a cheerful scepticism regarding the schemes which have blossomed beautifully and furnished no measurements of fruitage. Having established effectively that you must watch your step the circumstantial author treats steps in making a salary schedule, estimating the cost, computing the community's ability and conducting the salary campaigns.

In my list of names I expect to ask St. Peter expressly to note as worth attention after me, I have Willard Elsbree near the top for the very timely service to my country rendered by this practical presentation of a fundamental basis of national prosperity.

HELP IN TIME OF DANGER

In another place I let loose some enthusiasm over the editorial work of the National Education Association in its annual volumes of proceedings. Within an hour the mail brought one of the workman-like bulletins, such as the association has been issuing lately. Are you not gratified by the publication service of your society? At from 25 cents each to $1.00, it has produced studies by the ablest researchers in the country and covering salaries, tenure, school reports and accounting, health, schoolhouse planning, to which is added the constructive yearbooks of the superintendents, the principals, the teachers and the researchers. The latest offer-

18 J. C. Jessop, "Education in Angus." University of London Press. 328 pp. $1.50.

19 Willard S. Elsbree, "Teachers Salaries." Bureau of Publications, Teachers College, New York. 286 pp. $2.50.

ing[20] is the report of Burdette Buckingham's committee and the findings of the National Education Association research division, aided by Commissioner Cooper's survey, all studying the question of over-production of poor teachers. Buckingham caution stiffens the bulletin throughout. Don't you let your school board go cutting salaries because so many persons are willing to take positions at much less money. Proved ability, not willingness to cut wages, is the main thing due the community in teacher supply. Training at public expense more teachers than can get places is an injustice to public and to would-be teachers as well. The number of states which have no statistical facts as a basis for adjusting supply to demand is a sign that the problem needs attention at once. Over-supply has driven valuable teachers into other work. Teacher shortage has opened the school door to the poorly trained. The children and the community suffer from failure to bring supply more even with demand. Research and adjustment are imperative. This report is composed remarkably well. It outlines the preparedness essential to ward off the growing criticism against wasteful mismanagement of public education. It gives educational executives distinct assistance in laying before their boards the details of a much needed reform.

HAPPINESS OF MEN

MAYBE teachers don't think about happiness more than other people do. They talk about it more. John Stuart Mill held that it is the prime end of education. Carlyle sneered at those who prate of being unhappy. Edison remarked that nobody attains felicity. Randolph Sailer[21] tries some of the modern methods of research to make a summary of what a large number of selected males think of their own good fortune. He had five hundred young men of Oakland, Buffalo, Washington, Boston, Philadelphia and other places fill his question blanks. The answers are not vitiated by a particular personal equation, for every man wrote his own diagnosis under cover of anonymity. "And," remarks Dr. Sailer, "the attitude of a man toward himself is one of the most important things about him."

How measures of happiness for reducing records to comparative scales are devised is set out in an interesting manner. In these young men a high worry score is not inconsistent with happiness. Perhaps you know school people who get a high degree of pleasure from worrying aloud. Possibly worriers are not unhappy, because of unloading the distress on others. Lincoln used to say that Chase was never so happy as when he was making everybody miserable. Dr. Sailer considers it notable that less than a quarter of the unhappy persons can attribute their state to poor health. But give the other three quarters of the downcast ones time enough and they'll evolve as fine an assortment of physical complaints as you could ask for. In this study the experimenter reaches no conclusion as to health and happiness. "Perhaps there is no direct relation between them at all, but merely a connection of each with some third factor such as adequate sex adjustment."

An abnormally high proportion of the married men fell within the most happy group.

Harboring dislike of working associates is an element in unhappiness. Dr. Sailer estimates that this tendency is due more to the nature of the disliker than to any other cause.

It reminds me of a group of crape-hangers we had among the teachers in one of the annexes of the Washington Irving High School. The district superintendent advised transferring them at the beginning of a new term to annexes in newer buildings. We separated them. The branch principals soon began reporting them as immune to sunshine, modern ventilation and up-to-date conveniences. They longed for the old barracks from which they came. At length the increase of pupils made necessary the creation of a new high school. Mr. Maxwell acted in accordance with a favorite plan. He transferred all the disconsolate to the new school before selecting a principal. Within six months the whole bevy of seek-sorrows sent a petition to the superintendent, asking him to dismiss the principal he had put over them. Mr. Maxwell,

[20] Wm. G. Carr, Margaret Alltucker Norton, Frank Hubbard, Richard Foster, Ivan Booker, "Teacher Demand and Supply." National Education Association, Washington, D. C. 102 pp. 25 cents.

[21] Randolph C. Sailer, "Happiness Self-Estimates of Young Men." Teachers College Press, New York. 116 pp. $1.75.

whose fondness for hearing teachers' objections to their principals was the subject of much comment, might have been helped by Dr. Sailer's estimate that workers' dislike of their supervisor springs more from their own attitude and disposition than from his. I have seen a capable woman principal fussed and fretted by continued insinuation of a mischief-maker that the teachers were unhappy. I knew a man of genial disposition whose school developed a nest of this sort who broke it up by assuming the punctilious courtesy and dignity of the dramatic stage. The bearers of sad tidings couldn't break through his reserve. The infection, not being able to spread to its objective, soon atrophied.

Charting the Spirits

Sailer's push of statistical methods into a matter about which most of us like to talk without being called to book is a new departure. Goodwin Watson, who had done something along this line with questionnaires for students put him up to it. The happiness tests will interest you. Are you sensitive to opinion of others? Do failures depress you? Do you tell jokes poorly? I read through the scores of these self-tests and can see that according to statistics I should be very unhappy. But I learned my tricks before the days of the researchers.

Ernest Fenelosa told us all at Pratt Institute that we needn't bother about happiness, but we should get rid of hatred and fear and their minor forms, dislike and worry. "How do you get rid of them?" some one in the audience asked. "Why," said Ernest, "you just get rid of them." Harvey Shepherd told me he divided his spirits into "very high," "high," "medium," "low" and "very low" and charted them every night. He found that he had thirty-seven occasions of low or very low spirits during the year, most of them due to dislike of his superintendent. When he made up his mind he wouldn't record any spirits as "low" nor as "very low," his range being from "medium" to "very high," the amount of high spirits he experienced increased, John Stuart Mill notwithstanding. When a man or woman is mature-minded enough to keep the negative emotions out of the brainpan and to conclude that happiness is not at all a necessity of living, then there's a grown-up attitude worth while.

When you sting beneath an unfair blow or one that seems such, don't, by thought or speech, condemn some one for destroying your happiness. Rather blame yourself for having a happiness that is destructible.

There comes to me the memory of a passage in Xenophon. We read it together in Ann Arbor, forty-eight years ago: "He is the best man who is always studying how to improve. He is the happiest who feels that he is improving."

Happiness, according to all the preachers I ever heard, is not from without.

To ask a teacher whether he is happy or not seems to me an insult to his intelligence. Nobody would have dared to ask Washington, Franklin or any of the authentic Americans whether they were happy or not. John Wesley recorded that so long as he blocked out his daily stint in the morning and didn't neglect to give it reasonable attention up to nightfall, he never had an unhappy moment.

Suppose we leave the subject with the remark of Elbert Hubbard: "A good way for an unhappy man to become more so is to think of how to make himself happy."

HAPPINESS AND OLD AGE

Two cheerful women philanthropists,[22] aided by interested social workers, make an intensive study of over two hundred men and women who came into the world at about the time I did. What proportion of them do you think are recorded as happy or even as content? One and one half per cent.! Their unhappiness is set down as having little to do with physical conditions. Well does happy author Martin, who is seventy-eight, say these people need to adopt the newer ideals. The book is full of valuable experience and sound advice. I, for one, am sorry that the best preservative of the life that satisfies is open only to limited numbers. It is the occupation of teaching. You might advise your friends who are not in the ranks to behave as nearly like a teacher as they can.

22 Lillien J. Martin and Clare DeGruchy, "Salvaging Old Age." The Macmillan Company, New York. 173 pp. $2.00.

SCHOOL AND SOCIETY

EDITED BY J. McKEEN CATTELL

WITH WHICH IS COMBINED THE

EDUCATIONAL REVIEW

EDITED BY WILLIAM McANDREW

Volume 35 SATURDAY, JANUARY 9, 1932 Number 889

TRAINING TEACHERS FOR CHARACTER EDUCATION

By Dr. HENRY NEUMANN

ETHICAL CULTURE SOCIETY, BROOKLYN, NEW YORK

In one sense there is no special technique required for the work of character training. Every possible interest which broadens the outlook of the teacher or in any other way contributes to the elevating of personality in him is that much to the good in his profession.

Hence there is much to be gained, in the first place, when teachers have a riper and richer knowledge of the subjects now taught than many at present possess. In view of the difficulties attending a regularly scheduled direct moral instruction, it may often be found better that teachers utilize for moral ends subjects which are already set down in the curriculum. Abundant moral values are there for those who have the eye to see them, in literature, geography, history, science. A deeper and more loving acquaintance with these subjects would make every teacher a better teacher of morals.

Consider why. Arnold Bennett tells a parable about a man who every day studied pages in a manual of carpentry but in whose home there were no tables, or shelves or closets—only orange boxes and a few rickety chairs. Visited one day by a friend, he was asked, "Why don't you put your manual to use and make some furniture?" He replied loftily, "I am a student." Mr. Bennett was thinking of the crying need to put into practical self-management what is told in the books on psychology. The parable hits just as truly the other subjects taught in classrooms. They can be put to better uses than merely getting promotion or a degree. Not that these uses must always be of the grosser kind. A study is useful if it fills a child's life with some enriching interest. It is most useful when such interests are worked over into high-grade ethical personality.

In many rooms it would assuredly make a great difference if this were kept in mind. Much teaching is utterly dead because the instructors themselves have no moving sense of what makes their efforts genuinely important. They need to feel "in their hearts" a better reason for teaching the given subjects than the mere fact that these happen to be set down in the school syllabus. A high and broad conception of the moral opportunities of the school will inspire the day's work with new life. Curriculum is Latin for chariot. It pays to keep asking just where the chariot is expected to take its riders. If the journey itself is a delight, we may more confidently expect that, as adults, our pupils will enjoy further trips in the art studies, in history, in science. If, in addition, the journey brings them to some deeper understanding of a life truth and to a better application in practise, all the better.

Instances of where the study of literature, for example, may be of high ethical value, lie on every hand. Children in comfortable homes will not be harmed by hearing occasionally "the still, sad music of humanity" recorded in such poems as Kingsley's "The Three Fishers," Untermeyer's "Caliban in the Coal Mines" or collections like Gibson's "Fires" or "Daily Bread." Their outlooks over life can be expanded when the teacher of "Ivanhoe" takes the one hundred per cent. scorn of old Cedric for everything Norman as the starting point of a discussion, "Are there people like that in America now?" Hamlin Garland's "Son of the Middle Border" and Ole Rolvaag's "Giants in the Earth" tell the story of pioneers in the trans-Mississippi territories and tell it beautifully. Attention may be called to the way in which both writers treat the special hardships endured by the women. The stories then become even more interesting; and surely it pays to be reminded of the part played in America's pioneer life by the mothers. Galsworthy's "Mob" and his "Loyalties" are excellent studies in moral courage and in the need to flood our group-attachments with light. His "Escape"—especially with its closing thought, "It's one's decent self one can't escape"—is a wise introduction to the problem of fundamental self-respect.

We need not multiply instances here. Every subject now taught offers abundant opportunities to enlighten moral judgments, quicken worthy appreciations, and feed healthy interests. Unfortunately many teachers are not particularly awake to the moral resources in literature, history, science. Their own acquaintance with these subjects is neither ripe nor loving enough.

Necessary, therefore, as the usual courses in methods are, still greater is the need for an ampler culture—as more and more normal schools are showing by becoming four-year colleges. While it is true that the teacher, as distinguished from the specialist, is expected to be interested mainly in the children rather than in the matter to be taught, teaching in these United States will move ahead faster when the teachers themselves are better educated persons. Many a lover of nature who has never taken a single course in pedagogy is able to arouse and to feed an interest which teachers better trained but less informed about nature (or possibly less enthusiastic) can not get. In general, teachers will mean more to their pupils and be able to offer more of the moral help there is in enriched life-interests, when their own reservoirs are fuller.

Ideally, it would also be expected that in view of the supreme importance of the ethical motive in education all teachers without exception be students of ethics. Though this subject as handled in some college courses is often very dry and academic, it can be made one of the most fruitful in the whole curriculum.[1] It can invite the student to share the reflections of the world's keenest intellects upon the fundamental problems of human life and destiny. It can help him to interpret his own problems in the light of whatever he finds helpful in these experiences of more mature minds.

All teachers likewise need courses on today's social problems. Character is shaped best in the attempt of people to remold their environment on nobler patterns. What social conditions interfere with the emergence of the best life in men, women and children? What challenges to the

[1] For recommendations on this head see chapter "Ethics," in P. Klapper's "College Teaching"; World Book Co., Yonkers, N. Y. See also chapter "History of Education," by H. H. Horne, in the same volume.

creative energies do these offer? Especially what place has the school among the other forces for reconstruction? How is it influenced by the children's housing, their parents' work-conditions, the political life of the community, immigration, race attitudes, the peace movement, to-day's changing family life? What can the school contribute toward the meeting of these problems? All teachers need to know far more than most know now about the burning social questions of our age. The chief obstacle, which progress here encounters, is not human badness, but indifference. Not enough people know the needs or care to know them. That is why many a good cause must struggle along on contributions of dimes and quarters, where other appeals, less deserving, get the big sums. Those who are teaching the builders of the future should be the first to feel the needs and get light upon them.

But teachers, like other folk, vary in their loves and interests. Some are more enthusiastic than others about the moral values to be striven for in their occupation. For these the training for work in character-building will include the broad education expected of the others and in addition certain special requirements.

They will study the present stage of man's ethical development in the light of its long and checkered past. They will know something of the history of moral practises and of the ethical philosophies that went with these. What light is thus shed on the ethical problems of to-day? Particularly when in many quarters the accent is now put upon change, and college students grow aware how often morality is only the peculiar custom of some one time and region, a thorough study of the problems raised by this fact can do much good. What is custom? What is conventional morality? What do we mean by right and wrong? Granted that morals change, what is there which stays and which deserves to stay? Or granted that human motives are a mixture of high, low and in-between, what has been done in the past to encourage the higher? What can still be done? What is the difference between change and progress? Apply these considerations to typical problems of personal and group conduct to-day.

Practice is essential. In view of the fact that the true teacher of ethics can not coerce but must lead, it is invaluable experience to lead a club where attendance is uncompelled. If it is good training for a public speaker to speak out-doors where auditors who lose interest move on freely, it is beneficial for teachers to have pupils who are perfectly free to walk out. Long ago educators saw that the use of the rod spoiled the teacher by exempting him from any need to improve his methods. Every teacher, and particularly the ones who specialize in character-training, should learn to handle classes or clubs where the only coercion is that exercised by the genuine interest of the members.

Of more than ordinary benefit is such work among groups where problems of maladjustment are acute. For instance, the usual problem of clash between child and parent is complicated where the parents are immigrants. What can be done to bring the older and the younger together? Or how can persons of varying religion, nationality, race, be harmonized? Or what can be done to set delinquents on the right paths? Work in clubs or settlements where these questions are foremost has its special importance for the teacher. Out of the successes, he learns in a new fashion how there is a moral power at work in people which raises some of them above the most unfriendly of outward circumstances. From the failures the teacher may be helped to grasp, without necessarily losing hope, something of the bigness of the problem. Why do people fail? What can a better social order do for such folk?

Why, for that matter, do people fail who do not live in slums? What light can the psychologist give us? The clinician?

There is ample work for teachers who want their profession to offer its best contribution. So high is the demand that teachers who are asked to direct clubs or to take Sunday classes will sometimes plead that for so serious a business they are quite unfitted. They are partly right. The more seriously we conceive the aim of character-education, the more we appreciate how little fit anybody is to promote it. In the strictest sense, nobody is fit to be a parent either. But partial fitness at any rate is learned by lifelong practise; and one step toward the learning is to appreciate how necessary it is. A whole world needs to be re-made for the better, to-day, to-morrow, in endless years ahead. The true teacher is the one who feels the need and wants to do his full share toward meeting it by means of his daily work and by every experience which will make that work more effective.

The supreme aim must be kept with all vividness before the minds of teachers no less than before the children's. What are we to make of the gifts, in all their endless variety and profusion, with which past and present have endowed us? Ordinarily we are not tempted, most of us, to commit the grosser outrages. More often we are tempted either to waste our lives in triviality or to live parasitically at the expense of those who do the good work of the world without adding our own. It makes all the difference what we keep foremost as the thing to be striven for. We can have our youth go through life with eyes open for every chance to grab what they can get and without a thought of whether, wittingly or not, they are hurting other lives or neglecting their share of the collective business. We can, on the other hand, have them go through life scorning to live on such terms. We can train them from their earliest years to know in their hearts that the best way to square their accounts with life honorably is to do their full share in promoting the march of mankind upward.

Plainly much depends on how genuinely all this is part of the living philosophy of their teachers. When we say that character-building should be the main objective in home, school, community, we mean much more than teaching little children to stop lying, or to "succeed" without hurting others. Certain superlatively worth-while creations are to grow in the garden of the human mind; a more ideal type of person is to inhabit this globe of ours; and teachers, parents, boys, girls, young and old, all together, are to give meaning to their lives in the effort to make these potential grandeurs actual. There is an ampler justice than people have yet done to one another, a richer, warmer charity, than the world has yet achieved. To become conscious of one's self as a being capable of a part in promoting this object is to become aware of what is most genuinely one's self. The best help we can give our youth to find themselves is to aid them to exercise that creative self-fulfilment which honors the selves most worth respecting in the others.

THE WORK OF BERTHOLD OTTO

By Dr. ADOLPH E. MEYER

NEW YORK UNIVERSITY

AT Lichterfelde, a suburb of bustling Berlin, there was founded in 1906 a school which eventually became known as the Berthold Otto Schule. This school, curiously enough, got its name through the efforts of both its friends and foes. The former baptized the new institution in honor of its founder, in whom they beheld a progressive educational reformer of the first magnitude. The school's opponents, on the other hand, named the school after its creator because they were determined to impress upon the world their conviction that the Lichterfelde Academy was simply the private venture of an eccentric pedagogue whose ideas at best were impractical. Since those early days the currents of pedagogy, as every one knows, have shifted considerably. Berthold Otto's school, starting existence in a precarious and uncertain way, gradually gained strength, until finally it has matured into one of Germany's well-known schools. Berthold Otto's work itself has taken on significance. True, it still sets off streams of corrosive criticism; yet without question it has earned for its inspirer a front place in the ranks of modern German educators.

Born in Silesia in 1859, Otto sprang from a family of land-owners. His father was a pastor who in the war of 1867, however, exchanged his sacerdotal robes for the more wordly uniform of a Silesian officer. Otto's parents were a cultured couple. Both took great pains to develop a questioning, critical attitude in their offspring. Berthold's father and mother, it seems, preferred to raise their children with love and understanding rather than with rattan and ironclad discipline. These happy, youthful days at the domestic fireside, I believe, are largely responsible for the important place that Otto assigns to the family as an educative force.

Like so many ambitious and intelligent German youths young Otto enrolled in a classical gymnasium. This was at Rendsburg. Here the boy attended classes until he reached the *untertertia.* Curiously enough, Otto was not particularly incandescent as a student. Endowed with a fairly active mind, and accustomed to do his own thinking, the boy naturally could not thrive in a school which specialized in memorization and drill. The classics in particular were converted into a horrendous nightmare for Otto. "The strong interest I originally manifested in Latin and Greek," he has since told us, "was tortured and almost destroyed, less by the teacher's ineptness than by the whole method of instruction."[1] The boy's health, moreover, wasn't any too good. Subject to nervous attacks, he was twice compelled to suspend his secondary schooling. Fortunately for the boy his family left Rendsburg, migrating in 1873 to Schleswig. Here young Berthold entered the celebrated Domschule. Compared with his former school, Otto's Schleswig school was a paradise where reason and not memory was in style. "I still well remember," writes Otto, "my Horace and Cicero periods, which encouraged my independent thinking . . . I believe that the name of Gidionsen will bring forth memories of the most beautiful hours of intellectual youthful enthusiasm to everyone who, like myself, was a member of the Schleswig *prima* during the seventies."[2] Another teacher to stimulate Otto at this time was Ostendorf, under whose direction the young student became privy to the works of Steinthal. Through Ostendorf, moreover, Otto also became familiar with the *Zeitschrift für Völkerpsychologie.* It was through the guidance of this gifted teacher that Otto's interests were steered into the channels of education.

In 1878 Otto matriculated at the University of Kiel. Here he came in contact with the philologian Lübbert under whose tutelage he began to specialize in the classics. But Lübbert lacked the necessary spark to set off Otto's enthusiasm. Instead of dealing with broad and fundamental matters in language, Lübbert con-

[1] "Volksorganisches Denken," No. 5, p. 54, 1917.

[2] "Schulreform im 20. Jahrhundert," 2nd edition, p. 19.

cerned himself with such hair-splitting questions as to whether this or that letter of the alphabet occupied such and such a position. Disgusted with the microscopic attention bestowed upon such academic trifles, Otto returned to his early loves in the domain of Hebrew, Arabic, Gothic and Old High German. It was in philosophy under Erdmann, however, that he finally found the open gates to original thinking.

After a year at Kiel Otto went to the University of Berlin. Here he continued his work in philology and philosophy, but he also plunged into the mysteries of economics, finance, politics, history and education. Privately, moreover, he undertook a detailed study of the Faustian literature, which even in those days had reached a vast magnitude. It was at Berlin that Otto came under the influence of Friedrich Paulsen.

> I remember no other course of lectures which influenced me nearly as strongly as those of Paulsen on education. The ideas that in instruction the main thing was not the subject but the child, that childhood was not merely a period of preparation, but that it possessed value of its own, and hence was not to be let carelessly to go to waste, made a great impression on me. In everything connected with educaiton, I do not believe I ever went a step beyond the limits sketched for us by Paulsen.[3]

Another Berlin professor who exerted considerable influence on Otto was the gifted Steinthal. He it was who kindled in Otto a scientific interest in the instructional process. He it was too who convinced his student of the value of child psychology in teaching. From Steinthal Otto also learned to recognize the value of child linguistics. This influence is clearly perceptible in Otto's pedagogics to-day in which he lays such tremendous stress on the importance of approaching the child on his own linguistic level.

While studying at Berlin Otto also undertook some private tutoring. His activity in this domain had in fact started while he was still in the secondary school. Oddly enough, Otto looked upon his charges as "hopeless dolts." The instruction which he gave in those days Otto has since characterized as "coercive instruction of the worst sort." Paulsen, who wanted Otto to concentrate on his own studies, advised his student against the addition of such extra burdens. But Otto, it appears, looked upon his teaching with an experimental eye. "Every hour I learned more than I taught," he has since said.

Otto left the halls of higher learning in 1883 without taking his degree. His career now becomes somewhat checkered. Thus for several years he earned his hire as a tutor. Then in 1889 he betook himself to Hamburg to accept a night editorship on a local journal which worked him hard and paid very little. After slightly more than a year at Hamburg he migrated to Leipzig to join the editorial staff of the well-known Brockhaus. During this time Otto was also personally teaching his four daughters. Upon this practise the Saxon school authorities looked with grave suspicion. Indeed, they even sent several warnings to Otto to make him cease his nefarious doings. But these official bulls, I regret to report, were without effect: Otto continued to refuse to send his girls to the public schools. Finally the school authorities, tiring of being forever flouted by this stubborn Silesian, got an order for his punishment. Otto, however, countered by appealing to the Saxon Ministry of Education, which, after long and judicious deliberation, decided in the end to side with the appellant. Much to the chagrin of the amazed pedagogues of Leipzig the triumphant Otto now received official permission from the Kingdom of Saxony to instruct his children himself and at home.

This battle with the Saxon obscurantists brought Otto to the crossroads of his ca-

[3] "Psychologie des Unterrichts," p. 113.

reer. If heretofore he had harbored any doubts as to which vocation his heart really belonged, it was now quite plain that his life work was to be in the field of teaching. It was during those stormy days, moreover, that he fashioned his incisive blast, "The School of Force and Punishment,"[4] in which he pounded a mighty tocsin of revolt against the traditional education as he saw it. From now on the tide of Otto's pedagogical activities was definitely on the rise. Particularly does fortune seem to caress him when Jentsch, a publisher, became interested in his work. It was Jentsch who, in 1898, launched the weekly *Deutsche Schulreform* and invited Otto to assume its editorial direction. The magazine aimed to investigate political and educational problems under the rays of psychology. Here at last was a splendid outlet for the vast reservoir of pedagogical ideas that had been rising in Otto's mind for the past two decades. Otto plunged into his editorial duties with vigor. Soon several significant educational articles emerged from his pen. In addition he wrote a number of small texts which were particularly commended by some critics for the simple and lucid way they succeeded in presenting the most profound subjects.

Even more important than his work with *Schulreform* was Otto's connection with the *Hauslehrer,* a magazine which came into being in 1901. This was a joint venture on the part of Otto and a Leipzig medico. It sought to stimulate parents to educate their children along the lines employed so successfully by Otto in the instruction of his own youngsters. The *Hauslehrer,* however, was intended not only for parents but for the children themselves. All sorts of topics bedizened its interesting pages—from the Faustian legend to self-instruction in Greek. Oddly enough the magazine drew salvos of applause from one of the least expected quarters, namely, from a group of secondary school teachers. Indeed, the head of a Magdeburg gymnasium shed considerable enthusiasm for Otto and his work. Eventually the Prussian Ministry of Education, under the direction of Dr. Althoff, became cognizant of Otto's efforts. The Prussians must have held these efforts in high esteem, for soon they offered Otto an annuity of 3,000 marks to transfer his activities to Berlin. The offer came in 1902, and, since no unusual strings were tied to it, Otto accepted.

Four years later, as I have said, Otto launched his school at Lichterfelde. This was more or less due to a growing need. The material which had been set down in the *Hauslehrer* had been based in the main on Otto's work with his own children. But since these were now rapidly growing up, Otto, as he said, "had to look for pupils with whom I could enter into the same intellectual relationships as with my children." The school was started in Otto's own home with an enrolment of seventeen children. In the fall of 1907, however, Otto's school was closed by the Prussian school authorities because it did not, as they thought, meet the official requirements. The Prussian ministry, however, after a thorough inspection of the Otto school and its master's methods, rescinded the order. After the war the Prussian government even began to subsidize Otto. By 1911 the school had grown so far beyond its original limits that it was moved into a new building, the money for which had been donated by one of Otto's admirers.

What now are the main pedagogical postulates of Berthold Otto? Fundamentally, he is opposed to what he has called the "coercion and standardization" of the old school. This he would replace by a school of "organic growth," which is to

[4] "Die Zwangs- und Strafschule," *Deutsche Schulreform,* 1899.

stimulate the development of the child's individual mind and spirit as well as his body. Education is not to be fashioned and imposed upon children from above by adults; education is rather to be *vom Kinde aus;* that is to say, it is to be child-centered. The relationship between teachers and pupils is to be patterned on the relationship existing between parents and children at home. Here of course Otto is holding the mirror up to his own home. By nature, Otto believes, children seek to adjust themselves to the world about them through their senses; their inquisitiveness leads them everywhere. Only when they reach difficulties which they can not solve for themselves do they turn to adults for help. This situation Otto would reproduce in school. Instruction, he feels, should be generated by the questions of pupils and the answers of their fellow-pupils and teachers. This is the basic idea underlying Otto's so-called *Gesamtunterricht,* a form of integrated group instruction.

This *Gesamtunterricht* is perhaps the chief feature of Berthold Otto's school. The entire school, composed of some fifty to sixty children, as well as the faculty, participates in it. This group meets in an assembly after school three or four times a week. For this purpose a large room has been reserved. When the weather is mild, the meeting is held out of doors. In the assembly-room there are no fixed benches. The children—boys and girls between the ages of six and seventeen—seat themselves around the walls, thus forming a large circle where everybody can see every one else. The teachers sit in the midst of the pupils. Here the schoolmasters are not guardians but comrades. Indeed, as one watches the youngsters happily seek their places, as one hears them toss friendly greetings to their fellow-pupils and teachers, one can hardly believe that this is a school. When the business of the assembly is finally launched the chairmanship is usually assumed by Otto. The children seem to have mastered the art of self-control. To get order no bells have to be rung; no orders snapped; no warnings issued. The children whisper and move if they feel so inclined—but never in a disturbing way. In a word, the youngsters have real liberty, and they use this like responsible men and women. The assembly begins with routine business of common interest. Thus, plans for a hike may be brought up and discussed. Once these matters are out of the way, one proceeds to the "order of the day." A pupil may now bring up any subject he wishes. This topic is discussed as long as it holds the interest of the group. These discussions usually are started by questions. Sometimes they get their beginnings from a composition presented orally by one of the group. In answering, the youngest pupils are given the right of way; then come the older children; and finally the teachers are allowed their say. Just as in Otto's *Hauslehrer* a vast array of topics is discussed in the long run. A glance at the minutes of these meetings reveals such items: the speed of airplanes; explosions; wireless telegraphy; language; sound; alcohol; nicotine; revenge; talking pictures; orthography; lies; Russian log cabins; and so on. In the average assembly from three to four topics are usually considered. A careful analysis of the topics discussed during the school years shows that not only all the so-called "subjects" come up for discussion, but also a great many other significant matters which usually are not considered in the average class.

Pupils at Lichterfelde are divided into four groups—beginners, elementary, intermediate and advanced. Each of these groups has *Gesamtunterricht* of its own, the advanced group getting about two hours a week and the other groups much more. Instruction, interestingly enough, is given in any subject that the children may want. Theoretically, if sufficient children craved a knowledge of Chinese, such instruction would be given. Some of the most popular subjects, marvelous to say, are mathematics and the classics. In all this instruction formalism is reduced to a minimum. Free discussion, individualization and learning by doing are the desiderata, though in the domain of self-activity Otto varies considerably from the orthodox.

Berthold Otto's school has also bestowed considerable attention on the development of the so-called pupils' court. This court, be it noted, is not a faculty creation. Developing out of a natural need, it started with Otto's refusal to interfere in the disputes of his pupils. With their teachers on the sidelines, the pupils naturally took the settlement of such matters into their own hands. At the outset, as might be expected, right usually went to might. Gradually, however, the youngsters themselves became dissatisfied with this primitive way of settling things. They agreed to select an arbiter to settle their disputes. He was to have a corps of assistants. The next step was to make laws. Then, obviously, came the task of enforcing these laws. As time slipped by, the pupils evolved a form of court trial. In some ways this imitated adult procedures; in others it blazed its own way. To-day this form of self-government has reached such heights of efficiency that Berthold Otto is able to entrust all matters of school discipline to the pupils' court. Its success is due, I feel, in a large way to the fact that it is really run by the students themselves. The teachers really resist the temptation to play a leading part.

Berthold Otto, being a pioneer, has often tramped the hard and lonely road. The army of his opponents, of critics and scoffers, being mainly of the conventional herd, has always been vast. Indeed, opposition to Otto's fundamental ideas and practice still is large. Yet ever since the birth of democratic Germany, the work of Otto has drawn more and more devotees. In the main Otto's dream of the *Zukunftsschule* is still only a dream; but some of its main aspects have become reality. Certainly with the rise of progressive education in Germany, Otto's ideas may be expected to attract more and more followers.

EDUCATIONAL EVENTS

THE OATH OF ALLEGIANCE TO FASCISM IN ITALIAN UNIVERSITIES

THE correspondent at Rome of the London *Times* reports that the announcement that 12 university professors out of 1,225 have refused to swear the oath of allegiance to Fascism has been corrected by a further *communiqué,* which gives the number as 11. Professor Orlando, the former prime minister, is absent. He had already handed in his resignation, which therefore can not be regarded as a consequence of a refusal to accept the oath. The list of those professors who have resigned is as follows: Bartolo Nigrisoli, of the University of Bologna; Giorgio Errera, of the University of Pavia; Ernesto Bonaiuti, Gaetano de Sanctis, Giorgio Levi Della Vida, and Vito Volterra, of the University of Rome; Mario Carrara, Francesco Ruffini and Lionello Venturi, of the University of Turin; Piero Martinetti, of the University of Milan; Edouardo Ruffini, of the University of Perugia.

Perhaps the best known name is that of Professor Volterra, who holds the chair of physical mathematics at the University of Rome. Another important name is that of Professor Bonaiuti, who is a professor of history of Christianity and a former priest of the Roman Catholic Church. Professor Francesco Ruffini, a former minister of education and professor of law at Turin University, has been one of the most outspoken critics of the Fascist Government in the Senate.

The oath which the professors are required to take reads: "I swear to be faithful to the king and his royal successors and to the Fascist régime; to observe loyally the statute and the other laws of the state; to exercise the teaching function and to fulfil all academic duties with the purpose of forming citizens active, bold and devoted to the fatherland and to the Fascist régime. I swear that I do not belong and will never belong to any association or party the activities of which are not in harmony with the duties of my office."

A group of leading Harvard professors, headed by Dr. Roscoe Pound, dean of the Harvard Law School, has requested the Institute of Intellectual Cooperation of the League of Nations to consider ways and means by which Italian university professors may escape the obligation to take the oath of allegiance to the Fascist régime. Committees of professors have been formed in France, Switzerland, Spain, Germany and England to devise means of helping their Italian colleagues.

The letter written by the Harvard professors reads:

> We, professors and members of the various faculties of Harvard University in Cambridge, Massachusetts, United States of America, take the liberty of bringing to the attention of the Institute of Intellectual Cooperation the Royal Decree of the Italian Government of August 28, 1931, No. 1227.
>
> This decree imposes upon all university professors of the Kingdom of Italy—and among all state officials of the Department of Education it is applicable to university professors alone—the obligation to take an oath which implies complete adherence without reservation or discussion to a particular system of political ideas.
>
> Since political doctrines no less than all others should be the subject of discussion and revision, it seems to us that this oath involves an intellectual coercion which is incompatible with the ideals of scholars. As such, we feel that the Institute of Intellectual Cooperation among Nations can not ignore it. In no other way can the peoples of the world better promote intellectual cooperation than by extending mutual assistance to each other to secure to all scholars those conditions of freedom under which disinterested search for truth alone becomes possible.
>
> We, therefore, request the Institute of Intellectual Cooperation to consider ways and means by which the Italian university professors may best be helped to defend their intellectual liberty.

CIRCULATING COUNTY LIBRARIES IN CANADA

The Christian Science Monitor reports that circulating public libraries have been established in 13 of the 18 counties of Nova Scotia within three years and that the Department of Education expects to have one in each county before next September.

There is great demand for these libraries, and the number of books read by all classes of the communities is already large. Some books were worn out by constant use in less than a year.

These libraries, each containing from 1,200 to 3,000 books, are intended to supplement the school libraries. The department is naturally pleased with the reception of the books; it expects them to have a wide-spread effect on the reading habits and on the general standard of information.

The American Library Association in 1926 pointed out that 93 per cent. of the rural population of Canada was without access to public libraries. At that time there was one circulating library in Cape Breton County, established by the Sydney Rotary Club through the efforts of Dr. W. A. Creelman, inspector of schools. Three years ago a similar library for Halifax County was endowed by Mr. W. A. Black. Last year the Department of Education put five more into circulation, and this year six are being organized.

The libraries are packed in boxes, each containing 25 books. Each box has a carefully selected cross-section of the whole library, divided approximately as follows: 10 juveniles, 7 fiction and belles-lettres, 2 poetry, 2 history, 1 science, 1 art, 1 travel, 1 biography. The inspectors of schools take charge of the libraries and the teachers act as librarians. In June the boxes are collected and stored at the county seat.

Nova Scotia has thus made progress since 1926 toward supplying the people of the rural districts with an adequate library service. Acadia University three years ago sent out "bookmobiles," trucks fitted up as libraries.

THE WORLD CONGRESS ON RECREATION

THE first world congress on recreation will be held in Los Angeles from July 23 to 29, just prior to the Olympic games. The congress will be held under the auspices of the National Recreation Association.

President Hoover has accepted the honorary presidency of the congress and the State Department of the Federal Government has issued invitations to the diplomatic offices of the various countries. In England the Right Honorable Earl of Derby is serving as a member of the International Advisory Committee. The National Playing Fields Association, of which he is chairman, has named Sir Henry Bowden, Bart., and Noel Curtis-Bennett, C.V.O., as its delegates. This association is also announcing the congress among many societies in England.

In Denmark a committee, of which General H. Castensciold is chairman, is promoting interest in the congress. Colonel H. P. Langkilde, director of physical education in the Copenhagen public schools, is a member of the international committee. The Pan-American Union is actively cooperating in arousing interest in the gathering in Mexico, South and Central America.

Mr. Albert Thomas of France, director of the International Labor Office at Geneva; Dr. Theodore Lewald, chairman of the German National Committee for Physical Training; Count de Baillet Latour, of Belgium, chairman of the International Olympic Committee; Captain G. Van Rossem, Holland; Dr. Ricardo C. Aldao, Argentina; Dr. Alice G. Masarykova, head of the Czecho-Slovakian Red Cross; Mr. Lauri Pihkala, president of the Intercollegiate Amateur Athletic Association of Finland, and Miss Wanda Prazmowska, of the Women's Division of the Polish Government Board of Physical Education, are the other members of the International Advisory Committee. Delegates from twenty-two countries have already been designated.

The objectives of the congress are: (1) To provide an international exchange of information and experience on play, recreation and the recreational use of leisure; (2) to build interest and support for the movements in all countries; (3) to provide one further means of developing international good will.

Discussions will be held on topics of facilities and activities such as parks, playgrounds, community recreation buildings, games, athletics, music, drama, arts and crafts, camping, hiking and other leisure time activities organized and developed upon a community basis. Both rural and urban activities are to be considered.

The announcement of the congress committee points out that: "Recreation is an important human problem because it makes a definite contribution to education, character development, happiness, health, safety and citizenship. Recreation is of growing importance because it offers one means of using wisely the increasing leisure which science and invention are making possible for mankind."

A limited amount of space will be available for educational exhibits for which there will be no charge. There will also be commercial exhibits. A special tour *en route* to Los Angeles with stop-overs in a number of cities is being planned. Admission to the congress is open to any one.

All correspondence should be addressed to Mr. T. E. Rivers, administrative secretary, International Recreation Congress, 315 Fourth Avenue, New York City.

HANDICAPPED CHILDREN

THE study of facilities for the special training of handicapped children made by the White House Conference on Child Health and Protection has recently issued a volume on "Special Education." This is one of the studies conducted under the chairmanship of Dr. F. J. Kelly, of the U. S. Office of Education, who headed Section III on Education and Training, and represents the investigation of the subcommittee dealing with special classes under the immediate chairmanship of Dr. Charles Scott Berry, of the Ohio State University.

According to the official summary of this bulletin, the 10,000,000 or more handicapped children in the United States include: 14,400 blind children under 10 years of age; 50,000 partially seeing children; 3,000,000 with hearing impaired in various degrees; 1,000,000 school children between the ages of 5 and 18 who are defective in speech; 300,000 who are crippled, of whom 100,000 need special education; 382,000 children who are tuberculous; 1,000,000 who have weak or damaged hearts; 675,000 who present behavior problems, and 450,000 children in the elementary grades who are so retarded mentally that they require special education.

From its investigations the conference finds that there is a surprisingly large number of handicapped children who need special education, and a comparatively small number are receiving it. For example, of the 50,000 partially seeing children enrolled in schools, but 5,000 are enrolled in special classes; of the 1,000,000 children suffering from defective speech, but 60,000 are at present receiving the proper corrective training and remedial treatment. It was also found that adequate vocational guidance and training along with placement and follow-up work are seldom found in connection with the special classes of the public schools.

While much is being done in special classes to remove the handicap or reduce it, little is being done to discover and develop special aptitudes. A marked variation in the laws of the different states relative to the organization and support of special classes exists. There are many cities in the United States with population in excess of 10,000 in which no provision is made for special education of any type. The majority of principals of elementary schools have little interest in the handicapped child. No large city in the United States is providing special education for all its handicapped children.

Cities differ in a remarkable degree in the annual *per capita* cost of special education for the same type of handicapped child. For the blind costs range from $120 *per capita* to $590; for the deaf, from $204 to $517; for the child of lowered vitality, from $100 to $305; for the mentally retarded, from $83 to $454; for the delinquent, from $162 to $741, and for the crippled, from $187 to $593.

As a special recommendation, the conference calls for the organization of a National Council for Handicapped Children consisting of representatives of appropriate groups. Also the immediate creation in each state of a State Advisory Council for Handicapped Children is recommended to cooperate with the National Council and with the White House Conferences, both state and national.

EXPENDITURES OF AMERICAN COLLEGES AND UNIVERSITIES

AMERICAN colleges and universities are now spending more than $500,000,000 annually for the advancement of learning, according to a statement made to a representative of the *U. S. Daily* by Dr. E. M. Foster, chief of the Division of Statistics at the Office of Education.

For the first time, the Office of Education has compiled a relatively complete table of expenditures, public and private, for all colleges and universities throughout the United States.

H. G. Badger, statistician in the Office of Education, has just compiled a tabulation of expenditures which shows that publicly controlled institutions of the college grade spent in 1930 $225,816,040 compared with $337,731,030 spent by privately controlled ones. For higher education, a grand total of $563,547,070 was expended in 1930.

The outlay is divided into eight or nine groups, with the highest single item covering the cost of instruction. This amounted to $191,066,825. Publicly controlled institutions spent for this item more than $81,700,000 while privately controlled ones spent nearly $110,000,000. For organized research the public institutions spent over $13,500,000 and the private institutions nearly $4,500,000.

A total amount of $93,674,726 was laid aside by the institutions for new buildings and grounds, over $27,100,000 by the public and over $66,500,000 by the private institutions. These colleges at the same time bought new equipment to the amount of approximately $16,000,000. A total of $46,000,000 was spent on the physical operation and maintenance of the physical plants.

The smallest single item set aside by the colleges was for libraries. Of the entire amount spent by them, only $9,600,000 went for libraries. For this the public libraries spent $3,200,000 and private libraries $6,300,000.

California led all states in its public outlay for higher education. Publicly controlled institutions there spent a total amount of $18,807,000. Michigan was next with $15,551,000, and Ohio third with $14,518,000. Minnesota spent $11,337,000 and Iowa $9,639,000. In Illinois the amount for publicly controlled institutions ranged next with $8,500,000, in Indiana it was $8,200,000, and in Virginia, $7,000,000.

Privately controlled institutions made the greatest expenditures in six states. Those in New York led the list with an outlay of $68,-

600,000. Those in Massachusetts followed with expenditures amounting to $42,800,000. Private colleges and universities of Pennsylvania spent $39,800,000, those of Illinois, $29,700,000 and those of Connecticut, $17,800,000. California ranked sixth among the leading privately controlled institutions in expenditures with an outlay of more than $14,800,000.

THE MASTER OF SCIENCE DEGREE AT THE MEDICAL SCHOOL OF COLUMBIA UNIVERSITY

THE University Council of Columbia University has adopted the degree of master of science for postgraduate students in the Medical School. Dean Willard C. Rappleye characterizes the step as "having important significance of a public character." He says:

The university has adopted a standard of training in each of the clinical specialties, successful completion of which will carry the degree of master of science. The university, however, will not grant recognition for postgraduate training for less than that which will qualify the man as competent in the specialty concerned.

The time will come in this country, as it has in others, when the public and the profession will demand that only those who are properly trained to do major surgery, for example, will be permitted to do so. At the present time large numbers of doctors are doing surgery who are quite incompetent and untrained.

It is possible now for a physician to come to New York or to go to another medical center and watch operations and attend clinics for a period of a few months and return to his own community as a self-labeled specialist with complete freedom to practice a surgical or any other specialty. The action taken by Columbia University is in the direction of helping to correct this situation.

The requirements for the degree are:

A period of study, after the internship, of not less than three years in the university or in hospitals and laboratories recognized by it, at least one calendar year of which must be spent in the university.

Such intensive graduate training in the basic medical sciences of anatomy, embryology, physiology, biochemistry, pharmacology, pathology, bacteriology and in the other fields of science as shall be recommended by the departments concerned and approved by the administrative board on postgraduate studies in medicine.

An active experience during the three-year period of not less than eighteen months in the hospital, clinics and diagnostic laboratories of the specialty elected.

Written, oral and practical examinations and a dissertation may be prescribed in the specialty elected and in clinical, laboratory and public health fields to which the specialty is related.

Students admitted to the university for this training may become candidates for the degree of doctor of philosophy if they meet the prescribed requirements for that degree.

BROADCASTING CLASSICAL MUSIC TO THE SCHOOLS

THE Board of Education of St. Louis, Missouri, has adopted unanimously a vote of thanks to the St. Louis Symphony Orchestra, to the National Broadcasting Company and especially to Mr. Walter Damrosch, for his work in connection with the NBC Music Appreciation Hour broadcast each Friday for the special benefit of school children. The resolution follows:

The broadcasting of programs of classical music is bringing to an increasing number of persons, both adults and juveniles, the educational benefits and pleasures that are derived from them by attentive listeners.

Such programs as those given by the St. Louis Symphony Orchestra on Sundays, and, particularly, the programs given on school days by the national orchestra conducted by Walter Damrosch, contribute much to the development of higher standards of music appreciation in children. The world's best music is carried into the homes and also into the schools; the children are given an opportunity, made use of in a number of our schools, by hearing this music to become familiar with the leading masterpieces.

Furthermore, the interpretations which the noted orchestra leader, Walter Damrosch, is broadcasting regularly in explanation of the music broadcast under his direction, tend greatly to increase the community's and the children's knowledge of the constituent elements of the compositions and also of the conditions which inspired the composers to produce them.

Be it Resolved, therefore, that the Board of Education of the City of St. Louis, recognizing the educational advantages that broadcasting has introduced into the schools, commend this activity and express to the St. Louis Symphony Orchestra and the National Broadcasting Company Orchestra, and especially Walter Damrosch, its appreciation of the aid they are giving to the schools in elevating the musical standards of the children.

Dr. Damrosch wrote in appreciation to Mr. Charles A. Roe, secretary and treasurer of the board, as follows:

Needless to say, I am immensely touched and deeply honored to receive a copy of the resolution adopted by the Board of Education of your great city of St. Louis. What a privilege for me at a time of life when I feared that I could not do much more than repeat what I had done in the previous forty years, to have, thanks to the radio, such a marvelous new field of endeavor opened up to me.

During those many years when I tried to instill a love for music in the young people of New York, limited by the capacity of Carnegie Hall, I had dimly hoped that some plan might evolve by which I could continue this work on a larger scale, reaching especially the children who were not located near one of our few great cultural centers.

The magic of the radio has permitted me to do this, and our audience of one and one half million of three years ago has grown, like the bean-stalk of the famous fable, to gigantic proportions—over six millions. From the thousands of approving letters received from educators, as well as from the children themselves, I feel that not only have we succeeded in awakening a love for music among the children, but have induced them to take up the study of music for self-expression, both instrumentally and vocally.

All this would have been impossible without the hearty and understanding cooperation of the officials of the National Broadcasting Company, and the supervisors and teachers of music in the many thousands of schools that are now listening in to our concerts.

For me, for Mr. John W. Elwood, vice-president of the National Broadcasting Company, and for my assistant, Mr. Ernest La Prade, as well as for the members of the National Orchestra, this has been truly a labor of love.

Please present my humble and heartfelt thanks to the members of your board for their very encouraging message.

THE NEW LECTURE SERIES OF THE ADVISORY COUNCIL ON RADIO IN EDUCATION

FORTY authorities on economics, psychology and related fields will speak over a National Broadcasting Company network in its weekly coast-to-coast educational feature for the spring term of 1932. The series will continue twenty weeks, closing the last week in May.

The speakers will be presented by the National Advisory Council on Radio in Education as a continuation of its "Listen and Learn" lecture series inaugurated last fall. An economist and psychologist will speak for fifteen minutes each every Saturday over an NBC–WEAF network at 8:30 P. M., E. S. T.

Dr. Robert M. Hutchins, president of the University of Chicago, inaugurated the series on January 2 when he and representatives of the council outlined the courses.

The lectures on psychology are divided into four groups of five lectures each covering "Our Changing Personalities," "Animal Behavior," "Psychology of Education," and "Psychology and Industry." The lectures are given by well-known leaders in psychology, those in the Psychology of Education being as follows:

March 19—"The Psychology of Reading": Dr. Charles H. Judd, professor of psychology, University of Chicago.

March 26—"Difficulties in Learning": Dr. Walter F. Dearborn, professor of education, Harvard University.

April 2—"The Bases of Learning": Dr. Frank N. Freeman, professor of psychology, University of Chicago.

April 9—"Psychology of Musical Skills": Dr. Carl E. Seashore, professor of psychology, University of Iowa.

April 16—"Individual Differences: Their Measurement and Significance": Dr. V. A. C. Henmon, professor of psychology, University of Wisconsin.

EDUCATIONAL NOTES AND NEWS

DR. JOHN J. ABEL, professor of pharmacology at the Johns Hopkins University, was elected president of the American Association for the Advancement of Science at the meeting held last week in New Orleans. Dr. S. A. Courtis, professor of education at the University of Michigan, was elected vice-president of the section of education; Dr. Walter S. Hunter, professor of psychology at Clark University, for the section of psychology, and Dr. William F. Ogburn, professor of sociology at the University of Chicago, for the section of social and economic sciences. At the joint meeting of the sections of education and psychology, Professor Leonard V. Koos, of the University of Chicago, and Professor Edwin G. Boring, of Harvard University, gave the addresses of the retiring vice-presidents for education and psychology.

MR. HARRY MILLER LYDENBERG, assistant director of the New York Public Library, has been officially nominated for the presidency of the American Library Association for 1932–33.

PROFESSOR HERBERT E. BOLTON, of the University of California, was elected president of the American Historical Association at the recent meeting in Minneapolis. He succeeds Professor Carl Becker, of Cornell University. Dr. Charles A. Beard, of New Milford, Connecticut, was elected first vice-president, and Professor William E. Dodd, of the University of Chicago, second vice-president.

PROFESSOR E. G. SPAULDING, of Princeton University, was elected president of the eastern division of the American Philosophical Association at a banquet concluding its recent two-day convention at New Haven. He succeeds Professor A. N. Whitehead, of Harvard University. Others elected were Mrs. Grace A. Delaguna, Bryn Mawr, *vice-president;* Professor F. S. C. Northrop, Yale, reelected *secretary-treasurer;* H. B. Smith, University of Pennsylvania, and H. T. Costello, Trinity, *members of the executive committee.*

DR. WILLIAM WARREN SWEET, professor of American Christianity at the University of Chicago, was elected president of the American Society of Church History at its annual meeting at the Union Theological Seminary. Other officers were chosen as follows: Conrad Henry Moehlman, professor of church history at the Colgate-Rochester Divinity School, *vice-president;* Frederick William Loetscher, *secretary;* Robert Hastings Nichols, *treasurer,* and Matthew Sinka, *assistant secretary.*

AT the Minneapolis meeting of the American Association of Schools and Departments of Journalism, Professor Frederick J. Lazelle, of the Iowa State University, was elected president, succeeding Professor Ralph D. Casey, head of the Department of Journalism at the University of Minnesota. Dr. Vernon J. McKenzie, of the University of Washington, was chosen vice-president. H. H. Herbert, of the University of Oklahoma, was reelected secretary-treasurer. The next convention will be held at Washington and Lee University, Lexington, Virginia.

MISS JESSIE M. PANGBURN, head of the department of education at the Spearfish Normal School, has been elected president for 1932 of the South Dakota Education Association. Miss Pangburn has been recording secretary of the association since 1924.

MR. GEORGE T. MILLER, head of the art department of the State Teachers College at Slippery Rock, Pennsylvania, was elected president of the Southwestern Arts Association at its recent meeting in the Fine Arts Department of Carnegie Institute, Pittsburgh.

HECTOR L. BELISLE, superintendent of schools at Fall River, Massachusetts, has been elected president of the New England Superintendents' Association.

MR. FRANCIS KELLY NEMECK, graduate of the University of Arizona, was elected on December 31 president of the National Student Federation of America in the closing business session of a four-day congress at Toledo. An invitation from Tulane University, New Orleans, for the 1932 congress was accepted.

THE *Journal* of the National Education Association states that as it is going to press with its January issue word is received that United States Commissioner of Education, Dr. William John Cooper, and Superintendent Robinson G. Jones, of Cleveland, are recovering in health. They are at their offices a part of each day.

MR. JAMES H. RICHMOND, of Louisville, Kentucky, became State Superintendent of Public Instruction on January 4, succeeding Mr. W. C. Bell.

DR. DAVID HARRISON STEVENS, director of the Division of Education of the General Education Board, has been appointed director of work in the humanities of the Rockefeller Foundation. Dr. Stevens assumed his new duties on January 1. This is one of the five fields in which the foundation is interested, the other four being public health and the medical, social and natural sciences.

DR. AUGUSTUS O. THOMAS, president of the World Federation of Education Associations since its organization in 1923 to the present year, has now accepted the position of secretary-general with headquarters in Washington, D. C.

MISS ISABELLA ROSE, supervisor of probationary teachers in Fife County, Scotland, has been appointed supervisor and special consultant of the Child Education Foundation, New York City.

THE REV. LOUIS J. GALLAGHER has been appointed president of Boston College as successor to the Reverend James H. Dolan, who has been transferred to Georgetown University on leave of absence.

THE REV. VAUGHAN DABNEY was installed as dean of Andover-Newton Theological School on January 7. The Rev. Frederick H. Page, president of the trustees, presided, and President Beavan, of the Colgate-Rochester Divinity School, gave the main address.

MR. E. R. HAMILTON, lecturer in education at the University College of North Wales, has been appointed principal of the Borough-road Training College, Isleworth.

DR. NORMAN WALLACE FRADD, instructor in physical education at Harvard University, has been promoted to be assistant director of physical education for three years from September 1, 1931.

MR. GEORGE SIMPSON KOYL, of New York City, has been elected professor of architecture and dean of the School of Fine Arts of the University of Pennsylvania. Mr. Koyl, who will begin his work at Pennsylvania in July, will succeed Dr. Warren Powers Laird.

MISS GRACE DOUGHTY, co-director of the summer nursery group at Clark Neighborhood House, New York City, has become director and instructor of the nursery school in the Alabama Institute of Technology at Auburn.

MR. JOHN F. MEENAN, who recently resigned as football coach at New York University, has been appointed director of physical education and football coach at Manhattan College.

M. M. WALTER, associate professor of industrial education at the Pennsylvania State College, has been appointed director of the Bureau of Rehabilitation of the Pennsylvania State Department of Labor and Industry, Harrisburg. As director of this bureau, Mr. Walter will have charge of civilian rehabilitation as carried out in accordance with the state plan for rehabilitation and the Federal Act of 1920.

MR. WILLIAM S. DAUGHERTY, president of the Board of Education of Indiana, Pennsylvania, resigned on November 12. In 1883 Mr. Daugherty was first elected to the board and he served continuously, except for part of one term, until he resigned. During these forty-eight years he acted as president for forty-six years.

PROFESSOR ELLIS PERSING, of the Cleveland School of Education, has leave of absence which he is spending as assistant in natural science at Teachers College, Columbia University.

PROFESSOR ROBERT N. BROOKS, head of the department of church history at Gammon Theological Seminary, has been awarded a fellowship from one of the foundations which makes possible for him a year of study at the University of Oxford. He will specialize in the European backgrounds of American church history and will travel on the continent during his vacation periods.

PRESIDENT JOHN A. COUSENS, of Tufts College, who has had six months' leave of absence, reached the United States on December 20 after a trip abroad.

PRESIDENT DAVID A. ROBERTSON, of Goucher College, has been elected a member of the Senate of Phi Beta Kappa to succeed the late Senator Dwight Morrow. At the meeting of the Senate of Phi Beta Kappa in New York on December 16 when this action was taken, President Robertson was made a member of the new Phi Beta Kappa committee charged with studying the standards of colleges in which chapters of Phi Beta Kappa will be established. Other members of this committee are President Frank Aydelotte, of Swarthmore College; Dr. Henry Suzzallo, president of the Carnegie Foundation; Dean Theodore H. Jack, of Emory University; Professor Adam Leroy Jones, of Columbia University, and Dean Guy Stanton Ford, of the

University of Minnesota. The membership of the Senate of Phi Beta Kappa includes among others Dr. James Rowland Angell, Dr. John William Davis, Dr. John Huston Finley, Dr. Frank Pierrepont Graves, Dr. John Grier Hibben, Dr. Robert A. Millikan, Dr. Albert Shaw, Dr. Henry Suzzallo and Mr. Owen D. Young.

DR. JOHN HOLLADAY LATANÉ died suddenly at New Orleans at the age of sixty-two years. Dr. Latané had been a member of the faculty of the Johns Hopkins University since 1913, serving as professor of American history and head of the history department until a year ago, when be became a member of the Walter Hines Page School of International Relations at the university. He was dean of the College of Arts and Sciences Faculty from 1919 until 1924. Dr. Latané had been on the West coast delivering a series of lectures at the University of Southern California, and on his way back to Baltimore with Mrs. Latané had stopped at New Orleans to attend the annual meeting of the American Association for the Advancement of Science.

THE REVEREND DR. J. KNOX MONTGOMERY, president of Muskingum College, New Concord, Ohio, since 1904, died on December 30. He was seventy-one years old.

PETER CHRISTIAN LUTKIN, dean emeritus of the Northwestern University School of Music and founder of the North Shore Music Festival, died on December 27 at the age of seventy-three years.

BY the will of the late Elmer A. Darling, Lyndon Institute, Lyndon Center, Vermont, will receive $100,000; St. Johnsbury Academy and Brightlook Hospital, both at St. Johnsbury, will each receive $10,000. The University of Vermont, the Bennington College for Girls and Middlebury College, each receive $5,000.

WESLEYAN UNIVERSITY has received a check for $150,000 from the Carnegie Corporation for the endowment of the Wesleyan University librarianship. The Carnegie Corporation has made grants to Wesleyan at various times in the past; in 1920, $75,000 was donated to the library. It is understood that this is one of three college librarianships for which the corporation has given similar endowments.

ACCORDING to a United Press despatch, Chicago, which owes $20,000,000 in back pay to its 14,000 teachers, has announced it will hold school by radio if its appeal to the State Legislature, reconvening at Springfield, fails to provide money to keep its schoolhouses open. Schools of three suburbs closed on January 4 and nine night schools remained dark. Mayor Anton Cermak in addressing 30,000 teachers, pupils and parents at the huge sports arena held out no hopes for immediate relief. If the legislature acts too late, 500,000 pupils would be without schools, so plans for radio instruction were made. For families without radios neighborhood groups would be formed.

AT Akron, Ohio, the public schools did not reopen after the Christmas holidays. The 54,000 pupils have an enforced two weeks' vacation which may be extended, unless the board of education can borrow $350,000 a month. The 1,500 teachers and general office and staff employees will receive no pay for the compulsory "vacation," Superintendent Thomas W. Gosling is reported to have said. "But we are most anxious not to duplicate the Chicago situation. We must live within our income and I see no other way to do it."

THE daily papers reported in December that one third of the schools of Tennessee would not be able to continue their term after the Christmas holidays.

FIRE destroyed the main block of buildings of the university at Johannesburg on December 24, including the library, which contained 30,000 books and many historical documents.

A CORRESPONDENT writes: "Constantinople Woman's College, under the direction of Dr. Marion Talbot, has taken steps to recognize more fully fine standards of achievement in scholarship. At the recent convocation the members of the different classes who completed last year's work with honors were formally presented to the assembly and congratulated by Dr. Talbot. Great interest was shown by the students and it is thought that the effect will be stimulating and encouraging."

ONLY a few out of the hundreds of applications from American students received at Edinburgh and Aberdeen Universities are being approved, according to a dispatch to the *New*

York Herald-Tribune. Far from being pleased by the growing popularity of their institutions with Americans, university officials are making strenuous efforts to stop a so-called "invasion" from the United States. Nearly all American students who go to Great Britain to finish their training in one of the Scottish or English universities return home to practice. While there they absorb a part of the government grant to those schools. Naturally, when they return, the government has no chance to get it back. The university officials do not attempt to discriminate against Americans, though in recent years they have outnumbered the students from other countries.

PLANS are being made to inaugurate in July, 1932, a summer school at San Marcos University in Lima, Peru. The summer school will be conducted in the same way as those held in the United States, *i.e.,* a six weeks' session with daily periods for each course during five days of the week. The courses offered will include elementary and advanced Spanish, Latin American literature, Peruvian archeology and one on current Latin American affairs (politics, sociology and economics). Arrangements will be made for the students to visit the Amazon basin, also historical Cuzco. A summer school at Lima will offer an exceptional opportunity to study at the oldest university in the Western Hemisphere. The climate is cool in July and August, as it is winter in Peru at that time. Persons interested in this project are requested to communicate with the Institute of International Education, 2 West 45th Street, New York, N. Y., for the further details, which will be available before January.

DISCUSSION

SHOULD ARITHMETIC BE A REQUIRED STUDY IN THE SENIOR HIGH SCHOOL?

FAR-REACHING changes have been made in the school curriculum of the United States during the past half century. Education had gone quite beyond the three R's stage at the beginning of the period, but the number of branches was still small. In this period many new studies were added to the few at the beginning, and a considerable amount of time was devoted to them in the elementary school. But, strange to tell, no additional years were added for elementary or secondary education, nor was either school year or school day lengthened. It follows self-evidently that the time for these new branches had somehow to be taken from the older ones. In the earlier times arithmetic was receiving more than its fair share of time and effort. This was because the public, especially the rural public, attached great practical value to this study. Probably two fifths of the pupils' whole time went to their arithmetic.

In the hearings before Congress on the metric system in 1904, an expert testified that two thirds of a year's time could be saved in arithmetic study by the adoption of the new weights and measures. Twenty years later this claim was shown to be rather absurd by directing attention to the fact that only a year and a quarter were assigned to arithmetic in the elementary curriculum of the New York City schools. Thus we see in the early part of the half century arithmetic was having rather more than three of the eight years' time devoted to it, while in the later portion it had only a year and a quarter. For one thing, the so-called mental arithmetic, which was reasoning and calculating without the aid of a pencil, had been taken completely out of the course.

Naturally, during the half century, improvements were made in methods of instruction, and, besides this, topics of little or no value were removed from text-books, the selection of subject-matter being improved. But there were losses as well as gains. Thus, in the earlier period, pupils were thrown more and more on their own resources, while in the later one they fell into the way of depending too much on teacher aid, probably because of poorer preparation.

Returning to the disparity in time devoted to arithmetic, sharp attention should be directed to the fact that mental power and agility are increased in a geometrical rather than an arithmetical ratio. Thus a pupil learns twice as much, say, the second year of study as he does the first year, and twice as much the third year as in the second year; and so on. Hence it becomes very apparent that to cut the time materially would result in a large reduction in the amount of arithmetic learned, and lower the quality of the work done. This is exactly what has happened.

The conclusion just reached can be checked up in several ways. One way is by examining the changes in the text-books in arithmetic and algebra in wide use. It will be found there has been a steady lowering of standards throughout the period. Perhaps the algebras present a better gauge than the arithmetics. If the arithmetic is not so well done, the effect will be even more marked in the algebra. Another test may be found in the amount of mathematical work required in physics. This has been going steadily down. Manifestly the quality of work done in physics would depend in large measure on the quantitative relations studied.

Another test is found in the judgment of individuals who have lived through this period and who have had opportunity to measure the preparation of pupils when they come out of our schools. A certain superficial smartness is observable in the later product, but examination quickly reveals its weakness.

Let us agree at once that neither the pupils nor their teachers are to be blamed for this result. It is all the outcome of evolution, and we have a right to expect losses as well as gains.

A remedy for the situation described would be to revise the curriculum, cut out the least important portions of the new matter, and combine related branches. The American Bar Association is asking that the constitution be taught in or with history. Ex-President Eliot, before his death, advocated this combining of courses. But such improvement will be hard to effect. A much simpler and in some respects a better remedy for the deficiency in arithmetical training is to make arithmetic a required subject in the senior high school. It is needed there on its own account as training in reasoning; as a preparation for more advanced mathematics; as a preparation for the study of science and technical studies; and as an essential preparation for meeting the multifarious situations, business and other, that are constantly coming up in the lives of all of us. For one thing the pupil should learn far more than he now acquires in the elementary and junior high school courses of the way business is done, since he finds this in no other study. Thus he should be taught all the steps in the sale of real estate; he should know how the Federal Reserve Banking System is conducted in some quantitative way he can understand; he should be trained in the calculations of the Federal Income Tax; he should go to some length in the study of installment buying; he should be taught the use of many interest, sinking fund, insurance, etc., tables; he should learn the fundamental principles of double entry bookkeeping; these and many other like topics should be taken up. Besides the foregoing, students should be trained up to a good standard of speed and accuracy in calculations, and should be taught *general* methods for solving all sorts of problems.

At present only commercial course pupils are required to take a course something like that just described. But for both cultural and practical reasons should not all take it? Notice the maturity of mind of senior high school pupils is almost essential to a proper understanding of the work outlined.

Added to the above course should be sets of classified problems designed to give special training along certain lines; as business, industry, agriculture, science, engineering and home economics (for girls). For the corresponding class of pupils each class of problems would have great value.

In heaven's name why teach the intricacies of history, literature, etc., and Greek and Latin and Norse mythology and not teach the foregoing?

The answer to the question, "Should arithmetic be made a required subject in the senior high school?" is "Unquestionably, yes."

JOS. V. COLLINS
STATE TEACHERS COLLEGE,
STEVENS POINT, WISCONSIN

WHAT A FRESHMAN EXPECTS OF A LIBERAL EDUCATION

"WELL, I think, sir, a liberal education ought to teach you about the things everybody talks about, so that you could talk to people about anything. You know, sir, politics and economics

—everybody talks about economics now—or literature, or chemistry." I have found, in my dealings with freshmen, that they want a liberal education to give them material for conversation.

In getting acquainted with the new class every autumn I often ask them, "Now that you have enrolled in a liberal arts college, what do you understand by a liberal education?" Their answers are, I think, truthful, for they are not applying for admission. Their reasons are probably representative of the popular opinion of what is meant by a liberal education. They show why thousands of boys and girls come to college every year, since we may well suppose that their parents, in general, hold the same views.

"I went to a dinner once," one freshman said, "and there was a real estate man there who couldn't talk about anything but real estate. Then I decided that I should come to college." Another said that he had known a number of college men as well as many non-college men in his father's business, and he thought that the college men "knew about the things people talk about" more than the others did; they were better able to hold up a conversation. One freshman said thoughtfully that he was not sure that the college men actually knew more than some of the non-college men, but he was sure that they talked as if they did. All the freshmen seem to be convinced that aptitude in conversation is necessary for success, and they think of success with the capital "S."

There may be behind this desire for conversational agility a desire for knowledge for its own sake; I always hope so, at least. And indeed there is an occasional student who has a genuine thirst for knowledge for its own sake. I think there was in the boy who said, "I came to college because I found out in prep school how much there is that I don't know." I regret that he is not typical. More representative is the boy who said, "In a liberal education you mustn't worry too much about books." Each freshman wants to talk like an educated man, if possible, but he does not want to have to work too hard in acquiring the necessary knowledge, for he wants the education for its prestige value—he wants it, not for itself, but for display purposes.

The average freshman wants not only the materials of conversation, but the method as well. "You get to talk to educated men in college," one freshman said to me, "and you learn how they put things." Another put the same thought, "In college you learn about things and you learn how to discuss them intelligently." Over and over they have told me of the value they put upon talking with other students, getting their points of view. There is no harm in that, of course, but they seem to think that there is a type of educated man which they are seeking, and that they will know him by his talk.

Not much different from the desire for topics of conversation is seeking "background," whatever that is. Among my freshman students the word appears as frequently as "democracy" appears in the speeches of politicians. One freshman told me that, although he could not define background, he could tell a man who had it. Probably the catchword represents another aspect of the prestige value which freshmen seek in a liberal education.

Another word which appears frequently is "contacts." They want a liberal education, they say, for the contacts they will make in the process of getting it. "I wasn't sure what I wanted to do when I got through college," a freshman told me, "and I thought I might make some valuable contacts in a liberal arts college." There is the utilitarian motive quite bare: a liberal education may be used as a highly respectable employment agency. Sometimes the freshmen couple "contacts" with "associations," as one member of the class of 1935 said to me, "The contacts and associations which one makes in college are sometimes the most valuable things a college has to offer."

Very few of the freshmen of my acquaintance have come to college primarily to study. They all expect to study, of course, but most of them do not want to study more than necessary. "It is just as important," one of them said, "to have a good time, to play in athletics, and to make friends, as to study." The making of friends—there must be some difference between friends and contacts—seems to be a major reason for enrolment in a liberal arts college. One freshman put it in this way, "You'll forget most of what you learn in college after you have been out a few years, but the friends that you make will last all your life." Again and again when I have asked, "What do you expect to do in college?" the answer has begun, "Well, I hope to make friends, and—"

College friendship and fellowship, freshmen feel, are promoted by participation in athletics and "activities." I have found freshmen much more ready than upperclassmen to defend athletics and activities, because, perhaps, they do not see as well as they will later that participation in them is largely a waste of time. A candid senior will admit that the hours and hours he spent indexing the year book or issuing sweat shirts to the team were wasted hours; but as a freshman he looked forward more keenly to becoming manager of the team or the year book than he did to any subject in the curriculum.

Spirit and sportsmanship come next to friendship, according to my freshmen, as being desirable parts of a liberal education. All three are admirable qualities, beyond doubt, but they are not inseparable from a liberal education. College spirit is a rather ephemeral emotion, and excellent colleges have existed without a trace of it. Sportsmanship may be found outside college walls; indeed some recent critics of college athletics insist that there is rather more to be found outside than inside. No college, so far as I know, was ever founded to promote spirit and sportsmanship. One freshman, however, went so far as to tell me that "No man who does not have the true college spirit can be said to have a real liberal education." Freshmen seem to think that spirit and sportsmanship are essentials of the A.B., even though no examinations are taken in the fields.

The largest number of freshmen frankly say that they hope to make more money in later life because of the liberal education they expect to get. They are observant youths, and they have followed the careers of college men. A future business man said to me, "In the company my father works for only college men are placed in the good positions. Father says it's much easier for a college man to get ahead." Another said quite frankly, "I don't know if the four years in college are wasted or not, but I do know that it's easier for a college man to get a job." For these boys the faculty struggles over majors and minors, requirements and prerequisites, are nearly, if not entirely, in vain; for them one subject is as good as another.

A great many students have been, I think, misled by the statistics about the number of college men in "Who's Who," in Congress, or with such-and-such incomes. These figures or stories are always coming back to me as I talk to the freshmen in the autumn. The college men are in "Who's Who," of course, but perhaps not entirely because of their college training; there may have been other reasons. But the fact that there is this concrete evidence of the success of college men is enough for a boy of college years; one dose of these inspiring figures, and he is off to get an A.B.

Freshmen who expect to go into one of the professions will tell me, "Why, I've got to have an A.B. to get into the Harvard Law School," as if that were the only sensible excuse for getting one. The years in college are, such students are often frank to say, wasted; and I have found this attitude very common among those who do not plan to get their degrees. When I asked one barrister-to-be what he expected to do in college, he responded easily, "I expect to get forty-five semester hours." As freshmen, very few students see the reasons for the requirements made by the professional schools; they tend to regard them as hurdles, and nothing better. In later years they probably understand the reasons and view the requirements sympathetically.

The explanations freshmen give for coming to a particular college bear out the conclusion that they expect two things from a liberal education, social prestige and increased earning ability. My acquaintances among the freshmen put the location and prestige of the college as their most impelling motives, and after these, the wishes of the family or the advice of friends. I have yet to meet the freshman who knows as much about the kind or quality of the liberal education in the college as he does about the social standing of the institution, the record of its football teams, or the success of its graduates.

Of all the freshmen I have talked with, the prize candidate for the higher learning appeared this autumn, in the year of grace 1931. I tried to lead him out with the usual questions. At length he said, "I couldn't find a job, and there didn't seem to be much chance of one this winter. The family and I thought that I might as well come to college as do nothing." I assured him that I thought no harm would result from his decision.

DAYTON D. MCKEAN
PRINCETON UNIVERSITY

SPECIAL CORRESPONDENCE

EDUCATION IN THE OPEN

THE show of hands was three to one in favor of a six o'clock rising gong, an advance of half an hour in the day's schedule of the camp school. This surprised the director, for the session was but just starting, and, unacclimated, every one was shivering at breakfast time with a morning chill which sweaters and leathers could only externally assuage. Even in August the nights are generally cold at seven thousand feet; and since it is particularly difficult to accommodate the imagination to the idea of cold anywhere in mid-summer New Mexico, the students, heedless of warning, will come up with insufficient bedding,—with the consequence that the traders at Jemez Springs usually sell out their stock of blankets a few days after the camp is opened. And as for six o'clock, under ordinary circumstances no impossible hour, well, the mesa to the east, which the morning sun must surmount, is high enough to leave the camp in shadow (and chill) until near seven, although we have all found out that a very brief exposure to his rays puts us into such hale comfort as mountain air and morning sunshine should give. But we must shiver at breakfast—the camp has voted it, three to one, and the Director knew at once that the Field School for 1931 was to be a success.

Can any location on earth equal ours for an outdoor school? Down toward Rio Jemez—one of those ever-singing mountain streams which in August floods and subsides daily with the torrents that fall now up the east, now up the south fork—stands the old lumber-camp cook-house, a log barrack which we have made over into the camp kitchen. A roof-and-canvas extension, with board tables and seating, serves alike for commensal and for lecture-hall—indeed, for the "edifice" and "front" of our collegiate campus. As for the remainder, tentage is all that is necessary, be it for library, laboratory, office, or such dormitory system as is disclosed here and there where the "Jemez red" of the canvas breaks visibly through the rich greens of spruce and fir and yellow pine. For while there is a splendid plaza ("campus," if you like) rising southward from the cook-house toward the foothills of Mount Redondo—a space cleared by the lumbermen, we suppose, but gloriously useful to the whole camp—we are forest-enclosed, everywhere magnificent timbers the better part of which, fortunately, are in the National Forest, whose boundary mark is in the open of our plaza.

The presence of the cook-house we can ascribe to luck, but the site is surely predestined for our purpose. We are six miles above Jemez Springs; perhaps four above the Soda Dam, with its perpetual boiling of mineral waters, the fame of which drew a scouting party of Coronado's men up from Tiguex on the Rio Grande in 1540. At the Springs are hot baths, warmed by the senescence of the great volcano; but for that matter, there is a hot bath not two miles above our camp, where the boys go when the nearer plunge into the cold seems out of friendship. As for the girls, they have wonderful pools at the foot of Battleship Rock, up the south fork. Perhaps most of all chancy is the drinking supply. Over the volcanic tuff, on the flank of Battleship and less than a half-mile from camp, comes such a spring-fall of water, a forty-foot leap at the least, as only the genii that satisfy thirst can devise, clear, chill, pure, and veritably the nymphan shrine of a sprite Parnassian. Actually the place is a wonder! The approach is by a meadow glamorous with flowers, with primroses in sheer golds, with Indian paintbrush, penstamen ruby-red, and all about scores of the shy blossoms, the blues, the purples, the whites. One follows the brook through every greenery, laced and interlaced, with glimpses of the sky-high mesas through and under branches, and then, as by a curtain disclosed, the froths and veils of the fall! And all the adoration that has gone to living springs since the world began! Practically this beauty means a perfect water supply, and that is the beginning of camp sanitation.

But the real glory of our camp site is the west mesa. It is this, rising monumentally eighteen hundred feet or more above us, that brings from first-comers an involuntary, "Magnificent!" Just as a spectacle, by morning sun, in evening shadow, or spectrally under the moon, it is a tyranny to the eyes, built vast, but *built* and with such architecture as only the Earth-Makers could plan,—just over the forest-tops the long horizontal laminations of the Pennsylvanian limestones, which, near-viewed, are a tapestry of marine fossils recording life as it was toward three hundred million years ago; above this the russets and reds of five-hundred feet of Jura-Trias, stratum over stratum, perhaps an hundred million years of them; and on such a sea-laid foundation, the volcanic verticals, gray basalt worn into buttressing cones and columns, and over all the buffs and pinks of the perfectly perpendicular walls of tuff, crystallized there where the tides left it when Earth's hugest eruption blew out the Jemez crater some sixty million years ago. Yes, the west mesa is a spectacle, but more than that, it is such a chart of Earth-making as no eye can see without question, and for our geologist it is class-room and laboratory, and the library of time.

As our schedule goes the first work-gong sounds at seven-thirty and the hour we choose to call a "nature walk." Geology, with the mesa for demonstration, is the first subject. But when the biologists take their turn, we find that flora and fauna are as speaking as are the rocks. Two thousand feet above us and two thousand below represent very little in linear space, even by our mountain roads, but within this we pass from a Sonoran vegetation, subtropical and arid, on zone by zone into the Canadian, by a mere climb traversing the whole longitudinal measures of our United States. There are even little islets of residual trees and plants from farther north and farther south, how carried or preserved who can say, through their exotic generations. The really fascinating problems of natural life, for the youngster at all events, are those that deal with colonies and kinds, with the natural drama which ecology discloses; and here is our camp at a very center of ecological strategy with the ancient life-forms of the North, clinging on since glacial times brought them southward, besieged in their mountain heights by the more opulent southrons, plant and insect, bird and reptile, all following their zonal habits—so that the lines of militant pines that crest the mesa suddenly assume a new character, transformed into spearmen and stalwarts formed for the attack, while a half mile below camp the alligator-bark is seen as a lurking scout, surreptitious from the south. Our "nature walk" not only introduces kind and character of tree and rock and woods-dweller, but it has as well its thrill of event, fighting or friendly.

Our camp is in two divisions, one for the biologists and geologists who follow their own peregrine adventures after the morning hour, but the other, which is the parent of the school, for the archeologists. And of course, no matter how lovely or fortunate our site, it could never have been chosen for a school of Man and Nature, if before ourselves other men had not chosen it for their habitation. So that our real reason, after all, for being in these natural fashions blessed, is the fact that Unshage is only ten minutes and Nonoshage another ten down the road from where the forks unite into Rio Jemez. These are names the living Indians give to the sites of pre-Columbian pueblos which form our archeological laboratory—just as mesa and canyon are laboratory for the naturalists. The excavations go slowly, year by year, but this is only to the good, for every year's, and indeed every day's digging, turns up something of sudden interest, and adds, as a mosaic bit, to that picture of life past which it is the essential idea of our course to create. Not, mind you, just for the sake of becoming familiars with the dead whose poor bones the trowel lays bare, nor for any empty antiquarian curiosity, but for the sake of the conception of what an education should give—for this is the real core of our endeavor. "Man's place in Nature" is the title of a famous book, and it is just this which in the end is the subject of any schooling worth having, of any education worthy its effort. Our camp school has no other teaching in view. What the natural world must mean to human life, and how life shall find its adjustment, even as time flows and continents shift, these are our problems. The dead pueblos are eloquent of such a problem; as in brilliant miniature they proclaim—plaza and kiva and communal house, olla and metate, flint and bone awl. Daily they tell how thought and nature could meet in a men's society, and solve (surely with some gain of beauty) the tremendous problems which for every form of life condition its vitality. Our students, we intend, shall go from their summer in camp with some gain of lucidity in their understanding of what it means to be human beings in the midst of a Nature to which every civilization, no matter what its pride or power, must in the great finality be an accommodation. So our laboratory is chosen not for any dilettante curiosity, nor yet for the zest which it undoubtedly gives to the youngster out for discovery, but seriously and effectively for thought and understanding, cleared of the artifices of book and theory and face to face with the man-fact of the thing.

Eight-thirty is second gong and another lecture under the mess-roof, this time on the rituals and ceremonials of the olden peoples, which must be understood if any digging is to be clear-headed, and also that we may keep in mind that all, even material walls and floors, which we unearth is as a writing out of the minds of men gone. We can not forget that thought builds towns, and that all values return into the mind's house—so the second hour tells of mind, as the first of the natural world. By nine-thirty the sun is up, and down at the "dig," under direction, the Navaho and Jemez Indians are doing honest work with spade and pick; and thither go the shifts of students who are assigned to the morning hours—till the dinner gong calls them in, dusty and exhilarated. After dinner a second shift, and in the latter afternoon, when all, presumably, have had their go at "dig," at library, and at the ever-popular baths, stream-provided, come the two lectures on the local archeology and on the broad problems of social adjustment which finish our assigned day. Supper, twilight sports, finally campfire and its discussions, tales, songs, occasional dances by the Indians whom the day seems never to tire beyond the drum's arousing, and ten o'clock, which is camp "taps"—this is the long and short of it, program-wise.

But the real thing is that without any vastness of plant or apparatus, without officialdom or show, with no material beyond Nature's gifts and a few books, we conduct a month of schooling which defines unforgettably "man's place in nature," be it as problem or image. Many a student passes through his college with this center of all education undisclosed, or even with balks and dams to its understanding erected midmost of his mind's channels. Certainly—as before it has been made—the field session above Jemez Springs of the School of American Research and the University of New Mexico has made the discovery that the apparatus of education need not extend beyond a group of students camped in the open for that teaching where curiosity asks and Nature gives answer. Does the program work? It is a small student group, less than a hundred are received; but they come from universities and colleges Atlantic to Pacific, and seldom indeed do they come without returning clean in record. In the plateaux and mountains of western North America there are sites for scores of such field schools as ours, and there are whole years of to-morrows which may become illumined by education in the open.

HARTLEY ALEXANDER

SCRIPPS COLLEGE

THE EDUCATIONAL CHANGES IN GREECE

THE inclination of the Greek people to acquire education was strong even under the Turkish subjection. It was realized that education is the best means to regain liberty. After the revolution, the school system was organized on the basis of the systems of other states; in general, the schools were divided into general and professional. Subsequently, numerous changes, dictated by the changing conditions and especially by those resulting from the world war, were introduced. The present Government of Venizelos is especially interested to realize substantial reforms. Some of them have been realized; but the complete materialization of the plan will take about ten years.

The attendance of primary schools was made compulsory already in 1834. The development of the elementary schools can be observed from the following figures: In 1830, there were 71 schools with 6,721 pupils; in 1858, 754 schools with 51,596 pupils; in 1879, 1,035 schools for boys and 137 schools for girls with 67,108 and 12,310 pupils, respectively; in 1901, 3,123 schools with 189,903 pupils. The latest statistics state that there are 7,850 schools, which required six years of attendance, of which 1,558 are for boys, 958 for girls and 5,334 mixed; they take care of 711,474 pupils; in addition there are

149 private schools with 14,611 pupils and 407 kindergartens. While in 1879 the pupils numbered one twentieth of the inhabitants, in 1901 they numbered one twelfth, and now about one eighth.

We must notice in this connection a peculiar fact. While these schools require six years for the pupils who, after their graduation, can enter the third year of the so-called "Hellenic" (intermediary) schools, in reality those who complete the fourth year of the elementary school enter the first year of the "Hellenic" schools. The consequence is that most of the elementary schools have only four-year classes.

In spite of the growth of the number of pupils, the number of illiterates is rather great; this is due to the lack of enforcement of the law for the compulsory attendance. But the recent measures seem to show that the government is determined to enforce the law.

There are about 8,200 male teachers and 4,347 female teachers. In 1858, 440,630 drachmae were spent; in 1877, 1,612,000; in 1901, 6 million; to-day the sum is more than 363,000,000 drachmae.

Secondary education is given in the lower, so-called "Hellenic" and in higher schools or gymnasia, "classic" and "real." The "Hellenic" schools accept the pupils from the fourth grade of elementary schools, if they pass special examinations. The course lasts three years. There are 435 of this type of schools, 24 being for girls, others for men or mixed. In this class also belong 21 secondary schools for girls, introduced in 1914, with three years' attendance; they accept only graduates of the sixth grade. In 1929 there were 68,113 in all these schools, 16,211 of whom were girls.

Most of the "gymnasia" specialize in classic education. The graduates of "Hellenic" schools spend four years there. While there are 207 state "Hellenic" gymnasia, only 13 are "real" gymnasia, in addition to 78 private institutions of both types. The pupils in the state institutions number 29,651, in private only 1,703. The teachers of theoretical subjects must be university graduates, and their number reaches the figure of 2,767. The state spends about 135 million drachmae yearly on these secondary schools.

The whole educational system of Greece is headed by two universities. The University of Athens was founded in 1837, and is also known as the National and Capodistrian Universities. The reason for it is that a rich Greek left a sum of money for the purpose of founding a university in Greece. As one has already existed, it was decided to apply the bequeathed sum to the National University, which was then divided into these two universities. In 1925 a second university was established in Salonica, but does not possess all faculties at the present time. The universities admit the graduates of gymnasia and "real" gymnasia. They are administered autonomically, as other European universities. The examinations are held annually; the whole field is again covered by the examinations for diplomas. The doctorate is given to those who write a dissertation. The University of Athens comprises the following faculties: law, theology, medicine (with a dental school), philosophy and natural sciences and mathematics. The law students predominate; altogether there were 6,500 students in 1929, 88 full professors, 23 "docents" and 9 others.

The teachers in secondary schools receive practical training in the "State Institutes for Teachers in Secondary Schools"; about 50 teachers are called every year to attend here. The physical training teachers are taught two years in the "Teachers' Institute For Physical Training." The teachers in grammar schools come from state and private schools (recognized by the state). The priests are trained in 12 theological seminaries. They accept the graduates from the "Hellenic" schools; the students study five years; after 15 years of service as teachers in elementary schools they are entitled to serve as priests as well as teachers. The number of the students in seminaries is about 1,400 yearly.

There is also a polytechnical school in Athens which has the university standing, with about 450 students, and "The High School of Commercial and Financial Sciences." Between 2,000 and 2,250 students attend 19 state business schools; there are also 23 other business schools, adjusted more or less to the state schools.

Agricultural education is really insignificant. The same is true about the industrial and trades' schools. The recent reforms undertook to improve and develop these phases of education.

The whole educational system of Greece suffers from the excessive development of theoretical education. The graduates of the elementary and secondary schools are not prepared directly to enter an occupation which would offer them a career. For the lack of the elementary practical schools the students keep themselves busy by going to the "Hellenic" schools; for the same reason they go to the gymnasia, which again train only university students or the graduates who always look for positions in the state service.

The situation has many dangers from the economic, social and political view-points. The Government of Venizelos has its program of reform, which contains the following points: (1) The reorganization of the elementary schools; (2) the upbuilding of lower trade and occupational schools; (3) the creation of more secondary schools with practical education.

Some of the details of the reform are as follows. The compulsory attendance of the elementary school is increased from four to six years. Each elementary school also has "kindergartens" with voluntary attendance. In most cities there are now schools for adults.

All elementary schools for male and female students are replaced by the attendance of both in the same classes. There will be separated classes according to sex in the secondary schools only if the state finances will be able to finance them. The subjects taught in the elementary schools are now more practical and are to build up the foundation for further practical studies. Instead of the "pure" language, the teaching language of the elementary schools is now the language as it is spoken by the masses. The changes reflect in the foundation of new teachers' training schools.

The existing "Hellenic" schools and about 500 of the gymnasia (which were incomplete) will be gradually abolished within ten years and replaced by the following schools: agricultural, commercial (for small business men), artisans' schools; and agricultural schools for girls. The admission requirement is the graduation from the six years' grammar school.

Concurrently with the gradual abolition of the "Hellenic" schools, new reforms have been planned: their basis is the introduction of the gymnasia with six classes; these will absorb the "Hellenic" schools and the gymnasia (with four years' attendance). The first two years are for all students; from the third year on the students will enter for the next four years either of the following: Classical gymnasia; realistic gymnasia; commercial schools; agricultural schools; and the institute for grammar school teachers (five years' attendance). The length of the studies for the graduation from the classical, realistic or commercial schools will now take 12 years instead of 11, because two years have been added to the elementary schools and two years to the secondary schools, instead of the abolished three years of the "Hellenic" schools.

All these schools represent a novelty for Greece and are the most serious step toward the adjustment of the educational system to the needs of the Greek state. As far as the girls are concerned, another novel introduction is the creation of four-year schools for the graduates from the six-year elementary school; the teaching schedule is to provide education corresponding to the nature and duties of women.

Formerly the university graduates could teach without any practical training. Now they receive their practical training under the direction of the pedagogical faculty in Athens and Salonica. A special training in field agriculture is now obligatory for the grammar school teachers. The period of training for the physical training teachers was lengthened from two to three years.

A very useful reform seems to be the creation in the ministry of education of the advisory committee of forty members, composed of educational experts and the representatives of commercial, industrial and agricultural organizations. Special advisory councils were established in the ministries of communications, national economy and agriculture for the study of the questions concerning the technical, commercial and agricultural education. Two autonomous educational councils in the ministry of education were changed into three five-membered councils; the first is to approve the textbooks and regulate the teaching in general; the two others are to have the administrative and disciplinary powers over the teachers.

JOSEPH S. ROUCEK
CENTENARY JUNIOR COLLEGE,
HACKETTSTOWN, N. J.

QUOTATIONS

THE HIGH COST OF ATHLETICS

THE financial statement of the Harvard Athletic Association for the year ended June 30, 1931, provides much food for reflection. The grand total of income exceeds $1,000,000. It may be compared with other (approximate) totals for the same year, such as: Harvard College and the Graduate School of Arts and Sciences, $3,000,000; the Medical School, $1,275,000; the Graduate School of Business Administration, $1,275,000; the Law School, $900,000; the University Library, $435,000; the School of Public Health, $365,000; the Engineering School, $330,000; the Graduate School of Education, $230,000; all other department totals for the year being smaller. Examination of the athletic accounts yields the following items: Gross receipts from football, $900,000; expenses of teams engaged in major sports, $249,504.51; "administrative and other expenses," $130,795.05.

As has been the case for many years, football earns a surplus which supports other sports, intercollegiate and intra-mural, maintains playing fields and other athletic plant and equipment, and pays for physical education. This goose undoubtedly lays golden eggs. It is easy to argue that such a goose should be treated with care and respect, and that there is no harm in expending lavishly what is so plentifully supplied. It is true that it would be short-sighted to diminish the public appeal of football so long as one is dependent on the revenue which it yields, but this very fact contributes to the essential viciousness of the present situation.

Most of the universities and colleges in the country have allowed themselves to drift into a situation in which they are not really free to deal with football as their better judgment might dictate. They have either pledged the gate-receipts in advance to pay for athletic plant, or they have developed a highly commendable system of "athletics for all" and physical education which would have to be curtailed if gate receipts diminished. The uses to which the money is put being imperative or unquestionably good, it is not easy to question the methods by which the money is obtained. The legitimate expenses met from football earnings are now so great that an alternative source of revenue is not at present conceivable. Thus there is no immediate prospect of dispensing with the gate-receipts of football.

It does not follow, however, that an advance may not be made in this direction. No one would wish to see a reduction either of physical education or of facilities for wholesome and health-building recreation on the part of the general student-body. But the layman may be pardoned for believing that there might be some reduction elsewhere, as for example, in the expenses of administration and of the major sports. Every such saving of costs reduces the burden that must be carried by gate-receipts, and opens the way to such reforms as are at present rejected for fear of reducing them.

It may be asked why if competitive sport can more than pay its way it should not be allowed to live high. The reason, of course, is that an educational institution has a peculiar obligation to emphasize values of a totally different sort. It owes this both to its own students and to the public. At present the universities and colleges in the United States are systematically engaged for two months of every year in catering to the public taste, and in creating a powerful counter-attraction to their own educational activities. Money received and expended is a rough but reliable measure of the attention and emphasis which an enterprise receives. So long as intercollegiate football is a million-dollar business, it is bound to seem correspondingly important. In helping to create this illusion, institutions of higher education are denying their own professions and working against the very purpose to which they are dedicated.—*Harvard Alumni Bulletin.*

SOCIETIES AND MEETINGS

ANNUAL MEETING OF THE AMERICAN ASSOCIATION OF UNIVERSITY PROFESSORS

THE eighteenth annual meeting of the American Association of University Professors, held at the Hotel Stevens in Chicago on Friday and Saturday, November 27 and 28, was well attended, more than 150 delegates and members representing 105 institutions being present, and proved unusually profitable. Contrary to custom, the sessions were not held in conjunction with one or more of the learned societies, and hence the interest of members was undivided. This was the third subsidized-delegate meeting in the history of the association.

Among the more important subjects of discussion, the one particularly featured was the comprehensive survey of college teaching to be undertaken by the association during the coming year and financed by the recent grant of $20,000 by the Carnegie Corporation through the Carnegie Foundation for the Advancement of Teaching. The entire session on Saturday morning was devoted to this problem, being introduced by the presidential address of Professor W. B. Munro on the "Advancement of Teaching," followed by the addresses of Professor Lester B. Rogers, president of the National Society of College Teachers of Education, on "College Teaching from the Standpoint of Relations and Contributions of Schools of Education," and by Professor C. H. Judd on the "Psychology of the Learning Processes at the Higher Levels." The discussion of the projected survey of teaching was introduced by Professor Homer L. Dodge, of the University of Oklahoma, who outlined the problems, procedure and desired results of the project.

At the first session on Friday, the perennially important problem of academic freedom and tenure was presented in the report of the association's committee in the form of the annual report read and discussed by the chairman, Professor S. A. Mitchell, of the University of Virginia. This report showed the grave increase in the number of cases brought to the committee during the past year, no less than seventy-two formal complaints being presented, in comparison with thirty-eight during the previous year. The conditions brought out by the report were extensively discussed, and representatives of Ohio State University and of the University of Mississippi, where serious situations have recently arisen, spoke encouragingly of anticipated improvement at both institutions. At the same session, the preliminary report of the committee surveying conditions of tenure at higher institutions throughout the country was presented by Professor W. W. Cook, president-elect of the association. This investigation, it was announced, will be continued with a view to the publication of results as soon as practicable.

Closely related to these reports was that of the committee on the economic status of the profession, prepared by the chairman, Professor Alzada Comstock, of Mount Holyoke College. Reflecting similar findings in Professor Mitchell's report, Dr. Comstock pointed out that from information received from all parts of the country salary reductions are creating a more and more serious problem. "The policies of the colleges and universities which have suffered income losses," the report observed, "either through reduced appropriations or through falling investment yields, range all the way from a carefully graded set of percentage salary reductions which applies least severely to low-salaried men, to erratic discharges and salary reductions which can not fail to suggest that two birds are being killed with one stone; that local political aims are being served in the guise of salary slashes." The situation will be carefully watched by this committee and by the officers of the association.

Informal reports were presented by the committees on junior colleges, cooperation with Latin-American universities, pensions and requirements for the master's degree.

The annual dinner on Friday evening, attended by more than 100 persons, was addressed by Professor Yandell Henderson, of Yale University, on "University Maintenance Costs: Buildings versus Instruction," and by President R. M. Hutchins, of the University of Chicago, on "The Professor Pays." Dr. Henderson cited the financial statistics of various institutions to show how a decreasing percentage of income is devoted to instruction in comparison with the erection and maintenance of buildings. President Hutchins made the sweeping and challenging assertion that nothing should affect the professor's tenure except his effectiveness as teacher and scholar.

Among the resolutions passed at the meetings were the following:

Resolved, that when a duly authorized Committee of the American Association of University Professors finds, upon investigation, that a given college or university has been guilty of a serious breach of the principle of the freedom of teaching, involving the dismissal of one or more of its teachers, that upon recommendation of such committee, and the endorsement of the Council of this Association, and a vote of the Association itself at its Annual Meeting, such college or university be placed upon a "non-recommended" list, this action to be published in the next issue of the Bulletin;

Resolved, further, that such institution shall remain on this list until it has given satisfactory evidence of a change of policy in this respect;

Resolved, furthermore, that a record of such action be printed in the January issue of the Bulletin of the Association for as long a time as the institution in question remains on the non-recommended list.

Resolved, that this Association views with concern the inauguration of post-season "charity-games" in intercollegiate sports, and concurs in the opinion expressed by the presidents and other administrative officers of our leading educational institutions that such a practice tends to prolong the dislocation and confusion incident to the beginning of collegiate work in the fall and establishes an undesirable precedent in that there will always be some charity or other wholly worthy object which can be brought forward as an excuse for continuing such games even after the present depression shall have passed.

In the report of the general secretary of the association, Professor H. W. Tyler noted the increase of more than one thousand members during the current year, the total now numbering more than eleven thousand, in spite of the increase in dues from three to four dollars a year, voted at the last annual meeting.

The following officers were elected for two years:

President: W. W. Cook, Law, Johns Hopkins University.

Vice-presidents: E. G. Conklin, Biology, Princeton University, and F. K. Richtmyer, Physics, Cornell University.

Members of the council: R. A. Budington, Zoology, Oberlin College; Barry Cerf, Comparative Literature, Reed College; F. W. Coker, Political Science, Yale University; Marian E. Hubbard, Zoology, Wellesley College; G. F. Reynolds, English, University of Colorado; W. J. Robbins, Botany, University of Missouri; Thorndike Saville, Engineering, University of North Carolina; L. M. Terman, Psychology, Stanford University; Oswald Veblen, Mathematics, Princeton University; Carl Wittke, History, Ohio State University.

H. W. TYLER

EDUCATIONAL RESEARCH AND STATISTICS

PRACTICAL "EDUCATIONAL ENGINEERING" IN A TEACHER-TRAINING COURSE

MIDWAY between educational research in the strict sense and every-day educational practice is an area of effort where scientific methods are employed, but very immediately in dealing with some specific local practical problem—an area where work might be described perhaps most aptly as "educational engineering." Such work does not have the clean-cut character of the purely research undertaking. Nevertheless, findings of some rather general interest may often be obtained. And the progressive adaptation of methods to practical problems is of special interest as suggestive of methods of attack which other "educational engineers" might use in dealing with their own difficulties.

It is work of a character above indicated which is described in this present paper. The immediate practical situation was this, that the writers were in charge of a five-hour one quarter required course in educational psychology enrolling about 200 students a quarter and taught, in sections of about 30 students each, by some five different part-time instructors (graduate students working for the doctor's degree). Three outstanding problems were here involved: (a) the work of the different instructors needed to be unified, (b) the work of all needed to be improved, and if possible better methods of instruction developed, (c) some general training of these student instructors for their future careers as college teachers was desirable.

In this situation, and with these general problems in mind, the following general experimental set-up was arranged: (a) It was first agreed that all sections should, at the beginning of each quarter, take a pre-test covering important points of the course, and an end-test of 250 multiple choice questions; (b) at the beginning of the course all students were to fill in a rather elaborate class census card covering such points as previous related courses, teaching experience, professional plans, and so on; and at the end of the course each student was to fill in an inquiry blank giving his judgment regarding various characteristics of the course, the instructor, and the methods of instruction used. Finally, (c) the "open door policy" was agreed upon; it was agreed that the writers were to feel free to visit any class at any time, and (more important) the instructors were to visit each other's classes.

In this general set-up the following special experimental procedures were tried: (1) During the three quarters of the regular year a total of seven control sections taught by informal lecture-discussion method were arranged for; (2) there were five interview and re-interview sections, the important differential element here being that each instructor, early in the course and again toward the end, had a personal interview with each student in which he attempted to achieve understanding of the student and his work; (3) a test-teach-test method was also used in five sections, the distinctive element here being that at the beginning of each one of the seven divisions of the course an objective test was given, the results used diagnostically as basis for discussion and remedial work, and a check test given at the end of the time allotted to that division; (4) finally, five sections used what was known as the committee technique. This consisted of having the students meet in groups of four or five, with a rotating student chairman, two out of the five days each week instead of meeting with the instructor every day. The purpose was to permit more free discussion among the students; there was also the notion that perhaps a rotating chairmanship would give in a way a little experience in teaching.

Having tried these four teaching procedures it was then possible, because of the general experimental set-up above described, to compare them (and study the total situation) on the basis of objective test data, student reports, and direct observation. On these bases the following questions were considered:

(1) *What was the initial status of these students with reference to this course?*

The findings obtained here were the usual findings; but these usual findings are so important, and so little is usually done about them, that mention is nevertheless desirable. Most clean-cut evidence was obtained from results on a "core" of 150 questions included in both pre- and end-tests for all three quarters. Distribution of scores on these 150 items, for the 527 students in all three quarters for whom complete data were obtained, ran as follows:

Score:															
25	30	35	40	45	50	55	60	65	70	75	80	85	90	95	100
3	13	18	35	47	75	99	72	53	47	37	13	7	5	2	1

Total 527; median 58.6

The range is from 25 to 103 or twice the average gain of the entire group at the end of the course. Four students scored at the beginning of the course above the median of the entire group (all quarters) at the end. When one turns now to the census blank above mentioned, for some elucidation of factors here, it appears that the class was made up of students all the way from freshmen to graduates; about 50 per cent. of the students had had only five hours of psychology previous to this course while 20 per cent. had had from 12 to 39 hours; about 50 per cent. had already had a course in methods or philosophy of education, 30 per cent. a course in school administration, and 25 per cent. a course in history of education. Chiefly transfers from other colleges and institutions, but also schedule difficulties and a variety of other factors, had caused these variations in sequence of courses. About 20 per cent. of the students had taught; 50 per cent. were headed for high school teaching, 15 per cent. for elementary school, 10 per cent. for college teaching, 10 per cent. for supervisory or administrative work, while 15 per cent. did not intend to go into teaching of any kind. And in the background were differences in intelligence, interest, total life experience, even more important than these gross factors. The total resultant heterogeneity presented an extraordinary problem of instructional and curricular adjustment to individual differences. It is a problem almost universal at the college and university level (probably even more acute in such subjects as English and history) and beside which the much talked of heterogeneity of the elementary school seems like uniformity—a problem so difficult that the writers have found many college teachers angry when it was brought up![1]

[1] And the problem can not be solved off-hand by requiring rigid sequences of courses and special curricula. The necessity is for such organization of material, and such method, in each course as will permit adjustment to such differences. The work here reported has been the basis for various changes in this direction and important further developments are under way.

(2) *What was the progress made by these students?*

Table I, showing scores on the 150 "core" items at the end of each quarter, summarizes the situation.

TABLE I

Score	45	50	55	60	65	70	75	80	85	90	95	100	105	110	115	120	125	130
Fall	2		5	12	31	40	38	31	29	18	7							
Winter			1		1		3	10	8	13	26	25	17	22	8	8		
Spring						1	1	5	9	16	20	30	21	30	18	15	5	1

Medians: autumn 77, winter 102, spring 106

The especially interesting feature was this, that the gain in the winter and spring quarters was approximately twice that in the fall quarter. The probably most important factor here was simply this, that the instructors suddenly woke up, when the fall quarter's results were presented and discussed, to the facts that the experiment was being seriously considered, that it showed many lacks of agreement among the instructors as to points of view and subject matter, that the students' comments on their work (on the inquiry form filled out at the end of the quarter) clearly pointed the finger toward weaknesses. The value of the objective test technique came out strikingly in connection with the first issue; the objectivity made possible definite determination of the divergencies of fact or point of view. And many hours, some rather hectic, were spent in discussion of the various examinations used, coordination of points of view, formulation of a detailed outline so that no important points would be overlooked, and so on. As a measure of the divergencies among instructors these discussions were exceedingly interesting; it is unfortunate that no check was at the time made of the number of items under discussion, as a measure of the needed coordination. Another factor possibly having an influence here was the class visiting.[2]

The correlations in Table II are also of interest; they show correlations of the university intelligence test percentile, final grades assigned by the instructors, and total score on all the objective tests (mid-terms and final).

TABLE II

	Fall quarter	Winter quarter	Spring quarter
Intelligence and grades	.33	.56	.59
Intelligence and test scores	.26	.50	.57
Test scores and grades	.42	.63	.84

Apparently there was an increase in accuracy of grading. Inspection of the scatter tables indicated that the rise in correlation with intelligence in the winter and spring quarters was due also to more stimulation of the brighter students. And there was better coordination of the marking of the various instructors.

(3) *What was the comparative efficacy of the different methods of instruction?*

A variety of comparisons were made between sections taught by the different methods previously described, on the basis of scores on the final objective examination, the two objective midterms, student reports. Great exactness of statistical handling seemed hardly possible. The general run of the findings is fairly well indicated, however, by comparative gain on the end test over the pre-test on the 150 "core" questions (with a slight adjustment for differences in intelligence between the groups). If the gain on the control sections be taken as a base then it appears that the gain on the interview section was 18 per cent. greater, on the test-teach-test sections substantially the same, and on the committee sections 12 per cent. less.

Light for the further interpretation of these

[2] The cynical reader may query whether there was not "teaching for the test" as an important factor. But it must be remembered that the instructors were appraised not on the 150 "core" questions but more on the two mid-quarter tests, which were changed from quarter to quarter, and that the final test consisted not only of the 150 "core" questions but of other questions which were also varied from quarter to quarter. Since there were these changes on mid-terms and total final, direct comparisons from quarter to quarter on these tests could less readily be made. But there were marked gains on all these tests. Moreover, the student ratings of the instructors at the end of the winter and spring quarters indicated improvement in teaching. . . . That there *was* substantial improvement would seem hardly questionable.

findings is furnished by the student reports. In the committee sections 82 per cent. of the students felt the two days a week in committee less profitable than two days in class would have been. The visits of the instructors to their committees served to illuminate the situation somewhat here. It appeared that all too readily the discussion in committee tended to be simply with reference to "what will probably be asked on the next quiz," or campus gossip, trends of discussion which the instructor had constantly to block. This procedure had previously been tried in a more advanced class by one of the writers (Dr. Luella C. Pressey) and had been highly successful. The immaturity of the students in the present course and the unselected character of this group were apparently the important factors. In the interview sections there was much range on the part of the students in the judgments concerning values the interview had contributed, many of them feeling that it had been especially profitable in connection with issues of vocation or other matters outside of the content of the course—but there was a general feeling of the profit of personal contact. Concerning the diagnostic or test-teach-test procedure the comment was generally favorable; 60 per cent. reported that the pretest helped them locate their weaknesses and that they liked frequent examinations because they could check up often on their mastery of the material. They were almost unanimous (96 per cent.) in stating that the diagnostic system was a time saver. Apparently here is to be found one significant explanation of the fact that this procedure effected no extra gain; the students reached safety with less work and did not try to go beyond.

CONCLUSIONS

From this work the following inferences seem important:

(1) It would seem clear that such "educational engineering" can as a matter of fact serve in many ways to improve instruction. The writers would suggest that in time such practices will become as common in education as an accounting system in business.

(2) They would also point out (in contrast to the usual opinion in this matter) a decided worth, in connection with any such program, of graduate student part-time instructors.[3] They would venture the assertion that, in most institutions and with the usual faculty attitude, such a program could not be satisfactorily put through in a course taught entirely by permanent members of the staff. But these young instructors were willing to cooperate. Since their future depended in part upon the satisfactoriness of their teaching they were eager to improve. And the class visiting and other checkups seemed under the circumstances natural and proper.

(3) In the third place the program was to these young instructors (and this surely does not need to be elaborated upon) a very valuable factor of their training for the profession of college teaching. And it is in this connection a natural outcome that a continuance of important phases of this research (aiming to develop a procedure which would take more adequate account of individual differences, develop a more intensive system of measurement, and systematize still more the routine "engineering") has been in the hands of a graduate student[4] as his doctor's thesis.

S. L. PRESSEY
L. C. PRESSEY
THE OHIO STATE UNIVERSITY

NEW BOOKS IN EDUCATION

ABBOTT, ARTHUR P. *A Loving People.* Pp. xi + 147. Illustrated. Arthur P. Abbott. $1.50.

BLACKIE, JOHN H. *Thought and Feeling in English Verse.* Pp. ix + 80. William Heinemann, Ltd., London. 1s. 9d.

COIT, MARJORIE C. *Projects in Science and Nature Study.* Pp. 64. Illustrated. American Museum of Natural History.

GRAY, HORACE and J. G. AYRES. *Growth in Private School Children.* Pp. xv + 282. University of Chicago Press. $3.50.

THORSMARK, THORA. *George Washington.* Pp. 293. Scott, Foresman and Company. $.52.

[3] The department of psychology has a distinctive system of part-time instructors developed by Dean George F. Arps as head of the department. Part-time instructorships are available at sufficient salary that it is possible to select exceptionally able men, of previous teaching experience. And the program of combined teaching and graduate work which these men take can be made, as here indicated, to give unusually effective teaching, exceptional training for future college teaching—and also (the writers believe) added significance to the graduate studies.

[4] Dr. C. H. Smeltzer, now of Temple University, Philadelphia. Dr. Smeltzer has done a decidedly vigorous and able piece of work, which it is hoped will be published shortly.

SCHOOL AND SOCIETY

EDITED BY J. McKEEN CATTELL

WITH WHICH IS COMBINED THE

EDUCATIONAL REVIEW

EDITED BY WILLIAM McANDREW

Volume 35 | Saturday, January 16, 1932 | Number 890

THE STATE UNIVERSITY—A SERVICE INSTITUTION[1]

By President JAMES MONROE SMITH

LOUISIANA STATE UNIVERSITY

THESE ceremonies mark my official entrance upon the duties of a high office, in the actual discharge of which I have now been engaged for one year, lacking five days. The presence here of this large company — distinguished representatives of state and national governments; of universities, colleges and learned societies; of the Army and the Navy; of the Louisiana public-school system; and of the board of supervisors, faculty and students of the university, together with this group of distinguished citizens—adds materially to the impressiveness of the occasion but can not make me more keenly aware of the seriousness of the task which I have undertaken. By their presence I am made more conscious of the fact that upon me has been conferred a great honor and upon my shoulders has been placed a great responsibility, towards the acceptable discharge of which I have dedicated my life and whatever of my talents and abilities may serve the office.

The present Louisiana State University had its beginning as the Louisiana State Seminary of Learning. The state constitution of 1845 availed itself of the grant of public land already made by the national government for the establishment of an "institution of higher learning." In 1853 a site on the east bank of the Red River near Alexandria was selected and a plan of organization adopted. The seminary opened on January 2, 1860, in an atmosphere surcharged with the conflict of opinion which was soon to culminate in the clash of states. In 1861 nearly all the faculty and students resigned to enter into the struggle, among them William Tecumseh Sherman, the first superintendent, who left his college duties to enter the Union Army. After the war, notwithstanding the poverty-stricken condition of the state, the seminary again opened its doors, in October, 1865. Under the presidency of David French Boyd the institution weathered the reconstruction period and in spite of small attendance, meager support and a fire which necessitated moving the whole school to new quarters in Baton Rouge, the instructional activities continued. Outgrowing these quarters—the building which is at present occupied by the State School for the Deaf—by 1886, the university secured the loan of the site and buildings of the United States Army post, just north of the city of Baton Rouge, from which regular troops had been withdrawn. The generos-

[1] Inaugural address of the president of the Louisiana State University, given at Baton Rouge, Louisiana.

ity of the United States Government in making this loan resulted in acts by Congress in 1902 and 1928, converting the loan into a gift to the university, with absolute title. As is well known to all who are familiar with the recent history of the university, these historic quarters were occupied until the beginning of the session of 1925–26. At this time most of its activities were transferred to the present plant, and in 1931–32 the transfer become complete.

During the period of more than seventy years, in which the university has occupied four distinct sites, important changes have taken place in its organization. In 1870 its name was changed by the Legislature to the Louisiana State University; and on January 2, 1877, the university and the Agricultural and Mechanical College, which had been chartered in 1873, and which had been in operation at New Orleans since 1874, were combined. Thus the two state institutions, "united and constituted into one and the same institution of learning," became the Louisiana State University and Agricultural and Mechanical College. The action of the Louisiana State Legislature of 1877 was not only significant; it was perhaps momentous. It meant the creation of one state university and the uniting of public opinion in its support. The continuance of the Agricultural and Mechanical College as a separate institution would have been conducive to the development of two inadequately supported, weak and competing universities attempting to serve the same area. The policy of developing the university and the Agricultural and Mechanical College as separate institutions has been followed in some of the states and can be justified, I feel, in more populous and wealthier commonwealths; but for a state with the population of Louisiana it would have been disastrous. One state university—one institution sufficiently broad in scope to serve the needs of all the people—has been always the hope and the aspiration of the statesmen and educational leaders of the state. This hope, then, is the foundation upon which Louisiana has built for more than seventy years and upon which with full confidence and abiding faith we stand to-day.

Rising gradually from this foundation the Louisiana State University has had a glorious past. It has rendered a tremendous service, not only to the people of this state, but in a measure to neighboring states and to foreign countries. Its student population has been more or less cosmopolitan from the beginning and much more so since the organization of the College of Agriculture, the College of Engineering and the Audubon Sugar School, all of which have attracted students from a wide area; the Audubon Sugar School, particularly, has drawn hundreds from Cuba, South America and other tropical and semi-tropical countries. The place of the university is not only well fixed in the fundamental law but also in the affection and regard of the people. Its campus is coextensive with the whole territory of the state, and in every community of the sixty-four parishes its representatives may be found. In shops and on farms; in government and in commerce; in industry and in education, its alumni have played an important part. There are among them jurists of high repute, lawyers of ability, engineers of note, teachers of distinction and scholars of renown.

We, however, are not here concerned primarily with the university's interesting and glorious history nor with its past or present achievement. We regard ourselves still, if not founders, at least as builders. We look upon the past, not as a source of complacent satisfaction but of inspiration, as we concern ourselves, in the true American spirit, with what is and what is to be. It is our task to turn our eyes toward the future and build as constructively as possible upon the heritage which has been transmitted to us. The test of the fitness of the president of this university has been, is and always will be measured in terms of what he has been able to build upon this foundation and what he has been able to contribute in providing wider opportunities for those who are now facing or must later face the future. This is a stern test and one that can not be met by any man alone, although one man must always accept the responsibility. An institution created and supported by the state for the purpose of serving the needs of the people of the state must take cognizance of their needs. Its leader must translate these needs into an educational program which is worthy of their aspirations and which challenges their intellect. Into such a program, with the whole-hearted cooperation of the faculty and officers of the university, he must breathe the spirit of lofty ideals, liberal scholarship, unstrained loyalty and willing service.

A university is the expression of the age in which it exists. It reflects not only the type of government, but, broadly speaking, the social ideals of the people both in its scheme of organization and in the conception of its functions and purposes. The Legislative Act of 1877, which constitutes the charter of the university, sets forth in Section 12, the organization, as follows:

> That there shall be maintained in the Louisiana State University and Agricultural and Mechanical College, First: Schools of literature, including the languages of the principal nations of ancient and modern times; philosophy, logic, rhetoric and elocution, history, ethics, metaphysics, and such other and special branches of learning as the board of supervisors may determine; Second: Schools of science, including mathematics, astronomy, engineering, drawing, physics, chemistry, botany, zoology, agriculture, mechanics, mining, navigation, and commerce, and such other special branches of learning as the Board of Supervisors may determine; Third: Schools of the useful and fine arts, and of military science and art; Fourth: Schools of medicine and law; Fifth: Such other schools as the Board of Supervisors may establish.

In accord with the purpose for which it was designed by its founders and the interpretation of present and future social needs, the following colleges and schools have been created from time to time and now constitute its organization: The colleges of arts and science; of agriculture, engineering and pure and applied science; of education and commerce; the schools of law and medicine; of music, geology, journalism and library science, and finally, the graduate school. In addition to these there should be perhaps added two other divisions; namely, a college of fine arts and a school of social welfare administration, as they would entirely complete the organization and furnish the machinery for rendering a complete educational service to the people of the state.

There are, however, men, held in high esteem, who insist that a state university, if it has been so unfortunate as to acquire them, should immediately divest itself of all those colleges, schools and divisions; those subjects, students and professors engaged in any type of work that smacks of the vocational or utilitarian—that is tainted in any way whatsoever with the practical or useful; that the introduction or continuance of such work as an integral part of its program should be resisted or discontinued on the ground that it lowers academic standards. With this point of view I find myself at variance. I am in full accord with the principle that strong colleges devoted to the humanities, and schools and departments devoted to teaching and research in pure science must be maintained and strengthened. Undoubtedly, these divisions constitute the core of a modern university. But, as President Coffman, of the University of Minnesota, points out:

> A university that fits for nothing, that lays only broad bases with no objective in view, that has no ideal but that of understanding and interpreting knowledge, searching for truth and training others

who are to understand and interpret knowledge and search for truth will . . . find it rather hard sledding in this practical world of ours. . . . Universities, certainly state universities, are not merely places for the living of an intellectual life; they are definitely designed and maintained to train practitioners for higher levels of service.

The broad scope and diversity of interests of a state university, particularly one embodying within its organization the agricultural and mechanical college, is shown by the following statement from the pen of President William Neilson, of Smith College:

The knowledge of fact and theory in agricultural, economic, and domestic fields that is called for by the people of a state, is theirs by right if they are willing to pay for it, and the state university with its complex organization, its varieties of research, its academic and non-academic methods of instruction, is the institution which has grown up to meet these needs. It may well be that the various divisions of the university would do their work better if they were separated; but this is a matter of organization and terminology. The professors of classics are not seriously disturbed in their philological labors because a colleague in the agricultural department gives advice to farmers on the best breeds of cattle for milk or beef, though the president might welcome a simplification of his functions.

A university should seek to understand and to interpret the movements and changes which are constantly taking place in our social order and to concern itself with the training of individuals for the vocations growing out of these changes. The entire history of higher education, as practiced in state universities at least, has been decidedly in the direction of this broader conception. Every expansion of the curriculum within recent years has grown out of some definite social need. New studies have come in—will continue to come in—as new needs and social shortages manifest themselves. As our population grows more dense and social relationships more complex new demands will be made and the university, I think it safe to say, will continue its policy of curriculum expansion. It is as undesirable as it is impossible for such a university to maintain its existence in an atmosphere of sheer intellectual isolation. As a public institution it is, as former President Kinley, of the University of Illinois, has stated, "the developmental arm of the state."

A state university is essentially, then, a service institution. There are but few people, I believe, in this country who, understanding its origin and being familiar with its growth and development, would take issue with this conception. There are certain specific functions and services which, it seems to me, are peculiar to a state university and which the people of the state may reasonably expect this institution to render. They may be summarized as follows: The conservation and transmission of the accumulated knowledge of the race, with some attempt at the interpretation of values; the extension of the boundaries of knowledge through research; the extension of the boundaries of applied science; and the discovery and training of students who possess marked ability or qualities of leadership in an unusual degree.

It will be readily recognized that the conservation and the transmission of knowledge is not peculiar to the college level. For this purpose the elementary and secondary schools exist primarily and fundamentally. Nevertheless, instruction is an important function of the university. The transmission of the social inheritance of the race is accomplished largely through formal instruction and inasmuch as the activities of the undergraduate college, particularly in the first two years, have to do almost exclusively with teaching, the instructional function looms large. Generally speaking, it has been the history of educational reform that it has worked from the bottom up. In the earlier days attention was chiefly centered upon the improvement of elementary education, and much is still being done in this field. Later, with the growing popularity of the high schools the problems of secondary education challenged the attention of the leaders of educational thought. Their vigorous attack upon the problems of curricula expansion and improvement of instruction on the secondary level resulted in many reforms and in improved service. With the enormous increase in college enrolment during recent years many problems heretofore of little importance have made their appearance in the institutions of higher learning. It is scarcely necessary to point out that reforms similar to those that have taken place in education in the elementary school and in the secondary school are now taking place on the college level. The training of college teachers still tends toward too narrow specialization. The individual so trained finds himself not only out of sympathy with the point of view of departments other than his own but likewise out of sympathy with those students who evidence an interest beyond the confines of his own field. That this problem has been recognized by university officials is shown by the number of articles appearing recently in educational journals and by programs sponsored by certain associations and institutions, notably the Institute for Administrative Officers of Higher Education, held at the University of Chicago. The graduate schools in the great universities of the country constitute the source of supply of college teachers. It is therefore to them that we must look for improvement in this field. The problem of increasing efficiency in instruction is not peculiar to any one type of college. The teachers engaged in unravelling the intricacies of a profession or the difficulties involved in interpreting problems in technology are as much concerned as those who are attempting to transmit knowledge of a general and cultural type. It is a problem that concerns the whole university and certainly one that will challenge the best minds in the field of higher education.

While the function of instruction is of primary importance, interest in research must always form a part of the university's offering and must absorb the attention and energies of at least a certain proportion of its faculty and staff. Any modern university accepts as a part of its service program the burden of attempting to extend the boundaries of knowledge. In performing the research function it is serving in a most acceptable manner not only the state which supports it but the nation which encourages it and the civilized world of which it is a component part. In this intricate and increasingly more complex civilization it is imperative that the work of research should be continued and its methods constantly refined. In fact, as a recognized authority in the field of higher education claims, "Intensive study of phenomena under the most favorable possible conditions—the phenomena of the physical world, of the social world, of the aesthetic world, and the ceaseless struggle to see things in relation, constitutes the most important function of a modern university."

While research in the field of pure science is of tremendous importance it must be borne in mind that our material civilization has advanced hand in hand with the application of science to such processes as manufacturing and refinement of material and to such problems as transportation, communication and commerce. It is then of paramount importance for the people of our own times that capable scholars shall devote their attention, energies and skill also toward the continual widening of the scope of applied science. The knowledge of electricity—its origin, nature and quality, as a theoretical problem—was of great interest to scientists of a half century ago, but the world was lighted with a tallow candle. Communication by the posted letter has now been supplemented by the telephone, telegraph, cable, wireless and radio. All the tremendous strides which have been made in the improvement of live stock, the subject of horticulture and the control of human diseases have come about through the efforts of that faithful group of workers who may be referred to as applied scientists. Whatever may be the faults of state universities, it is safe to assume that they have at least one saving virtue—they are responsive to social needs. They will continue to operate experiment stations, industrial research institutes and other research divisions whose avowed and publicly proclaimed object is the discovery of new methods and the application of new principles to the problems of our social order. This process—the process of socialization of science and invention—constitutes the very core of our modern civilization and is the basis of its continuance. There are, then, as will be readily recognized, two fields of research: one interested in the discovery of knowledge, *per se,* and the extension of its boundaries; the other in the discovery of new applications of known principles to the improvement of the various processes by which civilization is maintained and by which its continued progress is assured. The university should give equal protection and encouragement to the two types of research.

What is the responsibility of the university to the students who enter its doors? There are two views, widely divergent, on this question. One view is that the university is essentially interested in the conservation and the transmission of knowledge and in research as an impersonal objective. This view is clearly stated by Dr. Flexner as follows: "The university professor has an entirely objective responsibility—a responsibility to learning, to his subject, and not a psychological or paternal responsibility for his students." This is typically the attitude of the graduate school and of the professional school in this country. The former, from the very nature of the case, must take an objective, impersonal view of its functions, while the latter must recognize its responsibility to the profession for which it trains and to the public which is to be served by its votaries. But the graduate and the professional schools do not constitute the whole of the university. Should their philosophies then be permitted to permeate the whole institution? The trend in the United States has been decidedly toward a refutation of this theory. Evidence of this may be seen in the tendency to separate undergraduate work into junior and senior colleges; the establishment of personnel organizations for the social, educational and vocational guidance of students and the recent wide-spread interest already referred to, in the problem of improving instruction in the undergraduate college. It is, it seems to me, impossible for an educational institution to refuse to be concerned about the individual welfare of its students. As Dean Hawkes, of Columbia University, has pointed out, "Most colleges recognize the fact that in admitting a boy and girl the whole individual is involved." That our status in this matter is far from satisfactory, however, may be indicated by the following quotation from Dr. Little: "It is far easier," says he, "to administer an institution if the students are considered as so many logs of pulpwood to be turned into a certain number of paper degrees at the end of the senior year."

Certainly the university owes to the state a careful consideration of the many problems presented by incoming students. They come from all walks of life and they are interested in the variety of offerings and activities which are sponsored by the institution. The least that can be done for them is to assist in every way possible in their orientation in a new environment and their adjustment to new conditions, methods of instruction and modes of living.

There is another function of the university which must not be overlooked and which I feel has been, in the past, too often neglected: Students possessing qualities of leadership in a marked degree should not only be discovered but more attention given to their training. This is one of the fundamental purposes of the graduate school. Perhaps the greatest criticism that can, at the present time, be levelled at the graduate school is its uniformity of requirements for graduation. Students who expect to become primarily research workers and those who hope to become leaders in politics, social welfare work or as college teachers are put through exactly the same routine. The professional school has found that the most important factor in getting a high type of work from its students is not maturity nor excessive preparation but segregation. Would it not be better, then, to differentiate, in the graduate school, between those who expect to become research workers on the one hand and those who are preparing for social leadership on the other? Undoubtedly better research students could be trained by releasing them from the necessity of taking too many formal courses and by encouraging them to devote more of their time, with such direction as may be necessary, to the technique of research. And would it not be better to provide for those whose interests lie, primarily, in the field of social leadership, a curriculum made up of courses and problems which may be considered as fundamental to the adequate preparation for such work? It is an indisputable fact that America has produced a high type of technical leadership, as will be shown by a survey of such fields as finance, technology and commerce. It can, however, boast of few great statesmen, diplomats and leaders of social thought. We are to-day facing a crisis in our civilization because the socialization of our technology has fallen behind in the race of human achievement. It is imperative, therefore, that our graduate schools should recognize their responsibility to train students who "see life steadily and see it whole"; whose background of knowledge is rich, whose sympathies are broad, whose understanding is profound and whose ideals of service are built upon a high plane.

There is still another type of service which it is incumbent upon a state university to provide. In addition to its work in research, in instruction, in training for the professions, it must provide the equipment and the leadership for the training of its students in the artistic and esthetic. The aim is not primarily to train artists in the technical sense, while that is important and should be provided for, but to make of all its students, without reference to the curriculum being pursued, intelligent and appreciative consumers of the artistic, whether in nature or works of art.

It is not true that the state university is built upon a foundation of low artistic ideals, nor is it true that it is concerned only or primarily with the purely intellectual and practical. I believe that state universities will continue to be responsive to the needs and demands of the public that supports them; that when new needs arise they will be administered to; and as new social problems make their appearance new solutions will be sought. They will continue to disseminate information, not only through campus instruction, libraries and laboratories, but through divisions of extension and bureaus of information. I accept with seriousness the responsibility which I am assuming and I look forward with happy anticipation to the part which I hope to play in the continued interpretation of the spirit of the Louisiana State

University. I believe the university will continue to hold high the purposes and strive to attain the lofty ideals stated by its founders in its charter "to become an institution of learning in the broadest and highest sense, where literature, science and all the arts may be taught; where the principles of truth and honor may be established, and a noble sense of personal and patriotic and religious duty inculcated; in fine, to fit the citizen to perform justly, skillfully, and magnanimously all the offices, both private and public, of peace and war."

SCIENCE AND FAITH—THEIR CLAIMS IN CONTEMPORARY EDUCATION

By Professor EDWARD HARTMAN REISNER
TEACHERS COLLEGE, COLUMBIA UNIVERSITY

It would be of considerable interest to know what meaning the topic of this paper possesses for those whose eye it catches. To some, the juxtaposition of the words "science" and "faith" may imply that here at last has come forth a champion of the good old ways—some one to say, in effect, that science has its very definite limitations, beyond which we must fall back upon the factor of faith. Science may do very well with respect to things that can be weighed and measured, but there is a vast range of intangibles which it knows nothing about. In that realm we must have recourse to faith—and faith means the view of life and reality which our fathers accepted and which represents the classical orthodoxy in religion.

To others, the suggestion may occur that faith is in for a spanking. Faith, they might think, is out of date. The conquests of science have been so spectacular and extensive that we have come to be satisfied with what we know and can demonstrate. Every day science presses farther outward the boundaries of knowledge and control and we shall go with it. What we do not know at present, we shall wait for. Faith is the refuge of ignorance. It is the sign of muddleheadedness. No, faith is out, and science is in. Scientific methods are being applied more and more effectively every day in the procedures of education. Soon science will be everything in education. And if the writer knows his sigmas, that is the position which he is going to take.

One of the difficulties that is bound to arise in contrasting science and faith lies in the fact that each of these words is ordinarily thought of as possessing a single meaning. The meaning attached to faith is ordinarily—almost universally that of belief in the quantities made sacred in the traditional theology. These include a god who is a perfect being and who created, and rules from on high, the physical universe and the race of men. He gave laws for the government of man's moral life and holds him responsible through eternity for failure to keep the divine commandments. The vehicle of man's eternal existence is his undying soul, which was created in God's image with full responsibility for living up to his opportunities. Faith is thus identified with far-away, intangible existences which continue to hold the loyalty of millions, but which science finds no warrant for by any of the procedures which it employs.

On the other hand, science means the tested and respectable intellectual procedures of the present day. Science looks for law in everything. It depends upon experience. It asks for demonstration and proof. Its conquests have already gone so far as to supersede almost entirely the conception of the universe of man which one's father held. Revelation, miracle, the soul, and practically all the nomenclature of orthodox religious faith are meaningless or non-existent for the scientific spirit of to-day.

If one speaks of faith he is taken to mean the attitudes of the intellectual age which science has superseded. If one speaks of science, he can be taken to signify no intellectual method except that which has experienced such spectacular development in the Western world during the last three centuries and a half. He means the application of mathematics to the movements of celestial bodies, to the action of molecules, atoms, electrons, protons and ions, which has been instrumental in creating the imposing sciences of astronomy, physics and chemistry. Or he means the type of observation and description which has resulted in modern biology, botany, zoology, bacteriology, physiology and psychology.

This very simple contrast between science and faith has the great disadvantage of not being altogether sound—in fact, of being decidedly inaccurate. Science is by no means a single thing. That which we call science is a newcomer—it is the successor to that intellectual method coming out of Aristotle which up to the seventeenth century was itself regarded as science—science pure and undefiled. Aristotle was master of those who know, even as since the seventeenth century Newton, Darwin, Pasteur and Einstein have at successive periods been outstanding leaders of the respectable and dominant method of knowing.

The conceptions which to so many of us at the present time seem incomprehensible, but which live on vigorously in the orthodox statements of religious belief among us, at one time seemed to be perfectly justifiable in the light of the most rigorous intellectual method available. Aristotle's philosophy found a place for God—a conception amazingly like the Perfect Being of religious belief. His formulas of science fitted into the religious estimation of the relative lowness and vileness of human character and mundane affairs when they were placed in comparison with the perfect being who drew all creation up toward the thin ether which was his abiding place. For the man who took his point of departure from the philosophy of Aristotle and Plato, modified into closer conformity with the needs of the Christian religion by the great medieval leaders of thought, the shading off of science into faith was so gradual and imperceptible as to cause no difficulty. Faith was logical, easy, inevitable. The intangibles had to be where they were and what they were in order to fill out the picture. God, the soul, absolute truth and goodness, the immortal life not only were not inconsistent with the dominant intellectual attitudes, but they were the logical developments out of those attitudes and of the existing body of what passed in that age for science.

The story of the development of the new science, which began with Copernicus in the middle of the sixteenth century and has gained in authority with the passing of the centuries, is too long and complicated to recall even in its barest outlines in this connection. Neither will it be possible to describe the ever-widening hiatus between the new attitudes and findings of science and the old intangibles of faith, which had been so respectable and secure in the intellectual world of the middle ages. It is probably historically sound to say that the publication of Darwin's "Origin of Species" in the middle of the nineteenth century once and for all cut the thin thread which had kept the old faith in precarious touch with the new science. After Darwin the breach was complete, for the hypothesis of organic evolution destroyed the last lingering hold of the science of Aristotle upon which that faith was intellectually built.

No less interesting than the gradual separation of science and religion during those centuries is the rise from time to time of new faiths, more consistent with new intellectual standards, which philosophers and scientists declared and which were accepted by successive generations. The record of the wishful thinking of those three centuries is almost as complicated and luxuriant as is the record of scientific discovery. Man is apparently a believing animal, who almost inevitably goes a little beyond that which he can see and clearly knows. All that he asks is that his excursions into the land of faith be of a piece with the world which he knows in sober and undoubted fact.

Even so in our own day the aspirations, the will to believe, the faith of mankind run beyond the clearly marked limits of scientific knowledge. Much of that which gives life point and meaning—much of that which supplies dynamic power in our lives is of the tissue of dreams and hope and faith. Science describes the given; faith sees the potentialities of the matter of fact. Science is instrumental; faith is creative. Science is the servant; faith is the executive that recognizes worth-while objectives and furnishes the motive to attain them.

To be sure, the new intellectual conditions from which faith takes its departure in our generation profoundly change the things beyond knowledge in which we believe. A list of faiths consistent with the modern intellectual temper set down side by side with a list of the classical, orthodox faiths will exhibit a great deal of contrariety, even as modern science is extremely different from Aristotelian science. If, in the latter, God was the perfect being standing at the apex of a graded universe, in the former, which is the modern, God, in whatever way he may be conceived, if at all, is in and through the entire tissue of material and human existence. If the old faith disparaged earthly existence as relatively unworthy and unimportant and expended its energies on the life to come, the new faith sees the excellence and importance of this life and draws up plans to make it more satisfying and rewarding. Where the old regarded sickness, poverty and misery as inevitable and looked to heaven for compensation, the new sees the possibility of greatly lessening these drawbacks to human welfare and plans effective means of curtailing their empire. If orthodoxy viewed man's biological self as a collection of moral pitfalls, the faith of this day's science sees it as the basis of rich and triumphant personality. If the old and now discarded intellectual viewpoints encouraged men to believe in the inevitableness and sacrosanct quality of human institutions as they were and as they provided the support and sanction of injustice and oppression, the new temper of science breeds in mankind a faith that institutions are a product of social evolution and that they should be remade and changed so as to serve human needs the better. The old faiths were largely concerned with belief in a superexperiential reality which in some mysterious way laid its hand upon the world of human experience. The new faiths represent in great degree belief in things that ought to be done, and can, without too great strain on credulity, be seen as accomplished. In other words a modern faith is a program of desirable and feasible action.

It is a sign of our cultural dividedness and immaturity that the new faiths consistent with the spirit of modern science are not recognized as faiths at all. That word is applied almost exclusively to the faiths that are obsolete among educated folks, or rapidly becoming so. If one were to seek a reason for this inconsistency it probably is to be found in the fact that the spirit and methods of science have been applied in so small degree to human nature and institutions while they have been very thoroughly and consistently applied to the description, understanding and control of physical forces. When the scientific spirit is applied to economic, political, family and personal life as thoroughly as it has been to the stars and to coal tar, there is strong probability that man's vision of potentialities just around the corner from the actual will be greatly enhanced. In other words, new faiths pointing the way to desirable human reconstructions just beyond the present actualities will flourish in the atmosphere of scientific treatment. At present, however, our faiths have not as yet caught up with our science. Our generation is long on "how to do," but distinctly short on "what is worth doing."

The failure of the present age to develop its impulses on a parity with its techniques results in a noteworthy slackness and uncertainty in education. In sharp contrast with our fathers' fathers we are not sure about the objectives which we ought to seek. They had a definite conception of reality and clear blue prints for the way of life which was in accord with that system of reality. Everything in their world hung together. Even science lifted its voice in proof and praise of God. The light that glowed upon terrestrial concerns from the world of pure existence, pure truth and pure goodness showed the way to definite and exacting paths of conduct.

In contrast with the unity of that old world of faith our own is sprawling, disintegrated and wavering. The old faiths are dead and we have found no new ones to take their place. Accordingly, our education is lacking in direction. It possesses no sureness of touch. It is not integrated. It lacks punch and power.

Under the circumstances, what may be done? Certainly we can not force a mechanical union between the old faiths that are out of touch with our scientific knowledge and methods. The only alternative is to explore our experience, clarify our knowledge of our own impulses and set them in a position to guide our activities. It is impossible here to undertake any extensive enumeration of the faiths that are consistent with our new world of science and which more or less unrecognizedly are controlling our actions. However, it may be worth while to point out a few major lines of human impulse and aspiration which are at present operating and of which we deserve to be made more acutely conscious.

Of these the first that may be mentioned is a faith in the possibility of improving the larger political relationships among mankind. Such a faith comes up to the specifications that it be of a piece with experience and reasonably possible of realization. The thoughtful study of international affairs reveals the desirability of new attitudes and new political and economic ties among the nations of the world. Moreover, the first steps in the realization of such a consummation have already been taken. The dominance of the nineteenth century pattern of nationalism is being threatened. Its power over the impulses of mankind is being weakened. The possibility of change from universal competition to a measure of cooperation among nations has been demonstrated in fact. With a clear consciousness of further desirable developments of international good-will, the world may be carried far in the direction of a real community of nations. War, the dread scourge of humanity in the past, may be all but eliminated from human experience and its cost in life and health and wealth may be applied during the centuries to come in works of social constructiveness. Faith in the possibility of improving social organization in its more comprehensive patterns is a legitimate faith for educators in this generation. It is not a dream of distant and unattainable things, but an impulse to action with respect to something that is visible in its larger outlines even to-day. It is a faith that is already passing into the stage of being instrumented and put into operation. That faith ought to be at the core of every curriculum and of all the attitudes of every school in the Western world.

Another item in the catalogue of living faiths is a belief in the possibility and desirability of substantial improvement of the condition and welfare of mankind through change and adjustment in the economic order. Through the improvements of technology and of the means of production which modern science has brought about, the world has reached the point where it is even embarrassed by its riches in goods and commodities. Science applied to the problems of production and distribution, insurance, wages and leisure has already changed the economic scene until it is very different from that which our forebears knew. But only the beginning has been made. What is needed even more at present than the further improvement of technology is the presence in the minds of human beings of the impulse to apply available means to the improvement of human existence. We need faith, steady and unwavering, in the potential improvability of human society through the wiser and more equitable distribution of the products of collective activity. Faith in a better management of the economic life represents the dynamic impulse to bring such improvement about. Such faith should be placed squarely in the midst of the current school experience.

Still another major aspect of modern faith must be the belief that better citizens can be created who will manage better the civic affairs of the community. The impulse to the creation of citizens has up to now been almost exclusively devoted to setting up in the young attitudes of narrow and provocative nationalism. The future must expand the impulse of citizenship and vitalize it with reference to the daily necessities of honest, efficient, public-spirited management of community affairs. At present, by and large, we do not seem to believe in the possibilities of political health and efficiency. We are supine before the organized forces of corruption and personal advantage. And that condition will never change until the conception of what it means to be a citizen will be made to take its place with compelling force and power in the minds of citizens, young and old. Full appreciation of what citizenship means, full understanding of its effective exercise and dynamic impulse toward its realization represent an element of faith which deserves to be stimulated and vitalized.

There are other items in the modern catechism of faith which might be called to mind, but it will have to suffice if but one other is mentioned. This other, however, represents the inward reference of all the objective impulses which may be catalogued as items in a list of constructive human impulses. It is faith in human personality, which is the organizing core of experience in general. Just as a person is made up of impulses which represent the objective reference of his own self, just so the kind of person one is depends upon the kind of impulses which go out from him. The chief end and business of all education is the creation of human personalities. The chief item of educational faith is the belief that personalities can be constructively conditioned by the experiences which education may provide. The teacher, the curriculum and the methods of instruction employed are for nothing else than for the creation of persons who can and will be competent and effective in the good works of social administration and individual functioning. Personality can be improved through the means of conditioning the individual that are available—that must serve as one of the major tenets of a modern faith.

At present education with us is hindered from attaining more than a formal efficiency because the purposes and impulses of education are not clear. The old faiths have largely lost their hold. New ones to take their place have not yet been created. With all the wealth of scientific knowledge of the educative process which is available we are going no place in particular because we aren't sure of the larger objectives that we ought to seek. The most urgent thing to be accomplished in education to-day is not the extension of technical knowledge of the processes of education, but a clear delineation of the direction in which the procedures of education are to lead. In other words we need to discover and affirm and put into operation those programs of social improvement which are discoverable, with good intention, in the world about us and make them the direction posts for teacher and pupil in the schools. In short, we need to rediscover those dynamic impulses of experience which an older generation has called by the name of faith.

EDUCATIONAL EVENTS

EDUCATION IN CANADA

The Dominion Bureau of Statistics has issued preliminary statistical summaries of education in Canada for 1930. The totals for the year show 2,490,623 pupils enrolled in 32,209 schools or colleges, taught by 83,144 teachers; the entire cost was $165,361,198 or about $66 for each person enrolled. The average daily attendance was 77 per cent. of the enrolment; for every 32 pupils there was a teacher; the proportion of teachers with second-class or higher certificates in eight provinces was 95 per cent.; and the percentage of children in the upper grades was 13. Ordinary day schools, public and private, accounted for 2,199,153 of the enrolment; technical and vocational schools, 188,163; normal schools, 7,360; colleges and universities, 78,440 of which 19,783 were studying on preparatory levels; schools for the blind and deaf, 1,764, and Indian schools, 15,743.

The Dominion statistician makes the claim that of an equal number of Grade VIII pupils in the United States and in Canada, for every three in the United States that will study in Grade IX, four in Canada will. He attributes the high proportion in Canada to the fact that many children there find it possible to carry on high-school studies for one or two years in the rural schools. A school-life table of Canadian children based on age-grade tables that have been compiled for seven provinces for the past eight or ten years shows that of 100,000 boys and girls beginning school the following reach the grade specified:

Grade	*Boys*	*Girls*	*Both*
I	100,000	100,000	100,000
II	99,168	99,401	99,284
III	97,924	98,624	98,274
IV	95,368	96,956	96,112
V	90,895	93,579	92,237
VI	83,543	88,328	85,936
VII	73,413	80,914	77,163
VIII	61,845	71,812	66,829
IX	42,684	53,798	48,241
X	28,762	37,895	33,329
XI	17,382	23,000	20,191
XII	5,020	6,397	5,708

In explanation of the table the statistician writes, "The number shown in Grade XII (upper school in Ontario) does not fully represent the proportion taking the post-graduate high school year, for it is also taught as 'first year' in the universities. But it is to be noted from the above that 61.8 per cent. of boys and 71.8 per cent. of girls, or two thirds of the oncoming population, are getting as far as entrance to high school. Almost half of all are doing some high-school work—42.7 per cent. of the boys and 53.8 per cent. of the girls; and one-fifth are reaching the final or matriculation year—17.3 per cent. of the boys and 23.0 per cent. of the girls. The advantage of the girls is greatest in the advanced years, but it exists in smaller degree all the way through school. Its cumulative effect is to give the average girl half a year's more education than the average boy—8.5 years as compared with 8.0 years for the boy."

THE RETIREMENT FUND FOR TEACHERS IN VIRGINIA

An Associated Press dispatch printed in the Baltimore *Sun* states that the retirement committee of the Virginia Education Association has asserted that the state is under a definite and recognized obligation to Virginia's teachers, who have contributed $3,000,000 to the retirement fund.

In a formal report, which will be circulated among members of the General Assembly, the committee urges that the state guarantee an annual appropriation of $262,500 to the fund, to be matched by five per cent. of the salaries of all teachers in the public-school system.

Mr. Fred M. Alexander, of the *Newport News,* in making public the report, pointed out that the General Assemblies of 1912, 1916 and 1930 made adequate appropriations to cover deficits.

To-day the retirement fund which was established in 1908 on an admittedly unsound actuarial basis has been depleted. Education officials say that teachers have paid into the fund $2,000,000, which, with compound interest, amounts to $3,000,000.

They point out that not only will 17,000 teachers now in service lose their contributions to the fund unless aid is forthcoming, but assert that 1,022 retired teachers will be reduced to destitution.

The purpose of the act of 1908 "to provide a retirement fund for public-school teachers" is clearly set forth, the committee said. Under this act any teacher who had taught an aggregate of twenty years might be retired, provided he has maintained a good record and "by reason of physical or mental infirmity or old age is incapable of rendering efficient service."

That act further provided that a teacher might be retired for old age alone after twenty-five years of service, and further provided that the State Board of Education "may, of its own motion, place any teacher on said list who has served for twenty years if said board shall deem it best for the good of the school system."

The law provided for an annual appropriation of $5,000 by the state, plus one per cent. of the annual salary of all school teachers. It provided that each retired teacher should receive quarterly an amount equal to one eighth of the annual salary earned at the time of retirement, in no case to exceed $500.

By amendment in 1910, the retirement for old age was raised from twenty-five to thirty years and the age of retirement was fixed at 58 for men and 50 for women.

Another amendment deducted from the first annuity of each retired teacher an amount equal to thirty per cent. of the average annual salary earned during the last five years of service, thereby creating a permanent endowment fund. The annuity was based on the average annual salary for the last five years of service.

When a deficit existed in 1912 the General Assembly raised its appropriation to $8,000 and again in 1916 met a deficit by increasing the appropriation from $5,000 to $10,000. In 1930, when the fund was $60,000 in arrears, the General Assembly "appropriated the corpus of the permanent endowment fund to pay annuities," the report continues. This permanent endowment fund then amounted to $278,000.

The report asserts that as further proof of the state's "obligation" to the teachers, the General Assembly in 1930 provided for the appointment of a legislative commission "to make a scientific study of teacher retirement and to report to the assembly of 1932."

Of the 1,022 teachers now on the retired list, ninety-nine receive the maximum allowance of $500, eighty-four get from $400 to $500 per year and 839, or eighty-two per cent., receive annuities varying from $50 to $400 a year.

Condemning the present system as unsound actuarially, the committee announces that it will propose a "sound law" at the next assembly, "virtually all" the cost of which would be borne by the teachers, "in fact," the committee adds, "a male teacher who enters the plan at age 25 or under (female teacher 21 or under) will purchase his entire annuity without cost to the state."

The committee proposes that the teachers contribute five per cent. of their salaries, or approximately $750,000 annually. Of this amount they would turn over to the state for a period of eight years twenty per cent., or $150,000. This would be used to pay out the present pension roll, to provide past service annuities for teachers who soon will retire, and to provide disability allowances.

The remaining eighty per cent. of each teacher's contribution, the report asserts, would accumulate at interest to purchase his own annuity.

NEW YORK CITY'S PUBLIC SCHOOLS

THE New York *Times* reports that although New York City's public schools again became a battle-ground for civic debate in 1931, with the result that the State Education Department will begin its inquiry this month into their "pedagogical efficiency," the past year has been one of considerable achievement for the city's schools.

The biggest school budget on record, calling for an expenditure of $146,338,848, was adopted by the Board of Education last year for 1932. This represented an increase of almost $6,000,000 over the 1931 budget.

Oddly enough, this rise in education cost was attributed largely to the depression. Never before has there been such a sudden increase in demand for admission to the high and other secondary schools of the city. The record high-school register here of 194,000 is a gain of 22,000 over the previous year. More than 1,000 additional high-school teachers were provided, and several new high schools were projected.

The heavy enrolments in the city's forty-two high schools, caused by unemployment, brought a shifting of the short-time problem from elementary to secondary schools. There was no appreciable gain in the grammar school enrolment, so, with new buildings completed, the percentage of elementary pupils on part time was reduced to about 3 per cent. At the same time the figure for high schools rose to 15.8 per cent. last year from 12.6 per cent. in 1930. Two new high schools were opened during the year.

Another phase of the depression's effect was the sudden demand for free adult education. The emergency was met by throwing open to adults the city's continuation schools.

A more enlightened policy in the treatment of maladjusted and other special-problem children also was a feature of the year in the school system. The Board of Education established a "behavior clinic"—known as the Bureau of Child Guidance—to study and correct, if possible, cases of maladjusted pupils.

The school for truant boys in Queens was reorganized. The penal note was removed and a home atmosphere substituted, and 150 special classes enrolling about 3,600 handicapped children, including crippled, cardiopathic and tuberculous pupils, were regrouped.

The needy children of the city's public schools, in most cases, were cared for by the teachers and other employees of the Board of Education through contributions to the School Relief Fund, which reached almost $500,000 at the end of the academic year in June. With donations doubled, the administrators of the fund expect the current school year's fund to total $1,000,000.

Although the school board adopted a $68,000,000 building program early in the year, calling for erection of about ninety school buildings and additions over a three-year period, comparatively few of these projects were begun during 1931, because of disagreement among city officials as to the best method of acquiring sites. It was said at the board's offices on January 1, however, that thirty-four buildings were under construction at a cost of about $20,000,000.

SCHOOL SCHOLARSHIPS

THE American Child reports that the Vocational Service for Juniors, New York City, is appealing to the public for $50,000 to provide scholarships of $3.00 to $6.00 a week to New York City children whose parents can not afford to keep them in school without aid. This amount will be enough to keep 200 children in school until next June, who would otherwise be out of school and looking for work. The children will be carefully selected from applicants at juvenile employment offices and will be aided in the choice of studies. Those who need medical care will be sent to the proper clinics.

The New York Child Labor Committee is raising a scholarship fund for the benefit of children between 14 and 16 years who are still in elementary school, to enable them to complete the educational requirements for work permits.

In Chicago there are two organized scholarship offices in the Board of Education to take care of the children who can not stay in school without financial help. The budget for the combined offices during the present school year is between $50,000 and $60,000. In addition the

Chicago Tribune has collected some $25,000 for the "Hungry School Children's Fund" which is used to furnish free lunches in the schools for children of needy families.

A Louisiana Scholarship Association in New Orleans furnishes school facilities to hundreds of children, enabling them to go to high school as long as they maintain certain standards.

According to information received from the President's Organization on Unemployment Relief in Providence, in Rhode Island the Parent-Teacher Association has been very helpful in raising money for high-school scholarships, and local organizations and foundations have increased their aid for this service.

Indianapolis has tried to make it possible for every child under 16 years of age to attend school, regardless of the economic condition of his family. Funds have been provided by the Indianapolis Federation of Parent-Teacher Clubs, the Indianapolis Foundation, the Altrusa Club, the Exchange Club and a number of individuals. It was possible by this means to keep 346 additional students in school during the 1930–1931 school year.

FELLOWSHIPS AT COLUMBIA UNIVERSITY

COLUMBIA COLLEGE has established fellowships which will enable graduating students of merit to continue their studies at either the University of Oxford or the University of Cambridge, according to an announcement made by the *Columbia Alumni News*. The new honors are known as the Euretta J. Kellett Fellowships and have an annual minimum stipend of $2,000.

The faculty of Columbia College will nominate for the fellowships the graduates who have shown exceptional proficiency in the study of the humanities. The number of scholarships to be given will be determined by the trustees of the university and the appointees of the college will be passed upon by them.

The recipients of the awards will spend one year or more at either of the two English universities. The first Kellett fellowships will be given to members of the graduating class of 1932.

The Alumni News in an editorial states that the fellowships are similar to the Rhodes Scholarships.

For one thing, they will bring further to the front the importance of the college in the university and will help to keep it from being submerged among the many departments of the institution. They also will be a splendid gesture toward binding the knot of friendship between Columbia and Oxford and Cambridge.

Although the new Kellett Fellowships will lack the tradition and nation-wide scope of the Rhodes Scholarships, it is believed that within a few years the importance and honor that are attached to the former will become known far beyond the confines of Morningside Heights.

Another scholarship for Columbia College was established in honor of the late James H. Killough and will be awarded annually to the member of the graduating class of Erasmus Hall High School, Brooklyn, who is most distinguished among his classmates in literary and scholastic ability and attainments, manhood, character, public spirit and leadership. The student selected must enter Columbia as a candidate for the bachelor of arts degree. The stipend is $1,400 for four years.

Two other scholarships were founded, one in the name of Harriet S. Phillips and the other to be called the Lydig Fellowship. The Harriet S. Phillips Scholarship is designed as a financial aid for women students in the School of Journalism and will be awarded every year, with the recipients eligible for reappointment. The Lydig Fellowship will be given for work in the graduate faculties of political science, philosophy and pure science.

THE HEALTH OF STUDENTS AT YALE UNIVERSITY

THE annual report of the director of the Department of University Health at Yale outlines the efforts being made to safeguard the students' physical and mental health. The report shows that there were 5,322 routine medical examinations, 1,507 orthopedic examinations, 30,973 office consultations, 4,248 dental examinations and 1,245 vaccinations of all kinds.

Under the direction of Dr. Willard B. Soper, stereoscopic x-ray films were taken for the first time of the lungs of all members of the entering classes of all departments of the university with a view to determining the presence of tuberculosis in any of its manifestations. A total of 1,602 routine examinations of new students was made. The findings indicated that 30, or 1.9 per cent. of the new students had shadows of threatening character. A total of 283 students, 17.7 per cent. of those examined, gave evidence of infection potentially dangerous but in most instances destined not to cause trouble.

All students who showed shadows of a threatening character are carefully followed during their college courses and x-rays of the chests will be made at least once a year. It is pointed out that a certain number of them should be saved from a breakdown, and a single one so saved would justify the expense.

A meeting of the representatives of a number of universities was held in July under the auspices of the National Tuberculosis Association, at which there was discussed the formulation of a plan for the early diagnosis of tuberculosis practical and economical enough to be recommended to educational institutions generally.

The Division of Student Mental Hygiene has had a number of out-of-town visitors, many of whom have represented other universities wishing to develop a program for their student body. In line with this general interest of universities in student mental hygiene, a committee has been appointed by a joint conference of the American Student Health Association, the National Health Council, and the President's Committee of Fifty on College Hygiene. This committee aims to establish desirable minimum standards with respect to mental hygiene service in universities and colleges.

In the field of nutrition, it was found that sixty-two members of the freshman class were 10 per cent. or more below standard weight. These students were given individual instruction relative to their particular problems, and fifty-six made a distinct gain in weight.

The appointment of a full-time dental surgeon has resulted in a much broader service to the student body. In addition to the inspection and charting of the teeth of 4,248 students, emergency treatments and treatments for Vincent's infection have been given and restorations and extractions have been made for self-supporting students.

THE DEATH OF RANDALL J. CONDON

RANDALL J. CONDON, nationally known educational leader, died on December 24 at Greenville, Tennessee, where he had gone to spend the Christmas holidays with his daughter, Mrs. Frank C. Foster, and her family.

Dr. S. D. Shankland, secretary of the Department of Superintendence, in tribute to the past president of the department writes:

Dr. Condon stood for the finer things in life. His was a spirit which could not be satisfied with anything that bordered on the sordid or the mean or the low. He was a militant leader in righteous causes. When for policy's sake others held their peace, Dr. Condon was wont to assume leadership in aggressive fashion. He knew, too, how to bring things about in conference and in personal contacts with his associates. Leadership is an intangible thing; but whatever it is, he possessed it.

Superintendent Condon spent a lifetime in promoting the interests of the children of America. His services as superintendent of schools at Templeton, Massachusetts; Everett, Massachusetts; Helena, Montana; Providence, Rhode Island, and Cincinnati, Ohio, covered a period of exactly forty years. In each of these cities the permanent imprint of his personality was left for good.

Dr. Condon found time for many outside activities. Among other responsibilities of a busy life, he was president of the Department of Superintendence of the National Education Association, 1926–1927; a delegate to the Geneva Convention of the World Federation of Education Associations; president of superintendents' associations in New England, Montana and Ohio; a member of the Ohio State Board of Education; a trustee of Colby College, and an author of text-books and magazine articles. He was in constant demand as a public speaker.

Death called him in the midst of his work. With a light heart he had gone to spend the Christmas holidays with his daughter and the grandson of whom he was so proud, after completing a tour of more than thirty states to press the campaign against illiteracy. His mind was active with plans for the Committee on Financing Educational Research of the Department of Superintendence, of which committee he was chairman, and for enlarging the activities of the National Congress of Parents and Teachers, of which organization he was vice-president. He was a man of the type whom the schools sorely need just now. He was an educational missionary. As he left my office just before the holidays, he wished all of us a Merry Christmas and paused to say, "These are critical times for the children. We must stand by our guns."

EDUCATIONAL NOTES AND NEWS

THE California State Superintendent of Public Instruction, Dr. Vierling Kersey, has announced his resignation to become effective next August. He will become superintendent of schools of Long Beach, at a salary of $10,000 a year, which is double the salary of the state position.

MAJOR GENERAL W. D. CONNOR, superintendent of the Army War College, Washington, D. C., has been appointed superintendent of the Military Academy at West Point effective on April 30. He succeeds Major General William R. Smith, who retires.

DR. JAMES D. BRUCE has been appointed vice-president of the University of Michigan, in charge of university relations. This is a newly created position in which Dr. Bruce's duties will be to centralize all requests made to the university for outside aid and meet them so far as the university's resources allow. Dr. Bruce for the last three years has been director of the department of postgraduate medicine.

DR. M. E. SADLER, professor of science, has been appointed to succeed Professor C. L. McPherson as dean of Lynchburg College, Virginia. Professor McPherson has served as dean for five years.

DR. J. G. FITZGERALD has been appointed dean of the faculty of medicine at the University of Toronto to succeed Dr. Alexander Primrose. Dr. E. Stanley Ryerson, secretary of the faculty and assistant professor of surgery, has become assistant dean.

MR. HERBERT BRUCKER, of the editorial board of *The Review of Reviews,* has been appointed assistant dean of the Columbia University School of Journalism. Mr. Brucker takes up his new work on January 15.

DR. WILLIAM LYON PHELPS will retire in June, 1933, from the Lampson professorship in English at Yale University, which he has held since its establishment in 1901. Dr. Phelps will sail for a tour of the Mediterranean within a few weeks.

DR. JAMES R. ANGELL, president of Yale University, on whom the University of Liverpool proposes to confer the honorary degree of Litt.D., was unable to be present at the congregation of the university held in December in connection with the jubilee celebrations.

A DINNER and reception was tendered to Dr. Charles E. Mackey, newly elected member of the Boston School Committee, at the Hotel Bradford on January 6, more than one thousand persons being present. Among those who spoke were Governor Ely, Commissioner William G. O'Hare, of the Institutions Department, School Committeemen William A. Reilly, Maurice Tobin and Joseph J. Hurley, Superintendent of Schools Patrick J. Campbell, District Attorney William J. Foley, the Reverend Richard A. Burke, former Mayor Nichols, Dr. Edward J. Denning, Robert S. Atkins and James H. Brennan. Dr. Mackey was presented with a watch by Daniel J. Tyne, who acted as toastmaster.

THE REVEREND LOUIS J. GALLAGHER, S.J., the newly appointed head of Boston College, was recently tendered a dinner by the Community of the Dorchester (Massachusetts) High School Center. Dr. Gallagher's address was on "Soviet Russia and World Conditions."

SIR EDWARD DENISON ROSS, director of the London School of Oriental Studies, who has been on a lecture tour in the United States under the auspices of the American Institute of Persian Art and Archeology, New York City, was the guest of honor on December 28 at a farewell dinner given by the institute at the Waldorf-Astoria. Mr. Franklin M. Gunther, formerly Minister to Egypt, president of the institute, presided. The speakers included Professor John Coss, of Columbia University, toastmaster; Dr. John H. Finley, of the New York *Times;* Mr. Arthur Upham Pope, director of the institute, and Sir Edward.

AT the national convention held at New Orleans from December 28 to 31, of the National Social Science Honor Society, Pi Gamma Mu, Incorporated, Dr. Charles A. Ellwood, professor of sociology in Duke University, was elected national president and the society was completely reorganized on a higher plane with the definite purpose of promoting scholarship in the social sciences, including sociology, economics, political science, history, philosophy, ethics, psychology, education, religion, etc. The other officers elected were: Dr. George Harris Webber, Georgia State College for Women, *first vice-president;* Dr. Gordon S. Watkins, University of California at Los Angeles, *second vice-president;* Dr. S. Howard Patterson, University of Pennsylvania, *treasurer,* and Dr. Leroy Allen, Southwestern College, *executive secretary.*

AT the recent meeting in Minneapolis of the American Historical Society the George Louis Bier prize of $250 was awarded to O. J. Hale, assistant professor of history at the University of Virginia, for his "Study of Germany and the Diplomatic Resolution, 1904–1906"; the Herbert Baxter Adams prize, of the value of $200, to V. W. Puryear, of Albany College, Oregon, for an essay on "England, Russia and the Straits Settlement," and the John H. Dunning prize of $200 to Frances B. Simpkins and R. H. Woody for their joint book "South Carolina during Reconstruction."

AT Rutgers University Mr. Herbert D. Bixby has been appointed associate professor of education and Mr. George A. Osborn, for more than thirty-five years connected with the Rutgers library, has been raised from the rank of associate professor to a full professorship.

THE REVEREND DR. HOWARD TILLMAN KUIST, of the faculty of the Biblical Seminary in New York, will join the staff of Princeton Theological Seminary for the second half of the current academic year as visiting professor during the absence in the Far West of the Rev. Dr. Charles R. Erdman, professor of practical theology.

MR. MASON HAMMOND, of the department of classics at Harvard University and for a year and a half head tutor at Lowell House, has resigned on account of his marriage. He will be succeeded by Dr. G. C. S. Benson, who has been tutor in government at Harvard for the last two years.

PROFESSOR FRANK L. SHEPARDSON has resigned as treasurer of Colgate University to become effective on August 1. He has been associated with the university for the last thirty years as professor of Greek and has held the treasurership for twenty years.

MISS OLIVE TORGENSON, who was recently elected dean of women in Carthage College to succeed Miss Adah Livingston, has taken up her new work. Miss Livingston has been associated with the administrative matters of Carthage College since 1918, when she served as registrar and instructor in history. In 1922 she became instructor in Latin for a year, and in September, 1929, she returned as dean of women.

CANON R. D. BUDWORTH has announced his intention of retiring at the end of the summer term from the head mastership of Durham School, England, a position he has held for a quarter of a century.

AN educational committee headed by Dr. Paul Monroe, director of the International Institute of Teachers College, Columbia University, sailed on January 12 to investigate the educational system of the Iraq government with particular reference to the application of education to the present problems of industry. The survey will be made at the request of the Iraq government. The other members of the committee are Professor W. C. Bagley, head of the department of teachers training, Teachers College, and Dr. Edward W. Knight, head of the department of education of the University of North Carolina. Miss Janet Monroe, daughter of Dr. Monroe, will accompany the committee as secretary.

DR. and MRS. HAROLD RUGG will spend the next six months conducting studies of cultural changes in China. These studies are the first of a series to be carried on in collaboration with associates in Nankai University in Tientsin, under the auspices of the Institute of Pacific Relations. Dr. Rugg will also collaborate with the Japanese and Chinese leaders in organizing branches of the New Education Fellowship. Returning through Siberia and eastern Europe, Dr. and Mrs. Rugg will take part in the sixth World Conference on the New Education at Nice, in August, 1932. They plan to return to the United States in September.

DR. WILLIAM L. BURDICK, vice-president of the University of Kansas and professor of law, has leave of absence for the academic year beginning in September. Dr. Burdick plans to visit European countries with a view to completing manuscripts upon which he is now working.

Professor D. D. T. Jabavu, of the South African Native College, Fort Hare, Alice, Cape Province, is visiting the United States.

Clark P. Bissett, professor emeritus of the University of Washington, Seattle, died on January 9 in his fifty-sixth year. Dr. Bissett was professor of law for sixteen years and dean of the law school until his retirement in 1929.

The Rev. Dr. Walter Bowman Yount, head of the classical language department of Western Maryland College since 1912, died on January 5 at the age of seventy-two years. Dr. Yount was president of Bridgewater College, Virginia, for a period of sixteen years.

The death is announced at the age of sixty-three years of Miss Lida Shaw King, professor of classical literature and archeology and from 1905 to 1922 dean of the women's college in Brown University.

The death at the age of eighty-two years is announced of John Frederick Eliot, head master of the East Boston High School for thirty-one years until his retirement in 1920.

Dr. William Kershaw, head master emeritus of Germantown Academy, Philadelphia, with which he was connected for fifty-seven years, died on January 6 at the age of eighty-eight years.

Miss Sarah Comly Norris Bogle, assistant secretary of the American Library Association, died on January 10. Miss Bogle was assistant librarian for the Queensboro Library of New York in 1909, and from 1909 to 1911 was librarian of the East Liberty branch of the Carnegie Library at Pittsburgh. She also served with the main Carnegie Library at Pittsburgh and later was principal of the Carnegie Library School. When a member of the American Committee for Work in Devastated France in 1923 Miss Bogle was director of a summer library course in Paris. She also was director of the Paris Library School from 1924 until it was closed for lack of funds in 1929.

Miss Anna Beach Pratt, since 1916 director of the White-Williams Foundation and one of the two women members of the Philadelphia Board of Education, died on January 3 at the age of sixty-four years. Before going to Philadelphia she was active in social service work in Elmira and organized the first welfare federation group in the city. In June, 1929, she was appointed a member of the Philadelphia Board of Education. For five years, until 1930, she served as president of the Philadelphia County Council of Home and School Associations.

Arthur S. Somers, a manufacturing chemist, member of the New York City Board of Education and at one time its president, died on January 6. He was sixty-five years old. Except for two brief periods, Mr. Somers had been continuously active for forty years in the direction of the public school system, first of Brooklyn and then, after the consolidation of the five boroughs, of the whole city.

The Inglis Lecture of the Harvard Graduate School of Education was delivered by Dr. William Setchell Learned, of the Carnegie Foundation for the Advancement of Teaching, on January 13. The title of the address was "Realism in American Education." The Inglis Lectureship in Secondary Education was established by the Harvard Graduate School of Education in honor of the late Professor Alexander Inglis, a member of the faculty of the school, who at the time of his death in 1924 had become a leading scholar and writer in the field of secondary education.

At the Christmas meeting of the American Political Science Association, Washington, D. C., four representatives of teacher-training institutions were invited to appear on the program to discuss certain aspects of the problem of the work in civics in the secondary schools. The representatives were: Dr. George Counts, Teachers College, Columbia University; President J. O. Engleman, Kent State College; Dean J. B. Edmonson, School of Education, University of Michigan, and Dean Charles H. Judd, University of Chicago.

The cornerstone of the new building of the Enoch Pratt Free Library, Baltimore, was laid on January 12 by Mayor Jackson. Mr. William G. Baker, Jr., president of the board of trustees of the library, and Mr. Joseph L. Wheeler, librarian, were the principal speakers.

The twentieth annual conference of British educational associations was held from January 4 to 11 at University College, London, under the presidency of Sir William Rothenstein. The presidential address was given on January 4. On the same day, Dr. Emmanuel Miller delivered a lecture on "The Difficult Child: Sociological *versus* Individual Interpretation." Other lectures include Mr. J. Howard Whitehouse on public schools and public life, and Mrs. C. B. S. Hodson on the desirability of including biology in the school syllabus. On January 6, a popular lecture on comets and shooting stars was given by Sir Richard Gregory. A discussion was arranged on the film in education.

THE following addresses were given at the recent national convention of Pi Gamma Mu held at New Orleans during Christmas week: "Pi Gamma Mu's Obligation to the Coming Generation," by Dr. James Elliott Walmsley, Virginia State Teachers' College, Farmville; "The Functioning of Social Ideals," by Leroy Allen; "New Economic Ideals for Old," by Dr. S. Howard Patterson; "Scholarship in the Social Sciences," by Dr. Charles A. Ellwood; "Russia in Retrospect," by Dr. Gordon S. Watkins; "The Task of Higher Education in a Social World," by Dr. Hamilton Holt, president of Rollins College, and "The Social Mission of Humor," by Dr. George Harris Webber.

DR. WILLIAM TRUFANT FOSTER, director of the Pollak Foundation for Economic Research, formerly president of Reed College, has left for the West for a lecture tour lasting three months. He is expected to lecture at the following institutions: the University of Kansas, Washburn College, Kansas State, the University of Oklahoma, the University of Colorado, the University of Utah, the Utah State College, Pomona College and Scripps College, Stanford University, Mills College, the University of California, the State Normal School, the Bellingham, Washington, the Washington State, State Normal School, Cheney, the University of Idaho, the Montana School of Mines, North Dakota State, Minneapolis and Carleton Colleges and Purdue University.

DISCUSSION

1932 AS A CENTENNIAL YEAR IN THE HISTORY OF EDUCATION

IN continuation of previously published lists[1] of centennial dates in the history of education, the following group of important 1932 dates is presented. Additional details regarding the events and persons mentioned may be found in the standard encyclopedias and histories of education.

469 B. C.

Birth of Socrates, whose guiding principle in education and philosophy was ''Know thyself.''

A. D. 732

Battle of Tours, assuring the continuance of European government, law, education and civilization.

A. D. 1432

Founding of the Sevenoaks Grammar School in England.

A. D. 1632

Birth of Locke, English educational philosopher, who set forth the disciplinary theory of education and profoundly influenced later educational philosophy.

Publication of Galileo's *Dialogo dei due massimi sistemi del mondo*, expounding the Copernican theory.

Banishment of Comenius from Moravia to Poland where he worked out in practice his great work on method, *The Great Didactic*.

A. D. 1832

Establishment of first school for crippled children, at Munich, Germany.

Address of Guizot, ''The Gladstone of France,'' to the Chamber of Deputies in introducing the law which became the foundation of national elementary education in France.

Death of Andrew Bell, one of the creators of the widely known ''Monitorial System'' of schools.

Organization of the ''Western Literary Institute and College of Professional Teachers'' at Cincinnati, making that city the center of educational propaganda in the west.

Opening of first public school in Chicago.

Opening of the first American institutions for the blind in Boston and in New York.

Enactment of special legislation to provide free public schools for New York City.

Publication of Noah Webster's ''History of the United States,'' marking the beginning of the study of civics in American grammar schools.

[1] SCHOOL AND SOCIETY, Oct. 9, 1926; Feb. 5, 1927; Feb. 25, 1928; Jan. 12, 1929, Feb. 1, 1930; Jan. 3, 1931.

Opening of Wabash College, Indiana.
Opening of New York University, New York.
Opening of Lane Theological Seminary, Ohio.
Opening of Lafayette College, Pennsylvania.
Opening of Randolph-Macon College, Virginia.
Opening of University of Richmond, Virginia.
Benjamin Pierce became professor of mathematics and natural philosophy at Harvard, marking an epoch in the history of mathematics teaching at Harvard and in the United States.
Thomas H. Gallaudet became professor of the philosophy of education at the University of the City of New York, probably the first effort to train teachers in higher collegiate institutions in America.

W. C. EELLS

STANFORD UNIVERSITY

COUNSELING SERVICE IN THE SMALL PUBLIC SECONDARY SCHOOL

WHAT does the future hold for counseling in the small public secondary school? What opportunities are there for efficient application of our counseling practices now in vogue in many of our high schools of 300 to 500 enrolment? It is true we have developed a guiding philosophy of secondary education whereby greater relationships between the individual and society have been brought about through a counseling program. We have also become aware of the general functions of the counseling work, developed certain techniques, and, to a certain degree, have been able to evaluate and measure the results of counseling.

But with all our general and specific knowledge of the aims and practices concerned with the task of counseling, we have not by any means reached the point of efficiency that could be obtained when it comes to applying this knowledge to individual counseling in the average size high school. Most of the counseling outside of the large city school systems is being carried on by the part-time counselor, who is allowed to devote only one or two periods of the day's program to this work. Such a counselor even in the small high school is handicapped from the start in attempting to make counseling an individual matter. A secondary school which has an enrolment of less than 500 students offers a serious problem to the counselor who is limited in both time and resources towards efficient application of the principles of his profession. His job of counseling consists for the most part of giving attention to problem cases which are ever present in a public institution of learning. The counselor, as a result, has neither time nor energy to extend a liberal guidance program to the average or superior type of student who many believe should be given greater consideration than the weaker student, who figures very largely in the group that leaves school before the completion of their course. A large part of the counselor's duties are of routine nature which have to do with the compilation of records, testing and its interpretation, placement and follow-up work, which are an additional burden to the adviser.

If we wish to apply our principles of counseling in a democratic fashion we can not afford to give less attention to the moron than to the genius because of the public nature of the secondary school itself, which more or less dictates that we proceed with the policy of equality in the treatment and guidance of those of high-school age. Since it is apparent that the majority of high schools can not afford to provide full-time counseling service, what changes or solutions to the problem can be made to the best advantage of all concerned?

In an inspiring address given at one of the sections on counseling at the recent National Education Association convention in Los Angeles, Professor G. Watson, of Teachers College, Columbia University, after acknowledging certain difficulties which arise in administering a guidance program, offered the suggestion that the public schools could well afford to devote a full week at the beginning of school for purposes of establishing a counseling program in respect to the freshman students. What a great advantage there would be if the advisers and other members of the school staff could get better acquainted with the freshmen during this first week in assisting them to become aware of the actual aims and practices of the high school where they are to spend a whole or part of their four years of schooling! The splendid opportunities which it would provide the counselor in making a case record for every beginning student to be utilized throughout his school career are self-evident. This, in the writer's judgment, is an opportunity that should be seized upon and applied, for the time spent on the pupil, parent and school would unquestionably be justified as sound educational achievement. The idea of Freshman Week is not a new one in the field of education, as it has been successfully applied in many of our universities and colleges, but the use of this plan in the high school has not for some reason or other been given much serious consideration and trial. The practice of the high school in assisting the pupil to make his social adjustment has often been its primary function, while the practice of aiding the student to adjust himself from an educational or vocational standpoint has received only secondary attention. Proper organization and application of practices which tend to assist the pupil in the way of educational and vocational guidance should be attempted before and not after the school year is under way. The necessary machinery for efficient guidance should be set in motion during the first few weeks of school in order to prevent wasteful methods and procedures which always follow in the wake of poor planning.

Whether a particular school can afford to give as much time as a week to the incoming students is a matter of local concern, but certainly at least three days could be well spent in establishing a machinery for educational adjustment and for a counseling service. Assuming that the plan is accepted as being educationally sound and that time and resources are available, what should constitute an economical program for the beginning student? The following is a suggestive outline for a program of adjustment covering the first three days of school:

I. First day
- A. General assembly
  - 1. Address of welcome by the principal
  - 2. Introduction of important members of the school staff, *i.e.*,
    - a. Vice-principal
    - b. Boys' and girls' deans or counselors
    - c. Heads of departments
  - 3. A talk giving outline of course offerings in the school
    - a. Requirements and nature of college preparatory course
    - b. Same for general, commercial and shop courses
  - 4. Brief instructions for registration
    - a. Where, how and when to register
- B. Tour of the high-school campus
  - 1. Visit to classrooms, gymnasium, shops and athletic field
- C. Registration
  - 1. Registration by subjects
  - 2. Registration with deans or counselors
    - a. To provide such persons with personal information bearing upon social and economic conditions which are necessary to the counseling service.
- D. Student conferences in respect to:
  - 1. Program of studies
  - 2. Part-time employment
  - 3. Other information or services
- E. Conferences with parents
  - 1. To obtain further information of a personal nature concerning student
  - 2. To discover home conditions
  - 3. To establish means of cooperation between parent and school

II. Second day
- A. Intelligence testing
  - 1. Group testing
- B. Aptitude testing
- C. Physical examination
- D. General assembly
  - 1. Health talks
    - a. To be given to students collectively or to boys and girls alone
- E. Conferences with students or parents

III. Third day
- A. General assembly . . . for instruction in regard to:
  - 1. Discipline
  - 2. School traditions
  - 3. Advantages of scholarship
  - 4. Extra-curricular activities
  - 5. Student body government
  - 6. Use of the library
- B. Class sessions
  - 1. Distribution of books and supplies
  - 2. Use and care of texts and equipment
  - 3. Preliminary instructions and assignments by teacher
- C. Conference with students or parents

IV. Fourth day
- A. Registration of old students
- B. Class work begins

The above outline of a three-day program to be sure is an ambitious one, but with proper planning and necessary cooperation of the administrative and teaching force, it should prove to be one of the most helpful aids towards pupil-adjustment than perhaps has been experienced in any other form of educational endeavor. In respect to the testing program indicated in the outline, the writer does not feel that a rigid scheme of testing should necessarily follow in every school. If the high school is fortunate in securing the intelligence test scores from the elementary school and the results are satisfactory to the school counselor, a repetition of a testing program would be both necessary and expensive to the school. If, however, resources are available, it would be perhaps advisable to retest the entire group of incoming students in order to obtain more satisfactory results under similar testing conditions. The giving of aptitude or similar tests rests entirely with the school officials, who may desire additional information for their particular educational scheme or organization.

The above plan of preregistration or educational adjustment might of course be extended over the entire first week of school depending upon its size, and upon the resources at hand for the application of a more extensive program. Whether the beginning period be three or five days, there at least has been a start in the right direction for an orderly, wise and efficient administration of pupil-adjustment through the agency of a limited counseling service in the small high school.

Richard M. Benson

San Mateo, California

SPECIAL CORRESPONDENCE

NEW SCHOOLS IN OLD MEXICO

Last summer through the kind cooperation of Dr. Manuel Baranco, head of the Secondary Education division in the Ministry of Education, and through the cooperation of the various heads in other departments I enjoyed visiting Mexican schools and observed them at close range in their normal functioning. My visits were centered chiefly in the new schools in the capital. Summer being the rainy season in Mexico, all the schools were in session. The long summer vacation comes during the sunny months of December and January.

Primary Education

The new kindergartens in the capital attracted my attention first. They are located in old convents, remodeled especially to house the children of kindergarten age. In their philosophy, curricula, methods and arrangement they do not represent the kindergartens of the old Froebelian type. They embody the spirit and methods of the new modified type of kindergartens, the first model of which was originated under the auspices of Teachers College, Columbia University, under the leadership of John Dewey. They represent the actual activity school. Children work in real gardens, plant seeds, cultivate the land and harvest crops. They take care of animals, raise chickens, rabbits and goats. They indulge in all types of physical activity under the boughs of dark green trees. One must admit at once the fact that these kindergartens are not housed in modern buildings for lack of money (*por falta de dinero*), but they enjoy a compensating advantage, namely, groves and gardens of unrivalled verdure and beauty. The directress of the school told us again and again that children spend almost all their time in the open air, except during the rain. I can not forget the enthusiasm of young Mexicans in presenting to their visitors a bunch of radishes (*rebanitos*), the product of their care and toil.

Elementary Education

Through the kind permission of Señor Esquivel, then the head of the division of Elementary Education and Teacher Training, we visited the elementary schools in the city. Mexican elementary schools have six grades only. They are coeducational. They, too, embody in their objectives, curricula and methods the spirit of modern progressive education. The elementary school authorities believe in creative activities. They teach reading through word and story methods. Children write original compositions and work in shops attached to their schools. As to organization, classes are divided into various groups—from three to seven, according to intelligence quotient and achievement of the pupils. The proficiency of each student is determined by mental tests, objective standard tests of achievement (*pruebas mentales*). Teachers seem to be familiar with new-type testing and examination. We have witnessed such tests given in the fifth grade to determine the grammatical knowledge of individual students. Members of the sixth grade publish a monthly magazine. Through the generosity of the director of the elementary school attached to the *Escuela Nacional de Maestros,* we were given a collection of back numbers of this magazine, *"Mieses, Organo de los Alumnos."* Even a rapid perusal of it will convince the visitor with the earnestness of Mexican children, their love for self-expression and their fondness of the *belles lettres.*

There are quite a few of these new elementary schools in the capital. The Ministry of Education is planning to spread a network of such schools throughout the country. In the rural sections the elementary schools emphasize agriculture, and vary their programs according to the needs of the local community. These rural schools (*escuelas rurales*) are very important in Mexico.

SECONDARY EDUCATION

In Mexico there are two types of secondary schools. The old type, *Escuela Preparatoria,* the preparatory school, a classical school attached to the university. It embodies the spirit of the old classical preparatory schools. Select few are given admission to this school. It does not meet the needs of common people for secondary education. Four or five years ago, after a long struggle, Mexicans have been able to organize a new type secondary school, *Escuela Secundaria,* which embodies the spirit of modern democracy. It is open to all. It is under the jurisdiction and supervision of the Ministry of Education. It does not emphasize classical subjects. Science and modern languages occupy prominent places in the curriculum. It is not coeducational. There are separate high schools for girls. These are not yet numerous. But those that are in actual operation are very efficient. Its course of study includes three years of secondary education beyond the elementary school.

For days we visited classrooms and listened to the recitations. Social sciences are being taught chiefly by discussion method, and sciences by laboratory method. The teachers are well selected and well trained, either in the United States, Canada, or in European countries. The salary schedule seems to be satisfactory. The high school teachers receive from 15–20 pesos daily (a peso normally is worth 48 cents) throughout the year. The elementary school teachers receive from 7–15 pesos daily, likewise throughout the year. The salary given the teachers in normal schools and in the university is a little higher than that given to high-school teachers. The teachers are paid by the government and if the government lacks funds they suffer just the same as other functionaries in the government.

NORMAL SCHOOL TRAINING

Escuela Nacional de Maestros offers a three year course. Unlike the secondary school it is coeducational. It trains teachers for the elementary school. It is attached to the model elementary school where practice teachers receive their training. The course of studies includes content subjects taught in the elementary schools, as well as professional subjects, such as educational psychology, principles of education, methods of teaching, etc. We observed a class in educational psychology. A well-trained teacher, educated in the United States and Germany, taught without a text-book, the principles of Educational Psychology. Reaction hypothesis, conditioning, laws of learning, transfer of training, and similar modern topics are discussed. Students are eager to learn. They seemed to us too young to grasp some of the complicated problems in modern psychology. The members of the senior class on the average are eighteen to nineteen years of age. They have attended six years in elementary school, three years in high, and, with the three years' additional work in the Normal School, they will have completed upon their graduation twelve years of training, in years an equivalent training to which the high-school graduate in the American school system has been exposed. The same lack of maturity in judgment, due to the very young age of these prospective teachers was obvious in a class in principles of education. In this field the teachings of John Dewey reign supreme. In the *librerias* one can easily see all the volumes of John Dewey's literature displayed in its Spanish version. Next to John Dewey, Decroly occupied a prominent place. The works of two Swiss progressive educators, Adolphe Ferrière and Claparède, also are held in high esteem. This gives an idea as to the fondness of the Mexican educational leaders of our modern progressive philosophy of education. The sub-secretary of the Ministry of Education in a genial conversation told us the ardent faith of the new Mexican educational leadership in the democracy of education. They are aiming to bring education within the reach of all, white, Mestizo, and Indian, alike. They are tending to lift the general level of culture of the entire population. They believe that the salvation of the Mexican people lies in the education of all, free for all, supported and supervised by the state, and attendance made compulsory for all.

We are inclined to believe that Mexico is in the right path toward progress. With our encouragement and neighborly assistance Mexican educational leaders will continue their great work in leading the Mexican populace to the broad field of culture and civilization.

K. A. Sarafian
La Verne College,
California

VALPARAISO UNIVERSITY

In 1873 H. B. Brown established the Northern Indiana Normal School, which was later to become Valparaiso University.

An opportunity for every one sums up the educational philosophy of Brown. It made no difference how much or how little former education one had on coming to Valparaiso. There was room for all. The only considerations were moral fitness and willingness to work.

Brown's educational philosophy was especially adapted to the pioneer conditions of the Mississippi Valley. In the newly established civilization there was little time or opportunity for the satisfaction of man's cultural wants. Education, even long after the Civil War, was of the simplest, most elementary nature. Schools, where they existed at all, were really a makeshift. Thousands of men and women grew up without even getting by the A.B.C. stage of reading, writing and arithmetic. But hosts of them had the inner urge to advance and believed that more education was the ladder on which to rise. Valparaiso University, as established by Brown, was their opportunity.

And so they came, first in dozens, later in hundreds and at last in thousands, to get at Valparaiso what was denied them elsewhere. All in all, the records show that 75,000 students attended Valparaiso. Some spent but a semester and went back to the farm, humble apostles of culture and apostles of a better day in education. Some stayed and completed an education which led them to leadership in state and nation. The history of the American frontier is not complete without the part played in it by Valparaiso University.

A little over a decade ago conditions which had favored Valparaiso's growth and created its opportunity of service were over. Educational opportunities in the Middle West had become fairly general. The frontier generation had passed. A new generation inherited the results of their privations in greater ease from economic pressure, in the larger outlook to give their children an education as part of the obligation of parenthood. Furthermore, Brown died and the ship which he guided so well for decades had lost its captain.

For a number of years Valparaiso declined and found growing difficulties. In 1925 a group of Lutheran laymen bought the physical property and took over the institution. They saw clearly from the beginning that the chance for continuing Valparaiso on its old basis was forever gone and that only a standard, high-class educational institution had the chance to live and serve.

So their first goal was Valparaiso's educational reorganization. By the spring of 1929 this was completed. The college of liberal arts was accepted as a member of the North Central Association of Colleges, the colleges of engineering, of pharmacy and of law likewise became accredited.

While this reorganization was going on the enrolment dropped to 325 in 1929. With accreditation a new student body has come in nearly faster than it was possible to provide for them. Last year the enrolment reached 599. In the coming year it will probably reach 700.

While the old frontier service of Valparaiso is passed, the new Valparaiso is rendering a frontier service in a different way. It was taken over by a Lutheran group not only to serve any young man or woman desiring a higher education but to serve especially one of the larger Lutheran Church bodies which till then had taken no part in general lay higher education.

O. H. P.

QUOTATIONS

PUBLIC EDUCATION IN NEW JERSEY

PUBLIC education in New Jersey has maintained its standards during the past year. Significant improvement has been made in teaching in the elementary schools. About 650,000 children are enrolled in these schools, which for many offer nearly all of the education which they will receive. These facts define the importance of the problem of the elementary schools and our obligation to spare no efforts to make them as efficient as possible.

The high schools of New Jersey place large emphasis upon training for citizenship and it is of more than passing interest to note that 21.4 per cent. of the registration is enrolled in courses in American history and problems of democracy, as compared with only 13.8 per cent. in 1925–26. Enrolment in the public high schools of New Jersey for the year ending June 30, 1931, increased 17,126, which was 13.2 per cent. over that of the previous year.

Preliminary reports indicate that the 1931 enrolment exceeds 1930's by 20 per cent. This increased enrolment has placed a serious strain upon the facilities of our high schools, since sixteen months ago classrooms, libraries, laboratories and shops were used almost to capacity. Teachers are cheerfully making their contribution by accepting heavier schedules and added responsibilities.

The depression has had a marked effect upon industrial education. The number of applicants for the all-day trade and industrial schools has exceeded the facilities and we have waiting lists for those schools. Through trade extension courses given in these schools and in other public schools after the day school hours, many opportunities are offered adults for further trade training and for retraining.

Such courses contribute to the solution of the unemployment problem of the present depression. Due to the depression, the enrolment in the continuation schools declined last year to 12,706, a loss of 4,197 from the previous year. For the most part, the youth dropped from industry have returned to school.

The health supervision in the schools is maintained at a high standard of efficiency—this is of the greatest importance in a time such as the present. During the prevalence of infantile paralysis the health service of the schools proved itself alert and most efficient.

The teachers of the state have given freely of their time and energies to community work. In many school systems, generous contributions have been made by the teachers to the end that food may be served free at school to the children who need aid and that aid may be given also to their families. Newark has furnished an outstanding example of what can be accomplished by the teaching staff in work of this character.

One marked effect of the depression has been reflected in the item of capital outlay for lands and school buildings. For the state, as a whole, for the year ending June 30, 1931, the expenditure was $16,759,063. This was less by $7,392,053 than that for the preceding year, which indicates that building programs are being deferred and that only very necessary parts of a projected program are being undertaken.

These items summarize some of the things taking place in the schools. In general, the high standards of New Jersey schools are being maintained and we enter the new year with these projects and problems, confident that the schools will continue to serve the communities efficiently.—Charles H. Elliott, Commissioner of Education, State of New Jersey, in the *U. S. Daily*.

SOCIETIES AND MEETINGS

THE NATIONAL COUNCIL OF STATE SUPERINTENDENTS AND COMMISSIONERS OF EDUCATION

How to finance the schools, a subject of extreme timeliness in this era of depression, was the chief subject before the National Council of State Superintendents and Commissioners of Education at their annual meeting in the auditorium of the Department of the Interior, Washington, D. C., on December 7 and 8.

Dr. Paul R. Mort, associate director of the National Survey of School Finance, recently launched by the Federal Office of Education, clearly outlined the four-year study of school expenditure, stressing the need for organization of local education tax districts so as to secure economic use of funds and to gain most effective education results.

"A worth-while survey of school finance," Dr. Mort told the nearly two score state education leaders attending the meeting, "can not limit itself to finding facts as to how much we spend and the nature of the expenditures for education. It should seek, out of the varying experience of forty-eight sovereign states and of thousands of communities almost sovereign in their control of education, facts bearing on the question of how much education should be financed by public taxation, how much expenditure we can afford, and danger points below which such expenditure may not safely go. We must not only seek out the dangerously underschooled areas," he said, "but we must also gather facts which will be helpful in raising the level of schooling in such areas. We must seek out the shortcomings in the financial system which explain how the educational program remains meager in some communities even in times of prosperity, and those explaining the breakdown of educational support in able communities in such times as these."

Dr. Mort's address was the forerunner of school finance discussions led by Commissioner James M. McConnell, Minnesota, Superintendent Vierling Kersey, California, and reports on equalization funds in Arkansas by Commissioner C. M. Hirst, Arkansas, and in Missouri by Superintendent Charles A. Lee. Most of the other superintendents and commissioners of education entered whole-heartedly into the discussion and exchange of ideas.

Insistent public demand is responsible for most of the "fads and frills" in the school of to-day, and not the school authorities, state or local, said Commissioner McConnell in explaining the reason for increasing education costs in recent years. "Curricula have been improved, text-books modernized, teacher qualifications advanced," he said. "In many states extensive provision has been made for the special instruction of children with mental or physical defects. Rural school terms have been lengthened, attendance improved, satisfactory courses are being completed. . . . Health and sanitation have become matters of public concern, education for adults has received much attention, and illiteracy has been greatly reduced. After a period of such unprecedented development, the time is ripe for a full and fair evaluation."

Superintendent T. A. Allen, North Carolina, told how his state finally decided to pay the entire cost of local education for six months, out of state funds. Communities which desire more than six months' school term may increase their school programs beyond the six months at their own expense.

The reports of equalization funds in Arkansas and Missouri by Commissioner Hirst and Superintendent Lee, respectively, brought forth considerable discussion on school district consolidation and cost of eliminating the one-teacher (ofttimes one-room) rural schools. "During the past two years," said Commissioner Hirst, "the number of school districts in Arkansas has been reduced from 4,200 to approximately half that number." Superintendent Lee, who incidentally reported Missouri as having some 9,000 school districts and from 30,000 to 35,000 school board members, said that his state urges consolidation by giving $3 for transportation per child transported two miles or more to school. The state also appropriates $110,000, to districts, for construction of new buildings to further the consolidation movement.

"In a single state this winter, 150,490 school children will need food and other care from relief organizations," said Dr. David E. Weglein, superintendent of schools, Baltimore, Maryland, in discussing the additional demands and responsibilities being placed on the schools. Reporting the work of the Department of Superintendence committee on school costs, he said, "The number of pupils in public schools has approximately doubled in the past 30 years. . . . Two thirds of the public school systems are now operating on reduced budgets. . . . As a result of the dilemma imposed by reduced resources and increased demands, many school systems are now curtailing or entirely abandoning important educational services, some of which are particularly essential during a period of economic hardship."

Agricultural education, rural education, the work of national and state surveys, committees and other organizations, and national problems were also discussed at length during the two-day meeting.

The recently completed report of the National Advisory Committee on Education as to federal relations to education was given by Dr. Charles R. Mann, chairman of the committee. The presentation of the findings of this national education survey and analysis of public reaction to the published report was received with eager attention by the state education leaders. No action was taken on the report.

Comprehensive reviews were made of the National Survey of Secondary Education by the associate survey director, Dr. Leonard V. Koos, and of the National Survey of the Education of Teachers, by Mr. Ben W. Frazier and Dr. Guy C. Gamble, of the Federal Office of Education. Mr. Fred C. Croxton, assistant director of the President's Organization on Unemployment Relief, addressed the meeting on "The President's Organization on Unemployment Relief"; Dr. Randall J. Condon, on work of the National Advisory Committee on Illiteracy, and Superintendent John Callahan, Wisconsin, on work of the committee on state guidance programs of the National Vocational Guidance Association. Dr. Francis W. Kirkham, educational director of the National Child Welfare Association, expressed the need of state "White House" Conferences on Child Health and Protection. "At this time of economic stress and strain when expenditures of money for all purposes are being curtailed, it will be increasingly easy to neglect the child," he said. "The hope of the child against such neglect lies in an aroused and intelligent public interest in his welfare. President Hoover's national White House conference, supplemented by a state conference, may well be an effective method to provide a backfire against selfish interest." He commended the creation of a state child health and protection committee in Iowa by Governor Dan W. Turner.

Mexico's methods of improving education were explained by Mrs. Katherine M. Cook, chief, division of special problems in the Federal Office of Education, who studied education in that country this year. She illustrated her address with slides of Mexican schools, children, street scenes and homes. Superintendents W. F. Bond, Mississippi, M. L. Duggan, Georgia, and F. G. Blair, Illinois, spoke on the rural one-teacher school. "Condemning of all one-teacher rural schools is wrong," said Superintendent Blair. "I believe that some are and can be made fine vehicles of public education. Some should be discontinued, but others can not and should not be discontinued. Many of them offer a quality of public education which can not be excelled by any other type of school."

Other addresses were made by Dr. Wm. John Cooper, U. S. Commissioner of Education, who presided at the meetings; Dr. C. H. Lane, chief agricultural education service, Federal Board for Vocational Education, on "The Future Farmers of America Movement"; Dr. James N. Rule, Pennsylvania state superintendent, on Pennsylvania Studies Itself"; Superintendent A. T. Allen, North Carolina, on "The New School Law in North Carolina"; Dr. Ben D. Wood, Columbia University, "Some Reflections on School Records," and Superintendent Chas. W. Taylor, Nebraska, on "Nebraska's Efforts in Character Education."

The council went on record as opposed to national school essay and declamation contests in connection with the George Washington Bicentennial Celebration in 1932, and passed a resolution to request registrars of state universities or land grant colleges in the various states to confer with their respective state superintendents or commissioners of education in the formulation of a law which will preserve the student records in institutions of learning which become defunct.

W. F. Bond, state superintendent of Mississippi, was elected president of the council to succeed John Callahan, state superintendent for Wisconsin. Other officers elected were Charles A. Lee, state superintendent of Missouri, vice president, and W. H. Pearce, state superintendent of Michigan, secretary.

Secretary of the Interior Ray Lyman Wilbur, in his message of welcome to the state superintendents and commissioners of education, said: "Education is starting to undergo a renaissance. . . . A part of this renaissance is the conception that health, recreation and education are inseparable in the training of youth. To amalgamate the functions associated with them in the public school system, to make full use of every educational dollar, and to secure additional dollars through the development of public understanding is, as I view it, the function of the present day leaders in education."

JOHN H. LLOYD

EDITORIAL DIVISION,
OFFICE OF EDUCATION,
WASHINGTON, D. C.

EDUCATIONAL RESEARCH AND STATISTICS

ESSAY EXAMINATION QUESTIONS CLASSIFIED ON THE BASIS OF OBJECTIVITY

WRITTEN examinations are typically classified as traditional or essay examinations and new-type or objective tests. Such classification implies distinct demarcation between the two types, implies that examinations can always be placed in one or the other category. Further, one is prone to interpret it to mean that however much they may differ in difficulty, in subject-matter, in thought processes evoked, essay examination questions are all alike in that any attempts to evaluate the pupil performances are, and of necessity must be, subjective. In all probability such dogmatic classification is not justified. Common sense would suggest that no clear-cut distinction could be made between essay examinations and objective tests, and that there were wide differences in the inherent subjectivity of essay questions.

It is the purpose of this paper to report an attempt to classify typical essay examination questions on the basis of their objectivity, that is, on the basis of the extent to which one would expect disagreement among competent judges as to the correctness of the pupil responses. Such a classification should throw light on two problems rather intimately tied up with the "objective versus traditional" examination controversy. First, it should furnish evidence of the similarity or dissimilarity between the traits or abilities measured by the two types of examination; secondly, it should assist in determining the extent to which the demonstrated subjectivity of the essay examination is inherent in the nature of the pupil response, and to what extent it is the result of extraneous factors such as disagreement as to what is being measured, lack of scoring rules, differences in the weighting of elements, variations in standards of grading, etc.

Theoretically, one would name the factors determining the intrinsic objectivity of a particular question as the extent of the response called for and the freedom permitted in the making of the response. That is, the more extended the response, and the more freedom allowed the testee in making this response, the greater the subjectivity. Inspection of typical essay examination questions leads us to believe that they may be classified on the basis of objectivity into three more or less roughly defined groups or types:

(1) *Simple-recall questions:* Questions demanding a very brief response that may be scored as right or wrong. (A number, a date, a name, a place, an event, etc.) Such questions are almost entirely objective and are invariably named as one of the major types of "objective" tests.

(2) *Short-answer questions:* Questions demanding a response that consists of a single statement, a phrase or a sentence. (Define, identify, list, find, state, etc.) These questions have a high degree of objectivity and are commonly listed among the "types of objective tests."[1] Simple scoring rules make for close agreement as to the score a particular answer should receive.

(3) *Discussion questions:* Questions demanding a more or less elaborate and detailed response. (Discuss, explain, describe, compare, outline, etc.) Such questions have a minimum of objectivity. Because of the relatively large opportunity for the introduction of personal judgment, it is probably impossible to construct a set of scoring rules that would lead to very close agreement among competent judges as to the score a particular performance should receive.

The extent to which teachers' essay questions are made up of the first two types suggested should be an indication of the degree to which traditional examinations and new-type tests measure the same thing, and it seems that it might also be taken as a rough measure of the inherent objectivity of the typical essay examination. In order to determine the extent to which essay examinations are made up of the respective types, a number of examination questions taken from different elementary and high school subjects were analyzed. The questions used were reported by Odell (and were collected by Monroe) as being a "selection of distinctly good questions made according to the judgment of a single person, but one who had made a study of examinations. They were chosen from a rather large number of final examinations given in the elementary and high schools of Illinois."[2] They were collected before the vogue for objective tests (1922) and certainly may be

[1] For example, see G. M. Ruch, "The Objective or New-type Examination," pp. 189 and 194. Scott, Foresman and Company, 1929.

[2] C. W. Odell, "Traditional Examinations and New Type Tests," pp. 221–233, Century Company, 1928.

taken as typical of questions actually used by teachers.

Nominally there were 165 questions on twelve different school subjects listed by Odell, but usually the questions consisted of several parts (occasionally indicated as (a), (b), (c), etc., but oftentimes not so indicated). Since the different parts of many of the questions did not necessarily fall under the same type, they were treated as separate questions. When so divided there were 458 questions. Each of these was classified as belonging to one of the three types mentioned above. The following examples of the different types represent random samplings from the total group, and may be used as a check on the objectivity of the classification:

Simple-Recall Questions:

(1) What people settled Jamestown, Virginia?
(2) Who was the first president of the United States under the constitution?
(3) Name the officers of the President's cabinet.
(4) Name and give the dates of our greatest English dramatist.
(5) Name the authors of the following: (ten titles follow)
(6) When did the constitution of the United States go into operation?
(7) Name two great mountain systems of our continent.
(8) Name at least eight branches of the animal kingdom and an example of each.
(9) Extract the cube root of 5882.
(10) What is the lateral surface of a cylinder 15 inches high and 10 inches in diameter?

Short-Answer Questions:

(1) What was the ordinance of 1787?
(2) Identify the following: (names of five men and events follow)
(3) Define *verb*.
(4) Give five facts concerning the life of Poe.
(5) For what were each of the following noted? (names of ten literary men follow)
(6) How may a bill be passed over the President's veto?
(7) What is a democracy?
(8) What is the heat of fusion?
(9) Why are the porifera a step higher than the protozoa?
(10) Define *circle, radius, diameter, circumference.*

Discussion Questions:

(1) Tell the story of William Penn.
(2) Discuss five powers or duties of Congress.
(3) Why was Europe better fitted than Asia to develop the highest civilization?
(4) Why is the study of Latin important to us?
(5) Describe the theater of Shakespeare's time or characterize Shylock carefully, illustrating your points.
(6) Compare our government to a ball team.
(7) Write an interesting paragraph about the Eskimos.
(8) How do the facts of fusion and vaporization affect our lives?
(9) Describe either the phone or the telegraph.
(10) What is your opinion of the theory of evolution?

Table I presents the number and percentage

TABLE I
SHOWING THE NUMBER AND PERCENTAGES OF ESSAY QUESTIONS CLASSIFIED IN EACH OF THREE TYPES

	Number of Questions	Simple-Recall		Short-Answer		Discussion	
Elementary School		Number	Per cent.	Number	Per cent.	Number	Per cent.
Amer. history (7th. gr.)	61	22	36.0	24	39.0	15	25.0
Amer. history (8th. gr.)	47	9	19.0	27	57.0	11	24.0
Grammar (8th. gr.)	44	30	68.0	11	25.0	3	7.0
Civics (8th. gr.)	48	22	46.0	16	33.0	10	21.0
Geography (8th. gr.)	18	6	33.0	8	44.0	4	23.0
Arithmetic (8th. gr.)	25	14	56.0	11	44.0	0	0.0
Total	**243**	**103**	**42.0**	**97**	**40.0**	**43**	**18.0**
High School							
Amer. history	29	5	18.0	12	41.0	12	41.0
Anc. history	32	6	19.0	8	24.0	18	54.0
English	72	30	42.0	14	19.0	28	39.0
Civics	33	6	18.0	14	42.0	13	40.0
Physics	28	0	0.0	12	45.0	16	57.0
Zoology	21	7	33.0	3	14.0	11	53.0
Total	**215**	**54**	**25.0**	**63**	**29.0**	**98**	**46.0**
Grand total	**458**	**157**	**34.5**	**160**	**35.0**	**141**	**30.5**

of questions, for each subject and for the total, that were classified under each of the three types. The questions for elementary school subjects are separated from those for high-school subjects, and the total for each of these groups is also reported.

Examination of the table shows that 34.5 per cent. of the questions were simple-recall, that is, almost purely objective; 35 per cent. were short-answer, have a rather high degree of objectivity; and only 30.5 per cent. were classified as discussion questions. In other words, approximately 70 per cent. of the questions have the same inherent objectivity as new-type test items, and apparently measure the same thing that typical recall types of objective tests measure. When we compare questions from the elementary school level with those from the high-school level we find more of the discussion type and fewer of the simple-recall used in the high schools. Forty-six per cent. of the high-school questions as compared with only 18 per cent. of those from the elementary school were classed as discussion; and but 25 per cent., as compared with 42 per cent. from the elementary school, were classed as simple-recall. The number of questions in each subject was so small that the differences among subjects can scarcely be considered significant, but it is interesting to note that physics, usually considered a highly objective subject, had the highest percentage of discussion and no simple-recall, while English, usually considered a subjective subject, had the lowest percentage of discussion and the highest percentage of simple-recall of any of the high-school subjects. Such facts would cause one to question the practical significance of a common theoretical argument advanced against the new-type test.

The interpretation of the findings seems rather obvious. To the extent that the examination questions used here may be taken as typical of essay questions, the differences between essay questions and new-type items is not so great as commonly believed, and the subjectivity of a large part of the traditional examination is not due to the nature of the subject-matter but is seemingly due to such extraneous factors as disagreement as to scoring rules, differences in standards of grading, etc.

When, in the light of these facts, one attempts to recommend a testing procedure the way is not so clear. Certainly a "mongrel" type, such as the typical essay examination seems to be, is unsatisfactory. Not only does adequate scoring become very difficult but one is apt to violate principles of good measurement common to both types. By recommending the elimination from the examinations of the 30 per cent. of discussion questions one would presumably increase the objectivity of the measurement, but in so doing would but make crude new-type tests of them, and it would surely be more satisfactory to develop the usual new-type technique. Further, assuming the discussion questions measure desirable outcomes of instruction not measured by the other types of tests, in excluding these questions from the examinations we would narrow the range of testing and to a degree invalidate our measurement. On the other hand, one certainly could not recommend the elimination of all objective questions. To omit questions concerning matters of importance simply because the answer was objective would be surpassed in ridiculousness only by the attempt to test for this information in some subjective manner.

Probably the wisest procedure would be to definitely distinguish between the two types, to develop more satisfactory methods of marking discussion questions and to differentiate such measurement from that of the objective sort. Although the general principles underlying both types of measurement would perhaps be the same, the details involved in working out the scoring procedures would differ radically. Practical experience in other realms of human measurement where we have as yet been unable to evolve objective instruments suggests that for questions of the subjective sort a rating procedure is the most satisfactory, while the objective questions could certainly be improved by taking advantage of techniques developed by students of the more formal new-type tests.

VERNER MARTIN SIMS
UNIVERSITY OF ALABAMA

NEW BOOKS IN EDUCATION

JONES, WALTER B., editor. *Basic Units in Vocational Guidance.* Pp. xvii + 194. McGraw-Hill. $1.50.

MERRIAM, GEORGE E. *More Precious Than Fine Gold: Washington Commonplace Book.* Pp. ix + 428. Illustrated. Putnam. $5.00.

SHOWERMAN, GRANT. *Rome and the Romans.* Pp. xxi + 643. Illustrated. Macmillan.

SCHOOL AND SOCIETY

EDITED BY J. McKEEN CATTELL

WITH WHICH IS COMBINED THE

EDUCATIONAL REVIEW

EDITED BY WILLIAM McANDREW

Volume 35 | SATURDAY, JANUARY 23, 1932 | Number 891

TEACHING GOVERNMENT IN PUBLIC SCHOOLS[1]

By Professor CHARLES H. JUDD

UNIVERSITY OF CHICAGO

THE purpose of this paper is to persuade the members of the American Political Science Association, if it is possible to do so, that a program of instruction designed to make young people intelligent regarding government can never be genuinely successful unless it becomes a part of a larger program of broad social training. It ill behooves me as a mere layman in political science to venture any comments on what views about the nature and functions of government should be taught in the schools. The content of instruction should be determined in this field, as in all fields, by experts. It may be that government has gone too far in its efforts to control economic forces, or it may be that we are in the early stages of a vast extension of governmental controls. Whatever our partisan disagreements with regard to government, one fundamental principle will, I am sure, be accepted without dissent. Government is only one of the institutions which make up the composite pattern of civilization. If we did not have language, we should have no civilized government. If we had no number system, we should not be able to calculate the annual deficit. If we had no factories, we should not need a flexible or an inflexible tariff.

It is this fundamental principle that government is only one phase of civilization which furnishes the starting point of my argument. The larger whole to which government belongs is that which the school was organized to pass on to the new generation. By long struggle the race has built bridges across rivers and invented the ingenious devices used to-day in securing the necessities and luxuries of life. The child born to the race is to enjoy the benefits of architecture and machine industry, but, in order that the child may use the instruments put at his disposal, he must be taught how to behave as a civilized person. It is no simple task to transform a child into a civilized person. Society has therefore set aside a part of the energy and wealth of the community for the purpose of transmitting civilization.

If all this argument be accepted as obvious and even commonplace doctrine, we come with something of a shock to the discovery that in our American society many elements of civilization are transmitted to oncoming generations with a certain careless assumption that preparation to use these acquisitions of the race is of slight importance. Again and again it has been

[1] Read before a section of the American Political Science Association, Washington, D. C., December 28, 1931.

pointed out that American schools do little or nothing to make people intelligent about money. Our schools deal with money only in arithmetic. We tell children how to count money, how to subtract and add and even multiply money, but we never tell them the romantic story of primitive barter and half-civilized, half-standardized exchange.

Or, to use another illustration, we teach pupils in the schools how to calculate the premium on insurance, but we do not make them intelligent about the vast cooperative social enterprise through which modern society has transferred its losses to the broad shoulders of collective groups.

If one asks why some of these vital subjects are omitted from the ordinary program of studies in the schools, one finds the answer in the history of our educational system. This system was originally very meager in its equipment because seventy-five years ago, when the outlines of the curriculum were determined, society depended on many teachers outside the schools. The home taught children the simple lessons of rural thrift. Religion exercised its authority over a very large fraction of the population and dictated its precepts in a form which permitted no neglect.

The school system was meager in equipment for another reason. The pattern of civilized life was simple enough to be fairly open to direct observation. The spatial extent of any individual's environment was comparatively narrow. There were only limited facilities for transportation and intercommunication.

With the changes in civilization that seventy-five years have witnessed, the school has acquired responsibilities of a wholly new order. Unfortunately, however, the school has not been able to keep pace with changing social conditions. This statement will be construed by many as an attack on the efficiency of the schools. I wish to make the point as vigorously as I can that the school is no less efficient than is society in general. The banker who was teaching thrift to children a few years ago in a pompous and abstract way was not efficient. He did not himself understand how to deal with the savings that he lured into his vaults. He used words that he did not intellectually compass. He played with emotions that he had no right to arouse and use to his own advantage. He was a propagandist, not an educator. Whoever is disposed to blame the schools for not teaching young people to be intelligent about money will have to include the bankers of the generation in his indictment.

Perhaps I have gone far enough in my efforts to define the schools as society's agency for the transmission of civilization to justify me in coming directly to the plea which I am here to present. I am quite sure that the American Political Science Association is right in its contention that American schools must make pupils intelligent about government. I am equally sure that it is impossible to accomplish the end desired by injecting into the curriculum a new course on government. We must devise some method of making pupils conscious of the meaning of civilization long before we introduce them to the special problems of government and the political system.

Let us consider an illustration which will make clear what I am trying to say. We teach little children very early in life that they must pass people on the street on the right. What we say to children in this connection sounds, when one stops to think of it, like an arbitrary dictum. It is indeed arbitrary in the form in which it is passed on to children, but it is not arbitrary in its origin. If a child who is told to pass on the right should ask "Why?" it would be very difficult to give any satisfactory answer except in terms of racial history. If the child knew enough to reinforce his question by the statement that in England people pass on the left, he would make it clear that he is justified in characterizing the demand that he pass on the right as an arbitrary order. No better opportunity can possibly be found than that which is here presented for a lesson in the fundamental social origin of governmental regulation of individual behavior. Not only so, but the literature of childhood will be greatly enriched by putting into children's hands the story of the origin and evolution of the rules of the road. No one can read this story without gaining a new and vivid appreciation of how exacting are the demands of the group and how advantageous it is for the individual to act in accord with group conventions.

The illustration which I have just presented was selected with a view to arriving by the shortest possible route at the goal of my discussion. The sympathy of pupils for government must be cultivated if the lessons of government are to be really understood and appreciated. I said a few minutes ago that no course dealing with government and neglecting the other facts of civilization will accomplish the ends at which I believe this association is aiming. There must be from the earliest years of the pupil's schooling a steady instillation of the concept of government. The pupil must come naturally to a mature understanding of government through many immature stages of acquaintance with the evolution of governmental forms. The rules of the road must grow out of the direct experience of a few minor collisions.

From the simple illustration presented let us progress to a somewhat enlarged view of the school program. The laws of the nation and of the state are only a small part of the social inheritance. If we could inspire in pupils some appreciation of the effort which has gone into the production of science or literature, we could, I believe, give a wholly new tone to our whole educational system. As the school program is administered to-day, the pupil too often gets the impression that a course in science is a succession of adult pronouncements forced on his acceptance by dire threats. The fact is, of course, that science, both in its refined techniques and in its suggestive and highly useful results, is a gift of enormous value made by the race to the individual. Science is as much a part of the pattern of civilization as is government. The relation between science and law is very intimate when we think of the two as products of cooperative human endeavor. I am sure that we could give young people a wholly new attitude toward natural science if we could induce the scientists to think of themselves as part of the social pattern, which is expressed also in civil order. Conversely, I am sure that government will be in far safer hands when a generation is trained to recognize that the teachings of science are the safest guides in the formulation of statutes.

The foregoing statements are offered as a basis for the plea that this association join in an effort to bring into the American educational system a new and radically different general social content. This plea is presented with some assurance that it is legitimate because there are evidences that we are entering on a new era in education. For many years past the specialist has been in full possession of instruction in the schools and colleges. The specialist has cultivated his subject with the single-minded energy of a narrow enthusiast. It can not be denied that the world owes a great debt to the specialist, but it must also be admitted that the very success of the specialist is a threat to the solidarity of society.

Not only has the specialist cultivated his chosen field with intense devotion, but he has tried to make every one with whom he came in contact a specialist. We have set bounds upon the areas of intellectual endeavor as rigid and as jealously guarded as the bounds which mark national domains. The result is that civilization as a whole has been unnaturally disrupted. We all know, if we are willing to stop pursuing our special interests and think in broad terms, that our specialties are very insignificant strands in a complex and colorful pattern, but this comprehensive view is difficult to keep before our limited thinking.

There are hopeful signs that the era of extreme specialization is over. Universities are beginning to set up administrative devices for the combination of departments into larger units of organization. Courses are being offered in all the centers of aggressive thinking which transcend departmental specialization. The orientation or general-survey courses are sometimes criticized as crude, but they are here in such numbers that it is evident that their crudeness is not fatal. They are crude because the extreme specialization of the past has made it almost impossible to find the proper personnel to conduct a broad, inclusive course.

Not only so, but the lower schools recognize that the curriculums which they have been administering are inadequate. For the past ten years there has been an effort to rework the contents and methods of teaching in elementary schools and high schools in all parts of the country. It must be admitted that the net outcome of the curriculum revision which has been going on is disappointingly small. There does not seem to be any fundamental guiding principle which can be appealed to in the selection and arrangement of new contents. New contents are introduced and withdrawn; old contents are rearranged and rejected in whole or in part. Again we note that, while the results of experimentation seem crude, the striking fact is that experimentation continues, impelled by a realization that something new is needed.

The movement for curriculum revision has finally reached the stage where the ordinary parent is restless and desirous of seeing a transformation in the school and college program. The nation has given its support and the prestige of its control to vocational education. On the other hand, vigorous contentions are presented in the public press in favor of training for leisure. The fine arts are praised as refining forces and as correctives for the evil effects produced by too much devotion to material civilization.

There never was a more promising opportunity than that which now offers for intelligent leadership to assert itself to the great advantage of our national program of education. If all the specialties which are to-day seeking recognition and all the forces which make for synthesis can be reconciled so that a single unified movement may be started, the new era will have arrived. I am quite aware that this statement seems extravagant, but I hold to it as an accurate description of the present possibility.

Let me sketch in a general way the program which I think we should try to have adopted. All persons who teach or administer schools and all citizens who support schools should be led to see clearly that the purpose of education is to give young people the fullest possible equipment of civilized ideas and civilized methods of thinking and behavior. It should be recognized that it is only through an acceptance of these gifts of civilization that the individual can achieve in a short lifetime the goals of personal existence. The individual can make his contributions to civilization only when he has command of the best techniques of life that are contributed through racial effort.

The school under the proposed plan becomes a place of individual training in the arts and adjustments of civilization. At first, pupils in the lower schools will learn the simpler adjustments, such as punctuality and social regard for the rights of others. They will also learn the art of reading and the art of counting. Too often reading and counting have been taught as ends in themselves rather than as highly refined methods of using one's mind. The list of pupil acquisitions in the reconstructed school does not seem at first sight to be different from the list aimed at in the ordinary school of the day, but the spirit of the program will be quite different if the subjects taught are recognized as introductions to the arts of civilization. The pupils will have arduous tasks to perform, to be sure, but the teachers will little by little transmit the feeling that these tasks are arranged for the purpose of giving to the pupils something of great value.

By the time the pupils reach the upper levels of the primary school the lesson that social cooperation is desirable can be made explicit. In the third and fourth grades children should learn why we call our numerals "Arabic." They should learn something of the curious efforts made by ancient and primitive peoples to write. They should be taught why weights and measures came into existence and why in modern times weights and measures are under the control of the federal government. All this explicit training in ideas about social cooperation can be made the central coordinating theme of the full program of instruction in the early grades, and it can serve at the same time to prepare the pupils for later initiation into the higher forms of social thinking.

I pause to repeat what I said at the beginning of this paper. No course dealing with the political system which is inserted into the curriculum of the upper grades can be more than a partial success if it is not preceded by some such cultivation of a general social understanding as I am advocating. Ideas must have a background. As the schools of this country have been conducted in the past, there has been no remotest intimation given to the pupils of the social meaning of the Arabic numerals and of their absolutely unique character. The schools have taught Roman numerals as a kind of added arithmetical luxury without calling the attention of pupils to the uselessness of these numerals for calculation and without confessing to the pupils that the Roman numerals are the best that the European mind was able to devise.

Coming back to our school program, I recommend that the fifth and sixth grades be made opportunities to learn about other civilizations and also about our own. Industry, with its fascinating machinery and its systems of transportation, with its story of recent rapid evolution, should be given attention. Reading matter about industry and transportation should displace some of the trivial reading material which now finds its way into these grades.

Somewhere in these upper grades there should be introduced an account of national government. It is my firm belief that the explicit study of national government should not concern itself at first with the legislative aspects. Instead of telling pupils about Congress in the early stages of instruction about national government, I should tell them about the Bureau of Standards. In my judgment, pupils will have more respect for government if the early discussions deal with the Bureau of Standards or with some other scientific branch of the government.

Such a sketch as I have tried to draw has perhaps become as complete as it is profitable to make it at this time. I turn to the discussion of the practical operating machinery necessary to effect the reform which I am advocating.

The necessary information to be used in instructing children along the lines indicated is not now possessed by teachers in the lower schools. It is not possessed by the teachers who give instruction in teacher-training institutions. It is in the possession of scholars of the type commented on a short time ago—the specialists. These specialists must be induced to supply the information.

As a second step, the information must be put in a form which will make it presentable to pupils. For the execution of this second step, writers must be found who have full knowledge of the vocabulary which children can understand and of the literary style which children enjoy. In short, skilful teachers must be employed to formulate the social material.

It should be noted at this point that there is a definite intention to include in this program of reformulation of information the conventional subjects now currently taught in schools, such as science and arithmetic. Would it not be an experiment well worth trying to rewrite the arithmetic text-books so that they can be read? Arithmetic is at the present time a barren skeleton. This and other subjects now represented by dry bones could be made into living realities if the economic information were supplied which would enliven all teaching in elementary courses. Instead of being required to calculate interest in arithmetic, pupils might be made at least somewhat intelligent about investments. In time, even a chapter on speculation might be introduced, to the great advantage of the public purse. When taxation, which is now studied as a case of percentage, is rewritten in the kind of book on arithmetic that I am advocating, there will be an account of how taxes were levied in the time of Caesar, whose image on the coin was pointed out as the legal justification for the collection of tribute. There will be a definition of the duties of the assessor and like entertaining materials.

In short, text-books in all school subjects should be rewritten by competent writers equipped with information supplied by wise men who know the facts as only the specialists do. These text-books should go into the normal schools and into the hands of pupils. There will be a new curriculum with a social core. Ultimately the periphery as well as the core will be socialized. The school will become in a much fuller sense than it is to-day the agent of civilization charged with the duty of transmitting its highest achievements to the new generation.

It remains to ask: Who is to engineer this reform? A partial if not a complete answer to this question can be supplied as follows: On October 11 of this year there came together a group of men, including your subcommittee on political education, Professor George S. Counts, who is the active agent of the Commission on Social Studies of the American Historical Association, Director C. R. Mann, of the American Council on Education, and the present speaker, representing the committee on supplementary materials of instruction of the American Council on Education. This group of men talked at some length of the possibilities which I have attempted to review before you. It was decided that a joint effort would be made by all the organizations represented at that meeting to promote a movement to bring to full realization the project of socializing the whole body of instructional material in schools and colleges. It is confidently expected that in the near future a concrete exhibit can be presented of what the projected change in the curriculum means. It is hoped that the American Political Science Association will lend its support not only to the launching of the enterprise but to the far more arduous task of helping it through its critical experimental stages.

TEACHING VERSUS RESEARCH

By Professor NEWMAN I. WHITE
DUKE UNIVERSITY

"There is but one God, and Allah is his prophet." But whoever reads educational or scholarly journals or listens to the conversation in faculty clubrooms knows that in American academic circles there are two, besides the great Anti-Christ, Athletics. These two gods, Research and Teaching, have each their local prophets who tend—occasionally—to prophesy each others' confusion and indulge in scornful references to each other as mere pedants or mere pedagogues. In Texas the last expression has even undergone a picturesque distortion of pronunciation, to which the former is likewise unfortunately vulnerable. This Holy War has as yet hardly passed the sniping stage even among professional groups, but it has its effect beyond these groups in the policies of presidents in engaging teachers and in the instruction (and hence, we fondly imagine, the whole outlook on life) of millions of American youth. Thus it constitutes an element in that grave perturbation as to what is wrong with our colleges, the gravity of which is attested by the fact that most of the analysts—professors, journalists and undergraduates alike—grant the initial assumption without question.

The fundamental opposition of teaching and research, like the faults of the American college, is too readily taken for granted, and for fairly obvious reasons. Scores of scholarly journals and societies advance the special interests of research, and several large foundations grant it financial endowment. Scores of educational journals and societies advance their own special interests. With very little mutual antagonism, each of these two groups of interests pursues its own highly specialized affairs in a way that constitutes a powerful *argumentum ex silentio* that they have nothing in common. The weaker individuals of each group have developed enormous defense-complexes. Bad teachers discover that they can get articles printed and fancy that they are therefore entitled to neglect teaching for research. It is just possible they are, if they turn out to be extraordinarily good research men, but that seldom happens. Even so, they are not justified in demanding that all others stand and deliver a list of published articles. Christ and Socrates also failed to publish. On the other hand, teachers who have never had time for research or who do not know how easily bad articles are published magnify their own importance by sneering at research. These familiar facts suggest a conclusion that the antagonism of teaching and research is not a natural, but a manufactured one. Even if it were wholly artificial, however, it would still be real, as real as the acrimonies and mistaken educational policies and theories that spring from it.

Research may be readily defined as intensive study in a restricted field, usually with the intention of publishing the results to the learned world. Practical research, in the sciences, is not always conformable to this definition, but even the practical research maintained by big industrial corporations emphasizes the theoretical rather than the purely utilitarian much more than is commonly supposed. Teaching might require more wary definition at a convention of educational specialists—one educator has just produced a book defining the good teacher on the basis of over a thousand questionnaires—but essentially it is certainly no more than imparting knowledge to the unlearned. Although many mere teachers may and often do have more learning than many mere researchers, it is obvious that one may be a good teacher and still be ignorant of many things the researcher must know. The converse is equally obvious. It is also obvious that teaching is not preaching—there is a difference between expounding and exhorting. Fortunately, the confusion of teaching and preaching touches the present subject only tangentially.

The research worker is much too prone to work simply for the purpose of publishing, when his ideal purpose should be the attainment of truth. Publishing should be regarded ideally as merely the means of disseminating the scholar's findings for the benefit of other scholars and of mankind in general; actually it is too often merely the means of gratifying personal vanity or of increasing the writer's salary. College presidents, not being universal scholars, have a habit of judging scholars by the amount of their publication, taking the quality for granted on the editor's say-so. Scholarship is so varied and technical that the editors themselves are not always fit judges of quality. Thus it commonly happens that what college presidents and the world in general recognize as scholarly research is in reality mere publication. It may or may not be research. Salesmanship is rewarded more often than scholarship. This abuse of research is too natural to be susceptible of utter abolishment. Where it proceeds from vanity it may be partly corrected by a more truly critical attitude on the part of the readers and the editors of scholarly journals. Where its course is the desire for an increase in salary it may be partly corrected when and if professorial salaries reach a proper level.

The teacher who does not do research work finds a salary just as much a practical benefit as the research worker. His system also calls for vitamins and carbohydrates. Unfortunately, he is not born with a conventional strawberry mark by which his merit is attested. The college president can know only a few of his faculty sufficiently well to judge of their teaching ability from his knowledge of their characters and common sense. He must depend on others—deans, student opinion, public opinion. The deans have the same difficulty as the presidents. Student opinion, generally right in the long run, goes off at wild tangents in the beginning and is extremely difficult to apprehend truly. Public opinion is vague and generally wrong. Deans and presidents, partly realizing the unreliability of these sources of information, must nevertheless use them. The mere teacher, lacking the leverage of a reputation for scholarship, realizes not only the weaknesses of student and public opinion, but also realizes the extent to which they influence the administrative mind. Lacking confidence that they will function truly if unaided, he too uses them. Thus we get the back-slapping professor who specializes on meeting student interest more than halfway, the dinner-club professor who impresses local business men with his "humaneness" that they may impart this startling fact to presidents and trustees, the professor who specializes in ladies' clubs or church speeches, the professor who has a genius for occasioning little paragraphs in local or student newspapers that will reach the presidential or decanal eye. It would be a gross libel to say that all the activity just described has the salary check as an ultimate object, but much of it surely does. Such is the mere teacher's method of salesmanship, paralleling that of the scholar who publishes merely for advertisement. If, in both cases, salaries depended more on merit than on salesmanship there would be less talk of the conflicting interests of teachers and research men. No such salary basis can be achieved, however, until administrative officers develop better means of judging both teachers and research men and until teachers and research men are themselves convinced that better means have been developed.

These arts of salesmanship are not limited to the more petty and mediocre types of research workers and teachers. They are too much a part of normal human nature for that. Naturally they find their most extreme expression in such types, but no professor, conventional fiction to the contrary, is entirely artless. The really significant point is that the good men, of both classes, have enough character to regard the quality of their goods as much more important than the salesmanship.

If we consider the qualities most essential to the real value of both research men and teachers we find them surprisingly similar. By common agreement, they are honesty, tolerance, industry, mental alertness. Parenthetically, the same may be said of preachers. The good teacher, however, needs one quality that is not essential to the research worker, namely, a pleasing personality, since his contribution depends largely on personal contacts. But when we analyze this quality we find its chief ingredient to be a kind of imaginative sympathy, something that is also necessary to the good research worker. The teacher must be a man who can apply this imaginative sympathy to his students as well as to his studies, whereas the research man, to the extent that he is purely a research man, is not concerned with students.

For this reason the excellent teacher is an even rarer bird than the excellent research man and is more valuable to his employers. College presidents themselves say the same thing and profess a desire to reward good teaching as well as good research work. Few teachers can be persuaded that they actually do so, or can do so. Adequate means are not at hand for discovering the good teacher, either to engage him or after he has been engaged by accident, and we must discover him before we reward him. There are no national academies to give him official recognition. The research man enjoys an economic advantage in that his advertisement is national, while the teacher's is merely local. This explains why a man may be actually recognized as a good teacher and still be paid less than he is known to be worth. There is no competitive demand for him, because his worth is known only locally. Thus he is in the position of that gifted character who made a better mousetrap than his neighbor. Only in this case the world neglects to wear a path to his door. He may feel the necessity of peddling his traps. Hence an overeagerness for local publicity.

Another avenue to recognition would be productive scholarship. If he is really a good teacher he has already the most essential traits of the productive scholar. He could write, with ridiculous ease, better articles than those published by many mere research men. Then it would be observed with surprise—and probable financial reward—that here was a scholar who, *mirabile dictu,* could teach! One reason why textbooks are too often unsatisfactory is that where they are written by research men they are sound but not always teachable, and where written by teachers they are not always sound. The writing of better texts is another avenue open to the teacher that also leads in the direction of research.

The common impression that a research man can not be a good teacher is just as fallacious as the one that a good teacher can not become a good research man. In both cases they not only can be, but often are. In fact, by actual observation, they generally are, unless they elect to devote themselves exclusively to one object. The research man needs to do some teaching in order to keep in contact, not only with human nature, but with aspects of his own field of scholarly interest from which highly specialized research tends to lead him away. The teacher needs to keep in touch with research because research is constantly modifying the material he teaches. He may keep in touch with research without becoming himself a researcher, but if he should do some research work of his own, he would find it a valuable insurance against that time when the man who is nothing but a teacher will surely go bankrupt. His actual fund of knowledge has a habit of leakage and must constantly be replaced. Worse still, he goes dead intellectually unless he applies the only stimulus to which fading knowledge is susceptible—namely, more knowledge.

The teacher and the research man, in the long run, must stand or fall together, not in opposition. They employ the same qualities to achieve success and they are mutually dependent on each other in the practical management of academic affairs.

The preacher is not so essentially related to either. It is necessary to mention him, however, because of the plausible theory that education has for its prime purpose the molding of character, with its somewhat shaky corollary that the teacher should be a moral exhorter. The great universities are not so much affected by this idea as the denominational colleges and smaller universities attended by the great majority of American students. If by education we mean the whole training of life in which college instruction has only a small part, the theory is at least respectable. The proponents of the idea, however, generally seem to assume that education is bounded by the limits of what we call our educational "system." Their disciples, with the inevitable tendency of discipleship to misunderstand and distort, will certainly so assume. The effect will be to set the teacher more in opposition to the investigator and to divert him from his own and his students' best interests. A more disastrous effect, extending far beyond the concerns of teachers and research workers, is the cheapening of the idea of character.

Character is the most valuable possession, in fact the only inalienable possession, the individual has. This is true whether we think of it in the old idealistic terms or under the most hard-boiled behavioristic interpretation. If it is a mere complex of habits it is still a trifle too implicated to be a promising subject even for educational tinkering. We might reasonably suspect that the only possession that can never be really filched from a man is something that might also be difficult to impose upon him. We might have suspected, too, that modern life had already achieved the ultimate in the presumptuous invasion of privacy, but apparently not. Should the humanists wish to erect a theology, here, ready made, is their sin against the Holy Ghost.

The character builder will no doubt protest that this is not only off the subject, but misrepresents his intentions. He merely wishes to "lead out" character. Quite probably this is what he thinks. The time will come, however, when he ceases to think, and acts mechanically. Moreover, most people professionally engaged in "building" or "leading out" character have not the faintest notion of what they intend to make of it—if they can. Least of all do they suspect that they are trying to fashion replicas of themselves.

We may waive the question of whether such patterns would be uniformly acceptable. A much greater difficulty that would eventually defeat the whole scheme lies in the fact that the characters so formed would necessarily be character-builders themselves. In time there would be plenty of character-builders, but a great scarcity of genuinely virgin character to be "built." In a world thus thrown out of equilibrium the character-builders would perforce begin remodeling each other, and chaos would be at hand.

Character-building, in the sense in which children fashion mud pies, is happily beyond the educator's ability and should be beyond his ambition. But according to another theory of character, the good teacher and the good research man are already accomplishing all that the character-building theorist can reasonably expect. It is imitation, rather than exhortation, that evokes character. Character breeds character as unconsciously and mysteriously as in medieval theory money bred money.

Your really good teacher or earnest research worker stresses honesty, tolerance, industry, mental alertness, because they are the traits by which he has become what he is. They shine out in his very presence. This may seem like mere lyric rapture, but there is scarcely a college graduate who has not felt it in the presence of the teachers and researchers he most admired, and who does not know it to be true. Teach a student how to think straight and fairly, furnish him with the means and technique of acquiring knowledge, see to it that his teachers are men whose characters furnish an acceptable model—and we may dispense with exhortation. The really good teacher and the really good research man need give no conscious attention to character-building.

There still remains to be considered the more extreme types of both teacher and research man. Among these are the radical self-advertisers of both groups who naturally seek to elevate themselves by decrying their fancied competitors. Though they are very important in forming the opinions of executives and the public, they misrepresent their groups. Nothing more need be said of them here. There are, however, some exceptional cases. Some very good research men have been led so far into technicalities by the detailed nature of modern research that it is doubtful if they are well adapted to ordinary teaching. The best thing to do with such men, if they are producing valuable results by their research, is to excuse them from teaching altogether. There is also, of course, the extremely limited, dogmatic teacher who thinks that everything consists in the machinery of instruction. "Old Blank," an undergraduate was recently overheard to remark with a tinge of amused admiration, "starts up and runs his class like a sewing machine. Don't you try to stop him." College executives recognize this teacher more often than their faculties suppose, but there is little to be done short of dismissal, and general incompetence is, strangely enough, one of the most genuinely difficult of all grounds for dismissal from the faculty of a modern American college or university.

Meanwhile, the stress upon salesmanship rather than research or instruction has resulted in an accentuation of both extremes and in a growing neglect of a very valuable region of interest. Between the extreme that is interested in mere formal instruction and the extreme that is interested only in remote detailed research, there lies a broad, general field of knowledge, the lack of which makes much of our pseudo-research work almost uncivilized and much of our specialized pedagogy simply horrible. It has little perceptible market value. One cultivates it largely for his own satisfaction. Its more extensive cultivation is one of the most crying needs of all. Unluckily, it is neither pedagogy nor research. The Victorians, whom we so unfortunately patronize, called it culture, but the very tendencies just discussed have led us to call it general culture. The smug, unconscious tautology of that phrase is the significant measure of our deficiency.

EDUCATIONAL EVENTS

LONDON EDUCATION

THE annual report by the education officer, Mr. Gates, to the London County Council for 1930 has just been published and is abstracted in the London *Times Educational Supplement*.

Among the facts relating to elementary education one of the most interesting is that the fall in the birth rate, which from the "peak" year of 1920, when the number rose to 111,388, had continuously declined to 65,094 in 1929, has been arrested, and a small increase of 244 is shown this year. During the years 1929 and 1930, teachers and head teachers have increased by 78 in the council's schools and decreased by 16 in the non-provided schools, the total staff amounting to 17,309. A striking table of the average attendance and size of classes and average number of children per teacher brings home the progress made in the increase of teaching power and the decrease in the size of the classes. In 1914 there were in the council's schools 511,962 pupils in average attendance, with 12,416 teachers, the average size of the class being 45.4 and the number of children 36.6. (In 1908 the figures were 45.4 and 40.0, respectively.) The corresponding figures for the non-provided schools exhibit parallel progress. Another interesting figure is the number of teachers who left the service in 1930, which amounted to 924, and represents a wastage of about 5 per cent. There were on an average 25.14 teachers per 1,000 absent through illness on the 213½ working days of the year. This is equivalent to a total absence of 476 teachers per diem.

The central schools system continues to grow. In 1920–21 there were 50 schools with 15,613 (average roll), in 1928–29 the schools had risen to 77 and the average roll to 24,488. Last year the schools totalled 80 and the average roll 26,273; or, in other words, the number attending central schools had increased 63 per cent. in the decade. The course of instruction is four years, with an extension in some schools to five years. Differentiation takes place after a course of two years in a commercial or technical direction. Thirty-nine schools have a commercial bias, six a technical bias and 36 a clerical one. The council has now three schools with classes for myopic children.

EDUCATION IN NEW ZEALAND

ACCORDING to information sent us from the U. S. Office of Education the total expenditure, including endowment revenue, for education in New Zealand for the year ended March 31, 1931, is given by the minister of public instruction in his annual report as £4,174,855, an increase of £36,278 over that of the previous year. Of this, £501,344 was capital outlay spent on buildings. The remainder was equal to £2 9s. 3d. per person of the population (1,492,376) of New Zealand in 1930.

The distribution among the different services, of the £4,101,933 spent under the control or supervision of the minister was: General administration, 1.0 per cent.; elementary education, 61.8; secondary, 12.8; technical, 7.4; training colleges, 4.2; higher education, 4.6; native schools, 2.4; child welfare, 3.2, and other services including physical education and schools for defectives, 2.6 per cent.

The total number of persons that on July 1, 1930, were receiving instruction at recognized institutions was 292,374, not including 1,753 attending the 32 kindergartens, a registration of 4,801 in the four affiliated colleges of the University of New Zealand, and 276 students at the two agricultural colleges. The organization of instruction in New Zealand is on the plan of a primary school of five classes named, respectively, primer and standards I., II., III. and IV., followed by standards V., VI. and VII. of the advanced primary school or forms I., II. and III. of the lower departments of secondary schools or junior high schools. The secondary school has four forms III., IV., V. and VI., form III. overlapping that of the junior high school. The attendance at primary instruction up to and including standard IV. was 191,516; at the levels of forms I., II. and III., taught in advanced primary classes, junior high schools and lower departments of secondary schools, it was 53,958, a total of 245,474. The regularity of attendance was remarkable, 92.2 per cent. of the average weekly roll number. In none of the nine education districts was it below 91.5 per cent.; in one it reached 93.1.

Secondary instruction, *i.e.,* forms III. to VI., inclusive, counted on attendance of 25,523; technical day schools, 8,002; technical (part-time) classes, 11,829; training colleges, 1,155, and special schools, 391.

The Department of Education does not attempt to set up and maintain kindergartens. It does, however, aid recognized kindergarten associations to do so through a capitation grant of not more than £4 per pupil and subsidies for building and maintenance. Of the 2,593 public primary schools, 1,523 are sole-teacher schools each with an average attendance of less than thirty-six pupils. This is being changed some by uniting schools, but all applications for school consolidations for the year 1930 were held over because of the financial stringency. In many cases pupils are conveyed to and from school at public expense either in motor-buses owned by the department or by rail under free school-ticket regulations. The department's correspondence school for children in isolated places enrolled 860 primary and 166 secondary pupils.

THE ABOLITION OF THE NEW YORK INSTITUTE FOR CHILD GUIDANCE OF THE COMMONWEALTH FUND

THE Institute for Child Guidance, one of the pioneer psychiatric clinics for children in New York City, is soon to pass out of existence owing to withdrawal of financial support by the Commonwealth Fund, which has been forced by the economic depression to curtail its activities.

The institute was established by the fund five years ago to serve primarily as a training center for psychiatrists, psychologists and social workers in child guidance clinics.

The Commonwealth Fund, of which Edward S. Harkness is president, is financing the institute on a current budget of $220,000 for the year, but will reduce this appropriation to $140,000 at the opening of its next fiscal year on July 1. Financial support of the institute will then be discontinued and the clinic will close its doors on July 1, 1933.

The closing of the institute will affect its staff of six psychiatrists, three psychologists and fifteen social workers, as well as an officer and custodian force of about twenty men and women. There are forty-five students receiving training at the center now and about 400 cases, all children, are being treated, according to Dr. Lawson G. Lowrey, director of the institute, who is a psychiatrist of eighteen years' experience.

A statement issued by Mr. Barry C. Smith, director of the Commonwealth Fund and chairman of the institute's administrative board, said that the present economic depression had made it necessary for the fund, "in common with other philanthropic foundations," to decrease its commitments.

"After a careful study of the various projects which the fund is financing," Mr. Smith said, "it appeared that the least damage would be done by discontinuing support of the Institute for Child Guidance. The institute was established primarily for the purpose of training psychiatrists in the special techniques of preventive work with children, and for the training of psychiatric social workers. When the institute was established five years ago facilities for the training of workers in the mental hygiene field were far less numerous than at the present time. With the addition of anticipated training facilities under auspices other than that of the fund, it seemed possible to bring to a conclusion the work of the Institute for Child Guidance without greatly decreasing the necessary training facilities."

Mr. Smith said that with the closing date a year and a half away, ample time was provided for completing the work already undertaken and for the development of other facilities. The institute, he added, has done "a most necessary work and, in the judgment of the fund, has done it well." Mr. Smith said that the London Child Guidance Clinic, a similar center maintained by the fund in England, would not be discontinued.

ECONOMIES TO BE EFFECTED IN THE NEW YORK CITY SCHOOLS

AFTER a conference of members of the Board of Education and city officials the sum of $1,380,000 has been cut from the budget of the New York City schools and $3,300,000 in construction contracts of the Board of Education are tied up in a wide retrenchment program recently adopted by the Board of Education. Three hundred and forty high-school teachers are affected, the status of nearly 1,200 scheduled for elementary and junior high school appointments and transfers is uncertain.

The board was scheduled to approve the appointment and promotion of 595 elementary and junior high-school teachers, needed as a normal replacement force for the new term beginning on February 8, and to transfer 593 teachers to new posts. Their appointment was left instead to Dr. George J. Ryan, president of the board.

Dr. Ryan later explained that the appointments would be made in time for the new term, but certain difficulties had to be "straightened out" first. He announced, however, that 340 new high-school teachers, who had been scheduled for permanent appointments would be given positions as substitutes instead until next fall, when their appointments probably would be made permanent. Their pay will be $7.50 a day. The board thus will save $330,000. The 222 high-school teachers already appointed for next term will not be affected.

To this saving will be added a cut of more than $1,000,000 on small repair jobs, consisting largely of labor, so that the total budget slash will be $1,380,000. Dr. Ryan stated that repairs, although badly needed, did not involve the safety of pupils. Such work as painting is included. The jobs will be deferred until May, when the city collects its tax revenues.

Dr. Ryan announced also that the comptroller's office was holding up $3,300,000 in school construction contracts, financed from corporate stock issues, of which $2,643,000 was for new buildings. Thus the building program, already several months behind, is to be delayed further.

The board approved $500,000 in contracts for supplies and a few small emergency contracts for construction, as well as plans for $286,800 in mechanical equipment for the Staten Island Vocational School.

THE USE OF FILMS IN EDUCATION

EXPERIMENTS with the use of talking films in education are being carried out in the junior high schools of Lynn, Quincy and Revere, Massachusetts. These tests, designed to show whether instruction in science can be improved through the aid of films, are, it is believed, the first attempted anywhere. The tests were devised by the Harvard Graduate School of Education, to which the Carnegie Foundation for the Advancement of Science has made a grant of $25,000 "for determining the value of mechanical aids in education." The experiment continues for six weeks. During that period 300 students will be instructed with both films and text-books, and an even larger "control group" will be instructed with text-books alone. At the end of the period both groups will have tests to determine the effectiveness of the instruction.

Material has been prepared for eight units of study, six from the University Film Foundation in Cambridge, and two from the Western Electric Company. The films deal with physiography and biology as presented in the last-year course in general science in junior high schools. Each unit consists of a chapter of text, together with a talking film presenting the fundamentals of the subject.

The three films on physiography were prepared under the supervision of Professor Kirtley F. Mather, chairman of the Department of Geology at Harvard, and the three Harvard films on biology under the direction of Dr. A. E. Navez, lecturer on general physiology. The two Western Electric films are the work of Electrical Research Products, Incorporated, a subsidiary of the Western Electric Company; one deals with the growth of plants, and the other with the growth of animals. Preliminary tests of the students, to determine their knowledge of general science, etc., were prepared by Dr. Phillip J. Rulon, instructor in education at the Harvard Graduate School of Education.

THE BOARD OF EXAMINERS AT THE UNIVERSITY OF CHICAGO

A BOARD of Examinations to determine policy has been appointed at the University of Chicago. This board will consist of Dean George Alan Works, chairman *ex officio;* Dean Chauncey Boucher; Dean William H. Spencer; Dean Basil C. H. Harvey, and Professors H. W. Prescott, M. M. Knappen, G. S. Monk, K. S. Holzinger, Walter Bartky and Henry Schultz. This group includes representatives of all the university divisions under the reorganization plan, the two professional schools which have adopted the comprehensive examination idea, and three presidential appointees.

The university's plan of setting up an examining group which is distinct from the instructors teaching the various courses is partly based on the idea that under older systems the students merely fed back to the instructors in examinations as much of the lectures as they could memorize. Partly it is based on an attempt to break down the old antagonism between student and instructor in the battle for grades, and foster an atmosphere of mutual effort, and each is striving to prepare the student for the examinations.

Five technical experts who will aid in the formation of the University of Chicago's comprehensive tests, have been attending all sessions of the four freshman survey-courses, participating in the incidental conferences and reading all the books recommended for the students. They have thus been getting the student viewpoint, and at the same time cooperating with the instructors in discussing the possibilities and limitations of the new plan of education at the university. They will collaborate with the faculty in framing the examination questions, the form of which constitutes an important phase of the plan.

Dr. Louis L. Thurstone, professor of psychology, has been appointed chief examiner, working with Dr. George Alan Works, dean of students and general director of examinations.

According to Dr. Thurstone, sample sets of the kind of questions which will be typical under the new system will be published in pamphlet form within three months, and made available to all students. The questions will emphasize thinking ability in each of the various fields, and will minimize mere factual information. Largely, the questions will call for short answers which necessitate the understanding of concepts and general ideas in the humanities, the social sciences, the physical sciences and the biological sciences.

Experts working under Dr. Thurstone are Dr. John M. Stalnaker, formerly instructor in psychology at Purdue University; Dr. James T. Russell; Professor R. W. Tyler, of the Ohio State University, and Miss Ruth Peterson and Miss Carol McCamman, graduate students. After the examination questions have been prepared by the instructors, working with these technicians, the tests will be submitted to the faculty in general and all ambiguities will be removed on the basis of the faculty version of what the right answer should be.

In all, examinations for eight one-year courses will be prepared, four for the first-year general courses and four for the second-year courses. Students who expect to receive the college certificate must, at one time or another, pass the four first-year examinations and any two of the second-year tests. The first-year tests will be available for the first time this June and will be administered regularly thereafter. Later the board of examiners will send its work to the upper divisions of the university and will provide an examination service for the bachelor's degree.

THE NORTH CAROLINA STATE COLLEGE AND DEAN CARL C. TAYLOR

THE dismissal of Dr. Carl C. Taylor, dean of the Graduate School at the State College of Agriculture and Engineering of North Carolina on June 8, 1931, is found by the committee on academic freedom and tenure of the American Association of University Professors to be "unusual" and to have been caused by other motives than the officially announced necessity of reduced budget, according to the report to be published in the February *Bulletin* of the association.

The summary action of the trustees of the college in discharging "the most distinguished member of the faculty" is analyzed by Professor Holland Thompson, of the College of the City of New York, a native of North Carolina, who made the investigation at the request of the committee, and is described by him as arising from several possible causes. The determining factor, however, is declared to be the personal "tension which had developed" between President E. C. Brooks and Dr. Taylor over several years. Such action is implied by the report as constituting a breach of the accepted principles of academic tenure.

Dr. Taylor's prominence throughout the state has made the case widely discussed, and most of the newspapers of North Carolina have condemned this action. According to the report, "the action of the trustees was not unanimous either in the executive committee which first considered the matter or in the full board which met later in the same day." Some of the issues involved are the effort of Dr. Taylor to develop an elaborate graduate school, the possible opposition to his religious views, and his liberalism on industrial and social questions. Professor Thompson, however, was unable to find any of these possible causes to be influential factors in the decision of the trustees made upon the recommendation of President Brooks.

EDUCATIONAL NOTES AND NEWS

Dr. Arthur Stanley Pease, since 1927 president of Amherst College, has presented his resignation to take effect at the end of the current college year. He has accepted a professorship of Greek and Latin at Harvard University. Dr. Pease was elected tenth president of Amherst on June 18, 1927, to succeed the late George Daniel Olds. He had been called to Amherst three years before from the University of Illinois to hold a professorship of Latin. The trustees have addressed a letter to Dr. Pease expressing their appreciation of his services and their regret at his resignation.

Dr. Henry Lefavour has presented his resignation to the Simmons College Corporation. It is understood that until his successor is appointed he will continue to administer the affairs of the college of which he has been head since its inception thirty years ago. Before becoming president of Simmons College Dr. Lefavour was dean of Williams College.

At the meeting of the Montana State Board of Education on December 14 the contract of Dr. Melvin A. Brannon as chancellor of the Greater University of Montana was extended for another term of four years. Dr. Brannon is completing his ninth year as chancellor.

Dr. Frank L. Babbott, Jr., was installed as president of the Long Island College of Medicine in Brooklyn on January 14. The principal address was delivered by Dr. James R. Angell, president of Yale University.

Mr. Jay William Crofoot has been installed as fourth president of Milton College, a Wisconsin institution.

Dr. Charles M. Snelling, chancellor of the University of Georgia, has been elected president of the state system of higher education, which comprises twenty-six institutions in different parts of Georgia. This appointment was made at the initial executive meeting of the recently appointed board of regents which, in accordance with a reorganization bill enacted into law by the last Legislature, succeeds the former boards of trustees of the various institutions. The presidents of the twenty-six separate institutions were reelected by the board.

A dinner in honor of Dr. Mary Emma Woolley, delegate by appointment of the President to the Geneva Disarmament Conference, national president of the American Association of University Women, president of Mount Holyoke College, was tendered on January 19, on the eve of her sailing, by fourteen women's colleges, joining with the Mount Holyoke College Club and the American Association of University Women. In addition to the college clubs the Foreign Policy Association, the League of Nations Association, the Women's City Club, the Women's University Club, the New York League of Women Voters, the American Woman's Association, the Panhellenic, the National Board of the Young Women's Christian Associations, and the National Federation of Business and Professional Women's Clubs joined in paying honor to Miss Woolley. A luncheon in honor of Dr. Woolley was given at the Boston City Club on January 14, at which one of the principal speakers, in addition to Dr. Woolley, was Dr. Karl T. Compton, president of the Massachusetts Institute of Technology.

Yale University has announced the establishment of the Josiah Willard Gibbs Professorship of Mathematics and the William Graham Sumner Professorship of the Science of Society. Dr. Ernest W. Brown, professor of mathematics, has been elected Josiah Willard Gibbs Professor, and Dr. Albert Galloway Keller, professor of the science of society, William Graham Sumner Professor.

Mr. Herbert E. Winlock, curator of Egyptian art at the Metropolitan Museum, New York City, has been made director of the museum to succeed the late Edward Robinson.

Dr. Eliot Carr Cutler, professor of surgery in the Medical School of Western Reserve University and director of surgery at the Lakeside Hospital, Cleveland, has been appointed Moseley professor of surgery at the Harvard Medical School and surgeon-in-chief at the Peter Bent Brigham Hospital, to succeed Dr. Harvey Cushing, whose resignation takes effect on September 1, after a service of twenty-one years.

Dr. William R. Shepherd, Seth Low professor of history at Columbia University, has been appointed visiting Carnegie professor at the University of Vienna.

Miss Jean Slavens has been made dean of women at the University of Utah, effective at the opening of the fall quarter of 1932, and Dr. LeRoy E. Cowles has been appointed dean of lower division students. Dr. Cowles, beginning in the fall of 1932, will have charge of all students in the freshman and sophomore classes.

Mr. Milton J. Fletcher has submitted his resignation as superintendent of schools at Jamestown, New York, to take effect on August 1. He has been connected with the Jamestown public schools for 33 years, having been principal of the high school for 20 years and superintendent of schools for 13 years.

Mr. William W. Shirley has resigned as librarian of the Hamilton Smith Library at the University of New Hampshire to accept a position in the economics division of the New York Public Library. The resignation will be effective February 6.

Dr. Harold W. Foght, president of the University of Wichita, was appointed director of an educational survey at Omaha, Nebraska, in connection with the establishment of the new municipal university there. Associated with Dr. Foght will be a number of other scholars and educators, including Dr. George Works, of the University of Chicago, and Dr. W. Carson Ryan, Jr., of the Office of Indian Affairs, Washington, D. C.

Miss Blanche McCarthy, retired president of the Wisconsin Teachers Association, has been appointed chairman of the committee on international relations of the Wisconsin State Board of the American Association of University Women.

Leave of absence from Princeton University for the entire academic year, 1932 to 1933, has been given to Professor Howard Crosby Warren, chairman of the department of psychology, and to Professor Thomas Marc Parrott, of the department of English. Associate Professor Carl Einar Hille, of the department of mathematics, received leave of absence for the first term of the next academic year and Associate Professor Alpheus Mason, of the department of mathematics, for the second term.

Dr. F. W. Hart, professor of education in the University of California, has been granted leave of absence from January 1 to June 30. Drs. R. B. Wiley and A. B. Murphy have been appointed lecturers in the department of education.

Dr. Harry D. Kitson has returned from a sojourn in Europe where he spent his sabbatical leave from Teachers College, Columbia University. He attended the Seventh International Conference on Psychotechnique in Moscow, Russia, and visited a number of the psychological laboratories in other countries.

Dr. Lucius W. Elder, librarian and professor of English at Knox College, has been granted leave of absence during the second semester for a European tour and study. He will sail from this country in February for Naples and from there will make a tour of the libraries and museums of Europe, making a special study of the history of printing and bookmaking.

At the recent dedication of the new Lincoln Elementary School, built at the cost of $100,000, at Ventura, California, Dr. William M. Proctor, of the department of education of Stanford University, made the dedicatory address. Mr. E. L. Van Dellen is superintendent of the Ventura schools.

Dr. Albert W. Beaven, president of the Colgate-Rochester Divinity School, will be the commencement speaker at Pennsylvania State College.

Mr. Archie M. Palmer, associate secretary of the Association of American Colleges, will speak on "The College and the Community" before the Association of Georgia Colleges, which will meet at Atlanta on January 30. The meeting will be attended by the presidents, deans and faculty members of the colleges of Georgia.

IN the winter and spring, Professor Thomas R. Garth, of the department of psychology of the University of Denver, has engaged to give a lecture on "Race Psychology" at various institutions in the Middle West and East. His itinerary will include the University of Iowa, Wellesley College, Smith College, the New School of Social Science of New York, Davidson College in North Carolina and Washington University, St. Louis.

PROFESSOR MICHAEL V. O'SHEA, of the department of education of the University of Wisconsin, died on January 14 at the age of sixty-five years. Professor O'Shea graduated from Cornell University in 1892 and had been at the University of Wisconsin since 1897.

CARL M. COTTON, for ten years superintendent of schools at Derry, New Hampshire, was found dead on the floor of his office on January 14.

AN Institute of Adult Education will be held in Spokane, Washington, on April 6, 7 and 8, under the auspices of the Inland Empire Education Association, an organization which draws its membership from Idaho, Montana, Oregon and Washington. The institute will be conducted in round tables, discussion groups from the various agencies of formal and informal adult education whose leaders, national and local, will be in attendance. The adult education movement in its several aspects, its agencies, methods, purposes, instruments and trends will present the problems the institute will consider. The committee of the Inland Empire Education Association in charge of calling the institute are Principal James A. Burke, of Spokane, Washington; Superintendent L. C. Robinson, of Sandpoint, Idaho, and the chairman, Dean Rhoda M. White, of Spokane.

THE first Institute of Urban Problems will be held at Pennsylvania State College, from July 26 to 29 for city and borough officials and any others who are interested in problems arising in the development of urban life in Pennsylvania. Dr. C. V. Hasek, head of the department of economics and sociology, has been named chairman. Other members of the committee are Thomas F. Chrostwaite, Hanover, president of the Pennsylvania Association of Boroughs; George E. Foss, Harrisburg, secretary of the State Chamber of Commerce; Adrian O. Morse, executive secretary to President Ralph D. Hetzel; Dr. Will Grant Chambers, dean of the School of Education; Jacob Tanger, acting head of the department of history and political science, and E. L. Keller, assistant professor of engineering extension.

THE laying of the cornerstone of the new Enoch Pratt Free Library building in Baltimore occurred on January 12. This building, which covers one acre of ground, and contains 4,500,000 cubic feet, is being built from a municipal loan of $3,000,000 voted by the public in May, 1927. $600,000 was spent for additional land, so that the library could maintain its downtown location on Cathedral Street, running from Mulberry to Franklin Streets. Lengthy delays involved in a condemnation suit to secure one of the properties and an injunction suit as to the letting of the contract, delayed actual work until June, 1931, at which time the old buildings were demolished. The building contract was let to the George A. Fuller Company for $1,998,000; the architectural fee and furnishings and equipment will consume the other $400,000. It is expected that the new building will be ready for occupancy next Christmas.

AT the last meeting of the New York City Board of Education Dr. William J. O'Shea, superintendent of schools, and chairman of the School Relief Fund, said that the teachers and principals in the public schools are prepared to increase their contributions to the fund for the relief of poorly clad and undernourished children and their families if the Board of Estimate is unable to appropriate $5,000,000 for the Home Relief Bureau. A report of the fund from October 1 to December 31 showed that the teachers and principals had swelled the balance left over from the last school term—it was less than $100,000—to more than $422,000. In December more than $147,000 was spent for relief. According to a report issued by the board, a record number of unemployed men and women have returned to school since the beginning of the year, 5,320 unemployed adults are enrolled in retraining courses in thirteen continuation schools.

ACCORDING to the *School Board Journal,* Dr. Frank P. Graves, commissioner of education for New York State, has rendered a decision in which he upholds the contract of a superintendent of schools. In the case of the school board of Buffalo versus Dr. E. C. Hartwell, superintendent of schools, Dr. Graves has ordered that the resolution reducing the salary of the superintendent, be vacated, and that the board pay the superintendent's salary of $15,000 per annum during six years from August 1, 1930. The commissioner's decision is final. Under the New York laws, boards of education are required to elect superintendents in first-class cities for a term of six years. Superintendent Hartwell was serving under a six-year contract tendered him at a salary of $15,000 a year. He had drawn this salary for eleven months, when, under a change in the personnel of the board, it was voted to reduce the salary from $15,000 to $12,000. Superintendent Hartwell offered to take the reduction as a matter of economy, provided other city executives would also accept reductions, but none followed his example. Suit was thereupon brought.

THE Assembly of Wisconsin has passed a resolution providing for the appointment of a committee of educators to study and determine the veracity of history text-books giving statements placing blame for causing the world war. It was sent to the Senate for final consideration. The resolution provides for the appointment of nine presidents of Wisconsin colleges and universities to study text-books on the war. Books which the committee finds make inaccurate statements would be stricken from the list approved for use in Wisconsin public schools. The resolution replaced one passed by the Senate which claimed that more than 13 text-books placed the blame on Germany.

THE Buffalo Board of Education voted on January 8 to declare a one-year postponement of the promised rises of $175 each in the salaries of 3,350 school teachers. The action will effect a $500,000 saving in the board's $40,000,000 budget for 1932. The proposed increase was part of a rise promised in 1929 to each instructor over a period of years. The board's action does not affect about 1,200 teachers who are scheduled to receive from $25 to $100 under terms of the state education law.

IMMEDIATE reduction of their salaries will be asked shortly by 1,500 school teachers of Akron, Ohio, according to an announcement made by a committee of the Teachers Association. The amount of the cut has not yet been determined. The Board of Education was without power to reduce salaries until after the present school year, so the teachers decided to make the reduction voluntarily. The offer was described as a contribution toward maintaining uninterrupted school activities which faced a $1,065,000 shortage in 1932 revenues.

ACCORDING to an Associated Press dispatch from Lowell, Massachusetts, Mr. Hugh J. Molloy, superintendent of schools, has urged 500 public school teachers to oppose a 20 per cent. reduction in salaries proposed by the finance commission. Mr. Molloy said he opposed the proposal because it did not distribute the city's retrenchment burden equitably, and that the burden of responsibility rested on all people of the city and not merely on teachers and other municipal employees. The city treasurer, Mr. Abel Campbell, has announced that there were insufficient funds in the city treasury to meet the teachers' monthly payroll of $106,000, the principal cause of the shortage being that $149,000 of municipal funds are tied up in the closed Lowell Trust Company. Mr. Molloy planned to sell short term obligations of approximately $300,000 to meet the two weeks' payroll.

SUCH large numbers of adults, mostly unemployed, have sought admission to the public day schools of New York and other cities during the depression of the last two years that the place of the grown-up in day classes as well as night classes of the state's educational system was officially recognized yesterday for the first time by the State Board of Regents. A meeting held in the State Office Building, 80 Centre Street, amended the board's rules to permit adults to attend classes in this city's continuation schools and in vocational schools of other types in up-state cities. These institutions already have been opened to unemployed persons above the normal age limit, about 15,000 adults now being enrolled in day classes throughout the state, according to the regents. In most cases, as in New York City, this provision was made about a year ago after thousands of unemployed persons asked to be allowed to take the vocational courses offered to boys and girls not over seventeen years of age in the city's fifteen continuation schools. Under an emergency provision the Board of Education has allowed the enrolment of between 8,000 and 9,000 adults in day classes throughout the city. Most of these older pupils are out of jobs and are retraining themselves in their chosen vocations or learning other trades. The regents also adopted a resolution calling upon local attendance boards of school systems to enforce rigidly the section of the state education law requiring minors to attend continuation schools twenty hours a week, instead of four, while they are not employed.

DISCUSSION

UNIVERSITY MAINTENANCE COSTS: BUILDINGS VS. INSTRUCTION[1]

REPORTS coming to the association from universities and colleges all over the country show that many are facing deficits and are discharging a part of their teaching staff or proposing considerable decrease of salaries. In every case the reason given by the college authorities is that the general depression has impaired income. But in some universities this is really only a part of the whole story. For several years past universities have been administered as if the funds that have poured particularly into the richer institutions were limitless. The personnel, however, has profited comparatively little. New schools and institutes, non-teaching, non-investigative departments have been set up. The administrative organization has been enlarged and vast building programs are under way. As a result the percentage of university income devoted to salaries for teachers and investigators during the past decade, especially in the richer universities, shows a very general and marked decrease, and is almost certain to go still lower. The overhead expense has increased correspondingly.

There are three principal causes for this subordination of teaching and scholarship to the material side of our universities. These causes are, first, the mounting cost of running the plant and the drain which this expense involves upon income from general funds. The second cause is the swollen administrative expenses. The third cause is the practice of large donors and particularly of the great foundations, from which the universities draw a considerable part of their new funds, to refuse to contribute for schools and departments already established in the universities, but insufficiently endowed, and to make their donations in large part to new and bizarre undertakings. The present financial trouble in universities is largely due to this unwise practice of these foundations.

The heavy load that an immense plant imposes upon general university endowment is not generally understood even by members of university faculties. In some institutions a maintenance fund of 33 per cent. of the erection cost of each new building, except dormitories, is now set aside. This amount is, however, wholly insufficient. Investigations which I have been making, and which are as yet incomplete, indicate that the expenses of use of university buildings, such as heating, lighting, insurance, cleaning, repairs, janitors and the unavoidable additional secretarial staff when a department moves into a new building throw an expense upon the general funds of a university which often amounts to the income of a sum equal to the original cost of the building. At one university a particularly tragic situation has arisen from the expenses associated with the new buildings; for this expense has absorbed an amount of income from general endowment virtually equal to the entire interest from a fund of $20,000,000, subscribed by the alumni four years ago and three quarters paid in, particularly for the purpose of raising salaries. Now the authorities of that university announce an estimated deficit for the current year of $500,000 to $700,000. In many universities the acceptance of a few more millions for buildings will produce virtual insolvency. Even if their incomes were unimpaired a few more years of the present policy would bring them to a condition in which their entire income would be absorbed

[1] From an address at the meeting of American Association of University Professors at Chicago, Illinois, November 27, 1931.

by plant and administration, with no funds for teachers.

The obvious, if partial, remedies for this situation are that universities should open no new buildings, even if they are completed, until times improve. No donation in future should be accepted for a building that does not carry an equal amount for the expenses of using the building; in other words 50 per cent. for building and 50 per cent. for endowment. Administrative and non-educational, non-investigative departments should be reduced as much as possible. And finally the great foundations should be forced by an aroused public opinion to throw the whole of their remaining funds if necessary to the support of those essential but unsensational parts of universities and colleges to which they have heretofore contributed comparatively little.

YANDELL HENDERSON
YALE UNIVERSITY

DEPRECIATION IN SCHOOL BUILDINGS

FOR the first time since becoming a "charter member" of the family of readers of SCHOOL AND SOCIETY I find myself unable to refrain from registering a complaint. It seems to me that the article entitled "Should Depreciation Be Accounted for in Public School Buildings?" under the heading "Discussion" in the issue for December 26, 1931, exhibits the usual confusion of ideas in regard to the subject and gives no concrete or usable information, that is, anything which would be of service to one not better acquainted with the subject than the author of the article.

In the first place, depreciation is that loss of value which occurs in spite of repairs, however adequate they may be, and should not be confused with obsolescence or inadequacy, which are much more difficult to foresee than depreciation. And depreciation does not constitute "another financial difficulty" in addition to the "retiring of bonded indebtedness," since any proper amortization of indebtedness must be based on estimated depreciation and automatically provides for such depreciation when carried out.

As to the methods of computing depreciation, I suspect that his first and third methods are substantially the same, though he does not point out in either case that the yearly depreciation charge should be applied on the indebtedness, thus keeping it at all times approximately equal to the remaining value of the building. If this be done, and there is no other legitimate use for the money, the interest charge on the remaining indebtedness will reduce each year. Incidentally, serial bonds automatically apply the straight-line method of figuring depreciation and their amount and terms should be found by using this method.

The depreciation charges found by the second, or percentage method, should also be applied to the indebtedness. This method is not adapted to structures likely to be worn out in service but is sometimes used for such things as construction machinery which may have to be thrown on the market at any time.

In the sinking fund method it is not a question of comparing return on invested capital with return on sinking fund but of comparing rate of interest which has to be paid on borrowed capital with rate of interest received on deposits in the sinking fund. If the two latter be the same there is no financial difference between the methods. That is, if the present worths of all the payments on account of capital, *i.e.,* depreciation plus interest, be found, the totals will be identical whichever method be used. Of course, if the sinking fund method be used, the interest paid each year on indebtedness remains constant, since nothing is paid off until the end of the period of accumulation, or life of the structure.

Hence with the sinking fund method the yearly charge on account of capital, interest plus depreciation, is constant, while with the straight-line method the interest charge decreases from year to year. This change from one year to the next is comparatively small and there is little to choose between the two methods if the same rate of interest can be obtained on sinking fund as is paid on the debt. Even some sacrifice in this respect may be worth while if payments into sinking fund can be made obligatory, though the use of serial bonds should accomplish the same purpose with the use of the straight-line method.

Since the cost of repairs is likely to increase as the building grows older and the use of a school building would also normally increase with increase in population it would seem fair to use whichever method seems more expedient.

Certainly there is nothing unfair in the fact that "our present generation in the midst of a depression is paying back money borrowed in more prosperous times" provided such payments are in proportion to the present use of the buildings.

The climax of confusion is "capped" in the last paragraph of the article where it is intimated that paying for a farm is similar to providing for depreciation. In the first place a farm often appreciates in value rather than depreciates, and in the second place it surely "wouldn't be good business" if "his sons and daughters" did not earn interest on the value of the plant they used regardless of whether they were compelled to because of borrowed capital or owned the plant themselves. Failure to appreciate this fact has caused many a farmer to work hard for a bare living when he might better have sold his farm, invested the proceeds and taken it easy.

F. A. BARNES

SCHOOL OF CIVIL ENGINEERING,
CORNELL UNIVERSITY

SPECIAL CORRESPONDENCE

TURKISH ADULT EDUCATION

Two daring but far-sighted reforms have won for Turkey the interest and respect of other nations. These are the change from the Arabic to the Latin alphabet, and the order that all illiterates between the ages of 16 and 40 must learn to read and write. It is natural to ask now, after a lapse of two years, whether she is making these much talked of changes an actual fact.

The first reform, that of the alphabet, is accomplished beyond the shadow of a doubt. One rarely sees the Arabic writing any more. School books, newspapers, signs, everything are in the new phonetic letters. To quote from an editorial in the Turkish "Milliyet," "The revolutions in characters transformed our libraries which were full of Arabic and Persian works for so many centuries into museums, left their use to a handful of scholars and opened the doors of the treasures of modern science to the new Turkish generation."

As to the second reform, it is known in general that a great deal has been accomplished in wiping out illiteracy, and especially in arousing a spirit of ambition among the common people. Moreover, the actual statistics of work done verify the impression that one gets from observation. The figures make one enthusiastic about the possibilities that lie in the new Turkey. During 1928–29 a total of 946,552 men and women learned to read and write. The next year 549,858 more received the literacy certificate. In addition to the last figures, most of the preceding numbers attended classes in simple arithmetic, hygiene, civics and reading for a second year.

Of these last mentioned classes, the ones in health are especially significant. One of Turkey's big problems is that of public health. Ignorance of hygiene, even among the educated classes, is astonishing. The literacy schools, however, are attacking the problem and making a special fight against the five great enemies of Turkey's health—infant mortality, malaria, syphilis, tuberculosis and alcohol.

These adult schools have been for the most part night schools. Teachers are drafted from the day schools and receive extra pay for their service. In general there are as many night schools in a town as there are head teachers. Some villages have no day school at all, so to these a traveling teacher is sent for a few months at a time. In actuality the demand for teachers exceeds the supply, so there are still many villages which are not touched by a teacher. However, another effort is being made to meet the need of the isolated village by establishing boarding schools. There are in all fifteen in the country. To these boarding schools some villagers come for a few months and then return to relay their knowledge.

In about 130 villages reading rooms have been established. To these are sent a few magazines, books and pamphlets. For the most part the books and pamphlets are circulated by traveling libraries. According to the director of education 65,000 copies of these pamphlets have been published. These deal with health, citizenship and other practical subjects. For the graduates of the first section of the folk schools, a simple, highly illustrated newspaper called "The People" is published. Pictures of scientific farming and better ways of doing other tasks are featured.

Recently I visited a civics class in a night school. It was indeed a thrilling sight to see the eager faces of those grown men, cooks, farmers, watchmen as they read from their simple book and listened to the explanations of the teacher. A sense of pride and self respect of course will come to the villages with accomplishment but a real effort is being made by the government to instil these qualities in the erstwhile ignored classes. For example the opening day of the folk school is always celebrated as a memorable occasion. A speech is made on the purpose of the schools and the value of education. Recently at the biggest student event of the year at International College in Smyrna, an American institution, the Turkish governor awarded literacy diplomas to about 20 villagers at the same time that he awarded silver medals and athletic cups to college students. Before he gave the certificates he made a stirring speech in which he addressed them as brothers and equals. He went on to say that in the new democracy the service of everyone was necessary and valuable. The rousing cheers of the boys, and the sincere words of the governor will long be treasured by these men who had previously considered their fate settled from birth. International College has had successful night classes for the past two years, taught by upper class college students.

The director of education in outlining the policy for the coming year recently said:

> We have many dreams in our imagination for the future of the night schools, but what we can really accomplish in the coming year is as follows:
>
> (1) The organization of the folk schools and reading rooms will be improved.
>
> (2) The number of traveling village teachers will be increased.
>
> (3) Traveling cinemas and libraries will be increased.
>
> (4) The head man of each village must attend the folk schools and learn how to read and write. (This last item is maybe over-confident, for the village heads are usually venerable men).

The editor of "Milliyet," a Turkish newspaper, shows the spirit of the new Turkey in this quotation from an editorial:

> Our aim is to present ourselves as an altogether new nation to the civilized world. There is no more need for a past history full of all sorts of evil deeds. If the nations wish a new type of history, we shall make one. The opinions which Europeans have held about us for centuries have been nourished by their numerous publications, both just and unjust. To change these impressions we must show that Turks, just like themselves, are striving after human ideals. This will take time and hard work on our part.

HELEN VROOMAN

INTERNATIONAL COLLEGE,
SMYRNA

QUOTATIONS

THE EXCESS OF MEDICAL STUDENTS

PROFESSOR DUGGAN, director of the Institute of International Education, has sounded a warning that should have wider reach than the bulletin of the institute gives it. The gist of it is that though there seems to be no immediate need, according to figures recently published by the *Journal* of the American Medical Association, for a larger number of medical graduates than the American colleges are able to supply, American students are applying in such numbers to medical schools abroad that it has become necessary to establish "American quotas."

If only the most promising students went abroad in search of what could not be had at home, the situation could provoke no unfavorable sentiment in European University centers. As it is, they are now aware, says Dr. Duggan, that "a large percentage" of the American students who make application to them were rejected by the medical schools at home. In 1930 the number of applicants for admission to the first class of the Medical School of Columbia University (the College of Physicians and Surgeons) was 1,000, of whom only 115 were admitted. Somewhat similar conditions obtain in other American universities. The British universities are obliged to adopt a like policy. At Edinburgh University, whose medical school has a world fame, there were 800 American applicants in 1929–30. This year it has been necessary to reject seven-eighths of them.

The situation is described as bad in every respect. There is, first of all, an imputation of inferiority in the institutions to which applications are made after rejection at home. In the next place, student fees do not support the medical schools abroad, as they do not at home. This means that the students from America absorb a part of the governmental grant and return to America when their training is finished to practice, if, indeed, they succeed in passing the examinations at home. Inquiries continue to come in unprecedented numbers, but it is to be hoped that through a wider acquaintance with actual conditions this disservice to our own country—which already has the largest relative supply of physicians—and to the universities abroad may be prevented or at least abated.—*The New York Times.*

THE SCHOOLS DURING A CRITICAL PERIOD

IN a period of business depression when the federal, state and municipal governments generally are meeting with deficits in their incomes and are unable to balance their budgets without additional taxation, it is right and proper that economies be exercised along all lines of governmental activity. It may even be necessary in parts of the country to curtail some governmental projects or duties to some degree. Whatever may be the exigencies, whatever may be the reasons for drastic reductions in appropriations, one thing must not happen. There must be no curtailment of educational facilities, The school systems for the education of our children in every state must be kept up to 100 per cent. efficiency.

A state can afford to lose time on the construction of a road, a bridge or a building and by speeding up construction at a later time possibly catch up, but education must be continuous. Time lost in preparing our children to take their places in the world can not be made up.

There are only certain years in which the great majority of them can attend school, and during that period it is the solemn duty of every state to provide full and complete education.

At no time in our history was there greater need for the influence of education upon our future citizens. It goes without saying that at this critical period it would be a great mistake to weaken the services of any of our educational institutions. On the other hand, they should be strengthened, no matter what the drain may be. Let the watchword be therefore—not only will we not permit them to fall back in their educational services, but we will, in spite of the demands upon us, do what we humanly can to improve them.—*Alfred E. Smith in the New York World-Telegram.*

REPORTS

WORK OF THE SOCIAL SCIENCE RESEARCH COUNCIL

DURING the year 1930–1931 the Social Science Research Council received six new grants. Otherwise, its work has been continued with funds previously assured.

For the general administration of the council during 1930–1931, a total amount of $80,761.08 has been expended. This sum includes expenses for the committee on problems and policy as well as advisory and various other committees. The administration of the council's fellowships in the social sciences and in agricultural economics and rural sociology, and the Southern fellowships, as well as the administration of the council's grants-in-aid are separately financed, with total expenditures amounting to slightly over $11,000. The joint committee on materials for research expended $1,784, contributed jointly by the council and the American Council of Learned Societies.

On June 30, the council completed its sixth year of research fellowship awards in the social sciences, with payment of $82,325 to thirty-five fellows. For the ensuing year the work continues with an appropriation of $90,000.

The committee on fellowships in agricultural economics and rural sociology awarded and paid $33,320 to twenty-four fellows in 1930–1931, and begins its new year with a balance of approximately $55,800, out of a total amount of $150,000 available over the five-year period ending June 30, 1933, but with present fellowship commitments amounting to $29,000 for 1931–1932.

The committee on Southern fellowships completed its first year of awards out of a five-year appropriation of $50,000 with payments during the fiscal year to twenty-six fellows, amounting to $21,730. For the new year, twenty fellows are receiving $14,450. The committee on grants-in-aid for the year ending June 30, 1931, paid grants totaling $22,825 to forty-nine individuals. This brings the total grants paid by the Council to nearly $76,000, with $15,000 pledged to twenty-two individuals payable in 1931–32.

The work on projects and other work financed out of the research grant of $750,000 has gone forward, with total net commitments amounting to almost $730,000 as of July 1, 1931. Social Science Abstracts, Inc., reported expenditures for the council's fiscal year amounting to $81,568.

The council held a conference in Hanover, New Hampshire, in the late summer of 1930 under a special grant, with expenses of $13,111. This year the summer conference was held on Nantucket Island, and was likewise separately financed, costing approximately $8,300. The President's Research Committee on Social Trends, for which the council acts as fiscal agent, expended during its fiscal year the sum of $192,946.

A new series of grants-in-aid of research to Southern social scientists has been established during the year with an appropriation of $15,000 available through June 30, 1934. With an amount of $40,000 available in instalments through June 30, 1935, for special instruction in agricultural economics the work has begun with expenditures of $3,138.37 reported through June 30, 1931.

During its early years extending through 1927, the council had at its disposal nearly $250,000 for projects. In that year the council was assured of a fund of $750,000 to be expended over a series of years for the support of research. Through June 30, 1931, a total of nearly $400,000 has been used and reserved toward the support of projects developed by the council's committees or submitted by investigators throughout the country; the cost ranging from approximately $1,000 to a maximum of approximately $100,000, the greater number lying between $5,000 and $25,000.

A further sum of approximately $115,000 from the total of $750,000 has been set aside for grants-in-aid, and this sum is allotted to individual research workers in sums usually not exceeding $1,000.

Beginning in the fall of 1929 the new emphasis on comprehensive planning for research has necessitated the husbanding of unpledged funds, with something over $100,000 reserved for this important side of council activity.

"How far it will be possible or even desirable in the future to finance miscellaneous projects from council funds remains at the moment an unsettled question. Nevertheless, the staff of the council wishes to maintain contacts with investigators seeking financial support for sound scientific projects."

Gifts to the council during the past year amounting to nearly $130,000 have come from the Rockefeller Foundation, the Russell Sage Foundation, the Carnegie Corporation and the Julius Rosenwald Fund.

SOCIETIES AND MEETINGS

THE CHICAGO MEETING OF THE AMERICAN LIBRARY ASSOCIATION

THE task before librarians of entering upon a wider sphere of service in response to the demands of an unprecedented era furnished the central topic for discussion at the midwinter meeting of the American Library Association held in Chicago from December 28 to 31, 1931. The conference which was attended by librarians from all sections of the country, representing many branches of library work, was presided over by Josephine A. Rathbone, president of the association and director of the School of Library Science, Pratt Institute, Brooklyn, N. Y.

Reflecting the theme of the conference in his paper before the council, Matthew S. Dudgeon, of the Milwaukee Public Library, pointed to the greater opportunity for educational extension to found among two classes of readers—the employed, who find under conditions of keener competition the necessity for advancing their educational qualifications, and the unemployed who are "anxious to attain higher qualifications for the relatively few existing jobs."

Outlining further the various new demands of the times, Mr. Dudgeon finds that there is an impetus toward reading along the lines of industrial and economic questions, connoting a desire to educate for more intelligent and purposeful citizenship, and that the increase of leisure among persons financially unable to attend schools is creating a wider interest in subjects of cultural nature such as travel, biography and history, philosophy, religion, literature and art.

In a paper entitled "Some Observations on the Reading of University Students" presented to the college and reference section of the conference, Samuel W. McAllister, associate librarian of the University of Michigan, notes that opinions differ widely as to whether the college student really reads beyond curricular requirements. He expresses the belief that the student is "a reading being in so far as his opportunities permit." "I believe the average student to be conservative in his taste," said Mr. McAllister, "at least to the extent of wanting to read what other people are reading. Like his elders the college man may be somewhat prone to want to talk about books rather than to read them, which discourages his pioneering spirit into fields of literature which might possibly interest him more."

From observations based upon a voluntary reading experiment conducted at the University of Michigan, Mr. McAllister presented a further point of interest in comparing the subject matter of reading done with the topics listed as "preferred by all men college students" in Waples and Tyler, "What People Want to Read About." The experiment disclosed little similarity in subjects, and led to his expressed opinion that "selection of books plays little part in encouraging college students to read, and by the same token that there are few students with well-defined interests along the lines of which they want to read. . . . I believe we do attract the rank and file of the student body who will read what we put before them in such scant time as can be snatched from innumerable tasks and activities, and who are willing to trust us not to put in their way that which will utterly waste the precious moments." Subjects mentioned as finding favor during the experiment were biography, adventure as represented by the accounts of explorers and travelers, foreign affairs chiefly as related to Russia and Germany, and books on the American scene.

"Unemployment in the Library Profession" as an aspect of the times, was discussed by James I. Wyer, of the New York State Library, Albany, in a paper before the council. Contributory causes to unemployment Mr. Wyer finds not only in the economic situation, but also in the existence of too many second- and third-rate library courses providing a supply of partly trained persons, and of too lax entrance requirements on the part of other schools.

The problem of "Economizing to Meet Budget Cuts," when libraries throughout the country are faced by a greater demand for service than ever before, was the subject for a paper by Jessie Welles, of the Toledo Public Library, and of discussion by a number of group meetings during the conference.

That state governments should set certain standards for the fundamental services of education and culture such as libraries and schools, was the conclusion expressed by Professor A. R. Hatton, of the Department of Political Science of Northwestern University in his address on "Current Trends in State Government and Taxation." He believes that state funds provided by state-wide taxation should be used to maintain such a level, supplementing the efforts of local communities. He drew attention to the fact that state governments have in the past fallen short of the responsibilities belonging to them with the result that there is an increasing tendency to seek federal aid in every department. He sees in the state income tax a more equitable mode of taxation to provide state revenue than the present system of taxes on real property.

The name of Mr. Harry Miller Lydenberg, assistant director of the New York Public Library, has been placed in nomination for the presidency of the association for 1932–1933.

EDUCATIONAL RESEARCH AND STATISTICS

IMPROVEMENT IN SCHOLARSHIP DURING THE PROBATIONARY PERIOD

A STUDENT who is placed on probation in the college of education at the University of Minnesota is disciplined in this manner for ostensibly one reason. He has failed to meet a given standard that requires him to attain satisfactory grades in one half or more of his work if he is to remain free from the probationary status. If he does not maintain this standard, he is automatically placed on probation, his parents are notified that he is doing unsatisfactory work, and he is apprized of his standing by letter, and by a special conference with a member of the Students Work Committee. This action is considered as a warning. If his work does not improve during one or two quarters his registration in the college is likely to be cancelled. When he secures an average grade of C, he is removed from probation.

Although the probation students are alike in failing to meet a given standard, they differ considerably in the reasons for their unsatisfactory work. Some are definitely of such inferior ability that their chances for a successful college career are extremely slight. Others are lazy and shiftless and therefore do not succeed even though they may have the requisite ability. A few are experiencing some cataclysmic event in relation to a home situation or love affair. A number have recently transferred from a junior college or small college and have not been able to make the necessary adjustments to a complex university environment. Several are deficient in reading habits, academic background or incentive. Without doubt, some of these students are capable of doing satisfactory work if they are given the proper aid. Perhaps they need counsel, perhaps drills in certain of the so-called fundamentals, perhaps encouragement. Each year a considerable number of students are removed from probation. For some unknown reason their scholarship has improved. In most of these cases the success has been derived through personal effort rather than through sagacious counsel on the part of faculty members.

In past years, members of the Students Work Committee have interviewed all probation students in order to ascertain, if possible, the causes for the deficient scholarship. During the course of the interview, the student was advised in regard to the manner in which he might improve his standing. The effectiveness of this counsel has never been determined.

Throughout the academic year of 1930–31 an additional effort was made to aid the probation students. Each quarter they were required to assemble for three class periods of each week. The time during the fall quarter was devoted largely to tests and exercises. Reading, intelligence and achievement tests were given. The students were notified of their standing on these tests and an attempt was made to have them fully appreciate the significance of their scores. The exercises included practice in reading against time, writing summary sentences, outlining, reviewing, vocabulary, studying to pass an examination, and practice in other types of study situations. While no absolute rules for study were laid down, numerous suggestions were given relating to reading and study habits. The relative merits of such suggestions were discussed, and the members of the class were urged to give them a trial. Students also kept time budget sheets for a period of one week. For at least one class hour each week the students studied their regular lessons under supervision. During the winter quarter the exercises, tests and supervised study were continued. Throughout the spring quarter, however, practically all the class time was used for supervised study.

It is evident that a program of this type is extremely difficult to evaluate objectively. If it were possible to judge the effectiveness of the exercises and supervised study by the improvement in scholarship during the period of investigation the task would be a simple one. It would be necessary first of all to determine the scholarship of the students at the beginning of the probation period and again at the end of one or two quarters of special training. The difference between the average scholarship at these two periods could be evaluated in terms of its reliability. With such an index it would be possible to state whether or not there was a significant gain in scholarship during the period of probation. If a reliable difference were

TABLE I

Committee Action in Regard to Probation Students 1929–30 and 1930–31

Quarter	Removed from probation		Continued on probation		Dropped		Voluntarily withdrawn		Total on probation	
	N	Per cent.	N	Per cent.	N	Per cent.	N	Per cent.	N	Per cent.
Fall 1929	5	7	44	59	10	14	15	20	74	100
Fall 1930	21	23	50	56	4	4	15	17	90	100
Winter 1930	20	20	52	53	6	6	21	21	99	100
Winter 1931	14	13	46	42	11	10	39	35	110	100
Spring 1930	16	16	48	49	8	8	27	28	99	101
Spring 1931	23	25	34	37	5	5	31	33	93	100
Total 1929–30	41	15	144	53	24	9	63	23	272	100
Total 1930–31	58	20	130	44	20	7	85	29	293	100

found the tendency would be to attribute that difference to the period of special training. A number of such studies have crept into the literature, and in practically all cases the conclusion has been derived that the training period has been exceedingly valuable.

In analyses of this type an important factor has been overlooked. That oversight can be appreciated best if it is stated in question form as follows: Would the students have made similar gains during the probation period had they not been given the special training? Perhaps the improvement is due wholly to the fact that they were placed on probation, and is not related in the slightest degree to the exercises and supervision. Such methods of evaluation, therefore, must be scrutinized closely in order to observe whether all the several factors that may have been influential have been taken into consideration.

Another means of evaluation that has sometimes been used in studies of this type involves an expression from the students to indicate if they feel that the special training has been valuable. Obviously such a method is too subjective to aid one in drawing any sweeping generalizations concerning the benefits that may be derived from supervised study.

In view of these and similar difficulties, it was decided to make as many types of comparisons as seemed feasible and in each case attempt to compare the group with special training with another group without training but similar to the first group in one or more respects. The first of these comparisons is based upon the action that the Students Work Committee has taken with reference to probation students. In Table I a summary of the action appears for all probationers throughout a period of two academic years. The individuals with whom the committee were concerned in 1929–30 were given no special supervision. They conferred with advisers in regard to their work, and the advisers, in turn, recommended to the committee the action that should be taken. The second group (1930–31) received the special training. It is readily observable that a larger percentage (23 per cent.) of the students were removed from probation at the end of the fall quarter during which the special class was in session than during the same quarter one year earlier (7 per cent.). At the end of the winter quarter a greater proportion were removed from probation following the period without training (20 per cent.) than following the period with training (13 per cent.). The net effect, then, of the training period in terms of the proportion of students removed from probation is probably very near zero. The percentage of students who were dropped was greater for the group without supervised study during the fall quarter than for the group with special direction. This condition is reversed for the winter quarter. Again the result is probably very near zero. A similar observation may be made with reference to the students in the group who voluntarily withdrew. During the spring quarters, the proportion of students removed from probation was greater in 1931 than in 1930. The totals for the three quarters of each year show that a larger proportion of the students with special training are removed from probation, a smaller proportion are either continued on probation or dropped, and a larger proportion have voluntarily withdrawn. While the trend is definite, the differences can not be described as "statistically significant."

To afford another type of comparison the probationers were matched with a group of students in terms of percentile ranks on the Miller Analogies Test, sex, major subject and college classification, *i.e.,* freshman, sophomore, junior or senior year. The members of this second group were apparently more successful in their scholarly attainments, for none was on probation. Frequently the deduction is drawn that probation students are unsuccessful because they have low ability. The alacrity with which generalizations of this nature are made precludes the consideration of other students who have comparable ability but yet do succeed. A comparison of these matched groups may offer evidence relating to the scholarship of students with low ability as well as indicate the efficacy of the supervised study.

The first section of Table II presents the differences between the probation group for the fall quarter 1930 and the group matched on the bases indicated above. The Miller Analogies Test was one of the measures on which the groups were equated. No significant differences would be expected, therefore, between the averages of the two groups on this test. The mean for the probation group is 22.85, whereas that for the matched group is 25.35. The difference of 2.50 ± 3.25, which is only .77 times its probable error, may be attributed wholly to the fact that the individuals were matched within deciles rather than on percentile points.

The average percentile rank of the probation students on the Minnesota reading examination is 26.75. For the matched group, the average is 39.25. The difference of 12.50 ± 3.83 is more than three times its probable error and does, therefore, approach significance. This noteworthy observation indicates rather clearly that effectiveness in reading is a factor attributing to the scholastic success of the members of the matched group. In spite of the fact that intelligence has been kept constant in the two groups through the process of equating, the students who have succeeded show a definite trend to obtain higher scores on the reading test. With this observation apparent it might be assumed that if the probation students could improve their reading abilities, higher scholarship is likely to ensue.

With a relatively small number of cases the differences between the groups on the Meier-Seashore art judgment test are negligible. This is not true, however, when the scholarship records are summarized. The average honor point ratio (.49) of the probation students during the quarter just prior to the probation period of 1929, is .75 ± .08 honor points lower than that of the matched group (1.24). The data clearly indicate that the difference in scholarship was considerable. For the probationers, the average is approximately half way between a grade of D and a grade of C. For the other group, the average is substantially above the grade of C.

During the quarter of special training in reading and study, the probation group increased its average honor point ratio by .28 ± .09 for at the end of the quarter the average was .77. This gain is almost three times its probable error, whereas the gain of .03 for the other group is only .3 times its probable error. While neither gain is decidedly significant, the increment for the probation students is considerably greater. It is sufficiently greater to reduce the differences between the two groups at the end of the quarter by one third, or to .50 ± .11.

Similar facts are available in the second and third sections of the table, which summarize the data for the winter quarter group and for a small group of students who were in the special class throughout a two-quarter period. In both sections the differences are consistent with the foregoing. The winter quarter probation group has a decidedly lower average honor point ratio (–.01) for the quarter prior to probationary period than was true for the fall quarter group. While the gain is twice that of the first quarter probationers it does not place these students at the same level for the average honor point ratio at the end of one quarter of special training is only .53. The gain, however, is 9 times its

TABLE II

DIFFERENCES BETWEEN PROBATION STUDENTS AND NON-PROBATION STUDENTS MATCHED ON THE BASIS OF INTELLIGENCE TEST PERCENTILES

	Probation group				Matched group				Difference		
	N	M	PE_M	S.D.	N	M	PE_M	S.D.	D	PE_D	D/PE_D
Fall quarter group 1930											
Miller analogies	42	22.85	2.29	22.00	42	25.35	2.30	22.10	2.50	3.25	.77
Minnesota reading	40	26.75	2.53	23.70	40	39.25	2.87	26.90	12.50	3.83	3.26
Meier-Seashore	17	38.95	4.60	28.10	17	45.45	4.49	27.45	6.50	6.43	1.01
*H.P.R. quarter prior to probation	26	.49	.06	.47	26	1.24	.06	.43	.75	.08	9.38
*H.P.R. quarter of probation f 1930	26	.77	.07	.53	26	1.27	.08	.58	.50	.11	4.55
Difference		.28				.03					
PE_D		.09				.10					
D/PE_D		3.11				.30					
Winter quarter group 1931											
Miller analogies	72	18.35	1.29	16.25	72	19.05	1.27	16.00	.70	1.81	.39
Minnesota reading	72	22.50	1.54	19.40	72	30.55	2.00	25.15	8.05	2.52	3.19
Meier-Seashore	15	54.15	4.35	24.95	15	59.85	3.95	22.70	5.70	5.88	.97
*H.P.R. quarter prior to probation f 1930	49	–.01	.04	.38	49	1.10	.05	.48	1.11	.06	18.50
*H.P.R. quarter of probation w 1930	49	.53	.05	.54	49	1.18	.05	.55	.65	.07	9.29
Difference		.54				.08					
PE_D		.06				.07					
D/PE_D		9.00				1.14					
Fall-winter quarter group 1930–31											
Miller analogies	15	17.15	2.95	16.95	15	18.15	2.73	15.65	1.00	4.02	.25
Minnesota reading	15	19.85	2.90	16.65	15	36.15	4.96	28.45	16.30	5.75	2.83
Meier-Seashore	9	55.85	6.08	27.05	9	58.05	5.60	24.90	2.20	8.27	.27
*H.P.R. quarter prior to probation	10	.40	.09	.40	10	1.30	.12	.57	.90	.15	6.00
*H.P.R. quarter of probation F–W 1930–31	10	.65	.04	.18	10	1.23	.12	.54	.58	.13	4.46
Difference		.25				–.07					
PE_D		.10				.17					
D/PE_D		2.50				–.41					

* H.P.R. refers to the honor point ratio that was obtained by dividing the total number of honor points earned by the total number of credits for which the student was enrolled. The honor points were assigned as follows: One for each credit of A, two for B, and three for C. One honor point was subtracted for each credit hour with a mark of F.

probable error and unquestionably significant. It is evident that students make a pronounced gain in scholarship while on probation whereas the matched students make practically no gain. It would be premature to generalize at this point with a statement that the significant gain for the probationers was due to the special training they received. Before such deductions are warranted additional comparisons must be made.

Since it did not seem feasible to divide the probation group for a single quarter into two

TABLE III

PROBATION STUDENTS WITH SUPERVISED STUDY COMPARED WITH PROBATION STUDENTS WITHOUT SUPERVISED STUDY

	Supervised study group 1930–31				Matched group 1929–30				Differences		
	N	M	PE_M	S.D.	N	M	PE_M	S.D.	D	PE_D	D/PE_D
Fall quarter group											
Miller analogies	40	20.10	2.00	18.75	40	19.85	1.89	17.70	.25	2.75	.09
H.P.R. quarter prior to probation	40	.32	.05	.43	40	–.03	.04	.42	.35	.06	5.83
H.P.R. quarter of probation	40	.70	.07	.64	40	.47	.06	.55	.23	.09	2.56
Difference		.38				.50					
Pe_D		.09				.07					
D/PE_D		4.22				7.14					
Winter quarter group											
Miller analogies	43	17.62	1.55	15.08	43	17.50	1.55	15.10	.12	2.19	.05
H.P.R. quarter prior to probation	43	.00	.05	.44	43	.14	.05	.47	.14	.07	2.00
H.P.R. quarter of probation	43	.58	.07	.67	43	.53	.07	.64	.05	.10	.50
Difference		.58				.39					
PE_D		.08				.08					
D/PE_D		7.16				4.87					

equivalent groups and provide special training for one but not for the other, the individuals required to study under supervision were matched with probation students of the previous year, 1929–30. The bases used for matching were intelligence as measured by the Miller analogies test, sex, major subject and college classification. The data for these comparable groups are presented in Table III. A glance at the first row of figures and particularly the ratio at the end of the line shows clearly that no difference existed between the averages on the Miller analogies tests for the matched groups. There is a significant difference between the two groups in the average honor point ratio for the quarter prior to probation. The supervised study group begins with an average that is $.35 \pm .06$ higher than the second group. At the end of one quarter of probation the difference between the two groups is less ($.23 \pm .09$). Although the gain for the supervised study group ($.38 \pm .09$) is less than that for the matched group, the average for the first group (.70) at the end of one quarter of probation is greater than the average for the matched group ($.47 \pm .06$). Both groups made significant gains. The evidence does in no way indicate that the supervised study groups were especially benefited by the period of special training. Apparently the chief factor that seems to be operating is the fact that these students are on probation. Such disciplinary action seems to be effective as a means of producing improvement in scholarship. The data for the winter quarter group are similar, with the exception of a somewhat greater gain for the supervised study group. At the end of the quarter, however, the difference in the scholarship of the two groups is insignificant.

It would be audacious to infer from these results that students with inferior scholarship could not be given any type of special training to aid them in improving their records. The very fact that students succeed to a greater degree during the probationary period is clearly indicative that certain of the causes operating to produce low-grade work prior to the time of the disciplinary action are removed by that action. Aside from the improvement in scholarship, the changes that take place are not perceptible in the present stage of the analysis. That these students can and do improve is proof in itself that conditions can be arranged to assist them. Whether an attempt should be made to establish those conditions at the college level is an academic question with which the present considerations do not deal.

The ineffectiveness of the program for special training that has been evaluated may be due to a number of unfavorable circumstances. Chief among these is probably the compulsory arrangement under which it was conducted. The probation students were required to attend the special class. They came, therefore, with an antagonistic attitude which many of them nourished throughout the period of supervision. It would probably be more advisable to place the special training on a voluntary basis. The number of probation students who would take advantage of the special training would be difficult to ascertain without actually putting the schedule into effect. The fact that certain of them would be willing and anxious to participate may be a significant indication of an attitude that is essential for satisfactory scholarship.

Another difficulty encountered is allied to the number of students in the class. Throughout the three-quarter period the registration varied between 60 to approximately 100. Obviously the amount of individual attention that could be given by one instructor was decidedly limited. It has already been inferred that the reasons for inferior scholarship are probably individual. While group measuring instruments may be used to aid in the diagnosis of the difficulties, any remedial work that is attempted should be placed almost wholly on an individual basis. This statement does not imply that marked improvement would be observed if considerable individual attention were given. It is offered purely as a limitation of the present study.

A condensation of the observed facts seems to warrant three concluding statements: (1) The reading ability of probation students is inferior to that of other students of equal mental ability who are succeeding with their college work; (2) poor students improve their scholarship during the probationary period; and (3) the improvement that was found does not seem attributable to the program of special training. If, through experimentation and study, a large number of similar facts might be accumulated, the whole question of what should be done with inferior college students would not always remain in a quagmire of uncertainty.

Summary

(1) The action taken by the Students Work Committee reveals a slight trend favoring the probation students with special exercises and supervised study.

(2) When students who have not been placed on probation are matched with probation students on the bases of intelligence, sex, major subject and college classification, there is a marked difference between the two groups on the Minnesota reading examination. This indicates that effective reading habits vary concomitantly with scholarship when intelligence is held constant.

(3) Students of equal ability, of the same sex, pursuing the same major subject, and with the same college classification as probation students do succeed with college work. Ability, therefore, as measured by the Miller analogies test is by no means the only factor that determines scholarship. Without question, additional unknown factors are operating to reduce the scholarship of students.

(4) Gains made by students in average honor point ratios for the quarter of probation are considerably greater than those made by the matched group not on probation. Even so, the probation students do not attain the same scholastic standing at the end of one quarter.

(5) When probation students with supervised study are matched with students without special training who were on probation one year earlier, the differences in the scholarship of the two groups do not indicate that the period of special training was particularly efficacious.

Alvin C. Eurich
University of Minnesota

NEW BOOKS IN EDUCATION

Achilles, Paul S., Editor. *Psychology at Work.* Pp. xiii + 260. Illustrated. Whittlesey House, McGraw-Hill. $2.50.

Boome, E. J. and M. A. Richardson. *The Nature and Treatment of Stammering.* Pp. ix + 135. Dutton. $1.50.

SCHOOL AND SOCIETY

EDITED BY J. McKEEN CATTELL

WITH WHICH IS COMBINED THE

EDUCATIONAL REVIEW

EDITED BY WILLIAM McANDREW

Volume 35 — Saturday, January 30, 1932 — Number 892

THE "TEACHING DEGREE"

By Professor OTTO HELLER

DEAN OF THE GRADUATE SCHOOL, WASHINGTON UNIVERSITY, ST. LOUIS

Academic degrees in this country are by way of becoming a plague. Although, together with their rarity value, they have forfeited their social luster, while at the same time they have ceased to be positive evidence of learning or proficiency, they are coveted by an abnormal number of people, and mostly for utilitarian reasons. And yet, as far as real uses go, they might as well be done away with and the ornate engrossment on parchment of "these presents" and the "privileges and prerogatives thereunto appertaining," supplanted by a straightforward statement of the owner's qualifications for a job, legibly written out in plain English on ordinary paper.

To expect such a sweeping abolition of time-hallowed frills and fiddle-faddle is impossible in sight of the lusty spread of academic pomp and pageantry. Our scholastic world remains unimpressed by the fact that in most foreign countries the two lower degrees have gone out of existence, and that even the surviving degree of doctor is neither a *sine qua non* nor, on the other hand, a guarantee, for high-grade educational placement. In England, to be sure, where academic life is so firmly incrusted in archaic forms, the bachelor's and master's degrees have not been interfered with; but there, too, they have largely lost their nimbus. What seriously counts to a collegian's credit among Britons is not the bare degree but the kind of supererogatory distinction with which it was earned.

Since the bachelor's degree by reason of its ubiquity has dwindled in prestige, it seems strange that no thought of its abolishment is ever entertained. Certainly one glance at the degreeless yet overcrowded colleges of continental Europe should allay any fear lest the removal of so slight a premium should stop the universal scramble for a college education. One wonders at the retention of the bachelor's degree in such a reorganization as is now going forward at the University of Chicago.

If the bachelor's degree has fallen below par in value as a first naturalization paper in the Republic of Letters, neither does the master's degree pass unchallenged as a certificate of full citizenship. In President Lowell's opinion, the A.M. to-day represents just about what the A.B. used to represent in its better days. That is indeed a "rough" estimate, but if it is fairly correct, then we have been guilty of tying the label to the wrong package, and it is time to rectify the mistake. For my part, ringing a slight change on Mr. Lowell's postulate in relativity, I venture to guess that the master's degree stands for about as much as the bachelor's degree would stand for, if the concern for higher education were really as strong as is popularly supposed. Anyway, the master's degree is no more vital to the advancement of learning than the bachelor's. Functioning, as it does chiefly, as a ticket of admission to the medium range of the teaching field, it could be satisfactorily commuted to an unambiguous testimonial of competency and perhaps a graded designation like the French *licencié, diplomé, agrégé*.

However, I am not Quixotic enough to crusade against university degrees. Assuming, on the contrary, that they will continue to flourish and multiply, my main design in this paper is to plead in favor of a revised routine whereby, at least for the master's degree, a fuller protection of its proper standards might be secured. Reference was made a moment ago to an alleged shifting of values. I am not ready to admit that in the broad view either the bachelor's or the master's degree has intrinsically deteriorated. They have merely lost caste. However, the status of both should be raised, for it has always been too low. I completely dissent from the gloomy anticipation of certain defeatists that in the precarious relativity of things the Ph.D. in its turn must eventually come to mean only what the master's degree ought to mean. Neither do I subscribe to the prediction that when confidence in the A.M. as a voucher for efficiency is wholly lost, the Ph.D. shall be exacted from high-school teachers, nor acquiesce in the proposal to convert the Ph.D. into a "teaching degree," in time-serving readiness against that event. Some of these prophets, in moments of brighter outlook, have discovered a compensation remedy for the threatened avolation of the spirit of science. Namely, they would top the existing academic step-ladder with an additional degree to whose holders the world may confidently look for the increase of aggregate human knowledge.

The idea of the separate research degree or super-doctorate takes its rise from the new-fledged superstition that teaching and research, the communication of assured knowledge and the quest for new, are wholly disconnected and incompatible activities, when in effect their unity of aim can not be reasonably denied. The project repeatedly put forth of late to differentiate sharply the training of teachers and of scientists smacks of naïveté. Surely it is on the steady transmission of knowledge from master to pupil, rather than on any other single factor, that the progress of science has ever depended. The torch of knowledge will burn no less brightly at the goal for having kindled other lights on its way, and a new handle will not enhance its flame. The Ph.D. and the M.D. have served science too long and too well to be relegated to a partial and impliedly inferior utility.

Be that as it may, it is the master's degree to which just now the lion's share of our vigilance is due. This degree is awarded on such heterogeneous conditions that its meaning rather baffles definition, yet the incentive to its acquisition is nearly always the same. To turn up one's nose at this prime motive and denounce it as mercenary is very foolish. Even the staunchest lover of science must keep his eye on his livelihood. Institutions of learning can not blink this all-important fact nor repudiate all responsibility for their students' future.

Now it chances that of the annual output of 16,000 masters or so, probably more than 14,000 are either active or prospective teachers, and that the degree has been almost universally adopted, explicitly or tacitly, as a criterion of placement and preferment. Naturally, those in search of positions are eager to get the A.M. in quick order and on easy terms. They will spar desperately for points of academic credit and, topographic convenience apart, pick a graduate school less for its quality than for the reach of its patronage, the efficiency of its appointment bureau and its largess toward students.

Since to all practical effect the A.M. or M.S. is thus established as the "teaching degree" *de facto,* let us see whether it would not be the part of wisdom frankly to acknowledge it as such. My hypothesis is that this could be done without injury to its position as a halfway station between baccalaureate and doctorate and with decided benefit to the cause of teaching.

According to my conception, the work for the master's degree should fit the student to teach competently one or possibly two subjects in secondary school and junior college, without putting the full stop to his studies and damping his ardor for original research. Clearly a goal set as high as that can not be honestly reached by racing against time, nor indeed should it be pursued at all except from a proper starting point. Normally, therefore, graduate work should be grounded on a full course of study in a regular college of arts and sciences.

The imperfect design of our educational system admits not a few ill-prepared students to the graduate school through loopholes that seem to be dilating rather than contracting. A special source of damage is the considerable ingression of teachers college graduates. By degrees, the functions of three distinct types of school—the junior college, the liberal arts college and the teachers college—have fallen into a deplorable confusion in which the fate of the graduate school is none too indirectly involved. Unquestionably all these institutions have a strong reason for being, and they would be equivalent in civic importance, if each of them loyally looked after its own affairs. The junior college, I fancy, should be a finishing school of sorts, giving to the high-school graduate who does not care to go all the way through college an epitome of sorts of collegiate education, an abstract of contemporary knowledge, together with a tincture of letters, or maybe instead of these things a specific preparation for certain non-professional or semi-professional careers. There can be no question that a real need of such schools does exist. As for the teachers colleges, they were originally training-schools of elementary teachers, and should by all means be restored to their sadly neglected task. For as long as they are engaged in a wasteful competition with the regular colleges, of which the net result is a grievous intermixture between cultural and professional ends, they offend against their ordained mission. An undesirable corollary of their attitude is that the standard colleges retaliate by conforming their education courses to local eligibility rules to assist their graduates in obtaining public-school appointments. The fact is, however, that an enormous number of college graduates wish to pursue graduate work, at once, or later, and that teachers colleges are not constituted for the business of preparing students for graduate work, save in the vocational subject of education. Almost never are their students completely equipped for graduate work, even in the branch of study they want to take up at the university. Many graduate schools are liberal enough to admit this class of students, only imposing a supplemental amount of work to balance the deficit. Far from realizing the advantage of the provision for such students, teacher college officials are apt to denounce it as an unfair discrimination against their institutions and to bear down loudly on the moderate entrance requirements of the graduate school.

Under the plan broached in these pages, the functional difference between the teachers college or normal school and the college of arts would be expressed by the removal of practice teaching and all other pedagogical specialization from the program of the latter. In that way the responsibility for elementary teacher training would squarely revert to teachers colleges, and college students in order to qualify for elementary teaching would have to do so outside of regular sessions, perhaps in the summer, or by joining regular or special classes at a teachers college in convenient location. With good-will on both sides, the required practice teaching could also be adjusted to such a plan.

The duty of training elementary teachers assigned to where it actually belongs, the graduate school could no longer temporize with its responsibility for the preparation of secondary and college teachers. Hence, unless my statement that the master's degree is almost mandatory for them be wide of the mark, candidates for the degree should learn something about teaching their subjects.

Under present conditions I side unequivocally against any division of graduate work between objective study and study of method, for the simple reason that there is not time for both. But a removal of this objection would leave little ground for disputing to education its legitimate place in the graduate school. For we must square ourselves with these incontrovertible facts: first, that the overwhelming majority of masters of arts and masters of science do intend to teach, and second, that acquaintance with educational principles and routine is sure to expedite the working of classroom experience. That minority of students who do not care to qualify for teaching appointments can, of course, do without any pedagogical training. Under my plan, the educational propaedeutics would have to be firmly rooted in philosophical and psychological foundations. Meticulous occupation with administrative matters, or the statistical and experimental concern with tests and measurements, now usually on the front page of the educationist program, would hardly serve the purpose. The work ought to be in part of the most generic, in part, however, of a quite specific sort: that is, it should consist, on the one hand, of education *per se,* on the other, of education *ad hoc.*

And here a practical difficulty springs into view. It is relatively easy for any university to provide courses in the history, philosophy and psychology of education; but it is fiscally impracticable for each graduate school to offer method courses in each separate discipline. Hence, students would necessarily avail themselves of special advantages where they are offered, and graduate schools would attract students to particular departments by the existence of those opportunities. Thus, a chemist might be swayed in favor of Johns Hopkins, where a special chair for the teaching of chemistry exists, while for a corresponding reason a Germanist might prefer the University of Wisconsin. Similar possibilities are found in other places, but under suitable provisions it should be feasible for a student to pursue his substantive studies at one institution, and his method work at another; to illustrate, he could take his mathematics at his own university in regular residence and the incidental method courses at, say, the University of Iowa, which specializes in that field during a summer session of eleven weeks. It can not be my design here to go into the details of the incident problem of student migration.

In conclusion I would forestall the insinuation that a plan such as mine might imperil the solidity of graduate work. It goes without saying that graduate work must under no circumstances allow itself to be weakened. On the contrary, if methods are to have a more than perfunctory effect on the quality of teaching, the work in the subject itself should be still further intensified through the correlation with teaching. For this reason, the division of the student's time between two fields during his first year of graduate study is to be discountenanced if the degree is earned, as is usual, in one postgraduate year. The combination of two disciplines into "major" and "minor" may, of course, be defended on the ground that a "minor" is subsequently required for the doctorate. My contention is that the formal election of a "minor" in a program embracing preparation for teaching is impossible on the one-year basis without a lowering of standards which even now are none of the highest. If the student extends his residence beyond a single year, he need not be restricted to a single field. At my university we have made a move, not unwise in my belief, to check the inordinate haste of students for the degree. We allow the "splitting" of the "major" if the candidate will do a compensatory amount of additional work involving some prolongation of residence. Also, it is feasible with us for a student to do some work outside his official subject, in a related field of study, without an explicit "minor" and without an extra load of credit-units. Concessions and makeshifts of this sort exist nearly everywhere, and seem to indicate that the schools are becoming conscious of a fundamental difficulty which as yet they do not dare to attack at the root. That fundamental difficulty is simply this, that one year's time is not enough if the degree is to denote a genuine achievement together with readiness to teach in a special field. I should be reluctant to fix the requisite period definitely, because under the system of qualifying and final examinations for both the master's and the doctor's degree, to which I think we shall generally resort before long in lieu of the credit-unit system, the residential requirements are apt to be radically revised. But if, for the present, an average residence of from three to four semesters were imposed upon aspirants to the master's degree, they would promptly learn to use a part of their summers for study and in the end would have shortened instead of prolonged their graduate residence.

Three other beneficial results should follow from the suggested reform. The transfer of education courses from the collegiate to the graduate level of instruction would remove a load of from 15 to 18 credit-units from the undergraduate schedule of future teachers, representing work which in the consensus of their opinions is at that stage uncongenial and uninteresting. It would distinctly raise the ancillary importance of education in the academic scheme and put an end to the disdain in which it is held under present conditions. At the same time it might conduce to some desirable reconstruction of education itself, with a lessened emphasis perchance on administrative and statistical procedures, and a heightened stress on the vital elements of teaching.

With four semesters of residence ahead of them students could start in both major and minor subjects, although even then they should not be discouraged from concentrating on a single field, so as to gain time for making up any deficiencies in their collegiate antecedents. For it is deplorable that at present they are often permitted to carry serious handicaps into their professional careers. For example, in the division of letters, thousands now receive the master's degree in English or Latin without previous study of any other language. In the division of science, it is a very common complaint that the study of physics is carried on with an inadequate knowledge of mathematics. To remedy these faults universities should avoid the lure of short cuts as well as the temptations of devious paths and resolutely lay out a way leading definitely to the desired goal. They can do a larger share toward producing competent teachers and also competent scientists, though they will never be able to predetermine the individual vocation. That lies on the knees of the gods. Anyway, even if it took two full years to acquire the master's degree, students could still make their professional début without undue delay. They would attain the master's degree at twenty-two or twenty-three years of age, and surely that is neither too late to begin teaching nor too early to embark in research.

SELECTING GOOD COLLEGE RISKS

By HARL R. DOUGLASS

PROFESSOR OF EDUCATIONAL ADMINISTRATION, UNIVERSITY OF MINNESOTA

In no age or among no people has higher education reached the masses to the extent that it does in the United States to-day. Approximately a million boys and girls, men and women, are enrolled in public or in private colleges and universities. Since 1910, enrolments in institutions of higher learning have mounted astonishingly. Twenty years ago fewer than 275,000 individuals, constituting approximately 3.7 per cent. of the population of the country of ages 19 to 22 inclusive, attended colleges and universities. By 1920, these figures had become 462,000 and 6.3 per cent., respectively. In 1926, according to U. S. Commissioner of Education Wm. J. Cooper, 763,000 students or 10.4 per cent. of the population of ages 19 to 22 inclusive were attempting higher education. The percentage of people of college age who are attending college to-day is approximately 14 per cent., or one in seven as compared to one in sixteen in 1920, one in twenty-seven in 1910 and one in thirty-six in 1900.

That this rapid increase in the number of young people seeking college degrees is not uniformly regarded as an unmitigated blessing may be noted in the complaints by members of college and university faculties that the quality of college entrants has been perceptibly lowered. By economists and heavy taxpayers the question is bluntly raised as to how far we may safely go in providing higher education at public expense.

Ordinarily it has been assumed by those protesting the admission of inferior students to college that the large increase in numbers has resulted in recruiting the college student body in greater proportions from the lower levels of ability. A conventional concomitant of this assumption is the charge that secondary schools are, for one reason or another, deteriorating in accomplishment and are permitting less able students to graduate.

While what few objective data supplied by careful investigations as are available do not offer much encouragement to these assumptions, nevertheless applications for admission to institutions of higher learning have become so numerous that we can now much better afford to consider possibilities and means of selecting the better college risks and of rejecting the less promising ones.

Space will not be taken here to outline the history of the various methods employed to select college entrants. Until the seventies, each institution required every applicant to submit to an entrance examination, the content and standards of which varied widely among different institutions. Dating from 1871, and first employed at the University of Michigan, the accrediting system, by which graduates of approved secondary schools presenting credits in specified subjects are admitted, has grown until to-day it is by far the prevailing method of admission to college.

The development of the uniform College Entrance Examination Board examinations, beginning in 1900, has served to preserve that route for a small minority of college entrants, confined largely to the New England and Middle Atlantic States. Even in these regions, it is not the predominant method.[1] Only in a very small number of institutions, half of which are colleges for women, is it impossible for students to enter without having passed college entrance examinations.

With the exception of a small minority of institutions, students entering by means of transcripts from their high-school records are required to present from five to twelve credits in specified subjects conforming to prescribed patterns of minimum credits in each of a number of fields. Some idea of the extent to which these subjects are favored may be obtained from the following summary based upon the comprehensive study of college entrance requirements by Edwin J. Brown and William M. Proctor, of Stanford University.

(1) *English:* At every institution, some credits in English were specified, 93 per cent. requiring three or more year units and 18 per cent. requiring four units.

(2) *Mathematics:* Two units in mathematics were required at 94 per cent. of the institutions.

(3) *Foreign Language:* Two or more units in some foreign language (a few schools specifying Latin) were required at 75 per cent. of the colleges and universities.

(4) *History and Social Studies:* One or more units was specified by 75 per cent. of the institutions—usually one unit of history.

(5) *Natural Science:* A minimum of one unit of science was required in 54 per cent. of the schools—usually one unit of a laboratory science.

(6) *Vocational Studies:* Not more than four units of credit in vocational subjects were accepted towards entrance in 73 per cent. of the institutions.

Other standards have been set up which directly or indirectly determine who shall be permitted to enter college; with certain of these standards we are concerned here. Within recent years, there may be noted a tendency to qualify the acceptance of high-school credits upon the basis of the marks attached to the credits. Perhaps the most popular form of this practice consists of setting up an arbitrary dead line, credits presented with marks below the minimum so established not being accepted towards entrance. At a number of institutions, the lowest passing secondary school mark is not acceptable.

All these standards have been based upon empirical evidence and are largely the creatures of opinion more or less expert. Good logic requires that their validity as bases for acceptance of the entrants be measured by the degree to which they differentiate between students who will succeed in their scholastic endeavors and those who will not.

It should be obvious that with the exception of the minimum high-school mark the standards mentioned in the foregoing paragraphs are such as permit judgment upon the school as a whole or upon the pattern of the courses studied in schools as distinct from measurement of the capacity or ability of the individual student. It is equally certain that students coming from a given school and students following the same high-school curriculum differ as widely in ability to succeed in college as do groups of students who come from different schools and who have followed different patterns of high-school courses.

These facts serve to raise the legitimate question whether such methods are effective in differentiating between good and poor college risks. The basic data for the com-

[1] See E. J. Brown and W. M. Proctor, "Methods of Admission and Matriculation Requirements in Three Hundred and Thirty-One Colleges and Universities." *Seventh Yearbook of the Department of Superintendence*, 1928, pp. 331–58.

parisons and conclusions presented in the following paragraphs were gathered in connection with a study involving the 387 students of the class of 1930 of the University of Oregon, all the class entering the university in the fall quarter of 1926 and remaining in continuous residence for five successive quarters, with the exception of some 60 individuals for whom complete data were not obtainable.

Zero order coefficients of correlation representing the relationship between number of units of high-school credit in the various fields and average college were calculated. These indicate conclusively that knowledge of the number of years any subject is pursued is of very little value for the purpose of predicting college success. The coefficients range from –.04 for social studies to .17 for foreign languages. When percentile rank on the American Council psychological test is held constant, the partial coefficients of correlation between average college mark and number of units of credit in a given subject were even less, ranging from –.12 for social studies to .11 for vocational studies, that for foreign languages dropping to .05. It was obvious that by no combination could a multiple correlation of any significant magnitude be obtained.

Students who presented two units of credit in foreign language did no better on the average in college than students who presented no units in that field. No effective threshold to bar poor students may be set at less than five units of foreign language. Setting such a threshold at any number of units in foreign languages operates to bar almost as many superior students as poor ones (see Table I).

Students presenting fewer than two units of mathematics achieve as well in college as do those having spent two more years in the study of high-school mathematics.

It is interesting but not significant to note that of the four students having more than four years of high-school mathematics but one achieved a college average above the median for all students. While the median is slightly higher, the average college mark of those having had four years of high-school mathematics is less than that of those having had one, two or three years (see Table II).

The absence of negative correlation between number of units of high-school credits in vocational subjects and college marks invites closer analysis (see Table III). Inspection of the scattergram reveals no relationship between amount of credit in these subjects and scholastic success in college. Of the students presenting in excess of four units of credit in vocational subjects, very few were distinctly inferior or distinctly superior students. Fourteen students presented five or more units of vocational credit. The average college mark of these fourteen students was about .18 of a grade step on a six-step scale better than the average of all students included in the study.

One may be expected to suspect that these students constituted a select group. They were slightly more mature than the average as represented by a difference between 19.6 and 18.2 years. One only was more than 21 years of age. Eight were students in the school of business administration, for entrance to which more than four units of vocational credit are accepted. They pursued, however, few courses in technical business administration and the percentage of failure is rather high in those subjects. In percentile rank on the Council of Education mental test they were slightly inferior to the average student included in the study, as represented by difference of percentile ranks of .472 and .513. Their average high school mark was slightly superior, 86.4 as compared to an average of 83.6 for all students in the study. Thus they prove upon examination to be in no way an abnormal group.

Inspection of the other scattergrams reveal no significant relationship not suggested by the negligible coefficients of correlation. Students who presented but three units of English did not fare quite as well in college as did those who completed four years of work in that subject. The difference in median average college mark was .25 of a grade step on a six-point marking scale. That this difference may be attributed at least in part to difference in ability rather than to the college preparatory training provided by fourth year English is evidenced by the superior rank in intelligence of those having had four years of high school English, .553, as compared to .506 for those having had but three years of high school English.

Students who have had more than three years of high school work in history and social studies on the average do definitely inferior work in college and those having less than three units of credit in that field achieved definitely higher averages. These differences may likewise be attributed to differences in intelligence of the two groups of students. Of the fourteen students having less than two units of history and social studies, twelve ranged in percentile rank from .706 to .952 with a mean rank of .778 as compared to a median rank of .513 for all students included in the study.

Not only was there little or no relation between pattern of high school credits and college success, but apparently there is little relation between the mastery of any particular subject and college success. As a reasonable though arbitrary measure of mastery, the number of units in each field was multiplied by average mark received and the resulting products referred to as subject indices. While the correlations between high-school marks and college marks ranged from .38 in vocational subjects to .54 in science, the correlations between subject index and average college mark ranged from −.04 for vocational subjects to .23 for foreign languages. With percentile rank in intelligence held constant the coefficient for foreign languages diminished from .23 to .06 and that for mathematics from .12 to .04.

TABLE I

COLLEGE MARKS RECEIVED BY STUDENTS CLASSIFIED ACCORDING TO THE NUMBER OF YEARS OF CREDIT IN HIGH SCHOOL IN FOREIGN LANGUAGE

Units of foreign language	0	1	2	3	4	5
Upper quartile	3.0	3.3	2.8	2.7	2.6	2.7
Median	3.3	3.7	3.3	3.4	3.1	3.1
Lower quartile	3.8	4.0	3.8	3.6	3.7	3.3

TABLE II

COLLEGE MARKS RECEIVED BY STUDENTS CLASSIFIED ACCORDING TO THE NUMBER OF YEARS OF CREDIT RECEIVED IN HIGH SCHOOL IN MATHEMATICS

Units of mathematics	Less than 2	2	2.5	3	3.5	4
Upper quartile	2.6	2.6	2.8	2.7	2.6	2.6
Median	3.2	3.2	3.3	3.2	3.2	3.1
Lower quartile	3.5	3.7	3.7	3.6	3.6	4.0

TABLE III

COLLEGE MARKS RECEIVED BY STUDENTS CLASSIFIED ACCORDING TO THE NUMBER OF YEARS OF CREDIT RECEIVED IN HIGH SCHOOL VOCATIONAL SUBJECTS

Units of vocational subjects	0	.5	1	1.5	2	2.5	3	3.5
Upper quartile	2.7	2.8	2.6	2.9	2.8	2.7	2.9	2.7
Median	3.1	3.4	3.3	3.3	3.2	3.3	3.2	3.1
Lower quartile	3.5	3.9	3.7	3.8	3.7	3.9	3.4	3.5

	4	4.5 to 5.5
Upper quartile	2.8	2.8
Median	3.3	2.8
Lower quartile	3.6	3.8

HIGH-SCHOOL CREDIT REQUIREMENTS AS A MEANS OF BARRING POOR STUDENTS

When an analysis is made of the records of those students who should have been barred because of having had less than a certain set minimum of units in specified subjects, very interesting light is thrown on the relative value, for purposes of selecting good college risks, of entrance requirements in terms of specified units of credit in certain favored fields on the other. If, for example, those individuals who presented less than two units of foreign language had been barred, fifty individuals would have been affected. The median average college mark of these people was 3.5, as compared to an average of 3.4 for the entire class.[2] But ten (20 per cent.) of them failed to obtain an average better than 4.0. Twenty-six (52 per cent.) averaged as well as 3.5 and ten (20 per cent.) higher than 3.0, three (6 per cent.) higher than 2.0 and one ranked among the ten best students of the entire class.

Only nine individuals presented less than two units of credit in mathematics. The median of the average college marks of this group was 3.1, distinctly better than that of the entire group, which was 3.4 Not one of them averaged as low as 4.0, only one as low as 3.5. Three of the nine averaged better than 2.75, ranking in the upper quarter of their class.

There were twelve individuals who did not present one or more units of science for entrance. But one of these received an average as low as 4.0 and but three as low as 3.5. Four of the twelve averaged better than 3.0, two better than 2.25 and one as high as 1.7, ranking among the ten best students in the group of 387 individuals.

If the 26 students presenting more than four units in vocational subjects had been barred, 16 individuals would have been rejected who received five-term averages better than 3.4, the average for the entire class. Eleven of the 16 averaged better than 3.0, one ranking among the ten best students in the group of 387 people. Only one of the 26 averaged as low as 4.0, while 51 or one in seven of the other 361 students with less than four units of credit of vocational subjects averaged as low as 4.0.

Though no fine accuracy may be safely assumed from so few cases, in general, it is clear that those students entering with less than the conventional entrance prescriptions in terms of high-school credit in certain favored fields contributed to each of the various levels of scholarship in about the same proportion as those who met the requirements. To be sure most of these people were admitted on condition that their entrance deficiencies be made up. This does not seem to constitute a likely explanation, especially in view of the comparable percentage of these people ranking as honor students, nine of the seventy-one, or 13 per cent., averaging 2.5 or better, as compared to 16 per cent. of the entire group of 385 students. One seems forced to conclude that, at best, pattern of high-school units as a means of selecting good college risks is but another way of measuring intelligence and industry, and a distinctly inferior one at that.

In distinct contrast to the operation of average high-school marks and intelligence test scores, the requirement for entrance of specified high-school credit bars as many superior as inferior individuals and admits as many inferior ones as superior ones.

DATA FROM CONCLUSIONS BASED ON OTHER STUDIES

It is all the more convincing that the conclusions of each of the other studies which throw light on the question of relation of pattern of high-school credits to academic success in college are in fairly close agreement with those of this study. As early as 1923, Gebhardt[3] reported a study in which the relation of the weighted credits earned at Colorado State Teachers College to the number of units of credits earned in cer-

[2] In the six-step marking system employed at the University of Oregon, 1.0 is the highest mark and 6.0 (failure) is the lowest.

[3] G. L. Gebhardt, *The Relative Value of College Entrance Subjects,* A.M. thesis, Colorado State Teachers College, 1923.

tain high-school subject fields was the subject of study. He found no significant evidence in this investigation to show that one subject or group of subjects is of greater value than any other as an aid to successful college work.

Proctor and Bolenbaugh[4] compared the academic records of two groups of students entering Stanford University in 1921 and 1922. The students of one group had each received credit in high school for two or less units of vocational subjects, and those of the other group had earned 3 or more units of credit in one or more vocational fields. The data reported by these authors indicate that there is no significant relation between amount of credit in vocational subjects in high-school and subsequent college success. While those of fewer vocational credits earned a slightly higher median in honor points, the difference is almost negligible, being not as great as would be expected in view of the difference in median score on the Thorndike intelligence examination.

Brammell[5] reports conclusions similar to those of Bolenbaugh and Proctor. The average freshman mark of 163 students entering the University of Washington in 1925 with five or more year-credits in non-academic subjects was 2.08, as compared to 2.22 of 353 students who entered at the same time with not more than one year-credit in non-academic subjects, the difference being but .14 of the difference between a B (B = 3) and a C (C = 2). Corresponding average marks for the class entering in 1928 were 2.19 and 2.23—a difference of but .04 of a grade step. Similar figures for the four-year scholastic average of the two groups of the entering class of 1925 were found to be identical to the second decimal place—2.38.

A more recent investigation conducted by Stinnette at the Colorado State Teachers College supports Gebhardt's earlier study.[6] Entrance to the college is contingent upon completing 15 units of credit in high school and recommendation of the candidate by the principal of the school from which he is graduated as being in the upper three quarters of the candidate's graduating class. No set distribution of credits is required. Among those entering the college in 1926 were 183 students whose high-school credits did not include all the set pattern required for entrance to the University of Colorado or the University of Denver and 128 students who for the same reason could not meet the entrance requirements of Colorado College. These two groups of students were slightly inferior in Thurstone (American Council on Education) psychological test scores, in the classification test (based on elementary and secondary school subject-matter and in the English test given to all entering students).

Clark,[7] at the University of Southern California, compared the university marks of two groups of freshmen entering that institution in 1923, one group entering with 12 or more "standard" preparatory school units and the other with less. The former group passed in 93 per cent. of their work and the latter in 90 per cent. The Bi-serial r between groups with first semester marks was but .09.

Sorenson[8] studied the relationship of

[4] L. Bolenbaugh and W. M. Proctor, *Relation of Subjects Taken in High School to Success in College, Journal of Educational Research,* xv: 87–92, February, 1927.

[5] Paris R. Brammell, *A Study of Entrance Requirements in the University of Washington,* Ph.D. dissertation, University of Washington, 1930. Pp. 319.

[6] Ray L. Stinnette, *An Evaluation of the Present College Entrance Requirements at Colorado State Teachers College,* A.M. thesis, Colorado State Teachers College, August, 1930.

[7] W. W. Clark, *Status of University Students in Relation to High-School Course, Journal of Educational Research,* xiii, 36–42, January, 1926.

[8] Herbert Sorenson, *High School Subjects as Conditioners of Collegiate Success, Journal of Educational Research,* xix: 237–54, April, 1929.

units of high-school credit in various fields to the college marks of students earned at Northwestern University. He concluded that only in the case of Latin was there any significant difference which could not be attributed to selection in intelligence. He then studied the relationship between units of Latin taken in high school and college achievements of the groups of students falling into the four different quarters of intelligence as measured by the Scott Mental Alertness Test. These tabulated data seem to show rather conclusively that the percentage of students making superior college marks increases slightly with the number of years' credit in high-school Latin.

One of the most extensive studies of this problem is that of Yates,[9] involving students at the Universities of Kentucky, Indiana and Cincinnati. While a higher percentage of those following the classical curriculum ranked above average in college achievement, the difference was not as great as should be expected of that group in view of their superior high-school record and the greater ability that may be therefore implied. From that standpoint the "scientific" group shows outstanding achievement as compared to the other three groups.

Students of equal ability, as judged by mental test scores, were paired, one of each pair having followed in high school one pattern of curriculum and the other having followed another. From 11 to 86 pairs of students were included in the various units of the study. The academic success of students following vocational patterns was compared with that of those having pursued studies of a non-vocational pattern in two of the units, vocational versus Latin in another, science versus non-science in two instances, classical versus non-classical in two, social studies versus non-social studies in two, mathematics versus non-mathematics in two, and English—3 units versus English—4 units in two.

His data indicate clearly that students having taken Latin or classical curricula are likely to make slightly higher marks than those who have taken vocational or non-classical curricula, but that the differences between averages (2 per cent. to 10 per cent. superiority) are so small that when compared to the extent of overlapping, but slight correlation exists, certainly not sufficient to constitute a fair or effective basis for differentiating good college students from poor ones.

Not only do the results of the study based on the Oregon students indicate that entrance requirements based upon minima of high-school credits in specified subject-matter fields are practically useless in differentiating between good and poor college risks, but there is general agreement with the conclusions of all other scientific investigations with bearing upon the question. It would seem that no more striking example of the application of fallacious untested theories to educational administration may be mentioned than in the prevailing method of selecting students for higher education.

One can not but be impressed with the certainty that thousands of able and a considerable number of outstanding minds have been barred from attending college or university by the administration of worse than useless means of selecting college entrants, set up in arm-chair committee meetings, and in all probability the creatures of the prejudices of those who saw no need of quantitive investigation of the dicta of the "best minds." The interests of colleges and universities and of the conservation of human intelligence, genius and scholarly traits would seem to demand an early abandonment of the practice of requiring for general entrance to college specified minima of credits in traditionally

[9] J. A. Yates, *The Type of High School Curriculum Which Gives the Best Preparation for College.* Bulletin of the Bureau of School Service, University of Kentucky, Vol. 11, No. 1, September, 1929.

favored and vested secondary school subjects, and that careful and scholarly investigation be made to determine what high-school studies contribute sufficiently to success in the various schools and colleges to warrant their prescription as prerequisites to entrance to those divisions.

Compared on the basis of predictive usefulness to psychological test scores, high-school marks and principals' ratings on college promise, the pattern of high-school credits is obviously and definitely inferior. The author of this study feels certain that, a few decades hence, our present practice of selecting college entrants on the basis of minimum credits in certain fields of high-school credits will seem a curious and inexplicable anomaly.

EDUCATIONAL EVENTS

A NEW SCHOOL IN FLORENCE FOR DIPLOMATS

SPECIAL courses for students who wish to train for the diplomatic service of Italy were recently inaugurated at the Reale Istituto Superiore "Cesare Alfieri," Florence, with the sanction of the Fascist government. These are intended as a further means of developing the diplomatic and consular service and making it a career organization similar to the army and navy. These courses, the only ones of their kind in Italy, will be under the auspices of the Italian Foreign Office. Students of them will be able also to take courses in jurisprudence, and political and commercial sciences at the University of Florence.

A circular issued by the Reale Istituto Superiore "Cesare Alfieri" concerning this "School of Advanced International Studies" states that its purpose is to prepare graduate students in the advanced study of international problems so that they may enter the diplomatic and consular service. The degree granted is the "Diploma di perfezionamento in studi politici internazionali."

The course covers one year and follows the programs fixed by the Ministry of Foreign Affairs for the examinations of admission to the foreign service. The subjects of study are: (1) Problems of public international law in peace and war (year); (2) problems of private international law, of administrative, industrial, labor, and penal law (half-year); (3) theory and practice of commercial treaties (year); (4) international economic problems, with special reference to monetary and banking problems (year); (5) diplomatic and consular history (year); (6) The League of Nations (half-year).

Admission to the school is open to persons who have graduated in the political and social sciences. It will be granted also to graduates of other faculties, as well as to foreign graduates, whose preparation is considered adequate by the School Council.

To be admitted to the examinations for the "Diploma di perfezionamento in studi politici internazionali," the student will be required to pass a first examination in at least five of the subjects of the course as listed above, and to prove in written and oral examinations his knowledge of either the English or the German language.

INSTITUTE ON NEAR EASTERN AFFAIRS AT BROWN UNIVERSITY

BROWN UNIVERSITY will hold its Institute on Near Eastern Affairs on March 11 and 12. Participants in the program will include Henry Morgenthau, former American Ambassador to Turkey; Louis Van Norman, of the U. S. Department of Commerce; Dr. James L. Barton, chairman of the Near East Relief; Professor George Grafton Wilson, of Harvard University; Felix M. Warburg, the New York banker, and Dr. Willis J. Abbot, editor.

According to the official statement issued, in selecting the Near East as the topic for special study, Brown University felt that American attention, all too often, is directed to a quarter of the world only after a crisis has occurred there. The Near East, always a potential trouble spot, as the recent election riots in Syria show, is now, however, undergoing in peaceful fashion a thorough reconstruction, politically, economically and socially. The time seems opportune for a study of this important section of the world.

The institute, which has been made possible by a gift from Chester D. Pugsley, of Peekskill, N. Y., will open in Sayles Hall on the Brown campus on Friday evening, March 11, with an address by Mr. Morgenthau. Next morning the scene will shift to Alumnae Hall, the student center of Pembroke College, whose Dean, Margaret Shove Morriss, is a trustee of Constantinople Women's College. The members of the institute, approximately seventy in number, all specialists in the financial, economic, diplomatic and educational affairs of the Near East, will hear addresses by Mr. Van Norman, Dr. Barton, Wallace Murray, chief of the Division of Near Eastern Affairs of the Department of State, and Dr. David Mitraney, visiting professor at Harvard University.

Mr. Van Norman will deal with "American Economic and Financial Interests in the Near East"; Dr. Barton will discuss educational and philanthropic interests; Mr. Murray's subject will be "Modernization Movements in Turkey and Persia," and Dr. Mitraney, whose knowledge of Near Eastern affairs has given him a wide reputation in England, will speak on "Diplomatic Rivalries in the Near East." Professor Wilson, graduate of Brown and a member of the Brown Board of Trustees, will preside.

In the afternoon there will be a round table in the lounge room of the Little Theater and various other rooms of Faunce House, the student center at the university. The major topics of discussion will be three: educational and philanthropic; economic and financial; political and diplomatic.

At the dinner on Saturday evening, Dr. Stephen P. Duggan, director of the Institute of International Education, will preside, and the speakers will be Mr. Warburg, Dr. Willis J. Abbot, who is a director of the American Schools, Sofia, and the Minister from Albania.

In connection with the institute, the Brown authorities are planning special exhibitions at the John Carter Brown Library, famed for its collection of Americana; the John Hay Library, which will show the Wheaton Collection of International Law and Lincolniana; the Annmary Brown Memorial; the Faunce House art gallery, and the Rhode Island School of Design, which is associated with Brown.

TEACHER TENURE IN RURAL AREAS

THE rapid change in teacher personnel in rural areas of the United States constitutes a serious educational problem, Dr. G. C. Gamble, research consultant for the National Survey of the Education of Teachers, stated orally at the Federal Office of Education to the representative of the *U. S. Daily*.

According to statistics compiled by the investigating committee, of every five elementary teachers employed in sparsely settled areas, it is necessary to select two new ones annually. Cities of over 100,000 population afford a sharp contrast. In 1930–1931, there was only one new elementary teacher for every 20 employed. This situation shows a high degree of stabilization. The following additional information on the fluctuation of teachers was supplied:

The survey has tabulated returns from data for the year 1930–1931 involving 244,647 elementary teachers, 36,251 junior high school teachers, and 84,882 senior high school teachers. The purpose of the inquiry was to ascertain what are the reasons creating a demand for new teachers. The term "new" is applied to any teacher who holds a position in her present school system for the first time.

The demand for new elementary school teachers is specifically associated with the social factor "size of population." In areas sparsely settled, the school administrator in 1930–31 found it necessary to select two new elementary school teachers for every five teachers employed in one and two teacher schools in the open country, and three new teachers for every 11 elementary school teachers employed in villages of less than 2,500, or in three or more teacher schools in the open country.

In cities of 2,500 to 10,000 population, only one out of every six elementary school teachers was holding her present position for the first year. In cities of 10,000 to 100,000 population, only one out of every 10 was new. In cities of over 100,000 population, there was only one new elementary teacher for every 20 employed, showing a high degree of stabilization.

The greater cause of the rapid turnover of teachers in the elementary, junior high schools arises from the fact that the predecessor of the new teacher goes elsewhere in the state to teach.

For example, 42.2 per cent. of the new elementary teachers listed this as the reason for their selection, 28 per cent. of the new junior high-school teachers and 33.3 per cent. of the senior high-school teachers.

Marriage constituted the next single demand of importance. The demand for new elementary teachers in 16.4 per cent. of the cases was because a vacancy occurred through marriage, for new junior high-school teachers in 13.6 per cent. of the cases, and for new senior high-school teachers in 12.7 per cent. of the cases.

The creation of new positions gave 8.8 per cent. of the elementary teachers their jobs, 20.8 per cent. of the junior high-school teachers, and 16.2 per cent. of the senior high-school teachers. Death of a predecessor was the least important cause demanding a new teacher. But 0.7 per cent. of the new elementary teachers acquired their jobs for this reason, 1 per cent. of the new junior high-school teachers, and 0.8 per cent. of the senior high-school teachers.

But 6.5 per cent. of the new elementary jobs were due to a change of profession by the former occupant, 7.2 per cent. of the new junior high-school teachers, and 9.8 per cent. of the new senior high-school teachers.

THE MOTION PICTURE DIVISION OF THE NEW YORK STATE EDUCATION DEPARTMENT

THE Motion Picture Division of the State Education Department reviewed 1,698 miles of motion picture film during the fiscal year ending on June 30, 1931, according to the report of Dr. James Wingate, submitted to the Commissioner of Education, Dr. Frank P. Graves.

The Motion Picture Division is charged with the review and licensing of motion pictures, except news releases, previous to exhibition in New York State. It is also charged with the duty of inspecting theaters or any place where motion picture films are exhibited, stored, kept or used, for the purpose of ascertaining whether such films have been licensed, the license leader is displayed on the screen in accordance with the statute and the eliminations have been made pursuant to directions of the division.

A total of 2,149 different subjects made up the 1,698 miles of film reviewed and licensed by the division. Eliminations were made in 366 of these subjects. The total number of eliminations made was 3,031, as compared with 2,116 of the previous year. Fourteen pictures were rejected in their entirety, of which three were revised and later approved with eliminations. The 3,031 eliminations are classed as follows: scenes eliminated, 1,687; titles eliminated, 1,344. The grounds on which eliminations were made are classed as follows: indecent, 468; inhuman, 243; tending to incite to crime, 1,129; immoral or tending to corrupt morals, 1,165; sacrilegious, 26.

The great majority of films submitted during the year were talking pictures, 1,913 of 2,149 films reviewed being of this type. The division not only reviews the pictures but reads all dialogues before issuing a license.

The statistical report submitted by Dr. Wingate shows that total receipts for the year were $237,867 and expenditures were $88,804. The net revenue to the state for the fiscal year amounted to $149,072.

The total receipts since the organization of the Motion Picture Commission in 1921 to June 30, 1931, amounted to $1,991,724. The amount expended during this period, including salaries, was $796,538. The net profit to the state over and above all expenditures since the creation of the commission is, therefore, more than one million dollars.

RESOURCES OF THE AMERICAN LIBRARY ASSOCIATION

THE American Library Association has in the general endowment fund $1,050,000. One million of this was given by the Carnegie Corporation in 1926 and the $50,000 represents the endowment which increases slightly from year to year from life memberships.

The second million dollars of endowment, which the association hopes to receive upon presentation of a satisfactory program may not be in hand in its entirety until late in 1933. The promise of this second million dollars, contingent upon the association's accomplishing certain definite tasks, carried with it no specific time of fulfillment. It should be remembered that this second million, when received, will provide an income which will offset, in part at least, the decrease in the annual grants which were made by the Carnegie Corporation.

When the Carnegie Corporation in 1926 voted a million dollars to the endowment of the association, it voted also to decrease, and eventually discontinue, its annual grants. They at that time were about $1,555,000. This sum was reduced to $15,000 in 1931, and ceased altogether, with the exception of certain special grants, on October 1 of last year. This represents a decrease of $15,000 in income for 1932.

The association is faced consequently with a period of one year, possibly part of two years, during which its income for general purposes will be less than in 1931. It can not continue a campaign for special memberships in order to qualify for a million dollars. That has been done. But, if it does not retain its present—or an equivalent—special membership enrolment, some of the present work must abruptly cease.

The amount received for special memberships in 1931 was $5,000 less than the estimated receipts. There were two main reasons for this: (1) the endowment fund was completed at New Haven before the year was half over and the efforts of the association members relaxed accordingly; (2) the nation-wide drive for unemployment relief made it necessary practically to suspend special membership solicitation during the autumn months. However, to avoid losing ground in 1932, the effort to keep the special membership enrolment intact will now be renewed.

ACADEMIC SALARIES

EIGHTEEN state universities and colleges cut salaries last year from 2 per cent. to 23 per cent., according to information made public at the Office of Education. A small number, however, increased the remuneration of the staff.

The decrease in salaries of professors and instructors was necessary probably because of financial retrenchment resulting from adverse economic conditions and a falling off in revenues.

In its current statistics on state universities and colleges, the Office of Education finds a wide variation in salaries from the presidents down. The University of Wisconsin, for example, pays its president the highest salary of any state-supported institution. The annual income of this president is $20,400, with an additional $2,400 set aside for rent and miscellaneous expenditures connected with maintaining his home. In contrast, Arkansas State College pays its president $4,000 annually with an additional $620 for maintaining the home.

The University of Illinois ranks second in presidential salary with $20,000 straight income and an additional $2,500 house expenses. Michigan ranks next with $18,000. The Ohio State University rewards its president with $15,000 and an additional $5,000 for house expenses. Purdue, Iowa State, California, Pennsylvania State, Virginia and West Virginia pay $15,000 apart from additional grants for house maintenance. Thirty other state-supported institutions pay annual incomes ranging from $10,000 to $15,000.

On the other hand, salaries of deans range from $3,000 to $12,000. They would average probably $5,000. Michigan College pays its dean $12,000, while the University of Michigan ranges from $8,500 to $12,000 with $10,500 as the most common salary for the dean. The most common salary for the dean in Arkansas State College is $1,800. Deans at Cornell University, on the other hand, receive between $7,000 and $10,000.

The most common salary paid full professors varies from $1,800 in Arkansas State College to $5,500 in the State College of Washington. The University of Virginia has the highest common salary of any state-supported institution of higher learning, the income being $6,000. Full professors receive incomes at Virginia ranging from $4,000 to $10,000. In the same state, those at William and Mary range from $3,000 to $4,200. The salary range in the University of Illinois, for full professors, ranks with Virginia, but the most common salary is $5,000. The range in the University of California is from $4,000 to $8,000, and Wisconsin from $3,900 to $8,000.

Associate professors receive less, but the variation from institution to institution is equally noticeable. The most common income for the associate professor ranges from $2,250 in Alabama College to $4,000 in the University of Illinois and Rutgers University. Instructors receive probably an average of $2,250. They vary from $1,900 to $3,300.

STUDIES OF INDUSTRY BY GRADUATE SCHOOLS OF BUSINESS

SPECIAL industry studies by graduate schools of business will be fostered by the Social Science Research Council. Four projects, each intended to continue for several years, with annual budgets ranging from $25,000 to $75,000, have already received the council's approval.

The automobile industry will be studied at the University of Michigan, the bituminous coal industry at the University of Pennsylvania, distribution in the book industry at Columbia University, and the motion picture industry at Harvard University.

The work will be under the general direction of a new committee on industry and trade appointed by the council with Dr. Benjamin M. Squires, of the Trade Board of Men's Clothing Industry, Chicago, as chairman. The council's committee on business research, of which Professor Edwin F. Gay, of Harvard University, is chairman, has, it is announced, been adopted into the organization of the new committee in the hope of further promoting comprehensive studies of selected industries.

Other members of the committee on industry and trade are: Henry S. Dennison, Dennison Manufacturing Company, Framingham, Massachusetts; Professor Clare E. Griffin, University of Michigan; Professor Alvin H. Hansen, University of Minnesota; Dr. Leverett S. Lyon, Institute of Economics, Brookings Institution; Professor Frederick C. Mills, Columbia University; Mr. George Soule, *The New Republic;* Professor Leo Wolman, Columbia University; Dr. Meredith B. Givens, Social Science Research Council, secretary.

"For the better integration of its activities," the announcement says, "the council has set up a committee on industry and trade to carry out the purposes of the council in this whole broad field. As at present constituted the committee includes representatives of economic theory, statistics, labor, marketing, business administration, industrial management and journalism. Representatives from other fields will be added.

"The plan of organization has been developed around this central committee, assisted by the council staff and supplemented by specialized working committees and conferences on specific problems. The central committee is an initiating, planning and reviewing body responsible for the general direction and balance of the research program.

Under the general supervision of the committee on industry and trade a series of special or technical committees will carry out much of the detail of the program in this field. The technical committees thus far set up, and their chairmen, are as follows:

Unemployment, Colonel Arthur Woods, New York City; public utilities, Professor James C. Bonbright, Columbia; savings and capital formation, Professor James Harvey Rogers, Yale.

An exploratory committee on economic statistics has already been named. The well planned collection of raw data, it is asserted, remains the greatest single need of social research in spite of the rapid development of economic statistics in recent years.

EDUCATIONAL NOTES AND NEWS

DR. WALTER SCOTT ATHEARN, formerly dean of Boston University School of Religious Education and Social Service, will be inaugurated president of Butler University, Indianapolis, at a two-day academic celebration on February 6 and 7. Dr. Athearn will succeed Dr. Robert Judson Aley, who last year became president emeritus.

THE inaugural ceremonies in honor of Dr. John Scholte Nollen as the fifth president of Grinnell College will be held on February 11, beginning with the inauguration proper in the morning, followed by a formal luncheon, a conference on education, tea at the president's house, a faculty dinner, and an address in the evening.

MR. W. F. CONN, of Miltonvale, Kansas, has been elected president of Marion College, Indiana. He will succeed Mr. Henry A. West, who died recently. Professor A. Jones, dean of the college, has been named acting president until Mr. Conn assumes office.

DR. HOWARD D. NEWTON, professor of chemistry, has been appointed dean of the Division of Arts and Sciences of Connecticut Agricultural College. He succeeds the late Professor George H. Lamson, Jr. Dr. Newton was graduated from Massachusetts Agricultural College and received his doctor's degree from Yale University. He has been on the faculty of the college since 1909.

DR. FRANCIS LANDEY PATTON, president of Princeton University from 1888 to 1902 and president of Princeton Theological Seminary from 1902 to 1913, celebrated his eighty-ninth birthday at his home in Bermuda on January 22.

DR. CHARLES HALL GRANDGENT, professor of Romance languages at Harvard University since 1896, will retire at the end of the academic year to become professor emeritus. From 1915–16 Dr. Grandgent was Harvard exchange professor in Paris; in 1925 he was president of the Harvard Alumni Association.

DEAN EVERETT V. MEEKS, of the Yale School of the Fine Arts, has been made a Chevalier of the Legion of Honor by the French Government. Dean Meeks has been professor of architecture at Yale University since 1919, and dean since 1922.

DR. IRVING MAURER, of Beloit, Wisconsin, was elected president of the Association of American Colleges at the recent Cincinnati meeting. He succeeded Dr. Ernest H. Wilkins, president of Oberlin College. Dr. Frank L. McVey, president of the University of Kentucky, was chosen to be vice-president.

THE officers of the Liberal Arts College Movement, elected at a recent meeting at Cincinnati, are: *President,* Dr. Harry M. Gage, president of Coe College, Cedar Rapids, Iowa; *Vice-president,* Dr. Albert C. Fox, dean of John Carroll University, Cleveland; *Treasurer,* Dr. John E. Bradford, general secretary of the Board of Education of the United Presbyterian Church of North America; *Secretary,* Dr. George L. Omwake, president of Ursinus College, Collegeville, Pennsylvania.

MR. EARL V. MOORE, director of the School of Music of the University of Michigan, was elected president of the National Association of Schools of Music, which he helped to organize in 1924.

DR. EDWARD S. SOPER, president of Ohio Wesleyan University, was elected president of the Educational Association of the Methodist Episcopal Church at the recent convention of the Council of Church Boards of Education.

MR. GLENN G. STEELE, superintendent of schools of the first supervisory district of Oneida County, was elected president of the New York State Association of District Superintendents at the annual meeting held at Syracuse.

THE REVEREND JAMES H. DOLAN, formerly president of Boston College, has become assistant to Jesuit Provincial Father Kilroy and will supervise studies in New England Jesuit schools and colleges.

MR. JOHN W. SWEET has been elected superintendent of schools of the fourth supervisory district of St. Lawrence County, New York. He succeeds Mr. Virgil C. Warriner, who has been acting as district superintendent pending the election of a successor by the board of directors.

PRINCIPAL E. E. EVANS has been made superintendent of the Winfield, Kansas, schools, succeeding the late W. W. McConnell.

PROFESSOR REXFORD B. HERSEY, of the industrial research department of the Wharton School of the University of Pennsylvania, is the recipient of a fellowship for foreign study from the Carl Schurz Memorial Foundation.

PROFESSOR JAMES F. HOSIC, of Teachers College, Columbia University, was the guest of honor at a luncheon on January 21 of Massachusetts school supervisors and administrators. Dr. Hosic gave an address on "Supervision for Schools."

THE holder of the Russell Lectureship for 1932 of the University of Michigan, awarded in recognition of outstanding achievement during the year, is Professor Jesse Siddall Reeves, of the department of political science. In addition, he is William W. Cook Professor of American Institutions for the present year.

PROFESSOR LEONARD J. RUSSELL, of the University of Birmingham, England, will be acting professor of philosophy during the summer session at Stanford University.

Dr. Livingston Farrand, president of Cornell University, returned on January 25 after a brief tour of Spain and Italy.

Dr. Frederick P. Keppel, president of the Carnegie Corporation, and Mrs. Keppel have left for the British West Indies, where Dr. Keppel will make a study of economic conditions in reference to the work of the Carnegie Corporation.

Dr. Robert J. Trevorrow, president of Centenary Collegiate Institute, has been granted a leave of absence and will sail for Europe on March 4, returning early in April. He will be accompanied by Mrs. Trevorrow. They have been invited by the Governments of Czecho-Slovakia and Roumania to deliver a series of lectures on American education.

Professor M. P. McNair, of the Harvard Graduate School of Business Administration, has returned from London where he cooperated in setting up a department of business administration at the London School of Economics and Political Science.

At the University of Michigan, sabbatical leaves of absence for the second semester have been granted to Professor Arthur B. Moehlman and Professor Orlando W. Stephenson, of the school of education, and to Professor Robert C. Angell, of the department of sociology. Leave of absence, without salary, for the second semester, has been given to Professor Henry C. Hutchins in order that he may finish the editing of the biography of Professor William P. Trent and also the editing of Professor Trent's bibliography of Daniel Defoe.

Professor and Mrs. Walter M. Horton, of Oberlin College, leave New York on February 9 on a trip around the world. They plan to be gone eight months. Dr. Horton plans to gather first-hand information on the philosophical and religious conditions in India, China and Japan. He will give a series of lectures at several educational centers, including the Shansi Schools, Yenching University, Cheeloo University and Doshisha University. Invitations have also been received to speak in several Indian cities.

Mr. Frank Ernest Hill, author and editor, will visit Knox College this year on the William Honnold Lectureship. His subject will be "What is American: a search for a national character in our life and literature." The lectureship was established by William L. Honnold and under its terms a well-known man or woman is brought to the college each year for a series of lectures.

The death is announced of A. A. Stearns, president of the Cleveland Public Library Board, formerly professor of law at Western Reserve University, at the age of seventy-three years.

The Reverend Dr. James Gore King McClure, president emeritus of the Presbyterian Theological Seminary at Chicago, formerly the McCormick Theological Seminary, died on January 18 at the age of eighty-three years.

The Reverend Dr. Lewis B. Paton, professor of Old Testament exegesis at the Hartford Theological Seminary, died on January 24 at the age of sixty-seven years.

Dr. George Kerschensteiner, professor at the University of Munich, died on January 15. Dr. Kerschensteiner was at one time superintendent of the Munich school system, in which he instituted various reforms. At the time of his visit to the United States he made an extensive lecture tour, speaking on industrial education and allied topics.

An Ohio sequel of the White House Conference on Child Health and Protection was held, January 21 and 22, at Columbus at the call of Governor George White. Honorary chairmen who presided at the sessions were Dr. John H. J. Upham, Columbus, representing the section on child health; John Eisenhauer, superintendent, Cleveland Boys' Farm, the section on child welfare; Charles S. Berry, Ph.D., director of the bureau of special education and professor of psychology at the Ohio State University, Columbus, the section on child education.

An Institute of Adult Education will be held in Spokane, Washington, on April 6, 7 and 8, under the auspices of the Inland Empire Education Association, an organization which draws its membership from Idaho, Montana, Oregon and Washington. The institute will be conducted in round tables, discussion groups from the various agencies of formal and informal adult education whose leaders, national and local, will be in attendance. The adult education movement in its several aspects, its agencies, methods, purposes, instruments and trends will present the problems the institute will consider. The Committee of the Inland Empire Education Association in charge of calling the institute are Principal James A. Burke, of Spokane, Washington; Superintendent L. C. Robinson, of Sandpoint, Idaho, and the chairman, Dean Rhoda M. White, Spokane, Washington.

The Carnegie Corporation, upon recommendation of its Advisory Group on College Libraries, has made a grant to the Knox College Library of $10,000 for the purchase of books, the money to be paid in three annual instalments. This grant is given as part of a project on which the advisory group has been engaged during the past three years, the ultimate purpose of which is the standardization of college libraries.

To aid in training Negroes for business careers, the Carnegie Corporation of New York has made a $100,000 grant to Atlanta University, Atlanta, Ga., for a professorship in its graduate department of business administration.

An Associated Press dispatch reports that southern college professors plan to make an investigation with particular reference to their economic status as compared to that of their colleagues in universities and colleges in northern and western sections, under the direction of Dr. Benjamin B. Kendrick, professor of history in North Carolina College and chairman of the southern regional committee of the Social Science Research Council. The study will be made under direction of Dr. Wilson Gee, professor of rural sociology at the University of Virginia. This information will be sought: Comparison of annual salaries; comparison of teaching loads; comparison of cost of living in university communities; comparative attitudes of college and university presidents toward research by professors in their institutions; use made by professors of their leisure time, and the extent to which more able southern professors are drawn out of the region by offers of better salaries and conditions of work.

The Michigan Alumnus writes: "Led by the literary college faculty, members of the teaching staff were up in arms for a while just before the holidays as the result of the distribution of administrative information sheets which requested detailed data on where and how the faculty spends its time. Immediately upon hearing of the questionnaires, the faculty instructed its representatives to the university council to bring the matter up and definitely oppose its approval at the next meeting of the council. Since that time, however, the council has met and approved the new measure. Scores of indignant protests have been pacified with the explanation that answers to the questions asked are not compulsory but are merely being gathered for statistical purposes. However, the council suggests that members of the faculties cooperate in providing the information desired regarding hours spent in class, in consultation, in research, in lectures, etc.

At their recent annual meeting in Boston, the trustees of Massachusetts State College at Amherst voted to omit the summer school session at the college this year as an economy measure. With a 20 per cent. increase in student enrolment this year and the prospect of a decrease in state appropriations, the trustees felt that some curtailment in the program of the institution was necessary. The omission of the summer school was the major economy measure adopted at this meeting. The summer school has long been an established institution at the State College, having been started in 1907. In acting to omit the session in 1932, the trustees expressed the hope that this would be the only year in which this omission would be necessary and that the school would be re-established in 1933.

An Associated Press dispatch reports that shrinking college finances, with the accompanying difficulty of maintaining standards, present the biggest problem for consideration at a meeting of the Council of Church Boards of Education in convention at Cincinnati. It was announced that a nation-wide survey, just completed, showed that 233 institutions established a net saving of $1,483,331, over 1929, but that, despite the economies, budget deficits at the end of the year just closed aggregated $1,998,097. Attendance showed a slight increase. The survey, made under auspices of the Liberal Arts College movement, which represents a majority of the denominational and privately supported schools, showed Eastern colleges with the greatest tendency toward expansion of budget and the least tendency toward contracting budgets in the last two years. Southern colleges showed the least expansion and the greatest curtailment of budgets, while Mid-Western colleges showed the largest expectation of deficits. Ohio colleges were classed in the Eastern group. The council is made up of twenty religious denominations, representing approximately six hundred colleges, universities, schools and seminaries.

MANY school teachers in Tennessee have received no pay or only a part of their salaries since last July. The State Funding Board has now arranged to sell $2,000,000 of a $5,000,000 bond issue authorized recently by the legislature. Comptroller Roy Wallace is reported to have said that the $2,000,000 with $700,000 now on hand, will be used immediately to pay some $2,600,000 of school obligations.

MORE than two hundred classes in adult education are being organized in Los Angeles and surrounding cities this month by the Extension Division of the University of California, according to announcement by Director Leon J. Richardson. The subjects include accounting, advertising, economics, interior decoration, pottery, lettering, social problems, municipal administration, personnel management, land economics, banking and foreign trade, visual education, radio telephony, the English novel, dramatic interpretation, writing courses, poetry, correct English, French, German, Spanish, backgrounds for foreign travel, current history of modern Europe, history of California, commercial law, mathematics, philosophy, development of the speaking voice, botany and others.

A STUDY of the education of Mexican and Spanish-speaking children, financed by the University of Texas Fund for Research in the Social Sciences and directed by Dr. H. T. Manuel, professor of educational psychology, is now in its fourth year. The first extensive report, primarily a survey entitled "The Education of Mexican and Spanish-Speaking Children in Texas," was published by the university in 1930. Some of the current projects, in various stages of completion, are as follows: a study of the population of Texas from the standpoint of national origin and home language, an experiment with English and Spanish editions of the Stanford-Binet test, a study of physical measurements of Mexican children, preparation of standards and a score-card for the educational treatment of Mexican children, construction of a scale for measuring attitudes toward the Mexican child, and a study of the achievement of Mexican children in reading and arithmetic.

DISCUSSION

ENROLMENT IN JUNIOR COLLEGES

IN Dean Raymond Walters' admirable compilation and analysis of "Statistics of Registration in American Universities and Colleges, 1931," occurs the following brief comment on the junior college situation:[1]

> The junior colleges doubtless reduce somewhat the attendance at liberal arts colleges. However, other studies have shown that, from 1929 to 1930, the rate of increased attendance in junior colleges was lower than that of the present approved list of higher institutions from 1929 to 1930.

This statement seems hardly in accordance with the facts regarding the growth of this relatively new and vigorous movement in the field of American collegiate education.

No reference is given as to the source of the "other studies" mentioned. The most reliable and extensive statistics on a comparable basis, however, are those which have been collected annually over a five-year period by Dr. D. S. Campbell, secretary of the American Association of Junior Colleges. They show the following increases since 1928:[2]

[1] SCHOOL AND SOCIETY, 34: 784, December 12, 1931.

[2] The directories for 1928 and 1929 were issued in mimeographed form by the association; that for 1930 was printed by the association; those for 1931 and 1932 were printed in the issues of the *Junior College Journal* for January, 1931, and January, 1932.

Year	Number	Enrolment	Increase	Per cent. increase
1928	408	50,529	....	....
1929	405	54,438	3,909	7.7
1930	429	67,627	13,189	24.2
1931	436	74,088	6,461	9.6
1932	469	97,631	23,543	31.8
Average annual percentage increase				18.3

The data for 1932 should be modified somewhat, since the enrolment there reported includes 9,895 special students in the California junior colleges, a classification only partially reported in the 1931 directory. If the "specials" are omitted in both 1931 and 1932 the percentage of increase is 23.2 instead of 31.8 and the modified average is 16.2 per cent.

The only other junior college statistics collected regularly on a nation-wide basis are those of the U. S. Office of Education. These are admittedly incomplete, and are collected only at two-year intervals. They have the merit, however, in spite of their incompleteness, of extending back to 1918. A summary of growth in number and enrolment of junior colleges as indicated in the latest published *Bulletin* of the Federal Office is as follows:[3]

Year	Number	Enrolment	Increase	Per cent. increase
1918	46	4,504	....	....
1920	52	8,102	3,598	79.9
1922	80	12,124	4,022	49.6
1924	132	20,559	8,435	69.6
1926	153	27,122	6,563	31.9
1928	248	44,855	17,733	65.5
Average annual percentage increase				26.6

The percentages of increase (or decrease) over the preceding year for the more than four hundred American universities and colleges which Dean Walters uses as a basis for his summaries are given in the following table.

Year	Full-time students	Total students[5]
1929	+ 1.5	+ 2.0
1930	+ 3.5	+ 1.0
1931	+ 0.6	− 1.5

Whether the figures from the junior college directory or those from the Federal Office are taken, they indicate in either case that the rate of increase for any year for which data are available, or the average of such rates, is strikingly greater for the junior colleges than for the four-year colleges and universities for any of the past three years. Even in years of severe depression the junior college continues to increase rapidly until now it enrolls almost one hundred thousand students in all parts of the country. Possibly the economy of collegiate education in the local junior college is a factor. Perhaps some of the large universities are beginning to experience the relief from inordinately large freshmen and sophomore enrolments which many of their administrators have been seeking. If university enrolments have not decreased, at any rate the junior college has certainly been a potent factor in preventing their continued increase at the rate which prevailed for a few years following the war. As a matter of fact Dean Walters' figures indicate a slight decrease from 1930 to 1931 in the enrolments of the large universities—those having 3,000 students or more.

WALTER CROSBY EELLS
SCHOOL OF EDUCATION,
STANFORD UNIVERSITY

THE HIGH COST OF INEFFICIENCY

FIVE years ago, as a school superintendent, the writer of this article criticized the college rather severely for not turning out better-prepared high-school teachers. Now, as a head of a department of education in a liberal arts college, he has come to realize that the professors are just as anxious to turn out well-prepared teachers as the public-school man is to get them. But he has come to the conclusion that effective training, which includes a period of practice teaching, is difficult without the united effort of both the college and the public school system.

Any activity that deals with the control of human beings is complicated. The mastery of such involved processes must be gained by prac-

[3] "Statistics of Universities, Colleges and Professional Schools: 1927–28," *U. S. Office of Education Bulletin No. 38*, 1929. Washington, D. C., p. 1.

[4] SCHOOL AND SOCIETY, 32: 787, December 13, 1930; and 34: 783, December 12, 1931.

[5] Includes special students and summer students.

tical experience in addition to theoretical training. Teaching is one of these complicated activities. One who has completed a theoretical course in pedagogy without some practical experience, is no better fitted to cope with the problems involved than is a physician who has not served a period of internship. The physician cannot get into his profession without a period of practical experience, but the teacher can. Hence, pupils are subjected to the errors and blunders of the inexperienced teacher, and the public, in the end, pays dearly for the product of such teaching. Every teacher should have a period of practical experience under competent guidance before entering upon the regular duties of the profession.

The beginning high-school teacher is particularly lacking in this special kind of training. For several years the state teacher's colleges and normal training schools have been able to supply a major portion of the grade instructors who have had a period of practice teaching. On the other hand, most of the high-school teachers have come from the liberal arts colleges where facilities for practice teaching have been very inadequate. The liberal arts colleges will continue to produce secondary school teachers because no other institution is so well prepared to give the necessary broad and extensive background. What is needed is an efficient and economical plan of student teaching. There are at least three fundamental principles involved in any workable plan.

First, the student teaching should be done under conditions that are as nearly like actual situations as possible. Classes of unselected pupils in a public-school system are the most ideal. Here the student teacher comes in contact with all of the problems that he will encounter later. The good and the bad are there and must remain, which might not be the case in the private training school. Because of identical situations the public school offers the best opportunities for student teaching. In most cases it is also the only alternative because few colleges could afford to build and maintain a separate training school.

Secondly, this work should be done under expert supervision. The critic teacher, as she is sometimes called, must be a competent and well-trained expert in order to protect the children from the blunders of the beginning teacher. She must be able to teach a class of pupils effectively through a group of inexperienced teachers. Pupils suffer no hardships from practice teaching if it is done under proper supervision. In one of the best school systems in the middle west the pupils in the student teaching rooms rank equal to other pupils on all standardized tests. The critic supervisor will not only protect the children but will also make the novice see and correct her own errors in much less time than if left to work out her own problems. Expert supervision insures the welfare of the children and makes for rapid development on the part of the student teacher.

The third principle to be considered in any plan of practice teaching is the cost to the agencies which are in a position to give such training. There are only two possible agencies, the public school or the college, but conditions are such that it makes it impractical for the former. Few districts which employ beginning teachers take in enough new ones each semester to warrant the services of a critic supervisor. Even if they took in ten or twelve new ones each semester, they would still be so widely distributed over the system as to make systematic supervision impractical. Real systematic supervision of this kind requires that the critic read and O. K. all lesson plans at least two days before the lesson is taught. She must do demonstration teaching herself, observe much of the teaching of the student, and hold many group and individual conferences. The student teachers need to be centralized to make the administration of the program possible. If the plan were workable, the public school could best afford to pay the salary of the critic because the public already pays more dearly for inefficiency. The other agency and the one that is in the best position to give such training is the college, but it is less financially able to do it. Here the students who desire to enter the profession are still grouped. But the problem is to get children for the students to teach and to raise money to pay the salary of the supervisor. Ordinarily, the tuition from the students in the college classes will pay the major portion of a professor's salary but not so with practice teaching. The income in tuition from twenty students for three hours' college credit each will not exceed three hundred dollars per year while the salary of an expert supervisor is not less than two thousand. Most colleges can not afford to pay out seventy-five dollars more per student than the income from the three hours' tuition, hence cheaper methods have been devised. The most common of these is to assign the students to teachers that need assistance in a public-school system. While care is exercised to place them with good teachers, practically none of these are trained supervisors. Instead of getting a definite course of training, the student is apt to fall into routine work. Cases are not uncommon where most of the time is spent in some form of clerical work. This is a cheaper method for the college but it always shows up in cost to the public school.

What means of systematic practice teaching can be devised that will take the above principles into account, namely, having the student teaching done under conditions that are like actual situations, having work done under expert supervision, and providing for a plan that can be financially afforded by the agencies involved? The public school in conjunction with the college can work out a program with a minimum of cost to each. Regular classes in a public school system in the proximity of the college should be used and an expert supervisor should be placed in charge. The critic will replace the regular classroom teacher. If the work is done efficiently and the pupils make normal progress there would be a minimum cost to all concerned because the public schools should pay that amount toward the salary of the supervisor that would be paid normally to the replaced teacher. In fact, there would be no cost to the public school and the college could afford to pay the difference between the regular salary and that of the expert. Obviously the public would realize a saving in the end in more efficient teaching and the college would realize an immediate saving in dollars and cents. This would make it unnecessary for the college to resort to some less efficient plan of practice teaching.

The administration of this program should have no serious difficulties. An efficient supervisor is imperative. She must feel responsible to the public school for the general welfare of the pupils under her charge. She must feel responsible to the principal for carrying out the course of study and other activities of the school. She must feel responsible to the college for the proper development of the student teachers. Candidates for practice teaching should be selected on a basis of hours in education, scholastic standing, character and general fitness for the profession. With a careful understanding on the part of both agencies, with an efficient supervisor, and with a well selected group of student teachers, there need be no serious administrative problems.

The problem of training efficient secondary school teachers should be faced squarely by all agencies concerned. The public school is anxious to secure well-prepared high school teachers and the colleges are anxious to produce them. This can be done by a proper allocation of cost between the college and the public school.

V. E. STANSBURY

MORNINGSIDE COLLEGE,
SIOUX CITY, IOWA

TRAINING RURAL TEACHERS

IN the October 17, 1931, issue of SCHOOL AND SOCIETY, Mr. Walter W. Ludeman has presented quite clearly the problem that the inexperienced teacher faces in attempting to obtain a position. His point that the rural school furnishes diversified training is well taken from the standpoint of the teacher. However, the question arises, "Should the rural pupils be expected to serve as training material to prepare teachers for service in city schools?" This question has been asked many times before. Its theoretical answer does not coincide with practical experience. In spite of the fact that many city schools are recognizing their responsibility of training a few inexperienced teachers each year, the fact remains that, to an increasing extent, inexperienced teachers are forced to go to rural schools to obtain the much-coveted experience so necessary for admission to service in the city schools. Are the teacher-training institutions recognizing this tendency, and preparing the embryo teachers for the positions that they most likely will fill while obtaining their initial experience? In other words, should we abandon our practice of specialization, training these students in primary work, in the intermediate methods and for the junior high school, and give them instead a more comprehensive, if less thorough training, involving work in all these fields?

Supervisors and administrators in the Bemidji State Teachers College report several instances in visiting rural schools, where they found a teacher doing splendid work teaching primary children, but succeeding poorly with the upper grades, while in other situations the reverse was the case. Obviously the preparatory training of these teachers lay at the seat of the difficulty. As a result of these observations, this year this institution is attempting to give a broad training, both in the methods classes and in the practice teaching. Instead of giving the beginning teacher special training in either primary, intermediate or junior high school methods, an attempt is being made to give some training in all these fields. Students enroll for a class in "Technique of Teaching" taught by various supervisors in the training school. Thus a student may be taught for a few weeks each by a primary, an intermediate and a junior high school supervisor. Likewise each two-year student is expected to take a course in rural methods.

In obtaining their practice teaching experience, students enrolled in the rural course must spend a part of their time teaching in one of the affiliated rural schools. Other two-year students are not permitted to do all their practice teaching in one field, but teach six weeks in the lower grades, and six weeks in the junior high school, for example. Thus they are given a broad training in theory and in practice teaching. Young men who make a splendid success teaching in the junior high school often find themselves somewhat ill at ease in the primary grades. They are accepting the challenge, however, realizing that their first positions will probably be in rural schools, and that later promotions will depend to some extent upon their success in the rural situations.

From the standpoint of the teacher in training, and from the view-point of the rural pupils who are "practiced upon," it seems that this is a logical method of approach.

C. V. HOBSON

STATE TEACHERS COLLEGE,
BEMIDJI, MINNESOTA

SPECIAL CORRESPONDENCE

PUPIL PROCTORS IN STUDY HALLS

IT has become a common practice among school principals to encourage pupil participation in administrative affairs of a minor nature. This is considered a part of the program in the teaching of citizenship. As a result of this tendency, we have all kinds of student organizations whose functions range all the way from policing the school yard to supervising corridor behavior and even examinations. From the principal's point of view, the success of such student activities depends too frequently on their outward appearance in the attainment of the administrative objective. Frankly, the duties assigned to pupils in such cases are a relief to teachers and principals. Seldom, however, have school administrators paused to ask themselves whether their assignments are not by the same token a burden on the pupils.

There are well defined rules against the "exploitation" of public school children in the performance of such tasks as the making of school furniture or the preparation of cafeteria foods, as part of the manual training curriculum. This kind of "school work" should not, of course, be confused with the practical assignments occasionally given to pupils in the commercial course, nor with those projects undertaken by the pupils in several departments cooperatively in the promotion of a general school activity such as a play or the publication of a school magazine. Entirely in a different class, however, belongs the practice of assigning pupils to supervisory duties under the guise of teaching them self-government when, as a matter of fact, they are really relieving teachers and vice-principals from irksome responsibilities.

The high school which is under the writer's administration is run on a six period basis and has four large study halls. In order that instructors may have a "breathing" spell, two are assigned to each study hall during their free period, with instructions that they may either alternate, one being in charge one week and one the next, or that they may relieve each other during the same period. The supervision of these four study halls consumes the free periods of 48 teachers during each term.

It occurred to the writer to inaugurate pupil supervision of the study halls in order that these teachers might have their free periods to themselves to spend either in the library, in pupil conference, or in complete relaxation. Therefore, in January, 1931, the teachers who were given study hall assignments were informed that after they had organized their study halls they were to appoint pupil proctors to take their places. Two pupils were to be appointed for each period and they were to serve through the entire term. It was suggested that the best behaving and the most respect-commanding pupils should be selected. Teachers were advised to leave the study halls a few minutes after the opening of each period, but they were to return once or twice during the hour to make sure that perfect order reigned.

The writer kept in close contact with the teachers and made occasional visits to the study halls in order to assure himself that the system was working satisfactorily. And indeed it did. There were times when on entering the study hall unobserved by the pupils he found them so quiet and preoccupied with their lessons that he thought surely the teachers must be seated somewhere among them. But no, this splendid order reigned solely under the influence of the two young pupil proctors seated at the teacher's desks.

But the system worked altogether too well. It was satisfactory to the teachers, who were relieved, because it gave them a completely free period. It was satisfactory from the administrator's point of view, because from outward appearances it showed what a splendidly organized school he had, and how well disciplined and cooperative the pupils were. But during all the months that this system was in operation the question kept coming up in his mind: How did it affect the pupils who were placed in charge of the study halls? If the teachers who were relieved were happy because the burden had been removed from their shoulders, was it not likely that this burden was just a wee bit too heavy for the tender shoulders of the boys and girls upon whom it fell?

At the end of the term, therefore, the pupil proctors were called together and asked to answer very frankly and honestly certain questions pertaining to their responsibilities, without signing their names to the papers. Thirty-seven proctors reported at the conference without knowing why they were called together.[1]

The first question put to them was whether they ever had to report pupils for disturbing the study hall. Only 4 out of 37 replied in the affirmative. This was rather surprising, for it proved that either the pupil proctors were able to maintain better discipline than some of the teachers, or that considerable disturbance went on without being reported. For who wanted to be a squealer? The teachers have a weapon with which to maintain discipline. If pupils misbehave, teachers can give them demerits which affect their permanent school records and might lead to suspension. The pupil proctors, however, were not given this power for obvious reasons.

In response to the question whether they ever had to speak to pupils for disturbing the study hall, 19 replied in the affirmative and 18 in the negative. This is not so bad for it is quite likely that teachers themselves might have been obliged to speak to disturbers more frequently than that. Curiously enough, of the 19 proctors who had to issue warnings to disturbers, 13 were boys and 6 were girls. Apparently, the male of the species, at least during high school age, is less timid than the female about telling one "what's what."

In reply to the sub-question as to whether they felt that they secured satisfactory results when they spoke to those who were disturbing the study hall, only 8 answered affirmatively, while 11 admitted that they did not. Here, then, arises the question: Are we justified in placing pupils in situations where their authority is challenged and their purpose defeated while, at the same time, they are compelled by the code of youth to keep quiet about the matter? For we must not forget that while 11 issued warnings to pupils who created disturbances without securing satisfactory results, only 4 actually reported the matter to teachers.

In response to the query as to whether the study hall was just as quiet under their supervision as under the teachers', only 13 declared that it was, while 23 frankly admitted that it was not. Obviously, the replies to this question are in direct contradiction to the conclusion that one might be inclined to draw from the fact

[1] The freshman study hall was not assigned to pupil proctors.

that only 4 out of 37 ever had to report pupils for creating disturbances, as well as from the reports of the teachers and the observation of the principal himself.

It might be argued that the 23 pupils who thought the study halls were not as quiet under their supervision as under that of the teachers were laboring under misapprehension due to the nervous strain incident to their unusual responsibilities. If such is the case, then the question arises whether it is proper pedagogy, even under the pretext of teaching self-government, to place upon pupils duties that are fully as enervating as the study of mathematics or languages, to which so many proponents of citizenship teaching raise strong objection.

Another question asked was whether they could do as much homework while proctoring as when they used their free periods for study purposes exclusively. Only 13 answered in the affirmative while 23 gave negative replies. Here, then, it seems is the strongest objection to the system of assigning to pupils functions properly belonging to teachers. Pupils are sent to school primarily to study and to be instructed in matters which require the guidance and advice of professionally trained people. If they are assigned duties which interfere with their ability to devote themselves fully and freely to their studies, then, no matter what the pretext may be, such assignments are wrong and should not be made without the voluntary consent of both pupils and parents. Obviously, the outward appearance of success in gaining an administrative objective is not enough in school management.

That not all pupils who are appointed to supervisory duties are happy, though they may perform them without complaining, is indicated by the fact that to the question whether they liked to proctor, 10 out of the 37 frankly answered that they did not while 4 were silent on the matter. Eight admitted that they had been "razzed" by other pupils for proctoring, though none of them ever reported their "razzing," be it said to their credit.

Most of the proctors did not want the teachers to pop in and out of the study halls to see how matters were going. As one declared, "teachers should either stay in the study hall all of the time or else not come back at all." Again, most of the proctors felt that they could discharge their duties better if they had more power, such as giving their fellow pupils demerits.

It appears, therefore, that the attempt to teach self-government through the assignment of administrative responsibilities to pupils involves one of two dangers: Either they develop the habit of mental indifference to social ills because of the futility they experience in possessing "office" without power—and we see plenty of that in public life; or, by being clothed with powers for the proper exercise of which they are insufficiently mature they develop an exaggerated ego which in later life is just as likely to lead them to the obstruction of the social good as to its enhancement—and we see plenty of that also.

What, then, is suggested? A return to first principles.

GUSTAVE A. FEINGOLD
PRINCIPAL OF THE BULKELEY
HIGH SCHOOL,
HARTFORD, CONNECTICUT

QUOTATIONS

BRITISH EDUCATION IN 1931

THE Report of the Board of Education issued in May deals with the year 1930, but it shows the lines upon which the undoubted progress of 1931 has been based, and especially on the great school building activities of the local education authorities, which have had their first-fruits in the year now ending, and in the steady progress of the worst "black list" schools, a policy which the economy legislation of last autumn has not stopped. Indeed in August the Board of Education issued revised suggestions for school building. Last month there were only 295 schools of the worst type left, and the new President of the Board of Education, Sir D. Maclean, hopes that the board will approve grants to help in the work. A large number of new secondary schools (such as the new Dover County School for Boys, opened last month by Prince George) have been opened, and the necessary growth of school buildings, though checked on grounds of economy, will go forward, since actual contracts are to be carried out. The report last month of the Committee of

Officers of the Board of Education on educational facilities in the South Wales coal field lays special stress on the need for secondary education and declared that "the time has come when technical education must be carried on with the utmost efficiency, and this can not be unless it is soundly based on a good general education." The growth of technical education for persons leaving the secondary schools and adults is very encouraging, and many local authorities are developing this side of their work.

The political history of the year is less satisfactory. The Labor Government, as far back as December 17, 1929, introduced a bill for raising the compulsory age to 15 and to provide maintenance allowances under conditions. This bill was to come into force on April 1, 1931. The bill was withdrawn on May 12, 1930, and a new bill was introduced on May 22 to the same effect, but which also gave power to the local authorities to contribute to the cost of enlarging and improving voluntary schools. The bill was given a second reading by 280 votes to 223, but it was withdrawn on June 25, the prime minister stating that a third bill would be introduced. This third bill was published on October 31, 1930. It omitted the Concordat between the denominations (to the disappointment of many Anglican and Roman Catholic members of the House of Commons), and settled allowances for parents on an income-tax basis. An amendment was accepted in the House of Commons deferring the raising of the school age till September, 1932, and another amendment was carried by which the raising of the school age would be deferred until a further act was passed authorizing expenditure on voluntary schools. This clumsy bill was rejected by the House of Lords on February 18, 1931, but Lord Hailsham gave a pledge that the Conservative Party would support a bill embodying the clause relating to voluntary schools. The raising of the school age was not to be abandoned, and, in fact, it has the support of most educationists in the country, while the principle of the Concordat is getting to work. The whole country is tired of inter-denominational disputes about education.

But a storm, long brewing, broke before any further action could be taken. The state of the national finances was becoming more and more threatening. The report of the Committee on National Expenditure, appointed by the Labor Government, was issued at the beginning of August, and recommended a reduction of £13,000,000 on the education estimates and the reduction of teachers' salaries by 20 per cent. A minority report suggested 12½ instead of 20 per cent. In the last week in August the Labor Government resigned, and the National Government was formed. Mr. Snowden's famous budget followed, and Circular 1413 in consequence dealt with the questions of teachers' salaries and the general educational financial position. The deduction was to be 15 per cent. from the aggregate total of the teachers' salaries, while the statutory 50 per cent. minimum limit imposed in 1921 was to be repealed by statute and the grant in respect of expenditure was to be reduced from 60 to 50 per cent. The National Government decided, in the cases of the defense services, the teachers, and the police, to make the aggregate reduction of salaries in each case 10 instead of 15 per cent., and by Order in Council under the National Economy Act, 1931 (which came into force at the end of September), power was given to vary agreements with teachers made before October 1, 1931, so as to carry into effect any reductions in salary, while the lessening of the statutory 50 per cent. minimum paid to local education authorities was legalized. Despite very extensive and expensive propaganda undertaken by the National Union of Teachers, the profession accepted with a good grace the necessary reductions. It was seen that if Mr. Snowden's budget had not been balanced worse things were in store, both for the teachers and the country generally.

Shortly after the settlement of the salary question it was found that it had solved automatically another problem. In the earlier part of the year difficulties as to the scale system, which was due for a new settlement on April 1, 1932, were feared between the local authorities and teachers' panels, but when, on November 20, the Burnham committees on the salaries of teachers in elementary, secondary, and technical schools actually met it was decided to let the 1925 scales stand for another year. The resolution to continue the awards of 1925 was subject to the maximum reduction of 10 per cent.

provided by the local agreements as varied by the provisions of the Order in Council under the National Economy Act, 1931, but the resolution also provided that the continuance of the 1925 scales is subject to the grant regulations of the Board of Education not being further altered to the financial disadvantage of local education authorities. The general position in education has now settled down, and progress, though somewhat slower progress than in 1931, in national education will be looked for in 1932.—*The London Times Educational Supplement.*

BOOKS AND LITERATURE

Education and the Philosophy of Experimentalism. By JOHN L. CHILDS, Ph.D., with a foreword by William Heard Kilpatrick. The Century Company, XIX, 264 pp., 1931.

THIS volume is mainly a clear setting forth of the educational philosophy of Dr. John Dewey. The author's "sympathies are frankly with the experimentalists" (p. 179). The experimentalists are said to be Peirce, James and Dewey, but Dewey is quoted sixty-five times, James five times and Peirce only once. Apart from James and Peirce there is only one quotation from a non-living philosopher, John Stuart Mill, to whose memory James dedicated his work on "Pragmatism." The volume is really concerned only with Dr. Dewey's form of experimentalism. In all there are some thirty-five pages of quotations from as many current sources.

The total argument hinges about the following seven main points: Experimentalism is "indigenous" to the American scene; it has a metaphysic of its own; it is regardful of the humane as well as the biological phases of human nature; it emphasizes experience and hypotheses; it has its own view of freedom as the intelligent guidance of response; it defends democratically the capacity of the rank and file of men to think for themselves; and it maintains a just balance between the interests of the individual and society. Under these cardinal views the various subordinate arguments are grouped. The arrangement is good, the style readable and the treatment light and suggestive, and far from exhaustive. Students using the book as a text would need to read widely in the Dewey writings to realize their mammoth, if not majestic, proportions.

Let us take a look at each of these seven points. The characterization of the pragmatic philosophy as "indigenous" is dubious in view of the facts that James expressly assigns it to the English and that Dewey asserts Peirce derived the idea from Kant, and that Dewey himself began as a Neo-Kantian. James also wrote: "There is absolutely nothing new in the pragmatic method. Socrates was an adept at it. Aristotle used it methodically. Locke, Berkeley and Hume made momentous contributions to truth by its means ("Pragmatism," p. 50). Dewey has also rejected expressly the criticism that pragmatism is the voice of American industrial efficiency. In what sense then is experimentalism "indigenous" to America. It was first a European importation and is now a naturalized, husky and growing American philosophy. What the author probably means is that experimentalism is a conscious and appealing formulation of a philosophy implicit in the procedures of American frontier life.

Has experimentalism a metaphysic? The author undoubtedly correctly defends the view that it has, that as a method it implies a system. What is this system? The universe of experimentalism has "the lid off," is unclosed, in the making, indeterminate, adventurous, implicating man in its perils; it is possessed of uncertainty, novelties, creativeness, inventiveness, possibilities, irregularities, whose order is uninsured; in it no absolute security is attainable in science, esthetics, logic or ethics, but a process of real change goes on in real time; and in it mind emerges within social experience, and values are our felt interests made intelligent. Existence is a mixture of the precarious and the stable. "Hence life itself is inherently experimental," as Childs says (p. 55). Here is metaphysics enough indeed.

The author correctly implies, without distinctly asserting, that the views of Dr. Dewey to-day on this question are either different from, or inconsistent with, earlier views of his. Once he held pragmatism was only a method and wrote his "Reconstruction in Philosophy" (1919) to lead to the abandonment of classical philosophy. Ten years later appear "Experience and Nature" and "The Quest for Certainty," as solid metaphysical treatises. They defend "naturalism," certainly one of the "classical philosophies."

In dealing with the nature of man the author adopts the naturalistic point of view and does not suggest that the intelligence of man relates him to a rational world-order, such as Morris Cohen and Marie Swabey have recently shown, nor does he take the trouble to refute this view. Intimate familiarity with the history of philosophy or with the systems displaced by experimentalism is not indicated, despite the fact that Dr. Dewey advocates using the past in thinking about the present. He does so himself.

There is no recognition of the *progressus in infinitum* of experimentalism. If all ideas are hypotheses, then knowledge is never reached, we never arrive. And also it must be only an hypothesis that no idea is more than an hypothesis. We can not even be certain that we are uncertain. Relativity needs some permanence to which to be relative. Neither Dr. Dewey nor his followers utilize his own recognition of the element of stability as well as precariousness in the universe.

The new approach to the old problem of freedom and determinism does not show clearly how the new solution, though called freedom, really differs from the old determinism. Both Socrates and Plato would insist on intelligent and reflective behavior and the "capacity to learn," but they did not call it freedom. They were intellectual determinists. Aristotle gave us the conception of freedom, not as directed activity, but as self-directed activity.

In dealing with "the rank and file," Finney, with his regimented mentality, is rejected, and Woodworth, with his purpose, is deftly substituted for Thorndike's "S–R Bond" psychology without any direct criticism of Thorndike's position as his. The work gives internal evidence of being a Ph.D. thesis (an excellent one, be it said) with its cautious reserve in attack.

There are a few gingerly criticisms on experimentalism, not as a philosophy but as an educational theory. These are as follows: the experimentalist has "possibly" some responsibility for the failure in "progressive" education to recognize adequately the basic importance of personal attitudes and the need for far-reaching social purposes (p. 124). Again, the principle of education as its own end "seems to be a somewhat ambiguous doctrine" (p. 129). Again, as Dewey himself says, "in some progressive schools the fear of adult imposition has become a veritable phobia" (p. 144). That is all, and it is meager, in view of what critics like Bagley and Mrs. Ward (see *Harper's*, February, 1931) have said of the movement.

On the other hand, experimentalism is defended against three classes of critics, the metaphysicians who hold some things are changeless, the behavioristic psychologists, and the ethical regimentarians. The defense against the metaphysicians of the changeless is purely social and so misses the point in part. The other two defenses are much needed and are well made.

In the final chapter the author defends Dr. Dewey's views against the interpretations of Lewis Mumford, Margaret Naumburg, Henry Hazlitt and Santayana. The important views of Waldo Frank are not introduced. The views of the first three named critics are correctly shown to be based on misunderstandings of Dr. Dewey (who is not easy to understand). The point of Santayana is missed in the reply. To restate the position attacked or to show that it has worked well in the schoolroom is not an adequate defense.

The philosophy or experimentalism has here been expounded ably, criticized slightly, and sympathetically defended. It has not been translated into educational procedures. Perhaps that is too much to expect of a non-pragmatic philosophy but a pragmatic philosophy might naturally be expected to point out in more detail the differences it makes.

The volume has an index of subjects and of sources. The bibliography is somewhat inconveniently gathered at the end of each chapter. The printing is good and the typographical errors are few. With a critical instructor and a supplementary bibliography, the volume is very usable as an introductory text in the philosophy of education. As Dr. Kilpatrick says in the foreword: "Hard is that reader to please or instruct who from these honestly argued pages does not find himself upbuilt in fruitful outlook."

HERMAN H. HORNE
NEW YORK UNIVERSITY,
SCHOOL OF EDUCATION

EDUCATIONAL RESEARCH AND STATISTICS

A CONTINUATION STUDY OF OVERLAPPING OF COURSES IN DEPARTMENTS OF EDUCATION

IN SCHOOL AND SOCIETY,[1] the writer presented a limited discussion on the evergreen subject of overlapping among courses in departments of education. Therein, she reported the initial findings from a simple experiment made for the purpose of investigating the extent of duplication in the content of her course in educational measurements as given in the State Teachers College, Milwaukee. The present article reports the cumulative results from a continuation of the study which was carried through the two years, 1928–1930 inclusive.

The set-up of the experiment continued the same as that observed in the initial stage of the investigation. It was, briefly, as follows: A list of seventy-five true-false statements was submitted at the beginning of each semester of the two years to students enrolled in the writer's classes in educational measurements. This same list was a part of the final examination given these students at the close of the course. The fall semester, 1928–1929, which was the first semester of this experiment, educational measurements was a three-hour course. At the opening of the following semester, it had been changed, by administrative action, to a two-hour course and so continued throughout the duration of this study.

In the initial stage of the experiment, as reported in the previous article, the distribution of scores made by the beginners was compared with the distribution of scores made at the close of the course by a control group made up of educational measurements students from the previous semester who were selected on the basis of equal mental ability, student for student, as that trait is measured by the Thorndike Intelligence Examination for High School Graduates.

[1] Vol. xxix, pp. 776–778.

This procedure, that is, use of a control group, made possible an early and valuable, but certainly quite tentative, analysis of results. Although such procedure is perfectly sound, it is, obviously, less desirable, the results therefrom are regarded less conclusive than the findings from a comparison of the distributions of scores made by the same students who wrote the test "before and after taking" the course. However, these distributions show virtually the same characteristics as did those reported for the first semester of the investigation. The tabulated results are as follows:

	N	Range	Md.	Sigma	Percentage below other Md.
Before	217	0–40	22	9.0	100
After	217	9–68	41	8.5	2

Again it may be said that the comparison of the data shows such a minimum of overlapping as is almost incredible. The simple fact, reported in the last column above, that all scores at the beginning were below the median of the scores made at the close of the course and, vice versa, that only 2 per cent. at the close fell below the median of the first distribution, is quite significant evidence that this course did much that had not been accomplished previously in the education of these students, either, (or both), it gave them new subject-matter, or training in clear thinking. Certainly any instructor should aspire, and every administrator should expect, even demand, that a course justify its right to continued existence on one or both of these grounds.

Inspection of the class records of these 217 students shows that 77 per cent. of the failures in the course made a score on the test at the beginning of the course, below the median of that distribution. This fact has significant bearing on a question aside from the main purpose of the study, namely, the prognostic value of a pre-course test to determine the knowledge a student brings to the study of this subject. The results of this unpretentious investigation raise the question whether there is not something, fundamental to success in the study of measurements, that is lacking in the college junior or senior who has failed to pick up a modicum of general information in a subject that permeates all professional study and literature.

The results herein reported which tally so closely with the results first reported are regarded as trustworthy evidence that we, who teach professional subjects, need not continue under the odium that the overlapping of our courses is so gross as to justify the attacks commonly made upon their credit value. It is our responsibility to learn the degree of truth or falsity in the accusation and, having learned, to act according to that knowledge.

There is no gainsaying the fact that there is a reprehensible amount of duplication in professional courses in departments of education. The condition is recognized throughout the teacher training world from classroom teachers to administrators of full or more limited authority. The fact is not only recognized but it is acknowledged where intellectual honesty prevails over the too universal tendency to ignore sinister facts which disturb the *status quo* or which, above all, may reflect adversely upon professional training as now organized and administered.

The condition is not confined to the smaller and weaker schools, but likewise permeates our best known teacher training institutions. It is often concealed under dignified but deceptive titles of courses so worded as to obscure, to the unsophisticated, the pitiful dearth of new material possible to present therein. Reorganization, combination or outright elimination of courses is, perhaps, the outstanding need in the curricula of these professional departments. This is not to imply that this need is confined to departments of education, but it is to say emphatically that, with possible, rare exceptions, departments of education have a full job of housecleaning right at home. Wherever this corroding condition prevails, it entails an irreparable loss of cultural, educational opportunities for the students and inestimable waste throughout the institution in both administrative and instructional affairs.

Overload for instructors, excessively large classes, scarcity of classroom space, inflation of course credits, financial stringencies—who will presume to contend that these and other conditions that impair the effectiveness of professional courses for teachers in training would not be materially improved did the administrative heads of these colleges have the courage and the wisdom to rally their faculties in support of a real housecleaning job—not a rough and tumble affair and not one to be concluded with the speed and transitory effects of a week-end excursion, but a comprehensive, professional undertaking, seasoned with common sense and committed to the acceptance of facts, empirical evidence, to be collected with a degree of scientific procedure commensurate with the importance of the undertaking and analyzed with impartiality, with an eye single to the development of efficiency throughout the institution. This, unquestionably, represents a high standard as compared with the prevailing methods and motives for determining curricula, but it is becoming the goal of those professional schools that are destined to head the list of teacher training institutions which will be recognized, throughout the academic world, as colleges in fact as well as in name, worthy of public confidence and support.

LILIAN HUNSICKER
MILWAUKEE, WISCONSIN

NEW BOOKS IN EDUCATION

BAZAN, EMILIA P. *Los Mejores Cuentos.* Edited by Willis K. Jones. Pp. 208. Doubleday, Doran. $1.25.

FAUBEL, ARTHUR L. *Principles of Economics.* Revised edition. Pp. 522. 125 illusrations. Harcourt, Brace. $1.60.

KIRKPATRICK, J. E. *Academic Organization and Control.* Pp. xxiii + 246. Antioch Press. $3.00.

POULTON, ETHEL M. *The Teaching of Biology.* Pp. ix + 244. 96 figures. Methuen, London. 6/6.

SMITH, WILLIAM A. *Secondary Education in the United States.* Pp. xvi + 429. Macmillan. $2.50.

SMITHBERGER, ANDREW and CAMILLE MCCOLE. *On Poetry.* Pp. 160. Doubleday, Doran. $1.00.

WEISINGER, NINA L. and MARJORIE C. JOHNSON. *A First Reader in Spanish.* Pp. 143. Doubleday, Doran. $.80.

SCHOOL AND SOCIETY

EDITED BY J. McKEEN CATTELL

WITH WHICH IS COMBINED THE

EDUCATIONAL REVIEW

EDITED BY WILLIAM McANDREW

Volume 35 | Saturday, February 6, 1932 | Number 893

THE LIBERAL ARTS COLLEGE

By President FRANKLIN W. JOHNSON

COLBY COLLEGE

The liberal arts college is under fire. Resting on the aristocratic traditions of New England, with a curriculum at first drawn mainly from Old World sources and based upon an educational theory now commonly discarded, this ancient institution finds its one-time independence challenged and its respectable complacency rudely shaken. It is now asked to give reasons for its continued existence.

The tremendous increase in the number of students attending institutions above the secondary level in recent years was at first naïvely hailed as evidence of the increasing recognition of the worth of these institutions. Maturer thought, however, assigns this increase rather to an unprecedented growth in wealth, to the social prestige associated with a college education, and to the diminished opportunity for profitable employment brought about by the technological and managerial improvements in industry and commerce. Hundreds of thousands of youth thus have found themselves with nothing to do but to continue their education, and the social ambitions of young people and their parents have found in the college a satisfying solution of what otherwise would have been a baffling problem. But the insistent question remains whether the liberal arts college is the type of institution in which they may spend four years most profitably to themselves and to society.

The increased number of students has perplexed both the smaller colleges and the larger universities. The rise and rapid development of the junior college has furnished some relief to the latter and perhaps some added anxiety to the former. The present situation may be described as one of flux, not of chaos. The proponents of the junior college look upon this new type of organization not merely as supplementing the opportunities already existing for education above the secondary school, but as soon to supplant the four-year college itself. The burden of proof rests upon the junior college as to whether this is likely or desirable. As yet, the junior college certainly has not taken over the functions of the liberal arts college. A few years ago some of our outstanding educators urged a shortening of the time devoted to secondary and collegiate education. This is now plainly contrary to social tendencies easily discernible. Within the four-year college itself there is the growing conviction that for many students some other form of education is more desirable. Many of these colleges lack the facilities and financial resources necessary to provide collegiate training of sufficiently high order to justify their continuance unless their present inadequacies are removed. The combination of several hundred small colleges in the so-called "Liberal Arts College Movement" indicates the concern which they feel over their present situation and is aimed almost solely at arousing public interest and financial support for the large number of institutions which find themselves slipping in their competition with others more favorably circumstanced.

The times demand that the liberal arts college take account of its educational stock and determine its policies. This may necessitate the writing off completely of some shop-worn material that has occupied the shelves and the substitution of other goods that have a real demand. In spite of much popular clamor to the contrary, I am inclined to think that good-will, not merely of alumni but of society at large, is one of the most valuable assets of the liberal arts college. We shall do well, however, not to assign to this item a fictitious value nor to count too confidently upon its indefinite continuance.

What do we mean by a liberal education? This is difficult to define in exact terms. Etymologically, it would seem to mean the education of a free man, *liber,* in distinction from a slave. Among some peoples it came to mean the education of the gentleman, who lived without the necessity of manual labor. Both these distinctions have gradually lost their force. Attempts to define a liberal education as one that frees the mind lead to high-sounding statements, more confusing than definitive. Equally difficult is the distinction between liberal and vocational studies. The study of the drama may be vocational for the playwright, but liberal for the lawyer or the doctor. Perhaps we can do no better and can safely go no further than to say that liberal education is concerned chiefly with the meaning of facts and skills, and that professional or vocational education is concerned with the uses to which these may be put. Since free man and slave, gentleman and worker, are gradually disappearing as terms that distinguish individuals or groups; since leisure is no longer the coveted possession of a few, but is increasingly forced upon us all, the present demands a wider extension of the opportunities for learning the meanings of life rather than the limiting of education, in respect to those who are to receive it or to its contents, to the means of earning a living. The methods of organization and instruction of the college may and should be improved. The curriculum is undergoing vigorous change. But if the liberal arts college is to preserve its original purpose and justify its continuance, it must furnish a broad foundation on which to build a full and effective life under the prevailing conditions of the times.

I am aware that this statement of purpose is too general and furnishes no guarantee of results. Secondary education has gained immeasurably in recent years by a revision and clearer statement of its aims. The promise of greater effectiveness in higher education lies in the same direction. In the main, above the elementary school, the difference in the aims of different levels and types of schools is one of emphasis. The aims of the secondary school and the college are for the most part identical, except that the former emphasizes the vocational subjects for a considerable number of its pupils. The liberal arts college, however, can not ignore this in its guidance program and in its offering of pre-professional courses. The professional school shows a distinct tendency, in its requirements for admission and in its own curriculum, toward the inclusion of more of the so-called cultural courses.

The liberal arts college not only provides foundation for professional work, but increasingly emphasizes the aims of preparation for a worthy use of leisure and for an enlightened social cooperation. Perhaps the general aim of culture has always had in mind the ennobling use of leisure time, but to-day the scope of this objective has gone far beyond its original limited application to artistic appreciation and enjoyment. It now includes all the desirable activities of the home and civic life in which one engages apart from his occupation or profession as well as those which are usually thought of as recreational.

In training for enlightened and morally guided social cooperation, the college finds its greatest opportunity and obligation. The knowledge of our physical environment and the ability to control it have far outrun our ability to direct this knowledge to the common good. The crowning event in the process of evolution has been the emergence of personality. The goal of education must be the ability and the desire of persons to cooperate in securing the highest social good in human society. Scientific discoveries, inventions, and new uses of knowledge will surely continue to be made, but greater than the need of extending the limits of human knowledge is that of devising ways of applying the knowledge we already have to the improvement of human living.

The small liberal arts college has peculiar advantages for attaining this most important aim.

(1) It is a self-contained unit, organized for the single purpose of giving a broad general training to undergraduates. The university must have a variety of aims and of emphases. Its more extensive equipment of libraries, museums, and laboratories is not necessarily of advantage to the undergraduate. Much of this is concerned with research activities and serves no directly useful purpose for the college student. In these respects it is possible for the small college to provide as adequately for the real needs of its students as does the great university.

(2) The greater similarity of the students in respect to age, experience and interests makes the life of the small college more homogeneous. The teaching staff, whose activities are related primarily to undergraduate life and instruction and who are interested only incidentally in research, may center their attention more closely upon the common and more definite problems of the small college. The closer associations and more intimate contacts of students with each other and with their instructors are an important factor in the understanding of widely varying personalities and in the development of socially desirable ideas and habits of life. The college community furnishes a laboratory of unique possibilities for training young people in the art of living together as human beings. Several of our great universities are attempting to secure the democratizing influence of smaller groups through the introduction of the house plan. Very large sums of money are thus being spent to secure an improvised approximation of certain highly important advantages which the small college, by its very nature, already possesses.

(3) The typical small college is situated in a small community, usually at considerable distance from large centers of population. This is again a distinct advantage. The surroundings amid which one lives exert a real, although subtle, influence. Men, who can, still lift their eyes to the hills and find added strength in so doing. The Empire State Building offers a poor substitute for this invigorating experience. The beautiful campus with its shaded walks and ivied buildings, its far view of valleys and wooded hills, its intimate contacts with elemental features of life, is itself a potent educative force. The opportunities which a large city affords for the graduate professional school are of doubtful value to the undergraduate, for whom such an environment is largely diverting and works against the social solidarity which is so essential a feature of undergraduate student life. The country boy or girl of to-day is not unlike the city boy or girl in appearance or experience. Both types mingle freely and on

equal terms in the small college. There is little that either could gain from receiving his general education in an urban environment. Neither is wholly unacquainted with the good or bad features of city life. Indeed, some of the most serious problems of the college are due to the ease with which, under modern methods of transportation, students migrate to the city for their week-ends.

(4) Most of our small colleges, in their beginnings, were associated with some religious group. This is fortunate, for while many of them never erected any barriers of creed or practice and few, if any, now emphasize the beliefs of a particular denomination, they are still permeated with the ideals we associate with religion. It is this fact that more than anything else gives them their distinctive tone and influence. The traditions of the past are cherished and have made religion a motivating force which finds its abundant expression, though in changed form, in the present-day life of the college.

(5) The individual student is less likely to be submerged in the small college. The obvious fact that individuals differ widely in their interests and capacities and in their corresponding needs has arrested the attention of educators. It is no longer thought to be desirable, as it was never possible, for each student to learn the same subject in the same amount as every other. The teacher now realizes that he must learn his student before he can teach him. Detailed methods of personnel study are being introduced to determine the selection of students who may profitably enter college and to direct the work of individuals toward the maximum achievement of which each is capable. Curriculum and course requirements are becoming more flexible and special effort is being made to develop the ability of students to work independently and without the mechanical pressure which has hitherto placed a premium upon mediocrity. Some of the most promising results in this direction have been secured in the small colleges which for rather obvious reasons seem to be better adapted for setting up an effective program for this purpose.

In the confusing situation in which education in common with other social institutions finds itself, there still is a highly important place for the small college. There is no reason to doubt that the number of those whose education will be continued beyond the secondary school will increase in years to come. Most of the professions are already overcrowded and the requirements for admission to the professional schools are properly becoming more exacting. It is unlikely that these schools will admit students with shortened periods of preparation. Other types of schools will doubtless be required to provide educational opportunities for those whose needs will be better served than in the liberal arts college. But if the college were to disappear, its place would have to be filled by another institution whose aims would be identical with those so briefly outlined in this paper. The liberal arts college will survive, unchanged in purpose, but with form, curriculum, and method modified to meet the demands of new knowledge and changed conditions. Under wise and progressive guidance the liberal arts college in the years ahead should surpass the achievements of its long past.

EDUCATIONAL EVENTS

LONDON TECHNICAL SCHOOLS

ACCORDING to the London *Times Educational Supplement*, technical education in London in 1930 showed marked progress on the figures of 1929. The number of students rose over 12,000, and the student-hours, on a total of 25,972,345, were over 1,750,000. The day continuation schools accounted for over 2,000,000 student-hours.

The figures for the evening institutes are said to be the most satisfactory of all. Since 1926–27 there has been every year a rise in students from 138,159 to the present figure of 152,462, and this in spite of an actual reduction in the number of institutes. The student-hours have risen over 1,250,000, and the average of hours per student has risen over three hours, from 61.5 to 64.8. In 1920–21 the average was only 54.9, and at that date the session was a fortnight longer. The drop in the birth-rate has mainly affected the junior institutes. The largest of the institutes is the City Literary, which, with its 5,660 students, is almost a university in itself; the Hugh Myddelton Commercial Institute has 3,242; the largest women's institute is Sayerstreet, with 2,197, and the largest men's is Bethnal Green, with 1,972. No fewer than 50 institutes have an enrolment of over 1,000 students. The statistics for schools for mothers and clubs are not included in the figures for evening institutes, though the council supplies instructors. In 1929–30 they amounted to 70, with 3,961 students and 110,781 attendances. One of the most interesting developments has been the creation of men's junior institutes for students of the difficult age of 14–18, who do not attend the ordinary evening classes. There are seven of these, with an enrolment of about 5,000, and the council has now decided to stabilize this very useful type of institution.

The junior instruction centers for unemployed boys and girls were extended during the session. The number of students enrolled was nearly 8,000, the boys numbering about two to one to the girls; the work was made as practical as possible, with physical exercises, and English taught on the broadest lines.

In secondary education a new school was opened by the council for boys, which brought up the number of council secondary schools to 28, against 52 receiving grants from the council. The number of pupils attending the schools was 31,717, of whom practically a third were in the maintained schools. The grants to the aided schools were over £400,000, or £500,000 if fees and the expenses of the Council scholars are included.

FELLOWSHIPS OF THE COMMONWEALTH FUND

For the sixth consecutive year, a group of British students has been brought to the United States for postgraduate study. The new appointees to these Commonwealth Fund Fellowships, 35 in number, were assigned to sixteen schools and universities, as follows: California, 6; California Institute of Technology, 2; Chicago, 1; Columbia, 3; Cornell, 1; Harvard, 4; Johns Hopkins, 1; Massachusetts Institute of Technology, 1; Michigan, 1; New York, 1; North Carolina, 1; Pennsylvania, 1; Princeton, 3; Stanford, 2; Wisconsin, 3; Yale, 4. Among them were six government officials from various parts of the British Empire, including two from South Africa, one from Southern Rhodesia, one from New Zealand, one from Palestine, and one from India. These men and women, selected by a British committee of which the Prince of Wales is honorary chairman, were appointed for a two-year term of study and will travel in the United States, at the expense of the fund, during the summer vacation.

Forty per cent. of the fellowship holders of previous years, who have returned to Great Britain or the Dominions, are engaged in teaching or other academic work which gives them an opportunity to spread their knowledge of the United States to younger men and women. The next largest groups are in government service and industrial research.

According to the annual report of the Commonwealth Fund, from which this information is taken, these students are asked to record their impressions. Their comment on American educational methods varies from praise to sharp criticism. One student reports his opinion that "there is much that commends admiration under the American system, notably its general efficiency in keeping the maximum possible number up to a certain average standard, and the undoubted keenness of the majority of the students." Another says of undergraduate teaching, "The American system seems to encourage a student not to think for himself if he can possibly get a professor to think for him."

USE OF MOTION PICTURES IN PUBLIC SCHOOLS

"More than 60 per cent. of schools represented by approximately 6,000 principals and superintendents use motion picture films in some way for educational purposes," according to a statement recently made by Mr. J. O. Malott, of the Office of Education.

Questionnaires on the administration of film service in public elementary and high schools throughout the United States distributed through the Motion Picture Division of the Department of Commerce, with the cooperation of the Office of Education, were returned by this number of school administrators.

Many city and a few state departments of public instruction have organized administrative units to render motion picture service to the schools. Visual education departments with full-time employees have also been provided in numerous cities.

Mr. Malott points out that of 44,186 presentations of films reported in one school year, more than 32,000, or 73 per cent., were for curricular activities. Forty per cent. of the total motion picture offerings were in the social sciences, and 26 per cent. in the natural sciences. More than 25 per cent. of the total showings were in the fields of physical education, manual and industrial arts, home economics, English and commercial education, although approximately 2,500 presentations not specifically related to school subjects were reported.

Nearly 18,000, or 41 per cent. of the showings were in elementary schools; 12,000, or 27 per cent., were in junior high schools, and 14,200, or 32 per cent., were in senior high schools." In most instances films were obtained at low cost, by rental, or free "from educational centers, including city, state and federal agencies, extension divisions of universities, and various other types of educational organizations.

Five out of six teachers using motion pictures for instruction state that they are not able to make a sufficiently detailed study of the film to get the maximum value from it. The inquiry shows, however, that motion pictures were reported by 98.9 per cent. of teachers as being helpful or very helpful in creating an increased interest in school work and a sustained interest in topics studied.

THE JUNIOR HIGH SCHOOLS OF CLEVELAND

FIFTEEN years of experimentation with the junior high school in Cleveland have been reported in the annual report of Mr. R. G. Jones, Superintendent of Schools of Cleveland, Ohio, recently published by the Board of Education. Describing minutely the various activities of the modern junior high school, the author, Mr. Jones, makes some conclusions and predicts future developments in this comparatively new branch of the public school.

Mr. Jones reports that "The junior high school finds itself with a population so diverse in interests, capacities and probable future that it must consider this diversity as of first importance in attaining any goals whatever." The chief goals are apparently (1) to increase the child's command over fundamental facts and processes, (2) to help the child build up, maintain, and enjoy good health, (3) to help him choose, and in the case of the older child, facilitate his start in a vocation, (4) to help him form interests that will lead to worth-while recreative activities in leisure time, and (5) to assist him in learning how to get on with people, developing a spirit of cooperation and recognition of rights of others, individually and in social groups, large and small.

Mr. Jones predicts that new inventions, including television, will exert a great influence on the curriculum of the junior high school. He believes, according to the report, that visual aid will continue to become an increasingly important medium for broadening and enriching the scope of the pupil's experience. He says, after several years of experimentation with radio in Cleveland junior high schools, that "It is the opinion of those connected with the experimental work that certain desirable educational outcomes reasonably may be expected from radio lessons."

The social civic program of Cleveland junior high schools is the subject of a long chapter in the report. Changing social conditions in an industrial city make it imperative for the school to assume many obligations formerly taken by the family. The homeroom, clubs, student council, newspapers, social events, assemblies—all are described in this social civic chapter.

Results of revisions of courses of study in mathematics, the social studies and English are described in the report. After several years of study a committee of teachers of mathematics, under the supervision of the chief of the Bureau of Educational Research, reports that "arithmetic will continue to be the backbone of the seventh and eighth year work but there will be an increasing tendency to make this work more practical."

ADVANCED DEGREES AT THE UNIVERSITY OF PITTSBURGH

The University of Pittsburgh will in the future confer the degree of doctor of education, particularly designed to serve the needs of supervisory officials in education. Practically the same requirements hold for this degree as for the doctor of philosophy. Students working toward either degree must earn a total of seventy-two credits beyond a bachelor's degree.

The major difference comes in the type of research that is required for the two degrees. The plan in part states:

> A student must present, within his major field of study, a dissertation representing scholarship of a high order. The two degrees are similar in their requirements for scholarship; they may be differentiated in the nature of the contributions through research which candidates are required to make.
>
> The degree of doctor of education stands for the ability to organize materials and to test educational theory and practice through application to actual school situations. Research for this degree is of a service type. The degree of doctor of philosophy stands for discovery or production in educational theory and practice. Research for this degree should make a contribution either to technique or to knowledge.

Under the regulations for the degree of doctor of education, students, instead of being required to be certified in two languages or in one language and advanced statistical method as instruments of research, may meet certification requirements by any two of the following: (a) French, (b) German, (c) advanced statistical method, (d) mental measurements; and (1) a thesis prepared for a master's degree, or (2) a formal paper describing some phase of school practice.

Curricula leading to four different advanced degrees are now offered in education at the University of Pittsburgh. These degrees are: master of arts, master of education, doctor of philosophy, and doctor of education. The master of education degree was first offered in 1930.

THE GRADUATE EDUCATION BUILDING OF THE UNIVERSITY OF CHICAGO

The new Graduate Education Building of the University of Chicago has been erected with a part of the $1,500,000 given to the university by the General Education Board for the support of the scientific study of educational problems.

It has usually been assumed that teachers, school administrators and students of the science of education can be trained in recitation rooms of the simplest type. The Graduate Education Building of the University of Chicago shows that an entirely new idea with regard to the science of education is beginning to be accepted. This building has a statistical laboratory, a fully equipped apparatus workshop with a skilled mechanic, dark rooms for photographic work, laboratory rooms, record rooms, work rooms for members of the staff engaged in school and college surveys and other studies in the field of school and college administration, and a library with work space for 200 students and stack space for 100,000 volumes. The stack now contains 60,000 volumes on education. There is a special-collection room, where reports of school systems and colleges are made available for students of educational administration.

In addition to the equipment described, there are office workrooms for the fifteen professors and the fourteen staff members of lower academic rank who give instruction in the department. The building is devoted strictly to graduate work. It stands between the two buildings which house the laboratory schools. With the older buildings now occupied by the laboratory schools and with the school gymnasium, the department of education has a plant which is not surpassed by any of the plants provided for the natural and social sciences, which were recognized in universities before the science of education came into being.

PROPOSED FOUNDATION IN NEW YORK CITY FOR CHAMBER MUSIC

Plans are reported in *The New York Times* for the establishment of a foundation for chamber music that will serve for music the same purpose that a public library does for literature, that will support free public concerts, and encourage and instruct musical talent. The announcement was made on January 28 at a testimonial luncheon and concert given in honor of Adolph Lewisohn in the auditorium of Hunter College, New York City.

The proposed foundation, said to be the first of its kind in the country if not in the world, will have a building of its own in the Bronx on a site for which funds have been in part subscribed, and for which it is hoped to obtain an endowment large enough to perpetuate its work. Eventually, if arrangements made by Dr. Henry T. Fleck, head of the department of music at Hunter College and originator of the proposal, are consummated, the foundation will become international in scope.

The new institution, of which Mr. Lewisohn is the chief patron, will be opened within a year, and it is hoped to begin building in the fall. The site is in the neighborhood of the new Hunter College buildings. Dr. Fleck will be in charge of the institution and other sponsors will be Mr. George Gordon Battle, Lieutenant-Governor Herbert H. Lehman, Mr. Clarence Mackay, Mr. McAneny, Dr. Nicholas Murray Butler and Messrs. Harry Harkness Flagler, Grover A. Whalen, Felix Warburg, Otto Kahn, Theodore Steinway, Samuel Levy and Albert Goldman.

Facilities for instructing students will be available and advanced students who show promise will receive opportunities to make public appearances at the free concerts. The present chamber music concerts, which have been held at Hunter College for some years under the patronage of Mr. Lewisohn, will be continued and expanded in scope.

THE NEW YORK CITY SCHOOL RELIEF FUND

CONTRIBUTIONS from school teachers amounting to 5 per cent. of their salaries are necessary to meet the needs of school children and others aided by the School Relief Fund, according to Dr. William J. O'Shea, Superintendent of the Schools of New York City, who last week made an appeal for additional contributions at a meeting of district superintendents.

Dr. O'Shea told the superintendents that they might inform the teachers that a 5 per cent. contribution was necessary to raise the amount needed for relief work, but he made it clear that the teachers should not be given the impression that they were being compelled to contribute to the fund.

In a circular sent to all members of the supervising, teaching, extension, administrative, attendance, technical, custodian and mechanical staffs of the Board of Education, it was pointed out that

> concerted effort and self-denial are as necessary in this war on poverty and want as they were in the world war period.
>
> During the last two months the demands made on our school relief fund have far exceeded the estimates made in October when we resumed our contributions. It is now known that over 60,000 families are in dire need. The following carefully prepared estimate of our monthly needs is submitted for your consideration:

For out-of-school or family relief supplied by the schools	$150,000
For 50,000 free lunches for pupils per day	100,000
For shoes	30,000
For clothing	20,000
For salaries of workers for 80 new lunch centers	15,000
For relief to be supplied during the summer months	85,000
Total	$400,000

> This program will require a considerable sacrifice from all of us, but it is beyond neither our ability nor our inclination to help in the present crisis. Our large numbers and the security of our positions lay upon us the obligation to carry it through.
>
> We are now contributing about $108,000 each month. We need at least $400,000 each month for the next five months. A 5 per cent. contribution is necessary to raise this amount. We have full confidence that all of us who are in the employ of the Board of Education, in any activity, will respond to this appeal. There is no doubt of the moral obligation to do so.

The circular was signed by George J. Ryan, president of the Board of Education, as well as by Dr. O'Shea.

THE WASHINGTON BICENTENNIAL IN NEW YORK STATE

To guide the schools in the observance of the celebration of the two hundredth anniversary of the birth of George Washington, the State Education Department has issued a 36-page Washington Bicentennial Number of its Bulletin to the Schools which is distributed to all schools in the state.

The *Bulletin* includes an article by Dr. Alexander C. Flick, state historian, on "Washington's Relations to New York State." It also includes a statement by Mr. Edward P. Smith suggesting a plan for the celebration in the schools of the Bicentennial including special anniversary programs on Washington's Birthday, February 22, Inauguration Day, April 30, Flag Day, June 14, and Constitution Day, September 17. Also included in the publication is a bibliography for elementary and secondary schools prepared by the Library Extension Division of the department and a statement regarding the lantern slides which the Visual Instruction Division will lend to schools.

The following statement by Commissioner of Education Frank P. Graves regarding the observance of Washington's Birthday is printed in the *Bulletin:*

> The 200th anniversary of the birth of George Washington this year offers to schools of the state an unusual opportunity not only to pay honor to the Father of our Country, but also to draw many helpful lessons from the personality, the character and the achievements of George Washington. Although the law permits the closing of the schools on Washington's Birthday, I urge that this year the schools remain in session on February 22 and that at least part of the school period be devoted to special exercises in commemoration of this important anniversary. In no better way can we properly show our gratitude to the man who won our independence and founded our nation.

EDUCATIONAL NOTES AND NEWS

DR. ROBERT MAYNARD HUTCHINS, president of the University of Chicago, and Dr. Ray Lyman Wilbur, Secretary of the Interior, will address the general session of the Department of Superintendence at Constitution Hall, on Thursday morning, February 25. The general plans for the Washington meeting of the department are given in the issue of SCHOOL AND SOCIETY for January 2.

THE honorary degree of doctor of science has been conferred by the University of Chicago on Dr. William Wallace Campbell, president emeritus of the University of California, and formerly director of the Lick Observatory.

AT a dinner given in honor of Dr. Albert Einstein at the California Institute of Technology at Pasadena, Dr. Charles A. Beard and Dr. Jacob Gould Schurman, formerly president of Cornell University and ambassador to Germany, were the principal speakers.

DR. WALTER DAMROSCH, composer, conductor and leader in musical education, celebrated his seventieth birthday on January 30. A breakfast and a dinner were arranged in his honor, and congratulatory messages were received from all parts of the country and from Europe.

AN Associated Press dispatch reports that K. C. Chatterjee, education officer of the Calcutta Corporation, was arrested on January 26. The corporation controls three hundred schools and charges were made that many of them were "breeding places of sedition."

MISS ADELAIDE NUTTING, professor emeritus at Teachers College, Columbia University, will receive a portrait of herself at a reception at Teachers College on February 10. The portrait is the work of Stanislav Rembski. Miss Nutting, who was appointed professor of institutional administration at Teachers College in 1907, was the first nurse to be appointed to a chair in any American university. She retired from active work in 1925.

PROFESSOR WILLIAM R. SHEPHERD, of Columbia University, who was recently appointed visiting Carnegie professor to the University of Vienna, was the guest of honor on January 27 of Dr. Friedrich Fischerauer, consul-general of Austria in New York.

THE William H. Nichols medal of the New York section of the American Chemical Society for 1932 has been awarded to Professor James Bryant Conant, chairman of the division of chemistry at Harvard University. Dr. Conant was presented with the Chandler Medal of Columbia University on February 5, when he discussed "Equilibria and Rates of some Organic Reactions." The Nichols Medal will be presented to him on March 11, when he will speak on "An Introduction to the Chlorophyll Molecule."

Dr. Walter L. Bullock, associate professor of Italian at the University of Chicago, has been elected president of the American Association of Teachers of Italian.

Dr. Francis B. Haas, formerly Pennsylvania state superintendent of public instruction, now president of the State Teachers College at Bloomsburg, has been elected president of the Pennsylvania State Education Association.

At the annual meeting of the Board of Directors of the Kansas State Teachers Association, Superintendent Ira J. Bright, of Leavenworth, was chosen as president of the association. He will preside at the sixty-ninth annual session to be held on November 4 and 5, 1932, in the cities of Kansas City, Topeka, Salina, Dodge City, Hutchinson and Pittsburgh. The vice-presidents are: Principal Charles O. Wright, Atchison, for the Kansas City session; Superintendent G. A. Swift, Blue Rapids, for Topeka; Superintendent Wm. McMullen, Phillipsburg, for Salina; Superintendent L. L. Thompson, Ness City, for Dodge City; Superintendent J. F. Hughes, El Dorado, for Hutchinson, and Superintendent Glenn A. DeLay, Neodesha, for Pittsburg.

Albert Lindsay Rowland, superintendent of schools of Cheltenham Township, Montgomery County, Pennsylvania, and formerly director of the Teachers Bureau of the State Department of Public Instruction, has been elected president of the State Teachers College, Shippensburg. Dr. Rowland succeeds Ezra Lehman, who died recently.

Dr. Thomas Nixon Carver, professor of economics at Harvard University, will become professor emeritus in September, 1932.

Professor James B. Pollock, who for approximately thirty-five years has been a member of the department of botany of the University of Michigan, has presented his resignation, to take effect at the end of the present semester.

Dr. Joseph S. Ames, president of the Johns Hopkins University, has been elected a lay member of the standing committee of the Protestant Episcopal Diocese of Maryland.

Dr. Robert C. Binkley, acting head of the department of history of Flora Stone Mather College of Western Reserve University, has become chairman of the joint committee on materials for research of the Social Science Research Council and the American Council of Learned Societies.

Dr. W. S. Taylor, dean of the College of Education of the University of Kentucky, has been appointed by the president of the National Education Association as delegate from Kentucky to the World Federation of Educational Associations.

Dr. Louis A. Pechstein, dean of the School of Education of the University of Cincinnati, will lecture during the summer quarter of the Stanford University School of Education, which opens on June 24.

Mr. Langdon Warner, lecturer of fine arts at Harvard University, has been appointed guest lecturer at the College of Fine Arts of New York University, beginning with the spring semester. Mr. Warner will fill the place of Professor George Rowley, of Princeton University, who resigned recently because of illness.

Dr. Clarence C. Little, formerly president of the University of Michigan, spoke on January 23 on "Higher Education as I See it" at a public meeting of the Ethical Society at Boston.

Dr. Albert D. Mead, acting president of Brown University, was on January 29 the principal speaker at the fifty-ninth annual dinner of the Brown Alumni Club of Boston. Those present had the privilege of listening to the voices, as reproduced upon phonographic records, of two late presidents of Brown, Dr. E. Benjamin Andrews, who died in 1917, and of Dr. W. H. P. Faunce, who died two years ago.

Dr. Sidney Turner Moreland, formerly president of Washington and Lee University, died on January 29 at the age of seventy-nine years.

The death is announced of Dr. H. C. Pryor, formerly dean of education at Northern State Teachers College, South Dakota, and later dean at Kansas State Teachers College, Pittsburg.

Charles Sheldon Hastings, professor of physics emeritus of Yale University, died on January 30, in his eighty-third year.

DR. EMIL CARL WILM, professor of philosophy at Stanford University, died suddenly on January 31, at the age of fifty-four years.

LOUIS GUERINEAU MYERS, treasurer of the Rockefeller Foundation, of the General Education Board and of the Rockefeller Institute for Medical Research, died on January 28 at the age of fifty-eight years.

THE Graham Memorial, the new student union building of the University of North Carolina, was dedicated on January 29, in exercises in honor of the late President Edward Kidder Graham. The building is of three stories and was erected by the alumni at a cost of $250,000. Charles W. Tillett, Jr., of Charlotte, a former student and close associate of the late President Graham, delivered the dedication address.

PLANS for the dedication of the Folger Shakespeare Memorial in Washington on April 23, and for its formal presentation at that time to Amherst College by Mrs. Henry Clay Folger, widow of the donor, have been made public. Mr. George A. Plimpton, president of the corporation, will make the speech of acceptance. Dr. Joseph Q. Adams, formerly professor of English at Cornell University, supervisor of research in the Shakespearian Library once owned by Mr. Folger, will deliver the dedication address. The memorial building was erected at a cost of $2,000,000; the Shakespearian collection that it contains is valued at $4,000,000. The building, which stands opposite the site of the proposed Supreme Court building, near the Library of Congress, is classical in exterior architecture, and bears bas-reliefs of notable Shakespearian scenes. It contains an exhibition room, a reading room, private studies, offices and a theater.

A SETTLEMENT for $160,000 of the action to break the will of William Wilson Cook, corporation lawyer, who left the bulk of his $11,300,000 estate to his alma mater, the University of Michigan, was authorized on February 2 by an order signed by Surrogate James A. Foley. The contestants are Mrs. Ida C. Cook, of Los Angeles, divorced wife of Mr. Cook, and a nephew. Mr. Cook died on June 4, 1930, at Rye, New York. During his life time he made donations to the university which, with his testamentary bequest, brought his benefactions to the institution to about $20,000,000. The trust fund created for the university in the will was to create a law center "so as to produce superior lawyers, judges, legislators and executors; in other words, intellectual and reliable leaders."

THE board of trustees of Northwestern University have named the Evanston campus in memory of two benefactors of the institution. The south part, extending as far north as Willard place, will in the future be known as the Milton H. Wilson campus; and the section north of the Garrett Biblical Institute to Lincoln Street, on which are Patten gymnasium, Dearborn Observatory and the men's dormitories, will be called the James A. Patten campus. The late Milton H. Wilson, of Wilson Bros., manufacturers of men's furnishings, was a member of the board of trustees continuously from 1897 until his death in 1929. His gifts to the university up to that time had amounted to more than $1,500,000. In his will he bequeathed the bulk of his estate, valued at approximately $8,000,000, to the university as an endowment for the College of Liberal Arts. Mr. Patten also was a member of the board of trustees and served as its president from 1917 to 1920. For more than twenty years he made Northwestern University one of his vital interests.

A FUND which will ultimately amount to $210,000 and which will be known as "The E. D. Farmer International Scholarship Fund" has been established to finance fellowships for students from the University of Texas at the National University of Mexico and from the National University of Mexico to study at the University of Texas.

To enable Atlanta University to develop its work in the training of Negroes for business, the Carnegie Corporation of New York has made a grant of $100,000 for the establishment of a professorship in the university's graduate Department of Business Administration. Graduate work was inaugurated at Atlanta University two years ago following an affiliation agreement with Morehouse College for men and Spelman College for women. Under this agreement undergraduate instruction is confined to Morehouse and Spelman Colleges, while graduate work is undertaken by Atlanta University. First emphasis has been placed on the development of a department of education and the department of business administration. According to President John Hope, the graduate department of business seeks to give students a sound general knowledge of economics and an understanding of the technique of modern business. Because Negroes have little opportunity under existing conditions to learn business procedure at first hand as clerks and apprentices, it is necessary to provide them with technical training if they are to engage successfully in business. In addition to general business training the department proposes to give individual students of exceptional promise opportunities for more specialized work in the fields of investment, banking, insurance, merchandising and the like.

ACTING under a grant from the Carnegie Corporation, the committee on fellowships and scholarships of the American Library Association has announced that a limited number of grants is available for the school year, 1932–33. The purpose of these grants is to enable those who have shown promise of contributing to the advancement of the library profession to pursue a year of special study or research in library problems. In general applicants should be graduates of approved colleges or universities and should have had one year's work in a library school and satisfactory experience, although these requirements may be varied for exceptional cases. The stipend for a fellowship will be $1,500 or more, varying according to the requirements of the recipient, and may be renewed for a second year. Scholarships will vary in amount from $750 to $1,000, and will be awarded to persons with less extensive experience and training. Applications should be filed before February 15, and should be addressed to the chairman of the American Library Association Committee on Fellowships and Scholarships, Mr. Harrison W. Craver, Engineering Societies Library, 29 West 39th Street, New York, N. Y.

AN International Catalogue of Educational Films, to be issued in five languages, is to be compiled and published by the International Institute of Cinematography, with offices in Rome. The commission therefore request all distributing firms, educational societies, and other organizations interested in the production of educational films to communicate with them immediately. The lists sent in should show date of production, length of film (standard or substandard) and whether silent or talking, title, name of firm or organization responsible for the production, and if intended for general or special circulation.

DISCUSSION

ON THE OVERSUPPLY OF TEACHERS

"THE general picture . . . is that the profession of teaching is getting seriously and increasingly overcrowded." This is the summary of "fourteen factual investigations of supply and demand in teaching," presented by Eliassen and Anderson in a recent number of the *Educational Research Bulletin* of the Ohio State University. The evidence is rather conclusive that more persons are preparing to teach than there are positions available, and it seems to be generally felt that this situation is undesirable. At any rate, the situation gives point to the whole question of raising the requirements for entering the teaching profession, and in connection with this the further question of restricting enrolment in teachers' colleges and colleges of education. It is the purpose of this article to make two suggestions—one tending to show that the statistics on oversupply should not be taken at their face value and the other suggesting that a certain liberality in allowing students to select teacher-training courses is desirable.

The oversupply of teachers is at least not a unique situation. Millions of workers in other fields are unable to secure jobs. Conditions in teaching are but a part of a wide-spread socio-economic maladjustment. The reason for pointing out this fact is not to brush the problem lightly aside but to ask that it be considered in its larger setting. Perhaps education needs more, as well as better, workers.

As a starting point let us assume that every

willing and able worker is entitled to a job—somewhere. At the present time, however, millions are unable to secure a job of any kind. It must be apparent, therefore, that, unless society is to resort to some kind of wholesale slaughter of the unemployed, a way must be found to make more jobs available. It is hardly conceivable that we shall be willing to leave conditions as they are. Where, then, shall these jobs be found? This is the practical question. In any kind of serious social planning, education as well as industry and business must be examined to see whether it is not an area in which part of the readjustment should be made.

Let us not be guilty of dealing merely with symptoms and accepting the *status quo* without any intelligent contribution to the solution of the general problem. It is a task that will require fundamental social engineering. To the educator, certainly, it appears reasonable that in a society in which material production has apparently outrun demand and in which profound readjustments must be made in human relations—or, looking at it from the other side, in a school system so inadequately staffed—to an educator it appears reasonable that society can well afford to make greater investments in its schools, and thus incidentally reduce a part of the oversupply of those who want to teach. One of our greatest advances will come, it is true, in increasing the quality of our staff, but we need numbers as well; and we should not meekly accept the suggestion that society is now paying about all that it may be expected to pay for education. Now that we have learned how to produce wealth with less human labor, why may we not turn more time and energy into the improvement of human nature?

The second suggestion is that in our present social structure a certain excess in the number of persons prepared for teaching is necessary and desirable. This desirable oversupply is largely in the field of women workers, and the desirability rests not on the needs of the teaching profession but on general social conditions. As society is now constituted, married life commonly restricts outside employment. Whether this is as it should be, opinions will vary; but it is a fact. Coupled with this is the fact that the possibility of a desirable marriage is often uncertain, as is also the possibility that at some time after marriage a woman may be forced to work outside the home. The net result is that either women must be left without specific preparation for outside work or else many of them must be trained for jobs which they will fill temporarily or not at all. There is much to be said in favor of the latter alternative.

If, then, many women are to be prepared for jobs which they will fill only temporarily or not at all, for what jobs—from the standpoint of the general welfare—should they be prepared? It is obvious that no single answer can be given; many fields are and should be open. From the standpoint of society at large, however, there are some reasons why teaching makes an especially happy choice for a large number who have the requisite ability and interest. A great deal of the preparation for teaching is also a preparation for parenthood, for the parent is the first—and in some ways the most important—teacher. There are few vocations which present so much overlapping between outside employment and home-making, and consequently so little waste in changing from one to the other. By a proper selection of courses the loss can be reduced to a reasonable minimum.

No attempt has been made in this article to discuss the apparent oversupply of teachers at all exhaustively. As is usually the case with social problems, the situation is extremely complicated. While two suggestions have been offered, the main point of the discussion is to urge that the problem be considered, not narrowly, but in its relation to the welfare of society at large. In the reconstruction which follows the depression, if we do any social planning at all, some one should see that the service of education is both improved and enlarged. In the meantime we need not feel that it is a greater waste to prepare teachers who will never have classrooms than it is to prepare others who will never follow their professions, or indeed than it is to invest in the ordinary liberal arts course without specific goal.

H. T. Manuel

University of Texas

INCREASING THE I. Q.

Does a child's ability to read make a significant difference in his I. Q., as determined by a group intelligence test?

This problem presented itself many times last year in connection with an experiment in teaching the mechanics of silent reading. All the children in grades four to eight in the public schools of Latrobe, Pennsylvania, about 900, were used in the experiment. In December five reading tests, a test in reading arithmetic and one in reading history and two group intelligence tests were given. A drill procedure was instituted during the first week in January and continued for three months. Most of the children made rapid progress. Those who did not make proper progress were studied individually. In this connection, Binet tests were often given. It was soon evident that some children in the intermediate grades were rated as feebleminded on both group tests, but as normal on the Binet test. These children could pronounce words with good expression, but they could not read.

After the second forms of all reading tests had been given and scored, the writer chose 25 children from each of two buildings and gave the Otis Intermediate Examination, Form B to them. They had previously been given Form A. It was the afternoon of the last day of school when Form B was given. Nevertheless, these children increased their I. Q.'s an average of 11.76 points.

None of the 50 children chosen had been given a Binet test, and none of them was personally known to the writer. They were chosen because they had made considerable progress in reading, particularly in speed. Some had very low reading ability at the beginning, some very high; some had low I. Q.'s as indicated by the December tests, some had high I. Q.'s. But all had made significant progress in some phase of reading ability. The average reading ability of the group at the beginning of the experiment was a grade score of 5.22 and the average gain, as indicated by the five tests, was 1.36 grades. The average gain in speed, two tests, was 2.72 grades.

The following table indicates the gains made in the I. Q.:

TABLE I

Gains Made in I.Q. After Increased Reading Ability

Points gained	Number of cases
–4 to 0	8
1 to 5	5
6 to 10	10
11 to 15	12
16 to 20	7
21 to 25	4
26 to 30	1
31 to 35	1
36 to 40	2
Average 11.76	Total 50

The highest 10 per cent. made an average gain of 32 points; the highest 25 per cent. made an average gain of 24 points. This would seem to indicate that an I. Q. made on a group test may be largely a reading score.

Ellsworth Lowry
Pennsylvania State College

SPECIAL CORRESPONDENCE

A COURSE FOR AMERICAN WOMEN AT OXFORD UNIVERSITY

In the midst of depressions and rumors of war, education goes on. Oxford University has seen systems and personalities come and go, and through the centuries has continued its quiet work of education. As recently as 1926, in the face of disorganization attendant upon the general strike in the spring, a vacation course for American women was inaugurated. Some three hundred gathered that year to live in the Oxford Women's Colleges and to drink in the spirit of English learning under the guidance of many of England's greatest living scholars. The course was repeated in 1928 and now is offered again for 1932.

The subject around which three weeks of lectures will be organized in 1932 is "Eighteenth Century England." The era will be approached from the angles of literature, history, philosophy, religion, education, music and art. The lecturers are drawn from various universities of England, and the American student would ordinarily have to expend much time and effort to hear all of them. To take literature as an illustration, the lecturers announced on that subject are Ernest de Sélincourt of Oxford, F. P. Wilson of Leeds, Lascelles Abercrombie of London, D. Nichol Smith of Oxford, Caroline F. Spurgeon of London and H. F. B. Brett-Smith of Oxford. In addition, there will be writers whose books are well known in the scholarly literature of the period—J. L. Hammond, economic historian; Hilaire Belloc, biographer and religious historian, and Sir Richard Lodge, president of the Royal Historical Association.

The academic program will include two lectures each morning and frequent evening lectures in addition to the discussion classes which will be held in the early evening. Excursions are planned to places of historic interest in the neighborhood, and invitations will be extended to members of the course to meet residents of Oxford in their homes.

The dates of the course are July 8 to 28. The triennial conference of the International Federation of University Women at Edinburgh will follow the course immediately, and it is hoped that many members of the American Association of University Women will plan to attend both the course and the conference. For those who wish to spend a little longer in the university atmosphere of England, there will be an opportunity to go to Cambridge, where a University Extension Summer Meeting will be in progress from July 28 to August 17. Women graduates of accredited American universities are eligible to the Oxford course, as well as teachers in secondary schools, whether or not they have obtained university degrees. Application should be made to Miss Marion Day, 39 W. 54th St., New York City.

The women who have attended the earlier courses have returned expressing happy satisfaction with their experiences at Oxford. They speak of the men and women who bring the results of years of scholarship to the students of the course; they remember with joy the visits to Stratford-on-Avon, to Warwick Castle and the Sulgrave Manor, when they reveled in history and the atmosphere of literature; and they tell you of unforgettable afternoons when they took tea in Oxford homes. Few American women can spend two or three years as students at Oxford, but because of the special vacation courses that are planned there for them, they can have a taste of Oxford life and come to understand its mellow flavor.

ESTHER CAUKIN BRUNAUER,
International Relations Secretary,
American Association of
University Women

QUOTATIONS

GIFTS BY TEACHERS

No voice was heard in opposition to Superintendent O'Shea's appeal at the meeting of district superintendents, principals and directors for contribution by the teachers of 5 per cent. of their salaries to the relief of school children. Yet the Teachers' Union has written to President Ryan in strong protest against "the assumption of authority and responsibility" involved in the effort to make what is looked upon by them as a "levy." Dr. O'Shea would employ no coercion, but at the same time his reproach of those who declined to give was such as to suggest that they were not worthy of being in the school system—in the position of foster-parents to these children in want.

Teachers have no responsibility beyond others of like means in providing for those in need, whether in the school or the community outside. They are, however, closer to the children than any others except parents, and are under constant appeal from the helplessness of those under their care, and are likely to do even more than their obligations to others would approve. To be condemned for not making a fixed contribution is virtual coercion, especially if the failure to make it is known. The more sensitive would feel it as such, even if their refusal were known only to themselves.

There is also the question whether an educational system should assume so great a relief obligation. Granted that food is more essential than a knowledge of arithmetic or geography, should not the schools do what they are established to do and let relief workers do what they are better prepared to do than even the teachers? They do not derive their living from those whom they teach, as has been urged. It is probable that teachers give under the pressure of the need with which they are intimately acquainted and out of their devotion to the children in their care more than they ought to give in fairness to themselves and others. They should be entirely free from other coercion than that of their own consciences.—*The New York Times.*

SOCIETIES AND MEETINGS

ASSOCIATION OF AMERICAN COLLEGES

A MESSAGE from Principal L. P. Jacks, of the University of Oxford, and an address by Charles P. Taft, 2nd, both presented at the annual dinner, were features of the eighteenth annual meeting of the Association of American Colleges, held at the Netherlands Plaza Hotel, Cincinnati, on January 21 and 22. Of the association membership of about 450 institutions somewhat more than half were represented by a total of about 350 presidents, deans and professors. It was hardly an outstanding meeting, but it had interest and value in the discussion of certain problems of wide importance and indefinite action upon several of them.

There were four sessions and a dinner, with a total of twenty-five listed speakers. The program included a visit to the Cincinnati Art Museum, and musical numbers at the dinner by students of the Cincinnati Conservatory of Music.

President Ernest H. Wilkins, of Oberlin College, president of the association, announced the appointment of committees at the opening session on the morning of January 21. Giving his annual report, Dr. Robert L. Kelly, executive secretary, said that "the largest proportion of time, both of the executive and associate secretary, is given in the office and in the field to consultative and advisory service." He told of the study of the smaller college now being conducted by Archie M. Palmer, associate secretary, in which 117 colleges are cooperating. "Among this number are eight colleges affiliated with the Society of Friends, which have contributed financially so as to make possible a more intensive tilling of certain areas than the general survey calls for. The office has carried on extensive correspondence both with member institutions and with others, especially deans of graduate schools with reference to constructive use and distribution of questionnaires."

Expenditures of the association for the year ending January 1 were $32,236, as reported by President William Mather Lewis, of Lafayette College, treasurer. The balance for the year was $4,250.

The report of the commission on the enlistment and training of college teachers was summarized by President James L. McConaughy, of Wesleyan University, printed copies of the full text being distributed to those in attendance. It was revealed that

> approximately 5 per cent. of all the graduates in the colleges represented in this association during the last decade are teaching in colleges, or preparing therefor. The intellectual quality of these present and future teachers is high; over one half of those who have chosen college teaching as their life work graduated in the upper quarter of the class. Furthermore, approximately one tenth of all the honor graduates chose to become college teachers. Where separate figures for men and women are given, no noteworthy differences between the two groups were found, in numbers, percentage of total graduates, or quality of the recruits. Although the figures were given for each of the last ten years, the commission could find no observable trend, toward either a decrease or an increase in the number of recruits, nor any evidence of a change in quality.

President McConaughy emphasized that recently there has been a marked change in economic conditions in the profession. Believing that "these conditions are temporary," the commission recommended "that a book or booklet be prepared, under association auspices, for the benefit of undergraduates interested in the possibility of preparing for college teaching." The association later adopted a report of the resolutions committee authorizing such a publication "provided that funds can be secured to cover the cost."

President Frank L. McVey, of the University of Kentucky, chairman of the commission on educational surveys, gave a résumé of certain surveys conducted during the past year, including the study of the smaller college by Associate Secretary Palmer.

Dean Raymond Walters, of Swarthmore College, presented a classification he had been asked to devise, grouping institutions of higher education in the United States. He stressed that "this is distinctly not a new accrediting list and that the several groups are not differentiated or ranked in respect to educational excellence." The purpose is to classify the leading types of institutions "so that statistics regarding them may be presented in as convenient and illuminating a fashion as possible. For administrators to have financial and administrative data about institutions of like character and to know enrolment trends in these and other colleges and universities have become increasingly necessary in these difficult days." Mimeographed copies of the proposed classification were distributed and certain suggestions were received. At the morning session next day, the resolutions committee recommended the adoption of this classification in principle and a committee was appointed "with power to assign the institutions to their respective places and to report these assignments to the association and to such other educational associations as can make proper use of this material." The committee includes Dean Walters as chairman, Chancellor S. P. Capen, of the University of Buffalo, and Dr. F. J. Kelly, of the U. S. Office of Education.

President Donald J. Cowling, of Carleton College, reported briefly for the National Committee on Standard Reports for Institutions of Higher Learning. At the luncheon conference of January 22, the report of this committee on standard financial reports for colleges and universities was given by Lloyd Morey, comptroller of the University of Illinois. "Colleges and universities are facing the most critical time in their history. Income from endowment and from public appropriations is shrinking and student enrolment is decreasing very little and in some cases increasing. Every means possible must be devised to aid in the administration of these institutions under such conditions. A sound system of budgeting, accounting, and financial reporting is particularly valuable to this end." The National Committee has recently published a booklet, under support from the General Education Board, "in which principles of accounting and reporting are set forth and forms of published financial reports presented for guidance of institutions." "The Present Financial Status of the College" was discussed by Dr. Alfred W. Anthony.

Commission on College Athletics

"Mere discussion of collegiate athletics has for the moment gone far enough; the next steps of progress lie in action—immediate, decisive, and courageous action to put into effect those principles at our colleges and universities which have generally been agreed upon as beneficial."

The report of the commission on college athletics began with the foregoing statement by an educational leader who has practiced what he preaches, President Thomas S. Gates, of the University of Pennsylvania. President Gates made only a brief reference to the reforms now in effect in Pennsylvania's athletics, concentrating in this preliminary report upon twelve points which, in the judgment of the commission, are "essentials of a program and policy which would be in accord with the most sincere thought on the subject of physical education in college life to meet modern conditions":

(1) The trustees, the officers, and especially the president of a college or university are responsible for the type of athletics and physical education that an institution has.

(2) Athletics and physical education should be coordinated administratively, and in detailed functioning, with student health services, preferably under a single directing head.

(3) A program of physical education and athletics should be operated for the benefit of all students and not merely for those proficient enough to win positions on teams engaging in intercollegiate competition.

(4) Responsibility for the physical welfare of athletes should rest with the college or university health service both as to qualifications for participation and as to continuance in any contest.

(5) When athletics cease to be fun and become drudgery, there is something wrong with the system.

(6) Not only subsidizing, but also recruiting and proselyting of athletes, as defined by the Carnegie report, are contrary to the amateur system which should prevail in college athletics. Most of our institutions need more funds for scholarships

and loans to students. Such aid should be distributed impartially upon the basis of need, ability, and promise, and should be neither given nor withheld because of athletic accomplishment.

(7) Full publicity should be given to all that our colleges and universities do in athletics, for the willingness to have full publicity is a test of honesty.

(8) The shortening of the football season to six or seven games for the first team, with the elimination of pre-season practice is a desirable development which will do much to place football more nearly in its proper relationship to the whole program of physical education and the educational process. All athletic events should be studied for effects on health, which might lead to shortening of crew races and elimination of the longer track events.

(9) The elimination from our schedules of all but natural rivals—teams from those institutions not too far distant and approximately of the same size, whose codes of academic and athletic work are approximately on a parity. . . .

(10) There is a growing belief that coaches should be of faculty caliber, of faculty rank, paid in accordance with the general scale of faculty salaries. . . .

(11) The actual control of the playing of games must be returned more and more to the students. . . .

(12) Finally, we believe that the colleges and universities have a considerable task to perform in the education of their constituencies as to what constitutes real merit in an institution's physical education system. If we can educate our alumni and the public to have respect and admiration for an institution which lays greater store by a well-developed program of athletics for all than by a lop-sided development of one sport, and for teams which are honest though they may not be able to win more than half the time, so-called over-emphasis will have become only a growing pain of the past.

President Gates then indicated certain problems which the commission proposes to consider during the coming year: "Is there a possibility that through informal treaties we may bring about athletic disarmament among a certain number of institutions which can set the pace for the country?" "Should we consult our medical authorities for advice as to the habits of exercise best in youth for one who in a few years is to be an adult leading a different kind of life from that of student days?"

After giving his report as chairman, President Gates proceeded to an address on "The Character-Building Function of Higher Education," in which he said that "athletics are but one link in the chain." He discussed the spiritual development of undergraduates, which he did not think could be left by the universities entirely to the churches. He advocated a curriculum based upon the words of Herbert Spencer, "How to use our faculties to the greatest advantage of ourselves and others—how to live completely."

THE SECOND SESSION

At the second session on the afternoon of January 21, addresses were given by President Wilkins and by Director Walter H. Siple, of the Cincinnati Art Museum.

"Society and College" was the subject of the presidential address by Dr. Wilkins. He contrasted school and college attendance to-day with that of 1890. Many students "have gone to college not because the existing college was really adapted to their needs, but because they found no institution other than the existing college to which they could go." For men and women "headed for some sort of non-professional employment" there should be created a new type of college which President Wilkins would call "the General College." This would "give these students what society really wants them to have, namely, a training which will enable them to live well as members of society."

President Wilkins proposed training in health; training in the use of "general mental tools (English, logic, etc.)"; instruction and some experience in five fields: "Home life, the field of earning, citizenship, leisure, and the field of philosophy and religion"; and, finally, "the encouragement of social-mindedness."

A college course carefully designed for this purpose could be completed in three years. New institutions might be founded as three-year general colleges; those separate two-year junior colleges which want to expand would do well to become three-year general colleges; and those four-year colleges which, through lack of endowment, can not stand the cost of maintaining specialized work, would also do well to become three-year general colleges. The establishment of such colleges would mean that the four-year college could be more exacting than it now is in its admission requirements and might thus secure a more homogeneous body of students.

As to the four-year college, President Wilkins declared that all the work of its upper half should be of "the character of honors work." He highly recommended a fifth year in the stronger colleges, leading to a master's degree.

Preceding the visit of the association members to the Cincinnati Art Museum, Director Sipple spoke on cooperation between art museums and universities. He referred to conditions in Germany to illustrate what relations may be developed between industries and art schools or art departments of universities and museums. Ways in which the museum and the university may cooperate were indicated, as the use of the x-ray and ultra-violet ray in the detection of forgery; technical processes in restoring art objects; the chemistry of pigments; and the lighting of a museum. A properly organized museum can serve in the education of university undergraduates. Students, as well as the general public, need fundamentally to realize that "a modern museum is not an aggregation of objects but a living organization."

THE ANNUAL DINNER

A message to the association from Principal Lawrence Pearsall Jacks, Oxford philosopher and editor of the *Hibbert Journal*, was read at the annual dinner by Secretary Kelly. It is here printed in full.

I much regret my inability to attend your great conference at Cincinnati. If I had been able to do so I would have taken the opportunity to speak of those fundamental things which are common to educators all over the world; the ultimate things which give to our work its dignity and value. In this message I will tell you briefly what they are as I conceive them.

I believe that our civilization has now to choose between two things—education and catastrophe. Unless we can succeed in raising the quality of human beings to a higher level, both mentally, physically, and morally, it seems to me certain that sooner or later, and sooner rather than later, the fabric of our civilization will collapse. All our other problems, political, industrial and economic, are centered in this great problem of raising the quality of this human material which forms the living substance of our civilization. But this can be done; our work as teachers is to find out how it can be done—and to do it. Every teacher and educator, from the beginner in a grade school, to the President of a University, has a part to play in getting it done. We teachers should think of ourselves as a great army in active service, fighting the battle on the issue of which the fate of our civilization depends. We are doing our work injustice when we think of it as merely a *profession*. It is a *mission to humanity*, the great mission of the age. We bear the central responsibility of the civilized world; we are all soldiers in that cause and brothers in arms, no matter what nation we belong to.

I look upon education as the great adventure of the twentieth century. Unlike those who exploit the riches of the material world we are engaged in exploring and developing the far greater riches that lie hidden in human nature. It has dawned upon the modern world that of all the precious things that exist and grow upon this earth by far the most valuable is man himself. We are beginning to explore his vast possibilities, just as our forefathers, centuries ago began to explore this vast continent. We are beginning to see that man, in his haste to develop the material world, has neglected to develop himself. And now we are turning to this new human continent and finding there a task which will surpass in splendor all the past achievements of our race—the task of educating man to the full stature of his possibilities. Nothing so hopeful, nothing so fascinating, nothing so adventurous has ever been attempted before. It calls of the service of the best men and women of every land. There was a time when the calling of a school teacher was despised. I believe the time is coming when it will be regarded as the most honorable and important calling in the world, a calling which gives larger room than any other for the competence of the wise man, the courage of the brave man, and the faithfulness of the true man.

It is of course upon the young that the work of education will mainly operate. The hope of the future lies with them. I do not think that the course of the world can ever be greatly changed for the better by appeals addressed only to grown up people, whose habits are already formed. If we would have a new and a nobler civilization we must lay the foundation of it in the young and begin to do so from earliest childhood. Unless we catch them while they are young we shall never change the habits of the people for the better either in regard to their labor or in regard to their leisure. Their labor might be made far more excellent than it is, and their leisure might be made a hundred times as enjoyable. But we shall do neither thing unless we liberate and train the creative part of them while they are young. The happiness of the individual, and the values of civilization are impossible without a high degree of creative activity. The education which is to save our civilization from catastrophe must follow the creative line from the very first.

Two great principles have been discovered which may help us to achieve this object. Both were discovered long ago by the ancient Greek; but unfortunately they were forgotten by those who established our traditional system of education, and it is only of late that they have been revived and brought to bear on educational policy.

The first is the principle that the best approach to the minds of young people lies through the medium of their bodies. Young people should be taught to think with their whole bodies. Sane thinking must always be expressed by the whole body. In practice this means that a genuine physical education, which of course is a very different thing from mere gymnastics, should be made accessible to every child in the community on exactly the same terms as reading, writing, and arithmetic.

The second is the discovery that the play instincts of the young have a high educational value and can be made use of, under wise training, for wider and beneficial cultural purposes. These play instincts, which sometimes take the direction of active games, and sometimes the direction of arts, crafts and hobbies, are the first form which creativeness takes in the life of the young. By giving them opportunity and skillful guidance this creative spirit can be established as a permanent possession for later life and led on to great heights of excellence and beauty.

I would recommend both principles to the earnest attention of your conference. It is the merit of the so-called "Recreation Movement" (so well represented in this country by the National Recreation Association) to have brought both these principles into prominence on the educational field. I regard it as a contribution of the utmost importance to the New Education which the modern world requires.

In conclusion I would express my fervent hope that your conference will inspire every member of it with new ardor for the great adventure of the twentieth century—the work of education.

The address of the evening was delivered by Charles P. Taft, 2nd, militant participant in Cincinnati's reform movement, who attacked what he termed "defeatism":

We are told that this is a world economic depression, with so many complex influences that no one can solve the problem. We are told that there will always be unemployables who can't work and never could work. We are told that clean politics are impossible, that you can't have honest and effective government. Men say there will always be war. In this battle, thank God, the colleges are always on the foreground on the side which says, "This can be done!"

You and the social workers stand together in saying, "We can make these things better," and your graduates are leading in the right.

So far as peace and disarmament are concerned, it is significant that one of the outstanding members of the American delegation to Geneva is a member of your association and president of an old and honored institution. It is the school and college that are turning the minds of the present and the rising generation to the determination that we must have peace.

Mr. Taft, in discussing "how colleges can be increasingly useful in fitting men and women for the tasks of life," asked whether colleges teach their students "how to maintain their physical health when they leave college," whether they teach them to express themselves "through the written or spoken word?"

When a man has left college for five or six years and the freshness of his new occupation has worn off, it will be strange if he does not begin to wonder what use his job is anyway, and what life is all about. If a few fundamental principles are pounded into him during his educational experience, they will return to help him when he reaches that stage.

BUSINESS SESSION

The business session of the association, held on the morning of January 22, was opened with the submission by President E. D. Soper, of Ohio Wesleyan University, of the report of the resolutions committee. Beside the two resolutions earlier referred to, there was a third providing for the appointment of "two members of a committee of six to clarify and define the relationship between the Liberal Arts College Movement and the Association of American Colleges." All of the resolutions were passed unanimously.

Dean John R. Effinger, of the University of Michigan, reporting as chairman of a special committee including President W. A. Neilson, of Smith College, and Deans Radcliffe Heermance and L. P. Eisenhart, of Princeton University, presented the following resolution.

Resolved, that the Association of American Colleges recommends: (1) That two or more units of Chinese or Japanese be included in the list of subjects accepted for college admission. (2) That each college approving this recommendation indicate in its catalogue the manner in which these units will be accepted.

Dean Effinger explained that this resolution (which was unanimously passed by the association) was the outcome of study of a situation to which attention was called a year ago by the American Council of the Institute of Pacific Relations and earlier by Dr. Frederick P. Keppel in a paper read before the Association of American Universities. The allowance of credit for Chinese and Japanese is designed for American boys and girls in the American schools of the Far East (estimated at 1,650 in 1930). It will permit them, in preparing for college study in the United States, to acquire a literary knowledge of a language which they frequently speak in the vernacular, and hence increase the group of American citizens familiar with the Chinese and Japanese languages, a group needed "from the points of view of scholarship, business and professional activities, and diplomacy."

Dean Herbert E. Hawkes, of Columbia College, gave an account of the work of the committee on personnel, American Council on Education. After reference to the five projects of the committee from 1926 to 1929, he outlined the present development of one of these projects, under further subvention from the General Education Board,—the preparation of new-type examinations in a large variety of subject-matters. "This work is going forward under the directorship of Professor Ben D. Wood. It is anticipated that, in the course of a year, tests in certain of the subjects will be available." Dean Hawkes told also of the new-type comprehensive examinations to be given in more than two hundred colleges this spring under the auspices of a subcommittee of the Cooperative Test Service under the chairmanship of Dean J. B. Johnston, of the University of Minnesota. The whole subject of examinations should be studied, Dean Hawkes maintained. "There should be a collection and accurate analytical description of the various examinations as related to their various functions as, for example, the oral examination, the written examination, the essay type, the comprehensive, and the new-type examination." Furthermore, he concluded, "the whole question of education for leisure, and what our colleges ought to do about it, is bound to be an increasingly serious and important question in the years just ahead of us."

Chancellor Samuel P. Capen, of the University of Buffalo, read a paper on "Vital Educational Measures Applicable to Colleges." Saying that the success of any social institution "can be gauged only with reference to its purpose," Dr. Capen declared: "We can not now get agreement as to the purpose colleges should serve. Consequently efforts to measure colleges deal only with external characteristics and are unsatisfactory."

Pending agreement as to the purpose of the colleges, why do we not stop trying to measure them and measure students instead? There is a wealth of instruments for the measurement of students. We are now in a position to apply on a nation-wide scale psychological tests, subject examinations, and general examinations. The application of these measures will enable us to judge the accomplishments of the student population, and to compare the efficacy of the different types of college education. Such general measurement of the results of college education will help us toward ultimate agreement concerning the purpose of the college.

Dr. Edward S. Jones, of the University of Buffalo, who is director of the study of the comprehensive examination for the Association of American Colleges, gave a short informal statement of his work thus far.

Greetings to the association were presented by three representatives of kindred organizations, Professor Homer L. Dodge, of the American Association of University Professors; Dr. Kathryn McHale, of the American Association of University Women; and Dr. Stephen P. Duggan, of the Institute of International Education.

There was a brief talk by Dr. Irving Maurer, president-elect of the association.

Twenty-five colleges were elected to membership in the association, their names being presented by Associate Secretary Palmer in behalf of the executive committee. In the discussion Executive Secretary Kelly brought out the principle of the association that "it is not a standardizing agency and that membership is inclusive, not exclusive."

Upon motion of the nominating committee, of which President W. G. Clippinger, of Otterbein college, was chairman, the following officers, commissions and committees were elected for 1932–33:

President: President W. Irving Maurer, Beloit College.

Vice-President: President F. L. McVey, University of Kentucky.

Executive Secretary: Dr. Robert L. Kelly, New York City.

Associate Secretary: Archie M. Palmer, New York City.

Treasurer: President William Mather Lewis, Lafayette College.

Executive Committee: President E. H. Wilkins, Oberlin College; President J. L. McConaughy, Wesleyan University; President W. P. Few, Duke University; Dean William Cunningham, St. Thomas College.

Representation on Standing Committees and Commissions: American Council on Education: President Guy E. Snavely, Birmingham-Southern College (one year); President J. Edgar Park, Wheaton College (Mass.) (two years); Chancellor S. P. Capen, University of Buffalo (three years).

National Advisory Committee on Education: President W. M. Lewis, Lafayette College; Dr. Robert L. Kelly, Association of American Colleges; President Frank Aydelotte, Swarthmore College; President R. E. Blackwell, Randolph-Macon College; Rector James H. Ryan, Catholic University of America.

National Committee on Standard Reports for Institutions of Higher Learning: President Donald J. Cowling, Carleton College; Professor Floyd Reeves, University of Chicago; President E. E. Rall, North Central College; Assistant Secretary, J. C. Christensen, University of Michigan; Controller G. C. Wintringer, Princeton University; Professor E. S. Evenden, Teachers College, Columbia University; President George F. Zook, University of Akron.

National Research Council: Professor Arthur H. Compton, University of Chicago.

Commission of College Architecture and College Instruction in Fine Arts: President Frederick C. Ferry, Hamilton College, Chairman; President F. P. Keppel, Carnegie Corporation; President John Erskine, Juilliard School of Music; J. Frederick Larson, Dartmouth College; President Meta Glass, Sweet Briar College; Sister Anna Coulet, College of St. Catherine.

Commission on the Cost of College Education: President Donald J. Cowling, Carleton College, Chairman; Controller C. C. Wintringer, Princeton University; Controller Lloyd Morey, University of Illinois; Auditor N. C. Plimpton, University of Chicago; Secretary Alex. H. Sanda, Jr., The Duke Endowment; Auditor T. L. Hungate, Teachers College, Columbia University.

Commission on Educational Surveys: President D. A. Robertson, Chairman, Goucher College; President G. F. Zook, University of Akron; Executive Secretary, M. C. Huntley, Association of Colleges and Secondary Schools of Southern States.

Commission on Enlistment and Training of College Teachers: President Albert Britt, Chairman, Knox College; President J. R. Angell, Yale University; President Lucia Briggs, Milwaukee-Downer College; President H. F. Rainey, Bucknell University; President L. W. Boe, St. Olaf's College.

Commission on Faculty and Student Scholarship: President Henry M. Wriston, Lawrence College, Chairman; Dean C. S. Boucher, University of Chicago; Dean Julian Park, University of Buffalo; President C. D. Gray, Bates College; President Katherine Blunt, Connecticut College.

Commission on Permanent and Trust Funds: Dr. A. W. Anthony, New York City; President Rees E. Tulloss, Wittenberg College; Assistant-Treasurer Raymond L. Thompson, University of Rochester; President James Ross McCain, Agnes Scott College.

Commission on Athletics: President T. S. Gates, University of Pennsylvania, Chairman; President D. L. Marsh, Boston University; President W. M. Lewis, Lafayette College; President E. H. Wilkins, Oberlin College; Acting President J. M. Newcomb, University of Virginia.

Committee on Form of Classification of Institutions of Higher Education: Dean Raymond Walters, Swarthmore College, Chairman; Chancellor S. P. Capen, University of Buffalo; Dr. Frederick J. Kelly, U. S. Office of Education.

SECTIONAL LUNCHEON CONFERENCES

The closing session of the meeting comprised six sectional luncheon conferences at 12:30 P. M. All were largely attended. The subjects of discussion and the chairmen of the various conferences were as follows: "Credits and Credit Systems," President W. M. Lewis, of Lafayette

College. "Objective Indices of Faculty Scholarship Obtainable through the Library," President H. M. Wristom, of Lawrence college. "Standard Financial Reports," Comptroller Lloyd Morey, University of Illinois. "Faculty and Student Relationships," Dean Christian Gauss, of Princeton University and President Katharine Blunt, of Connecticut College for Women. "Individualization in Teaching," President H. P. Rainey, Bucknell University. "The Comprehensive Examination," Dr. Edward S. Jones, director of special study.

RAYMOND WALTERS

SWARTHMORE COLLEGE

EDUCATIONAL RESEARCH AND STATISTICS

AMOUNT OF HIGH SCHOOL LATIN AS AN INDICATOR OF SUCCESS IN COLLEGE WORK

AT least one article has recently been published maintaining that the amount of foreign language taken in high school is positively related to a student's success in his first semester of college work, and that this relationship is close enough to be used in forecasting college success.[1] There can be little doubt concerning the desirability of more adequate methods of selecting applicants, but there is some reason to be suspicious about the contribution made by a knowledge of the amount of high-school language.

As a part of a much larger survey of students in the College of Liberal Arts of Northwestern University, notation was made of the amount of high-school Latin, as well as other languages, presented by each entering freshman. This was studied in relation to the first and second semester average grades. Grouping the students according to the amount of high-school Latin presented at college entrance and keeping the sexes separated, we find that the average grades, both for first and second semester, of these groups coincide very nicely with the amount of high-school Latin. In Table I we see that those having the most Latin tend very definitely to have, on the average, the highest grades.

With such data as these one is tempted to speak of the close relationship existing between the two variables. However, such averages, because the variability of each group is not known, may be very deceptive and indicate only a slight positive relationship. The relationship will be quite low if the variability within each group is great. By working coefficients of correlation between the amount of high-school Latin and grades in college it was found that the relationship was quite low. These coeffi-

[1] C. F. Ross, "A Method of Forecasting College Success," SCHOOL AND SOCIETY, 34: 862, July 4, 1931.

TABLE I

AMOUNT OF HIGH-SCHOOL LATIN AND MEDIAN POINT AVERAGE IN COLLEGE

Units of High-School Latin	Median Point Average in College			
	Women		Men	
	1st sem.	2nd sem.	1st sem.	2nd sem.
4 or more	1.46	1.48	1.44	1.40
3 or $3\frac{1}{2}$	1.17	1.24	1.03	1.04
2 or $2\frac{1}{2}$	1.07	1.14	.90	.88
1 or $1\frac{1}{2}$	.94	1.11	.80	.91
0 or $\frac{1}{2}$	.93	1.05	.72	.90

Students here considered are 1,431 women and 1,182 men who entered Liberal Arts as freshmen. The top row shows the median grades of those who had had four or more units of Latin, the second row the grades of those having had 3 or $3\frac{1}{2}$ units of Latin, etc.

TABLE II

AMOUNT OF HIGH-SCHOOL LATIN AND COLLEGE GRADES

	Men		Women	
	1st sem.	2nd sem.	1st sem.	2nd sem.
Freshmen of 1919	.234	.108	.254	.162
Freshmen of 1923	.180	.321	.377	.252
Freshmen of 1925	.142	.094	.342	.236
Freshmen of 1927	.125	.129	.184	.168
All classes	.162	.129	.258	.199

Relationships are here expressed by Pearson's r. Probable errors range from .02 to .05.

cients, presented in Table II, indicate that the typical correlation is perhaps somewhat less than .20. The coefficient of alienation for such a correlation is about .98; that is, the error of estimate of the predicted college grades is with a knowledge of the amount of high-school Latin taken at best about 2 per cent. smaller than it would be with no information concerning the amount of high-school Latin. Thus it appears that the data of Table I are misleading in respect to their predictive value.

Granting that the amount of high-school Latin taken has only very slight value in forecasting college success, we may still raise the question as to whether this be information which can be gained in no other way. If the amount of Latin shows something other than zero correlation with intelligence tests scores, then there must be some overlapping of these two indicators of college success. Although the tests used with the earlier classes of this study were short and not so valuable as some now available, there is a positive correlation between the tests results and amount of Latin as shown in Table III.

TABLE III

	Men	Women
Freshmen of 1919	.014	.189
Freshmen of 1923	.172	.198
Freshmen of 1925	.229	.234

Coefficients of correlation (Pearson's r) between amount of high-school Latin and intelligence test scores. Probable errors range from .03 to .05.

Table IV shows the correlations between test results and grades. The low correlations found among those for the first two classes are due probably to the relatively short intelligence tests used and possibly also to the fact that a small percentage of the students avoided taking the tests. With these coefficients it is possible to partial out the test to get, perhaps, a better idea of the usefulness of the amount of high-school Latin for forecasting college grades. This gives twelve partial coefficients, which are on the average a little more than .04 less than those presented in Table II. While this does not remove the positive relationship existing between Latin and college grades it does trim somewhat an already meager relationship.

TABLE IV

	Men		Women	
	1st sem.	2nd sem.	1st sem.	2nd sem.
Freshmen of 1919	.363	.194	.418	.249
Freshmen of 1923	.165	.180	.356	.232
Freshmen of 1925	.519	.415	.445	.383

Coefficients of correlation (Pearson's r) between intelligence test scores and college averages. Probable errors range from .03 to .05.

As a corollary to this study of Latin we examined the relationship existing between varying amounts of other high-school languages and college success. French, German and Spanish for the men and women of two college classes were correlated with first and second semester grades. This gave 24 coefficients of correlation, which averaged minus .001 and ranged from plus .10 to minus .13 with 10 of the 24 within the probable error of a zero correlation. Although none of these correlations shows any significant relationship, it is interesting to note that the average for French was plus .10, for German minus .022 and for Spanish minus .042.

In conclusion we may say that these data indicate that the amount of Latin taken in high school is the only language which shows any traceable relationship with the quality of college work done during the first year and that, in this group at least, a knowledge of the amount of high-school Latin is of little value for forecasting college success.

EDWARD L. CLARK
NORTHWESTERN UNIVERSITY

NEW BOOKS IN EDUCATION

CARVER, GEORGE. *Elements of English Composition.* Pp. 150. Doubleday, Doran. $.80.

GOULD, ADRIAN G. and JOSEPH A. DYE. *Exercise and its Physiology.* Pp. xi + 434. 54 figures A. S. Barnes. $3.00.

HILL, VICTOR D., editor. *Bulletin on First-year Latin.* Ohio Latin Service Committee, Cincinnati.

RAGSDALE, CLARENCE E. *Modern Psychologies and Education.* Pp. xviii + 407. Macmillan. $2.25.

RAMEY, ANDREW R. and WINIFRED JOHNSTON. *Readings in English Prose.* Pp. 600. Doubleday, Doran. $2.00.

WOODS, GEORGE B. and CLARENCE STRATTON. *Drills in English.* Pp. 208. Doubleday, Doran. $.80.

WOODY, THOMAS. *New Minds: New Men?* Pp. xiii + 528. Illustrated. Macmillan. $4.00.

EDUCATIONAL REVIEW

Edited by WILLIAM McANDREW

EDITORIAL COMMENT

APPRAISING RADICAL TEACHERS' UNIONS

Criticism of protesting teachers' organizations rarely takes middle ground. In the New York investigation of questionable activities of a local organization, School Board Member Leventritt expressed the opinion of the trustees that instead of a chip on the shoulder the reputed leader of a local organization of teachers carried a whole lumber yard. "Soreheads," "Publicity seekers," "Bolshevists," "Educational under-world," are some of the unpleasant words that have been applied to various organizations in the New York, Chicago, Milwaukee, Minneapolis and Columbus school systems.

On the other hand, Dr. Dewey, Professor Merriam and other high-class speakers at the conventions of these lively people call them "glorious rebels" or "unafraid progressives." Professor M. V. O'Shea has published an unexcited appraisal of the policies of the American Federation of Teachers. This organization takes its stand for freedom from school-board control over teachers' extra-classroom doings, for political and social liberty, for unrestricted use of all resources available to obtain a high level of wages, permanence of tenure, pension allowances and disability payments, for independence from organizations of vested interests. Thoughtful educators and unprejudiced laymen, remarks Professor O'Shea, will probably approve these standards. What the professor criticizes is the absence of professional ideals: promise of high grade devotion to educational and social service, not stressing the intention to cooperate in raising the standards of teaching. Other professions, says Dr. O'Shea, put more emphasis on ethical and professional attainments than they do upon the rights of members. The impression is often created that teachers are more keen for themselves than for their cause. If the public were convinced that teachers desire and intend to make themselves as necessary for the welfare of society as are physicians and sanitary engineers, the establishment of good salaries, tenure and pension would be easier.

Not the Time to Irritate the Public

Elsbree, Alexander, Charles and other students of the status of teachers cite instances of failure of teacher campaigns lost by exhibitions of the lumber yard on the shoulder, and of successful outcomes secured by praise of education and expression of gratification at being engaged in it. When William Ettinger was chairman of the committee that worked for the protection of New York City teachers' incomes by state law, his committee workers were warned: "Leave out the tired teacher, the downtrodden and neglected public servant. Crack up the value education is to the community. Tell how glad you are to be permitted to have these delightful children in charge and how much better you can teach them if you have the means wherewith to make yourselves more fit." Ettinger recommended keeping sad-eyed sisters out of the delegations to Albany but selecting men and women whom the legislators would like to have as companions to their children. John Tildsley, who put a high quality of brains into the successful New York salary campaigns, insisted that pugnacity was a risky luxury for teachers when seeking support of public or legislature. "Keep your selfish interests down. This is a community advantage we are working for. Whether you or I as individuals live in cheap houses and wear poor clothes doesn't matter. The question is, how can the public best be served?" Tildsley's theory was that a citizens' committee is the most efficient medium for presenting pleas to school boards and legislators. "Of course every one will know that we are furnishing such a committee with facts and arguments. Every one will know that it is legitimate that we should. The committee of citizens and parents can be trusted to sift the ultra-selfish demands and leave a sound statement of public policy."

These are times that call for clear brain work. Every board intending to cut educational costs expects the hysterical outbreak, the oratorical furor. In this situation, mannish, contentious women, fed by a long diet of adulation of teachers who have enjoyed the excitement of anticipated skirmishes, men teachers with a record of publicity as leaders of protest, are handicaps because they are the expected. In normal times these people serve as a necessary mustard plaster. Just now they are a risk. School boards are worried and rasped by money troubles. The agitator grates on their raw flesh. They need calm argument and sympathetic coaxing.

A Fresno Example

It seems to me the teachers of Fresno, California, set a splendid example. Their council, led by President Alice Smith, has issued to the public a forty-two page book wherein they tell definitely what they are trying to do for Fresno. They raised, in ten days, $1,377 for the Red Cross relief fund, gave luncheons to civic clubs, organized pupil self-government, gave a "Community night" entertainment, extended the service for handicapped children, beautified school grounds on the street front, boomed beautification of front yards of homes, set up health centers, involved many citizens in the celebration of public school week, pushed thrift in the school banks and got into many community services such as no doubt your schools are aiding effectively. But the topping feature of the Fresno year is the issue of the book telling the taxpayers what the schools are doing, even to popular accounts of reading, writing and so forth, by which the teachers talk shop interestingly to their public. The last page is detachable; it invites you to write on it what better things the teachers should undertake. You send the sheet to Teacher Aspinwall and his committee of seven on professional advancement.

There's not a whine or a boast in the whole book. The teachers dedicate it to Father Hubbard, the superintendent, "who has faith in us and whom we admire and respect."

If every school system set itself to an annual account of its stewardship in this temper, especially excluding the chance of basis for accusation of bragging; if the soreheads, of which our ranks have their share, are given tasks of describing some successful project of the year, if the failures, which every system makes, are taken up and the intention of correcting them is recorded, what effect upon the safety of the educational system do you think it would have? Your answer will be tinged somewhat by the condition of your liver.

What Our Critics Ask

Truly this is a good time for persuading the public into considering the large aspects of the educational service which they support. Criticism of the upper reaches of the public school system increases in volume. The economic crisis turns attention to the dearth of economic teaching. Commissioner Cooper is convinced that we must teach economics, political science and sociology. Impatient at the slowness of their schools to do this, Michigan citizens get their legislature to force it into the schools. University of Chicago editors protest. I try to spank them for it. An unconverted friend among them writes me that laws compelling schools to do something are generally ineffective because they do not supply teachers with the material necessary. Such laws are usually passed to get rid of a bothersome minority group coming to the capital. "You are right that something more should be done about citizenship. Several vigorous efforts are now being made in the direction of preparing material. I am clear in my own mind this is a call for intelligence and not for legislation."

Very good. Better do this thoroughly in the schools than be pushed into it from the outside.

For respectable Bakers, Smiths, Hugheses, Allens and editors are saying that we have fallen down as far as this duty is concerned. I could fill the magazine with criticisms of our failure. It is not pleasant reading. But, as Walter Lippmann observes, it is not the time to pamper schoolmasters as if they were invalids. History shows how real leaders of men have talked to their people in time of trouble, how false it is to offer mere optimism and reassurance. The officer doesn't tell his men the enemy's guns aren't loaded. The captain of a ship in a storm doesn't say the gale isn't blowing.

The true morale lies in facing the menace, in complaining not at all, in finding what is needed and doing it.

Come on, therefore, and take your monthly medicine; doses of counter-irritant and tonic.

MORE BREVIARY

Continuing the verses to be read in the closet by brothers of the major and minor orders of public educational service here is sober reading for you.

32. PURPOSES NEGLECTED. Educational policy makers have neglected essential objectives; they center on subject-matter instead of the legitimate civic aim. PROFESSOR DAVID SNEDDEN. "What's Wrong With American Education?" 1927.

33. AMERICA A BY-WORD IN THE WORLD. Our politics are notorious; our lawlessness, a by-word. If we are not each concerned with the public weal our education may train prospective pirates and cutthroats. Humanizing the social order is tied up with humanizing the curriculum. Our education, aiming at culture, has not provided leadership in a democratic society. PROFESSOR BOYD BODE. Modern Educational Theories. 1927.

34. NOT GOOD ENOUGH. We schoolmasters must produce a better type of citizen. FRANK BOYNTON. President Nat. Assn. of School Superintendents. 1929.

35. THE NEED IS GREAT. Education has for ages aimed at leadership by the few. The political boss is robbing the many of their inheritance from the Revolution. DEAN JAMES RUSSELL. "The Nation's Schools." Nov., 1930.

36. SIDE ISSUE. We're only scratching the surface yet. The planting of civic virtue, the cultivation of it, will never amount to much if the schools keep on considering it a side issue. PROF. GEORGE STRAYER. "The Nation's Schools." Sep., 1930.

37. DISAPPOINTMENT. The public schools, organized and supported to keep democracy healthy, are conducted as though the patriot fathers proposed a plan that God would take care of, somehow. Meantime more and weightier thinkers are becoming dissatisfield with the failure of education to address itself to the problems of democracy. Few educators realize their own fatuity. CHARLES PROSSER, CHARLES ALLEN. "Have We Kept the Faith?" 1927.

38. SCHOOL'S NEGLECT OF THE MAIN DUTY. School has forgotten what it was charged with. It is not educating boys and girls to government. They grow up, easy marks for hoodwinking by political bosses. HENRY RYAN, American Legion address to teachers. Des Moines. 1921.

39. MUST MAKE EVERYBODY CARE. We have run up the flag on the schoolhouse but we are saying nothing of what should be done. We must see to it that every citizen cares. RUTH BRYAN OWEN, M.C. To Nat. Ed. Assn. 1922.

40. NO RATIONAL PATRIOTISM. Critics of the products of our schools have not failed to point out that these young people have not, as a rule, acquired a rational patriotism or a capacity to view problems from other than a local point. It is small wonder that agencies find in the minds of our citizens a fertile field for the seeds of discord. WILLIAM G. CARR. "Education for World Citizenship." 1928.

41. THE FORMALISM USED IN CIVIC TRAINING PRODUCES AVERSION. Educators might well memorialize legislatures and school boards to put an end to the frequent salutes to the flag. Reiteration is not educational. Commanders have learned that it causes indifference and even antipathy. They avoid too much repetition of oaths of allegiance. LEWIS A. MAVERICK, University of California. "Guidance in Citizenship." 1931.

42. THE FORM, NOT THE PRINCIPLES OF GOVERNMENT IS TAUGHT. Nearly everybody agrees that citizenship must be continuous throughout the school but too often it is tucked away in the corner of the high-school senior year to which the fewest children arrive and is a lifeless description of form not of principles. ARTHUR DUNN, American Red Cross, at convention of National Education Association. 1921.

43. MUST MEET RESPONSIBILITIES OF A DEMOCRACY. Democracy without education for citizenship is a failure, schools may help the participant earn a living but they must meet the responsibilities of democracy. EDWARD GAY, Editor, N. Y. Evening Post in "The World's Work." Oct., 1923.

44. THERE IS MORE NEED AT PRESENT. In every generation there is a need of examining anew the foundations of government. At the present time this duty is more imperative than usual. For we are passing through a period of criticism upon our institutions that has created an unwarranted depreciation of their value and of solicitude for their preservation. DAVID JAYNE HILL. Former Asst. Sec'y of State. Diplomat and historian. "The People's Govt." 1915.

45. LACK OF CONCRETE PLAN. The school's obligation is to train its pupils to be good citizens, the difficulty in fulfilling this demand has been due to lack of adequate concrete presentation. GEORGE D. STRAYER. Introduction to "Citizenship Through Education." 1929.

46. DEMAND FOR BETTER POLITICAL TRAINING IS INSISTENT. More than a million men and women have entered the high calling of teaching. Their obligation is that citizenship may become better. There are insistent and sustained demands that citizenship be better taught. CLYDE B. MOORE. "Citizenship Through Education." 1929.

47. SCHOOL GIVES A FANCIFUL PICTURE. School gives the child a fanciful picture of popular government. To him is revealed the people authorizing persons to carry on public business. These delegates work for the people. An amazingly large number of Americans grow up without bothering to revise these ideas. Simple investigation uncovers the fact that the people have very little to do with choosing public officials. Only when one is caught with his fingers in the till is any one aroused. The recital of a creed, the knowledge of the theoretical form of government, have gotten us nowhere. The responsibility of the single citizen is not felt. The people, as a whole, presume they are living in a democracy. As a matter of fact it is an oligarchy of machine-made statesmen. HEINRICH E. BUCHHOLZ. "U. S. a Study in Democracy." 1926.

48. MERE UNIVERSAL EDUCATION WILL NOT INSURE DEMOCRACY. Americans are accustomed to hear the public school lauded as the foundation of democracy. They fall into the mistaken belief that any scheme of universal education is democratic. The example of imperial Germany refutes this belief. The goal toward which it led should awaken us to a national consciousness and a new devotion to democracy. What is needed is a thoroughgoing reform, not compromise. CHARLES HUBBARD JUDD. "The Evolution of a Democratic School System." 1918.

BOOKS OF BENEFIT

THE purr of the presses that print professional books goes cheerily on, albeit Ann Arborite New Yorker Cheney, in his master study of publishing, shows money lost alarmingly and high-schools weaning possible readers from love of literature. Here is a varied ration for you for this month: politics more and more, increasing insistence that high schools must mend their ways, problems of boys, praise of teaching, college crises, teaching different subjects, supervision, measuring it, and an American symphony.

POLITICS FOR SCHOOLS

"WE must wake 'em, Mr. Lumley," "Positively, Mr. Bode." Thus may these two authors have sung each other into action writing their big civics.[1] Not so much by the assembling of acres of facts and miles of details, but by real samples of engagements in the actual business of living must the idea of democracy be developed. This is the writers' creed.

Their plan covers the candidate for citizenship, his heredity, environment, habits and growth. The candidate is everybody.

Institutions and how to live with them, labor and capital, schools, movies, churches and government are discussed.

The book is in the mood of straight talk to the reader quoting numerous respected masters on the duties and satisfactions of courage, generosity, industry, unselfishness, progress and maintenance of ideals. Too many of you dislike stirring things up. You dodge discussion

[1] Frederick E. Lumley, Boyd H. Bode, "Ourselves and the World. The Making of an American Citizen." McGraw-Hill Book Company. 591 pp. $3.00.

of the liquor law. This is not the way to live in a democracy. The democratic way of progress is through discussion, agitation and thinking.

Our authors give attention to corrupt government in New York, Philadelphia, Cincinnati and other cities. They compare the types of city organizations and see the outlook full of hope. They describe the weakness of courts, the difficulty of getting justice, and conclude with 50 pages of present-day political problems that schools should incline all their beneficiaries toward settling.

AS WE ARE AND WHAT WE SHOULD BE

The National Arts Club sponsored a proposition of Mr. John G. Agar, former member of the New York City Board of Education, to offer a prize of $3,000 for the best book on "The Soul of America." Professor Bowden, Youngstown College, Ohio, won the award. His book[2] offsets the literature of despair which has increased since the war. The soul of civilization, of culture, of politics, of education, of art and literature, the indictments against us, the integration going on, are the contents of this engaging essay.

We began, ruled by a privileged class inherited from the old world. The masses supplanted soon the American aristocracy and wild politics roared. Ostensibly an extension of the second phase, but really the rise of a small class to political and economic power, is our present situation, not dissimilar to the conditions that ruined Rome. On hearing of the election of Jefferson, the brother of the President of Yale College exclaimed, "America now has a government of knaves and block-heads." As property and other limiting qualifications for suffrage were wiped out, voting and office-holding lost much of its attraction for large numbers of the former ruling class. As they withdrew, novices on the make assumed control. Now, the small group who govern are no longer aristocrats but politicians dominated by bosses. The better class of professional men have withdrawn. The commercial class has done the same. The Republican party is the champion of wealth, prosperity, the strong, the smug, but has not forgotten how to appeal to the small-town ego and to rural simplicity. The Democrats are a party of protest. The demagogue is in his glory. But, in a way, he is a gain, for he is a vaccine against revolution. In a rich and undeveloped country, busy people could create a comfortable life and let their political duties alone. That day is over. Our national evils and scandals are our own fault. The founders of the republic had no illusions of virtue in office-holders, even elected by the people instead of named by the king. They warned again and again that eternal vigilance, honest suspicion, perpetual scrutiny of the doings of representatives is the price of safety. Big business, a corporate press, bossism, crooked politics, tax iniquities, were promoted by American citizens, acquiesced in by millions of them. There was prosperity enough in spite of robbery. Prohibition has not increased our disrespect for law; it has merely revealed it. It has not created the wild high school or college revels: it has served to call attention to parental neglect. There is no revolt of youth; it is copying its elders.

Appraiser Bowden lists, on the other hand, a large collection of gains and promise. No circumstances lead to a conclusion that our democracy is doomed. Popular government can be made effective by a competent school system. Education has come to be largely by formula. Ancient wisdom has been imported to be used occasionally as ornament but is of little use in modern, changing life. Much of our school machinery is geared to old habits of a fixed order. But an improvement is under way.

These bits, taken from various pages of Professor Bowden's book, give you a taste of him. He is head of the social sciences department in his college. He sees the progress America is making; he does not blink the failures now persisting. His dissatisfaction with you is decided, but not peevish. You are the appointed of history to bring America to what your fathers called its destiny and you had better not put off the task a single day.

ATTACKING THE GANGRENE OF DEMOCRACY

A red-hot preface to a text book is Chester Maxey's.[3] He has just written a notable civics.

[2] Robert Douglas Bowden, "In Defense of Tomorrow." The Macmillan Company, New York. 210 pp. $2.00.

[3] Chester Collins Maxey, "You and your Government." D. C. Heath and Company, Boston. 593 pages. $1.76.

I remember this young Lochinvar, fourteen years ago, training folks for public service right here in New York, then doing the same for Cleveland. Now he is back in his native country of the Chinook, the Evergreen State, professor of politics in his own Whitman College. I should guess him to be growing on to forty years by this time and he certainly has learned how to write. Listen to bits from his reasons for his book:

No one is sorry the old civics has dried up and died. It was doomed by its own lack of sap. The current "social civics," triumphant, is romanticizing the educational process. It is not making the culture of political-mindedness a primary objective. The real problems of community life are not emphasized. Some of the worst-governed cities are notable pioneers in the new civics. That racketeering, bossism and corrupt alliances between business and politics are complacently tolerated by multitudes whose minds have been nurtured on the new civics in their school days is something for you, the schoolmaster, to ponder. Political apathy is the gangrene of democracy. Not only is the new civics weak but it is growing weaker.

So, my remonstrant Maxey makes a book stressing problems, responsibilities, duties, conscious of the popularity of the community civics which works upon wonder and pride for our accomplishments. He falls below none of the new books in varied and attractive pictures of fire engines and Hoover dams, but your responsibility to pay back for all the benefits cooperative living has given you is skilfully and persistently kept prominent.

The author's manner of working up your recognition of the need of laws, constitutions, cooperation and sacrifice is singularly effective. His discussion of force as an essential of community action and as a right of only the community is masterly. Your rights, benefits and duties are brought together all through the book. Health, education, vocation, the ills of community life, your political laziness, how the bosses are able to rob you, the politics of your town, state and nation, world citizenship, are some of the major topics mettlesome Maxey makes you discuss by means of his frequent "little adventures in civic thinking," found at the end of each chapter.

HIGH-SCHOOL TEACHERS' DEMOCRACY

On two postulates, that the large purpose of the secondary school is preparation for citizenship and that democracy, therefore, is the true relationship of teachers and supervisors, Alberty and Thayer[4] build a remarkably high-class body of counsel for improving high school teaching. They have a healthy skepticism for current scientific applications to education. They have gathered into compact space a wealth of prevailing dogma which they undermine in a workmanlike manner: teacher rating, pupil testing, lesson planning, line-and-staff organization, efficiency formulas.

It may be good business organization or military advantage that has subordinates do as they are told, but the imposition of a supervisor's will upon his colleagues is not in accordance with the democratic ideal. Teachers can not be turned into regiments nor mass-workers. Hamilton showed that the most efficient soldier had no right to think. But a teacher, alone with her class, knowing its members as no one else can, is meeting situations every hour that require adjustment, new resource, thinking. The best supervisor is the one who gets teachers to realize their highest potentialities. Only by a democratic cooperation of the supervisor and teachers can the school more fully contribute to the preparation of boys and girls for an effective participation in democratic citizenship. If he is to instil democracy, the teacher must get some from his own experience.

Ably developed, well fortified by sound principles, a body of usages is offered by the authors covering faculty organization, teacher committees, councils, curriculum making, professional study clubs and the general field of teachers' work at the high school level. A characteristic permeating the work is a largeness of spirit with which teaching is regarded.

HELP FOR HIGH SCHOOL

Half the boys and girls who should be in high school are now there. In 1890 only 4 per cent. of eligibles were attending, and superintendent Maxwell, then of Brooklyn, was saying

[4] H. B. Alberty, V. T. Thayer, "Supervision in the Secondary School." D. C. Heath and Company, Boston. 471 pp. $2.00.

in his official reports that many were in who ought to be out. It is now well established that all children of high school age should be in. The wail of the colleges that a parallel demand from all sorts and conditions of youth is being made upon college, the highest unit of the public education service is only forty years behind the times. With an opening chapter upon such interesting changes as have bewildered the secondary teachers in our generation, Dean Edmonson, Professor Roemer, and Principal Bacon[5] set out to record the steps by which the high-school chaos is being reduced to order.

How shall you organize your high school teachers, attend to office routine, care for the building, make a program of recitations, control the pupils, run a guidance program, make the assembly worth while, supervise teaching, get study done, organize examinations and marks, establish college relations and keep the extra-curriculars on a worth-while basis? These problems, with an abundance of concrete instances, relation of usages to logical justification, and comparison of values are treated by the three authors.

They will have it that citizenship is logically the chief aim of schools maintained by a democracy. When these men go into the vexed problem of college influence upon high school they want a recognition of the civic duty. "Citizenship requirements for admission to college should be emphasized in order that the high school may encourage its students toward a high quality." "The college should ask for full information regarding an applicant's rank in school citizenship. It should reject an applicant whose record in this is unsatisfactory." This is pretty good, but a principal worth his salt need not throw this burden higher up. Let him refuse recommendation. The Evansville high schools will not issue diplomas unless and until the boy and girl show, by their civic knowledge and conduct, promise of worthy citizenship.

Practice in cooperative government gets in their book much merited attention. Set up as a promoter of honest democracy, filled with youth at the time when social and political problems begin to be of vital interest, a high school marked by the continuance of rule by scholastic monarchs is a tragic anomaly. Government, studied and practiced, general welfare, economics, politics, defects of our management of civic affairs, investigation must be an essential of high-school work.

It is a forward-looking book, mindful of changes that must be made, but careful not to discourage the dear old scholiasts by nagging them on too rapidly. Be considerate of the dead.

[5] James B. Edmonson, Joseph Roemer, Francis Bacon, ''Secondary-School Administration.'' The Macmillan Company, New York. 483 pp. $2.25.

HIGH SCHOOLS FACING A CRISIS

THAT scouting troop in Teachers College—Monroe, Counts, Kandel, Alexander, Wilson, Del Manzo, and Miss McMurray—who for eight years have been questioning the nations of the world as to the state of education, deem the current criticism of high-school policies of such moment as to warrant devoting the whole of the current year-book[6] to the condition of secondary education in different countries. The situation abroad is startlingly like affairs with us. "What are you going to do with your traditional course," asks Australian Teachers-College Executive Percival Cole, "now that the thousands unfitted for it are coming in?" "The high school is not fitted for the newcomers," comments Austrian Viktor Fadrus, of the Ministry of Instruction. Professor Maurice Weber, of the Versailles Lycée, notes the conviction of France that her education is organized in a conception of culture outmoded for all except limited groups. So speaks Argentina, Chile, Czecho-Slovakia, Hungary and Japan. You may well be amazed at the similarity of views of these scattered observers. You wonder at the persistence of our English brothers in hoping that the beloved tradition of their secondary schools, *viz.*, the training gotten chiefly through games, is going to satisfy the problems of the people. Another surprise is the glow of universal interest the sixteen contributors have put into their descriptions, problems and perplexities of local situations.

[6] I. L. Kandel, editor, ''Expansion of Secondary Education.'' Sixth Year-book of the International Institute of Teachers College, Columbia University, Bureau of Publication. 543 pp. $3.50.

Dijon's Problems Read Like Detroit's

Harold Clark is a newcomer in the year-book company. He certainly comes in with a stride. He marches directly into the trouble American high-school people have approached with averted eyes. "Up to this present no one has made out the case for providing secondary education for all on economic grounds. It would cost two billion dollars a year. High school expansion has been enormous but it has mostly meant doing more of what was already being done rather than meeting the new needs. There will be a steady growth of high school applicants. They are being forced into institutions unfitted to serve them. A large portion of the population can not profit by the sort of education available. In Illinois high schools over 50 per cent. of the seniors were found intending to go into four professions, only two and a half per cent. of the employed can make a living in these callings."

High Schools Need Revising

These are some of the hard facts set out by Dr. Clark in a strong and nervous style likely to cause considerable disturbed blinking of eyes.

It is absurd to expect to revive the old high school policy of rejecting and driving out all except "good students." Good student and poor student are the product of an educational system and an assumption that a substantial portion of the children are going to fail. Is there any inherent reason why every student may not be a good student if he is doing the educational task appropriate to him? Every student can not make a good record in the academic sense. For many good boys the academic sense is nonsense.

Really, you must read Clark's brilliant essay if you are superintendent, high-school teacher or member of the school board. After collecting the universal facts about high schools he shows how they lead to a solution which, if suddenly presented to a conservative educator, would seem wild indeed. Then he slips in an observation of our most widely accepted leader, John Dewey, which shows the Clark proposition to be inevitable. What the prophets have foretold as a far-off perfection this comprehending Clark shows to be pushing towards us and close at hand.

A CHEERY HIGH-SCHOOL VIEW

Everybody enjoys Fretwell's talk. You can now have many profitable hours of it in a cheerful five-hundred pages on what the school-masters used to consider the odds and ends of high-school life.[7] He lays down the purpose of his essay as a gentle protest against permitting a phase of school, in which so much of pupils' and teachers' life is put, to go on unplanned. Often the extra activities have been tolerated or suppressed. Some have been foolish; some of high value. All can be immensely improved by making the most of the human drive behind them. Accordingly, Fretwell, in the light of a distinctively wide experience as high-school principal and supervisor, boy-scout official, army recreation provider, and college professor, retaining an unspoiled sympathy with youth, discusses the usage in hundreds of designated schools. He analyzes a great number of books and articles on the extra-curriculars, the list alone occupying 65 pages. So important have these once rejected affairs become.

These are his themes: Seven principles to work by, the home room, class organizations, pupil participation in government, councils, assemblies, clubs, high-school newspaper, magazine, hand-book, annual, commencement, athletics, finances. Both junior and senior high schools are covered.

Permeating his presentation is Fretwell's incurable optimism for youth and the country. We have a democracy, he says. Our pupils will live in one. Their injection of their own inventions into the autocracy of the high school shows that they are set on living on democratic principles. It is our plain duty to see that their respect and affection for democracy becomes a delight.

AN INANE INSTITUTION

According to the best and latest usages it is now rather late to plan the commencement exercises for next May or June. Whether yours are under way or not, Professor McKown's lively treatise[8] will help. In selecting him to

[7] Elbert K. Fretwell, "Extra-Curricular Activities in Secondary Schools." Houghton Mifflin Company, Boston. 552 pp. $2.75.

[8] Harry C. McKown, "Commencement Activities." The Macmillan Company, New York. 310 pp. $2.50.

write this book the Macmillan Company made a happy choice. He has a keen sense of the ridiculous and a talent for sharing it with you.

His concept of educational aims are high. His indignation at neglect of them is deep. His exposure of persisting stupidities in graduation ceremonies is vivid. His substitutes for them are easily attainable, are employed in hundreds of good schools and seem such that, once described, they will be adopted henceforth.

For both high and elementary schools he gives a convincing presentation of the purposes and values of commencement and promotion exercises. He quotes scathing protests of persons worth listening to who score the meaningless waste of many persisting programs. Page after page of definite plans and usages are here offered by an enthusiastic and sympathetic educator who summarizes a study and analysis of more than six thousand programs from every part of the United States.

PASSING PHASE DOESN'T PASS

VERY much out of the ordinary is Head Master O'Neil's discussion of the present day change in youth.[9] The smug dictum that its problems are no more serious now than before, that there is only a temporary aberration is wicked and dangerous. The motor car, the movies, the press, the hip-flask, the "new" girl, and, most of all, the twentieth century parent have injected profound damage and disturbance into young humanity. So, Foster-Father O'Neil, who has taught under the same roof all sorts and conditions of boys, talks knowingly of the home, youth's cleverness, its view-points, its parentage, its misdemeanors, its promising qualities, and offers remedies that he has found good.

COLLEGE CONFLICT

LET us hope, for your sake, that you know the H. W. Wilson Company,[10] compilers, classifiers, makers of abstracts, summaries and lists, for they are savers of the schoolmaster's time. Their attractive books, in the series called "The Reference Shelf," continue to come along: one on "Soldiers' Bonus," others on "Academic Freedom," "Prohibition," "School and College Athletics," "Unemployment," "Disarmament," "Federal Department of Education," etc.

It is a library of current controversy, of public problems moving toward settlement, a provoker of thought, a Thesaurus for debaters.

Vol. VII., No. 4, contains fresh criticism and defense of college procedure by Gilman, Butler, Snedden, Association of University Professors, and others. Arguments are formulated in the shape of "resolves" and briefs. There is a bibliography of three hundred titles and a summary of recent experiments in university administration.

A PHELPS PHYLACTERY[11]

ANY teacher can force any pupil to attend classes, to hand in written work, in other words, to keep engagements. This kind of discipline can be enforced and not necessarily disagreeably, and it is certainly preparation for the art of living.

If a teacher tells a boy or girl that work for others is ridiculous, that they ought to get all they can for themselves and not bother about public service, he will not be believed. They know better.

Universities, like monasteries, should not be of the world. They serve an ideal which the world has never understood and never can—pure learning without regard to its practical value.

But there is only one department of the modern university where there is an intellectual atmosphere. This is the graduate school.

The best way to deal with youth is not by a new system but rather by obtaining the best teachers.

A football coach is in many instances the ablest teacher connected with the "institution of learning."

But there is nothing spectacular about teachers. The only way one of them can attract public attention is by doing something scandalous.

Many think teaching is a dull affair. On the contrary, it is wildly exciting, adventurous, romantic, with no two days alike.

[9] Jerold O'Neil, "That Problem Called the Modern Boy." Sears Publishing Company, New York. 233 pp. $2.50.

[10] James G. Hodgson, compiler, "Trends in University Education." H. W. Wilson Company, 950 University Ave., New York. 163 pp. 90 cents.

[11] William Lyon Phelps, "The Excitement of Teaching." Horace Liveright, New York. 80 pp. $1.50.

These are a few blossoms plucked from Philosopher Phelps's 1931 garden of flowering philosophy. A neat little work, the third of Horace Liveright's Delta Kappa Pi lectures on education, John Dewey and Dorothy Canfield Fisher being two other gardeners with "Sources of a Science of Education" and "Learn or Perish," respectively. Professor Phelps cheered the profession with a glad morning song almost twenty years ago. We used to open teachers' meetings with verses from his "Teaching in School and College." His humor, gayety, understanding and solidity is perennial and in full flower here.

EDUCATIONAL IDEALS

A MAXIMUM chance that everybody shall have opportunity for richness of life, a necessity that society continually improve, a political philosophy recognizing individual rights, are the three essentials of education as Professor Valentine sees America from his classroom window in San Francisco State Teachers College.[12]

That science is not enough, that the other qualities that go to make an art are needed, what they are, how they may be come at, basic ideals, higher technique, development of thinking, social participation, personality, are the themes of the author's discourse.

COMPASSED WITH A CLOUD OF WITNESSES

THIS then is the foretelling of Joseph the Prophet.[13] Education will get on the road marked for it. It will be put there not by its leaders but by its times. Eventually it will leave its leaders behind. It will get to new leaderships and new objectives, perhaps of the sort indicated by the readings in my books, or some such sort at any rate. The community needs a center of intelligence. For this the first school grew up. A fallacious psychology came along and the school grew "academic," shut itself in the schoolhouse. Its intelligence became a thing embalmed in books with no concern of the community's work. The result is seen in the graduate, an irrelevant fellow who might perhaps adorn the world but otherwise is of little use. It remains for the school to escape the classroom and become of the community.

Hart's is a documentary interpretation of the history of education. In their turn, in their own words, Thucydides, Socrates, Plato, Virgil, Cicero, Tacitus, Anselm, Tertullian, Bacon, Luther, Milton, Locke, Spenser, Huxley, Eliot, James, Butler, Dewey, many other masters, expound in these pages the high aims. Their shots that fell short of the mark are not here recorded. Who cares for misses? Their yet unrealized ideals are ordered in battalions marching toward a great objective clearly mapped.

Historian Hart has found a school achieving its destiny at least in a preliminary way. It has sloughed off academicism. It is tackling community problems. It is the center of usable knowledge and high endeavor.

Come on, ask your question: "Where is this school, this community?"

To which the circumspect witness answers. "I, myself, have visited it but I shall not name it, because dull humans finding a great thing being done, breathe a sigh of relief exclaiming, 'These people can do that in their town but it can't be done in our part of the country.'"

Dear me, it reminds you of what Colonel Parker said his visitor concluded in Quincy, or what Wirt's said in Gary, or Caldwell's in the Lincoln School, or Miss Parkhurst's in Dalton. Old Hallsworthy used to say, "If men can think a Utopia they can make one."

PULLING DOWN THE BALLOONS

NEARLY all the current writers on educational theory that Professor Snedden[14] reads are "excessively deductive, abstract and vague. They are over-ready with facile generalizations and over-shy of concrete example. The foundations of education are still resting far more on faith and prepossession than on clear knowledge. This is especially true in respect to what is called cultural training. Culture has had a long use in designating decorative, embellishing qualities which seem to many furthest removed from utilitarian life."

With this introduction Dr. Snedden goes back to foundations and brings into the realm of cul-

[12] P. F. Valentine, "The Art of The Teacher." D. Appleton and Company, New York. 299 pp. $2.00.

[13] Joseph K. Hart, "Creative Moments in Education." Henry Holt and Company, New York. 476 pp. $3.00.

[14] David Snedden, "Cultural Educations and Common Sense." The Macmillan Company, New York. 324 pp. $2.00.

ture such things as good citizenship, American traits, practical science and skill, health gains, nature knowledge and vocations. Culture means all the achievements of a people, no less. He analyzes and classifies cultures. He collects an anthology of famous definitions of it and appraises them: Mathew Arnold's, Eliot's, Nietzsche's, Mencken's, Will Durant's, Kuno Francke's, Bernard Shaw's, John Dewey's, Alsworth Ross's, Herbert Spencer's, Kenneth Macgowan's and more. He surveys advancing culture in America and gives you a tonic chapter to read when you are blue. When Examiner Snedden takes up cultural education through schools his characteristic pertinence intends to make you uneasy, and does. Our foolish high schools, our lack of appraisal, our neglect of training for better civic, social, political America, a list of definite changes required, are masterly handled. Collegiate education gets a similar diagnosis. After this comes constructive treatment of culture through reading, fine arts, science and personality refinements.

If you were given a test question, "What living man comes nearest to a Socrates?," I imagine you would at once write the name of this American Athenian. In his manner and spirit at the search for truth, in his demand that ideas be thoroughly and accurately defined, in his detection of specious error, in his gadfly sting into wild assumption, this California-born philosopher could suitably have an "S" put between his two names. This latest book is one of the best bracers in the list of educational therapy works.

INTERLUDE FOR MENTAL REST

BERTRAND RUSSELL was visited by an enthusiast who desired to study Russell's system of philosophy.

"But I have to confess," he said, "that in the only book of yours I have read there is only one statement I can understand and that one isn't true."

"What is the statement?"

"It is the assertion that Julius Caesar is dead."

"Why do you not accept that?"

The guest drew himself up and replied with dignity, "Because I am Julius Caesar."

Being alone with this visitor in a flat, Russell got to the street as quickly as possible and found a keeper looking for an escaped inmate.

SOLID FOOD

"THEY have read some books and are able to recall from them incidents and some ideas. They are not able to use what they recollect. They stop at the recall or the naming of facts. They have no power to indicate significance of them. To them a book is a book. Reading has not been for them a genuine experience. Literature is to them apart from real life. It is something to be mastered for an examination." Who are these lost souls? The applicants for college who fail in the English entrance examination. What Dante here pictures them? The college entrance board's commission on English.[15] Their book is one of those few that are to be chewed and digested. The commission method of research, a history of English examination, comparisons, reproductions of answer papers, their marks and appraisals, discussion of the causes of failure, relations of examination marks to later achievement, critique of present secondary-school English teaching, the educational value of the examinations, recommendations, bibliography, are some of the pertinent chapters. The investigators who write this report weave no garlands for themselves, for the makers of the tests, nor for the markers. They early uncover the trick most of us perform of making a decision intuitively and thereafter fitting the constituent figures to sum into our chosen answer. They bewail our failure to require good English in other than English classes. They have produced a manual that must seem to the careful reader an indispensable text to be studied by teachers of English, whether preparing pupils for examinations or "for life."

STUDIES OF STUDIOUSNESS

PROFESSOR EURICH'S investigation,[16] carried on independently, makes a good companion to the Harvard report on English. Likewise, it is treasure trove for English teachers everywhere. It describes the diagnosis made of numerous students, the special exercises given to help them read and study effectively, comprehension and retention tests, and vocabulary gains. The 100 items in the self-rating scale for studious-

15 Charles Swain Thomas, Chairman, ''Examining the Examination in English.'' Harvard University Press, Cambridge. 295 pp. $2.00.

16 Alvin C. Eurich, ''Reading Ability of College Students.'' University of Minnesota Press, Minneapolis. 208 pp. $2.00.

ness is a masterpiece. When I consider how my days were spent in the blindness of my college years, when I recall the real desire we youngsters had to learn how to use our minds, when I remember the unscientific hints coaxed out of classmates and older students and from Todd's "Students' Manual" and Hamerton's "Intellectual Life," when I review the utter lack of teaching how to study—not a member in the whole faculty ever opened his head upon the subject—I rail at the fate that brought this Eurich into my ken just fifty years late. But, Son Alvin, that's not your fault. I'll make the most of you. From now on I am resolved to lead a better life, thanks to the hundred guide-posts you set up on the straight and narrow trail.

POETRY FOR SCHOOL

DR. LAW[17] gathers poems to fill 345 pages, sorts them as tellers of stories, as showing the sacrifice and tragedy of war, as exhibiting the beauty of speech, as picturing the past, as painting nature, and as featuring the inner life. He subjoins brief biographies, writes of the teaching usages he has found successful, gives questions for aiding appreciation and encouragement for poetical composition by pupils.

A BELOVED LIBRARIAN

AT times when consulting the catalogue of a well-organized library, especially if you have ever attempted getting at anything in a Paris collection, you feel a desire to place a wreath on the unknown and unsung benefactor who has worked out the details for your getting what you want when you want it. Arthur Bostwick, former Montclair teacher, now head of the St. Louis Public Library, is bringing out a series of biographies to save these benefactors from oblivion. The third book[18] is the life and work of Charles Ammi Cutter. By making a catalogue on a new plan he unlocked the treasuries of the Boston Atheneum Library and set a model followed by other collections. He formulated rules for cataloguing which were successfully printed for thirty-nine years. He was a charter member of the American Library Association. He suffered under the resistant attitude of the Atheneum trustees and plunged joyfully into the management of the new Forbes Library in Northampton. He devised classifications of titles, edited the *library journal,* taught library management, made friends and at the age of 66 passed from earth. The book is full of incident and human touches.

LITERARY EXCURSIONS: ENTERTAINING GUIDE

YOU remember Carl Holliday for his excursions into our colonial literature and his gathering of the flowers of Southern poetry. Here he comes with a beautiful bouquet of exotics,[19] Egyptian, Babylonian, Assyrian, Hindu, Persian, Chinese, Hebrew. It is a comparative literature. The gardens are of the least familiar to the well-read American.

The every-day philosophy of Egypt, the lush poetry of Persia, the fascinating tales of India, the humor of the ancient Chinese, the grandeur of the Old Testament, the charm of the New, the homely comfort of Talmud, are illuminated by the high light of Dr. Holliday's appreciative comment.

"If one rails and insults thee, answer not. Even thus shalt thou conquer him," advises Ptah-Hotep, sixty centuries ago in Egypt. "Grant honor to thy wife and love her exceedingly. Give her ointments and cosmetics galore. Fail not to caress her every day."

"To-day," comments Carl, "psychologists, judges and thinking men in general are seeking to discover the cause of failures of marriage." The "Precepts of Ptah-Hotep" should be prominent in the Reno Public Library, or rather in the one back home.

From Sadi, the Persian: "Some one asked a muezzin of atrocious voice how much he was paid for reciting the prayers. " 'Paid? I am not paid. I recite for the sake of God.'

" 'Then, for God's sake, don't?' "

Mark my words, some rascal is going to twist the following tale from an old Yuan Chinese classic into a slander upon a commendable quality of a modern canny race.

A frugal father, nearing his end, enjoins his son not to waste his patrimony on an expensive coffin, but to use the old watering trough.

[17] Frederick Houk Law, ''The Stream of English Poetry.'' The Century Company, New York. 383 pp. $1.10.

[18] William Parker Cutter: ''Life of Charles Ammi Cutter.'' American Library Association, Chicago. 67 pp. $2.75.

[19] Carl Holliday, ''The Dawn of Literature.'' Thomas Y. Crowell Company, New York. 367 pp. $3.50.

"But, father, it's too short."

"No matter, you can chop off enough of me to get a fit. But, attend to this: don't use the good axe I paid to have sharpened; borrow a neighbor's."

Even at the moment of death, too weak to speak, the old man held up two fingers to show the watchers they were wastrels in burning two candles rather than one.

Superb flashes of poetry, penetrative fables, fascinating tales, exalted ideals, every-day philosophy, live in these pages, enriched by the comments of a professor who has spent thirty years discovering literary treasures and passing them to others, making some of his own.

PIERCING THE MISTS OF HISTORY

Gathering and comparing traditions, art movements, language peculiarities, of the great peoples, Eugen Georg,[20] taking care not to be stampeded into the fascinating field of too easy conclusion, describes the probable origin of the civilizations on earth at the beginning of recorded history. Vividly he pictures the Asiatic onrush, the birth and decline of the Orient, the Aryan Odyssey, world commerce six thousand years ago, the behavior of the moon, and events seen as "rhythm" and "spiral."

The tremendous buildings on islands of the South Seas, in Yucatan, in other places which the world forgot, the author subjects to examination. The similarity of form in these to structures in ancient Egypt he can not reconcile with a theory that the line of connection was across Asia and by way of Alaska. The Atlantis legend he examines anew and finds it the more probable. The science of the Yucatan Mayas, their use of zero and logarithm amaze him as he makes them do us. His tracing the pedigree of the bogie man, the Schwarzenmann, the bête noire, his incursions into biology, ethnology, astronomy, archeology and history make entertaining reading.

SCIENTIFIC ATTITUDE

Houghton Mifflin Company offer a revised and enlarged edition of "The Science of Everyday Life."[21] Arranged in learning units this junior-high-school text, with narrative, pictures, projects, reports and questions, teaches how we use air, water and foods, how we control the forces of nature in building, lighting and heating our homes. There is "Clothing and its Care," and "The Work of the World."

The workbook guides the boy and girl first to get a clear notion of the problem, then to observe with care, to experiment intelligently, to criticize results, to arrive at a conclusion. To fit individual needs, the problems are designated as required, optional, and for advanced credit. Tips to the student are many and direct. The separate objective tests: true-false, completion, multiple choice, etc., are accompanied by fool-proof directions for the teacher.

BRITISH EDUCATIONAL CLASSICS

Professor J. Dover Wilson, who assembled the specialists on British education in the volume reviewed here last year, is, from his chair in King's College, University of London, editing, in collaboration with Professor F. A. Cavenagh, chair of education, University College, Swansea, a series of Landmarks in the History of Education. The Cambridge University Press is bringing it out. In preparation are: Newman's "Idea of a University," Arnold's "Culture and Anarchy," Spencer's "Education." The design is to reprint scarce but important texts making educational classics available for students. The first of the series[22] contains a spirited introduction by Professor Cavanagh putting the Mills in a historical setting and criticizing them in comparison with present-day ideas. James Mills' Encyclopedia Britannica article is more than a hundred years old. It was a text-book at Cambridge. The Cavanagh volume reprints also so much of John Stuart Mill's Autobiography as bears on education, reproduces his famous Inaugural Address as Rector of St. Andrews, and carries a generous offering of informative and critical notes.

SUPERVISION BOILED DOWN

Supervision isn't visiting schools, nor making inspirational addresses, nor community work, nor planning specifications for buildings, nor

[20] Eugen Georg, "The Adventure of Mankind," translated from the German by Robert Bek-Gran, E. P. Dutton and Company, New York. 395 pp. $5.00.

[21] Edgar F. Vanbuskirk, Edith Lillian Smith, Walter L. Nourse, "The Science of Every-day Life." 638 pp. $1.50. "Workbook." 220 pp. 72 cents. James R. Wilson, "Objective tests in General Science." 48 pp. 24 cents. Houghton Mifflin Company, Boston.

[22] F. A. Cavanagh, Editor, James and John Stuart Mill on Education." Cambridge University Press. The Macmillan Company, New York. 207 pp. $2.00.

hiring nor firing teachers. It is the improvement of instruction. With this unpalavering declaration of principles Professor Burke Fitzpatrick opens his boiled-down rations for the sustenance of the supervisor of elementary schools.[23] Principles, activities, practices, and details of supervision are covered tersely, as are keeping up to date, criticism, rating, examinations, etc.

TIME-SAVERS

PRINCIPAL GEORGE RYAN used to claim that he was the only one of 3,499 Brooklyn school people to use a comptometer. The rest of us were spendthrifts of time and gray matter adding the columns of our monthly reports and computing the numerous averages, while he merely touched keys and saved what he called his brains. Every now and then I hear allegations that we schoolmasters are behind other business men in time-saving, error-preventing devices. Since I read the Duke of Buckingham's book on school statistics I floor these slanderers by saying, "What per cent?" "Who are they?" "When did you make your count?" In a moment I have the loose talkers floundering and say, "With all your advocacy of mechanical numerators you are a very vague arithmetician."

By this prelude I introduce you to a book that will soon save you many times its cost.[24] Professor Holzinger, School of Education, University of Chicago, offers twenty quick-reference tables, the paper, print, and binding being in the good style of the University Press. From the samples, lists of products, quotients, squares and square roots, the tables run through probable errors of the product, moment coefficient, facilitation of Spearman's rank formula, and other time-savers for measures in education.

HAPPY LAND

MARIE LAWSON, painter, designer, artist, brings a vibrant color into United States history.[25] Her splendid adventure is no less than an American saga, a stately prose poem, moving like a symphony. As tone motifs recur in certain musical compositions, here the caravel, the Indian, the slave, the musket, the arrow, the grenadier, the clipper-ship, a score of other master designs, mark the return of essential notes in new phases. You have to let yourself go when you describe the work of this book. It has a pomp and a glory.

It is "the story of the pioneer nation of the western world, of wide lands and many waters, of struggle and aspiration, of luxury and log cabins, of sails and skyscrapers, of buffalo and big business, documents and dreams, war and peace, progress, the march of Columbia's children, the people of this, the United States of America."

The dedication is a ceremony, a salute, "to ships and sailors and new men."

The chapter headings are poetry: "Dreams and Ventures," "Flags," "Calls of the Wilderness," "Many Inventions."

Each era is opened with a sentiment, a pledge, a toast, a viva, a salvo: "to the lonely mariners of the Santa Maria," or "to the heroes of 1917 and the hope of everlasting peace."

"I mean to stress our romance," says the Lady Lawson. "There is nothing important in our history which, taken with its background, is dull. Roads, machinery, farming, woman suffrage are as full of thrills as Captain Kidd or Stonewall Jackson."

Example: "Another voice, not new. It was heard since the founding—the voice of the women of America. You see long, long lines of women, in silk and calico, in sunbonnets and Paris hats, in log cabins on the wilderness edge, as busy, hospitable mistresses of mansions. You see them on the forest road, in the lowly patches of the hill country, in the covered wagons on the plains. Slim, white hands guiding the affairs of huge households, strong work-worn hands, gentle hands binding wounds of wars.

"The age changes. Clear voices ring out. Emma Willard's for better education of women. Elizabeth Cady Stanton's, Susan Anthony's, for rights to their own earnings, for a voice in the care of the nation."

Brava, Marie, your black-and-yellow pirates, your virile pioneers, your homely Lincoln, your adorable towns with hedges and spires and masts of ships, your lovable little locomotives, your swaggering sailors, are irresistible.

[23] F. Burke Fitzpatrick, ''Supervision of Elementary Schools.'' F. A. Owens Publishing Company, Dansville, New York. 758 pp. $1.25.

[24] Karl J. Holzinger, ''Statistical Tables for Students in Education and Psychology.'' University of Chicago Press. 101 pp. $2.00.

[25] Marie A. Lawson, ''Hail, Columbia, The Life of a Nation.'' Doubleday, Doran and Company, Garden City, New York. 387 pp. $5.00.

SCHOOL AND SOCIETY

EDITED BY J. McKEEN CATTELL

WITH WHICH IS COMBINED THE

EDUCATIONAL REVIEW

EDITED BY WILLIAM McANDREW

Volume 35 | Saturday, February 13, 1932 | Number 894

THE MEDIEVAL UNIVERSITY AND THE AMERICAN COLLEGE

By WILLIAM E. NICHOLL

DEAN OF THE COLLEGE AND ASSISTANT PROFESSOR OF EDUCATION, POMONA COLLEGE

In his "Ethics" Aristotle says: "The true nature of a thing is that which it will become when its growth is completed." If this is true, it would seem rather futile for any one to attempt an analysis and interpretation of the American college, for the changes that are going on within it at the present time and the warfare going on about it, as to what the new changes or next experiment should be do not indicate any immediate settling of that ancient and peculiar institution into the final form for which its destiny may have intended it. The American college certainly is not what it was in the beginning and "it doth not yet appear what it shall be," but nevertheless I am daring to join that vast and steadily increasing company, which no man can number, who attempt to say, with at least some conviction, what it is and what it ought to be.

Now, although it may not appear so on the surface, there is a sense in which it is much easier to say of any given institution what it ought to be than what it is, for the standards of oughtness are, alas, largely subjective and, therefore, easily "swayed by every wind of doctrine" and prejudices of every kind, whereas to determine the actual status of an institution, particularly one whose evolution seems in rapid progress, requires a more sane and perhaps a more prosaic viewing and interpreting of the facts—a mental process, the labor of which is not nearly so alluring and for which not nearly so many of us are by nature and inclination properly fitted as deem ourselves fully competent of doing the more spectacular thing of setting up categories of judgment as to what ought to be.

However, if the changing status and function of the American college preclude the possibility of determining its true nature, according to the standard set up by Aristotle just quoted, perhaps a brief review of some of the factors in its evolution thus far may help us to a clearer understanding of its present unstable position.

The college as we know it has, of course, its roots reaching back into the medieval university but, although there is much in the offshoot with which we are familiar that is like the parent tree, there is also much that is quite different. It is a far cry in time, space and general function from the early university of over a thousand years ago in sunny Italy to the American liberal arts college of our day.

Originally the terms "college" and "university" had the same connotation and were by no means, as now, limited to designate institutions of learning, but rather any group of people associated or bound together for any purpose whatsoever. During many generations of the Middle Ages the common manner of addressing any group such as an association of merchants or monks or even soldiers was *"Universitas Vestra"*—"the whole of you." Even the whole body of Christian people was often thus addressed in papal announcements. The term "university" was therefore never used alone but always with a defining word, as "University of Scholars," "University of Masters and Scholars," etc. There is an interesting incident out of medieval lore discovered in an old manuscript by Hastings Rashdall, which furnishes a somewhat extreme example of this general use to which the term was put: A Pisan vessel, with its crew and cargo, had been captured by a ship from Genoa. The cargo was confiscated and the crew held for ransom. Though given considerable freedom about the city, they were nevertheless prisoners and for purposes of promoting mutual welfare during the period of their captivity they organized themselves into what they called a "Universitas carceratorum"—a "University of Prisoners." (Some might draw a cynical parallel at this point, but I shall refrain.) A modern survival of this more general use of the term "college" is to be found in our electoral college, and judges of the Supreme Court of Scotland are still designated as "Senators of the College of Justice."

In its earlier connotation the term "university" never signified a place, but only an organization. When a place of higher learning was referred to, the term used was "Studium," "Studium publicum" or "Studium Generale," signifying a place of study open to all. Inasmuch as the other institutions where some of the more advanced subjects were studied—the monasteries and cathedral schools—were usually closed except to members of the particular order or chapter for which they were the headquarters, the development in the later middle ages of these *studia* where universities of scholars from all lands and without monkish or ecclesiastical restrictions could come together for the promotion of their common interest was a great boon to those who found in the pursuit of learning the *summum bonum* of life.

In our day we depend too much upon buildings and equipment and the general impedimenta of a location. It has become too easy for us to identify the college or university with these things. We could learn something here from the medieval university which recognized that the university is where the scholars are, and that the structure of true learning and culture is a "house not made with hands" and herein consists its truly enduring nature.

We have also lost something—much, I think—in the discontinuance of the medieval custom of strong emphasis upon the idea of membership in the college or university. We think of ourselves too much as separate groups of trustees or regents, who constitute the legal corporation; of faculty who do the teaching; of students who receive instruction, and of alumni who have been awarded the degree (each more or less distinct and without much interest in or provision for cooperation or correlation). When in the days of its beginning, under the presidency of William Harper and the patronage of John D. Rockefeller, the students of Chicago University used to paraphrase the doxology thus—

> Praise John from whom oil blessings flow,
> Praise also Bill who spends the dough.
> Praise John, praise Bill, praise all the host,
> Praise Bill a little—John the most.

they were giving expression, in a very clever way—and with proper emphasis on comparative importance—to a separateness of interest and function between two of the parts of a university which modern education has come to take for granted to its very great loss—with references to all the functions which in the medieval university were jointly shared and jointly promoted by all who had membership in it.

When in the course of time the terms "college" and "university," particularly the latter, came to have a more restricted meaning and were applied more or less exclusively to groups of scholars, there developed two types of institutions more or less distinct, with only one of which the American college has close relationship. In Southern Europe the interest of scholarship centered largely around the subjects of medicine and law and attracted more mature students, who retained a great deal of the control and administration of the university in their own hands. Bologna became the type of this "student university," which spread through Southern Europe and finally from Spain to Mexico, whose university is the oldest on this side of the Atlantic and in a sense is only a cousin and not a sister of the institutions in our United States.

In these student universities, as the name indicates, the government was in the hands of the students. They determined what the tuition fees should be, when and where lectures were to be held and what was a fair price for board and lodging in the town.

However, in Northern Europe the interest was more largely in the so-called "liberal arts," which attracted a younger group of students—sometimes very young—who were not so capable of administration and were not allowed to exercise government in any large degree. Moreover, the northern universities were more directly under church control and fostered by theological interest and this fact also tended to emphasize control by hierarchal authority rather than the more mutual sharing of it by the whole group of scholars themselves. It was from this northern heritage that our American college has descended, and it represents a less mature type of higher education than that developed in an earlier day in Southern Europe. Paris was the mother institution of this master-controlled university. From Paris the tradition passed to Oxford, from Oxford to Cambridge, from Cambridge in the old land to Cambridge in the new, and by a series of steps easily traced and dominating in their influences from Harvard, in Massachusetts, to one or more colleges in nearly every state of the Union.

There is another consideration which has tended to emphasize this comparative immaturity of students and of method as the college developed in America. In the Paris-Oxford type, though the students were less mature than in universities of Southern Europe, they nevertheless came quite fully prepared to carry on more or less independent study of an advanced kind. They had, before matriculation, mastered the tools of scholarship and did not need to be instructed in them by the university and were ready in a greater or less degree, to "go it alone." When Harvard was founded, it was the intention also to found many secondary schools of the English Latin grammar type that would as fully prepare the student for his later college work as did the corresponding great "public schools" in the mother country. The Massachusetts General Court passed a law in 1647 requiring "that every town having one hundred households must provide a grammar school to fit youths for the university, under a penalty of five pounds for failure to do so." This law, like many another, though looking well in print, did not work out so well in practice. Town after town paid the fine rather than bother with the establishment of a Latin grammar school, the utility of which the descendants of the first colonists, who knew not so much about the culture of the old land as the rigors of the new, found it difficult to appreciate. This lack of real provision of adequate secondary schools made it necessary for the American college itself to teach secondary school subjects and adopt secondary school methods—a function and practice which it has continued to this day, thus making it the peculiar institution that it is, since it combines, in large measure, functions exercised by two quite distinct institutions in all other countries of the western world. Of some two hundred courses of instruction offered by Pomona College in this year's catalogue, approximately seventy are of distinctly secondary school content.

Failure to clearly recognize and definitely plan for this double function of the American college has led to many grave and sometimes ridiculous errors and glaring blunders in the operation of our so-called institutions of higher learning. I think it might be shown that one result of our groping attempt to make provision for this dual nature in our colleges led us to invent, with characteristic American ingenuity, the credit and hour system of academic bookkeeping, unknown elsewhere in time or place, whereby it seems we hoped to stimulate and check those less mature students who were doing work of a preparatory or secondary grade. Of course, the brighter minds and more advanced students found little in this system to challenge intellectual effort, and so, on their part, and with equally characteristic American ingenuity, they developed or rather greatly expanded the so-called collegiate "activities" in comparison with which scholarly interests often became "passivities."

It would, however, be an unwarranted interpretation of the facts to infer that all the members of the medieval university were any more "eager, thoughtful and reverent" than are all those who register year by year in any of our institutions of higher learning. The inherent nature of youth is probably not much different now from what it was a thousand years ago—or will be a thousand years hence—the oldsters have always found fault with the youngsters, and *vice versa,* and always will. I ran across not long since this complaint of an adult of the twelfth century whining about the flaming student youth of his day: "The scholars," he wrote, "are accustomed to wander throughout the whole world and visit all the cities; that their many studies bring them understanding. For in Paris they seek a knowledge of the liberal arts; of the ancient writers at Orleans; of medicine at Salernum; of the black art at Toledo; and in no place decent manners." He was probably right. It was his generation of students who produced the song that has come down even to our time:

Gaudiamus igitur juvenis dum sumus.
Post jucundam juventutam, post molestam senectutem
Nos hababet humus.

Wherever and whenever some hundreds or thousands of the youth of the land are gathered together, there will spring into being what some of us may too critically allude to as "noisy activities," but, believe me, time has not—nor will not greatly change this—if these should hold their peace, the stones would cry out.

But with a more or less mechanical and unstimulating academic offering on the one hand and in consequence a greatly over-developed and over-emphasized offering of so-called "collegiate activities" on the other it followed, in many instances, that zeal for learning and comradeship in intellectual endeavor, which was the soul of the earlier universities, almost perished, like many another notable human endeavor, crucified between two thieves.

However, we are taught to believe that severe afflictions do not arise out of the ground, and, although this struggle of interests within the college would probably not be hailed as a celestial benediction, there is a sense in which it has nevertheless been a means of grace to our beloved institution, the American college. This struggle, it is true, has made serious problems, but serious problems constitute challenges and by this continual challenge those interested in the American college have been stimulated to activity that has helped to keep it a living organism when otherwise it might have gone the way of many other social institutions which have become too complacently adjusted to a deadening routine of existence.

Chaucer paints a vivid word picture of representatives of two of the great social institutions that had their origin in the Middle Ages, one at the very beginning of that period and the other toward the end, when the signs of a new day were beginning to be evident. The monk represents the older institution, the monastery which had about run its course, and the clerk of Oxford, the new institution, the university, which was just growing into general recognition. The monastery had begun with seriousness of purpose and through many generations of loving labor had served mankind, but by Chaucer's day it had grown rich and comfortable and unresponsive to the needs of humanity and is well represented by the fat and worldly companion of the Canterbury Pilgrims. The decadence of the institution is clearly expressed by the description of its representative who "was a lord full fat and in good point" who loved hunting and had many a fine horse in his stable and fast hounds in his kennel. The Benedictine rule was for him too strict and old fashioned. Why should he study, poring over a book in his cloister? That rule he considered of no more value than an oyster, but when he went hunting, men might his bridle hear, "jingling in a whistling wind as clear and eek as loud as doth the chapel belle."

How different the representative of the new institution! Almost unduly serious in his attitude toward life and his feeling of responsibility for it. He will tell no lively tale such as the other pilgrim. His face will hardly relax into a smile at the stories of the others. The "Burden of the Valley of Vision" is upon this young man who would "leefer have at his bed's head twenty books clad in black or red, of Aristotle and his philosophye, than rich robes or high living . . . full of moral virtue was his speche . . . and gladly would he learn and gladly teach." He represents the free institution of higher learning just then in its youthful years of promise. It is a long time since Chaucer's day. The university of the liberal arts is about as old now as the monastery was then, and I have often wondered if it might not be that we, like the fat monk in Chaucer's tale, are representatives of a decadent institution—and do not know it. Many arguments could be presented in support of the thesis that other agencies in society to-day are more potent educational influences than the organized school system—even the crown of it, the college and the university. If this be true, there is no power that can save it from the fate that society metes out to institutions that have ceased to serve. The same social forces that eliminated the monastery are ready to carry the college into oblivion if it ceases to give value received: not wealth, nor fine buildings, nor noble history will save it if it does not serve.

However, the very fact that the college, in our day, is finding itself in difficulty, and is aware that it is being called upon to justify itself, is the most hopeful thing about the whole situation.

> Never on custom's oiled grooves
> The world to a higher level moves,
> But grates and grinds, with a friction hard,
> On granite boulder and flinty shard.
> The heart must bleed before it feels,
> The pool be troubled before it heals,

Ever by losses the right must gain,
Every good have its birth of pain.

Booker T. Washington used to tell the story of the colored mammy whom he met one morning and greeted with the question: "Good morning, mammy, where are you going?"

To which the good woman made answer: "I ain't gwine no place, I's been wha I's gwine." Let us hope that this may not be true of the American college, and indeed there is evidence in all the agitation of recent years that it is not true.

The Swarthmore plan—the new honors courses, the Meiklejohn College, the Chicago plan, the liberal arts college movement, which is sponsoring a broadcast on a national hook-up with an address by the President of the United States early this fall and many other proposals and ventures of recent years, however futile many of them may be, are nevertheless indications that the college is alive and anxious to reshape its offerings and its methods so that as an institution it may serve the needs of society to-day at least as well as its predecessors did in the society of long ago.

Unrest is indeed a sign of progress—but it is not always and necessarily progress. To quote Chaucer again, who thus characterizes the man of law: "Nowhere so bisy a man as he there was—and yet he *semed* bisier than he was." Not in unrest merely, but in sanely guided unrest, may we hope to find solutions for the problems of the American college. In the attacks we have made upon our college problems I have sometimes wondered if there was not a good deal of puttering that has made us seem busier than we really are, and I am sometimes reminded of the nursery story of the general who, upon being informed that the enemy was approaching, "rushed from his tent, mounted his horse, and galloped madly in all directions." The college must be alive to the needs of this changing world, and we must not allow the ignorant past to bully the intelligent present, but though we should think of readjustment and reorganization in perhaps very radical terms, we should act with due conservatism. We should be willing to experiment but experiment upon a sound scientific basis and not merely unintelligently tinker with grave questions—and after all is said and done we must remember that no single scheme can be the cure-all of the ills of any institution. No plan will rise much above those who administer it. It can be as truly said of the good college, as it was long since of the kingdom of heaven, that "it cometh not by observation, men can not say of it, 'Lo, here it is, or, lo, there it is,' " but the good college, like the kingdom of heaven, is within us, students, teachers, trustees, alumni and all who have the high privilege of membership in it.

TEACHER DEMAND AND THE SUPPLY

By ALONZO F. MYERS
PROFESSOR OF EDUCATION, NEW YORK UNIVERSITY

In 1927 the National Education Association appointed a committee to study the economic status of the teacher. As one of its first projects, this committee chose to study the status of teacher demand and supply. The data which they collected relate to the demand for and the supply of public school teachers for the school year 1929–30. The study is published as a research bulletin of the National Education Association.[1]

[1] Research Bulletin of the National Education Association, "Teacher Demand and Supply," Vol. IX, No. 5, November, 1931.

The National Education Association and the committee are to be congratulated upon the timeliness of the study. Reliable information on this subject was greatly needed. At this point, however, congratulations cease. The need was for a careful, accurate study. Admittedly this would have been a costly and laborious procedure, and adequate funds were not available for the use of the committee. Consequently, the committee depended upon figures and estimates supplied by state departments of public instruction for their principal source of data. In view of the fact that only 15 states were able to supply data relative to teacher demand and supply and that 16 states did not even hazard guesses on the subject, it should have been apparent to the committee that their data were so incomplete as to make it inadvisable to draw any important conclusions on a nation-wide basis. The only positive conclusion which one would have been justified in drawing from this study is that state education departments do not know the essential facts relative to teacher demand and supply.

The first important pronouncement of the study (page 312) is the statement: *"Demand for teachers tends to be fixed."* This statement, like many others contained in the study, will not stand critical scrutiny. If there is any positive statement which one would be justified in making relative to the demand for teachers it is that the demand tends to vary rather than to be fixed. The two factors which determine the demand for any given year are the following: (1) The number of new teaching positions created. This factor will be influenced by such factors as changing birth rate, rate of increase in number of students enrolled in high schools, compulsory attendance laws and general economic conditions. (2) The number of teachers who leave the profession each year. This factor will be influenced by such considerations as general economic conditions, which, if good, will encourage large numbers of teachers to enter commerce and industry, or to leave the profession through marriage, and which, if bad, will discourage them from doing so; salary schedules; retirement provisions; tenure laws. Careful consideration of the significance of Table 2 (page 313), should have caused the committee to be wary of the statement that the demand for teachers tends to be fixed. This table presents data secured from the volumes of the Biennial Survey of Education in the United States by the U. S. Office of Education, showing the number and biennial increase of teaching positions in elementary and secondary schools. The increase for the biennium 1924–1926 was 47,436. For the biennium 1926–1928 it was 26,008.

The second important announcement was that at the present time "a conservative estimate is that the annual demand in the United States is for 110,000 to 120,000 new teachers." How this "conservative" estimate was reached was not made clear, but it certainly did not grow out of any data presented in the study. For example, Table 8 (page 339) endeavors to show the annual demand for new teachers. Figures based on data and estimates supplied by state education departments were presented for 32 states and the District of Columbia. They showed an annual demand for 69,181 new teachers. This figure included for any given state all teachers teaching in the state in 1929–30 who were not teaching in that state in 1928–29. Obviously, it included inexperienced teachers, experienced teachers from other states, and experienced teachers from that state who returned to teaching in 1929–30 after a period of absence from teaching of one year or more.

The states which reported a demand for 69,181 new teachers for the school year 1929–30 represented approximately 70 per cent. of all the teachers in the country. If the demand for new teachers in the 16 states not reporting was the same in relation to their total number of teachers as in those states which reported, the annual demand would have been for approximately 98,830 new teachers, a mere 11,000 under the conservative estimate. At this point, however, it is necessary to examine this definition of a new teacher. For certain purposes in any given state it may be appropriate to define a new teacher as any teacher who was not teaching in that state during the year preceding the study. However, for the purposes of determining the number of new teachers needed by the country annually, a teacher who merely transferred from one state to another is not a new teacher at all. Furthermore, for the purpose of determining the number of new teachers needed annually, with reference to the number who must be trained each year, the only significant figure is that which represents the demand for inexperienced teachers.

Fortunately, certain information was available on this subject. The states which reported a demand for 69,181 new teachers reported that of this number 53,363 were inexperienced. If the demand for inexperienced teachers in the states which did not report was the same in relation to their total number of teachers as in those which reported, the total demand for inexperienced teachers in this country was approximately 76,200. Compare this figure with the statement quoted above: "A conservative estimate is that the annual demand in the United States is for 110,000 to 120,000 new teachers."

The committee requested the state education departments to answer this question, "On the average, how long do teachers remain in service in your state?" The median of the guesses of the 33 states which supplied the information was 5.77 years. The committee then proceeded to show in Table 8, column 3, the annual demand in each of the 48 states, on the basis of this estimated six-year teaching life. The total, and note that this would necessarily be for replacement only, and not for expansion, was 145,291. This should be very comforting to all placement officers in teachers colleges.

The committee made no apology for this procedure except to state that "No doubt column 3 is very inaccurate when applied to specific states" (page 338). Neither did they attempt to explain how 33 states with a total teaching population of approximately 606,000 could report an annual demand for 69,181 new teachers for replacements and expansion and at the same time report an average teaching life of 5.77 years. If we admit the possibility of the consistency of these figures with each other, then we could not possibly admit the correctness of the technique employed by the committee in dividing the total number of new teachers by the estimated average teaching life for the purpose of establishing the annual demand.

The data presented by the committee, and the conclusions drawn, relative to teacher supply are equally questionable. One must admit at the outset that reliable information on this point is exceedingly difficult to obtain. The committee used such information as was readily available. They can be criticized in that they were not sufficiently critical of their data, and that they drew strong and important conclusions which their data did not warrant.

An example of their uncritical use of data, and an example, as well, of the unreliability of some of the data supplied by the U. S. Office of Education, was the reference to students in teacher-training classes in high schools in connection with sources of supply. The statement is made on page 313 that "In 1928 there were 46,565 students enrolled in teacher-training courses in high schools." Again, in a footnote on page 340: "Most of students enrolled in high school teacher-training classes are qualified for certificates in one year or less.

In 1927–28 there were 50,286 students in such classes according to page 5 of Statistics of Teachers Colleges and Normal Schools, 1927–28, Bulletin, 1929, No. 14, U. S. Department of the Interior, Office of Education, Washington, D. C."

Perhaps the committee should not be criticized for accepting without question data coming from such a high source. Certainly the principal responsibility for the data rests with the Office of Education. On the other hand, it should require only superficial acquaintance with the sources of teacher supply in this country to persuade one that the statements quoted above are not correct. The reader is referred to Table 2, page 8, of the bulletin of the Office of Education, previously mentioned, which is part of the Biennial Survey of Education in the United States, 1926–1928. The information which follows is contained in the table.

STUDENTS IN TEACHER-TRAINING COURSES IN PUBLIC HIGH SCHOOLS

State	Boys	Girls
Connecticut	318	1,872
Massachusetts	337	3,406
New Jersey	767	3,395
Pennsylvania	1,591	3,587

The writer has given examples from the table of states in which it is generally known that there were no high-school teacher-training classes, for the purpose of showing the incorrectness of the information contained in the table.

There are several instances (in the N. E. A. study) of strong and unwarranted conclusions drawn from incomplete and unreliable data. The most important of these as well as the most misleading and the most widely quoted, is the one which occurs on page 349: "If we accept two years of training beyond high school as the minimum professional training for teaching, there was in reality a *wide-spread shortage of trained teachers in 1929–1930.*" Let us examine the data which were presented in substantiation of this conclusion.

Table 14 presents "The Number, Training, and Sources of Teacher Supply." It includes data, chiefly estimates, secured from 37 states and the District of Columbia. According to this table, in these states there were 93,334 persons who completed teacher-training in 1928–29. Of these, 23,578 were trained less than two years. Thus, there were reported for these states 69,756 *trained teachers.* It should be noted that this number can not be compared with the demand figures quoted above from Table 8, since those figures included data from only 33 states.

Table 17 presents a comparison between demand and supply in the 33 states which supplied data on both demand and supply. This table compares the demand with the total supply, and also the demand in relation to the trained supply. It shows that in these states the total supply was 96,674, the demand 69,181. It shows a surplus of 31,736 in 24 states, a shortage of 4,423 in 7 states, and an even balance in 2 states, a total surplus of 27,493. When considering the trained supply, the figures show a shortage of 17,185 in 18 states, a surplus of 9,797 in 13 states, and an even balance in 1 state, a total shortage of 7,448. It was this last comparison which provided the justification for the conclusion that "there was in reality a wide-spread shortage of trained teachers in 1929–30."

Let us examine the tenability of this positive and important announcement. It leaves entirely out of account the fact that information relative to supply was incomplete. For New York, for example, there is credited a total shortage of 3,461 teachers, and a shortage of trained teachers amounting to 4,732. New York is one of those states in which the data on supply did not include graduates of colleges and universities. It specifically included only graduates of state teachers colleges. It may be stated positively that New York has no shortage of teachers, and that no shortage existed in 1929–30. On the contrary, it had a surplus.

Consider the situation for New York in the light of additional information, not included in the study, relative to the number of students in teacher-training courses in colleges and universities and in city normal schools in that state. The figures used are taken from Bulletin, 1929, No. 14, Department of the Interior, Bureau of Education, Statistics of Teachers Colleges and Normal Schools, 1927–1928, Tables 1 and 2.

Students in teacher-training courses in colleges and universities under public control in New York, 1927–1928	3,678
Students in teacher-training courses in colleges and universities under private control in New York, 1927–1928	19,359
Students in teacher-training courses in city normal schools in New York, 1927–1928	7,498
Total not included in the N. E. A. study	30,535

It should be noted that the figures presented above relate to the number of students enrolled in teacher-training courses, rather than graduates. The number of graduates, however, should more than account for the shortage of 4,732 trained teachers reported for New York in the N. E. A. study.

In the comparisons of demand and supply the study compares for each state the supply with the demand for experienced as well as inexperienced teachers. It is this faulty comparison which results in the finding that there was a shortage of 7,448 trained teachers in the 33 states for which data and estimates were available, and which provided the sole justification for the most important conclusion of the study, that *"there was in reality a wide-spread shortage of trained teachers in 1929–30."* Let us examine the method employed in the study of computing the relationship of the demand to the trained supply.

(1) Total demand, involving demand for:
  (1) Inexperienced teachers
  (2) Teachers from other states
  (3) Experienced teachers within the state returning to teaching after an absence of one year or more.

(2) Trained supply:
  (1) Trained teachers trained with the state who completed their training in the school year, 1928–29, exclusive, in certain states, of teachers trained in colleges and universities
  (2) Teachers from other states.

Criticism of the method:

(1) It fails to take into account in sources of supply experienced teachers within the state returning to teaching after an absence from teaching of one year or more.
(2) It fails to take into account inexperienced teachers, previously trained, who entered, or were prepared to enter the teaching service at the time of the study (1929–30).
(3) In several states it fails to take into account teachers trained in colleges and universities.

We know that there were at the time of the study considerable numbers in each of these groups.

Consider the data contained in the study for a comparison of the newly trained supply with the demand for inexperienced teachers, a highly significant comparison which the study did not make. The demand for inexperienced teachers in the 33 states which supplied data on this subject was 53,363. The newly trained supply reported in the study for these 33 states was 52,066, giving an apparent shortage of 1,297. Please note that this supply specifically excludes in the following states graduates of colleges and universities, and includes only graduates of state teachers colleges and state normal schools: Connecticut, Maine, Massachusetts, New Hampshire and New York. The number of students in teacher-training courses in colleges and universities and in city normal schools in 1927–28 in these five states as reported in statistics of teachers colleges and normal schools in the

Biennial Survey of Education for 1926–1928 was as follows:

State	Student enrolment in teacher-training courses: Colleges and universities	City normal schools	Total
Connecticut	85	90	175
Maine	659	23	682
Massachusetts	3,141	22	3,163
New Hampshire	634	13	647
New York	23,037	7,498	30,535
Totals	27,556	7,646	35,202

It should be noted that the figures reported above represent not graduates, but students enrolled in teacher-training courses. However, the number of graduates must have been several thousand in excess of the number (1,297) that the trained teachers as reported in the N. E. A. study fell short of the reported demand for inexperienced teachers.

The writer would not be consistent with the point of view expressed earlier in this article if he drew positive conclusions from the additional data presented above relative to teacher demand and supply. Sufficient additional data have been presented to demonstrate that the principal positive conclusion contained in the N. E. A. study that *"there was in reality a wide-spread shortage of trained teachers in 1929–30"* was entirely without justification. To the extent that the data, for the most part estimates and highly unreliable, indicate anything, they indicate that there was a *surplus of trained teachers in 1929–30* as defined in the N. E. A. study.

Additional conclusions and recommendations of the writer, growing out of a careful study of the N. E. A. Research Bulletin, "Teacher Demand and Supply," are the following:

(1) There is urgent need for a careful, nation-wide study of teacher demand and supply.

(2) There is a need for studies and constructive action looking toward the strengthening of state education departments to the end that they may: (1) know the needs in the respective states for trained teachers; (2) determine and enforce adequate requirements for admission to the teaching service; (3) regulate the output of teacher-training institutions in the light of the need for beginning teachers.

(3) It is recommended that the National Education Association through its research division undertake only such research studies as its financial resources and research staff enable it to conduct in a satisfactory manner.

EDUCATIONAL EVENTS

INSTITUTE AND MUSEUM OF INTERNATIONAL EDUCATION IN GERMANY

To American teachers the new institute gives an opportunity for a permanent display of progressive educational material to be shown to teachers in Europe. A great exhibition of the educational efforts of the different nations will be built up by the "Institut für Volkerpädagogik" which was established during this year in Mainz.

The "Institut für Volkerpädagogik" is in the historic citadel of Mainz, a fortress which for nearly two thousand years has weathered the storms of warfare, high above the city, commanding a magnificent view of the Rhine Valley. Here teachers of all countries may meet for the discussion of pedagogical practices and ideals.

The institute is under the direction of Dr. Feldmann and Dr. Niemann. The board of trustees includes the names of many leaders in

German education. The board will also have foreign members. The institute is neither a state nor a municipal undertaking, and maintains its independence unhampered by official regulations.

Various permanent exhibits will prove attractive to all interested in education. The German pedagogic exhibit gives in forty-five rooms a survey of German schooling. In two special houses are shown models and drawings of new school buildings, as well as examples of new school furniture. In another house there is an extensive exhibit of modern school apparatus, toys, grammophone records, films, etc.

As a basis for studies in comparative education, the permanent international exhibit, which now contains sections for other European countries, will be enlarged by a really representative section.

In about twenty rooms a selection of the best achievements of American education from preschool to university will be brought together, including examples of education in health, citizenship, leisure, vocational education, skills and curriculum activities. Material for this exhibit is now being gathered under the auspices of the International Institute, Teachers College, Columbia University.

The old citadel, which is now the "Institut für Volkerpädagogik" has also two guest houses and a students' hostel, where visitors may live inexpensively, to receive individuals, or groups of teachers, students and children. The institute offers various courses which are arranged in close cooperation with the Teachers College in Mainz and with the near-by Universities of Frankfort, Bonn and Heidelberg.

Dr. Richard Mönnig, of the International Institute at Mainz, is visiting the United States to seek contacts and materials to help the institute in its establishment of an educational museum.

AMERICAN SUMMER SCHOOL IN PERU

THE Institute of International Education has completed plans for an American Summer School at the University of San Marcos in Lima, Peru. The Institute, the headquarters of which are at 2 West 45th Street, New York City, has arranged with Dr. Albert A. Giesecke, of Cornell University, formerly director general of public education in Peru, to supervise personally the activities of the new school. The Peruvian Government and the Pan American Union have cooperated with the institute in establishing the project, and the Grace Steamship Lines have reduced the round trip fare from Lima to New York from $550 to $375 for American students intending to enroll in the school.

The summer school at San Marcos is intended primarily for graduate students and teachers whose interest lies in South American history or culture. Especial attention will be given to the study of the numerous remains of the early Inca civilization which are centered around Lima. A special ten-day field trip to visit the ruins near Cuzco has been arranged for the students in the course on Peruvian archeology. This course will be presented by Dr. Julio Tello, the Peruvian archeologist and will be given in English. There will also be courses in elementary and advanced Spanish, a course on Latin-American literature given by Professor Luis Alberto Sánchez, professor of that subject at the University of San Marcos. Dr. Victor Andrés Belaúnde, formerly professor of history at the University of San Marcos, and since 1926 professor of Latin-American history and Institutions at the University of Miami, Florida, will give a course on Latin-American affairs.

In order to provide direct contact with Peruvian life, the institute has arranged for excursions to surrounding places of interest on Saturdays and Sundays. They have also made provisions for excellent living quarters in Lima houses. Dr. Giesecke, the director of the school, who has long been prominent in Peruvian affairs, will devote much of his efforts to establishing valuable and intelligent contacts between the students and important Peruvians.

The general plan of the school will be similar to that of the American summer school with daily periods for each course during five days of the week for four weeks. At the close of this period there will be the ten-day trip to Cuzco for the students of archeology. It is estimated that living expenses should not exceed thirty dollars a week, thus bringing the cost of the summer school up to about five hundred dollars.

The University of San Marcos was founded in 1551, the oldest university in the Western

Hemisphere. It is situated within the city of Lima and is similar in organization to European universities. Student life there is considerably affected by the fact that the university consists entirely of professional schools, a degree from which entitles the holder to a government position. Most of the prominent Peruvian statesmen have graduated from the University of San Marcos.

As a result of this practice, the students take a keen interest in politics, and frequently make pronouncements on government affairs which carry considerable weight with the political officials. Occasionally the situation has become so tense that there are student strikes such as that in Santiago in which the students alone practically overthrew Dictator Ibañez and successfully ran the government for three days. Another feature of student influence in South America is the fact that they have a one third vote in the management of the university.

The result of this serious student attitude to national affairs has been that the universities have a more mature scholastic tone. The University of San Marcos has little of the so-called college life. The students live in private houses and the university itself consists chiefly of class rooms, libraries and an excellent museum of Inca remains. The present buildings of the university were built in 1571.

The University of San Marcos was selected by the Institute of International Education for its summer school because of the easiness of access, its high rating among South American universities, the richness of archeological remains in the vicinity, and the excellence of the Spanish spoken in Lima.

The city itself was founded by Pizzaro, in 1535, the oldest Spanish city in South America. The cathedral on the Plaza Mayor contains his mummified body. Lima is five hundred feet above sea level and has an exceptionally fine climate from June until September, the winter season. Because it is the cosmopolitan center of Peru with broad boulevards once said to have been paved with silver, race courses, an opera house, many fine old buildings and numerous seaside and pleasure resorts, it was considered by those arranging the summer school to be the most advantageous spot in South America.

The foundation of this school is a part of the general program of the institute to further friendly relations through an exchange of students. It cooperates with foreign student exchanges such as the Franco-American Student Exchange, and the American-German Student Exchange, Inc. It is also the agent for fellowships and scholarships provided by the American Field Service Fellowships for French Universities, Inc., Germanistic Society of America, Inc., Committee on Junior Year Abroad, and the New York Committee on Foreign Travel and Study. The institute selects the recipients of these awards, and supplies information and aid to foreign students in this country.

The institute has for its general aim the development of international understanding, good will and education through such activities as the exchange of professors; the establishment and administration of international fellowships; the holding of conferences on problems of international education, and the publication of books and pamphlets on the opportunities for study in the different countries.

CREDITS FOR THE JUNIOR YEAR ABROAD

A report on what grades should be given in this country for scholastic work done in France by students who are members of the authorized Junior Year Abroad groups has just been issued through the Institute of International Education by Professor B. E. Young, chairman of the subcommittee on evaluation of credits of the Committee on the Junior Year Abroad. The report says:

According to the French system of grading, on a scale of 20, a grade of 10 is a passing grade, and a grade of 12 to 14 is very satisfactory or even high, and frequently no more than fifty per cent. of those taking an examination are passed. It is evident that correct equivalents in the United States can not be obtained by simply transferring these numerical grades to the scale of 100. The director of the Foreign Study Bureau of the University of Delaware in his reports now gives the approximate American equivalents, A, B, C, D, for the French numerical grades, taking the difference in standard into account, on a very conservative basis.

The Committee on Evaluation of Credits has examined these grades in the case of a number of superior students who have returned to this country. It has discussed the whole system with some judicious and observant members of various groups. The members of the committee are all familiar, by personal observation, with the strenuous work required of the students, all of whom come from the upper levels in American colleges.

The conclusion of the committee is that the grades A, B, C, D, as reported by the foreign director, on the basis of the numerical grades of each student given by the French universities, are fully equivalent to the similar grades in the best colleges and universities of the United States, and that they can be accepted with confidence by Phi Beta Kappa membership committees and other honor committees.

Naturally the various faculties and chapters of honorary fraternities will have their own rules for determining scholastic honors. Some American institutions, for one reason or another, eliminate the junior year abroad in computing grades for Phi Beta Kappa and base their estimate entirely on grades given in residence here. Perhaps each case involving foreign study should be treated as an exception. The committee strongly urges, however, that no student, who might otherwise be eligible, be deprived of academic honors because of having spent the junior year abroad, and that whenever it is necessary to take this year into account the record made there be given its full value, or reckoned on the basis of comparison with the record made by the candidate in his own institution.

1932 SESSIONS OF THE SUMMER SCHOOL FOR ENGINEERING TEACHERS

The Society for the Promotion of Engineering Education announces an important development in connection with its Summer School for Engineering Teachers. Heretofore sessions of the school, which has as its purpose the improvement of methods of teaching, have been devoted to the more technical divisions of engineering education. Engineering mechanics, electrical engineering, mechanical engineering, civil engineering, chemical engineering, physics, engineering drawing and mathematics have been studied at previous sessions. Beginning with the year 1932 the scope of the school is to be broadened to include the more liberal subjects of the curriculum, thus making it inclusive of all the divisions of engineering education.

The two sessions of 1932 are to be devoted to English and to economics. The session on English will be held at the Ohio State University, from July 11 to 29, inclusive, and the session on economics at Stevens Institute of Technology from July 5 to 22, inclusive. The program of the session on English will be divided into a number of principal parts, in accordance with the type of work in English commonly provided for engineering students. Emphasis throughout the session will be upon methods of teaching and course content. The teaching of composition, literature, technical writing and speaking, as well as advanced courses in English for engineers, are among the topics to be considered. There is also to be a series of lectures by prominent men from the field of letters. The English session will be under the direction of Professor Sada Harbarger, chairman of the committee of English of the Society for the Promotion of Engineering Education, and in charge of English work for the College of Engineering at the Ohio State University.

The program of the session on economics comprises four principal divisions: (1) course content and methods of teaching general economics, engineering economics and subjects relating to economics, such as industrial engineering, engineering administration and accounting; (2) a series of lectures on basic economic principles; (3) a series of lectures dealing with the applications of economic laws to engineering problems; (4) a series of lectures on current economics trends. The economics session will be under the direction of President Harvey N. Davis and Professor William D. Ennis, of the Stevens Institute faculty.

SUMMER SESSION OF THE UNIVERSITY OF MICHIGAN

More than 500 students of education, including thirty-three visiting professors prominent in their fields, will serve on the staff of the 1932 summer session of the University of Michigan, giving seven hundred and twenty-seven courses in all departments of the university, according to a statement made by the dean of the school, Professor Edward H. Kraus. Most of the courses are eight weeks in length, but there are some six-week courses in the Medical School and four- and eight-week series in education, as well as week-end institutes in public health and short institutes in engineering. Courses in the Law School are of five and ten weeks.

The practice of inviting leading educators from other universities to serve upon the summer faculty has long been a custom at Michigan, and is valuable in encouraging new points of view and arousing critical discussion among both faculty and students, Dean Kraus states. Among the visiting professors this year will be, Edward Gleason Spaulding, philosophy, Princeton; Antonio G. Solalinde, Romance languages, University of Wisconsin; Agnes E. Wells, dean of women at the University of Indiana and formerly with the Helen Newberry Residence for Women at Michigan; Harald M. Westergaard, theoretical and applied mechanics, Illinois; Thomas Marc Parrott, English, Princeton; Fred Carleton Ayer, educational administration, University of Texas; Ellsworth Faris, chairman of the Department of Sociology, University of Chicago; Albert C. Jacobs, law, Columbia University; Herbert Baker Hungerford, entomology, University of Kansas; Henry S. Vedder Jones, English, University of Illinois; G. Watts Cunningham, philosophy, Cornell; and Edgar Holmes McNeal, European history, the Ohio State University.

REGIONAL CONFERENCES OF THE PROGRESSIVE EDUCATION ASSOCIATION

The first of four regional conferences conducted under the auspices of the Committee on the Relation of School and College of the Progressive Education Association was held at the University of Chicago on Saturday, February 6. The invitation to attend went out from Director Wilford M. Aikin, of the John Burroughs School, Saint Louis, chairman of the committee; Dean C. S. Boucher, of the University of Chicago; and the chairman of the North Central Association Committee. The purpose of the conferences is to bring about a closer relationship between colleges and the Progressive Education Association, particularly in regard to admission of students from progressive schools.

For the Chicago conference, representatives were invited from the University of Michigan, University of Wisconsin, University of Minnesota, University of Illinois, Northwestern University, Oberlin College, Wabash College and Knox College.

The second conference will be held at Columbia University on Saturday, February 27. Dean Herbert E. Hawkes and Dr. Adam LeRoy Jones signed the invitation which was sent to Princeton University, Cornell University, Vassar College, Wells College, Rochester University, the Elmira College for Women, Skidmore College, Barnard College, Colgate College and the New Jersey College for Women.

The third conference will be held at the University of Pennsylvania on Saturday, March 5. Vice-president G. W. McClelland and director of admissions Karl Miller have joined in the invitation to that conference and the following colleges will send representatives: Johns Hopkins, Bryn Mawr, Haverford, Swarthmore, Lafayette, Lehigh and Goucher.

A fourth conference will be held at Harvard University on Saturday, April 16. Dean A. C. Hanford, of Harvard College is inviting representatives of the New England colleges for men to meet with us at that time. This group will include Yale, Brown, Williams, Bowdoin, Amherst, Dartmouth, Wesleyan, Tufts and Massachusetts Institute of Technology.

Two other conferences are now being arranged, one for the representatives of New England Women's Colleges, and the other to include representatives of some of the more southern institutions, chiefly those located in Virginia and North Carolina.

GOVERNMENT EDUCATIONAL EXHIBIT AT THE MEETING OF THE DEPARTMENT OF SUPERINTENDENCE AT WASHINGTON

The most extensive United States government educational exhibit ever assembled awaits superintendents and other educators coming to Washington for the meeting of the Department of Superintendence on February 20–25.

Thirteen government agencies which have services and publications important to schools are planning exhibits in the Interior Department reception hall. They are:

Office of Education
National Park Service
The White House Conference on Child Health and Protection

Reclamation Service
Geological Survey
Illiteracy Commission
Children's Bureau
Federal Board for Vocational Education
Department of Commerce
Indian Service
Department of Agriculture
Government Printing Office
George Washington Bicentennial Commission

The exhibits will depict the activities of these bureaus and commissions. Attendants will be present at each booth during exhibit hours to answer questions and to show various publication, maps and motion pictures available to schools.

The government educational exhibit, sponsored by the federal office of education, will be convenient to all attending the convention, as the Interior Department is within a block of the general meeting hall and the exhibits.

The Interior Department reception hall will also contain a display of floor plans, specifications and photographs of seventy-five outstanding new elementary school buildings selected from every section of the United States by the National Advisory Council on School Building Problems.

EDUCATIONAL NOTES AND NEWS

AT a meeting of the convocation of the University of London on January 19 the Earl of Athlone was elected chancellor of the university. The installation ceremony will be held on February 18.

DR. LOUIS R. WILSON, librarian at the University of North Carolina, has accepted a position as dean of the graduate library school at the University of Chicago. Dr. Wilson is president of the North Carolina and Southeastern Library Associations and a former vice-president of the American Library Association.

MR. PERCY GRAINGER, pianist and composer, has been appointed head of the music department of the New York University College of Fine Arts.

DR. JUSTIN H. MOORE, counselor of economic conditions for the Irving Trust Company, has been elected to succeed Dr. George W. Edwards as dean of the School of Business and Civic Administration at the College of the City of New York.

MAJOR ALEXANDER M. PATCH, JR., who was commandant of Staunton Military Academy, Staunton, Virginia, from 1921 to 1924 and from 1925 to 1928, will return to that institution for duty in June.

PROFESSOR WILHELM KOHLER, director of the state art collection at Weimar, Germany, comes to Harvard University in September as professor of German art and culture. He will succeed Professor Friederich von der Leyen, of the University of Cologne.

MR. RUDOLPH D. LINDQUIST, professor of education in the Ohio State University, was elected national president of Phi Delta Kappa, professional education fraternity, at its recent meeting in Chicago.

MR. MILTON J. FLETCHER, who recently resigned from the superintendency of the schools of Jamestown, New York, has been elected superintendent emeritus. Mr. Fletcher served the schools of Jamestown for thirty-three years, during the last thirteen years as superintendent.

DR. CARL OTTO SCHOENRICH, formerly professor of French and German at the Baltimore City College, celebrated his eighty-fifth birthday on February 5.

MR. E. M. HOSMAN, secretary of the Nebraska State Teachers Association for the past ten years, has resigned his position to accept that of director of extension and publicity in the Municipal University of Omaha.

DEAN JAMES B. MUNN, of the Washington Square College of New York University, has been appointed professor of English at Harvard University.

DR. LAURENCE MCKINLEY GOULD, associate professor of geology in the University of Michigan, has resigned to become head of the department of geology at Carleton College, Northfield, Minnesota. His resignation takes effect on June 1.

Dr. S. M. Troxell, of the University of Illinois, lately on a research fellowship at the U. S. Bureau of Standards, has joined the science department of the Trenton, New Jersey, State Teachers College.

The *School Board Journal* states that Superintendent G. N. Child, of Salt Lake City, has been reelected for a new term, beginning with July, 1932. Mr. Child, who was reelected for a seventh consecutive term, is at present completing his twelfth year of service in the schools.

Dr. John Ruhräh, a physician specializing in pediatrics, has been appointed a member of the School Board of Baltimore to succeed Mr. Lewis W. Lake, whose term expires on March 1.

At Indiana State Teachers College, Terre Haute, Professor D. A. Glascock, of the department of physical education for men, has been appointed by the state superintendent of public instruction, Mr. George C. Cole, to take charge of a survey of physical education in the eight hundred high schools of the state. Miss Florence Curtis, head of the department of physical education for women, is working with a special committee to revise the requirements for teachers of physical education in Indiana and Professor E. E. Ramsey, head of the department of education, has been appointed a member of the sub-committee directing the illiteracy campaign in Indiana.

Professor Milo H. Stuart, assistant superintendent of schools of Indianapolis, and Dr. D. H. Eikenberry, of Ohio University, have been appointed on a special committee which is to conduct a survey of the Chicago high-school system. The committee will work under the direction of Dr. George D. Strayer, director of the survey.

Dr. J. T. C. Noe, head of the department of the history of education at the University of Kentucky, was the speaker at the second annual mid-year commencement exercises, held at the university on January 29. Dr. Noe has been a teacher at the university for twenty-six years.

The Board of Trustees of Cornell University has granted partial leave for the second semester to Professor Madison Bentley, of the department of psychology, to enable him to direct a study of the present state of the subject of mental disorders. The study is undertaken by the National Research Council and is supported by a grant from the Carnegie Foundation.

Dr. David Kinley, president emeritus of the University of Illinois, left for Tokyo on February 8 to obtain assurances that Japan would participate in the 1933 World's Fair.

President Wallace W. Atwood, of Clark University, has left Worcester to join the Carnegie Institution expedition in Guatemala, where Mayan ruins are being uncovered.

Dr. Gerhardt Hauptman, the German dramatist, will speak at several American universities in connection with celebrations of the hundredth anniversary of the death of Goethe.

Dr. Donald M. Erbe, of the department of economics of the University of Oregon, has been given leave of absence to lecture at Stanford University.

Through an exchange arrangement between the University of Cincinnati and Northwestern University, Professor W. H. Bucher, of the University of Cincinnati, presented in January a series of lectures at Northwestern University. Dr. Bucher's lectures included one on "Life in the Cincinnati Seas" before the Geological Society at Northwestern, and a lecture on "The Interpretation of Joints," one on "Cryptovolcanic Structures," and three on aspects of megatectonics before the class in structural geology. Under this arrangement Professor C. H. Behre, Jr., of Northwestern University, will give the exchange lectures at Cincinnati. Before the class in economic geology he will give three dealing with phases of ore deposition, one on the "Geology of Leadville," and one on "Slate Deposits." He will also speak before the Geological Society at Cincinnati on "Physiographic Research in Central Colorado."

Dr. F. B. Pearson, formerly California state superintendent of schools, is spending the winter in California.

Dr. John L. Johnson, for twenty years president of Mississippi Women's College at Hattiesburg, died on February 1, in his sixty-third year.

Dr. Reginald Heber Howe, head master of the Belmont Hill School at Belmont, near Boston, died suddenly on January 28, at the age of fifty-six years. Dr. Howe was a lecturer and writer on ornithology and biology. He had been curator at the Thoreau Museum of Natural History and instructor in natural sciences at Middlesex School in Concord. From 1921 to 1923 he was with the Bussey Institution of Harvard University.

Miss Marie Antoinette Ward, until her retirement in 1929 for many years principal of Public School No. 31 in Jersey City, died on February 1 at the age of seventy years.

John Hay, superintendent of schools at Mt. Carroll, Illinois, died on January 6 following an automobile accident. He was seventy-four years old.

The death is announced of Clinton S. Marsh, who from 1910 to 1918 was superintendent of public schools at Summit, New Jersey. Mr. Marsh served as superintendent of schools at North Tonawanda and Auburn, New York, and at Wallingford, Connecticut.

The fifth triennial International Congress on Commercial Education will be held in London during the last week of July. The Prince of Wales is patron of the conference and will address its closing session on the morning of July 29.

"Education and Changing Society" is to be the theme of the sixth World Conference of the New Education Fellowship which will be held in Nice, France, next summer. The dates are July 29 to August 12, 1932. Professor Paul Langevin, of the Collège de France, is the president of the conference. The vice-presidents are Dr. C. H. Becker, formerly Minister of Education for Prussia, and Sir Percy Nunn, of the University of London. Delegates from all over the world will attend. Representatives from China, Japan and Russia are expected. In America, the work of organizing the American delegation for the conference is under the auspices of the American Committee on International Education composed of members of the Progressive Education Association and other organizations. Further information can be obtained from Frances Fenton Park, secretary, 425 West 123rd Street, New York City.

The John W. Lieb Memorial Library, which will form a part of the main library of the Stevens Institute of Technology in Hoboken, has been dedicated. Among the speakers were President Harvey N. Davis, Walter Kidde, chairman of the board of trustees, William B. Barstow and Samuel Insull. The west end of the main library building has been rebuilt to provide for a memorial entrance to the three rooms in which will be placed the library assembled by Mr. Lieb, who at the time of his death in 1929 was senior vice-president of the New York Edison Company. He was a graduate and trustee of the institute.

The will of the late Lewis Cass Ledyard bequeaths $2,000,000 to the New York Public Library and $250,000 to the Morgan Library. Mr. Ledyard's right and interest as a fellow in perpetuity of the Metropolitan Museum of Art go to Junius S. Morgan, described as "the grandson of my friend John Pierpont Morgan." In making his bequest to the New York Public Library Mr. Ledyard expresses the desire that "this legacy shall be added to and become part of the permanent endowment fund of the Library" and that the income shall be used for the maintenance and support of the institution. The sum of $40,000 each is left to Mr. Edwin H. Anderson, director of the public library, and to Mr. Harry Miller Lydenberg, assistant director.

Two appropriations amounting to three hundred thousand dollars to Vanderbilt University for the benefit of the School of Medicine have recently been announced. Of this amount, two hundred and fifty thousand dollars was granted by the Rockefeller Foundation as a fluid research fund for the School of Medicine, with the understanding that a supplementary amount shall be secured by the authorities of the school. An appropriation of fifty thousand dollars was made by the General Education Board for the medical library. The research fund will be divided and distributed over a period of eight years, while the medical library grant will be distributed over a period of four years.

Alumni of New York University have established an Alumni Meritorious Award which will include the presentation of a medallion designed by Thomas Hudson Jones. A suitably inscribed certificate also will be presented to those alumni who have rendered unusual service. The first awards will be made at an all-university dinner on March 1. Presentations will be made by Chancellor Elmer Ellsworth Brown. After this year the honor will be limited to a maximum of two from each degree-conferring unit of the university. It is planned to make the presentations a part of the annual commencement exercises.

THE Board of Regents of the University of Wisconsin has restored to Germans and German-Americans the honorary degrees taken from them during the world war.

THE current number of *The American Oxonian,* quarterly publication of the Association of American Rhodes Scholars, includes the first comprehensive bibliography of American Rhodes Scholars, prepared by Dr. George Emerson Barnes. Nearly 150 pages of the magazine are required to present the list of books and articles written by 120 scholars. Pointing out that additions remain to be made, A. C. Valentine, editor of the magazine, makes the comment that "even as the list stands, its breadth and bulk can not fail to be impressive. Those who have wondered what influence former Rhodes Scholars have brought to bear upon their communities and the nation have here food for thought."

THE trustees of the Massachusetts State College at Amherst as an economy measure have voted this year to omit the summer school session.

ATLANTIC CITY'S public school teachers voted on February 4 to turn back 10 per cent. of their 1932–33 term salaries into the treasury of the Board of Education. This will save about $120,000 during the next school year without jeopardizing tenure, pensions and wage scales. Following this action, the Board of Education adopted a budget reducing the amount to be raised by taxation by $157,034 under the amount of the present school term.

IT is reported to the *United States Daily* from Harrisburg that Dr. James N. Rule, superintendent of public instruction, in an address before the annual convention of the School Directors Association, stated that never before "have public-school officials been confronted with such vital and such far-reaching problems of economy and public education. To cut teachers' salaries unless and until every other measure of necessary economy has been taken is unsound and unsafe. It will further reduce their buying power. Greatest of all, however, will be the loss of confidence on the part of those who direct the spiritual and educational development of our children." The answer for lower school costs, Dr. Rule said, does not lie in a "disruption of salary schedules and the public school program." Dr. Rule suggested a comprehensive study of the situation and for appropriate adjustments in conformity with the findings.

ACCORDING to an Associated Press dispatch, Dr. Sidney B. Hall, Virginia state superintendent of public instruction, on February 3 informed the governor that owing to lack of funds hundreds of public schools in Virginia will have to close this session much earlier than usual. The statement filed with the governor is based on a report made to the Department of Education by the various division superintendents. It shows that even in many of the counties which will run their schools for a full term they will only be able to do so by borrowing money or by making drastic cuts in the salaries of teachers.

THE immediate closing of the vocational schools of New Jersey is asked in a resolution received by Governor A. Harry Moore, from the Mount Ephraim local of the United Brotherhood of Carpenters and Joiners. The governor stated that he plans to confer with the state education commissioner on the subject. It was pointed out in the resolution that the vocational schools are graduating boys skilled in various crafts who compete in seeking work with married men with families. Another argument advanced was that tax costs would be cut by the closing of the schools.

THREE fourths of the aggregate of all poll taxes collected in North Carolina counties must be forwarded to the state treasurer with the proceeds of the newly levied 15-cent *ad valorem* tax for the support of the public schools. Mr. Dennis J B.rummitt, attorney-general, has ruled that the per capita tax is $2, levied on men over 21 years old.

According to the *Journal of Education* the Cuban National University, which has been closed since September, 1930, will be reopened under an entirely new plan which will remove it from the direct supervision of the government, according to the proposal of Dr. Carlos Miguel de Cespedes, Secretary of Public Instruction, who is working out the details of a proposal to be submitted to Congress. The plan is to turn over all buildings and grounds now owned by the state to the university, which will become a separate organization governed by a board of directors composed of twenty-six deans and professors who were appointed to the faculty in 1900 after competitive examinations. The government will arrange an endowment of $2,000,000. The matriculation fee will be set at $200 and the government will each year purchase 1,500 scholarships to be distributed among men and women who would be otherwise financially unable to attend the university.

DISCUSSION

THE STUDY OF BIBLIOGRAPHY

The importance of bibliography as an adjunct to learning and scholarship is altogether too much neglected in the educational scheme. When freshmen first arrive in college it is an annual curiosity to discover that fully half the class can make no intelligent discrimination between biography and bibliography. When the same boys become seniors it is a matter of concern to those of us who have labored with them for four years to find so many of them making blind approaches to subject-matter in assembling material for their theses. Nor is this ignorance of the technique of research work confined to undergraduates alone. Many who have passed on to the rôle of teacher are maimed in the regions of higher scholarship by unfamiliarity with fundamental bibliographical tools. Even the specialist who is adept in handling the apparatus of research in his own field is unaware of much related bibliography that would be ancillary to his investigations.

A governmental report in England of a decade ago arrived at the conviction that " . . . in every University where research work in English is undertaken provision should be made for instruction in bibliography."[1] The conclusions of this report would doubtless be applicable to other subjects. Looking back a very few years to a three-year concentration on "The History and Literature of England" and to a senior thesis on "The Influence of the *Edinburgh Review*" the writer can now see how much the quality of that work would have been improved by instruction in bibliography.

Of course there is more than one type of bibliography. There is the kind which has to do with the history and descriptions of books and the comparison of texts. This is for the genuine scholar and requires a precision which is not easily imparted. The other kind bears the same relation to research as tools to the work of a carpenter and oil to a machine. It provides a method of attack and facilitates approach. Training in it is an elementary prerequisite of any productive research. Occasionally, it is self-acquired satisfactorily; generally, ignorance of it is the cause of much imperfect work.

Here and there in the last decade, bibliography as a subject of study has come in for distinguished, if sporadic attention. In 1926, Cambridge University established the Sandars Lectures, the first fruit of which was a series of lectures on the sources of English literature. The following year the lectures catered to a much more esoteric group on the subject of "Binding Before 1500." Similarly, lectureships of this nature have been established at London University, where Mr. Pollard is the distinguished incumbent, and in modified form at various American universities.

Important as such recognitions of bibliography are, they are not particularly fruitful as a method of instruction to students. In 1926 the American Library Association listed[2]

[1] "The Teaching of English in England," London, 1921, p. 242.

[2] "Survey of Libraries in the United States," Chicago, 1926, v. 2.

seventeen American colleges which offered elective courses in bibliography. These courses provided valuable training in the use of books and libraries, but insofar as they are divorced from the special field in which the student is interested, they do not refine his ability as a scholar capable of original research. *A priori* training that comes with the lectureship method can not equip the student with the necessary technique. In fact, it is frequently impossible to explain to an individual student the clear distinction between primary and secondary source material without supervising investigation of a particular problem.

Clearly, instruction in bibliography is a laboratory problem. One or two universities in the country have met it by introducing "bibliographic seminars," in which the student is asked to compile a bibliography in his special field. However, even closer contact between the work of the student in his own history or economics seminar and his technique of research is doubtless desirable. Fundamentally, probably the best point for instruction would be his own tutor, but unfortunately too many of the tutors have traveled the same unilluminated course as their pupils, even if they had the will to work with students in the library.

The immediate solution of the problem, therefore, finally narrows itself down to the need for closer cooperation between tutor and library. Definite appointments must be arranged for a small group of students in a particular field to come to the library and spend one or more intensive sessions studying the apparatus applicable to their own research work. Of course many individual students invite such help of their own free accord, but a more formal appointment is necessary to reach even a majority of the "honors" students. In the normal course of events, the departments are enthusiastic to avail themselves of any instruction the library is willing to give along these lines. The interest of the student runs the usual gamut from absorption to diffidence, although a good deal depends as always upon the person supervising the work. If, for instance, his subjects are making a special study at the time of appointment of seventeenth century American history, he has a very definite region of bibliography in which to stimulate their interest.

Administratively, instruction of this type is a problem for the college and the library. It is the business of the first to put at the disposal of the librarian funds for the hire of some one who can free himself at times from routine and has the training and qualities requisite for the work. The library itself must provide a bibliographical workshop, preferably its regular bibliographical room where the locale and appearance of the books may become permanently fixed in the students' minds. Then the work is done in fact under the conditions of a laboratory.

The emergence of bibliography as a subject for study has always been slow. Latterly, demand for it has proceeded from scholars who desire assistance from research workers in the compilation of bibliographies. It has become their opinion that the scholar should no more be called upon to "handicap his ideas with details of library research," as one scientist recently put it, than that "the chemist should do all his glass-blowing, the astronomer his lens-grinding." This is another angle to the same problem. Some may even see a suggestion of contradiction between the training up of students to self-help and the demand of scholars for assistance. But there is no real conflict. The instruction of the immature student is essentially a training in the method and technique of research, without which no mature scholar can hope to be forth-putting. The appeal of the latter for research librarians who will prepare bibliographical lists is a legitimate demand for relief from drudgery. Nor is such labor distasteful to those whose business it is. They realize that they are a desirable link in the creative process, although their name may not appear even in the preface to the finished product. In fact, some scholars there are who will not forego the pleasure of doing all their own bibliographical work, but to a large majority it is understandable that such work is mentally dwarfing and obstructive. Freedom from the trammels of routine has always been considered an enhancement to creative power. It is one additional fact in the accumulating evidence that bibliography as an adjunct to scholarship will sooner or later probably emerge into fuller usefulness.

Arnold K. Borden

Dartmouth College

BACK TO READERS

SEVERAL of our educational publishers have embarked lately on one of those compilation schemes for which America has always been noted, or perhaps it would be more accurate to say notorious. The idea is to collect in a series of volumes, generally one for each school year, all the reading required for college entrance and such other material as the editors deem suitable for high or junior high school use, presenting it as a complete literature "course." "Back to Readers" the movement has been called, and certainly from the standpoint of a librarian "back" is the correct word. Since the librarian is supposed to be by profession an expert in that gentle art of bringing books and readers together, the ultimate aim of all courses in literature, it may be of interest to consider how this new movement accords with the principles that have been worked out in modern library science.

In the first place the mere physical appearance of such books is against them. Every librarian finds that when a book is physically heavy, the average person leaps to the conclusion that the contents are heavy, too; and young people are particularly prone to be influenced by such considerations. Those big, beautifully illustrated classics, which are so popular with fond relatives as gift books, may be looked over in the library reading room but are seldom carried home. Even magazines are so evidently turned into dead wood when bound in large volumes that most public libraries have abandoned the idea of binding back numbers, piling them on storeroom shelves instead. Accordingly, it seems more than likely that the average high school pupil, confronted at the beginning of the year by one of these weighty tomes, will feel tired before he starts, and his required reading will not have a fair chance to win his interest. The teacher will be handicapped. And even the very bright student, who may at first enjoy having so large a literary meal spread before him, will probably find before the end of the year that it was unfortunate that the whole *menu* was presented at once. He will soon skim the book through, forming his own ideas as to what is interesting and what is "punk," and thereafter the freshness will have been lost and he will approach with prejudice those more difficult selections for which he needed and should have had a little preparation.

In fact one serious disadvantage of such compilations is the absolute impossibility of including adequate introductions and notes for those selections that lie far outside the experience of our boys and girls. Granted that the present trend is happily away from textual criticism, sources and the like in high school literature courses, it requires a remarkable teacher to plunge a freshman class into a Shakespeare play and make them enjoy it if they have not been provided with any background such as a cultured person normally brings to his reading. The supposition that the usual teacher or school library can supply such a background is quite unwarranted. It should be provided by a carefully prepared text-book given out when the class is ready to begin it.

The separate text-book has the added advantage of variety. There is a deadly monotony in putting out all kinds of literature in the identical print, paging and cover design which reminds one of the dull and unattractive shelves of those old-fashioned public libraries where the books used to stand in uniform covers of brown paper. The modern librarian not only shows up the publishers' alluring bindings as effectively as possible but has rebound books put into cheerful covers of gay and varied colors, knowing that the pleasant anticipations aroused by outside attractiveness do much to make the contents of books appear attractive also. In such matters the schools may well take a leaf from the modern librarian's book of methods. It is psychologically bad policy for them to throw such helps overboard when they are tackling a task preeminently important and at best difficult. The aim is to give our young folks a love of good literature, and in the whole school course they will hardly find anything outside the three Rs which will be of greater value in their future lives. We can not afford to prejudice them at the start by offering them their whole four years' reading bound up in a set of heavy, uniform volumes whose contents resemble nothing so much as those Elks' benefit performances of blessed memory, when the scene from "Hamlet" or "As You Like It" was sandwiched in between Gilbert and Sullivan and the performing seals. All three were excellent entertainments, but they did not synchronize, and surely this is not the way to present the classics to our young people, who need all the help we can give to induce them to appreciate the product of past generations.

What the advantages of these compilations are supposed to be we can only guess. One may be that they reduce the labor of book-buying to a minimum, for when once such a set has been purchased, the literature department is off the minds of the book committee. And possibly they may be a little cheaper than the separate books would be, although this can only be determined after several years of experiment. Heavy books get hard usage, and each volume being in continuous use throughout the year would need to be replaced much oftener than the individual books contained in it. In any case, such small savings of time or money are negligible. The only point to be considered is whether it is better for the student to have the books he is asked to read bound up together in such collections or treated as the separate entities they are.

Pauline W. Leonard

Accord, Mass.

CONFERENCE OF WOMEN MEMBERS OF BOARDS OF EDUCATION

The writer has communicated with all women members of boards of education in cities of over 30,000 in all states east of the Mississippi with a view to organization of such women into a permanent association, which will probably affiliate with the National Education Association. My idea in organizing such an association of women is for the purpose of enabling interchange of ideas and aims among board members from all parts of the country, with the object of establishing a better understanding of the functions of boards of education and the improvement of our educational systems throughout the country. Believing that women are freer than men from the restraints of business, and that therefore they could more easily attend conferences and discussions which might be held at some distance from their respective cities, women board members are invited to attend an organization breakfast and round-table conference in Washington, D. C., at the Hotel Hamilton, on February 22, 1932, at noon.

Ruby Crampton,

Member of Board of Education, Toledo, Ohio

SPECIAL CORRESPONDENCE

MODERN EDUCATION IN GERMANY

No one familiar with the German schools of pre-war times can fail to be surprised at the many changes made during the past decade in the system of German education. It is really difficult for Americans, who went to Germany in large numbers in pre-war days to do graduate work at the great universities, to realize fully the modern trend of educational reforms. But what is most astounding is to learn that the youth of Germany are among the real leaders in the work.

A movement was started by them a few years ago which had as some of its characteristic features: Intense love of nature and a natural life; self-expression; respect for the personality of others; and the demand for the respect of one's own personality, faith, simplicity and unity. These proved to be something more than mere catchwords as they found attentive and willing ears among educational reformers who were eager to give the younger generation a share in the work. For instance, they sanctioned the organization of student councils, composed of pupils of the three upper classes who meet periodically with the authorities to discuss questions of instruction, educational matters, discipline, etc. As yet, they may only propose reforms; but they have been alert to point out the defects and weaknesses of the old system and many of their suggestions have been adopted. For example, under the old régime, several distinct disadvantages were apparent: firstly, not all boys and girls had the same right to education and culture; secondly, if one type of school was entered, it was very difficult to transfer to another; thirdly, little use was made of self-activity, and consequently there was a failure to develop originality and initiative.

These were some of the serious defects which were remedied by the Federal Education Council, which met in Berlin in 1920. Its plans, which form the basis of present-day education in Germany, are essentially as follows: in order to promote democracy, all pupils between the ages of six and ten are compelled to attend a "foundation school" which forms a part of the elementary school. (This is a new departure, as those who could afford to do so used to send their children to a private school for preparation to enter the secondary schools. These private schools were abolished at the end of 1929. The private secondary schools, however, continue their own existence.) At the age of ten, a boy may continue four more years in the elementary school or enter a six-year course at the *Mittelschule,* which prepares for positions in commercial life, etc. Admission to the secondary schools is possible for those who pass their examinations. Another type of school, the *Aufbauschule,* permits entrance to the secondary school at the end of the seventh year, thereby saving three years. It is worthy of mention that the chief test for education in these schools and others in Germany is whether a boy has developed responsibility and the essential power of achievement.

Now that a boy is ready to enter a secondary school, he is faced with the problem of making a choice among several types of schools: (1) The *Gymnasium,* which offers a nine year's course, making an extensive study of the classics; (2) the *Realgymnasium,* where Latin is required and where great emphasis is laid on the modern languages "to familiarize the student with the creative thought of western Europe"; (3) the *Oberrealschule,* stressing mathematics and the sciences; and (4) the *Deutsche Oberschule,* a new type of school which makes the study of German, history, geography and the culture of the German people its main purpose. There is not a lack of unity in these types of schools, as might be supposed, for unity is preserved through a number of subjects common to all schools: *e.g.,* religion, German, history, geography, civics, physical training and music. In all the secondary schools, boys remain from six to nine years.

The German boys devote more time to study than American boys. The latter have time for study during the school hours, whereas a boy at a *Gymnasium,* for example, has a recitation nearly every hour of the day. As he usually has seven recitations a day, except on Wednesdays and Saturdays, it is impossible for him to "prepare" them, as we understand the term. The Germans call them "instruction hours," and the boys take notes on the subject under discussion. Home study has certain fixed limits, ranging from one hour a day for the two lowest classes to approximately three hours per day for the two highest classes, and such study concerns itself chiefly with rearranging notes and memorizing material indispensable for class work, and reviewing what has been learned.

Personal ambition, family pride and restricted means prevent the German schoolboy from taking his education quite as casually as American boys do. It is really a serious business which fits a boy for positions in the state as well as for the professions. Education for simply the cultural values is not the main objective in Germany. Nor is this necessary. The older European civilization through the aid of wonderful art galleries, theaters (where the masterpieces of literature are played) and the strong influences of the great universities meet the demands for culture, the value of which is by no means underestimated.

German instruction, above all, puts a high premium on the development of the intellectual faculties of a boy. He must get more than a real grasp of the subject. He must also learn its relation to other subjects and learn how to work with scientific method; how to study in a free, independent manner and to be responsible for the conduct of his life if he hopes to succeed in the higher institutions of learning. At the universities the aim is to realize the ideal of education through the highest degree of freedom of study and instruction. For example, there is no system of points and credits, and there are no examinations either at the beginning or the end of a semester. At these universities, therefore, unusually great demands are made upon the self-discipline of the student who generally reacts favorably to the great confidence placed in him.

This article covers only a few aspects of the extensive subject of modern education in Germany, but the writer would like to stress again the significance of the so-called "Youth Movement," which has brought a new form of student life to the universities through the agency of student houses, which have comprehensive departments for sport, economic self-help and the furthering of art and social intercourse. Student houses have already been built at five universities, and students, native and foreign, are meeting there for joint work, social events and festivals, and thus, together with teachers and friends of the university, they are striving to bring into existence that community life which is the ideal of the younger generation of German students.

LESTER C. NEWTON
PHILLIPS ACADEMY,
ANDOVER, MASS.

THE INTRAMURAL ATHLETICS PROGRAM AT SYRACUSE UNIVERSITY

LAST June the trustees of Syracuse University approved a transfer of all control over athletics from an athletic governing board to the administrative authorities of the university. They voted, further, that immediate direction of all athletics of any sort should be through an athletic manager responsible directly to the chancellor and that he should be assisted by an athletic council made up of representatives from the undergraduates, the faculty and the alumni. The program provided for two other definite steps, the giving of academic rank to athletic coaches, and the extension of academic control over their activities; and the immediate expansion of an intramural program of athletics. College opened in September without the appointment of the new athletic manager, Mr. H. Harrison Clark was appointed director of intramural sports, and he began at once upon an intensive program. Mr. Clark is a graduate of Springfield College, has been a director of physical education in public schools, a member of the Central Committee of the New York State Athletic Association, and state chairman of cross country. He is an instructor in the physical education department and his program involved the utilization of all students majoring in physical education, training themselves for the work of high school coaches and Y. M. C. A. athletic directors and similar positions. With a staff of such men, Mr. Clark has been able to show progress within the two months already past, which many advisers believed would be impossible in view of lack of equipment and endowment for such work.

In the past the only form of athletics open to the young men who did not "go out" for a team, were "pick-up" games of ball, or an occasional interfraternity competition or intramural meets in track, boxing or wrestling. The latter were initiated spasmodically by athletic coaches to find material for their teams. There was no organized baseball, football, basketball or other team play for the average student.

It was found impracticable to play football, as there was too much danger for untrained players. But a fast, lively game, "touch" football, in which the player is tackled by merely being touched instead of being pulled to the ground, was substituted. Thirty-five teams entered the tournament and enthusiasm ran high as class, college, fraternity and rooming house leagues battled through their schedules.

Seventy-eight teams and almost a thousand students played intramural basketball. On a single afternoon early in December twenty-four basketball games and twice that many teams played on the courts of Archbold Gymnasium.

Nor are football and basketball the only popular games. Even horseshoe pitching has achieved success as an intramural activity. A game need not be spectacular to find a place in intramural competition. Because they lead the student toward the wise use of leisure time, both now and in later years, such sports as bowling, swimming, handball, golf and tennis have been selected. Volley ball, track and foul-shooting complete the list of sports planned for the first year of campus athletics at Syracuse. As demand arises other games will be added. The next steps will be campus-wide ice-hockey and fencing.

Besides these sports there is a mountain-climbing club led by Dr. Ernest S. Griffith, dean of the lower division. At regular intervals trips are made to the Catskills or Adirondacks. During the week-end excursions one or more mountains are scaled. By the use of private automobiles for transportation and by other economies, the cost of the two-day trip is brought within the reach of the average student.

Syracuse University enrolls more than 5,000 students, and approximately 3,000 of these are men. The great majority of these men students not already forced into out-of-door work by reason of the curriculum of such schools as Forestry and Applied Science are brought out into the open air. The women students already have a well organized intramural program which includes rifle-shooting, archery, basketball, baseball, hockey and even horseback riding. So that the officers of Syracuse University now feel that while a great deal remains to be accomplished, they are well on the way toward a solution of the serious problem, due to over-emphasis of inter-collegiate sports.

A CORRESPONDENT

QUOTATIONS

MUSEUMS

IN the "Memorandum on the possibility of increased cooperation between Public Museums and Public Educational Institutions," just issued by the Board of Education and summarized on another page, it is stated that, though there are more than 400 museums in England and Wales accessible to the public, only about twenty have organized arrangements for lending exhibits to the public elementary schools. The Memorandum compares this with the thousand museums in the United States, all of which have been "deliberately created as auxiliary to the education system of the country." That system is admittedly inferior, except in some favored areas, to the English system, which, by the unifying control of the central Board of Education, keeps definite educational standards on foot everywhere. But in the matter of the use of museums as part of the educational system, America is in advance, and the same may be said—or might have been said very recently —with respect to the relationship of the public libraries and the schools. France, Italy, and even Germany, share our backwardness, if it is backwardness, in this respect, and the writer of the Memorandum is anxious to link more closely our elementary and secondary schools with the museums, and incidentally with the English library system. The writer mentions the Deutsches Museum at Munich, opened in 1925, devoted solely to pure and applied science (other than biology), and says that about 2,000 parties of children (including 800 from other countries and other parts of Germany) visit the museum each year, and these include members of school journey parties. On the other hand, no mention is made of the fact that the British Museum at Bloomsbury is visited by innumerable school children in the course of the year and that the National Gallery and the National Portrait Gallery in London are also popular.

The Memorandum seems to understate the indirect use of the great museums other than the Museums of Science and Art at South Kensington, and dwells upon the failure to use the local museums in the past. It adopts the finding of Sir Henry Miers that, with certain important exceptions, they were failing to serve the needs either of research or of popular education. This is true in many cases, though since the Museums Act, 1845, the museum movement throughout the country has slowly been growing since the war. The museums are beginning to federate into an organized public service, "in which each unit will have a definite function and act in regular cooperation with other units, both national and local, and with the public service of education." No doubt the better selection and arrangement of exhibits will make museums educationally and technically more efficient, and where there is a technical end to serve, in the case especially of art schools and craft schools, and, of course, universities and university and technical colleges, the proper arrangement and coordination of museums are vitally important. But despite former weakness, and in some cases the present weakness of local museums, there must be some other reason that teachers and educationists generally have not adopted, as their colleagues in America have, a very obvious educational service. In the past, English and German teachers have left the museums to the attention of school journeys or their equivalents, and have treated the school proper as the scene of ordinary class work as understood by the older generation. In the ordinary elementary school the children were too young to take educational interest in museums, however well their contents were exhibited, and in the ordinary grammar or secondary school it was deemed impossible in most cases to use the museum in direct class work. The Memorandum advocates the use of "traveling museums" and loan collections in the class room. The London loan collections for a quarter of a century have in fact been so used, and in 1930 the loans from the Victoria and Albert Museum comprised 39,312 works of art, 18,544 lantern slides, and 519 books issued to thirty-seven training colleges, 359 secondary schools, and 261 art schools besides other institutions. That is the line on which development can best take place. For students of history photographs from the British Museum and the National Portrait Gallery might be more used. Teachers are increasingly using material of that type—even from the Record Office—and the teaching of local history would gain stimulus by the use of reproductions from local museums. The museum, in fact, can stimulate the educational sense in both teachers and pupils, and that is its chief use.—*The London Times Educational Supplement.*

REPORTS

PROGRESS OF THE NATIONAL SURVEYS OF EDUCATION AMONG NEGROES

THE three national surveys being conducted by the U. S. Office of Education are: The National Survey of Secondary Education, the National Survey of the Education of Teachers and the National Survey of School Finance. Each of these surveys is giving special attention to problems of the education of Negroes in the states which have separate schools for the white and colored races. Although much general interest has been shown by many persons concerned with the advancement of Negro education which these surveys are likely to effect, there is need of increased interest and activity if the surveys are to have the greatest possible value in the improvement of educational conditions for the more than 2,000,300 Negro pupils, and 50,000 teachers in the Southern states. It seems desirable, therefore, to make a report at this time on the progress of the surveys as they pertain to the Negro.

SECONDARY SURVEY

The National Survey of Secondary Education was begun on July 1, 1929, and will be completed on June 30, 1932. During the school year 1929–30 Mr. H. C. Russell spent several months devising plans and making certain preliminary investigations in connection with the study of Negro secondary schools; and Dr. John M. Gandy, president of Virginia State College, was appointed as the Negro representative on the general advisory committee. During this time general policies and plans were formulated and the main objective of the phase of the survey dealing with Negro schools was decided upon.

The national survey is "devoted chiefly to inquiries concerning current efforts to improve secondary education rather than merely to a description of its present status. Studies of status should be made chiefly to provide the background against which innovating practices may be made to stand out." Since there were considerable data on the status of secondary education for whites, the directors of the survey and the group of consultants were justified in emphasizing innovating and noteworthy practises as the main objective. For the Negro, however, very little was known concerning the status of secondary education; and it was believed by many persons that too few Negro schools would be found with constructive and innovating practises to yield sufficient comparable data to make any real contribution to the advancement of Negro secondary education. It was decided, therefore, that the chief objective of the section of the survey dealing with Negro education should be to ascertain status, at the same time to collect and report all the evidence possible which will show noteworthy practices, the facts regarding status being used frequently to throw in relief those techniques and procedures which are out of the ordinary.

This special study will not preclude the participation of certain Negro schools in the general study. About fifty different forms have been sent out to a large percentage of the 25,000 public secondary schools. Some of the schools received one or two inquiry forms, while others received as many as five or six, the number depending on the extent of constructive or noteworthy practices in a given school. Thus several Negro schools were included among those receiving any given form. However, these schools will not be reported on the basis of race, but rather with respect to regional and other classifications.

This decision respecting the major objective having been made, the first task of the writer, after being appointed specialist in the education of Negroes in the U. S. Office of Education, was to begin the construction of an outline for the study and the development of a special inquiry form. The outline included all the major topics of the general outline, namely: (1) Organization of schools and districts, (2) secondary school population and related problems, (3) administration and supervision, and (4) the curriculum and extra-curriculum. Two additional topics were included in the special outline for Negro schools: Teachers and teaching, and housing and equipment. Inquiries with respect to each of these topics will be made chiefly to ascertain status, while for the general survey, as explained above, the chief objective will be to find innovations.

Some of the subjects which will be studied in this special section are:

(1) Availability of high-school facilities, including transportation provisions.
(2) Trends in reorganization of secondary schools for Negroes.
(3) Trends in enrolment, attendance and elimination.
(4) Special provisions for secondary work.
(5) Organization of schools and length of term.
(6) Types of student personnel records.
(7) Policies and practices in administration and supervision.
(8) Professional status and duties of principal.
(9) Average number and length of recitation.
(10) Pupil load and provisions for individual differences.
(11) Curriculum offerings, electives, and graduation requirements.
(12) Extra-curriculum offering and supervision.
(13) Teachers, teaching problems, teaching load, and salaries.
(14) Housing and equipment.

The state departments of education of the states having separate schools were requested to send us a list of all schools for Negroes doing one or more years of secondary school work, including junior high schools. A total of 1,315 such schools was reported. The commissioner of education sent a letter to the principal of each of these schools, explaining the need and nature of the special section of the survey dealing with Negro schools and requesting his cooperation. We have not received up to the present as large a percentage of returns from these schools as is desired. However, it is believed that the follow-up procedures which have been adopted will bring in a sufficiently representative sampling to make valid whatever conclusions may be drawn from the study.

In order to obtain first-hand information and to assure a correct analysis and truer interpretation of the data, the writer has visited fifty-four Negro high schools in fourteen different states, including Alabama, Arkansas, Illinois, Indiana, Kansas, Kentucky, Maryland, Missouri, New Jersey, North Carolina, Oklahoma, Tennessee, Virginia and West Virginia.

The survey must be completed and the report written by June 30, 1932. As in the case of the outline, the check list and the administrative procedures, the counsel of the National Advisory Committee on the Education of Negroes will be sought in the interpretation of some of the data and concerning certain conclusions, and also in the manner of reporting the findings. The major facts and interpretations regarding the status of secondary education among Negroes will be reported in one of the series of monographs. It is believed that such a plan will insure the widest possible audience among the various groups who are likely to be interested and who are able to effect an improvement in the situation.

TEACHER EDUCATION SURVEY

The National Survey of Teacher Education, which was begun in July of 1930, has special phases devoted to Negro teachers, which are being studied by the specialist in the education of Negroes, and which, in all essential respects, are identical to the studies being made of white teachers. Unlike the secondary survey, it has no special outline or separate questionnaire for Negro teachers and schools. The personnel data sheet sent out to all the teachers of the country reached the Negro teachers through the same channels that were used for other teachers, and the data furnished by these questionnaires will be sorted and tabulated in the same manner and at the same time as all the other data.

Similarly, the inquiry form to be sent to a selected number of teacher-training institutions for white students will also be sent to a group of selected Negro schools doing significant work in the training of teachers. This form is designed to collect data concerning students, the curriculum and curriculum policies, and certain other facts with reference to general educational philosophy and policy of the institution.

Nearly a million personnel data blanks were sent through the state and county superintendents to the teachers of the entire country. Replies were received from 460,000 teachers. Something over 13,000 of these replies were from Negro teachers, which is about 26 per cent. of the 50,000 Negro public-school teachers in the states maintaining separate schools. Some of the data gathered through these personnel blanks will be used in the Secondary Survey and the Survey of School Finance. Since, therefore, such wide use is to be made of these data, and because of the necessity of having representative samplings from each state, especially those maintaining separate school systems, a special effort is being made to secure additional returns.

The value of the three surveys now under way in the improvement of Negro education will largely depend upon the representativeness of the returns of these personnel blanks. Every Negro public-school teacher, therefore, who has not sent in a questionnaire reply will make a real contribution to the progress, the profession, and to Negro education in general, by immediately securing a blank from his superintendent or the state director of Negro education, filling it out and returning it to the U. S. Office of Education in Washington.

The group of Negro schools selected for special study was chosen in the following manner: All Negro colleges, normal schools and teachers colleges were classified into five groups according to certain geographical regions, giving approximately equal representation to the various sections of the country in terms of Negro population, number of teachers and number of higher institutions. A jury of competent educators, acquainted with these schools, assisted in selecting the five schools in each group that are representative of the better practices in the education of Negro teachers. Some of the bases upon which the schools were considered were: Size of enrolment, library facilities, physical plant, equipment and income.

Personal visits will be made to most of the schools selected in order to secure first-hand information concerning the teacher education facilities for colored students.

While separate inquiries will be made concerning Negro teachers and Negro teacher-training institutions and departments, the general studies and conclusions will be just as applicable to Negro teachers and their education as to others; and it is the hope that the survey will make as significant a contribution to the improvement of the teaching profession among Negroes as among whites.

SURVEY OF SCHOOL FINANCE

On July 1, 1931, another survey was begun by the Office of Education, a National Survey of School Finance. The question of finance is perhaps the most important and dominant educational problem to-day in most states and communities, and is of special significance in the education of Negroes where separate schools are maintained. Some of the more vital school problems which are closely related to finance, and which are of great significance to Negro education are: Enrolment, retention and elimination, high-school offering, curriculum enrichment, provisions for individual differences, number and salary of teachers, pupil-teacher ratio, and equipment and facilities. It is hoped that this survey will do much toward the solution of these problems.

While details of the survey have not yet been worked out, it is the plan to give thorough consideration to those special problems of the various phases of the survey which have important implications for Negro education. Commissioner Wm. John Cooper, director of the survey, and Dr. Paul R. Mort, associate director, are seeking advice and counsel on the matter, and it is believed that the facts revealed by this school finance study will do much in creating a public opinion calculated to promote a fair approach toward the equalization of educational opportunities.

ADVISORY COMMITTEE

In December of 1930 the National Advisory Committee on the Education of Negroes was appointed by Dr. Ray Lyman Wilbur, Secretary of the Interior. The purpose of this committee, the personnel of which was nominated by Commissioner Cooper, is to cooperate with the Office of Education, through the specialist in the education of Negroes, in its general work concerned with Negro education and give advice and counsel in connection with major problems and questions which will arise in connection with the national surveys.

There are twenty-four members of the committee. They come from the various sections of the country and represent different phases of education, such as elementary, secondary and teacher training. Seven members are specialists in secondary education and are teachers or administrators in that field. Five are specialists in the preparation of teachers and are engaged in that particular line of work.

Four members of the National Advisory Committee on the education of Negroes are also members of the general advisory committee of the teacher-education survey, acting as liaison agencies between the two committees. They are: Miss Fannie C. Williams, of the Valena C. Jones School, New Orleans, Louisiana; Dean D. O. W. Holmes, college of education, Howard University, Washington, D. C.; President B. F. Hubert, Georgia Agricultural and Mechanical College for Negroes, Savannah, Georgia; and Dean W. T. B. Williams, Tuskegee Institute, Tuskegee, Alabama. Likewise, as explained earlier, Dr. Gandy, who is a member of the advisory committee on Negro education, is also a member of the general advisory committee on the secondary survey, serving in a similar capacity as those persons on the teacher-education advisory committee. It is the plan to have persons especially qualified in school finance and related problems to represent the Negro interest on the advisory committee on the School Finance Survey. Such persons will also become members of the advisory committee on the education of Negroes and serve in a liaison capacity as the other members similarly situated.

It is the plan of the commissioner of education to call regional conferences upon the invitation of the persons concerned, for the purpose of discussing the results of the findings of the surveys and to assist the states and local communities in evaluating their own situation in the light of national conditions and trends.

Thus it is believed that the continual publicity given the facts relating to education and the additional light thrown on the subject and information furnished as a result of conference discussions will contribute much toward the advancement of education.

No such procedure can be practiced without greatly affecting the education of Negroes under the American system. It is, therefore, hoped that full cooperation on the part of all concerned will continue to be given in the present and future surveys to the end that the Negro may receive that education and training which will adequately fit him to make the greatest possible contribution to American civilization.

AMBROSE CALIVER
U. S. OFFICE OF EDUCATION

EDUCATIONAL RESEARCH AND STATISTICS

PRESIDENTS OF STATE TEACHERS COLLEGES

THIS is a study of sixty-one state teachers college presidents, selected as follows: (1) All institutions rated as Class A four-year teachers colleges by the American Association of Teachers Colleges in 1925 were listed; (2) all private and municipal institutions were eliminated, as also were any state institutions whose names failed to appear in the Class A rating of the association for 1931; (3) the incumbent president of each of the institutions remaining is included in this study, provided a biographical sketch of him appeared in "Who's Who in America" for 1931, which is the sole source of the data assembled. Of course the sixty-one presidents so selected are not accurately representative of the whole class from which they are drawn. They merely afford a basis for the study of the species in sixty-one institutions which have been rated as reputable degree-granting colleges for at least six years. These institutions happen to be distributed in twenty-five states, scattered on the map from California to Maine.

The present ages in years of the presidents range from 36 to 80, the median being 58. Their tenure in their present positions ranges from 1 to 39 years, the median being 12 years. Fourteen, or nearly one fourth of them, had previously held a teachers college presidency or normal school principalship. For the group as a whole, the total length of service as head of an institution for the training of teachers ranges from 1 to 43 years, with a median of 14 years. These data appear in Table I.

TABLE I

The Presidents of Sixty-one State Teachers Colleges

Present age in years		Years in present position		Total years as a teachers college or normal school head	
80–84	1	35–39	1	40–44	1
75–79	0	30–34	2	35–39	2
79–74	3	25–29	4	30–34	2
65–69	8	20–24	8	25–29	3
60–64	16	15–19	12	20–24	10
55–59	11	10–14	11	15–19	12
50–54	9	5– 9	11	10–14	11
45–49	7	0– 4	12	5– 9	13
40–44	3			0– 4	7
35–39	2				
Totals	60*		61		61
Ranges	36–80		1–39		1–43
Medians	58		12		14

* One age not given.

Among the positions held by these presidents during their earlier careers, educational work predominates very heavily. The only non-educational employment reported was as follows: Two reported having been engaged in business, one had been a lawyer, one had been a public officer, and one had been an editor. Two reported having been engaged as lecturers, and all others had apparently spent their entire professional careers as teachers or administrators. The previous positions occupied, in descending order of frequency, appear in Table II.

TABLE II

Previous Positions Held

Professor or instructor in college or normal school	46
Public school superintendent (city, county, village, rural)	41
Principal or teacher in high school or academy	38
Principal or teacher in elementary school	36
President of teachers college or head of normal school	14
State superintendent of schools or assistant	10

The subjects taught by those who had been teachers in college or normal school are likewise shown in Table III. For the purpose of affording easy comparison with the results of Rainey's study of 190 college presidents,[1] the distribution of subjects taught as found by him is inserted as columns 4 and 5 of Table III. It

TABLE III

Subjects	61 state teachers college presidents		Rainey's 190 college presidents	
	No.	Per cent.	No.	Per cent.
Education or psychology	15	33	26	15
The social sciences	9	20	32	18
Mathematics or sciences	7	15	39	23
English	5	11	20	12
Foreign languages	3	7	30	17
Philosophy	2	4	13	8
Bible or theology	0	0	11	7

readily appears that professors of education, psychology or the social sciences have been called to teachers college presidencies in greater proportion than to the presidencies of the liberal arts colleges studied by Rainey. The proportion of former teachers of English is nearly the same for each group, but in the case of the liberal arts college presidencies the former professors of mathematics, science, foreign languages, philosophy and theology are all relatively more numerous than their confrères among the teachers college presidents.

[1] Homer P. Rainey, "Some Facts about College Presidents," School and Society, 30: 580–584, October 26, 1929.

The sixty-one teachers college presidents hold a total of 116 earned degrees, granted by 52 different institutions. All institutions granting a bachelor's or master's degree to more than one of them, together with all institutions granting an earned doctor's degree to any of them, are shown in Table IV.

TABLE IV

INSTITUTIONS GRANTING DEGREES

Bachelor's	
Indiana	7
Wisconsin	3
Nebraska	3
Iowa	2
Kentucky	2
Bowdoin	2
Hamline	2
Missouri	2
Valparaiso	2
32 others, each	1
Total degrees	57
Institutions	41
Master's	
Columbia	10
Harvard	5
Indiana	4
Chicago	3
Iowa	2
21 other institutions, each	1
Total degrees	45
Institutions	26
Doctor's	
Columbia	3
Stanford	2
Iowa	2
Johns Hopkins	1
Washington (at (Seattle)	1
Harvard	1
Yale	1
Chicago	1
Pennsylvania	1
Peabody	1
Total degrees	14
Institutions	10

Only ten institutions granted three or more degrees of any grade to this group of presidents. These institutions, with the number of degrees of each grade granted by each, appear in Table V.

TABLE V

INSTITUTIONS GRANTING THREE OR MORE EARNED DEGREES

Institutions	Degrees	Bachelor's	Master's	Doctor's
Columbia	14	1	10	3
Indiana	11	7	4	0
Harvard	6	0	5	1
Iowa	6	2	2	2
Chicago	5	1	3	1
Stanford	4	1	1	2
Wisconsin	4	3	1	0
Missouri	3	2	1	0
Kentucky	3	2	1	0
Nebraska	3	3	0	0
Totals	59	22	28	9

Thus ten institutions granted 50 per cent. of all degrees, 39 per cent. of the bachelor's degrees, 62 per cent. of the master's degrees and 64 per cent. of the doctor's degrees earned by the group.

The percentage of the selected group of state teachers college presidents holding earned doctor's degrees (23 per cent.) is low in comparison with the percentage (36 per cent.) found by Rainey among the 190 college presidents he investigated. No doubt the proportion of holders of earned doctor's degrees may be expected to increase rapidly in the future, as the profession of education approaches the status of such learned pursuits as that of medicine, wherein there are no reputable practitioners without the doctor's degree.

Another tangible evidence of scholarship is the authorship of books. In this field the teachers' college presidents appear in considerable force. Twenty-four of them have written at least one book. Of these, eight have written two, and seven report as many as three publications in book form.

It is probably true that our teachers colleges would benefit by an increased emphasis upon standards of intellectual attainment, and that improvement in this respect is conditioned largely upon better scholarship on their faculties. It may also be true that the securing and holding of scholarly teachers depends largely upon the scholarship of the incumbent of the executive chair. At any rate, the academic histories of teachers college presidents should not escape observation. These men are in very important key positions, where sound scholarship and intellectual independence can do much toward the advancement of our civilization.

M. M. CHAMBERS

TEACHERS COLLEGE
OF KANSAS CITY, MO.

NEW BOOKS IN EDUCATION

ANDERSON, C. J. and I. JEWELL SIMPSON. *The Supervision of Rural Schools.* Pp. xiii + 467. Illustrated. Appleton. $2.50.

DRAPER, EDGAR M. and ALEXANDER C. ROBERTS. *Principles of American Secondary Education.* Pp. xxiii + 549. Century. $2.25.

SCHOOL AND SOCIETY

EDITED BY J. McKEEN CATTELL

WITH WHICH IS COMBINED THE

EDUCATIONAL REVIEW

EDITED BY WILLIAM McANDREW

Volume 35 | SATURDAY, FEBRUARY 20, 1932 | Number 895

IS THE COUNTY UNIT NECESSARY FOR EFFECTIVE RURAL SCHOOL DEVELOPMENT?

By Professor FREDERICK E. BOLTON

UNIVERSITY OF WASHINGTON

(1) Usual Arguments for the County Unit

During the last two decades much has been written concerning the county unit of school organization and administration. It has been argued by many that the county unit is absolutely necessary for efficiency in rural school organization. The old district system is considered to be a hindrance to educational progress. It is assumed that the only remedy is in the complete abandonment of existing rural school districts and the substitution of the county unit as a single school district.

This change would eliminate all the numerous district board members or trustees; take from the local school district the power to determine school revenues, to construct school buildings, to employ teachers and to manage their local schools. All these functions would be vested in a single board of education chosen at large from the entire county. This board would have the power to determine the school revenues to be raised and their apportionment; to employ the county superintendent and all the teachers for each of the districts; to construct and modify school buildings; and to manage all the affairs of all the local schools.

It is argued that a county unit with a single board in control of the financial and educational policies of the schools would secure greater uniformity, greater unity and greater efficiency. By this plan every child would be insured adequate educational facilities, and with the county superintendency removed from politics higher professional standards would result.

It is believed by many educators that the school buildings provided by the district trustees are often miserable makeshifts, cheap in construction, with poor lighting arrangements, no facilities for special types of work and almost no sanitary arrangements. When funds depend upon district taxation the money is so limited that only a poor and inadequate school is maintained and taught by cheap teachers and providing inferior education.

In painting this picture of the wretched condition of rural education one writer depicted the rural school buildings in the following depressing language: "The rural school, from the standpoint of health and general fitness for its important use, is the worst type of building in the whole country, including not only all types of buildings used for human beings, but also those used for live stock and all domestic animals. Rural schools are, on the average, less adequate for their use than prisons, almshouses, stables, dairy barns, pig pens, chicken houses, or dog kennels are for their use.''

The conclusion reached by many is that the district system is the cause and that the remedy lies in the substitution of the county unit. It is maintained that the district system and the township system are no longer adapted to the needs of the present or the future. The district organization should be abandoned in favor of a unit more in harmony with business methods and one better designed to meet the educational needs of rural people. Nothing less than a fundamental reorganization of rural education can transform the rural schools into the type of educational and social institutions demanded by present-day needs. This can be accomplished only by the establishment of a larger type of administrative organization than the district or the township. Many maintain that the district system is absolutely incompatible with the development of an efficient educational system. They say that the hordes of district boards, each with different ideals, purposes and plans, make any unity of operation impossible. Each board works at the problem in a limited way and each produces about the same limited and unsatisfactory results. Often there are from forty to two hundred district boards in a single county.

(2) County Unit Recommended in Recent State Surveys

Eleven recent state school surveys have been made and in eight of them the county unit for school administration is recommended. That cities should be excepted is recommended in seven of the reports. The usual arguments for the county unit are advanced in all the reports. The states surveyed include Florida, Indiana, Kansas, Mississippi, New Jersey, New York, North Carolina, Texas, Utah, Virginia and West Virginia. The probability is that most of these surveys were made by persons with the same sort of training and background. Probably several of the surveys included the same individual surveyors.[1]

(3) Are the Foregoing Conclusions Justified?

If the county unit contributes to educational superiority a comparison of the county unit states with an equal number of district unit states ought to verify the theoretical conclusions. Accordingly I have arranged the ten states having a county unit organization in one group and have selected ten other states still under district organization and have analyzed them from the standpoint of six criteria of school success. The individual statistics are taken from various recent studies made by the U. S. Office of Education. The facts are set forth in the accompanying table.

The table assembles statistical measures of educational success concerning: (1) The ratio of school enrolment to total population; (2) the number of days annually that school is maintained; (3) the average number of days attended by each pupil enrolled; (4) the percentage of the total enrolment in the high school; (5) the per capita expenditure for education in the state; (6) the amount expended for each pupil annually. It may be fairly assumed that the higher the number in each case the greater the success.

The first ten states constitute the county unit group; the last ten are under the district system.

[1] W. S. Deffenbaugh, ''School Administration in State Educational Survey Reports.'' U. S. Office of Education Bulletin, No. 35, p. 13–19, 1930.

TABLE I

COMPARISON OF THE EDUCATIONAL EFFICIENCY OF 10 DISTRICT UNIT STATES WITH 10 COUNTY UNIT STATES (THE FIRST 10 ARE THE COUNTY UNIT STATES)

State	Ratio of pupils enrolled to population	Days in session	Average number days attended by each pupil enrolled	Percentage of enrolment in high school	Average annual cost per pupil	Average per capita cost to population
Alabama	.749	147.9	108.3	.86	$25.29	$ 7.82
Florida	1.121	154.1	117.5	11.3	64.89	21.59
Georgia	.691	148.0	112.4	10.2	23.07	5.54
Kentucky	.799	164.9	120.8	9.5	32.19	8.82
Louisiana	.702	153.3	119.7	11.5	42.18	11.09
Maryland	.713	187.1	155.8	13.4	66.75	13.31
North Carolina	.891	149.4	111.6	12.1	35.20	13.26
New Mexico	.722	180.0	125.2	10.4	58.08	13.34
Tennessee	.900	164.0	115.6	9.7	27.74	9.10
Utah	.867	164.1	142.4	20.5	67.03	20.04
California	1.115	181.1	152.8	19.8	110.48	31.66
Texas	.781	152.9	127.3	17.5	43.40	20.04
Minnesota	.834	177.8	145.8	16.2	81.18	18.21
Illinois	.802	186.8	159.3	19.5	84.96	19.83
Indiana	.877	174.0	160.7	20.1	89.25	22.39
Iowa	.904	173.0	144.9	19.9	84.81	20.52
Michigan	.817	186.7	171.0	15.5	102.37	23.81
Missouri	.791	175.7	150.8	18.4	58.46	14.99
Wisconsin	.753	176.1	157.9	17.8	75.64	16.20
Washington	.939	180.0	145.2	23.1	82.82	20.51
United States	.815	171.5	140.4	15.5	71.39	18.17

A very cursory examination of the two groups reveals convincingly that the states that rank highest according to these criteria are the states with the district system. In none of these cases is a district system state of low rank and in only two cases do the county unit states rank high. There was some intentional selection of high ranking states under the district system just to show that high rank may be attained under the district system. However, nearly every one of the district system states not included in the table ranks fully as high as the average county unit state.

The data are not assembled to prove that the district system is a superior form of school organization, but rather to show that in spite of the district organization high rank is possible of attainment. A general evaluation would cause any one familiar with all the states to assign them about the same rank revealed by the statistical information. But no one familiar with the conditions would attribute the relative positions to the organization under the district or the county unit. A multitude of other factors enter in, most of them economic. Most of the states ranking low have been handicapped by a tremendous race problem and economic conditions dating back a half century which make the states rank low educationally, even though they have many individual schools of unexcelled quality. Another study should be made, if possible, to ascertain whether the county unit states have improved more rapidly since changing to the county unit plan than the district unit states have during the same period.

It has been quite the vogue to lay most of the defects of rural education to the district organization and to praise the county unit. It is not the purpose of this article to criticize the exponents of the county unit. I have been an ardent advocate of the county unit for more than two decades, urging legislation to secure its adoption in two different states. Study of the problem in several states and from new angles has led me to a very much modified view.

A fair appraisal of educational outcomes does not bear out the conclusion that education is a failure in the states still under the district system nor that all the successes are in the ten county unit states. Most of the failures or successes can be attributed to other causes, generally social or economic.

There is no question but that the old type of school district with the one "little red school house'' has outlived its usefulness in most localities. Any one who has struggled with his A, B, C's in one of those schoolhouses—or still worse, in the old log schoolhouse with the home-made desks—would not contend that the old type of school was efficient. It was decidedly primitive and grossly inefficient, suited only to the crudest pioneer times. Too many of the one-room schools still survive. Too many are taught by relatively inefficient teachers. In some, the equipment is meager and out of date. All that must be acknowledged.

(4) A More Reassuring Picture

But are those conditions typical to-day? When we study the whole of American education does it not present a very different picture? It is true that there are approximately 145,000 one-room schoolhouses in the United States. But when one says that about three fifths of all school buildings are of the one-room type, while true, it is grossly misleading. As a matter of fact, less than 15 per cent. of all teachers are in one-room buildings. More than seven eighths of the approximately one million teachers (public and private) are teaching in decidedly comfortable and hygienic structures. Probably twenty-six million of the approximately twenty-nine million of pupils are reasonably well, or even luxuriously housed in the 100,000 multi-room structures, while only about three million are in the 150,000 one-room buildings. Not a few of these one-room structures even are architecturally pleasing, hygienically arranged and supplied with up-to-date equipment. In a good many of these only the first five or six grades attend and the higher grades are transported at public expense to the centralized junior and senior high schools.

While recognizing that rural school education as a whole has not kept pace with education in the cities and with general industrial progress we should not become obsessed with the belief that rural education has been at a standstill for the last half century. Neither should all the defects be attributed to the district system and the lack of the county unit of organization. The picture drawn by many writers is especially depressing. It is true that in some areas much is to be desired. But any one whose memory reaches back fifty years will recall vividly the short terms of school, the irregularity of attendance, the lack of compulsory education laws, the absence of a definite curriculum in the county or even in a given school, the lack of uniform text-books even by pupils in the same class, the teachers without professional training and no education beyond that afforded by the country school in which they were teaching. The average length of the school year then was 132 days, and now it is 171.5 days. A half century ago each pupil between 5 and 18 years of age received annually an average of 78.5 days of schooling, while now the average is 140.4 days. The total number of days' schooling received then by each child was less than half the number received now. Now almost every rural teacher has at least a high-school academic education and on an average more than a year in a normal school.

Much is still to be desired in rural school housing, but even in that progress has been made. Then there were no ''patent'' desks and seats, all were home-made, and, oh, how uncomfortable! There were no heating plants except the cast-iron stove in the center of the box-like room. In the winter some pupils scorched, while others froze. Slate blackboards, sanitary drinking fountains and indoor toilets were unknown. Library books, adequate maps and apparatus were never a part of the equipment. It is a rare school in which there are any such conditions at the present time.

An automobile trip through most any of the states now gives one the impression that the old type of one-room isolated country schoolhouse is becoming rare. Those that are still to be seen are mostly in disuse. A recent automobile trip of 4,000 miles taken through seven Western states disclosed only a relatively small number of one-room country schoolhouses along the way. They were very scattering, and most of them abandoned. Instead, along the wayside between eight and nine o'clock in the morning happy children were at the roadside in twos and threes and singles waiting for the big bus to gather them up and take them to the village or sometimes to the real countryside consolidated school. Every morning we met the bus loads of twenty to fifty laughing mirthful youngsters speeding to the school plant. In the evening the same troops were carried back to their respective home domiciles. Always they appeared well groomed and happy. Every few miles we passed through the villages and small cities. Always the finest buildings in the community were the school buildings. They are generally of pleasing architecture, commodious, sanitary, the grounds well kept. So common is the sight of from one to ten school buses that they no longer excite a comment. They are standard equipment everywhere. In every one of these states the elementary teachers are trained in the high and normal school, generally with a minimum of two years of normal school training. The high-school teachers without exception are college trained, generally with a bachelor's degree and a goodly percentage with master's degrees, many others with considerable graduate training. The superintendents are usually men of several years of experience and with special training in administration and supervision in the best graduate schools of education.

Just as I had finished writing the foregoing impressions the morning paper came carrying a feature column by Brisbane on "California's Public Schools." Some of Mr. Brisbane's observations are reproduced here. Keep in mind that California is still under the district system of educational organization.

> In modern California, and many other states, to their honor, the public schools surpass in beauty and importance all other buildings. High schools here are surrounded by beautiful parks, each public school has its athletic field. In California *Every Child* must be educated at public expense.
>
> Mr. Whitney, secretary of the Barstow (out on the desert) school board, was discussing, yesterday, the case of an unfortunate child, crippled by infantile paralysis, unable to walk up the steps of any school. Must such a child go without education or be educated at its parent's expense?
>
> Not in California.
>
> A teacher will be appointed to attend solely to that child's education, in its own home, and the cost of books and teacher will be divided between the county and the state.
>
> That will make some taxpayers roar "Bolshevism," but it must make the angels smile, if they ever do smile. And, more Bolshevism. Barstow, a small town (population 2,455) on the Mojave Desert, spends $51,000 a year for public education, more than for all other purposes combined, and sends school buses as far as fifty-two miles, bringing children at public expense to the high school, 104 miles every day for the round trip. That costs the taxpayers for every child more than one hundred dollars a year extra.

(5) Betterment Occurring Rapidly

The elimination of the one-room schools and corresponding districts is taking place amazingly fast without legislation establishing the county unit. Good roads, transportation and school consolidations are effecting the change. The new districts are formed to meet local needs of what Commissioner Cooper calls "economic and social provinces." New York emphasizes the "community district." In 1917 there were approximately 7,500 consolidations, in 1922 there were 13,000, and by 1928 the number had increased to 17,000. There are now probably about 21,000. In 1920 a total of 356,000 children were transported; in 1928 there were 1,250,574; and at present considerably over a million and a half are carried daily at a cost of approximately forty-six million dollars annually. California, Indiana and Ohio each transport more than 100,000 daily.

According to Frank M. Phillips, until recently chief of the division of statistics in the U. S. Bureau of Education, the number of one-room schools in the United States decreased between 1920 and 1928 from 189,227 to 153,306, a reduction of approximately 36,000 in the eight-year period, or 4,500 annually. He said that "These small schools have been replaced by larger consolidated or union schools. The consolidated schools numbered 9,752 in 1920, and 16,050 in 1928. Approximately 6,300 consolidated schools did away with thirty-six thousand one-room schools, which indicates that a single consolidated school replaced more than five one-room schools."[2] According to Timon Covert,[3] of the U. S. Office of Education, the number of consolidations average well over a thousand annually. That means the abandonment of more than 5,000 one-room schools every year. There are now about 21,000 consolidated schools and the number of one-room schools is probably not in excess of 145,000.

During recent years there has been a strong effort on the part of educational leaders, backed by state teachers' associations, to establish the county unit in various states. The movement has gained but little momentum, judging by the small number of actual changes accomplished. The attachment of the people to the "little red schoolhouse" and the fear of undue centralization of government in general has served to defeat almost every attempt to secure a change. This outcome has not been confined to any particular region but has been witnessed in every part of the United States.

[2] Frank M. Phillips, "Statistics of State School Systems, 1927–1928," p. 4, U. S. Office of Education, Bulletin No. 5, 1930.

[3] Timon Covert, "Rural School Consolidation." U. S. Office of Education, Pamphlet, No. 6. June, 1930.

With those results in mind would it not be well to recognize that there is something vital to the idea of democracy and of universal education in retaining and stimulating local initiative in the development of free education. Democracy and education were cradled in the New England town and district and grew to mighty proportions under those crude forms of organization. Foreign countries developed more perfect machinery under centralized government, but the highest fruits of civilization, material or social, could never have been produced under the bureaucratic conditions of the old world. Can we not, therefore, conserve the social values of the somewhat cumbrous, heterogeneous organization and evolve some plan for securing greater unity and efficiency without removing direct management too far from the people in whose interest the schools are maintained and established?

Several of the survey commissions recognize the importance of local initiative and therefore would not abolish all the districts or all the district boards. New York advises some unit intermediate between the district and the county. The New Jersey commission said: "The nearer the control can be kept to those who send their children to school and who bear the burden of cost, the better it would be. It is essential that there be fostered a pride in the schools of a district so that adequate buildings may be erected, qualified teachers appointed, and high standards of instruction maintained. This would be impossible with as large a unit as the county."[4]

(6) Suggested Legislation

If the counties could take just one step, *viz.*, the establishment of a county board authorized to employ the county superintendent instead of having him elected by popular vote, a great advance would be accomplished. For awhile, at least, prob-

[4] *Loc. cit.*, p. 16.

ably it would be best to retain the district boards and the present financial organization. Almost everything desirable from an educational standpoint would be secured through the one change. The nomination of teachers should be included in his duties. Let the district boards still elect the teachers.

Possibly the entire membership of the district boards could be empowered to select an executive committee from their membership who would be authorized to employ the county superintendent. Possibly election by the people would be a more desirable method. The levying of funds, the determination of amounts to be raised, the type of school to be maintained, the construction of buildings, the actual employment of teachers, the salaries to be paid, could all remain exactly as at present and no fundamental principle would be sacrificed. In proposed school legislation omit financial reorganization. Its inclusion is almost sure to spell disaster. The fear that some centralized bureaucracy will saddle new taxes upon them or control the expenditures of all their revenues is usually the one idea that causes the people to defeat any county unit system. The one thing necessary for furthering educational progress in the rural areas is not primarily the control of funds but rather the opportunity for professional direction and supervision. The people can be trusted to provide the revenues if they can be shown that they are receiving better education. With the opportunity to secure the right kind of leaders all the rest can be accomplished.

There should be no attempt to secure absolute equalization of school funds. Most states have gone about as far as desirable in the centralized distribution of school funds. To insure good schools it is not necessary that school funds should be levied and allocated by the state or even by the county. Some states, like Iowa and Wisconsin, for example, have almost no state school funds. The bulk of their school revenues is raised and disbursed by the local districts. They have just as efficient schools as those states which have comparatively large state school funds or those which levy and apportion most of the school funds through the county machinery. If centralized state or county funds are provided which will insure the minimum essentials and then each community is left free to add to those funds according to its best judgment local pride will usually insure reasonable provision and often even lavish opportunities. Imitation is more potent than legislation in providing school opportunities. Arrange for professional leadership and stimulation and local pride will do the rest.

POLITICAL INTERFERENCE IN HIGHER EDUCATION AND RESEARCH[1]

By Professor JOHN DEWEY

COLUMBIA UNIVERSITY

IT is not easy to define political interference in higher education. It may cover anything from meddling with a particular appointment, so as to do a favor to a friend, to a deliberate attempt to control the personnel and educational policies of an institution in the interest of a party or a faction. It is not easy to draw the line between interference for economic and

[1] Presented as a part of the symposium program under the Committee of One Hundred on Scientific Research at the New Orleans meeting of the American Association for the Advancement of Science.

other social reasons and political interference.

The alleged reason for dismissal of Professor Miller at Ohio State University was a supposed indiscreet remark made in India, tending to cast discredit on Great Britain. This certainly was not a case of domestic politics. Since the British Government made no diplomatic representations it was hardly a case of foreign politics. What was it? Or if, as was indicated by some evidence, domestic prejudice about race and color entered in, under what heading does that come?

The activities of the "Power Trust" in subsidizing a certain number of college instructors by a variety of means were primarily economic in nature; they did not proceed from any political office, but their intention was admittedly to discourage consideration of public ownership of utilities and to secure a public opinion favorable to legislation in behalf of private ownership and management. Economic in origin, it was political in effect.

Under a somewhat similar heading would come the organized efforts of persons connected with the War Department to prevent speakers suspected of pacifism from getting a hearing by students, and similar efforts by persons influential in the community to prevent socialists or others holding radical economic views from being heard. For while these latter moves do not concern regular classroom instruction, they do affect students' access to ideas and information having a bearing upon legislation and political administration.

If I mention these cases which seem to lie upon periphery, it is for two reasons. One is that direct interference from state officers, from those clothed with evident political authority, and having an evident political aim in view, is universally reprehended, and is for the most part confined to those parts of the country which are admittedly backward. On the other hand, the cases of mixed origin and motive are much more common; they are found in states which pride themselves upon their educational and cultural advancement, and in institutions of high academic status. Because they operate indirectly, employing relatively subtle means, they are much more dangerous in the long run than direct attacks upon educational integrity undertaken for obvious political reasons. They are, moreover, often condoned by university instructors and by the educated public who would be indignant at interference proceeding from a governor of a state or some political board responsible to the governor.

In political matters, even of the narrower sort, indirect interference is much commoner, more insidious and more injurious than the overt cases which attract public attention. The Board of Regents of one state university adopted the following bylaw: "If any professor or teacher of the university shall become a candidate for any public office or for a nomination thereto, or be a delegate to any political convention, or openly seek a nomination thereto, he should be taken and considered as having resigned his position." Inquiry has not disclosed that any other state has a similar regulation on the books. But pressure accomplishes the same result in other cases. A professor of one of the largest and most populous states in the union is on record to the following effect:

> There is not an institution of higher learning in the state supported by the taxes of the people where any member of the faculty from the president to the humblest instructor would be permitted to engage in any kind of political activity, at least of such a character that it would be pronounced or conspicuous. . . . If a professor has political convictions that he wishes to express in an effective manner there is only one course open to him, and that is to give up his job. . . . Institutions of learning under the auspices of religious groups have their shortcomings and disadvantages, but in this state their presidents and faculty members take a much more active part in public affairs,

especially where the question of politics may be involved, than is the case in state institutions.[2]

That cases of direct political interference are more readily and effectively dealt with than the covert and indirect cases is seen in the instance of the educational institutions of the state of Mississippi. During June and July, 1930, wholesale dismissals and demotions were made at the four chief state-supported educational institutions. This action, instigated from political sources, stirred up an immediate reaction of the public. Various professional bodies of educators took action. The Southern Association of Colleges and Secondary Schools suspended the four state institutions from membership as a manifestation of "disapproval of political interference with state-owned schools"—a courageous action which was much resented locally, but which, coming from the neighboring states, had great influence. The American Society of Civil Engineers took similar action as far as engineering schools were concerned. The Association of American Medical Colleges placed the School of Medicine of Mississippi on probation for one year. Such organizations as the American Chemical Society, the Association of American Universities, the Association of University Professors, passed resolutions of condemnation.

The case of Mississippi is especially cited because it demonstrates so clearly that obvious overt political interference will call out wide-spread protests which are pretty sure in the end to be effective. Professor Bates, chairman of the committee on academic freedom of the Association of University Professors, states in the report for 1923, that cases of "open and clear interference with freedom of speech will be few. The more baffling cases are those in which a steady and powerful, but almost invisible and impalpable pressure of an academic hierarchy suppresses, discourages and seriously interferes with the usefulness and development of the independent and original thinker."

[2] Bulletin of the American Association of University Professors, for 1931, pp. 572–3.

We might add to the list of cases in which the political activities of teachers are curtailed, the cases of suppression of liberal clubs among students and of extreme censorship of college publications when their utterances seemed to have a radical tinge, economic or political. Such instances do not directly affect instruction in the classroom. Many persons, including some university teachers who strongly resent interference with their freedom of research in their own special lines, are not sensitive to interference with activity outside the classroom. Permission of such outside activity involves, as does all free action in any line, some risk. But its denial, whether by direct action, as in the case of the by-law cited above or by indirect pressure, sterilizes thinking on the part of a class to whom, by reason of their especial education, a democratic community might be supposed to look for guidance; it lowers the whole tone of political opinion and action; it reacts unfavorably in classroom instruction by producing a type of teachers who have the habit of suppressing their real views and who finally cease, in consequence, to have any significant convictions.

Teachers and investigators in the more developed and exact branches of science are sometimes so aware of the relative crudity of the state of the social and political subjects that, because of personal economic and political conservatism, they tend to condone restrictions placed on outside activities of teachers in other branches. But they should recall the struggle their own sciences once underwent in order to get a hearing, and be convinced that the social subjects can not attain a more scientific status so long as those who teach them suffer from suppression.

Upon the whole, direct political interferences will, with growth of popular enlightenment in the backward states, tend to become fewer. Local sentiment always resents outside criticism and yet almost always modifies local action because of such criticism when it is fair. At the same time, I do not think the time has come when scientific men through their organizations can afford to be quiescent. If our different professional organizations are alert for infractions upon the integrity of inquiry and teaching of a direct sort, they may profitably extend their activity to take more cognizance than they have done in the past of indirect infractions. Public opinion among educators is tending, as far as I have been able to observe, in the following direction. Let the American Association of University Professors institute a list of accredited colleges and universities. Membership in the association should be confined to those teaching in the accredited institutions. Violation on the part of any institution of the principles of freedom of inquiry and expression should, when proved after investigation, be sufficient cause for removing the institution in question from the accredited list; this would automatically carry with it the dropping from the rolls of the association of members from that institution. All the more special organizations, having scientific and professional aims, should adopt the same course. Both the professors and the scientific associations should have suitable and stringent rules regarding the conditions under which an institution once dropped could be restored to the list.

If the public opinion of the profession could be organized first for its own enlightenment and then for express action along the lines indicated, there would be every prospect, I believe, that cases of infringement of freedom of investigation, speech and writing, including those of political interference, would be reduced to a minimum.

EDUCATIONAL EVENTS

OCCUPATION OF STUDENTS LEAVING SCHOOL IN NEW ZEALAND

DATA on the destination of pupils that leave the primary, junior-high and secondary schools of New Zealand are regularly gathered by the Department of Education of New Zealand. The minister of education in his latest annual report gives the following percentages for 21,175 pupils (11,120 boys and 10,595 girls) that left the public primary schools in 1930. These children were mostly about 14 years of age and had attended school at least 7 years.

Destination	Boys Per cent.	Girls Per cent.
Further education	53	53
Commercial occupations:		
(a) Clerical, including typing	1	1
(b) Shop and warehouse	2	1
Trades:		
(a) Engineering	1	......
(b) Building	1	......
(c) Other	2	......
Agricultural and pastoral	22	2
Other occupations	6	4
Home	9	36
Not known	3	3
	100	100

The tables for the 9,565 students (4,923 boys and 4,642 girls) that had completed their secondary education in either general or technical high schools or day technical schools show the following occupations:

Occupation	Boys Per cent.	Girls Per cent.
Attend university	4	2
Teach or attend training college	3	6
Clerical:		
Government or local office	4	......
Banks, insurance	2	......
Commercial	7	13
Engineering, surveying and architecture	4	......
Various trades and industries	14	2

Shop and warehouse	12	8
Farming	27	......
Home	8	57
Other occupations	2	4
Not known	13	8
	100	100

When the percentages for the primary schools for 1930 are compared with those of the two previous years slight increases toward further education and agricultural pursuits are shown. The figures for five years for the secondary schools show a drop in the percentages of boys entering the clerical, professional, shop and warehouse, and trades and industries occupations, while the percentages of those entering the farming occupations are definitely increased.

SCHOOL ATTENDANCE IN THE UNITED STATES

A STATEMENT has been issued by the Office of Education summarizing the enrolments in the public schools of the United States during the last ten years. Seven out of every ten Americans between 5 and 20 years of age attend school. For the United States as a whole, of the 17,209,566 persons from 7 to 13 years of age, 16,398,400, or 95.3 per cent., attended school at the end of the decade. This was an advance from 90.6 per cent. in 1920.

Those between the ages of 14 and 15 numbered 4,678,084, while 4,156,378 or 88.8 per cent., were enrolled in school. In 1920, only 79.9 per cent. of this group was in school. Turning to those between the ages of 16 and 17, which numbered 4,663,137, 57.3 per cent., or 2,669,857, were enrolled. In 1920 only 42.9 per cent. of this group entered school.

There are 6,815,710 persons within the country between the ages of 18 and 20, of which number 1,456,784, or 21.4 per cent., go to school. In 1920 this group, the lowest of all, constituted but 14.8 per cent. of that age population.

One of the significant increases has been among adults above 21 years of age in turning toward organized education. The number of students 21 or over increased during the decade nearly 300 per cent. In 1920 but 344,789 adults attended school. In 1930 the number had increased beyond 1,034,000.

According to geographic division, New England, with 98.2 per cent., has the highest percentage of children between 7 and 13 years of age in school. All other divisions have 97 per cent. or over of their school population within this age group actually enrolled except the West South Central, the East South Central, the Mountain and the South Atlantic States, which muster between 90 and 95 per cent.

With 98.4 per cent. of its children in school, Nebraska leads all other states in enrolment in ratio to this population age group. Massachusetts, Rhode Island, New Jersey, Michigan, Wisconsin, Kansas, and Wyoming enroll over 98 per cent. of their children from 7 to 13 years old. South Carolina enrolls but 86.4 per cent. of hers and thereby ranks lowest in percentage.

Louisiana, which had only three fourths of its 7 to 13 year old children in school in 1920, had nearly nine-tenths of them in the classrooms by 1930. Arizona raised its percentage enrolment in this age level from 78.8 in 1920 to 90.8 in 1930.

CONFERENCE OF THE CAMP DIRECTORS ASSOCIATION OF AMERICA

PLANS for carrying out recommendations of President Hoover's White House Conference on Child Health will be developed at a four-day convention under the auspices of the Camp Directors Association of America at Buck Hill Falls, Pa., beginning on March 3. Mr. Frank S. Hackett, head master of Riverdale Country School, Riverdale-on-Hudson, N. Y., is president of the association.

The Hoover Conference urged a better organization of the camping movement as imperative. The camp directors, aided by leaders in education, religion, child welfare and other groups, will, according to Mr. Hackett, make the first concerted effort to attain this aim.

For the first time, delegations will be present from the Boy Scouts, Girl Scouts, Young Men's Christian Association, Young Women's Christian Association, Camp Fire Girls and the Children's Welfare Federation, as well as from numerous private camps. Economists and health experts will also participate. In general meetings and in seminars, the delegates will discuss the whole problem of organized camping.

The first formal session, on Friday morning, March 4, will be devoted to a discussion of "The Organized Camp of the Future." Speakers and their topics are: Dr. F. W. Maroney, Teachers College, Columbia University, "Physical Education"; Raphael J. Shortlidge, head master of the Storm King School, Cornwall-on-Hudson, N. Y., "Intellectual Contributions"; Dr. C. E. Grave, psychologist, Sleighton Farm School, Philadelphia, "The Emotions"; Mrs. Edward L. Gulick, director of the Aloha camps, "Spiritual Contributions."

Open forums will be conducted at the afternoon sessions, where delegates will further discuss the subjects covered by speakers in the morning lectures.

An address on "Economic Trends and their Possible Effects upon Camping," will be delivered on Friday evening by Merwin K. Hart, of Utica, New York, president of the New York State Council on Industrial Economics. Pendleton Dudley, New York publicist, will lecture on "How Shall we best Interpret Organized Camping to the American People."

For Saturday morning the following talks on "The Camp of the Future, its Relationship with Organized Education" are scheduled: Dr. L. B. Sharp, of the University of Chicago, "Public Schools"; Dr. Richard M. Gummere, head master of the William Penn Charter School, Philadelphia, "Independent Schools"; Professor Elbert K. Fretwell, Teachers College, Columbia University, "Colleges and Universities."

A business meeting will be held on Saturday preceding the afternoon seminars. On Saturday evening there will be reports on "Camping in Russia," by Julien H. Bryan, Young Men's Christian Association executive who spent last summer in Russia, and on "What the Forester can do for the Camp Owner," by Professor Henry R. Francis, of the New York State College of Forestry, Syracuse University.

The theme of the Sunday morning conference, the final session of the convention, will be "Organization of the Camping Movement." The speakers will present the view-points of various groups interested in the camp movement.

A PHI BETA KAPPA MAGAZINE

TAKING as its name the title of Emerson's famous address at Harvard in 1837, the United Chapters of Phi Beta Kappa have launched a new magazine, *The American Scholar*. The first number of this quarterly, issued recently as of January, 1932, exhibits an attractive format, with gray-green cover, book paper, and large Caslon type for the main articles and smaller type in double columns for departmental news and discussion.

To the 63,000 living members of Phi Beta Kappa and to "all who have general intellectual interest," the editor, Dr. William Allison Shimer, and the editorial board address a statement of the objectives of the new quarterly as follows.

The promotion in America of liberal scholarship.

A medium for scholars and all persons who are interested in intellectual pursuits, higher learning and the cultural development of America.

A synthesis of the arts and sciences essential to liberal education and a guiding philosophy of life.

An *esprit de corps* among the educated.

The scholar's responsibility for major social tendencies.

A whole diet for the whole mind.

In the first issue there are contributions by sixteen writers, ten of them men and women who are prominent in American universities and colleges and six who are prominent in varied professional fields. The opening article by John Erskine reproduces paragraphs from Emerson's address on "The American Scholar" and gives Dr. Erskine's own comments upon the abandoning by American colleges of "the lovely architecture with which many of them began and putting on instead the Gothic garment," and "the Medieval aspects of American scholarship which show themselves in the social organization of our colleges."

The educational leaders contributing articles include Dr. Paul Shorey, President Mary E. Woolley, Dr. F. J. E. Woodbridge, President Frank Aydelotte, Dr. Julius Seelye Bixler and Dr. Karl T. Compton. Professor George Lyman Kittredge is represented with a humorous poem, "The Critical Alumnus," and there is a poem, "The Three Pharaohs," by Herman Hagedorn. Other contributors are Alvan E. Duerr, Joseph H. Beale, Owen D. Young, Dorothy Canfield Fisher, John W. Davis and John H. Finley.

FELLOWSHIP AWARDS OF THE AMERICAN ASSOCIATION OF UNIVERSITY WOMEN

THE American Association of University Women have announced the following fellowship awards for 1932–1933. They are:

Sarah Berliner Research Fellowship: CAROL JANE ANGER, Radcliffe College fellow, Harvard College Observatory; alternate, LAURA EMILY KREJCI, fellow of the American-Scandinavian Foundation, Uppsala University.

A. A. U. W. European Fellowship: LUCY WESTON PICKETT, instructor, Mount Holyoke College; alternate, MARY KARPINSKI STAUBACH, Graduate School, University of Michigan.

Margaret E. Maltby Fellowship: RUTH WILLARD HUGHES, graduate student, Cornell University; alternate, HELEN GWENDOLYN BRIDGES, teaching fellow in English, University of California.

A. A. U. W. International Fellowship: FRANCESCA BOZZA, doctor of laws, University of Naples; alternate, HILDA MARGARET LYON, research assistant, department of aeronautical engineering, Massachusetts Institute of Technology.

Northwest Central Sectional Fellowship: LUCILE KATHRYN DELANO, instructor in Spanish, University of Iowa; alternate, LUCILE GAFFORD, head of the English department, Starrett School for Girls, Oklahoma City.

Boston Alumnae Fellowship: FAITH PRINDLE BALDWIN, Bryn Mawr College; alternate, HELEN WOOD, graduate student, Columbia University.

Alpha Xi Delta Fellowship: MARY SHAW SHORB, the Johns Hopkins University; alternate, ASSUNTA VASTI, graduate student, the Johns Hopkins School of Hygiene and Public Health.

Latin-American Fellowship: PAULINA GOMEZ-VEGA, National Institute of Hygiene, Bogota, Colombia; alternate, MRS. SARAH YSALGUE DE MASSIP, instructor, University of Havana, Cuba.

THE TWELFTH ANNUAL OHIO STATE EDUCATIONAL CONFERENCE

THE Twelfth Annual Ohio State Educational Conference will be held in Columbus on April 7, 8, 9. An attendance of 6,000 is anticipated. "Education as Social Investment" will be the keynote of the two general and the thirty-six sectional meetings. The names of thirty-six well-known out-of-state speakers and the sections in which they speak follow:

Anderson, John E. (University of Minnesota), Adult Education, Clinical Psychology, Home Economics.

Ayer, Adelaide (State Teachers College, Milwaukee, Wisconsin), Teacher Training.

Ballou, Frank W. (Washington, D. C., Public Schools), Attendance Officers.

Barr, A. S. (University of Wisconsin), County Superintendents.

Bobbitt, Franklin (University of Chicago), High School Principals, Junior High School Principals.

Bristol, Ruth (University of Michigan), Kindergarten.

Caseman, Juvenilia (Hutchinson High School, Buffalo, New York), Commercial Education.

Chamberlain, C. J. (University of Chicago), Biological Science.

Clapp, Elsie Ripley (Ballard Memorial School), Art, Elementary Teachers.

Clark, Harold F. (Teachers College, Columbia), School Business Officers.

Cole, Robert D. (University of North Dakota), Modern Languages.

Ehrenfeld, Louis (Museum of Science and Industry, Chicago), Physical Science.

Hartshorne, Hugh (Yale University), Religious Education, Educational Tests.

Hatfield, W. Wilbur (University of Chicago), English.

Heyl, Paul R. (U. S. Bureau of Standards), Physical Science.

Holt, Nellie Lee (Stephens College), Religious Education, Physical Education.

Johnson, B. Lamar (Stephens College), School Librarians.

Jones, Arthur J. (University of Pennsylvania), Guidance Counselors.

Judd, C. H. (University of Chicago), Higher Education, City Superintendents.

Lippman, Walter (*The New York Herald-Tribune*), Journalism.

Lomax, Paul S. (Haire Publishing Co.), Commercial Education.

McGinnis, Esther (American Home Economics Association), Home Economics.

McKown, Harry C. (University of Pittsburgh), Village Superintendents.

Milliken, Carl E. (former Governor of Maine), Visual Education.

Morgan, Joy E. (National Education Association), Teacher Training, County Superintendents.

Oldfather, W. A. (University of Illinois), Latin.

Otto, M. C. (University of Wisconsin), Social Study.

Reavis, W. C. (University of Chicago), Attendance Officers, Guidance Counselors.

Reed, Mary M. (Teachers College, Columbia), Kindergarten.

Schlauch, W. H. (New York University), High School Principals, Mathematics.

Scott, Harry A. (Rice Institute), Physical Education.

Snedden, David (Teachers College, Columbia), Industrial Arts, Social Study.

Stetson, Paul C. (Indianapolis Public Schools), City Superintendents, Elementary Teachers.

Stull, DeForest (Teachers College, Columbia), Geography.

Thurstone, L. L. (University of Chicago), Educational Tests.

Weet, Herbert S. (Rochester, New York, Public Schools), Special Education, Elementary Principals.

THE AMERICAN LIBRARY ASSOCIATION

"Libraries in a changing world" is the theme of the fifty-fourth annual Conference of the American Library Association, which will be held in New Orleans, from April 25 to 30. Miss Josephine Adams Rathbone, president of the association, and vice-director of the Pratt Institute School of Library Science, will preside during the conference which it is estimated more than 2,000 representatives from libraries in the United States, Canada and Mexico will attend.

Dr. Edwin R. Embree, president of the Julius Rosenwald Fund and author of "Brown America," will speak at a general session, on Tuesday morning, April 26, on "Cultural Problems and Prospects in the South." Mr. Embree has conducted extensive studies in secondary education in the United States, on the education of Negroes and the relation of white and colored races in America. During the last several years he has studied conditions in Europe and the Far East.

"The Public Library in American Civilization—New Ideas in Education" will be the subject of an address by President Frank P. Graham, of the University of North Carolina, at a general session Tuesday evening. Miss Edith O. Lathrop, of the U. S. Office of Education, who has been conducting a survey under a grant from the Carnegie Corporation, will speak before the School Libraries Section on "New Library Service for Rural and Village Schools."

Miss Mary Mims, community organizer for Louisiana and author of "The Awakening Community," soon to be published by the Macmillan Company, will also be a speaker during the week.

Several problems of the junior college library will be discussed at round table meetings of the section for junior college librarians. The library from the standpoint of the administrator and his faculty, the problem of securing desirable results in recreational reading among students, and the question of training for librarianship in the junior college will be considered.

Group meetings will be arranged for discussion of work in adult education, problems of elementary school libraries, library work with children, county libraries and other phases of library service.

The award of the John Newbery Medal for the outstanding work of the year in children's literature will be announced at a meeting of the section for library work with children, at which Count René d'Harnoncourt will be the speaker. Count d'Harnoncourt, who is an illustrator, has recently published a volume of "Mexicana," a series of drawings of life and customs of modern Mexico. The Newbery award, which is made annually at the conference of the American Library Association, is given in honor of John Newbery, one of the first publishers to recognize the value of books for children, and was established in 1922 by Frederic G. Melcher, of New York. In 1931 the medal was presented to Elizabeth Coatsworth for her book, "The Cat who Went to Heaven."

EDUCATIONAL NOTES AND NEWS

Dr. George Norlin, president of the University of Colorado, will be visiting Roosevelt professor from Columbia University at the University of Berlin for the academic year 1932–1933.

Dr. Frank J. Goodnow, president emeritus of the Johns Hopkins University, on February 11 resigned from the Baltimore School Board after twelve years of service, on account of ill health, and Dr. Joseph S. Ames, president of the university, was named by Mayor Jackson to succeed him.

THE New York State Senate and Assembly, in joint session, on February 10 reelected Dr. James Byrne, of New York, as member of the State Board of Regents for a term of twelve years. Dr. Byrne is vice-chancellor of the University of the State of New York.

DR. CYRUS ADLER, president of the Jewish Theological Seminary of America, will be honored with a public reception marking his completion of thirty years' service in the institution. The reception will be held at the seminary at a date not yet announced.

A BANQUET was given in honor of Dr. Richard R. Smith on January 14, at Grand Rapids, in recognition of his appointment as a regent of the University of Michigan. Dr. Alexander G. Ruthven, president of the university, was among the speakers. Dr. Smith spoke on "The Privileges and Responsibilities of the Doctor of To-day."

DR. JAMES S. STEVENS, for forty-one years professor of physics at the University of Maine and for thirty-seven years dean of the College of Arts and Sciences, has retired from active service.

DR. GEORGE COLEMAN GOW, head of the department of music and for thirty-seven years a member of the faculty of Vassar College, will retire at the end of the academic year.

THE installation of Mr. Compton Mackenzie as Lord Rector of the University of Glasgow took place on January 29. Mr. Compton Mackenzie was presented by the dean of the faculty of law, Professor John Girvan, for the honorary degree of LL.D., and was afterwards invested by the principal, Dr. R. S. Rait, with his robes of office. Mr. Mackenzie's rectorial address was devoted to the subject of "Nationalism."

MR. J. F. DUFF has been appointed professor of education and director of the department of education at the University of Manchester as from next September.

DR. P. S. BURGESS, professor of agricultural chemistry at the University of Arizona, has been appointed dean of the College of Agriculture and director of the Experiment Station.

MR. FREDERICK ALLEN REPLOGLE has become the dean of McPherson College, Kansas, after three years of graduate work in the University of Chicago. During this time he also served as associate director of research for the Methodist Board of Education.

DR. MERTON E. HILL, professor of education, has been appointed to the newly established position of director of admissions in the University of California. Dr. Hill succeeds Mr. Dwight C. Baker, whose title was university examiner, who resigned to become head of the Modesto Junior College. Professor Clarence H. Robison, of the University of California at Los Angeles, has been appointed associate director, and Miss S. M. Love, assistant director.

MAJOR GENERAL CHARLES P. SUMMERALL, former Chief of Staff of the army, has withdrawn his resignation as president of The Citadel, the South Carolina State military college at Charleston. General Summerall sent his resignation to the Board of Visitors last week after becoming annoyed at a question asked him by a member of the Senate Finance Committee regarding a $19,000 deficit at The Citadel.

MR. GEORGE A. HASTINGS, administrative assistant to President Hoover, has been granted leave of absence for a year to serve under the Secretary of the Interior, Dr. Ray Lyman Wilbur, to direct the activities of the White House Conference on Child Health and Protection.

MISS BEATRICE MCLEOD, formerly state director of special education in Wyoming, has been appointed specialist in the education of physically handicapped children in the division of special problems of the Office of Education. Miss McLeod is a graduate of the University of Oregon and has done graduate work at Columbia University and the University of Washington.

MR. BRUCE W. DICKSON, adviser of foreign students at the University of Chicago for the past nine years, has been appointed director of the new International House now being completed on the university quadrangles at a cost of $2,000,000.

MR. OSCAR F. SHEPARD, who has been since 1929 president of Oahu College, Honolulu, has been elected vice-president and chairman of the education committee of the Hawaii Council of the Institute of Pacific Relations.

Professor C. W. Savage, head of the department of physical education of Oberlin College, has been for the third successive time chosen to head the Ohio Conference Managers' Association at its meeting in Columbus.

Professor Harold Chapman Brown, of the department of philosophy of Stanford University, was recently elected president of the Pacific division of the American Philosophical Association.

Dr. Ellen C. Potter, of the New Jersey Department of Public Welfare, was elected on February 10 president for 1932 of the Conference of Superintendents of Correctional Institutions for Women and Girls.

Charles A. Sink, president of the School of Music of the University of Michigan and for many years Michigan state senator, is proposed for the lieutenant-governorship of Michigan.

Associate Professor Arthur F. Whittem, dean of special students and director of University Extension at Harvard University, will be on leave during the second half of the current academic year, and those two offices will be filled during that period by Philip P. Chase, director of the Summer School. Assistant Professor Newton H. Black will be director of the Summer School from March 1 to September 1, 1932.

Professor William Alpha Cooper, head of the department of German at Stanford University, has returned from a six-months leave of absence which he spent in Europe. Professor Cooper consulted with leading men in Germany interested in the international academic exchange of both students and professors, particularly after his appointment as a member of a new committee of the German Academy set up to supervise such exchanges.

Dr. William Trufant Foster, formerly president of Reed College, now director of the Pollak Foundation for Economic Research, gave a lecture at the University of California on "The Present Economic State of the World," on February 12.

Dr. George W. Knight, professor emeritus of history at the Ohio State University from 1914 to 1920 and formerly dean of its college of education, died on February 10, at the age of seventy-three years. Dr. Knight had been professor at the university since 1885.

William W. Fry, for fifteen years president and principal of the Palmer Business School in Philadelphia and since 1905 its chief owner, died on February 8 at the age of sixty-two years.

On January 16, 1932, a group of educators, representing many types of adult education in every part of Ohio, met at Columbus, at the invitation of Dr. B. O. Skinner, state director of education, and organized the Ohio Conference on Adult Education. Officers were elected as follows: *President,* Dr. H. J. Arnold, director of extension, Wittenberg College; *vice-president,* Dr. F. D. Slutz, educator and author, Dayton; *secretary-treasurer,* Mrs. Mary Hill Kern, state chairman, Better Homes in America.

The summer Institute of Euthenics will hold its seventh annual session at Vassar College from June 29 to August 10. It offers courses in child development, mental and physical health, interior decoration, household technology and parent-education leadership. There will be also lectures and discussions on problems of family living and family adjustment. A nursery school is run in connection with the institute. Teachers will find it an unusually fine opportunity to study and discuss with experts the methods of handling children, to observe the twenty-four hour care of children in a nursery school and to study the parent-child relationship. For full information write the Director, Institute of Euthenics, Vassar College, Poughkeepsie, New York.

The third conference of the National Advisory Committee on the Education of Negroes will be held in Washington during the convention of the Department of Superintendence, National Education Association. The conference has been called by Dr. William John Cooper, Commissioner of Education, for February 23. As at previous conferences the committee will advise with Dr. Ambrose Caliver, senior specialist in the education of Negroes in the Office of Education, respecting the educational surveys being conducted by the office as they pertain to Negroes in states which have separate schools. A report of the progress of the special Negro sections of the Secondary Education and Teacher Education Surveys will be made. A special conference will also be held with Dr. Paul R. Mort, associate director of the Survey of School Finance. Other features will include addresses by Dr. Edwin C. Broome, president, National Education Association Department of Superintendence; by Dr. Leonard V. Koos, associate director, National Survey of Secondary Education, and by Mrs. Katherine M. Cook, chief, Division of Special Problems, Office of Education, and Commissioner Cooper.

A gift is announced of $300,000 from R. T. Miller, Jr., educator and encyclopedia publisher, to the American School, Chicago, which he had a large part in founding thirty-five years ago, for a student loan fund. The entire amount will be loaned to promising needy students. Mr. Miller had previously established a $100,000 student loan fund at Oberlin College and at the University of Rochester and one of $50,000 at Berea College.

The University of Kentucky announces a five weeks course in psychology to be given under its auspices in Vienna, Austria, during the summer of 1932. This course will consist of a series of lectures given (in English) by prominent members of the faculty of the University of Vienna and will be supplemented by independent work under their guidance in laboratory or clinic. University credit will be granted, if desired, upon satisfactory completion of the course, provided the requirements for credit are met. Full details may be obtained from the Educational Director of the Study Tour, Dr. Henry Beaumont, University of Kentucky, Lexington, Kentucky.

After a debate in which Senators James G. Moran, of Mansfield; Frederick E. Judd, of Southampton; Donald W. Nicholson, of Wareham, and Charles A. Stevens, of Lowell, took part, the Massachusetts state senate on February 11 substituted a bill that would require Massachusetts school teachers to take the oath of allegiance to the United States before being allowed to serve.

After a month of enforced idleness through the strike of some 600 teachers at Jerusalem for non-payment of salaries, 24,000 Jewish pupils returned to their classrooms on February 10. The strike gained the teachers only individual contracts with the Jewish agency and recognition of the important sacrifice involved in their voluntary surrender of one month's salary to help the agency balance its education budget. Lost work is to be made up by shortening the summer vacation.

The Board of Directors of Shanghai College has decided to change the English name from "Shanghai College" to the "University of Shanghai." During past years, friends and alumni of the institution have urged the administration to change the English name to "university" in conformity with the Chinese name adopted a long time ago. Among the reasons which they advanced are these: The general practice in China is to call an institution of higher learning "Ta Hsueh" (university). All the government and private institutions which have the same standing as Shanghai College are known as universities. Then the word "college" is used rather loosely in China. It is widely adopted by secondary institutions and technical schools. Many of these are feeders to Shanghai College. Furthermore, there are many institutions in Shanghai whose English names are almost the same as Shanghai College. In addition to the College of Arts and Science, the University of Shanghai is conducting a school of commerce, a school of education, post-graduate work, preparatory schools and a social center. This does not include the affiliated Theological Seminary, which is not registered with the Ministry of Education. There are altogether more than 1,800 students enrolled in all divisions of the work. The institution has been jointly supported by the Northern and Southern Baptists in U. S. A. and the Chinese Baptists. The government has recognized it as one of the Class A institutions of higher learning in China.

The total number of London school playgrounds open during the recent summer holidays shows a decrease on the two previous years (398 against 434 and 418 respectively). This decrease is partly accounted for by schools being closed for repairs, but is mainly due to the fact that the London County Council decided in July to close the playgrounds of 63 schools where the attendance was small. On the other hand, the wide publicity given to holiday playground facilities has resulted in an actual increase for the year, 15,877 as against 15,855 in 1930 and only 9,422 in 1926. The average attendance is also up, being 40 as against 37 in 1930 and 25 only in 1926. The play centers organized by the Play Centers Committee were held at 31 schools, and the average attendance per center was 322.

THE *News Bulletin* of the Institute of International Education quotes the following extract from one of its correspondents in Germany: "I have become rather doubtful if it might be advisable for me to come over next year. Conditions in Germany are going from bad to worse. Especially our teaching profession and our whole educational system have become a heap of ruins. There is such a surplus of teachers and such a shortage of money that out of one hundred and nine thousand teachers in Prussia, all fully trained, more than twenty thousand are out of work, a great number of them being over thirty and waiting ten years and longer to be employed. Recently the number of teaching hours for each teacher has been increased, and at the same time the number of lessons fixed for each class has been reduced and the size of the classes has been enlarged. All this means that many thousands more teachers will be superfluous. Not enough with this, the fees for high school instruction have been increased. In my own school situated in an industrial district where mostly workmen and craftsmen live who on the average earn only nine to twelve dollars a week, the annual fee amounts to twenty-four dollars and in addition to this the parents have to buy all text-books and exercise books. Since yesterday the wages have been shortened by four and one-half per cent., but at the same time the town has raised the fees from twenty-four to thirty dollars a year. All this seems to be only a beginning. Winter has not yet begun. As soon as the farm work has come to a standstill, short labor and unemployment will become more general. There is no money to support the unemployed and to pay the obligations due to our creditor states. Everywhere there is restlessness, life has lost its value, every year we have sixteen thousand suicides, and those who prefer to live are determined to risk the utmost to better their conditions. Everyone feels a sudden turnover is near at hand, and no one knows what the future will bring. It may even happen that I lose half of my teachers and nearly all of my pupils next Easter when our new scholastic year begins, not to speak of all the political changes which will come next spring with the election of a new Reichspresident and a new Chamber of Deputies."

THE Berlin correspondent of the *Journal* of the American Medical Association reports that the German Pediatric Society issued at its recent meeting the following proclamation: "With great anxiety German pediatricians look forward to the future of the German people. Already they observe in Germany and Austria conditions similar to those seen during the worst years of the war and post-war period: general debilitation, reduced resistance to disease, and increase of tuberculosis. As a result of economic distress, the birth rate has declined considerably. But—worse still—the small number of children born are seriously threatened in their development. And under these conditions, the organizations that have been slowly and laboriously built up to supply aid to sick children are to retrench? Are also hospitals to be closed; are sick children to be dismissed from hospitals before they are well, and are welfare centers to be abolished? In the face of such threatened action, the Deutsche Gesellschaft für Kinderheilkunde can not remain silent. It warns against the great dangers that threaten the life and health of our children, and protests most decidedly against any ill planned restrictions on the aid to be given children in need. To be sure, retrenchments will be necessary; but they must not be introduced at the expense of our children, in whom lies the hope of the German people."

THE fourth session of the summer school for adults, a cooperative enterprise of the University of California, the State Department of Education and the California Association for Adult Education, will be held at Berkeley beginning on June 23. Courses will include controversial problems and the technique of discussion, public opinion and adult education, methods of teaching English to foreigners, methods of teaching social science to adults, arts and crafts for adult amateurs, human relations, and an unpublished review. Students will reside with members of the faculty at Hansford Hall, one of the college dormitories, and Monday night discussion meetings open to the public will be held there. Excursions to points of educational interest are being arranged. The director of the school will be Mr. Lyman Bryson, who succeeded Dr. Harry Allen Overstreet in that position last year. Members of the faculty will include Professor William F. Adams, of the University of California; Miss Ethel Swain, of the Los Angeles Public Schools; Mrs. Lucy Wilcox Adams, of the California Association for Adult Education; Mr. John Dale, of the State Department of Education, and others. The session lasts six weeks and university credit will be given for most of the announced courses. Information can be obtained from the office of the California Association for Adult Education at Los Angeles, or from the dean of the summer session of the University of California, Berkeley.

DISCUSSION

WILL DEPRESSION LEAD TO EQUALITY OF OPPORTUNITY IN EDUCATION?

FOR too long Americans have looked upon equality of opportunity in education as necessitating the grinding of all the children of the land through the same mill, regardless of their interests, their capacities or their future occupations. We set up a curriculum of traditional subject-matter with little regard to the social, political, economic, spiritual or cultural value that it might have, employed teachers on the apparent theory of selling the interpretation of the curriculum to the lowest bidder, and satisfied ourselves with prating about democracy in education. As a result we have brought forth a generation without regard for the laws of either God or man, not trained to think in terms of the problems of the day, and often actually prevented from learning to reason through having the entire emphasis of conventional education placed upon learning "facts," most of which have no other use than to be forgotten as soon as possible. The vital education has been gotten on the streets and in the alleys, in the pool halls and the movies, out of sensational and filthy magazines. What of value for practical citizenship purposes, of the entire public school curriculum of the first eight years, could not be taught to the average twelve-year-old child in a year?

Will the depression do for other communities what it has done for Chicago, where twenty millions of dollars are due in back salaries to its teachers? The situation is tragically serious in many more places. When the smoke of the depression has blown away will the public demand their money's worth in education? Will they demand equality of opportunity in education and will they demand education that is vital to their civilization? These are the questions that will be answered within the next ten years.

Will America come out of the depression with an entirely new philosophy of social rights and social obligations? Will society concede the right of every able-bodied man to be employed an amount of time which will represent his proportion of the labor required to produce the goods that can be disposed of, and receive for it a living wage for himself and his family, regardless of whether that amount of time is 48 or 4.8 hours per week? Without committing suicide by outlawing machinery and new inventions, the working hours must inevitably be shortened unless the entire social wealth is increased sufficiently and distributed uniformly so that the purchasing power of every individual is raised to a point where sufficient luxuries will be consumed to require the present length of working week for their production. This increase of purchasing power is not to be anticipated in the near future. Rather, we may look for an increase of leisure time instead.

Granted, that the reorganization following the depression will shorten the working week and leave humanity the blessing or curse of more leisure, the task of education will become more and more that of preparing humanity to live sanely. When men worked twelve or sixteen hours per day the devil and his associates were unemployed most of the time. With the advent of the eight-hour working day he has had to work overtime, and if the working day goes to four or six hours Old Nick will have to put on another shift to handle the job. In educating for leisure the schools are faced with a bigger task than was ever undertaken before because they must train individuals to follow their own inclinations rather than an arbitrarily set-up program. At least if a semblance of liberty is maintained the occupation of leisure hours can not be dictated by society. Interests and hobbies that are not anti-social must be developed for human nature rebels at being forced to do anything. The school of the future will have to adapt its program to cultivating the real interests of individual children and directing those interests into socially worth-while channels. In fact, education must develop a philosophy of life that is compatible with a state of liberty if personal freedom is to be maintained. There will probably be very little drudgery or heartache in the new program. There will, likewise, be very little if any standardized "measuring" of results. Social harmony in the group may be the measure of a teacher's success, and teachers will hold their places only as they can command the love and respect and confidence of the children. What a tragedy for some teachers!

When the work of the adult is shortened it is only logical that the school time of the child will be shortened. Is it possible that the child may attend school only one day a week and practice what he has learned about living the other six days? It is not unthinkable. It is probable that even now the adults of most communities need to be educated more than do the children. When leisure time is squandered less there will be more educational cooperation from the homes of children.

Equality of opportunity in education can mean in practice but one thing—the opportunity for every individual to develop his own latent capacities and interests to the utmost. It means that the one whose interests and capacities lie in digging ditches has not been discriminated against when he has been prepared to find happiness in that work, and to live as a peaceful citizen. It likewise implies that equality of opportunity to the one who has the interest and capacity to become a skilled surgeon shall be given every advantage that society can confer toward that end. The program and the time consumed in the educative process are not the measures of equality of opportunity in education.

C. E. HAGIE

NEW YORK, N. Y.

PHILADELPHIA HIGH-SCHOOL LOCKERS

READING the report in the *Public Ledger* for January 20, that one of our high-school teachers, Dr. Henry G. Maeder, had made charges that high-school students keep liquor in their lockers, I sent for Dr. Maeder, with the principal of the school, Mr. J. Ellwood Calhoun, to come at once to my office for an explanation. Following is a stenographic account of the interview:

Dr. Broome: Dr. Maeder, in your address before the Reformed ministers yesterday, did you make a statement that you knew high-school students to keep liquor in their lockers?

Dr. Maeder: I did not.

Dr. Broome: What did you say to the ministers?

Dr. Maeder: "You are doubtless conversant with the reports in the papers that high-school students are said to carry hip flasks."

Dr. Broome: Did you ever, in your experience as a teacher in Philadelphia high schools, know of a single case of liquor in a student's locker?

Dr. Maeder: No.

Dr. Broome: Did you ever have reliable evidence that such was the case?

Dr. Maeder: None whatsoever.

Dr. Broome: Then, you were merely stating to the ministers a general rumor in the newspapers?

Dr. Maeder: I was.

Dr. Broome: Of course you regret, then, that a wrong interpretation was placed on your remarks?

Dr. Maeder: I most assuredly do.

Dr. Broome: Mr. Calhoun, you were teacher in the Germantown High School for 10 years, you were principal of the Roxborough High School for 3 years and have been principal of the Gratz High School for 4 years; altogether you have been 25 years in the Philadelphia Public Schools. Have you ever in your experience known of a case of liquor in a student's locker?

Mr. Calhoun: I have not.

Dr. Broome: Have you ever had any reliable evidence that liquor was kept in a student's locker?

Mr. Calhoun: I have not.

Dr. Broome: Do you, personally, and other members of your staff frequently examine the lockers?

Mr. Calhoun: The lockers are continually supervised.

Dr. Broome: Do you think it would be possible for the practice of keeping liquor in lockers to prevail without your discovering it?

Mr. Calhoun: I am sure I would know of it and if there was any liquor in lockers, I would hear of it.

Dr. Broome: Thinking people who know youth and have their interest at heart are getting very tired of this constant berating of the young people of our community. If all the adults in our community would behave as well as the young people do, and would set the right example, much of the difficulty that we are having with youth would disappear. This seems to be an open season for attack on the schools, and the church, and the courts, and on the other American institutions which we have taught our children to revere. How can we expect the rising generation to have respect for our country and its institutions if they are to be exposed to a constant barrage of flippant and irresponsible criticism?

EDWIN C. BROOME
SUPERINTENDENT OF SCHOOLS,
PHILADELPHIA, PENNSYLVANIA

SPECIAL CORRESPONDENCE

CUSTOMS AND PRACTICES IN THE GERMAN SCHOOLS OF TO-DAY

THE organization of schools in Germany and America is in many respects similar. Any one who tries to discover points of similarity and contrast between the schools of the two countries is sure to reach this inevitable conclusion. This is necessarily true, as the schools of both lands face the same problem of preparing students for the universities and of creating for them the best conditions under which their studying may be done. Yet there are enough variations in procedure to make a study of the practices in German schools worthy of our attention.

The fundamental differences between school systems are due primarily to the amount of emphasis laid on certain studies and the methods by which they are taught. Take, for instance, the study of modern languages. If you were to stop a German schoolboy on the street and ask him in English how to reach a certain place, you would probably be surprised to have him understand you at once and direct you in your own language. There is nothing so remarkable in this if you stop to consider that boys in German secondary schools regularly devote six to nine years to the study of languages, both ancient and modern. By way of analogy, it is interesting to remember that only 85 per cent. of the students in the private and public schools of the United States study modern languages for a period of two years during their secondary school career.

Other subjects besides modern languages receive more attention and are studied along more progressive lines than is generally the custom with us. Take, for example, art.[1] It is taught through the medium of experience. A class of students is supplied with sketch books and goes into the country in charge of an instructor who casually draws attention to certain beauties of nature, such as an unusual tree, a bird or a bit of attractive landscape. The instructor does not "become the eyes" of the class by asking questions about the thing under observation, but he permits them to see objects through their own eyes and to express ideas in their own original way. So they sketch, then and there, whatever appeals to their artistic sense or, if they prefer, they do their sketching later from ideas held in their memory. The same method is used to cultivate an appreciation of architecture. Cities like Nuremberg with its many fascinating old buildings are visited and the interesting towers, doorways or picturesque woodwork are studied and developed into sketches.

Then, too, a new musical culture is coming into existence, chiefly through the potent influence of the "Youth Movement." The youth of the land claim that they can only appreciate music by feeling, creating and expressing themselves in music. With the folk-song as a basis, they are composing music of their own which they use as a stimulating accompaniment on their hiking excursions. Of course, Germany is unusually blessed with a rich store of old songs, but new zest has been given to the singing of them during the extensive wanderings afoot, by boat or by train. It may here be noted that school orchestras flourish now to a greater ex-

[1] For a fuller discussion of modern methods, see the excellent book of Parker and Day (The John Day Company) called "The New Education in the German Republic."

tent in the secondary schools than in former years.

The increased interest in art and music is developing a kindred growth of interest in dramatics. Rather elaborate representations of classic dramas are now given in the schools, and German students enjoy the further advantage of attending municipal theaters where traveling amateur companies, corresponding to the Little Theater movement in this country, give excellent drama and opera at low prices.

While there has been a noteworthy impetus given to these subjects, the greatest and perhaps the most ambitious program is being carried out in the educational travel movement. O'Donnell Bennett made the statement that "travel, if men use it shrewdly, is a book in action." This seems to be strikingly true of the educational policy in Germany to-day. One is tempted to inquire whether there are any German pupils left inside of the schools, particularly the elementary schools. Boats loaded with students ply up and down the Rhine during the spring, summer and autumn months; boys clad in rough coats, knee breeches and carrying knapsacks make their way through beautiful forests. On arriving in cities, they visit museums, parks, cathedrals, village market places and other places of interest.

As an aftermath of the war, the youth of Germany were under-nourished, and the morale of the nation generally was very low. Some inexpensive form of recreation was needed to restore the nation physically and mentally. The best solution of the problem lay in utilizing the general mania for outdoor life which had seized the country. With this in view, the number of stopping places called hostels, which had existed in Germany since 1900, was greatly increased and their sphere of usefulness extended. The emblem of these homes is D. J. H. Board and room can be secured for hiking-parties at very low prices: five cents for a bed and ten cents for breakfast! The house-father provides lunches for the hikers' knapsacks, sees to the enforcement of the rules of the house and acts as adviser to his guests.

The types of buildings used for these purposes are most interesting. They are often woodcutters' huts located in the beautiful forests, fishermen's shacks by the sea, moss-covered cottages on the heath, or even magnificent medieval castles. Many of the latter fell into the hands of these hiking associations during the inflation period of 1922–1923. Of course, these castles are rich in legend and in many instances they afford fine examples of architecture. It is one of the duties of the house-father to acquaint the traveling youth with the historic setting of these old landmarks.

The equipment of the hostels is quite adequate for entertaining their guests: light, airy bedrooms, modern, sanitary kitchens, and frequently a stage for dramatics. A lantern and screen are usually at hand to provide interesting diversion for the evenings.

Such a program of outdoor life would hardly be feasible in this country, where towns are often so far apart and roads are crowded with automobiles. In Germany many towns are within two or three miles of each other and automobiles do not yet constitute a problem. It is well to remember that it is possible to travel from one corner of Germany to the other in twelve hours.

By law, ten full days are reserved each year for school journeys. In many secondary schools it has gradually become the custom to round out the course, at least once before graduation, with a vacation trip to some foreign country like England, France or Italy to get acquainted with some features of foreign life and to promote a spirit of international good-will. These trips are carefully planned with particular reference to the geographical and historical study of various regions, to the use of the foreign language and to the study of art and architecture.

The sudden abolition of military training has redoubled interest in athletics. Apparatus work and formal gymnastic drills are being replaced by other forms of exercise. There is a growing fondness for track athletics, swimming (required in all schools) and rowing. The latter is extremely popular, and it is said that there is more rowing than in either England or the United States. Football has never made much headway. Stadiums have been built for holding competitive track meets to determine the best material for the Olympics. Judging from a photograph of the beautiful stadium at Dresden, I should say that the Germans are taking their track athletics very seriously. They look to us for guidance in training methods and they send men to this country to study our ways of training athletes.

To return to the scholastic side of a student's life, let us assume that the German boy is ready to "come up" for his final examination, which is held at the end of his secondary school days. This is the most important examination in the German schools, and the written part of it may be compared to the "new plan" examinations offered by the College Entrance Examination Board. First, the candidate must have good scholastic standing to gain admission to the examination and he must also write an acceptable thesis. Then he is ready to face the all-important written, oral and physical examinations. The written part tests him in four subjects: German, mathematics and two other subjects, depending on the type of school he is attending. The student's own teachers make out the question papers, which are submitted for approval to a provincial school board. The examinations are held in the candidate's own school and are conducted by teachers of the senior class, the director of the school and a state representative acting as chairman.

A few favors are shown the candidate when he appears for his oral examination. He may choose his "pet" subject, and he is made to feel as comfortable as possible on the momentous occasion. Those who examine him are expected to familiarize themselves with his previous record and his outstanding characteristics so that, after all, it is the complete personality of the candidate which is an important factor in the final analysis.

LESTER C. NEWTON

PHILLIPS ACADEMY,
ANDOVER, MASS.

QUOTATIONS

THE NEW YORK CITY SCHOOL INQUIRY

THE legislative committees eliminated the item of $50,000 for the investigation of the schools of New York City, which was included in the Governor's budget at the instance of the Board of Education and upon the recommendation of the Director of the Budget. There is now only one chance left—its possible inclusion in the supplemental appropriation bill. The steps taken in advance by the State Education Department have given assurance that the inquiry would be disinterested and thoroughgoing. The advisory committee chosen by Commissioner Graves consisted of men of the highest qualifications. The survey was to be made by men of technical competence directly under the supervision of the department. There would have been this advantage, as compared with earlier surveys, that the authorities making the investigation would be charged with carrying out any constructive suggestions resulting from it.

It was at first proposed that the investigation of the school system should be by the Hofstadter committee but, as the matters involved would be largely of a pedagogical or technically administrative nature, it was urged and planned that the State Education Department should undertake it, except that purchase of sites, erection of buildings, buying supplies and the like should be kept within the purview of the legislative committee. Appropriations for the continued activity of the Hofstadter committee have with public approval been made. It can hardly be less important that this school investigation should also proceed. The appropriation needed is slight compared with the total amount spent yearly for the schools—$120,000,000 exclusive of what is appropriated for buildings—the State contributing approximately one third of this total. The State's interest is as great as that of the city itself, since nearly half of the children in the public schools of the State are in this "school district."

The Constitution requires the Legislature "to provide for the maintenance and support of a system of free common schools wherein all the children of this State may be educated." The free schools have been provided. But there is the added obligation of finding out whether the children are being "educated"—actually given the instruction which the State through its educational authorities wishes them to receive. It is earnestly to be hoped that the Legislature will do its full duty in making this possible.—*The New York Times.*

REPORTS

THE DEVELOPMENT OF THE SECONDARY SCHOOL IN THE WEST BETWEEN 1890 AND 1920[1]

PUBLIC education in this country evolved out of a general dissatisfaction with the teachings and practices of the early private school, whose program of education was inadequate in both its content and objectives to satisfy the varying needs of the students. The private school, particularly of secondary grade, failed to provide a rich program of instruction because it held to the one sole objective, that of college preparation. Early private school growth in America was to a large extent a product of church endeavor which followed the advancing lines of territorial expansion during the period of the westward movement in the nineteenth century. Failure of the private secondary school to keep pace with the rapid progress of the public high school since the beginning of the twentieth century resulted in strengthening the popularity and support of the latter institution more than ever.

Interest by the people in the advancement of the public school idea in the more populous sections of the East and West soon brought about an agitation for state interest in education as against the private school, particularly those schools operating under denominational auspices. Such a change of attitude in the public mind toward the question of the right to educate all the children of all the people soon won many supporters to the public schools, causing the church, in many instances, to drop its narrow educational aims in order to compete with the rapidly growing public high school.

In order to determine the extent to which the public high school had gained in its popularity and support in the secondary school field, a comparison was made showing the growth and development of the public and denominational secondary schools in the states west of the Mississippi during the period from 1890 to 1920.

[1] Report of the commissioner of education for 1890, 1900 and 1910, Vol. 2; Biennial Survey of Education for 1918–1920, Bull. 1923, No. 29; reports of the U. S. Bureau of Census for 1890, 1900, 1910 and 1920.

Three factors were employed in tracing the educational history of the two types of secondary institutions namely: (1) growth in the number of schools, (2) growth in enrolment, and (3) the number of secondary students per one thousand general population.

The results of the study as indicated by Table I shows that the growth in the number of public secondary schools in the West during the period from 1890 to 1920 represented a gain of 3,866 schools contrasted to an increase of 255 church secondary institutions. The public high schools of the West had increased in numbers by 568 per cent. compared to a gain of only 114 per cent. in the number of denominational secondary schools established during this period. The greatest percentage of increase in the number of public high schools took place in the decade 1890 to 1900, at which time a gain of 166 per cent. occurred, while the largest percentage of increase in the number of denominational secondary schools was reported for the two latter decades of the thirty-year period with an increase of 31 per cent.

TABLE I

NUMBER OF PUBLIC AND DENOMINATIONAL SECONDARY SCHOOLS IN THE WEST, 1890–1920

	1890	1900	1910	1920	Per cent. gain 1890 to 1920
Public	680	1,812	3,624	4,546*	568
Denominational	224	278	365	479	114

* Includes four-year high schools only.

Of the two types of churches which comprised the denominational group of secondary schools, Table II shows that the Catholic Church reported a gain of 250 schools, representing an increase of 263 per cent. during the period from 1890 to 1920. The increase in the number of Protestant secondary schools amounted to only five institutions, having gained but three per cent. The greatest increase in the number of Catholic secondary schools occurred during the period from 1910 to 1920, having gained 66 per cent., while the largest percentage of increase in the number of Protestant secondary schools took place in the decade, *i.e.,* 1890 to 1900, with a gain of 15 per cent., and since that time the secondary schools of the Protestant order have shown a decrease in the percentage of growth.

TABLE II

DISTRIBUTION OF DENOMINATIONAL SECONDARY SCHOOLS IN THE WEST, 1890–1920

	1890	1900	1910	1920	Per cent. gain 1890 to 1920
Protestant	129	148	151	134	3
Catholic	95	129	214	345	263

The growth in public secondary school enrolment, as shown by Table III, offered a greater contrast during this period when the public high schools of the West reported a gain of 567,938 students, or an increase of 1,259 per cent. The denominational secondary school enrolment in the West showed an increase of 19,010 students, representing a gain of only 113 per cent. The public high schools of the West reached their highest percentage of growth in enrolment during the decade from 1890 to 1900 with a gain of 221 per cent. The peak of growth on the part of the denominational secondary school enrolment occurred in the decade

TABLE III

ENROLMENT OF PUBLIC AND DENOMINATIONAL SECONDARY SCHOOLS IN THE WEST, 1890–1920

	1890	1900	1910	1920	Per cent. gain 1890 to 1920
Public	44,647	142,743	288,726	606,585	1,259
Denominational	16,800	15,321	22,773	35,810	113

* Includes four-year high schools only.

of 1910 to 1920, with a gain of 57 per cent., due in the main to large Catholic secondary school increases for that period.

There were also wide differences in the gain in secondary school enrolment reported for the two religious faiths during the thirty-year period. According to Table IV, the increase in Catholic secondary school enrolment amounted to approximately 160 per cent., compared to a gain of about 70 per cent. in Protestant secondary school enrolment in the Western states. The Catholic secondary school reported its greatest percentage of growth in enrolment during the decade from 1910 to 1920 with an increase of 148 per cent., while the largest gain in Protestant secondary school enrolment occurred during the decade from 1900 to 1910 with an increase of 39 per cent.

TABLE IV

DISTRIBUTION OF DENOMINATIONAL SECONDARY SCHOOL ENROLMENT IN THE WEST, 1890–1920

	1890	1900	1910	1920	Per cent. gain 1890 to 1920
Protestant	8,613	10,211	14,222	14,541	70
Catholic	8,167	5,019	8,551	21,269	160

The extent to which this extraordinary growth in public secondary school enrolment in the West has had an effect upon the denominational secondary school enrolment during the three-decade period is shown to an effective degree by the relationship between the total number of public and denominational secondary students per one thousand general population. The number of public secondary school pupils per one thousand general population in 1890 according to Table V was approximately three students per thousand, and by 1920 this number had increased to twenty per thousand, representing a gain of seventeen students, or an increase of about 566 per cent. for the entire period. The gain in the number of denominational secondary students between 1890 and 1920 amounted to considerably less than one student per thousand population, with an increase of only nine per cent. The holding power of the public secondary school is clearly shown by the increasingly large number of its students per one thousand general population in the Western states between 1890 and 1920, and far outdistanced the enrolment of the denominational secondary school for the same period.

TABLE V

NUMBER OF PUBLIC AND DENOMINATIONAL SECONDARY SCHOOL STUDENTS PER 1,000 GENERAL POPULATION IN THE WEST, 1890–1920.

Year	Total population	Public high-school enrolment	Per cent. per 1000	Denominational enrolment	Per cent. per 1,000
1890	16,345,598	44,647	2.72	16,800	1.10
1900	19,532,442	142,743	7.31	15,231	.78
1910	25,384,152	288,726	11.37	22,773	.89
1920	29,891,029	606,587	20.29	35,810	1.20

The reasons for the superiority in the growth of the public secondary school of the West over that of the denominational secondary school were attributed to many factors namely: (1) That the public high school is offering to-day a broader curricular content in respect to the newer objectives than ever before, while the denominational secondary school has just begun to enter a period of curricular readjustment to meet the newer conceptions of modern education. (2) The reorganization of our secondary school system has resulted in the formation of two types of public secondary branches of learning, those of the junior high school and junior college. The fact that these new types of schools make provision for greater articulation between the elementary and the high schools on the one hand; and the college on the other, has resulted in a large increase in public secondary school enrolment. (3) The progressive attitude of the Federal government in financing public education through its system of land grants and aid towards the promotion of vocational education has been another important factor in public high-school growth. The history of private-school support on the other hand reveals an unstable development due to the lack of endowment funds to finance a program of education for a sufficient number of years, and also indicates the failure of tuition fees or rates to adequately cover operating expenses. These factors have considerably hampered private and denominational school growth. (4) During the past fifty years or more, there has been a gradual disappearance or withdrawal of the secondary school from the denominational educational field. In a questionnaire received from 128 denominational colleges of the West, sixty-four, or 59 per cent., of these colleges reported that they had dropped the secondary school from their institutions for various reasons, the chief reason being the growth and development of the public high school. (5) Practically all the churches of the Protestant order, with the possible exception of the Lutheran church, have taken the attitude of favoring public secondary education. This has resulted in the transfer of many of its secondary school students over to state institutions. The Catholic church, on the other hand, has from the beginning maintained the policy of educating the young people of that faith in its own schools. This undoubtedly accounts for the rapid growth of the Catholic secondary schools during the past quarter century.

SUMMARY

(1) The public high school has shown a marked superiority over the denominational secondary school of the West between 1890 and 1920 in the number of schools established, growth in enrolment, and in respect to the number of secondary students per one thousand general population.

(2) The Catholic church in the West between 1890 and 1920 reported larger increases in both the number of secondary schools established and in secondary school enrolment than was reported by the secondary schools of the Protestant faith.

(3) The most important factors attributed to the extraordinary growth of the public high school were found to be: Broader educational outlook in terms of curriculum and school organization, greater opportunities for financial support, and the attitude of the Protestant churches to favor public school development.

RICHARD M. BENSON

SAN MATEO, CALIFORNIA

SOCIETIES AND MEETINGS

STUDENTS' PAN-AMERICAN CONGRESS

A CONGRESS of students from universities in Latin American countries, Canada and the United States will be held in Miami from April 11 to 14. The object of the congress is to establish brotherly relations through an intimate discussion of such topics as the national debt of Bolivia, the question of the Pacific, boundary disputes, overproduction of coffee in Brazil, trade relations and the Monroe Doctrine.

Mayor Gautier and the City Commission of Miami expressed their enthusiasm in pledging the support of the city. Foreign delegates will be guests of Miami and will be accommodated at the finest hotels.

The Munson and Grace Steamship Lines and the Pan-American Airways have cooperated in reducing transportation rates.

The cooperation of the Pan-American League has been pledged, and Hon. Ruth Bryan Owen is favorably impressed and is endorsing the congress in her usual forceful and effective way.

A highly specialized student committee of forty-five members has been mobilized and the mass of intricate preparations has been assembled and assigned to various chairmen and their committees.

Identification of the congress with the National Student Federation has given it national scope. A Miami University delegate attended the National Federation's Convention in Toledo during the Christmas holidays, at which time the plans for the congress were given its approval and support.

Distinguished speakers are addressing the student committee on subjects relative to the proposed congress and every means has been used to prepare delegates for such a vital experiment.

Rafael Belaunde, Joseph Eggum and Meldrin Thomson, Jr., the three originators of the plan, made a trip to Washington to contact Latin delegates to the Pan-American Chamber of Commerce Convention. Very encouraging results were obtained through those consultations. It was remarked that the students from Latin America would undoubtedly be leaders in their respective countries.

American delegates will receive valuable experience in cultivating friendships among the Latin and Canadian students. These friendships will be molded through the mutual efforts of delegates who want to understand each other.

Discussion of problems among all the delegates will establish international understanding of problems that formerly were confined to their respective areas. Students who attend the congress will be better prepared through such intimate contact, to represent their countries in international affairs should they be called upon a few years hence.

About sixty delegates are expected, forty representing South American universities and twenty from universities in Canada and the United States.

The social and business calendar for the congress is active from morning to night. The first day is set aside for committee meetings and general arrangements.

There will be an opening breakfast on Tuesday morning, April 12, with Mayor Gautier, of Miami, host. At the official opening in the afternoon of the exhibition at Bay Front Park, booths will be so grouped as to form a map of North, South and Central America, representing twenty-one Pan-American nations and Canada. The schools will exhibit displays of all the nations.

The Pan-American Day Committee will sponsor a ball which will be held in the evening for distinguished guests and their friends.

On Wednesday, April 13, there will be held the official Pan-American Day luncheon, which will be broadcasted over a national hook-up and the low wave set. In the evening there will be a program in Bay Front Park. Speakers will inform the general public of the meaning of Pan-American Day.

Thursday, April 14, will feature Pan-American Club day. A luncheon honoring all the Pan-American Clubs will be held at noon and in the afternoon there will be a float parade representing each nation of the Pan-American Union. At eight o'clock at Bay Front Park a pageant will glorify the Pan-American Union, and a magnificent ball at one of the leading hotels will bring the Pan-American Congress celebration to a happy close.

The Latin American and Canadian universities may be depended upon to send students of outstanding ability who by character are gifted with the power to express themselves convincingly and eloquently.

The universities of the United States will also be adequately represented by students with the vision and tenacity to establish the student nucleus of future political brotherhood.

Whatever youth unanimously dictates will eventually be accepted, for the youth of to-day is the governing body of to-morrow. So in our modern trend, education tends to blend the past in an emphasis of the future. Our youth has grasped the significance and in its bold and admirable way has spanned the Pan-American spaces with a peace-bridge, riveted in student relationship and understanding.

GLADYS E. NELLENBOGEN

MIAMI, FLORIDA

EDUCATIONAL RESEARCH AND STATISTICS

THE BENEFACTIONS OF PHILANTHROPIC FOUNDATIONS AND WHO RECEIVE THEM

INTRODUCTION

SUCH rapid growth has taken place in the establishment of general foundations that approximately two hundred of these organizations with capital assets exceeding two billion dollars are now existent in America.[1]

Five of the older and more prominent of the foundations are: (1) The General Education Board, organized in 1902; (2) The Carnegie Corporation of New York, in 1911; (3) The Rockefeller Foundation, in 1913; (4) The Commonwealth Fund, in 1918; and (5) The Laura Spelman Rockefeller Memorial, in 1918.[2] Their contributions to the discovery and dissemina-

[1] Edwin R. Embree, "The Business of Giving away Money," *Harper's Monthly Magazine*, 161: 322, August, 1930.

[2] The Rockefeller Foundation and the Laura Spelman Rockefeller Memorial were consolidated in 1929.

TABLE I

AMOUNTS OF FUNDS AUTHORIZED TO PRIVATE AND PUBLIC INSTITUTIONS OF HIGHER LEARNING BY FIVE GENERAL FOUNDATIONS DURING THE PERIOD 1923–1929

Character of institution	Year authorized							
	1923		1924		1925		1926	
	No.	Amount	No.	Amount	No.	Amount	No.	Amount
Private Institutions								
Private Universities	13	$ 5,352,017.00	11	$6,089,250.00	16	$5,781,050.00	15	$12,350,849.00
Private Colleges	64	4,701,416.00	14	1,245,133.00	15	1,590,583.34	16	351,939.23
Total:								
Private Institutions	**77**	**$10,053,433.00**	**25**	**$7,334,383.00**	**31**	**$7,371,633.34**	**31**	**$12,702,788.23**
Public Institutions								
State Universities	1	$ 1,125,000.00	3	$ 672,000.00	5	$ 734,000.00	5	$ 1,355,200.00
Municipal Universities	......	....	1	40,000.00	......	....	......	....
State Colleges	......	....	......	....	1	22,500.00	2	112.500.00
Total:								
Public Institutions	**1**	**$ 1,125,000.00**	**4**	**$ 712,000.00**	**6**	**$ 756,500.00**	**7**	**$ 1,467,700.00**
Grand Total:								
Public and Private	**78**	**$11,178,433.00**	**29**	**$8,046,383.00**	**37**	**$8,128,133.34**	**38**	**$14,170,488.23**

tion of knowledge in medicine, health, education, social science and other fields have been of outstanding importance.

The principal concern of the investigation reported here has been to determine the channels through which the contributions of the five mentioned foundations have run. More especially, attention has been directed to the activities carried on by these foundations in conjunction with colleges and universities. For purposes of comparison these institutions have been divided into two main categories—private and public.

THE SOURCES OF DATA

The sources of the data presented were the available annual reports published by the respective foundations for the years 1923–1929, inclusive.[3] These data were not in all cases unequivocal, but with limitations to be pointed out the findings are presented.

THE FINDINGS

The principal recipients: The composite data for the five foundations studied are presented in Table I. It is apparent that:

(1) Of the total amount, consisting of $112,031,306.22, there was authorized $102,808,256.22, or 91.7 per cent., to private and $9,223,050.00, or 8.3 per cent., to public institutions.

(2) Of $102,808,256.22 authorized to private institutions.
  (a) $88,579,104.48, or 86.2 per cent., was distributed among 36 different private universities.
  (b) $14,229,151.74, or 13.8 per cent., was distributed among 106 different private colleges.

(3) Of $9,223,050.00 allotted to public institutions:
  (a) $8,712,550.00 or 94.5 per cent., was distributed among 23 state universities.
  (b) $452.500.00, or 4.9 per cent., among 9 state colleges.

[3] (1) Annual Reports of the General Education Board for the years 1923–24–25–26–27–28–29. General Education Board, 61 Broadway, New York City; (2) Reports of the President and the Treasurer for the years 1923–24–25–26–27–28–29. The Carnegie Corporation of New York, 522 Fifth Ave., New York City; (3) Annual Reports for the years 1923–24–25–26–27–28–29. The Rockefeller Foundation, 61 Broadway, New York City. (4) Annual Reports for the years 1923–24–25–26–27–28–29. The Commonwealth Fund, 57th Street and Madison, New York City; (5) Annual Reports for the years 1923–24–25–26–27–28. The Laura Spelman Rockefeller Memorial, New York City.

TABLE I

AMOUNTS OF FUNDS AUTHORIZED TO PRIVATE AND PUBLIC INSTITUTIONS OF HIGHER LEARNING BY FIVE GENERAL FOUNDATIONS DURING THE PERIOD 1923–1929

Year authorized									
1927		1928		1929		Total		Per cent. of total	Per cent. of grand total
No.	Amount	No.	Amount	No.	Amount	No.	Amount		
16	$22,466,266.68	15	$11,423,825.97	23	$25,115,845.83	36	$ 88,579,104.48	86.2	79.0
20	2,348,537.50	18	2,944,950.00	19	1,046,592.67	106	14,229,151.74	13.8	12.7
36	**$24,814,804.18**	**33**	**$14,368,775.97**	**42**	**$26,162,438.50**	**142**	**$102,808,256.22**	**100.0**	**91.7**
10	$ 1,714,000.00	10	$ 1,858,000.00	17	$ 1,254,350.00	23	$ 8,712,550.00	94.5	7.8
......	....	1	15,000.00	1	3,000.00	2	58,000.00	.6	.1
3	175,000.00	3	39,500.00	2	103,000.00	9	452,500.00	4.9	.4
13	**$ 1,889,000.00**	**14**	**$ 1,912,500.00**	**20**	**$ 1,360,350.00**	**34**	**$ 9,223,050.00**	**100.0**	**8.3**
49	**$26,703,804.18**	**47**	**$16,281,275.97**	**62**	**$27,522,788.50**	**176**	**$112,031,306.22**		**100.0**

(c) $58,000.00, or 0.6 per cent., between 2 municipal universities.

A consideration of individual institutions leads to the following arrangement in order of the amount authorized to each:

1.	The University of Chicago	$21,255,500.00
2.	Vanderbilt University	11,610,992.64
3.	Yale University	10,713,950.00
4.	Cornell University including New York Hospital	9,179,000.00
5.	Columbia Univ. $3,238,683.34; Teachers College 4,899,150.00	8,137,833.34
6.	Johns Hopkins University	5,916,740.00
7.	Harvard University	5,218,828.83
8.	Washington University, Mo	4,306,500.00
9.	Princeton University	3,487,150.00
10.	California Institute of Technology	3,390,416.67

From this list it is observed that there is no public institution that attains a rank among the first ten.

With respect to the allotment of funds to private and public institutions by any particular foundation, it may be said that:

(1) The General Education Board, which contributed $77,830,583.00, or 69.5 per cent., of the total amount authorized by all five foundations, distributed:
- (a) $74,084,083.00, or 95.1 per cent., to 100 private institutions;
- (b) $3,782,500.00, or 4.9 per cent., to 12 public institutions.

(2) The Laura Spelman Rockefeller Memorial, which contributed $13,336,182.53, or 11.9 per cent., of the total, distributed:
- (a) $9,997,682.53, or 75 per cent., to 19 private institutions;
- (b) $3,338,500.00, or 25 per cent., to 12 public institutions.

(3) The Carnegie Corporation of New York, which contributed $8,198,449.69, or 7.3 per cent. of the total, distributed:
- (a) $7,717,399.69, or 94.2 per cent., to 67 private institutions;
- (b) $481,050.00, or 5.8 per cent., to 21 public institutions.

(4) The Rockefeller Foundation, which contributed $12,181,941.00, or 10.9 per cent. of the total, distributed:
- (a) $10,647,441.00, or 87.4 per cent., to 15 private institutions;
- (b) $1,534,500.00, or 12.6 per cent., to 5 public institutions.

(5) The Commonwealth Fund, which contributed $484,150.00, or 0.4 per cent. of the total, distributed:
- (a) $397,500.00, or 82.2 per cent., to 10 private institutions;
- (b) $86,500.00, or 17.8 per cent., to 7 public institutions.

From these data it is again noted that, whereas some variation exists among the percentages of funds authorized by the respective foundations to public and private institutions, the latter are by far the chief recipients of the major portions.

The character of activities: The extent of which these foundations attain their projected purposes is reflected in the types of activities in which they engage. While it was not possible to locate these activities into discrete categories, Table II gives some description of their character. A tendency is shown to authorize funds in most cases for specific projects. Wide diversity is revealed in the fields fostered, but, in general, education, health and scientific research appear to be the most popular subjects. Dominance in funds authorized is indicated for public over private institutions only in such fields as child welfare, teacher training, public education (buildings), public welfare and rural education.

Funds to special insitutions: Although this investigation has been primarily concerned with the relation between specified foundations and private and public institutions of higher learning, it is recognized that colleges and universities are not the only recipients of funds from these foundations. This is apparent from the data presented in Table III, which indicates the extent of authorization of funds to certain institutions other than those previously considered.

Funds to unclassed institutions: In the allocation of funds authorized to public and private universities and colleges, there were certain institutions for which available data did not permit a classification. The total allotment to twelve such institutions and three unassigned funds or unspecified institutions was $2,378,666.68.

SUMMARY AND IMPLICATIONS

This investigation has dealt chiefly with the authorization of funds by five general foundations to specific private and public institutions

TABLE II

FUNDS AUTHORIZED TO PRIVATE AND PUBLIC INSTITUTIONS OF HIGHER LEARNING DETAILED AS TO ACTIVITIES FOR WHICH ALLOTTED (1923–1929)

Character of activity	Funds authorized to Private: Universities	Private: Colleges	Public: State universities	Public: Municipal universities	Public: State colleges
1. Buildings					
Medical	21,843,000.00		3,050,000.00		
Science, General	2,250,000.00				
Institute of Human Relations	1,500,000.00				
Library	1,385,000.00	75,000.00	100,000.00		
Chemistry	1,000,000.00				
Physics	400,000.00				
Psychology	385,000.00				
Astronomy	200,000.00				
Public Education			15,000.00		100,000.00
Not Specified	1,987,667.00	750,000.00			
Total	**30,950,667.00**	**825,000.00**	**3,165,000.00**		**100,000.00**
2. Medicine, Medical Education, Health Education	18,369,300.00	250,000.00	522,000.00	40,000.00	
3. Research and Teaching:					
Sciences, General	3,542,500.00	2,500,000.00	15,000.00		
Biology, Zoology	281,000.00	15,000.00	77,500.00		
Physics, Anthropology, Geology, Astronomy, Chemistry	765,000.00	55,000.00	15,000.00		
Social Sciences, Humanities	4,658,967.33		565,000.00		
Economics	312,500.00				
Public Welfare		8,700.00	212,000.00		
Psychiatry, Mental Hygiene	2,354,600.00	47,800.00	27,000.00		
Medicine	894,115.00	10,000.00	153,500.00		
Psychology	428,500.00		5,000.00		
Honors Course		915,000.00			
Public Education		245,000.00			
Vocational Guidance	39,150.00				
Agriculture (Study of Graduate Work)	15,000.00		15,000.00		
Rural Education					5,000.00
Study of Compensation for Automobile Accidents	70,000.00				
Legal Education	750,000.00				
Law	160,000.00				
City Planning	240,000.00				
Architecture	250,000.00				
Not Specified	1,000,000.00	600,000.00			
Total	**15,761,332.33**	**4,396,500.00**	**1,085,000.00**		**5,000.00**
4. Salaries, Additions to Staffs	3,944,500.00	1,444,083.00	75,000.00		
5. Music, Art	1,111,928.83	609,200.00	163,200.00		3,000.00
6. Child Welfare	537,550.00	36,000.00	1,131,000.00		22,500.00
7. Library Development	473,166.68	381,833.34	24,850.00	3,000.00	25,000.00
8. Teacher Training			490,000.00		180,000.00
9. Schools of Nursing	1,552,750.00	20,000.00			
10. Adult Education	109,000.00		12,000.00		22,500.00
11. Lincoln School	3,500,000.00				
12. Not Specified	12,268,909.69	6,266,535.40	2,044,500.00	15,000.00	94,500.00
Grand Totals	**88,579,104.48**	**14,229,151.74**	**8,712,550.00**	**58,000.00**	**452,500.00**

TABLE III

Allotments during the Period 1923–29 to Special Institutions by the Five Foundations

Institution	Allotment
Carnegie Institution of Washington	$ 6,006,500.00
New York Academy of Medicine	2,630,040.60
American Law Institute	1,075,000.00
Marine Biological Laboratory	1,000,000.00
Robert Brookings Institute of Economics and Government	490,000.00
Carnegie Institute of Pittsburgh	255,000.00
National Academy of Science	105,000.00
Marine Biological Station, California	100,000.00
Regents of the University of New York	80,500.00
Association of American Universities	14,000.00
Association of American College	10,000.00
American Academy of Teachers of Singing	5,000.00
University of the State of New York	5,000.00
Total	$11,776,040.60

of higher learning. The findings reveal that these funds are predominantly allotted to private institutions.

Information has been given about conditions as they are, but this presentation has not afforded an understanding as to what produces them or what they signify. The object has been to describe rather than to explain. If the circumstances as described indicate a policy on the part of foundations then certain issues arise of special importance to state institutions. Of these a few will be listed.

(1) What relationship does this policy bear to securing and retaining staff members of eminence?

(2) Do conditions to insure the most satisfactory conduct of a projected activity obtain in state institutions?

(3) (a) Will the introduction of new and diverse activities pervert the institutional program?

(b) Is provision made for the maintenance of certain types of activities after their introduction so as to prevent a diversion of institutional funds needed for other purposes?

(4) Is the institution prevented from the acceptance of certain funds for research because of the basis upon which its research program rests; *i.e.*, the needs of showing each year completed results or those of a practical bearing? This is likely in some cases a short-sighted policy. Investigation of the most recondite type may be prerequisite to the solution of many practical problems.

(5) Are state institutions either through policies imagined or real less inclined than private institutions towards trying out new procedures in teaching or research?

If an inference can be drawn from the data presented it would likely be that appropriations have not been withheld from public institutions as a result of a discriminating policy. If this were true of an earlier period it is somewhat abating. This is supported by the increasing number of public institutions that are granted funds. Each year of the period under review bears witness to the increasing proportion the public institutions constitute of the total to which allotments are made. The successive percentages for the respective years of the period, 1923–1929, are 1.3, 13.8, 16.2, 18.4, 26.5, 29.8 and 32.3. The percentages of increase in number, however, do not synchronize with corresponding increases in the proportions the funds authorized to public institutions bear to the total. The percentages for the respective years are 10.1, 8.8, 9.3, 10.4, 7.1, 11.7 and 4.9. A partial explanation of this discordance may possibly be found among the answers to the issues raised.

Palmer O. Johnson
The University of Minnesota

NEW BOOKS IN EDUCATION

Almack, John C. and Elmer H. Staffelbach. *The Stanford Speller. For grades two, three, four, five, six, seven and eight.* 80 pages each. Laidlaw. $.24 each.

Comfort, Mildred E. *Peter and Nancy in Europe.* Pp. 208. Illustrated. Beckley-Cardy. $.75.

De Schweinitz, Dorothea. *How Workers Find Jobs.* Pp. xvi + 199. Illustrated. University of Pennsylvania Press. $2.50.

Kinneman, John A. *Society and Education.* Pp. xii + 558. Macmillan. $2.00.

Lyford, Carrie A. *The School Dormitory.* Pp. vi + 200. Barrows. $2.00.

Taylor, Frances L. *Adventures in Fact and Fancy.* Pp. 304. Illustrated. Beckley-Cardy. $.84.

SCHOOL AND SOCIETY

EDITED BY J. McKEEN CATTELL

WITH WHICH IS COMBINED THE

EDUCATIONAL REVIEW

EDITED BY WILLIAM McANDREW

Volume 35 SATURDAY, FEBRUARY 27, 1932 Numbe

THE MONTANA SYSTEM OF ADMINISTERING HIGHER EDUCATION

By Dr. M. A. BRANNON

CHANCELLOR OF THE UNIVERSITY OF MONTANA

THE map of practically every state in the Union teaches that state institutions of every kind, governmental, eleemosynary, custodial and educational, have been located by political barter. Questions of efficiency and economy in subsequent state service seem to have had little or no significance in determining location. Personal and provincial objectives apparently dominated legislative action. Legislators were motivated by such questions as "How can I secure some revenue-producing institution for my community, my constituents?" and "How can I, myself, secure permanent recognition for my legislative service?" rather than, "How can I achieve the greatest good for the greatest number?" Such questions seem always to have been answered politically, with the result that there is to be found on every state political map an institutional mosaic. This traditional political procedure is responsible for the development in many states of two or more separated universities instead of one staunch university. This unfortunate multiplication of higher educational institutions in a commonwealth frequently penalizes its economics, its interest in cultural and scientific work, and the development of its state consciousness. So expensive and unsatisfactory has this competitive educational product of political barter become in many states that earnest efforts are being made to secure a reorganization of higher educational institutions in order that tandem, constructive educational procedure may be substituted for head-on collisions. Several of these states, looking toward readjustment of higher educational policies, have sought information regarding Montana's system of administering her state-supported collegiate institutions. In order that Montana's experiences may be examined and possibly prove helpful I shall endeavor to sketch the evolution of the plan and the techniques employed in its operation, and shall present some of the manifest results, together with the comparative costs of higher education in twelve Western and Rocky Mountain states.

Following the lead of older states, Montana reacted affirmatively to political forces which determined the location of all her state institutions. In 1893 the legislature established and located the State University at Missoula, the College of Agriculture and Mechanic Arts at Bozeman, the School of Mines at Butte and the State Normal College at Dillon. Running true to the separatists system followed by many other states, intensive competition among the four institutions of higher education and the respective communities in which they were located developed at once and from year to year, was augmented. Faculties, students and friends of each unit [illegible] higher education industriously capital- [illegible] every available economic, social and, [illegible]ical interest for their own institution [illegible] worked directly or indirectly against [illegible] other unit of higher education in the state. Naturally, during every session of the legislature competition reached fever heat. Vigorous and hostile lobbies sought appropriations for each educational institution. Educational lobbying became so intense during the early sessions of Montana legislatures that it was difficult for the legislators to consider important state matters in other divisions of government. This educational competition and head-on collision of state teaching units operated positively within the legislature and throughout the state. It interfered with the development of service and the building of state consciousness. Effort, energy and money which should have been employed constructively for the enrichment of institutional life and the improvement of public service were wasted in legislative and state-wide rivalries.

As the cost of government advances, it becomes increasingly evident that subsequent generations must bear the increasing burdens resulting from the use of purely political procedure in locating state institutions. The burden is indeed becoming so acute that society is seeking vigorously for relief. If reduction and scientific relocation of institutions are impossible, the quest is next directed toward amelioration of the situation and the lightening of burdens without cheapening and reducing educational service. Manifestly the more vital the state service, the more significant and serious become the questions of modification. A careful analysis of the four arms or divisions of government, legislative, executive, judicial and educational, indicates that society will be seriously penalized by unscientific and crude procedure in dealing with the institutions built for service in the educational or fourth division of government. It happens, moreover, that this is the governmental division in which local and provincial interest always expresses itself most actively and effectively. This is doubtless true in part because education is intimately related to the interests of the home, in the training and development of the child. Universally the desire for educational advantages near the home, that is, accessibility, stimulates citizens in different communities to work feverishly for the establishment of an institution of higher education within their own area of the state. It is natural that this competition for higher educational service near home should merge and be capitalized by politicians, with the result that institutions are divided and multiplied and that their location and sites are determined by political expediency and not solely in relation to needs and opportunities of a long-time program of efficient and economical educational state service. This multiplication and separation of institutions of higher education indubitably leads to bitter competition for appropriations among the separated institutions and the communities in which they are built. This competition is usually expressed by wasteful and unnecessary duplication of work, by lobbying for state support, and by unfortunate institutional and local rivalries. After twenty years of educational guerilla warfare, thoughtful leaders in Montana determined to secure release from a situation which was definitely wasteful and unstatesmanlike. One of these thoughtful leaders, Dr. John S. Durston, a son of Yale and Heidelberg, devised a cosmopolitan plan for the control of institutions of higher education and successfully advocated its substitution for the provincial policy which had prevailed in the state. Dr. Durston in his scholarly travels had observed that large business organizations operating plants in widely separated areas of the country, and even operating in different countries, had devised efficient coordinating agencies located in remote cities, New York, London or Paris, with the result that high efficiency and economy replaced the inefficiency and wastefulness of separated organizations. This world scholar and educational statesman reasoned that if good-will and understanding were possible and desirable in highly competitive business enterprises, they should prove helpful and salutary in the altruistic, non-profit-making service of higher education. He set forth his ideas in a proposed legislative act which was discussed and accepted by the 1913 session of the legislature. The statute reads in part as follows:

SECTION 1. From and after the first day of July, 1913, the State University at Missoula, the College of Agriculture and Mechanic Arts at Bozeman, the School of Mines at Butte, and the Normal School at Dillon, and such Departments of said institutions as may hereafter be organized, shall constitute the University of Montana, under the name and style of the University of Montana.

SECTION 2. The control and supervision of the University of Montana, as hereinbefore constituted, is vested in the State Board of Education, which must appoint a president and faculty for each of the various State institutions constituting The University of Montana, as hereinbefore provided, and such other officers, agents and employees for said University of Montana, and for its component state institutions as the State Board may deem necessary, including, a Chancellor of the University of Montana, and whose powers and duties shall be such as may be prescribed by the State Board of Education, which shall also prescribe the powers and duties of the presidents, faculty, officers, agents, and employees of said institutions, composing said University of Montana, and shall also establish for the government of the University of Montana and for its component institutions, and for the instruction given therein, such rules and regulations, not inconsistent with the laws of the State, as may be necessary for the proper government and control of the University of Montana, and its said component institutions.

SECTION 4. It shall be the duty of the State Board of Education, in the exercise of its discretion, in the government and control of said University of Montana, and its component institutions, as conferred upon it by the Constitution of the State, to take such steps and prescribe such rules as may be necessary to prevent unnecessary duplications of courses of instruction in the various educational institutions composing the University of Montana; to investigate carefully the needs of each of said institutions with referen[illegible] [illegible]ldings, equipment and instruction; [illegible] necessary appropriations required [illegible] and to make recommendations to [illegible] Assembly accordingly. . . .

SECTION 6. The presidents of eac[illegible] cational institutions constituting the U[illegible] Montana, as herein prescribed, in conne[illegible] their respective executive boards of the [illegible] institutions, as now prescribed by law, sha[illegible] the immediate direction, management and co[illegible] of their respective institutions, subject to the general supervision, direction and control of the State Board of Education, as now prescribed by law, and no one of the presidents of any of said institutions shall have any direction, control, management or authority in or over any of said institutions, except his own.

Approved March 14, 1913 (see Session Laws of Montana, 1913, Chapter 92).

The dominant principle of this legislation was centralized, coordinating control granted to the State Board of Education and exercised by its executive officer, the chancellor of the university. It was hoped that this plan would minimize the unfortunate results of prior competition among the local communities within which the units of higher education had been established, that unnecessary misunderstanding and ill will among faculties, student bodies and alumni would be greatly reduced, that "*unnecessary duplications*" would be eliminated and thereafter prevented among the units of the consolidated university, and that the units of higher education would move tandem in serving the state unselfishly, economically and efficiently.

As might be expected, this legislative measure was sharply opposed both by institutional and community interests. It was generally feared that outside and dictatorial control would be imposed upon the institutions composing the University of Montana. Resistance against the legislative measure was so stubborn that the state board of education was disposed to move slowly against institutional and community opposition and did not, during the biennium of 1913–15, deem it advisable to appoint a chancellor. Stimulated by the institutions and communities affected by the legislation written in chapter 92, the legislature of 1915 repealed the act. Governor S. V. Stewart, who was chairman of the state board of education, realizing that the Act of 1913 had great merit, vetoed the repeal. The opponents of the measure were unable to secure further action on the part of the legislature of 1915, and the governor's veto was unquestioned during the remainder of the session. During 1915 the board of education instituted its quest for a chancellor and in October of that year elected Dr. Edward C. Elliott, of the University of Wisconsin, the first chancellor of the University of Montana.

The legislative act of 1913, providing for the consolidation of the State University at Missoula, the State College of Agriculture and Mechanic Arts at Bozeman, the State School of Mines at Butte, and the State Normal College at Dillon, prescribed also the duties of the presidents of the several institutions. Prescription of the duties of the chancellor were wisely omitted. It was evident that Dr. Durston, the author of the consolidating university statute, recognized the wisdom of leaving this highly important function to the state board of education. Manifestly the harmonious administration of this interesting experiment in coordinating institutions on separated campuses depended upon a proper adjustment of the powers and duties of the chancellor and the presidents and upon the development of scientific technique in the exercise of the authority delegated by the state board of education to the chancellor. After experimenting for two years with the complex questions involved in administering the four separated institutions—each having gone its own competitive way—the state board of education adopted the following resolution relative to the powers and duties of the chancellor:

I. *Relation of the Chancellor to the State Board of Education:*

The Chancellor is the chief executive officer of the University and as such performs the duties prescribed by law, and carries out the orders of the Board. He is responsible to the Board for the prompt and effective execution of all policies determined upon for the proper enforcement of the rules and regulations adopted for the several institutions of the University. He shall act as the medium of communication between the Board and the officers and organization of the University. He shall attend and participate in all meetings of the Board at which matters relating to his office, or to any of the institutions or affairs of the University are under consideration. He shall make nominations and reports of appointments, promotions, salaries, transfers, suspensions, dismissals, and resignations of administrative officers, members of the instructional and scientific staffs, and other employees of the several institutions of the University. As prescribed by law, he shall sign all diplomas, degrees, papers, instruments, and documents executed by the University. It is also his duty to report to the Board, at reasonable intervals, on the general condition of the University and to make recommendations concerning general policies that will promote the development of the higher educational system of the State.

II. *Relation of the Chancellor to the University.*

The Chancellor is a member of all legislative bodies within the University organizations and decides all questions of jurisdiction, not specifically defined, of the several councils, faculties, and officers. He may refer any question of institutional or general University policy to any council, faculty, committee, or to any member of the instructional or scientific staffs for investigation and report. He may call special meetings of any council, faculty or committee at any time. The Chancellor shall afford every opportunity, consistent with sound administration and educational policy, to every officer and member of the instructional and scientific staffs to present suggestions for the general welfare of the University or of any of its institutions.

The Chancellor may veto any act of any council, faculty or committee within the University, but in so doing he shall transmit with the veto a written statement of the reasons for such action. A copy of each veto statement shall be transmitted to the Board. Any council, faculty, or committee may appeal from a veto of the Chancellor to the Board and may be represented before the Board by one of its members for this purpose.

III. *General Powers and Duties of the Chancellor.*

The Chancellor shall prepare and submit to the Board such annual and special reports concerning the University as the Board may require. He shall also prepare and present annually to the Board, the University budget. When approved by the Board, this budget shall govern all expenditures, subject to the provisions of the law and to the regulations of the State Board of Examiners.

IV. *Incidental Powers of the Chancellor.*

As the Chief Executive Officer of the University, the Chancellor is especially charged with the duty of securing harmony and cooperation among the institutions of the University, and the economical coordination of their instructional and scientific work. To these ends he has such powers as may be definitely delegated to him by the Board; and in addition such incidental powers as are necessary properly to perform the duties of his office.

An examination of the outline of the chancellor's powers and duties indicates that the state board of education recognized the complex and wide-sweeping responsibilities of their executive officer and delegated authority commensurate with the responsibility imposed. By the same token, the chancellor naturally recognized the high responsibilities of the presidents of the various units of the university and endeavored to secure authority for each president commensurate with the responsibility to be discharged. This policy of keeping authority and responsibility in even and judicial balance has steadily characterized the actions of the state board of education, the chancellor and the presidents who are charged with administering this exceedingly interesting educational experiment of coordinating separated institutions into one integrated university.

Chancellor Elliott, during his administration, which continued for six and a half years, elaborated and established effective and economic coordination of four university units situated on campuses hundreds of miles apart. In place of four separate, competing institutions, operating without budgets, employing different methods of accounting, encroaching wherever possible upon the work of one another, and each feeling more or less that it possessed vested rights, Dr. Elliott left a coordinated university composed of four units, with business offices thoroughly modernized and operating with budgets; with vital, experimental and enterprising faculties; with duplication of courses minimized and eliminated and with a consuming desire to give higher educational service to students and to improve steadily in all public service relations. The Montana system is unique in America. Dr. Elliott had no precedents to study or follow. He built exceedingly well and displayed unusual foresight and wisdom in elaborating the details and techniques of an enlarged and coordinated institution.

Since the conclusion of Chancellor Elliott's administration, the legislature has authorized the establishment and development of two additional teaching units of the University of Montana—the Eastern Montana Normal School at Billings and the Northern Montana College at Havre. The two new units were established in response to many factors, of which accessibility was the major. It was easier in 1922 for students in northern and eastern Montana to travel to the University of Minnesota, six hundred miles to the east, than it was to reach the nearest unit of the University of Montana. Legislative provision for refund of railroad fares in excess of $10.00 ameliorated the situation but did not compensate adequately for the loss of time, the inconvenience of a circuitous journey and the fatigue of traveling from remote points in far eastern Montana to any unit of the University of Montana.

When the Eastern Montana Normal School was located, there was a notable exception to the use of traditional political barter. In 1925 (see Session Laws of Montana, 1925, Chapter 160, Section 6) the legislature of Montana made permissible the appointment of a commission of educational experts in order that the various communities petitioning for the location of a new institution of higher education might be surveyed. After a thorough survey the commission submitted to the state board of education a report incorporating its findings in the several cities seeking to become the home of the new institution. This commission investigated the educational, the economic, the social, the sanitary, the recreational, and other factors which should be evaluated in determining the location and site of an institution of higher education. This procedure caused Dr. John J. Tigert, then U. S. Commissioner of Education, to write me the following:

> The step which Montana has taken to insure the establishment of a higher educational institution in a location to secure the best results interests me very much. This is the first instance of the kind that has come to my attention. I think the State is to be congratulated on the wisdom it has shown in going about the matter in this scientific way. It has set an example which other States might well follow in establishing new institutions.

The success or failure of Dr. Durston's plan to consolidate the various units of higher education and develop a single cooperating university depended upon many factors. Unless the legislature recognized clearly that its field of action was legislation and not administration, conflicts with university administration would unquestionably result. This was a highly important factor to consider, and credit must be given to subsequent legislatures of Montana for general recognition of this basic principle in government—that is, that there must be no conflict among the legislative, executive, judicial and educational divisions. Otherwise, serious impairment and possible destruction of efficiency in the division of government whose field is invaded by the representatives of any other division will result.

The Montana system of administering higher education through a centralized coordinating agency might fail also if the governing board of education did not discriminate sharply between responsibilities concerned on the one hand with financing higher educational units and on the other hand with administering expertly and effectively educational policies. Happily for the success of the Montana system the state board of education has uniformly recognized the wisdom of delegating the formulation and administration of educational policies to faculties and administrative officers. They have reviewed and accepted, with minor changes, educational policies proposed and have given their major attention to university finance. The importance of this procedure can not be overestimated. Unless a state board of education wisely delegates authority to highly trained administrative officers and highly trained students of education and research, mediocrity of performance and almost certain failure in higher education will result. Because the legislature has largely refrained from invading the field of service prescribed by the state constitution for the state board of education and because the state board of education has consistently encouraged administrative officers and faculties to discharge the responsibilities concerned with the techniques and the experimental problems of education, it has been possible to write in Montana a record of definite improvement and progress of higher education during the sixteen years that the present system of a coordinated and integrated university has operated.

The success or failure of the Montana system has been dependent not only upon a wise policy of "hands off" in the legislature and a wise delegation of authority to educational experts by the state board of education, but also upon two additional factors: first, an enthusiastic and sympathetic support of faculties; and second, a clear and cordial cooperation upon the part of the administrative heads of the individual institutions. Positive support of these last two factors has been secured in a large measure by an executive council, or chancellor's cabinet, composed of the presidents and certain directors and deans from the different units of the Greater University, and the chancellor's associate in the central office, the executive secretary of the university. The different faculties have worked with a large freedom under the guidance of the presidents and with the advice of the chancellor, in detailing proposed educational experiments and developing cordial cooperation of students, alumni and citizens of the community. They have presented their conclusions and recommendations to the executive council for consideration, amendment and final approval. This has insured wise cooperation on the part of the faculties and administrative officers and has given the higher educational system an integration and an enrichment which would be impossible without a liberal policy encouraging experimentation and the exercise of vital and constructive enterprise on the part of the faculties which must carry the heavy responsibilities of teaching and research. Meetings of the executive council are called by the chancellor to his office, located in the State Capitol, Helena, or to the executive office of one of the unit institutions of the university for the consideration of interinstitutional administration, the discussion of educational policies, the presentation of budgets and the proposals for appropriations and other legislative matters. At the council meetings the proposals of faculties and the plans of each institutional head are presented, and criticisms and suggestions are invited. After decisions are reached by the council and approved by the chancellor, the recommendations and requests are presented by the chancellor to the state board of education for acceptance or rejection. This open and democratic procedure has made for fine understanding, good-will and fraternal cooperation among all the presidents of the six units of higher education now composing the University of Montana.

Inasmuch as the Montana system was devised for the dual purpose of increasing efficiency and reducing cost of service, it is desirable to submit comparative statistics relative to the extent and cost of service in higher education in Montana at the time the Montana system was inaugurated—that is, in 1915–1916—and the last year of record, 1930–1931. In 1915–1916 there were enrolled in the four teaching units then comprising the University of Montana 2,133 students. The legislature appropriated for the operation and maintenance of the four institutions $520,182.00 of state money, a per capita cost of $243.87. In the year 1930–1931 there were enrolled in the six teaching units now comprising the University of Montana 4,909 students. The appropriation from state funds was $1,035,000.00, a per capita cost of $210.83—a saving of $33.04 per student. This amounts to a reduction in the appropriation of state money of over 13 per cent. per student in the fifteen years that the present system has been in operation. While the per capita cost of education is a very unscientific and unsatisfactory unit of measurement, it is perhaps the most suggestive measure which can be employed in the operation of the same collegiate units during different collegiate years. Allowance for the variable purchasing power of the dollar and for the respective offerings in the departments and in professional schools during each of the collegiate years considered must have proper evaluation.

In 1928, at the request of the chancellor, an educational statistical survey of twelve northwest Rocky Mountain states was made by Dr. Charles H. Clapp, president of the state university. The twelve states studied were Arizona, Colorado, Idaho, Montana, Nevada, New Mexico, North Dakota, Oregon, South Dakota, Utah, Washington and Wyoming. It should be noted that in but two of these twelve states investigated—Nevada and Wyoming—is all higher educational service centralized on one campus. In the synopsis on higher education, Dr. Clapp's survey contains the following statements:

> Montana ranks eighth in the twelve states considered in maintenance expenditures from state revenues for teaching in institutions of higher education. Montana's expenditures represent 5.5 per cent. of the total for twelve states, whereas she has 7 per cent. of the population and approximately 8½ per cent. of the resources, as shown in Part 1.
>
> Expenditures from state revenues for teaching in institutions of higher education amount to $1.23 per capita of population as compared with $1.83 in twelve states; in relation to material resources, expenditures average more than thirty per cent. less than in other states.

Three years later, a corresponding survey of the same twelve northwest and Rocky Mountain states shows that the average expenditure per student from state revenue is $261 and that Montana's expenditure per resident student from state revenue is $219. As previously stated, per capita costs are not truly comparable on account of the variation used in registering students and in institutional accounting and also because of different institutional objectives. However, in so far as this measure may be employed, it is interesting to note that the Montana system, which now includes the administration of six teaching units with differentiated schools and divisions, totaling twenty-eight, is done at a 19.9 per cent. lower cost per capita than the average of the twelve states in the northwest Rocky Mountain area. Mr. Lloyd Morey, comptroller of the University of Illinois and an outstanding certified public accountant in American education, examined the survey and reported as follows:

> I have examined the Fiscal Section of the Montana Educational Survey. The material is drawn from sources which I believe to be accurate, and in my opinion is correctly exhibited to properly present the facts concerning the subjects dealt with.
>
> In my opinion, the conclusions presented are justified by the facts as set forth.

President L. D. Coffman, of the University of Minnesota, also examined the records and made the following statement:

> *The educational statistical survey, comparing higher education in Montana with that in eleven other Northwest and Rocky Mountain states,* is a notably complete and impartial effort to determine the real facts concerning the demand for higher education and the support of state colleges and universities in Montana and the neighboring states.
>
> With these facts before them, all the people of Montana now can see their higher educational problem and, with the knowledge of the facts, can be expected to solve this problem in a way that will be a credit to the State of Montana.

The discussion of the Montana system of administration of higher education on separated campuses has been presented with no thought that it is a perfect system, that it has achieved the measure of success desired by its creators or present administrators, or that it would prove a success in every state now operating higher education in two or more separated institutions. The record of fifteen years does show, however, that it has justified itself in Montana because it has made possible unified, efficient, cooperative and steadily improved higher educational service; it has permitted educational experts to eliminate unnecessary duplications in curricula; it has made possible the training of students for intelligent and friendly participation in public service, and in the development of a state consciousness; and it has substituted budgets prepared by administrators, reviewed by the executive council, and accepted after exacting analysis by the state board of education, for the former traditional lobbying in the legislature. This system of coordinated, centralized administration has also made it possible to reduce the per capita cost of higher education more than 10 per cent. in fifteen years, and to achieve a high rank among the twelve northwest Rocky Mountain states with which Montana is associated. The system is being steadily improved and strengthened and has the enthusiastic approval of all informed and intelligent leaders in the state.

SOME CURRENT ISSUES IN NURSERY EDUCATION[1]

By Dr. GEORGE D. STODDARD
UNIVERSITY OF IOWA

I

IN nursery or preschool education, as elsewhere, not all issues are of the same size. Only a few years ago the major issue was, should nursery schools be established in this country under any conditions? A great issue of this type is said to be resolved when a categorical yes or no is accepted as true. If the answer is in the positive the attack shifts to a study of conditions, of kinds and qualities.

It is a real tribute to pioneer workers in the field of nursery and kindergarten education that this paramount issue of earlier days was not sidestepped. And it must be a source of immense satisfaction to them that hypothesis, theory, observation and experiment all seem to point in the same direction—to a strong need for organized, professional public- and private-school education for children, three or four years below the conventional primary age.

Of course we shall still be concerned about the terrible wrench given mother love by the separation of parent and child each day for three or more consecutive hours. But calmer reflection will sometimes find economic drives or selfishness at the base of extreme opposition. Where such motives are not too strong, a few weeks' trial in a good nursery school usually convinces the most conscientious of mothers that love of little children has nothing to do with the case. You can love them and leave them in the nursery school (they don't seem to mind), or love them and abandon them just as effectively by retreating to the kitchen, the card room, the novel or the theater. Separation of some kind is bound to take place, else we have a situation pathological to one and harmful to both.

But the vast majority of parents are not pathological cases, nor are they so enamored of a perpetual child-parent contact as to refuse, under any circumstances, to relinquish their offspring to the expert ministrations of other people. What they learn to do and hope to do when the child is six, they can learn to do and hope to do when the child is two. Why is it, then, that the nursery school movement meets passive resistance, is sluggish, a force of small con-

[1] A paper read before the biennial conference of the National Association for Nursery Education, Philadelphia, November 12, 1931.

sequence in our national educational scheme? An answer to this question leads to a whole series of issues on which I shall venture a few opinions.

II

In the first place, parents distrust the nursery school. This is to be expected. It took the medical profession hundreds of years to reach an order of competence and of control over its membership such that people could place high faith in its practices. The public school was bitterly assailed at first, both as to the legality of its support and the efficacy of its methods. Those issues are not completely closed, even to-day. Medicine must keep up its fight against quackery, while preventive medicine battles a tremendous lethargy, not only of individuals, but of city and state governments. Meanwhile public schools, especially in rural areas, are often so impoverished that the higher aims of education appear pathetically irrelevant.

Nursery schools, too, can fall so far below minimum standards as to damage the whole movement, and with probably greater harm to the children involved. Hence when parents reject the whole idea of nursery education, we should try to locate specific grievances: they may be protesting against an educational malpractice which we, ourselves, would be the first to condemn.

Educators will not win the confidence of parents by asserting the right of eminent domain over their preschool children. Compulsory school laws are accepted chiefly because they are generally in accord with the wishes of parents. A family has every instinctive and social sanction for retaining the complete educational independence of its preschool children until the scales are definitely balanced in favor of a proposed nursery school régime. And the showdown is not easy! Old-time school teachers bested parents in open competition when it was a matter of teaching reading, writing, arithmetic, spelling and history. The decision is not likely to be so one-sided in such matters as nutrition, mental and social development, music, art and language stimulation.

III

Second, the nursery school is costly. The groups are small; the equipment needed is extensive; the staff requires special training; a playground is essential. Moreover, the required professional attention for each child is relatively great. In all-day sessions the preparing and serving of meals is not simple.

There are two ways of meeting these difficulties: first, by reducing costs, and second, by justifying a larger per capita expenditure for children so young.

What can be done about costs? A recent survey of sixty nursery schools shows that the median number of children per teacher is seven. Nursery procedures to-day are almost as intimate as the affairs of a large family! Reduction of the child-teacher ratio through better techniques would result in an enormous saving.

The other hurdles do not appear real. Interviews with hundreds of parents reveal that the amount spent annually for toys, games, candy and movies is far in excess of nursery school demands along these lines. Poor families are surprisingly lavish in this respect. Similarly, in most towns, outdoor space is adequate, although transportation, equipment and supervision rarely are. In the largest cities, space on roofs and in parks could be allocated to approved nursery schools.

Of course these restrictions need not retard the growth of private nursery schools conducted for families of greater means, and many of these are doing notable work. But these schools will be a prototype for public education only to the extent that less expensive correlates are discovered for their activities and surroundings. Similarly, the elaborate research preschools of universities belong to the era of custom-built models.

Nutritional, medical, dental and psychological services pay for themselves in the long run. Any state, town, community chest, service organization or alliance of private citizens could well afford to subsidize preventive work of this kind when it is properly organized and administered. Nevertheless, nursery education will be thrown into economic competition with cars, good roads, radios and what-not. It must deliver some economic goods and services if people are to pay for it. This leads us to the third troublesome question.

IV

Nursery education does not meet an apparent need. Fundamentally, needs are general, not specific. Usually they can be met in a variety of ways. Nobody asked for the telephone, the motion picture or the vacuum cleaner. But man has long had a strong desire to communicate, to escape reality, to reduce drudgery. Similarly, in whole cities, nobody seems to want nursery schools as such, or at least the want is so feeble as to be submerged by others. To what underlying human need, then, can we attach this new venture? I believe to a need centering about the mother and to a closely allied one which centers about the child.

There is to-day a strong desire on the part of the mother for personal freedom: freedom to work for pay or to develop more intensively various cultural and recreational activities. This desire is coupled with a recognition of the shortcomings of mother love as a complete guide to child development or to parent-child relationships and of the home as the sole milieu for preschool children. Nor does the dearly bought freedom which comes from childlessness or from passing children indiscriminately to servant girls, other children or relatives prove to be a satisfactory solution for most people. Beneath all this lies the vague, but powerful, human desire to have children and to do well by them. It can be shown that the nursery school assists definitely in securing additional freedom for women and in providing certain influences essential to the all-round development of children. At its best, it can be made to enrich the lives of both children and parents.

V

A fourth difficulty is really a corollary of public inertia; namely, an almost complete lack of educational sponsorship. Few schools will touch nursery education at the present time. Executives are busy trying to balance their budgets. School appropriations are often included in the general hatred of taxes. The need for extending the schools downward need not be apparent, but the cost is. We must not expect too much of school superintendents. First, they must survive; then, if progressive, they will wedge in some constructive planning which takes the community only slightly beyond its depth. If we believe in nursery schools we shall need to educate whole communities.

VI

These four great deterrents—distrust, high cost, inertia and administrative neglect—have certainly not been unmitigated evils. They have saved us from the reformers' zeal by permitting a period of research and small-scale experience of the highest value. It is not too much to say that leaders in this field are carrying forward the most intensive program ever undertaken in advance of a specific educational practice. The Froebelian kindergarten had no such period, nor did the high school or the junior high school. Junior colleges were born over night and some are in danger of dying the same way. The contagious enthusiasm of a single professor has plunged more than one university into an ill-starred program of educational reform.

It should be a source of pride to nursery school people that they have heavily weighted the early days of their work with scientific inquiry and genuine self-criticism. I should be distressed if anything in this paper were construed to suggest a reduction in such activity. Without constant inquiring and philosophizing any educational endeavor is likely to degenerate. On the other hand, we need not wait for completion or perfection before taking action. There comes a time when a new régime is established as better than the old, although far from its ultimate goals. In my opinion, that time has come now, with respect to nursery schools of the highest class.

A word should be said about current conditions. A time of depression, when new educational buildings or increased staff are not likely to be approved, is perhaps the best time of all for a careful consideration of the next step in a planned educational program. If we are serious about this matter of universal nursery education we must be prepared to recommend an expenditure of possibly a half billion dollars per year on the systematic education of five million preschool children. Such an item involves a major economic readjustment. If only we could be sure that the government really wanted to extend its public works, we might propose such a plan as a contribution to the national economy. It would lead to new construction, new employment, new careers. It could be made permanent and beneficial. We could give the plan a substantial dowry of research and experience, with more to come.

VII

Clearly enough, this conference on nursery education, to the extent that it epitomizes thought and action in the field, is engaged in pattern-making on a scale potentially huge. If the whole structure is to crumble and decay, let us make sure that we shall have willed it so: that full experience will have adjudged nurseries and nursery schools as unnecessary or harmful. But if ever-increasing knowledge and experience point to unique values inherent in good nursery education practice, let us determine what that practice is, and then so arrange matters that every child will have an opportunity to be nourished by it. The primary issue is, in a word, the critical evaluation of what nursery education holds in store for the child and his parents.

EDUCATIONAL EVENTS

HOURS OF WORK OF YOUNG PEOPLE IN GREAT BRITAIN

THE fourth report of the National Advisory Council for Juvenile Employment (England and Wales) recommends, according to the *London Times Educational Supplement,* that further steps should be taken to regulate the hours of employment of boys and girls in unregulated occupations; that a maximum working week for boys and girls in unregulated occupations should be fixed by Parliament, and that, within the limits set by statute, powers should be given to local authorities to make by-laws prescribing shorter hours and additional conditions.

On the first recommendation the council think that in most occupations the hours worked by the majority of boys and girls can not be regarded as open to serious criticism, but they consider that the number of working hours which should be regarded as excessive is sufficient to require some regulative action.

An appreciable proportion of the 127,000 juveniles dealt with in the returns were covered by the Shops Act and therefore subject to some regulation of hours, but the committee adds, "The maximum limit of hours for juveniles under those acts is as high as 74 per week."

The council states that probably there has been some improvement as compared with the conditions before the war. The report says: "The progress made has, in our opinion, been slow. It may be that with the diminishing supply of juvenile labor during the next few years, due to the low war-time birth rate, and the falling birth rate in more recent years, boys and girls may be able to secure better conditions by the ordinary laws of supply and demand, but it must be remembered that the occupations in which those boys and girls are employed are not only unregulated, but also largely unorganized and outside the scope of collective action. The force of public opinion is in consequence slow to make itself felt, because the facts are difficult to discover and escape public attention. Boys and girls under the age of eighteen are still in the formative stage of their lives. They should have leisure to devote both to continued education and to healthy recreation."

The majority of the boys and girls, it is pointed out, were employed in subsidiary occupations, and it could not be claimed that some limitation of their hours of employment would have any appreciable effect on the cost of production or the competitive power of British industry.

Some members of the council add a note that they think that the recommendation does not go far enough, as it does not specify that the maximum number of hours should be forty-eight a week. The case for this particular maximum number of hours appears to them to be irresistible.

A minority report by five members states that legislation for governing the hours of work of juveniles in unregulated occupations would impose further regulations on trade, the keeping of additional records, and expenditure of public funds. The grave national situation demands that the whole energies of the nation should be concentrated on matters of urgent importance and "does not permit of public effort, time and money being devoted to matters of this order."

REPORT ON THE EXPERIMENTAL COLLEGE OF THE UNIVERSITY OF WISCONSIN

Two recommendations of the advisers of the Wisconsin Experimental College asking that further educational experimentation be made at the university are as follows:

(1) There should be set up to study the problems of freshman and sophomore instruction four experimental units. One of these would be, as at present, for men, and should be lodged, in the same way, in one of the men's dormitories, as in the experimental college. A second should be for women, and should be lodged in a women's dormitory. A third should be for men, but without dormitory arrangement. A fourth, also without dormitory arrangement, should enroll both men and women.

(2) There should be set up a corresponding unit to study the problems of instruction in the junior and senior years, since the issues here involved are radically different from those of the earlier years but they are in the same way vital and significant, and there is need of at least testing the merits of plans which would radically modify our present procedures rather than attempt to improve them at this point or that.

The committee recommends that, if possible, the experimentation which the advisers have been allowed to begin should be continued. It points out that "what has been done thus far is very incomplete and fragmentary. It is only a first step—the formulating of one possible way of teaching. But with the taking of that step there has been developing a point of view, a framing of questions and suggestions, which leads on indefinitely along the road of experimental inquiry. It would seem to us very desirable that the university should go on further along the road."

Four suggestions and observations furnish the basis for the new plan of organization for the College of Letters and Science. They are as follows:

1. Student social life and student education might profit greatly if the 3,600 freshmen and sophomores in the college of letters and science were divided into 15 or 20 smaller colleges, each with its own social organization and social interests.

2. There would be very great gain if the teach-

ers of the lower college could act, not only as one body, but also as 15 or 20 smaller faculties, each considering the educational problems as a whole, each working out its own aims and methods in relative independence.

3. The experience of the experimental college suggests a way in which college teachers might, much more satisfactorily than at present, be trained for the art of teaching.

4. It seems clear that the cost of teaching in smaller units, and along lines analogous to those followed by the experimental college, would not be, other things being equal, greater than that of the present system.

The experimental college had its birth in the report of the university committee in 1925, in which it was claimed that there was need for a revision of teaching methods and social arrangements within the state university, especially in the freshman and sophomore years. The college was founded two years later in 1927. Dr. Alexander Meiklejohn, formerly president of Amherst College, had been brought to Wisconsin as a professor of philosophy, and he was chosen to administer the new college. In February, 1931, the faculty acted to bring the experiment to a close in June, 1932, and to call for the report of its results.

THE BUILDING PROGRAM OF THE UNIVERSITY OF CINCINNATI

The University of Cincinnati is engaged in a building program covering several years, in the course of which approximately five million dollars, provided by municipal bond issues and private sources, will be spent for improvements and additions to the university plant. The most recent building to be completed is that of the Teachers College, funds for which were secured by a bond issue voted in 1927.

In keeping with a campus plan worked out under the direction of President Herman Schneider, the Teachers College building is constructed in Georgian style, and has been built between the administration building and the University Library. It comprises five stories, and houses all the units of work for which the college is responsible.

Four major divisions comprise a memorial given by the friends of Miss Annie Laws (1855–1927), of Cincinnati to perpetuate her memory. The first of these is an assembly room in eighteenth century style, seating 450 persons. Two units of the memorial are planned primarily for the training of teachers of little children. The physical activities room houses training in plays, rhythms, dramatic games and festivals. Adjoining this is the manual activities room, a workshop center for training in industrial, applied and fine arts work. Completing the memorial is a reception room furnished in the style of the late colonial period. This room and an adjoining dining room provide for social events under the auspices of the college and its student organizations.

The administrative offices provide quarters for the dean and five directors, of graduate, undergraduate, extension, student teaching and placement divisions, respectively. Separate suites of ten offices each for men and women faculty members are supplemented by faculty rest rooms. Laboratory facilities are provided for educational psychology, including the comparative psychology of learning; for clinical work in psychology and school subjects, and for public school art, public school music and school administration, in addition to the facilities for the training of teachers of young children. Other features include a faculty room, a study room for students and two seminar rooms, in addition to nineteen classrooms of various sizes, and provisions for lockers for one thousand students.

For the present semester the Teachers College has a registration on the campus of 1,088 students, including 388 graduate students and 376 teachers in service. Away from the campus there is an extension registration for the semester of 1,036. Dr. L. A. Pechstein is now serving his tenth year as dean of the college.

THE SUMMER SCHOOL OF YALE UNIVERSITY

Yale University will hold the second summer seminar in education under the direction of the Department of Education of the Graduate School from July 5 to August 6. The subject of the seminar will be "What can Philosophy, Psychology and Administration Contribute to the Advancement of Education?"

The faculty will consist of Professor Henry W. Holmes, dean of the Graduate School of Education of Harvard University; Professor V.

A. C. Henmon, for ten years director of the School of Education, now chairman of the department of psychology at the University of Wisconsin, and Dr. Frank W. Ballou, superintendent of schools, Washington, D. C. They will serve daily throughout the five weeks' session of the seminar. Their work will be supplemented by that of several other educators of distinction who will lecture and conduct conferences.

The student body will be limited to one hundred. It will include teachers in normal schools, teachers colleges, departments of education, public and private schools—secondary and elementary; head masters, principals, supervisors, directors, superintendents, and graduate students preparing for educational work. The student body represents all parts of the country, many types of educational experience and many educational institutions.

The purpose of the seminar is to offer an opportunity for a small group of educational leaders and potential leaders of ability to meet and, under the guidance of a small faculty of nationally recognized distinction, to study and discuss together problems of significance for the advancement of education. The resources of the Sterling Memorial Library will be available, including seminar and lecture rooms; the Penniman Memorial Library of Education; the Penniman Reading Room, and new and important books and magazines, not only in education but in related subjects.

The student body will be divided into three approximately equal groups. Each group will meet in turn one of the three regular instructors for a two-hour lecture and discussion each morning in the week, except Sunday. Following this two-hour session, on alternate mornings each week, there will be a second two-hour session for the whole student body and faculty meeting together. These sessions will be presided over once a week by a member of the permanent faculty, and twice by outside lecturers chosen on the basis of their ability to make some special contribution to the program. Afternoons and evenings will be at the disposal of students for reading, personal conference with members of the faculty and informal discussions. The formation of small discussion groups will be promoted and arranged to suit the desires of students.

In the organization and conduct of the seminar, credits are an incident, not a controlling factor. Many will be in attendance who have no desire for credits. Those working for an advanced degree, however, may receive credit acceptable at Yale University and presumably at other universities.

AWARDS FROM THE GENERAL EDUCATION BOARD'S APPROPRIATION FOR STUDIES IN THE HUMANITIES AT HARVARD UNIVERSITY

The Committee in charge of the awards of the General Education Board for the pursuit of "Studies in the Humanities" at Harvard has recommended the following assignments for 1931–32:

Marston Stevens Balch, instructor in English: English plays and playwrights in France in the Eighteenth Century.

Robert Pierpont Blake, professor of history, and Kirsopp Lake, Winn professor of ecclesiastical history: Photography of dated Greek Manuscripts.

Huntington Brown, instructor in English: Gargantua and King Arthur.

Arthur Burkhard, assistant professor of German: Life and Work of Hans Burgkmair, and of Conrad Ferdinand Meyer.

Jeremiah Denis Matthias Ford, Smith Professor of the French and Spanish Languages: Harvard Council on Hispano-American Studies.

Jeremiah Denis Matthias Ford: Letters of the Royal Family of John III of Portugal.

Charles Hall Grandgent, professor of Romance languages, and John Albrecht Walz, professor of the German language and literature (for the Division of Modern Languages): Studies and Notes in Philology and Literature, Vol. XIV.

Arthur Kent Griffin, lecturer on Greek and Latin: To complete the publication of "Aristotle's Psychology of Society."

Mason Hammond, instructor in history and in Greek and Latin: The Augustan Principate.

Richmond Laurin Hawkins, associate professor of French: Little Known French Letters of the Seventeenth, Eighteenth and Nineteenth Centuries.

Carl Newell Jackson, professor of Greek and Latin: Harvard Studies in Classical Philology, 1932.

George Lyman Kittredge, Gurney professor of English literature: Elizabethan Literature.

David Mason Little, Jr.: Letters of David Garrick.

Kenneth Ballard Murdock, associate professor of English: Literary and Intellectual History of the American Colonies, 1700–1765.

John Tucker Murray, professor of English: Harvard Studies in English.

Chandler Rathfon Post, professor of Greek and of fine arts: History of Spanish Painting, Vol. IV.

Benjamin Rand, librarian in charge of the Philosophical Library: Berkeley's American Sojourn.

Edward Kennard Rand, Pope professor of Latin: Photographs, etc., for four projects.

Maxwell Isaac Raphael, instructor in Romance languages: For aid in preparing his Historical Grammar and Chrestomathy of the Rumanian language.

Fred Norris Robinson, professor of English: Hanley's Atlas of American Speech.

Hyder Edward Rollins, professor of English: for work in preparing for publication: "Poetical Rhapsody," "Pepys Ballads," Vol. VIII and two other works now in progress, and publication of Vol. II of "Poetical Rhapsody."

Herbert Weir Smyth, Eliot professor of Greek literature, *emeritus:* Text of Aeschylus.

Arthur Fisher Whittem, associate professor of Romance languages: Fable Literature in French and Spanish.

George Kingsley Zipf, instructor in German: Relativity of Language.

DEGREES CONFERRED AT THE BICENTENNIAL CONVOCATION OF THE GEORGE WASHINGTON UNIVERSITY

TWENTY-THREE alumni of the George Washington University received honorary degrees at the bicentennial convocation of the university on the evening of February 22. The degrees were conferred by Dr. Cloyd Heck Marvin, president of the university and chairman of the District of Columbia Bicentennial Commission, who gave the convocation address on "Washington's Political Leadership in the Modern World." Among the degrees were:

Doctor of Laws

Albert Norman Ward, A.M. 1900 (George Washington); A.B. 1898 (Western Maryland); D.D. 1920 (Adrian); D.S. 1920 (Otterbein); LL.D. 1921 (Kansas City). President of Western Maryland College.

Will Carson Ryan, Jr., Ph.D. 1918 (George Washington); A.B. 1907 (Harvard). Director, Educational Division, Bureau of Indian Affairs; formerly professor of education, Swarthmore College and educational editor, the New York *Evening Post.* Dr. Ryan has conducted educational surveys for Province of Saskatchewan, Porto Rico, etc.

Walter Collins Clephane, LL.B. 1889, LL.M. 1890 (George Washington). Professor of law, the George Washington University; author of standard law texts. Dr. Clephane served on important arbitration tribunals.

Doctor of Science

Ray Smith Bassler, M.S. 1903, Ph.D. 1905 (George Washington); A.B. 1902 (Cincinnati). Head curator of geology of the U. S. National Museum and professor of geology in the George Washington University; president of the Paleontological Society of America and vice-president of the Geological Society of America.

Charles Napoleon Moore, M.S. 1905 (George Washington); A.B. 1903 (Cincinnati); Ph.D. 1908 (Harvard). Professor of mathematics, University of Cincinnati.

Joseph Fels Ritt, A.B. 1913 (George Washington); Ph.D. 1917 (Columbia). Professor of mathematics, Columbia University; author of original contributions in the field of mathematics.

Sterling Ruffin, M.D. 1890 (George Washington). Professor emeritus of medicine and consulting physician of the hospital.

Daniel Kerfoot Shute, A.B. 1879, M.D. 1883 (George Washington). Professor emeritus of clinical ophthalmology, formerly professor of anatomy, the George Washington University; author of articles and texts on anatomy and ophthalmology.

Doctor of Engineering

David Albert Molitor, B.S. in C.E. 1908 (George Washington). Structural engineer; designing engineer on Panama Canal; works connected with Saulte Ste. Marie Falls Canal and the Channels through the Great Lakes, and other engineering projects; professor of civil engineering in Cornell University from 1908 to 1911.

Doctor of Education

Stephen Elliott Kramer, B.S. 1906, A.M. 1909 (George Washington). Assistant superintendent of schools of the District of Columbia; alumni trustee of the university.

Jessie Fant Evans (Mrs. Joshua Evans, Jr.), A.B. and T.D. 1913 (George Washington). Member of the board of trustees of the university; prominent in the civic life of Washington.

ADDRESS OF PRESIDENT HOOVER AT MOUNT VERNON

PRESIDENT HOOVER addressed members of the Department of Superintendence of the National Education Association at Mount Vernon on February 22 as part of the George Washington bicentennial celebration. After placing a wreath on Washington's tomb, Mr. Hoover spoke from the front veranda of Washington's home. His address follows:

It is a signal event that the representatives of teachers of our whole country should meet at Mount Vernon this day. Because our teachers more than any other group have both the privilege and the duty to guide the steps in each new generation on the road of democracy, to instruct them with understanding and reverence for the spiritual benefits which flow from the history of this great man, and to instil our children with the accomplishments of the men who have made and guided our nation.

We meet here to-day in one of the places which physically, in itself, is enchanting and beautiful in its grounds, buildings and associations. But it is not those which attract hither the steps or thoughts of millions of Americans. It is the memory and the spirit of the greatest man of our race which pervades these grounds; it is a national shrine, the very name of which swells our hearts with pride and gratitude. It has been preserved and cared for all these many years by the women of America in whose trusteeship the nation can find no greater assurance of its meaning, its sanctity and reverence.

You have come from every part of the country, from homes, towns, cities and states unknown to Washington's life, yet each and every one of which received untold blessings from his life and his public service. To you, more than any one else, we entrust the translation of Washington to our children, and that is a trusteeship which the nation can find no greater assurance of its meaning, of its sanctity and reverence.

EDUCATIONAL NOTES AND NEWS

THE inauguration of Dr. Aymer Jay Hamilton, formerly associate professor of education at Claremont Colleges, California, as president of the State Teachers College at Chico, California, took place on January 22. Among the speakers on the occasion were Dr. Vierling Kersey, state superintendent of public instruction; Dr. Edward L. Hardy, president of the California State Teachers College at San Diego, and Dr. Allison Ware, formerly president of the college.

DR. SEBASTIAN CHARLÉTY, rector of the University of Paris, who is visiting the United States as the guest of the Carnegie Endowment for International Peace, gave an address at the unveiling of a bust of Lafayette at the Hall of Fame of New York University which took place on Washington's birthday. M. André-Louis Chevrillon, the French historian, member of the Institute of France, also spoke on this occasion. At a private ceremony the university conferred the degree of doctor of literature on M. Charléty.

AMONG the honorary degrees conferred at the Founder's Day exercises of Rollins College were the doctorate of humanities on Miss Jane Addams, and the doctorate of laws on Dr. Irving Fisher, professor of political economy at Yale University.

THE honorary degree of doctor of laws was conferred at the celebration of Founder's Day at Temple University on February 15 on Dr. James N. Rule, state superintendent of public instruction of Pennsylvania.

AT the exercises commemorating the fifty-sixth anniversary of the Johns Hopkins University on February 22, portraits of four past and present faculty members were presented to the university. Dr. Joseph S. Ames, president of the university, presided, and Sir Wilmott Lewis, Washington correspondent of the London *Times,* was the principal speaker. Mr. George F. Baker, Jr., New York, presented a portrait of Dr. William H. Wilmer, since 1925 professor of ophthalmology in the school of medicine and head of the Wilmer Ophthalmological Institute of the Johns Hopkins Hospital. The painting is the work of Mr. Frank O. Salisbury, London. Dr. William H. Welch, professor emeritus of the history of medicine, presented a portrait of the late Dr. William S. Halsted, first professor of surgery in the school of medicine. Dr. William S. Thayer, professor emeritus of medicine, presented a portrait of Dr. Frederick H. Baetjer, professor of clinical roentgenology. Both of these portraits are the work of Eric Haupt. Dr. William Seifriz, professor of botany in the University of Pennsylvania, presented a portrait of Dr. Duncan Starr Johnson, professor of botany and director of the Botanical Laboratory and the Botanical Garden.

MEMBERS of the faculties of Northwestern University gave a dinner in honor of their colleagues who have taught in the university twenty-five years or more at the North Shore Hotel in Evanston on February 19. Fifty-three men now on the faculty have taught for more than twenty-five years. The oldest in point of service at Evanston is Dr. James Taft Hatfield, professor of German language and literature, who has served for forty-one years. Dr. Frank T. Andrews, professor emeritus of gynecology, is the oldest in point of service at the medical school. He has been on the faculty forty-six years. Dr. Thomas F. Holgate, dean emeritus of the college of liberal arts, Dr. John H. Wigmore, dean emeritus of the law school, and Professor Henry Crew, professor of physics, are among those who have been on the faculty for more than thirty-five years.

AN anonymous donor has given funds for a special international fellowship in honor of Dr. Alice Hamilton, professor of industrial medicine at the Harvard University Medical School, for the year 1932–33. This fellowship will be awarded to a member of the foreign federation of the International Federation of University Women by the Committee of Awards of International Fellowships of the Federation, with Dr. Hamilton serving in an advisory capacity.

CANON ANSON PHELPS STOKES, of Washington Cathedral, for more than twenty years secretary of Yale University, will be the Carnegie visiting lecturer for 1932 to the universities of South Africa. He will leave in May to be gone until the summer of 1933, and intends visiting mission centers in Egypt, Uganda, Kenya, Tanganyika and the Belgian Congo. He will later spend six months working on a history of universities in Europe.

PROFESSOR GIUSEPPE A. BORGHESE, of the University of Milan, Italian literary critic, author and journalist, was guest of honor at a luncheon given in Boston on February 8 by the Italian Historical Society. For the first semester of this year Professor Borghese was exchange professor in the chair of Italian culture at the University of California. He recently lectured at Harvard University on the "Spirit of Poetry" and planned to speak at Wellesley and to lecture at Columbia and Yale Universities. He has been for many years a member of the staff of the *Corriera della Serra* of Milan.

PROFESSOR S. G. MORLEY, of the department of Spanish and Portuguese of the University of California, was elected president of the American Association of Teachers of Spanish at the recent meeting held in Madison, Wisconsin. This association consists of college and high-school teachers of Spanish throughout the United States. The next annual convention of the organization will be held in San Francisco, probably in December.

DR. HARRY P. SMITH, of Syracuse University, was elected president of the New York Educational Research Association at its annual meeting in Syracuse. Other officers are: Dr. Julian Butterworth, Cornell University, *vice-president;* Arthur L. Maxon, Schenectady, *secretary-treasurer;* Dr. Ethel L. Cornell, State Education Department, *director.*

MR. LLOYD K. GARRISON, of New York City, has been selected to succeed the late Harry S. Richards as dean of the University of Wisconsin Law School. The formal appointment will be made at the March meeting of the Board of Regents.

DR. CHARLES UPSON CLARK, since 1929 special historical research investigator in Spain for the Smithsonian Institution, has been appointed director of the summer session of the College of the City of New York.

DR. J. W. JONES has succeeded the late Professor Frank Smith Bogardus as dean of the faculty of the Indiana State Teachers College at Terre Haute. Dr. Jones came to the college in the fall of 1927 as director of the division of research. He was formerly secretary to the dean of the School of Education of Indiana University. Dr. Waldo F. Mitchell has succeeded Professor Bogardus as head of the department of social studies.

The contract of A. L. Threlkeld, superintendent of the Denver Public Schools, has been renewed for a period of five years by the unanimous vote of the Board of Education. The new contract begins September 1, 1932. It provides for the present salary of $10,000 per annum. Mr. Threlkeld came to the Denver schools in 1921 as assistant superintendent; he became superintendent in 1927.

Dr. Silas O. Rorem has been named associate superintendent of schools in Port Chester, N. Y., where Mr. Alvah G. Frost is superintendent. Dr. Rorem is a graduate of the University of Chicago and received the degree of doctor of philosophy at New York University last year. He has been engaged in educational work since 1912 and has recently been on the faculty of the Institute of Education at New York University.

Miss Henrietta Flaum, for the last several years head of the reference library of the New York City Board of Education's bureau of reference, research and statistics, has been appointed secretary to the Board of Superintendents.

On account of the general financial situation the Baltimore School Board and Public Improvement Commission have been compelled to dispense with the assistance of Professors George Drayton Strayer and N. L. Engelhardt, of Teachers College, Columbia University, as advisers in the expenditure of about two million dollars during the year on school construction.

Dr. Milton E. Loomis, assistant dean of the School of Education and director of the Summer School at New York University, has sailed for the Virgin Islands, where he will make an educational survey at the invitation of Governor Paul M. Pearson. Governor Pearson, formerly professor at Swarthmore College, is said to be considering the establishment of a six-weeks summer school course under the auspices of New York University.

Dr. Henry S. Drinker, formerly president of Lehigh University, is spending the winter in Florida.

Professor V. C. Miller, of the English Department of the Indiana State Teachers College, Terre Haute, Indiana, who has been on leave studying in Germany the last two years, has extended his leave until August.

The National Land Use Planning Committee appointed by the Secretary of Agriculture will consist of fifteen members, five to represent the Association of Land Grant Colleges; five the U. S. Department of Agriculture; three the Department of the Interior, and one each from the Federal Farm Board and the Federal Farm Loan Board. The committee held its first meeting at Washington on February 15. Members of the committee representing the Association of Land Grant Colleges are: Provost A. R. Mann, of Cornell University; President H. A. Morgan, of the University of Tennessee; President H. L. Shantz, of the University of Arizona; Dean C. B. Hutchison, of the University of California, and President F. D. Farrell, of Kansas State College.

The newly revised constitution of the Kansas State Teachers Association limits the membership of the Board of Directors for the year 1932 to the eight members elected by congressional districts. These eight members are as follows: Superintendent A. J. Stout, Topeka; Superintendent M. E. Pearson, Kansas City; Professor D. M. Bowen, Pittsburg; Superintendent E. R. Sonnenberg, Council Grove; Superintendent W. S. Heusner, Salina; Superintendent Fred W. Meyer, Jewell City; Superintendent M. F. Stark, Greensburg, and Superintendent G. H. Marshall, Augusta; Superintendent Ira J. Bright, Leavenworth, president of the Kansas State Teachers Association; Superintendent Caleb W. Smick, past president, and State Superintendent Geo. A. Allen, Jr. They constitute an advisory committee, and will sit with the Board of Directors during the year 1932.

Dean Roscoe Pound, of Harvard Law School, who served on the Wickersham Commission, on February 18 opened a series of twelve lectures on the ideal element of the law, at the New School for Social Research, New York City.

Dr. Ben D. Wood, of the Bureau of Collegiate Educational Research at Columbia University, was the guest of Bethany College on February 3. He addressed the students, members of the faculty and the public school men of that area.

The Reverend Dr. Horatio Oliver Ladd died on February 16 at the age of ninety-three years. Dr. Ladd was the founder of the University of New Mexico, which he served as president until his retirement in 1889. He was later for fourteen years rector of Grace Church, Jamaica, Long Island, N. Y.

Mr. Gordon L. Berry, who acted as assistant director of the Institute of International Education from November 1929 until last November, when he left to become secretary general of the League of Red Cross Societies in Paris, died in Paris on January 6.

The National Council of Teachers of English will hold its annual meeting in Memphis, Tennessee, from November 24 to 26. This is the first time the council has met in the far South since the meeting in Chattanooga in 1922. The council has a membership of more than six thousand high-school and college teachers, representing every section of the United States. The officers of the National Council are: *President,* Dr. Stella S. Center, of Georgia and New York; *First Vice-president,* Dr. C. J. Campbell, University of Michigan; *Second Vice-president,* Dr. Francis R. Dearborn, the Johns Hopkins University; *Secretary-Treasurer,* W. Wilbur Hatfield, Chicago Normal College; *Auditor,* Dr. Ward H. Green, Tulsa, Oklahoma.

The New York City Board of Education has decided to revive the position of "executive manager" with an annual salary of $7,500 a year. The executive manager will act as confidential investigator for the president of the board, Mr. George J. Ryan. The position of executive manager, created by law in 1917, has been vacant except for a few months fifteen years ago. It is exempted from civil service requirements.

Dr. Elizabeth Cassidy has made a further gift of $300 to Knox College for the Lysander Cassidy room of the Henry M. Seymour Library. This money is to be spent for the purpose of keeping the Cassidy collection abreast of modern thought on matters relating to international affairs.

Canadian colleges and universities have been offered $125,000 by the Carnegie Foundation of New York for the purchase of books of special interest to undergraduates. The sum will be divided in a fixed ratio which depends upon size, equipment, attendance and other qualifications.

Mr. Frank Ball, of Muncie, Indiana, has made a conditional gift of $100,000 to the Ball State Teachers College, Muncie, for a fine arts building.

The Children's Museum of Hartford, Connecticut, has received a bequest of $2,000 by the will of Miss Emma G. Allen. This bequest is the nucleus of an endowment fund for the museum.

Antioch College has announced a scholarship of $500, to be used at any college in the United States and to be awarded to the winner of an essay contest on "What Is College For?" open to high-school seniors throughout the country. The successful contestant may choose the school at which he wishes to use the money. Blanks can be obtained until March 15, from the Scholarship Secretary, Antioch College, Yellow Springs, Ohio.

The International Institute of Teachers College will proceed at the end of March to the appointment of an American graduate student with some teaching experience to the Scottish Exchange Scholarship. Information and application blanks may be obtained from Mrs. Nancy Reger, Secretary, International Institute of Teachers College, Columbia University, New York City.

Fire on February 19 destroyed Wesley Hall, which housed the student dormitories and faculty apartments of the Vanderbilt University School of Religion. Four upper stories and a basement were damaged by flames. The library, containing 15,000 volumes, many of them rare, was destroyed. Chancellor J. H. Kirkland is reported to have said that the university carried $145,000 insurance on the building and $15,000 on the library equipment, and that it will cost about $350,000 to replace the building and equipment.

THE W. K. Kellogg Foundation has provided for the establishment of a permanent fresh air camp for physically handicapped children, involving an expenditure of about $100,000. The plans of the W. K. Kellogg Foundation Pine Lake Camp, as it will be known, call for the erection of an administration building, staff quarters, small emergency hospital building and twenty-four unit cottages, and will provide accommodations for 200 handicapped children for an eight or nine weeks' camping period every summer; July 1 is the date designated for its opening. The site chosen on Pine Lake is desirable, it is reported, because of the ideal shoreline, particularly suitable for sunlight and air bath treatments for handicapped children. The staff of the camp will include physical therapists, chief and regular counselors, secretary, quartermaster and dietitian. Dr. Matthew R. Kinde, medical director of the Barry County health unit, will act as medical director of the camp.

THE Washington State Normal School at Ellensburg, Washington, is cooperating with the Open Road, Inc., of New York, in sponsoring a Progressive Education Tour for the summer of 1932. The group will leave New York on June 25 and will spend nine weeks in visiting schools of note and the sixth World Conference of the New Education Fellowship at Nice. The itinerary includes London, Paris, Cologne, Lachersee, Mainz, Munich, Heidelberg, Vienna, Venice, Nice and Geneva. The group will be under the supervision of Miss Amanda Hebeler, director of training.

A NEW series of educational programs was inaugurated over an extensive National Broadcasting Company network on Sunday, January 17, under the direction of Miss Florence Hale, president of the National Education Association, under the title of "Our American Schools." Nationally known authorities on education will discuss problems confronting schools and universities during the weekly broadcasts, at 6:30 P. M. eastern standard time. The series is designed to cover the entire field of education from the first grade to the final year of college. Speakers will endeavor to explain to parents the problems confronting educators and ways in which parents may cooperate in furthering the training of their children.

OBITUARY

MICHAEL VINCENT O'SHEA[1]

MICHAEL VINCENT O'SHEA was born at Leroy, New York, September 17, 1866. He obtained his education at Cornell University, receiving the B.L. degree in 1892. In 1894 he married Harriet Frisbie Eastabrooks. Following his graduation from Cornell, he was professor of psychology and education from 1892 to 1895 at the State Normal School, Mankato, Minnesota. Then followed two years as professor in the Teachers College at Buffalo, New York. In 1897 he came to the University of Wisconsin as professor of education, remaining here until his death, January 14, 1932.

He was a prolific writer in the field of child and adolescent psychology. Among his contributions in this field were:

[1] Minute of the faculty of the University of Wisconsin on the death of Professor O'Shea. The memorial was presented on January 18, by Dean C. J. Anderson, chairman, and Professors Philo Buck, W. J. Chase, Frank L. Clapp and V. A. C. Henmon, and was made a part of the faculty records.

Suggestions for the Observation and Study of Children, 1894.
Linguistic Development and Education, 1903.
Social Development and Education, 1909.
The Child and His Spelling, 1914.
Mental Development and Education, 1920.
First Steps in Child Training, 1920.
The Trend of the Teens, 1920.
Faults of Childhood and Youth, 1920.
Everyday Problems in Child Training, 1920.
The Child—His Nature and His Needs, 1925.
Newer Ways with Children, 1929.

He was chairman of the Educational Board of the Children's Book Club.

In the field of general education his contributions were:

Education as Adjustment, 1913.
Dynamic Factors in Education, 1906.
Everyday Problems in Teaching, 1912.

As a text-book writer he contributed partly or in whole to the following publications:

The Health Series of Physiology and Hygiene, 1915.

Everyday Spelling Series, 1915.
How Much English Grammar, 1925.

He was nationally recognized for his ability to evaluate the work of school systems and directed surveys of the All Year Schools in Newark, New Jersey, in 1925, the Mississippi Educational System in 1926, and the Virginia Educational System in 1927.

His activity and success as an educational author brought him many editorial responsibilities. He was editor-in-chief of The World Book Encyclopedia, The Experimental Education Series, The Childhood and Youth Series, *The Junior Home Magazine* and *The Nation's Schools Magazine*. For many years he was editor of the *Wisconsin Journal of Education*.

Professor O'Shea was a close student, at first hand, of both European and American educational practice, and especially in the field of genetic psychology made both important investigations and distinct enrichment to professional literature. With a talent for clear and lucid statement, he possessed an unusual gift for popularizing educational theory and pedagogical principle, and, on the public platform, his powers of interpretation were of high order and in wide demand. For this form of service his intellectual resourcefulness and readiness, his native wit, his dynamic vigor and charm of personality were invaluable assets. Such did his repute for professional expertness become that his professional counsel was widely sought for by parents, teachers, school boards, and both city and state boards of education. On various occasions, he was appointed official representative and delegate at professional gatherings in Europe as well as in the United States. In 1905 he was chairman of the American Commission at the International Congress of Education in Belgium and in 1910 of the International Congress of home education at Brussels.

As a teacher his methods were unique. He loved to present problems for solution by the students in his classes. He did not think of a class exercise as having for its chief function the imparting of knowledge, but rather the exchange of opinion, the stimulation of thinking. The enrolment in his classes was large, and the personnel was cosmopolitan. Hundreds of students were attracted to Wisconsin by his work, especially during the summer session. His classroom manner was that of a fellow worker with his students—all searching for the truth. He was never dogmatic. His views were always fresh and wholesome.

But it is his own community that will most keenly feel his loss. It was here in Madison and in the faculty of the university that he had his most intimate friends and displayed his happiest characteristics. As a member of clubs of congenial friends, as colleague, as associate in the larger community, he was always the same restless and happy inspiration. Few persons are as widely or as cordially welcomed as was Michael Vincent O'Shea. Few have the vital imagination and genial curiosity, that were his, to draw out the best in a conversation and illuminate the commonplace. He had a scholarly theory of values, but one which he had brought into intimate relation with the whole of life. The friendships that he created and maintained, the groups, large and small, of which he was an intimate part, these will feel increasingly the irreparable loss of his death; but the inspiration also of his happy and vital life.

DISCUSSION

SHOULD THE COURSE IN FRESHMAN COMPOSITION BE ABOLISHED?[1]

THE issue raised by the title of this paper might be proposed for any course listed in a college bulletin. Certain subjects are obviously professional in nature. These are designed to give the student specific training for the profession he desires to enter. Others are cultural. If one believes that college training should be principally for the purpose of broadening the student's intellectual horizon, he is generally skeptical in regard to the professional subjects. If, on the other hand, one is steadfast in his opinion that the chief purpose of a college is to prepare a student for a vocation, the so-called cultural subjects appear as annoying appendages or embellished trappings of a college education.

[1] Based on an address delivered on November 28, 1931, at the annual convention in Milwaukee of the National Council of Teachers of English.

The study of English composition falls in neither of these categories. It strides on middle ground and is, therefore, open to the animadversions as well as the approbations of the proponents of each point of view. Since English composition has a definite bearing upon a wide range of professions, it may be regarded as essentially vocational. When it is thought of as a study that develops appreciation of literary masterpieces or as a subject that opens the possibilities for creative work of the highest order, it becomes cultural and professional. Since it serves this dual purpose, only the lack of ordinary prudence would permit one to propose that freshman composition be abolished without submitting a counter proposal for training college freshmen to write.

In the face of insufficient evidence, the counter proposal must be limited to a suggestion for experimental attack. The plan that the writer wishes to submit entails instruction in English composition through the cooperation of all departments within the university. Instead of the formal instruction in composition that is now being offered in freshman classes, it is proposed that English be taught in all courses for which the student enrolls but principally in relation to the major subject he has selected.

In brief, the plan would require the following administrative procedure. The English department would make arrangements with departments in which majors are offered so that an instructor in English composition would cooperate with each departmental division. For some of the larger departments several English instructors might be required. Then, at the beginning of the freshman year, all students would be given extensive examinations to measure their ability to express themselves. When those students who are particularly deficient in English expression are discovered, it is proposed that they be arranged in special groups within the major department for the study of composition. Thus, students who are deficient in composition and are pursuing history as a major subject would be classified in one group. The instructor who is cooperating with the history department would meet these individuals two, three or even four times a week until the rudiments of composition have been acquired. In addition the instructor would work with all other students majoring in the department. For the better students, the method of instruction in composition would be essentially the tutorial plan. All papers written for any course in history would be checked and the student would not be permitted to be graduated with a major in history unless he satisfied certain requirements in composition.

Obviously such a plan would be confronted with numerous obstacles, but certainly not insurmountable barriers. The advantages that might accrue make the proposal worthy of trial. In the first place, the students would be studying composition as related to the subject of major interest. Secondly, the study of composition would not be limited to the freshman year, but would extend throughout all the college levels even into the graduate school. In other words, the plan involves not less work in English composition but a more intensive study for those who require it. Furthermore, if the proposal were put into effect, it would undoubtedly make other members of the staff more careful of their own written and oral expression. That is to say, there would be a veritable consciousness of English expression permeating the entire student body and faculty. Perhaps such a scheme may make the product of our colleges more worthy of the designation generally attached to their names.

ALVIN C. EURICH
UNIVERSITY OF MINNESOTA

A MORAL EQUIVALENT FOR THE CLASSICS

IN a recent number of SCHOOL AND SOCIETY Mr. J. S. Cleland called for a moral equivalent for the classics. His particular claim to high moral value for the classics left the present writer unimpressed for two reasons; first, because the theories of transfer of training involved in his assumptions of value have not been supported by any of the considerable body of available experimental evidence on the questions at issue, and, second, because, even if one were to grant that the classics did possess the power of generating habits of industry, accuracy and lucidity, they could hardly claim superiority in these respects to such subjects as physics, economics and chemistry, fundamental sciences that are sufficiently difficult and precise and usually a part of any modern curriculum.

There is, however, a sense in which the abandonment of the classics may actually be involving us in a decided moral loss, particularly upon the upper levels of educated leadership. This loss, if it occurs at all, occurs in the realm of ideas rather than in the realm of discipline. The student of an older generation, when he was clever and able, stayed with his Latin and Greek long enough so that it eventually gave him access to and forced him to think through some of the great literature of the classical period. This literature has had the advantage of two thousand years of sifting by men of learning and discrimination, until that which remains to be selected for use in the schools represents only the noblest of all the great volume of material that must have been produced. The result was that the abler students during the classical period were nourished upon literary materials of high quality, infused for the most part with the most lofty of social and ethical ideals.

The modern student, in contrast, unless he majors in literature or philosophy, spends most of his time upon text-books of very low literary quality and quite devoid of any lofty ethical ideals. Consider the vast output of decidedly second-rate material which is ground out to nourish the mind of the modern student in a college of commerce or medicine or education, and imagine its effect upon his literary taste and social ideals. It is possible that a certain deterioration in the average quality of modern educational and social leadership may be attributed to the fact that a man may secure a Ph.D or an M.D. without having the least familiarity either with the thought and spirit of classical antiquity or with that of his own age as it expresses itself outside his own narrow specialty. Scientific beyond a doubt he is, a first essential, to be sure, but intelligent about human values he is not. For the would-be specialist of an elder day, Plato and Cicero and Vergil provided some essential educational values that it is now possible for an ambitious young specialist to miss entirely.

If there be anything to these speculations at all, they do not imply that there is any value in the miserable grubbing at the classical languages which still persists for a year or two is the modern high school, nor do they call for a return to six or seven years of labor on either or both of these languages. The implication would seem to be rather that the study of the languages themselves for any but potential specialists should be abandoned entirely, and the time now given to a miserably poor mastery of the tools should be devoted to a study of the vital content of the classics in English translations. Whatever may be done about classical thought, it would appear obvious that any individual who expects to equip himself for leadership in any sphere of learning should be required to acquaint himself with that which appears most illuminating in modern thought, with such writings, say, as those of William James, of Dewey, Russell and Bergson, of the more thoughtful novelists and poets, and whatever others there may be who can illuminate modern life with clear thinking upon high levels.

There is some cause for thinking that the modern high school, in its compromise between the old disciplines and the new understandings, has missed the real values of both. In order to introduce smatterings of physical and social science, and beginnings of vocational guidance, it has reduced the time given to the older subjects of ancient languages and mathematics to the point where the only possible values they could have are not even approached, and they have degenerated into utterly sterile disciplines that can only be justified with discarded theories of mystic mental training. On the other hand, so much of the old has been retained that time does not remain to carry the sciences and the guidance activities to a point where they have any real functional value for most of the pupils.

The ultimate solution, of course, will be the complete elimination of the older subjects in their present character. When this change is complete, the substitute for the classics will take the form of an attempt to introduce the pupil to the high and lucid thought of all ages, without any long and largely fruitless struggle with the languages in which that thought happened to be first expressed.

Roscoe Pulliam
Superintendent of Schools,
Harrisburg, Illinois

SPECIAL CORRESPONDENCE

PACIFIC COLONY SUMMER SCHOOL OF CLAREMONT COLLEGES, CALIFORNIA

To meet the need of school systems and institutions in the way of training personnel for the teaching of mentally deficient children a summer school is to be developed by Claremont Colleges, Claremont, California, in cooperation with the Pacific Colony, a state institution for mental defectives near Pomona, California, and a short distance from the college campus at Claremont. The development of this school is in the line of the policy of Claremont Colleges, while carrying on a general summer school, to organize specialized schools for the more intimate and practical advantage of students in particular fields. By this arrangement academic work will be carried on at Claremont, and the clinical work and practice teaching will be supplied by the opportunities furnished at the Pacific Colony. Work done in the teaching of subnormal children will receive regular academic credit at Claremont Colleges.

The opportunity for clinical work furnished by Pacific Colony is very unusual, as it is the only state institution for the training of the mentally defective in Southern California. Moreover, these advantages will doubtless steadily increase as it is the purpose of the administration now in charge to develop the program at this institution so that it will equal the most progressive training schools for the feebleminded anywhere in the world. Cooperation with Claremont Colleges in the summer school has therefore been welcomed, and the combined facilities should not only make for progress in carrying out this purpose but should also set this experience at the service of all officials and teachers occupied in this type of work.

The direction of teacher training in the summer school will be in charge of Dr. Norman Fenton, director of Juvenile Research Bureau of the state of California, who will be related as a member of the faculty of Claremont Colleges.

In addition to the opportunity for classroom contacts with mental defectives, the school will offer opportunities to students in the social sciences—psychology and kindred subjects—for research investigations under expert guidance and for other interesting and valuable experiences with the children at Pacific Colony. Assistance will be rendered by the staff of Pacific Colony as occasion may offer. Additional related subjects will be offered by the staff of Claremont Colleges, thus affording the usual summer school privileges, as may be desired.

The proposed program will also have the special advantage of the cooperation of the California Bureau of Juvenile Research, an organization of the State Department of Institutions, under the immediate charge of Dr. Norman Fenton, who is so well known as an educational authority and who will direct teaching and research for the students of the summer school. The plan has also the approval of the director of state institutions, Dr. J. H. Toner, and the active cooperation of the superintendent of the colony, Dr. James B. Cutter, these authorities having placed the facilities of the colony at the service of this undertaking.

Claremont Colleges, in offering this opportunity for summer training to teachers, psychologists, social workers and others, believes that it will meet a need for communities and institutions in the West, and that a considerable number of students will avail themselves of this privilege of six-weeks' first-hand contact with the feeble-minded and their problems. The only other summer program of this sort in the United States is at the Vineland Training School, Vineland, New Jersey. The program at Vineland is offered in association with Rutgers University. The Summer Session at Pacific Colony, which is about six miles from the campus of Claremont Colleges, will thus be an opportunity for institutional personnel and teachers not only in the state of California but also in the other states of the West.

Summer school will begin the latter part of June, and inquiries regarding the program can be made to the Director of Summer Session, Claremont Colleges, Claremont, California. Applications for admission to the school are now being taken. Information will be available in pamphlet form, giving a detailed account of the academic courses of Claremont Colleges and the concrete description of the teacher training and psychological and sociological program at Pacific Colony.

KENNETH DUNCAN

QUOTATIONS

THE POLICIES OF THE CARNEGIE CORPORATION

THE past few years have witnessed an increasing spirit of cooperation among American foundations. Problems common to two or more are studied together. Information is freely exchanged, and joint programs undertaken, as, for example, by the General Education Board, the Julius Rosenwald Fund and the Carnegie Corporation in the library movement in the southeastern part of the United States, particularly with reference to the school library.

It is not expected or desired that this tendency will lead toward uniformity of policy or procedure. There is wide variety in the basic policies of the different trusts.

There is one matter, however, in which uniformity is most desirable and it has not as yet been achieved. It is unfortunately true that there are still a number of trusts, some of large capitalization, which publish no reports and furnish no information as to their activities. It must be assumed that these organizations realize neither the essentially public nature of their responsibility as evidenced by exemption from taxation, nor the degree to which the attitude which they have adopted may tend to threaten public confidence in the foundation as an instrument of social usefulness.

In general, the relations between the foundations and what may be called the grant-consuming public have been steadily improving. It is no longer felt by applicants that obeisance need be made as a condition of receiving attention, for it is recognized that the foundation is quite as anxious to find outstanding opportunities for carrying out its trust as the applicant is eager to receive financial aid. It is also recognized by reasonable people that only a small proportion of new applications can possibly receive favorable consideration, not only because of their number, but because in the distribution of the limited funds at its disposal, a foundation must recognize continuing responsibilities toward activities to which it has contributed in previous years.

There remains, however, one real difficulty in these relations, namely, the delay in receiving a definite response to an application falling within the recognized field of activity of the foundation in question. In most instances, the executive has a shrewd idea as to what the ultimate answer must be, but he has no right to anticipate the action of his trustees, and if he is wise, he will not permit himself to do so. The boards themselves meet seldom, in some cases only twice a year, and when they do meet, their members naturally desire, and they should have, entire freedom of action within the terms of their charters. Just what solution will be reached is still problematical with many foundations.—*Dr. Frederick P. Keppel in the Annual Report of the Carnegie Corporation.*

CHANGING EMPHASIS

THE report of Dr. Frederick Keppel as president of the Carnegie Corporation calls attention to the reaction against lavish grants by foundations of wide scope for general research programs and surveys, in favor of specific enterprises conducted by individuals of recognized ability. This amounts to the endowment of persons with particular problems on their hands or in prospect. In pioneering days there was more daring in making use of men of promise, but the tendency has grown to demand credentials of academic respectability in the fear of picking the wrong man, with the result that there is danger of reducing the chances of picking the right one. Against this a distinct effort is being made to give recognition and support to the highly gifted individual who fits into no predetermined category. Certain foundations have already shown courage in making such selection and have in some instances been richly rewarded.

Another change in emphasis is likely to show results in another five years as a consequence of giving more aid relatively to tax-supported institutions. During the last few years 92 per cent. of the contributions to higher education by the five large foundations went to privately endowed universities. That only 8 per cent. went to state universities was due, probably, in large degree to the feeling that their funds are adequate. On the other hand, it is often more difficult to get funds for testing or demonstrating "the vitality of a new idea" in tax-supported institutions. Yet some of the most fruitful groups of scholars and research workers are to be found in them. It is to be inferred from the report that there will be a change in the percentage of distribution in their favor.

Of wider interest is the emphasis given by the Carnegie Corporation to adult education. Less than a decade ago the first conference on this subject in this country was held in response to a call which it issued. This led to the organization of the American Association for Adult Education, which has since served as a clearing house for information and as a sponsor of studies and experiments in this field. The growth of this idea has been due not to any contention that it is a panacea for all political or social ills, but to the belief that study beyond the traditional period of schooling may prove "not only profitable but pleasurable." This is significant not only as lengthening the period of intellectual growth and creative interest, but also as having its retroactive effect upon the teaching of the earlier years.

To be especially noted this year is the attention given to problems of reeducation arising from unemployment, "especially technological unemployment." "Opportunity schools" and like ventures are also receiving special notice. The corporation still keeps at heart the library, which was of vital interest to Mr. Carnegie, and its new ventures relate themselves closely to that and seek to respond to the intellectual and practical needs of the many.—*The New York Times*.

REPORTS

ACTIVITIES OF THE CARNEGIE CORPORATION

GRANTS amounting to more than three and one half million dollars were voted by the Carnegie Corporation of New York during the fiscal year 1930–31, according to the report of the President, Frederick P. Keppel, issued on February 20. Library interests, adult education, the fine arts, educational and scientific studies, research and publications benefited by the grants. During the year eight hundred and twenty applications for grants were considered. Of these, one hundred and ninety-six received favorable consideration and six hundred and twenty-four were declined.

The library was of vital interest to Andrew Carnegie, the report states, and the corporation which he created has been, since its organization, and doubtless will continue to be, more closely identified with the library than with any other single activity falling within the term of its charter.

During the year, at the request of the corporation, a group of librarians and others interested in libraries surveyed the library field and presented a report analyzing modern conditions and trends.

The distribution of funds for the enrichment of college libraries in the United States was continued. During the year, a total of $797,000 was voted to sixty-three institutions, these institutions being widely scattered geographically, as is shown by gifts averaging $10,000 each to Mills College, California; Read College, Oregon; Rockford College, Illinois; Millsaps College, Mississippi, and Trinity College, Connecticut.

Since the idea of adult education is new in this country, on recommendation of the American Association for Adult Education, the corporation grants have been voted to organizations willing to try out new methods of teaching and new approaches to students. During the last year the association, with the financial assistance of the corporation, has addressed itself particularly to problems arising from unemployment, especially technological unemployment. At the present time a series of studies of opportunity schools and similar ventures is under way, the results of which will be made available to school boards, school officials and others interested.

To encourage the recent interest of state universities in the arts, the corporation made a grant of $100,000 to the State University of Iowa. Colgate University, Lawrence College, Monmouth College, Skidmore College and Tufts College were among the institutions receiving grants for the support of the fine arts. The College Art Association, the American Federation of Arts, the American Institute of Architects, the American Institute of Graphic Arts also received grants amounting to $200,000.

The corporation has continued its study of the educational services of American museums. The largest grants made were of $45,000, spread over a five-year period, to the Pennsylvania Museum of Art at Philadelphia, and of $50,000, likewise over a five-year period, to the American Association of Museums. A contribution of $30,000 was made to enable the Museums Association (British) to conduct a much needed general survey of the museums in the British Dominions and Colonies.

Typical of the publications for which the corporation has been directly or indirectly responsible are the following: A List of Books for College Libraries, by Charles B. Shaw; The Education of Adult Prisoners, by A. H. MacCormick; A Report on Architectural Education; A Study of Technical Institutes, and a Report on College Library Buildings. Twenty or more other studies financed in whole or in part by the corporation are now under way.

President Keppel says in regard to non-degree granting technical institutes: "With few exceptions we have failed to stabilize this type of institution in the United States. Some, like the Worcester Polytechnic Institute or the Carnegie Institute of Technology, Pittsburgh, have changed their original purpose and have become degree-granting institutions. Few of those remaining in the field have received adequate financial support, either from the communities in which they are situated or from general agencies. Meanwhile, we have been extravagantly using our engineering colleges to provide the routine parts of engineering and industrial service, although the example of England and the Continent proved that the training offered by the technical institute, which is relatively inexpensive both in money and in the time of the student, is quite sufficient to provide the personnel for maintenance and operation of industry, as contrasted with engineering design and other high forms of profession activity. It has been found that there are, at present, approximately one fiftieth as many technical institute men in manufacture as the employers say they should have. An output of from 15,000 to 20,000 technical institute men could probably be absorbed annually in manufacture alone. Less comprehensive estimates from the public utility and transportation industries indicate demands in proportion."

Grants amounting to $400,000 were made in Canada and the British Colonies from a special fund provided by Mr. Carnegie. By means of this fund, books on education and psychology have been distributed to educational institutions in Australia and New Zealand, a demonstration of the possibilities of public library development in the Province of British Columbia has been supported, and an adult education project has been carried on in Newfoundland. The fund has supported a library school at McGill University and five "Jeanes" schools for the training of native supervisors in British Africa. Grants amounting to $1,200,000 have been made to Dalhousie University, King's College and Acadia University. The fund has also supported the activities of the Australian Council for Educational Research. Forty-four visitors have come to the United States as guests of the corporation, and eleven have gone from this country to different parts of the British Empire.

A grant of $250,000 was made in 1931 to the Emergency Unemployment Relief Committee of New York, $75,000 was contributed toward a cooperative study, under the auspices of the University of Minnesota, of the re-education of the unemployed. Smaller grants were also made to the National Urban League, the New School for Social Research, Frontier Nursing Service, Church Peace Union, and other institutions.

A PROFESSIONAL AND PATRIOTIC OBLIGATION[1]

CONDITIONS that caused the world war and that have contributed to so many other wars have not been destroyed by the peace treaties. National lust for power and prestige, economic rivalries, competition in armaments, imperialism involving the exploitation of weaker peoples, secret diplomacy and secret treaties, limitation of freedom of speech and freedom of the press,

[1] Statement prepared in connection with the resolutions introduced at the annual meeting of the Department of Superintendence.

calculated appeals to fear and hatred, propaganda to conceal from the citizens of all nations the real motives behind many governmental acts and policies, are still active influences in international relations, and are still full of menace to the peace of the world.

Historians of high standing have studied and analyzed the thousands of new documents that have come to light since the close of the war, with the result that it is now certain that no one nation was solely responsible for the war. Moreover, it is plain that the masses of the peoples of all the various nations were unaware of much that their respective statesmen were doing and are not to be held responsible for the great catastrophe. There is a growing body of opinion that in the interests both of fairness and of the general peace of the world the Versailles treaties should be revised. This change of sentiment is itself a historic fact that any work on contemporary history should record.

Enlightened public opinion based on accurate information is essential if future wars are to be avoided. No other nation is in a better position than our own to accept and to disseminate the facts about the world war and about international conditions which may bring on war as they have made wars in the past.

When the world war began, most Americans had little understanding of its underlying causes, for the conventional history courses in our schools had done little to give them an adequate understanding. Nor do most of them even now present with adequate realism the factors responsible for wars. Text-books in history and other subjects used in most of the public and private schools of the United States still reflect more or less the distortions of wartime propaganda. They fail to reveal that millions of citizens in all nations were moved again and again to acts of supreme idealism and unselfishness by propaganda of interested groups controlling national policies. Not yet has the selfishness and the falseness of much of that propaganda been exposed in history texts.

The duty of educators is clear. True patriotism is not served by ignorance and refusal to face facts and problems. The patriot can truly serve his country only if he is intelligent enough to know how to meet the problems that confront him as a citizen. School history should, therefore, include an intelligent effort to arrive at essential facts involved in the significant crises of the past in order to prepare our people to deal intelligently and justly with the crises of the future. Intelligent patriotism and consideration for our true national interests, as well as sound ethics, therefore, make it a professional obligation of the administrators of American schools to see that the text-books in history and other appropriate fields present truthfully and adequately the chief factors and influences operating in world affairs and producing the problems of peace and war, that they emphasize such fundamental facts as the foregoing paragraphs set forth, that they make it clear that economic crises and unemployment usually follow wars bringing insecurity and suffering to millions, and that they record the existence of a conviction on the part of many Americans that the United States has an obligation with respect to leadership in the reduction of armaments by international agreement.

These facts are known to the well-informed citizens of the United States and of other nations. In the face of the present perils to the economic welfare of all the world and to the peace and security of all nations, it is both a patriotic duty and our special obligation as educators to face all the facts honestly and courageously. Only enlightened public opinion, based on accurate information and full and free discussion of facts and issues, can give to our nation real and adequate security. Dissemination of vital facts with honest discussion of the issues they involve is a major responsibility of the nation's schools.

To aid in meeting that responsibility at this critical time is the high obligation of every teacher and school administrator in the nation.

(*Signed*) Charles A. Beard
William C. Bagley
Boyd H. Bode
Jesse H. Newlon
Clyde R. Miller
Heber Harper
J. Montgomery Gambrill
Frank E. Spaulding
Philip W. Cox
James T. Shotwell
Frank P. Graham
Rollo G. Reynolds

EDUCATIONAL RESEARCH AND STATISTICS

PRECAUTIONS AND PROCEDURE IN NORMAL GRADING[1]

IT is generally conceded that sounder theory and more painstaking and systematic procedures than those current are necessary if the application of the normal distribution to student grading is to be a valid and effective device for the improvement of instruction. The present reference is to two precautions that seem to be especially needed.

First, students should not be graded solely on the basis of their class rank, as is often done. (That is, the first 5 per cent. are given grade A, the second 25 per cent. are given grade B, and so on). The error is that no relation is established between the proportion of students placed in any grade group and the spread of achievement for the group. In statistical language, there is no connection between the divisions of the area of the normal curve and the divisions of its base line. Such arbitrarily assigned proportions obviously can not indicate whether or not students are achieving according to their native abilities, and they can not serve as an index or guide of instruction, either for teachers or for administrators.

Second, even when the above objection is met, each class should not be taken as sufficient to itself, and its average used as a basis for the distribution of grades within the class, as is frequently recommended. The reason is that the standard of achievement and difficulty of tests must be kept constant from class to class, in order that the disturbing factors which must be watched (*e. g.*, lack of student effort, poor teaching, student selection, etc.), may be detected and controlled.

To avoid these and other fallacies in the use of the normal curve, the following steps are suggested: (1) Students are graded according to clear-cut (chiefly true-false) standardized tests that, when other factors are properly controlled, have been found to distribute grades in agreement with the normal curve, corrected for selection, among large numbers of students in many similar classes, using a percentage scale say from 0 to 100; (2) the students' numerical grades are arranged in descending order; (3) they are divided into groups represented by letters (E, D, C, B, A) corresponding to specified divisions of the grading scade, say 0 to 60, 60 to 70, 70 to 80, 80 to 90, 90 to 100, respectively; (4) when the number of students is large, the proportion falling within each grade group is compared with the proportion of the area of the corrected normal curve lying above the corresponding scale division, say 5 per cent., 25 per cent., 40 per cent., 25 per cent., 5 per cent., respectively; (5) if there is then a close agreement between the sets of actual and theoretical proportions, the indications for good teaching and good grading are favorable, otherwise unfavorable. But before deciding that the distribution of grades is abnormal, several things should be done.

(1) Allowance must be made for the number of students in the class. It is advisable for administrators to furnish instructors with a table, like Table I, showing permissible variations in the proportions of students that should receive each grade in classes of different sizes.

TABLE I

VARIATIONS IN THE NUMBER OF STUDENTS WHO SHOULD GET EACH GRADE IN CLASSES OF DIFFERENT SIZES, DUE TO CHANCE ERRORS OF SAMPLING

Number of students in class	F, E	D	C	B	A
5	0 to 1	0 to 2	1 to 3	0 to 2	0 to 1
10	0 to 1	1 to 4	3 to 6	1 to 4	0 to 1
15	0 to 1	2 to 5	4 to 8	2 to 5	0 to 1
20	0 to 2	3 to 7	6 to 10	3 to 7	0 to 2
25	0 to 2	4 to 8	8 to 13	4 to 8	0 to 2
30	0 to 3	5 to 10	9 to 15	5 to 10	0 to 3
35	0 to 3	6 to 11	11 to 17	6 to 11	0 to 3
40	1 to 3	7 to 13	13 to 19	7 to 13	1 to 3
45	1 to 4	8 to 14	15 to 21	8 to 14	1 to 4
50	1 to 4	9 to 15	17 to 24	9 to 15	1 to 4

(2) If non-standardized tests are used, shift all grades by an equal amount that gives the most normal distribution possible, keeping equal scale divisions (say 10 points) for each grade letter. A sliding scale can easily be made to expedite this step.

(3) Revise grades slightly (not over 5 points) by personal estimate of students further

[1] Research Paper No. 275, Journal Series, University of Arkansas.

to improve the normal distribution, if necessary.

(4) If grades still do not agree with a normal distribution, the following hypotheses should be tested:

A. Examination too hard or too easy: Indicated by too high or too low grades, other factors controlled. *Remedy:* Standardized tests, so that 90 to 100 per cent. of questions are answered correctly by 5 per cent. of students, 80 to 89 per cent. by an additional 25 per cent. of students, 70 to 79 per cent. by an additional 40 per cent. of students, 60 to 69 per cent. by an additional 25 per cent. of students, and 0 to 59 per cent. by an additional 5 per cent. of students, under properly controlled conditions.

B. Students a selected sample: Indicated by skewed distribution of grades over several tests, other factors controlled. Check by mental tests (IQ's) and average grades of students secured from examiner's office.

C. Lack of student effort: Indicated by poor showing of those guilty, by grade lapses and pick-ups, by easy misses, by contrast with students known to be trying, etc. Inconsistency of students' grades is shown by rank correlations, and by disagreement between grades in this class with the IQ's and average grades of its members obtained from examiner's office. Suspected students will often admit lack of effort. *Remedy:* Special efforts to arouse interest; personal conferences; accurate grading; etc.

D. Course too hard for students, due to poor preliminary training: Indicated by poor showing, and by inquiry into or test of students' earlier training. *Remedy:* Make up deficiencies before going further.

E. Poor teaching: Indicated by poor showing of this and other classes, when other factors are accounted for; by inquiry into pedagogical methods; etc.

F. Other Causes.

THOMAS C. MCCORMICK
UNIVERSITY OF ARKANSAS

ATHLETICS AND ACHIEVEMENT IN HIGH SCHOOL

THIS paper reports the results of an investigation attempting to reveal any relationship existing between interschool athletic participation and scholastic achievement among boys graduating from University High School, University of Minnesota. Data have been collected on 174 boys who were graduated during the seven year period ending June, 1931.

Records of athletic participation have been taken from the school annual, published by the senior class. Five athletic sports have been included, namely, football, basketball, baseball, track and swimming. One point has been assigned to a boy for each team on which he played for one season.

As a measure of scholastic achievement, an honor point average for each individual has been computed from quarter marks earned throughout high school. The rather common practice of assigning 3 honor points for an "A," 2 honor points for a "B," 1 honor point for a "C," none for a "D," and –1 for a "failure," has been followed.

As a measure of intelligence, scores on five group tests administered to each individual at or just prior to the time of high-school entrance have been employed to compute I.Q.'s. These I.Q.'s have been equated by Miller's method[1] to obtain values comparable to Terman group I.Q.'s. Of the five equated I.Q.'s available for each boy, the mid-score has been taken as the best measure of intelligence.[2]

Despite the fact that the athletic participation scores form a truncated distribution of relatively narrow range, as will be seen from Table I, the product moment correlation formula seems to furnish the best means of discovering what relationships exist between extent of participation in athletics, achievement and intelligence. Zero order coefficients obtained are as follows:

Extent of participation and honor point average	$-.08 \pm .05$
Extent of participation and I.Q.	$-.21 \pm .08$
Honor point average and I.Q.	$+.53 \pm .03$

When partial correlation is employed to eliminate the effect of intelligence, the first order co-

[1] W. S. Miller, "The Variations and Significance of Intelligence Quotients Obtained from Group Tests," *Jour. of Ed. Psych.*, 15: 359–366, 1924.

[2] In case of eight boys, Stanford-Binet was employed instead of the 5 group tests.

efficient between participation and honor point average is found to be +.03. Zero order coefficients computed for the group of 101 boys who were members of at least one athletic team during their high-school career, differ little from those given above. They are:

Total participation and honor point average	$-.07 \pm .07$
Total participation and I.Q.	$-.33 \pm .06$

TABLE I

EXTENT OF ATHLETIC PARTICIPATION OF 174 HIGH SCHOOL BOYS

Total season's participation 5 sports	0	1	2	3	4	5	6	7	8	9	10	11	12	13	14	15	16
N	73	32	16	17	13	8	7	2	4	1	0	0	0	0	0	0	1

A further analysis of the data has been made by grouping athletes according to the sport in which they engaged. Members of each of these groups were then matched on I.Q. with boys who had taken no part in interschool athletics. That a comparison of honor point averages of these paired groups reveals no significant differences between participants in any sport and non-athletes of equal mental ability is seen from Table II. A similar comparison of boys engaging in two or more sports with non-athletes reveals only a slight difference in honor points. When the 21 boys who have taken part in at least 3 sports are matched with non-athletes, the difference in achievement is still such as might readily occur by chance.

TABLE II

A COMPARISON OF HONOR POINT AVERAGE OF GROUPS OF ATHLETES AND NON-ATHLETES OF EQUAL MENTAL ABILITY

	N	I.Q. Mean	Mean H.P. av.	Diff. in H.P. av.	σ_D	$\frac{D}{\sigma_D}$
Football	65	115.3	1.117	–.031	.09	.034
Non-athletes	65	115.8	1.148			
Basketball	35	113.0	1.136	–.003	.12	.0025
Non-athletes	35	113.8	1.139			
Baseball	19	113.5	1.138	+.131	.15	.87
Non-athletes	19	112.8	1.007			
Track	31	113.5	1.181	–.138	.15	.92
Non-athletes	31	113.1	1.319			
Swimming	25	116.7	1.075	–.070	.17	.41
Non-athletes	25	117.1	1.125			
2 sports or more	51	112.4	1.101	–.122	.11	1.11
Non-athletes	51	112.9	1.223			
3 sports or more	21	112.2	1.161	–.154	.20	.77
Non-athletes	21	112.3	1.315			

While generalizations upon these data must be subject to the limitations imposed by the small numbers of cases, and also to any constant error in marks favoring either athletes or non-athletes, the following conclusions may be advanced for situations such as that existing at University High School.

(1) There is a slight tendency for boys of high intelligence to engage least in interschool athletics.

(2) Boys who play on teams engaging in interschool athletic contests receive marks approximately equal to those received by boys of equal mental ability who are not members of such teams.

(3) Boys engaging in more than one sport receive marks approximately the same as those of non-athletes of equal mental ability.

(4) There is no evidence that boys engaging in any particular sport differ markedly in achievement from boys engaging in any other sport.

F. H. FINCH

COLLEGE OF EDUCATION AND
INSTITUTE OF CHILD WELFARE,
UNIVERSITY OF MINNESOTA

NEW BOOKS IN EDUCATION

FISHBEIN, MORRIS. *Health.* Pp. 158. Lippincott. $1.00.

GATES, ARTHUR I., and JEAN Y. AYER. *Magic Hours.* Pp. viii + 408. Illustrated. Macmillan. $.80.

GRAY, WILLIAM S., and others. *Number Stories, Book One.* Pp. 144. 109 figures. Scott, Foresman. $.60.

JERNEGAN, MARCUS W. *Laboring and Dependent Classes in Colonial America.* Pp. xiii + 256. University of Chicago Press. $3.00.

National Society of College Teachers of Education. The Direct Contribution of Educational Psychology to Teacher Training. Year Book No. XX. Pp. v + 154. University of Chicago Press.

PALMER, IRENE. *Tests and Measurements.* Pp. xii + 143. A. S. Barnes. $2.00.

WEBB, L. W., and ANNA M. SHOTWELL. *Standard Tests in the Elementary School.* Pp. xiv + 532. Illustrated. Long and Smith. $2.75.

SCHOOL AND SOCIETY

EDITED BY J. McKEEN CATTELL

WITH WHICH IS COMBINED THE

EDUCATIONAL REVIEW

EDITED BY WILLIAM McANDREW

Volume 35 SATURDAY, MARCH 5, 1932 Number 897

THE PRESENT CRISIS AND PUBLIC EDUCATION[1]

By EDWIN C. BROOME

PRESIDENT, DEPARTMENT OF SUPERINTENDENCE

THE most important duty of society is the proper nurture and education of its children. President Hoover expressed this thought in much better language when he said of education: "It is our biggest business. It is our only indispensable business . . . if we were to suppress our educational system for a single generation the equipment would decay, the most of our people would die of starvation, and intellectually and spiritually we would slip back four thousand years in human progress." During the world war, a catastrophe that threatened the continuance of civilization itself, H. A. W. Fisher, Minister of Education of Great Britain, with England's back to the wall, courageously said: "Education is the eternal debt of adulthood to youth." With thousands of their schoolmasters in the trenches, England's schools carried on, and made a mighty sacrifice to meet their "eternal obligation to youth." Minister Fisher made his statement in 1917. At no time in England's history did the future look more dismal. But, with undaunted faith in education, English statesmen were at that critical time formulating plans for the expansion of the school system when peace should again return.

Our country is passing through a serious social and economic crisis. Shall we continue to discharge our eternal debt to childhood and youth? Or shall we repudiate that debt, or declare a moratorium which will deprive the children of the depression of the advantages which the children of prosperity have of right enjoyed?

During the last twenty years the people of the United States have begun to understand and appreciate the importance of education for all the people as the surest guarantee of our success as a nation. School attendance laws for the protection of children have been adopted and enforced; and during this period illiteracy has been reduced to the vanishing point. The average attendance in the public schools has increased twice as much as the increase in the general population.

As prosperity became more generally diffused, the demand for more education for the children of all the people increased; and the attendance in the high schools grew tremendously, over six times as fast as the increase in the elementary school enrolment.

The curriculum has been expanded to provide for the education of the whole

[1] Statement before the Department of Superintendence, Constitution Hall, Washington, D. C., February 23, 1932.

child. To this end programs of health and physical education, of recreation activities, courses in music and art, and industrial arts have been established. Also education has been provided for adults who were so circumstanced in childhood that they were unable to receive the complete educational opportunities that others enjoyed.

Better, safer and more attractive school buildings have been built and provided with modern furniture and equipment.

The preparation of teachers has been greatly extended and the qualifications of teachers increased. The value of the teaching service has been tardily recognized by substantial increases in salary. But, even at that, when teachers' salaries reached their peak, about 1928, the average salaries of teachers were still over thirty per cent. below the average salaries of all other salaried employees. And at no time during the last twenty years has the average salary of teachers increased in proportion to the decreasing purchasing value of the dollar.

During the last twenty years, with some setbacks, such as that of the world war, education has gradually grown in strength, in service, and in public recognition. By 1929, popular education was approaching the goal which was so hopefully set for it by George Washington and his far-sighted contemporaries. Then came the economic depression. Practically every community and every person in the country has become reduced in circumstances. Bankruptcy faces many cities; and starvation faces thousands of people.

What is happening to the public schools in which we have invested so much of our resource, our enterprise, and our faith? A brief survey of the conditions facing the schools of the country was made last November by the Division of Research of the National Education Association. This is what was found:

(1) An unprecedented increase in school enrolment, due to lack of opportunities for employment, and a consequent increase in the demand on the public schools; but, in spite of a greatly increased demand, over two thirds of the city school systems are forced to operate on reduced budgets.

(2) Many schools closed, especially in rural districts, and the school year shortened in many other districts.

(3) Educational services that have been regarded necessary have been discontinued or curtailed; for example, kindergartens, night schools, summer schools, health work, playgrounds and recreation centers, supervision, special classes for handicapped children, and manual and industrial courses.

(4) The replacement of experienced and competent teachers by inexperienced ones at lower salaries.

(5) The reduction of teachers' salaries in many places to a point from which they will not recover for a generation.

(6) Increase in size of classes and of the teaching load to a point which threatens the efficiency of instruction.

(7) The suspension of building programs sorely needed in many communities to relieve overcrowding and to give the children decent and safe housing.

These are the most common devices that are being used at present to reduce the cost of the public schools. Needless to say, if they are applied unwisely or continued long, the standards of our public schools will be materially lowered and the children will pay the penalty in impoverished educational opportunities, and in an inadequate preparation for service in the generation to come.

All sensible educators realize that in this time of national distress the public schools must bear their proportionate share in any program of economic retrenchment. But the education of the children must not be the first point of attack, nor should the schools bear the major sacrifice. Mr. Alfred E. Smith, in a syndicated article on January 17, eloquently and forcefully emphasized this thought in the following words:

A state can afford to lose time on the construction of a road, a bridge, or a building, and by speeding up construction at a later time possibly catch up, but education must be continuous. Time lost in preparing our children to take their place in the world can not be made up. There are only certain years in which the great majority of them can attend school and during that period it is the solemn duty of every state to provide full and complete education.

A fine declaration of faith in our public schools is found in the following resolutions recently adopted unanimously by the school directors of Pennsylvania at their annual convention:

Social and economic unrest and uncertainty prevail throughout the world. The disturbed conditions of to-day can largely be charged to our inability to cope with and effect a solution of the problems of civilization. With an ever increasing complexity of our problems, one thing is clear—the oncoming generation must be better prepared than we are to shape their own destiny and the destiny of mankind. To do less than this for our children in the public schools is to invite utter and inevitable social collapse. Therefore, we urge that School Boards all over the State of Pennsylvania not only maintain standards of education as they now exist, but be on the alert to better adapt the schools to the needs of our time. Such a program does not necessarily involve more expense, but it does involve intensification of educational thought and effort all along the line. It also means that the future of our children must not be turned over to an inferior brand of teachers but that the school system must continue to attract outstanding talent and character to its teaching force.

The operation of the provisions of that part of the school code, commonly known as the Edmonds Act minimum salary law, has done more than any other legislation to improve the quality of teaching, place teaching on a high professional plane, and to stabilize teaching as a profession. Therefore, we urge all school districts to observe not only in letter but in spirit the statutory salary regulations and view the circumvention of the Edmonds Act by indirection as equivalent to open violation of the Act.

Whatever retrenchments are made in public education should be made by the friends of children, and not by those who would sacrifice the welfare of the schools to serve selfish ends or to promote their own political fortunes or those of their party, or who in this period of distress, seek to gain temporary and cheap popularity with the over-burdened taxpayers by loudly denouncing the public school as costly and extravagant—to be led first to the sacrifice as the chief offender among our public institutions. Economies in the administration of schools are being made and possibly further economies may be effected, but they should be made only after careful and sincere study by those, both educators and laymen, who honestly believe in the truth of the theme of our convention, that education is "our guide, and our safeguard, and one of the chief sources of our cultural growth, and our material power."

With this end in view the members of the Department of Superintendence at its meeting in Detroit a year ago unanimously adopted a resolution providing for the appointment of a joint committee of business men and educators to make a study of school costs and report at the next meeting. This committee was promptly appointed and has been at work throughout the year. Its membership is as follows:

Members representing the Department of Superintendence: David E. Weglein, superintendent of schools, Baltimore, Maryland, *Chairman;* G. Carl Alverson, superintendent of schools, Syracuse, New York; Frank W. Ballou, superintendent of schools, Washington, D. C.; W. G. Carr, director of research, National Education Association; Frank Cody, superintendent of schools, Detroit, Michigan; R. G. Jones, superintendent of schools, Cleveland, Ohio; John K. Norton, Teachers College, Columbia University; Frank G. Pickell, superintendent of schools, Montclair, N. J.; George D. Strayer, Teachers College, Columbia University.

Members representing Business: Marcus Aaron, president, Board of Education, Pittsburgh, Penn.; Russell Forbes, director, National Municipal League, New York City; Harry R. Freeman, director, Bureau of Municipal Research, Buffalo, N. Y.; Fred P. Keppel, president of Carnegie Corporation, New York; A. L. Moore, president, Board of Education, Pontiac, Michigan, and Chairman of Property Owners' Division of National Association of Real Estate Boards; Edward B. Passano, Chamber of Commerce, Baltimore, Maryland; H. P. Seidemann, Brookings Institution, Washington, D. C.; Lent D. Upson, director, Bureau of Governmental Research, Detroit, Michigan; E. M.

Williams, President, Board of Education, Cleveland, Ohio.

Ex-officio: Edwin C. Broome, president, Department of Superintendence; S. D. Shankland, executive secretary, Department of Superintendence.

Members representing National Council of State Superintendents: A. S. Cook, state superintendent of education, Baltimore, Maryland; J. N. Rule, state superintendent of education, Harrisburg, Penna.; Charles H. Elliott, state commissioner of education, Trenton, N. J.; Sidney B. Hall, state superintendent of education, Richmond, Virginia; H. V. Holloway, state superintendent of education, Dover, Delaware.

Members representing American Council on Education: Charles H. Judd, University of Chicago, Chicago, Ill.; David E. Weglein, superintendent of schools, Baltimore, Maryland; Edwin R. Embree, Julius Rosenwald Fund, Chicago, Illinois; Samuel P. Capen, president, University of Buffalo, N. Y.; Charles R. Mann, American Council on Education, Washington, D. C.

Ex-officio: William John Cooper, U. S. Commissioner of Education, Washington, D. C.; J. W. Crabtree, secretary, National Education Association, Washington, D. C.

School superintendents are practical men, not often carried away by their imagination. They realize that it is their duty to the public to be prudent in school expenditures, even in prosperous times, and they understand the importance of carefully assaying the value of educational activities. They have an intelligent comprehension of the educational needs of their communities. Instances of actual extravagance in school expenditures are rare, and instances of the improper use of school funds are still rarer. A nation whose people spend more on tobacco and chewing gum than on schools for their children can not be said to have an extravagant system of public education. We owe no apology to the taxpayers. They are getting good schools, but not too good, and at a cost that is reasonable in comparison with the cost of other forms of public services. Also the returns for money invested in schools are greater and of more lasting benefit to the community than the returns for an equal amount of expenditure for any other enterprise.

We appreciate the difficult problem that public officials everywhere are facing in their efforts to finance all branches of government. But we urge the citizens of every state and community to do their utmost to preserve the integrity of their public schools; to give immediate consideration to needed reforms in the methods of securing and distributing school revenues; and, while we realize that sane economy in school expenditures is desirable in times of prosperity, as well as in times of adversity, we know, and the public should know, that arbitrary and drastic reduction in school revenues is really a form of extravagance, piling up a deficit in the shape of ineffective citizenship, wasted human resources, and lowered standards of health. The resolution which established this committee quite appropriately said: "Curtailment in some other branches of public service occasions only temporary discomfort which later may be compensated. Abridged educational service is an abiding misfortune to this generation of children, the evil of which may reveal itself only in the next generation of youth."

THE WASHINGTON MEETING[1]

By WILLIAM DOW BOUTWELL

EDITOR-IN-CHIEF, UNITED STATES OFFICE OF EDUCATION

ON Tuesday afternoon I wedged my way into a crowd packed to subway train density in the U. S. Chamber of Commerce auditorium to hear Professor Boyd H. Bode, of the Ohio State University, argue against indoctrination and Professor George S. Counts, of Columbia University, contend for it. These stalwart adversaries

[1] A review of the annual convention of the Department of Superintendence, National Education Association, at Washington, D. C., February 20 to 25, 1932.

were seconded by Jesse H. Newlon, of Columbia University; Melvin E. Haggerty, of the University of Minnesota; Ernest Horn, of the State University of Iowa; Alexander Meiklejohn, of the University of Wisconsin; Frank N. Freeman, of the University of Chicago, and H. Gordon Hullfish, of the Ohio State University. Any one who has attended a sectional session of the National Education Association may gauge the meeting's zest by the fact that not more than half a dozen of the six hundred standees and sitters moved from their places for an hour and a half. Doggedly as the contending debaters argued against each other in this palace built by big business, they were one and all agreed that our capitalistic system has failed us in a pinch. Here, in the very citadel of capitalism, within a few feet of the offices of the leading public defenders of the sacred right of the ruggedest individuals to own steam yachts, this group of outstanding spokesmen of American education talked a remarkably strong brand of socialism.

Cropping up continually in this debate and in other meetings appeared an insistent demand for social planning, met by an equally insistent demand that full and free discussion of our problems—not a set program—is the democratic way to reach the same end. Planners included Professor Counts, who believes that thought palsies action and that the ship will sink while we weigh carefully the best methods to save it, and Ross L. Finney, of the University of Minnesota; Frank N. Freeman; Joy Elmer Morgan, editor, the *Journal* of the National Education Association, and L. B. Evans, superintendent, Augusta, Georgia. Among those who hold that free discussion, a realistic approach to American problems, and healthy doubting will bring us through are: Henry Suzzallo, of the Carnegie Foundation; John Dewey, of Columbia University; Herman H. Horne, of New York University; Melvin E. Haggerty; Lewis W. Lorwin, of Brookings Institution, and Jesse H. Newlon. Many of the latter are in favor of social control, but rest their confidence in its achievement through adherence to principles of equality and free speech, instead of specific plans.

Professor Ross put the case for the planners before the National Council of Education:

> This learning is not a think-for-yourself process, but a process of passive mentation. It is an imitative, absorbent, rote-learning process. Social progress is due to independent, creative thinking; but social *process* is due to passive mentation; and while progress is desirable, process is absolutely necessary to existence and survival—a fact seldom realized. Passive mentation is, accordingly, the usual, normal attitude of the human mind.
>
> Democracy is therefore an inference from the psychological illusion that the people think for themselves. The only successful civilization that is based upon the popular franchise must be, therefore, a government by echo. The problem is to get the masses to echo the right voices, namely, the voices of those intellectuals who know the culture mass most thoroughly.
>
> Hence the responsibility of public education to secure a popular echo for the best knowledge extant, as against selfish propaganda and the popular mythologies. Therefore, the wisdom and necessity for an open conspiracy upon the part of educational leaders to set up a dictatorial oligarchy for the intellect, to function through the curriculum. Such an oligarchy would, first, dictate a curriculum that epitomizes the world's best knowledge; second, develop a minority of first-class intellectuals to carry on; third, broadcast culture in epigrammatic form to the average mass, and, fourth, drill the dullards to a desirable echo. A problem-solving pedagogy for the masses, especially for the duller half, is an inference from the popular, democratic, think-for-yourself illusion.

Others in the ranks of the planners are not willing to go so far. Dr. Lorwin, speaking before the Department of Home Economics, on the other side, pointed out that we are conditioned toward situations and that when the situation changes, as it is constantly changing, we find it difficult to recondition our attitudes. Therefore, teachers must help students to be mentally flexible and to meet the changes when they come. What these changes will be no one can predict with exactitude.

Dean Haggerty asked that the principles of scientific thinking be extended to the field of social thinking. Science, he declared, is an intellectual ideal, while democracy is a moral ideal. As science identifies problems, gathers evidence and makes observations before reaching conclusions, so may democracy. Let us plan for the future, he declared, but let us plan with our tongues in our cheeks. Science did not foresee the revolution it wrought. Nor can we foresee what is ahead of democracy.

Belief that free discussion is the way out was implied in Dr. Dewey's trenchant statement: "Unless and until we permit or rather encourage the schools to abandon the following of traditions which have no relation to existing social realities, our thinking in matters of the greatest public concern, including peace and war, as well as industrial prosperity and depression, will continue to be thoroughly stupid and our leaders will be such only in the sense in which the blind lead the blind. . . . There has been a heavy pall of hush-hush imposed upon teachers, and the easy way for them, the way of inertia, has been to become yes men and women."

Dr. Dewey's cry for realism echoed again and again through the convention. None put the demand more strongly or with more knowledge of the cost than Jesse H. Newlon, who spoke on, "How Can the High School Stimulate the Intellectual Curiosity of American Youth?" "It may be dangerous," declared Dr. Newlon, "but we shall not measure up to our civic responsibilities unless we have the courage to meet this challenge. We are altogether more timid than the occasion warrants. Whatever may be the desires of the majority, there is a strong minority of liberal Americans who are ready to defend a school that dares to stimulate the intellectual curiosity of its pupils in the social realms."

This and many other addresses foreshadowed an extension of collegiate academic freedom down into the high schools. If listeners take seriously what many speakers advocated, a large crop of educational martyrs may be expected during the next few years, but the convention did nothing to guarantee the rescue of those whom it called on to welcome danger.

The frontal attack State Superintendent Butterfield, of Connecticut, made on ability grouping last year found new support this session from Dr. Henry Suzzallo and Professor James R. McGaughy, Teachers College, Columbia University. Dr. Roy O. Billett, of the National Survey of Secondary Education, however, found it, rightly or wrongly, one of the most widely used modes of providing for individual differences.

"It is probable," declared Dr. Suzzallo before the General Session, "that segregations of classes on the basis of ability will not be as popular as was once the case with us. The intellectual advantages have not proved to be as large as we had expected and the unsatisfactory emotional consequences have been far greater than we had anticipated. Probably a school class should be a society as mixed as cooperating groups are in life generally." Dr. McGaughy, in his address on "Fallacies in Homogeneous Grouping," challenged "any one to point out in real life, outside of our penal institutions, anything remotely approaching homogeneous grouping."

Large classes *versus* small classes became more of a rush than an argument. Principal William A. Wetzel, of Trenton Senior High School, predicted classes ranging from 150 down to 30. Superintendent M. R. Keyworth, Hamtramck, Michigan, speaking on

"Size of Classes and Teacher Load," held a similar point of view: "There is no available evidence to justify the small class. In 35 published experiments, 11 showed an advantage in larger classes, 20 revealed no differences in results, while only 4 showed the smaller classes as being superior." He adds, however, the significant comment, "In all these experiments the only measurement was that of subject-matter achievement." Assistant Superintendent McDade, of Chicago, took a middle position in this drift back toward Lancastrian class size, maintaining that there was no such thing as a standard class size. He told how Chicago has planned the new model elementary school for its World Fair to permit double classrooms for large classes and quarter size classrooms for small working groups. Increase of class size is apparently being widely accepted as a means of economizing. New methods which require a teacher to supervise learning instead of to teach students were used by many speakers to justify the change. One sour note in this chorus of larger classes appeared in a comment made at the board of consultants of the National Survey of School Finance that some parents in California, obviously dissatisfied with the effect of large classes, were themselves teaching their own children daily.

Differ violently as they did on these and numerous other policies, philosophies, methods and practices, practically all speakers were agreed that the schools should not be sacrificed on the grim altar of depression economy. The theme of "touch not a single bough" or if some boughs must be lopped, let us do the lopping, recurred again and again. Superintendents, depressed by demands for tax cuts, must have returned home with lighter hearts, because they carried with them a helpful word from President Herbert Hoover, the findings of their national committee on school costs, the solemn warnings of President Robert M. Hutchins and Dean Charles H. Judd, of the University of Chicago, Edwin C. Broome, superintendent, Philadelphia, and George D. Strayer, of Columbia University, and the comforting advice from many others that the blame for lack of funds could be laid chiefly on the taxing system.

Dean Judd, in a speech widely acclaimed, attacked the attackers:

> I confess that I am filled with resentment when I hear the criticisms of those who say that the American schools are failures. There are the smug exploiters of society who have been driving communities to the brink of ruin by their greed and self-seeking. They have refused to adopt new taxing systems. They have refused to study social movements. They have been parsimonious with the schools, and they have had the effrontery to pass adverse judgment on the experiments which the schools have been trying in the effort to prepare society for its new day. There are the exasperating critics who belong to our own fraternity, seekers after a little cheap notoriety, carping and complaining, but doing nothing to clarify the situation. If the worst that our critics say were true, there would still be ample ground for pride in what has been achieved.

That there may be another side to the question of economies in education during the depression was brought out by Dr. Robert M. Haig, professor of political economy, Columbia University, who, speaking before the superintendents for the first time since the last depression, repeated his warning of nine years ago, that a "tax system is not in itself productive in the economic sense. . . . At best, it is only a pump and a new pump is no cure for a dry well." Dr. Haig estimated that the "water" in the United States income well had dropped from 90 billions of dollars in 1929 to 50 billions in 1931. While holding out great hope for aid arising from improvement in taxation methods, he declared:

> If the present reduction in the social income persists for any considerable time, severe retrench-

ment in dollar outlay for education is inevitable. If the present level of prices persists for any considerable time, the maintenance of existing salary scales will amount to a substantial increase in compensation. In the course of any retrenchment which may be necessary, the intelligence and skill of the administrative officers of our school system must be exercised so as to preserve what is most valuable, and standards of compensation stand high in the scale. But this is no time for a truculent show of political power. Let me bespeak at this juncture a spirit of helpful cooperation with the harassed public official and the distressed taxpayer.

There were other important themes that ran through the convention. Miss Florence Hale, president of the National Education Association, made a strong plea that there be no retreat from the enriched curriculum. Dr. John H. Finley, of *The New York Times,* Lorado Taft, Walter Damrosch (paper read) and others reviewed the remarkable recent achievements of education in the arts and counseled further advance. Other speakers charted the progress of public education's endeavor to meet the health, leisure, creative and moral needs of the child in addition to his need for information and tool subjects.

Chief among the results of research and investigation reported to the convention was the two-year study of character education that went into the Department of Superintendence Yearbook on Character Education just released. It was evident from the interpretations by A. L. Threlkeld, superintendent, Denver, Colorado, *chairman;* Professor Frank N. Freeman; Mrs. John K. Norton, associate director of research, National Education Association, and Charles B. Glenn, superintendent, Birmingham, Alabama, that the compilers had walked a difficult path with great skill. Said Mrs. Norton:

Character education is not a program to be "put over," but an outcome of our philosophy of education, our school organization and supervision, our selection of curriculums, our methods of teaching, our skill in living with and guiding children, our ability to quicken and guide the growth of boys and girls. . . . The Yearbook recognizes master teachers as a guiding force. The teacher who has understanding of the complexity of modern life, courage to face its issues and faith in the possibilities which human personality has for growth will see to it that the school is always a place of growth.

Professor Arthur I. Gates, of Columbia University, announced that recent studies showed that new methods of teaching conventional subjects—reading, writing, spelling and arithmetic—reveal that improvements will produce an optimum degree of skill in a fraction of the time now required. Principal S. N. Ewan, Jr., of Lansdowne, Pennsylvania, and Professor T. C. Holy, of the Ohio State University, reported recent studies that indicate larger classes practicable. Earl W. Anderson, Bureau of Educational Research, Ohio State University, reviewing teacher supply and demand, said that 90 teacher training institutions reported placing only 42 to 75 per cent. of their 1931 graduates.

The rising tide of the Office of Education's contributions to the progress of education in the United States was clearly evident in the convention. More than 25 members of the regular and survey staffs participated in the programs. The end of the National Survey of Secondary Education in June was foreshadowed by many reports of preliminary findings reported by Dr. Koos and his assistants. Members of the National Surveys of Teacher Training and School Finance, respectively, reported progress and future plans. Each of the three survey groups held meetings of their consultant boards during the convention. U. S. Commissioner of Education William John Cooper spoke before the General Session on "The National Advisory Committee Report and the Office of Education," and Assistant Commissioner

Bess Goodykoontz addressed the Department of Supervisors and Instructors on "One Phase of Supervision in Progressive Schools."

The Office of Education also sponsored the first U. S. Government Educational Exhibit. Twenty government agencies which have special services, publications, maps, pictures or movies useful in schools revealed in displays that extended along the main corridor of the Interior Department, a distance of a city block, the many aids available to schools from Uncle Sam. In the hall also were drawings, photographs and specifications of 75 new outstanding elementary schools erected throughout the United States.

Commercial exhibits to the number of 372 packed the Washington Auditorium from cellar to garret. This, as ever, was one of the most interesting and profitable features of the convention. The Eastman Company was showing the new Washington film. Three other companies revealed remarkable progress within the year in improving talking picture equipment for school use. Harcourt, Brace and Company showed some alluring maps of English literature in connection with their book exhibit. Development of tests and measurements in education was reflected in numerous exhibits. Card forms for more complete child accounting are also appearing. Trends toward freeing classes of regimentation are conspicuous in new types of desks offered by supply houses. One of the most welcome newcomers was The Medici Prints. It is a pleasure to discover that drops in prices bring these splendid prints within the range of more schools.

Attendance, affected by the depression, fell off about 700 as compared with the Detroit meeting. Still greater decreases were noted among some of the other organizations meeting simultaneously.

Among the other organizations holding meetings during the week in Washington were the National Council of Education, the American Educational Research Association (which had a very full program), the Department of Elementary School Principals, the Department of Rural Education, the Department of Secondary School Principals, the Department of Supervisors and Directors of Instruction, the Department of Vocational Education, Municipal Normal School and Teachers College Section, the National Association of Deans of Women, the National Association of High School Inspectors and Supervisors, the National Council of Childhood Education, the National Council of State Superintendents and Commissioners of Education, the National Society for the Study of Education, the National Society of College Teachers of Education, the Department of Adult Education, the Department of Special Education, the American College Personnel Association, the National Academy of Visual Instruction, the National Advisory Committee on School Building Problems and the Department of Supervisors and Teachers of Home Economics.

To the newly elected president of the Department of Superintendence, Superintendent Milton C. Potter, of Milwaukee, President Hoover on the last day of the convention wrote:

I congratulate the Department of Superintendence of the National Education Association most cordially upon the success of its conference just closing in Washington, and the Nation upon the inspiration in the high service of education that flows out to the people from its deliberation. These serve again to remind our people that, however the national economy may vary or whatever fiscal adjustments may be made, the very first obligation upon the national resources is the undiminished financial support of the public schools. We can not afford to lose any ground in education. That is neither economy nor good government.

EDUCATIONAL EVENTS

SAVING ON LONDON EDUCATION

THE London *Times* reports that the Education Committee of the London County Council has considered estimates for the year 1932–33 submitted by the general purposes subcommittee. It is pointed out that the estimates have been prepared in circumstances of exceptional financial stringency. Under the National Economy Act, 1931, and the Order in Council of October last, the 50 per cent. Exchequer grant towards elementary education was withdrawn, and teachers' salaries were reduced by 10 per cent.

The problem in preparing the 1932–33 estimates was how to obviate throwing so large a burden on the rates while maintaining existing educational services. By stringent economy in every direction it had been possible to make a reduction of £1,539,939 in gross estimated expenditure compared with the estimates of 1931–32. That included £830,000 in respect of the 10 per cent. reduction in teachers' salaries. It did not, however, fully compensate for the loss of the Exchequer grant. This grant had been reduced by £1,898,180 (1932–33), leaving an additional burden on the rates of £353,216. If no savings had been effected apart from the 10 per cent. reduction in teachers' salaries the additional burden on the rates, as compared with 1931–32, would have been some £900,000.

Of the estimated total expenditure of £14,307,054 in 1931–32, the salaries of teachers (including superannuation contributions) (£8,332,000) and staff (£1,645,000) accounted for £9,977,000. Of the remainder certain items, such as rates and taxes and insurance (£385,000), debt charges (£802,000), superannuation and provident fund and pensions (£185,000), could not be reduced by the Education Committee. The subcommittee proceeded to estimate for an expenditure of £12,767,115, compared with £14,307,054 in 1931–32. Of the former sum £9,025,510 is for elementary education, £3,036,025 for higher education, and £705,580 for general and special county and public assistance accounts. The ratepayers will have to find altogether £7,768,455, compared with £7,415,239 last year. The percentage to be borne by the ratepayers in 1932–33 will be 61 per cent., against 52 per cent. in 1931–32; by the Exchequer 35 per cent., against 44 per cent. last year, and other receipts 4 per cent. in each year.

Apart from the 10 per cent. reduction in teachers' salaries; £90,425 is saved by economies in staffing; £331,135 by general economies, mainly in materials, and £175,790 from minor alterations. Against reductions, which total £1,554,190, are set unavoidable increases amounting to £50,980, leaving the net decrease £1,503,210.

The expenditure on education in London, which in 1904–05 was only £4,307,630, rose to nearly £10,000,000 in 1919–20, became £14,175,000 in 1921–22, fell to £12,078,000 in the following year, and had risen again to £14,307,054 last year. The ratepayers, who contributed £2,792,422 in 1904–05, will next year, as already stated, pay £7,768,455.

COLLEGE FINANCES

THE Commission on Permanent and Trust Funds of the Association of American Colleges made a report at the educational meetings in Cincinnati based upon a review of a study made by that commission of college finances for the two years 1929–1930 and 1930–1931, with a comparison of results and figures. The salient facts brought out by the commission are as follows:

The worst of the depression had not struck the colleges before the close of the fiscal year ending in the summer of 1931. Doubtless the fall and winter brought more discouraging and depressing effects upon income and capital than appeared in the preceding year.

Reports from 277 institutions showed that the diminution of income between the two years compared are from 5.26 per cent. to 5.06 per cent., practically one fourth of one per cent. The colleges were divided geographically into five groups—the New England, Atlantic, Southern, Middle Western and Far Western districts. The largest default in interest and in principal was shown to be in the Southern and Mid-Western areas, where colleges had invested their funds more largely in real estate and mortgages. In the other areas, where bonds, preferred and common stocks were more in evidence in the portfolio of the institutions, the defaults and losses were less. The far western states, including Montana, Idaho, Colorado, Utah, New Mexico and the Pacific slope, had no default whatever in common stocks, although their holding of common stocks was more than 12 per cent. of their total invested funds.

Of all the colleges reporting, 49.26 per cent. of the investments are in bonds, 21.7 per cent. in mortgages, 10.4 per cent. in real estate, 5.13 per cent. in common stocks, 5.6 per cent. in preferred stocks, 5.6 per cent. in miscellaneous holdings and less than 1 per cent. in notes.

Receipts from tuition in most of the institutions had increased. Of 227 colleges reporting this item, 127 showed a decided increase, 29 reported a practically static condition, and 71 showed some decrease of receipts for tuition.

Gifts reported from the areas for running expenses, permanent improvements, capital and other purposes during the last of the two fiscal years, were in the New England states $3,809,-007, in the Atlantic states $33,626,892, in the Southern states $4,401,772, in the Mid-Western states $10,627,500, and in the Far Western states $2,335,774, making an aggregate sum of $54,800,945.

While these figures represent a cross section of the country as a whole, and show that no alarming misfortunes had fallen upon the financial structure of the colleges as a whole, yet certain single individual institutions came to the attention of the commission. One college, for example, had mortgaged its entire property, sold bonds secured by the mortgage and had consumed the proceeds of the bonds in debts and running expenses, and yet this institution was not reported as about to close its doors. Despite the fact that interest on the bonds was in default, the holders of the bonds had no disposition to foreclose the mortgage because a college campus and buildings have little marketable value. Furthermore, the institution may run by resources drawn from (a) teachers who may work for little or nothing; (b) students whose tuition fees may carry along at least major interests, and (c) supplementary gifts sufficient to keep the wolf from the door while not closing the door permanently. Since this concrete instance was reported, the name of another institution in a similar condition has been reported to the committee and indications have been given that yet two other institutions are in a similar plight.

Information came to the attention of the commission which showed that two colleges had actually profited by the depression. One, with $600,000 already in hand and about to build, expected to expend the entire sum upon a new building, then found that contracts could be and were written for less than $500,000. Another institution with a building to erect which was supposed to cost $250,000 or perhaps as much as $300,000, found this building could be built for less than $200,000.

THE EMPLOYMENT OF CHILDREN

MRS. CLARA M. BEYER, director of the Industrial Division of the Department of Labor's Women's Bureau, in a statement issued by the bureau, gives the facts in regard to the employment of children during the depression, which are printed in the *United States Daily*.

In September and October of the past year, 5,549 boys and girls of 14 and 15 took out their first working papers in New York City alone. In Philadelphia the corresponding figure for September was 1,182.

The 1930 census shows for the 18 states and the District of Columbia, for which figures are available, a total of 102,503 children 14 and 15 years of age at work, a decrease of 22 per cent. as compared with 1920 figures. The number of employed children 16 and 17 years of age was 231,322, or 5 per cent. less than in 1920. The children between 10 and 14 years of age in these states (75,649), who, according to all our standards should not be at work at all, have decreased 42 per cent.

The 178,152 children between the age of 10 and 15, inclusive, reported as gainfully employed in 1930 constitute one out of every 12 children of this group in the 18 states and the District of Columbia, for which information was available. Of the boys and girls 14 and 15 years old in these states, 1 out of 7 was employed, and of the 16 and 17, 1 out of 3.

These figures are incomplete and are not to be regarded as a reliable basis for an estimate for the country as a whole. They show, however, that in a large group of states, and these do not include large industrial states like Pennsylvania and New York, employment of children is still a serious problem.

Not only are large numbers of young persons employed—many more are out of school. The last census statistics of school attendance, which are complete for all the states, show that more than 1,300,000 boys and girls of school age—7 to 15, inclusive—were not enrolled in any school during the school year 1929–1930. In addition, nearly 2,000,000 of their brothers and sisters of 16 and 17 had already severed their school connections.

Laying aside consideration of the 800,000 children from 7 to 13, inclusive, who were not attending school—a number somewhat disconcerting in view of the theory that all our children have the advantage of schooling at least up to 14, 2,500,000 boys and girls, 14, 15, 16 and 17 years of age, are missing the chance for education in these most impressionable and most difficult years.

In addition, nearly 2,000,000 of their brothers and sisters of 16 and 17 have severed their school connections. One child in 12 between the ages of 10 and 15 in 18 states was employed at the time of the census, while one in 7 was employed between the ages of 14 and 15. One in 3 between the ages of 16 and 17 was at work in those states.

PSYCHOLOGICAL TESTS TO DETERMINE THE EFFECTIVENESS OF THE TALKING PICTURE

A SERIES of extensive experimental psychological tests to determine the effectiveness of the talking picture as a supplementary aid in education were inaugurated in February in a large number of the public schools of New York City; Camden and Elizabeth, New Jersey; Schenectady, New York, and Baltimore, Maryland. The tests involve 2,538 pupils and 64 teachers and will extend over a period of eight weeks.

The testing programs are being administered by the local school authorities in each city. The pictures and the tests were developed by a group of educational research specialists of the educational department of Electrical Research Products, headed by Colonel Frederick L. Devereux, general manager.

Pupils of the fifth and seventh grade levels are being given the tests, 1,190 of the former and 1,348 of the latter. In each course studied five thirty-minute periods of instruction are given in two weeks. Pupils participating are evenly divided into two groups, one forming the control group, the other the experimental. The control group receives instruction in the courses studied with every modern means of instruction available to the teachers and pupils, with the exception of talking pictures. The experimental group receives similar instruction in the same subjects and for the same length of time with the inclusion of educational talking pictures based on the courses.

Following the period of instruction, each group will be tested with the same questions covering the subject-matter in which instruction was given. Comparison of the results achieved by each group should indicate the measure of effectiveness of the talking picture as a medium of education.

Eight pictures are being used in the experiment. For the seventh-grade experimental groups four pictures designed for use in music appreciation courses, "The String Choir," "The Woodwinds," "The Brass Choir," and "The Percussion Group," are being used. The fifth grade experimental groups are being shown four natural science films, "The Frog," "Butterflies," "Beetles" and "Plant Growth."

A group of research students from Columbia University, now receiving special training for the work, will score the test papers. Two years of preliminary research work by the Research Department, during which more than 2,000 pupils were involved have been devoted merely to preparing the tests, which are said to have reliability coefficients ranging from 86 to 95.

THE ALLEGANY SCHOOL OF NATURAL HISTORY

THE sixth season of the Allegany School of Natural History in Allegany State Park opens on July 5 and closes on August 24. This "Summer School in the Forest" is conducted by the Buffalo Society of Natural Sciences in cooperation with the New York State Museum and is affiliated with the University of Buffalo from which its students receive college credit. Registration should be made with Harold T. Clement, curator of education at the Buffalo Museum of Science, or Dr. R. E. Coker, director of the Allegany School of Natural History, Box 950, Chapel Hill, North Carolina.

Courses will be given in field zoology by Dr. Robert E. Coker, professor of zoology, University of North Carolina; in field geology by Frederick T. Thwaites, lecturer in geology at the University of Wisconsin; in field botany by Dr. Robert B. Gordon, instructor in botany at the Ohio State University; in the Natural History of Birds by Aretas A. Saunders, teacher of biology in the Central High School, Bridgeport, Connecticut, and in nature study by Mr. William P. Alexander, field naturalist and assistant curator of education at the Buffalo Museum of Science.

The Allegany School of Natural History is nine miles from Quaker Bridge, New York, and well above it, being situated on a hillside bordering Quaker Run in its upper part at an altitude of about 1,900 feet. It is a feature of the setting of the School in Allegany State Park that within an area of some 65,000 acres under the care of the state much of the wild life is protected, and so one may occasionally see in wild state bear, deer, raccoon and porcupine, besides observing daily the abundant smaller mammals—squirrels, chipmunks, field mice and, less frequently, jumping mice, shrews, weasels, mink and others. There are few places, in fact, where small animals in great variety can be so readily observed or collected. Nor are there many sites in which nature can be studied at such close contact.

Teachers in public schools and colleges, particularly those who have had little opportunity for field studies, university and college students, scout and camp leaders of various kinds, young and amateur naturalists, and those interested in the nature work of museums, public forests and parks, are expected to find in the Allegany School of Natural History "the opportunity to broaden their experience, advance their training and receive fresh stimulus."

THE CLEVELAND NATIONAL CONFERENCE OF MUSIC SUPERVISORS

FIVE thousand teachers and supervisors of public school music, and others interested in music education, will be in Cleveland from April 3 to 8, to attend the Music Supervisors National Conference. This is the silver anniversary of the organization which was founded twenty-five years ago in Keokuk, Iowa.

In addition to the 5,000 teachers and supervisors expected at this meeting there will be 700 high-school boys and girls who will constitute the national high school orchestra and chorus. Students from thirty-one states, Porto Rico and Alaska already have signed up for these groups. They will arrive in Cleveland, on Sunday, April 3, and will rehearse every morning, afternoon and evening until the gala concert at the public auditorium, on Friday of that week.

Teachers attending the convention have certain aims they wish to further. One of the most important is the continuance of music interest after the student leaves school. Amateur groups of instrumentalists and vocalists should, it is held, be encouraged to continue their music after they are graduated.

School bands, teachers' orchestras, singers and all manner of music will be presented. Among well-known musicians and educators going to Cleveland will be: Dr. John Erskine, of the Juilliard School of Music and Columbia University; F. Melius Christiansen, director of St. Olaf's Choir; Mr. Eugene Gossens, conductor of the Cincinnati Symphony; Mr. Ernest Fowles, music critic and lecturer of London; Dr. Peter W. Dykema, professor of music, Teachers College, Columbia University; Taylor Branson, conductor, U. S. Marine Band; Mr. Joy Elmer Morgan, editor of the *Journal* of the National Education Association; Dr. Thomas Briggs, of Teachers College, Columbia University, and Dr. Howard Hanson, director, Eastman School of Music, Rochester, N. Y.

COMMITTEES OF THE AMERICAN LIBRARY ASSOCIATION

MR. SYDNEY B. MITCHELL, director of the School of Librarianship of the University of California, has been appointed chairman of a preliminary committee of the American Library Association for Research Studies, Surveys and Special Projects. The need for a committee which should consider and recommend research projects, and through library schools and other channels foster and develop interest in research, has grown out of several recent developments in library work. The establishment of advanced graduate library schools, of *The Library Quar-*

terly and the gradually increasing interest of the library profession in research have indicated the usefulness of the present committee whose task will be to consider the desirability of a permanent committee, and to define its methods of operation and functions. The personnel of the preliminary committee on research studies include the following librarians: George F. Bowerman, District of Columbia Public Library; Harold F. Brigham, the Public Library of Louisville, Ky.; Carleton B. Joeckel, department of library science, University of Michigan; Charles H. Brown, Iowa State College Library; Adam Strohm, Detroit Public Library; H. M. Lydenberg, assistant director, New York Public Library; Douglas Waples, Graduate Library School, University of Chicago; C. C. Williamson, director of the School of Library Service, Columbia University; Louis R. Wilson, of the University of North Carolina; Eleanor M. Witmer, Teachers College Library, Columbia University, and P. L. Windsor, University of Illinois.

A temporary committee has been appointed to consider the matter of a board which should act in an advisory capacity to a department of library work with children in and out of school, which it is the purpose of the association to establish at its headquarters. The committee has been chosen as follows: Grace D. Rose, librarian, Morristown, N. J.; Anne Carroll Moore, superintendent, work with children, New York Public Library; Mary S. Wilkinson, director of work with children, Enoch Pratt Free Library, Baltimore; Mabel Williams, supervisor of work with schools, New York Public Library, and Eleanor M. Witmer, librarian, Teachers College Library, Columbia University.

Mr. Donald B. Gilchrist, librarian of the University of Rochester, has been appointed chairman of a College Advisory Board whose duties will be to prepare for the council of the American Library Association a statement as to college library services which might be performed at the headquarters of the American Library Association. It is intended that this statement shall be based on one prepared by Mr. Francis L. Goodrich, librarian of the College of the City of New York while chairman of the college and reference section of the American Library Association. Mr. Gilchrist has been asked to serve for a period of five years.

Other librarians of the College Advisory Board with the term of their services are: William W. Bishop, University of Michigan (one year); Fanny Borden, Vassar College (two years); Charles H. Brown, Iowa State College Library (three years), and Julian S. Fowler, Oberlin College (four years).

The 1932 midwinter meeting of the American Library Association will be held in Chicago.

IN HONOR OF SEBASTIEN CHARLÉTY

THE degree of doctor of laws was conferred in camera by Columbia University on February 29 on Dr. Sebastien Charléty, rector of the University of Paris, and the degree of doctor of letters on Dr. Gerhart Hauptmann, poet and dramatist. Professor Howard Lee McBain, dean of the Graduate Faculties of Columbia University, in presenting Dr. Charléty for the degree spoke in part as follows:

Out of the dim years of the early twelfth century there still shine down to us luminous shafts of the intellectual quickening which then stirred in the City of Paris. It was the era of the magnetic teaching of the renowned dialectician, the dynamic and tempestuous Peter Abelard. Throughout all the world ran the fame of the church school that nestled in the shadow of Nôtre Dame and of the schools that he founded upon the Montagne Ste. Geneviève. Out of this intellectual awakening, out of these schools on the Île de la Cité and the left bank of the Seine there emerged around the middle of that far-off century the great University of Paris.

Then, as now, scholars were the university. Then, as now, students came in thousands from near and distant lands to be touched, to be taught, to be fired by living scholars. Over a splendid company of such scholars the distinguished guest from France whom we honor here to-day now presides.

Though not as old as the university itself, the office of recteur is none the less of very ancient origin. The name of him whom we now celebrate adds the luster of a brilliant career to a long list of illustrious predecessors.

In conferring the degree President Nicholas Murray Butler said:

Born at Chambery, in Savoy; always eager scholar in the field of history; successful administrator of education in succession at the University of Lyons, in Tunis and in Alsace-Lorraine; serving since 1927 in the distinguished post of rector of the ancient University of Paris, which for some eight centuries has been a gladly accepted leader of the world's learning; historian and interpreter of the life of modern France; outstanding representative of the culture and public service of her people, I gladly admit you to the degree of doctor of laws.

EDUCATIONAL NOTES AND NEWS

SUPERINTENDENT MILTON C. POTTER, of Milwaukee, has been elected president at the Washington meeting of the Department of Superintendence of the National Education Association to succeed Superintendent Edwin C. Broome, of Philadelphia.

DR. WILLIAM SCOTT GRAY, professor of education and dean of the College of Education of the University of Chicago, was elected president of the American Educational Research Association at the Washington meeting. He succeeds Dr. John L. Stenquist, director of research in the Baltimore schools.

DR. C. J. GALPIN, in charge of the division of farm population and rural life in the Bureau of Agricultural Economics, was elected president of the American Sociological Society at the recent annual meeting.

MR. ELWOOD W. SHAFER, principal of the Riverhead, New York, High School, was elected president of the Associated Academic Principals at the annual meeting which was held recently at Syracuse.

A TESTIMONIAL dinner in honor of Mr. James J. Colgate was given on February 25 under the auspices of the New York district of the Colgate University Alumni Corporation to celebrate Mr. Colgate's fifty years of association with the university as student, alumnus and patron. Messages were received from Mr. Hoover and from Chief Justice Charles Evans Hughes. Mr. Colgate inherited his position of patron to the university as the son of James B. Colgate and the grandson of William Colgate.

DR. ALLEN WINTER ROWE, director of research at Evans Memorial, Massachusetts Memorial Hospital, and professor of physiological chemistry in Boston University School of Medicine, has been nominated for president of the Alumni Association of the Massachusetts Institute of Technology for the term beginning in June, when Mr. Bradley Dewey will retire.

MR. DAVID J. MALCOLM, superintendent of schools in Clarksburg, Monroe, Florida and Savoy, Massachusetts, has been made a trustee of the Massachusetts State College.

THE REV. A. T. P. WILLIAMS, head master of Winchester College, England, has been elected a member of the Athenaeum under the provisions of the rule of the club which empowers the annual election by the committee of three persons of distinguished eminence in science, literature, the arts, or for public services.

MR. P. E. MEADON, the director of education for Lancashire, England, has been invited by the governing body of Columbia University to deliver a course of lectures upon the organization and administration of education in England.

THE REV. A. SIDNEY LOVETT has been appointed chaplain of Yale University. He is now pastor of the Mount Vernon Church, Boston. Mr. Lovett succeeds the Rev. Elmore M. McKee, who resigned last year to become rector of Trinity Episcopal Church in Buffalo.

DEAN PARVIN WITTE, for eleven years head of the College of Fine Arts of Nebraska Wesleyan University, will retire at the close of the academic year.

PROFESSOR DONALD P. COTTRELL, of Teachers College, Columbia University, has visited the University of Maine to confer with officers of the university and certain faculty committees with reference to a program which is now under way for the improvement of instruction in the university. The program calls for the special counsel of Professor Cottrell over a period of two years.

PROFESSOR GEORGE D. STRAYER, of Teachers College, Columbia University, has announced the staff of the Chicago School Survey to include the following from the staff of the college: Professors E. S. Evenden, J. R. McGaughy, Jesse H. Newlon, Carter Alexander, Jesse F.

Williams, Paul R. Mort, H. B. Bruner, John K. Norton, E. H. Reeder, L. Thomas Hopkins, F. B. O'Rear, W. S. Elsbree, Jean Betzner, and Dr. F. W. Maroney. In addition the staff will include: Professor Frank W. Hart, of the University of California; Professor Fred Engelhardt, of the University of Minnesota; Mr. George A. Womrath, business superintendent of the Minneapolis Public Schools; Professor W. W. Wright, of the University of Indiana; Mr. Milo Stuart, assistant superintendent of schools at Indianapolis; Professor D. H. Eikenberry, of the Ohio State University, and Dr. L. A. Wilson, assistant commissioner for vocational education in the New York State Department of Education.

Dr. James W. Norman, dean of the College of Education of the University of Florida and for eleven successive years dean of the summer session, has been granted three months leave of absence. Dr. T. McN. Simpson, head of the department of mathematics, has been appointed director of the summer session.

Professor J. J. Findlay, professor of education at the University of Manchester from 1903 until 1925 and author of numerous publications on education, is visiting the United States.

Dr. Elmer Ellsworth Brown, chancellor of New York University, sailed on March 4 for a six-weeks stay in Europe.

Professor George H. Blakeslee, Frank B. Weeks, visiting professor at Wesleyan University, has been appointed by the United States Government a special assistant to the American Legation at Peiping, to assist in the present Far Eastern crisis, and particularly to be available for assistance to General McCoy, the American member of the League Commission of Inquiry. Professor Blakeslee sailed for Peiping at the end of February.

Dr. Frederic T. Blanchard, professor of English and chairman of the department of English at the University of California at Los Angeles, has returned after a half-year leave of absence during which he did research work in Europe.

Dr. Clarence Cook Little, director of the Roscoe B. Jackson Memorial Laboratory at Bar Harbor, Maine, and formerly president of the University of Michigan, will be the speaker at the commencement exercises of the University of New Hampshire.

Dr. Ralph C. Hutchison, the newly elected president of Washington and Jefferson College, addressed more than one hundred and fifty members of the Washington and Jefferson Alumni Association of New York on February 29 at the Century Club.

Dr. Albert Bushnell Hart, professor emeritus of history at Harvard University and historian of the George Washington Bicentennial Commission, was the principal speaker at the three-day bicentennial celebration at Syracuse University.

Dr. Edward M. Lewis, president of the University of New Hampshire, attended the meeting of the executive committee of the New England Association of Colleges and Secondary Schools at Boston on February 26. On the following day he spoke to a gathering of the Manchester-New Hampshire Rotary. An address to the University Club of Stamford, Connecticut, was delivered on March 4, and the following day Dr. Lewis attended a meeting of the New England Council at Hartford.

Robert Lincoln Kelly, president of Earlham College, 1902–17, and now permanent secretary of the Association of American Colleges and the Council of Church Boards of Education, has been invited to speak on the program of the World's Conference of Educational Associations at Honolulu, Hawaii, in July; to deliver the oration at the annual dinner of the Phi Beta Kappa Chapter in Cincinnati, Ohio, and to give the address at the annual dinner of the American Association of Military Colleges and Schools at Washington, D. C., on "Vitalizing the Military College Curriculum."

Fred Herbert Dodge, director of physical education at Rutgers University since 1898, died on February 20 at the age of seventy-two years.

Harold Barnes, since 1911 supervising principal of elementary and junior high-school education at Girard College, Philadelphia, died on February 26 at the age of sixty-four years.

Daniel Webster Abercrombie, teacher of

Latin and Greek and principal of Worcester Academy, Massachusetts, from 1882 until his retirement as emeritus principal in 1918, died on February 24 in his seventy-ninth year.

EMMIT M. SIPPLE, for seven years advisory director of the Park School, Baltimore, and treasurer of the Progressive Education Association, died suddenly on February 22 at the age of fifty-three years.

FERDINAND BUISSON, one of the founders of the third French Republic's free public-school system and a former director in the primary instruction division of the Ministry of Education, died on February 16 at the age of ninety-one years.

THE second General Congress on Child Welfare will be held in Geneva, Switzerland, from July 18 to 21. The first congress was held in 1925, with over a thousand in attendance from fifty-two different countries.

AN institute of Adult Education will be held in Spokane, Washington, from April 6 to 8, under the auspices of the Inland Empire Education Association.

THE School Board of Cleveland has voted to discontinue all summer school classes to enable it to make a saving of $185,000.

THE Education Board of Atlanta, Georgia, has adopted a budget providing for a ten per cent. pay cut for employees paid less than $100 and sixteen per cent. for others, thus assuring funds for teachers' salaries unpaid since January 1.

THE will of the late Dr. William H. Nichols has been appraised and it is announced that half the residuary estate (less certain legacies) bequeathed to New York University amounts to $3,670,401. Other bequests amounting to $795,000 include $250,000 to the Polytechnic Institute, Brooklyn, and $50,000 to the American Chemical Society.

THE *World-Telegram* reports that bills pending in the New York State legislature to increase school attendance requirements have been disapproved by the New York Board of Education. These bills would have (1) raised the minimum age for obtaining working papers to 16; (2) increased hours of required attendance at continuation school from four to eight a week; (3) allowed minors to substitute evening school for continuation school attendance. The board also went on record against bills making the State Education Commissioner the final resort of appeal from decisions of the Teachers' Retirement Board, requiring teachers to be residents of New York State, lowering the restrictions on use of school buildings after school hours and eliminating charges to organizations using the buildings. It also opposed a bill providing for the election, instead of appointment, of members of the Board of Education.

IT is reported that on account of lack of funds, the Institute of Law at the Johns Hopkins University, founded four years ago, may be discontinued. The institute has never had an endowment but has been supported by gifts received from time to time. Funds, however, will be exhausted at the end of the present college year and unless further gifts are forthcoming soon, the institute will have to operate at a deficit. This deficit, it is said, would have to be paid out of the operating expenses of the rest of the university and so result in the curtailment of other work, or be carried as a debt against unrestricted endowment funds of the university.

PRESIDENT JAMES L. MCCONAUGHY, of Wesleyan University, speaking before a gathering of alumni on February 27, reported that the business depression has not had a marked effect at Wesleyan University. Larger gifts for current income have been received this year than in any recent year, and instead of decreasing expenditures, increases amounting to $25,000 are to be made in professors' salaries. The faculty and student body are the largest in history, although about one third of the undergraduates have applied for scholarships and loans. $200,000 was expended for buildings in 1931 and the endowment was increased more than $150,000. The expenditures in 1931 were greater than the previous year, but the total income was decreased by only about $3,000.

VASSAR COLLEGE maintained its sound financial condition and increased its student fund last year by $36,500, according to a report to the alumnae association by President Henry Noble MacCracken. The budget for 1931–32 was increased by $53,000 to an aggregate of $570,000 and the number of the faculty remained the same. The pension system would continue, the maintenance program being carried out and the wages of the working staff would be unchanged. Student aid for the past year aggregated $160,000, and assistance was given to 28 per cent. of the students.

ON January 2, the University of Würzburg celebrated its three hundred and fiftieth anniversary. The university was established in 1402 but was closed in 1413 and was not reopened until January 2, 1582. In contrast with most other schools of higher learning that were the outgrowth of the Reformation, this university was designed as a stronghold of Catholicism. The university retained its ecclesiastical character until the end of the eighteenth century. When, however, in 1803, it came under the control of Bavaria, it took on a more liberal character.

THE formal celebration of the fiftieth anniversary of the foundation of the University College of Liverpool was held on December 18, 1931, the Chancellor (Lord Derby) presiding over the degree ceremony at St. George's Hall. An address of commemoration was delivered by the vice-chancellor, Dr. Hetherington, and the principal, Canon Rendall, gave a formal recital of the long roll of nearly sixty benefactors to whom the college and the university owed so much of their material existence. In his address the vice-chancellor said that the University of Liverpool could trace its real origin to the foundation of a medical school in the town in the earlier part of the eighteenth century. The school was able to conduct official examinations, and there was certainly organized medical teaching in the city before 1800. By 1900 there were nearly 600 students, and in 1903, when the college became an independent university, it had 645 day students. The students now numbered 2,200, and the annual expenditure was over £200,000.

A HIGHER institute of physical education has been organized as a department of the faculty of medicine at each of the two government universities at Ghent and at Liége, Belgium, respectively. The degrees of licentiate of physical education, agrégé of physical education, and doctor of physical education are conferred.

IT is announced in the London *Times* that the members of the Royal Society of Teachers will presently proceed to the quinquennial election of the Teachers' Registration Council, a body created by Parliament with authority to form and keep a Register of Teachers. The council has laid down conditions of admission, covering attainments, professional training and experience, and all teachers admitted to registration thereby attain professional standing. By command of the King, the whole body of registered teachers is now known as the Royal Society of Teachers, and members are entitled to use the designation, M.R.S.T.

A SURVEY of education in the Province of Ontario is being sponsored by the Ontario Men Teachers' Federation. One of the problems to be undertaken will be the overburdening of pupils with activities creeping into the school system. The survey will probably take two years to complete, when its findings and representations will be presented to the Department of Education.

A UNITED PRESS dispatch from Brazil states that the Minister of Education, Dr. Francisco Campos, has informed the Foreign Ministry that he was ready to sponsor a cultural interchange between Italy and Brazil which would include scholarships for Italian students. Free transportation will be given to Italian students aboard Brazilian boats, according to the plan. Teaching of Italian in official educational institutions in Rio de Janeiro, Sao Paulo, Porto Alegre and Bello Horizonte, is included.

DISCUSSION

AN IMMEDIATE PROBLEM

EDUCATION is an optimistic profession. We speak in our educational researches, journals and books only of those pupils with whom we have succeeded. The failures are relegated into the limbo of the maladjusted. With these nothing is to be done beside keeping them in the warm school away from outside mischief and from under their parents' feet, and occasionally sending them down to be examined by the school expert in mental hygiene. At these pupils we shrug our shoulders, thereby confessing the failure of the school to cope with extraordinary conditions and to correct the deficiencies of the home environment.

In the average high school the teacher soon gives up the attempt to impart knowledge to such pupils and concentrates on bridling their unruly spirits, preventing them from throwing spitballs, erasers and other projectiles, and from annihilating one another with the bare fist. The teacher must also be concerned with the probability that they will contaminate the well-behaved.

Imagine teaching the intricacies of Latin syntax to a class of forty Marx Brothers, each a specialist in his own particular brand of monkey business and loudly appreciative of the performances of his "brothers." With such, the ordinary recourse to sending home for the parents has long since been tried and found useless. The parent, needless to say, shrugs his shoulders, too, and there the matter ends. If we, the teacher and the parent, resign—as we must—for the boy can not be expelled, his madness is reaffirmed. He glories in the evident discomfiture of his teachers and parents and regards the incident as an official imprimatur to his badness. At least, he is recognized as being a hopeless case and it becomes a matter of pride to maintain the desperate position. Providing he does not go too far, the run of the school or the special annex to which such pupils may be sent is his.

And now for some actual examples. Take the sturdy, colored six-footer whose canary-whistle is the delight of the study-room. In the same room we have a specialist in barnyard noises and a ventriloquist whose *forte* is impressions of angry dogs and love-sick cats—not to forget the young kleptomaniac who must be made to surrender at the end of each period the chalk and erasers he has managed to purloin in the course of the hour. Truly, Topaze's torture was a pin-prick compared to the pain of one who supervises such a room! None of these antics warrants expulsion, even though they continue to be performed term after term, in the same progress grade.

In the case of confirmed truants, after ten cents a week has been wasted on them for ten weeks in the form of absentee postal cards and telephone calls, and after the truant officer has spent three weeks rounding up the neighborhood Loew theaters, a lenient judge, eyeing the disproportionate sizes of the burly attendance officer and the shrinking culprit with his mother crying behind him, permits himself an *obiter dictum* on the school's lack of sympathy for these poor, misunderstood children and discharges the case with a warning. And there is something to be said for the judge!

Undoubtedly, one of the causes of this situation is the degeneration of the home brought about by unemployment. The father has been gradually losing the little control he had over his children, and his continued presence in the home leads to the usual contempt a family feels for a bread winner who fails to win bread. At the same time, the parent, conscious of his own plight, does not bother the boy to seek a job that does not exist for him or for anybody else. In other words, these times of unemployment and hunger increase the burden of the school, which is turned into an asylum for the boys who would normally work after completing the elementary school course. The result is that the dreaded problems of the continuation schools are now piling up on the high schools.

For such boys we have neither effective curriculum nor proper educational equipment. They do not belong in an academic environment. Nor will they learn bookkeeping and typewriting. What remains for them is the vocational school and a gymnasium in which to play ball. If those whose business it is to supervise a vocational school tell us that just as much brains are required to make a good mechanic as is necessary to conjugate the verb "avoir," we shall be first to agree. But the condition we are faced with is not so much to turn out model mechanics as to give these so-called "maladjusted" boys an opportunity to work off their tremendous vitality, even if it consists only in donning a "monkey" suit and lugging pig-iron castings up and down the stairs until they drop exhausted when the final bell rings. If in the four years they learn only the rudiments of a trade, the school will have been of some material assistance to them. The school will have done something to prepare them for practical living.

It must be understood that we are no longer preparing every Tom, Dick and Harry to become a doctor or a lawyer. We must accept in education the conclusions Frederick Taylor found in industry; that we have various types of mentality among which the "ox-type" is frequently to be met. For such the education of the muscles precedes that of the mind. During the last twenty years, we have been thinking primarily in terms of college-entrance and secretarial courses. In the next five years, we must hastily recast our planning and make provision for an unprecedented demand for vocational schools to accommodate the new influx of pupils. We must accept our pupils for what they are and cope with the problem, not from our knowledge of the past development of our high schools, but from the costly lessons that have followed our failure to plan for the future of the raw material entering our schools. Education in the past has been entirely too willing to follow catastrophe; it should occasionally anticipate it.

JULIAN ARONSON
F. K. LANE HIGH SCHOOL,
BROOKLYN, N. Y.

SPECIAL CORRESPONDENCE

THE NEW COLLEGE PLAN OF THE UNIVERSITY OF CHICAGO IN OPERATION

OUR new college plan has been in operation four months. Though definitive judgments can not be made at this time, those of us most vitally concerned with the plan in operation have found much of interest and value in the reports from members of the instructional staff, from student advisers and from staff members of the health service, who have daily contacts with many students individually. These reports indicate student reactions quite accurately and make possible some comparisons and contrasts between conditions under the old plan and conditions as they now seem to be shaping under the new plan.

During the first three weeks of last October more of our students were confused and uncertain about what they were doing than during the corresponding period in previous years; in each succeeding week the number of such students became steadily less among those interviewed, and by the end of December the number and percentage of students not satisfactorily oriented seemed to be no greater than under the old plan at the corresponding date. Furthermore, the number of students who were positively enthusiastic about their work was greater than under the old plan. Thus, as far as the orientation of our students into their college life and work is concerned, the dark side of the picture seems to be no darker, while the bright side seems to be brighter.

Each week of operation of the new plan seems to add preceptibly to the number of students and faculty members who are enthusiastic in their praise of the basic features of the new plan and the accompanying results. Faculty members, relieved of police duties, are studying more critically than ever before the effectiveness of their different types of instructional methods and efforts. Students, given increased responsibility for their own education, with their attention directed solely to educational opportunities rather than to compulsory disciplinary devices, are working harder and more effectively, are reading more books with greater profit, are attending classes faithfully and more purposefully, are interested in tests, quizzes and examinations for instructional purposes rather than for marks, and are learning how to work effectively much earlier in their college career than under the old plan.

Since faculty members and advisers are interested in doing all that they can to assist the student who is vitally interested in his own educational advancement, and since our freshmen under the new plan are showing more intellectual curiosity and more concern about their own intellectual development than was the case under the old plan, this year's freshmen are provided classroom activities better designed and conducted with greater verve and enthusiasm, and find more individual attention available whenever they need or desire it, than were ever before provided under our old plan.

Of course we have a small minority of students who have interpreted freedom to mean license without responsibilities. These students are being informed that we shall not permit the standard for satisfactory completion of the college requirements to be lowered by the failure of a minority to realize their responsibilities in a cooperative undertaking.

Though we have already changed some details of our plan as a result of experience in operation, and shall continuously be ready to change details in the light of experience, our experience to date has converted our previous belief into a conviction that the basic features of the new plan are soundly conceived and eminently practicable.

That the distinguishing features of our new educational program are attractive to a highly desirable type of student is testified by the fact that the scores on scholastic aptitude tests, the reports from the health service staff and the opinions expressed by faculty members show that this year's freshmen have higher intellectual capacity, are better specimens of humanity physically, and are more attractive beings socially than any previous entering class.

C. S. BOUCHER

DEAN OF THE COLLEGE,
UNIVERSITY OF CHICAGO

BOOKS FOR BOYS AND GIRLS

DR. EDWIN D. STARBUCK, director of character research in the school of philosophy, University of Southern California, announces the completion of a book including short summaries of 647 biographies for juveniles, Volume III of a series of eight "Guides to Books for Character."

Cooperation of thousands of Los Angeles high-school students made possible a practical test of the biographies selected by a staff of literary critics working at S. C. under Dr. Starbuck's direction. "Students at Lincoln and Manual Arts senior high schools, and at Mt. Vernon and Hollenbeck junior high schools made frank, discriminating comments about which books they liked or disliked and why, and their opinions were not only interesting but of great value to the critical staff at Southern California," states Dr. Starbuck. "This is the first time that any similar check of California children's actual reading interests has been attempted scientifically on a large scale."

The staff in character research at S. C. also has had the cooperation of the Los Angeles Public Library since this literary enterprise has been carried on in Philosophy Hall for the purpose of giving parents and teachers reliable data on literature for the direction of children's reading. During the past two years, work on Volume III has entailed the reading of 5,000 biographies and autobiographies, of which 647 were included in the recommended list.

Among these are "Boyhood of a Naturalist," by John Muir; "Abe Lincoln Grows Up," by Carl Sandburg; "Benjamin Franklin," by E. Laurence Dudley; "Personal Recollections of Joan of Arc," by Samuel Langhorne Clemens; "Against the Current," by Edward A. Steiner; "Everybody's Boswell," by James Boswell, and "Mark Twain's Autobiography," by Samuel Langhorne Clemens.

Work in character research under Dr. Starbuck first received recognition before he came to Los Angeles as a result of its winning a $20,000 national prize for the best plan of character education for public schools. Since 1928 the enterprise has been supported financially by the Payne Research Fund of New York.

Volume 1 of the "Guide" series treats of fairy tales, myths and legends, and consists of 380 pages. Volume II classifies fiction for young people between the ages of six and sixteen, and is a book of 579 pages. Three collections of stories for boys and girls selected from those so far recommended in the "Guide" have also been published, "Familiar Haunts," "Enchanted Paths," and "Far Horizons."

World poetry is to be the subject of Volume IV. A group of six literary critics, a statistician, and a clerical staff is now organized for the new project. They are to examine all poetry which might prove enjoyable and valuable for children of all school grades through high school. This staff includes writers, critics who have had experience in teaching, in literature, philosophy, psychology and library management. Some of them are parents.

"While it is true that it will probably be

much more difficult to apply objective standards to the appreciation and selection of poetry than it has been to prose for children, the present staff of critics has worked out an original satisfactory technique," Dr. Starbuck states. "The result of its application should satisfy the exact requirements set by literary craftsmen and critics, as well as the qualities most valued by teachers, parents, children and the poets themselves."

Methods of judging literature for children by the character research staff at S. C. and results have been internationally endorsed by educators, librarians, teachers and parents. Enthusiastic recommendations have been given by Roger W. Babson, W. H. Kilpatrick, Clarence M. Case, George A. Coe, Goodwin B. Watson and many others.

Standards of value used include: fitness for school grades, high literary quality, values tending to promote character and situations which are true to nature and to human nature.

A Correspondent

Los Angeles, Calif.

QUOTATIONS

THE CHILDREN BILL IN PARLIAMENT

The Children and Young Persons Bill should go a long way to remedy the imperfections of the laws dealing with the protection of neglected children and the treatment of youthful offenders. It was introduced with great ability by Mr. Oliver Stanley; it was welcomed by Mr. R. J. Davies on behalf of the Opposition, and given a second reading with the consent of the whole House; none of the critics was partisan or destructive. Their one object was to make suggestions for its improvement, so that the House of Commons may be able to feel, when the bill passes into law, that a determined effort has been made to fulfill more faithfully than ever before their duty to the children, unable to speak or fend for themselves, the care of whom ought to be an especially sacred charge to the community. The country has moved far since the bad old days when, in 1849, as Mr. Stanley reminded the House, the full majesty of the law sentenced over 10,000 children under seventeen to imprisonment and even to transportation. In more recent times there has been what Mr. Davies called a gratifying fall in juvenile offenders. Between 1917 and 1929 the number of young offenders charged has diminished from over 50,000 to less than 24,000, and the number convicted from 27,290 to 5,936. Moreover there has been a great improvement not only in the statistics of youthful offences but in the conditions of children's employment.

Yet, even to-day, as Lady Astor pointed out in the debate, many of the children employed in unregulated trades, estimated at 400,000, are working for seventy-two hours a week, and these figures appear to be an under-statement of the case. It is to be hoped that the omission of the bill to deal with this particular blemish, which is not strictly relevant to its purpose, will be repaired before long by other means. On the whole, however, though the measure still leaves much to be desired before it can be regarded as the perfect Children's Charter, there is, as Major Jesson remarked, evidence of a warm heart in the bill. Those of its clauses which aim at revising the law with which young people find themselves in conflict all tend to give them a better chance of avoiding a life of crime, and those which provide means of removing children from undesirable surroundings and making suitable arrangements for their education and training show a wise regard for their welfare and happiness. The bill, in short, is a good bill, and will undo much of the harm that has been tolerated in the past by successsive governments. But there is still room for further improvement, and this, to judge from the temper of yesterday's debate, it is likely to receive during its passage through the House.—*The London Times.*

The enlightened measure now before the British House of Commons for dealing with young offenders deserves general attention as being the outcome of experience carefully recorded by many earnest child welfare workers.

Twenty-four years have gone by since a bill of this kind has been passed in Britain. In 1908, when the existing law was enacted, special courts for dealing with juvenile offenders were largely experimental. Now these valuable institutions have proved their worth, and one of the provisions of the bill is to extend their scope and to separate them more nearly completely than they hitherto have been from places in which grown-up persons are brought to trial.

Juvenile courts would deal with young persons up to the age of 17. Up to now their jurisdiction has ceased in cases of neglect when the child was 14. In other matters it has ended at the age of 16.

The object of the bill throughout is to give children and young persons who are led astray better opportunities of getting back to the straight course. No child of eight would be regarded as capable of cognizable crime. At present seven is the age limit. No child under 10 would be sent to a reformatory school, and none under 18 would receive a capital sentence. Increased powers would be given to local education authorities so that neglected children might not come into the hands of the police merely because they are not being properly looked after.

Numerous other changes are proposed in the existing law. Voluntary homes for difficult children would be brought under registration and inspection, and regulations regarding street trading revised. New and salutary rules are outlined to prevent abuses in connection with adoptions.

All this is to the good. Improvements may be introduced in the bill as the result of debate. But as the measure stands, it is already a valuable contribution to world effort to help the less happily situated sections of the rising generation.—*The Christian Science Monitor.*

REPORTS

MEASURING MENTAL ABILITY IN THE INTERMEDIATE GRADES OF THE ELEMENTARY SCHOOL

THE traditional approach to classifying pupils has involved the use of measures of mental ability. Such instruments, usually called "intelligence tests," measure the ability of pupils to learn.[1] Each such test has some claim to validity by virtue of its standardization.[2] Studies by the writer,[3] by Kuhlmann,[4] and by Witty and Taylor[5] indicate that validity coefficients of correlation, involving the paired quantitative scores yielded by the several instruments, range between positive 0.50 and positive 0.75, with an occasional coefficient reported above or below these extreme values. Hull has pointed out that modern aptitude tests have forecasting efficiency defined by validity coefficients between positive 0.50 and positive 0.70.[6] The validity coefficients obtained in the several studies are below the level of Hull's concept of "decided value."

The evidence concerning the relationship between school achievement, as measured by marks, and quantitative scores yielded by measures of mental ability is somewhat similar in character. Ruch and Stoddard assembled data from several studies, showing that coefficients for these paired variables range, normally, between positive 0.30 and positive 0.60, with relatively few above positive 0.50.[7] A wealth of data is available to support this finding. Unfortunately, little or none of it is directly related to educational work in the intermediate elementary grades. The majority of such studies have been carried out in the secondary schools or in the colleges and universities.

[1] R. Pintner, "Intelligence Testing—Methods and Results." (New Edition.) New York: Henry Holt and Co., p. 49, 1931.

[2] For a discussion of validity, see G. M. Ruch, "The Objective or New-Type Examination." Scott, Foresman and Company, Chicago, pp. 27–30, 1929.

[3] M. E. Broom, "The Validity of Four Individual Tests of Mental Ability." *Los Angeles Educational Research Bulletin,* 8 (No. 7): 9–10. March, 1929. (A second study by the writer involving group tests in the intermediate elementary grades has not been published.)

[4] F. Kuhlmann, "The Pearson Formula, and A Further Note on the Kuhlmann-Anderson Tests." *Journal of Applied Psychology,* 13: 32–45. February, 1929.

[5] P. A. Witty and J. F. Taylor, "Some Results of the Multi-Mental Test." *Journal of Applied Psychology,* 20: 299–303. April, 1929.

[6] C. L. Hull, "Aptitude Testing." World Book Company, Yonkers-on-Hudson, New York, p. 274, 1928.

[7] G. M. Ruch and G. D. Stoddard, "Tests and Measurements in High School Instruction." World Book Companv Yonkers-on-Hudson, New York, p. 221, 1927

With the evidence which has been presented in mind, it is now possible to consider somewhat different data. In October, 1929, the writer directed the administration of the McCall Multi-Mental Scale, Form 1, and of the New Stanford Achievement Test, Advanced Examination, Form V, in a small elementary school system in southern California. The mental and educational age scores obtained by using these tests, when paired, yielded a coefficient of correlation of positive 0.732 (N = 273). The data were obtained in grades four to six inclusive. Subsequently, the work was repeated in this school system. Additional testing in October, 1929, and in September, 1930, made scores for both of the tests available for 324 additional pupils. The coefficient obtained by pairing the mental age scores yielded by the McCall test and the educational age scores yielded by the New Standford Test for these 324 pupils was positive 0.752. These results check closely with those reported by Witty and Taylor (footnote 5.) Witty and Taylor, in grades four to six, obtained a coefficient of correlation for paired McCall mental age scores and Stanford educational age scores which was positive 0.78 (N = 522.)

In September, 1930, the writer conducted a school achievement survey in a second school system in southern California. The Public School Achievement Test, Form 1, Batteries A, B, and C, and the McCall Multi-Mental Scale, Form 1, were used. The grade placement measures yielded by the group of achievement tests were correlated with the McCall mental age scores. The resulting coefficient was positive 0.805. Records of 575 pupils in grades four to eight inclusive were considered in this study.

The correlation coefficients involving the paired derived quantitative measures of achievement and of mental ability indicate a higher degree of agreement than either those between paired measures of mental ability or those between paired marks (measuring school achievement) and mental test derived measures. It appears that we can use grade placement measures or educational age scores yielded by batteries of achievement tests instead of mental age scores for purposes of forecasting academic success in the intermediate grades of the elementary school. The "intelligence tests" devised for use in the intermediate elementary grades validate the batteries of school achievement tests in the same grades as measures of the academic phases of intelligence better than they validate each other.

It is perfectly logical to regard batteries of achievement tests as excellent tests of mental ability. Some years ago Calvin pointed out that "we never measure inborn intelligence; we always measure acquired intelligence, but we infer from differences in acquired intelligence, differences in native endowment when we compare individuals in a group who have had common experiences and note the differences in the attainment of these individuals."[8] Pupils in the intermediate grades of the elementary school undoubtedly have had similar opportunities to learn the subject content of an educational achievement battery, and, since they have progressed through the schools to the intermediate grade level, it is to be assumed that they have demonstrated some interest in learning.

It has been shown in this brief report that measures yielded by mental tests and by batteries of school achievement tests in the intermediate grades of the elementary school validate each other to a higher degree than do mental age scores yielded by mental tests. The obvious conclusion is that it is unnecessary to administer mental tests in such school grades to obtain a measure of the pupils' ability to learn, when they have reacted to a battery of school achievement tests. This situation might be changed by the improvement of the mental tests devised for use in the elementary school intermediate grades.

M. E. BROOM

STATE TEACHERS COLLEGE,
SAN DIEGO, CALIFORNIA

NEW BOOKS IN EDUCATION

LYMAN, R. L. *The Enrichment of the English Curriculum.* Pp. viii + 251. University of Chicago Press. $2.00.

MIMS, MARY and GEORGIA W. MORITZ. *The Awakening Community.* Pp. xxvii + 273. Macmillan. $2.00.

[8] S. S. Colvin, "Principles Underlying the Construction and Use of Intelligence Tests." Chapter II, Part I, in "Intelligence Tests and Their Use," edited by G. M. Whipple. Public School Publishing Company, Bloomington, Illinois, p. 19, 1922.

EDUCATIONAL REVIEW

Edited by WILLIAM McANDREW

EDITORIAL COMMENT

FRANK LOESCH

WALTER FORD writes from Chicago, "Your review of 'Citizen Cole' is tip-top. Your urge that schools study heroes who fight, *now,* for the things schools ought to be stressing is tremendously important. The text-book heroes, dead and gone, are of not much help in present problems. Why don't you feature Frank Loesch?"

Thank you for the hint.

Who is Frank Loesch? A quiet, dignified Chicago gentleman of eighty years, who, having attained financial competence, legal distinction and personal respect, might, with general approval, be now sorting and scrap-booking souvenirs in a country house library and directing the cultivation of roses and persimmons in his private greenhouse.

Instead, he is the president of a commission of Chicago citizens engaged in fighting crime and struggling to give the city a good name. This is his fifth year in this strenuous and dangerous service. Had he retired at the end of any of the other four terms, who could have blamed him? Had he chosen to keep out of it altogether and to enjoy a leisure earned by a strenuous life at the bar and in the prosecution of election frauds, he would have made a good subject for an essay on "Success."

But to see this superb old citizen sacrificing ease and safety to root out crime from one of its vast intrenched strongholds, to see him showing the legal profession who its crooks are, to note his fearless criticism and logically constructed provisions for betterment, suggest that he is the example our youngsters ought to study, to know, to enjoy and to follow. I hope some of our favorite text-book writers will get before schoolboys the civic adventures of such patriots of peaceful times as John Quincy Adams, Grover Cleveland, Rutherford Hayes, Thomas Nast, Henry Raymond, Lucius Swift, Tom Johnson, William Dudley Foulke, George Cole and Frank Loesch. Our political history has them sprinkled all along the road, men who fought successfuly or without victory against evils that are now, after a hundred and fifty years, as full of peril as in the heroic age of American pioneering.

THE LIBRARIANS'LL BEAT YOU IF YOU DON'T WATCH OUT

JOSEPHINE RATHBONE, former Ann Arborite, now president of the American Library Association, summoned leaders in the library field to meet and discuss the library's duty in these hard times. For long hours the lady Josephine held the experts together, transforming the old familiar "What might be done if—" to the unqualified "We will do these."

Reading rooms have customers as never before. "Our old professional ways will not do," resolved the shepherds of books. "We must also work outside the walls. We will be part and counsel of community responsibility for lifting the depression." You should send a stamp to the association office, 520 North Michigan Avenue, Chicago, asking for the pamphlets, "The Library and Depression," and "For Thinking America."

Commissioner Cooper keeps telling us that the depression, the crime wave, the crooked courts, are the teachers' challenge. Dean Russell notes a sad fact that the percentage of teachers who can manifest an interest in a political problem such as the present evils represent is smaller than the proportion of laymen discussing such things. This has remained true notwithstanding the uncontradicted assertion of Coolidge, Roosevelt, Taft, Cleveland and Hayes that the public-school teacher is maintained to provide for civic affairs to be managed so as to secure general welfare now at low ebb.

It will occur to you that present circumstances require you and the teachers associated with you to instigate community meetings for discussion and action appertaining to the depression. You have halls to offer. You have influence with the speakers best qualified to think and to advise. You are called a community leader by every layman who addresses educational meetings. Live up to your reputation.

Insomuch as our best people say your schools must train the next generation to keep the nation out of such a crisis as it now is in, you will do well to get the teachers exposed to economics, government and politics. The community meeting is a potent means for such contacts.

LOS-ANGELES LANE

THAT noise coming from the West is Robert Lane, assistant superintendent of Los Angeles schools, shouting that because social studies have gotten themselves a place everywhere the promoters of them musn't think the time has come to rest. Hear him. What you have done is good, fine, superior, and it is not good enough. You have a delightfully easy attitude toward citizenship. Savage tribes manage better. Their youth can't enter manhood until they have proven themselves worthy. We should see to it that no one is allowed to become an American citizen either through the courts or by mere growing up until subjected to rigid scrutiny as to fitness by knowledge and past performance. This is the school's business. The elementary record should show that for seven years John Jones has acquired American ideals suitable to his age. The added testimony of junior and senior high schools should be satisfactory. University or employer should be the final witness and be called on to stand sponsor in the civic baptism. We are comic, we Americans. We are greatly concerned about the foreigner who wants to become a citizen. It's time to Americanize the American born.

YOUTH AND MR. MORRELL

OUR local paper, *The Long Island Chronicle,* commends the recommendation of Gerald Morrell, a New York City attorney, that high-schools, colleges and universities should include in their courses requirements that all students should attend a designated number of meetings or conventions of organized political parties.

The *Chronicle* editor is for the scheme. Unnumbered thousands of citizens, he says, are disgusted with the type of persons now prevalent in and ruling the political service. The visiting foreigner is amazed at the riff-raff hanging around our city halls or county court houses and occupying positions of trust. Politics today is based largely on essential dishonesty, on the submergence of personal ideals and clean ethics. It is an opportunistic calling where men bend to the boss, playing a game according to rules neither honest nor intelligent. Principle in politics yields to expediency.

Politicians are in disrepute, though politics has been called by the best minds the most noble of man's pursuits. Among Americans the cultured avoid public affairs. They leave the duty of governing to other hands rather than to contaminate themselves. This is contentment and stupidity.

It is a waste to blame the politicians. They are, by and large, a band of merry men, honest when they have to be or when it pays. They are interested in profitable jobs. Business men are hardly more ethical.

The roots of the evil are apathy and ignorance.

Mr. Morrell would take youth when it is beginning to use its own mind, when it is receptive to ideas. He would make young people, as the founders of the educational system proposed, a part of political life. He would essay to bring back to politics the respectability our fathers at the birth of the Republic ascribed to common affairs.

Mr. Morrell sees that schools are not preparing youth for the great adventure—the making of a nation. Schools avoid politics.

On first thought, continues the editorial writer, one wonders why the New York State Board of Regents does not require a more intimate knowledge of political affairs than is involved in the dry civics text-books. Principals, presidents and professors can not help but be in sympathy with the movement.

To be sure, there will be many who will heartily dislike politics, just as, now, many have no taste for Latin, algebra or literature. But should Mr. Morrell's plan succeed in interesting a fraction it will accomplish wonders.

Such is the comment of the editor of a small town paper. In 1923, French Strother canvassed the editors of the great dailies, North and South. They were amazingly unanimous that the most important service the schools should undertake is honest and efficient government. Franklin, Washington, Rusk, Madison, Webster, Clinton and Mann, proposed this as the paramount purpose of schools. But Webster, in 1787, thought the schoolmaster too ignorant of the meaning of the Revolution to carry out its principles unless compelled by law to observe them. Attorney Morrell, in 1932, has this same idea. I do not know of any public high-school that makes the knowledge of politics and intent to purify government its chief concern. If you do, for the land's sake name it, and we'll turn the spotlight on it that its good works may be seen of man.

BREVIARY AGAIN

The Persian king at times grew murderous toward the man he had hired to harp on "Sire, remember the Athenians." The Roman senators were often bored to death by Cato's perpetual "Carthage must be destroyed." The themes lacked variations. Not so the verses in this Schoolman's Breviary which comes to you here, each month, from the mouths of no hired men but as carefully considered truths spoken by eminent respectables. Let us unite in reading the verses beginning with 49.

49. PRESENT SCHOOL TRAINING MISSES THE MARK. The training received in school does not fit for democracy. Insufficient time and effort are devoted to it. The citizen is not taught to think for himself on political and other social questions both of which are always current in the community. Study and practice must be cooperative. SEBA ELDRIDGE, Prof. Sociology, U. of Kansas. "Major Problems of Democracy." 1928.

50. MORE SCHOOLS, MORE CRIME. That which available statistics demonstrate beyond dispute is the low standard of public security in the United States as compared with any other country of parallel civilization. According to Hoffman, statistician of the Prudential Insurance Co., homicide in the United States, from 1919 to 1923, was 16 times that of England and Wales. Chicago had a longer list of killings than all England. Burglary insurance was fifteen to twenty times as high as in England. PRESTON WM. SLOSSON. "The Great Crusade and After." 1930.

51. IDEALS GONE FROM PUBLIC SCHOOLS. Our American idealism is increasingly disparaged and forsaken by the public schools. We have turned our backs on altruism once cherished. We are materialists. Vocational training, business, and athletics are in the curriculum. Ideals have departed. REV. WM. G. THAYER, Headmaster, St. Marks, Southboro, Mass., as reported in N. Y. Times. June 5, 1931.

52. ONLY AUTOMATONS. Our teachers are little more than automatons. If education is to be a creative civic force it must play a tremendous part in the thinking that will establish a civilization. JESSE H. NEWLON. N. Y. Times. July 18, 1931.

53. LAG OF THE SCHOOL. Our present situation is a tragic absurdity. We have the requisites for an almost ideal civilization. Not once in its life has the American school caught up with its obligation. Education, the potential giant, is, in fact, an impotent weakling, failing to repair current ignorance and indifference to our mutual responsibilities of government. HAROLD RUGG. "Culture and Education in America." 1931.

54. EDUCATION NEEDS RECONSTRUCTION. The present high school, with the exception of its extra-curriculum activities, might well pass as an institution of more than a century ago. Nine-tenths of what is taught is in need of reconstruction. There should be in every high school a department of citizenship. PROF. GOODWIN WATSON. "The World Tomorrow." Oct., 1930.

55. POLITICAL CRIME. The neglect of public obligations is the great American crime. PROFESSOR TAEUSCH. "Professional and Business Ethics." 1930.

56. OUR UNSATISFACTORY DEMOCRACY. What America needs is a passion for justice. The average citizen would like to feel that he can trust his government. He can't. It does not operate in a spirit of fair play. What we ask is a public conscience. For this we look to you young men of the colleges. DR. JOHN H. McCRACKEN. Address, Lafayette College. Oct. 17, 1930.

57. OUR EDUCATION UNFRIENDLY TO DEMOCRACY. We must deal with the problem of making education prepare for a democratic social system. Too much of our curricu-

lum is unfriendly to democracy. If we believe in it, why don't we make the course of study around it? PROF. BOYD BODE. "Modern Educational Theories." 1927.

58. CIVIC TEACHING NOT POPULAR WITH TEACHERS. In "The Nation's Schools," Nov., 1930, in an analysis of the annual conventions of the Michigan Educational Association, meeting in six sections in different cities, a few more than fifteen hundred programmed speeches, papers, etc., are examined. Three are found on civic teaching. "Ninety-nine and four-tenths per cent. of the program is devoted to matters that hardly entered at all into considerations that warranted establishment of schools at public expense."

59. ALL SCHOOL WORK SHOULD SHOW THE CIVIC ELEMENT. All the exercises of the public school should be directed to promoting the general, not the individual welfare. PROF. EDWARD THORNDIKE. "Principles of Education." 1926.

60. WHY ARE SO MANY CORRUPT POLITICIANS PRODUCTS OF THE PUBLIC SCHOOLS? Democracy must rest on a system of free, public, universal education if it is to succeed and be permanent. If education helps good government why is it that well educated people are often found among corrupt and selfish politicians, and that notorious political bosses (Tweed, Wood, Barnard, Platt, Payne, Quay, Barnes, etc.) are usually men who have had a good education? WILLIAM BENNETT MUNRO. "Our Democracy and Its Problems." 1931.

BOOKS OF THE MONTH

IF the ladies and gentlemen will step into the refectory a collation will be served, consisting of college dishes, Canadian food, confections *a la* Washington, Cleveland punch and more. There will be conversation upon sex, youth, courage, success, myth, measurement, supervision, studies, waste, leaders, birds, personality and radioistic education.

THE GREAT TRADITION

ALBERT JAY NOCK is as sure as he is sparkling. In a brilliant series of lectures delivered at the University of Virginia and now offered in a handsome volume[1] he discourses with vigor and enthusiasm producing a spirited classic.

Those who first set up education in America said education is the establishment of certain views of life, the direction of certain demands on life, views and demands which take a proper account of the fundamental instincts of mankind all in due measure and balance: the instinct of workmanship, the instinct of intellect and knowledge, of religion and morals, of beauty and poetry, of social life and manners. To aim at an inculcation of these views and demands is The Great Tradition.

[1] Albert J. Nock, "The Theory of Education in the United States." Harcourt, Brace and Company, New York. 160 pp. $2.00.

What were the disciplines of The Great Tradition?

Latin, Greek and mathematics. By the time the young scholar reached the college all his language difficulties with Greek and Latin were forever behind him. He was prepared to deal with both literatures purely as literature. In four years he covered practically the whole range of Greek and Latin thought.

What was the purpose, asks our lecturer, and makes a bold presumption that we admit the disciplinary value of these studies, since it has never been seriously disputed. Thus, by a sentence, are Montaigne, Dr. Porson, Sydney Smith, Franklin, Bain, Huxley, Spencer, A. C. Benson, Justin McCarthy, Hammerton, Stanley Hall, Thorndike, Snedden and the intelligence testers waved aside. Also, calmly declares the professor, the literatures of Greece and Rome comprise the fullest record of what the human mind has been busy about in practically every department of spiritual and social activity except music. The record covers twenty-five hundred consecutive years of operations in poetry, drama, law, agriculture, philosophy, architecture, natural history, philology, rhetoric, astronomy, politics, medicine, theology, geography, everything.

Dr. Nock's faith is that an education consisting of a canvass of this imposing record forms a disciplined mind, an experienced mind, a mind able instinctively to view any contemporary circumstance from the vantage point of an immensely long perspective.

The charm and flow of this scholar's discourse carries one along so smoothly that it requires an effort to stop and ask why this great perspective, in the days when The Great Tradition was in full swing, failed to get the world quit of serfdom and slavery, plagues of black death, scourges of famine, burnings for heresy, imprisonment for finding that the earth moved. When in the history of man the largest number were reading Greek and Latin, was civilization the most advanced and progress most promoted? The lectures need footnotes citing the blessings existent when The Great Tradition was in flower. Too many readers of this doubting generation have been told that The Great Tradition bakes no bread, cures no diseases, unlocks no secrets of physics or chemistry, or of the attainment of the good life by the majority.

Dr. Nock assures you that the education of The Great Tradition is not for every one. We can be considered as of two classes: The educable and the nons. Our pioneer statesmen made a sublime mistake in proposing equality of educational opportunity, in advocating democracy and in assuming that honest government depends on literacy. At present we are reaping rewards of these wild theories. The mature person, bred in The Great Tradition, could at any time have reached into his accumulation of experience and have found a match for each of our present economic difficulties and for every circumstance of each, every sequence of cause and effect.

Good Lord! Where were such persons in the economic crises of the epochs when The Great Tradition bloomed? What studies in the seats of its learning in Oxford, Cambridge, Paris or Göttingen furnished solution? European systems, says our author, have a sound theory; ours do not. To which the doubting reader must inquire: How comes it that Germany, with so many shrines of The Great Tradition, failed to block The Great Calamity? She and France, Dr. Nock informs us, keep turning out a better educated product than we. We revolutionized our education, so he says, about thirty-five years ago. Foreign visitors remark that our really educated men are over sixty years of age. Coolidge, Hoover, Owen Young and many of those on whom we have counted to help us through are, I am afraid, products of the decadent schooling. Their draughts from the great well, twenty-five centuries deep, of the human mind's operations in poetry, rhetoric, philosophy, politics, everything, have been too meager. See, says the professor, what comes out of Bonn, Poitiers, Montpellier, and what comes out of our institutions of learning! But we ask "Show us, Doctor, we want cases." The experienced mind is aware, says the author, that all the progress in actual civilization that society has ever made has been brought about not by political programs, platforms, parties, not even by revolutions, but by right thinking. Our society can get along for periods by muddling through, but gets nothing permanent.

It occurs to you, perhaps, that muddling through, as phrase and process, comes to us from a country that is so much more wedded to The Great Tradition than we are that the entire thesis of the Nock lectures is damaged by speaking of muddling through.

I heartily recommend this book. Its recitation of the failures of instruction and training cuts into complacency like a keen blade. Nock isn't afraid of anything, Columbia, Butler, Coolidge, Hoover, Henry Ford, vocational educationists and the Declaration of Independence have no immunity. No inspired Mather ever sacrificed heresy with more withering anathema or showed more unquestioning faith in his own cherished doctrine. You degenerate free-thinkers must read him from beginning to end. He is an eloquent antithesis to the preface which the twenty-two untraditional professors put as the start to their "Higher Education in America," to wit—"First place can not be given to opinion and theory. Taught by a regime that discredited the application of the methods of science to the study of education we have been traditionally predisposed by early training to shun that which annihilates pet theories."

Against destroyers of the old tradition, our chivalrous defender comes to the bar, a Burke, a Taine, in denunciation of the cheap and nasty, a Bayard in elegance and knightly charm.

LEARNED'S CONSTRUCTIVE CRITICISM

Seventy pages of as meaty a discourse as you will find in many a day make William Learned's 1932 Inglis Lecture, just issued in the same natty form as make the preceding seven volumes of other addresses a delight.[2] It is, of course, criticism. All educational lectures are that, now. The most obvious defect of our school system, says Secretary Learned, is lack of plan. We have a traditional seventeen-year course, divided into kindergarten, elementary, secondary and higher education, like a seventeen-story building put up by wholly different architects, contractors with different designs for the first floor, second to fifth, sixth to ninth, and top four. Each of these parts is managed with less regard for the inmates than with intent to have the mechanism of the structure escape impingement.

The "articulation" sought by committees of state and national associations, the "integration" exhorted to by Dewey and Burnham get consideration at the hands of Mr. Learned that makes their importance clear and the realization of them immediately possible.

Our education is blanketed by a formalism that friendly attitudes of teachers toward pupils and helpless good wishes of deans for the students do not correct. Our educational institution is interested in students only when they happen to interfere with the formal operations of the machine. We set enormous store by curricula and instruction as though they were essentials instead of finding out what the student is, what he wants, what he can master, what he probably should do. We fit him to the suit instead of fitting the suit to him. Without ideas that to him seem important a boy loses morale. Give him such ideas adapted to his own personality and you can, with proper guidance, marshal behind them all the emotional resources and moral qualities of his nature.

In Mr. Learned's discourse the current discussions of individual differences take on a vitality and importance of the highest level. The effect of grades, marks, and imagining youth as classes and sections, is covered here with startling outcome. Fresh from conducting one of the most extensive surveys of educational processes and products, Mr. Learned depicts the divergence between marks and abilities calmly enough, but to any one who is concerned about the future of intelligence among those now in school the conclusions are alarming. Our departmentalized instruction in high school and college is mass production, but as if an automobile manufacturing concern should go through the idiotic process of making multitudinous parts, leaving them unassembled and the complete machine untested. We give studies a time schedule. There is no corresponding fact in the composition of the classes. My learning time is not yours nor any one's but my own. Class conception, class spirit are bogus and demoralizing to character.

Examinations, as we have them, are sudden spasms to generate spurts of learning. They are too inadequate in scope to evaluate a man. The great majority of college teachers make no attempt to find out what their students are. They do not care. The boy's faulty ideas and half lights, which are prime factors in deciding how he is to be taught, are not interesting to his instructor. Rather he is disposed to rail at faulty preparation.

The whole affair of college admissions could be revolutionized to-day and placed on a basis more just to the individual, more trustworthy for the college, and promising more to the welfare of the country.

Mr. Learned is, in these pages, enheartening in his constructive proposals. Whatever loyalty to college traditions he may have had in Brown, Berlin, Leipzig and Harvard (I accuse him of none), he is here most for the student and little for the professor. He sees an astounding public demand that more and more young persons be given what, a short time back, was the educational portion of but a few. He sees the enormous waste of life resulting from the continuance of educational administrations devised for situations now no more. No one has put the absurdity of the theory better than he in this illustration. I ask you how tall are you? You answer "five feet three." We prescribe gymnasium exercises, reaching, stretching and so on. At the close of the course we say, "you are now four gymnasium years tall."

[2] William Setchel Learned, "Realism in American Education." Harvard University Press, Cambridge. 70 pp.

A CRUSADER GONE

FROM the Antioch College Press comes a significant volume on the decadence of faculty influence upon the government and policy-making of higher institutions of learning.[3] Dr. Kirkpatrick, as a perusal of this notable volume can not fail to reveal, drove himself to scorn delights and live laborious days among dusty archives hunting the facts which he has cleared of cobwebs and fashioned into a connected narrative, bright and clear.

The college and university began as a syndicate of scholars. Their councils formed, ruled, and, as circumstances required, modified the university. America founded her higher education on this model. How the layman crept into control is related in the Kirkpatrick book by means of extracts from the enactments of governing boards of Harvard, William and Mary, Yale, Princeton, Columbia, Brown, Bowdoin, Dartmouth, Pennsylvania and Michigan.

By steps pointed out, education has reached a situation in which the vested rights are in the trustees. The students have the powers of minor children, the faculties those of hired servants. Finally the feeble remonstrances of university teachers have allowed the situation to become that in which the common concept is such that the decisions of courts protect authority of governing boards at the expense of the professional body. The college is a cosmos incarnate in the corporation and is, by the courts, given first consideration when in conflict with officers of administration and instruction.

In other words, the American academic constitution has slowly come to provide for a forming, controlling, governing body from which has been eliminated almost every resident officer and teacher. The board may remain inactive and let principal or president exercise powers, but authority is not permanently committed to teachers and professional officers.

When school interests outgrew selectmen or town councils, their overburdened bodies have not turned to the school people. They have, on the contrary, created other lay boards to take over the responsibilities. It is a situation developed in the days of Jackson's deerskin-shirt democracy, dominated by a philosophy that had no room for professional or expert leaders in any social or political field. America had little regard for the specialist, least of all for the professor.

We have in America no opportunity for studying at first hand a strong academic institution which finds little use for centralized authority and management, for efficiency, for quantity production of a standardized article, for the factory model in general. Too many of the teaching profession are pleased to continue the system of lay government. No other system has ever been present to their minds. They can not visualize a college or university in which the resident professional body is itself authorized to carry on its business. So foreign is this concept of the college to present-day American collegians, especially to the administrative mind, that it is difficult to gain a patient and understanding consideration of the problem. Indeed, to such people there is no problem.

Dr. Kirkpatrick keeps the complaining tone out of his book. He is rather a physician tracing the causes of a disease. He is persuaded that a Renaissance of our American college is well under way and that in due time the burdensome features of government will be removed. This author's field has been the traditional obstacles to educational progress. His "Force and Freedom in Education" was a general survey of administrative antiquities which hold education back. The present volume was to be only a beginning of his brave crusade. But death has taken him from the ranks. These two books are monuments to a fair-fighting warrior, devoid of personal animosities, but inspired by the faith that in education as in religion, and indeed in all life, the cultivation of the spirit should be the aim of teachers. Come that, and the ancient swaddling bands of administration will burst asunder. He hoped to aid school and college in the campaign for "athletes of the spirit."

He surely devoted his life to it. We shall have killings in this cause to swell the lists of Ettingers, Finegans, Suzallos, Chadseys, Bordens, Carsons, Englemans, Wests, Rosses and Millers. Why not? Out of this nettle, danger, pluck the flower.

[3] J. E. Kirkpatrick, "Academic Organization and Control." The Antioch Press, Yellow Springs, Ohio. 246 pp. $3.00.

TIPS FROM A NEIGHBOR

You will not be far astray in crediting Supervisor Marshall, of the schools of Yarmouth, Nova Scotia, with performance of a piece of singularly valuable educational statesmanship.[4] He has surveyed the schools of Nova Scotia, portrayed the sources of their strength and weakness, and outlined the measures which, within the financial abilities of the province, would advance them to a higher efficiency. It would, indeed, be a dull school man of any of the United States to whom a perusal of this study of the social setting of communities, of state policies, of local attitudes, of teacher disposition, of training school usages, of methods of improvement in service, would fail to give a wealth of valuable suggestion.

A COMPLETE WASHINGTON

Young Louis Sears—it is hardly more than yesterday that he was teaching our Chicago high-school boys and girls that history is awake —offers a very live Washington in a majestic Crowell production.[5] Here is adventure, romance, politics, statesmanship, psychology, economics, ethics, personality, in an unbroken stream of history and biography. From his diaries, letters and official papers the foremost American is made to paint a self-portrait. From the mouths and pens of his intimates he is portrayed at home, in camp, on journeys, at battle, in council, as boy and man.

Historian Sears is not of the guild that turns heroes into common clay. The worshippers from 1780 onward counted Washington the greatest man of his time. The Sears biography subjects this appraisal to exhaustive scrutiny, weighs the opinions of enemies, measures the surmises of muckrakers, gives ample quotation of derogatory libel, and brings you to the end with the conviction that here was a character with will and temperament directed toward the successful creation of a great republic. The book establishes as fact that Washington's character assured the success of the Revolution.

[4] M. V. Marshall, "Education as a Social Force." Harvard University Press, Cambridge. 161 pp. $1.50.

[5] Louis Martin Sears, "George Washington." Thomas Y. Crowell Company, New York. 560 pp. $5.00.

Love affairs are in this biography treated with unusual frankness. Outdoor life, Western expeditions, relations with mismanaging superiors, experiences of a country gentleman, sacrifices in joining the revolutionists, defeats and imminence of complete failure, criticisms and cabals, cowardice of patriots, victory and peace, prospects of national dismemberment, growth and triumph as a statesman are revived here with a unique realism.

Steeped in the atmosphere of many societies of historical and political research, rescued from archival dulness by the daily duty of keeping classrooms awake, practiced by the making of six previous histories and by frequent work for magazines, Author Sears, when bulletined as soon to issue this book, won the rare compliment from famous Historian Charles Beard, "best man in the world to do it."

A WASHINGTON MIRROR AND MAGNISCOPE

Collecting Washingtoniana for a lifetime, Dr. Merriam[6] renders a timely service in this year of years by offering 428 pages of word-pictures, estimates, comments, compliments, character studies, maxims and exhortations, in prose and poetry, concerned with the Father of Our Country. They are short, three or four to the page. They are by notables: Washington himself, Adams, Ames, Bancroft, Byron, Coolidge, Depew, Emerson, Franklin, Hart, Holmes, Hoover, Irving, Kipling, Lossing, Lodge, Madison, Monroe, Marshall, Paine, Roosevelt, Thackeray, Webster, Wilson—more than four hundred authors in all. They are grouped in these classifications: gentleman and sportsman, friend and relative, Christian if not churchman, farmer and man of affairs, soldier, hero, citizen and patriot, statesman, leader and ruler, prophet, exemplar, man. The continuous joy Dr. Merriam must have had in collecting these treasures through the years is surely multiplied by knowing what a boon he has conferred upon you by making them so handily available. They furnish you texts for the speeches you have to make this year, they supply instantly the extracts your boys and girls wish to print upon the blackboards. There are

[6] George Ernest Merriam, "More Precious than Fine Gold. Washington." G. P. Putnam's Sons, New York. 428 pp. $5.00.

ten pages of a list of books in which extended readings may be taken. There are sixteen full-page reproductions of the famous Washington portraits, the Peales, the Trumbull, the Houdon, the Stuarts and others.

Bravo, Merriam! Fifteen hundred wreaths to you, one for each quotation.

WASHINGTON IN BRIEF

THE Houghton Mifflin Company offer two short Washington books.[7] The first is Senator Lodge's spirited summary of judgments as to why Washington is a great inheritance and exemplar. The other is a collection of short stories about the First American by John Fiske, Washington Irving and other authors, to which are added nine poems.

FAVORITE SCHOOLROOM WASHINGTON

THE American Book Company's tribute[8] is a crisp reprint of the schoolroom favorite, "Story of George Washington," by James Baldwin, with frequent pictures of events in the first president's career. It is a familiarly told set of tales to be read by children from the third grade up.

MAN FOUR SQUARE

I'D put Denis Tilden Lynch's "Grover Cleveland"[9] in my high-school library and in every collection for older students. Our boys crave the real thing in preference to denatured biography. Lynch paints Cleveland as he was, roistering youngster, Bible reader, fighter of crooks, preacher of eternal vigilance to prevent the people's representatives from maintaining a tyranny worse than in the good old colony days.

Here you will learn to know the politician who started public life with the declaration that there is no difference in obligation whether you are charged with the money of one man or of many, though an office-holder assumes that a different rule of fidelity prevails between him and taxpayers than that which would regulate his conduct if entrusted with the money of his neighbor. You will see the politician growing to the statesman. An old truth was the core of Cleveland's speech to the Buffalo common council on taking his place as mayor. A majority were crooks. He shot at them the old maxims he had been taught—and you are teaching—in public school. He set up the watchword, "A public office is a public trust," which, put into practice in governorship and presidency, occurs as the Cleveland contribution to memorable utterances included in collections of quotations since his day.

Author Lynch has the skill of unstrained vividness, giving you the sense of accompanying his man into the inner councils of the manipulators.

John Manning had faith that money could do anything. Cleveland acted in accordance with the Sunday-school claim that, win or lose, we must be honest. Jay Gould told him that to win there must be Gould payments to both parties and if there was a third he'd buy that, too. Cleveland beat him "because the majority of the people are too honest to be bought."

Mr. Lynch takes you through the happenings of private life and public struggles. You meet and know Dave Hill, James Blaine, George William Curtis, Richard Watson Gilder, Jo Jefferson, Daniel Manning, William McKinley, Theodore Roosevelt, Henry Ward Beecher, William Jennings Bryan, Jay Gould, Charles A. Dana, Dan Lamont, Father McGlynn, J. Pierpont Morgan, Alton B. Parker, Samuel J. Tilden, all the Tammany bosses, and most of the American notables of the generation closing in 1908.

You learn why Cleveland declined the degree tendered by Harvard University. "I am not suitable for it. My education is scanty; I can not figure as a man of letters nor as an eminent lawyer." You hear him in an address at a Harvard anniversary, telling the collegians there is no excuse for their neglect of their political duties. "The destiny our country may achieve through united service will be sooner attained if our educated men shall deem it a solemn duty of citizenship to engage in political affairs, actively and practically."

In his address to Cornell students he said:

[7] Henry Cabot Lodge, "George Washington, The Man." 94 pp. 44 cents. Frances Jenkins Olcott, "Stories about Washington." 60 pp. 28 cents. Houghton Mifflin Company, Boston.

[8] "James Baldwin's George Washington." American Book Company, New York. 65 pp. 36 cents.

[9] Denis Tilden Lynch: "Grover Cleveland, a Man Four Square." Horace Liveright, New York. 581 pp. $3.50.

"A college man's diploma is evidence that he owes service to the nation."

In his Chicago speech on Washington's birthday, 1907, he warned those easy-going citizens that it isn't safe to leave public affairs to the party of one's choice. No one knew this better than Washington himself, urging his countrymen to realize that electing honest men must be followed by constant vigilance and holding to account.

Mr. Lynch begins his biography with Lowell's estimate: "Cleveland is the best representative of the higher type of Americanism we have had since Lincoln." Temptation there must have been to Author Lynch to omit everything not strictly in line with an appraisal like Lowell's. But the biographer has chosen to paint the young Cleveland as he was. Fidelity to fact gives the book the strength of epic story tracing the growth of a great character.

UNAPOLOGETIC TALK ON SEX

YOU will be wide of the mark in your guess as to how a minister of religion will treat sex problems.[10] The Macmillan Company will set you right if you send for Leslie Weatherhead's frank book. Mystery, pussyfooting, reticence, are supplanted by a straightforward account of the information needed to drive away an enormous amount of derangement and unhappiness due to ignorance of sex affairs and disinclination of the experienced to give information. The author is a social worker of wide observation with standard books on psychology, complexes and self-control to his credit. He has associated with himself in this volume physicians, clergymen, psychologists and a schoolmaster.

Shame at having a sex and sex instincts is calmly reproved in the first straightforward chapter. There follow sections upon comradeship and flirting, the true approach to marriage, unhappy mating, silence and ignorance, healthy-mindedness, and others. Frequent accounts of experiences confided to the author give an atmosphere of reality to the book.

A generation ago only a medical publisher would print this material. Police would have seized it if put on the counter of a general book store. Now, a highly reputable publisher issues it and the *Methodist Recorder* says that tens of thousands of young and old will be grateful for this solid and most valuable contribution to one of the chief problems of the time.

Every school ought to have a teachers' library. Every such should have this book in it.

COURAGE-CULTURE

A NEW JERSEY normal school professor of psychology, in demand as a popular lecturer on education, is Dr. Leon Mones. He has done us all a service by a practical presentation of the psychology of fear.[11] It takes him less time to get down to concrete prescriptions than the most of our wandering boys to-night. He knows how to compose paragraphs and how to give them heads. Grown-ups' fears, men's, women's, children's benefits, damages, remedies, stupid and wicked attempts at cures, make this little book one of the best printed missionaries you will see in many a day. Mothers must have it; babies cry from lack of it. Classes in parenthood should use it as a text.

PERSONALITY MEASUREMENT

WHAT'S your type, theoretical, economic, esthetic, social, political or religious? Or mixed? If the last, with how much of each temperament? By means of the simple, rational and ingenious measuring scale[12] devised by Doctors Allport and Vernon, you can compare with a norm yourself or any one who will answer a set of easy questions. For a teacher of high-school or college students the device must accomplish valuable results for instructional and vocational guidance. It concentrates in a few minutes essential truths about dominant interests of personality that are usually picked up only on long acquaintance.

TEACHER RESPONSIBILITY FOR SUCCESS AND FAILURE

ARE there any schools or teachers left that pride themselves on standards so tough that a large number of failures are a cause for pride?

[10] Leslie D. Weatherhead, "The Mastery of Sex through Psychology and Religion." The Macmillan Company, New York. 246 pp. $2.00.

[11] Leon Mones, "Why Be Afraid?" The Stratford Company, Boston. 103 pp. $1.00.

[12] Gordon W. Allport, Philip E. Vernon, "A Study of Values." Houghton Mifflin Company, Boston. 23 pp.

Authors Brueckner and Melby[13] think there probably are, judging from the large number of pupils who are not promoted at the end of the term. Teachers who allege responsibility for all failure to lie in the laziness or incompetence of the failing child are not yet extinct, according to the book before me. By 1900, it tells me, democracy had come to look upon an elementary education as the right of every boy and girl. By 1925, high-school education had been claimed for all. The battle is climbing into the colleges of liberal arts, fighting for training, compulsory or otherwise, that will make of the 65 per cent. of youth which the deans deem unfit something more valuable than it would be if left to itself.

What the Frazers, Rices, Burkes, Boks and other protesters reiterated thirty years ago, "find out what ails 'em and how to cure it," finds modern echo in patient, laborious working out of a practice of diagnostic and remedial teaching. Instead of a staff of passers of standard rations from behind counters, a modern demand for something like a mental and physical sanitarium or health farm, with mind-doctors and brain-dietary experts, is taking shape.

The Brueckner-Melby book is a manual for such an institution. It presents the different promotion and classifying plans, serving individual needs, uses of standard tests, interpretation of results, diagnosis and remedial teaching in arithmetic, reading, language, spelling, handwriting, social studies, character education and in health culture.

The care with which the multitude of tests on the market are criticized in this book can not fail when these appraisals are called to teachers' attention, in mitigating the readiness so many mortals have to swallow anything in print. This kind of caution regarding standard tests grows as the book leaves the old subjects and passes into civic and moral training. Elgin plan, Iowa scheme, Hartshorne and May, Wickman, Olson, their diagnoses and remedies, are described, and criticized, as is meet; but in this citizenship and character education—the field for which the founders of the common schools promised most—the objective tests for finding definite results are still the most wobbly of all. But practically all the books that come to this magazine for review insist that you must not give up. Trial, record, hypothesis, trial and record, again, until a method can stand up and say, "I make a manhood that the measurers can find," is a task before you.

13 Leo J. Brueckner, Ernest O. Melby, ''Diagnostic and Remedial Teaching.'' Houghton Mifflin Company, Boston. 598 pp. $2.75.

THE TEACHER'S ALMA MATER

What other productive organizations do in appraising the results of their plans and performances should be imitated by the institutions that purport to make efficient teachers. This is the thesis of Dr. Effie Bathurst's[14] published study. No one is doing this with sufficient thoroughness. What could and should be done, what the graduates say they need, what the supervisors feel would save an immense amount of the influence of the training schools from wasting away, are set out in convincing style.

MYTH AND MEASUREMENT

The way Donald Paterson[15] wades into present myths and superstitions, whether it be in the matter of big heads, long heads, blondes or the overfat, is to take some current piece of alleged wisdom or some widely advertised conclusion of a cocksure writer and subject the statement to a measurement in the case of a few hundred or thousand individuals.

These are the topics covered in his book: necessity for accurate measuring, the temptation to classify us as types, the relation of bodily facts to intellect, the influence of social status, inferiority complexes, glandular theories, temperaments.

You come through the book immensely relieved of a lot of bugaboo. The inevitability of human handicap is like the premature reports of Mark Twain's death—awfully overdone.

Dr. Paterson is professor of psychology in the University of Minnesota. You will expect to find his book a valuable aid to school people responsible for the development of children. You will not be disappointed.

STIFFENING SUPERVISION WITH SCIENCE

Seventh in the series of Appleton's supervisors' library comes Professor Wisconsin Barr's

14 Effie G. Bathurst, ''A Teachers College Follow-up Service.'' Bureau of Publications, Teachers College, New York. 89 pp. $1.50.

15 Donald G. Paterson, ''Physique and Intellect.'' The Century Company, New York. 297 pp. $2.50.

work-out[16] of most of the recent investigations in effective management of classes and in the productive methods of improving instruction. Inspection, direction and improvement are essentials of all productive management. Education has lagged behind its possibilities from insufficient use of these means. Heavy among the obstacles thrown in the way of using them has been the objection that supervisors are guided by personal likes and the contrary. We have enough impersonal, objective standards now to enable us to evaluate good and poor teaching without incurring the charge of favoritism or personal dislike. We have enough variety in school programs to afford play for the inspirational personality of the teacher even though training in the multiplication table is held to a cut-and-dried method that in hundreds of experiments has proved itself the least wasteful. The businesslike Barr gets his proposals for better supervision condensed to seven points:

(1) Formulate objectives.
(2) Survey the product.
(3) Search the probable causes of its deficiency.
(4) Check measurements and results for validity.
(5) Harmonize the work of teachers to the best practices.
(6) Measure the improvement.
(7) Use science.

Author Barr's first chapter is a review of the progress of scientific method in education, a summary of its gains and of next steps to be taken. The rest of the book is a fertilizing treatment of the seven points.

If a manager of a hospital, gathering the experiences of the institutions which have the highest percentage of successes, were to formulate a line of management for his organization in the manner of this Barr book, and were to guide himself and all his staff by it, the usual board of trustees would engage him in perpetuity. If there are school boards that make retention of a superintendent conditioned upon good and progressive teaching service, let them be exalted. The fact that an author will undergo the hard labor of gathering and interpreting the facts of a masterpiece like this and that a publisher will print it, and that intending supervisors are fed this kind of rations in the college, seems, doesn't it, to show that we are certainly coming into the class of producers who know what can be done and know how to do it. Even politically debilitated Brooklyn once had a superintendent of water supply who reviled the bosses but held his post through Republican and Democratic upheavals because he turned on the most water for the least amount of taxes. Let a superintendent, invited to assume control of a system of schools, hand the board a copy of Barr on supervision and get a promise of support in carrying it through. There would be an exploit worth while, my countrymen!

[16] A. S. Barr, "An Introduction to the Scientific Study of Classroom Supervision." D. Appleton and Company, New York. 399 pp. $2.50.

THE ESSAY FOR THINKING

THE Hale-and-Tobin plan[17] for mitigating this persistent dread of teachers for using essays in the English course is to select such pieces and to take them up in such sequence as will make thinking come more readily. Here are thirty-six essays between the times of Montaigne and James Truslow Adams arranged in pairs, reinforced by short sketches of the authors and chosen on a basis of current interest and wide variety.

DEBATING BOILED DOWN

SEVEN professors of public speaking join Raymond Howes in bringing out a book of minimum essentials in debate.[18] Result: a direct and compact manual for coach and team; a presentation of aims, training, gathering material, organizing the case, preparing and delivering the speeches, judging advertising, suggested topics, helpful books.

LIVING LATIN

HERE is a well-told story[19] of the pervasive Romans carrying their language to Britain and Gaul, of the Normans getting and changing this speech and taking it to England, of the flood of Latin words coming with the Renaissance. With copious lists and illuminating comment Professor Johnson argues that Latin is not dead.

IT'S A GRAND WORLD

AUTHOR, publisher, illustrator, printer and binder have conspired in Gertrude Hartman's

[17] Charles Brockway Hale, James Edward Tobin, "Contrast and Comparison." Prentice Hall, Inc., New York. 476 pp. $2.00.

[18] Raymond F. Howes, Editor, "Debating." D. C. Heath and Company, Boston. 182 pp. $1.00.

[19] Edwin Lee Johnson, "Latin Words of Common English." D. C. Heath and Company, Boston. 337 pp.

story of our world[20] to give geology, anthropology, sociology, geography and history the charm so long claimed by myth and fiction. Here is a superb gallery of clear, fresh pictures tied together with instructive talk entertainingly sustained.

Who is Gertrude Hartman and whence came this engaging talent of description and narration? It seems to me this must be the cheerful young rebel who broke out of curricular bounds and went over to the Progressive Party in education. That's right; now I remember. This is the Gertrude Hartman who enlivened "Progressive Education" by her exposition of the philosophy of the new learning when she was editor of that magazine. If books like this are furthered by membership in that party, we're for it.

A BEAUTIFUL BIOLOGY

DR. GEORGE HUNTER'S Biology is an alluring volume.[21] Its text, pictures and diagrams are crisp and clear. The author offers more than any pupil will cover because the modern demand for fitting individuals and localities requires a variety of problems, demonstrations, projects and work-book material.

Planned as a classroom and laboratory manual the lessons are so well done that I find them entertainment for evenings by the fireside. Even the problems entice the reader into working them out.

OUR OWN FAMILY ALBUM

NELLIE VAN DE GRIFT, now Mrs. Sanchez, of Oakland, California, is one of the Indiana literary crop. For the past twenty years her researches into the romance of American history have furnished her and readers much delight. At the cheery age of seventy-five, Mrs. Sanchez puts out a fresh and colorful compendium of the lore of each of the United States territories and dependencies.[22] You will want this book in your school library. In alphabetical order each commonwealth is presented in story form, informing you of its exploration and settlement, how it got its name, what its capital, motto, nickname, flower and seal are, and what great names and events are associated with it. It will be much used in classes in geography, history and current events.

IRRIGATING AN EDUCATIONAL SAHARA

LOUIS BENEZET'S researches ten years ago disclosed that the number of persons who would read a school superintendent's report was two: the superintendent and the proof-reader. Dr. Zenas Clark[23] holds the long-distance record. He has read, dissected and tabulated ninety-five superintendents' reports to the public. He has studied sixty-six previous studies. He comes through with definition of purposes, contents, understandability, illustration, charts, timeliness, use, display, legibility and rules for hitting the mark, all conducive to a pulling of these dreary documents out of the limbo.

BLOWING TWO AND A HALF MILLIONS

ONE of the last places you would consider in looking for interesting reading would be in a report on ventilation.[24] The composer of the findings of the New York Commission on School Ventilation agreeably disappoints you. Here, in a snug little book, is one of the most airy, vivacious stories you can read on a winter's day.

Forty-five years ago, in the Hyde Park High School, the school board was reprimanding us teachers for trying to get a breath of refreshment by opening the windows. Did we not have a battery of expensive fans in the basement forcing perfectly scientific atmosphere upon us? Who were we to dare to say we were not comfortable? The installing company brought school boards from far and near to look at pretty ribbons fluttering from the registers, to sniff the peppermint essence wafted in 4½ seconds from intake to outlet. Eminent education signed puffing recommendations to legislators. Scores of states, their lawmakers warmed by the persuasive blowings of manufacturers, passed statutes for the fans.

Eighteen years ago the Milbank Memorial

20 Gertrude Hartman, "The World We Live in and How it Came to Be." The Macmillan Company, New York. 357 pp. $5.00.

21 George W. Hunter, "Problems in Biology." American Book Company, New York. 706 pp.

22 Nellie Van de Grift Sanchez, "Stories of the States." Thomas Y. Crowell Company, New York. 380 pp. $2.50.

23 Zenas Read Clark, "Recognition of Merit in Superintendents' Reports." Bureau of Publications, Teachers College, New York. 123 pp. $1.75.

24 Commission, Milbank Memorial, "School Ventilation, Principles, and Practices." Bureau of Publications, Teachers College, New York. 73 pp. $1.00.

fund had a Missourian member who said, "I wonder." In experimental chambers, in classrooms in New York, New Haven, Cleveland, Chicago and elsewhere, its scientists studied comfort, health, drafts, radiation and moisture. The present book concludes that the grand air played by the combined ventilating organs in school basements is to the tune of $2,500,000 wasted each year. State laws in force and school regulations are based on antiquated propaganda utterly disproved. Retrenchment and economy in the field of school expense are demanded up and down the country. You're wasting money on hot air. Education is blowing itself shamefully. Instead of aiding health with the mechanism you proudly show to visitors you are hindering, you are—oh, get the book and read it! Your ideas need fresh air. The narrative not only tells you what's wrong but what a long list of scientific tests have shown to be better and cheaper.

APOSTLE OF AFFECTION

DR. REISNER'S series of educational classics has reached fourteen volumes. This last, "Pestalozzi,"[25] shows the Swiss pioneer, while primarily a philanthropist and not a professional educator, to be, really, the beginner of a movement that is raising teaching from a traditional and empirical process to a science. There are given sixteen extracts from his writings.

A MODERN OLDSTER

PROFESSOR PAYNE taught us, fifty years ago, that John Amos Komensky, rechristened Comenius, taught that school is life. Patriotic Americans will claim John Amos got this idea from John Dewey. The eminent Moravian also taught that schools should be organized so that the scholar should be occupied with only one object of study at any given period of his life. This idea he may, by projective clairvoyance, have taken from Don Seitz of the *New York World*, for Don has written many articles in defense of it.

An attractive collection of typical principles and practices recommended by the great reformer, with comments by Dr. Keatinge, is a late issue expanding Editor Reisner's "Education Classics."[26] Dr. Keatinge's translations have a smack to them such as the old educator will enjoy if he reads current literature. How he would be warmed to find what an abundance of his precepts are urged upon us by progressive apostles to-day, 275 years after him.

BIRDMEN'S ADVENTURES

HERE are exploration, adventure, danger, courage, science and success for you. Curator Crandall[27] tells a thrilling tale of the expedition of the New York Zoological Society through the enormous island of New Guinea in search of birds of paradise. He treats of wild life, human and animal, of the mysterious interior, of isolated missionaries, of wild ceremonials, of anthropophagi (the men that do each other eat), of natural liars and of thieves by education, of schools that run from 7 A. M. to 9 in the morning, of buying and stealing wives, of safe loading the cages of living treasure on a steamer homeward bound, of its shipwreck, of rescue, birds and all, and of the safe delivery of two hundred forty chirping feathered prizes to the Bronx Zoo.

RISING RADIO

IN handsome red and black binding, printed handsomely on high-class paper, comes the account of the first annual assembly of the National Advisory Council on Radio in Education.[28] Livingston Farrand presided and rejoiced that education is more acutely criticized by outsiders and our own family than ever. General Soltzman was there, chairman, Federal Radio Commission, and described its work. This volume gives his entire address. So does it for Dr. Bellows, of the Columbia Broadcasting System, and for William C. Bagley, Joy Morgan, Walter Damrosch, Ray Lyman Wilbur, Robert Millikan, Werrett Charters and other eminences. The discussions after each speech are prime: mostly cross-questioning of the previous speaker and spurring him to clear the mist. In the offerings are treatises on music by radio, chemistry, economics, history, library, psychology, vocational guidance, education for parents and other adults, science, Spanish, rural service and politics. Brother Bagley gives a brilliant prophecy of what future broadcasting may do for the schools. The speakers seem to have been on their best behavior. Result: an up-to-date and really readable review.

[25] Lewis Flint Anderson, "Pestalozzi." McGraw-Hill Book Company. 283 pp. $2.00.

[26] M. W. Keatinge, "Comenius." McGraw-Hill Book Company, New York. 255 pp. $2.00.

[27] Lee S. Crandall, "Paradise Quest." Charles Scribner's Sons, New York. 226 pp. $3.50.

[28] Levering Tyson, Editor, and thirty contributors, "Radio and Education." University of Chicago Press. 271 pp. $3.00.

SCHOOL AND SOCIETY

EDITED BY J. McKEEN CATTELL

WITH WHICH IS COMBINED THE

EDUCATIONAL REVIEW

EDITED BY WILLIAM McANDREW

Volume 35 SATURDAY, MARCH 12, 1932 Number 898

THE NATIONAL ADVISORY COMMITTEE AND THE OFFICE OF EDUCATION[1]

By Dr. WILLIAM JOHN COOPER

UNITED STATES COMMISSIONER OF EDUCATION, WASHINGTON, D. C.

THE National Advisory Committee on Education formulated its report on Tuesday, October 6, 1931, and shortly thereafter transmitted it to the President. It was released to the general press on November 16. In it are the findings and recommendations with regard to education of a committee of fifty-one persons, professional and lay. These I would consider with you briefly this morning and try to show in what ways the plans outlined have been so far realized.

It was found that there are seven important relationships of the Federal Government to education. They are:

(1) The relationship to education of the people in the various states, a matter which has had a long and changing history. Beginning with land grants without any restrictions whatever, each great war in which we have been involved has witnessed an ever-increasing federal control. In 1862 the Congress charged the Interior Department and the Federal Office of Education with the administration of moneys granted colleges by the Morrill Act. Through this act and acts amendatory thereto at the present time we distribute to the Land Grant Colleges in the various states and territories $2,550,000. As a matter of fact, the office is only the custodian of these funds and passes them on when the terms of the law have been met, a matter largely cared for by affidavit.

Much of the statistical work of our office is concerned directly with this topic. It was assumed when the law creating the Department of Education was passed that if the people of each state knew what other states were doing they would do similarly. Consequently we publish statistics: first, on universities and colleges; second, on the school systems of states; third, on city school systems, and fourth, on high schools.

In 1917 during the world war the Smith-Hughes Act was passed under which the Federal Board for Vocational Education distributes to the states at the present time about ten millions of dollars.

The Smith-Hughes Act was responsible for the creation of new administrative organizations—both federal and state. Thus there has developed—separate from the land-grant college system with its subordinate experiment stations and extension work—a second important federally-aided administrative system.[2]

In accordance with this act all plans of

[1] Address before General Session, Department of Superintendence, Constitution Hall, Washington, D. C.

[2] Federal Relations to Education. Report of the National Advisory Committee on Education, Part II, Basic Facts, pp. 55–56.

vocational education which expect to receive federal funds are subjected to the approval of the board. In addition to this approval there must be an equal sum raised by state or local taxation.

(2) The education of persons resident on special federal areas such as government reservations, the National Capital, and other districts lying outside of the various states.

The Constitution itself gave Congress exclusive control over a district not to exceed ten miles square for the seat of government. This district is governed under a commission of three persons. A board of education consisting of nine members is appointed by the courts to operate a system of schools. The budget for the support of these schools is prepared by the superintendent and his deputies, adopted by the board of education, passed on to the commissioners of the district, and then to the Budget Board and Committee on Appropriations of the House of Representatives. Each body feels free to cut off something. But even so a rather good school system is now provided for the approximately half a million people who live under the jurisdiction of the District of Columbia.

Likewise in the Panama Canal Zone there is a central system of schools organized according to the act of 1914 and having complete accountability to Washington rather than dependence upon local initiative. Although the white population has two high schools in the Zone, the colored have none and the Columbia University survey reports a serious situation for those children who graduate from the eighth grade and are not allowed to work until they reach the age of twenty-one.

In the other federal possessions involving a population of over thirty-three thousand people no provision whatever is made by the Federal Government for the pupils who are in the 481 lighthouse reservations nor for those on the fifty reservations of the Bureau of Fisheries, nor for such persons as are employed by the Department of State, Treasury, War, Navy, and Commerce, in various parts of the world. The Office of Education, in an effort to minister to these children, has sought the right to give them correspondence instruction, but so far Congress has not seen fit to give either the appropriation or the authority.

(3) Education of the American Indians and other indigenous peoples within the national territories. This is cared for by the Federal Government. Until recently the Office of Education provided the school system for the native peoples of Alaska. Since the fifteenth of March, 1931, this has been turned over to the Commissioner of Indian Affairs who also handles the schools for the natives in the western states. It is recommended that these Alaskan schools be handled by the Territory of Alaska in line with the plans to have all Indian affairs handled locally.

(4) Education of the people of the territories and outlying possessions. This has been a duty of the Federal Government until the people have been organized on a regular territorial basis. In both Alaska and Hawaii schools are operated in accordance with territorial acts. In the dependencies generally the matter of education rests with appointees of the Governor who is appointed by the President.

(5) The training of persons in the service of the National Government. Almost every department maintains some schools. In the State Department is a foreign service school; in the Treasury Department are some schools designed to train personnel for the peculiar work of the department; in the War Department there is a National Academy at West Point, the War College in Washington for the training of officers, and some fifty schools for the training of men attached to the different posts. This does not include the school work done in the civilian military training camps. In

the Navy Department also are about a hundred schools for the training of different vocations in the Navy. There are also training stations at Newport, Rhode Island, Hampton Roads, Virginia, San Diego, California, and Great Lakes, Illinois, for new recruits. All of these are in addition to the Academy at Annapolis for the training of officers for the U. S. Navy and a war college at Newport, R. I. In fact, some schools are maintained by each of the departments of the Federal Government excepting the Labor Department.

(6) Scientific research and the collection and diffusion of information regarding education. Scientific research is conducted primarily by the Departments of Agriculture, Commerce and Labor. The diffusion of information is carried on extensively by all departments. In the Interior Department research and diffusion of information regarding education are the chief responsibility of the present Office of Education. At the present time the cost to the government of the Office of Education proper is higher than at any previous date in its history. The regular staff costs about $290,000 to the Federal Government for salaries, approximately $25,000 for general expense, and some $62,000 for printing. At the beginning of the present administration the Office of Education was without a librarian. Shortly thereafter the editor died, and more recently the chief of the division of colleges and professional schools resigned to become professor of higher education at Ohio State University, and the chief of the statistical division transferred to other government work. Now all these places have been filled and in addition to them the following offices have been created:

First, an assistant commissionership has been created freeing the commissioner from much of the routine work of the office and permitting him to devote his time and energies to the nation-wide surveys and to work in the field. This place is ably filled by Miss Bess Goodykoontz, a graduate of Iowa State University and a professor of education in Pittsburgh University. She is assisted by Dr. J. F. Rogers, M. M. Proffitt and Dr. David Segal, the latter an expert on tests and measurements who came to us the first of last November.

Second, a section on the education of Negroes, which was only beginning to receive attention in 1929 in the survey of Negro colleges. There are in this office at the present time Dr. Caliver and his secretary on regular status and two temporary employees.

Third, a section on special education. A year ago we created this section with Dr. Elise Martens, well versed in the education of those mentally deficient and subnormal. This year we have added another specialist in the education of those physically handicapped, the blind, the crippled, the deaf, etc. Miss Beatrice McLeod is this specialist.

Fourth, the section on foreign schools, which was formerly in the Division of Adult Education, has been taken out and raised to a division in charge of Dr. James F. Abel. To it has been added Dr. Alina M. Lindegren, who has a working knowledge of the Germanic languages. There should be added to this division two more specialists, one an authority on the languages of China and Japan and the other an authority on the languages of Latin America.

Fifth, a section on radio education. This section, which was created when the National Committee on Education by Radio reported, was run for a year and four months on part-time basis through the generosity of the Payne Fund. It is now operating on a full-time basis with Dr. Cline M. Koon as specialist.

In addition to these changes the following are worthy of note: Mr. Timon Covert has been assigned the position of specialist in school finance. He is now working with the Survey of School Finance. Miss Mina M. Langvick has been assigned to a position in charge of elementary education in the American Schools Division. Miss Edith A. Lathrop has been put in charge of the relationships which should exist between the school and the library and is this year holding a grant-in-aid from the Carnegie Corporation which takes her most of the time in the field. With just a few more specialists scattered throughout the divisions the office will reach its maximum enrolment.

In addition to this, there are three surveys of major importance, (1) a survey of Secondary Education begun in 1929 and finishing June 30 of this year. This survey has been under the direction of Dr. L. V. Koos, of Chicago, and will bring to the front all the new practices in secondary education. (2) The Teacher Education Survey, which was begun a year later than the secondary survey and will be completed a year from this June, will bring out all approved practices in connection with the education of teachers. Dr. E. S. Evenden is in charge. (3) The Survey of School Finance, begun last July under the direction of Dr. Paul R. Mort, of Teachers College, Columbia University, is expected to run four years. On this study there have been but two meetings of the consultants, one held only last week.

(7) Intellectual and educational cooperation of the United States with other nations. There are now several committees at work on intellectual cooperation, some with the European nations and some with Latin America. In the State Department the Divisions of International Conferences and Protocol have charge of our dealings with other nations. We have had very pleasant relations in the Office of Education with this division of the State Department and have received a great many bulletins from it. Also the Pan American Union has a division of intellectual cooperation which handles the matter of international cooperation with the Republics to the south of us.

In order to accomplish the recommendation of this report, Mr. Reed, of New York, has introduced into the House of Representatives a bill, H. R. 4757, which creates a Department of Education with a Secretary and three assistant secretaries. There is transferred to the new department from the Secretary of the Interior the Office of Education, the authority over Land Grant Colleges, Columbian Institution for the Deaf and Howard University. The Federal Board for Vocational Education is abolished and its offices are entrusted to the Department of Education. In order to coordinate activity there is also created an Interdepartmental Council on Education which will consist of one representative and an alternate appointed by the head of each department.

THE YOUNG EDUCATOR AND THE DEPRESSION[1]

By Dr. CARTER ALEXANDER

Professor of Education, Teachers College, Columbia University

The relationship suggested in the title compels much thought these days from those of us engaged in training or advising schoolmen professionally. Young educators give it plenty of thought on their own account. But much of such thought by both groups has so far been futile because it has treated the depression like the weather.

[1] Delivered at the banquet of Kappa Phi Kappa, Washington, D. C., February 21, 1932.

Mark Twain long ago observed that while a good deal was said about the weather, nothing much appeared to be done about it. To be at all profitable, this talk must certainly try to show what the young educator can do in the depression to advance himself professionally or what the older ones of us can do to help him advance. Any attempt at this of course involves prediction.

Now prediction is so hazardous that even the experts, from economists to educators, shy at it. Furthermore, the little book "Oh Yeah"[2] has made prediction decidedly less attractive than formerly. And yet prediction is what most people really wish. In fact, they desire it so earnestly that when men who ought to know will not venture opinions, they will give ear to rogues if the latter but speak of the future with assurance. They will heed any one who can give reasonable grounds for definite and clear-cut expectations. So in making my predictions about the young educator and the depression, I am well aware of the dangers involved. But the knowledge and observations of over twenty years devoted to training school administrators have given me certain convictions and evidence. It is on this basis that I outline the changes in the professional careers of young educators that it seems to me this depression is making, or will make.

In the first place, the young schoolman is going to reach an administrative position like a principalship or a small superintendency far more slowly than formerly. From the way research work is being cut down, he will have fewer opportunities to start as a research assistant to a superintendent. Such things mean that often he must start his field work in a teaching position. In most regions the steady cash income of teaching during the depression has made the occupation much more attractive than formerly. The competition for even teaching positions is going to be far harder for the inexperienced man. He will all the time face competition from older teachers and from former teachers who are moving heaven and earth to get back on the school payroll. Many of these competitors will be men with families who will count heavily with board members also serving on unemployment committees. Against such competitors the beginner will stand little chance, unless he is unusually well prepared to teach valuable subjects over a fairly wide range. Furthermore, he must show far more evidence of successful practice teaching over a reasonable length of time than formerly.

This state of affairs means that the young educator is going to have to regard his teaching experience as part of his professional preparation for administrative work. The preparation is thereby stretched out by just so much. He must be willing to secure this extension, even if he can make little more than expenses during the period of teaching. In the long run, if he aspires to administrative positions, this will not be a bad thing for him. He will make all the stronger principal or supervisor for having had some teaching experience. But it also means that if he is to get any administrative experience during the first two or three years in the field, he must get it on the side by assisting the principal or superintendent, often by doing extra work in outside hours. A live and ambitious young teacher who will keep himself physically fit can do this. But it is no program for bluffers, lazy youngsters or physical weaklings. It means as well that a young educator will be wise to put off his courses in administration and supervision until after he has had some teaching. He can then really apply what he gets from such courses because it is learned nearer to the time for applying it. This of course means a fifth year or summer sessions equivalent to such an extra year, of professional preparation. But in

[2] Edward Angly, The Viking Press.

my judgment the competition of the depression is going to extend the preparation demanded of the young school administrator by that much at least. The young educator who does not recognize this is liable to be caught without oil in his lamp when he needs to light up for the job-hunting season on administrative positions.

A willingness to work and mental and physical capacity for long hours and application that will show results are going to count for much more than formerly. We hear a lot about four- and five-day weeks, a few hours a day for factory workers, and the like. But I foresee nothing of this nature in educational work carrying any responsibilities. Classes are going to be much larger. The teachers being let out now are the ones who can not handle modern subject-matter in large classes successfully. A teacher is going to be called on to take more classes a day. He is going to be expected to assume more student activity responsibilities. It is easy to pick out the young man who is going to get the chance to start teaching under these conditions. He is the one who can convince a superintendent that he can do more work and stand more work than the average man, and yet keep up standards by his superior command of testing techniques and by his knowledge of how to reach individuals in large classes quickly and effectively. The chaps with notions about doing ordinary amounts of work, with ordinary inclinations to exert themselves and with sloppy ideas of performance quality, will not get chances to teach. Instead, they will continue to warm the student chairs of the training institutions or live off their kinfolks.

A knowledge of how to do school work economically is going to be a great asset to a beginner, although formerly this was of little importance. He is not going to have much of a chance at the start to show what he can do except in the way of making the pitifully small allowances for equipment and instructional materials go as far as possible. If I were advising a young man going out to teach, on this point, I would try to give him detailed knowledge of the minimum books, equipment, tests and the like necessary for satisfactory work with large classes in his subjects. He ought to know how and where to buy these things most economically. I should also like to see him know how to make simple apparatus and equipment with inexpensive materials. In particular, I should advise him to make himself fairly proficient in typing, stencil cutting and mimeographing. With large classes and more of them, the difference between an enriched course of study, with good teaching, and a barren offering, with low grade instruction, is going to be a matter of using a mimeograph. If the young man knows how to use one, he can direct cheap clerical service on it profitably, get students to help him or in a pinch do some of the work himself.

Acute specialization in work pursued solely because of the young educator's interest in the subject is not likely to bring him quick returns during the depression. Specialization in some highly desirable work is, of course, always advisable. But as the employer determines this desirability, the young educator for some years to come should insure his future by having several strings to his bow. For examples, he should be able to teach science, not simply zoology or botany; modern languages, not simply German; the following combinations and not merely one of the items—mathematics and one or two sciences, several extra-curricular activities, both supervision and administration. The old, old recipe for success, being equipped to do one desirable thing better than any one else, still holds. But if the young educator changes the recipe by being equipped to do his specialty only well, or by omitting the specialty ingredient, he can't expect the results guaranteed by the use of the correct recipe. The young man sure of a job will be the one who can do surpassingly good work in such things as teaching his subjects, personnel work with boys, leading choruses or coaching athletics on the side. For him enough other work to fill out a program can always be scraped up by employers desiring him because of his special talent.

But avoidance of too acute specialization in his school work will not alone be sufficient for the young schoolman aspiring to rapid promotion. The depression is forcing all people to realize that human affairs under modern conditions are inextricably interwoven throughout the country, and indeed throughout the world. I believe the time is over when a young man can count on rising rapidly in education if he is an ignoramus outside his specialty. He will be expected to know the outstanding movements in other fields like business, finance, government and social welfare. Moreover, people will expect him to understand and interpret for them the movements in other countries in these fields that have a decided bearing on American affairs. The change I am emphasizing is well typified by Will Rogers. He started out with his humorous comments on rather narrow American interests. But now he often devotes his attention to world matters because he considers these of greatest importance to Americans. All this points clearly to one thing. From now on, the valued young educator will be the one who does a fair amount of intelligent reading of substantial articles and books about other lines of education, other occupations and general conditions for both this country and Europe. Those of us in teacher-training institutions will have to see that our students start such reading before they leave us, and that they know where to find the best brief treatments.

Some special equipment is necessary here for the young educator if he is to play any real part in the successful maintenance of the public school program. The prized young educator will be the one who can see the educational system as a whole, the relation of his work to it, the relation of both to the community's needs, and above all can bring citizens and taxpayers to see these things clearly. The young man who can present these things so as to secure public confidence and steadily maintained financial support will be particularly valued. This means that the young educator must not be content with merely academic or school interests. It means also that we in the training institutions must show him these outside relationships, start him to cultivating these outside interests, and in some way give him training in public speaking and in writing for the public. So far we have only too often fallen down on the job here.

To have the worth of his work recognized for advancement, the young educator must avoid hiding his light under a bushel far more than formerly. In any effort to gain recognition, work so good that if known it will command recognition, of course, comes first. But such merit alone is not enough. In the competition of the times the violet blushing unseen merely wastes its sweetness on the depression air. The people who count in the young educator's professional advancement must more than ever be kept informed of his real growth and his increasing capacity to take on responsibilities. By this I do not mean ballyhoo, sly reminders that he is ready for promotion and should not be forgotten or incessant appeals to be helped to a better job. Rather I mean talks, articles and reports of significant work accomplished, so worded as to carry conviction that the man has definite and clear ideas of unusual worth, or that he has done exceptionally good work. I mean writing that carries acceptable evidence of real work well done, and that is not manifestly put out merely to advertise the writer.

The young educator and those training him of course wish to know the fields in which there are the fewest competent persons awaiting positions. It is hard to make pronouncements on this matter at any time, the situation is so complicated. But at present there seem to be extremely few competent men in commercial education, elementary education, the supervision of elementary schools and adult education. There are plenty of commercial teachers, but few with four or more years of standard training above high schools, including good courses in education. For young men willing to teach a few years in elementary schools and then to take adequate graduate training in elementary education and supervision, the opportunities are very great. They will have chances at fine elementary principalships. Many a superintendent wishes some men principals, so that, if they are well prepared, they can be easily placed. The economy measures of the depression are retaining only the strongest teachers, those who can handle large classes. These teachers are demanding real leadership in supervision by supervisors with enough ability, mastery of subject-matter and professional training, to command their respect. Any young man of high native ability who will equip himself with elementary school teaching experience and adequate graduate work in elementary education, ought to be sure of an unusually fine career. The changing times of which we hear so much are throwing many adults out of work, and giving even the employed much leisure time. This makes educational provision for adults of all ages loom up as one of the educational fields sure to expand greatly before long. Any young man of ability who will make adequate provision for working in adult education can hardly fail to have chances to go up rapidly in that field.

Does all this seem too large an order for the young educator? Certainly it is not a small one. But then this depression is no Sunday-school picnic. It seems clear to me that for years to come only young men of evident ability who are willing to get really ready for large orders are going to be sure of good seats at the educational position's table. This same view appears in a recent New York *Times* editorial on the number of men in educational work: "Broad educational qualifications, together with specialized training, are now demanded, and keen administrative ability in executive positions."

The young educator can not change the depression any more than he can the weather. But he can use his head in making adjustments to the situation. In particular, he can act on the fact that the depression accents preparation. If he does these things, the economic slump ought to hold him back in his professional career no more than the weather hinders a man whose work must take the weather into account.

EDUCATIONAL EVENTS

THE APPOINTMENTS BOARD OF THE UNIVERSITY OF CAMBRIDGE

THE sixth quinquennial report of the Appointments Board of the University of Cambridge for the years 1927 to 1931 states that the work of the period has in its latter part been overshadowed by the world-wide economic and industrial crisis. That the results should show a very sensitive reaction to economic conditions is a proof of the actuality of the board's relation to trade and industry. Conditions in the Far East have curtailed the number of entrants to the great merchant houses and producing bodies which trade with the East. Further, the very low prices fetched by primary products have resulted in a serious fall in the revenues of the Crown Colonies, and the recruiting of the administrative and the scientific staff of these colonies has in consequence been much diminished. The recruitment to manufacturing firms at home has suffered, but not to the same extent.

The average number of appointments of all kinds in each year in the period 1922–26 was 389. The numbers during the present period were: 1927, 438; 1928, 483; 1929, 499; 1930, 501; 1931, 365. The largest number of appointments in business made in any one year was 258 in 1929. The number fell to 206 in 1930, and to 147 in 1931. The total number of appointments in 1931 was kept at the high level of 1929 mainly by an exceptional number of educational appointments (which included an unusual number of appointments in the Crown Colonies) and by an increase in the number of appointments to the scientific staffs of those colonies. A number of regular clients, including some of the largest firms or combinations, have in the last year suspended recruitment or reduced it to a minimum. The fall in the number of industrial and commercial appointments would have been still greater were it not that even in these times fresh names are continually added to the list of firms which apply to the board. For example, of 151 firms asking for graduate recruits in the last two years, 50 were making applications for the first time. Consequently, when the position becomes normal the recovery, so far as the employment of Cambridge men is concerned, should be rapid.

The distribution of the appointments gained in the last year of the period under review were as follows: Government departments, mainly scientific, 12; administrative appointments in commerce and industry, 66; manufacturing and technical appointments, 81; colonial administration, 14; agriculture and forestry, 25; Indian, colonial and foreign railways, public works departments and surveys, five; railway traffic, eight; journalism and publicity, eight; articled clerkships, six; librarians, one; hospital administration, two; medical, two; miscellaneous, three; educational appointments, 132.

THE INFANT MORTALITY RATE

THE lowest infant mortality rate ever attained by the cities of this country was that of 1930, according to the "Statistical Report of Infant Mortality," based on the records of 860 cities in the birth registration area of the United States, issued by the American Child Health Association. The 1930 rate—62.2 deaths for every thousand live births—is four points lower than that of the preceding year, when it was 66.2.

Inclusion in the birth registration area depends on registration laws accepted as satisfactory by the U. S. Census Bureau and on assurance that at least 90 per cent. of the births are registered. All but two states are within this area. The 860 cities reporting had a population of 10,000 or over in 1930. The report gives also infant mortality rates for 14 cities outside the area, 8 of them in Texas and 6 in South Dakota.

Seattle, with an infant mortality rate of 37, leads in the list of cities with a population of over 250,000. San Francisco ranks next, with 40, and Portland, Oregon, is third, with 41. In the preceding year, 1929, Portland led, Seattle was second and Minneapolis third.

Among the 10 largest cities in the country in 1930, two are tied for first place, Chicago and St. Louis, each with an infant mortality rate of 54. Cleveland stands next with 55, and New York follows with 57. Boston and Pittsburgh foot this group with 69. Nine of these ten cities, however, show lower rates in 1930 than in 1929.

Long Beach, California, with a rate of 43 leads the cities in the 100–250,000 class. Oak Park, Illinois, stands at the top of the 50–100,000 class with a rate of 28. Alameda, California, with 21, ranks first in the 25–50,000 class.

Among the smallest cities, with populations from 10–25,000, Shorewood, Wisconsin, is at the top with its infant mortality rate of 0.

As in other years, the states on the Pacific Coast and in the Rocky Mountains offer to babies their best chances for survival. The lowest urban infant mortality rate is in the State of Washington, where the figure is 41. Idaho comes second with a rate of 44, Oregon third with 48 and then three states each with 50, Utah, Nebraska and Montana.

It has been customary to publish this report in the middle of the year, according to Dr. Samuel J. Crumbine, general executive of the American Child Health Association, but a delay was necessary this time because of the work involved in the decennial census of 1930 which prevented the Census Bureau from issuing as early as in previous years its summary of provisional birth, death and infant mortality figures. The purpose of this statistical report, prepared under the direction of Dr. George Truman Palmer, director of the association's division of research, is to stimulate public opinion to support the work being done by the health officials and voluntary health agencies of the country in endeavoring to reduce the number of infant deaths.

THE SUMMER SESSION OF THE UNIVERSITY OF HAWAII

INTERNATIONAL understanding, the theme of the Pacific regional conference of the World Federation of Education Associations which will convene in Honolulu from July 25 to 31, 1932, will be emphasized in the University of Hawaii Summer Session, which begins on June 29 and ends August 9, 1932. Delegates to the conference have been advised by Dr. Paul Monroe, the president of the World Federation, that they will find these summer session courses useful in providing a background for the conference discussions.

Three noteworthy features of the Honolulu summer session deserve mention. Under the direction of Dr. Charles E. Martin, of the University of Washington, the first School of Pacific and Oriental Affairs will offer a number of lecture courses, seminars and round table discussions concerning Pacific international and educational problems. Serving with Dr. Martin on the guest faculty of this school will be Dr. Arthur N. Holcombe, of Harvard University; Dr. William Bennett Munro, of the California Institute of Technology; Dean Henry Grady, of the University of California; Mr. Chester Rowell, of Stanford University; Professor Wilfred J. Hinton, of the Bankers Institute, London, England; Dr. Kenneth J. Saunders, of the Berkeley School of Religion, and Dr. Kokichi Morimoto, of Hokkaido Imperial University, Japan.

A second feature is the coordination between the summer session and the World Federation Conference. Not only will university students be encouraged to attend the conference meetings, but several leaders in the World Federation will give special lectures at the university and some will be members of the summer session faculty. Professor Charles H. Williams, of the University of Missouri, the secretary of the federation, and Dr. Clair E. Turner, of the Massachusetts Institute of Technology, who played an active part in the Denver meeting of the federation last summer, will offer summer classes in the University of Hawaii, while Dr. Paul Monroe will give special lectures.

The other visiting professors on the summer session faculty will be Dr. Lester Wilson, of the International Institute, Teachers College, Columbia University; Dr. Arthur J. Jones, of the University of Pennsylvania, and Professor Virginia Van Norden Woodbridge, of the University of California at Los Angeles.

A third feature of the session will be the educational recreational program which will supplement the class work. Visits to Shinto and Buddhist shrines, inter-racial dinners, Oriental theatrical entertainments and Hawaiian celebrations will afford the students first-hand glimpses of the inner lives of the various Pacific peoples.

SCHOOL FOR TEACHERS OF ENGLISH AT ENGINEERING COLLEGES

TEACHERS of English in engineering colleges in all parts of the United States visit the Ohio State University next summer to study their own subject at a special school sponsored by the Society for the Promotion of Engineering Education. The session will be held from July 11 to 28.

Plans for the session are being made by Professor H. P. Hammond, of Brooklyn Polytechnic Institute, director of the society's summer schools for engineering teachers. Miss Sada A. Harbarger, of the English faculty at Ohio State, is chairman of the committee on English. Miss Harbarger will be local director of the session. Mr. Wilson R. Dumble, instructor in English, will be the secretary.

The general purpose of the school is the improvement of the teaching of engineering. The enterprise is the outgrowth of the general investigation of engineering education conducted by the society from 1924 to 1929. The sessions began in 1927 with those on engineering mechanics at Cornell University and the University of Wisconsin.

Since then, schools have been held as follows:

1928, electrical engineering, University of Pittsburgh; physics, Massachusetts Institute of Technology; 1919, mechanical engineering, Purdue University; 1930, civil engineering, Yale University; engineering drawing and descriptive geometry, Carnegie Institute of Technology; 1931, mathematics, University of Minnesota, and chemical engineering, University of Michigan.

Concurrently with the session on English at the Ohio State University this year, there will be a session on economics at Stevens Institute of Technology, Hoboken, New Jersey.

Members of the faculty of the Ohio State University have been active in the work of the society. Dean E. A. Hitchcock, of the College of Engineering, is a past officer. Professor W. T. Magruder, of the department of mechanical engineering, is a past president and charter member of the society.

THE AMERICAN COUNCIL OF LEARNED SOCIETIES

THE fourteenth meeting of the American Council of Learned Societies, being its thirteenth annual meeting, was held in Washington on January 29–30. The eighteen constituent societies were represented by forty-four delegates and secretaries.

The treasurer, Professor William E. Lingelbach, reported receipts during the year of $271,-467 and expenditures of $240,666. The expenditures had been for the following purposes: for administration, meetings, executive offices, etc., $31,925; for expenses incidental to affiliation with the International Union of Academies, $376; for publications of the Council, $1,882; for activities of planning and development, $9,-926; for projects of research and publication, including projects specially financed, with the exception of the "Dictionary of American Biography," $134,254; for grants-in-aid of research, to individual scholars, $20,735; for post-doctoral research fellowships in the humanities, $41,567.

The treasurer reported that support for general purposes, projects, grants-in-aid and fellowships, available until July 1, 1934, had been received since last annual meeting in the amount of $481,500, bringing the aggregate of all direct support secured since the organization of the council in 1920 to $1,820,366; additional indirect support made available over the same period amounted to $185,685.

The permanent secretary, Dr. Waldo G. Leland, announces the appointment, on part time, of Mr. John Marshall, of Cambridge, Massachusetts, as editor, bringing the strength of the executive staff to seven full-time and two part-time positions. The total budget of the council, for 1932, including fellowships and grants-in-aid, the "Dictionary of American Biography," and other specially financed projects, amounts to approximately $370,000.

Officers for 1932 were elected as follows: *Chairman,* Edward C. Armstrong, Princeton University; *Vice-chairman,* J. Franklin Jameson, Library of Congress; *Secretary-treasurer,* William E. Lingelbach, University of Pennsylvania; *Members of the Executive Committee,* in addition to the officers, Alfred V. Kidder, Carnegie Institution of Washington; Robert P. Blake, Harvard University; *Members of the Advisory Board,* Joseph P. Chamberlain, Columbia University; Edwin F. Gay, Harvard University; William H. Hammond, Library of Congress.

Upon invitation of the delegates of the American Philosophical Society, the council voted to hold the next annual meeting in Philadelphia on January 27, 28, 1933.

THE PRESIDENCY OF THE UNIVERSITY OF CINCINNATI

DEAN RAYMOND WALTERS, of Swarthmore College, was elected president of the University of Cincinnati on March 7 to succeed Dr. Herman Schneider. He will assume office on September 1. Dean Walters has been a member of the department of English and dean of Swarthmore College since 1921. He was graduated from Lehigh University in 1907 and after spending four years in newspaper work became successfully instructor and assistant professor of English. He was registrar of the university from 1912 to 1921 and has been associated with the editorial work of SCHOOL AND SOCIETY since 1918. Since 1921 Dean Walters has assisted President Aydelotte in building up the Swarthmore system of honors work.

In making public his acceptance of the presidency, Dr. Walters is reported to have said: "I am sorry indeed to leave Swarthmore. I have accepted the presidency of the University of Cincinnati, however, because I feel there is a marvelous opportunity there. I understand the university, which has 4,000 full-time students and a total enrolment of more than 10,000, wants to increase the liberal arts work. It has honors work now, but wants to emphasize and better it."

Dean Schneider is said to have been persuaded to accept the presidency early in 1929 with the understanding that the position was to be temporary. His resignation was presented and accepted at a special meeting of the university directors, who were unanimous in expressing their regret.

Dr. Schneider pointed out that his duties as president, director of the School of Applied Arts, director of the Institute of Scientific Research and dean of the College of Engineering and Commerce were too great a drain upon his health. He will continue in the three latter posts.

THE NEWLY ELECTED PRESIDENT OF THE DEPARTMENT OF SUPERINTENDENCE OF THE NATIONAL EDUCATION ASSOCIATION

MILTON C. POTTER, superintendent of schools, Milwaukee, Wisconsin, was elected president of the Department of Superintendence at its sixty-second annual convention held in Washington, D. C., February 20–25.

"It seems rather absurd that we should come here to eulogize a superintendent whom we all know so well," said William J. Bogan, of Chicago, in seconding the nomination of Dr. Potter made by Paul C. Stetson, of Indianapolis. "However, Frank Cody says an audience on an occasion like this demands its pound of flesh from so-called orators; therefore I am going to give an ounce or two. Dr. Potter has in Milwaukee the most wonderful collection of radicals and conservatives to be found in any city of the world—except Chicago—and in his eighteen years he has made them like him. He tells the truth to the radicals and to the conservatives, and he never bends his convictions to expedience. It may be that that is the cause of their liking for him. I maintain that any man in this great democratic nation who can retain his poise and his job, in such a position for eighteen years deserves something—perhaps the presidency of the National Education Association, who knows?

"Moreover Dr. Potter has a literary knack that I think is very becoming in a superintendent, president of this great department. He is one of the newer school that still has a liking and a love for the old classics. If you don't believe this, take a trip with him sometime and you will learn much about the classics that you never knew before—perhaps these things never were before for all I know—but you will learn much."

Following the second of Dr. Bogan, a dozen additional seconds followed each other in rapid succession, all of whom called attention to the high character of Dr. Potter's service to the association for many, many years.

"He has remained in the background when his place was at the front, but modesty has held him there and now at last some of his friends think that modesty has served all its ends, and we bold ones are going to try to push him over," was one of the tributes paid him.

Dr. Potter is a native of Allegan County, Michigan, where he attended the rural schools and taught in several towns before his graduation from Albion College in 1895. He secured his master's degree from the University of Chicago in 1905, and the honorary degree of Litt.D. from the University of Denver in 1915. For several years before going to Idaho Springs, Colorado, as superintendent of schools, Dr. Potter served at different times as elementary and high school principal in Oak Park, Illinois, and in Superior, Wisconsin. He was superintendent of schools in Colorado Springs, and later in Pueblo, Colorado, 1908–1912, and in St. Paul, Minnesota, 1912–1914.

Dr. Potter went to Milwaukee in March, 1914, as superintendent, and was reelected last January for another three-year term. This is, with few exceptions in the entire country, the longest continuous service of a superintendent in a city comparable in size to Milwaukee.

EDUCATIONAL NOTES AND NEWS

DR. ROBERT C. CLOTHIER, formerly dean of men at the University of Pittsburgh, who was recently elected the fourteenth president of Rutgers University, took office on March 3. He succeeds Dr. John M. Thomas, who resigned in October, 1930, to engage in business. Dr. Philip M. Brett, a trustee, has since then been acting president.

DR. JOHN JETER HURT, pastor of the First Baptist Church, Jackson, Tennessee, has been elected president of Union University, Tennessee. He succeeds Dean A. W. Prince, who has been serving as acting president since the resignation of Dr. H. E. Watters last spring.

DR. PAUL J. MACKENSEN was recently installed as president of St. John's Junior College, Petersburg, West Virginia. Dr. C. C. Hein, president of the American Lutheran Church, conducted the installation.

DR. RICHARD H. BENNETT, president of Lander College, at Greenwood, South Carolina, has tendered his resignation to become effective on June 1.

DR. WARREN WEAVER, professor of mathematics at the University of Wisconsin, was on February 1 appointed director for the natural sciences in the Rockefeller Foundation and in the General Education Board. He succeeds Dr. Herman Augustus Spoehr, who has resumed work with the Carnegie Institution of Washington.

MR. S. M. STOUFFER, superintendent of schools at Wilmington, Delaware, formerly superintendent at Pottstown and Hanover, Pennsylvania, has been elected president of the Delaware State Education Association.

DR. E. A. HOLBROOK, dean of the School of Engineering and Mines, University of Pittsburgh, has been elected president of the Coal Mining Institute of America.

MR. CHARLES S. DAVIS, superintendent of schools at Steelton, Pa., received in January a medal from his Kiwanis Club for outstanding service in the community. His service there covers fifty years as teacher, principal and superintendent. He is a director of the Kiwanis Club and chairman of its committee on vocational guidance.

THE silver medal of the Ling Foundation of Los Angeles, established as a memorial to Pehr Henrik Ling, founder of formal and corrective gymnastics, and awarded for distinguished service in the health education of children, was bestowed on March 1 on Miss Signe Hagelthorne, professor of physical education at New York University. The citation of Miss Hagelthorne by the foundation's governors read in part: "Through her efforts a program of formal gymnastics and corrective gymnastics has been organized for thousands of children to benefit them and to aid them so they may grow up to be healthy men and women. Her work has not only been recognized in this country but in her native land, Sweden, where she is known as one of the great leaders of physical education. As a scholar, as an educator and as a teacher she has proved herself a wonderful friend to all children."

THE eighteenth award of the Spingarn Medal of the National Association for the Advancement of Colored People for achievement by an American Negro has been made to Major Robert R. Moton, head of the Tuskegee Institute.

MR. CHARLES P. TAFT, 2nd, son of the late President Taft, has been appointed a trustee of Miami University.

DR. IRVING W. FAY, for thirty-five years professor of chemistry at the Polytechnic Institute of Brooklyn, will become professor emeritus on September 1. Professor Fay has been invited by the corporation of the institute to assume charge of the chemical museum and collections, and at its request will spend a considerable part of next year in Europe visiting museums and collections in foreign universities.

MR. WORTHINGTON C. FORD has resigned as lecturer on historical manuscripts at Harvard University. His resignation will take effect on September 1. He has held that post since 1910. From 1885 to 1889 he was chief of the Bureau of Statistics in the Department of State, from 1893 to 1898 chief of the Bureau of Statistics in the Treasury Department, both at Washington, D. C., and from 1897 to 1902 chief of the statistical division of the Boston Public Library. From 1902 to 1909 he served as chief of the division of manuscripts in the Library of

Congress, and from 1909 to 1929 as editor of the Massachusetts Historical Society.

Dr. Livingston Farrand, president of Cornell University, has been appointed a member of the Public Health Council of New York State by Governor Roosevelt to succeed Dr. Jacob Goldberg, whose term of office has expired.

Sir F. Gowland Hopkins, professor of biochemistry at the University of Cambridge, has been granted leave of absence with stipend for such one term as the general board may approve in each academic year in which he holds the office of president of the Royal Society.

The March issue of the *Yale Journal of Biology and Medicine* has been published as a "Mendel Anniversary Number" in honor of the sixtieth birthday of Professor Lafayette B. Mendel, professor of physiological chemistry. It has as a frontispiece an engraving of the portrait of Professor Mendel recently presented to him.

Dr. Eugene L. Pearson has been appointed director of the division of research and statistics in the Tennessee State Department of Education. The funds for the support of this department, including a director with a clerical assistant, are furnished by the General Education Board of the Rockefeller Foundation. The work in Tennessee will be similar to the work maintained by the General Education Board in the departments of education in other southern states.

Mr. John Lund, superintendent of schools of Norwalk, Connecticut, has been appointed to succeed Mr. Ulysses G. Wheeler, of Newtonville, Massachusetts, who will retire on September 1, having reached the age limit.

Mr. Charles Bowers, superintendent of schools of Holdrege, Nebraska, has been elected executive secretary of the State Teachers' Association, to succeed Mr. E. M. Hosman, who has resigned to become director of publicity for the University of Omaha.

After serving for more than twelve years as college editor and director of public information at the Pennsylvania State College, Mr. D. M. Cresswell has resigned to accept the invitation of Superintendent James N. Rule to direct similar work for the State Department of Public Instruction. Pending action by the college authorities, Mr. W. W. Dunlap will be acting director of the Penn State department and college editor. Mr. Dunlap has been a member of the staff in the department of public information for five years.

Dr. Evda Tillie Hankamer, of the University of Cologne, exchange professor at Wellesley College, has joined the faculty of the department of adult education of the Boston Young Women's Christian Association and is teaching second and third year German.

Governor Paul Martin Pearson, of the Virgin Islands, formerly professor of public speaking at Swarthmore College, is visiting the United States to plead for favorable action on various Virgin Islands bills before congressional committees at Washington.

Dr. Albert Einstein, who has been visiting professor at the California Institute of Technology, sailed from San Francisco for Germany on March 4.

Dr. J. Enrique Zanetti, professor of chemistry at Columbia University, will represent the Chemical Foundation of New York and the synthetic nitrate interests in the United States in a survey of the Chilean Nitrate Industry.

Dr. Quincy A. W. Rohrbach, professor of the history and principles of education and head of that department at the University of Pittsburgh, will spend the next semester in visiting educational institutions in the eastern part of the United States.

Dr. Payson Smith, Massachusetts commissioner of education, was the principal speaker at the dedication on March 4 of the new high school at Hamilton, which was built at a cost of $125,000.

The Dodge lectures on the Responsibilities of Citizenship, founded at Yale University in 1900 by William E. Dodge, of New York City, are being given by Dr. David Mitrany, writer on international politics and this year visiting professor in European government and international relations at Harvard University. Professor Mitrany is giving a series of four lectures on the general subject of "The Progress of International Government." The dates of the individual lectures, and their subjects, are as follows: March 3, "International Government in Perspective"; March 10, "Realities in State Equality"; March 17, "Communal Organization of World Affairs," and March 24, "Authority in the Modern State."

THE annual Howison Lecture in Philosophy at the University of California was delivered on March 11 by Professor Walter G. Everett, for many years head of the department of philosophy at Brown University.

THE REV. DR. GEORGE LEWES MACKINTOSH, for more than fifty years connected with Wabash College, at Crawfordsville, Indiana, as student, instructor, president and finally as president emeritus, died on February 29, at the age of seventy-two years. Dr. Mackintosh was president of Wabash from 1907 to 1926.

DR. ARTHUR BUFFUM CHACE, trustee and for twenty-five years chancellor of the corporation of Brown University, a leader in the Rhode Island textile industry, died on February 28. He was eighty-six years old.

OSCAR W. FIRKINS, professor of comparative literature at the University of Minnesota, author and literary critic, died on March 7 at the age of sixty-seven years.

WINWOOD PRESCOTT, professor of English at the Massachusetts Institute of Technology, was killed on March 1 when a pistol that he was cleaning was discharged. He was forty-seven years old.

THE ninth Annual Conference of the Faculties of the State Teachers Colleges of Pennsylvania will meet in Harrisburg on March 21, 22 and 23, in the Education Building. The program is now being planned by a committee of which J. Linwood Eisenberg, president of the State Teachers College at Slippery Rock, is chairman, and Henry Klonower, director of the Pennsylvania State Teacher Certification Bureau, is secretary. Other members of the committee are: William R. Straughn, president of the State Teachers College at Mansfield; T. T. Allen, president of the State Teachers College at East Stroudsburg; Carrie Belle Parkes, State Teachers College, Indiana; Elsie Bull, State Teachers College, West Chester, and Helen Ganser, State Teachers College, Millersville.

THE fifth annual meeting of the Mid-west Education Conference sponsored by the department of education of Washington University, St. Louis, will convene on April 1 and 2. At the general meeting on Friday evening Mr. Cameron Beck, personnel director of the New York Stock Exchange, will speak on the topic "The Cost of Leadership." Themes for the round table discussions on Friday afternoon are: Character research; problems relating to the elementary school teacher; parent-child relationships; guidance in the secondary school; education for the hard of hearing. The speakers on Saturday are Dr. Lois Hayden Meek, director, Child Development Institute, Teachers College, Columbia University; Dr. Melvin E. Haggerty, dean of the College of Education, University of Minnesota, and Dr. Otto Heller, dean of the School of Graduate Studies, Washington University.

THE third summer school will be held from June 11 to 20 in Prague, Czechoslovakia, under the auspices of the American Institute and the British Society of Czechoslovakia, at the Department of English, Charles University. The aim of the courses is to outline Central European, particularly Czechoslovak, civilization to the English-speaking students and visitors. The lectures will be combined with tours conducted by experts to historical places of interest, and with social evenings. Additional information can be secured from the Institute of International Education, 2 West 45th Street, New York City.

BY the will of Mrs. Frederick Courtland Penfield, New York University and the University of Pennsylvania receive $100,000 each for the establishment of scholarships.

A FUND of $50,000 from the estate of Agnes L. H. Dodge, widow of Professor Fred H. Dodge, of Rutgers University, has been received by Bowdoin College. The fund is in memory of Mrs. Dodge's father, the late Moses Mason Hastings, of Bethel, and will be known as the Moses Mason Hastings Fund. It will be used for endowment of scholarships, preference being given to "needy and deserving students from Bethel and Bangor."

THE Virginia House of Delegates on February 17 passed the bill providing for the conversion of the Fredericksburg State Teachers College into a college for women coordinate with the University of Virginia. The bill for a Liberal Arts College for Women passed the House by a vote of 72 to 21.

The School Board Journal reports that the board of education of Chicago at a recent meeting adopted a resolution placing in effect salary cuts for teachers and civil service employees beginning with February 1, and amounting to $6,801,000. The amount is included in the total of more than $14,000,000 eliminated from the 1932 school budget. Of the salary reduction, a total of $4,174,212 is taken from the regular teachers, who have received only two months' salary since April 1. A total of $817,000 in the salary saving has been effected with the discontinuance of night schools, summer schools and vacation schools. The remaining $1,810,400 will come from the civil service employees, including clerks, janitors, engineers and others, who will donate a month's work without pay.

THE members of the teaching staff of Atlantic City, New Jersey, have effected a saving of $120,000 in the budget by agreeing to donate 10 per cent. of their annual salary to the municipality's economy program.

OWING to lack of funds hundreds of public schools of Virginia will have to close their doors this year much earlier than usual, according to the report of Dr. Sidney B. Hall, state superintendent of public instruction, who has filed with Governor John Pollard a statement detailing the situation in every county. The statement, based on a report made to the Department of Education by the various division superintendents, shows that even in many of the counties which will run their schools for a full term, they will only be able to do so by borrowing money or making drastic cuts in the salaries of teachers.

DISCUSSION

THE LIBERAL ARTS COLLEGE AND SOCIETY

No less a person than the President of the United States, in a recent national broadcast, lauded the smaller liberal arts college as the institution which furnished the leaders of the nation in the past and to which the people would have to look for leaders in the future.

That brings up for discussion a matter which has been disturbing social-minded observers for a long time: the liberal arts colleges of our big institutions are not as effective, spiritually, as they should be, considering their prominence, their wealth and facilities. Upon examination one will find that the spirit pervading these colleges is quite different from that to be found in the smaller ones. In the latter, the teacher is still primarily a teacher; here teaching can still be practiced as a fine art, as an act of devotion, and the teacher has a deep interest in the young people coming to his classes. In the liberal arts colleges of the big institutions, teaching is generally looked upon as secondary, at least in practice; research comes first, as a means to success. The teachers are either beginners working for a higher degree, or they work for the higher ranks through publishing research. Those who are "mere" teachers are not welcome, and are treated accordingly. The younger teachers will gradually leave as they obtain their higher degrees, if they are not outstanding in scholarship; if they are promising "scholars," they will be retained. Like their superiors they will work in turn for an impressive list of "publications." Is it any wonder that the majority of undergraduates who have no scholarly interests are looked upon, and treated, as an unteachable horde, just cluttering up the venerable halls of learning? The fault, however, lies not with the students, but with the maladjustment of the teachers. The latter imagine themselves to be chiefly scholars and teachers of the graduate schools, when they actually should be, first and foremost, teachers of young America during its college years. In short, the liberal arts colleges of the big institutions have become untrue to their original purpose; they have allowed their vision to become obscured by two powerful influences:

(1) From Germany they have taken over cer-

tain standards of research, forgetting that the German universities were class institutions and graduate schools; that they were not interested in developing leaders of the nation, but rather experts for the multifarious civil service positions of an autocratic state. Their training produced great efficiency of a technical sort and shed much light, but radiated little warmth. The German people realize now that an entirely new structure must be reared to meet the needs of the times. In fact, modern Germany is looking to America for spiritual guidance because its own lights have failed.

(2) The spirit of the scientific colleges clustering around the liberal arts colleges has helped to keep this ideal of research on the pedestal. But the liberal arts college with its courses in arts and literatures has spiritually nothing in common with the colleges of weight and measurement and microscopic observation. In the scientific colleges teaching and research easily go hand in hand; the impersonal attitude of mind can successfully prevail where the facts of the experiments speak for themselves. The liberal arts college, on the other hand, should minister to the spiritual needs of the community; it should constitute the secular church in the cluster of human activities. The arts and literatures should not be turned into another set of vocational and professional courses. Here the great messages of the past, the aspirations of the human race as expressed by the very flower of the human mind should find their reverend and humble interpreters. In these courses, the teacher, like a true priest of the spirit and a firm believer in the perfectability of human institutions, should be happy to have the youths of the land, irrespective of their economic interests, flock about him. The more he can reach, the better for the land, and, in due course of time, for the world. Instead of that, not a few try to keep the students away by artificial restrictions and kill their joy in the spiritual messages of the poets and sages by routine procedure and tricky examinations.

The difference in spirit pervading these two groups is exemplified by the fact that the professors in the scientific colleges usually are also the leaders and discoverers in their respective fields; the professors in the field of letters, on the other hand, at best are great interpreters, but never creative poets and artists, such as form the subjects of their courses. The majority, by force of their petty research, are turned into the Wagner-type, as exemplified in Goethe's "Faust," smugly clinging to the parchment and the letter of the text.

Far be it from us to deny due credit to the great critics and investigators in the field of arts and literatures; they have shed much light. But teaching should never be sacrificed. Teaching in these courses should always hold a place of eminence as a high duty toward society and its future progress.

Business is waking up to the fact that it has no right to speak of "rendering service to mankind" by merely doing business in the haziness of "selfish enlightenment" of nineteenth century economic theory. To be of service, its leaders now realize, plans must be made with that goal definitely in mind. Likewise, scholarly efforts and research can only be helpful to society when directed by the proper spirit. "Research" *per se* is "not enough," no more than patriotism. The state universities have a particular obligation in this respect by cause of their origin and popular support.

Russia and young Italy have a passion and feel a keen joy in helping to build what they consider a better world. But they had to tear down much, particularly in Russia, and with great loss. No doubt, a fairer world must be built. It is our ambition that America lead the way in this, as it did throughout the nineteenth century, in the matter of political and religious freedom. The pliability and looseness of our social-economic structure, the absence of rigidity and class prejudices place it in an advantageous position to make those basic adjustments in social ethics and social practices which the twentieth century will irresistibly demand. It can do that magnificently and without destroying anything valuable, but its young generation must become more spiritual. The courses in the arts and literatures are the very ones where the spiritual elements can be got in their purest form, while the pick of the land is at the age where it can be most lastingly impressed for the common good. If we teachers of these courses throughout the nation fail to rise to this opportunity, if we conceitedly limit our radius of influence, if we give our students stones instead of bread, we truly become derelict in our responsibilities toward the great spirits of the past which we pretend to interpret. But we also sin against our students, and thereby against the future, for by our dulness or indifference we shall have wastefully retarded the coming of the day when there will be peace on earth and good-will among men.

FRANZ SCHNEIDER
UNIVERSITY OF CALIFORNIA

RECEIVERSHIPS FOR COLLEGES AND UNIVERSITIES

SHALL colleges and universities be forced into receivership or into bankruptcy? This question is confronting the educational world to-day and has already been answered in the affirmative in at least two cases. The danger is real enough to demand the attention of educators throughout the United States. For, if our institutions of higher learning do not receive relief from the effects of the long-continued economic depression (I use the word with some hesitation), not only will many more of them close their doors, but it is to be feared that some of them, at least, will likewise be subjcted to the very undignified and unusual procedure of receivership or bankruptcy.

Within the past sixty days two cases have been brought rather forcibly to my attention in this connection.

Case No. 1: On December 12, 1931, two former members of the staff of Atlantic University, who had been dropped by the board of trustees on December 10 as a measure of economy and for other reasons, applied through their attorney to the judge of the Circuit Court of Princess Anne County, Virginia, for a receivership for the institution. At the same time they were granted an injunction, which prohibited the board of trustees and other officials of the university from disposing of any of the institution's assets or disbursing any of its funds whatever. It is true that the university was financially in arrears so far as faculty salaries were concerned and that it had outstanding obligations, other than faculty salaries, to the extent of something like $25,000. The indebtedness to the faculty would have been almost entirely cancelled by voluntary action of the great majority of the faculty members themselves. But it appears that the two ex-members of the staff, who brought the court action, were actuated not only by motives of recovering the salary due them but also by the idea of eventually getting control of the institution and obtaining vengeance or something akin to it against the president and certain others.

As a result of these legal proceedings and in order to prevent the consummation of the very questionable desires of the two plaintiffs in question, the board of trustees of the university voted unanimously on December 19, 1931, to place the institution in voluntary bankruptcy. The result was the immediate closing of the university, although it had been planned to reopen on January 4, 1932, and possibly to continue through the session; the transfer (somewhat hurriedly, of course) of the students to other institutions on as favorable a basis as possible; and the ultimate sale of all the books, laboratory equipment and office furniture of the institution, so that the proceeds might be distributed among all the creditors. This has now been accomplished, and it is quite unlikely that the university will reopen at any time in the immediate future.

So far as I am aware, this is the first time in the history of American education that an institution of higher learning has been forced into bankruptcy or receivership. The lawyers, the trustees in bankruptcy and the referee in bankruptcy all assure me that there is no law covering an educational institution in these circumstances, and they have been compelled, therefore, to make such adaptations of the existing law as they could in this particular case.

Case No. 2: A newspaper dispatch from Mexico, Missouri, under date of January 15, 1932, carried the intelligence that fifteen members of the faculty of Hardin College, a Baptist institution located at that place, had applied for a receivership for the institution and that their applicaion had been granted, apparently with little question. A receiver was accordingly appointed and placed under the usual bond as required by law. His first announcement was to the effect that he would attempt to operate the college for the remainder of the present session, if possible. The alleged reason for the action of the fifteen faculty members involved is that "60 per cent. of the income from the endowment fund of $117,000 was pledged for the payment of teachers' salaries and other running expenses of the college under the terms of the incorporation of the institution." It is stated by the petitioners that a building program begun in 1924 interrupted the payment of teachers' salaries.

It is clear from a study of the above two cases that the immediate objective was the same in each instance, that is, the collection of back salaries on the part of the plaintiffs. Even admitting that the motive can not be impugned, the method of accomplishing the objective is open to grave question. Up to this time the church and the college were usually regarded in the public mind as being exempt from the methods ordinarily employed in dealing with businesses and individuals whose assets were admittedly smaller than their liabilities. But here we have something new in the educational field, which, if it has not already happened before, will certainly set a precedent for the future. And, as all the world knows, the law moves almost entirely by precedent.

It is not denied by any one that a college or university faculty has a right at any time to "redress of grievances." Heretofore, it has been the custom to petition the president or board of trustees of the institution involved for the adjustment of such matters as were open to complaint. Individuals and groups of faculty members have followed this course since time immemorial. Generally, the relief asked for has been obtained through these channels. Occasionally a faculty member, who was unsuccessful here, has carried his case to the courts in the form of a suit against the institution for the collection of so much in the way of back salary or damages as was due under the terms of a contract. Such agencies as the American Association of University Professors have always been ready to champion the cause of a professor and to investigate the grounds for any complaint referred to them.

But here we have something new under the sun. College faculties have discovered a way to bring about a change in the administrative and governing bodies of any institution, whose financial difficulties in times like the present make it impossible to pay salaries according to schedule. Imagine the appointment of a receiver for some church or religious denomination, which could not pay the instalments on money borrowed for buildings, educational work, missionary enterprises, and the like! One could hardly conceive of a lawyer, who was appointed as receiver for an institution of higher learning, carrying on the "business" of education in a very satisfactory way.

Surely there is much food for reflective thinking here so far as the future of higher education in America is concerned. Have we merely run into a passing fancy or will receivership and bankruptcy proceedings become a regular part of educational administrative procedure in the future?

WILLIAM MOSELEY BROWN
ATLANTIC UNIVERSITY
VIRGINIA BEACH, VIRGINIA

SPECIAL CORRESPONDENCE

EDUCATION IN FRENCH INDO-CHINA

THE school system in French Indo-China is portrayed by the direction general of public instruction in its report, "Le Service de l'Instruction Publique en Indochine en 1930," as young, multilingual, rapidly growing, and already in its first results justifying the hopes in which it was founded. The present scheme, the report states, was set up in 1917 by Governor-General A. Sarraut to (1) give French children in Indo-China education through the second cycle of the secondary school fully equal to that offered in France, (2) provide the mass of the indigenous population with a minimum of indispensable knowledge taught in the native tongues, (3) furnish to an indigenous élite a classical training given in the French language and based on the Far Eastern humanities, (4) offer opportunities for special physical and vocational training, and (5) provide Indo-Chinese higher education, general or technical, open under proper conditions of age and capacity to students from any country.

The French schools in 1930 numbered 33 primary, 6 superior primary and 3 lycées. They enrolled on these respective levels 2,977, 397 and 953 pupils. These schools carried on in the usual French way and following the official programs of France were fairly easy to establish and maintain in the larger cities; very difficult to handle in rural districts and small towns where but few French children are residing. Recourse is had to internats, bus transportation and the annexation of primary to superior primary schools and to lycées. The comparatively small number of schools and pupils has made coeducation rather general in this system, a plan not common in France. Indigenous and foreign children are admitted to the lycées if places are available after all the qualified French children have been accommodated.

For the great mass of the children, the Franco-indigenous schools offer a unit three-year course taught in the native language and closing with the examination for the certificate of indigenous elementary studies. The use of the mother tongues as vehicles of instruction greatly complicates the task. Annamite is used in Annam; khmer in Cambodia; laotien in Laos; and even for the small minority groups in the mountain regions teaching is carried on in their particular dialects. In 1930 the Service of Public Instruction issued 4,884,000 school manuals printed in the native languages. These mass schools in that year enrolled 338,379 pupils—a good showing, since compulsory attendance is in force in none of the five states but Cochin-China, and there only in part, and the education of girls is opposed in many sections of the Union.

In the three-year course no child need study a foreign language, but those that expect to continue their training in the Franco-indigenous classical courses elect either Chinese characters or French. From these pupils and others, selection by strict examination determines those that are to be the indigenous élite. They are then taught, through French as the medium, in the two-year primary, four-year superior primary and three-year secondary school courses. The studies are planned and purposed to give a broad, general, bilingual culture in French and the indigenous language both ancient and modern, and in science. Specialization is avoided. The final diploma is the local baccalaureate, now accepted in Indo-China for some purposes as the equivalent of the French baccalaureate. These classical courses in 1930 enrolled 45,139 pupils, of which 40,367 were in the primary cycle, 4,615 in the superior primary and 157 in the secondary. This system is just coming to fruition; the first examination session for the local baccalaureate was held in 1930.

Sending young Indo-Chinese to universities in France had proved unsatisfactory, and Governor-General Sarraut included in his scheme plans for a university open on a footing of equality to both French and Indo-Chinese and requiring the baccalaureate for admission. That university, the University of Hanoi, now comprises for general training the schools of medicine, higher studies, law and pedagogy; and for technical instruction, the schools of public works, fine arts, commerce, agriculture and veterinary science. It registered 551 students in 1930, most of whom live in the Cité universitaire de Hanoi, planned and regulated much like the Cité universitaire de Paris.

The expenditure for education from both the general and state budgets in 1930 was 10,558,224 piasters, or $4,136,712, counting the piaster at par, $.3918. This was 6.13 per cent. of the total budgets. The credits for education written in the different state budgets were in the following proportions of the totals: Tonkin, 14.23 per cent.; Cochin-China, 12.47; Annam, 14.45; Cambodia, 6.16, and Laos, 8.76 per cent.

J. F. Abel

U. S. Office of Education

QUOTATIONS

THE TEACHERS SCHOOL RELIEF FUND OF NEW YORK CITY AND THE HOFSTADTER COMMITTEE

Samuel Seabury, counsel to the Hofstadter committee, revealed to-day that his preliminary investigation of the school relief fund had disclosed evidence that coercive methods had been applied by certain district superintendents to compel contributions, that threats were made to reluctant teachers and that a mild state of terror existed in more than one school district.

Robert Davidson, special investigator for the Hofstadter committee in the School Relief Fund inquiry, gave his opinion to Mr. Seabury to-day that there is enough evidence of coercion to justify a thorough inquiry by the legislative committee, and he recommended also that the committee subpoena the records of the fund and ascertain not only how contributions were obtained and from whom, but to study all expenditures from the point of view of possible waste of money.

Beginning last October, the Department of Education, working through its organization of district superintendents and school principals, has collected approximately $500,000 for the relief of poor and needy children. Possibly half of that sum has been expended for shoes, clothing and other necessaries. About half, or $250,000, was turned over to the various district superintendents throughout the city for emergency use—cash on hand to be applied as circumstances demanded.

There was some grumbling among the more poorly paid teachers and among the $6-a-day substitutes—all of whom were required to contribute their money at the rate of 1 per cent.—but little real resistance except in isolated cases. But last January the department inaugurated a broader scheme of building up the fund. Contributions of 5 per cent. were asked of every teacher in the common and high schools, teachers of all classes. When that edict was given out rebellion raised its head as much as it dared. The Teachers Union protested vigorously, and other teaching associations added their protestations. Nevertheless the work of collecting the 5 per cent. went busily ahead.

Finally reports began to trickle into Mr. Seabury's office that collection methods were becoming rigorous. The reports had it that certain principals were threatening to "show up" teachers who had continued to give 1 per cent. instead of 5 or of some percentage less than the demanded 5.

There were reports also that principals mentioned were "taking it out" in classroom on teachers who were unwilling or reluctant, and that these methods were affecting the classwork report cards which eventually are filed in the offices of the Board of Education and upon which a teacher's standing altogether depends. When sufficient rumors piled up about these phases of the school relief fund Mr. Seabury concluded it was time to get to work and assigned Mr. Davidson to the preliminary inquiry.

Mr. Davidson questioned Frederick J. Reilly, principal of the Creston High School, at Creston avenue and 181st street, the Bronx, for three quarters of an hour to-day. He asked Mr. Reilly particularly what he knew about the collection activities of District Superintendent Anthony J. Pugilese, who is in charge of Districts 21 and 22 of the Bronx. In substance Mr. Reilly told the investigator that while he had a great admiration for Superintendent Pugilese he disagreed with the superintendent's methods. He himself did not hold with coercive methods, he told the investigator.

The name of another district superintendent, Charles E. O'Neill, in charge of Districts 43 and 44 of Brooklyn, has been brought into the inquiry, and Mr. O'Neill, together with all of his principals, will be called before Mr. Davidson to explain or give their version of charges regarding collection methods.

Mr. Seabury indicated that the inquiry into the School Relief Fund will be wide-spread and that a number of district superintendents and principals will be called to testify, along with scores of teachers. The records of the fund, both as regards income and outgo, will be scrutinized to ascertain if there is any basis for charges of waste and improper expenditures. One thing Mr. Seabury is anxious to find out is what limit has been set on the fund. Information reached him that $2,000,000 is the goal and that this must be attained before the close of the schools this June.—*The New York Sun.*

STARVING THE SCHOOLS

The recent meeting of the National Education Association superintendents in Washington brought out in disquieting tones a situation confronting the American school system. The closing of 750 schools in Arkansas, turning 36,000 pupils out of classrooms, indicates the depression's effect upon schools closed, colleges placed on short rations, educational budgets pared to below the subsistence level.

This is dangerous and it is unnecessary. We

are still the richest nation on earth, worth about three hundred billions in dollars.

Of our estimated national income in normal times of ninety billions we spend only two and a half billions on public schools. It is pertinent to remind ourselves that we spend more than two billions annually on tobacco; nearly the same on soft drinks, ice cream, candy and chewing gum; one billion on theaters and movies; nearly as much on jewelry, perfumes and cosmetics; half a billion on sporting goods and toys.

For every dollar we spend on schools we spend $2.61 on these luxury items. Out of every $100 of national income we spend $2.74 on schools, but $13.98 on passenger autos.

Compared with other nations, we spend little of our great wealth for public purposes. Great Britain uses 22 per cent. of her income for public purposes, Germany 20.1 per cent., France 17.1 per cent., Japan 14.4 per cent., the United States 10.4 per cent. Yet our per capita wealth and incomes are far greater than any of these nations.

It is axiomatic that the price of democracy is education, that the quantity and quality of our democracy is in direct proportion to the quantity and quality of our education. With machines giving us more and more leisure we must absorb this in the schools or pay the price in crime, degeneracy, deterioration and, hence, autocracy.

We can not afford to starve the nation's schools.—*The World Telegram, New York.*

REPORTS

REPORT OF THE COMMITTEE ON RESOLUTIONS OF THE DEPARTMENT OF SUPERINTENDENCE OF THE NATIONAL EDUCATION ASSOCIATION[1]

BECAUSE we believe that our convention theme, "Education: our guide and our safeguard, and one of the chief sources of our spiritual life, our cultural growth and our material power," expresses the ideals, the scope, and the function of the work which the Department of Superintendence fosters, and because we believe that this theme, to be of real value, should find expression in the policies of our department, we offer the following resolutions for your approval:

NEED FOR NATIONAL LEADERSHIP

Because of the serious situation with which Boards of Education and administrators are faced, there is a wide-spread demand and need for a continuance and an extension of national education leadership by the National Education Association, by the Department of Superintendence, by all other departments of the National Education Association, and by the Office of Education. Although the many and fundamental differences in the administration of our local public school units make uniformity of action during this crisis neither possible nor desirable, there are many services which these agencies could and should render.

Therefore, we recommend that the Executive Committee of the Department of Superintendence, as a temporary and emergency measure, be authorized to request of the National Education Association such additions to the Division of Research of the National Education Association necessary to assure the active members of this Department constant, accurate, and timely information on practices and trends in administrative procedures arising out of our present financial situation:

And that the officers of our Department confer with the officers of other allied organizations of the National Education Association and with the Office of Education for the purpose of determining what further national services these organizations can and should render.

[1] These resolutions were adopted, as also one presented from the floor which reads:

WHEREAS, The current emergency reemphasizes the fact that the financing of public education is a responsibility which should involve the technical advice of experts in taxation, the cooperation of professional school people, and the educational policy of the public;

Be it resolved, That the Department of Superintendence recommends that there be constituted in every state a group of citizens, including expert economists, competent school people, and representative laymen, to make a careful study of the existing system of taxation; and,

Be it further resolved, That since a comprehensive national study of school finance is under way under the direction of the United States Office of Education, the utmost cooperation should exist between such groups as may be established in the several states and the National Survey of School Finance.

SOCIAL STUDIES CURRICULUM

We recommend that the Executive Committee appoint a committee which shall prepare and send to the active members of this Department, at the earliest practicable moment, suggestive changes for such adjustments in the social studies curricula in our junior and senior high schools as our present social and economic situation has made necessary and vital:

SCHOOL AND BUSINESS

Because of the interdependence of our social, economic and educational life we urge that, when feasible, Boards of Education and administrators cooperate with other state, county and municipal officials to the end that, during this period of economic distress, ways may be found to effect economies in governmental administration which will not cripple the education of the children.

EDUCATION OF YOUTH SHALL NOT BE SACRIFICED

The welfare of the nation demands that the education of its youth shall not be sacrificed. To this end we call the attention of Boards of Education and of all legislative bodies, who find themselves confronted with the necessity for economy, to the imperative need for the maintenance of instructional standards. Let economies be made in the material programs of government, but let America not falter in the training of her youth.

FINANCIAL SUPPORT FOR OFFICE OF EDUCATION

We urge that increased financial support be given to the Office of Education in order that it may continue to render its valuable services to the schools of this country. We particularly wish to commend the present Commissioner of Education for his keen, active and intelligent interest as shown by the commissions appointed to conduct research in various phases of public education.

The report of the President's National Advisory Committee on Education has presented to our profession and to laymen an adequate consideration of federal relations to education. Their report is a document which deals with fundamental principles which should govern the relations of the federal government to the several states in the establishment and development of our system of public education. It is a state paper of first importance. It proposes that the control and administration of education be left to the states, and that there be established in the federal government a Department of Education with a Secretary of Cabinet rank. We concur in these proposals and recommend the study of their report to the members of our profession and to the lay public.

CITIZENSHIP TRAINING

Your committee endorses the resolution relative to citizenship training adopted February 28, 1929, at the meeting of the Department at Cleveland, Ohio.

"Again we remind ourselves that our state systems of education were established in accord with the proposals of Washington, Franklin, Jefferson, and a long line of far-seeing statesmen for the purpose of preserving and improving our political institutions. Again we recall that our wages are paid and our equipment provided by a tax on all the people whether or not they be parents. Thus reminded, we pledge ourselves anew to the direct teaching of the duties of citizenship in all the school grades. Not culture, nor scholarship, nor self-support, nor compliance with the entrance requirements of more advanced schools shall turn us from the duty of teaching our youth the needs of our civic life and from inspiring our citizens with a determination to improve it."

We recommend that increased emphasis upon citizenship training be given in all curricula reorganizations.

HISTORY TEACHING

We believe that true patriotism is not served by ignorance and refusal to face facts and problems. Therefore, the history taught in our public schools should include an intelligent effort to arrive at essential facts involved in the significant crises of the past in order to prepare our people to deal intelligently and justly with such crises in the future. We urge that instruction in history and other social studies shall present impartially the chief factors and influences operating in domestic and world affairs, and producing problems in peace and war.

Because we believe that only an enlightened public opinion, based on accurate information arrived at after a full and free discussion of facts and issues, can give to our nation real and adequate security, we feel that the dissemination of vital facts with honest discussion of the issues involved is a responsibility of the nation's schools.

RESPECT FOR CONSTITUTION OF THE UNITED STATES

The Department of Superintendence urges teachers to continue to impart respect for the Constitution of the United States and for all of its various amendments. We urge the continued, vigorous and impartial enforcement of the entire Constitution of the United States as the supreme law of the land and we reaffirm our belief in the principles of the Eighteenth Amendment and in the habits of life and conduct which it is intended to inculcate.

Children's Charter

We trust that the influence of this Department and of those organizations with which we are allied will be directed toward the realization of the high ideals set forth in the "Children's Charter" adopted by the White House Conference on Child Health and Protection so that our educational system may insure "For every child these rights, regardless of race or color or situation, wherever he may live under the protection of the American flag."

Parent-Teacher Organizations

The Department of Superintendence acknowledges with gratitude the splendid spirit of cooperation and of helpfulness shown by the national, state, and local Parent-Teacher Organizations and urges upon Boards of Education and superintendents of schools the necessity for even closer relationships with this splendid organization.

Standards of Department of Secondary School Principals, Etc.

We commend the high standards set by the Department of Secondary School Principals; the Department of Elementary Principals; the Department of Classroom Teachers; and other allied organizations and departments of the National Education Association and the Department of Superintendence; and we pledge to them our cooperation to the end that the high ideals of preparation before and during service of the members of these departments may be encouraged and maintained. If education is to realize its ideal as one of the "chief sources of our cultural and spiritual life," it will be realized only through the type of services rendered by the principals and teachers in the buildings and classrooms of our public schools.

Department of Public Relations

At no time in the history of public education has it been more important that the relationship between the public and the schools shall be one of sympathy, cooperation and understanding. We recommend, therefore, that extraordinary efforts be made to continue courteous, tactful, and considerate public relationships; that administrators gain and keep the confidence of the community through the increased efficiency of the school system, the impartiality of its officials, and the far-sightedness and justness of the policies of Boards of Education; and that Departments of Public Relations, whether in a system so small that the superintendent is the department, or in a city large enough to have its own organization, be established. Such a policy will be a legitimate and necessary source of friendliness between a public school system and the community which it serves.

Relationship Between Boards of Education and Superintendents of Schools

We go on record again as approving the findings and recommendations of the committees on relationships between Boards of Education and Superintendents of Schools as reported at earlier meetings of this Department by the late Dr. Charles E. Chadsey and Dr. E. C. Hartwell. Because we feel that the theme of this convention will be realized more effectively through a redefinition of these relationships, and because throughout the country there is still a wide difference of procedure in this important matter, we recommend that the Executive Committee of the Department of Superintendence be asked and authorized to have compiled by its secretary a statement of these relationships as reported by these committees and to have such statement included in the next annual printed report of the proceedings of this Department.

Lay Relations Committee Formulate Methods for Protection of Members of Department of Superintendence

Other professional bodies have adopted and put into practice methods of procedure which have been a safeguard to those in other professions against unjust assaults from within and from without their own membership. We recommend that the Lay Relations Committee be charged with the formulation of such practicable methods of procedure as will give to the active members of the Department of Superintendence the same adequate protection now afforded to the members of the Legal and Medical professions and to the professors in our universities and colleges.

Committee on Lay Relations—Size of Annual Convention

We acknowledge with gratitude the work of the "Committee on Lay Relations" and subscribe heartily to its findings. It is our belief that the best interests of the Department of Superintendence are served when the number of affiliated groups is reduced so that the "Department itself may be assured of its own place in its own national convention." The point has been reached where it is scarcely possible for any city to supply adequate facilities for the annual winter meeting with any degree of comfort to its own membership. Various social functions, numberless breakfasts, luncheons and dinners and a wide variety of extraneous interests combine to defeat the purpose of our annual meeting. We protest against the practice of those organizations, not affiliated with the Department of Superintendence, of holding their meetings in the same city and at the same time as the annual meeting of the Department of Superintendence and thus, still further, increasing the problem of taking care of the winter meeting.

We ask that the Executive Committee forward to each unaffiliated organization a copy of this resolution.

COMMERCIAL, SEMI-COMMERCIAL, ETC., ENTERPRISES

Commercial, semi-commercial, and philanthropic enterprises have long sought, and in many cases gained, access to the school children and teachers through the schools. The schools should promote only those enterprises which represent the best interests of the children in their charge and should refuse to allow them to be exploited in any way whatever.

CONTESTS

We view with disfavor the tendency toward the multiplication of district, sectional, state and national contests. These contests now embrace every conceivable activity—some conducted by professional organizations with a high purpose, but many representing only thinly veiled commercial interests. Regardless of sponsorship these state contests involve almost certain disorganization of school work, the solicitation of funds for their financial support, special preparation and great nervous strain on the part of the contestants. Therefore, we feel that such district, state, and national contests should be discouraged, and eventually, unless of proved social and educational benefit, abolished. We also go on record as opposed to prize essay contests and other individual competitions for material rewards.

OBSERVANCE OF SPECIAL DAYS, WEEKS, ETC.

The increasing demand upon the schools for the observance of special "days," "weeks," holidays and half-holidays has increased to the extent that it presents a real problem in school administration. Many of these observances have little or no educational value and represent an attempt of commercial interests to advertise in the schools. Others, with more respectable sponsorship, do not make a contribution to the educational life of the schools commensurate with the effort and the energy required properly to administer them. When the relatively short time that pupils are in school, the cost of each school day, and the difficulty of finding time to carry out the school program are considered, it is apparent that administrators and Boards of Education must take steps to discourage such encroachments upon the work of the schools. This department recommends that school administrators set up standards by which to measure the value of these requests and that a definite limit be placed upon the number of school projects to be undertaken in any one school year.

EXCHANGE OF STUDENTS, PROFESSORS—INTERNATIONAL CONFERENCES, ETC.

We endorse the resolution adopted by the National Education Association, July, 1931, favoring "the exchange of students and professors, the formation of international education associations, and the holding of international education conferences, for all of these promote world understanding, friendship, cooperation and peace."

WORLD FEDERATION OF EDUCATION ASSOCIATIONS—WORLD COURT

We commend and endorse the World Federation of Education Associations program for world understanding. The Department of Superintendence once again goes on record favoring the prompt adherence of the United States to the Permanent Court of International Justice as a means of stabilizing world relationships.

APPRECIATION OF TEACHERS

In closing we pay tribute to those teachers, principals, and others connected with our public schools who, under most difficult and trying conditions and at great self-sacrifice, have demonstrated unusual devotion and loyalty to their tasks. In spite of an uncertain future; of reduced salaries; of payless pay days, they have remained at their posts; they have performed their duties conscientiously; they have, from slender savings, given generously to the support of public relief measures; and they have provided thousands of school children with food and clothing. Their example is an inspiration to all of us. They have proved anew that the true teacher is concerned primarily, not with money, but with the welfare of the children under his care.

APPRECIATION OF HOSTS, ETC.

To the President of the United States for his graciousness in appearing on this program; to the citizens of Washington for their hospitality; to the local and national Press for their splendid publicity service; to the National Broadcasting Company, Columbia Broadcasting Company and Station *WRC*, Washington, for their very effective cooperation in broadcasting our programs; to the Boy Scouts, the Girl Scouts and all allied organizations; to Superintendent Frank W. Ballou and his assistants for the effectiveness of the arrangements made for this convention; to President Broome for his inspiring leadership and for the high plane upon which he has placed this meeting; for all of these things and to all of these people and organizations and to many, many more, we express our deep appreciation and our gratitude.

EDUCATIONAL RESEARCH AND STATISTICS

THE REPRESENTATION OF THE COLLEGES IN GRADUATE AND PROFESSIONAL SCHOOLS

METHODS of measuring the colleges are, of course, very numerous and have proven useful to various accrediting agencies in recent years. The number of professors relative to students, the degrees of the faculty members, the number of volumes in the library, the endowment, are all useful criteria of colleges. They all fall short, however, in that they measure the machine rather than the product, and it is the product of the college which is important to society.

Measures which describe more accurately the product are much more difficult to apply. Requirements for admission or graduation can be accurately expressed on paper, but their administration may be a totally different matter. The standing made by students in a general examination like that recently applied to the colleges of Pennsylvania by the Carnegie Foundation gives a picture, imperfect to be sure, of the intellectual qualities of the students at different periods of their formal education. The quality of graduates is also indicated by the frequency with which the alumni are met with in certain lists of notables, such as "Who's Who in America," or "American Men of Science." The measure of the intellectual interest of the undergraduate colleges which is applied in the present study is the representation of the colleges by recipients of the bachelor's degree in certain types of graduate and professional schools.

This measure of the product of the colleges is naturally imperfect. The quality of the representatives, for example, is not taken into account. Many students in the graduate and professional schools fall by the wayside before attaining their higher degrees. It is assumed that the number of students aspiring to these more advanced institutions reflects the intellectual quality of the undergraduate body. A further imperfection arises from the fact that the number of graduate and professional schools is only partial. The list has been arbitrarily limited to graduate schools of arts and science, medical schools, law schools and schools of theology as representative of the traditional learned professions. No attempt has been made to gather data from graduate schools of business administration, education, journalism, dentistry, forestry, etc., although it is not to be inferred that these schools are in any way less worthy. But even in this restricted group of higher institutions it has not been possible to gather all the data desired because of the limitations of time and the incompleteness of the published records of some of the higher institutions. Apparently such institutions as the Graduate Schools of Michigan, Wisconsin, New York University and the Law School of Minnesota do not publish the academic antecedents of their students. In all, the academic antecedents of the students of 30 graduate schools of arts and science, 21 medical schools, 16 law schools and 12 theological schools have been obtained. I am under obligations to all those administrative officers who have generously supplied me with the necessary data for completing this study and wish to acknowledge the data presented in this study.

To draw conclusions from the data here presented might be premature. Certainly it would be more fitting for the administrators of our educational institutions to do this. It is hoped, indeed, that those who direct the policies of our colleges may find something of value in the data presented in this study.

The graduate schools of arts and science the academic antecedents of whose students have been investigated are as follows: Brown, Bryn Mawr, California, California Institute of Technology, Chicago, Clark, Columbia, Cornell, Duke, Harvard, Indiana, Iowa State, Johns Hopkins, Kansas, Massachusetts Institute of Technology, Minnesota, Missouri, North Carolina, Northwestern, Pennsylvania, Princeton, Rochester, Smith, Stanford, Stevens Institute, Texas, Virginia, Western Reserve, Worcester Polytechnic, and Yale. The medical schools upon which this study is based are as follows: Chicago, Columbia, Cornell, Harvard, Indiana, Jefferson, Johns Hopkins, Johns Hopkins School of Hygiene, Michigan, Minnesota, Northwestern, New York University, Pennsylvania, Pittsburgh, Rochester, Stanford, Temple, Virginia, Washington University (St. Louis), Western Reserve, and Yale. The law schools upon which this study is based are as follows:

California, Chicago, Columbia, Cornell, Harvard, Iowa, Maryland, Michigan, Northwestern, Pennsylvania, Pittsburgh, Stanford, Southern California, Western Reserve, Wisconsin and Yale.

It is with some hesitancy that the data from the theological schools are here presented for several reasons. In the first place, the list of schools from which data have been obtained is quite restricted. In addition, religious belief and moral qualities play so large a part in the determination of the students that the theological schools usually have a different standard for admission from the other types of professional schools. Besides, the students of some of the more strictly denominational theological schools come from a greatly restricted number of sectarian colleges, so that the omission or inclusion of a single theological school may affect unduly the representation of certain colleges. The institutions upon which this study is based include: Auburn, Boston University, Chicago, Chicago Presbyterian, Colgate-Rochester, Drew, Hartford, Harvard, Lutheran Seminary of Philadelphia, Princeton, Union and Yale.

The numerical representation in the post-graduate institutions of some 240 undergraduate institutions was determined. Table I shows the representation of all the institutions which have twenty or more alumni in the graduate and professional schools which have been investigated; 173 in number. The numbers followed by an asterisk are probably too small because of the lack of data from graduate schools located in neighboring territory which no doubt draw heavily from the nearby colleges. Some institutions are possibly omitted because of the lack of data from institutions of which they may be important feeders.

The University of Minnesota has the largest number of representatives, in graduate schools of arts and science, 1,075, followed in order by Chicago with 1,044, Stanford with 1,034, University of Pennsylvania with 674, Columbia with 665, Harvard with 652, Iowa State University with 546, Indiana with 478, Cornell with 397, California with 342, Texas with 335, and Yale with 303.

In the number of alumni who are enrolled in the medical schools studied, New York University leads with 292 graduates, followed by Michigan with 252, University of Pennsylvania with 241, Columbia with 233, Chicago with 216, Harvard with 204, Indiana with 184, Stanford with 173, Pittsburgh with 164, Yale with 157, Cornell with 142, College City of New York with 125, and Princeton with 102.

In the number of alumni who are enrolled in the law schools studied, Michigan stands first with 498, Pennsylvania second with 322, Harvard third with 315, California fourth with 260, Stanford fifth with 240, Princeton sixth with 203, Columbia seventh with 186, Yale eighth with 171, Southern California ninth with 158, and Chicago tenth with 156.

The representation of the undergraduate colleges in the schools of theology is not as completely determined as is desired. A number of institutions did not respond to requests for information so that the number of theological schools from which data have been obtained is small. Besides, the strong denominational affiliation of many colleges often makes their student bodies rather local in origin, with the result, as already pointed out, that the representation of alumni is seriously affected by the list of theological schools included in the study. In the number of alumni who are enrolled in the theological schools studied, Chicago heads the list with 130, followed by Ohio Wesleyan with 73, Boston with 60, Muhlenberg with 57, Yale with 55, Columbia with 49, DePauw with 36, Syracuse with 30 and Wooster with 26.

In order to obtain a more accurate picture of the intellectual qualities of undergraduate bodies regardless of size, their representation in graduate schools of arts and science is expressed in Table I also as a percentage of the undergraduate enrolment. The figures for the undergraduate enrolment upon which the percentage is based are those published by Raymond Walters in his paper in SCHOOL AND SOCIETY for December 13, 1930. In the case of the larger institutions with many special schools the combined number of college men and college women and engineers as given in his Table I was used; in the case of other institutions not included in this table, only the full-time students enumerated in his Table III have been used. The omission of a percentage for the tables is because of the omission of the figures of college enrolment from Walter's study.

The variations in the relative numbers of

TABLE I

In the Following Table, the Columns Headed *a* Show the Number of Graduates Enrolled in the Higher Institutions; Those Headed *b* Show the Number Expressed as a Percentage of the Undergraduate Enrolment

Institution	Grad. Schools Arts and Sci.		Med. Sch.		Law Sch.		Theol. Sch.		Totals	
	a	b	a	b	a	b	a	b	a	b
Adelphi	35*	5.9	1*	0.2					36*	6.1
Akron	15*	1.4	7	0.7	6	0.6			28*	2.6
Alabama	36*	0.9	30*	0.8	6	0.1	2	0.1	74*	1.9
Albion	18*	2.4	14	1.9	10	1.3	10	1.3	52*	6.9
Allegheny	25	4.0	17	2.8	19	3.1	10	1.6	71	11.5
Amherst	71	10.5	37	5.5	44	6.5	11	1.6	163	24.1
Arkansas	25	1.5	6	0.3	6	0.3			37	2.2
Augustana	19	4.8	1	0.3	2	0.6	5	1.3	27	6.9
Baker	35	9.3	3	0.8			19	5.1	57	15.1
Bates	37	5.8	6	0.9	2	0.3	9	1.4	54	8.4
Baylor	67	6.7	9	0.9	1*	0.1			77*	7.7
Beloit	32*	6.6	4	0.8	16	3.3	18	3.6	70*	14.5
Boston	21	1.2	11	0.6	21	1.2			53	2.9
Boston Univ.	72*	1.3	4*	0.1	6	0.1	60	1.1	142*	2.5
Bowdoin	33	5.9	26	4.6	17	3.0	5	0.9	81	14.5
Brooklyn P. I.	21	4.5	1	0.2	1	0.2			23	4.9
Brown	174	9.5	45	2.4	50	2.7	7	0.4	276	15.0
Bryn Mawr	78	16.9	7	0.2	3	0.1	1	0.1	89	19.3
Bucknell	49	4.2	41	3.5	15	1.3	14	1.2	119	10.2
Buffalo	20	1.2			1	0.1			21	1.3
Butler	61		6		4		11		82	
California	342	3.1	38*	0.3	260	2.3	5	0.1	645*	5.5
Calif. I. T.	69	10.5	1*	0.1	6	0.9			76*	1.5
Calvin	11	3.1	13	3.7	4	1.1	7	2.1	35	10.0
Carleton	83	9.0	11	1.2	10*	1.1	6	0.7	110*	12.0
Carnegie I. T.	18	0.7			2	0.1	1	0.1	21	1.0
Case	20*	2.6	2	0.3					22*	2.9
Cath. U. of Amer.	15	1.4	11	1.1	10	1.0			36	3.5
Center	4	1.0	7	1.8	4	1.0	1	0.2	16	4.1
Chicago	1,044	35.0	216	7.2	156	5.2	130	4.4	1,546	48.4
Cincinnati	24*	0.9	2*	0.1	6*	0.3	5	0.2	37*	1.0
Clark	57	18.1	2	0.6	2	0.6	6	1.9	67	21.2
Coe	92	11.6	4	0.5	4	0.5	4	0.5	104	13.0
Colby	17	2.8	13	2.1	6	1.0	6	1.0	42	6.9
Colgate	41	4.1	43	4.3	27	2.7	23	2.3	134	13.4
C. C. N. Y.	289	5.4	125	2.4	133	2.5	2	0.1	548	10.3
Colorado Col.	33*	6.3	3	0.6			3	0.6	39*	7.5
Colorado	65*	2.0	6*	0.2	8	0.3	1	0.1	80*	2.5
Columbia	665	18.1	233	6.4	186	5.0	49	1.3	1,133	30.0
Cornell Col.	86	16.5	2	0.4	4	0.8	12	2.3	104	20.0
Cornell Univ.	397	13.0	142	4.6	83	2.7	7	0.2	629	20.5
Dartmouth	111	4.8	59	2.5	118	5.1	7	0.3	273	12.7
Davidson	34	5.5	19	3.1	6	0.9	5	0.8	64	10.3
Delaware	28	3.8	7	0.9	13	1.8	2	0.2	50	6.7
Denison	37*	4.5	7	0.8	10	1.2	14	1.7	68*	8.2
Denver Univ.	22*				6		5		33*	
DePauw	95	6.0	23	1.5	15	1.0	36	2.3	169	10.8
Dickinson	35	6.4	26	4.7	20	3.6	21	3.8	102	18.5
Drake	46	3.9	4	0.4	5	0.4	9	0.8	64	5.4
Drury	12	3.0	6	1.5	2	0.5	2	0.5	22	5.4
Duke	154	6.8	16	0.7	3	0.1	5	0.2	178	13.8
Earlham	47	11.1	9	2.1	3	0.7	5	1.2	64	15.1
Elmira	19	3.3	2	0.3			5	0.9	26	4.5
Emory	47	4.0	10	0.9	1	0.1	11	0.9	69	5.9
Franklin and Marshall	54	7.4	37	5.1	10	1.4	10	1.4	111	15.3
Furman	25	6.0	3	0.7	1	0.2	5	1.2	34	8.1
Florida	14*	0.6	15*	0.7					29*	1.3
Fordham	15	0.4	23*	0.6	15*	0.4			53*	1.4

Institution	Grad. Schools Arts and Sci.		Med. Sch.		Law Sch.		Theol. Sch.		Totals	
	a	b	a	b	a	b	a	b	a	b
Geo. Washington	42*	2.3	2*	0.1	9*	0.5	3	0.2	56*	3.0
Georgetown	7	0.3	2*	0.1	35	1.3			44*	1.7
Georgia	9*		6*		9*				24*	
Gettysburg	35	6.0	15	2.6	8	1.3	8	1.3	66	11.3
Goucher	55	6.3	13	1.5	5	0.6	2	0.2	75	8.6
Grinnell	85	12.9	8	1.2	10	1.5	4	0.6	107	16.2
Gus. Adolph	36	8.6	2	0.4	1	0.2	3	0.7	42	9.6
Hamilton	35	7.7	21	4.6	14	3.1	5	1.1	75	16.6
Hamline	62	13.6	2	0.4			9	2.0	73	16.0
Hanover	21								21	
Harvard	652	18.6	204	5.8	315	9.0	20	0.6	1,191	34.1
Haverford	44	14.7	14	4.7	27	9.0	1	0.3	86	28.1
Heidelberg	7	2.2	9	2.8	3	0.9	11	3.4	30	9.3
Hiram	30*	8.8	3	0.9			7	2.0	40*	11.7
Hobart	16	4.8	8	2.4	4	1.2	1	0.3	29	8.8
Holy Cross	17	1.7	27	2.7	50	4.8			94	9.1
Hope	21	5.1	35	8.5	7	1.7	8	1.9	71	17.2
Hunter	316	6.9	10	0.2	1	0.1			327	7.1
Illinois	296*	5.3	40*	0.7	64	1.2	11	0.2	411*	7.4
Ill. Wesley	27*	4.3	10*	1.6	3	0.5	2	0.3	42*	6.7
Indiana	478	20.2	184	7.9	16	0.7	3	0.1	681	28.9
Iowa	92	3.1	4*	0.1	15	0.5	3	0.1	114*	3.7
Iowa St. Col.	86	2.0	3*	0.1	3	0.1	5	0.1	97*	2.3
Iowa St. Univ.	546		1*		87		1		635*	
Iowa Wesleyan	30								30	
Johns Hopkins	83	11.4	73	10.0	60	8.2	2	0.3	218	29.0
Juniata	13	2.7	8	1.7	2	0.4	4	0.9	27	5.7
Kalamazoo	19*	4.7	10	2.5	3	0.7	5	1.4	37*	9.4
Kansas	234	7.7	29	1.0	15	0.5	6	0.2	284	9.4
Kentucky	45*	1.5	11*	0.4	8	0.3			64*	2.1
Knox	21*	3.1	3	0.4	9	1.3	5	0.7	38*	5.6
Lafayette	41	4.1	37	3.7	43	4.3	12	1.2	133	13.3
Lawrence	40*	5.5	3	0.4	7	1.0	3	0.4	53*	7.3
Lebanon Valley	22	6.1	6	1.7			1	0.3	29	8.0
Lehigh	22	1.4	15	1.0	22	1.5	2	0.1	61	4.0
Luther	24	7.3	2	0.6	2	0.6			28	8.6
Macalester	45	9.0	4	0.9			13	2.6	62	12.4
Manhattan	10*	1.3	15	2.0	6	0.8			31*	4.1
Maryland	15*	0.5	10*	0.3	28	1.0	1	0.1	54*	1.9
M. I. T.	240	7.5	11	0.3	5	0.1	1	0.1	257	8.0
Mass. State Col.	24	3.7	2	0.3	2	0.3	2	0.3	30	4.5
Miami	26*	1.2	5	0.2	11	0.5	1	0.1	43*	1.9
Michigan	224*	4.0	252	4.5	498	9.0	11	0.2	985*	17.5
Michigan State	17*	0.5	14	0.4	1	0.1			32*	1.0
Middlebury	20	1.2	9	0.5	5	0.2	4	0.2	38	2.2
Minnesota	1,075	16.1	38	0.6	25*	0.4	8	0.1	1,146*	17.2
Missouri	183	8.9	46*	2.2	12	0.6	11	0.5	252*	12.2
Monmouth	21	4.6	3	0.6	4	0.9	9	2.0	37	8.2
Mt. Holyoke	103	10.1	17	1.7	1	0.1	12	1.2	133	13.2
Muhlenberg	47	10.4	18	4.0	14	3.1	57	12.6	136	30.1
Muskingum	26*	3.4	11*	1.4	3	0.4	8	1.0	48*	6.2
Nebraska	151*	6.4	15*	0.6	16	0.7	8	0.4	190*	8.1
Nebraska Wes.	29*	5.1					21	3.7	50*	8.8
Nevada	27	3.4	10	1.1	8	0.9			45	5.4
New Hampshire	14	0.9	4	0.3	4	0.3	1	0.1	23	1.5
N. Y. U.	163*	3.0	292	5.3	73*	1.3	14	0.3	542*	9.8
N. Car.	93	3.4	52*	1.9	13	0.5	2	0.1	160*	5.8
N. Dakota	43*	2.7	22	1.4	8	0.6	1	0.1	74*	4.6
Northwest.	270	10.0	67	2.5	151	5.5	22	0.8	510	18.8
Notre Dame	31	1.0	28	0.9	50	1.6			109	3.5
Oberlin	131*	7.8	34*	2.1	23*	1.4	16	1.0	204*	12.3
Occidental	34	5.0	4	0.6	13	1.9	8	1.2	59	8.7

Institution	Grad. Schools Arts and Sci.		Med. Sch.		Law Sch.		Theol. Sch.		Totals	
	a	b	a	b	a	b	a	b	a	b
Ohio State	175*	4.6	28*	0.7	24*	0.6	9	0.2	**236***	**6.3**
Ohio Univ.	39*	1.8	10*	0.5	1	0.1	2	0.1	**52***	**2.3**
Ohio Wesl.	90*	4.9	28*	1.5	27*	1.5	73	4.0	**218***	**11.9**
Oklahoma	73	1.4	6*	0.1	6	0.1	7	0.1	**92***	**1.2**
Oregon	73	2.3	8*	0.3	12*	0.4			**93***	**2.9**
Otterbein	14	3.9	4	1.1	8	2.2	10	2.8	**36**	**10.0**
Park	30	6.0	6	1.2	11	2.2	16	3.3	**63**	**12.8**
Penn. St. Col.	101	2.3	149	1.1	48	1.1	10	0.2	**308**	**7.0**
Penna.	674	46.2	241	16.5	322	22.1	8	0.5	**1,245**	**85.5**
Pittsburgh	52*	1.8	164	5.7	152	5.3	7	0.2	**375***	**13.1**
Pomona	83	11.0	12*	1.6	16	2.1	5	0.7	**116***	**15.4**
Princeton	163	7.3	102	4.6	203	9.0	21	0.9	**489**	**21.7**
Purdue	66	1.5	11	0.2	1	0.1	1	0.1	**79**	**1.8**
Reed	20*								**20***	
Rice	29	2.4	5	0.4	10*	0.8			**44***	**3.6**
Richmond	41	7.1	3	0.5	2	0.3	10	1.7	**56**	**9.1**
Ripon	24*	6.7	3*	0.8	4	1.1	1	0.3	**32**	**8.9**
Roanoke	13	5.0	8	3.1	1	0.4	2	0.8	**24**	**9.2**
Rochester	168	17.3	23	2.4	7	0.8	16	1.6	**214**	**22.0**
Rutgers	33	1.4	32	1.4	19	0.8	8	0.3	**92**	**3.9**
Smith	181	9.1	21	1.1	4	0.2	2	0.1	**208**	**10.5**
South Dak.	48*	4.8	15	1.5	4	0.3			**66***	**6.7**
St. Johns (Md.)	7	2.6	3	1.1	13	4.5	1	0.4	**24**	**8.4**
South. Cal.					158				**158**	
Stanford	1,034	26.5	173	4.4	240	6.2	1	0.1	**1,448**	**37.1**
Swarthmore	58	9.8	11	1.9	12	2.0	1	0.2	**82**	**13.9**
Syracuse	70*	4.2	8*	0.4	14	0.7	33	1.7	**135***	**7.2**
Temple	87	1.8	19	0.4			2	0.1	**108**	**2.3**
Tennessee	25*	0.8	6*	0.2	2	0.1	3	0.1	**36***	**1.1**
Texas	335	7.4	19*	0.4	3	0.1	4	0.1	**361***	**8.0**
Thiel	8	3.4	3	1.3	2	0.8	19	8.1	**32**	**13.6**
Trinity (Conn.)	18	5.1	20	5.7	8	2.3	2	0.8	**48**	**13.7**
Tufts	49*	2.6	10*	0.5	16	0.8	2	0.1	**77***	**4.0**
Tulane	87	6.6			3	0.1	1	0.1	**91**	**6.9**
Union	27	3.3	10	1.2	10	1.2	2	0.2	**49**	**6.0**
U. of Wash.	125*	3.8	29*	0.9	13*	0.4	6	0.2	**173***	**5.3**
Ursinus	36	7.7	14	3.0	4	0.8	9	1.9	**63**	**13.5**
Utah	49*	1.3	42	1.3	16	0.5	2	0.1	**109***	**3.4**
Vanderbilt	44*	2.9	6*	0.4	12	0.8	3	0.2	**65***	**4.3**
Vassar	105	9.1	15	1.3	6	0.5	4	0.2	**130**	**11.3**
Vermont	20*	1.6	3	0.2	9	0.7	1	0.1	**33***	**2.7**
Virginia	87	6.3	32	2.3	28	2.0	1	0.1	**148**	**10.7**
V. M. I.	17	2.3	12	1.7	9	1.2			**38**	**5.3**
Wabash	44	11.5	12	3.2	10	2.6	4	1.0	**70**	**18.4**
Wake Forest	31	4.7	24	3.6			2	0.3	**57**	**8.6**
Washburn	12	1.8	3	0.4			2	0.3	**17**	**2.6**
Washington Mo.	50*	2.9	47	2.7	4	0.3	6	0.3	**107***	**6.2**
Wash. and Lee	24	2.6	18	2.0	16	1.7	5	0.5	**63**	**6.9**
Wash. and Jeff.	12	2.7	32	7.2	29	6.5	8	1.8	**81**	**18.2**
Wellesley	125	8.1	22	1.4	3	0.2	8	0.5	**158**	**10.2**
Wesleyan	58	9.6	18	3.0	17	2.8	23	3.8	**116**	**19.2**
West. Res.	250	14.6	28	1.6	103	6.0	6	0.3	**387**	**22.4**
West Va.	38*	1.5	33*	1.3	10	0.4	4	0.2	**85***	**3.4**
Wheaton (Ill.)	17*	2.8	6	1.0	1	0.1	12	2.0	**36***	**5.9**
Whitman	28*	5.4	7	1.4	1	0.1	2	0.2	**38***	**7.3**
Wm. and Mary	29	2.0	11	0.8	4	0.3			**44**	**3.1**
Wm. Jewell	21	5.2	4	1.0	1	0.2	4	1.0	**30**	**7.5**
Williams	55	6.8	22	2.7	58	7.2	8	1.0	**143**	**17.6**
Wisconsin	264*	3.8	79*	1.1	84	1.2	12	0.2	**439***	**6.3**
Wittenberg	22*	2.3	9	1.0	11	1.2	3	0.3	**45***	**4.7**
Wooster	56*	6.2	20*	2.2	16	1.8	26	2.9	**118***	**13.2**
Worcester P. I.	20	3.2	1	0.1					**21**	**3.3**
Yale	303	13.7	157	7.1	171	7.7	55	2.5	**686**	**31.0**

students who go on to graduate schools of arts and science from the various undergraduate colleges are very striking. On the basis of undergraduate enrolment, the University of Pennsylvania evidently sends the largest number of students to such institutions with an index of 46.2 per cent; Chicago follows with 35 per cent.; Stanford is third with 26.5 per cent., and Indiana is fourth with 20.2 per cent. In how far these indices serve to measure interest in scholarly affairs on the part of the undergraduates can not, of course, be determined accurately. It is probably safe to say that they show to what extent the graduates of a particular institution will find themselves in research or teaching in colleges and higher institutions generally. Those who are in close touch with individual institutions may be able to explain the significance of these indices in special cases. For instance, the representation of colleges which permit the completion of the first year of the professional school to count toward the bachelor's degree may be greater than would be the case if the four years of undergraduate study were required before the granting of the bachelor's degree. The extremely high rating of the University of Pennsylvania may be explained in part by the fact that the Wharton School absorbs a large number of the students of the University of Pennsylvania who do not contemplate professional careers. The enrolment of the Wharton School was not included in the undergraduate enrolment of the university. In general, it is the large institutions with graduate schools which send the largest percentage of students to the graduate schools of arts and science, although there are several notable exceptions: Amherst, Bryn Mawr, Coe, Cornell College, Earlham, Grinnell, Hamline, Haverford, Mt. Holyoke, Muhlenberg, Pomona and Wabash, which have indices of 10 per cent. or over.

If the undergraduate institutions are grouped according to their size and organization, their indices show some interesting contrasts. The ten great privately endowed universities, Chicago, Columbia, Cornell, Harvard, Johns Hopkins, Northwestern, Pennsylvania, Princeton, Stanford and Yale, have an aggregate undergraduate enrolment of 26,524 and have 5,283 representatives in graduate schools, a collective index of 20.2 per cent. The nine state universities for which the necessary data were obtained, California, Indiana, Iowa, Kansas, Minnesota, Missouri, Nebraska, Texas and Virginia, have an aggregate undergraduate enrolment of 36,544 and have 2,977 representatives in the graduate schools, a collective index of 8.1 per cent. Forty independent colleges with an enrolment of 500 or more each have together 43,925 students. These institutions are represented by 2,544 graduates in graduate schools, so that their collective index is 5.8 per cent. Finally, 54 small colleges, with an enrolment of less than 500 students each, have an aggregate enrolment of 19,974 and have 1,069 alumni in graduate schools, a collective index of 5.3 per cent. It is obvious that as a group the independent colleges making no attempt to conduct a graduate school do not send as many of their alumni to graduate schools as do the larger institutions with affiliated graduate schools.

The representation of the colleges by their graduates in medical schools expressed as a percentage of their undergraduate enrolment is also shown in Table I. The University of Pennsylvania stands first in this list with an index of 16.5 per cent. Johns Hopkins stands next with 10 per cent., followed by Hope with 8.5 per cent., Indiana with 7.9 per cent., and Chicago and Washington and Jefferson each with an index of 7.2 per cent.

Comparing different types of institutions, as was done above for the graduate schools, it is found that ten leading endowed universities having an aggregate undergraduate enrolment of 26,802 have 1,414 graduates in medical schools and an index of 5.3 per cent. Eight state universities for which adequate data were available have an aggregate enrolment of 24,869 with 614 graduates in medical schools and a collective index of 2.5 per cent. Fifty-one colleges of over 500 enrolment each have an aggregate undergraduate body of 59,776 and 1,058 graduates in medical schools, a collective index of 1.8 per cent. A group of forty colleges of less than 500 enrolment each have an aggregate enrolment of 15,238 and 335 graduates in medical schools, a collective index of 2.2 per cent.

The number of graduates expressed as a percentage of the undergraduate enrolment of the colleges who are pursuing the study of law in the institutions studied shows much variation, as is indicated in Table I. Pennsylvania again leads with 22.1 per cent., but her nearest competitors are Harvard, Haverford, Michigan and Princeton, each with an index of 9 per cent. Johns Hopkins stands third with an index of 8.2 per cent., Yale stands fourth with 7.7 per cent., Williams fifth with 7.2 per cent., Amherst and Washington and Jefferson sixth with 6.5 per cent., Stanford seventh with 6.2 per cent., Western Reserve eighth with 6.0 per cent., Northwestern ninth with 5.5 per cent., and Pittsburgh tenth with 5.3 per cent.

Comparing, as before, the different types of undergraduate colleges, ten great endowed universities, having an aggregate enrolment of 26,524, are represented in law schools by 1,887 graduates, a collective index of 7.1 per cent. Eleven state universities having an aggregate enrolment of 46,254 undergraduates have 1,021 alumni in law schools, a collective index of 2.2 per cent. Fifty-two colleges of more than 500 enrolment each, with an aggregate enrolment of 54,631, have 809 alumni in law schools, a collective index of 1.5 per cent.; and forty-six small colleges, each with less than 500 enrolled, have an aggregate enrolment of 17,282 and 262 alumni in law schools, a collective index of 1.5 per cent.

The number of representatives of the undergraduate institutions on the basis of enrolment pursuing work in theological schools shows comparatively little variation. Muhlenberg and Thiel stand out preeminently above all the other institutions for which data have been obtained, and it may be that their high index is to be explained in part by the fact that practically all these students were in a single theological school which furnished the necessary figures. It may be, that had the selection of theological schools been wider, other distinctly denominational institutions would have presented much larger indices. It is with some trepidation that these indices are presented. Muhlenberg heads the list with an index of 12.6 per cent. Thiel stands next with 8.1 per cent. Baker is third with 5.1 per cent., Chicago is fourth with 4.4 per cent., Otterbein fifth with 4.0 per cent., Wesleyan and Dickinson sixth with 3.8 per cent., Nebraska Wesleyan seventh with 3.7 per cent., Beloit eighth with 3.6 per cent., Heidelberg ninth with 3.4 per cent., and Park tenth with 3.3 per cent. No other institution in the table has as high an index as 3.0 per cent.

In order to measure still more completely the intellectual quality of the undergraduate bodies of the various institutions, the percentages have been combined of their undergraduate enrolment in graduate schools of arts and science, medical schools, law schools and theological schools. These figures are presented in Table I. Omitting from the comparison the institutions for which the data are insufficient because of the absence of the academic antecedents of the students in one or other of the postgraduate schools, the order of the highest twenty-five is as follows: Pennsylvania, Chicago, Stanford, Harvard, Yale, Columbia, Muhlenberg, Johns Hopkins, Haverford, Amherst, Western Reserve, Rochester, Princeton, Cornell, Clark, Cornell College, Wesleyan, Bryn Mawr, Northwestern, Dickinson, Wabash, Washington and Jefferson, Williams, Hope and Hamilton.

B. W. KUNKEL

LAFAYETTE COLLEGE

NEW BOOKS IN EDUCATION

ARNHEITER, THEODORE. *The Soul of a Christmas Tree.* Pp. 72. Christopher. $1.50.

CAMP, LOUISE S., EVA H. LYCAN and FREDERICK H. BAIR. *Creative Composition.* Pp. xiii + 446. Illustrated. Lippincott.

COBB, STANWOOD. *Discovering the Genius Within You.* Pp. 287. Day.

DE LA FONTAINERIE, F., editor and translator. *French Liberalism and Education in the Eighteenth Century.* Pp. ix + 385. McGraw-Hill. $2.25.

FOSTER, GEORGE S. and LEON G. KRANZ. *Health.* Pp. 218. Illustrated. Christopher. $3.00.

HUNTINGTON, ELLSWORTH, C. BEVERLEY BENSON and FRANK M. MCMURRY. *Living Geography.* Book One: *How Countries Differ.* Pp. vi + 346. Illustrated. $1.20. Book Two: *Why Countries Differ.* Pp. vi + 506. Illustrated. $1.60. Macmillan.

NATIONAL SOCIETY FOR THE STUDY OF EDUCATION. *Thirty-first Yearbook.* Part One: *A Program for Teaching Science.* Pp. xii + 370. Part Two: *Changes and Experiments in Liberal-Arts Education.* Pp. ix + 307. Public School Publishing Company.

YATES, DOROTHY H. *Psychological Racketeers.* Pp. 232. Badger. $2.00.

YOAKUM, GERALD A. *The Improvement of the Assignment.* Pp. xii + 398. Macmillan. $1.80.

SCHOOL AND SOCIETY

EDITED BY J. McKEEN CATTELL

WITH WHICH IS COMBINED THE

EDUCATIONAL REVIEW

EDITED BY WILLIAM McANDREW

Volume 35 | SATURDAY, MARCH 19, 1932 | Number 899

EDUCATION AS A NATIONAL ENTERPRISE[1]

By Dr. ROBERT M. HUTCHINS

PRESIDENT OF THE UNIVERSITY OF CHICAGO

I WISH this morning to insist upon a paradox. The first half of it is that there is an educational system in the United States; and the second half of it is that the parts of that system should be independent of one another.

There is an educational system in the United States. The separate origin of its various parts has obscured the fact of its existence. We have heightened the impression of its non-existence through that mutual disdain with which we have customarily treated one another. That you have asked the presidents of two privately endowed universities to address you on education as a national enterprise suggests that we here to-day, at least, realize that our work is interdependent, that our financial interests are identical, and that our problems are the same. In this sense, the sense of joint occupation in a common enterprise, we are all parts of the educational system of the United States.

Our work is interdependent. The universities may develop ideas in higher education of striking symmetry and beauty; they are futile unless they penetrate the public schools. At seventeen or eighteen or nineteen, the student is, from my point of view at least, far too old to effect radical changes in his habits and attitudes. The schools may experiment to their hearts' content; their accomplishment must fall short of complete success if they are unable to dislodge the ancient prejudices of universities. Even privately endowed universities have been able to restrict the scope of high schools managed by their own departments of education through solid indifference to their work and rigid adherence to requirements framed as though they did not exist. There is, moreover, a twilight zone between the college and the high school, the zone of general education. We do not know what to do with it. We shall never find out unless we are prepared to engage in a cooperative attack on its problems. The integration of the elementary school and the high school has resulted in great savings of time and money. Only through similar integration of the high school and the college can the problems of general education be solved. If we can regard the educational system as a unit, we can expedite and direct this process.

Our financial interests are identical. If the schools are cut to pieces this year, the state universities will be next year. If the schools are crippled now, the colleges will be later, either through reductions in their funds or through gross defects in the prep-

[1] Address before the Department of Superintendence of the National Education Association, Washington, D. C., February 25.

aration of their students. If our work is interdependent, the universities can not without protest watch a major operation performed on the schools which, to judge by its present rate and direction, seems more likely to kill the patient than to profit him or the community. The president of the University of North Carolina has taken a position for which he deserves the thanks of every one in education. He has said that since the university is part of the educational system of the state, it must receive in this emergency the same financial treatment as the public schools. This position is as sound as it is courageous. In self-defense the universities must defend the educational system of which they are a part.

Undoubtedly in the hysteria of inflation the schools, like the colleges and universities, did some things that they can now do without. But the things that communities propose to do to them in the hysteria of economy far surpass the wildest aberrations of bull-market days. We hear a great deal about frills. What are frills? Teachers' salaries appear to be frills in some cities. The health of school children is a frill in others. Since night schools are a frill in one community, we close them and throw 75,000 people into the streets. The plain fact is that the schools are under attack because it is easier to get money from them than it is to correct the fundamental iniquities and antiquities of local government. Only a people that had no conception of the place of education in its national life could contemplate the ruin of the next generation as the best remedy for governmental insolvency.

Our work is interdependent; our financial interests are identical; our problems are the same. The present effort of universities to solve their problems is comparatively new. In the flood of money and students that has poured into these institutions in the past thirty years the intellectual processes of administrators have been almost wholly directed to accommodating the students and spending the money. As long as both continued to roll in we did not have to care very much what we did with them. Now that the flow of both is diminishing, we are wondering about our methods, our standards, our organization, our curriculum, our research work, our building programs—and some people are even beginning to wonder about athletics. The consequence has been all kinds of experiments, studies and surveys. They have revealed principally how little we know about what we are doing.

The public schools face the same problems for the same reason. The tremendous increase in student numbers, the vast amount of new equipment they required, the money that came in almost unsought—all these things have diverted schools, colleges and universities from the main issue, which is, what are we trying to do? We must admit that our own inability to answer this question with a unanimous voice, our very divergent views of what we are about, seriously weaken our efforts to enlighten the public and to secure from it the support that education deserves. What is the place of the private university, the state university, the college, the junior college, the high school, the preparatory school and the technical institute in our educational system? We can only find out by breaking down the barriers that separate those in charge of these various units. We can only find out by recognizing our community of interest and by facing our problems as the problems of us all. We can only find out, in short, by starting with the assumption that there is an educational system in the United States, and that it is our business to run it as a system for the benefit of the community as a whole.

And yet I must at this point insist on the second half of my paradox: the parts of this system must be independent of one another. Because students at different stages require different treatment, separate organizations of specialists have grown up, each designed to care for the special needs of students at a given stage. Each of these organizations requires complete freedom to work out its own program. It must devote itself to meeting the needs of its students rather than to meeting the demands of some other organization.

One reason why there is confusion in universities as to the function of the junior college, the senior college and the graduate school is that no one of these groups has had this freedom to work out its own program. The tendency is always for the organization above to regard the organization below as merely preparatory to its own efforts. The organization above, therefore, will always seek to dominate the organization below in order to secure students who will fit readily into its machinery. But it must be clear that as long as the junior college is controlled by the senior college and the senior college by the graduate school, no one of them can make its full contribution to the advance of education in America. No educational institution can flourish unless it is free to determine its own ideals and its own methods of achieving them.

It must follow that the public schools must have this freedom. The forces of experiment and progress latent in them can never be released if they are compelled to think chiefly of meeting the requirements imposed upon them by institutions of higher learning. If one thing is clear it is that the primary purpose of the high school is not to prepare students for the colleges and universities. By behaving as though it were, the colleges and universities repress the high schools, and to that extent weaken themselves by weakening the educational system to which they themselves belong. The great task of educational administration in America is to take the organization above off the neck of the organization below. Our slogan must be cooperation, and not domination.

The problems of education are more complex and baffling than they have ever been before. The elaborate structure that has been rapidly erected is in danger from misunderstanding without and disagreement within. Much of the misunderstanding without results from the discord within. If we can envisage an educational system in the United States, built on cooperation and not on rigid central control, if we can grant to each organization that independence which its full development requires, we shall illuminate the educational scene for our people and for ourselves and in the light of a new day perform our common task.

ADEQUATE SUPPORT OF EDUCATION THE CONDITION OF AN EFFECTIVE SERVICE[1]

By Professor GEORGE DRAYTON STRAYER
TEACHERS COLLEGE, COLUMBIA UNIVERSITY

THERE is need in the United States today for an aroused public opinion in support of education. Those who believe that the battle for free public schools was won by the middle of the last century are living in a fool's paradise. That progress has been made, no one would deny. The reduction in illiteracy, the enrolment of more than one half of our boys and girls between 14 and 18 years of age in secondary schools, the increase in support of public education from less than $500,000,000 in 1910 to ap-

[1] Address before the Department of Superintendence, Washington, D. C., February 23.

proximately $2,300,000,000 in 1930, the introduction into the curriculum of science and of the fine and industrial arts, the expansion of the program to include kindergarten and nursery schools at the lower end and vocational education, continuation schools and adult education on the upper levels, the greatly increased provision for higher education both liberal and technical—all are evidences of progress.

There is danger that we may not be able to maintain the gains which have been made, much less develop the still more effective service which the present social and economic situation demands. Everywhere there is an attack upon public education expressed primarily in terms of retrenchment in the support of the schools. It is seriously proposed that we can not afford the program of education already established. There seems to be little appreciation of the fact that the need of the hour is for a richer education to be provided for an increasing percentage of the total population. The better we know the work that is done in our schools, the more certainly we are willing to acknowledge the necessity for the further development of our school system.

It is in this situation that in cities and in rural areas schools have been closed, terms have been shortened, teachers' salaries have been reduced, classes have been increased in size, some of the more significant offerings have been eliminated from the curriculum, adequate educational supplies and books have been denied, health service and physical education have been dropped, the attendance service has been crippled, proposals have been made for the lowering of the standards for entrance into the profession, building programs which were to provide adequate housing have been abandoned, night and continuation schools have been closed—in short, the whole program of education is being curtailed, if not indeed placed in jeopardy.

The realization in our practice of the ideal of equality of opportunity is the best single measure of progress in the development of our schools. Much has been gained, by way of providing for the personal development of boys and girls in skill, in knowledge, in appreciation and in vocational efficiency. Our population is more literate not only in the restricted sense in which we use that term but also in ability to appreciate music and the graphic arts, and in the understanding of applied science. We have gained in the knowledge and in the practice of personal and community hygiene. We are a more healthful people than were our grandfathers. We have applied science to industry, to agriculture and to commerce. We are justified in making the claim that our potential economic productive capacity is in large degree to be attributed to the program of education and of research which has been supplied in our higher educational institutions. We have achieved, primarily through education, a social solidarity which has enabled us to act as a unit in times of crisis. We have achieved "like-mindedness," the fundamental basis upon which a working society must be constituted, due primarily to the teaching of common knowledge, ideals and beliefs in our public schools.

But much remains to be accomplished. It is easy to point out the deficiencies in education if we measure them by the degree of social intelligence exhibited in our population. It is certainly true that learning to read, write and cipher, and the securing of a smattering of the subjects commonly taught in the elementary and secondary schools is not an adequate preparation for those who would maintain and develop our democratic society. That education has not yet produced a people who insist upon integrity in their political life is commonly acknowledged. That we have not yet attacked seriously the issues involved in the rapid development of our industrial society, nor yet understood the necessary interdependence of the nations of the world, must be admitted.

But the presentation of these facts, the argument that we have not yet secured these desirable results, is the best possible argument in support of the need for a more generously supported program. If our democracy is to endure, we must through education provide men and women with the knowledge, the insight and the ideals necessary to its perpetuity. We need not claim that the school alone is responsible, but we must acknowledge the fact that the school has been given a large responsibility in our society for the education of our people in the duties and responsibilities of citizenship.

We must have schools that do much more than provide opportunities for individual initiative and achievement. We must develop a curriculum which, while it adjusts educational opportunities to the needs and capacities of individuals, has for its objective the development of men and women who love liberty, who seek justice, who are willing to sacrifice personal advantage to the well-being of the whole group. We may not think less of the importance of guaranteeing to the individual the right of security of his person and property, but we must seek to develop as well his devotion to social justice.

And with this responsibility thrust upon the schools, we do well to ask how well we are equipped to render this surpassingly important service. According to the National Survey of the Training of Teachers, now under way, 26 per cent. of the teachers in the schools of the United States have less than two years of education beyond high school. One out of every five teachers is new to the job which he holds during the current year. The program of retrenchment which is everywhere being advocated, involving as it does reductions in salaries of from 5 to 30 per cent., promises to result in even less well-qualified teachers in our schools. Even more seriously, many of the more competent teachers already in the service are harassed by their inability to meet their financial obligations. Many of them view with uncertainty their economic security. Some of them have lost the high morale and professional enthusiasm necessary in those who would inspire the youth of the land.

Never before has there been such need as there is to-day for men and women of high intelligence, of broad training and of deep social sympathy and understanding to staff our schools. The situation demands teachers who are more than drill masters. The work of the teacher in our society must be measured by the degree of leadership which he is able to offer to young people in their attempt to understand our modern complex social life. He must be a student of society as well as a student of human nature. He must seek to lead boys and girls in their attempt to think straight with respect to the most difficult problems with which men have ever had to struggle. He must seek to develop those ideals which will make possible the regeneration of our society. Our plea is not for the maintenance of salaries but rather for the maintenance and development of our civilization and for the perpetuity of our institutions. It matters little in the long run what any particular teacher or group of teachers is paid; but we have in the support of public education or in the lack of it the destiny of our humanity.

There is need to call attention to the importance of the continued education of those who are no longer spending their full time in schools. Surely, if we are to maintain education at any level it should be for this group of young people and adults. Whether we like it or not, unemployment is here and, if we may trust the interpretation of the economists, is likely to continue and possibly to increase. There is an opportunity in the work with youth and adults for a more serious consideration of the problems fundamental to our political and social life than is possible with the lower age group. But it is equally important during this period of economic distress that the services of the school be made certainly available to all the children of the community. We must view with alarm any diminution in the effectiveness of the attendance service. Absence from the school is apt to contribute to delinquency. We need more certainly than ever before to inquire concerning the physical well-being of the children and to promote, by whatever measures the school may be able to take, their normal physical growth and vigor. Special opportunities for those who are handicapped are more certainly required now than during periods of prosperity. The issue before the people of the United States is not, "Can we afford to maintain the educational service?" but rather, "Can we afford not to maintain and to improve it?"

It is only fair to call attention to the fact that there are cities, counties and even states in which education is still being maintained at a high level of efficiency. Due to superior economic resources and to better procedures in the financing of their schools and sounder systems of taxation, retrenchment has not yet been found necessary in these more favored parts of the country. But even in these localities there are those who seek to reduce the support of education and to restrict the program of the schools. The maintenance of these school systems will require the vigilant support of those charged with the responsibility of leadership in education.

A state superintendent of schools, in the professional journal issued by his state for the month of January, 1932, reports as follows:

> Our program of education, always inadequate to our needs and always more or less restricted, stands in jeopardy of further and serious curtailment. Already in certain rural areas there have been shortened terms of school. Already the alarm is sounding that schools must close. Already city school authorities are pleading desperately that the state come to the rescue. Salary schedules very generally have become inoperative. Following the old paths of least resistance, those in authority have already reduced salaries that were always low enough. More is the pity that teachers have gone unpaid, some of them for months. In the cities, in the rural areas and at the institutions, our creditable building program has slowed up. Consolidation, transportation, supervision, standardization and teacher training, all on a praise-worthy and soundly progressive basis, if not in jeopardy, at least must await the return of a better day for further advances.[2]

I wonder in how many localities and in how many states the situation is described by the report which I have read?

I am persuaded that we are confronted with a serious crisis. I believe that we should go forth to proclaim to our public the necessity of maintaining the school service in order that we may preserve our social inheritance. I believe that we should call upon our people to bear the burden of taxation and, if need be, to suffer privation, in order that we may insure to ourselves and to our posterity life, liberty and the pursuit of happiness.

EDUCATIONAL EVENTS

THE TWENTY-FIFTH ANNIVERSARY OF THE UNIVERSITY OF HAWAII

The twenty-fifth anniversary of the youngest land-grant university in the United States was celebrated on March 24, 1932, by the University of Hawaii in Honolulu. In the twenty-five years that have followed the passage of the act of establishment by the territorial legislature in 1907, the institution has grown from an unbelievably small college with a faculty of thirteen and a student body of five to a respected uni-

[2] A. F. Harman, "Education and the Economic Depression," *Alabama School Journal*, January, 1932, p. 14.

versity with a research and instructional faculty of more than 200 and a student body of 2,000.

For the first twelve years of its existence the institution waged an up-hill fight. Founded as the College of Hawaii, for the purpose of instructing the island youth in the mechanical and agricultural arts, the school was handicapped by meager appropriations and the disfavor of the local citizens. In 1920, the college was expanded and became the University of Hawaii. In 1931, the Territorial Normal School was affiliated with the university as the university teachers college.

On its twenty-fifth anniversary, the University of Hawaii occupies a respected place in the collegiate world. With a faculty boasting more advanced degrees than the average land-grant institution, the only graduate school of tropical agriculture in the United States, its credits universally recognized by other universities and professional schools, the university has justified the optimism of the men and women who founded the College of Hawaii a quarter-century ago.

Seventy-seven research projects are under way in the laboratories, some of them of international importance. Dr. H. L. Shapiro, assistant curator for anthropology of the American Museum of Natural History, is directing a study of the environmental differences found between the Japanese and Chinese in Hawaii and those in Asia. The effect of racial intermarriage and the comparative reactions of different races are being studied. In the agricultural field, investigations in the hybridization of tropical fruits, methods of sterilization to kill insect pests and the development of sprays are progressing.

Located in the middle of the ocean separating Asia from America, the University of Hawaii is well placed for the study of the fusion of Occidental and Oriental cultures. Its student body, drawn from fourteen nationalities which work together in Honolulu, a more harmonious and smaller League of Nations, is in itself a laboratory.

PANAMA CONFERENCE OF THE INTER-AMERICAN FEDERATION OF EDUCATION

Dr. G. L. Swiggett, chairman of the organization committee of the Inter-American Federation of Education who has just returned to Washington from a brief visit to several Latin-American capitals announces that the second conference of the Inter-American Federation will be held in Panama the latter part of December, 1932, probably December 23 to 31. Twenty countries, including the United States, are now organized for effective participation in the purposes of the Federation.

The Panaman Conference will be organized and held under the auspices of the secretary of public instruction of that country, Dr. Jeptha Duncan, in cooperation with the Panaman National Association of Teachers which represents Panama in the Inter-American Federation of Education. Carlos Sucre C., a direct descendant of General Bolivar's famous aide, is president of the Panaman association. Other members of the organization committee for the Panaman meeting are Dr. J. D. Crespo, an outstanding Latin-American educator, Mrs. Esther Neri de Calvo, equally well known among the women educators of Latin America, and Max Arosemena, who is inspector-general of education.

The Panaman meeting will reemphasize the two major topics of the first organization conference of the Inter-American Federation of Education, namely, vocational and character training, through the repeated discussion of which, Dr. Swiggett says, the Inter-American Federation hopes to aid in the development of a practical popular understanding of the need for Inter-American cooperation in all matters that concern the daily living of the peoples of the twenty-one republics of the Western Hemisphere.

INQUIRY REGARDING THE ADMINISTRATION OF HOWARD UNIVERSITY

An investigation into the organization and operation of Howard University, Washington, D. C., was ordered on March 14 at a special meeting of the board of trustees of the university held in New York City. The situation is described in the *New York Times* as follows:

Although no official announcement of the reason for the investigation was made, it was reported that it was a development of the movement begun about a year ago to unseat Dr. Mordecai Johnson, the first Negro president of the school, after he had made a speech in which, according to his opponents, he had praised certain Negro groups alleged to have communistic tendencies.

The trustees yesterday adopted a resolution directing their chairman, General John H. Sherburne, of Boston, to name a committee of five trustees "who shall select a disinterested person or agency for the purpose of ascertaining and reporting to the board all the facts regarding the organization and operation of Howard University." The report is to be made to the annual meeting of the board on April 12.

General Sherburne appointed Dr. Abraham Flexner, Dr. Peter Marshall Murray and Dr. Thomas Jesse Jones, all of New York; George W. Crawford, of New Haven, Connecticut, and Dr. Sara W. Brown, of Washington, to the committee. Dr. Flexner said last night that so far as he knew the investigation was to be merely a routine survey of the institution, but he explained that he was not familiar with the situation, as he became a trustee only recently.

The charges against Dr. Johnson were investigated at the time by Oscar De Priest, Negro Representative from Illinois, who cleared the university president and since has been his ardent supporter. Mr. De Priest charged the whole affair to a disgruntled element which, he said, resented its failure to elect its own candidate to the presidency.

Representative Wood, of Indiana, then chairman of the House Committee on Appropriations, declared last year that he would vote for no more appropriations for the institution while Dr. Johnson remained at its head. Dr. Johnson's administration was approved at the annual meeting of the American Federation of Teachers, where it was charged that Representative Wood's opposition arose from Dr. Johnson's refusal to permit faculty posts to be used as political patronage.

THE CLAREMONT COLLEGES

THE recent dedication of Harper Hall as the central library and administration building of Claremont Colleges is another step in the development of a group of colleges at Claremont, California. This undertaking, which preserves the residential character and charm of the individual institution and at the same time assures the advantages of group facilities, has made notable progress since its organization in 1925. The dedication last September of Mabel Shaw Bridges Music Auditorium, one of the great concert halls of the United States, was another step.

In Harper Hall, the first building on the central campus, provision is made for the central library and central business office, the administration offices of Claremont Colleges, and important work in the graduate school. The building lies midway between Pomona College and Scripps College and fits harmoniously into the beautiful Mediterranean architecture which marks these campuses. The architect is Mr. Gordon B. Kaufmann, of Los Angeles.

The library quarters include working space for the staff of eight, in which is centralized the book purchase and cataloguing for the three libraries on the Claremont campuses. Pomona and Scripps Colleges continue their undergraduate working libraries in their own library buildings, while the new Claremont Colleges Library offers bibliographic and coordinating service for all and library facilities for advanced and graduate students.

On the occasion of dedication (February 19) a conference and symposium was held on the subject of the college librarian. Large sums have been invested in colleges, libraries and books, but the development of the college librarian in all his human, technical and scholastic interests has lacked attention. Dr. William Warner Bishop, librarian of the University of Michigan, and chairman of the recent Carnegie Corporation library committee which has assisted by grants over a hundred American colleges, realized so fully the need of such a conference that he traveled especially from Ann Arbor to share in the program at Claremont, at the invitation of Mr. Willis H. Kerr, librarian of Claremont Colleges. With the presence in California of Dr. Andrew Keogh, head of the Yale University library, himself a former president of the American Library Association, and with the ready acceptance of other college and university librarians and administrators from the Pacific Coast, an outstanding program was inevitable. Dr. Bishop spoke on "The American College Library and its Librarian," Dr. Keogh on "The debt of the college librarian to scholarship," and Mr. Kerr on "The Claremont Libraries." Participants in the symposium were Mr. Sidney B. Mitchell, director of the School of Librarianship, University of California; Mr. Matthew H. Douglass, librarian, of the University of Oregon, Eugene; Dr. Marcus Skarstedt, professor of mathematics, Whittier College, California, and President Aurelia Henry Reinhardt, Mills College, California. Over a hundred college librarians and administrators attended. The proceedings are to be published shortly by Claremont Colleges.

THE GRADUATE EDUCATION BUILDING AND EDUCATIONAL CONFERENCE AT THE UNIVERSITY OF CHICAGO

Nearly a hundred of the country's leading authorities on education gathered at the University of Chicago on March 14 and 15 for a series of conferences in connection with the dedication of the new graduate education building.

Thirteen addresses on various aspects of teacher-training were presented during the two-day program, five of them by college presidents. The conferences were held in the assembly room of the new building, which rises between Belfield and Blane Halls on Kimbark Avenue, near the Midway, completing the third side of the proposed education quadrangle. The dedication preceded the one hundred and sixty-seventh convocation of the university which took place in the university on the afternoon of March 15.

Several score men and women who had received the degree of doctor of philosophy from the department of education returned to open the exercises with a conference on the practical applications of the science of education in various types of institutions. The speakers included Dr. Homer Price Rainey, president of Bucknell University; Dr. James B. Edmonson, dean of the School of Education, University of Michigan; Mr. Douglas E. Scates, director of the Bureau of School Research, Cincinnati Public Schools, Dr. Ralph W. Tyler, professor of education, the Ohio State University, and Mr. Lloyd E. Blauch, executive secretary of the Survey of the Dental Curriculum, American Association of Dental Schools.

The Monday afternoon program was devoted to a conference on teacher training, the speakers including Frank E. Baker, president of the State Teacher's College, Milwaukee, and Thomas E. Benner, dean of the School of Education, University of Illinois. Dr. Edward L. Thorndike, of Teachers College, Columbia University, delivered the principal address in the evening, on "The Distribution of Education."

President Robert M. Hutchins presided at the Tuesday morning session, at which the speakers were Samuel P. Capen, chancellor of the University of Buffalo; Ernest Hatch Wilkins, president of Oberlin College and formerly dean at Chicago, and George A. Works, dean of students at the University of Chicago and formerly president of the Connecticut Agricultural College.

The new structure is described by Dean Charles H. Judd, of the department of education, as being in many respects unique among American university buildings, in that it provides scientific laboratories and work-rooms for the study of the learning process. In addition to office work-rooms for fifteen professors and fourteen staff members, the building contains a statistical laboratory, an apparatus workshop, photographic rooms, a library with room for 200 students and stack space for 100,000 volumes, and a large assembly room.

The cost of the structure, which was designed by Messrs. Armstrong, Furst and Tilton, was $610,000, part of a gift of $1,500,000 made to the university two years ago by the General Education Board of New York for educational research.

THE MICHIGAN SCHOOLMASTERS' CLUB

"An Appraisal of Current Opinion of our Secondary Schools and Higher Institutions," will be the keynote around which discussion will center at the sixty-seventh meeting of the Michigan Schoolmasters' Club, said to be the oldest organization of its kind, which convenes at the University of Michigan, at Ann Arbor, on April 28, 29 and 30. For the first time in recent years the meetings will be extended to include Saturday morning.

To make the conference function to the fullest extent as a forum for the practical discussion of current school trends and problems, the meeting this year will give less time to formal papers and will encourage free expression of opinion. Thirty conferences for educators in every field of instruction are scheduled, at which more than one hundred teachers will read papers and reports. The parent-teacher movement, long an active factor in Michigan education, will be represented as last year by the second annual Parent Education Institute which will meet on April 27 and 28. Besides addresses by members of the university faculty, this meeting will hear

Mrs. D. W. Stewart and Mrs. Hugh Bradford, presidents of the Michigan and National Congress of Parents and Teachers, and Miss Florence Hale, president of the National Education Association.

Other features include an address by President A. G. Ruthven, of the university, the annual university honors convocation, the final contest of the State High-school Debating League and a teacher-training conference sponsored by the School of Education. The Michigan Association of Collegiate Registrars will also meet during the conference, on April 30, and an exhibit of high-school text-books will be held in the University High School Library.

Founded in 1886 at Ann Arbor by a group of nineteen university and state students of education, Dr. John Dewey being an active member of the committee drawing up the articles of organization, the Michigan Schoolmasters' Club was at that time a new idea in educational organizations, but has since served as a model for similar societies in many other states. "We unite in forming the Michigan Schoolmasters' Club and aim to secure an opportunity to discuss matters pertaining to our common work, with particular reference to high-school and collegiate training," declared the resolutions of the Dewey committee, and the wish of the founders, to foster a close and congenial union in the whole educational system of the state, has been closely adhered to ever since. The club now has over 3,000 members. In 1894 three meetings a year were held, but as membership grew the number was cut to two, and in 1901 to a single comprehensive meeting—a series of round table presentations and discussions centering in the last analysis about the eternal problems of the teacher, if, when and how any subject should be taught. The president of the club is Professor C. S. Larzelere, of Central Michigan State Teachers College; the vice-president is Miss Ethel W. B. Chase, of the College of the City of Detroit, and the secretary-treasurer is Mr. Louis P. Jocelyn, of the Ann Arbor High School, who has held this post for thirty-five years.

ADVISORY COUNCIL OF THE MILBANK MEMORIAL FUND

AN experiment in "group thinking" and a discussion of public health problems were features of the program of the tenth annual meeting of the advisory council of the Milbank Memorial Fund, held on March 16 and 17 at The New York Academy of Medicine. The meeting opened with a general session of about fifty members addressed by Dr. William Henry Welch, chairman of the council, and John A. Kingsbury, secretary of the fund. Thereupon, departing from procedure in other years, the council was divided into five group conferences, each with a chairman to guide the discussion and a *rapporteur* to summarize it. These conferences continued through luncheon into the afternoon.

One group, presided over by Surgeon-General Hugh S. Cumming, of the United States Public Health Service, discussed health centers in New York City, Boston, and Los Angeles County, California. Dr. Shirley W. Wynne, commissioner of health in New York City, was one of the speakers. Another group dealt with the education of health personnel, school health education, and policies in public information regarding the prevention of venereal diseases. Dr. Linsly R. Williams, director of the New York Academy of Medicine, presided at the morning session, and Mr. Homer Folks, secretary of the State Charities Aid Association, at the afternoon session of this group. Dr. Thomas Parran, Jr., New York State Commissioner of Health was a speaker.

A third group discussed tuberculosis in children, particularly in New York City, Cattaraugus County, New York, and Baltimore, Maryland. The use, under carefully controlled conditions, of the bacillus Calmette-Guérin for immunization was reported on by Dr. William H. Park, of the New York City Department of Health. Dr. Charles J. Hatfield, executive director of the Henry Phipps Institute, Philadelphia, presided. Dr. James Alexander Miller, of the College of Physicians and Surgeons, was a speaker.

Studies of population absorbed the attention of one group, over which Dr. Robert E. Chaddock, of Columbia University, presided. There were reports on reproductive histories, differential fertility by social classes and modes of research into the factors affecting human fertility. Dr. Raymond Pearl, of the Johns Hopkins University, was a speaker. Public health nursing, particularly in Boston and New York, was discussed by a separate group, presided over by Miss Lillian A. Hudson, of Teachers College, Columbia University.

The *rapporteurs* summarized the group discussions for the respective chairmen, who made reports the following day to the council meeting in executive session.

During the afternoon of the same day Dr. Hsun-Yuan Yao gave an illustrated lecture on the health demonstration at Ting Hsien, China, which the fund is supporting. Following this the council heard a discussion of the economic aspects of medicine and health, the principal speakers being Dr. R. M. Atwater, commissioner of Health of Cattaraugus County; Dr. Louis I. Dublin, of the Metropolitan Life Insurance Company; Dr. E. R. A. Seligman, of Columbia University, and Dr. C.-E. A. Winslow, of the Yale University School of Medicine.

A dinner given on March 17 by the Board of Directors of the Milbank Memorial Fund concluded the meeting. Dr. William Henry Welch, of the Johns Hopkins University, formally resigned as chairman of the council, a position he had held since its organization in 1922. His successor is Dr. Livingston Farrand, president of Cornell University, who addressed the gathering. Mr. Albert G. Milbank, president of the fund, greeted the guests on behalf of the board. Dr. Ray Lyman Wilbur, United States Secretary of the Interior, delivered an address on the economics of public health and medical care. He presented and commented on some of the main findings of the committee on the costs of medical care, of which he is the chairman. While this dinner celebrated the tenth anniversary of the advisory council, the fund itself is twenty-seven years old, having been incorporated in 1905.

GEORGE EASTMAN

George Eastman, inventor of the photographic film that created the modern camera and the motion picture, founder and chairman of the directors of the Eastman Kodak Company, a $250,000,000 corporation, died by suicide on March 14. He was seventy-seven years old, in ill health, unmarried and with no near relatives except a niece. He asked his physician to leave the room while he wrote a note which reads:

> To my friends:
> My work is done, why wait?
> G. E.

Mr. Eastman inaugurated the system of wage dividends and the company is said to have paid employees more than $50,000,000 in money and stock. His donations to charitable and educational institutions amount to more than $75,000,000. They were made without ostentation. Mr. Eastman gave $11,000,000 to the Massachusetts Institute of Technology under the name of "Mr. Smith," and admitted the gift reluctantly. He later increased the amount. The larger gifts are:

University of Rochester	$35,500,000
Massachusetts Institute of Technology	20,000,000
Tuskegee Institute	2,362,000
Hampton Institute	2,000,000
Kodak stock distributed to employees	6,000,000
Chamber of Commerce Building	1,350,000
War chest, 1918	600,000
General Hospital	500,000
Mechanics Institute	625,000
Y. M. C. A.	300,000
Red Cross, 1917	250,000
War relief	225,000
State and municipal research bureau	300,000
Highland Hospital	100,000
Genesee Hospital	75,000
Rochester parks	100,000
Stevens Institute of Technology	50,000
Friendly Home	50,000
Eastman Visiting Professorship, Oxford	200,000
Waterville Memorial	50,000
Dental Clinic, London	1,300,000
Dental Dispensary, Rome	1,000,000
Dental Dispensary, Stockholm	1,000,000
Dental Dispensary, Paris	1,000,000
Dental Dispensary, Brussels	1,000,000

EDUCATIONAL NOTES AND NEWS

A farewell dinner in honor of Dr. John Grier Hibben, president of Princeton University, whose resignation after twenty years of service takes effect in June, was given at the Hotel Roosevelt, New York City, on March 11. President James Rowland Angell, president of

Yale University; President Abbott Lawrence Lowell, of Harvard University, and President Livingston Farrand, of Cornell University, were among the speakers.

A COMPLIMENTARY dinner on the anniversary of his seventy-second birthday, to Dr. George Lyman Kittredge, Gurney professor of English literature at Harvard University, was given at the Somerset Club, Boston, on February 27.

DR. FREDERICK L. GAMAGE, head master at the Pawling School at Pawling, N. Y., was the guest of honor on March 17 at a dinner which the school's alumni association held at the Hotel Gotham in celebration of Dr. Gamage's fifty years as a schoolmaster. From 1885 to 1893 Dr. Gamage was principal of Oxford Academy, when he became head master of St. Paul's School at Garden City. In 1907 he, with several other members of the St. Paul's faculty, established Pawling School.

THE Washington Award for 1932, "in recognition of devoted, unselfish, and preeminent service in advancing human progress," was presented to Dr. William David Coolidge, associate director of research in the laboratory of the General Electric Company at Schenectady, following a dinner and reception on February 24 at the Hotel Sherman, Chicago. Dr. Coolidge is the eleventh to be so honored by the Washington Award Commission, the first presentation being to President Hoover, in 1919. Dr. Harry Woodburn Chase, president of the University of Illinois, delivered the principal address of the evening, evaluating the importance of research in the present social order.

DR. IRVING LANGMUIR, associate director of the research laboratory of the General Electric Company, at Schenectady, N. Y., has received the *Popular Science Monthly* annual award of $10,000 for notable scientific achievement. The award, together with a gold medal commemorating it, was presented to Dr. Langmuir on February 29 at the Engineers Club in New York City.

THE appointment of Dr. Vannevar Bush as vice-president of the Massachusetts Institute of Technology was announced by President Karl T. Compton following the regular meeting of the corporation on March 9. Dr. Bush has been a member of the faculty of electrical engineering since 1923. Dr. Bush was also elected a member of the corporation and will be dean of engineering. Plans have been made for the subdivision into the School of Science, the School of Engineering, the School of Architecture, the Division of Humanities and the Division of Industrial Cooperation. Dr. Samuel C. Prescott, head of the department of biology and public health, will be dean of science, and Professor William Emerson, head of the department of architecture, will be dean of architecture.

APPOINTMENTS to the administrative board of the new Institute of International Affairs at Columbia University have been made as follows: Huger W. Jervey, director of the institute and professor of law; Howard Lee McBain, dean of the Graduate Faculties; Young B. Smith, dean of the Law School; James T. Shotwell, professor of history; Robert M. Haig, McVickar professor of political economy; Roswell C. McCrea, Hepburn professor of economics; Robert Herndon Fife, Gebhard professor of Germanic languages and literatures; Parker T. Moon, professor of international relations; Lindsay Rogers, Burgess professor of public law; Joseph P. Chamberlain, professor of public law; Charles Cheney Hyde, Hamilton Fish professor of international law and diplomacy; Milton C. Del Manzo, provost of Teachers College and professor of education, and Philip C. Jessup, associate professor of international law. Mr. Harlan F. Stone, associate justice of the United States Supreme Court, has been appointed a member of the administrative board. Justice Stone was dean of the Columbia Law School from 1910 to 1924, resigning before he was named Attorney General. The establishment of the institute was made possible through the bequest of the late Judge Edwin B. Parker, who died in 1929. The amount available for the maintenance of the undertaking will eventually be about $2,000,000.

DR. WARREN WEAVER, professor of mathematics at the University of Wisconsin, was on February 1 appointed director for the natural sciences in the Rockefeller Foundation and in the General Education Board. He succeeds Dr. Herman Augustus Spoehr, who has resumed work with the Carnegie Institution of Washington.

PROFESSOR REXFORD NEWCOMB, of the department of architecture, has been appointed dean of the College of Fine Arts of the University of Illinois.

DR. HOWARD E. ENDERS, head of the department of biology in Purdue University and a member of the staff since 1906, has been made dean of the School of Science to succeed the late Dr. Richard B. Moore, who died early last year. Dr. Enders has been acting dean for some months.

DR. KENNETH BALLARD MURDOCK, dean of the faculty of arts and sciences of Harvard University and master of Leverett House, has been elected professor of English, the appointment to take effect next September. Dr. Robert Silliman Hillyer has been appointed associate professor.

PROFESSOR BOIES PENROSE, of Devon, Pennsylvania, son of the late Dr. Charles B. Penrose and nephew of the late U. S. Senator Penrose, has been appointed professor of history at St. John's College, Annapolis, Maryland.

ACCORDING to press reports, dated March 11, a proposal has been made that the student council of Amherst College should go on record as advising the trustees that they desire the appointment as president of Dr. Alfred Ernest Stearns, head master of Phillips Andover Academy.

MR. GEORGE A. PERSELL, for more than ten years assistant superintendent of schools in Jamestown, N. Y., and for nearly twenty-nine years connected with the schools there, has been elected superintendent of the Jamestown schools to succeed Superintendent Milton J. Fletcher when he retires on August 1. Since 1921 Mr. Persell has been assistant to Superintendent Fletcher. For 25 years he has taken an active interest in the evening school work in Jamestown, during most of that time having been principal of the school. He has also had charge of developing the continuation school and junior high-school activities of the city.

MR. DANIEL MORNET, professor at the Sorbonne, will be visiting French professor at the University of Chicago from March 28 until June 12.

PROFESSOR WILLIAM A. ROBSON, of the London School of Economics, has arrived in New York for a brief lecture tour of the colleges, including Princeton, New York University, Wisconsin and Minnesota.

DR. ANNA SELIG, who is now a guest lecturer in Dr. Rabindranath Tagore's University at Santiniketan, India, has been appointed a reader in Calcutta University to deliver a series of lectures on German educational institutions and German student life. Dr. Selig at one time studied in the United States under the American German Student Exchange and was later associated with the Institute of International Education in its cooperation with the Deutscher Akademischer Austauschdienst of Berlin.

PROFESSOR GEORGE S. COUNTS, of Columbia University, spoke recently on "Education for an Industrial Age," at a luncheon of the Administrative Assistants Association of New York City.

PROFESSOR FREDERIC A. OGG, chairman of the department of political science at the University of Wisconsin and editor of the *American Political Science Review,* is spending the second semester in Washington and has recently completed a series of sixteen lectures at the Johns Hopkins University on some problems of representative government in Great Britain and France.

DR. W. V. BINGHAM, director of the Personnel Research Federation, gave the fourth Aldred Lecture of the year at the Massachusetts Institute of Technology on March 18. The title of his address was "Adventures in Industrial Psychology."

ARCHIE MACINNES PALMER, associate secretary of the Association of American Colleges, will deliver the commencement address to the combined graduating classes of Cumberland University on May 25. The Honorable James V. Allred, Attorney General of Texas and a graduate of Cumberland, will deliver the address to the law graduating class on May 24. Dr. Monroe G. Everett, chaplain of the University of Pennsylvania, will deliver the baccalaureate sermon on May 22.

DR. GEORGE J. RYAN, president of the Board

of Education of New York City, will be the principal speaker at the annual convention of the Eastern Commercial Teachers' Association to be held on March 23, 24, 25 and 26 in the Hotel Pennsylvania, New York.

PROFESSOR JOHN DEWEY will lecture on "The Philosophy of Education" at the summer school of the University of Cincinnati during the intersession from June 6 to June 18.

To perpetuate the peace ideals of the late David Starr Jordan, for many years president of Stanford University, the "World Unity Memorial to David Starr Jordan" has been established by a number of his friends and associates in this country and abroad. Sponsored by Mrs. Jordan, the memorial is being promoted by an international committee, of which Dr. Hamilton Holt, president of Rollins College, is chairman, other members being Miss Jane Addams, Dr. Manley O. Hudson and Mr. Salmon O. Levinson, representing the United States; Sir Norman Angell, representing England; Dr. Hans Wehberg, Germany; Dr. Joseph Redlich, Austria, and Baron Y. Sakatani, Japan.

A MEMORIAL vesper service in memory of Dr. Randall J. Condon, for nearly seventeen years superintendent of schools in Cincinnati, Ohio, was held on the afternoon of Sunday, March 6. The exercises were held in the auditorium of Withrow High School, to the planning and construction of which building Dr. Condon gave much attention. The exercises were arranged by a committee of which Superintendent Edward D. Roberts was chairman. Mr. Roberts also presided at the exercises. Music was provided by the Withrow High School orchestra, by Dr. Sidney C. Durst, an organist who designed the organ installed in the Withrow auditorium, and by Mr. Dan Beddoe, a soloist whose singing made especial appeal to Dr. Condon. Addresses were made by the Honorable Russell Wilson, mayor of the City of Cincinnati; by Principal C. M. Merry, of Hughes High School, who was associated with Superintendent Condon throughout his term, and by Miss Georgia W. Aiken, a teacher in the Twenty-third District School, whose presidency of the Cincinnati Teachers Association occurred during Dr. Condon's superintendency. Mrs. Condon was prevented from being present, but Dr. Condon's daughter, Mrs. Frank C. Foster, and her husband were present. There was a large attendance of friends and admirers of Dr. Condon.

BISHOP THOMAS JOSEPH SHAHAN, rector emeritus of the Catholic University of America and for many years one of the country's distinguished Catholic educators, died of heart disease at his home at Holy Cross Academy on March 9. He was seventy-five years old. Connected with the university for more than forty years, Bishop Shahan had been its rector from 1909 until 1928, when he retired to become rector emeritus.

DR. ROBERT SHAW WILKINSON, president of the State Agricultural and Mechanical College at Orangeburg, South Carolina, died on March 13 at the age of sixty-seven years.

DR. KENDRIC C. BABCOCK, for eighteen years dean of the University of Illinois College of Arts and Sciences, died on March 11 at the age of sixty-seven years. He retired from the faculty last year. For seven years prior to 1910 Dean Babcock was president of the University of Arizona. He also served on the faculties of the universities of Minnesota and California, and for three years was with the United States Bureau of Education.

DR. WILLIAM WALLACE FENN, formerly dean of the Harvard Divinity School, died on March 6. He was seventy years old.

DR. JAMES V. STURGES, for seventeen years principal of the Geneseo, New York, State Normal School, died on January 17 in Geneseo, at the age of sixty-seven years. He resigned from the principalship in 1922 because of ill health.

THE death is announced of Dr. Stanford McLean, clinical professor of children's diseases at the College of Physicians and Surgeons, Columbia University. He was forty-six years old. As an associate of Dr. L. Emmet Holt, Dr. McLean was influential in the development of the babies hospital at the Medical Center.

THE forty-first annual meeting of the Harvard Teachers Association takes place on March 19. The topic for discussion is: "Education and its Responsibilities toward Crime." The speakers and their topics are as follows: "How Can an Educator Help to Combat Crime?"

Professor F. B. Sayre; "The Importance of Education during the First Decade," Dr. Douglas A. Thom, Habit Clinics, Boston; "The Responsibility of the Public Schools," Professor Frank E. Spaulding, Yale University. The luncheon of the association was planned in Memorial Hall with Dean Harry W. Holmes as toastmaster. At the luncheon Dean Roscoe Pound speaks on "Education and the Legal Order," and the Hon. George W. Wickersham, chairman, Commission on Law Enforcement, gives an address on "Is Education a Deterrent of Crime?"

THE second Intercollegiate Scientific Conference of Connecticut Valley Colleges will be held at Connecticut College on April 16. The colleges participating will be Mount Holyoke, Smith, Massachusetts State College, Connecticut Agricultural College, Wesleyan and Connecticut College. Exhibits and reports covering nine branches of science will be included in the program. Dr. Edmund W. Sinnott, professor of botany at Barnard College, will lecture on "Modern Trends in Biology." The first scientific conference of the Connecticut Valley group of colleges was held at Mount Holyoke last April. It was the outgrowth of a suggestion made three years ago by the Biology Club of Mount Holyoke that the student science clubs of five other colleges of New England organize an intercollegiate scientific conference to present reports and demonstrations of work being done in college in the various fields of science.

AN Educational-Economics Association was organized on January 7 at the High School of Commerce in New York City with a membership that includes some of the city's leading college and high school economics teachers. It has been established to promote (1) social contacts between high-school and college economics teachers for the exchange of information and criticism; (2) a better articulation of high-school and college instruction in the social sciences, and (3) a more effective contact between education and business. It is hoped that periodic discussions will throw light on the relations between education and economic life. At a recent meeting, which was held at the Men's Faculty Club at Columbia University, Dr. Willard Atkins, chairman of the department of economics of Washington Square College, New York University, spoke on "The Teaching of Economics from the Institutionalist Point of View."

THE Gamma Omicron chapter of the national honorary society, Kappa Delta Pi, has been established at the University of Miami. Only those who are in the upper fourth of their class are eligible for membership. Dr. Ava Chadbourne, of the School of Education, is sponsor of the chapter at the university.

A CHAPTER of Phi Beta Kappa was formally installed at Wheaton College on March 18. Professor William G. Howard, of Harvard University, representing the United Chapters, presided at the initiation ceremony, which was held at 4:30 P. M. The usual ritual was followed, by-laws voted upon, officers elected, and foundation members received into the association. A dinner for delegates and guests followed the meeting, and at 8:15 there was a lecture in the Cole Memorial Church by Dr. Emma P. Carr, head of the department of chemistry at Mt. Holyoke. Miss Carr's subject was "Scholarship in a Democracy."

FORTY pupils whose indifference to their studies caused them to fail in from three to five courses last term will be dropped from the Asbury Park, New Jersey, high school because, in the words of Amos E. Kraybill, superintendent of schools, "they are wasting their time, their teachers' time and the taxpayers' money." The Board of Education decided to dismiss the offenders, though there was some doubt of the legality of the step. "In spite of the fact that we may have to take them back," Mr. Kraybill is reported to have said, "their removal may make them realize that their education should be taken more seriously."

THE teachers of New York State, who made a protest against three bills before the legislature, have succeeded in preventing the passage of the Westall-Gamble and the Dunnigan-Steingut bills. The Westall-Gamble bill would have permitted removal of teachers without trial on charges involving their positions. Assemblyman Gamble had it killed on a motion to recommit. The Dunnigan-Steingut measure would have given municipal boards in charge of appropriations final say on all salaries, thus taking teachers' salaries out of the hands of the boards of education. The third bill, which it is hoped also to defeat, would make failure to vote at general elections for five years sufficient grounds to remove a teacher.

Refused amendments which he deemed essential, Governor Pollard of Virginia vetoed the bill to convert the Fredericksburg State Teachers College into a liberal arts college for women, and was sustained by the House. Governor Pollard told the assemblymen in a message that the bill, which made no appropriation for the new institution, would in his opinion, be interpreted as a moral obligation on future assemblies, destroying their freedom of action. He set forth definite amendments changing the wording, and when the House declined to adopt them, 50 to 39, he came back with a veto message. A debate followed and the delegates voted 50–36 to sustain the veto. The action postpones the establishment of the liberal arts college for women at Fredericksburg for the next two years. Establishment of the college by statute law, even though no appropriation is made at present, was favored by University of Virginia alumni who have opposed all efforts to establish coeducation at the university, or a "coordinate college for women" at Charlottesville.

A correspondent writes: "The article entitled 'Academic Salaries' published in School and Society for January 30, 1932, is based on a bulletin recently issued by the U. S. Office of Education. This article conveys the impression that the institutions mentioned are state universities or four-year agricultural and mechanical colleges or institutions of equivalent grade. It shows the so-called Arkansas State College to be paying the deans and professors a typical salary of $1,800 a year. Very possibly the financial statistics for this institution are correct, but it is a type of institution that should not have been included in a list of state universities and equivalent institutions. A letter from the U. S. Office of Education states that the institution mentioned in their circular as 'Arkansas State College' is the Negro agricultural and mechanical college at Pine Bluff. The work of this institution is chiefly of high school grade and below with a small amount of junior college work. The institution is in no sense to be placed in the same category with state universities and standard four-year agricultural and mechanical colleges. Apparently there are two state institutions in the state each having changed its name to Arkansas State College without legal authority."

DISCUSSION

KEEPING THE RECORD STRAIGHT

Fearing that the article from the pen of Professor Frederick E. Bolton, entitled "Is the County Unit Necessary for Effective Rural School Development?" and appearing in a recent issue of School and Society, might be misleading to readers, the writer feels that attention should be called to the several items upon which he based his contentions.

In the first place, the criteria which Professor Bolton set up for measuring the efficiency of a rural school are entirely inadequate and invalid. (1) The ratio of school enrolment to total population fails to give any indication of the quality of schools, except that the children enrolled. Many children enroll but never attend. Many attend but never come in contact with a teacher who can inspire and stimulate. (2) No one has contended that the county unit would operate to extend the school term unless the school finances were by some means increased. (3) Again, the average number of days attended by each pupil fails to give any indication of the school program. (4) The percentage of total enrolment in the high schools for an entire state would not give any indication whatever of how many were enrolled in the rural high schools, since the rural boys and girls are now leaving the rural schools and enrolling in the city high schools. (5) The per capita expenditure for education in an entire state might indicate two things, *viz.*, A very poor and wasteful system of schools or a highly efficient system. The writer knows many one-room schools where the teacher is receiving $150.00 per month for teaching as few as two children—the entire enrolment. This is a high expenditure per pupil. (6) This item depends on the fifth item. It is often the case that in small rural schools more is spent per pupil than in our best city schools.

Consequently, Professor Bolton's criteria fail to stand the test of school efficiency. If he will go out among the rural schools, as did the writer, with standardized tests and measure the educational achievement of the children in the small schools and compare their achievement with that of the children of the city schools he will find that the school achievement varies directly with the size of the school. He will find that in almost all small rural schools the pupils are one to three grades behind where they should be properly classified. Professor Bolton would find that practically all the poorest teachers are in the small rural schools getting experience; he will find that these teachers are drifting toward larger schools where they can sell their services for a larger annual stipend and where living and working conditions are not so impossible. Professor Bolton would find that the percentage of annual teacher turnover among the small rural schools is so large as to practically kill the influence of these schools; and he would find that the larger the school the smaller the teacher turnover. Professor Bolton would find among the small rural schools a teacher with an impossible daily schedule of work, sometimes with as many as forty recitation periods in one day. He would find a poverty-stricken course of study, he would find a high cost of teaching per pupil. He would find many schools with fewer than ten children enrolled, a situation that is not calculated to give children training in group activities.

The writer still contends that most of the ailments of rural schools are due to the district organization, because the district organization causes the schools to be entirely too small, too wasteful and too inefficient.

The county as a unit of administration gives opportunity for consolidating the schools into larger units and to eliminate waste and extravagance. If the small schools are to remain small under the county unit, then there would be no point to the adoption of the county unit. The county unit *per se* would not mean anything, but it does offer the opportunity to reorganize the schools into larger units, to eliminate extravagance and waste, to regulate the teacher load, to broaden and enrich the course of study, to promote more group activities and to give the teacher opportunity to do a real job of teaching instead of going through the motions from day to day.

W. L. HUGHES

TEXAS AGRICULTURAL AND MECHANICAL COLLEGE

THE MENTAL HEALTH OF THE ANTI-PROGRESSIVE

THE subject of this paper is a type, not a character. He or she represents a departing order of teachers, the last of whom are still in the service. There is at least one in every school. It is the ultra-conservative teacher. He can be recognized by his steadfast refusal to admit that new times are upon us. Have tremendous social changes fairly transformed our lives through these decades of the current century? Has an intensely dynamic environment sent a new child into the American public school, a child that is sensitive, restless and practical? No matter! His philosophy of education is perfectly static. He would teach the old-fashioned material and by the same old methods. Latin, geometry and history, swallowed by the yardful of outline, have for centuries sharpened the minds of men (witness himself); they should continue to constitute the simple menu of the modern high school. This quality of mind need not, of course, be associated with the teaching of traditional subjects or with advance chronological age. The teacher that stands out in my mind as one truly progressive is a teacher of Latin and on the threshold of retirement.

The ultra-conservative teacher finds in the modern high school an uncongenial environment. The pupils, stirred incessantly by live, pulsating extra-school interests, offer stubborn resistance to his inert abstractions. More often than not he mistakes this attitude for hostility and responds in kind. The atmosphere is charged with mutual antipathy. There is no teaching, save under strain, and there is no learning, save under compulsion. Little wonder, then, that the teacher afflicted with the extreme form of this malady appears sullen, seeks seclusion and is at odds with head master, fellow teachers, textbooks—everybody and everything that clashes with his own inertia. He has cultivated an attitude that preys on his mental health, and the hostility that he imagines lurking everywhere around him is merely a reflection of his own psychic unrest.

Is there a remedy? Probably not for him, since among his many delusions the strongest is to the effect that all is well with him. But there is a remedy. It is in the fact that the mental health of the child is the clue to the mental health of the teacher. They react alike and to the same favorable or unfavorable conditions. Let the teacher discover the secret of creating in his class an atmosphere of mental well-being and he has found the key to joyful and successful teaching. But it will not be achieved with the technique of 1890.

The present school situation does not yet call for the ultra-progressive teacher. The latter, who snatches at every new idea and swallows it raw, is, in fact, only a shade more desirable than the teacher who repudiates all. One, however, need not cling to a discredited philosophy simply because nothing strikingly constructive has as yet arisen from the newer creeds. The spirit of inquiry is with us, and every rational teacher joins the search. If the newer trends in education yielded us nothing but the courage to question, it yielded a good deal. We are in the midst of significant and far-reaching social changes and are, moreover, entrusted with the tremendous task of helping the young adjust themselves to a most fickle and unstable environment. To cope with the new and changing order of things every walk of life has broken with traditional procedure. It seems that we, too, must break the chains that hold us to the past.

Barnet Rudman

South Boston High School

SPECIAL CORRESPONDENCE

THE DEGREE OF DOCTOR OF MODERN LANGUAGES AT MIDDLEBURY COLLEGE

In August, 1931, the degree of doctor of modern languages was awarded for the first time at an American college. Four years ago, the president and trustees of Middlebury College, in Middlebury, Vermont, voted to offer this new degree. They believed that Middlebury College, through its summer schools of modern languages, could make this definite contribution to higher education in the United States. The degree of doctor of philosophy is recognized as a research degree, representing a training in the science of research, and guaranteeing that the scholar is able to contribute to pure knowledge. It was felt, however, that there was a need in the educational world for a degree carrying with it a guarantee that the holder could impart his knowledge to others; that he was not only a scholar, but a linguist and a teacher, with a perfect mastery of the spoken and written language of his special field; familiar by personal contact with the civilization and customs of the foreign country; and possessing the pedagogical training and experience necessary to interest a class of students.

The new degree of D. M. L. offered by Middlebury College is not, therefore, a rival of the Ph.D. It is not primarily a research degree but a degree combining both scholarly and professional training, and representing the ideal equipment of a successful college teacher of foreign languages. The Middlebury schools, upon whose work this degree is based, are the French School and the Spanish School at Middlebury and the German School at Bristol. There will also be a Casa Italiana on the Middlebury campus this summer. The French, German and Spanish schools were founded at Middlebury shortly before the World War. Their total enrolment last summer was approximately 450. Their faculties are composed of university professors and recognized authorities in their field, natives of the foreign country. The Middlebury organization is built around the principle of exclusive use of a foreign language in all the school activities for the entire session, and a concentrated training in the spoken and written language, literature, history, civilization and customs of the country. The courses are planned primarily for teachers; over 90 per cent. of the students registered are teachers or graduate students preparing to teach.

The principal requirements for the degree of doctor in modern languages are as follows:

(1) The master's degree in modern language from some recognized university.

(2) Residence at Middlebury College equivalent to a full year's work. This requires ordinarily four summers at Middlebury, but the requirement is really the fulfilment of a program, not merely the accumulation of a given total of points. The candidate is expected to complete the main groups of the school's curriculum—philology, literature, the written and spoken language, phonetics, teaching methods and use of "realia."

(3) Two semesters' residence in the foreign country of the major language. This time must be spent in study in approved courses or in equivalent research. The work must be done in accordance with a plan previously approved, and the results of study must meet with approval. It is noteworthy that such foreign residence is not usually required of the Ph.D. candidate.

(4) A major foreign language. The student's knowledge of this language and his ability to use it orally and in writing are tested by oral and written examinations. The candidate must have a thorough training in phonetics and a satisfactory pronunciation. This training includes work in the experimental phonetics laboratory. A scientific study of modern methods of teaching foreign languages is a part of the required program.

(5) The final oral examination of three hours is conducted entirely in the major language, before a board including native professors. This examination will cover all elements of the candidate's preparation for teaching, as well as the history of the major literature, phonology and morphology. A thorough knowledge of philology is required, not *per se*, but with a realization of the great help it affords to the teaching of the language.

(6) A minor language. If the major language is romance, another romance language is preferred. It is tested by an oral and a written examination. The candidate's knowledge should be sufficient at least to teach elementary courses successfully by the oral method. A reading knowledge of German is also required, as a guarantee of the ability to use German texts or editions.

(7) A dissertation written in the major language. This dissertation, which should approximate 35,000 words, is intended to prove a thorough and understanding study of some subject, literary, phonetic or pedagogical, which is worth a careful study. It must embody considerable original work and reflection, must show a mastery of the field, and the ability to use the tools of research. It must also show clearness of thought, coordination of detail, and must be written in correct and easy style. The subject must be chosen and preparation continued under the guidance of some member of the Middlebury faculty.

(8) Candidates are required to teach at least one year under supervision. Statements are requested from heads of departments, school superintendents, and others, as to the success of the candidate's teaching and professional ability. No student will be granted the D.M.L. who can not be unqualifiedly recommended as an experienced and successful teacher.

At the close of the summer session of 1931, the degree was awarded from the Spanish school to two candidates who had completed the required program of training at Middlebury and in Spain, and whose theses and final written and oral examinations were eminently satisfactory. There are about 40 students now definitely registered as candidates for the degree, and six of the candidates are at present in France and Spain, completing their foreign residence. It is evident that, in the long run, the new degree will be judged, not by the purpose of its creation, but by the results in the preparation of language teachers. Yet Middlebury officials are pleased by the reception accorded to the degree thus far, and are determined to justify the confidence placed in its standards.

Stephen A. Freeman

Middlebury College

QUOTATIONS

REDUCTIONS IN THE SALARIES OF TEACHERS

Arguments in favor of salary cuts for teachers in New York State are presented by the Associated School Boards and Trustees in a bulletin to members of the organization, "to assist them in reaching a decision" for their 1932–1933 budgets.

The arguments are in the form of answers by R. S. Jewett, head of the organization, to a recent circular by Dr. W. Howard Pillsbury, president of the New York State Teachers'

Association. Dr. Pillsbury's points, and Mr. Jewett's replies, in part, follow:

1. Teachers' salaries are not anywhere near equal to those of other occupations requiring like qualifications.

The answer will be evident by comparing the present income of teachers with the net income of the average professional man in the same community for ten months' service.

2. Since teachers' salaries were the last to go up they should not be the first to come down.

Other salaries have been coming down for the past two years.

3. It is the salaries of teachers and other government employees that have kept merchants going. Much of their trade has to be on long-time credit at the present time, but the teachers have been able to pay cash.

Many of our members are merchants and we doubt if one of them would subscribe to the truth of this statement.

4. The bulk of a teacher's salary goes for the necessities of life—the chief of which are board and room. There has been little, or no reduction in these items.

Does Dr. Pillsbury think a larger percentage of a teacher's salary goes for board and room than goes for rent, house furnishings, food, heat and light in the case of others? A majority of teachers have no dependents, hence such expenses do not form as large an item as they do in the budget of the head of a family.

5. Past experience has shown it would be a long time before schedules would be returned. It would mean a tremendous loss in professional morale. (Because of the bitter struggle that would be needed to win back the present schedule.)

One of the most remarkable aspects of the depression is the wonderful exhibition of courage shown by the millions who have reduced incomes or no incomes at all. We can not believe the teachers are so inferior to the rest of us that their morale would be seriously affected.

6. Approximately 60 per cent. of the cost of teachers' salaries is provided by the state. It seems evident there is no disposition on the part of the legislature to impair the amount of this state aid. Can the local district, therefore, afford to decrease its 40 per cent. contribution, in view of the fact it gets 100 per cent. of the benefits?

The legislature has impaired state aid for the coming year to the extent of about $5,500,000. But, regardless of this, the principle remains: Are teachers justified in expecting to retain their present salary schedules under present conditions?

7. There is no group of people whose efficiency is so quickly impaired by economic worry as the teaching profession.

There is no group of people who are so secure in their positions and have as little occasion for economic worry as the teachers in the public schools of New York State.

8. Cutting teachers' salaries should be the last resort. If our present conditions of financial stringency were to become permanent, then there is no doubt salaries should be scaled down. But no one believes present conditions to be other than temporary.

Conditions have been progressively worse during the past two years and the outlook for a return to normal during the next twelve to fifteen months is not bright. In the meantime it is absolutely essential that all public expenditures be kept down.
—*New York World-Telegram.*

THE USE OF SCHOOL AUDITORIUMS FOR PUBLIC MEETINGS

A CONSERVATIVE soul is Eugene C. Gibney, director of extension activities for the Board of Education. It is one of his duties to issue permits to organizations which desire to use school auditoriums for evening meetings, and he tries to see to it that no school building is used for a purpose which may endanger the safety or morality of the populace. Thus, when the Brooklyn Citizens Committee, a branch of the Committee of One Thousand, asked permission to use Erasmus Hall High School assembly hall for a discussion of the city manager plan of municipal government Mr. Gibney's official sense of propriety was shocked. He recommended that no permit be issued.

He pointed out to his chief, Superintendent of Schools O'Shea, that the Committee of One Thousand was organized to support the legislative investigation conducted by Judge Seabury. Moreover, wrote Mr. Gibney in his official memorandum:

> The city manager plan of Cincinnati has already aroused expressions of acrimony on the part of a portion of the citizenry of New York City. It is highly probable that the discussion . . . will be a reiteration of sentiments that will not be calculated to advance the best interests of the school system.

Judge Seabury not long ago said he thought the city manager plan might be a good way to rid New York City of political domination, but that, of course, had nothing to do with Mr. Gibney's recommendation. When he vetoed the application for use of the auditorium he probably visualized a debate in which brickbats would be thrown by the speakers for and against the city manager plan.

Superintendent O'Shea is less fearful than is Mr. Gibney. After thinking the matter over for a day or two he overruled his subordinate and decided—too late—the proposed meeting might be held. The 450 cities and towns in this country which have the city manager plan of government may now go about their business without fear of having their names deleted from the geography text-books used in the New York City public schools. The citizens who attend the discussion, now sheduled for the Brooklyn Academy of Music, may be depended on to do their deeds of violence outside the auditorium.—*The New York Times.*

BOOKS AND LITERATURE

GIFTED CHILDREN[1]

VOLUME III of *Genetic Studies of Genius* consists of a follow-up study of the thousand gifted children of California (or as many of them as were available) whose characteristics were described in the first volume of this series. The original group was composed of children whose intelligence quotient was 140 or over when they were first measured in 1921–22. The initial investigation established certain facts of importance concerning children of superior intelligence, and served to correct several erroneous notions which were widely prevalent not only in the popular mind, but among psychologists and professional students of education. Superior children were shown not to be one-sided freaks socially not adaptable and eccentric, but normal, healthy youngsters with general intellectual interests and a love of sports and companionship. They excel in physical and moral qualities as well as in intellect, and they frequently acquire positions of leadership among their school fellows.

What will become of this group of superior children is a matter of much interest. Prediction at this period is unsafe, but the facts brought together in the present volume indicate that the group as a whole is maintaining its position of marked superiority. Intelligence tests were applied to as many as possible of the original one thousand. The Stanford-Binet tests, which are not satisfactory for the older age groups, were administered only to the younger members (under 13), 54 in number, while for the others use was made of the Terman Group Test of Mental Ability. Both sets of tests showed that the scores averaged somewhat lower than they did in 1921–22. One cause of this drop in the IQ, the authors explain, is the higher standard of comparison for the older children. Norms based on seniors in the high school are naturally higher than those based on individuals of corresponding age in the general population, because the high-school seniors are a selected group whose average intellectual level has been raised by the elimination of individuals in the grades. Another factor, not clearly brought out in the volume, is the fact that, since the original lot was selected on account of a high score, it would be selected in part on the basis of a higher rating than was really deserved. To the extent that the high record of the original thousand was due to good luck to that extent one would expect to find a drop in the IQ in a second test.

But quite aside from changes due to the causes mentioned, there is good evidence in certain cases of genuine changes in the IQ. These changes are not improbably due largely to changes in developmental rate. Health, personality traits, race and environment were found to have little, if any, relationship to changes in intelligence. The causes of change, therefore, were probably mainly internal instead of external. One factor of importance, probably, is sex. The drop in the IQ of the girls, as shown by the Stanford-Binet test, was 17 points, as compared with 3 points for the boys. A corresponding superiority was shown by the boys in the Terman test. These results are noteworthy in view of the fact that intelligence tests in general show little difference between the sexes. Is it possible that in the higher ranks of ability the males tend to develop

[1] *Genetic Studies of Genius.* Vol. III. *The Promise of Youth.* By B. S. Burks, D. W. Jensen and L. M. Terman. Stanford University Press, pp. xiv + 508, 1930.

longer than the females? And does adolescence affect the females more unfavorably than the males?

In scholastic achievements the selected group has fully justified its early promise. "Subject failures in high school are practically never incurred by children of this grade of intelligence," and "nearly three fourths of the total marks earned in high school by gifted girls, and nearly one half of those earned by gifted boys are of the A grade." Those who have graduated from high-grade universities win Phi Beta Kappa or other graduating honors about three times as frequently as the rank and file of graduates.

There have been some failures in the gifted group. One unfortunate boy with a bad heredity and a broken home committed suicide. Another erratic boy was sent to the reform school for stealing an automobile; and there were a few others who presented behavior problems. But as a rule the behavior of the gifted group was exceptionally good. The few failures were more than counterbalanced by individuals who made a striking success, even in a very early part of their career. Six became very proficient in music; several evinced marked literary talent, and others have shown unusual ability in art. Whether or not any great genius will emerge from the group it is, of course, too soon to predict.

The one case of identical twins, Barbara and Margaret, is of interest on account of the fact that in all the psychological measurements that were taken there was not one in which the difference was statistically significant. One family contributed five sons whose IQs ranged from 135 to 155. Especial attention in the follow-up study was paid to the siblings of the gifted children. The average IQ in 139 siblings was 123. This resemblance is about equivalent to a correlation coefficient of .45 to .50 which has been found to obtain among siblings in the general school population.

It is planned to devote further study to this group, one to be made not later than 1940, and the last not earlier than 1950. The investigation is in many respects unique and has already yielded results of great value that has fully justified the expenditures (about $60,000) involved. It would indeed be unfortunate if the present investigation could not be continued, and it is to be hoped that adequate funds will be secured for the completion of this valuable research.

S. J. Holmes

COMENIUS AND THE INDIANS[1]

A little less than three hundred years ago the rapidly growing popularity of Comenius' "Janua Linguarum" was beginning to make his name familiar not only throughout Europe but in certain parts of Asia and even in the infant English colonies in America. That his fame was not only wide-spread but firmly established is evidenced by the fact that, notwithstanding its partial eclipse during the eighteenth and early nineteenth centuries, it seems in our time to be increasing rather than diminishing. A succession of notable books on Comenius has appeared within the last two or three decades and scholarly investigations continue either to bring to light additional records relating to his long and active life or to afford fresh and illuminating interpretations of those which have proven obscure or confusing.

Of the latter, perhaps, the best known to American students is Cotton Mather's statement in his "Magnalia" that Comenius at one time accepted from "our Mr. Winthrop" an invitation to become president of Harvard College. The improbability of this statement rests, of course, upon the fact that on neither of the two occasions when, so far as is known, the younger John Winthrop and Comenius might have met was there a vacancy in the presidency of Harvard College.

Mr. Robert Fitzgibbon Young presents in his interesting monograph, "Comenius and the Indians of New England," two novel and yet fairly plausible explanations of this much-discussed passage. Incidentally he points out that the statement was repeated by Mather in his "Ratio Disciplinae Fratrum Nov-Anglorum."

Like other investigators, Mr. Young is convinced that Mather's assertion has a factual basis of some sort. While Mr. Matthews, how-

[1] Robert Fitzgibbon Young, M.A. (Oxford), F. R. Hist. S., Member of the Royal Bohemian Society of Sciences, Prague, "Comenius and the Indians of New England." Published by the School of Slavonic and East European Studies in the University of London, King's College, 40 Torrington Square, London, W. C. 1. 1929. Price 3s.

ever, in his "Comenius and Harvard College" ("Publications of the Colonial Society of Massachusetts, Vol. XXI) suggests that Winthrop and Comenius may have discussed the appointment as a possibility in case of a vacancy, Mr. Young is inclined to the view that the appointment in question was to some other position than to the leadership of the New England college. It may have been, he believes, to a general superintendency of the education of children of Indian converts.

> It seems likely that Winthrop met Comenius at London in 1641 or in Holland in 1642 and tried to persuade him to come to New England to organise the education of the children of the Indian converts.

In support of this hypothesis Mr. Young cites the fact, hitherto largely overlooked, that in one[2] of his references to his visit to London Comenius states that he was invited there "on the advice of certain pious theologians and bishops" to confer regarding missionary work, particularly "in New England." He quotes also two other passages from the letters of Comenius which relate to the spread of Christianity among the American Indians. References to this are cited also from the journal of the elder Winthrop.

A second suggestion is that the invitation Mather refers to was to the headship of a proposed college or society of research which Winthrop, together with other founders of what became the Royal Society, were planning to remove to New England in case continued disorders in England rendered its establishment there impracticable.

This suggestion, Mr. Young shows, derives some measure of plausibility from a statement in the fortieth volume of the "Transactions of the Royal Society" that

> had not the civil wars happily ended as they did, Mr. Boyle and Mr. Wilkins . . . with several other learned men, would have left England, and out of esteem for the most excellent and valiant Governor, John Winthrop the younger, would have retired to his new-born colony, and there have established that Society for Promoting Natural Knowledge, which these gentlemen had formed as it were in embryo.

Apart from its value as an attempt to solve the riddle of the purported agreement of Comenius to come to New England, Mr. Young's monograph throws many interesting sidelights upon the activities, educational and otherwise, of the great Bohemian reformer.

L. F. ANDERSON

EDUCATIONAL BOOKS OF 1931[1]

THIS list is prepared annually, appearing later than usual this year in an attempt to make it as complete as possible. Instead of issuing a supplementary list in April as was done last year, the complete list of *Educational Books of 1931* has been held back to be published in March. The starred titles are those included in the "Sixty Educational Books of 1931," published in the *Journal of the National Education Association* for March, 1932.

This list contains no foreign books except those English books that have been imported and are for sale in this country. It has been limited to the field of education in its broadest sense, excluding courses of study from various cities and states, and books on religious education.

As a "barometer" of current trends of interest, the present list shows that "administration and supervision" are still in the fore, while "curriculum" and "junior high school" have had even less space than last year devoted to them. There are more titles on child psychology than the number of informal child study books in 1930. In fine arts, 1930 produced three similar and very useful books on creative drama, while 1931 has given us more material on music

[2] In his dedicatory letter to the Royal Society of London prefacing his "Via Lucis."

[1] Prepared by Joseph L. Wheeler and Rea J. Steele, Enoch Pratt Free Library, Baltimore, Maryland.

and art in the school than has appeared in the teaching field for some time. Several valuable books on college teaching have appeared. "Adult education" has a larger number of books and more outstanding ones this year than last. A worthwhile series has resulted as the work of the White House Conference on Child Health and Protection and herein are included its several publications regarding the welfare of children.

Every effort has been made to discover material, by checking the Cumulative Book Index, the Education Index and over a hundred current educational periodicals. Approximately 100 more titles were found in 1931, a total of 777 as compared with the 685 titles discovered in 1930.

The chief value of the following list is, we hope, its attempted completeness and its convenience as a key to pamphlet material as well as the better known books on special topics. In spite, however, of direct inquiries to every publisher, including universities and research institutions, careful scrutiny of government lists and catalogues, and requests to other libraries for additions, it is realized that the following list is probably not complete—no list can be.

LIST OF EDUCATIONAL BOOKS

(1) History, Principles and Philosophy of Education

Anderson, L. F. Pestalozzi. 283 p. 1931. McGraw-Hill. $2.00.

*Bagley, W. C. Education, crime, and social progress. 150 p. 1931. Macmillan. $1.20.

Bollig, R. J. The German Catholic schools in southern Russia. (Catholic univ. of Amer. Educational research monographs, Vol VI, No. 2) 30 p. 1931. Catholic Educ. Press. $1.00.

Botsford, E. H. Fifty years at Williams. Book III —Administrations of John Haskell Hewitt, 1901–1902; Henry Hopkins, 1902–1908. Ltd. ed. 1931. Alumni Office, 15–17 Jessup Hall, Williamstown, Mass. $1.50.

Brubacher, J. S. Henry Barnard on education. 298 p. 1931. McGraw-Hill. $2.25.

Buchholz, H. E. (Ezekiel Cheever, pseud.) Fads and fallacies in present-day education. 200 p. 1931. Macmillan. $1.50.

Burnett, C. T. Hyde of Bowdoin, a biography of William De Witt Hyde; with an introduction by G. H. Palmer. 364 p. 1931. Houghton, Mifflin. $4.00.

Carrington, W. T. History of education in Missouri. 141 p. 1931. State Supt. of Public Schools, Jefferson City, Mo. $1.00.

Cavenagh, F. A., *ed.* James and John Stuart Mill on Education. 208 p. 1931. Cambridge Univ. Press, Macmillan, N. Y. C. $2.00.

Cebollero, P. A. Education in Porto Rico, 1920–1930. (U. S. Office of Educ. Leaflet, No. 4) 13 p. 1931. Supt. of Doc. $.05.

Childs, J. L. Education and the philosophy of experimentalism. 264 p. 1931. Century. $2.00.

Clapp, F. L., Chase, W. J., and Merriman, C. A technique of study to accompany "An introduction to education." 134 p. 1931. Ginn. $.80.

Coade, T. F., *ed.* Harrow lectures on education: being a series of addresses delivered at the first junior public school masters' conference at Harrow school in January, 1930. 230 p. 1931. Cambridge Univ. Press, Macmillan, N. Y. C. $3.50.

Cole, P. R. A history of educational thought. 316 p. 1931. Oxford Univ. Press. $3.50.

Confrey, Burton. Secularism in American education: its history. (Catholic univ. of Amer. Educational research monographs, Vol. VI, No. 1) 153 p. 1931. Catholic Educ. Press. $1.50.

Council of Christian Associations. Education adequate for modern times: discussions and proposals of the National student-faculty conference on religion in education. 276 p. 1931. Association Press, 347 Madison Ave., N. Y. C. $2.00.

Dewey, John. The way out of educational confusion. (Inglis lecture) 41 p. 1931. Harvard Univ. Press. $1.00.

Doughton, Isaac. Syllabus in an introduction to a philosophy of education. 108 p. 1931. The Author, 101 Sherwood St., Mansfield, Penn. $1.25.

Ebaugh, C. D. The national system of education in Mexico. (Studies in educ. No. 16) 149 p. 1931. Johns Hopkins Press. $2.00.

Eby, Frederick. Early Protestant educators: the educational writings of Martin Luther, John Calvin, and other leaders of Protestant thought. 312 p. 1931. McGraw-Hill. $2.25.

Elliott, A. E. Paraguay: its cultural heritage, social conditions, and educational problems. (Cont. to educ. No. 473) 210 p. 1931. Teachers College, Columbia. $2.50.

Eurich, A. C., *ed.* The changing educational world, 1905–1930: papers read on the occasion of the twenty-fifth anniversary of the College of education, University of Minnesota. 311 p. 1931. Univ. of Minn. Press. $3.00.

Franklin, Benjamin. Proposals relating to the education of youth in Pensilvania. (Ltd. ed. books) 32 p. 1931. Univ. of Penn. $2.50.

Frasier, G. W., and Armentrout, W. D., *editors.* An introduction to the literature of education. 562 p. 1931. Scott, Foresman. $2.00.

Goodsell, Willystine, *ed.* Pioneers of women's education in the United States. 311 p. 1931. McGraw-Hill. $2.25.

Haney, J. L., *ed.* Barnwell addresses, vol. 1, 1922–1930. 436 p. 1931. J. Faltermayer, Sec'y, Central High School, Philadelphia, Penn. $1.00.

Hart, J. K. Creative moments in education: a documentary interpretation of the history of education. 476 p. 1931. Henry Holt. $3.00.

Hofstead, J. A. American educators of Norwegian origin: a biographical dictionary. 316 p. 1931. The Author, 854 68th St., Brooklyn, N. Y. $3.50.

Honeywell, R. J. The educational work of Thomas Jefferson. (Harvard studies in educ. Vol. XVI) 295 p. 1931. Harvard Univ. Press. $3.00.

Horn, H. H. This new education. 280 p. 1931. Abingdon. $2.50.

Hovre, Franz de. Philosophy and education: the modern educational theories of naturalism, socialism, and nationalism: a textbook for normal schools and teachers' colleges; tr. from French edition of G. Siméons by Rev. E. B. Jordan. 443 p. 1931. Benziger. $3.25.

Josephson, Matthew. Jean-Jacques Rousseau. 559 p. 1931. Harcourt. $5.00.

Kandel, I. L., *ed.* (Seventh) Educational yearbook of the Institute of international education, 1930. 544 p. 1931. Teachers College, Columbia. $3.50.

Keatinge, M. W., *ed.* Comenius. 255 p. 1931. McGraw-Hill. $2.00.

Keep, R. A. Fourscore years: a history of Mills college. (Ltd. no. ed.) 143 p. 1931. The Author, Mills College P. O., Cal. $3.00.

Kirkham, F. W. Educating all the children of all the people. (U. S. Office of Educ. Bulletin 1931, No. 11) 57 p. 1931. Supt. of Doc. $.10.

Leary, D. B. Living and learning: a philosophy of education. 477 p. 1931. R. R. Smith. $2.25.

Lepley, Ray. Dependability in philosophy of education. (Cont. to educ. No. 461) 96 p. 1931. Teachers College, Columbia. $1.50.

Maas, Andrew. Pere Girard, educator. (Franciscan studies, No. 9) 69 p. 1931. J. F. Wagner. $.50.

McCallister, W. J. The growth of freedom in education: a critical interpretation of some historical views. 589 p. 1931. R. R. Smith. $6.00.

Matzen, J. M. State constitutional provisions for education: fundamental attitude of the American people regarding education as revealed by state constitutional provisions, 1776–1929. (Cont. to educ. No. 462) 159 p. 1931. Teachers College, Columbia. $1.75.

*Messenger, J. F. An interpretative history of education. 387 p. 1931. Crowell. $2.00.

Murphy, A. J. Education for world-mindedness. 366 p. 1931. Abingdon. $2.50; $2.75 by mail.

National Education Association. Department of Superintendence and Research Division. Education discussed in lay magazines, February 1, 1931. (Educational research service. Circular, No. 2) *Mimeographed.* 8 p. 1931. The Association. With subscription to Educ. Research Service.

National Education Association. Department of Superintendence and Research Division. Education discussed in lay magazines, April 1, 1931. (Educational research service. Circular, No. 5) *Mimeographed.* 8 p. 1931. The Association. With subscription to Educ. Research Service.

National Education Association. Department of Superintendence and Research Division. Education discussed in lay magazines, June 1, 1931. (Educational research service. Circular, No. 7) *Mimeographed.* 11 p. 1931. The Association. With subscription to Educ. Research Service.

National Education Association. Department of Superintendence and Research Division. Education discussed in lay magazines, June 1 to October 1, 1931. (Educational research service. Circular, No. 8) *Mimeographed.* 17 p. 1931. The Association. With subscription to Educ. Research Service.

National Education Association. Department of Superintendence and Research Division. Education discussed in lay magazines, December 1, 1931. (Educational research service. Circular, No. 11) *Mimeographed.* 9 p. 1931. The Association. With subscription to Educ. Research Service.

National Education Association. National Council on Education. What are the major objectives of education? 24 p. 1931. The Association. $.20.

National Education Association. Research Division. Childhood and the depression: a look ahead. 42 p. 1931. The Association. $.20.

National Society for the Study of Education. Thirtieth yearbook, part II. The textbook in American education. 364 p. 1931. Public School Pub. Co. $2.50 cloth; $1.75 paper.

National Society for the Study of Educational Sociology. Third yearbook: education and economics; ed. by H. F. Clark and B. R. Andrews. 68 p. 1931. Teachers College, Columbia. $1.25.

Park, C. F. A history of the Lowell institute school, 1903–1928. 192 p. 1931. Harvard Univ. Press. $2.50.

Parker, Beryl. The Austrian educational institutes. 184 p. 1931. N. Y. Univ. Book Store, 81 Washington Square, East, N. Y. C. $2.50.

Quarter century of learning: 1904–1929; as recorded in lectures delivered at Columbia university on the occasion of the one hundred and seventy-fifth anniversary of its founding. 380 p. 1931. Columbia Univ. Press. $3.50.

Radtke, Bruno. Some observations on German and English education in elementary and secondary schools. (Kansas studies in educ. Vol. II, No. 1) 36 p. 1931. Univ. of Kan. No charge—available on exchange basis.

Raymont, Thomas. Education. 337 p. 1931. Longmans. $2.75.

Reisner, E. H. A syllabus for a historical introduction to the study of education. Part I—Education as a public policy. (Teachers College, syllabi, No. 16) 31 p. 1931. Teachers College, Columbia. $.40.

*Rugg, Harold. Culture and education in America. 404 p. 1931. Harcourt. $2.75.

Sadiq, I. K. Modern Persia and her educational system. (Studies of the International institute, No. 14) 125 p. 1931. Teachers College, Columbia. $1.50.

Snedden, David. Cultural educations and common sense: a study of some sociological foundations designed to refine, increase, and render more functional the personal cultures of men. 324 p. 1931. Macmillan. $2.00.

*Snedden, David. Towards better educations: some critical sociological examinations of a variety of current problems of coordinating purposes and methods in education. 427 p. 1931. Teachers College, Columbia. $4.00.

U. S. Department of State. Report of the United States commission on education in Haiti. (Latin Amer. series, No. 5) 74 p. 1931. Gov't Print. Office. $.15.

U. S. Department of the Interior. The Office of education: its duties, its history, its publications. 13 p. 1931. Supt. of Doc. Gratis.

Woody, Thomas, *ed.* Educational views of Benjamin Franklin. 270 p. 1931. McGraw-Hill. $2.00.

Wynne, J. P. Handbook in the principles of education from the standpoint of the teacher. 48 p. 1931. Clarion Pub. Co., Farmville, Va. $.50; $.2 postage.

(2) ADMINISTRATION AND SUPERVISION

(*See also Teachers and Teaching Methods*)

Abel, J. F. Information about the certificates issued by the Scottish education department. (U. S. Office of Educ. Circular, No. 38) *Mimeographed.* 8 p. 1931. Supt. of Doc. Gratis.

Alberty, H. B., and Thayer, V. T. Supervision in the secondary school. 471 p. 1931. D. C. Heath. $2.00.

Alexander, Carter. Educational finance studies: summaries and evaluations for school administrators of recent educational finance dissertations at Teachers college, Columbia university. 92 p. 1931. Teachers College, Columbia. $1.00.

Alexander, Carter. Educational research: suggestions and sources of data with specific reference to administration. 3rd ed. rev. and enl. 120 p. 1931. Teachers College, Columbia. $1.00.

American Educational Research Association. School organization. (Review of educational research, Vol. I, No. 3) 84 p. 1931. The Association, N. E. A. $1.00.

American school and university: a yearbook devoted to the design, construction, equipment, utilization, and maintenance of educational buildings and grounds. 559 p. 1931. The Amer. School Pub. Corp., 470 Fourth Ave., N. Y. C. $5.00.

Association for Childhood Education. Committee on Supervision. Supervisory practices: nursery—kindergarten—primary. *Mimeographed.* 49 p. 1931. The Association. $.15.

*Barr, A. S. Introduction to the scientific study of classroom supervision. 399 p. 1931. Appleton. $2.50.

Brown, J. F. State publications of schoolbooks. Rev. ed. 56 p. 1931. Macmillan. $.25.

Brunstetter, M. R. Business management in school systems of different sizes: a study of certain aspects of business management in nine New Jersey cities. (Cont. to educ. No. 455) 135 p. 1931. Teachers College, Columbia. $1.50.

Byrne, Lee. Check list materials for public school building specifications, covering the general specifications. (Cont. to ed. No. 492) 195 p. 1931. Teachers College, Columbia. $2.25.

*Carpenter, W. W., and Rufi, John. The teacher and secondary-school administration from the point of view of the classroom teacher. 460 p. 1931. Ginn. $2.40.

Chase, V. E. School building survey and program. 72 p. 1931. Fordson Public Schools. Bureau of Research and Statistics, Dearborn, Mich. $1.00.

Child Study Association of America. Disciplinary devices: punishment. 15 p. 1931. The Association. $.20.

Child Study Association of America. Disciplinary devices: rewards. 19 p. 1931. The Association. $.20.

Clark, Z. R. Recognition of merit in superintendents' reports to the public. (Cont. to educ. No. 471) 123 p. 1931. Teachers College, Columbia. $1.75.

Cochran, H. A. The status of the Superintendent of schools in Pennsylvania. 90 p. 1931. Temple Univ. Press. $1.00.

Cole, R. D. Educational achievement in North Dakota—town and rural schools. (Univ. of North Dakota departmental bulletin, Vol. XV, No. 2) 53 p. 1931. The University. Gratis upon request.

Covert, Timon. An annotated bibliography of studies on consolidation and transportation, 1923–1929. (U. S. Office of Educ. Circular, No. 9) *Mimeographed.* 26 p. 1931. The Office. Gratis.

Covert, Timon. State aid for school consolidation and pupil transportation. (U. S. Office of Educ. Leaflet, No. 3) 9 p. 1931. Supt. of Doc. $.05.

Dartmouth College. Amos Tuck School of Administration and Finance. Manual on research and reports with special application to investigations in the field of business, economics, and public affairs. 108 p. 1931. Williams and Wilkins. $1.25.

Deffenbaugh, W. S. School administration in state educational survey reports. (U. S. Office of Educ. Bulletin 1930, No. 35) 34 p. 1931. Supt. of Doc. $.10.

*Edmondson, J. B., Roemer, Joseph, and Bacon, F. L. Secondary school administration. 483 p. 1931. Macmillan. $2.25.

Educational Press Association of America. Educational market: an analysis for advertisers and their counsel. 32 p. 1931. The Association, 1201 Sixteenth St., N. W., Washington, D. C. $.10.

Elsbree, W. S. Teachers' salaries. 286 p. 1931. Teachers College, Columbia. $2.50.

*Engelhardt, Fred. Public school organization and administration. 595 p. 1931. Ginn. $3.60.

Engelhardt, N. L. Survey field book for the analysis of a high school building. 45 p. 1931. Teachers College, Columbia. $.50.

Essex, D. L. Bonding versus pay-as-you-go in the financing of school buildings. (Cont. to educ. No. 496) 101 p. 1931. Teachers College, Columbia. $1.50.

Eubank, L. A. Organization and administration of laboratory schools in state teachers colleges. (Bulletin, Vol. XXXI, No. 4) 89 p. 1931. Northeast Missouri State Teachers College, Kirksville, Mo. $1.00.

Fitch, H. N. An analysis of the supervisory activities and techniques of the elementary school training supervisor in state normal schools and teachers colleges. (Cont. to educ. No. 476) 130 p. 1931. Teachers College, Columbia. $1.50.

Fitzpatrick, F. B. Supervision of elementary schools. 128 p. 1931. F. A. Owen Pub. Co. $1.00.

Fowlkes, J. G., and Jones, L. F. State support for public high schools in Wisconsin. (Univ. of Wisconsin. Bur. of educational research bulletin, No. 12) 82 p. 1931. The University. $1.00.

Grossnickle, F. E. Capital outlay in relation to a state's minimum educational program. (Cont. to educ. No. 464) 67 p. 1931. Teachers College, Columbia. $1.50.

Harrison, W. K., and Dobbin, C. E. School buildings of today and tomorrow. 233 p. 1931. Architectural Book Pub. Co. $16.50.

Henzlik, F. E. School administration and the training of superintendents for small city school systems. (Univ. of Nebraska. Educational monograph No. 1) 35 p. 1931. The University. $.50.

Hillegas, M. B. The elements of classroom supervision. 224 p. 1931. Laidlaw. $1.76.

Horstick, S. M. A study of sources of revenue for public education in New Jersey. 140 p. 1931. Univ. of Penn. $1.50 paper.

Houston, Texas. Board of Education. The building program of the Houston independent school district. (1929–1930) 121 p. 1931. The Board. $.75.

Hunkins, R. V. Superintendent at work in smaller schools. 401 p. 1931. D. C. Heath. $2.00.

Huus, R. O., and Cline, D. I. Municipal school and university stadia. (Publication, No. 18) 33 p. 1931. Municipal Administration Service, 261 Broadway, N. Y. C. $.35.

Jensen, F. A. Current procedure in selecting textbooks. 157 p. 1931. Lippincott. $2.40.

Job, L. B., Reeder, W. G., and Heck, A. O. The school clerk and his records. Handbook for Part II of The uniform school accounting system. 80 p. 1931. Public School Pub. Co. $1.25.

Ketler, F. C. Reserve funds in public school finance. (Cont. to educ. No. 456) 77 p. 1931. Teachers College, Columbia. $1.50.

Klemmedson, G. S. Taxation and public school finance in Colorado. (Bulletin, No. 376) 38 p. 1931. Colo. Agricultural College Experiment Station, Fort Collins, Colo. Gratis.

Kyte, G. C. Problems in school supervision. 214 p. 1931. Houghton, Mifflin. $1.60.

Langford, H. D. Educational service: its functions and possibilities. (Cont. to educ. No. 509) 212 p. 1931. Teachers College, Columbia. $2.00.

Magee, H. J. Unit costs of salaries in teachers colleges and normal schools. (Cont. to educ. No. 489) 75 p. 1931. Teachers College, Columbia. $1.50.

Massachusetts. Department of Education. Salaries of teachers in the public schools of Massachusetts for the school year 1931. (Bulletin No. 9, Whole No. 229) 47 p. 1931. Dept. of Educ., Boston, Mass.

Michigan Education Association. School economics through efficient administration and management. 39 p. 1931. The Association, Lansing, Mich. Gratis. Ltd. supply.

Michigan Education Association. Department of Elementary-School Principals. Fifth yearbook: the principal as an educational leader. 112 p. 1931. The Association. $1.00.

Morrison, J. C. Standards for the preparation and certification of elementary school principals. 13 p. 1931. Univ. of State of N. Y. Gratis.

Nanninga, S. P. A plan of organization of the State department of education. (Univ. of New Mexico bulletin, Vol. V, No. 2) 19 p. 1931. The University. $.25.

National Education Association. Department of Elementary-School Principals. The tenth yearbook: the principal and supervision. 652 p. 1931. The Association. $2.00.

*National Education Association. Department of Superintendence. Ninth yearbook: five unifying factors in American education. 543 p. 1931. The Association. $2.00.

National Education Association. Department of Superintendence and Research Division. Preliminary figures on classroom teachers' salaries, 1930–31, in eighty-six large cities. (Educational research service. Circular, No. 3) 7 p. 1931. The Association. With subscription to Educ. Research Service.

National Education Association. Department of Superintendence and Research Division. Salary schedules for elementary school principals, 1930–31, eighty-eight cities over 100,000 in population. (Educational research service. Circular, No. 10) 26 p. 1931. The Association. With subscription to Educ. Research Service.

National Education Association. Department of Supervisors and Directors of Instruction. Fourth yearbook: the evaluation of supervision. 182 p. 1931. Teachers College, Columbia. $2.00.

National Education Association. Research Division. Flat-rate and percent-of-salary retirement systems. (Studies in state educational administration, No. 7) 10 p. 1931. The Association. $.25.

National Education Association. Research Division. Personal income tax and school support. (Studies in state educational administration, No. 8) 20 p. 1931. The Association. $.25.

National Education Association. Research Division. The principal at work on his problems. (Bulletin, Vol. IX, No. 2) 94–159 pp. 1931. The Association. $.25.

National Education Association. Research Division. Salaries in city school systems, 1930–31. (Bulletin, Vol. IX, No. 3) 162–227 pp. 1931. The Association. $.25.

National Education Association. Research Division. Salaries paid school administrative and supervisory officers, 1930–31, eighty-eight cities over 100,000 in population. (Special salary tabulations I–B through V–B) 14 p. 1931. The Association. $5.00 per set.

National Education Association. Research Division. Salaries paid teachers, principals, and certain other school employees, 1930–31, eighty-eight cities over 100,000 in population. (Special salary tabulations I–A through V–A) 27 p. 1931. The Association. $5.00 per set.

National Education Association. Research Division. Staffs and salaries in state departments of education. (Studies in state educational administration, No. 9) 61 p. 1931. The Association. $.25.

New York (State) University. Public school finances in cities, villages under superintendents and other villages maintaining academic departments; also tables showing total finances and other data for all public schools for the school year ending July 31, 1929. (Univ. of the state of New York bulletin, No. 965) 137 p. 1931. The University. $.10.

Nobel, E. H. Status and professional preparation of recreation center executives and workers in California, 1929. (Univ. of California publications in educ. VI, No. 4) 217–283 pp. 1931. The University. $1.15.

Pennsylvania. Department of Public Instruction. Rules and regulations for public school building construction. (Bulletin No. 57) 43 p. 1931. The Department. Gratis.

Perry, C. A., and Williams, M. P. New York school centers and their community policy. 78 p. 1931. Russell Sage Foundation. $.50.

Phillips, Velma. Evidence of the need of education for efficient purchasing. (Cont. to educ. No. 447) 114 p. 1931. Teachers College, Columbia. $1.50.

Prewett, H. O. The economic advantages of special promotions: the amount saved to the school system by permitting pupils to skip half grades. *Mimeographed.* 27 p. 1931. Public Schools, Fort Worth, Texas. $.50.

Pringle, R. W. The psychology of high-school discipline. 362 p. 1931. D. C. Heath. $1.60.

Proctor, A. M. Safeguarding the school board's purchase of architects' working drawings. (Cont. to educ. No. 474) 138 p. 1931. Teachers College, Columbia. $2.00.

Puckett, R. C. Making a high school schedule of recitations. 164 p. 1931. Longmans. $1.80.

*Reavis, W. C., and others. The elementary school: its organization and administration. 571 p. 1931. Univ. of Chic. Press. $3.00.

Skidmore, F. R. A cross section of supervision in Garrett County, Maryland. (Maryland school bulletin, Vol. XIII, No. 2) 70 p. 1931. State Dept. of Educ., Baltimore, Md. $.35.

Smith, S. L. Community school plans. Rev. ed. 39 p. 1931. Julius Rosenwald Fund, Nashville, Tenn. Gratis.

*Swift, F. H. Federal and state policies in public school finance in the United States. 472 p. 1931. Ginn. $3.80.

Thrun, F. M. School financing in Michigan: a plan to equalize the burden. (Special bulletin, No. 212) 79 p. 1931. Mich. Agricultural Experiment Station, East Lansing, Mich. Gratis while supply lasts.

U. S. Office of Education. Accredited higher institutions, 1930–31. (Bulletin 1930, No. 19, supplement) 9 p. 1931. Supt. of Doc. Gratis.

(3) REPORTS, SURVEYS, STATISTICS AND LEGISLATION

(For Surveys of Special Phases see other Headings)

American Association of University Women. Proceedings: fiftieth anniversary and seventh national convention (forty-third general meeting) April 8–11, 1931. 309 p. 1931. The Association. $1.00.

Association of Colleges and Secondary Schools of the Middle States and Maryland. Proceedings of the forty-fourth annual convention, Atlantic City, 1930. 109 p. 1931. G. W. McClelland, Sec'y, Univ. of Penn. Gratis to Association members.

Association of Urban Universities. Proceedings of the sixteenth and seventeenth annual meetings, 1929 and 1930. 190 p. 1931. The Association, C. S. Marsh, Sec'y, Univ. of Buffalo, Buffalo, N. Y. $1.00.

Bachman, F. P., and others. Public schools of Nashville, Tennessee. A survey report. 373 p. 1931. George Peabody College for Teachers, Division of Surveys and Field Studies. $1.00.

Barrows, A. P. School building survey and program for Warwick, Rhode Island: a study of a town in the path of an expanding metropolitan area. (U. S. Office of Educ. Bulletin 1930, No. 33) 77 p. 1931. Supt. of Doc. $.15.

Beaumont Public Schools. Annual report on tests and classification in Beaumont schools for 1929–31. 20 p. 1931. Board of Educ., Beaumont, Texas.

Buffalo. Municipal Research Bureau. Report of the Buffalo school survey. 2 vol. 271 p., 230 p. 1931. The Bureau, White Bldg., Buffalo, N. Y. $5.00.

Carnegie Endowment for International Peace. Division of Intercourse and Education. Annual report of the director for the year 1930—Nicholas Murray Butler. 79 p. 1931. Carnegie Endowment. Gratis.

Carnegie Foundation for the Advancement of Teaching. Annual review of legal education for the year 1930. 66 p. 1931. The Foundation. Gratis.

Carnegie Foundation for the Advancement of Teaching. Twenty-fifth annual report of the president and treasurer, 1930. 206 p. 1931. The Foundation. Gratis.

College Entrance Examination Board. Thirty-first annual report of the secretary. 205 p. 1931. The Board, 431 W. 117th St., N. Y. C. Gratis.

Comstock, L. M. Per capita costs in city schools, 1929–30. (U. S. Office of Educ. Pamphlet, No. 19) 13 p. 1931. Supt. of Doc. $.05.

Conference on Education for Negroes in Texas. Proceedings of the second annual conference, Prairie View state college, Texas, 1931. (Prairie View standard, Vol. XVII, No. 16) 47 p. 1931. The College, Prairie View, Texas. Gratis.

Educational Press Association of America. Seventh yearbook. 31 p. 1931. The Association. Committee on Standards, 1201 Sixteenth St., N. W., Washington, D. C. $.10.

Embree, E. R. Julius Rosenwald fund: review for the year. 38 p. 1931. Julius Rosenwald Fund, 900 S. Homan Ave., Chicago, Ill. Gratis.

Falk, A. T. Survey of collegiate instruction in marketing and advertising 1929–30: a quantitative study of instruction relating to commodity distribution as offered by 633 degree-granting collegiate institutions. (Bur. of research and educ. 1931 series, Bulletin, No. 6) *Mimeographed.* 62 p. 1931. Advertising Federation of America, 420 Lexington Ave., N. Y. C. $2.50.

General Education Board. Annual report, 1929–1930. 75 p. 1931. The Board, 61 Broadway, N. Y. C. Gratis.

George Peabody College for Teachers. Division of Surveys and Field Studies. Public schools of Nashville, Tennessee. 373 p. 1931. The Division. George Peabody College. $1.00.

George Peabody College for Teachers. Division of Surveys and Field Studies. All-year school of Nashville, Tennessee. (Field studies, No. 3) 60 p. 1931. The Division. George Peabody College. $.25.

Graves, F. P. Addresses and papers, 1926–31. 354 p. 1931. Univ. of State of N. Y. Gratis.

Hebb, Bertha. An indexed list of city school reports, 1929–30. (U. S. Office of Educ. Circular, No. 39) *Mimeographed.* 20 p. 1931. The Office. Gratis.

Heck, A. O. Study of the Ohio compulsory education and child labor law. (Ohio State Univ. Bur. of educational research monographs, No. 9) 210 p. 1931. The University. $2.00.

High School Conference. Urbana, Illinois. Proceedings of the high school conference of November 20, 21, and 22, 1930. (Univ. of Illinois bulletin, Vol. XXVIII, No. 16) 327 p. 1931. The University, High School Visitor's Office. Gratis.

Holy, T. C. Survey of the schools of Springfield, Ohio. (Ohio State Univ. Bur. of educational research monographs, No. 10) 84 p. 1931. The University. $1.00.

Illinois. University. College of Education. Proceedings of the annual conference of the faculty of the College of education, University of Illinois, with the superintendents of the schools of Illinois, Urbana, Ill., Nov. 20, 1930. (Bulletin, Vol. XXVIII, No. 26. Bur. of educational research bulletin, No. 54) 36 p. 1931. The University. $.30.

Illinois Vocational Association. Report of the convention at Hotel Sherman, Chicago, November 7–8, 1930. (Bulletin, No. 2) 63 p. 1931. The Association. Gratis.

Julius Rosenwald Fund. Report on schoolhouse construction, transportation, and school libraries to July 1, 1931. 3 p. 1931. Julius Rosenwald Fund, Nashville, Tenn. Gratis.

Keyworth, M. R. Legal aspects for the records of proceedings of boards of education. 171 p. 1931. Bruce Pub. Co. $2.25.

Lide, E. S. Constitutional basis of public school education. (U. S. Office of Educ. Leaflet, No. 40) 11 p. 1931. Supt. of Doc. $.05.

Minnesota. University. College of Educational Research. Report of the Committee on educational research for the biennium 1928–1930. (Univ. of Minnesota bulletin, Vol. XXXIV, No. 7) 148 p. 1931. The University, College of Educ. Research. Gratis while supply lasts.

Monroe, Paul, *ed.* Conference on examinations, held in Eastborne, England, May 23–25, 1931, under the auspices of The Carnegie corporation, The Carnegie foundation, and The International institute of Teachers college, Columbia university. 316 p. 1931. Teachers College, Columbia. $3.00.

Nanninga, S. P. Report of the survey of the Estancia public schools with suggestions mutually pertinent to other small schools systems in New Mexico. (Univ. of New Mexico bulletin, Vol. V, No. 3) 61 p. 1931. The University. $.25.

National Advisory Committee on Education. Report. Federal relations to education. Part I. Committee findings and recommendations. Part II. Basic facts. 140 p.—Part I; 448 p.—Part II. 1931. The Committee, 744 Jackson Place, Washington, D. C. $1.25 per set.

National Association of Public School Business Officials. Proceedings of the twentieth annual meeting, Richmond, Virginia, May 19–22, 1931. 84 p. 1931. The Association, J. S. Mount, Sec'y, Trenton, N. J. $2.00.

National Association of State Universities. Transactions and proceedings, Vol. XXVIII, 1930. 207 p. 1931. The Association, A. H. Upham, Sec'y, 205 Benton Hall, Miami Univ., Oxford, Ohio. $.50.

National Catholic Educational Association. Report of the proceedings and addresses of the twenty-eighth annual meeting, Philadelphia, Penn., June 22–25, 1931. (Bulletin, Vol. XXVIII, No. 1) 864 p. 1931. The Association. $1.00.

National Congress of Parents and Teachers. Proceedings of the thirty-fifth annual meeting, Hot Springs, Arkansas, May 3–7, 1931, Vol. XXXV. 566 p. 1931. The Congress. $3.00.

National Education Association. Annual report of the secretary. 31 p. 1931. The Association. $.25.

National Education Association. Proceedings of the sixty-ninth annual meeting held at Los Angeles, California, June 27–July 3, 1931. 1200 p. 1931. The Association. $3.00.

National Education Association. Report of the committee of one hundred on tenure problems: presented at the Los Angeles meeting of the National education association, June 30, 1931. 8 p. 1931. The Association. $.05.

National Education Association. Committee on Retirement Allowances. Report, presented July, 1931, at Los Angeles meeting. 22 p. 1931. The Association. $.25.

National Education Association. Department of Superintendence. Official report, Detroit, Michigan, February 21 to February 26, 1931. 316 p. 1931. The Association. $1.00.

National Education Association. Department of Superintendence and Research Division. Size of class in 47 cities over 100,000 in population. (Educational research service. Circular, No. 1) 36 p. 1931. The Association. With subscription to Educ. Research Service.

National Education Association. Department of Superintendence and Research Division. Size of class in 101 cities 30,000 to 100,000 in population and cities under 30,000 in population. (Educational research service. Circular, No. 6) 63 p. 1931. The Association. With subscription to Educ. Research Service.

National Education Association. Department of Superintendence and Research Division. Transportation of school children in 67 large school systems. (Educational research service. Circular, No. 4) 12 p. 1931. The Association. With subscription to Educ. Research Service.

National Education Association. Research Division. 1931 supplement to the bibliographies on eight problems of school legislation. *Mimeographed.* 26 p. 1931. The Association. Furnished with the "Study in state educ. administration." $.25.

National League of Compulsory Education Officials. Proceedings of the twentieth annual convention held in Hotel Seneca, Rochester, N. Y., October 20–21–22–23–24, 1930. 96 p. 1931. The League. $2.00.

National League of Compulsory Education Officials. Proceedings of the twenty-first annual convention held at the Royal York, Toronto, Ontario, Canada, October 26–27–28–29, 1931. 96 p. 1931. The League. $2.00.

New York (State) University. Proceedings of the sixty-sixth convocation of the University of the state of New York, Albany, N. Y., October 16 and 17, 1930. (Univ. of the state of New York bulletin, No. 976) 97 p. 1931. The University. $.40.

Ohio State University. Proceedings of the Ohio state educational conference: eleventh annual session, ed. by J. H. MacLatchy. (Ohio State Univ. bulletin, Vol. XXXVI, No. 3) 544 p. 1931. The University. Gratis. Ltd. distribution.

Philippine Islands. Bureau of Education. Thirty-first annual report of the director of education for the calendar year 1930. 213 p. 1931. The Bureau. Gratis.

Proffitt, M. M. Industrial education section of the survey of the Buffalo public schools. (U. S. Office of Educ. Pamphlet, No. 17) 34 p. 1931. Supt. of Doc. $.10.

Riley, E. J. Development of the Montana state educational organization, 1864–1930. 135 p. 1931. Catholic Univ. of Amer. $1.00.

Smith, J. H. Legal limitations on bonds and taxation for public school buildings. (Cont. to educ. No. 453) 117 p. 1931. Teachers College, Columbia. $1.50.

Southern Conference on Education. Southern conference on education: proceedings of the third conference, 1930. (Univ. of North Carolina. Extension bulletin, Vol. X, No. 9) 137 p. 1931. The University. $.50.

Strayer, G. D. Report of the survey of the schools of Watertown, Massachusetts. 196 p. 1931. Teachers College, Columbia. $1.50.

Taubeneck, O. C. Legal opinions of the non-high school district law of Illinois. 84 p. 1931. Public School Pub. Co. $.75.

U. S. Office of Education. Biennial survey of education in the United States, 1928–1930. (Bulletin 1931, No. 20) 1931. Supt. of Doc.

U. S. Office of Education. Record of current educational publications comprising publications from July–December, 1930. (Bulletin 1931, No. 3) 118 p. 1931. Supt. of Doc. $.20.

U. S. Office of Education. Record of current educational publications, quarterly, January 1–March 31, 1931. (Bulletin 1931, No. 9) 105 p. 1931. Supt. of Doc. $.15.

U. S. Office of Education. Record of current educational publications, April 1–June 30, 1931. (Bulletin 1931, No. 16) 106 p. 1931. Supt. of Doc. $.15.

U. S. Office of Education. Record of current educational publications, July 1–September 30, 1931. (Bulletin 1931, No. 22) 86 p. 1931. Supt. of Doc. $.15.

U. S. Office of Education. School building survey and program for Warwick, Rhode Island. (Bulletin 1930, No. 33) 77 p. 1931. Supt. of Doc. $.15.

U. S. Office of Education. Statistics of public, society and school libraries, 1929. (Bulletin 1930, No. 37) 365 p. 1931. Supt. of Doc. $.50.

U. S. Office of Education. Survey of public higher education in Oregon. (Bulletin 1931, No. 8) 298 p. 1931. Supt. of Doc. $.45.

U. S. Office of Education. Survey of state-supported institutions of higher learning in Arkansas. (Bulletin 1931, No. 6) 139 p. 1931. Supt. of Doc. $.25.

Waller, E. C. A survey of the church and independent schools and colleges of the southern Appalachians. 98 p. 1931. The Author, 1410 Magnolia Ave., Knoxville, Tenn. $1.00.

(4) CURRICULUM

American Educational Research Association. Curriculum. (Review of educational research, Vol. I, No. 1) 64 p. 1931. The Association, N. E. A. $1.00 paper.

Broady, K. O., and others. Practical procedures for enriching the curriculums of small schools. (Univ. of Nebraska. Educational monograph, No. 2) 88 p. 1931. The University. $.50 paper.

Class, E. C. Prescription and election in elementary-school teacher-training curricula in state teachers colleges. (Cont. to educ. No. 480) 92 p. 1931. Teachers College, Columbia. $1.50.

Coxe, W. W., and others. Courses of study and curriculum offerings in junior high schools in New York state. 330 p. 1931. Univ. of State of N. Y. $.75.

*Davis, S. E. Teaching the elementary curriculum. 549 p. 1931. Macmillan. $1.75.

Houston, Texas. Board of Education. Curriculum revision and development in Houston, Texas. (1924–1930) 108 p. 1931. The Board. $.75.

Langvick, M. M. Current practices in the construction of state courses of study. (U. S. Office of Educ. Bulletin 1931, No. 4) 84 p. 1931. Supt. of Doc. $.15.

Phillips, C. A. Modern methods and the elementary curriculum. Rev. ed. 521 p. 1931. Century. $2.50.

Rollins College Conference on Curriculum for the College of Liberal Arts. The curriculum for the college of liberal arts; being the report of the curriculum conference held at Rollins college January 19–24, 1931, together with the reports of Rollins college committee on curriculum. 40 p. 1931. The College, Winter Park, Fla. $.50.

Rooney, J. R. Curricular offerings of Catholic secondary schools: an examination of 283 institutions. (Catholic Univ. of Amer. Educational research monographs, Vol. VI, No. 4) 48 p. 1931. Catholic Educ. Press. $1.50.

*Stevens, M. P. The activities curriculum in the primary grades. 440 p. 1931. D. C. Heath. $2.00.

(5) CONDUCT AND CHARACTER FORMATION

Bowyer, V. L., and others. Sixth yearbook of the Chicago principals' club; character education. 292 p. 1931. Chicago Principals' Club, 315 Plymouth Court, Chicago, Ill. $1.50.

Earp, J. R. Student who smokes. 2nd ed. 64 p. 1931. Antioch Press. $1.00.

Gerwig, G. W. Emotion. (School betterment studies, Vol. III, No. 2) 107 p. 1931. H. C. Frick, Educ. Commission, 465 Union Trust Bldg., Pittsburgh, Penn. Single copies gratis.

*Haddock, Laura. Steps upward in personality: a source book of material for administrative officers, teachers, sponsors and pupils in elementary and secondary schools and civic organizations, cooperating with the schools in citizenship and character development. 357 p. 1931. Professional & Technical Press, 420 Lexington Ave., N. Y. C. $3.25.

Kansas City School Service Bulletin. Character building: elementary school procedures. (Vol. IV, No. 3) 121 p. 1931. Public Schools, Kansas City, Mo. $.50.

King, E. M. Fifty hints and helps in character education. 48 p. 1931. The Author, Fairport Harbor, Ohio. $1.25.

*McLester, Amelia. The development of character traits in young children. 126 p. 1931. Scribner. $1.25.

Mary Fidelis, Sister, and Mary Charitas, Sister. Character calendar. 236 p. 1931. Bruce Pub. Co. $1.50.

Mathews, C. O. Bibliography on the honor system and academic honesty in American schools and colleges. (U. S. Office of Educ. Pamphlet, No. 16) 18 p. 1931. Supt. of Doc. $.05.

Morrison, J. C., and Layman, A. E. Character building in New York public schools: an analysis of practices reported by teachers and supervisory officers for the school year 1928–1929. 96 p. 1931. Univ. of State of N. Y. $.10.

Pennsylvania. Department of Public Instruction. Foundations for character education. (Bulletin No. 58) 32 p. 1931. Penn. Dept. of Pub. Instruction. Gratis.

(6) CHILD STUDY

Ackerson, Luton. Children's behavior problems: a statistical study based upon 5000 children examined consecutively at the Illinois institute for juvenile research. 268 p. 1931. Univ. of Chic. Press. $4.00.

*Bolton, F. E. Adolescent education. 506 p. 1931. Macmillan. $3.00.

Child Study Association of America. Teasing—harmful and harmless implications. 13 p. 1931. The Association. $.20.

Child Study Association of America. What do children inherit? 14 p. 1931. The Association. $.20.

Child Study Association of America. When children eat together: educational possibilities of the lunch room. (Summer play schools. Pamphlet, No. 2) 11 p. 1931. The Association. $.20.

Gerwig, G. W. Everychild: an American ideal. 39 p. 1931. The Roycroft shops, East Aurora, N. Y.

Goodenough, F. L. Anger in young children. (Institute of child welfare monograph series, No. 9) 278 p. 1931. Univ. of Minn. Press. $2.50.

Goodenough, F. L., and Anderson, J. E. Experimental child study. 546 p. 1931. Century. $3.00.

Institute for Child Guidance, New York. Selected reprints, ed. by L. G. Lowrey. (Studies) 1931. Commonwealth Fund. $1.50.

Kelly, F. J. Education and training; a presentation and discussion of the section on education and training of the White House conference on child health and protection at the Detroit meeting of the National council of education, 1931. 34 p. 1931. Nat'l Council of Educ., 1201 Sixteenth St., N. W., Washington, D. C. Gratis.

Minard, R. D. Race attitudes of Iowa children. (Univ. of Iowa. Studies in character, Vol. IV, No. 2) 101 p. 1931. The University. Price—apply.

Monash, Louis. Know your child. 246 p. 1931. McGraw-Hill. $2.00.

Moore, E. S. The development of mental health in a group of young children: an analysis of factors in purposeful activity. (Univ. of Iowa studies, New series, No. 207. Studies in child welfare, Vol. IV, No. 6) 128 p. 1931. The University. $1.50.

*Morgan, J. J. B. Child psychology. 474 p. 1931. R. R. Smith. $4.00.

*Murchison, C. A., *ed.* A handbook of child psychology. 711 p. 1931. Clark Univ. Press. $5.00.

Myers, G. C. Developing personality in the child at school: practical mental hygiene for educators. 375 p. 1931. Greenberg. $2.50.

National Committee for Mental Hygiene, Inc. Behavior problems of school children. 20 p. 1931. The Committee, 450 Seventh Ave., N. Y. C. $.15.

Patri, Angelo. The questioning child and other essays. Rev. ed. 221 p. 1931. Appleton. $1.60.

Sadler, W. S., and Sadler, Mrs. L. (Kellogg) Piloting modern youth: a guide for parents, teachers, and others dealing with adolescents; introd. by M. V. O'Shea. 370 p. 1931. Funk and Wagnalls. $3.50.

Skalet, Magda. The significance of delayed reactions in young children. (Comparative psychology monographs, Vol. VII, No. 34) 82 p. 1931. Johns Hopkins Press. $1.50.

Stebbing, L. R. Child training and parent education: references to material in recent books. 51 p. 1931. H. W. Wilson. $.65.

*White House Conference on Child Health and Protection. Abstracts and addresses of committee reports, ed. by K. Glover and H. Moses. 365 p. 1931. Century. $2.00; $.50 boards.

(7) EDUCATIONAL PSYCHOLOGY

American Educational Research Association. Psychology of the school subjects. (Review of educational research, Vol. I, No. 5) 325–450 pp. 1931. The Association, N. E. A. $1.00.

Bassett, Clara. The school and mental health. 66 p. 1931. Commonwealth Fund. $.40.

Bird, Charles. Effective study habits. 247 p. 1931. Century. $1.50.

*Caldwell, O. W., Skinner, C. E., and Tietz, J. W. The biological basis of education. 534 p. 1931. Ginn. $2.72.

Collman, R. D. The psychogalvanic reactions of exceptional and normal school children. (Cont. to educ. No. 469) 88 p. 1931. Teachers College, Columbia. $1.50.

*Gifford, W. J., and Shorts, C. P. Problems in educational psychology. 728 p. 1931. Doubleday, Doran. $3.00.

Hanawalt, E. M. Whole and part methods in trial and error learning. (Comparative psychology monographs, Vol. VII, No. 35) 65 p. 1931. Johns Hopkins Press. $1.25.

Hicks, J. A. The acquisition of motor skill in young children. (Univ. of Iowa studies. Studies in child welfare, Vol. IV, No. 5) 80 p. 1931. Univ. of Ia. $1.35; $1.00 paper.

Jones, E. S., *ed.* Improvement of study habits. 118 p. 1931. F. C. Jeffery, 53 Sagamore Terrace, Buffalo, N. Y. $.50; $.06 postage.

Newark, N. J. Board of Education. Department of Child Guidance. Mental hygiene in the classroom. 44 p. 1931. Nat'l Committee for Mental Hygiene, Inc., 450 Seventh Ave., N. Y. C. $.15.

Pear, T. H. The art of study. 117 p. 1931. Dutton. $1.50.

*Pitkin, W. B. The art of learning. 409 p. 1931. McGraw-Hill. $2.50.

Pitkin, W. B. How we learn: a book for young people with emphasis upon the art of efficient reading. 263 p. 1931. McGraw-Hill. $1.60.

Pressey, L. C., and Ferguson, J. M. Students' guide to efficient study; a manual based on the results of scientific investigation into the study habits of college students. 39 p. 1931. R. R. Smith. $.35.

Ralston, Alene, and Gage, C. J. Present day psychology: an objective study in educational psychology. 404 p. 1931. Lippincott. $2.40.

Reed, H. B. The influence of training on changes in variability in achievement. (Psychological monographs, No. 185) 59 p. 1931. Psychological Review Co., Princeton, N. J. $.75.

Robinson, E. S. Learning and forgetting. 10 p. 1931. Univ. of Chic. Press.

Stephens, J. M. The influence of different stimuli upon preceding bonds. (Cont. to educ. No. 493) 83 p. 1931. Teachers College, Columbia. $1.50.

Stretch, L. B. The relation of problem solving ability in arithmetic to comprehension in reading. (Cont. to educ. No. 87) 47 p. 1931. George Peabody College for Teachers. $.50.

Strong, E. K., Jr. Change of interests with age: based on an examination of more than two thousand men between the ages of twenty and sixty, representing eight occupations. 235 p. 1931. Stanford Univ. Press. $4.00.

*Thorndike, E. L. Human learning. 206 p. 1931. Century. $2.25.

*Trow, W. C. Educational psychology. 504 p. 1931. Houghton, Mifflin. $2.80.

*Wheat, H. G. The psychology of the elementary school. 440 p. 1931. Silver, Burdett. $2.00.

Wilson, F. T. Comparison of difficulty and improvement in the learning of bright and dull children in reproducing a descriptive selection. (Genetic psychology monograph, Vol. IX, No. 6) 397–435 pp. 1931. Clark Univ. Press. $2.00.

Wrenn, C. G. Practical study aids. 16 p. 1931. Stanford Univ. Press. Price—apply.

(8) Educational Tests and Measurements

Atkins, R. E. Measurement of the intelligence of young children by an object-fitting test. 89 p. 1931. Univ. of Minn. Press. $1.50.

Barthelmess, H. M. Validity of intelligence test elements. (Cont. to educ. No. 505) 91 p. 1931. Teachers College, Columbia. $1.50.

Burr, M. Y. A study of homogeneous grouping in terms of individual variations and the teaching problem. (Cont. to educ. No. 457) 69 p. 1931. Teachers College, Columbia. $1.50.

Bursch, J. F., and Meltzer, H. New examination: its construction and use. 83 p. 1931. Southern Cal. School Book Depository, Los Angeles, Cal. $.75 one copy; $.50 two or more.

Camp, B. H. Mathematical part of elementary statistics: a textbook for college students. 409 p. 1931. D. C. Heath. $3.60.

College Entrance Examination Board. Sixth annual report of the Commission on scholastic aptitude tests. 31 p. 1931. The Board, 431 W. 117th St., N. Y. C. Gratis.

Conrad, H. S., and Harris, Daniel. The free-association method and the measurement of adult intelligence. 45 p. 1931. Univ. of Cal. Press. $.55.

Cornell, E. L. Effect of trait differences in ability grouping. (Univ. of the state of New York bulletin, No. 981) 26 p. 1931. The University. $.05.

Cureton, E. E. Errors of measurement and correlation. (Archives of psychology, No. 125) 60 p. 1931. Archives of Psychology, Columbia Univ., N. Y. C. $1.25.

Davidson, H. P. An experimental study of bright, average, and dull children at the four-year mental level. (Genetic psychology monographs, Vol. IX, Nos. 3–4) 119–289 pp. 1931. Clark Univ. Press. $3.00.

De Busk, B. W., and Leighton, R. W. A study of pupil achievement and attendant problems. (Univ. of Oregon publication. Educ. series, Vol. II, No. 6) 157–200 pp. 1931. The University. $.75.

Foran, T. G. The meaning and measurement of validity. (Catholic univ. of Amer. Educational research bulletin, Vol. V, No. 7) 27 p. 1931. Catholic Educ. Press. $.35.

Fryer, Douglas. The measurement of interests in relation to human adjustment. 488 p. 1931. Henry Holt. $4.50; $3.60 students ed.

Gilliland, A. R., Jordan, R. H., and Freeman, F. S. Educational measurements and the class-room teacher. Rev. ed. 400 p. 1931. Century. $2.25.

Gordon, H. C. The specific nature of achievement and the predictive value of the I. Q. 147 p. 1931. Univ. of Penn. $1.50 paper.

Henmon, V. A. C., and Holt, F. O. A report on the administration of scholastic aptitude tests to 34,000 high school seniors in Wisconsin in 1929 and 1930. (Univ. of Wisconsin bulletin, serial No. 1786, General series, No. 1570) 104 p. 1931. The University. $.50.

Keliher, A. V. A critical study of homogeneous grouping; with a critique of measurement as the basis for classification. (Cont. to educ. No. 452) 165 p. 1931. Teachers College, Columbia. $1.75.

King, L. H. Mental and interest tests: their evaluation and comparative effectiveness as factors of prognosis in secondary education. (Cont. to educ. No. 444) 124 p. 1931. Teachers College, Columbia. $1.75.

Nelson, J. F. Personality and intelligence: a study of some responses other than intellectual noted in a simple mental test situation. 62 p. 1931. Teachers College, Columbia. $1.50.

*Pintner, Rudolph. Intelligence testing: methods and results. New ed. 555 p. 1931. Henry Holt. $2.40.

Pressey, S. L., and Pressey, L. C. Introduction to the use of standard tests. Rev. ed. 266 p. 1931. World Bk. Co. $1.80.

Rogers, C. R. Measuring personality adjustment in children nine to thirteen years of age. (Cont. to educ. No. 458) 107 p. 1931. Teachers College, Columbia. $1.50.

Rust, N. M. The effect of resistance on intelligence test scores of young children. (Child development monographs, No. 6) 80 p. 1931. Teachers College, Columbia. $1.50.

Street, R. F. A Gestalt completion test: a study of a cross section of intellect. 65 p. 1931. Teachers College, Columbia. $1.50.

Stutsman, Rachel. Mental measurement of preschool children; with a guide for the administration of the Merrill-Palmer scale of mental tests. 368 p. 1931. World Bk. Co. $2.20.

Taylor, J. C. The reliability of quarterly marks in the seventh grade of junior high school, together with the value of certain standard tests in predicting them. (Studies in educ. No. 17) 54 p. 1931. Johns Hopkins Press. $1.15.

*Tiegs, E. W. Tests and measurements for teachers. 470 p. 1931. Houghton, Mifflin. $2.40.

Tyler, H. T. The bearing of certain personality factors other than intelligence on academic success: a study of tests made at Teachers College. (Cont. to educ. No. 468) 89 p. 1931. Teachers College, Columbia. $1.50.

Wallis, B. C. The measurement of ability in children. 36 p. 1931. Oxford Univ. Press. $.50.

Wood, E. R. A graphic method of obtaining the partial-correlation coefficients and the partial-regression coefficients of three or more variables. (Supplementary educational monographs, No. 37) 72 p. 1931. Univ. of Chic. Dept. of Educ. $1.00.

Woody, Clifford. Results of the May testing programs in the elementary and high schools of Michigan. (Univ. of Michigan. Bur. of educational reference and research bulletin, No. 140) 47 p. 1931. The University. $.35.

(9) Exceptional Children

Child Study Association of America. What can we expect of our children? Individual differences. 15 p. 1931. The Association. $.20.

Educational Records Bureau. The educational achievement and intelligence of independent school children, 1929–1930. 141 p. 1931. The Bureau. $2.00.
Kunzig, R. W. Public school education of atypical children. (U. S. Office of Educ. Bulletin 1931, No. 10) 160 p. 1931. Supt. of Doc. $.25.
Madden, Richard. School status of the hard of hearing child: an analysis of the intelligence, the achievement, and certain personality traits of the hard of hearing school child. (Cont. to educ. No. 499) 64 p. 1931. Teachers College, Columbia. $1.50.
Martens, E. H. An annotated bibliography on the education and psychology of exceptional children. (U. S. Office of Educ. Pamphlet, No. 23) 48 p. 1931. Supt. of Doc. $.10.
Odell, C. W. Provisions for mentally atypical pupils. (Univ. of Illinois bulletin, Vol. XXIX, No. 6. Bur. of educational research bulletin, No. 59) 73 p. 1931. The University. $.50 to bookstores. Free to individuals for one copy.
Osburn, W. J., and Rohan, B. J. Enriching the curriculum for gifted children: a book of guidance for educational administrators and classroom teachers. 408 p. 1931. Macmillan. $2.00.
Regensburg, Jeanette. Studies of educational success and failure in supernormal children. (Archives of psychology, No. 129) 150 p. 1931. Archives of Psychology, Columbia Univ., N. Y. C. $1.75.
Rogers, J. F. The speech defective school child: what the schools are doing for him. (U. S. Office of Educ. Bulletin 1931, No. 7) 31 p. 1931. Supt. of Doc. $.10.
*Scheidemann, N. V. The psychology of exceptional children. 520 p. 1931. Houghton, Mifflin. $3.25.

(10) EDUCATIONAL RESEARCH

Barr, A. S., and Rudisill, Mabel. An annotated bibliography on the methodology of scientific research as applied to education. (Univ. of Wisconsin. Bur. of educational research bulletin, No. 13) 129 p. 1931. The University. Dept. of Educ. $1.25.
Hockett, H. C. Introduction to research in American history. 168 p. 1931. Macmillan. $2.00.
National Education Association. Department of Superintendence and Research Division. Questionnaire studies completed, bibliography, No. 2, 1930–31. (Educational research service. Circular, No. 9) 20 p. 1931. The Association. With subscription to Educ. Research Service.
Schmitz, R. M. Preparing the research paper. 94 p. 1931. R. R. Smith. $.60.
Sheehy, M. S., *comp.* A decade of research at the Catholic university of America. 202 p. 1931. Catholic Univ. of Amer., The Survey Council, Washington, D. C. $1.00.
Virginia. Polytechnic Institute. Research and publication, January, 1929, to July, 1931. (Bulletin, Vol. XXV, No. 1) 107 p. 1931. The Institute, Blacksburg, Va.
Weersing, F. J., and Haynes, B. R., *compilers.* Annotated index of theses and dissertations in education. 91 p. 1931. Univ. of Southern Cal., School of Educ. $.75.
*Whitney, F. L. Methods in educational research. 335 p. 1931. Appleton. $2.25.
Wright, E. A. Bibliography of research studies in education, 1929–1930. (U. S. Office of Educ. Bulletin 1931, No. 13) 475 p. 1931. Supt. of Doc. $.85.
Wright, E. A. List of educational research studies in city school systems, No. 2. (U. S. Office of Educ. Circular, No. 42) *Mimeographed.* 71 p. 1931. The Office. Gratis.
Wright, E. A. Organization and functions of research bureaus in city school systems. (U. S. Office of Educ. Leaflet, No. 2) 14 p. 1931. Supt. of Doc. $.05.

(11) TEACHERS AND TEACHING METHODS

(*See also Administration, Special Subjects and Age Groups*)

American Educational Research Association. Teacher personnel. (Review of educational research, Vol. I, No. 2) 96 p. 1931. The Association, N. E. A. $1.00.
Avent, J. E. Excellencies and errors in teaching methods. 569 p. 1931. The Author, Univ. of Tennessee, Knoxville, Tenn. $2.50.
Avent, J. E. The excellent teacher: a volume about teachers, by teachers, for teachers, containing the composite judgments of 1,002 teachers as to what the excellent teacher is. 477 p. 1931. The Author, Univ. of Tennessee, Knoxville, Tenn. $2.40.
*Brueckner, L. J., and Melby, E. O. Diagnostic and remedial teaching. 598 p. 1931. Houghton, Mifflin. $2.75.
Campbell, D. S. Beginning teachers in the accredited secondary schools of the Association of colleges and secondary schools of the southern states. 34 p. 1931. Division of Surveys and Field Studies, George Peabody College. Gratis.
Carr, W. G., and Waage, John. The lesson assignment. 98 p. 1931. Stanford Univ. Press. $1.50.
*Case, R. D. The platoon school in America. 283 p. 1931. Stanford Univ. Press. $3.00.
Coxe, W. W., and Soper, W. W. Study of the high school teacher in New York state. (Univ. of the state of New York bulletin, No. 964) 42 p. 1931. The University. $.15.
Dix, Lester. The economic basis for the teacher's wage. (Lincoln School research studies) 114 p. 1931. Teachers College, Columbia, Lincoln School. $1.75.
Flemming, C. W. Pupil adjustment in the modern school. First volume of a new series of Horace Mann School studies in education. 100 p. 1931. Teachers College, Columbia. $1.50.
Fraser, C. E. The case method of instruction: a related series of articles. 165 p. 1931. McGraw-Hill. $2.00.
Hoffman, M. D. Status of voluntary teachers' associations in cities of 100,000 population or more. (U. S. Office of Educ. Bulletin 1930, No. 36) 42 p. 1931. Supt. of Doc. $.10.
Huffaker, C. L. Teacher supply and demand in Oregon. (Univ. of Oregon publication. Educ. series, Vol. II, No. 5) 93–156 pp. 1931. The University. $.75.
Kansas City School Service Bulletin. Ethics of the teaching profession. (Vol. III, No. 4) 13 p. 1931. Public Schools, Kansas City, Mo. $.10.
Kilzer, L. R. Supervised study for teachers and administrators in elementary schools, high schools, and junior colleges. 332 p. 1931. Professional & Technical Press, 420 Lexington Ave., N. Y. C. $3.25.
Kriner, H. L. Pre-training factors predictive of teacher success. 91 p. 1931. Penn. State College. $.50.
Kulp, C. L. The health of the teacher. (Vol. XIV, bulletin No. 5) 77 p. 1931. School Dept., Ithaca, N. Y.
Marshall, M. V. Education as a social force, as illustrated by a study of the teacher-training program in Nova Scotia. (Harvard bulletins in educ. No. 18) 161 p. 1931. Harvard Univ. Press. $1.00.
National Education Association. Department of Classroom Teachers. The sixth yearbook: the economic welfare of teachers. 244 p. 1931. The Department. $1.50.
National Education Association. Department of Superintendence and Research Division. Provisions for sick leave and other absences of teachers, 249 cities above 30,000 in population, 1931. (Educational research service. Circular, No. 12) *Mimeographed.* 15 p. 1931. The Association. With subscription to Educ. Research Service.
National Education Association. Research Division. Ethics in the teaching profession. (Bulletin, Vol. IX, No. 1) 92 p. 1931. The Association. $.25.
National Education Association. Research Division. Teacher demand and supply. (Bulletin, Vol. IX, No. 5) 306–405 pp. 1931. The Association. $.25.
Ohio State University. College of Education. Bureau of Educational Research. List of workbooks, teachers' manuals and other instructional aids in the textbook exhibit. *Mimeographed.* 66 p. 1931. The University. Gratis.
Patterson, W. H. Letters from a hard-boiled teacher to his half-baked son. 348 p. 1931. The Daylion Co., Box 1133, Washington, D. C. $2.00.
Phelps, W. L. The excitement of teaching. 80 p. 1931. Liveright. $1.50.
Quigley, Samuel. The integration of teaching. *Mimeographed.* 198 p. 1931. Edwards Bros. $2.00.

Reeder, E. H., and Reynolds, R. G. How to study a demonstration lesson: a manual and notebook for classroom observation. 62 p. 1931. Teachers College, Columbia. $.60.
Ridgway, C. W. Comparative study of the training and teaching combinations of Kansas high school teachers. (Studies in educ. No. 5) 31 p. 1931. Kansas State Teachers College, Emporia, Kan. Ltd. free distribution.
Schleier, L. M. Problems in the training of certain special-class teachers. (Cont. to educ. No. 475) 138 p. 1931. Teachers College, Columbia. $1.50.
Stratemeyer, Florence. The effective use of curriculum materials: a study of units relating to "the curriculum" to be included in the professional preparation of elementary teachers. (Cont. to educ. No. 460) 161 p. 1931. Teachers College, Columbia. $1.75.
Teachers' views on some problems in general educational theory. (Questionnaire) 1931. Teachers College, Columbia.
Thorndike, E. L. A teacher's word book of twenty thousand words found most frequently and widely in general reading for children and young people. 182 p. 1931. Bur. of Publications, Teachers College, Columbia. $4.00.
Ullman, R. R. The prognostic value of certain factors related to teaching success. 133 p. 1931. A. L. Garber Co., Ashland, Ohio. $1.50.
Valentine, P. F. The art of the teacher: an essay in humanism. 289 p. 1931. Appleton. $2.00.
Virginia. University. The unit method as a means for individualizing learning activities. (Univ. of Virginia record extension series, Vol. XVI, No. 5. Secondary educ. in Virginia, No. 14) 54 p. 1931. The University, Extension Dept. $.15.
Yoakum, G. A. Improvement of the assignment. 1931. Macmillan. $1.80.
Zeigel, W. H. Some factors affecting teacher supply and demand in Missouri. (Univ. of Missouri bulletin, Vol. XXXII, No. 33. Educ. series, No. 32) 62 p. 1931. The University.

(12) Preschool, Kindergarten and Elementary Schools

(See also Special Subjects and Teaching)

American Educational Research Association. Special methods in the elementary school. (Review of educational research, Vol. I, No. 4) 245–323 pp. 1931. The Association, N. E. A. $1.00.
Andrews, E. G. Development of imagination in the preschool child. (Univ. of Iowa, New series, No. 191. Studies in character, Vol. III, No. 4) 64 p. 1931. The University. $1.00.
Association for Childhood Education. Supplement to the bulletin on equipment and supplies: nursery—kindergarten—primary. 23 p. 1931. The Association. $.15.
Association for Childhood Education. Yearbook, 1931. 55 p. 1931. The Association. $.25.
Baker, F. T. Elementary school literature for school administrators. 1931. Bur. of Publications, Teachers College, Columbia.
Belser, Danylu. Conditions and practices influencing the elementary education of white children in the public schools of Alabama. 1931. Birmingham Printing Co.
Brookfield, T. C. Games for graders: primary games, dances and rhythms. 45 p. 1931. Scholastic Press, Box C, Fredonia, N. Y. $1.00.
Brookfield, T. C. Ideas from the junk pile: primary construction problems. 22 p. 1931. Scholastic Press, Box C, Fredonia, N. Y. $1.00.
Charlotte, N. C. City Schools. Classroom activities and creative work in the primary grades, 1929–1930. *Mimeographed.* Pages not numbered. 1931. Charlotte City Schools, Charlotte, N. C. $.50.
Coxe, W. W. Study of the elementary school teacher in New York state. (Univ. of the state of New York bulletin, No. 975) 20 p. 1931. The University. $.05.
Eng, H. K. The psychology of children's drawings from the first stroke to the coloured drawing. 223 p. 1931. Harcourt. $3.75.
Hahn, J. L. A critical evaluation of a supervisory program in kindergarten-primary grades. (Cont. to educ. No. 495) 148 p. 1931. Teachers College, Columbia. $1.50.
Hansen, Rowna. Report cards for kindergarten and elementary grades. (U. S. Office of Educ. Leaflet, No. 41) 24 p. 1931. Supt. of Doc. $.10.
Harbison, S. A. A fair and a study of milk. (Teachers' lesson unit series, No. 15) 19 p. 1931. Teachers College, Columbia. $.25.
Hosic, J. F., and Hopkins, L. T. The cooperative group plan for the organization of elementary schools: philosophy and applications. 70 p. 1931. Teachers College, Columbia. $.60.
Hungerford, F. A. Preschool equipment. (Univ. of Iowa. Extension bulletin, No. 263) 78 p. 1931. The University. $.50.
Kawin, Ethel, and Hoefer, Carolyn. Comparative study of a nursery-school versus a non-nursery-school group. 52 p. 1931. Univ. of Chic. Press. $.75.
Linnell, Adelaide. The school festival. 124 p. 1931. Scribner. $1.25.
Loomis, A. M. A technique for observing the social behavior of nursery school children. (Child development monographs, No. 5) 100 p. 1931. Teachers College, Columbia. $1.50.
Morrison, J. C., and others. Cardinal objectives in elementary education, some administrative phases of the program. 108 p. 1931. Univ. of State of N. Y. $.10.
New York (State) University. Cardinal objectives in elementary education: some administrative phases of the program. A third report prepared by the Committee of elementary education of the New York Council of Superintendents, October 1, 1931. 108 p. 1931. The University.
Reed, M. M., and Raymond, E. M. Preschool education in New York settlements: a survey of some phases of educational work with preschool children in eleven settlements in New York city. (Preprinted from the Welfare Council's study of settlements in New York city) 48 p. 1931. Welfare Council of N. Y., 122 E. 22nd St., N. Y. C. $.50.
Swift, F. H. Emma Marwedel, 1818–1893, pioneer of the kindergarten in California. (Publications in educ., Vol. VI, No. 3) 139–216 pp. 1931. Univ. of Cal. Press. $1.00.
U. S. Office of Education. Nursery education: a classified and annotated bibliography. (Circular, No. 32) 10 p. 1931. Supt. of Doc. Gratis.
Vaughan, G. T. A grocery store. (Teachers' lesson unit series, No. 20) 15 p. 1931. Teachers College, Columbia. $.25.
Waddell, C. W., and others. A six-year experiment with a nursery school. 178 p. 1931. Univ. of Cal. Press. $2.00; $1.00 paper.
White House Conference on Child Health and Protection. Committee on Medical Care for Children. Health protection for the preschool child: a national survey of the use of preventive medical and dental service for children under six. 275 p. 1931. Century. $2.50.
*White House Conference on Child Health and Protection. Committee on the Infant and Preschool Child. Nursery education: a survey of day nurseries, nursery schools and private kindergartens in the United States. 187 p. 1931. Century. $2.00.

(13) Junior High School

(See also Teaching, Administration, etc.)

Beu, F. A. The junior high school: an annotated bibliography. (Teachers college bulletin, No. 113) 76 p. 1931. Eastern Ill. State Teachers College, Charleston, Ill. Gratis.

(14) Secondary Education

(See also Curriculum, Teaching, etc.)

Becker, C. H. Secondary education and teacher training in Germany. 53 p. 1931. Teachers College, Columbia. $.60.
*Collings, Ellsworth. Progressive teaching in secondary schools. 528 p. 1931. Bobbs-Merrill. $2.40.
Coxe, W. W., and Cowen, P. A. Educational needs of pupils in small high schools. (Univ. of the state of New York bulletin, No. 969) 63 p. 1931. The University. $.20.
Diefendorf, J. W. The high school situation in New Mexico. (Bulletin, Vol. V, No. 1) 58 p. 1931. Univ. of New Mexico. $.25.
Hendrix, S. G. Teaching devices on the high-school

level. (Univ. of Illinois bulletin, Vol. XXVIII, No. 42. Bur. of educational research bulletin, No. 56) 42 p. 1931. The University. $.30.

Illinois. University. Report of the high school visitor for the year 1930–31. (Univ. of Illinois bulletin, Vol. XXVIII, No. 50) 15 p. 1931. The University, High School Visitor's Office. Gratis.

Koos, L. V. Private and public secondary education: a comparative study. 228 p. 1931. Univ. of Chic. Press. $2.50.

Michigan Education Association. Department of High-School Principals. Second yearbook: the non-adjusted pupil in junior and senior high school. 111 p. 1931. The Association, Lansing, Mich. $1.00.

Morrison, H. C. Practice of teaching in secondary school. Rev. ed. 688 p. 1931. Univ. of Chic. Press. $4.00.

National Education Association. Department of Secondary-School Principals. Abstracts of unpublished masters' theses in the field of secondary-school administration. (Bulletin, No. 34) 116 p. 1931. The Department. $.50.

National Education Association. Department of Secondary-School Principals. Abstracts of unpublished masters' theses in the field of secondary-school administration. (Bulletin, No. 36) 68 p. 1931. The Department. $.50.

National Education Association. Department of Secondary-School Principals. Proceedings of the fifteenth annual meeting of the Department of secondary-school principals. (Bulletin, No. 35) 235 p. 1931. The Department. $2.00.

National Education Association. Department of Secondary-School Principals. Secondary-school administration abstracts and directory. (Bulletin, No. 38) 112 p. 1931. The Department. $.50.

National Education Association. Department of Secondary-School Principals. A study of the influence of departmental specialization on the professional attitudes of high-school teachers toward certain administrative problems. (Bulletin, No. 37) 70 p. 1931. The Department. $.50.

Remmers, H. H. The achievement of our high schools—results of the state high school testing program, 1930–31. (Purdue Univ. Studies in higher educ. No. 18) 30 p. 1931. The University. $.50.

Snedden, David. American high schools and vocational schools in 1960. 122 p. 1931. Teachers College, Columbia. $1.50.

Stetson, F. L. The organization and administration of standard high schools. (Univ. of Oregon publication. Educ. series, Vol. II, No. 7. Studies in educ. in Oregon, I) 201–296 pp. 1931. The University. $.75.

Turosienski, Severin. Secondary schools in Poland. (U. S. Office of Educ. Circular, No. 37) *Mimeographed.* 39 p. 1931. Supt. of Doc. Gratis.

U. S. Office of Education. Accredited secondary schools in the U. S. (Supplement to Bulletin 1930, No. 24) 26 p. 1931. Supt. of Doc. Gratis.

Virginia. University. Research studies. (Univ. of Virginia record extension series, Vol. XV, No. 10. Secondary educ. in Virginia, No. 12) 100 p. 1931. The University. Extension Dept. $.15.

Virginia. University. Some research studies. (Univ. of Virginia record extension series, Vol. XVI, No. 4. Secondary educ. in Virginia, No. 13) 71 p. 1931. The University. Extension Dept. $.15.

Williams, L. A. The person-consciousness of a selected group of high-school pupils. (Univ. of California. Publications in educ. Vol. VI, No. 2) 85–138 pp. 1931. The University. $.65.

(15) SCHOOL LIBRARIES

American Library Association. School library yearbook, No. 4. 278 p. 1931. The Association. $2.50.

American Library Association. Education Committee. Handbook for teacher-librarians. 52 p. 1931. The Association. $.65.

Clevenger, A. W., and Odell, C. W. High-school libraries in Illinois. (Univ. of Illinois bulletin, Vol. XXIX, No. 4. Bur. of educational research bulletin, No. 57) 41 p. 1931. The University. $.30.

Fargo, L. F. The superintendent makes a discovery: the answer to the rural school reading problem. 32 p. 1931. Amer. Lib. Ass'n. Single copy gratis; 10 copies $1.00.

Wilson, Martha. School library management. 5th ed. rev. 209 p. 1931. H. W. Wilson. $1.25.

(16) READING, WRITING AND LANGUAGES

*Baker, F. M. The teaching of French. 286 p. 1931. Houghton, Mifflin. $2.00.

Ballenger, H. L. The validation of the Iowa elementary language tests. (Univ. of Iowa. Studies in educ. Vol. VI, No. 3) 59 p. 1931. The University. $.75.

Bamberger, F. E., and Broening, A. M. A guide to children's literature. 121 p. 1931. Johns Hopkins Press. $1.75.

Banks, Myra, and Coy, G. L. The class writes a serial story. (Teachers' lesson unit series, No. 2) 23 p. 1931. Teachers College, Columbia. $.25.

Blaney, Jessie. Mother Goose land. (Teachers' lesson unit series, No. 9) 21 p. 1931. Teachers College, Columbia. $.25.

Brooks, S. M. Vergil's Aeneid. (Teachers' lesson unit series, No. 10) 17 p. 1931. Teachers College, Columbia. $.25.

*Cole, R. D. Modern foreign languages and their teaching. 598 p. 1931. Appleton. $3.00.

Coleman, J. H. The written composition interests of junior and senior high school pupils. (Cont. to educ. No. 494) 117 p. 1931. Teachers College, Columbia. $1.50.

Coleman, W. H. A critique of spelling vocabulary investigation. (Educ. series, No. 12) 119 p. 1931. Colorado State Teachers College. $2.00.

College Entrance Examination Board. Examination questions in English, 1926–1930. 63 p. 1931. The Board. $.48.

College Entrance Examination Board. Examination questions in French. 1926–1930. 130 p. 1931. The Board. $.68.

College Entrance Examination Board. Examination questions in German, 1926–1930. 127 p. 1931. The Board. $.68.

College Entrance Examination Board. Examination questions in Latin and Greek, 1926–1930. 177 p. 1931. The Board. $.68.

College Entrance Examination Board. Resume of the report of the Commission on English submitted April 1, 1931. 19 p. The Board. Gratis.

College Entrance Examination Board. Commission on English. Examining the examination in Enlish: a report to the College entrance examination board. 295 p. 1931. Harvard Univ. Press. $2.00.

Connecticut. State Board of Education. Remedial measures for reading deficiencies: eighteen studies from current practice. 63 p. 1931. The Board, Hartford, Conn.

Cotham, Margaret. The teaching of Latin. (Bulletin, No. 291) 93 p. 1931. State Dept. of Educ., Austin, Texas. Free to public schools of Texas.

Cox, R. M. Self-aid devices for teachers of silent reading in the intermediate grades. 126 p. 1931. Johnson Pub. Co. $.67.

Davis, H. I. Practical English projects for the high school. 234 p. 1931. Pitman. $1.75.

De Sauze, E. B., and Condon, Vesta. The Cleveland plan for the teaching of modern languages, with special reference to Spanish. 81 p. 1931. Winston. $.32.

*Dolch, E. W. The psychology and teaching of reading. 261 p. 1931. Ginn. $1.80.

Fife, R. H., *comp.* A summary of reports on modern foreign languages, issued by the Modern foreign language study and the Canadian committee on modern languages, with an index to the reports. 261 p. 1931. Macmillan. $1.00.

Foran, T. G., and Rock, R. T., Jr. The reliability of some silent reading texts. (Catholic univ. of Amer. Educational research bulletin, Vol. V, No. 6) 23 p. 1931. Catholic Educ. Press. $.35.

Gates, A. I. Reading for public school administrators. 126 p. 1931. Teachers College, Columbia. $1.50.

Horine, Clara. Shelley's "Ode to the West Wind." (Teachers' lesson unit series, No. 8) 27 p. 1931. Teachers College, Columbia. $.25.

Huse, H. R. The psychology of foreign language study. 231 p. 1931. Univ. of N. C. Press. $3.00.

Krueger, Louise. Reading in the activity program: first grade. 87 p. 1931. Harold Rugg, 425 W. 123rd St., N. Y. C. $.54.

La Brant, Lou. The teaching of literature in the secondary school. 185 p. 1931. Harcourt. $1.25.

Miller, Helen, and others. Creative teaching in the field of spelling: a manual of instruction. 133 p. 1931. Wallace Pub. Co., 11th and Walnut Sts., Des Moines, Ia. $1.60.

Mirrieless, L. B. Teaching composition in high school. 386 p. 1931. Harcourt. $2.00.

Rinehart, A. C. What Pittsburgh junior high school pupils read. (School betterment studies, Vol. III, No. 1) 83 p. 1931. H. C. Frick Educ. Commission, 465 Union Trust Bldg., Pittsburgh, Penn. Single copies gratis.

Robinson, L. J. Creative verse writing. (Teachers' lesson unit series, No. 11) 27 p. 1931. Teachers College, Columbia. $.25.

Sartorius, I. C. Generalization in spelling: a study of various bases of generalization in teaching spelling. (Cont. to educ. No. 472) 65 p. 1931. Teachers College, Columbia. $1.50.

Scott, G. W. How to teach reading. 160 p. 1931. A. H. Cather Pub. Co., 931 N. 19th St., Birmingham, Ala. $.75.

*Seely, H. F. Enjoying poetry in school. 267 p. 1931. Johnson Pub. Co. $2.00.

Shepherd, L. A. A plan for teaching language and literature in the first and second grades. 72 p. 1931. Wallace Pub. Co., 11th and Walnut Sts., Des Moines, Ia. $1.20.

Simon, H. W. Poetry appreciation. (Teachers' lesson unit series, No. 4) 28 p. 1931. Teachers College, Columbia. $.25.

Slattery, K. F. Building the paragraph. (Teachers' lesson unit series, No. 16) 25 p. 1931. Teachers College, Columbia. $.25.

*Smith, D. V. Class size in high school English. 309 p. 1931. Univ. of Minn. Press. $2.50.

Terman, L. M., and Lima, Margaret. Children's reading: a guide for parents and teachers. 2nd ed. 422 p. 1931. Appleton. $2.00.

U. S. Office of Education. The activity program and the teaching of reading. (Bulletin 1931, No. 2) 95 p. 1931. Supt. of Doc. $.20.

Vernon, M. D. Experimental study of reading. 1931. Macmillan. $3.00.

Walker, L. J. Bookland and its people. (Teachers' lesson unit series, No. 18) 19 p. 1931. Teachers College, Columbia. $.25.

Wheat, L. B. Free associations to common words: a study of word associations to twenty-five words picked at random from the five hundred most commonly used words in the English language. (Cont. to educ. No. 498) 51 p. 1931. Teachers College, Columbia. $1.50.

Zyve, C. T. An experimental study of spelling methods. (Cont. to educ. No. 466) 86 p. 1931. Teachers College, Columbia. $1.50.

(17) Mathematics and Science

Bray, W. J. Achievement in general chemistry as it is related to certain learning abilities. (Bulletin, Vol. XXXI, No. 6) 85 p. 1931. Northeast State Teachers College, Kirksville, Mo. $1.00.

*Breslich, E. R. Problems in teaching secondary-school mathematics. 348 p. 1931. Univ. of Chic. Press. $3.00.

Brownell, W. A., and Stretch, L. B. The effect of unfamiliar settings on problem-solving. (Research studies in educ. No. 1) 86 p. 1931. Duke Univ. Press. $1.00.

Buswell, G. T., and John, Lenore. The vocabulary of arithmetic. (Supplementary educational monographs, No. 38) 146 p. 1931. Univ. of Chic. Dept. of Educ. $1.25.

Cairns, G. J. Analytical study of mathematical abilities. (Catholic univ. of Amer. Educational research monographs, Vol. VI, No. 3) 104 p. 1931. Catholic Educ. Press. $.50.

Coit, M. C., *ed.* Projects in science and nature study shown at the American institute children's fair, 1930. (School service series, No. 6) 64 p. 1931. American Museum of Natural History, Dept. of Educ. of the Museum, N. Y. C. $.25.

College Entrance Examination Board. Examination questions in mathematics, 1926–1930. 123 p. 1931. The Board. $.60.

*Curtis, F. D. Second digest of investigations in the teaching of science. 424 p. 1931. Blakiston. $3.00.

Exelby, C. L., and Gambill, L. B. Science club manual (with programs) 92 p. 1931. The National Club Manual, Box 222, Lansing, Mich. $.75.

Godfrey, Charles, and Siddons, A. W. The teaching of elementary mathematics. 322 p. 1931. Cambridge Univ. Press. Macmillan, N. Y. C. $2.50.

Holy, T. C., and Sutton, D. H. Lists of essential apparatus for use in high-school sciences. (Ohio State Univ. Bur. of educational research monographs, No. 12) 32 p. 1931. The University. $.75.

Horgan, J. M. Story of lighting. (Teachers' lesson unit series, No. 22) 27 p. 1931. Teachers College, Columbia. $.25.

Immaculata, Sister M. Permanence of improvement and the distribution of learning in addition and subtraction. (Catholic univ. of Amer. Educational research bulletins, Vol. V, Nos. 9 and 10) 81 p. 1931. Catholic Educ. Press. $.50.

Kasir, D. S. The algebra of Omar Khayyam. (Cont. to educ. No. 385) 124 p. 1931. Teachers College, Columbia. $2.00.

Kilander, H. F. Science education in the secondary schools of Sweden: a comparative study of Sweden and U. S. (Cont. to educ. No. 463) 166 p. 1931. Teachers College, Columbia. $1.75.

Monroe, W. S., and Engelhart, M. D. A critical summary of research relating to the teaching of arithmetic. (Univ. of Illinois bulletin, Vol. XXIX, No. 4, Bur. of educational research bulletin, No. 58) 115 p. 1931. The University. $.50.

National Council of Teachers of Mathematics. Sixth yearbook: mathematics in modern life. 195 p. 1931. Teachers College, Columbia. $1.75.

Neulen, L. N. Problem solving in arithmetic: a study of certain factors in the allocation of arithmetic problems involving one, two, three, four steps or processes in reasoning. (Cont. to educ. No. 483) 87 p. 1931. Teachers College, Columbia. $1.50.

Overman, J. R. An experimental study of certain factors affecting transfer of training in arithmetic. 235 p. 1931. Warwick & York. $3.00.

Rock, R. T., Jr., and Foran, T. G. A comparison of studies on the relative difficulty of the number combinations. (Catholic univ. of Amer. Educational research bulletin, Vol. V, No. 8) 26 p. 1931. Catholic Educ. Press. Price—apply.

Rohan, B. J. Exploratory science: a means of life guidance. 259 p. 1931. C. C. Nelson Pub. Co., 303 W. College Ave., Appleton, Wis. $1.50.

*Schaaf, W. L. Mathematics for junior high school teachers: a professional subject matter text. 439 p. 1931. Johnson Pub. Co. $2.00.

Seidlin, Joseph. A critical study of the teaching of elementary college mathematics. (Cont. to educ. No. 482) 107 p. 1931. Teachers College, Columbia. $1.75.

Shea, J. T. San Antonio junior schools mathematics experiment in comparative courses of study. 61 p. 1931. San Antonio Board of Educ. Gratis.

Stokes, C. N. A comparative study of the results of a certain individual method and a certain group method of instruction in ninth-grade mathematics. 140 p. 1931. Henry Holt. $1.60.

Stone, J. C., Hopkins, L. T., and Brownfield, M. L. The construction of arithmetic practice material. 30 p. 1931. Sanborn. $.25.

Webb, H. A. The high-school science library for 1930–31. (Reprinted from Peabody Journal of Education, Vol. IX, No. 1) 12 p. 1931. The Author, George Peabody College for Teachers. $.10.

(18) Geography and Social Studies

Booth, M. J. Material on geography, including commercial products, industries, transportation and educational exhibits which may be obtained free or at small cost. 5th rev. ed. 108 p. 1931. The Author, Eastern Ill. State Teachers College, Charleston, Ill. $.50.

Cahill, M. E. The story of wool. (Teachers' lesson unit series, No. 14) 17 p. 1931. Teachers College, Columbia. $.25.

Carmela, Sister M. A critical study of elementary school tests in United States history. (Catholic univ. of Amer. Educational research monographs, Vol. VI, No. 5) 46 p. 1931. Catholic Educ. Press. $.70.

Carnegie Endowment for International Peace. Library. History teaching and school text-books in relation to international understanding, comp. by M. A. Matthews. (Reading list, No. 29) 14 p. 1931. The Endowment. Gratis.

College Entrance Examination Board. Examination questions in history, 1926–1930. 106 p. 1931. The Board. $.60.

Crawford, M. I. Eskimos. (Teachers' lesson unit series, No. 6) 29 p. 1931. Teachers College, Columbia. $.25.

Davis, B. J. Transportation. (Teachers' lesson unit series, No. 1) 25 p. 1931. Teachers College, Columbia. $.25.

Gibbs, M. T. We create a history room. (Teachers' lesson unit series, No. 23) 11 p. 1931. Teachers College, Columbia. $.25.

Keelor, K. L., and Sweet, Mayme. Units of work; developing out of children's interests in local history, Indian life and the Dutch colonial settlement. 314 p. 1931. Teachers College, Columbia. $2.20.

Kenwood Hall School for Girls. Projects illustrating current events as an aid in teaching social sciences in high school. 42 p. 1931. The School, Los Angeles, Cal. $.50.

Kilcullen, M. T. Materials and methods of geography teaching; effective map usage simplified. 218 p. 1931. Webster Costello Co., Chicago Heights, Ill. $1.25.

Krause, Edna. Indians of Florida. (Teachers' lesson unit series, No. 17) 24 p. 1931. Teachers College, Columbia. $.25.

MacNeel, M. W. The Spanish trail. (Teachers' lesson unit series, No. 7) 29 p. 1931. Teachers College, Columbia. $.25.

Maryland. State Department of Education. Goals in social studies for primary grades I–III with suggestions for their achievement. A revision and enlargement of Tentative goals in geography and history, Grades I–III. (Maryland school bulletin, Vol. XIII, No. 1) 236 p. 1931. The Department. $.60.

*Merriam, C. E. The making of citizens: a comparative study of methods of civic training. 371 p. 1931. Univ. of Chic. Press. $3.00.

National Council for the Social Studies. First yearbook: some aspects of the social sciences in the schools. 176 p. 1931. McKinley Pub. Co. $2.00.

Niland, K. J. A trip to beautiful Hawaii. (Teachers' lesson unit series, No. 21) 15 p. 1931. Teachers College, Columbia. $.25.

Reeder, E. H. Geography for public school administrators. 100 p. 1931. Teachers College, Columbia. $1.50.

Shafto, M. E. Pupils' history of their community. (Teachers' lesson unit series, No. 12) 13 p. 1931. Teachers College, Columbia. $.25.

Smith, Harriet, and Mitchell, Adelphia. Some helps in the teaching of geography. (Bulletin, Vol. XX, No. 5) 22 p. 1931. Sam Houston State Teachers College, Huntsville, Texas. $.15.

*Storm, G. E. The social studies in the primary grades. 596 p. 1931. Lyons and Carnahan. $2.50.

*Thralls, Z. A., and Reeder, E. H. Geography in the elementary school. 441 p. 1931. Rand, McNally. $2.40.

Van Hise, Gertrude. The ancestral history of a class. (Teachers' lesson unit series, No. 19) 9 p. 1931. Teachers College, Columbia. $.25.

(19) ART, MUSIC AND DRAMA

Coleman, S. N. Children's symphony as developed in the creative music classes of Lincoln school of Teachers college with the themes composed entirely by children of elementary school, and played by them on instruments of their own making and other simple instruments. (Lincoln school research studies) 218 p. 1931. Teachers College, Columbia. $2.00.

*Dykema, P. W. Music for public school administrators. 171 p. 1931. Teachers College, Columbia. $1.75.

Gunther, T. C. Manipulative participation in the study of elementary industrial arts. (Cont. to educ. No. 490) 58 p. 1931. Teachers College, Columbia. $1.50.

*Lemos, P. J. The art teacher: a book for children and teachers. 491 p. 1931. Davis Press. $8.00.

*Mursell, J. L., and Glenn, Mabelle. The psychology of school music teaching. 378 p. 1931. Silver, Burdett. $2.40.

Music Supervisors' National Conference. Yearbook; twenty-fourth year, 1931. 508 p. 1931. The Conference, 64 E. Jackson Blvd., Chicago, Ill. $2.50.

Music Teachers' National Association. Piano classes and the private teacher. 43 p. 1931. Nat'l Bureau for Advancement of Music, 45 W. 45th St., N. Y. C. $.10.

National Bureau for Advancement of Music. Guide for conducting piano classes in schools. 31 p. 1931. The Bureau, 45 W. 45th St., N. Y. C. $.10.

*Pelikan, A. G. The art of the child. 123 p. 1931. Bruce Pub. Co. $3.00.

Todd, J. M. Drawing in the elementary school. 60 p. 1931. Univ. of Chic. Press. $.35.

(20) VOCATIONAL AND INDUSTRIAL EDUCATION

Alabama Polytechnic Institute. School of Education. Bureau of Educational Service. Exploratory occupational studies. (Studies in educ. Vol. I, No. 1) 62 p. 1931. The Bureau, Auburn, Ala. Gratis.

American Vocational Association, Inc. The obligation of vocational education to business. (Bulletin, No. 6) 13 p. 1931. Dr. Z. M. Smith, Sec'y, Room 225, State House, Indianapolis, Ind. $.05.

American Vocational Association. National Committee. Training objectives in vocational education in agriculture with suggestions as to ways and means of attaining these objectives. (Federal board for vocational educ. bulletin, No. 153. Agricultural series, No. 39) 31 p. 1931. Supt. of Doc. $.05.

Association of Teachers of Agriculture of New York. Record of twenty years vocational agriculture in New York state, 1911–1931. 79 p. 1931. H. B. Knapp, Director, State Institute of Applied Agriculture, Farmingdale, N. Y. $3.10.

Bomar, W. M. The education of homemakers for community activities. (Cont. to educ. No. 477) 135 p. 1931. Teachers College, Columbia. $1.50.

Brown, C. M. An evaluation of the Minnesota rating scale for home economics teachers. 29 p. 1931. Univ. of Minn. Press. $.50.

Commercial Education Association of New York and Vicinity. Use of projects in commercial teaching: first yearbook, 1930–1931. 208 p. 1931. A. S. Massell, Commercial Educ. Continuation School, 210 E. 42nd St., N. Y. C. $1.50.

Connor, Ruth. The scholastic behavior of a selected group of undergraduate home economic students. (Cont. to educ. No. 497) 71 p. 1931. Teachers College, Columbia. $1.50.

Currie, J. H. Teaching methods for technical teachers. 42 p. 1931. Pitman. $.75.

*Eastern Commercial Teachers Association. Fourth yearbook: modern methods of teaching business subjects. 301 p. 1931. The Association, Banks College, Philadelphia, Penn. $2.50.

Getman, A. K., and Weaver, W. J. Outline of content for vocational agriculture. (Bulletin, No. 983) 54 p. 1931. Univ. of State of N. Y. $.10.

Goldberger, A. M. Variability in continuation school populations: a study of the significance of the differences in the proportions of child workers. (Cont. to educ. No. 454) 52 p. 1931. Teachers College, Columbia. $1.50.

Hammonds, Carsie. The distribution of time of teachers of vocational agriculture in Kentucky—its relation to distribution of aid and to teacher training. (Univ. of Kentucky. Bur. of school service bulletin, Vol. III, No. 3) 113 p. 1931. The University. $.50.

Lattig, H. E. Practical methods in teaching vocational agriculture. 360 p. 1931. McGraw-Hill. $2.50.

Leighton, F. H. A basis for building a course in economics of the home: deriving desirable content by the use of local family case studies. (Cont. to educ. No. 459) 114 p. 1931. Teachers College, Columbia. $1.50.

Lyon, L. S. Education for business. 3rd ed. 586 p. 1931. Univ. of Chic. Press. $3.50.

Maryland. State Department of Education. Vocational rehabilitation in Maryland. (Maryland school bulletin, Vol. XII, No. 6) 14 p. 1931. The Department.

Metz, J. J., *ed.* Bruce's 1931 school shop annual. 300 p. 1931. Bruce Pub. Co. $2.00.

Newkirk, L. V. Validating and testing home mechanics content. (Univ. of Iowa studies, New series, No. 201. Studies in educ. Vol. VI, No. 4) 39 p. 1931. The University. $.50.

Pennsylvania. Department of Public Instruction. Analysis of book material in the field of industrial education. (Bulletin, No. 62) 15 p. 1931. The Department. Gratis.

Pennsylvania. Department of Public Instruction. Organization and administration of home classes for foreign-born mothers. (Bulletin, No. 63) 31 p. 1931. The Department. Gratis.

Rollinson, E. A. Diagnostic testing and remedial teaching of Gregg shorthand. 391 p. 1931. Gregg Pub. Co. $2.80.

Schmidt, G. A., and Ross, W. A. Teaching evening and part-time classes in vocational agriculture. 278 p. 1931. Century. $2.25.

*Sears, W. P. The roots of vocational education: a survey of the origins of trade and industrial education found in industry, education, legislation and social progress. 310 p. 1931. John Wiley. $2.75.

Smith, H. J. (Homer J.) One thousand problems in industrial education: a list of titles appropriate for term papers and theses by graduate students and for practical research projects by men active in administration and supervision. 90 p. 1931. Univ. of Minn. Press. $1.00.

Society for Promotion of Engineering Education. A study of technical institutes: a collateral project to the investigation of engineering education. 39 p. 1931. Lancaster Press, Lancaster, Penn. $1.00.

Stemmons, Walter. Connecticut agricultural college—a history. 258 p. 1931. Connecticut Agricultural College, Storrs, Conn. $1.00.

Stewart, W. F. Records and reports for state supervisors of agricultural education with special consideration to the needs in Ohio. 160 p. 1931. Enterprise Co-operative Co., New Concord, Ohio. $2.25.

Stine, J. R. Coordination in part-time education. A study by the Committee on part-time education of the American vocational association. (Bulletin, No. 7) 67 p. 1931. Amer. Vocational Ass'n, Z. M. Smith, Sec'y, Indianapolis, Ind. $.25.

Switzer, G. M., and Reeves, G. G. Home economics without a laboratory. (Teachers' lesson unit series, No. 3) 32 p. 1931. Teachers College, Columbia. $.25.

Taylor, W. D., Jr. Vocational information: a study showing the vocational opportunities obtainable through the academic channels of the University of Washington. 158 p. 1931. Univ. of Wash. $.50.

U. S. Federal Board for Vocational Education. Fifteenth annual report, 1931. 129 p. 1931. Supt. of Doc. $.15.

U. S. Federal Board for Vocational Education. Organization and teaching procedure to be followed in evening agricultural schools on the marketing of cotton. (Monograph, No. 13) 19 p. 1931. Supt. of Doc. $.05.

U. S. Federal Board for Vocational Education. Organization and teaching procedure to be followed in evening agricultural schools on the marketing of cream or butter and fluid milk. (Monograph, No. 12) 20 p. 1931. Supt. of Doc. $.05.

U. S. Federal Board for Vocational Education. Organization and teaching procedure to be followed in evening agricultural schools on the marketing of grain. (Monograph, No. 11) 14 p. 1931. Supt. of Doc. $.05.

U. S. Federal Board for Vocational Education. Organization and teaching procedure to be followed in evening agricultural schools on the marketing of livestock. (Monograph, No. 10) 16 p. 1931. Supt. of Doc. $.05.

U. S. Federal Board for Vocational Education. Teaching of art related to the home: suggestions for content and method in related art instruction in the vocational program in home economics. (Bulletin, No. 156. Home economics series, No. 13) 89 p. 1931. Supt. of Doc. $.25.

U. S. Federal Board for Vocational Education. The teaching of science related to the home: suggestions for content and method in related science instruction in the vocational program in home economics. (Bulletin, No. 158. Home economics series, No. 14) 128 p. 1931. Supt. of Doc. $.25.

U. S. Federal Board for Vocational Education. Vocational training and unemployment. A discussion of the question—What service can the public program of vocational education render to the unemployed? (Bulletin, No. 159, General series, No. 4) 29 p. 1931. Supt. of Doc. $.10.

Webb, R. F. Principles and methods in typewriting. 221 p. 1931. Prentice-Hall. $1.25.

Winchell, C. M. Home economics for public school administrators. 151 p. 1931. Teachers College, Columbia. $1.50.

(21) Vocational Guidance

Eikenberry, D. H., and others. Our American schools and their opportunities. (Guidance manual, No. 2, Part 2, Grade 8) 173 p. 1931. Ohio. Dept. of Educ. $.75.

Hager, W. E. The quest for vocational adjustment in the profession of education. (Cont. to educ. No. 491) 85 p. 1931. Teachers College, Columbia. $1.50.

Jones, W. B., *ed.* Basic units for an introductory course in vocational guidance. 194 p. 1931. McGraw-Hill. $1.50.

New York (State) University. Introduction to the study of educational and occupational opportunity. (Univ. of the state of New York bulletin, No. 985) 51 p. 1931. The University. $.10.

Proffitt, M. M., *comp.* Good references on vocational guidance. (U. S. Office of Educ. Bibliography, No. 2) 15 p. 1931. Supt. of Doc. $.05.

Stuart, M. H., and Morgan, D. S. Guidance at work. 104 p. 1931. McGraw-Hill. $1.25.

(22) Health and Physical Education

American Child Health Association. Health trends in secondary education. 161 p. 1931, rev. and annotated bibliography. The Association, 450 Seventh Ave., N. Y. C. $1.00.

American Child Health Association. Principles and practices in health education from the Sixth health education conference held at Sayville, Long Island, June 16–21, 1930. 485 p. 1931. The Association, 450 Seventh Ave., N. Y. C. $1.50.

Barnstead, B. L. A school health program: a guide for the teaching of health. Rev. ed. 71 p. 1931. G. Wahr. $.50.

Bode, Rudolf. Expression-gymnastics; tr. from the German by Sonya Forthal and Elizabeth Waterman. 161 p. 1931. A. S. Barnes. $2.00.

*Brock, G. D. Health through projects. 268 p. 1931. A. S. Barnes. $2.00.

Caulkins, E. D., *ed.* School athletics in modern education. Wingate memorial lectures, 1930–31. 689 p. 1931. The Foundation, 57 E. 56th St., N. Y. C. $2.00.

Chayer, M. E. School nursing: a contribution to health education. 292 p. 1931. Putnam. $2.50.

Collier, L. W. School health program for parent-teacher associations and women's clubs, revised by J. F. Rogers. (U. S. Office of Educ. Health education, No. 5) 9 p. 1931. Supt. of Doc. $.05.

Collins, S. D. The health of the school child: a study of sickness, physical defects and mortality. (U. S. Treasury Dept. Public health bulletin 1931, No. 200) 159 p. 1931. Supt. of Doc. $.35.

Dinwiddie, Courtenay. Child health and the community. 88 p. 1931. Commonwealth Fund. $1.00.

Gray, Horace, and Ayres, J. G. Growth in private school children; with averages and variabilities based on 3,110 measurings on boys, and 1,473 on girls from the ages of one to nineteen years. (Behavior research fund monographs) 282 p. 1931. Univ. of Chic. Press. $3.50.

Hyde, F. S., and Slown, R. C. Safety programs and activities, for elementary and junior high schools. 265 p. 1931. Beckley-Cardy. $1.25.

McCormick, M. G. The rural hot lunch as a health and social activity. 19 p. 1931. Univ. of State of N. Y. $.10.

Maryland. State Department of Education. Spring athletics. (Colored) (Maryland school bulletin, Vol. XII, No. 4) 12 p. 1931. The Department. Gratis while supply lasts.

Maryland. State Department of Education. Spring athletics. (White) (Maryland school bulletin, Vol. XII, No. 5) 16 p. 1931. The Department. Gratis while supply lasts.

*Nash, J. B. Administration of physical education:

with special reference to public schools. 491 p. 1931. A. S. Barnes. $3.00.

Nash, J. B., *ed.* Interpretations of physical education.

v. 1 Mind-body relationships. (Originally published entitled "Symposium on physical education and health" by N. Y. Univ. School of Educ., 1930).

v. 2 Nature and scope of examinations.

v. 1—276 p. v. 2—307 p. 1931. A. S. Barnes. $2.00 each.

National Bureau of Casualty and Surety Underwriters. A guide book for safety education. (Educational series, Vol. V) 89 p. 1931. The Bureau, 1 Park Ave., N. Y. C. $.50; $.75 cloth.

Nebraska. University. Agricultural College Extension Service and U. S. Department of Agriculture. Hot lunches keep school children healthy and happy. (Extension circular 9–51–2) 14 p. 1931. The University. $.05. Ltd. supply.

Neilson, N. P. (A score card for evaluating physical education programs for high school boys. (Bulletin, No. E–2) 45 p. 1931. Cal. State Dept. of Educ. Division of Health and Physical Educ., Sacramento, Cal. $.25.

Neilson, N. P. A score card for evaluating physical education programs for high school girls. (Bulletin, No. E–3) 47 p. 1931. Cal. State Dept. of Educ. Division of Health and Physical Educ., Sacramento, Cal. $.25.

New York. Commission on Ventilation. School ventilation: principles and practices. (Cont. No. 7) 73 p. 1931. Teachers College, Columbia. $1.00.

Ready, M. M. Requirements by state departments of education for teachers and supervisors of physical education in grade and high schools. (U. S. Office of Educ. Circular, No. 35) *Mimeographed.* 8 p. 1931. The Office. Gratis.

Rogers, F. R. Physical capacity tests: notes on testing techniques and the significance of tests. 50 p. 1931. A. S. Barnes. $.75.

Rogers, J. F., *comp.* School health activities in 1930. Summary of information collected for the White House conference on child health and protection. (U. S. Office of Educ. Pamphlet, No. 21) 33 p. 1931. Supt. of Doc. $.10.

Sandlin, R. N. Physical education program and suggestions. (Bulletin, No. 289) 23 p. 1931. State Dept. of Educ., Austin, Texas. Gratis to public schools of Texas.

Savage, H. J., and others. Current developments in American college sports. (Bulletin, No. 26) 58 p. 1931. Carnegie Foundation. Gratis.

Stevenson, Idabelle. Safety education. 157 p. 1931. A. S. Barnes. $1.00.

Towle, Carolyn. Safety education. (Teachers' lesson unit series, No. 13) 20 p. 1931. Teachers College, Columbia. $.25.

U. S. Office of Education. Health education publications. 7 p. 1931. Supt. of Doc. Gratis.

U. S. Treasury Department. Public Health Service. A study of illness among grade school children. (Reprint, No. 1497) 23 p. 1931. Supt. of Doc. $.10.

Williams, J. F., and Brownell, C. L. Health and physical education for public school administrators. Secondary school. 167 p. 1931. Teachers College, Columbia. $1.75.

Witty, P. A. Study of deviates in versatility and sociability of play interest. (Cont. to educ. No. 470) 57 p. 1931. Teachers College, Columbia. $1.50.

Zulauf, A. E. The history of health and physical education in the state teachers college and state normal school at Trenton, N. J. (Trenton studies in educ. No. 2) 32 p. 1931. State Teachers College, Trenton, N. J. Gratis.

(23) EXTRA-CURRICULAR ACTIVITIES

Borgeson, F. C. All-school activities: a statement of current practice. Elementary school life activities, Vol. I. 143 p. 1931. A. S. Barnes. $1.00.

Borgeson, F. C. Group-interest activities: a statement of current practice. Elementary school life activities, Vol. II. 135 p. 1931. A. S. Barnes. $1.00.

Fox, F. C. Helps for schools in celebrating the George Washington bicentennial in 1932. (U. S. Office of Educ. Pamphlet, No. 25) 23 p. 1931. Supt. of Doc. $.05.

*Fretwell, E. K. Extra-curricular activities in the high school. 552 p. 1931. Houghton, Mifflin. $2.75.

Houston, Texas. Board of Education. Some activities in the Houston schools. (1924–1930) 106 p. 1931. The Board. $.75.

Le Compte, Pearle. Dramatics. 163 p. 1931. A. S. Barnes. $1.00.

Leslie, John, assisted by Richard Dickson. The best college fraternity? 64 p. 1931. Gablo Partners, Central Nat'l Bank Bldg., Peoria, Ill. $.50.

MacDonald, M. A. Class organization and activities. 134 p. 1931. A. S. Barnes. $1.00.

McKown, H. C. Commencement activities. 310 p. 1931. Macmillan. $2.50.

Martin, I. S. The sorority handbook. 11th ed. 180 p. 1931. The Author, 5 Cobden St., Boston, Mass. $2.25.

Meyer, H. D. The school club program: organization, administration, activities. 178 p. 1931. A. S. Barnes. $1.00.

Morelock, T. C. School newspaper production. 224 p. 1931. Lucas Bros., Columbia, Mo. $2.50.

National Education Association and Department of Superintendence. Things to do; American education week, November 9–15, 1931; outlines and plans authorized by the N. E. A., U. S. Office of Education, and American Legion. 51 p. 1931. The Association. $1.00.

Pound, Olivia. Extra curricular activities of high school girls. 97 p. 1931. A. S. Barnes. $1.00.

Preston, E. E. The popular commencement book. 434 p. 1931. T. S. Denison and Co. $2.00.

Trenton, N. J. State Teachers College. The assembly in the teachers college. (Trenton studies in educ. No. 1) 22 p. 1931. State Teachers College, Trenton, N. J. Gratis.

Zyve, Claire, and Staff of Fox Meadow School. An old English Christmas. (Teachers' lesson unit series, No. 5) 41 p. 1931. Teachers College, Columbia. $.25.

(24) RURAL EDUCATION

Carr, W. G. County unit of school administration. (The reference shelf, Vol. VI, No. 10) 144 p. 1931. H. W. Wilson. $.90.

Gaumnitz, W. H. Availability of public-school education in rural communities. (U. S. Office of Educ. Bulletin 1930, No. 34) 53 p. 1931. Supt. of Doc. $.10.

Gaumnitz, W. H., *comp.* Good references on teachers of rural schools: status and preparation. (U. S. Office of Educ. Bibliography, No. 1) 9 p. 1931. Supt. of Doc. $.05.

Hoffman, U. J. Modernized teaching in rural schools. 143 p. 1931. F. A. Owen Pub. Co. $1.00.

National Education Association. Research Division. The outlook for rural education. (Research bulletin, Vol. IX, No. 4) 230–302 pp. 1931. The Association. $.25.

*National Society for the Study of Education. Thirtieth yearbook, part I. The status of rural education. 272 p. 1931. Public School Pub. Co. $2.50 cloth; $1.75 paper.

New York (State) University. Play for rural children: fall activities. (Univ. of the state of New York bulletin, No. 983, supplement) 23 p. 1931. The University. $.10.

Nuttall, L. J., Jr. Progress in adjusting differences of amount of educational opportunity offered under the unit systems of Maryland and Utah. (Cont. to educ. No. 431) 105 p. 1931. Teachers College, Columbia. $1.50.

Reynolds, Annie. Certain state programs for the improvement of rural school instruction. (U. S. Office of Educ. Bulletin, No. 18) 32 p. 1931. Supt. of Doc. $.10.

Reynolds, Annie, *comp.* Good references on supervision of instruction in rural schools. (U. S. Office of Educ. Bibliography, No. 3) 10 p. 1931. Supt. of Doc. $.05.

Reynolds, Annie. Supervision of instruction in rural schools: abstracts of certain addresses delivered at a conference called by the U. S. Commissioner of education at Hot Springs, Arkansas, December 14–15, 1930. (U. S. Office of Educ. Circular, No. 34) *Mimeographed.* 20 p. 1931. The Office. Gratis.

Texas. State Department of Education. Concerning state aid for training in agriculture, farm mechanics, and home economics in rural schools. (Bulletin, No. 288) 14 p. 1931. State Dept. of Educ., Austin, Texas. Gratis to public schools of Texas.

Tireman, L. S., and Austin, Mary. The rural schools of Mexico, and Rural education in New Mexico. (Univ. of New Mexico bulletin, Vol. II, No. 1. Training school series) 30 p. 1931. The University. $.25.

(25) Higher Education

Association of American Colleges. Addresses and proceedings of the seventeenth annual meeting. (Bulletin, Vol. XVII, No. 1) 168 p. 1931. The Association. $1.25.

Association of American Colleges. College theory and practice. (Bulletin, Vol. XVII, No. 2) 170–304 pp. 1931. The Association. $.50.

Bane, C. L. The lecture in college teaching. 128 p. 1931. Badger. $2.00.

Bathurst, E. G. A teachers college follow-up service: its factors and development in an unsupervised service area. (Cont. to educ. No. 478) 89 p. 1931. Teachers College, Columbia. $1.50.

Baugher, J. I. Organization and administration of practice-teaching in privately endowed colleges of liberal arts. (Cont. to educ. No. 487) 127 p. 1931. Teachers College, Columbia. $1.50.

Bohan, J. E. Students' marks in college courses. 133 p. 1931. Univ. of Minn. Press. $1.50.

Bossard, J. H. S., and Dewhurst, J. F. University education for business: a study of existing needs and practices. 578 p. 1931. Univ. of Penn. $5.00.

Brown, E. J. A study of the facts and conditions involved in the problem of college admissions. (Studies in educ. No. 4) 56 p. 1931. Kansas State Teachers College, Emporia, Kan. Ltd. free distribution.

Carnegie Foundation for the Advancement of Teaching in Cooperation with the Joint Commission of the Association of Pennsylvania College Presidents and the State Department of Public Instruction. Study of the relations of secondary and higher education in Pennsylvania: memorandum of proposals for the treatment of the secondary inquiry group in the senior high school, 1931–1934. (Progress report III) 20 p. 1931. The Foundation. Gratis.

Carnegie Foundation for the Advancement of Teaching in Cooperation with the Joint Commission of the Association of Pennsylvania College Presidents and the State Department of Public Instruction. Study of the relations of secondary and higher education in Pennsylvania. (Progress report IV) *Mimeographed.* 34 p. 1931. The Foundation. Gratis.

Chamberlain, L. M. The housing of thirty public junior colleges of the middle west and tentative standards and principles relating to buildings, equipment, and associated administrative problems. (Univ. of Kentucky. Bur. of school service bulletin, Vol. III, No. 4) 210 p. 1931. The University. $.50.

Cincinnati. University. Teachers College. Abstracts of graduate theses in education, 1927–1931. Vol. I. 396 p. 1931. The University. $3.00.

Clatworthy, L. M. Study of what the college student knows of his library. (Reprinted from the College and reference library yearbook, No. 3, Amer. library ass'n, 1931) 8 p. 1931. Univ. of Denver. $.15.

College Entrance Examination Board. Bulletin of general information for 1932. 28 p. 1931. The Board, 431 W. 117th St., N. Y. C. Gratis.

College Entrance Examination Board. Definition of requirements for 1932. (Document, No. 136) 115 p. 1931. The Board, 431 W. 117th St., N. Y. C. $.25.

College Entrance Examination Board. Examination questions in biology, botany, chemistry, drawing, physical geography, 1926–1930. 177 p. 1931. The Board, 431 W. 117th St., N. Y. C. $.92.

College Entrance Examination Board. Places of examination, June 15–20, 1931. 15 p. 1931. The Board, 431 W. 117th St., N. Y. C. Gratis.

College Entrance Examination Board. Questions set at the examinations of 1930. 226 p. 1931. The Board, 431 W. 117th St., N. Y. C. $1.60.

Conant, M. P., and others, *compilers.* A girl of the eighties at college and at home; from the family letters of Charlotte Howard Conant and from other records. 262 p. 1931. Houghton, Mifflin. $3.75.

Cook, H. M. The training of state teachers college faculties. (Cont. to educ. No. 86) 143 p. 1931. George Peabody College for Teachers. $1.50.

Cutler, J. E., and Davis, M. R. A study in professional education at Western Reserve university: the school of applied social sciences, 1916–1930. 208 p. 1931. Western Reserve Univ. Press. $1.50.

Douglass, H. R. The relation of high school preparation and certain other factors to academic success at the University of Oregon. (Univ. of Oregon publication. Educ. series, Vol. III, No. 1) 61 p. 1931. The University. $.75.

Drake, C. A. A study of an interest test and an affectivity test in forecasting freshman success in college. (Cont. to educ. No. 504) 60 p. 1931. Teachers College, Columbia. $1.50.

Eby, Frederick, and Pittenger, B. F. Study of the financing of public junior colleges in Texas. (Univ. of Texas. Bur. of research in the social sciences. Study, No. 1) 80 p. 1931. The University. Gratis.

*Eells, W. C. The junior college. 833 p. 1931. Houghton, Mifflin. $4.00.

Eurich, A. C. Reading abilities of college students: an experimental study. 208 p. 1931. Univ. of Minn. Press. $2.50.

Five college plans: Columbia, Harvard, Swarthmore, Wabash, Chicago. 115 p. 1931. Columbia Univ. Press. $2.00 cloth; $1.00 paper.

Garrison, N. L. Current practice in coordination of college and training school work. 26 p. 1931. The Author, Ypsilanti, Mich. $.50.

*Gray, W. S., *ed.* Recent trends in American college education. (Proceedings of the Institute for administrative officers of higher institutions, Vol. III) 253 p. 1931. Univ. of Chic. Press. $2.00.

Gregg, R. T., and Hamilton, T. T. Annotated bibliography of graduate theses in education at the University of Illinois. (Univ. of Illinois bulletin, Vol. XXVIII, No. 40. Bur. of educational research bulletin, No. 55) 80 p. 1931. The University. $.50.

Harper, H. R. What European and American students think on international problems: a comparative study of the world-mindedness of university students. 255 p. 1931. Teachers College, Columbia. $2.50.

Harris, Daniel. The relationship of college grades to some factors other than intelligence. (Archives of psychology, No. 131) 55 p. 1931. Archives of Psychology, Columbia Univ., N. Y. C. $.80.

Hawks, L. J. Certain relationships between scholarship in high school and in college. (Studies in educ. No. 15) 58 p. 1931. Johns Hopkins Press. $1.15.

Hodgson, J. G. Trends in university education. (The reference shelf, Vol. VII, No. 4) 163 p. 1931. H. W. Wilson. $.90.

Hyde, M. W. Standards for publicity programs in state-supported colleges and universities, derived from the institution's responsibility for reporting to its constituents. (Cont. to educ. No. 506) 80 p. 1931. Teachers College, Columbia. $1.50.

Iowa. University. Graduate theses, including schedule of dissertations of approved candidates for advanced degrees with major and minor subjects, January 15, 1931. (Univ. of Iowa studies, New series, No. 203. Series on aims and progress of research) 61 p. 1931. The University. Gratis.

Iowa. University. Trends in graduate work: a program commemoratng the thirtieth anniversary of the founding of the graduate college of the state university of Iowa, ed. by J. W. Ashton. (Univ. of Iowa studies, No. 194. Series on aims and progress of research, No. 33) 176 p. 1931. The University. Gratis.

Katz, Daniel, and Allport, F. H. Students' attitudes: a report of the Syracuse university reaction study. 408 p. 1931. Craftsman Press, Syracuse, N. Y. $3.50.

Keeler, L. W. Investigation of the effect of subject deficiencies upon accomplishment of students entering the College of engineering of the University of Michigan during the academic years 1927–28,

1928–29, and 1929–30. (Univ. of Michigan. Bur. of educational reference and research bulletin, No. 138) 68 p. 1931. The University. $.35.
Kiely, Margaret. Comparisons of students of teachers college and students of liberal-arts colleges. (Cont. to educ. No. 440) 147 p. 1931. Teachers College, Columbia. $1.50.
Kirkpatrick, J. E. Academic organization and control. 246 p. 1931. Antioch Press. $3.00.
Knode, J. C. Problems of freshman scholarship in a small state university. (Univ. of New Mexico bulletin, Vol. V, No. 4) 39 p. 1931. The University. $.25.
Kurani, H. A. Selecting the college student in America: a study of theory and practice. (Cont. to educ. No. 503) 124 p. 1931. Teachers College, Columbia. $1.50.
McCabe, M. R., *comp.* Good references on the education of women. (U. S. Office of Educ. Bibliography, No. 4) 13 p. 1931. Supt. of Doc. $.05.
MacNair, M. W., *comp.* List of American doctoral dissertations printed in 1929. 275 p. 1931. Supt. of Doc. $.40.
Manahan, J. L. Addresses delivered at the annual meeting of the association of Virginia colleges, held in the Jefferson hotel, Richmond, Virginia, February 13–14, 1931. 59 p. 1931. The Association. Gratis.
Massachusetts Institute of Technology. Abstracts of scientific and technical publications; including abstracts of doctors' theses, July 1, 1930–December 31, 1930, January 1, 1931–June 30, 1931. (Nos. 7 and 8) 56 p.; 81 p. 1931. The Institute.
National Education Association. American Association of Teachers Colleges. Tenth yearbook. 154 p. 1931. The Association, Charles W. Hunt, Sec'y, 2060 Stearns Rd., Cleveland, Ohio. $1.00.
National Society of College Teachers of Education. Practices of universities in granting higher degrees in education. (Yearbook XIX) 187 p. 1931. Univ. of Chic. Press. $1.50.
National Student Federation of the U. S. A. Yearbook for 1930. 104 p. 1931. The Federation, 218 Madison Ave., N. Y. C. $1.00.
Nelson, G. E. The introductory biological sciences in the traditional liberal arts colleges. (Cont. to educ. No. 501) 135 p. 1931. Teachers College, Columbia. $1.50.
Newman, J. H. Select discourses from the Idea of a university; ed. by May Yardley. 164 p. 1931. Cambridge Univ. Press, Macmillan, N. Y. C. $1.75.
Newmark, David. A study of a class in the Philadelphia normal school. 150 p. 1931. The Author, Dept. of Educ., Philadelphia Normal School, Philadelphia, Penn. $2.00.
Olmstead, J. G. Alumni achievement. (Handbook series, No. 3) 147 p. 1931. Amer. Alumni Council, Editorial Office, P. O. Box 105, Ithaca, N. Y. $1.00.
Osler, William. The student life and other essays. 145 p. 1931. Houghton, Mifflin. $2.00.
Peters, C. C., and Struck, F. T., *editors.* Abstracts of studies in education at the Pennsylvania state college. (State studies in educ. No. 2) 96 p. 1931. Penn. State College. $.50.
Pope, R. V. Factors affecting the elimination of women students from selected co-educational colleges of liberal arts. (Cont. to educ. No. 485) 110 p. 1931. Teachers College, Columbia. $1.50.
Powers, W. H., *ed.* A history of South Dakota state college. 144 p. 1931. The Book Store, South Dakota State College, Brookings, S. D. $1.00.
Remmers, H. H., and Stalnaker, J. M. A study of the class entering Purdue university in 1926. (Purdue univ. Studies in higher educ. No. 17) 31 p. 1931. The University. $.50.
Rice, S. A., *ed.* Methods in social science: a case book. 822 p. 1931. Univ. of Chic. Press. $4.50.
Schrammel, H. E., and Wood, E. R. Success and failure of college students: a follow-up study of the freshmen who entered the Kansas state teachers college of Emporia during the years 1924 to 1929. (Studies in educ. No. 3) 103 p. 1931. Kansas State Teachers College, Emporia, Kan. Ltd. free distribution.
Seeger, R. E., *comp.* Orientation courses: an annotated bibliography. (Bibliographies in educ. No. 2) *Mimeographed.* 39 p. 1931. Ohio State Univ. Bur. of Educational Research. $.35.
Shaw, R. W. Some aspects of self-insight, as found in students of a two-year normal school. (Cont. to educ. No. 448) 78 p. 1931. Teachers College, Columbia. $1.50.
Shaw, W. B. The bureau of alumni relations: a review of two years' effort in developing a program in alumni education. (Univ. of Michigan official publication, Vol. XXXIII, No. 10) 15 p. 1931. The University, Bureau of Alumni Relations.
Sherbon, F. B., and Ferris, Emily. The experience and opinions of 350 married women graduates of the University of Kansas with reference to the university curriculum and problems of the American home. (Kansas studies in educ. Vol. II, No. 2) 30 p. 1931. Univ. of Kansas. Bureau of School Service and Research. No charge—available on exchange basis.
South Carolina. University. Abstracts of theses for higher degrees, 1931. (Univ. of South Carolina. Bulletin, No. 213) 52 p. 1931. The University. Gratis. Ltd. supply.
Talbot, Marion, and Rosenberry, L. K. M. History of the American association of university women, 1881–1931. 479 p. 1931. Houghton, Mifflin. $4.00.
Teachers College. Columbia University. Preliminary plan for a demonstration teachers college, fall—1932. 7 p. 1931. Teachers College, Columbia. Gratis.
Thilly, Frank. Modern university problems; an address at a University of Missouri convocation, September 11, 1930. (Bulletin, Vol. XXXII, No. 3) 16 p. 1931. Univ. of Missouri. $.50.
Thomas, M. H., *ed.* Black book, or book of misdemeanors in King's college, 1771–1775. 17 p. 1931. Columbia Univ., 108 Library Bldg., (Columbiana) N. Y. C. $.25.
Umstattd, J. G. Student self-support, University of Minnesota. 200 p. 1931. Univ. of Minn. Press. $2.50.
U. S. Office of Education. Guidance leaflets. Architecture. (Leaflets, No. 10) 7 p. 1931. Supt. of Doc. $.05.
U. S. Office of Education. Guidance leaflets. Civil engineeing. (Leaflet, No. 11) 9 p. 1931. Supt. of Doc. $.05.
U. S. Office of Education. Guidance leaflets. Dentistry. (Leaflet, No. 7) 10 p. 1931. Supt. of Doc. $.05.
U. S. Office of Education. Guidance leaflets. Electrical engineering. (Leaflet, No. 12) 11 p. 1931. Supt. of Doc. $.05.
U. S. Office of Education. Guidance leaflets. Journalism. (Leaflet, No. 8) 6 p. 1931. Supt. of Doc. $.05.
U. S. Office of Education. Guidance leaflets. Law. (Leaflet, No. 5) 13 p. 1931. Supt. of Doc. $.05.
U. S. Office of Education. Guidance leaflets. Librarianship. (Leaflet, No. 9) 9 p. 1931. Supt. of Doc. $.05.
U. S. Office of Education. Guidance leaflets. Mechanical engineering. (Leaflet, No. 13) 11 p. 1931. Supt. of Doc. $.05.
U. S. Office of Education. Guidance leaflets. Medicine. (Leaflet, No. 6) 14 p. 1931. Supt. of Doc. $.05.
U. S. Office of Education. Guidance leaflets. Music. (Leaflet, No. 17) 15 p. 1931. Supt. of Doc. $.05.
U. S. Office of Education. Guidance leaflets. Pharmacy. (Leaflet, No. 14) 15 p. 1931. Supt. of Doc. $.05.
U. S. Office of Education. Guidance leaflets. Veterinary medicine. (Leaflet, No. 18) 9 p. 1931. Supt. of Doc. $.05.
U. S. Office of Education. Recent theses in education: an annotated list of 242 theses deposited with the Office of education and available for loan. (Pamphlet 1931, No. 26) 41 p. 1931. Supt. of Doc. $.10.
Wahlquist, J. T. Status of the junior college instructor. (U. S. Office of Educ. Pamphlet, No. 20) 29 p. 1931. Supt. of Doc. $.05.
Walters, J. E. Student development: how to make the most of college life. 195 p. 1931. Pitman. $1.75.
Weeks, H. F. Factors influencing the choice of courses by students in certain liberal arts colleges. (Cont. to educ. No. 465) 62 p. 1931. Teachers College, Columbia. $1.50.
Will, A. S. Education for newspaper life: an account of the cooperation of a university and the press. 314 p. 1931. Essex Press, 16 Lawrence St., Newark, N. J. $3.00.

(26) ADULT EDUCATION

Cartwright, M. A., *ed.* Unemployment and adult education: a symposium. 63 p. 1931. Amer. Ass'n for Adult Educ. $.50.

Child Study Association of America. When parents meet at school: parent education in summer play schools. (Summer play schools. Pamphlet, No. 1) 19 p. 1931. The Association. $.20.

Hanson, Marius. World workers' educational movements: their social significance. 594 p. 1931. Columbia Univ. Press. $5.00.

*Jacks, L. P. The education of the whole man. 155 p. 1931. Harper. $1.75.

*Lorimer, Frank. The making of adult minds in a metropolitan area. 245 p. 1931. Macmillan. $2.00.

MacCormick, Austin. The education of adult prisoners: a survey and a program. 477 p. 1931. N. Y. Nat'l Society of Penal Information, 114 E. 30th St., N. Y. C. $2.50.

National Congress of Parents and Teachers. Education for home and family: the proceedings of a conference held at Hot Springs, Arkansas, under the auspices of the U. S. office of education and the National congress of parents and teachers, May 1–2, 1931. 245 p. 1931. The Congress. $2.00.

National Congress of Parents and Teachers. Handbook for parent-teacher associations. 64 p. 1931. The Congress. $.25.

National Congress of Parents and Teachers. Parent education: the second yearbook. 222 p. 1931. The Congress. $1.00.

National Council of Parent Education. Papers on parent education; presented at the biennial conference of the National council of parent education, November, 1930, Washington, D. C. 146 p. 1931. The Council, 60 E. 42nd St., N. Y. C. $2.00.

National Council of Parent Education. Problems for parent educators, Vol. II. 48 p. 1931. The Council, 60 E. 42nd St., N. Y. C. $.50.

Noffsinger, J. S., *comp.* Home study blue book. 4th ed. 24 p. 1931. National Home Study Council, 839 Seventeenth St., N. W., Washington, D. C. Gratis.

Rogers, M. L. A contribution to the theory and practice of parents' associations. 83 p. 1931. United Parents' Ass'ns of N. Y. C., Inc., 152 W. 42nd St., N. Y. C. $.50.

U. S. Department of Labor. Women's Bureau. The industrial experience of women workers at the summer schools, 1928–1930. (Bulletin, No. 89) 62 p. 1931. Supt. of Doc. $.20.

Waples, Douglas, and Tyler, R. W. What people want to read about: a study of group interests and a survey of problems in adult reading. 312 p. 1931. Amer. Lib. Ass'n. and Univ. of Chic. Press. $3.50.

Whipple, C. A. Adult education. (Univ. of the state of New York bulletin, No. 972) 42 p. 1931. The University. $.10.

(27) VISUAL AND RADIO EDUCATION

Brown, H. E., and Bird, Joy. Motion pictures and lantern slides for elementary visual education. (Lincoln school research studies) 105 p. 1931. Teachers College, Columbia. $1.00.

Butler, N. M. Radio's new opportunity in education. 5 p. 1931. Univ. of Chic. Press. Gratis.

Charters, W. W. Research problems in radio education. (Information series, No. 4) 17 p. 1931. Nat'l Advisory Council on Radio in Educ., 60 E. 42nd St., N. Y. C. Gratis.

Fox Film Corporation. Sound motion pictures as a factor in education. 11 p. 1931. Fox Film Corp., 850 Tenth Ave., N. Y. C. Gratis.

Keith, Alice, and Johnson, Helen, *compilers.* American school of the air: teachers manual and classroom guide. 67 p. 1931. Amer. School of the Air, 485 Madison Ave., N. Y. C. Gratis.

*MacLatchy, H. H., *ed.* Education on the air: second yearbook of the Institute for education by radio. 301 p. 1931. Ohio State Univ. Press. $3.00.

National Academy of Visual Instruction. Visual instruction directory, 1931. (Vol. XII, No. 1) 44 p. 1931. The Academy, Univ. of Kan. $1.50.

The National Advisory Council on Radio in Education. (Information series, No. 1) 2nd ed. rev. 36 p. 1931. The Council, 60 E. 42nd St., N. Y. C. Gratis.

National Advisory Council on Radio in Education. The broadcaster and the librarian, by F. K. W. Drury. (Information series, No. 3) 28 p. 1931. The Council, 60 E. 42nd St., N. Y. C. Gratis.

National Advisory Council on Radio in Education. Research problems in radio education, by W. W. Charters. (Information series, No. 4) 17 p. 1931. The Council, 60 E. 42nd St., N. Y. C. Gratis.

National Advisory Council on Radio in Education. Committee on Engineering Developments. Present and impending applications to education of radio and allied arts. (Information series, No. 5) 94 p. 1931. The Council, 60 E. 42nd St., N. Y. C. Gratis.

Tyson, Levering, *ed.* Radio and education: proceedings of the first assembly on the National advisory council on radio in education, 1931. 271 p. 1931. Univ. of Chic. Press. $3.00.

U. S. Department of Agriculture. Motion pictures of the U. S. Department of agriculture. (Miscellaneous publication, No. 111) 26 p. 1931. Gov't. Print. Office. $.05.

(28) SPECIAL EDUCATION AND NEGRO EDUCATION

Abbott, Edith. Social welfare and professional education. 177 p. 1931. Univ. of Chic. Press. $2.00.

Caliver, Ambrose, and others. Bibliography on education of the negro comprising publications from January, 1928, to December, 1930. (U. S. Office of Educ. Bulletin, 1931, No. 17) 34 p. 1931. Supt. of Doc. $.10.

Caliver, Ambrose. A personnel study of negro college students: a study of the relations between certain background factors of negro college students and their subsequent careers in college. (Cont. to educ. No. 484) 146 p. 1931. Teachers College, Columbia. $1.50.

De Land, Fred. The story of lip-reading: its genesis and development. 232 p. 1931. Volta Bureau, 1601 35th St., N. W., Washington, D. C. $2.75.

Jones, R. G. The special schools and curriculum centers: report of the superintendent of schools to the Board of education of the city school district of the city of Cleveland, for the school year 1929–30. 206 p. 1931. Board of Educ., Cleveland, Ohio. $1.00.

McCuiston, Fred. The south's negro teaching force. (A brief study) 29 p. 1931. Julius Rosenwald Fund, Nashville, Tenn. Gratis.

Peabody Conference. Executive Committee. Education and racial adjustment. Report of Peabody conference on dual education in the south. 78 p. 1931. The Committee, 703 Standard Bldg., Atlanta, Ga. $.25.

Rogers, J. F. Speech defects and their correction, for teachers, parents, and pupils. (U. S. Office of Educ. Pamphlet, No. 22) 28 p. 1931. Supt. of Doc. $.05.

Texas. State Department of Education. Negro education in Texas. (Bulletin, No. 294) 32 p. 1931. State Dept. of Educ., Austin, Texas. Gratis to public schools of Texas.

Thompson, E. R. Subnormal child in pedagogy: a book for Binet teachers. 1931. Snell Press, Newark, N. J.

Waldman, J. L., Wade, F. A., and Aretz, C. W. Hearing and the school child: hearing, school progress, and achievement of public school children. 222 p. 1931. Volta Bureau, 1601 35th St., N. W., Washington, D. C. $2.00.

*White House Conference on Child Health and Protection. Committee on Special Classes. Special education: the handicapped and the gifted. 604 p. 1931. Century. $4.00.

Yale, C. A. Years of building: memories of a pioneer in a special field of education. 311 p. 1931. Dial Press. $3.50.

NEW BOOKS IN EDUCATION

LEWIS, WILLIAM M. *From a College Platform.* Pp. ix + 294. Dial Press. $2.00.

RICCIARDI, NICHOLAS and IRA W. KIBBY. *Readings in Vocational Education: Trade and Industrial Aspect.* Pp. xi + 570. Century. $3.00.

WILSON, J. DOVER, EDITOR. *Matthew Arnold: Culture and Anarchy.* Pp. xl + 241. Cambridge University Press, Macmillan.

SCHOOL AND SOCIETY

EDITED BY J. McKEEN CATTELL

WITH WHICH IS COMBINED THE

EDUCATIONAL REVIEW

EDITED BY WILLIAM McANDREW

Volume 35 | Saturday, March 26, 1932 | Number 900

SPECIALIZATIONS OF EDUCATIVE PROCESSES: SOME ANTICIPATIONS

By Professor DAVID SNEDDEN

TEACHERS COLLEGE, COLUMBIA UNIVERSITY

I

"A period of economic depression amidst a people not suffering from wasting social diseases often serves as a fallow year for land. Fertility is restored, moisture accumulated, and rich crops follow."

Let us hope that this interpreter of history is right in his finding. And, let us educators have faith that one or more kinds of "surges of growth" may follow in our fields the present economically and politically fallow years.

But is it likely that the United States is to experience any further great expansions of education in sheer quantitative senses—that is, in numbers at school or college, in days of school attendance made, in new buildings and equipment, in gatherings of teachers in associations and summer schools, in dollars raised by taxation or given by philanthropy? Growths in these matters will still go on, certainly—as they will in settlement of frontier lands, the construction of railways, the making of steel, the finding of gold deposits, the clearing of forests. But in all these areas of marvelous past history "booms" will probably not recur or even be paralleled.

American parents, taxpayers and philanthropists have "bought" (or, in commercial jargon, "been sold") educations during the latest five or six decades on prodigious scales—all statistics give evidence of that. But it has been quantity rather than quality they have obtained, in large part.

Hence it is here suggested for the consideration of American educators that our present best opportunities to forecast and press forward new and upward developments of American education are to be found in regions of quality rather than quantity.

All observant critics of American collective life to-day can show us pronounced needs for better school and college educations, rather than for just more schooling. In fact, if some of our critics had longer memories and wider social perceptions they could easily harry us with tales of unfulfilled promises—promises made from one to five generations ago that more schools and more colleges and more monies for both would greatly lessen our crime and vice and idleness, would give us wise and pure political leadership and refined culture and self-respecting democracy.

At any rate, no one will dispute the contention that upon our already splendid quantitative achievements of public and endowed educations, there still remain worlds to conquer of qualitative achievement—especially when conceived in terms of such relatively end functionings or social values as widely distributed political competencies of voters, better self-ministrations to health by men and women generally, higher standards of cultural utilizations of journals and drama and broadcasts, and the other distinguishable qualities which are the attributes of a people collectively to be approved and admired. We must hope, too, that ways and means will be found of so improving our educations at school or college level that in much greater degree than at present they will reduce criminality, give us abler leaders in the scores of fields where they are now so acutely needed, and open clear paths of optimum opportunity to well-meaning workers, voters, parents, self-culturing minds and altruistic spirits.

II

It is the purpose of this paper to discuss one type of means of improving qualities of educations in the future to which in the writer's estimation none of us are giving enough attention—that, namely, of further, and in some cases different, specializations of teaching and directing services in the total range of educative processes.

It is contended that, judging by results in nearly every modern field of human work, we are justified in expecting or planning for better qualities of education only at the price of increasing specialization of service among all those contributing to it.

To the present writer our conferences seem to be dodging that probability, even necessity—or, at any rate, it is not being brought into the open. As concomitants to such ignoring of a vital issue, it is contended that in all our educational writings to-day we attach mystical meanings to the term "education," and that we are tending to make excessively abstract such terms "the teacher" and "the child."

No one of us, of course, likes specialization any more than he likes machines or armies or storms or policemen or prisons or hospitals or oil-wells or large corporations or popular resorts or sessions of Congress—except when such things visibly serve his own personal needs for movement or wealth or comfort or protection. "Yale head criticizes over-specialization in the training of physicians," is a headline in yesterday's newspaper.

He would, of course—and his criticism will have no more effect than if he criticized the rising tides. Flexner criticizes *ad hoc* training in our universities. Business men criticize specialized training of engineers. Customers criticize the departmental specializations of great emporiums. Every member of the intelligentsia of at least Great Britain and the United States has for a century seemingly viewed with alarm mechanical specialization in manufacture. And who of our American leaders of thought does not deplore regional and "money-crop" specializations in American farming?

But, in spite of all protest and apprehension, specialization of function proceeds like a glacial movement in every field of productive service in civilized societies—in armies and hospitals, in banking and urban religious ministry, in engineering scientific research, in literary production and moving picture work. As men of personal culture and broad scholarship most of our recent doctors of philosophy are jokes—but large proportions of them are fairly effective specialists. The typical "realtor" is far more of a "social leader" than the modern urban physician—partly because the latter is so specialized that we, his patrons, feel safe in trusting our children to his specialized knowledge and techniques.

Subdivision and intensification of productive functions proceed apace because, like gunpowder warfare, "mechanicalization," peopling of the West, and the spread of moving picture entertainment, it derives from two sources which, as social forces, are still obscure in their collective aspects, but which are poignantly real to us as persons wherever they directly impinge on our own personal fortunes and comforts.

One of these is the ever-present demand for *more* or *better* production of goods—largely as judged by the market or our employers—in order to have more abundant resources ourselves whereby to live; and the other is our own desires for comfortable work, short hours, ease of achievement. How intensely we of American universities now specialize in our work—and how we deplore and detest such specializations in all other fields than our own! And how, as contributors to educational theory and policy, more serious than the ancient king, we bid the tide to stay its course!

But it would certainly be a foolish student of the social sciences who would pretend that modern societies are not paying heavy prices for specialization. They certainly are—no less than at sundry times societies have had to pay heavy prices for the introduction of fire or tillage, for the building of cities or the expansion of commerce, for the spread of Christianity or democracy, for the opening of frontiers or the harnessing of steam-power.

And, as in pursuit of those other things of net ultimate good (so far as human collective valuations can now judge), let us not think that particular societies have not at times decayed, or at least disastrously retreated, from too much specialization—and will again and again.

Nevertheless, the current moves finally in one direction in spite of momentary returns. He who to-day says of medicine or engineering or California farming or college teaching or public-school supervision that "specialization has gone too far" is commonly the victim of wishful thinking. He has not opened his eyes to social realities.

III

In every field of human work which is steadily yielding to obscure pressures for more specialization there are, of course, always hosts of possibilities of wrong kinds, even self-destructive kinds, of specialization. For example, in perhaps all early stages of intense evolution in specialization, subdivision of *primary* processes unaccompanied by corresponding specializations in supervisory and coordinating processes may easily lead to disaster. "Organize, deputize, supervise," is a slogan of late arrival in business.

Is it a fair inference that subdivisions of primary instructional processes in to-day's liberal colleges have run much too far ahead of the development of competently specialized agencies of coordination and supervision—with disastrous effects on large proportions of students? When a genius has built up a great department store or army or railway or newspaper his "machine" often runs well for only a few years after his death—not because the specializations he developed cease to function, but because of failure of coordinating powers equivalent to those given by the founder's genius.

It would certainly be rash to assume that most of the forms into which the directing services of American education have thus far, like Topsy, "jest growed"—principalships, supervisorships, superintendencies, curriculum research bureaus and the rest—represent at all sound forms of specialization.

And perhaps for secondary school and college educations one of the most wrong, even at times seriously destructive, forms of specialization which we have permitted because it seemed logical at first and has the merit of offering many easy paths to follow, is that of subject-matter specialization.

Specialization of teaching service around such areas of the social inheritance as the vernacular language, the histories, the chemical sciences, music and the rest we shall certainly develop more extensively in the future than in the past—but to produce really effective educations, such specializations must be, not in the fields of subject-matter themselves, but in the functional applications, the proven valuable learnings for life, derivable from the riches of such fields.

For example, our larger high schools are still greatly in need, not of specially equipped teachers of history, but of specialists in "Those Findings of Historians Which Will Prove Valuably Functional in Forming Good Political Citizens for American Conditions." Do we not now need in our over-rich geography fields specialists in "Those Takings from the Geographical and Allied Ecological Sciences Which Are of Proven Functional Significances in the Common Cultures of Men and Women?"

Every liberal college should have one or more specialized professors, not of English literature, or even of modern literature, but of "Those Appreciations and Other Uses of Literature Which Will Lead to Cultivation of Superior Tastes in Reading at Ages Thirty to Sixty."

IV

Certain kinds of specialization adapted to differentiated types of learners have already proceeded a considerable distance with us; but it is predicted that during the next three decades we shall see them proceed many times farther.

We already have specialized teachers of the blind, the hard-of-hearing, the crippled. Institutions provided for the custody of the abjectly mentally subnormal have developed some of their own specializations of training and instructional service.

But it is confidently predicted that presently we shall evolve specializations of teaching service for the duller 20 or 25 per cent. of our public school personnel—and different types of specialized teaching service for the mentally more gifted pupils, formed in temporary special classes just to learn the mathematics or music or civistics most functional for them.

Surely our means of social diagnosis will presently enable us to detect incipient "gangsterism" as relatively early as good medical diagnosis enables us to detect incipient tuberculosis. Next we shall undoubtedly find that only specially equipped teachers working with specialized means can effectively arrest and permanently cure in their incipient stages such contagious social diseases as incipient gangsterism—and, no less than tuberculosis, no one can cure it if it has gone far.

But even more far-reaching in their departures from present ideals and practises will be the specializations of teaching and directing service which, it is here again confidently predicted, we shall develop when we shall have definitely interconnected potential school educations with their expected actual, rather than only aspired-after, functional outcomes in collective extra-school life, and especially as tangibly functional at ages twenty to seventy.

Good political citizenship of adults is, for example, a composite of qualities which we adults now crudely appraise—and in which, appraising even in 1932, we find much to deplore. We educators still hope that our school studies of history or arithmetic, the new social science or the old study of civil government, are contributive to good political citizenship. Even more fatuously, perhaps, we trust that playground sports or extra-curricular activities or the intangibles of teachers' atmospheres can yet by some magical process be made to contribute to that good political citizenship—though for a century the more informed of us have no longer expected corresponding magical processes to serve as preventives of malaria or cures of smallpox.

No, it is predicted that ere long some enterprising leaders will set out to specialize a class of teachers in junior and senior high schools in the teaching of "political citizenship." Unless researchers have pioneered the way, they will, of course, have to make their own subject-matter—drawing upon histories or literatures or biographies or censuses or Seabury investigations or court practises or college football or yesterday's sermons or last year's debates in legislatures or the protests of this taxpayer's association or what League of Nations associations are saying, for materials.

And presently still further specializations are to be expected. Special teachers will be equipped and assigned to prepare for adult political citizenship all those learners of IQ less than 90. Another set of teachers will specialize in similar objectives for all those of IQ over 120.

V

Finally, the writer would strongly urge the contention that in all the future specializations of educative service—that is, in the economical and effective guidance of learnings towards foreseen goals of really functional service to the learner himself and to his fellows—foreshadowed above, it is just as Utopian to expect the armies of teachers either to contribute to, or even to be more than superficially cognizant of, the more basic policies of social purposes involved, as it is to expect the soldiers in an army to be sources of, or to be more than superficially appreciative of, the strategies of the state and of leaders. Above all, there must be developed specialists in the coordinations of educative specializations of process—coordinations chiefly expressed in programs, of course, but also kept vital through supervision.

Many laymen, and not a few articulate educators, it seems to this writer, are today becoming quasi-mystical in their uses of the term "education"—just as it has proven in recent years so easy to become mystical about liberty or democracy or economic success.

Furthermore, as earlier noted, we are over-idealizing abstract and unreal conceptions of the possibilities of "the teacher"—just as a few years ago we overworked abstract and unreal conceptions of "the child."

Perhaps, as in other areas of trouble, such trends to mysticism are a kind of "escape" reaction. But do they ever lead anywhere else than into quagmires?

WHITHER EDUCATION?

A SUMMARY OF MUCH READING

By WAYNE W. SOPER

STATE EDUCATION DEPARTMENT, ALBANY, NEW YORK

To understand the development of our public school system, one must look more definitely to the American people and their ideals of democracy than to the history of education or to theories of educational philosophy. A people

To understand the development of our public school system, one must look more definitely to the early history of education and to theories of educational philosophy. Schools of educational thought have left their definite impress upon it in a land of freedom, committed to the principle that all men are created equal in opportunity and possessed of certain inalienable rights of life, liberty and the pursuit of what they think is happiness would naturally throw to the winds old theories of education and erect upon a new foundation a system compatible with its ideals.

Naturally such a system was designed to educate all the children of all the people. As an assurance of securing such education, compulsory attendance laws were early enacted, guaranteeing to the state a prescribed schooling of a certain level for its future citizenry. This, together with the growing popularity of secondary education, has resulted in an attendance upon high school instruction never before witnessed in any nation. Prospects point to our soon becoming a nation of high school graduates. So great are its benefits that the age limits of compulsory attendance are being raised in some states.

From the kindergarten, through the elementary, the junior and senior high school and the great state universities, the American scheme of free education is a series of unified and articulated steps cemented together by one common purpose—to educate in terms of social needs. There is literally no break between these separate units for the child capable of passing from one to the other; no social barrier stands in the way of the poor but worthy and ambitious student. The workman's son may sit with the millionaire's under the same professor.

Standardization is the American idol. It is worshipped in business and in education. There is a standard grading scheme, standard courses of study, standard school buildings and standardized tests and measurements. All of which have resulted in a more uniform education for the nation's masses, an assurance that children in Skowhegan, Me., Pensacola, Fla., Tucson, Ariz., Great Falls, Mont., and Columbia, Mo., are exposed to the same and equal educational opportunities. Without standardization there is no progress. With it, a goal to achieve, a direction to take and a realization of arrival at a desired destination.

But all is not well with this new education. It has been discovered that it costs money—and

as have great educators, such as Barnard, Mann, Eliot, Dewey, Jordan and Kilpatrick. Such men have thought and written, not in terms of democratic ideals, but rather in terms of a deeper philosophy of education centering in and purposive of child development. In some sense our system is a borrowed one.

Naturally such a system, although purporting to be for all children, actually has been designed for the child best able to fit into its routinization. In order to assure the state an educated citizenry, compulsory attendance laws were early enacted which, at the present time, have had the deplorable effect of holding in school until a certain age thousands of boys and girls for whom the schools have nothing to offer and who chafe under restraint. Compulsory attendance has outrun the ability of the school to provide a suitable education for those compelled to attend. High school education may well be more selective.

From the kindergarten, through the elementary, the junior and senior high school and the great state universities, the American system of education may be accurately described as a series of disparate, inarticulate units. The junior high school was intended to bridge one gap, but actually made two. This lack of integration has been an insuperable barrier to many pupils. It is a great hurdle to leap from elementary school to high school and a greater one to break through the intellectual snobbery and social phalanx of college life,—educational stratification.

Variety is the American ideal. It is worshipped in business and in education. It is a fetish of democracy that people and things have a right to be different. The unbiased observer can not fail to note the great variety of American educational theory and practice. And all to the end that education may not produce a stereotyped democracy. Everywhere are different schools, different courses of study, a variety of building types and wholesale methods of classroom procedure. All to the end that education in this country does not know where it is going and would not stop if it got there: that people and things may be different.

But all is not well with this new education. Its votaries claim that without more adequate more money. It has been surmised that all the funds being spent for it are not wisely expended nor accurately accounted for. That the teachers and administrators of this great and glorious experiment are not adequately trained for the job entrusted to them—overpaid in some instances for what is expected of them. That knowledge is being stressed more than character—no doubt a contributing cause of the present crime wave. This education lacks thoroughness; it lauds the athlete and hoots at the scholar; and spreads a thin coat of superficiality over a half-baked superiority complex.

To restore confidence in this great scheme of democratic education, we should first of all undo much of the mischief already perpetrated in the name of Federal Aid so that the hydra of complete Federal control of our schools—a Secretary in the President's Cabinet—does not get a stranglehold on our schools. As proof of such reasoning one need only refer to current published educational literature ———

financial support no semblance of educational opportunity can exist; that a people who can spend 50 millions for cosmetics and 100 millions or more for chewing gum or cigarettes and several times that amount for automobiles can afford to pay more for education. Business men deplore the fact that knowledge is being scrapped for fads and frills; that the graduates of our high schools can not add a column of figures accurately or compute the area of a city lot, or figure the interest on a promissory note. Back to the fundamentals, is the cry. Give us graduates who can do the job.

To restore confidence in this great scheme of democratic education, we should first of all elevate education to its proper sphere in the affairs of government as it is in the peoples' hearts by creating a Secretary of Education to sit in the Cabinet as a safeguard to our cherished ideals. As proof of such reasoning one need only refer to current published educational literature ———

EDUCATIONAL EVENTS

NEW SITE OF THE UNIVERSITY OF ROME

A special correspondent of *The Boston Evening Transcript* writes that the Italian Chamber has approved a bill by which the University of Rome hitherto established in the center of the city, known for centuries as the Sapienza, will be removed outside the Porta Pia to a large territory of its own for which provision was made two years ago by a decree of Mussolini. The correspondent continues:

The Sapienza will become a mere memory of the Rome of the past, when it was made the seat of the university by Pope Alexander VII and stood practically on the same site on which Pope Boniface VIII had established a "Studium Urbis."

Rome, contrary to Bologna and Paris, was prevented from taking the lead among the universities founded in the Middle Ages, owing to the tumultuous periods through which it passed from the fall of the Roman Empire down to the occupation of the barons who tried to dominate over the Popes themselves, and the populace which was in continual riots and revolutions until the seat of the papacy was removed to Avignon. Schools existed in Rome, and in time became very numerous, but they were mostly religious schools and seminaries maintained by different nations for students of each nationality.

It was only about the time of Boniface VIII and under his successor, Pope Benedict XI, that what afterwards became the University of Rome was founded, and the date generally accepted was the year 1303. At the time of Pius IX, in 1870, the university had less than 700 students, but this was a number hardly exceeded by the great majority of universities in Europe. Rome certainly never boasted of such an army of students as did Bologna and Paris which in their most glorious days in the Middle Ages had from 15,000 to 20,000 students. But on the other hand the numerous schools and colleges made up for it, and to-day the increase in the students is about 300 every year. They numbered 2,000 last year. The ground outside the Porta Pia, which will be called the University City, covers 150,000 square yards and within five years most of the new buildings for the various faculties will be erected.

INTERNATIONAL CHILDREN'S EXPOSITION IN BUCHAREST

An International Children's Exposition is to be held at Bucharest, Rumania, in the Park Carol, during May of this year.

The exposition will be divided into two main parts: (1) scientific and (2) commercial. The former section will exhibit scientific methods employed in the care and nourishment of children, their teaching and discipline from birth to adolescence. In the commercial or industrial section, all types of products used by children such as clothes and textiles, school and home furniture and equipment, medicines and toilet requisites, foodstuffs, toys and musical instruments, and miscellaneous articles for their education and development, will be accepted for display.

Rates for space in the pavilions are 500 and 1,000 leu a square meter (28 cents and 56 cents a square foot). In the open air rental is 200 leu a square meter (12 cents a square foot) with a minimum allotment of 10 square meters (108 square feet). Exhibits will not be accepted later than April 27.

Special privileges will be accorded participants in and visitors to the exposition. Among these are a 50 per cent. reduction on Roumanian railways, special rates on foreign railroads, steamship and air lines, and free importation of merchandise destined to the exposition on the condition that it be reexported immediately after the close of the exhibition.

The exhibition committee cordially extends an invitation to American firms and child welfare organizations to participate. It is reported that the French Government will be officially represented and, as well, the National Children's Council of London, England.

Requests for space and for other information may be addressed to Rumanian Consuls in the United States or to the Commissariat General de l'Exposition International de l'Enfant, Clemenceau 6, Bucharest, Rumania.

THE TWELFTH INTERNATIONAL CONGRESS ON COMMERCIAL EDUCATION

THE United States Government has accepted an invitation extended by the British Government to participate in the twelfth International Congress on Commercial Education to be held in London during the last week of July, according to information received by Mr. J. O. Malott, specialist in commercial education, U. S. Office of Education, Washington, D. C. The Prince of Wales will address the congress.

The Federal Office of Education is bringing this invitation to the attention of interested individuals and education associations. Institutions and associations are invited to send representatives to the congress. This invitation is being called to the attention of trade associations and business men by the U. S Department of Commerce and the Chamber of Commerce of the United States.

The purpose of the congress is to bring together the leaders in secondary and higher education for business from the various countries to exchange ideas about outstanding problems and practices in business education. Among the topics to be discussed are: Cooperation between business and institutions offering business courses, training for foreign trade and other specialized fields, business ethics, business research, modern office equipment and commercial-teacher training.

Due to the rapidly changing social and economic conditions throughout the world, the congress proposes to emphasize the newer social and institutional factors affecting business education. Authorities of the respective countries will discuss the necessity of broadening the scope of business training, the causes and effects of the increasingly large number of women in business and the recognition that all citizens be provided with general business information. The interchange of business teachers and students to develop a better understanding among future business men and women will be discussed.

Sir Francis Goodenough, one of the leading business men in England and president of the British Association for Commercial Education, in a special invitation to American business men and teachers, says: "The subjects to be considered have at no time been of more general interest or more vital importance to the welfare of the world than they are to-day. The economic disturbances which are affecting all civilized countries have thrown sharply into focus the necessity for a clearer understanding of the forces governing international trade. Commercial education has acquired a new importance and a wider implication."

International congresses on business education began in 1886. Because of the war no meetings were held from 1913 to 1929. The

United States was officially represented for the first time at the 1929 congress held in Amsterdam which was attended by 750 delegates from 38 nations. The significance of the congress is evidenced by the fact that business training has recently become one of the major educational responsibilities of the leading commercial and industrial nations. The new rôle of the business man in social and economic life and the increased importance of commerce in our national and international relations are giving an impetus to business education.

In various countries, national chapters of the International Association for Commercial Education, which sponsors the congresses, have been formed. The American chapter is cooperating with universities in the offering of an educational tour to seven European countries and to the congress. Many leaders in business education have indicated their intention of attending the congress.

CAMP FOR VOCATIONAL GUIDANCE OF STEVENS INSTITUTE OF TECHNOLOGY

SEVERAL colleges and some of the major engineering and industrial organizations of the country are represented in an experiment in vocational or collegiate guidance for boys which, according to an announcement made by President Harvey N. Davis, of the Stevens Institute of Technology, will be made at the Stevens Engineering Camp in northern New Jersey from August 13 to 27. Dr. Willis R. Whitney, vice-president of the General Electric Company; Dr. Clarence F. Hirshfeld, director of research of the Detroit Edison Company; Mr. John C. Parker, president of the Brooklyn Edison Company and one time professor of electrical engineering at the University of Michigan; Commander E. E. Wilson, president of the Sikorsky Aviation Corporation; Dean Dexter S. Kimball, of Cornell University; President Clarence A. Barbour, of Brown University; Dr. Roy V. Wright, former president of the American Society of Mechanical Engineers, editor of *The Railway Age;* Dr. H. Foster Bain, formerly director of the Bureau of Mines and later secretary of the American Institute of Mining and Metallurgical Engineers, are among those who will lecture. Individual and group tests intended to help each boy to estimate his natural characteristics and abilities will be administered by Dr. Walter Van Dyke Bingham, director of the Personnel Research Federation of New York, and Professor Johnson O'Connor, formerly personnel officer in the General Electric Company, now a member of the faculties of both the Stevens Institute of Technology and the Massachusetts Institute of Technology. Boys now in high school and preparatory schools, preferably those who will enter college a year from next September, in 1933, are to attend the camp. Dr. Davis said that every effort had been made to assure the impartiality of the guidance offered through the camp. Although under the auspices of his own college, neither that college nor any other has any interest in the camp beyond an interest in it as an attempt to answer educational questions of some importance to colleges and to students.

The scene of the encampment is a tract of three hundred and seventy-five acres on the lower slopes of the Kittatinny Range, twelve miles from the Delaware Water Gap. The tract includes a natural lake of thirty acres on the shores of which are the camp buildings and athletic fields. The camp is used for six weeks earlier in the summer for surveying instruction under field conditions. It is therefore possible to permit the preparatory school boys during the two weeks of their encampment to make trial of one type of engineering work, surveying, and they will have from four to five hours in the field each day getting a rudimentary knowledge of the principles of surveying. Field and water sports are scheduled for the late afternoon hours, and Blair Academy at Blairstown offers the use of its facilities for tennis and golf. Previous experience indicates, however, according to President Davis, that work in the field with maps and surveying instruments is as likely as sports to hold interest. In a similar encampment last year, the first trial of the experiment, there were boys from thirty-six schools.

A NATIONAL EDUCATION INSTITUTE

A PROPOSAL for the establishment of a National Education Institute to function for education, as the Political Institute at Williams College and the Institute of Public Affairs at the

University of Virginia function in relation to government and economics, is now being studied by a committee appointed by the National Council of Education of the National Education Association. The United States Commissioner of Education is suggested to serve on the board of control.

The feasibility of the plan, which was announced orally March 18 to the representative of *The U. S. Daily* by Miss Adelaide S. Baylor, chief of Home Economics Education Service of the Federal Board for Vocational Education, who is also secretary of the council, will be studied and recommendations presented to the National Education Association for consideration. Dr. William C. Bagley, of Teachers College, Columbia University, is chairman of the committee studying the proposal, which was made by Professor W. A. Evans, of Cincinnati. The following additional information concerning the proposal was supplied:

It is proposed to utilize for education the method of the Williams College political institute so that "positive leadership in education" can be secured for the National Education Association. In plan, it is hoped that through this agency the best minds in education and in allied fields can be brought together for conference and round-table discussion.

It is planned that meetings of the institute will follow the National Education Association summer meeting and continue for several weeks. The location might be permanent or it might follow the National Education Association convention.

A faculty of leading educators of the United States and Europe is proposed for the institute. Some of these might serve full time, others part time. Lectures are contemplated for the general theme of the session.

The institute would be open to those it might serve on application, or to delegates sent by cities or institutions, but the number enrolled would be limited to permit the conference idea to function. Expenses would be borne by the student body at first with cost of attendance determined by quality of faculty, length of session and similar factors.

The proceedings would be published and disposed of by sale, to members of the National Education Association, and to educational libraries. It is further proposed that the institute should be the child of the National Education Association, because no other agency could adequately handle its far-reaching possibilities.

The board of control will consist of an executive secretary, the U. S. Commissioner of Education, two members elected by the board of directors, and the president of the National Education Association.

With an enrolment of 450 at $100 each, it is believed the institute could function at a cost of $45,000 distributed as follows: Fifteen instructors at $500 per week, or in all $15,000; 10 lecturers at $200, amounting to $2,000; administration at $10,000; board and room for 450 enrolled, amounting to $9,000; recreation, $1,000; advertising campaign, $5,000; miscellaneous, $3,000.

THE NEW YORK ASSOCIATION OF BIOLOGY TEACHERS

During the current year the New York Association of Biology Teachers has considerably expanded its activities. Started over thirty years ago in an organization meeting of twelve New York high-school teachers, it now numbers nearly six hundred. While most of its members are teachers from the forty-one senior and nearly seventy junior high schools, a considerable fraction represent university and research institutions, and an increasing number of its members work in institutions outside New York City. Its president for the current year is Mr. Paul B. Mann, chairman of the biology department at Evander Childs High School, and associate at the American Museum of Natural History.

Beginning in October, 1931, the association started the publication of a printed bulletin, *The Teaching Biologist,* under a newly appointed editorial committee. This is scheduled to appear in eight issues during the current academic year. So far, five issues have appeared, four 4-page and one 6-page. These contain abstracts of the addresses delivered before the regular monthly meetings, book reviews, brief notes on new demonstration methods, announcements, etc. Any one interested to obtain a sample copy should address Miss May-Eunice Emanuel, James Madison High School, Brooklyn, N. Y.

The association carries on a diversified series of activities. Its regular monthly evening meetings are usually attended by three to four hundred people. Working through special committees, a series of special field and institutional trips are carried out during the year. Other committees are working on equipment and pedagogy and new course syllabi. A committee of members serving as the official high school Hygiene Syllabus Committee has recently completed three new courses in hygiene, "Personal," "Home and Community" and "Personality Studies." The first two have been in print for two years; the third is now in press. Another syllabus committee has recently prepared a new syllabus for ninth-year biology which is being tried out widely in the city and state. Still another committee is working on an "advanced zoology" syllabus, and another on a revision of the "advanced biology" which is the present New York City tenth-year biology course. The new state syllabus in general biology was prepared by a committee, all the members of which are members of the New York Association.

MEMORIAL VOLUME FOR PROFESSOR BONSER

Friends and former students of the late Professor Frederick Gordon Bonser will be gratified to learn that a posthumous volume of his writings has been compiled by Mrs. Bonser and a committee of the Teachers College faculty, and will be published by the Bureau of Publications early in April under the title, "Life Needs and Education." This book is no mere collection of scattered articles, but a living expression of Professor Bonser's fundamental philosophy organized under four divisions: (1) the school as a means of enlarging life; (2) subject-matter that derives from life experiences; (3) curricula based upon life needs, and (4) teachers trained to interpret life experiences. In addition to the twenty-five professional articles classified under these heads the volume contains three examples of Dr. Bonser's more literary efforts, namely, "My Art Creed," "Meanings and Moods in Music" and "The Greatest Satisfactions." Professor W. H. Kilpatrick has written an introduction in appreciation and evaluation of Dr. Bonser "as man and educator." The volume will be beautifully bound in semi-flexible cloth with gold-stamped title and autograph. It will contain a full-page, frontispiece photograph of Professor Bonser, and is designed in every detail to make a fitting memorial for one of the most influential and best-loved educators of the present generation.

Copies of this book may be purchased at cost for two dollars each from the Bureau of Publications, Teachers College. It is hoped that those interested will forward their orders at once so that the committee in charge, consisting of the following members of the Teachers College faculty, may know how large an edition to have printed. Committee: Maurice A. Bigelow, Benjamin R. Andrews, Lois C. Mossman, Florence Stratemeyer, Cora M. Winchell, Helen Judy-Bond, Jean Broadhurst, Sara L. Patrick, Fred Strickler, Fannie W. Dunn and Mabel Carney.

ECONOMIES IN NEW YORK CITY COLLEGES

Mr. Mark Eisner, chairman of the Board of Higher Education in New York City, has appointed a committee to study possible economies in the operation of City College, Hunter College and Brooklyn College, the three institutions governed by the Board. The action was taken in recognition of the need of the city to keep expenses down in all departments and in preparation for a probable reduction in appropriations for higher education in next year's budget.

The research to be conducted by the committee, according to Mr. Eisner, will be, first, to determine how to keep expenses down to their present level, and, secondly, to determine whether the colleges might develop sources of revenue which would operate to reduce the annual budgetary requirements.

A limit may be imposed on the number of students entering these colleges next fall. The committee is to consider whether it would not be possible to reduce or at least to prevent an increase in the size of freshman classes. Admission to Brooklyn College would not be restricted as much as to the two others, because the Brooklyn institution is a new college, whose growth the board would not wish to hamper.

The committee will consider the practicability of charging students for text-books, and will examine the curricula of the three colleges in an effort to eliminate some of the courses.

In announcing the appointment of the committee Mr. Eisner pointed out the value of these colleges to the city:

The City of New York has been committed to the policy of the free higher education of its youth since the year 1847 and its policy in this regard has by now become fundamental in its civic program. These colleges have promoted the prestige of the city itself and their graduates grace the bench and bar, the teaching profession, as well as other professional and business walks of life. The return which the city has received in service from the graduates of these institutions exceeds to an immeasurable degree the pecuniary cost of maintaining them.

MODEL SCHOOL AT THE WORLD'S FAIR

The Chicago Board of Education is planning a model elementary-school building to be exhibited at the Century of Progress Exposition in 1933. According to a special correspondent of *The New York Times,* Chicago architects have asked for suggestions from twenty-nine leading school-building architects throughout the country and have incorporated many of their suggestions.

The most striking feature of the building will be the flexibility in the size of classrooms. The school authorities believe that the building will permit adequate experimentation to determine the most suitable size of classes for various forms of study. Rooms of five sizes will be available: the assembly hall, the double classroom, the classroom, the half classroom or double workroom, and the small workroom.

There will be eight small workrooms, each 11 by 16 feet, on the second floor of the building. These will be equipped for the use of from three to six pupils, so that from twenty-five to fifty pupils can be accommodated simultaneously. Some of these rooms will be fitted for art and construction projects and some for science, while others will be equipped with reference materials, blackboard and "round table" for group discussion. These rooms may be combined by twos into larger rooms, 16 by 22 feet, as every two rooms will be separated from each other only by a folding partition. These double workrooms will be of a size suitable for dramatics or other work requiring a separate room smaller than a classroom but larger than a small workroom.

Classrooms will be separated in pairs by folding partitions, so that two of these may be combined into one of double classroom size for larger audiences as well as for study-hall purposes or for individual work.

The plan of the building predicates diversified learning situations as contrasted with the traditional "platform teaching" of classes of equal size, and admits of flexibility of program. The large-group activities will release teachers for the direction of the small-group work, where one teacher can supervise simultaneous activities in at least four of the small workrooms. In the small workrooms the pupils' activities would be self-directed or of the "free-learning" type.

The building will be a sixth-grade elementary school, two stories high, without basement, of steel construction with either brick or stone exterior, and with a capacity for 742 pupils. It will be thoroughly equipped for such modern aids to teaching as the radio and sound films. Not only will the auditorium have talkie apparatus, but each classroom will have a plug at the rear, with a conduit underneath the floor to the front of the room for sound projection. The radio outlets in each room will have a central control in the principal's office. In the small rooms, also, there will be map racks, encyclopedia cases, globes and sinks.

The floors will be of linoleum, cases will be recessed and the furniture will be movable. Blackboards will be placed on the front and side walls, even on the panels of the folding partitions. A generous glass area has been allowed for light.

EDUCATIONAL NOTES AND NEWS

Dr. George Herbert Palmer, Alford professor of philosophy at Harvard University until he became emeritus professor in 1913, celebrated his ninetieth birthday on March 19.

Dr. Arthur O. Lovejoy, professor of philosophy at the Johns Hopkins University, has accepted the appointment as William James lecturer in philosophy at Harvard University for the first half of next year. In 1931 Dr. John Dewey was the first lecturer under this foundation, established under the large bequest for psychology of the late Edgar Pierce, formerly instructor in psychology.

HONORARY degrees were conferred on Chancellor Samuel Paul Capen, of the University of Buffalo, and on Dr. Edward Lee Thorndike, professor of education at Teachers College, Columbia University, at the one hundred and sixty-seventh convocation of the University of Chicago on the occasion of the dedication of the Graduate Education Building of the university. The degree of doctor of science was conferred on Professor Thorndike, "in recognition of the effective pioneer work which he has done in developing the new science of education and in disseminating and applying techniques of this science." Professor Frank N. Freeman made the presentation. He said: "Professor Thorndike has made notable contributions to psychology and to the educational applications of psychology, psychology of learning, to the development of exact measurement of educational products and to the use of statistical methods in educational research. As investigator, author and teacher, he has been a leading contributor to the science of education." Chancellor Capen received the degree of doctor of laws, "in recognition of the leadership which he has exercised in American higher education and of the conspicuous success of his administrative achievements." He was presented by Professor Henry C. Morrison as "pioneer in the scientific study of higher education, leader in our national councils, wise adviser in the practical administration of colleges and universities."

MR. ELIOT G. MEARS, director of the summer quarter at Stanford University, received the honorary degree of LL.D. from Grinnell College at the exercises held recently to inaugurate Dr. John S. Nolen as president of the college.

PROFESSOR PATRICK GEDDES, Montpellier, France, who has been president of the British Sociological Society, and Professor S. R. Steinmetz, of the University of Amsterdam, were unanimously elected honorary members of the American Sociological Society at the recent Washington meeting.

THE King of Italy has conferred upon Dean Homer Albers, of Boston University School of Law, the rank of knight of the Order of the Crown of Italy. The presentation was made by Commander Pio Margotti, Italian consul general in Boston. Last summer Dean Albers made an extended trip through Italy.

AT the recent meeting of the Harvard Teachers' Association, officers were elected as follows: William L. W. Field, head master of Milton Academy, *president,* to succeed Zenos E. Scott, superintendent of schools in Springfield; Professor John J. Mahoney, of Boston University, *vice-president;* Mr. Charles Swain Thomas, of the Harvard Graduate School of Education, *secretary-treasurer;* Dr. David T. Pottinger, Harvard University Press, *auditor,* and Mr. George F. Cherry, Derby Academy, *member of the executive committee.*

MRS. ADA L. SNELL, Mount Holyoke College, has been elected president of the New England Association of Teachers of English.

PROFESSOR JOHN A. JAMES, for the past 13 years assistant dean of the College of Agriculture of the University of Wisconsin, has been appointed dean. He will devote his entire time to the department of agricultural education in the capacity of full-time director. The position of assistant dean will be filled by Ira L. Baldwin, of the department of agricultural bacteriology at the university. Mr. Baldwin has been a member of the staff of the College of Agriculture and Agricultural Experiment Station since 1927.

DR. PRESTON W. SLOSSON, of the department of history in the University of Michigan, has been appointed 1932 Carnegie professor of history and has been granted a year's leave of absence, during which he will go abroad to teach at Bristol, Manchester and Glasgow Universities.

MR. JOHN J. BLAIR, during whose service with the North Carolina State Department of Education as supervisor of rural school construction nearly $100,000,000 was spent for the erection of buildings, has retired. Mr. Blair has done much for rural schools in North Carolina. More than 4,000 trucks transport 200,000 North Carolina children to and from school daily. The average length of the school term in 1909 was 92 days, as compared with 152 days at the present time. During his residence in Raleigh, Mr. Blair established an art gallery in one of the state buildings.

Dr. Johnson Brigham in May will complete thirty-four years as state librarian of Iowa, with headquarters in Des Moines.

Miss Lucetta Daniell will retire on January 1, 1933, as welfare directress of Teachers College, Columbia University, after forty-one years service as teacher and administrator. She has been granted leave of absence for the fall term.

Miss Katherine R. Kelsey, assistant principal at Abbot Academy, Andover, Massachusetts, and a member of the faculty for forty-four years, and Miss Nellie M. Mason, head of the science department, who has been on the school staff for forty years, have both resigned their positions.

Thomas McIntyre Cooley, for many years professor of law in the University of Michigan, chief justice of the Michigan Supreme Court, framer of the Interstate Commerce Commission and its first chairman and authority on constitutional law, is to be memorialized in a biography for which the university is now collecting material. A university committee under the chairmanship of Professor John S. Worley will be glad to correspond with any one having knowledge of letters, books, manuscripts or papers relating to Judge Cooley.

Dr. Albert Bushnell Hart, Eaton professor of the science of government, *emeritus*, at Harvard, and historian of the George Washington Bicentennial Commission, was the principal speaker at the recent celebration of Washington's birthday at Syracuse University.

Professor Lane Cooper, head of the department of comparative literature at Cornell University, will be the speaker at the ninety-ninth annual commencement exercises of Oberlin College on June 21.

Dr. W. H. Kilpatrick, of Teachers College, Columbia University, will be the principal speaker on Education Day at Bethany College on April 7. Public school officers and teachers of the area near Bethany College will be the guests of the college that day.

Professor E. Allison Peers, of the department of Spanish, of the University of Liverpool, will lecture at Harvard University on April 18 under the auspices of the Harvard University department of Romance languages and literatures.

Mr. Elliott D. Smith, professor of industrial engineering at the Sheffield Scientific School, Yale University, spoke on "Undergraduate Education in Business and Industry" at the annual "alumni day" exercises held on February 22.

Dr. Frederick Jackson Turner, historian, died at Pasadena, California, on March 14 at the age of seventy-one years. He was a research associate of the Huntington Library and professor of history emeritus of Harvard University. He was formerly professor of history at the University of Wisconsin and had been president of the American Historical Association.

Dr. Joseph Ragland Long, formerly dean of the Law School of Washington and Lee University, died on March 15 at the age of sixty-one years. He had been professor of law at the University of Colorado since 1923.

Dr. Stafford McLean, clinical professor of children's diseases at the College of Physicians and Surgeons at Columbia, died suddenly on March 18 at the age of forty-six years.

Dr. Frank H. Beede, who retired as superintendent of schools at New Haven, Connecticut, in June after having held the office for thirty years, died on March 15 in his seventy-fourth year. For two years, 1905–07, Dr. Beede lectured at Yale University on school organization and administration. He was president of the New England School Superintendents' Association in 1909, and of the Connecticut State Teachers' Association in 1907. He belonged to the Harvard Teachers' Association and the Massachusetts and Connecticut Schoolmasters' Clubs.

Dr. Louis Claude Purser, formerly vice-provost of Trinity College in Dublin, died on March 20. Dr. Purser was a former vice-president of the Royal Irish Academy and was the author of many classical works.

Dr. Dixon Ryan Fox, professor of history at

Columbia University and president of the New York Historical Society, spoke on "The Dignity of Local History" at the banquet which closed the program of the third annual History Conference at the University of Pittsburgh on March 19. Speeches by Professor A. S. Martin, of Pennsylvania State College; Dr. William H. Bristow, deputy superintendent, department of public instruction, Pennsylvania; Miss Charlotte Truby, of the Pittsburgh public schools, and Miss Irene Stewart, of Carnegie Library, on the subject of "Teaching State and Local History in Colleges, Secondary and Elementary Schools" were given at the morning session, with Dr. Ben Graham, superintendent of the Pittsburgh public schools, presiding. "Research in Regional and Local History" was the subject of talks made during the afternoon meeting, under the direction of Dr. W. F. Woodring, professor of history at Allegheny College, by Dr. Solon J. Buck, director of the Western Pennsylvania Historical Society, Mr. Nathan Shappee, department of history of Johnstown Junior College, and Mr. A. G. Field, research fellow of the Western Pennsylvania Historical Society. Dr. John W. Oliver, head of the history department, and C. Stanton Belfour, assistant director of the university extension division and of the summer session, were in charge of arrangements.

DR. WM. JOHN COOPER, U. S. Commissioner of Education, has called a National Conference on Home Economics to be held on May 16 at Minneapolis, in connection with the National Congress of Parents and Teachers. The following home economics interests have been invited to participate in the conference: The American Home Economics Association; Department of Supervisors and Teachers of Home Economics of the National Education Association; Federal Board for Vocational Education, and the Bureau of Home Economics, Extension Service, and Office of Experiment Stations of the U. S. Department of Agriculture. This conference is expected to concentrate on the contributions that home economics education makes to the well-being of home and family life, care and training of children, wise management of incomes and use of leisure time. Minneapolis school children will demonstrate at the national conference phases of home economics taught in their schools. Other interpretations of home economics education will be given by 4-H club leaders, home demonstration workers, home makers and parents.

DR. ALBERT A. GIESECKE, of Lima, Peru, formerly director general of public education in Peru, will this year supervise an American summer school at the University of San Marcos in Lima. The school has been arranged by the Institute of International Education. The Peruvian government and the Pan-American Union have cooperated in its establishment. The summer term is intended primarily for graduate students and teachers whose interest lies in South American history or culture. Field trips and excursions are being arranged for the study of the remains of early Inca civilization. The University of San Marcos, founded in 1551, is the oldest university in the western hemisphere.

THE name of the Mississippi Agricultural and Mechanical College has been changed to Mississippi State College, and the old name of the post office, also indicated, has been changed, effective on April 1, to State College, Mississippi.

THE International House of the University of Chicago will be opened on the first of September. The house has been placed in charge of a board of governors of twenty-five members, under the presidency of Mr. Charles S. Dewey.

UPON the expiration of six life trusts in the residuary estate, Columbia University will receive the residuary estate of Henry R. Seager, professor of political economy at Columbia, whose estate was appraised at $205,720 gross and $188,184 net. Professor Seager died in August, 1930, while on a tour of Russia. Professor Seager left the residue of his estate to the trustees of Columbia University, with instructions to pay the income to several relatives during their life. A son, Schuyler F. Seager, of Pasadena, California, is to receive the income from $58,654, which represents the value of one half the residue, besides a legacy of $50,000. Professor Seager's bequest to Columbia was made in memory of his father to establish a foundation to be known as the

"Schuyler Fiske Seager Endowment for the Advancement of Economics and Research."

THE Santamaria Foundation Technical School, the first unit in a $7,000,000 educational center made possible by the bequest of the late Federico Santamaria, has recently been opened in Valparaiso, Chile.

THE trustees of Howard University in Washington have ordered an investigation of its organization and operation. They have directed their chairman, General John H. Sherburne, of Boston, to name a committee of five trustees to select a disinterested person or agency to conduct the inquiry. No announcement of the reason was given, but it was reported to be a development of a movement begun about a year ago to unseat Dr. Mordecai Johnson, first Negro president of the institution. The movement was started after his opponents charged he made a speech praising certain Negro groups alleged to have communist tendencies. Oscar de Priest, Negro representative from Illinois, investigated and cleared the president. Those named on the committee of five included Mr. George W. Crawford, New Haven, Conn., and Dr. Sara W. Brown, Washington.

THE Board of Trustees of the University of Arkansas has ruled that faculty members can participate actively in state politics during the forthcoming campaign only under pain of dismissal. Participation in campaigns involving nothing more than county or municipal issues will be permitted. Former Governor Charles H. Brough, a special lecturer for the university, has resigned to enter the Senatorial race. Governor Parnell, chairman of the university trustees, is a candidate to succeed Senator Hattie Caraway. Dr. Brough has issued a statement in which he says: "The right to participate in politics, either as a candidate or as an elector, is an elemental right of every American citizen. For an alleged liberal university to dogmatically seek to nullify the constitutional rights of its faculty bespeaks official cowardice and intellectual corruption."

A BILL making it unlawful to inquire into the religion or religious affiliations of persons seeking employment as teachers or any official position in the public schools of New York State became law on March 17 with the formal approval of Governor Franklin D. Roosevelt. The Governor observed in a memorandum that the new law would be a reminder of the principle of religious freedom guaranteed under the Constitution. A similar bill failed last year. Passage of the bill by the Legislature this year was the direct result of agitation caused by the rejection of a teacher from Plattsburg who applied for a position in the schools of Harriman, Orange County, two years ago. It was alleged she was questioned about her religion, and when it was found she was a Roman Catholic she failed to obtain the position. The matter was taken to the Governor by a Harriman priest, and there was a hearing before Commissioner Frank P. Graves, of the Department of Education, which resulted in the school principal being removed.

A REPORT to the New York *Times*, under date of March 17, states that inability of Chicago's public school teachers to carry on longer without pay will force the public schools to close within a month, it was predicted by most of the 5,000 teachers who had responded on March 17 in a financial survey of the city's 14,000 teachers, which is being made by the Principals' Club. Since last April school board employees have been paid for only two and a half months' work. All the replies to the questionnaire revealed lowered standards of living, poorer food, no new clothes, little or no amusement, neglect of health through inability to pay for medical and dental service and the curtailment or elimination of magazine and book purchases. Loan sharks, bank failures and lapsed insurance policies figured prominently in a large percentage of the reports. Many reported loss of homes imminent; not a few had been threatened with eviction. One reported the death of a child for want of medical attention, which could not be provided in his straitened circumstances.

THE Sewickley Township School District, of Herminie, the Derry Township Schools, the Unity Township Public Schools, of Latrobe, and the Mt. Pleasant Borough School District, Pennsylvania, have adopted group life insurance. Under all four policies 226 lives are protected for a total amount of $235,500, the individuals being insured in amounts ranging from $1,000 to $2,500, the amount being determined by the rank or position held. The Prudential Insurance Company of America issued the policies, which are of the contributory type, the individual paying a part of the premium and the institution assuming the remainder of the expense.

DISCUSSION

THE FALLACY OF ABILITY GROUPING

THE principle of grouping pupils into sections according to their supposed ability was for some time pretty generally accepted. It looked plausible. If we were to adapt our courses of study and our methods of teaching to the widely variant learning powers of the pupils, in accordance with the recently recognized need for adjustment to individual differences, what better procedure could be found than to separate the quick from the slow, with the assistance of the newly developed testing instruments? After careful trial of such grouping, I abandoned it in my own school five or six years ago. Now there seems to be a growing tendency toward heterogeneous groups. The recent pronouncement of Dr. Reynolds, of the Horace Mann School, is only one of the latest and most authoritative statements.

I am, I hope, open-minded on the subject, but for the present I feel that the weight of evidence is against homogeneous grouping. In this paper I am considering the junior high school, the level with which I am most familiar. In that division it seems to me that the system of ability grouping breaks down on five counts, and these I shall attempt to analyze in this paper. (1) The groups can not, except in a very large school, be organized with statistical validity. (2) Administrative difficulties still further interfere with effective grouping. (3) The bases of classification are not satisfactory. (4) Teaching procedures can be better adapted to individual needs by a different method. (5) Whatever advantages homogeneous grouping may have for the learner are more than counterbalanced by inevitable losses.

(1) STATISTICAL INVALIDITY

The generally accepted grouping is into three categories of ability, by the normal curve of distribution. Though a large school may have many more than three sections, it is doubtful if there would be more than three separate courses of study or methods of instruction. Indeed, the practice of three-division grouping is indicated by the common use of the expression "x, y, and z groups." Now, the shape of the normal curve is not such as to justify this grouping. We can hardly make a significant point of division between the middle group and the superior group, or between the middle group and the inferior group, at a statistical distance from the midpoint of less than one standard deviation. But if we lay off one sigma from the median in each direction, we find that 68+ per cent. of the cases fall into the middle section and 16 – per cent. in each of the others. Hence, to follow a threefold grouping with statistical accuracy, we should need to have at least six groups: one x group, four y groups, and one z group.

Let us see how this would work out as applied to the enrolment on a given grade level. We shall assume a school having semi-annual promotions, and hence six half grades. It is often the case that the mid-year class is not more than half the size of the next half grade. In that case, a mid-year half grade would constitute one ninth of the whole school. If that grade is to be divided into six sections of, say, 30 pupils each, it would imply a school with a total enrolment of 1,620. Similarly, even if all half grades are equal, we should need a school of over 1,000 to apply a proper system of distribution.

(2) ADMINISTRATIVE DIFFICULTIES

Even if we accept a practicably workable approximation to the statistical ideal, we face the administrative problem of proper classification of the individual pupil. Wherever elective subjects are offered, any sectioning will be affected by that factor as well. If in a given half grade there is, for example, one section in Latin, it is in practice almost necessary that all pupils taking that elective be in one section in their required subjects. There are certain mitigations of that necessity. Two or more electives may be scheduled for the same period, and the other classes will then retain such flexibility as to permit organization on an ability basis. This device, however, is necessarily limited.

Again, the very choice of elective subjects has a large selective effect. Thus, there is a tendency for Latin pupils to be of higher ability, measured by tests in abstract learning, than those who elect industrial subjects. Such selection, however, is not a deliberate one, nor equivalent to a deliberate one.

The administrative problem is further complicated by the fact that partial failures, that is, promotion in certain subjects while the pupil must repeat certain others, throw the sectioning machinery all out of gear. I have examined the programs of a group of ninth grade pupils, who chose among a considerable number of electives, and among whom the factor of partial promotion has had an opportunity to work since the seventh grade. The scrutiny showed that among the pupils of a given home room, not more than forty in number, we may expect to find anywhere from six to ten different combinations of courses.

(3) Unsatisfactory criteria

We are coming to doubt the infallibility of general intelligence tests. The best of them have a high degree of probable error. Yet they are probably sufficiently reliable for purposes of grouping if we concede that what they measure is the proper basis for such grouping. Most of the tests that we use for determining so-called general intelligence emphasize verbal memory and modes of thinking, abstract reasoning, acquired information and experience. They do not adequately measure social and mechanical intelligence, nor do they tell us anything of the pupil's habits and volitional powers. It may be objected that a wide battery of tests, plus teachers' judgments, expressed in marks or otherwise, and information as to achievements, chronological and physiological age, home environment, and other aspects, will give a sufficient basis for classification. This is probably theoretically true, but in practice the gathering and evaluation of such data are almost impossible as grounds of a confident classification.

(4) Inadequate Curriculum Adjustments

If an administrator is satisfied, however, that in spite of all these difficulties, he has obtained a satisfactory classification by ability, the question still remains what he is to do about it. Such a grouping is merely a gesture unless the course of study is so modified as to provide for the differences thus recognized. There must be at least three different choices and organizations of subject-matter. That for the lowest group must consist of a minimum of material, qualitatively within the comprehension of any normal child in the grade, and quantitatively such that any normal child can accomplish it within the semester or other time unit in use. A larger amount of material of a higher degree of difficulty must be provided for the middle group, and the superior group must have material sufficient to provide for the profitable expenditure of the highest degree of ability to be found in the group. Such a trilogy of courses of study I have yet to find. The alternative provision for heterogeneous groups presents no more difficulties and has certain advantages. In each subject let there be a core of units which shall be required of all and the passing of which shall be requisite for promotion. To this core should be added supplementary units to the extent to which individual pupils can handle them. These must be chosen so as to have genuine worth in themselves, not merely repetitions of the same sort of thing contained in the core. They must have their own specific objectives, in additional skills, informations, or habits beyond the primary requirements. This organization of the material provides an opportunity for those who would be classified as slow to exceed expectations if they can, a difficult matter under the other system.

(5) Positive Disadvantages of Homogeneous Grouping

The strongest reasons, it seems to me, for rejecting ability grouping are social and ethical. I do not mean that I have any sympathy with those who talk of the branding effect and the undemocratic character of grouping. Such objections are simply silly. Nevertheless, the unnatural division is vicious. It sets up a situation not to be found in the world outside of school. Later, a youth must compete, not against those of his own ability group, but against an unselected population. It is unfair to the slow pupil to give him the experience of comparative success which can not be continued after school days are over. On the other hand, success with the minimum core of units among an unselected group, many of whom will surpass him, prepares him to do self respecting work within his own range of abilities. To this slow pupil, too, the quicker thinking of his comrades will be a stimulation as often as a discouragement. To the abler pupils is offered the opportunity to help others, and the experience of respecting the conscientious and thorough, if unspectacular, work of the slower.

All these desirable outcomes, like any other educational results, depend ultimately upon the experience, skill, sympathy and good sense of the teacher. None but a very good teacher can be very successful with dull pupils under any system of organization; likewise, the brighter pupils will do pretty well with any kind of teacher, or perhaps with none at all. But for the reasons outlined above, I should far rather have a fairly good teacher work with unselected groups, with a properly built course of study, than undertake the teaching of segregated groups with even the best of teachers.

Laurence B. Brink
Monticello Junior High School,
Cleveland Heights, Ohio

DEMOCRACY IN EDUCATION?

Democracy is commonly maintained as the ideal towards which all American government should progress, and the schools are the springs from which the currents of democratic idealism are expected to flow. Our educational philosophy says that out of the schools must flow the democracy of the future.

It is generally assumed that the ideals and habits of thought and action necessary for good democratic government in a republic are common to all public-school teachers. Much discussion, therefore, impinges on the questions: By what methods may the true democratic spirit be imparted to pupils? How may teachers give to young America those characteristics which are essential to progressive and enlightened self-government? Discussion which aims to answer these questions attempts (I take the liberty of altering an ancient phrase) to pull a cart without a horse. For one of the vital assumptions of such discussion is false and even absurd. The average American teacher, under present conditions, is not and can not be competent in rudimentary self-government, much less understand and interpret the complexities of city government and its politics.

A useful citizen and voter in our republic needs must have a reasonably critical mind, a capacity for independent judgment and the courage and force of character to express that judgment and, if need be, to express it repeatedly.

Why is the average American teacher incapable of and uninterested in democracy pure or diluted? The reasons stare us in the face. Perhaps that is why they are rarely noticed.

Reason number one inheres in almost every public educational system. The teacher works in an absolutism of which the superintendent is the monarch, the board of education the privy council and the principals and supervisors the aspiring nobility. Like the monarchies of history, this modern example of them is sometimes controlled by the monarch, sometimes by the privy council and infrequently by the aspiring nobility. Some of the monarchs are benevolent, some are despotic, but they are all none the less absolute. The system makes them that.

The unbecoming obsequiousness and sycophancy which this absolutism often engenders in the teachers subjected to it develop the contrary of an ideal citizen of a republic. In concerns of finance, building, provision and distribution of supplies none will deny the need for positive single-minded control. The destructive absolutism is that which dictates minutiae of educational policy, demands control over far-removed details, and commands how a teacher should act in circumstances where the teacher has the undeniable right to the utmost liberty.

Some will say, in refutation, that in teachers' meetings and gatherings of teachers' associations teachers are in practice given enough scope for the exercise of independent judgment and the parliamentary development of policies. My observations make such a conclusion seem ironically absurd. In how many teachers' meetings are any more important matters presented for the opinion of the meeting than how to collect money for the Junior Red Cross or what to do about study hall desks stuffed with waste paper? Or how often is a vote taken for the avowed purpose of determining a course of action only to be secretly disregarded and forgotten as soon as the meeting disperses? But I need not elaborate too poignantly what all participants in such meetings know well.

So in a teachers' meeting the individual simply lapses into the attitude of a mildly interested spectator, enduring what she abhors because somebody in authority demands it. The teacher sits silent and unresponsive because she knows that sincere disagreement and honest criticism produce only antagonism from the chairman (too often a chairwoman). Thus it happens that older members of a faculty will advise entirely new members: "Never criticize or try to change anything. You'll only get yourself into trouble." And if the new teacher is still courageous and proposes reform, she will hear from the oldsters: "You will get over that. It is fine to talk like that. We did too when we first came. After a year or two you'll learn to keep still." Then the new teacher, full of college-fed idealism, begins to see that democracy has yet to win its way in the schools.

Reason number two is that teachers rarely have a self-governing organization of their own. In theory the teachers association is self-governing, but in fact (at least in New York State) it is the facile tool of the educational administrators. Superintendents often allow their absolutism to assert itself outside of its proper domain; accordingly teachers feel under that same restraint in meetings of their own association as they feel in teachers' meetings. The pitiful result is best illustrated by a meeting which I attended last year.

More than two hundred teachers had convened for the monthly meeting of their association. They represented nearly nine hundred teachers in the schools of the city in which they met. One thought was in the minds of most of these teachers: Somehow to ask the board of education concerning the security of their positions, which recent events had caused them to question. After trivial, routine business had taken up most of the time, the motion was made and quickly seconded to have a committee of teachers wait upon the superintendent to ask what every one wanted anxiously to know. A vote was taken and a count of hands showed an unquestioned majority in favor of the motion. Immediately three members of what I have called the "nobility" arose to oppose the motion on the ground that teachers had no right to ask about their security. These objectors remembered that the motion had not been discussed, so on the basis of its being out of order it was revoked. The same motion was remade. The vote, which followed another short discussion, was this time clearly against the motion, but many did not vote at all. As it was then late and their efforts had been crowned with success, the three members of the "nobility" left. But once more the same motion in slightly altered form was put before the house. This time it once again passed with an overwhelming majority! What a commentary on our capacity for democracy that was! The same motion had been passed, rejected and finally overwhelmingly passed by the same meeting of mature teachers.

Once I would have considered such an example as the above as an extreme case. But experience has taught me differently. Only a few months later substantially the same occurrence was repeated. Closer observation of other systems causes me to suspect that a similar inability to use the democratic method effectively is wide-spread.

My third reason to explain why teachers are very deficient in democratic abilities is that they are almost never urged to take any part in municipal political life. They are, on the contrary, discouraged from participating in it. If public-school teachers attempt to take a conscientious part in municipal political affairs after their school work is over, they are looked upon with deep suspicion and soon either recalled from such reprehensible wanderings from the straight and narrow way or quickly ejected from the system as "poor teachers."

To those who have had any varied experience in the public schools the truth of what I have said needs no further elucidation. There are, of course, schools and systems where the opposite conditions obtain, but I doubt if they make more than a small minority of the total. Many teachers in both private and public schools wonder among themselves why it is that administrators take the greatest pains to procure the services of well-trained, competent teachers of unquestioned good character only to subject them to the meanest absolutism after they have been employed. It is as if a bank were to spend six months finding an honest, capable teller and then, after employing one, to detail secret police to watch over him.

My major purpose is to illuminate the true situation, but I shall briefly conclude by indicating where I think the blame lies. The greatest culpability seems to rest upon the public-school system, as ordinarily organized. Our educational systems usually put all final authority in the hands of principals, superintendents or boards of education, as the case may be, and make no provision for allowing the teachers, who naturally know most about class-room problems, to share in shaping educational policy.

Next to the systems, the superintendents appear to be most at fault. The superintendents compel subservience and obedience with all the harshness of an absolute monarch. Frequently they profess to be friendly to the interests of their teachers; yet in more than one case they protect themselves from criticism at the expense of those beneath them.

And last of all the teachers are culpable. Often when they are called upon to express an opinion they see threats where there are none, remain silent when they are free and ought to speak, and fail generally to exercise the freedom and rights which they do possess.

A change for the better will not come until the faults, wherever they lie, are recognized and corrected. This much is patently clear. Schools will never inoculate a living spirit of democracy in their pupils until it has been developed in the hearts and minds of their teachers.

E. L. B. Curtis

QUOTATIONS

THE EDGAR PIERCE BEQUEST

The report of a special committee of overseers on the Edgar Pierce bequest, which is appended to the latest of President Lowell's annual reports, is a noteworthy document. Signed by Judge Learned Hand, '93, Elihu Root, Jr., LL.B. '06, and Walter S. Gifford, '05, and manifestly prepared with care, its conclusions will be of permanent interest to benefactors of the university as well as to its officers of administration and the members of the governing boards for whom it was prepared.

The discussion about the Pierce bequest arose out of a complaint made by the department of philosophy and psychology that the income of the bequest was not being used in accordance with the wishes of the donor. Edgar Pierce, '92, bequeathed the residue of his estate, amounting to nearly $800,000, "for the uses and purposes" of the department, and requested in an accompanying letter that the income be used for additional instruction and for the development of the psychological laboratory. In fact, some $10,000 were used last year for salaries payable on account of existing instruction. The corporation did not divert to other uses any of the usual appropriation from its unrestricted income for salaries in the department, but it did not increase that appropriation as much as it presumably would have increased it if this bequest had not become available. The issue was, whether or not the entire income from the Pierce bequest should have been used for additional instruction or for the psychological laboratory, as the donor requested.

The opinion of the overseers' committee confirms the action of the corporation. This case will consequently stand as a precedent in support of a wider discretion in the administration of such gifts by the corporation than some department heads and possibly some benefactors of the university have supposed to exist. The discretionary authority, now recognized as vested in the corporation, makes for greater freedom in the appropriation of the unrestricted income of the university and confirms the power of the corporation to equalize the financial resources of different departments; but it may diminish the incentive for department heads to secure new funds for their departmental activities. It points towards a further separation between the functions of instruction and of administration. In an age of growing specialization, this result may be desirable, but the fact that ambitious and energetic department heads contested the issue is a gratifying symptom of academic vitality.

Future benefactors of the university can, of course, insure strict compliance with their wishes, if acceptable to the university, by writing such conditions into their wills or deeds of gift, instead of stating them in separate letters, as in the case of the Pierce bequest. But if it is desirable that the corporation should have the wide discretion recognized as proper by the overseers' committee, benefactors should be encouraged to follow the practice adopted by Edgar Pierce. To this end, something more needs to be said than the overseers' committee, which dealt primarily with the question of legal power, deemed it necessary to say. President Lowell's comment on the committee's report makes it clear that the corporation will endeavor to maintain a proper balance between the resources of the different departments. It may fairly be inferred from his comment that the corporation will also endeavor to secure for a particular department a reasonable advantage from the bounty of its benefactors.—*The Harvard Bulletin.*

THE CHILDREN'S BUREAU

BEHIND the cloak of economy the administration is trying to cripple another government bureau of which it disapproves. First came the Federal Trade Commission. Now it is the Children's Bureau.

The Senate Appropriations Committee has eliminated more than one fourth of the budget upon which this bureau has been operating and proposes that in the coming fiscal year its activities be curtailed to come within a total appropriation of $295,500. The chairman of this committee is Senator Wesley Jones, who has led the administration's persistent campaign to have the Children's Bureau consolidated with the Public Health Service and thus abolished.

The Children's Bureau and the Trade Commission are among the few departments of government to be cut so drastically.

It is hard to discover what service of the Children's Bureau has incurred administration disapproval. The President's Emergency Committee on Unemployment turned to the bureau last July as the one source from which it could obtain statistics on poor relief and other social projects.

Last year the Department of Justice also turned to the Children's Bureau for aid. It needed an adequate study of juvenile delinquency, and it turned to the bureau best equipped to do this work. The Children's Bureau is doing the job. In addition it is carrying out its general work, which concerns maternal mortality, child health studies, the study of state and local public welfare administration, mothers' pension work, accidents to children, statistics as to accidents of minors and many other matters.

This attempted destruction of the Children's Bureau should meet determined opposition. Its cause is the cause of every home in America.—*The New York World-Telegram.*

SPECIAL CORRESPONDENCE

THE INTER-AMERICAN FEDERATION OF EDUCATION

WHY do individuals and nations with normal development naturally seek wider and wider contacts? And why, in disillusion and disappointment, do they repeatedly turn in upon themselves and shun these very contacts to which they aspire in moments of expansion? Social vision through education in the social sciences will give us the answer to these questions. Until there is, therefore, a far wider spread of social information about human relations and reactions, we must expect setbacks in our international programs of mutual understanding and accords.

We have blundered greatly through lack of social understanding in our recent international efforts for friendly accord. Seldom have international meetings been inspired by greater national selfishness. Progressive internationalism, however, is based upon nationalistic concepts. Nationalism and internationalism are only apparently mutually exclusive or self-contradictory. Programs of world betterment may, therefore, safely begin at home or within more restricted contiguous and regional areas. Frankly, wisdom counsels regional programs for the present in most of our interrelated political economic and social work. It is in this belief that an Inter-American Federation of Education has been proposed and is being organized.

National cooperating committees from seventeen of the twenty-one republics of the western hemisphere are helping to organize this federation. Adherence of the remaining four countries has been promised. The members of these committees are well-known educators and represent progressive education associations in their countries. The ministers of education have shown naturally a keen interest in the federation. They constitute an ex-officio advisory council to assist the organization committee. The latter is made up of one person from each of the following countries—Uruguay, Brazil, Venezuela, Guatemala, Mexico, the Dominican Republic and the United States. Committee headquarters are in Washington at the National Education Association, which proposed the federation and sponsors its present activities. The United States committee consists of the executive committee of the National Education Association, the director general of the Pan-American Union, the commissioner of education of the United States, the commissioner of education of Porto Rico and the chairman of the organization committee of the federation.

The growth of the Inter-American Federation of Education will be slow if it remains true to its present purposes. It believes that dependable Inter-American accord can only come from a cordial continental popular desire for Inter-American understanding.. The latter is impossible until through education there can be established in these twenty-one democracies permanent bases for friendly social action. Fifty years of fairly fruitless efforts for Pan-American accord should convince us of the futility of methods to establish effective Inter-American agreements, many of which are social, by governmental agencies, acting separately or cooperatively through governmental conferences. Successful cooperation among these republics demands that there first be prepared ground for common action; otherwise, resolutions proceeding from conferences will continue meaningless and without ratification.

Inter-American accord must wait upon the building of a real public opinion; and the latter upon the education of our peoples by programs and methods that are continental in aim and purpose. Expanding and deepening opportunities for education will lessen illiteracy, improve the franchise and strengthen the sense of need among all Inter-American nations for friendly cooperation; in the understanding that mutual advantages are individual advantages. Continental political agreements, even based on economic interdependence, can not be assured of any great measure of permanence unless they rest upon a social urge or need coming from a well-informed public opinion.

Another reason for the slow growth of the Inter-American Federation idea or project lies in the fact that few Latin-American countries have one outstanding, nationally representative, educational association. Many of these countries will have several similar associations. In time these associations may merge into a great organization that will represent and speak for the teachers, one for each country, as may truly be said of the National Education Association of the United States. The Inter-American Federation was conceived in the hope that some time it may become a federation of these education associations. And it has already aided the development of the one national education association idea in the Latin-American countries. A former minister of Ecuador among others, for example, recommended to his country the formation of a national education association to cooperate with the federation. The Brazilian Education Association, encouraged by the federation proposal, has greatly expanded its work. Last month it held in Rio de Janeiro its fourth national education conference. The first, as I understand, was the immediate fruit of the federation proposal.

The first preliminary conference of the Inter-American Federation of Education was held in Atlanta, Georgia, in the summer of 1929 during the annual meeting of the National Education Association of the United States. Ten countries were represented at the conference. A purely educational program was offered, and solely with the federation purpose in mind. The conference considered only helpful ways and means for promoting in these countries character and vocational training, without which the practical understanding of Inter-American fellowship and friendly accord is impossible. A second preliminary conference, continuing more or less the set-up and discussion of the Atlanta conference, will be held in Panama, December 23 to 31, 1932.

The Panaman conference will be organized and held under the auspices of the secretary of education of that country, Dr. Jeptha Duncan, in cooperation with the Panaman national association of teachers which represents the Republic of Panama in the Inter-American Federation of Education. A committee from the association will have active charge, with the minister of education, of the organization of the Panaman conference. Among the members of this committee are: Carlos Sucre C., president of the association; Max Arosemena, inspector general of public instruction; J. D. Crespo, F. R. Cespedes, Alfonso Tejeiro, Otilia Arosemena and Esther N. de Calvo, all outstanding educators of Panama and well known in the Latin-American countries.

The Panaman conference will reemphasize the two major topics of the first preliminary or organization conference of the Federation which was held at Atlanta, U. S. A., in the summer of 1929. In the discussion of these topics, elementary vocational and character training, the Inter-American Federation hopes to aid in the development of a practical popular understanding of the need for Inter-American cooperation in all matters of concern in the daily living of the peoples of the Inter-American republics.

GLEN LEVIN SWIGGETT,
Chairman of the Organization Committee.

AN EXAMINATION INTO THE SPEECH HABITS OF FRESHMEN

THE division of public speaking[1] in the Pennsylvania State College has undertaken, this year, an experiment which we hope will lead, over a period of years, to some conclusions of worth, and which, more immediately, we know is making our work more useful to the students of the college. We have felt that to examine students at entrance for their physical defects and to omit any examination of their speech habits was not consistent. Accordingly, through the cooperation of the department of hygiene, we undertook this September just past the somewhat staggering task of giving a speech test to each of nearly 1,200 freshmen. We are now engaged in studying and tabulating the results of that test, and while conclusions are neither final nor complete, and we are not stating our findings categorically, we have been led to feel that teachers of language might find interesting food for thought in the tentative conclusions which we have thus far reached.

We set ourselves, through the medium of this test, to discover as accurately as possible, the following information about the entering freshman: (1) The amount and kind of his previous speech training; (2) the level of his enunciatory accuracy and skill; (3) the correctness of his pronunciation; (4) the general quality and character of his voice; (5) special disorders or defects of his speech or voice. Because of the fact that only two minutes of the time allowed for his physical examination could be given us, the securing of the desired information had to depend on the oral reading by the student of a predetermined body of material. The examiners had to be familiar with this material and to agree upon the desired standard of its rendering. They were also compelled to attend very closely to all utterances of the student.

Test cards were prepared on which were printed twenty-seven sentences, each of which contained a speech sound to be tested for, with each sound at least twice repeated in each sentence. While not remarkable for their thought content, these sentences were grammatically sound and "made sense." Examiners were provided with printed key cards, on which were indicated the sounds each sentence was aimed to test, as well as the symbols the examiners were to use in indicating their diagnosis and grading of the students examined. Thus, there were four qualities of voice to be watched for, *viz.*, Defective, Unpleasant, Pleasant and Superior, denoted by the symbols D, 0, 1, 2, respectively. Rate was, by a similar loose and somewhat arbitrary classification, to be observed under the headings, Normal, Abnormally Fast and Ab-

[1] It should be said that this test is the project of the Division of Public Speaking as a group, and not the work of one individual. After the members had decided through long consultation and, naturally, considerable argument, what were to be the objectives of the test, and precisely what data were desired, the actual compilation of the cards and blanks was made by Mr. Herbert Koepp-Baker, Speech Clinician of the Division. He has furnished the statistical data of this report. Besides Mr. Baker, the examiners for the test were Mrs. Calista B. Baker, Messrs Joseph F. O'Brien, and Clayton H. Schug, Instructors in Public Speaking, and Professor John H. Frizzell, in charge of the Division.

normally Slow (N, F, S). Pronunciation and enunciation were to be graded, Poor, Fair, Good or Excellent, denoted by 0, 1, 2 or 3, while under the heading of Defects and Disorders were to be noted, Lisping, Stuttering, Foreignism and Speech Fear, with a symbol corresponding to each.

The procedure of the examination was as follows: As each student came to the examiner, he presented a blank form, previously handed him, and by him previously filled in. The upper half of the blank showed his name, home, age, paternal occupation and parental extraction, the kind and amount of his previous speech training, and any suggestions he cared to make as to his need for speech improvement. The lower half of the blank, which was left with the examiner for filing, contained spaces for indicating the grading and diagnosis of the student under the heads noted above.

Students were, singly, handed the test card, and asked to read aloud and in their natural manner the sentences printed thereon. By means of his key card, the examiner followed each sentence as it was read, and indicated on the student's blank, by a check under the proper heading, the number of defective sounds or mispronounced words. Also, by the appropriate symbol, he indicated the quality of the subject's voice and his rate of speaking. Further, he listened carefully during the reading for any specific defects or disorders sufficient to make the subject's speech abnormally conspicuous to his auditors, and indicated the nature of such defects, by means of the proper symbol on the student's blank. The blanks of all students found to have defects of sufficient seriousness were marked for immediate attention and separately filed, while such students were urged to report at once or at earliest convenience to the speech clinic, for further examination, diagnosis and treatment. Students with lesser defects or with easily remediable speech faults were given suggestions for improvement, or urged to report later to the clinic. Five examiners were used, generally in pairs, and were on duty eight hours a day during the five days of Freshman Week. Two hundred and one women students were examined, and 983 men students, a total of 1,184.

What of the results? Incomplete as our study is thus far, we have found some matters on which the examiners agree, and which are possibly of wider interest.

(1) The ability to read aloud pleasantly, not to say with intelligence, was so rare as to be almost negligible. In a group of students selected as these were almost entirely from the upper two fifths of their high-school classes, it would seem that we have here a condition worth further study. Is such a condition but the natural outcome of attempting to teach children to read by the modern "silent" method, wherein they do not "read" but merely recognize printed symbols? As yet, we do not know; we merely raise the query.

(2) Enunciation was found to be only fair, mainly, we think, because of carelessness or indifference on the students' part, rather than from failure on the part of their English teachers to insist on enunciatory accuracy. Many pupils who would, from home training or teacher inspiration, articulate precisely are kept from it by fear of companion ridicule, just as throughout America accuracy of enunciation is by many regarded as an affectation. On the other hand, are not some teachers of language so over-precise in their articulation and in their demands on their pupils as to render imitation absurd? Or again, are not many teachers in other than linguistic subjects all too careless in requiring of pupils a high standard of enunciation? Again, we only ask.

(3) Pronunciation was, for the most part, surprisingly grotesque. This may be due to a number of causes: careless reading, *i.e.,* hasty but inaccurate recognition of a printed symbol; limited vocabulary and limited reading; unfamiliarity with the dictionary or with correct auditory models—all interdependent and interrelated. Again we refrain from specific assertion.

(4) Just how far the faults of poor speech and voice habits are due to a lack of the right sort of speech training in the grade and secondary schools, we are far from ready to say. We feel, however, that there is a very vital connection into which we propose further inquiry. We were, let it be said, both surprised and gratified at the number of students who had had some speech training.

(5) While our examination is entirely fragmentary in its findings along many lines, we feel that in the field of the discovery of more or

less serious defects and disorders, it has been entirely worth while. We have found twenty-eight students who are in need of immediate corrective treatment to get them into proper adjustment both as to speech and as to view-point. We have these students undergoing clinical treatment now, at the beginning of their college career. We have found nearly sixty others whose need for help is not so immediate, but who will, as rapidly as possible, be given such help as is needed. We find that slightly less than 8 per cent. of the entire group show some appreciable deviation from the normal, defects amounting to slightly less than 5 per cent., serious disorders to a trifle more than 2½ per cent. No serious disorders were found among the women students examined, while almost 3 per cent. of the male students showed marked disorders. Defects (less serious but appreciable) were about equally distributed between the sexes, the women students showing 4.47 per cent., the men students, 4.88 per cent.

(6) Finally, we feel that we have put into the minds of nearly 1,200 freshmen, however briefly, a consciousness of their own speech and made them feel its importance. Moreover, we have made a start upon the gathering of a considerable body of data which, through study over a period of years, should yield conclusions of import in the field of speech.

JOHN H. FRIZZELL

REPORTS

THE AMERICAN ASSOCIATION OF UNIVERSITY PROFESSORS

A PRELIMINARY statement of the program of the American Association of University Professors for its study of college and university teaching has been given by Professor H. W. Tyler, general secretary, who kindly permits publication in SCHOOL AND SOCIETY in advance of printing in the *Bulletin* of the association.

The procedure calls for visits to numerous institutions to be made by Professor H. L. Dodge, of the University of Oklahoma, field director of the study, or by members of the association's committee or members of local chapters commissioned for the purpose. Visits are to be arranged in advance with officers of local chapters.

Two objects are specified for these visits in Dr. Tyler's statement:

(1) To obtain all available material bearing on teaching practices in the institution.

(2) To enlist the interest of the members of the chapters in discussing general problems covered by the study with special reference to specific problems in their particular institution.

It is requested that "material and reports should be sent to the field director, Dr. H. L. Dodge, Norman, Oklahoma, as promptly as possible."

Twelve questions are set forth as covering the program of the association's study. They are as follows:

(1) What are the effective means for assisting the teacher in service?

(a) A definite understanding of what is expected of him.

(b) Visits to classes of younger teachers by experienced members of the department.

(c) Visits by the younger men to classes in the same department or other departments taught by successful teachers.

(d) Conferences among members of the staff.

(2) How can methods used in the selection and enlistment of teachers be improved?

(3) How can recognition of good teaching be increased?

(a) Placing excellence in teaching on at least as high a footing as successful research as a basis for promotion in rank and salary.

(b) Making the rewards for good teaching such that one need not be induced to become an administrator to secure advancement.

(c) Special salary provisions for superior teaching.

(4) Under what conditions, if any, can student and alumni rating of teachers be successfully employed?

(a) To improve teaching?

(b) To determine teaching success with a view to its reward by advancement in rank and salary?

(5) What is the effect upon teaching of activities such as the following:

(a) Committee work within the institution. Extension and correspondence work.

(b) Unremunerative work closely related to his field of scholarship, such as editorial work.

(c) Remunerative outside employment, such as serving as consultants for industries.

(6) Is there evidence that courses in education contribute to the making of a better college teacher?

(a) As a part of general college training.

(b) As a requirement for candidates for the doctor's degree.

(7) How much emphasis should be placed on background and general culture in the training of college teachers?

(8) How important is it that college teachers know something about the major problems of higher education? How can such knowledge be obtained?

(a) By teachers in service?

(b) During the period of preparation for teaching?

(9) What has been the effect of the comprehensive examination on teaching? Of the external examiner?

(10) Can new type tests be used to improve teaching?

(a) In the individual course.

(b) To determine the relative efficiency of teachers.

(11) How far is the gain derived from meeting students in small sections worth the cost? Is sectioning on the basis of ability worth while and practicable?

(12) What value attaches to such administrative practices as the following?

(a) Standing faculty committee on the improvement of teaching.

(b) Interdepartmental conferences for discussion of college teaching.

(c) Committee on educational research to foster cooperation between the department, college, or school of education and other departments, colleges, and schools on the campus.

(d) Research projects in the field of college teaching carried on independently by faculty members or groups of faculty members.

(e) Appointment of some official whose special position is to promote effective teaching.

(f) Visiting and exchange professors appointed because of their success as teachers rather than as research workers.

SOCIETIES AND MEETINGS

SCHOOLMEN'S WEEK AT THE UNIVERSITY OF PENNSYLVANIA

APPROXIMATELY 7,500 persons, of whom 4,010 were individually registered, attended the nineteenth annual meeting at the University of Pennsylvania, from March 9 to 12 of Schoolmen's Week, held jointly with the Southeastern Convention District of the Pennsylvania State Education Association. It was distinctly the largest attendance in the history of this joint educational convention.

Some forty topics relating to education in schools and colleges were presented at about the same number of general and sectional sessions, round tables and demonstrations spread over four days and evenings.

The programs on Conferences of Teachers in the University and Secondary Schools were: Art, commercial studies, English, geography, Greek and Latin, history, home economics, industrial education, modern languages, music, science, physical education, mathematics and social studies.

Among the speakers were: William H. Bristow, deputy superintendent, Department of Public Instruction, Harrisburg; Edwin C. Broome, superintendent, Philadelphia; John K. Norton, Teachers College, Columbia University; H. B. Chapman, Bureau of Research, Baltimore; Lightner Witmer, University of Pennsylvania; V. T. Thayer, Ethical Culture Schools, New York; James N. Rule, state superintendent of public instruction, Harrisburg; Clifford Woody, University of Michigan; G. A. Yoakum, department of elementary education, University of Pittsburgh; Ambrose L. Suhrie, New York University; President Thomas S. Gates, University of Pennsylvania; Timon Covert, specialist in school finance, Office of Education, Washington, D. C.; Ellsworth Worthington, Yale University; Leta S. Hollingsworth, Teachers College, Columbia University; Francis B. Haas, president, State Teachers College, Bloomsburg; Bess Goodykoontz, assistant commissioner of education, Washington, D. C.; Clyde L. King, secretary of revenue, Harrisburg; Edward Logan, director of the budget; V. V. Anderson, director, The Anderson School, Staatsburg, N. J.; James M. Glass, Rollins College; Vida

R. Sutton, voice and diction critic of the National Broadcasting Company; Joy Elmer Morgan, editor, National Education Association; S. A. Courtis, University of Michigan; Charles T. Loram, professor of comparative education, Yale University; I. L. Kandel, Teachers College, Columbia University.

A program was tendered to Dr. A. Duncan Yocum, commemorating his twenty-five years of service in the University of Pennsylvania.

The Schoolmen's Week meeting next year will be held at the University of Pennsylvania on March 29, 30 and 31 and April 1.

The members of the 1933 committee elected to represent the state are as follows: Louis Nusbaum, district superintendent, Philadelphia; H. C. Moyer, county superintendent, Lebanon County; Arthur W. Ferguson, superintendent, York; J. Baird Beatty, principal, Radnor Township High School, Wayne; J. Linwood Eisenberg, president, State Teachers College, Slippery Rock; Richard M. Gummere, head master, William Penn Charter School; Jessie B. Dotterer, director, elementary education, Cheltenham Township. The members of the 1933 committee representing the University of Pennsylvania will be appointed by Vice-President McClelland at a later date.

The officers for the Southeastern Convention District of the Pennsylvania State Education Association for 1933 are as follows: E. H. Snow, principal, Lower Merion Junior High School, *president;* Alice Thompson Miller, head art department, Simon Gratz High School, Philadelphia, *vice-president;* Winfield W. Menhennett, West Chester State Teachers College, *secretary.*

R. W.

EDUCATIONAL RESEARCH AND STATISTICS

PERSONALITY OF THE CANDIDATES FOR THE EDISON SCHOLARSHIP[1]

THE purpose of this study was twofold: (1) to make a comprehensive analysis of the results of the tests given to the candidates for the Edison Scholarship during the years 1928–29 and 1929–30; (2) to compare the results with those obtained from giving parts of those tests to other high-school students and high-school graduates. There were 98 candidates for the Edison Scholarship, including two members for each state and the District of Columbia. These candidates had been chosen in each state on the basis of rigorous examinations in which thousands of aspiring candidates participated. The students who were finally chosen from their respective states thus constitute a highly selected group. They probably represent those of the highest caliber among the half a million boys who graduated during these two years from high schools throughout the United States.

These 98 chosen candidates were assembled and examined by the Edison Scholarship Committee. The tests and records were composed of four parts:

(1) A questionnaire on the student's background.
(2) A character test including questions on attitudes and moral judgment.
(3) A series of science tests, chiefly on physics, chemistry and mathematics.
(4) Records of an individual interview and an intelligence rating.

The interview and intelligence rating were conducted by Dr. Hubert Howe. The character tests were scored by the committee, including the late Mr. Thomas A. Edison, Mr. Henry Ford and Mr. Harvey Firestone. The students were first selected on the basis of their scores on the science test and then on the basis of the other ratings. Complete records of the 98 students were analyzed for this study.

The author wishes to take this opportunity to acknowledge with thanks the splendid cooperation of Mr. C. J. Williams (vice-president of the Edison Company), Mr. Theodore Edison, Dr. Hubert Howe, Dr. Joseph Zubin and Dr. Otis W. Caldwell, director of the Institute of School Experimentation, Teachers College, Columbia University.

In order to compare the Edison scholars with other students, a condensed form of the tests was prepared, including all sections of the tests dealing with background and attitudes.

[1] This paper was presented before Section I, Psychology, of the American Association for the Advancement of Science, at New Orleans.

The condensed form of the tests was given to 119 high-school graduates in a school in New York City and to all high-school students who participated in the essay contest sponsored by the American Association for the Advancement of Science.

Comparisons will be presented between the candidates for the Edison scholarship, which will henceforth be referred to as the Edison scholars, the New York graduates, and, for several comparisons, the American Association for the Advancement of Science group.

I. COMPARISONS OF BACKGROUND

(1) *Age.* The average age of the Edison scholars was 17.7. Their age at graduation from high school was 17.1. The age at graduation of the New York group was 18.0. Thus the Edison scholars were about one year younger than the age at graduation of the New York graduates and probably more than a year younger than the graduates of the country as a whole. It has been found that there is a marked positive correlation between age at graduation and intelligence.[2] The younger age at graduation of the Edison scholars is thus an indication of their higher intelligence.

(2) *Home background.* Classification of the occupations of the fathers of the Edison scholars indicates that 56 per cent. were of professional rank, 14 per cent. commercial, 23 per cent. skilled laborers, 4 per cent. farmers and 3 per cent. unskilled laborers. Among the fathers of the New York graduates 49 per cent. were professional, 36 per cent. were commercial, 12 per cent. were skilled laborers, 3 per cent. unskilled laborers and, as expected, 0 per cent. farmers.

The extremely small percentage of farmers among the fathers of the Edison scholars is quite surprising if we consider the fact that many of these graduates come from states that are predominantly agricultural.

The tabulation of the occupations of the paternal grandparents of the Edison scholars revealed a slightly different picture. Only 36 per cent. were professional, 9 per cent. commercial, 21 per cent. skilled workers, 1 per cent. unskilled laborers, and fully 33 per cent. were farmers. The comparisons are shown in Table I.

TABLE I

OCCUPATION OF FATHERS OF HIGH-SCHOOL GRADUATES

Occupation	Fathers of N. Y. graduates	Fathers of Edison scholars	Grand-fathers of Edison scholars
Professional	49	56	36
Commercial	36	14	9
Skilled worker	12	23	21
Farmer	0	4	33
Unskilled labor	3	3	1
Total	100	100	100

(3) *Family.* 51 per cent. of the Edison scholars had scientists in the family. Among the A. A. A. S. group 32 per cent. and among the New York graduates only 18 per cent. had scientists in the family.

(4) *Place of birth.* Distribution by place of birth and residence revealed that 23 per cent. of the Edison scholars were born and raised in a large city, 52 per cent. in a town, 25 per cent. in a rural community. Apparently, the proportion coming from rural communities was smaller than what one would expect from the distribution of the population in the United States.

(5) *College.* Every one of the Edison scholars indicated the intention of going to college. Of the A. A. A. S. group 48 per cent. and of the New York graduates 54 per cent. intended to go to college.

(6) *Scientific apparatus.* The students were asked whether they own any scientific apparatus. Of the Edison scholars fully 70 per cent. answered this in the affirmative. Of the A. A. A. S. group 42 per cent and of the New York graduates only 35 per cent. stated that they own any scientific apparatus.

II. COMPARISON OF HABITS

Several items in the tests were concerned with the student's habits, how he spends the day, in what form of recreation he engages, what are his hobbies, etc. The answers pre-

[2] J. B. Maller, "Age Versus Intelligence as Basis for Predicting Scholastic Success in High School." Teachers College Record, February, 1932.

sent a picture of the habit patterns among these representative groups of high-school students and graduates.

(1) *Time schedule.* The students were asked to indicate how they ordinarily divide the 24 hours between (1) sleep, (2) work, (3) eating, (4) recreation. The answers revealed striking differences between the three groups in this respect. These are shown in Table II.

TABLE II
DIVISION OF THE DAY

Activity	Edison scholars	New York	A. A. A. S.
Sleep	8.2	7.8	8.8
Work	9.5	9.6	9.0
Eat	2.0	1.6	1.8
Recreation	4.3	5.0	4.4
Total	24	24	24

Table II indicates that the Edison scholars spent more hours per day on work and less hours on recreation than the other groups. The New York group spent less hours in sleep, only 7.8 hours compared with 8.5 hours for the other two groups combined. They also spent less time on eating, 1.6 hours compared with 1.9 for the others. But they spent more hours on work, 9.6 compared with 9.25, and more hours on recreation, 5.0 hours compared with 4.35. Combining the four divisions of activity into two, it appears that the New York graduates spend less time on sleep and food and more time on work and play than the other groups. The latter two differences were statistically significant, being more than three times their respective standard deviations.

(2) *Recreation.* The favorite form of recreation among the Edison scholars was swimming. Reading was the favorite form of recreation among the other two groups. Tennis ranked second as the favorite form of recreation.

(3) *Hobbies.* The most frequent hobby among the Edison scholars was experimentation; among the A. A. A. S. it was the collecting of stamps and other objects. Radio was the favorite hobby of the New York group.

(2) *Choice of vocation.* Engineering was the predominant vocational choice among the Edison scholars, teaching the most frequent choice in the other groups.

III. Study and Reading

A comparison of the results on the questions concerning study and reading revealed a number of differences:

(1) *Favorite study.* The subject of instruction which the Edison scholars considered their favorite was physics. The New York graduates chose chemistry, and the A. A. A. S. contestants chose mathematics as the favorite subject. Biology ranked second among the New York graduates, and fourth in the other groups. English ranked third among the New York group and the A. A. A. S. contestants, and fifth among the Edison scholars.

(2) *Choice of book.* The type of books considered as favorites among the Edison scholars was that of science and invention. The second place was given to books on economics, followed by mystery, adventure, fiction and travel. Books on biography and history were given the last place. The choice of the other groups was quite different. Fiction ranked first, followed by science, economics, travel and history. Then come books on biography and invention. Books on mystery and adventure were given the last place.

(3) *Choice of periodicals.* The periodicals chosen as favorites among the Edison scholars were *Popular Science* and *Science and Invention.* The New York groups chose the *Literary Digest* as their favorite. The A. A. A. S. group chose the *National Geographic* and the *Saturday Evening Post.*

IV. Comparison of Attitudes

A large number of questions dealt with the student's attitude toward various social problems.

(1) *Capital and labor.* The students were asked whether, in their opinion, the present relation of capital to labor is reasonably fair. Among the Edison scholars 86 per cent answered this question in the affirmative, 13 per cent. left this question unanswered, and only 1 per cent. answered it in the negative. In the A. A. A. S. group 49 per cent. answered it in the affirmative and 51 per cent. in the negative, while in the New York group only 37 per cent. answered it "yes" and fully 63 per cent. answered it "no."

It appears that the Edison scholars were most inclined to favor the *status quo* and the New York group least inclined in that direction with regard to the question of the relation of capital to labor. It should be added, however, that the conditions under which the tests were given to the various groups were not identical and may account in part for the differences.

(2) *Attitude toward work.* One of the questions read: "Assuming it were an engineering and financial possibility, and you were given the opportunity of devoting 20 years of your life to be in sole charge of digging a hole 30 miles into the earth's interior, would you accept it or turn it down?" One third of the Edison scholars and a similar proportion of the A. A. A. S. group answered this question in the affirmative. In the New York group only 12 per cent answered it in the affirmative, while fully 88 per cent. stated that they would decline the offer.

(3) *Attitude toward art.* In spite of the fact that the interest of the Edison scholars was definitely in the field of science their attitude toward art was not altogether negative. This was revealed from the answers to the question as to what their attitude would be toward a brother who wanted to be an artist or a poet. Only 4 per cent of the Edison scholars said that they would attempt to dissuade him, while 86 per cent stated that they would encourage him, and 10 per cent. left the question unanswered. Among the A. A. A. S. group 2 per cent. answered the question in the negative, while in the New York group there was not a single answer in the negative.

(4) *Attitude toward discoveries.* An interesting difference was revealed in the answer to the question as to what discovery or invention would, in their opinion, be of greatest benefit to mankind. Among the Edison scholars the most frequently mentioned discoveries were those dealing with the utilization of the power of the atom. Among the other two groups the most frequently mentioned discoveries were those dealing with cures for cancer and other diseases. In the New York group the utilization of waste was mentioned by 16 per cent. It should be noted that fully 9 per cent. of the high-school graduates believed that the discovery of greatest importance would be that of perpetual motion.

(5) *Attitude toward self-defense.* The students were asked: "If some acquaintance of yours unfairly accused you of cheating what would you do?" There was agreement among the groups that the best thing to do is to disprove the accusation or to prove one's innocence. This answer was given by 76 per cent. of the students. Among the Edison scholars 18 per cent. stated that they would ignore the accusation and 6 per cent. would demand satisfaction. In the other group 23 per cent. would ignore the accusation and only 1 per cent would demand satisfaction.

V. Comparison of Ideals

The following four items will illustrate the questions concerning the ideals of these students:

(1) *Great men most admired.* The question read: "Outside of the field of religion, what three men, not now living, do you think particularly deserve your respect and admiration?" The three men most frequently given by the Edison scholars were Lincoln, Pasteur and Washington. The A. A. A. S. group gave the names of Lincoln, Washington and Franklin. The New York group gave the names of Lincoln, Washington and Pasteur. It appears that in spite of the enormous differences between the environments of our three groups there was marked agreement as to the heroes among high-school graduates.

It is interesting to note that in spite of the direction to give the names of men not now living the name of Edison and that of Einstein were included by at least 7 per cent. of the students among the three greatest men.

(2) *Qualities admired in great men.* An interesting difference was revealed in the answer to the question concerning the qualities admired in great men. The Edison scholars gave mental ability as the most admirable quality. In the A. A. A. S. group courage was given the first place and ability the fifth, while in the New York group perseverance was given as the most admirable quality.

(3) *Quality needed for success.* There was agreement among the three groups in the answers to this question. Ambition and per-

severance were considered the most important qualifications for success in any pursuit. Ability was given only the fourth place.

(4) *Sacrifice for success.* One of the questions read:

Which one of the following would you be willing to sacrifice for the sake of being successful?

(1) Happiness	(5) Honor
(2) Comfort	(6) Health
(3) Reputation	(7) Money
(4) Pride	(8) Love

There is agreement among the three groups in answering this question. The items to be sacrificed for the sake of success were those of comfort, money and pride. Not a single one of the Edison scholars included health among these, while 4 per cent. of the New York group included health among the items to be sacrificed for the sake of success.

One more comparison will be presented. It is based on the answer to a problem which has attracted considerable attention as a problem of moral discrimination. It read:

You are the head of an expedition which has come to grief in the desert. There is enough food and water left to enable three people to get to the nearest outpost of civilization. The rest must perish. Place check marks in front of three names which you think should be saved:

a. A brilliant scientist 60 years old.
b. Two half breed guides, ages 58 and 32.
c. The scientist's wife—interested mainly in society matters, age 39.
d. Her little son, age 6.
e. The girl you are engaged to marry.
f. Your best friend, a young man of your own age, who has shown great promise in the field of science.
g. Yourself.

There was agreement among the groups as to the one most frequently chosen to survive—the best friend. The second and third places were given by the Edison scholars to the little boy and self, by the A. A. A. S. group to the little boy and sweetheart, and in the New York group to the sweetheart and self.

The writer has given this question, as part of a moral judgment test, to 500 graduate students of Teachers College, Columbia University. The answers of the graduate students to this question included the friend, self and guide.

Before drawing any conclusions it should be added that this paper dealt only with one phase of the comparative study, namely, with the records of background and attitudes.[3] No comparisons were made here with regard to achievement. There is ample evidence that the Edison scholars were markedly superior to the other groups in knowledge of physics, chemistry and mathematics.

SUMMARY

The Edison scholars were selected on the basis of extensive examinations in science and were chosen from thousands of examinees in every part of the country. In their attitude and habits they tend toward extraversion and practical mindedness rather than intraversion. The interest and abilities of these candidates lie definitely in the field of science and they may be considered as representative of the American young men of science. Their fathers were chiefly professional men and there were many scientists in their family. This is consistent with the findings of Dr. Cattell in his analysis of the background of American men of science.

Comparison with the other groups of high-school graduates can be made only with reservation in view of the relatively small number of cases. The differences in judgment, attitude and habits, however, are indicative of real differences. Equally interesting are the similarities between the various groups of high-school graduates with regard to some of the attitudes and ideals included in this study.

J. B. MALLER
INSTITUTE OF SCHOOL EXPERIMENTATION,
TEACHERS COLLEGE,
COLUMBIA UNIVERSITY

NEW BOOKS IN EDUCATION

AMERICAN COUNCIL OF EDUCATION. *American Universities and Colleges.* Second edition, revised. John H. McCracken, Editor. Pp. xiv + 1066. Williams and Wilkins. $4.00.

SMITH, LEWIS W., VINCENT H. OGBURN and HAROLD F. WATSON. *Ventures in Contemporary Reading.* Pp. viii + 147. Longmans, Green. $1.00.

WALLENROD, REUBEN. *John Dewey, Educateur.* Pp. 227. Jouve and Cie, Paris.

[3] The other sections of the study include a comprehensive analysis of the science tests, a follow-up of the Edison scholars in their college work, and the correlations between the various tests and ratings and scholastic success.

SCHOOL AND SOCIETY
EDITED BY J. McKEEN CATTELL
WITH WHICH IS COMBINED THE
EDUCATIONAL REVIEW
EDITED BY WILLIAM McANDREW

Volume 35 | Saturday, April 2, 1932 | Number 901

"THE GREAT AWAKENING" AND ITS EDUCATIONAL CONSEQUENCES

By Professor WAYLAND J. CHASE
UNIVERSITY OF WISCONSIN

"The Great Awakening," adequately conceived, was a world-wide evangelistic movement, a remarkable and complete change of attitude to religion on the part of thousands of men and women. Its first noteworthy manifestation was in Lutheran Germany, when under the leadership of the clergyman Spener, "collegia pietatis" developed with the purpose of fostering and promoting a more vital type of religiousness than that which then prevailed, and which seemed too much a matter of dogma, too little a matter of living and feeling. The members of these groups came to be known as pietists, and pietism spread widely. Spener died in 1705, and was succeeded in leadership by the Reverend August Francke, who was a Lutheran clergyman, the professor of oriental languages in the University of Halle and the founder of a great system of educational and philanthropic institutions that continue to flourish. Pietism with its protest against religious formalism both mightily influenced the Lutheran Church, and also spread to the various other branches of Protestantism in Germany. Of these the Mennonites, the Moravians and the German Baptists (Dunkers) were especially influential. From Germany to the American Colonies successive waves of migration were moving during this period of the rise and spread of pietism, that is the last of the seventeenth and the first half of the eighteenth century; and among the German settlers in America were many pietists. Pietism was spreading in other directions also at this time. John and Charles Wesley, while students at Oxford, were won over to pietism by the preaching of a Moravian clergyman, and religious treatises of Francke influenced George Whitefield as well as others, who became, with the Wesleys, leaders of the English Methodist movement.

This spread of pietism shows both the international extent of the movement and also the interdenominational character of it. It was not a new sect or new church, but a new attitude to religion, which, identifying religion with life and conduct in fuller degree, became a new force in old churches and a new leaven generally in society.

Our concern is with its workings in America. There the dispersion of its adherents, the various German groups, through a wide wilderness in Pennsylvania, at first greatly weakened the movement, especially as the hard conditions of frontier life necessarily monopolized the attention and energy of these settlers. Wretchedly poor at first as many of them were, in the course of time to these plodding, hard-working Germans material prosperity came. But pietism was not powerful among them until it had been acted upon from outside their limits. Close to these early settlers of eastern Pennsylvania were the Dutch of western New Jersey, then a wilderness untamed. The struggling little Dutch Reformed churches of that region applied to their mother-church in Holland for leaders. In response to this cry there was sent to them Theodore J. Frelinghuysen, a college graduate, by birth not a Dutchman but a German, who had come in his fatherland under pietistic influences. Under his leadership and preaching, which began in America in 1720 with a pastoral charge over four widely separated frontier churches in the Raritan Valley, a gospel new to many was taught, namely, that baptism and communion were not the sum and substance of religious duty, that the essence of religion was in spiritual fervor and uprightness of conduct, because outward performance of religious ceremonies apart from a suitable frame of mind was hateful to God. Before long a vigorous revival of religion was manifest in these churches and spread from them to others of the Dutch Reformed congregations in this colony. The year 1726 especially saw wide-spread fervor manifested. At that time this frontier, like others in Pennsylvania, New York and New England, was receiving its first influx of the Scotch-Irish, whom industrial, religious and political oppression was driving out of North Ireland. This stock was predominantly Presbyterian in religious faith, and drew its inspiration, like the adherents to the Dutch Reformed faith, from John Calvin. Frelinghuysen had again and again ministered to struggling Presbyterian groups who caught evangelistic fire from him. Soon there emerged from the Presbyterian clergy powerful preachers of the Frelinghuysen brand of religion. Almost all these Presbyterian evangelists were graduates of the Log College of William Tennent at Neshaminy in eastern Pennsylvania. In his early ministry in Ireland Tennent, a graduate of the University of Glasgow, had been a priest of the Episcopal church, but having later espoused Presbyterianism, became in America the foremost exponent of that doctrine. A great preacher, he was also a great teacher. First associating other youth with his four sons whom he taught in his study, he built in 1726 a log structure for the better housing of this developing school, and this came to have national fame as the Log College. It was academy, college and theological seminary all in one. This was the mother of many similar schools South and West and North. Though religion had chief place in its curriculum, its graduates demonstrated convincingly a thorough grounding in the classical and oriental languages, and the other accepted essentials of the higher education of that time. Through the powerful preaching of such Presbyterian clergymen as these, the revival movement spread throughout the churches of this denomination scattered along the frontiers of the Middle Colonies.

Almost contemporaneous with these happenings another religious revival was prevailing in the New England region where the greatest of all eighteenth century clergymen in America, Jonathan Edwards, was exercising influence over his fellow Puritans. 1734 and 1735 saw especially fervid manifestations of his power over the emotions of his fellow New Englanders. How much this New England revival was in its early stages influenced from the old world, it is difficult to measure, though beyond question at this time waves of religious influence were reaching from there across the Atlantic into all sections of the Colonial area. Cooperating with Edwards were other preachers of notable pulpit power, and in consequence Congregationalism was mightily stirred and quickened.

By the 1730's the Baptist churches in America were but very few. They had as yet no national organization in either the old world or the new, and were not a powerful force in the early stages of the revival movement, but, as we shall see, no denomination eventually profited more from the Great Awakening than they did.

To this religious movement the Quakers were friendly, and by it they undoubtedly profited. As, however, emphasis upon "the inner light," the spiritual aspect of worship, was a cardinal feature of their religion, their need of religious quickening was less significant than was that of other sects. The Anglican Church in America for the most part was hostile to this type of evangelism and remained aloof from it. The influence upon this church was, however, very great, but as we shall see of a weakening rather than a strengthening sort.

We have now seen that by the last of the 1730's a great increase in religious fervor had manifested itself among the Germans, the Scotch-Irish, the Dutch and the English in America. At that time there occurred that which swept together these separate manifestations into one great practically nation-wide movement. This unifying force was the remarkable preaching of George Whitefield, who began the first of his tours of the Colonies in 1739. Before that time he had already had a distinguished career as an evangelist in the British Isles, and accounts of this had preceded him and prepared the way for him. Converted to the English form of pietism while he was a student at Oxford, he had identified himself heartily and prominently with the movement which John and Charles Wesley led, and had become famous for his power to hold thousands under the spell of his preaching. Though ordained as a clergyman of the Church of England, he had been refused by many churches of that faith the privilege to preach in them, and had gathered together great concourses of worshippers in open fields. His voice had extraordinary clearness and carrying power, and Franklin in his autobiography witnesses to his ability to hold together open-air congregations of three thousand or more. His interest in America was two-fold. He had established an orphan asylum in the young colony of Georgia, and was zealous to promote its welfare and to collect funds for it. Also he felt that he had been divinely called to spread the gospel, as he understood it, in England's colonial world. He was but twenty-five years old when in 1739 he entered upon this missionary enterprise, and he continued it to the time of his death in 1770, just before our Revolutionary War, having by then preached ten sermons a week for thirty-four years. In that interval his visits to America were oft repeated, 1740, 1746, 1754, 1763, and once more in the year of his death. These visits were long extended, and on his preaching tours he traversed the colonies from Georgia to northern New England. His mission was not to proselyte for Anglicanism, but to preach to people of every faith. Quakers, Lutherans, Moravians, Mennonites, German Reformed, Dutch Reformed, Presbyterians, Congregationalists, Baptists and many connected with no church, all flocked to hear him. Many leaders of the various churches gave him cordial welcome, and to all religious workers of whatever faith who would accept it, he gave cordial cooperation. Under his preaching the revival movements already started gained vastly greater momentum, volume, extent and duration. His gospel was not nearly so much of the terrorizing type as that of some of his fellow-evangelists, notably

Jonathan Edwards, for his theme was more often divine love than divine wrath.

In 1740 when the authorities of the Anglican Church in Philadelphia refused to permit Whitefield to preach in it, some of his supporters launched the project of constructing through popular subscription a huge brick building to be used for his preaching and that "of orthodox experienced preachers of whatever denomination," and also for a charity school. Whitefield and Franklin were trustees of both this so-called "New Building" and the school.

Not only religion but all sorts of benevolences had his support. The misery of the poor deeply stirred him, and he spoke often in behalf of humanitarian enterprises, like those of the orphan, the Negro, the Indian and the untaught poor.

Thus, for more than thirty years Whitefield gave continuousness of life to the Great Awakening, and measurably helped to make it what to-day the chief authorities in our country's history recognize it to be, namely, one of the most important social forces of eighteenth century America.

Of the many thousands who professed conversion, there were beyond doubt very many who backslid and relapsed, many individuals on whom the influence of the revival was but temporary and transitory. But there were enough more whose attitude to life became permanently changed; and as a result enduring transformation was wrought in religious groups. Churches that before had been weak became strong in number of members, strong in leadership, and strong in spirit. This may well be illustrated by the Lutherans and the Baptists. In 1742 Heinrich M. Muhlenberg came as missionary to the German Lutherans of Pennsylvania. He found them about the most needy of our immigrants, their poverty being the result of generations of desolating warfare in the European regions whence they came. They lacked the means to build churches or support ministers or to provide schools and teachers. Muhlenberg's leadership, reinforced by the other agencies of the Great Awakening, put courage and self-respect into this people whom prolonged servitude had all but crushed. By the time of the Revolutionary War this sect, whose churches then extended from the Carolinas to the Hudson, had been firmly united into a single organization and their membership increased many fold.

At the beginning of the eighteenth century there were about a score of small Baptist churches in the American colonies, with some 800 members. By the time of the Revolution there were 471 churches with more than 35,000 members distributed through all the colonies.

In respect to the older denominations, as the Presbyterians and the Congregationalists, the movement seemed at times to be likely to divide and disrupt more than to unify. Old Lights and New Lights, Old Sides and New Sides arrayed themselves against each other in hostility to or in support of the revival, yet on the whole both of these denominations were greatly strengthened in numbers and were made national in their organizations and influence. Because of the intellectual stimulus which conflict over the revival supplied, a liberal party developed eventually within these denominations. From this, after the Revolution, Unitarianism took its organized form. But what numbers the orthodox churches thus lost were very much more than offset by the gains made.

The Anglicans, who were practically united in opposition to the movement, suffered material losses in membership. And church establishment met with a very severe blow from this drawing away from the Episcopal churches and from the contemporaneous strengthening of the various dissenting denominations.

There were no Methodist churches in

America in the period of the Great Awakening. It was not till about 1765 that the first immigrants of this faith arrived, and the first Methodist organization in our colonies was within the Church of England. In the year immediately following the Revolutionary War a schism developed, and the Methodist Episcopal Church became a separate organization. Thus the Great Awakening did not develop this denomination, but it effectively prepared the way for it.

Thus much as to its effect upon denominations. As to the effect upon religion as a whole, our chief historians of the Colonial period, Osgood, Channing, James T. Adams, are in agreement. The Great Awakening reestablished religion as a controlling force in society and made it far more vital than it had come to be. This awakened vitality thereafter expressed itself in humanitarian enterprises of many kinds. "The first word against slavery was spoken by men of the Pietist group. The anti-slavery movement in New England was originated by one of the great evangelical leaders then."

The impulse given by the Great Awakening to education was tremendous. To understand this it must be remembered that in eighteenth century America nowhere outside of the New England Colonies was education an affair of the secular government. And in New England, towns maintained schools because of the union of town and church. Throughout Colonial America, then, the school was the handmaid of the church, and educational zeal ebbed and flowed with the tide of religious fervor. Because the Great Awakening had increased church membership and multiplied churches, more ministers were needed, and the Evangelical ministers of the Presbyterian and Congregational groups, which possessed the tradition of an educated clergy, bestirred themselves to provide colleges that would train for their ministries the gifted young men who under the spell of this revival heard the call to preach.

In 1746, about six months before the passing of William Tennent and his Log College, the Philadelphia Presbyterian synod projected another institution which should supply instruction "in the learned languages and in the liberal arts and sciences," and secured a charter for it from the royal governor of New Jersey. At first called the College of New Jersey, this institution became Princeton College, since in 1756 it found a fixed home in the town of that name. Two of its first trustees were sons of William Tennent. Most of its first six presidents, among them Jonathan Edwards, had been prominent preachers in the revival movement. In Princeton was the notable educational response that Presbyterians made to the Great Awakening.

John Frelinghuysen, son of Theodore J., established at Somerville, New Jersey, a theological seminary for candidates to the ministry of the Dutch Reformed Church. From this developed Queen's College, chartered in 1766. Enriched about sixty years later by Colonel Henry Rutgers, an eminent member of that church, it took his name and became Rutgers College of New Brunswick, New Jersey.

Among the first leaders of the eighteenth century Baptist churches were many who were without college diploma or special educational training. But through the cordial aid and cooperation the Baptist preachers of the Middle Colonies received from the Presbyterian divines, they gained an appreciation of the advantages of special ministerial preparation. In consequence several schools were established by the Baptists upon the model of the Log College. Of these the most famous was that at Hopewell, New Jersey. Here James Manning studied, and then at Princeton. In 1762 he met with other delegates to the Philadelphia Association of Baptist Churches in deliberation about the project to found a Baptist college. Some favored locating it south of the James River, in which region no college existed. But consideration of the difficulty of obtaining a charter for it from any other colony than Rhode Island led to its being established there, where it was incorporated in 1764. James Manning was its first president. Its board of trustees was to be made up of Baptists, Quakers, Congregationalists and Episcopalians. Similarly, Princeton's first board of trustees comprised representatives from several churches, the Quakers and the Anglicans as well as from the Presbyterians. Such union of effort was a direct outcome of the practice of cooperation which characterized the Evangelical leaders.

One of the most eloquent preachers of the religious revival in New England was Eleazar Wheelock, a graduate of Yale and a Congregational clergyman in western Connecticut on the edge of the land of Oneida and Tuscarora Indians. For the training of picked youth of these tribes for missionary work he began a school. To such missionary endeavors the Great Awakening gave new life and vigor, and to them Whitefield's influence in England brought financial aid from there.

By the 1760's this school was receiving white youth as well as Indians, for what might be called a collegiate course was now given. When the Colonial legislature of Connecticut denied Wheelock's request for a charter, he applied to the governor of New Hampshire, by whom a charter was granted. Then the school was moved to Hanover on the edge of the New Hampshire wilderness, and log buildings constructed under Wheelock's supervision for long constituted the college plant. It was fitting that this institution, named for Lord Dartmouth, who had assisted materially in collecting funds for it, should have on its seal "Vox Clamantis in deserto," "The voice of one crying in the wilderness."

Even the non-sectarian University of Pennsylvania has a root-tendril that runs into this religious soil so fertile for educational beginnings. It is to be remembered that this institution began as "The Academy of Philadelphia," a project of Benjamin Franklin. In 1749 Franklin, already one of the trustees of the academy, was chosen as one of the trustees of the so-called "New Building" which we have seen constructed on the stimulus that Whitefield's presence in America supplied. Needing a building for their school, the academy trustees acquired that, and agreed "to keep forever open in it a large hall for occasional preachers" and also to maintain in the building a free school for the instruction of poor children.

As has been pointed out, religionists among the Germans, whether Lutherans, Reformed or of other sects, had a greater handicap of poverty than other American church groups. In consequence early movements among them for higher education did not fructify till late in the century. But these endeavors were visibly accelerated by the Great Awakening and eventually resulted in the founding, by the joint effort of Lutherans and the Reformed Church, with the aid of Benjamin Franklin, of Franklin College at Lancaster, Pennsylvania, in 1787.

The stimulus given by the Great Awakening to schools below the level of colleges is fully as discernible as that given to higher education. In thousands of individuals, new aspirations had been kindled, and new ambitions aroused. The determination to make something of one's self or to make more of one's self commonly expressed itself in a purpose to get an education. More schools became needed. This need revealed itself to men of wealth, in whom humanitarian purposes had been quickened, and to religious leaders, who realized the significance of educational opportunity. Thus there were born in this period many academies, some of which secular philanthropy engendered, and others which had their origin in denominational zeal. Their name literally is legion. Before 1800 there were twenty-five or more of them in Virginia alone. Such were Prince Edward Academy and Liberty Hall Academy, both founded before the Revolutionary War. The former has developed into Hampden-Sydney College of to-day, and the latter into Washington and Lee University. Samples of such in North Carolina founded in the same period were Clio's Nursery and Science Hall in Iredell County, and Zion Parnassus near the town of Salisbury. In Georgia, South Carolina and Maryland others sprang up. Among those of the Middle Colonies the educational achievements of the Moravians under the leadership of Count Zinzendorf were especially notable, like the seminary for girls, first at Germantown in 1742, and to-day at Bethlehem; and Nazareth Hall for boys in 1743. New England proved to be an especially fertile field for academies; Phillips Andover, 1778, and Phillips Exeter, 1781, were of this crop, and both are directly traceable to the influence of the Great Awakening.

Along with the academies, and often almost indistinguishable from them, were the many schools begun by clergymen, especially those of the Presbyterian Church, and frequently modeled on Tennent's Log College. Typical of these was that frontier log school of Rev. Moses Waddell near the boundary between South Carolina and Georgia. There John Calhoun got his preparation for Yale.

Into the field of elementary education there is no need to enter at this time, for it will be accepted without demonstration that these manifestations of zeal for education on the upper levels insure that there was a multiplying of educational facilities for elementary schooling as well.

EDUCATIONAL EVENTS

THE SEVENTH MEXICAN SEMINAR

The Seventh Seminar in Mexico meeting in Mexico City from July 3 to 23 is planned to be a "cooperative study of Mexican life and culture." Its membership is open to people who have an interest in international relations and who have a genuine desire to understand the Mexican people. The three week's program includes lectures, round table conferences and field trips.

The lectures, given by authorities in Mexico, present various phases of Mexican life in the fields of education, art, international relations, economics, music, folk lore, sociology and government. Among those who will lecture before the seminar are Moises Saenz, Carlos Chavez, Ramon Beteta, Diego Rivera and Rafael Ramirez.

The round tables give small groups the opportunity to study and discuss some subject in their particular field of interest. The leaders and their subjects in this year's session include Judge Florence E. Allen, on international relations; Dr. Ernest Gruening, on economics; Count René d'Harnoncourt, on arts and crafts; Dr. Charles W. Hackett, on the history of Mexico, and Miss Elizabeth Wallace on Latin American literature. Of special interest this year will be the round table on archeology led by Dr. Frans Blom. Among other subjects, this group will study the recent discoveries made at Monte Alban and at the close of the seminar a trip will be made to Oaxaca to study the pyramids themselves.

Field trips will be made to Puebla, Oaxtepec, Xochimilco, Cuautla, Cuernavaca and Taxco, where members of the seminar will be guests at the "casa" of the committee. The object of these trips is to visualize the historical background, to see the schools at work and to understand the indigenous culture of Mexico. The summer is cool and the country affords many opportunities for study and travel.

Inquiries and applications should be addressed to Hubert C. Herring, Committee on Cultural Relations with Latin America, 112 East 19th Street, New York City.

EDUCATIONAL TOURS OF THE INTERNATIONAL INSTITUTE OF TEACHERS COLLEGE, COLUMBIA UNIVERSITY

THE youth movement in Germany will be studied by American teachers in courses to be given in Europe by the 1932 summer session of Columbia University, according to a statement issued by Professor John J. Cross, director of the session. The teachers also will investigate and study the educational systems of Germany, France and England.

Three tours, one to each of these countries, will be backed by the International Institute of Teachers College, under the direction of Professors Thomas Alexander, M. C. Del Manzo, Ruth E. McMurry and their associates.

Every type of German education will be studied, including school organization, methods of instruction, playgrounds, juvenile welfare work, physical education, outdoor life, art and dramatic instruction.

Berlin, Magdeburg, Heidelberg, Dusseldorf, Essen, Dresden, Weimar, Stuttgart, Halle, Jena, Mainz and Koln will be visited. Each student will be required to prepare a written report on some special problem studied during the six weeks' trip. Students on the German study tour will sail from New York on June 15 and will leave Germany about August 1.

The group visiting France will have the opportunity to study "other important phases of French life and culture" besides its educational system. The course will begin in Paris about June 1.

The English trip will be the first organized study tour to the British Isles to be backed by the International Institute. The students will have the opportunity to observe various phases of English life, including music, art, drama, industry, agriculture and commerce. The course will begin in London about July 6.

Science and science education in Germany will be studied by a fourth group on a special field trip under the direction of Dr. Lois Meier Shoemaker, of the New Jersey State Teachers College. Walking tours in the Black Forest, the Bavarian Alps and Saxon-Switzerland, a trip up the Rhine and visits to various cities will be included. On its excursions the party will put up at the German "Jugendherbergen," or youth hostels, provided throughout the country.

A course for advanced students which will include field studies and research in problems of education in foreign countries, under the direction of Professors Paul Monroe, George S. Counts, I. L. Kandel, L. M. Wilson, Alexander, Del Manzo and McMurry, also will be offered.

INSTITUTE OF INTERNATIONAL RELATIONS OF THE AMERICAN FRIENDS SERVICE COMMITTEE

THE American Friends Service Committee will hold this year three Institutes of International Relations: at Haverford College, Pennsylvania, June 13 to 25; at Northwestern University, Evanston, Illinois, June 20 to July 2, and at Wellesley College, Massachusetts, June 23 to July 2. In the past two years, this Quaker organization has held at Haverford College similar institutes, which have met with decided success.

All three institutes will give opportunity for study under experts in their respective fields of world relationships, and the questions of the times such as war debts, disarmament, the Manchurian struggle and the like. Courses of college grade on the economic, political and spiritual phases of the struggle for world peace will run throughout the period of each institute, while shorter courses and single lectures will deal with special topics, or with methods of creating attitudes of international good-will.

Some of those who will serve on the faculty, or lecture at one or more of the institutes, are James G. McDonald, of the Foreign Policy Association; Norman Thomas, of the League for Industrial Democracy; Sidney B. Fay, of Harvard University; Kirby Page, editor of *The World To-morrow;* Devere Allen, editor of *The Nation;* Edward A. Steiner, of Grinnell College; Grover Clark, consultant on Far Eastern affairs; Harry D. Gideonse, University of Chicago.

These institutes, with their emphasis on international affairs of the moment, together with their material and spiritual backgrounds, give the information needed by teachers who want to keep up with the times and are interested in promoting world peace. Moreover, there will be special lectures for teachers.

The schedule will be, in general: Classes in the morning, recreation in the afternoon, lectures (open to the public) in the evening. Further information may be obtained from the American Friends Service Committee, 20 South Twelfth Street, Philadelphia, Pennsylvania.

CHILD HEALTH DAY

President Hoover has issued a proclamation setting apart May 1 as Child Health Day and calling upon all agencies and organizations interested in child welfare "to unite upon that day in the observance of such exercises as will awaken the people of the nation to the fundamental necessity of unremitting effort for the protection and development of the health of the nation's children." The proclamation, made public at the White House on March 21, follows:

Whereas, The Congress of the United States, by enactment of May 18, 1928, requested the president to proclaim May 1 as Child Health Day, for national consideration of this subject; and

Whereas, The children of this nation are our most precious possession, the causes and objects of our deepest affections, and in them is the promise of our future homes; and

Whereas, We have in them the constant and unfailing source of vitality, wealth and leadership, the future benefits of which to the nation depend upon the health and protection of children to-day; and

Whereas, The knowledge of how to protect and promote their health, physical, mental and spiritual, is more accessible than ever before, as the reports of the White House Conference on Child Health and Protection give tangible evidence; now,

Therefore, I, Herbert Hoover, President of the United States of America, do hereby proclaim May 1, to be Child Health Day, and do invite all agencies and organizations interested in child welfare to unite upon that day in the observance of such exercises as will awaken the people of the nation to the fundamental necessity of unremitting effort for the protection and development of the health of the nation's children.

HEALTH PROMOTION WEEK IN ILLINOIS

Governor Emmerson of Illinois has issued a proclamation calling upon citizens of the state to take part in "health promotion week and child health day," the week beginning on April 24 and the day of Sunday, May 1. The State Department of Public Health was designated by the governor as "the official agency to develop suitable program for these projects," and Dr. Andy Hall, director of public health, has accordingly addressed a communication with suggestions to the educators of Illinois.

Dr. Hall opens his letter with the declaration that, "if the prevailing hard times had occurred just forty years ago our experiences of the last two years would have been immeasurably worse. This is a known fact because there was a major economic depression in the early nineties and extensive epidemics made suffering and hardship much worse than what we have recently witnessed." He continues:

The experiences of 1890 were typical. In that year tuberculosis, typhoid fever and diphtheria caused an aggregate of 11,049 deaths in Illinois. Last year the same three diseases caused only 5,274 deaths, although the population of the state has doubled since 1890. Had the 1890 rates of those three diseases prevailed, there would have been over 150,000 more cases and over 17,000 more deaths in 1931 than actually occurred.

For this magnificent improvement the schools deserve no little credit. They have been of the greatest importance in making possible the general application of preventive medicine. A recent study showed that over one third of the time is given to general science and biology courses.

RETRENCHMENT AND ECONOMY IN THE PUBLIC SCHOOLS

Dr. Paul R. Mort, associate director of the National Survey on School Finance, announced before the Board of Consultants in session at the Department of the Interior on February 19 and 20, that methods of retrenchment and economy in maintaining the public schools throughout the nation because of reduced budgets will be sought and tabulated by the survey.

An attempt will be made, according to a report of the meeting in the *U. S. Daily,* to determine what economies are harmful to educational opportunities and what will not vitally affect them.

The board discussed four outstanding types of retrenchments and economies which already have been tried by many school systems. One is classified as a major retrenchment representing a definite curtailment of educational opportunities. Under this type of economy, the school year is shortened, nursery schools, kindergartens, health service, special teachers and typical classes, guidance personnel, vocational education, evening schools, summer schools, supervision, transportation and similar activities are eliminated. Another policy introduced has been to raise the minimum age for school entrance.

A second type of retrenchment, which may be justified in some instances, calls for an increase in pupil-teacher ratios, the elimination of small classes in larger schools, the curtailment of the school building program, and the curtailment of repairs. The purchase of new equipment is limited, salaries are reduced, and new teachers are engaged at lower salaries than the regular scale.

Certain economies may be a definite step in the wrong direction. For example, to eliminate school clerks, the employment of students for this work is regarded as a wrong move. Also the elimination of free texts and supplies, the reduction in transportation expenditures, the shortening of bus routes, and the increase in charges for tuition, gymnasium, locker, towel and similar fees are regarded as bad methods of economy.

Within the same type fall the policy of eliminating teachers' sick leaves, cutting salaries of beginning teachers to that of substitutes, and the limitation of extracurricular activities.

The fourth or miscellaneous type of economies, certain measures, which are "earmarks" of good administration, "but even more necessary now than in ordinary times," are listed. Members of the Board of Consultants reviewed those involving such policies as careful specifications for purchasing, careful check on deliveries as to amount and quality, and careful need of personnel, equipment and supplies. Attention was given to methods of safeguarding funds and to an efficient planning of building construction.

Other measures of economy within this category touched such administrative matters as careful study of insurance rates, amounts, coverage, etc., getting lowest interest rates possible, receipt of interest on bank balances, placing cafeterias on a self-supporting basis, and efficient organization of classes to eliminate small sections.

Tentative studies proposed by the research staff about which discussion centered also included such topics as predictable changes in expenditures for schools, school indebtedness, sources of school support and the ability to support schools.

STATUS OF THE CHICAGO TEACHERS

AN insight into the straits in which public school teachers in Chicago find themselves because of the inability of that city to pay their salaries is given in a communication received on March 23 by the group of New York City teachers which is sponsoring a move to assist their colleagues, as reported in *The New York Sun.*

The Chicago teachers, writing to the New York group, stated that they had received only ten weeks' pay in about eleven months. The letter continued: "The daily papers in Chicago to-day carry reports about a questionnaire circulated by the Principals Club. Five hundred teachers replied that they have absolutely reached the end of their resources and recite numerous instances of real suffering. The present outlook is quite unpromising. We can not believe but that Chicago will find some way to secure some money for the teachers, but nobody seems to know how this will be brought about.

The New York City teachers, according to the *Sun,* are planning to offer assistance which will probably, if effected, take the form of a loan fund. The offer of the New York teachers, the letter from Chicago said, "thrilled" the Chicago staff.

Whatever arrangements can be made along the lines suggested by the New York teachers will be made through an organization of Chicago teachers set up by Superintendent of Schools William J. Bogan.

The New York teachers are representatives of seven leading teachers' associations, including the Brooklyn Teachers Association, the Queensborough Teachers Association, the Bronx Boroughwide Association of Teachers, the Staten

Island Teachers Association, the High School Teachers Association, the New York Principals Association and the Junior High School Principals Association.

Augustus Ludwig, president of the Brooklyn Teachers Association, is chairman of the special committee negotiating with the Chicago staff, and Miss Margaret Mackintosh, president of the New York Principals Association, is secretary.

REORGANIZATION OF HIGHER EDUCATION IN THE STATE OF OREGON

MR. WALLACE B. WHARTON, who is an editorial correspondent of *The New York Times,* writes from Portland, Oregon, under date of March 17, that to assist the general program of Governor Julius L. Meier in reducing cost of government, the Oregon State Board of Higher Education has approved a drastic reorganization of the higher education system, to become effective when the fall term opens. The plan eliminates duplications in courses of major importance given at both the University of Oregon and Oregon State College. The saving in operation of the two institutions will be in excess of $1,000,000 annually and, according to the board, will be accomplished without loss of efficiency.

In the broad set-up the number of schools in the two state institutions is reduced from forty-one to twelve through incorporating many into one unit. There will be six schools at the university and six at the State College. The number of deans will be reduced to twelve.

The board has decided to select a president of higher education who will be the senior administrative officer for both major institutions and the three normal schools. The university, the state college and the normal school group will each have a vice-president or a senior dean in immediate charge.

Under the plan the university will have the schools of literature and arts, social science, business administration and commerce, fine arts and physical education. At the State College the schools will be home economics, agriculture, physical and biological sciences, engineering, forestry and pharmacy. The University of Oregon Medical School in Portland will be continued without material change. The school of journalism at the university and the schools of industrial journalism and mines at the State College have been abolished.

Contrary to expectations based on the rivalry between the two institutions, the plan has met with general approval. It is conceded that the move will result in lower taxes and that the state board has labored conscientiously to avoid impairment of actual efficiency of the general system.

Although not adopted formally, the board has recommended that all freshmen be required to live in dormitories, and that Greek-letter societies refrain from pledging until the end of the freshman year. This move, if adopted, as seems likely, will do much to maintain the integrity of the bond issues floated for construction of the state dormitories by concentrating student personnel.

The effect on the Greek-letter societies that have recently completed new houses, most of them financed by bonds or mortgages, has yet to be determined. It is generally felt that while the shoe may pinch for the first year the membership can be built up later through increasing the size of the pledge list of sophomores.

President Lyle Spencer, of the University of Washington, is said to have approved the plan in principle and said the State of Washington would soon have to follow suit.

The general plan will permit an interchange of work heretofore impossible, or accomplished at the expense of maintaining two duplicate units.

The university and State College are in the same sector of the Willamette Valley and only forty miles apart, making the interchange comparatively easy.

Under the new plan the president of the system will maintain headquarters at the state capital, Salem, with the vice-presidents or senior deans resident at their respective institutions. Selection of the new president of the system is now the major problem of the State Board of Higher Education and is expected to be made by July 1.

THE SUMMER SESSION OF THE UNIVERSITY OF CHICAGO

THERE will be six hundred and five courses offered by the University of Chicago during the coming summer quarter. These embrace work for undergraduates and graduate students in the university's four upper divisions and for professional students in seven schools.

The faculty will number 352, of whom 142 are full professors and 129 are associate or assistant professors. A modification of the university's policy this year has increased the proportion of regular members of the university staff who will continue to teach throughout the summer and has reduced the number of visiting faculty members to twenty-five.

The policy of confining the work of the summer quarter to ten weeks, which was inaugurated last year for the convenience of teachers who wish to study during the summer, will be continued this year. The first term will begin on June 20 and close on July 22, and the second term will open July 25 and close on August 26. Each term is credited toward a university degree as a minor, those registering for one term only being privileged to complete the major through the home-study department.

A total of 4,957 different students registered for either or both terms of the summer quarter last year, 3,273 having graduate status, 1,234 being undergraduates and 450 unclassified.

The School of Education headed by Dean Charles H. Judd, leads in the number of courses offered. Fifteen full professors, all members of the regular university faculty, and twenty-three staff members of lower rank, will offer sixty courses. The work is divided into nine subdivisions: Introductory courses; the school in the social order; educational psychology; educational administration; curriculum, methods and supervision; statistics and measurement; higher education; secondary education, and elementary education. The work of the school is housed largely in the new Graduate Education Building, erected at a cost of $600,000, which was formally opened on March 14 and 15.

Two conferences will supplement the academic work in education during the quarter, the seventh annual conference of administrative officers of institutions of higher education, to be held on July 13, 14 and 15, and the conference of public-school administrative officers to be held on July 18 and 22.

Three visitors will supplement the faculty of law: Robert L. Henry, Judge of the Mixed Court, Alexandria, Egypt; Sigvald Nielson, of Stanford University, and Roger J. Traynor, of the University of California. The Divinity School, which is headed by Dean Shailer Mathews, will offer 49 courses. The staff of 33 members, including 17 full professors, will include Dr. Edmund S. Conklin, professor of psychology at the University of Oregon; Leslie Blanchard, executive secretary, National Student Council, Young Men's Christian Association; Richard H. Edwards, executive director, National Council on Religion in Higher Education; W. Hubert Greaves, professor of public speaking, Yale University, and Justin W. Nixon, pastor, Brick Presbyterian Church, Rochester, New York. A Pastor's Institute will be held from August 1 to 10.

Carlton B. Joeckel, professor of library science at the University of Michigan, and Francis L. D. Goodrich, librarian of the College of the City of New York, will be members of the Graduate Library School faculty during the summer quarter. The School of Commerce and Administration will offer 21 courses and the School of Social Service Administration 27 courses, these offerings being supplemented by a large number of courses in closely related fields administered through other departments.

Of the four upper divisions, the Biological Sciences, which includes fourteen departments and the University Medical School, under the direction of Dean Frank R. Lillie, will offer 163 courses. The staff of 109 includes as visitors Katherine J. Densford, professor and director of the School of Nursing, the University of Minnesota; Harriet Frost, director of the department of instruction, the Visiting Nurse Society of Philadelphia, and Heinrich Siedentopf, privat-dozent, Universitäts-Frauenklinik, Leipzig.

One hundred and seven courses will be offered through the eleven departments in the Humanities Division, which is headed by Dean Gordon J. Laing. The staff of 52 faculty members will include as visitors under the Frederick Ives Carpenter Fund, Kemp Malone, professor of English at the Johns Hopkins University, and Baldwin Maxwell, chairman of the department of English at the State University of Iowa. Carl F. Tauesch, associate professor of business ethics in the Harvard Graduate School of Business Administration, will offer a course in the department of philosophy.

The Physical Sciences Division, embracing seven departments, will have a staff of 43 and will offer 93 courses. Visitors include Dr. Wilhelm Blaschke, professor of mathematics, University of Hamburg; Dr. Gerrit Bol, privatdozent in mathematics, University of Hamburg, and Dr. Aristide von Grosse, in chemistry. Dr. Henry G. Gale is dean of the division.

The Social Sciences Division, under Dean Beardsley Ruml, will include 61 staff members, 35 of whom are included in other divisions or schools, and will offer 63 courses. Dr. Ralph Linton, of the University of Wisconsin, will be a visiting professor of anthropology.

A program of nearly one hundred public lectures will be offered in addition to the regular courses. The university also provides an extensive program of social and recreational events. Physical facilities added during the current year include a series of residence halls providing unusual living accommodations for 400 men; the new Graduate Education Building, and the new Museum of the Oriental Institute.

EDUCATIONAL NOTES AND NEWS

Dr. J. L. Morrill, junior dean of the College of Education of the Ohio State University, has been appointed vice-president of the university, a newly established office.

Howard P. Savage, former national commander of the American Legion, has been elected business manager of the Chicago schools, with powers to aid in straightening out the system's tangled finances. Mr. Savage will serve four years at an annual salary of $12,000.

Mr. Donald H. Biery, formerly coordinator for the public schools in Oakland, California, has been appointed superintendent of Sherman Institute, Riverside, California, a non-reservation Indian boarding school.

Dr. Stephen P. Duggan, director of the Institute of International Education, New York City, will give the opening address at the Centennial Celebration convocation of Lafayette College on May 17. His subject will be "French Influences on American Education." Dr. Robert L. Kelly, secretary of the American Association of Colleges, will deliver the commencement address in June.

Dr. Harold W. Thompson, a member of the faculty of the New York State College for Teachers at Albany, has been elected to membership in the Royal Society of Edinburgh. The honor was bestowed in recognition of research work in Scottish literature.

Dr. James M. Kieran, president of Hunter College, New York, was the guest of honor on March 21 at a tea given at the college by the Student Council in celebration of the third anniversary of his inauguration as president.

Mr. Charles H. Cheney, superintendent of schools of the second supervisory district of Westchester County, was honored at a dinner on March 1 in New York City, in connection with the celebration of the centennial of New York University. He was one of 34 alumni who received medallions for meritorious service. The medallion is inscribed "To honor one who, through good deeds, has served his Alma Mater." On the other side of the medallion is a relief of the building of the Hall of Fame at New York University.

Dr. John C. French, librarian of the Johns Hopkins University, was elected president of the university chapter of the Phi Beta Kappa Society, at its annual meeting and election of officers on March 24. Dean Edward W. Berry, of the College of Arts and Sciences, was elected vice-president. Dr. Johannes Mattern, assistant librarian, secretary, and Dr. G. H. Evans, Jr., assistant professor of political economy, treasurer, were reelected.

The honorary degree of doctor of letters has been conferred by the University of Oxford on Professor Jérôme Carcopino, of the University of Paris, member of the Institute of France.

M. Henri Guy, in 1929–30 exchange professor from France, will return to Harvard University as lecturer on French and tutor in modern languages. His first visit to Harvard, in 1921, was also as exchange professor, while he was dean of the University of Toulouse. He is now rector of the University of Grenoble.

DR. JOHN ARCHIBALD VENN, Gilbey lecturer in agriculture in the University of Cambridge and junior fellow and bursar of Queens' College, son of the late president of Gonville and Caius College, has been elected president of Queens' College in place of the late Reverend T. C. Fitzpatrick.

ON the resignation, for reasons of ill health, of the Rev. G. H. Dix, principal of the College of St. Mark and St. John, Chelsea, England, Mr. James Herbert Simpson, head master of Rendcomb College, Cirencester, formerly assistant master at Rugby, has been appointed principal of the college.

MR. E. BRETT, of the City of Birmingham Education Department, has been appointed assistant secretary to the University of Birmingham, in place of Mr. C. C. Harris, who recently resigned.

THE correspondent of the London *Times* writes from Cairo under date of March 10: "Following the government's action in transferring Dr. Taha Husein from his position as dean of the faculty of arts in the Egyptian University to a subordinate position in the department of education most of the students of the four faculties of arts, law, science and medicine have gone on strike and Ahmed Lutfy Bey es Said, rector of the university, has tendered his resignation. The government has received vigorous protests against its action from European and Egyptian professors."

PROFESSOR EDWIN F. GAY, of Harvard University, will be on sabbatical leave during the second half of 1932 and the first half of 1933–34, in order to prepare a book on the industrial revolution in England. Leave of absence has also been granted to Associate Professor William Leonard Langer, of the department of history, and to Assistant Professor Rupert Emerson, of the department of government, for the academic year 1932–33, in order that each may carry on research work under a grant from the Bureau of International Research. Dr. Kuang-Ti Mei, assistant professor of Chinese, has been granted leave of absence for the academic year 1932–33.

PROFESSOR EDWARD T. LEE, dean of the John Marshall Law School of Chicago, is advocating before the Illinois State Bar Association the use of sound films to reproduce the trial record for consideration by appellate courts. The suggestion has received considerable support, but has been disapproved by the executive committee of the American Bar Association.

DR. ARTHUR N. HOLCOMBE, professor of government at Harvard University, will be a member of the faculty of the first School of Pacific and Oriental Affairs, which will be held as part of the coming summer session of the University of Hawaii.

MR. HIRAM A. JONES has been appointed chief of the Physical Education Bureau of the New York State Education Department. He has been serving provisionally in this position since last September.

DR. CORNELIA T. SNELL has been put in charge of the laboratory for pediatric research of the Fifth Avenue Hospital, New York City. Dr. Snell was previously engaged in the food research department at Columbia University under Dr. Sherman and since September has carried out pediatric research under I. G. Kugelmaas at the Fifth Avenue Hospital.

DR. FREDERICK B. ARTZ, associate professor of history at Oberlin College, has been appointed by the American Historical Association an editor of the *Journal of Modern History*.

AT the invitation of the president of the Municipal University of Omaha, Nebraska, Professor Donald P. Cottrell, of Teachers College, Columbia University, is conducting a study of the faculty of the university and of certain problems with reference to the relocation of the university buildings.

DR. FRANK W. HART, of the University of California, and Dr. Morse A. Cartwright, director of the American Association for Adult Education, have been appointed visiting professors of education at Teachers College, Columbia University. Professor Hart replaces Professor Nickolaus L. Engelhardt as associate director of the division of field studies of the

Institute of Educational Research. He is working on the Chicago school survey and serving as a member of the instructional group responsible for the courses for superintendents of schools.

DR. KENNETH C. M. SILLS, president of Bowdoin College, spoke on "The College of To-day and To-morrow" at a meeting of the Beverly unit of the American Association of University Women on March 17.

DURING the week of March 14, Dr. Anton J. Carlson, of the University of Chicago, delivered the following lectures at Bethany College, West Virginia, to the Medical Associations of the Upper Ohio Valley: "Reflections on the White House Conference on Child Health and Protection"; "New Knowledge of the Physiology and Pathology of the Endocrine Glands," and "The Appetite, Hunger and Thirst Mechanism."

MR. CHARLES B. SHAW, librarian of Swarthmore College, and Miss Vera Southwick Cooper, librarian of De Pauw University, will teach classes in library science during the summer session of 1932 at the University of Michigan. The visiting faculty will also include Mr. Rudolph H. Gjelness, executive assistant of the preparation division of the New York Public Library, and Miss Letitia Helen McQuillan, librarian of Kingswood School, Cranbrook, who will give a special course for teacher-librarians.

THE VERY REVEREND LIONEL FORD, dean of York and formerly head master of Harrow School, England, died on March 27 at the age of sixty-six years.

MYRON TAYLOR HALL, the new home of the Cornell Law School, will be dedicated on October 15 by the Honorable Cuthbert W. Pound, who was recently appointed chief judge of the New York State Court of Appeals. Judge Pound is a member of the class of 1887 and was professor of law at Cornell from 1895 to 1904. The building, which resulted from a gift of $1,500,000 from Mr. Myron C. Taylor, a graduate of the Law School in the class of 1894, who is chairman of the finance committee of the U. S. Steel Corporation, is now completed and is awaiting interior furnishing before being occupied. It is planned to make use of the new quarters for the coming summer session of the Law School before the formal opening this autumn, when Mr. Taylor will turn over the keys of the completed structure to the trustees of the university.

CREATION of a state university that would embrace all phases of public higher education is urged in a report submitted to the New Jersey State Legislature by the Board of Regents of Rutgers University. As outlined by the board, the university would consist of junior colleges, colleges of arts and sciences, technical schools, professional schools and probably in the future normal schools and teachers colleges. Suggesting that Rutgers University, which now receives state aid, be made the nucleus of the system, the board asked appropriations of $1,118,484 for 1932–33. Of that amount, $1,037,784 would go to Rutgers and the balance, with the exception of $30,000 for administration expenses of the board, to technical and engineering schools in Newark.

ON account of the prevailing economic conditions, Ozark Wesleyan College at Carthage, Missouri, will transfer its educational program to Baker University at the close of her fiscal year in June. The details of the transfer, which are being worked out by the authorities of the two institutions, plan for Baker University to take over the educational program of Ozark Wesleyan College and to serve her territory in the St. Louis Conference. Under this arrangement Baker University becomes the official Methodist college, not alone for the territory of the Kansas Conference, but also for most of the state of Missouri. More than a year ago, it was made the official Methodist college for the whole of Missouri north of the Missouri River. Besides carrying forward its educational program, Baker will perpetuate Ozark Wesleyan by adopting her alumni and caring for the records of the college. Under the new plan, however, the authorities of Ozark Wesleyan will work out their own financial problems, so that no obligation for any indebtedness or liabilities of that college will be assumed by Baker University.

MR. ARTHUR L. ENDICOTT, comptroller of Harvard University, has issued a financial statement in which he says: "As far as it is safe to make any prediction in such uncertain times as these, the situation, while calling for the practice of every economy, does not seem to necessitate at present a general reduction in salaries or wages. Some departments will be in a position to expand while others will be obliged to curtail or postpone some of their activities. If every departmental budget is balanced, as at present is expected, without drawing upon any accumulated reserves, the forecast is that the total operating expenses of the university will not fall below the total for the year 1930–31, which was $13,466,991, and that there will be no deficit for 1932–33."

ACCORDING to *The British Medical Journal* an Alfred Fripp Memorial Fellowship, endowed with the sum of £7,000, has been established at Guy's Hospital for promoting the advancement of knowledge and research in psychology through the study of children in health and disease. The fellowship will be awarded by a board of electors consisting of the physician for diseases of children, the superintendent and the dean of the medical school as *ex officio* members, and five others coopted by the *ex officio* members. It will be open to either sex, but candidates must be unmarried, not more than thirty years of age, and be qualified to practice medicine or surgery; they will be expected to submit with their application a scheme of advanced study or research work. The appointment will be whole-time—it may be held concurrently with a demonstratorship—for a period of two years, which may be extended for a further period not exceeding three years at the discretion of the board of electors. The Fripp fellow will be allowed opportunities for study in the children's department of the hospital, and the salary will be £300 per annum.

SIX members of the faculty of the Jacob Tome Institute, Port Deposit, Maryland, have resigned. The action follows that of Dr. Murray Peabody Brush, head master, who resigned on March 5. Dr. Brush had been at the school since 1919. Mr. Samuel C. Rowland, president of the board of trustees, is reported to have said that the resignations were in accordance with the policy of the institution to reduce its faculty to meet a decreased enrolment. All members of the faculty are appointed for a year.

MAYOR CHARLES H. SLOWEY, of Lowell, Massachusetts, has announced that the city has negotiated a temporary loan of $200,000 through a New York banking house; sale of tax anticipation notes brought $31,000 into the treasury, swelling the total from such sales to $230,000, and teachers in Lowell schools received their first pay since early in January, the amount being approximately $50,000, representing the school payroll for the latter half of December.

THE Hammond, Indiana, School Board has voted to close the city schools a month earlier this year because its funds are exhausted. The schools will close on May 15, giving 13,000 pupils another month of summer vacation. The failure of Hammond banks and deficiency of tax collections were blamed for the closing order. Teachers are to be paid in full to the date of the closing.

THROUGH the International Institute of Teachers College, Columbia University, New York, the Museum of International Education at Mainz, Germany, invites exhibits of achievements of American education from kindergarten to university. The museum has set aside twenty rooms for such exhibits. Material should be sent to Room 305, Teachers College, Columbia University, New York, where it will be accumulated and sent to Mainz during the summer. Research work plans, statistical material, educational publications, children's work, toys, text-books, tests, school periodicals, equipment, sketches, pictures and photographs of classrooms, playgrounds and schools are included in the wanted material.

DISCUSSION

MATHEMATICS A TOOL SUBJECT—AND MUCH MORE

THE place of any subject, such as mathematics, in the high school or college can be maintained only for reasons sufficient to justify that place. That it is a traditional subject is of no consequence, except in so far as other reasons have made and kept it traditional. Interested educators have listed numerous grounds on which it appears that there is a large value in the study of mathematics, as, for example, the ever-present need of the facts of mathematics in daily life (usually of an elementary character), the possible future need or the contingent value of mathematics in one's life, its large use as a tool in the physical sciences and its increasing use as a tool in the economic sciences and, in more abstruse form, its corrective influence in the organization of certain parts of philosophy, especially logic.

On these and similar grounds of a utilitarian nature mathematics has been appraised highly for the past fifty years that mark the great development of the present scientific age. And it is primarily the tool value that has been ascribed to this subject as justifying its study and its retention in our educational scheme.

And readily can this position be maintained. Commercial chemistry, chemical engineering, chemical research, medical research, are all demanding an increasingly extensive training in collegiate and post-graduate mathematics as an indispensable prerequisite. This is witnessed by the extension of National Research fellowships in medicine to similar fellowships in chemistry, physics and mathematics in succession. It is witnessed by the fact that our college professors of chemistry, biology and economics are insisting that their major students have a knowledge and a technical preparation in mathematics which they themselves never had, but which they covet. It is witnessed by the surprising growth of the study of statistics and the theory of probability in our colleges and universities, with applications to economics, education and the biological sciences. It is witnessed by the fact that increasingly many who are alert to the scientific problems of the day, but who have studied little or no collegiate mathematics, are seeking, and too often are seeking in vain, to gain a clear, exact apprehension of relativity, of the recently discovered cosmic rays, of the present contention over methods of cosmic evolution, of the intricate investigations of the past fifteen years into the nature and structure of the atom. There has never been a time when there was such a call for expository treatments of such subjects as these; yet the service of such books is necessarily limited, for these complex and abstruse subjects can be described only in mathematical terms and with mathematical processes which are studied in college or university or technical school; paradoxically and unfortunately, but all too truly, the better the exposition is adapted to the popular mind, the less accurately does it convey the facts. No more is it true in literature or art than in mathematics that the treasures of the realm are reserved for those who have toiled for them.

Mathematics does indeed furnish adequate tools whereby science may treat systematically and critically its observational data; as such it is "the handmaid of the sciences." It furnishes a language which is surpassingly exact and comprehensive. It does analyze and test the quantitative side of philosophy and other general fields; indeed, in logic it has afforded the only great advance since the time of Aristotle.

But much more must be said if one is to characterize accurately its place in the world of learning and its place in the curriculum.

(1) Scholars have in all ages appraised pure mathematics far above its applications. We are told that Archimedes, the greatest of ancient mathematicians, was in his lifetime praised chiefly for his mechanical inventions, such as his mechanical screw, his engines of war, etc., but that he himself prized far more highly his discoveries in pure science. He said that "every kind of art which was connected with daily needs was ignoble and vulgar." It is these discoveries of an abstract nature in the theory of numbers, in pure geometry and in hydrostatics for which he is known to the present day. Again, according to David Eugene Smith and others, the practical use of numbers "was looked upon by ancient scholars as a somewhat plebeian art"—"so humble was its status that it was taught chiefly by slaves"—while arithmetic, which was the abstract theory, "was considered an intellectual pursuit worthy of the attention of the philosopher."

The same relative rankings of pure and applied mathematics were made in the Middle Ages and are still made.

(2) It is more than a language. While much

effort must be given to the mastery of the technique of mathematics, and these difficulties often make the subject distasteful or put it beyond one's grasp, nevertheless the chief value of mathematics does not inhere in its study as a language. As a colleague says, "mathematical ideas, ever self-consistent however extended, become clearer and more easily transmitted through the invention of fitting mathematical language. Form, language, symbolism, are, however, the outer dress; within are the eternal laws of God."

(3) Quite apart from its applications, mathematics presents numerical and geometrical and logical relationships that very generally appeal to the educated person as having beauty and elegance; as such, it has always been studied for its own sake, with attention to matters of symmetry, completeness, generality, etc.

(4) The late President E. D. Burton said that "(the college) ought to help each student to acquire such a knowledge of the physical universe, of the history of the race, of the structure of society, and of the nature of the individual that, taking his stand at the center of his own being, he may have a sense of where he is." If we subscribe to this statement, then we must certainly agree that an adequately trained mind should have a broad knowledge of the domain of mathematics entirely apart from any of its uses. A science so fundamental as this, so universal and definite in its established facts, so sequentially and ideally and completely organized, should be denominated one of the large fields of thought for undergraduate study by the general student.

(5) Its hypotheses and methods can be controlled as can those of no other science; it is thus the ideal field of learning and affords a standard, a norm, a fine pattern for all learning.

(6) Not merely is it true, as Gauss said long ago, that "every science tends to become truly scientific to the degree to which it becomes mathematical," but we may say more than that: just as the great Greek teacher used mathematics to train the mind and to enable the soul to get a glimpse of truth (Sir Thomas L. Heath), so to-day the great philosophical problems of causation, determinism, the nature of space and time, matter and energy, as they are more exactly formulated, *become* mathematics. It has proved difficult or impossible for keen philosophers to make a clear distinction between logic and mathematics, so closely fused are these two fields. Mathematics has been an ever-present tool to physics and chemistry, but it is a striking fact that within the past six years the core of these two subjects, *viz.*, the study of the molecule, has *become* mathematics; the physicist has replaced a vibration in the ether by a mathematical symbol for a vibration and has dismissed from his mind the physical, material image.

For these reasons I claim that mathematics is more than a tool and more than a language; it is one of the separate main fields of thought, and should be so classified in the curricula of the college and associated schools where liberal arts have their sway.

This lays no light task on the teacher of mathematics. It brings with it the responsibility for realizing this high ideal to the utmost of our ability. It lays on our conscience and our professional pride the necessity of acquainting ourselves with the broad scope and the far-reaching character of mathematics and the need of making in our own minds an appraisal of the relative values of the various portions of the mathematical field (1) for the student who seeks general culture, (2) for the prospective worker in applied mathematics, (3) for the prospective specialist in pure mathematics. My concern in the present discussion is for the first of these three classes; the last two are adequately provided for in our present educational scheme.

It imposes on us, too, the task of examining the present plans in our high schools and colleges, to determine whether the high ideals which I have outlined are included in the purposes which guide our courses for the general student. And it is a task which in the long run we can not evade.

A fine tribute to mathematics from a remote field of learning was paid by a man of letters, a professor of English in one of our Ohio colleges, soon after the death of a colleague whose clear and steadfast mind was an honor to mathematics. "There must be something exalting," he wrote, "about the study and teaching of pure mathematics, for the subject is less colored by material considerations than almost any other that could be named. 'God ever geometrizes,' says Plato, and those who are engaged in mathematical speculation must feel that they are coming into as close contact as man may with the deepest laws of the universe. To have spent one's life in this companionship and to have helped even a few ardent young men and women—for they must always be few—to share the austere joys of it is to have done a rare and beneficent work. There are many, as Aeneas told the young Ascanius, from whom we may learn what constitutes success; there are few who can reveal to us the majesty of eternal law."

William D. Cairns
Oberlin College

FRENCH METHODS OF TEACHING COMPOSITION

In the last issue of the *Bulletin of the American Association of University Professors* there is printed an address by Dr. Charles H. Judd on the "Psychology of the Learning Processes at the Higher Levels." Two paragraphs in this address call for a supplementary statement. In these paragraphs he says:

The American college teacher of composition, with his attention directed to the products of student writing, classifies examples of writing in a purely objective way as description, narration, exposition, or argumentation. He treats rhetoric as a science of written forms. The French teacher of composition, on the other hand, realizes that the written product is nothing but a recorded result of more or less successful psychological processes. The French teacher of composition asks such questions as these: Is the writing indicative of careful observation? Has the writer exercised his imagination in the effort to supplement the experiences which he gained through observation? Has the writer added to the bare account of facts illuminating statements which show that he has reflected on the meaning of what he saw and heard? In short, the French teacher of composition does his thinking in terms of psychology rather than in the terms of an objective classification of rhetorical forms.

The result of the French system of teaching composition is known to all students of comparative education. When students leave the *lycée,* they are in possession of a style of writing and speaking incomparably superior in clarity and effectiveness to the utterly inadequate pattern of expression found among the majority of American college graduates.

While I am not a teacher of English or English composition, it seems obvious to me that one might emphasize the "objective forms" of description, narration, exposition and argumentation, and still ask those questions which are alleged to be the private property of French teachers of composition. I would venture to assert that a majority of our teachers of English composition do ask those questions. Then why do they not get results?

Dr. Judd must know that the students who go to a French *lycée* are a relatively picked group, with mental gifts far superior to the mental gifts of three fourths of the students who throng our American high schools.

Furthermore, he must know that the students who emerge from the French *lycée* have had more training in foreign languages, both ancient and modern, than 90 per cent. of the students who graduate from our American colleges and universities. There are some of us who still believe that Goethe was more than half right when he insisted that a man never fully understood his own language until he had mastered some foreign tongue. Emerson, Lowell, Hawthorne, Washington Irving, and Cooper, so far as they had any training in composition, were brought up on the old-fashioned rhetoric, yet somehow, by reading the best in English literature and by translating foreign masterpieces, they seem to have acquired an English style that was lucid, appropriate and effective. Is it too much to assume that any boy of really superior gifts may attain some of the secrets of style in a similar way? On the other hand, we can safely declare, without making any assumption, that no method of instruction can give clarity and effectiveness of expression to a boy of inferior gifts.

I have no thought of trying to discredit in any way the method of French teachers of composition. It seems desirable, however, to make it clear that even French teachers of composition using French methods, might fail to produce results, if they were compelled to teach the unselected and untrained groups that fill the freshman and sophomore classes in our American colleges and universities.

Charles N. Smiley
Carleton College

SPECIAL CORRESPONDENCE

CONTROL OF EXTRACURRICULAR ACTIVITIES IN HIGH SCHOOL

WITH more and more emphasis on shorter working hours, the five-work-day week, the machine-made article which is replacing the hand-made one, etc., it becomes necessary to provide for unoccupied time, for a worthy use of leisure. The place to begin training for this is in school, since the school is replacing the home. The schools have begun to realize that there is an urgent need for an extension of the curriculum. The traditional subjects no longer completely fill the need. The school population has changed in numbers and caliber within the last twenty years, and a progressive school must take cognizance of this fact. For this reason we find that extracurricular activities have been introduced as an outlet. In the high school we have the middle and late adolescent period, in which boys and girls want to meet each other. The instinct of gregariousness must be satisfied, and here the high school through its clubs has an excellent opportunity to direct boys and girls along the lines of their interests.

There is, however, a great danger in extracurricular activities, as with any new idea when first introduced. It is apt to make the pendulum swing too far to one side. There must not be an over-emphasis on the extracurricular activities, with the result that the curriculum itself is neglected. The time will come when the two parts will be merged into a unified whole so that the student, when leaving high school, has a well-rounded education, by which he has been able to "find himself." It therefore becomes necessary to have a qualified faculty member as director of extracurricular activities who will guide and advise students.

This implies a definite program and control of activities. Such an attempt has been made at the James Monroe High School, Bronx. All activities which do not fall under the curriculum have been grouped under five headings, A, B, C, D, E, according to the amount of time required of the student in the activity, the importance of the activity to the proper functioning of the school and the honor attached to the activity in the eyes of the student body. In Group A we have the president of the G.O., the president of the Senior Class, the president of the Service League, the editor-in-chief of the school publication, the captain of the Patrol Squad, and the principal part in a major school production. In Group E we find all office squads, traffic squad, clubs, etc. All other activities, of which there are more than one hundred, are in groups B, C or D. Group A receives five units, Group B four units, Group C three units, Group D two units and Group E one unit. Each activity is classified according to whether it is of a literary, executive, athletic, clerical or dramatic nature. The purpose of this classification and unit evaluation is to restrict and guide pupils in their choice of activities. All students are advised to participate in some activity, and to prevent the few from taking all the major positions and offices, the plan restricts the student to nine units of activity, of which not more than two may be of the same kind, *i.e.*, literary, executive, etc. Furthermore, no student may have more than one activity in Group A, two in Group B, three in C, four in D, and five in E, but in no term may the total exceed nine units, except those of Group A who may have twelve units. In this way many more students may enter the activities which train for leadership, because those who in former terms held all positions of honor and importance are now restricted. It has been found that leaders have been developed who formerly were too modest to try against a popular student. In the matter of guidance into the proper activity three things are considered of paramount importance, namely, the student's own interest, the scholastic record and the health record. Each student is checked for the latter two from the official school records.

Many colleges now require for new entrants a statement concerning participation in extracurricular activities. In order to make this more objective instead of a mere subjective statement, a plan for evaluating activities has been devised. Each activity has assigned to it a maximum point credit, based on two main factors: the amount of work required of the student in the particular activity and the value to the school administration. These points range from fifty for Service League president to five for club membership, all others being in multiples of five in between. The system for recording is very simple. Toward the end of each term, each teacher in charge of an activity is required to rate each pupil in his activity on a basis of one to five (five for excellent work). The teacher must take into account the amount of time devoted to the activity and the quality of the service rendered. These ratings are then interpreted in terms of the maximum credit allowed. This credit becomes a part of the student's permanent record. It is entered on the achievement card in the form of a fraction, the denominator showing the maximum obtainable for that activity and the numerator indicating the actual accomplishment of the student in that activity. The total numerators over the total denominators gives a clear indication of the student's all-round ability and also what kind of work he has performed in all his undertakings.

The clerical part of the routine work of recording is done by a selected group of the Service League under the guidance of the faculty director of extracurricular activities. The Service League is an honor organization of third- and fourth-year students who have rendered invaluable service to their school for a period of at least one year and who have demonstrated to the faculty that in character they are worthy of membership in this honor organization.

Eugenie C. Hausle,
In charge of extracurricular activities
James Monroe High School, N. Y.

AN ENGLISH PLAN FOR THE WHOLE TEACHING STAFF

The teacher of literature is not expected to permit habitual carelessness in the simple arithmetical processes or in the handling of whatever historical, scientific or other material students may need to use. Is it unreasonable, then, to ask teachers of other subjects to require of the members of their classes something more than occasional conformity to the fundamental principles and details of standard English usage?

Special measures for improvement adopted in the past have been used mainly with freshmen, apparently with the hope that young students could be so grounded in good English that acceptable speech and writing would follow them all the days of their lives. A more comprehensive and effective plan is needed. The one outlined below is passing through its second year of experiment at Davidson College and gives promise of success.

The first step was the adoption by the faculty of a requirement which is explained in the college catalogue in a paragraph reading in part as follows:

> Students whose oral or written English is at any time unsatisfactory to one or more professors are regarded as conditioned in the use of English. When a student is thus conditioned he is required to take each test given thereafter by the English Department for such conditioned students until he makes a satisfactory grade. When a student has removed his condition in the use of English, he may be conditioned thereafter as often as his speech or writing becomes unsatisfactory to one or more professors.

A short time after the midyear examinations the dean asks all members of the teaching staff to give him the names and the points of special weakness of students in their courses who are not meeting the requirement stated above. From the reports handed in a general list is compiled. The members of the English department then confer with those reported and suggest to them means of improvement. Toward the end of the academic year a practical test is given to all students on the list. In this test special attention is given to spelling, punctuation and other fundamental aspects of usage.

The advantages of the plan are several. Instead of being observed in only one or two departments of study, each student's use of English is under quiet supervision in all classes throughout his college course. Official responsibility is thus shared by all members of the faculty, though the burden actually borne by those who do not teach English is very light. Their duty is simply to report students to the dean. The student himself is held to strict accountability. Accurate writers are made as well as born, and almost any student worthy to be in college can and will measure up to a satisfactory standard of English usage if he is required—not merely urged—to write and speak acceptably. When the college seriously takes an official stand in the matter, the right use of language is effectively impressed upon the careless student, who learns at last that he is facing not a formal and artificial requirement of one academic department, but a body of doctrine to be mastered and regularly applied in daily communication.

Wherever the general plan outlined here may be adopted, it can easily be varied in its particulars according to the views of different teaching staffs. The one thing needful is coöperation, and the secret of securing it seems to lie in making participation easy for those faculty members who do not teach English.

Edwin F. Shewmake
Davidson College

QUOTATIONS

AN INSTITUTE OF EDUCATION IN LONDON

The development of the science and art of teaching is vital to our national well-being, and the stimulation of post-graduate work with this end in view will be encouraged by the fact that the London Day Training College will pass next September wholly into the control of the University of London, a university which has many direct links with Imperial life. The Board of Education agreed in November, 1930, to the transfer from the London County Council to the university, provided that by September, 1932, reasonable progress had been made in the provision of new buildings. This progress has now been made and eventually the college will have its place on the Bloomsbury site of the university. Meanwhile it will continue to occupy the present site in Southampton Row belonging to the London County Council, and doubtless it will always continue to use the London elementary and secondary schools as practice schools in addition to the demonstration schools attached to the college. In this sense the college has always had a special local value, but the transfer from the London County Council to the University of London in no way alters that position. Indeed from at any rate the year 1909 the relationship of the college and the university has been very close. It was admitted as a school of the university in the Faculty of Arts in Pedagogy in that year and nine of the fourteen teachers are what is called Recognized Teachers of the University. The college has always had a high pedagogical ideal. It equips teachers for any branch of the teaching profession, it fulfils all the requirements of the Board of Education for a day training college, and it enables students to take the London degrees of B.A. and B.Sc., and, in the case of post-graduate students, the Teachers' Diploma awarded by the university.

What is, then, the meaning of the change that will take place next September? Clearly the real change will be gradual, with the ultimate goal of creating an Institute of Education on a larger scale—possibly approximating to the scope of work done at Teachers College, Columbia University. It is certain that the college will continue to train teachers and will continue to provide facilities for educational research. But the scale will be Imperial as well as English. Already there has been an effort to develop the Imperial side of the college, and advanced students are at work. Indeed one of the present goals is to admit advanced students who wish to make a special study of some branch of educational method, history, or organization under the principal, Sir Percy Nunn, who has been for many years the fountain of new educational inspiration. The need of research in education is, in some senses, as necessary as the need of research in medicine, and indeed the two sciences overlap at various points and the new college will develop on every side this function of its being. But the original function, the actual provision of teachers to supply the demands of the London County Council and the Board of Education, will not be forgotten, and it may be that the training of Oxford and Cambridge men for service in the great Public Schools will form part of the work. The older universities to some extent now use the London Day Training College, but it is a strange thing that many old schools still have a preference for untrained teachers. It may be that there is something lacking in the training hitherto given, or that the freshness of the young graduate for teaching work is, in the eyes of some head masters, lost in the processes of formal training. That ought not to be so, and perhaps the new Institute of Education will show that the head masters are mistaken.—*The Times Educational Supplement.*

REPORTS

A STUDY OF THE DENVER OPPORTUNITY SCHOOL

Under the title "What is this Opportunity School?" the American Association for Adult Education, 6 East 42nd Street, New York City, has published for free distribution a bulletin of 86 pages which presents a study of the Denver Opportunity School at Denver, Colorado. The bulletin is the product of two authors, Dr. Fletcher Harper Swift, professor of education in the University of California, and Dr. John W. Studebaker, superintendent of public schools, Des Moines, Iowa.

To the title question the authors give the reply at the outset that the Denver Opportunity School is "undoubtedly one of the most unusual and successful experiments in adult education to be found anywhere in the world." It has been in operation for sixteen years. Throughout these years this school "has rendered and is still rendering three great services to the solution of the problem of unemployment as well as of many other social problems.

''First, in up-grading those who are regularly employed.

''Second, in sustaining the morale of those temporarily unemployed.

''Third, by contributing in a most remarkable way to the occupational, economic, social, intellectual and moral rehabilitation of the large and increasing group of unemployed in a prosperous and growing American city.''

The Denver Opportunity School had its beginning in the vision of "Emily Griffith, an eighth grade teacher in a school located in the midst of an industrial and foreign section of Denver." She carried her campaign to employers, organized labor and social agencies. The board of education was convinced that a trial should be given to the proposal of this social missionary. In September, 1916, Opportunity School was opened in an old school building. Instead of the meager numbers expected 2,398 enrolled the first year. For the past eight years the annual enrolment has exceeded 9,000. The daily average attendance in 1931 was 3,875 men and women.

The specific aims of the founders of Opportunity School were:

(1) To provide a working knowledge of many trades and industries;

(2) To offer opportunities to men and women already engaged in mechanical and industrial and commercial pursuits who have the ambition to become more efficient workers;

(3) To provide the fundamentals of an education for those persons who have been deprived of school advantages in youth;

(4) To give another chance to boys and girls who for various reasons have not fitted well into the regular public schools;

(5) To give people born in other countries a chance to learn English and also to prepare them for naturalization and citizenship.

About 73 per cent. of the students take trade or commercial courses. "Nevertheless the school is far from being merely a vocational school, for it provides classes in general or academic subjects in its elementary and high-school departments, classes for illiterates, and classes in citizenship." The student's program is "adjusted to his personal schedule." Some get the training they need in a short time, others attend for several years.

Courses are established or discontinued on the basis of demand. A class is rarely started for less than twenty applicants, although in a few instances ten or twelve have been deemed sufficient.

Messrs. Swift and Studebaker have chapters describing how the school cooperates with employers, with organized labor and with the social agencies of the city. Facts are given about the teaching staff, which in 1931 numbered 57 in the day school and 62 in the night school, with an actual total of 84 individuals.

As to finances, it is shown that in 1920–30,

"Denver spent for current costs of Opportunity School $225,668, which was 4.42 per cent. of the total spent for current costs of all public schools in the city. The annual cost per pupil in average daily attendance of all Denver schools was $108.06; of the senior high schools $145.26; of the Opportunity School, including day and evening classes, $131.30."

The bulletin has a closing chapter on problems and basic issues in which the authors give replies to various question including these:

Is a day school for adults necessary? Should opportunity schools be free? Should every city maintain an opportunity school? Shall states establish opportunity schools?

R. W.

EDUCATIONAL RESEARCH AND STATISTICS

THE STATUS OF PARENTAL EDUCATION IN THE COLLEGES OF OHIO

IN July, 1928, the new department of adult education at Ohio State University sent a letter to all colleges in Ohio listed by the state department of education as having approved teacher-training courses. This letter requested information concerning work in all phases of adult education, both intramural and extramural. A specific inquiry was made for information about any work for parents, such as credit or non-credit courses, extension courses, lectures or lecture series, psychological clinics open to parents with their children and off-campus clinics or guidance centers. The letter asking for this information was sent to each college president.

Thirty-eight catalogues were sent for examination; about a dozen letters, stating whether or not extension work was offered, supplemented the catalogues. Letters from Cleveland College, the University of Cincinnati and Akron University told in some detail about parental education programs in these three institutions.

The U. S. Office of Education sent a surveyor into Ohio in 1928 to make an investigation of the work in parental education in this state. The results were published in the Biennial Survey of Education in the United States, 1928–1930, Chapter ix, which is published as a separate Bulletin, No. 20. Miss Lombard, the author of the section on parent education, found two colleges in Ohio conducting work in parental education under appropriations allowed by the institution itself, or through the use of benefactions; and one other college which had the support of the Spelman Fund. The state department of education was at that time one of twelve state departments having state-wide work in the field.

In 1924 Miss Emeline Whitcomb, for the Bureau of Education, had made a study of work in pre-parental education offered by departments of home economics. When the data were collected only two centers in Ohio offered courses or nursery-school practice in the pre-parental field. These institutions were the University of Cincinnati and Ohio State University.

Because of interest in the education of parents in every part of Ohio, our department in 1928 adopted a program of cooperating with the colleges in the state so as to stimulate them to develop courses suited to the needs and interests of parents. Every college president was placed on our mailing list. By this means every president received at least the *Better Parents Bulletin* once a month, the news-release from our department at least once a month (sometimes oftener), announcements of courses, special conferences and samples of current materials.

In cooperation with the parent education committee of the State Parent-Teacher Association a conference of college representatives was invited to assemble on the Ohio State University campus to discuss the services which the colleges might offer to parents, either in courses, consultation clinics or as leadership training centers. This conference met on October 19, 1929. Nineteen colleges and 7 other organizations sent representatives. Thirty persons registered. A complete report of that meeting was compiled from the shorthand minutes of a stenographer, and was sent to all college presidents, as well as to the participants in the conference.

In pursuance of directions embodied in a vote before adjournment, a second conference was invited on February 21, 1930.

Forty persons attended this February conference, 14 colleges were represented by delegates; 7 college presidents, deans or other interested representatives sent letters in lieu of personal attendance.

No report was returned from this conference. The secretary's records of the discussion indicated hesitancy on the part of many of the delegates to push a service program in their colleges. This hesitancy appeared to result from two causes—(1) the absence of any clearly expressed local need for the work and (2) the impending financial depression. The parent-teacher association in Ohio had not developed any plan for throwing its pressure upon the colleges for reinforcement of its avowed policy of promoting parental education. Here and there city councils and individual groups were asking for help, but no impulse had been manifest throughout the state.

In the summer of 1931 the department of adult education decided to recheck the data obtained by the initial survey in 1928. A request was sent to 65 colleges in Ohio for their latest catalogues. Fifty of the colleges returned catalogues. Of the 15 colleges not replying the majority were technical schools, some of which probably do not print catalogues yearly. However, catalogues were not received from 3 colleges, which are included in this report. Information was given by officials of the institutions in personal conferences.

Of the 50 catalogues received, 8 came from technical schools which do not offer courses for parents.

The remaining 42 catalogues which supplied data for this survey were scanned with the following questions in mind:

1. What fundamental or elementary courses are offered which are basic to work in parental education?

2. What courses are offered specifically in the field of parental education?

3. Is any provision made for students not regularly enrolled in the college to take these courses? That is, does the college admit to its courses special students, or mature students who may not be able to fulfill the regular entrance requirements?

4. Is any provision made especially for parents in these courses; or, is any extension work offered to parents?

The findings from the catalogues are presented in the following tables:

TABLE I

General Foundation Courses. Colleges Contributing, 42

Courses	Colleges
General psychology	41
Educational psychology	39
Sociology	41
Elementary physiology	25
Home economics department	22

TABLE II

Courses Offered Specifically in the Field of Parental Education

Courses	No. of colleges
Character education	5
Psychology of childhood	18
Health education	3
Home management	15
Child care and training	9
Child development	9
Psychology of adolescence	14
The family	21
Child welfare	5
Religious education	10
Miscellaneous courses[1]	14

[1] Twenty-six miscellaneous courses are offered by 14 of the colleges. An example would be a hygiene course in the women's physical education department, the description of which suggests subject-matter useful to parents.

TABLE III

Provisions for Special or Mature Students

	Colleges
Mature students admitted as specials	24
No special undergraduate students admitted	1
Special students admitted only in music	1
Extension and correspondence courses specified	2
Nothing said	15

Note: One college is repeated, as it admits both special students and extension students.

A study of the catalogues did not reveal the informal offerings in parental education which were known to exist in several of the college centers. In order to supplement the formal catalogue statements a follow-up letter was mailed to the president of each of the 42 colleges returning catalogues. The letter briefly explained the study being made and asked the following questions:

Does any department in your institution offer any courses, either credit or non-credit, for parents? If so, what is the enrolment?

Conditions under which courses are offered: Is matriculation in the institution required? Fee? Course fee?

If included in the catalogue, please give the catalogue number. If not, please give a description of the course: title, hours per week, length of term, department, lecture, text-book, further description of course.

Twenty-seven colleges replied to the questionnaire. Of these, four colleges—Kent, Wilberforce, Wilmington and Wittenberg—stated that an informal program of parental education was offered. In three others—Defiance, Findlay and Heidelberg—committees are at work formulating plans and studying the local demand. One college (Western College for Women) stated that although it was in sympathy with an adult education program its organization did not make feasible such a program. Ohio State University, Cleveland College and the University of Cincinnati are not included in this report as each of them has a definitely developed program of parent education which is adequately described in special reports and announcements, available for any one interested. In this statistical analysis the inclusion of these well-developed departments would obscure the picture in the other colleges which may be considered typical of the resources now available in Ohio for parental education.

A summary of the data furnished by the colleges supplies the following facts and conclusions:

(1) Colleges, the potential centers of parental education, are easily available in every district of Ohio.

(2) Forty-two colleges now offer courses fundamental to the field of parental education.

(3) Thirty-four colleges offer additional courses which would be recommended to those interested in the field of parental education.

(4) Twenty-four colleges have provisions for admission of mature students who desire to enter as special students.

(5) In addition to the three large colleges with well-developed departments, 4 colleges have definite work in the field of parental education (Wittenberg, Wilberforce, Kent, Wilmington).

Any movement of parental education depends upon leaders; and in order to secure a supply of leaders over the state there has to be some plan for adequate training. In the absence of a salaried and professional status for leaders, a certain amount of supervision and training could be given by teacher-training institutions to local leaders.

The fact that 42 colleges in all parts of the state now offer suitable fundamental courses, and 34 of these offer more specific work in the field of parental education indicates that specialists are already in service who are equipped to give special work with very little, if any, extra expense to the colleges.

The vast majority of the colleges do not recognize the possibilities of utilizing their departments which are already in operation. Although the colleges express sympathy for a program of parental education and approval of the steps that have been taken in this field, only a few of them have any plans for providing such education for parents and leaders in their area. Many of their catalogues do not even state whether they will accept special students, which, of course, is the only practicable, and in most cases, possible, classification for a mature person desiring training in the field of parental education.

CARROL DAY TIBBALS
JESSIE A. CHARTERS
OHIO STATE UNIVERSITY

NEW BOOKS IN EDUCATION

GRILL, GEORGE W. *The Minutes of a Board of Education: A Handbook for Public School Executives.* Pp. xiii + 215. Bruce.

KNUDSEN, CHARLES W. *Evaluation and Improvement of Teaching.* Doubleday, Doran. $2.50.

JASPERS, KARL. *Die Geistige Situation der Zeit.* Pp. 191. Walter de Gruyter, Berlin.

VAN ALSTYNE, DOROTHY. *Play Behavior and Choice of Play Materials of Pre-school Children.* Pp. xii + 103. University of Chicago Press. $1.00.

EDUCATIONAL REVIEW

Edited by WILLIAM McANDREW

EDITORIAL COMMENT

RICHARD WELLING'S TRACTATE

Ernest Blair writes from Boston, "Your Cole and Loesch tributes are needed. Our youngsters should have examples not too remote. Let us have more mention of present-day patterns." Very well. How about Richard Welling? I see he is sending out, for thousands of civic classes, a short specific summary of the way our common business is warped and wasted by the spoilsmen. The stockholders, the owners, of any productive organization, says Richard, hunt for ability and put it in the positions where it reduces waste and increases company profits. People's government is always in danger, as Washington often remarked, of degradation by the interests of selfish men, eager for personal profit. After several generations of scandalous waste, men mindful of general welfare pushed the merit system into the civil service of government. Commander Welling's leaflet reviews the struggles to get this just and logical plan made an integral part of our self-governing machinery. He quotes facts bearing on the violation of the spirit and letter of the civil-service law by Republicans and Democrats. He shows why and how politicians preserve the spoils system, how it wastes fifty per cent. of the public money abstracted from you as taxes, how it takes toll of life in preventable fires and pestilences.

Three states have the merit system imbedded in their constitutions. All state, county, city, town and village governments are subject to the blight of spoils corruption. Public education was established as nurse and physician to keep the body politic clean and hale. What do your boys and girls know of this civic disease and remedy? Ask them what they're going to do about it.

This is the line of Welling's little essay.

Who is he and why should he bother?

Young and vigorous at 74 years, this obstinate crusader graduated from Harvard fifty-two years ago and has practiced law in New York forty-nine years. He was a charter member of the City Reform Club, an organizer of good government associations, and of the National Municipal League, commissioner of civil service, secretary of the Society for the Prevention of Cruelty to Animals, director of the Municipal Art Society, National Sculpture Society and of the New York Philharmonic, was ensign in the Spanish-American war and in command of the naval base at Montauk Point during the world conflict. Early convinced of the discouraging labor of teaching old dogs new tricks, he added to his civic program encouragement to schools in assuming their historic duty of producing a citizenry able and desirous of purifying its politics. He became president of the George Junior Republic, took membership in the Academy of Political Science, in the Society for the Experimental Study of Education, in the Progressive Education Society, in the National Society for the Study of Education and in the National Education Association. Tired of hearing speakers remark upon his proposals, "That is very well from the layman's standpoint, but one must consider the principles of education, etc., etc.," he resolved to delve into the sacred esoterics of the educator. At 50 years of age he matriculated in New York University and in two years answered his critics with his own earned degree of master of pedagogy.

With the quiet manners of a Virginia colonel, with the modesty of an Ogden Mills, with the unwearied persistence of a Grant, this generous preacher and practitioner of political honesty seems to me the one to whom I would give the civic crown. He is a constant shame to me that I don't do more and better.

SPICY MATTER FOR HISTORY AND ENGLISH TEACHERS

Six years ago a group of high-school teachers in and around Boston conceived the happy idea of pooling their interest in historical and cultural research. They arranged with "The Boston Bookshop for Boys and Girls" to print the rare and good things the participants found in the rich old libraries of Boston and to issue in the form of bulletins the discoveries appertaining to life and society especially in tenth to seventeenth century Europe, or in early American history, exploration of the Southwest, war songs of the revolution, and forgotten matters in Jefferson's purchase of Louisiana.

The six teacher pioneers have uncovered a vein of treasure which is found to be in wide demand. Libraries ask for the bulletins. Harvard, Columbia, Marquette and New York University professors coaxed their way into membership.

A good, true and beautiful friend has made me a present of a bound volume of bulletins and I have revelled in it. Here are medieval Paris and London, guilds, markets, schools, universities, hospitals, courts, reproductions of stained glass, early maps and wood cuts. Words and music of the old cantata, "Innsbruck, I Must Leave Thee," Franklin's satire, "Selling the Hessians," image carvers in Paris in 1268, building a castle in 1079, words and music of sixteenth century English rounds, and so on. The volume affords entertainment and instruction for hours at a time. And some good soul has added to each quotation a suggestive series of "Notes for Teachers."

I fancy you may wish to do a good turn for history and literature teachers by telling them they can get into this club by sending Bertha Mahoney, 270 Boylston St., Boston, fifteen dollars for a school membership bringing 21 bulletins as they will come for 40 successive weeks; ten dollars for a library membership securing three copies a week; five dollars for any one satisfied with one copy weekly.

PROTEST FROM PEORIA

ONE of my unconverted friends, beloved of his fellow citizens, in the regenerated city whose schools are managed by the four-square Fisher, writes me, "I'm reading your breviary. From several sources lately, including its penetrating observations, is coming the suggestion that educators should be more keenly aware of the social, political significance of their obligation, and, furthermore, should be doing something about it. I see no point in saying these things and nothing more. There is already enough generalizing. In what way can the teacher on the firing line do his work differently as a result of reading your quotations on the civic aspects of education?

"It hardly seems reasonable to expect the high-school teacher to change society or perhaps even to achieve any significant interpretation of the movements needed."

Dearly beloved, these are the very ones that will have to do it. They have the children at the age when thinking, when public-mindedness, when unselfish desires for the general welfare, begin to show. Are not these high-school teachers, as Thomas Balliet is used to say, the main reliance for preparing a citizenry with minds tuned to economic, cooperative, political thinking by which the problems of our common lot will be undertaken?

The cause why it "hardly seems reasonable" to my Peoria protester that high-school teachers will change things is parallel with the lack of enthusiasm of a corset maker for the new clothing of womankind.

Joy Morgan is broadcasting through the National Education Association a remarkable invitation to high schools to get out of bed. Joy calls the high-school teachers a great body of consecrated leaders taking eager youngsters through tasks that do not reach the compelling motives of life. The pressing needs of the time are not represented at all in any of the high-school subjects. Teachers are half-heartedly teaching unused languages and theoretical mathematics. The high-school curriculum is wooden, chained to a dead past. High-school ought to be a community college responsive to the needs of a distressed present. The old American civilization is gone. A new one must be guided. Editor Morgan concludes this appraisal with a claim that the high-school teacher is the main reliance for achieving the new day.

Comes Chicago Judd, asserting, "What is needed is not a compromise but a thorough-going reform." John Tildsley, high-school superintendent of our largest city, concludes we'll have to scrap the high-school and build a new system on the original but neglected proposition that, to preserve a nation established to continue by self-government, its citizens must be trained in the essentials of such government, which are economics, politics, law, justice, union, domestic tranquillity, common defense, blessings of liberty (with the accent on the blessings) and general welfare.

GETTING HIGH SCHOOL OUT OF BED

What Grover Cleveland, Charles Hughes and Calvin Coolidge have called a political laziness of us Americans may not be any more chronic among high-school teachers than in other citizens, but it is more noticeable there, as profanity would be among preachers, for the reason that these teachers are, according to the promises of those who got the community taxed for high schools, the ordained correctors of civic indifference.

Ultimately the protests of Seaburys, Robinsons, Russells, Kilpatricks, Watsons, Sneddens, Ruggs, Deweys, Strayers, Judds, Coffmans, Eldridges, Bodes, Thomases, Suzzallos, Morgans, Bakers and others will, in the persisting difficulties of our nation, effect a drastic upset of high-school practice.

Every schoolman ought to know how much better it is for education to blow her own nose than to have the people, through legislatures, blow it for her.

In what way, asks my Peoria prodder, can the teacher on the firing line do his work differently?

If he's already on the firing line he's ahead of the multitude. There's where every teacher, worth his salt, belongs. Let him, in this welter of extracurricular joy-riding pursuits, form a political service club and with the coming citizens study what ails the politics of his own city, state and nation. Let his club issue protests and praise where indicated. Let it attend political meetings giving something of the attention to civic matters as is given to Latin syntax, Caesar, Cicero and Vergil. Let him wage gallant war against what Joy Morgan calls the wooden curriculum of the high school tethered to the dead past, let him—oh come, Peoria, you could sit down with paper and pencil and, writing down "How can a high school teacher change the moribund civic sense of this country?" answer it with scores of directions so direct, practical and necessary as to make yourself seem ridiculous to the academic world.

Wherefore, turn again to the civic breviary which is given, in part, here every month, a service for morning hour ere the schoolman sets out to his daily duty. Prime, terce, sext and nones of the verses have appeared here since the fifth of December. So many more are coming through the mail one might think the revolution Noah Webster said in 1787 we schoolmasters need is on the way.

A SCHOOLMAN'S BREVIARY

To be read in the closet and at conventicles of the major and minor orders.

61. A REVOLUTIONARY CHANGE NEEDED. There must be a reorganization leading to social interests. I see no other way out of our educational confusion. The change will be revolutionary. Further extension of "the scientific method" may increase bewilderment. There should be an interrelation with social bearing and application. Much of the trouble is due to the attempt to follow tradition. JOHN DEWEY. "The Way Out of Educational Confusion." Inglis Lecture, Harvard. 1931.

62. STRESSING THE SELFISH NON CIVIC AIM. The generation has seen an unusual use of selfish advantage used as a lure to education. In 1917, the United States Bureau of Education, Department of the Interior, issued bulletin No. 22: "The Money-value of Education," showing how much more the high-school and college graduate can make than the one who fails to attend. School men use this argument to induce parents to send their children to high school. The conception of school as an individual advantage is strengthened. Bagley considers it responsible to some degree for the increase of crime. It is antipodal to the reasons urged in early days for establishing public schools. WM. H. STANLEY. "Dollar Scholars." 1924.

63. NO TRADITION OF HONEST PUBLIC SERVICE. We have no tradition of honest public service, rather of the contrary. Present boys and girls must start one. To you, boys and girls, is given a work as grand as is dying for your country. It is living for the interests of your country. You are the hope of the world. HERMAN HAGEDORN. "The World and Democracy." 1919.

64. GOOD GOVERNMENT ATTAINABLE ONLY BY TRAINING GOOD CITIZENS. The high school has had but a faint vision of its place in a democratic state. It must mobilize the entire youth of the nation for the ser-

vice of the democracy in peace. Boys and girls have one vocation in common: that of citizenship—soldiers of the common good. In America we have assumed good government attainable without sacrifice. But good government is had only through good citizens, good citizens are gotten only by training for citizenship. Whatever else it may do, the American high school must give every one definite training for civic duties. Reorganization is of little use unless the spirit of education is changed. The high school has been scrapping its children when it should have scrapt its aim, its methods, its organization. JOHN L. TILDSLEY, Supt. of High Schools, New York City. "DEMOCRACY IN SECONDARY EDUCATION." 1919.

65. THINKING STERILIZED. High schools of the country have permitted political morons to go out by the millions. High-school diplomas are sought as badges of distinction but thinking has been sterilized through the desire of education to escape from controversial subjects. Educators have avoided the certain problems confronting America. NORMAN THOMAS as reported in the N. Y. Herald-Tribune. July 24, 1931.

66. A REFLECTION ON SCHOOLS. We call meetings to protest against office holders who sell their votes. It ought to be as absurd as urging people to come and discuss the multiplication table. It is a reflection on our means for promoting civilization that we should do this. CLARENCE DARROW. "Citizen Cole." 1931.

67. THE SCHOOLS AND THEIR MAIN JOB. The problem of constructing an effective program of training for citizenship has not been vigorously and discerningly attacked. Our whole reliance on self-government assumes the proper education of the people in citizenship. Much of the failure of our politics and our government to be efficient and even honest is the result of inefficient education in rights and responsibilities. Editorial, CHICAGO TRIBUNE. July 26, 1931.

68. MUST THINK ON POLITICAL PROBLEMS. Schools are one of the most direct avenues of approach to the public mind. What is taught in them will profoundly affect the thinking of the next generation. No one can be really intelligent of his own life unless he has thought intently of his relations to his neighbors. Schools can not do their full duty unless they teach a great deal more of social institutions. It is important that the way be cleared for the broad treatment of economic and civic problems which will train pupils to judge for themselves rather than fall victim to biased propaganda. PROF. CHARLES H. JUDD, N. Y. News Review. Oct. 23, 1930.

BOOKS OF THE MONTH

YOU are a pantophagistic family. In making up this month's ration for you I am putting into the basket some things you will not like, but they are good for you, much solid and nutritious food, some roughage, a dainty or two, and, I think, the right amount of calories and vitamins.

EDUCATIONAL SHAKE-UP

BECAUSE two New York University professors, Doctors Cox and Long,[1] hold me to page after page of their reasonable discourse I want to go forth and find them and give each a hearty slap on the back for saying so cleverly, proving so completely, and urging so sympathetically to all of us that the demands of the country are that the high schools change their ways.

There is no sarcasm, nor reprimand, in this survey of the high-school situation. It is free of personal propaganda or whimsical obsession. The authors have marshalled the findings of researchers, psychologists and social investigators and have applied them to the secondary school as it is to-day. From John Dewey, John Withers, Thomas Briggs, Lewis Terman, Walter Lippman, Leonard Koos, Alexander Inglis, Werrett Charters, Harold Rugg, Charles Judd, William Bagley, Franklin Bobbitt, George Counts, William H. Kilpatrick, Henry Morrison, John Tildsley, Roscoe Pulliam, and other analysts of high-school aims and failures, they have summarized and criticized the most im-

[1] Philip W. L. Cox, Forrest E. Long, "Principles of Secondary Education." D. C. Heath & Company, Boston. 620 pp. $2.40.

portant observations upon the weakness of the secondary school. Many strictures they mollify, many they show to be true and of vital importance. The crisis that has come is not a bugaboo to laugh away nor a goblin to frighten teachers with. This is a time for cool taking of stock and hard-headed planning.

American secondary education began as a service to higher-class people. The effort of the academy to offset the snobbishness of the Latin school left the academy as another scarcely less aristocratic concern. The coming of the public high school was hailed as a great advance in democracy. Up to this present, secondary education has been primarily an offering to the upper social and economic classes. Standardization and autocratic conceptions have dominated it. The organization of the school, its rules of admission and promotion make the basic principle of it to preserve a form the student must fit rather than a service to the different capacities of its members. It is still more of a system than of a service.

Mistaken Conclusions

Any claim that the marvellous increase of its enrolment is proof of its superior fitness needs close examination. History has too many instances of phenomenal demands for tulip bulbs or for South Sea stocks to let us reason that increased membership means approval of school policy. Some of the most generous donors to higher education never had any. A canvass of successful merchants as to what they most regret in their schooling brings, from many, a wail that they never studied Latin. Obviously these men could not know the benefits of Latin if they had never studied it. Of course, this is not to say that Latin would not have made the greatest contribution to their business careers. But there is no evidence that it would have done so and common observation leads to the conclusion that they were mistaken. The brightest youth, when these merchants were children, studied Latin—an inevitable high-school fashion. Naturally enough, the absence of it from the others' boyhood is thought a deprivation. The high schools have a large sprinkling of teachers who prefer the unsubstantiated testimony of eminent public men rather than cold tables of researchers who have been unable to find a basis for the claims.

The authors present a formidable array of social changes adequate to explain the increase of high-school membership quite apart from the assumption that the high-school offering is satisfactory or it wouldn't be popular. Diverse forces have made enrolment increase without any reference to the curricular offering of the high school itself.

Persisting Promise-Breaking

Half of the money raised as taxes goes to education. This enormous sum requires the most careful attention to what is being given in return. Now, these two authors thrust into our faces the uncomfortable fact that as the tax is paid by all the people, most of whom have no children in the high school, the high school should be run for the general welfare of all the people, not for merely the economically favored. In point of fact it was the promise of the proponents of education at public expense that it would be devoted to general welfare rather than to the advantage of those children who attend. But this proposal stands unrealized. We have the very anomalous situation of a system of taxation which collects from the poor to educate the children of the rich or well-to-do. Any canvass of high-school membership, anywhere, compared with the nonattending children of high-school age shows this to be true.

It is startling but timely for professors of education to put it so baldly as that. It is not the demagogic howl of the soap-box orator but the calm statement of two cautious students. It is a thrust of a clean cold scalpel into the viscera of every superintendent and high school principal of my acquaintance—including me.

The old alibi, "We are training the leaders," can be based on no suggestion of the original proponents of the school laws. No one urged the people to be taxed to make some of their children the leaders of others. Nor can the argument, by which schools of medicine, engineering, etc., supported by public funds, justify their exclusion of students deemed unfit, be urged for high schools' right to confine themselves to a select enrolment. Messrs. Cox and Long carefully traverse these arguments and come out with the inevitable conclusion that, as the whole public pays, as no sanction exists for designating children of from fourteen to eighteen years of age as selections for picked professions, the high school can justly be nothing less than a service for all youth.

Now, it is not.

Its offerings and its methods are still for a chosen class. No one has yet indicated how algebra, geometry, Caesar, Vergil, third year French, or any of the formal subjects are justified in the light of the promise that school would prepare for the solution of the problems of civic, political life. The high-school course is a gentleman's exercise.

Boys and girls of the lower levels of academic ability will continue in larger numbers to get into the high schools. Agitators, thinking more of citizens than of curriculums, will secure more laws raising the compulsory attendance age, even though, as in the case cited by the authors, high-school principals maintain a lobby to prevent such legislation.

Our authors have no maudlin sympathy for the children of low I.Q.'s, but, with the wide civic views that Bagley and Davenport have made familiar, they demonstrate successful schemes worked out in progressive schools whereby the human crop is tended in proportion to its needs and capacities, not segregated into corn and weeds, but mingled in music, in gymnasium, in extracurriculars and assigned in other exercises where their companions and teachers will do them the most good.

Evidently these writers have the notion that we are in the youth business rather than posing as specialists in English, biology or any kind of scholarship, as if we were indentured to it to keep its standard high. These cheerful rebels would seduce teachers to break a rule rather than see a boy leave school. Cox and Long tell of an irate father coming to high school with the threat of removing his son if the boy were forced longer to study poetry. What would you, Mr. Principal, do? Support the teacher, of course. "Sir, this is a required study. Your boy must take it or get out." God forgive me for the years I went schoolmastering on this all-or-none fallacy, until a group of Washington Irving High School teachers lured me into the belief that we should keep the girl in our family if she had only brains enough for sewing, cooking or dancing.

That was thirty years ago. These teachers issued their then infamous manifesto that the school, like a hospital, should take, without sifting, all the patients it could hold. Dear Professor Parker, in his book on teaching in the high school, called the proposition extreme and extraordinary. But now, glory be, two hard-headed university professors, who have studied all the high-school manuals in the world, calmly prescribe, "When poetry stands in the way of a boy's continued stay in the high school, then poetry must be removed from his program and the boy retained."

I think you will find this book's presentation of the claims, failures, and possibilities of general discipline and transfer of training one of the clearest short discussions of this old nightmare you have met.

The authors also make short work of that old educational blister, inner resistance—the harder a subject is, the more good it does you. Only eight years ago I heard an assembly of New England schoolmasters applaud an old fuddy-duddy who solemnly expounded his belief in the doctrine. A year later a solemn corpse of a college president upheld the same hard-work theory before a room-full of high-school teachers in Ohio and no one objected. Elbert Teachers College Fretwell, who holds intimate consultation with high-school worthies from all parts of the United States and New Jersey, tells me that this tradition is as firmly fixed among high-school mathematics teachers as is the belief that the Republican party, or the Democratic, is the hope of the common man. To you the Cox-Long dissipation of this error, and their distinction between lazy study and pleasurable pedagogy, will be real refreshment.

It is a startling book without aiming to be so. It has a unique arrangement in that instead of Chapter I, II, etc., it is presented as Principle I, Principle II, up to XXV. Don't miss the "Learning exercises," sprinkled here and there. They will, as St. Peter said in his first epistle general, cause you to gird up the loins of your mind and be sober. The vast majority of the contents of the book is constructive, remedial, based on actual advances in high schools here and there, all tending toward realizing the truth that the American conviction of equality and democratic control will not much longer accept the present illogical tradition still bunking the high schools.

Present difficulties involving funds is likely to require you to be on your taps with a better plan than was available last year. Public permission for high schools to spend money has been cheerfully careless. You could get away with absurd and fantastic expenditures. Blind faith of the taxpayer, good-natured generosity of local boards, are getting shaky. Times are changing with a whiz. The delicious preface of this book suggests that it will take all the running you can do to keep in the same place. If you want to go ahead you must run twice as fast.

ROADS OUT OF THE SLOUGH

IN this year of disgrace, 1932, Professor Kinneman,[2] concluded a survey of American education does not find the time for boasting yet at hand. It is true society with us has, to a degree not approached elsewhere, been taxed to pay for the school. But the managers of schools have not addressed themselves wholeheartedly to devising a service based on society's needs. Revision we have had, but the lovers of subjects and methods have kept the curriculum warped away from the civic and political objectives which, if realized, would justify continued taxation of the commonwealth. Schools have gone gaily on increasing in number and cost. There can be no justifiable boast of their civic service if their failure to promote public-mindedness is evidenced by the decline in the percentage of citizens who take the trouble even to vote. In 1896 eighty-five per cent. of persons of voting age cast ballots. In 1920 this had fallen to fifty-two per cent. Four years later it was fifty per cent., recovering slightly in the highly personalized compaign of 1928, when Governor Smith was a candidate for the presidency. Until the school sets about eliminating from its activities those pursuits which can with such difficulty as now be utilized for competent citizenship, until public education addresses itself to the economic, governmental, political needs of the country, its justification will be on no logical basis.

Even the favorite slogan, "Equality of opportunity," has not brought what it claims. Everybody sees the glaring favoritism existent in law and politics. "Pull" and "influence" is too common. Teachers are selected on the basis of race, religion, sex, or marital state. This is the way a society educated in our public schools functions in a land where equality of opportunity is claimed to be.

Professor Kinneman does not scold nor wail, neither does he coddle. He reviews the ideals of a self-governing republic, arrays what we have gained, analyzes our failures, and blocks out the things that must be done to save America from increasing disaster.

His book is primarily a text in educational sociology for colleges and teacher-training institutions. It seems to me a necessary aid to the thousands of teachers to whom the desperate cry of the times has never come in its educational aspects. A teacher of teachers, himself, Kinneman is a good answer to a current criticism that the normal schools have failed to recognize that a main, an essential, a preponderating necessity of a teacher's make-up must be a determination to break the pre-Revolutionary tradition that the imparting of knowledge of a scholastic type is what is mostly the proper function of a public school. This masterly work comes from dear old Felmley's monument, the Illinois State Normal University, in which Dr. Kinneman is professor of sociology.

AGAINST FUTURE DEPRESSIONS[3]

OSCAR HANSEN'S researches have reminded the country that the group of eminences who devoted their brains in 1787 to devising a system of education for the newly formed republic demonstrated that a self-governing people must enlighten themselves on economics, law, government and politics. Toward this long-deferred duty the more far-seeing educators, up to Commissioner William John Cooper, are directing our attention more urgently, day by day. We always have a drive or two going on to keep education from going to sleep: project method, new-type examinations, effects of alcohol, six-three-three plan, platoons, or whatever can get a good presentation at the convention. Now, the whole world feels, as never in your day before, that its ills are not due to slant penmanship nor an irrational system of spelling but to failure of economic planning. As Mr. Balliet has so often remarked, public opinion can not

[2] John A. Kinneman, "Society and Education." The Macmillan Company, New York. 558 pp. $2.00.

[3] Arthur L. Faubel, "Principles of Economics." Harcourt, Brace & Company, New York. 522 pp. $1.60.

project economic relief unless we have a citizenry that is accustomed to think on economic lines. The generation now in school will have tougher economic problems to solve than we are now confronted with. The opportunities for going out into a frontier domain to grow up with the country are no more. Economic readjustment is inevitable. A competent jury to examine proposals must be a citizenry capable of thinking in the economic field.

Dr. Arthur Faubel, of New York University, professor of economics and, as the writers of college catalogues like to add, "sometime" chief economist of the U. S. Tariff Commission, brought out an elementary economics for high schools nine years ago, which won a welcome because of its freedom from the complexities and dullness which high-school teachers not uncommonly complain prevent the subject from engaging the interest of youth. The professor now appears with a new work retaining his original plan and manner and bringing the discussion up to the departure of England from the gold standard. Marketing, the Federal Reserve, agricultural banking, tariff, mergers, labor and wages, the Russian venture, are newly written and illuminating. Cycles, trends, reforms, needs, are treated with a view to throwing light into our present darkness. Pictures and charts are generously provided.

As I read these presentations of vital matters affecting our common duty and welfare and recall that I have never met a high-school teacher who could explain why such topics should be less considered in high school than the self-laudation of a Caesar or a Cicero or the fictions of a Vergil, who, all together, steal four years from an apprenticeship in citizenry due from millions of young Americans, I could shout with joy to think of the growing number of public schools and oncoming legislatures that are making the satisfactory completion of a course like Dr. Faubel's compulsory. We give every West-Pointer a stiffer dose than this. Our wars come once in a generation. Our economic thinking will need, from now on, to be active every year.

WASHINGTON AS A HUMAN BEING

NONE of the current Washington books[4] surpass the work of two bright California schoolmasters, Cloud and Kersey. They make the great American distinctly human and admirable. They have a rare ability in welding letters, documents, speeches and quotations into the story without showing the seams of juncture. They are singularly successful, too, in estimating what will especially interest young people, not forgetting the girls. Animated descriptions of home and social life, of Washington's courtship and marriage, of his mother, of Martha Washington's activities during the war and the presidency, are remarkably well done. An unusual chapter on education is one of the best of admirable features. To have encompassed so well known a biography with the freshness exhibited here is a real triumph of composition. The generous notes are as entertaining as the text and the pictures! They are a triumph, no less. You can't lay this book down until you have read it all.

HOLMES'S MASTERLY WASHINGTON BIOGRAPHY

THE WINSTON COMPANY'S Washington[5] is a colorful memorial, beautifully done, with a profusion of new pictures, photographs, reproductions of old paintings, original drawings, special maps. Dr. Holmes, the author, has followed the sympathetic and elegant "Life" by Washington Irving, modified by the scholarly researches of Fiske, Corbin, the Fords, Lodge, Wrong, and Hughes. He has made a continuous, animated narrative, skilfully contrived to be, in fact, a vivid history of the whole nation in its formative years.

Dr. Herbert Burk, president of the Valley Forge Historical Association, gave the book in manuscript a careful scrutiny and praises the the honesty of its statements and the sincerity of its spirit.

You will appreciate the merit of this compliment as you note the absence of the old spread-eagleism. Author Holmes is no magnifier of the revolutionary soldiers, whom we, as boys, seemed taught to believe were an army of heroes, any one of whom could whip a dozen red-coats. We see here a horde of careless youngsters, so used to shouting "liberty" as to be devoid of respect for discipline or authority. We see them sneaking off home at critical moments. We learn of their stealing baggage,

[4] A. J. Cloud, Vierling Kersey, "Episodes in the Life of George Washington." Charles Scribner's Sons, New York. 226 pp. 80 cents.

[5] M. D. Holmes, "George Washington: The Soul of a Nation." John C. Winston Company, Philadelphia. 383 pp. $2.00.

commissary stores, hospital supplies, and looting the tents of their officers. "They are more dreaded by our own people," reports Washington in his confidential letters, "than the enemy is." You learn of the heartbreaking disloyalty of the commander's subordinates, Conway, Gates, Mifflin, Charles Lee, Edmund Randolph. The patience and skill with which the commander, thwarted by Congress, turned his fluctuating and unreliable troops into a respectable army; his marvelous tolerance of unfriendliness; his constant persistence in seeing the better side of his enemies; his ultimate possession of the affectionate regard of the nation, develop in Dr. Holmes's quick-moving story.

He presents no perfect-born hero. There is no Weems, Everett, Daniel, Brougham, Byron, Webster, panegyric of a heaven-sent demigod, incapable of falsehood, fear, wrath or wrongdoing. The Washington who lives in this story is no statue. He is capable of fear and conquers it. He is subject to fits of terrible anger and teaches himself control. He moves through the stirring scenes or quiet phases of a country life as a human warm-hearted, modest, great character.

The movements of the war involving Boston, New York, Trenton, Philadelphia, Monmouth, Saratoga, West Point, The South, Yorktown, and so on, you have found, in many text books, complicated and confusing. Dr. Holmes, by emphasizing the fact that Washington's campaigns were conditioned upon watching and following an enemy has simplified his movements and given a sequence to the phases of the war that is unique. Arnold and Andre are presented with generous gallantry. The Howes, Clinton and Cornwallis are less of abstractions and more of living characters than in the usual school text.

Especially good are Dr. Holmes' nine chapters after Yorktown, into which he puts a vitality often much needed in the school treatment of those perplexing days.

The book deserves a wide circulation. My guess is that it will win its way and become a favorite with young and old.

UNUSUAL WASHINGTON PROGRAMS

Alma Laird[6] puts humor, color, movement and sturdy morality into a charming collection of Washington ceremonials for each of the eight grades of an elementary school. The author lives up to her name "Alma," giver of blessings, in that she is furnishing teachers with a bright substitute for laborious search through books to find something simple yet impressive, something easy, yet inculcating worth-while ideas, with which to do the added duty which this year has brought. The compiler of these picturesque performances devises pieces which will please whether the school has a theatrical stage or must be content with the bare front of the class room. A flag or two, some bright paper, very simple properties, are indicated. One or two star parts are provided for. The rest of the class are soldiers, citizens, colonial dames, or something just as good. Each child has the joy of being "in it." You will like the way this Alma lets the good old cherry tree come to fruitage without pretending that any young American would use the ax in hopes of hearing, "run to my arms you dearest boy, glad am I that you killed my tree for you have repaid me a thousand times." One of the Laird verses, recited by a second grade boy, has in it:

When Mother said ''Who ate the pie?''
I spoke like a man and said, ''It was I''
And she didn't say she'd rather lose the pie
And know her little boy would not tell a lie.
She just shut me up where I couldn't see,
Then sent me to bed without any tea.

If you are shocked by this you can find another one, a page or two distant in which a young reciter defends the tale of the hatchet, "I've met folks, and so have you, who say this story is not true. It makes no difference what they claim. The moral's in it, just the same."

The moral is in these stories, not slopping over, not hidden deep as to keep away from the participants and the audience. The outcome of each program impresses you as being well worth while, the lesson, impressively presented, the ideal, suited to the age of the company. You will see this in an eighth-grade play in which Washington and his cabinet are discussing the essentials of the United States Constitution. You can have a little thrill of it in hearing a first-grade kissable recite:

When Betsy Ross made our first flag
So carefully bar by bar,
I wish I might have been there
To sew on just one star.

[6] Alma Laird, ''Complete George Washington Programs.'' Noble and Noble, 76 Fifth Avenue, New York. 167 pp. $2.00.

Well done, Alma! I should like to go to school to you. Your hearty Americanism is spiced with a charming good humor. Your Washington is no marble statue, unapproachable, inimitable. He seems to be one of the understandables.

THE U. S. FOR CHILDREN

RAMON COFFMAN'S previous success in making history interesting and profitable to children will, I know, be repeated in his new elementary historical reader[7] covering The United States from the beginning of the revolution to the end of the war of 1812. It is a stout little book, full of pictures, and is written in a lively and engaging style.

WHAT FIVE COLLEGES ARE TRYING

WHAT the post-war educational ferment has produced in Columbia, Harvard, Swarthmore, Wabash and Chicago Universities is described and discussed by one president or dean of each institution, the essays all in one book.[8] It makes a collection of aims, methods and reasons that will prove stimulating to you whether your main interest is in cutting loose from university influence or in extending and improving it.

YOUTH AND LIFE PROBLEMS

HANDSOMELY suitable in purpose, form and content, to carry out a patriotic purpose of a modest Philadelphian, comes the first volume of Philadelphia Central High School Speeches.[9] President Haney tells how James Barnwell, graduate of the Central High School's class of 1850, schoolmaster, librarian and quiet philanthropist, dying in 1919, recorded in his will that his mother and his high school had been the two chief aids to his happy life. He, therefore, left an estate of $320,000 in memory of both, "for encouraging in that school high principles and practices." A committee—the president of the high school, the president of its alumni, the president of the Fidelity-Philadelphia Trust Company—selected as one activity to be supported by the fund, a course of addresses to be delivered by notable leaders in education, letters, science and civic affairs. At first in the school, then in the Academy of Music, and now in the ball room of the Penn Athletic Club, capacity audiences have listened to Glenn Frank, Dean West, Lewis Perry, Alfred Stearns, Cheesman Herrick, Senators Pepper, Fess and Moses, Hamlin Garland, John Finley, Parkes Cadman, Admiral Sims, Wilfred Grenfell, Henry Turner Bailey, Fielding Yost, Ralph Adams Cram, William John Cooper, Leopold Stokowski, Alonzo Stagg, Henry Fairfield Osborn, Michael Pupin, Edwin Slosson, James M. Beck, and others to the total number of thirty-two, whose discourses on things that matter are handsomely printed and bound, embellished with felicitously chosen quotations on life and work taken from ancient and modern seers.

"Why go to school at all?" asks Andrew West, and answers it in a way that will pain the advocates of letting a pupil study what he likes when he likes.

Senator Pepper portrays the true American as tolerant, free from local narrowness and that of class. He must not turn his back on the sisterhood of nations. He discovers his powers and drafts them for public service.

President Haney records a wide-spread feeling now that the schools are failing to stiffen the moral fiber of the younger generation and are thus falling short in the one outstanding service they might have rendered. The question remains, he says, "Can the needed result be attained by formal character training measured in terms of the decimal scale?" The book is a contribution toward answering the question. It features a quotation from Pennsylvania's old warhorse of education whose books fed schoolmasters of my age when we were young—James Pyle Wickersham: "American educators have in their hands the destinies of the nation. They may so guide the hearts of youth that our republic will stand as firmly as the Egyptian pyramids."

RETURN OF THE ESSAY

HOWEVER a teacher may dread the essay as a subject for class consideration it is coming into favor everywhere, says Rose Adelaide Witham.[10] Forty-four selections, all done since 1900, are

[7] Ramon Coffman, "The Founding of the Republic." Owen Publishing Company, Dansville, New York. 128 pp. 72 cents. Quantity price, 54 cents.

[8] Five Authors, "Five College Plans." Columbia University Press, New York. 115 pp. Paper $1.00, Cloth $2.00.

[9] John Louis Haney, Editor, "The Barnwell Addresses." Central High School, Philadelphia. 426 pp. For libraries mostly. Free.

[10] Rose Adelaide Witham, "Essays of Today." Houghton Mifflin Company, Boston. 398 pp. $1.16.

in Principal Witham's offering, including work of Morley, Marquis, Broun, Strunsky, McFee, Conrad, Galsworthy, Chesterton and Van Doren. Each is followed by questions for discussion.

I don't see why a teacher should find it hard to participate with children in the use of this book as a text. The work is effectively blocked out in it. The selections are such as to provoke worth-while discussion among young people. The biographical notes will save the conscience of the old-timer who may fear that the work will be too pleasant and easy. Even I could keep going with a book like this.

COPIOUS READING LIST

DEVELOPING good reading habits, observes Dr. Terman,[11] is a complex task. You must know different children's tastes and needs, you must know multitudes of books.

The Terman-Lima volume is based on a study of two thousand children, and on appraisals by parents, teachers and the pupils themselves. Result: 317 pages of titles with descriptions and appraisal, all classified as picture books, story books, history books, and so on, supplementary readers by grades, suggestions upon children's book shelves, indexes by authors and by titles, discourses on reading habits, the desirable book, the undesirable, and other matters directly pertinent to teaching. There are numerous pictures.

VOCATION BOOK

WITH pictures, helps to self-analysis, and insistence upon making a choice of life work if only for getting the proper drive into a study project, Professor Kitson[13] comes forward with his bright blue book, starting with the eminently suitable, unusual and startling admonition that, as every one is obligated to choose a vocation if he shares in the benefits society confers on him, he might as well begin practicing a choice by the time he reaches high-school age. The nature of occupations, the qualities and skills needed, the rewards, the lure of the white collar, rural opportunities, girls' chances, the delight of an avocation, general principles, are some of the themes presented with distinct attractiveness. It is a book for class use full of provocation to discussion, which William Lewis calls the mother of judgment.

TEACHING AS A MAN'S JOB

PURPORTING to be written by William Patterson but copyrighted by Frederick Miller, twenty-three snappy epistles[14] of a schoolmaster father to a schoolmaster son touch upon school boards, parents, neighbors, superintendents 'n everything, with humor, sentiment and blunt truth. "They'll tell you," writes Pop, "that you have a second-rate place in the work of the world. But opinions, Boy, need not give you the inferiority complex. A teacher must do his own thinking about his job. When the mob looks at the teacher they don't see him making any wheels go round nor piling up anything. All the same, the master of his art, as teacher, does make men and women out of raw material. If teaching is little esteemed let it be the public's fault, not yours." State Superintendent Holloway told me he found this book a refreshing work on practical pedagogy. The author is an optimist with brakes,—keeps on the track and gets to destination every time.

UNCLE SAM'S FARM TEACHING

FARMERS SMITH and Wilson treat of the new leaven at work in rural America,[15] and the educational work the people, through organized government, are doing to increase the farmers' wealth, health, happiness and worth. The book describes boys' and girls' club work, agricultural research, teaching methods, opportunities and future plans.

STUDY MUST BE TRAINED

WITH the handsome books in Carlos Ellis's executives' series comes Dr. Kilzer's large volume.[16] It is a frank confession of the lost time still perpetuated by the maintenance of the traditional recitation, and the inevitable driving of the children by it into habits of

[11] Lewis M. Terman, Margaret Lima, "Children's Readings." D. Appleton and Company, New York. 422 pp. $2.00.

[13] Harry Dexter Kitson, "I Find My Vocation." McGraw-Hill Book Company, New York. 216 pp. $1.40.

[14] Wm. Patterson, "Letters from a Hard-Boiled Teacher to his Half-Baked Son." The Daylion Company, Washington, D. C. 348 pp. $2.00.

[15] Clarence Beman Smith, Meredith Chester Wilson, "The Agricultural Extension System of the United States." John Wiley and Sons, New York. 402 pp. $3.50.

[16] Louis R. Kilzer, "Supervised Study." Professional and Technical Press. 420 Lexington Avenue, New York. 332 pp. $3.25.

memorizing for brief retention. With a wealth of experiences gathered from educational pioneers in directing the formation of valuable mental habits the author makes clear the difficulties and the satisfying successes which are attending one of the great educational reforms of the present era.

CHEERILY AFLOAT

The delight Jean Dukelow and Hanson Webster put into making this boat book[17] will sparkle in school as the youngsters in a geography project or at some reading-activity time learn the ways of those who go down to the sea in ships. There are boats that work and boats that play, rules of the water road, safety, light-houses, early vessels, famous craft, and a fascinating set of helps for young builders of toys and models. There are diagrams of knots, a small sailor's dictionary, and hints on sailing model racers and real boats. It is a book written by a teacher and a sailor for use in the middle primary grades. It is brightened by an abundance of rollicking pictures in colors.

FLYING FUN

Chelsea Frazer,[18] who has to his credit already twelve books for boys and who offers this new one in Crowell's Amateur Craftsman series where tools and electricity hold sway, has been a favorite teacher of manual training in Michigan for many years. He has a jolly time in these pages with diagrams, photographs and directions telling you how to make miniature airships that actually fly, autogiros, mosquito models, mooring masts and model airports. It is a boys' book de luxe.

SURPRISES FOR RELIGIOUS TEACHING

Unless you are very young the most of your religious education was given, in a Sunday school, by a good-natured girl whose teaching technique was born, not made. Here is a book[19] based upon the surprising proposal that religious teaching, like any other organized activity, needs preparation, knowledge of learning processes, definite objectives, supervision, visitation and correction. The author, Ernest Chave, is professor of religious education in the University of Chicago.

Few churches are teaching religion as well as they can. Radical changes are needed. What? Adoption of aims, organization of classes, inspection, central direction, testing, catching up with the improvements in public schools.

A NEW MYTHOLOGY

Beginning with the birth of the gods, Professor Sabin[20] presents hundreds of fascinating old stories of Greek and Roman mythology, linking them with our literature, our art and our common speech. A wealth of pictures, mostly new, aid in this service. Questions, exercises and reading lists abound. There is a "Who's Who in Mythology," and a long list of common expressions, mythological in origin.

WHAT, THE DEVIL?

My friend Rudwin has been chasing devils for at least ten years since he published the first of his eleven books dealing with by-paths of superstition. His latest[21] looks at Lucifer, Abadon, Apollyon, Abiron, Achas, Agares, Beelzebub, Satan, Mephistopheles, Old Nick, the Deuce, or the devil by any other name, smelling as sulfurous. They are featured here in song, story and ancient pictures. How many devils are there? How many forms? Who has believed in him? Who does, now? Is he the father of blondes or of brunettes? How much is he still in religion? These and a thousand other questions are answered in this enchanting work. It is a marvel of research and quotation and with one of the most complete indexes you have seen in the devil of a while. Your high-school students will revel in it. If I am to believe Otis Caldwell it will purge them of a surprising lot of superstition that never went out of America with the fading of witchcraft.

[17] Jean H. Dukelow, Hanson Hart Webster, "The Ship Book, an Elementary Reader in Social Science." Houghton Mifflin Company, Boston. 280 pp.

[18] Chelsea Frazer, "The Modern Aircraft Builder." Thomas F. Crowell Company, New York. 385 pp. $2.50.

[19] Ernest John Chave, "Supervision of Religious Education." University of Chicago Press. 352 pp. $2.50.

[20] Francis E. Sabin, "Classical Myths that Live To-day." Silver, Burdett and Company, New York. 432 pp. $1.92.

[21] Maxmilian Rudwin, "The Devil in Legend and Literature." The Open-Court Publishing Company, Chicago. 354 pp. $3.00.

SCHOOL AND SOCIETY

EDITED BY J. McKEEN CATTELL

WITH WHICH IS COMBINED THE

EDUCATIONAL REVIEW

EDITED BY WILLIAM McANDREW

Volume 35 SATURDAY, APRIL 9, 1932 Number 902

SCIENTIFIC STUDIES OF TEACHING[1]

By Dr. CHARLES H. JUDD

DEAN OF THE SCHOOL OF EDUCATION, UNIVERSITY OF CHICAGO

IT is clearly recognized in every psychological laboratory that the most difficult problem which confronts an investigator is the problem of ascertaining what is going on in the conscious experience of a person other than himself. Each individual lives in a world of ideas and emotions peculiarly his own. The most elaborate and ingenious experimental methods are often required to arrive at even an approximately accurate description of an individual's mental processes.

Consider, for example, the difficulty of discovering what the world looks like to a person who is color blind and confuses red and green. To the individual who has normal color vision it seems almost incredible that any one should be unable to distinguish these two sharply contrasting colors. To the color-blind person, on the other hand, it seems equally incredible that sensations which to him are alike should be described by most people as strikingly different.

The psychologist goes through a long series of experiments in color-mixing and finally comes indirectly to the conclusion that red and green are to the color-blind person something like that which the normal individual calls straw color. Even this conclusion is uncertain, however. The uncertainty of the conclusion emphasizes the fact that each conscious world is absolutely hedged in by its own boundaries.

It would be a very illuminating experience for every person preparing to teach if he could investigate a few cases of color blindness. Such investigations would help to prepare him to grasp the fact that there are numerous examples in every classroom of differences in mental life which are far more fundamental than the difference between color-blind individuals and normal individuals.

It should perhaps be noted in this connection that teachers are often quite as unaware of obvious distinctions as are students. If I may venture to draw on my personal experience as a student, I may say that I once knew a teacher who seemed quite oblivious of all human interests except those which are classified under the general heading "mathematics." My classmates and I did what we could to draw his attention to other spheres of thought but without success. He and the members of his class lived mentally as far apart as did the characters in one of Kipling's stories. You will perhaps recall that Kipling tells of a young American who found himself in trouble in England because he had committed a serious offense against British

[1] Convocation address, University of Chicago, March 15, 1932.

conservatism. The American tried to extricate himself by methods which the English regarded as altogether incomprehensible. Kipling entitles his story "An Error in the Fourth Dimension." The world of British conventions and the world of youthful American ideas are as utterly foreign to each other as the three-dimensional world is distinct from that strange world which is imagined as lying outside the boundaries of our commonplace three dimensions. If we could reach beyond the space which we know and could add even one dimension to our limited world, what wonders of necromancy we could perform!

We must come back, however, to our theme. Mental lives are closed circles, and the happenings within each individual circle are unique. The art of teaching consists in finding out, if possible, approximately what is going on in an immature mind and so influencing that mind by various devices that its performances will lead to intelligent forms of behavior.

Let us consider an extreme case in which an individual's mental processes were such as to make impossible the application of ordinary means of education. Some years ago the psychologists of Indiana University found a boy who was an arithmetical prodigy. He lived in a mental world in which all kinds of arithmetical operations seemed to go on in a most unusual fashion. If this boy was asked to multiply large numbers which most people can multiply only with the use of paper and pencil, he gave an instant answer. In like manner, he could give without hesitation the square or cube of any ordinary number. So different was his mental world from the mental worlds of most individuals that his performances seemed marvelous. They were partly explained by the fact that the boy carried around in his interior a multiplication table which did not stop at 12 but ran up to 150 or more. He also knew by heart the table of logarithms. It is perhaps needless to remark that such luxuries are dispensed with by most human beings. Ordinary individuals are limited in their mental calculations to comparatively primitive operations. One can hardly refrain from speculating on the emotional satisfactions which must attach to the possession of such a piece of mental furniture as a complete logarithm table.

The university which discovered this boy tried to teach him higher mathematics but without success. He was absorbed in his own ways of thinking and was too well satisfied with himself to be inspired with any interest in anything but his multiplication table and his logarithms. Despairing in their efforts to make him a mathematician, his discoverers secured for him a position in an actuarial office, where it was thought he might serve as an animated calculating machine, but he did not succeed because even in an actuary's office one must have some human interests.

All the statements which have been made up to this point are introductory to our main discussion. We are to inquire what contributions science can make to the art which schools and colleges cultivate—the art of teaching.

We may begin by considering in some detail a very simple case drawn from actual experience. A teacher of history whose mental world was full of ideas about medieval Europe found himself, in the course of his efforts to discharge his duties, in contact with a student whose mind seemed altogether unable to take on the pattern required for a comprehension of history. Teacher and student met day after day, and words passed between them, but these words did not seem to draw them closer to each other. Quite the contrary. In due time the teacher was called upon by institutional routine to report as accurately as possible a description of the student's mind. It is, on the whole, fortunate that institutions have hit on the device of employing single letters as the vehicles of expression of instructors' judgments about students. The teacher in question reached down the alphabet as far as the rules permitted and reported the student as utterly and hopelessly incompetent in medieval history.

The student, too, was aware of the difference between himself and his teacher, but he could never decide just what prevented him from turning his mental world in the direction in which his teacher's mind seemed to move freely.

At this juncture the student fell into the hands of an interested investigator, who soon discovered what was wrong. The student was a poor reader. To be sure, he had been using reading throughout his school career, but it was a dull tool. It worked fairly well so long as no exacting demands were made on the tool or its user, but, as soon as the teacher of history began to make large demands, the dullness of the tool showed itself in evil consequences. Perhaps some one will be disposed to remark that the student ought to have known what the difficulty was. Let us not forget the fact which was emphasized in our discussion of color blindness. The student did not know anything about fluent, intelligent reading because he had never had any experience with such reading. Reading means to a student that process with which he is personally acquainted. The poor reader is incompetent because he has never been competent. In the case in question the student and the teacher recognized only the final fact—that the required knowledge of history was lacking. They both made the mistake of diagnosing the difficulty as inability to learn history. The more the teacher and the student tried to correct the difficulty by adding history to history, the more the case was aggravated.

There is probably no respect in which college students differ from one another and from their teachers so fundamentally as in their ability to read. A recent investigation of the reading ability of 255 college students showed that only 86 of these students were thoroughly competent readers. Sixty-one were so deficient in reading that they were seriously handicapped in their college work.

Deficiency in reading among college students can not be attributed entirely or even chiefly to failure of the lower schools to do their duty. Reading is an art which has higher levels as well as lower levels. The common assumption that reading is a single kind of mental behavior which can be acquired in the elementary school has been completely refuted by scientific studies. There are a great many different kinds of reading, and, unless the student is trained in the mastery of some of the higher levels of reading, he will find it difficult to adjust himself to the demands made upon him during his college career.

Perhaps it will be well to make the foregoing statement more impressive by pausing long enough to give one illustration of what is meant when it is said that scientific studies have shown that there are a number of different kinds of reading. When a thoroughly competent reader becomes interested in a prose narrative, he looks at the successive phrases on the printed page with rapid, fluent movements of his eyes. Records of such reading have been secured for purposes of scientific study by photographing the reader's eyes. The movements of a reader's eyes are reliable indexes of the processes which go on in the reader's brain and experience.

While a student is reading in the fluent fashion described, let the teacher come into the situation by saying to him that, after he has read the next paragraph, he will be asked questions about what he has read. Instantly there is a complete change in the reading process. Instead of fluent sweeping movements, indicating rapid comprehension and attention to the flow of the narrative, there is a slow, halting attention to details, indicative of an effort to prepare for any questions that may be raised. A form of reading which may be called "analytical study" is substituted for the free, fluent reading which the student exhibited before he was threatened with questions.

When we remember that most of the reading of students required by schools and colleges is of the slow, analytical type, it is easy to understand why students sometimes have difficulty with such subjects as history. Students who are in possession of both the method of analytical study and the method of fluent reading sometimes fail to use the right method in a given case. They read rapidly when the instructor expects analysis, or, when the instructor expects rapid, fluent reading of long assignments, they conscientiously apply the slow, laborious type of reading and become confused and unable to meet the instructor's requirements.

If there is one conclusion which can certainly be drawn from the scientific study of the methods of reading employed by students, it is that instruction in reading must not stop with the completion of elementary education. The higher schools must contribute to the perfection of the training which is begun in the lower grades. If instructors in the higher schools are not willing to train their students in reading, it may be necessary to recognize the principle of division of labor and allow specialists in subject-matter departments to concentrate on their own lines of thinking while special personnel officers are appointed to train students.

An interesting example of the success of intelligent personnel work is reported from the University of Buffalo. Professor Edward S. Jones, of that institution, found that he could reduce the number of failures in the freshman class by training the students in certain very simple arts. He taught them how to take notes on lectures, how and when to use the library and how to read rapidly. He reports that the mortality in the freshman year was reduced from 40 per cent. of those who entered to 15 per cent., a saving of about one fourth of the entrants.

In our own institution the experiment was tried, with salutary results, of assembling a number of members of a history class for an hour a day to receive special instruction in reading. The group was made up of students who had been found by tests to be deficient in reading.

Deficiency in reading is not the only obscure cause of failure in college. Scientific studies have revealed the fact that there are many wrong methods of attacking intellectual problems. There are fatal omissions in a student's comprehension of the first elements of a subject which make impossible normal progress. There are emotional distractions which interfere with trains of thought. So obscure are many of these causes of failure that they are overlooked and teachers attribute the difficulties of students to general stupidity or incompetency in particular subjects. Good teaching calls for penetrating knowledge of human nature quite as much as for adequate knowledge of the subjects taught.

It is undoubtedly true that long before scientific studies gave clear and explicit statements of such facts as have been reviewed good teachers who were interested in their students were proficient in correcting immaturity in methods of study. Good teachers can be described, I think, as persons who have cultivated the power of interpreting sympathetically the mental efforts of those whom they instruct. Good teachers have explored the road to knowledge and know where the road is rough and where the by-paths are that lead the inexperienced traveler astray. Good teachers have an insight into students' minds.

Wisdom did not begin with science. It is, however, equally true that the wise do not do themselves the disservice of closing their minds to the discoveries of science.

There is some indication that the teaching profession is slowly coming to a recognition of the necessity of scientific studies of teaching which will supplement the unsystematic efforts of those who have arrived by their own individual endeavors at superior methods of dealing with students. The American Association of University Professors has organized a strong committee and has employed a competent staff for the explicit purpose of making a nation-wide study of college teaching. This move on the part of the American Association of University Professors was undoubtedly stimulated in some measure by the criticisms which have recently been expressed in many quarters regarding the quality of instruction supplied by institutions of higher education. Possibly there is also a growing recognition of the urgent demand that human energy be conserved more completely than seemed necessary in the leisurely days of the past, when life was less exacting than it is to-day.

The study inaugurated by the American Association of University Professors might be passed over as a mere incident if it were not for the fact that impressive indications are appearing on every hand of restlessness and uncertainty with regard to the nature and organization of education.

If one studies the older civilizations, one finds that educational practices are undergoing rapid and radical changes. The countries of Western Europe are opening the opportunities of secondary and higher education to ever-increasing numbers. Russia and Italy have made their educational systems parts of their programs of social reconstruction. In those countries the governments are deliberately indoctrinating the young people and are experimenting on as large a scale with the nurture of young human beings as with the development of industrial and agricultural systems.

One does not need to go abroad for evidences of stirrings in the field of education. There never were in the United States so many educational doctrines advocated by enthusiastic supporters and denounced by hostile enemies as there are today. The country is full of people who announce themselves as "progressives" in education, and there are some who really are progressive. The traditional subjects of the curriculum are engaged in a bitter rear-guard defense, and aggressive new subjects are advancing at a pace which is astonishingly rapid, if not dangerously headlong.

While educators are attempting to reconstruct the programs of schools and colleges, anxious taxpayers are beginning to raise the question whether the whole system of instruction in this country is sound and supportable. There are voices heard in influential quarters calling for a halt, or even a drastic retrenchment, in American education.

At the same time that these discussions are going on and retrenchment is being urged, the attendance on schools is increasing, and the scope of school and college instruction is enlarging. Most people do not realize the rate at which expansion of the educational system has taken place. The fifteenth census of the United States shows that there were 5,500,000 more young people in the schools and colleges of this country in 1930 than there were in 1920. The population of secondary schools has doubled every decade since 1880 and now includes more than half the young people of secondary-school age. The population of institutions of higher education has increased more than fourfold in thirty years—from about 285,000 at the beginning of this century to more than 1,200,000 at the present time. The increase in school and college population has been paralleled by an increase in the offerings of educational institutions. One summary statement must serve to show something of the extent to which the number of courses offered has increased. A recent canvass of the courses announced by ten representative independent colleges and the liberal-arts colleges of ten representative universities showed that in 1900 the aggregate number of courses offered by these twenty institutions was 4,231. In 1930 the number of courses offered had increased to 12,104.

These figures may excite our pride as educators, but we must not overlook the fact that they represent a social responsibility which is not always fully recognized. There was a time—and that within the memory of some of us in this gathering—when American education was very limited in its scope and highly selective with respect to the individuals whom it served at the upper levels. If there was waste in school and college administration and if there was inefficiency in teaching in those early days, the loss to the nation was almost negligible. To-day the situation is altogether different. The changes which have occurred within a single generation make it necessary to deal with education in a new way. Reliance on the accidental insights of individual teachers is no longer safe because the movement in education is rapid and the huge populations with which education is concerned contribute to a momentum which must be wisely guided or the wreckage will be overwhelming.

I might attempt to describe in detail some of the problems which arise in the effort to adapt methods of teaching to new conditions, but I assume that extended discussion of these problems is not necessary in a center, such as this, which is alive with experimentation and supplied with special agencies for the reconstruction of the curriculum and of the examination system.

I deem it more appropriate to support my plea for the scientific study of teaching by a brief consideration of the fundamental reasons for the great expansion of the educational system which has been illustrated in the statistics cited.

Educational developments are not detached happenings. They are phases of a change in the order of human life. The reasons for the expansion of education must be sought in the general evolution of modern society. There was an industrial revolution. There is a social revolution. There was a national mind absorbed in pioneering and in mastering the material world. There is a new national mind engrossed in insistent questioning about human life and social relations. Let us see whether we can express the change that is taking place in a formula which will give education its proper setting.

Human beings once developed in intelligence and skill largely through contact with things. Anthropology has traced the long road which was traveled by primitive man as he learned to fashion tools out of wood and stone and metal. Economics teaches how exchange began in simple barter. It was only after long centuries of barter that coins and credit came into existence. We see in all these facts how man has gradually made himself efficient by devising instruments which help him to cope with nature by dealing with it indirectly rather than with his own hands. The tools and systems of exchange which man has invented have a twofold effect on life. They make the conquest of the physical environment easy, but they also change in fundamental ways the mental lives of individuals. They impose on every one who uses tools or participates in exchange the necessity of a double training. He who uses a tool must learn how to employ the tool as well as how to seek the ultimate end toward which hand and tool cooperate.

The past few decades have witnessed an

accelerated multiplication of indirect instruments for satisfying the needs of human life. The individuals who make up modern society have gradually been pushed farther and farther away from direct manual contact with most of the things with which they deal. It is no adequate description of the situation to say that men have invented machinery and created a system of exchange. The far more fundamental fact is that men have changed their relations to their environment and, as a consequence, have changed their modes of thought. Men in this age see the world of things down a long vista of machines. They are absorbed in the kind of thinking which is concerned with social institutions—with devices of communication, with wages, with credit, with government and with international relations.

It is easy to apply the lessons which we learn from anthropology and economics to education. The necessity of an elaborate system of education arises directly from the fact that man has devised a complex system of instruments to aid him in mastering the world. It requires very little education to barter. It requires no extended curriculum to learn how to wield a club. The necessity of an education arises from the invention of double-entry bookkeeping and from the construction of machine guns.

As education becomes complex, teaching becomes increasingly technical in character. Teaching in a highly evolved educational system can not be directed by amateurs and casual experimenters. It must seek its guiding principles through systematic scientific studies.

I come back to my earlier illustration. Young people must be made proficient in reading. It is only during the past century that any one has had the temerity to propose that the arts of reading be made possessions of the common man. We know the history of the alphabet—so recently has the human mind devised this instrument of recording experience. We know the history of the Occidental adoption of the number system which we use and which we call the "Arabic" system in acknowledgment of our obligation to the Orient for its invention. Reading and the mastery of Arabic numerals have opened up infinite possibilities of individual mental development, but, by so doing, they and the other civilized arts have made a long and arduous apprenticeship necessary for every one who would take advantage of the intellectual tools which the race has invented. Furthermore, the possibilities that the learner will fall into inefficient methods of dealing with the elaborate inventions which he has inherited have increased so greatly that it becomes necessary for us to study the way in which apprenticeship in the use of the civilized arts may be conducted without waste and without harm to the apprentice.

The science of education, like every other science, is a systematic formulation of the best knowledge that we possess about the conditions which surround human life. If we ask children to master the alphabet and the Arabic number system, is it not desirable that we find out by systematic studies all we can about what goes on in an individual's mind when he attempts to use these instruments? When we require a so-called "reading knowledge" of two foreign languages as a condition antecedent to admission to candidacy for our highest degree, does it not seem appropriate that we should encourage the Modern Foreign Language Study to continue its investigations? When the Association of American Colleges memorializes the graduate schools, as it did in 1929, in a document which says that the present method of training college teachers is not satisfactory, does it not seem rational to advocate the turning of attention to a careful study of the situation? If elaborate experiments are required to determine that some people see a straw color when most of us see reds and greens, is it not the part of wisdom to set up somewhere a laboratory for the discovery of the reasons why some students succeed and others fail? Does it not seem reasonable that an institution like our own, which cultivates and disseminates the most highly matured knowledge on every subject about which men think, should turn some part of its energies to an examination of its own operations for the purpose of developing a body of scientific principles which will guide teaching?

MAKING THE PEOPLE LITERATE

By Dr. ROBERT T. HILL

THINGS may happen within ten years, as, for instance, the decrease of people in the United States who can not read and write. Census authorities report that whereas 6 per cent. of the population ten years of age or older were illiterate in 1920, the percentage in 1930 was 4.3. That is to say, of every hundred persons ten years old and older a little over four were unable to read and write. At least this is the report of the census-takers.

Compared with other decades, this decrease in reported illiteracy is fairly consistent. For instance, from 1910 to 1920 illiteracy declined from 7.7 to 6.0 per cent.; in 1900 it was 10.7; in 1890 it was 13.3; in 1880 it was 17.0; in 1870 it was 20.0. Thus, in a period of sixty years the number of people unable to read and write per each hundred of the population has dropped from twenty to four. As things go, this is a marked increase, apparently, in the literacy of the American people.

This increase of literacy in the United States, insofar as census enumerators can secure accurate information, coincides remarkably well with the results of investigations of the federal Office of Education which has been carrying on studies of secondary education. One of its investigators is reported to have stated recently that the level of educational attainment in the United States has reached seventh-grade experience; fifty years ago we are said to have been a nation of third-graders.

The number of persons ten years old and over who could not read and write, reported by the 1930 census enumerators, was 4,283,753. As mere figures go, that does not seem a considerable number in comparison with a total population of 122,775,046. But it is too many. When one considers the fact, moreover, that they are older children and men and women, the bare figures take on more life and vitality. A little more than half of those who can not read and write are boys and men; slightly less than half are girls and women. They are found among the population, scattered on the farms, through the villages and towns, and in the cities and industrial districts of the nation. The matter of illiteracy is exceedingly human because illiterates are people.

Some of the salient facts about illiteracy in the United States in 1930 are noted in the following table:

Total illiterates, ten years old and over	4,283,753
Male illiterates	2,198,293
Female "	2,085,460
Negro "	1,513,892
White "	2,407,218
Other than white and Negro illiterates	362,643
Native-born white illiterates	1,103,134
Foreign-born white "	1,304,084

Now where are these people who can not read and write? According to geographical divisions of the country they were recorded as follows:

States	
New England	245,270
Middle Atlantic	757,228
East North Central	442,064
West North Central	156,068
South Atlantic	1,012,523
East South Central	727,861
West South Central	675,791
Mountain	120,866
Pacific	146,082

Illiteracy of the white population in 1930 in urban territory was 2.5; in rural-farm territory 3.4; and in rural non-farm territory, 2.9 per cent.

Illiteracy among Negroes in the urban population was 9.2 per cent.; in the rural population 23.2 per cent.; in the rural non-farm population 20.5 per cent.

The high degree of literacy to be found in the North Central states is suggested by the fact that Iowa registered an illiteracy of but 0.8 per cent. That figure is striking when one considers the fact that the average for the country in 1930 was 4.3 per cent. Iowa dominantly has a white, native-born population and is one of the conspicuously homogeneous states.

But there are also other states where illiteracy is low. For instance, Washington and Oregon reported an illiteracy of 1.0 per cent. each; Idaho, 1.1; Utah, Kansas, South Dakota and Nebraska, 1.2 each; Minnesota, 1.3; North Dakota, 1.5; Wyoming, 1.6; Montana and Indiana, 1.7 each; Wisconsin, 1.9. The District of Columbia, which draws from all sections of the country, reported an illiteracy of 1.6 per cent.

At the other end of the scale is registered South Carolina, with a reported illiteracy of 14.9; Louisiana, 13.5; New Mexico, 13.3; Mississippi, 13.1; Alabama, 12.6; Arizona, 10.1; North Carolina, 10.1 per cent.

These and other figures bear out the usual assertion that illiteracy in the United States is largely a sectional matter.

In the North and West the percentage of illiteracy for the total population ten years old and over was 2.7; in the South, 8.2. Of the native white population six tenths of 1 per cent. were illiterate both in the North and in the West, and 3.7 in the South; of the foreign-born whites 10.5 per cent. in the North, 9.8 per cent. in the South and 5.1 per cent. in the West. In the North 4.7 per cent. of the Negroes were illiterate; in the South, 19.7 per cent.; in the West, 3.3 per cent.

Among white persons of native birth the percentage of illiteracy for the country as a whole was 1.5, though it is higher in particular sections. Among foreign-born whites it was 9.9; among Negroes illiteracy was 16.3. Among those of other races it was much higher, 25.0 per cent. This is accounted for by the fact that Mexicans, among whom illiteracy runs high, were included, in this last census, among "other races" instead of being enumerated, as they were in the 1920 census, in the white classification. This cut down the percentage of illiteracy among the foreign-born.

From these facts one may summarize certain conclusions which, incidentally, have not changed during the past ten years.

> Illiteracy is least among the native white people of the country.
>
> It runs high among the Negroes of the South.
>
> It runs high among the foreign-born whites, East, South and West.

Checking these well-known conclusions with facts relating to American and to educational policy one may venture to say that:

> Illiteracy among the foreign-born is revealed mostly among those from least educationally advanced foreign countries.
>
> Illiteracy among native-born whites and Negroes is found in the most educationally backward states.

These two statements suggest that illiteracy is largely a matter of "educational backwardness"; that popular literacy is due to educational opportunity.

Suppose these principles are accepted. How far may illiteracy be reduced? Obviously, in principle, all mentally competent persons may become literate. This, however, involves certain confusions which should be cleared.

First and foremost, there is the question of literacy itself. What do we mean by "literacy"? The term is used with much uncertainty and confusion. For instance, is a person who can merely write his name "literate"? If literacy means writing ability, how much writing ability is expected? If "literacy" means ability to read, what is the test for reading? How difficult should it be?

As a matter of fact, there is the widest kind of understanding or misunderstanding, rather, as to just what illiteracy means or implies. It did acquire a certain meaning during the early days of the war, following the draft when, to all intents and purposes, one quarter of the men called into service were "functionally illiterate" in the sense that they could not read or write to the degree necessary for the most efficient military service.

To immigration officials who apply a literacy test to immigrants "literacy" has one meaning within the provision of the law. To election officials in various states which require some sort of literacy for voting, it means various things. Schoolmen are divided also, not altogether certain as to the difference between literacy and "functional literacy" or how either should be measured. At the Atlanta convention of the National Education Association in 1929 it was agreed and a resolution adopted to the effect that fourth-year schooling was a sound basis for determining literacy. But the following year at Columbus it was decided that a sound program for the reduction of illiteracy should aim at sixth-grade schooling. An education supposed to be assured by the completion of the sixth grade or its equivalent educational experience is regarded by many as necessary for full-functioning literacy. In fact, the state of New York has substantially adopted this standard, to all intents and purposes, in its literacy test for new voters. This is the most advanced and perhaps the soundest step which has been taken anywhere to insure a reasonably competent vote, at least a vote that is as competent as fundamental education can make it. The question of an "intelligent vote" is something else.

Mental competency, with reference to the acquirement of the ability to read and write, obviously has some bearing upon the reduction of literacy. Since most people above twelve years attain a mental competency of a normal child of twelve years, it would seem that some considerable degree of literacy may be acquired by almost everybody. Less than 1 per cent. of the population of Iowa, for instance, are illiterate, according to the census. The reduction of illiteracy chiefly involves the extension of educational opportunity.

Manifestly standards and methods followed by the Bureau of the Census to record illiteracy are inadequate to secure accurate data. With decreasing illiteracy it might be much better and perhaps more to the point to attempt some way of ascertaining "literacy." This is the positive aspect of the matter, while illiteracy is negative.

The census defines an illiterate as any one ten years old or over who is unable to read and write. According to a statement of the Census Bureau, "the classification is based on the answers given to the enumerator in response to the question 'Whether able to read and write.' No specific test of ability to read and write was prescribed, but the enumerators were instructed not to return the answer 'Yes' (which would classify the person as literate) simply because a person was able to write his or her name. A person able to read and write in his native language was not counted as illiterate, even though he could not read or write English."

There is something naïve and indefinite

about this question from the standpoint of securing exact facts. The enumerator is hurried, and with a quickened social sense and a pride in the community may not like to register persons as illiterate when he may have reasons to believe that they are. On the other hand, he may err the other way and be too exacting. The chances are, however, that the enumeration of illiteracy as now practiced does not produce an accurate picture of facts, however much the "law of averages" may even up the enumeration. Some more definite and accurate way of securing such facts is desirable. Whether that is possible with limited funds and with the difficulties involved in expanding census schedules is another question. A more detailed and accurate census on illiteracy or "literacy," with the use of proper standards, may properly belong with the education authorities of the several states and their localities. Whatever method is used, it is desirable to have more accurate facts than apparently the usual federal census on illiteracy reveals. Such is desirable from the standpoint of educational program and policy.

The federal census on illiteracy emphasizes the fact that the extension of popular education is a matter of national concern; otherwise such a census would not be taken. Popular literacy is something of both national and local concern. It may be safely said that in the United States, notwithstanding the extent of illiteracy in many quarters, the educational ideal of the nation is universal literacy. The general tendency and desire is to make literacy one of the universal folk-ways and a definite part of the fabric of American culture. This is humanly desirable, possible and, from the standpoint of democratic institutions, essential.

The national cultural, industrial and political aspects of universal literacy are leading various nations to devote definite attention to the reduction of illiteracy. The rebirth of many old nations and the development of so-called new nations has been accompanied, during the past ten years or more, by an extraordinary outburst of enthusiasm and energy in reducing illiteracy. Turkey has its program; Italy hers; Poland hers; Egypt hers. Russia is carrying on heroic measures to extend popular literacy. One of the most vigorous and virile aspects of national movements in China and India is the promotion of literacy. Much of this is due to the extraordinary national and nationalistic movements throughout the world. Both the eastern and western hemispheres as well as the northern and the southern are marked by efforts to increase the literacy of the people. It is part and parcel of the world-wide movement toward more highly developed and integrated nations and peoples. It certainly is in keeping with the development and extension of democratic institutions. The dictum, "A people can not at the same time be ignorant and free," is increasingly recognized as sound politics and at the base of sound popular government. While literacy does not inevitably insure intelligence it goes a long way to reduce ignorance. And ignorance is dangerous wherever and however it may be found.

The reduction of illiteracy is brought about in two ways: by the exclusion of those who are illiterate; and by the increase of literacy through schooling. The latter method is primarily a responsibility, in the American system, of the states and their several localities. The exclusion of illiterates is primarily and from the national standpoint, wholly a matter of national government. According to reports, the national government has virtually stopped any legal increase of illiteracy through its stringent immigration policy. Immigrants may be admitted and are, but they are supposed to be literate in their own language. The test, however, is quite simple and there are some exceptions.

The reduction of illiteracy and to that extent the promotion of literacy, chiefly involves the education of adults. Of the total 4,283,753 enumerated illiterates in 1930 ten years old and over, 3,863,215 were 21 years of age or older. With the increase of popular and enforced schooling for children and the limitation of immigration, if this policy is maintained, there is a cutting at both ends in the reduction of illiteracy. As matters now stand, the reduction of illiteracy depends chiefly upon the extension of adult schooling. Experience proves that this is a feasible and successful method. The reduction of illiteracy in Georgia, North and South Carolina and in Delaware is due in part, perhaps a large part, to educational efforts in those states among adults. It is due to the fact that those states have done more than wish for the reduction of illiteracy. Appropriate plans and policies have been put into operation.

Efforts in these states and elsewhere have revealed the fact that men and women who can not read and write respond to opportunities to learn. Illiteracy in New York state has declined from 5.1 to 3.7 per cent. This is largely due to the activities of schools and other institutions and agencies during the past decade which have provided ways and means by which foreign-born non-English-speaking adults have been able to become, not only literate, but literate in English.

Illiteracy is an anachronism in the modern civilized world. It is inconsistent with the requirements of popular government, industrial proficiency and modern standards of living. It does not fit in with life as it is lived to-day, whether people live on farms or in the city. Doubtless, with all that may be done to reduce it, there will still be an irreducible minimum of illiteracy; yet that minimum may be and should be reduced as far as possible to the vanishing point. The public schools, with appropriate extensions of policy and service, may be expected to carry the chief responsibility and load. By giving thought to the problem school authorities, during the next decade, may throughout the country do much to reduce illiteracy still further. And what is desirable is not "bare literacy" but a full-functioning literacy which enables mature people to live more completely as workers, home-makers and citizens. This requires, not only a "beginning" of schooling for those who are unschooled, but also a continuance of schooling until more intellectual proficiencies are acquired.

EDUCATIONAL EVENTS

BEQUESTS IN THE WILL OF GEORGE EASTMAN

According to the will of Mr. George Eastman the University of Rochester, to which Mr. Eastman gave $35,500,000 while he lived, will receive the bulk of his estate, which is valued at $20,000,000. The share of the university proper is a bequest of $12,000,000, but Mr. Eastman also left $2,500,000 to the Eastman School of Music, which he founded in connection with the university, and his own home, valued at $600,000, as a residence for the university presidents. The will establishes a $2,000,000 fund for the upkeep of the property, its grounds and the trophies of hunting and scientific trips and experiments which it contains, but provides that it may be sold after ten years if the trustees of the university see fit.

Next to the University of Rochester, the Rochester Dental Dispensary will benefit most from Mr. Eastman's will, $1,000,000 having been left to that institution. Dr. Harvey J. Burkhart, director of the dispensary and Mr. Eastman's personal representative in the establishment of dispensaries in Europe, is to receive the equivalent of the income of $50,000 for life.

Bequests of $50,000 each were made to the Rochester General Hospital, the Genesee Hospital, the Rochester Young Men's Christian Association, the Rochester Orphan Asylum, the

Door of Hope Association, the Friendly Home, the Family Welfare Society of Rochester and the People's Rescue Mission.

The Rochester Community Chest will receive $100,000 for the first year following Mr. Eastman's death and $50,000 the second year, with no further provision made.

All unpaid subscriptions and commitments for educational institutions and philanthropies are to be carried out. Bequests to Cornell University, the Massachusetts Institute of Technology and the Young Women's Christian Association of Rochester were revoked in a codicil to the will signed just before Mr. Eastman's death. A statement given out by the executors explained that Mr. Eastman had made substantial pledges to each of these institutions between the time of execution of the will last July and the codicil.

SCHOLARSHIPS IN THE UNITED STATES

INFORMATION regarding scholarships and fellowships available at institutions of higher learning in the United States, which is of vital interest to many thousands of students who need financial assistance to enable them to complete their education, is contained in a new bulletin of the Office of Education, prepared by Ella B. Ratcliffe, chief educational assistant in the division of colleges and professional schools. The bulletin lists the scholarship offerings at 402 colleges and universities. It is estimated that there are more than 50,000 scholarships and fellowships available annually in the United States. The total money value of the grants is approximately $10,000,000.

Twenty-two states now furnish, by legislative enactment to institutions in the state, some sort of scholarship aid. These states are Arizona, California, Delaware, Florida, Illinois, Indiana, Iowa, Kentucky, Maryland, Montana, New Jersey, New York, North Carolina, Ohio, Pennsylvania, Rhode Island, South Carolina, South Dakota, Utah, Vermont, Virginia and Wisconsin.

Undergraduate as well as graduate grants are listed in the bulletin. Scholarships are indexed by subject, state and institution. The annual money value of scholarships and fellowships, whether service is required, the number of grants awarded to men or women, and Negro scholarships are also included.

Various states, institutions, alumni, patriotic societies, womens clubs, industrial organizations, churches and individuals annually give large sums of money to provide opportunities for higher education. The donation of funds for scholarship purposes is a form of philanthropy which has gained impetus since the war when a greater desire for college and university training was evidenced.

Scholarships offered in 1927 and 1928 ranged in value from less than $50 to $2,500. The greatest number of scholarships and fellowships were reported as ranging from $50 to $300 a year.

Only a few of the older colleges in the east record scholarships a century or two old. Harvard University has one nearly 300 years old, a scholarship given by Lady Mowlson of London, England, in 1643, when Harvard was only seven years old.

THE COST OF HIGHER EDUCATION IN WISCONSIN

A REPORT issued by the University of Wisconsin shows that the university has during the past year reduced the cost of higher education to the taxpayers of the state.

Since budget funds for the university have been set by the legislature for this biennium, it was possible to include in the report accurate figures for both this year and next. Beginning with the fiscal year 1923–24, the funds for operation and maintenance of the university, provided by the state, show in general a gradual increase for every year through 1930–31, but a sharp downward trend since then.

During the same period, the figures show practically the same situation in funds provided for buildings and land, except that here the amounts fluctuated to a much greater degree. During the entire eight-year period between 1923 and 1931, these capital funds never slipped below $210,000, and in three different years, 1923–24, 1926–27 and 1930–31, university expenditures for buildings and land were over the million dollar mark.

Gradually rising from $2,767,230 in 1923–24 to $4,197,025 in 1930–31, the operating and maintenance funds of the university provided by the state for this year were decreased to $4,-102,368. At the same time funds for buildings and land were decreased from $1,008,435 last year to $39,698 for this year, which is rather a lop-sided comparison since 1930–31 was a boom year in university building activity.

For next year, university operating and maintenance funds have been decreased still further to a figure below the four million dollar mark, to $3,960,857, while the funds for buildings and land have been slightly raised to $54,000.

Reductions offered to the state by the university have lowered the educational costs for both this year and next. The original legislative appropriations for 1931–32 amounted to $4,260,-080, and to this amount have been added several appropriations by the state emergency board amounting to $48,070, making a total for this year of $4,308,150. The university has offered savings of $166,086, reducing the total receipts from the state for all university purposes for this year to $4,142,064.

For next year the total legislative appropriation was $4,257,380, but here again the university has offered savings to the state of $242,523, making the total receipts from the state for all university purposes next year $4,014,857—a figure that is comparable with those of ten years ago, and less than any annual amount given the university by the state during any of the last six years.

These reductions in the cost of higher education have been gained through careful budget supervision and planning throughout every department of the university. Although the funds have been cut to a minimum, the educational standards of the university have not been greatly curtailed. Further reductions would probably lead to drastic curtailment of educational activities and services to the people of the state, however, and would undoubtedly place the state's leading educational institution in a dangerous financial position.

THE EDITOR OF THE COLUMBIA SPECTATOR

Mr. Reed Harris, editor-in-chief of *The Columbia Spectator,* the university daily, was dismissed from the university on April 1. According to press reports he has stated his case as follows:

I feel that the action of Dean Hawkes was unfair in that the decision to cancel my registration was made before I was given an opportunity to present any portion of my side of the case.

While I have long been aware that the administration of Columbia University felt that the *Spectator* was too strong in its criticism, I did not expect from an allegedly liberal university direct expulsion without hearing and with the consent of President Butler.

I was called into Dean Hawkes's office to-day and informed that my registration was to be canceled. Dean Hawkes then called me to a hastily convened meeting of the university committee on instructions. In addressing that meeting Dean Hawkes explained that his decision to expel me had already been made, but that President Butler had cautioned him to "give the appearance of holding a hearing."

The statement of Dean Hawkes that the *Spectator* has contained "misrepresentations" during my editorship is false. The authorities have been disturbed by my attitude on football and by criticisms of the university dining service. The *Spectator's* facts in these matters have been verified and its charges have been justified. No member of the editorial staff has ever had adequate opportunity to present information on which our editorial charges have been based.

Dean Hawkes has issued a statement in which he says:

From time to time during the entire year the columns of *The Columbia Spectator* have contained material reflecting upon individuals and upon the college. More than once I have asked Mr. Harris for evidence to support his assertions, but without success. I have tried to make it clear to him that I was ready and willing to attempt to remedy any situations that were not as they should be, and that if he were in possession of facts with which I was not familiar he should make them known to me.

On Thursday last Mr. Harris was requested to provide the dean with a memorandum substantiating his statement that the John Jay Dining Hall was conducted for private profit by the personnel in charge of its management. His response was wholly lacking in proof. Mr. Harris was then invited to appear for a hearing on Friday afternoon before a full and regular meeting of the committee on instruction. The committee on instruction has no responsibility for disciplinary action. Mr. Harris was invited to their meeting in order that he might have an opportunity to explain his position before a responsible group of the Columbia faculty. At this hearing Mr. Harris was afforded a full and final opportunity to establish the truth of his most serious allegation. He was, however, quite unable to do so, but did not withdraw his charge. After the hearing the registrar's office was instructed to cancel his registration.

The question of free speech does not enter the case in the slightest degree. The administration of the college has and will continue to welcome criticism and differences of opinion concerning its policies and practices.

In the opinion of the disciplinary authority of the college, and after a full hearing, Mr. Harris's behavior has been such as not to justify his further candidacy for the college degree.

SURVEY OF THE NEW YORK CITY SCHOOLS BY THE STATE EDUCATION DEPARTMENT

THE New York State Education Department has announced that it intends to continue its survey of the efficiency of New York City's schools, but upon a "decidedly reduced scale," because of the refusal of the legislature to appropriate $50,000 to defray the cost of the investigation.

Members of the State Education Department are devoting what time they can spare from an already crowded program of essential activities to this special study, but they will not be able to secure the assistance necessary for the survey, as originally contemplated.

Governor Roosevelt included $50,000 for the survey in his budget, but the Republican fiscal leaders of the legislature eliminated it, despite his protests.

The department stated that it is attempting to obtain financial aid from private sources so that the survey can be carried out as originally planned.

"It is unfortunate that, because of the lack of special supporting funds, the work has to be limited," said the announcement. "Every facility that can possibly be secured will be used, but at the best the broad type of study that would have been possible with the desired appropriations can not be forthcoming under present conditions."

The work, on the reduced scale, is being conducted by Dr. George M. Wiley, assistant commissioner for secondary education; Dr. J. Cayce Morrison, assistant commissioner for elementary education; Dr. Lewis A. Wilson, assistant commissioner for vocational and extension education, and Dr. Warren W. Coxe, director of the educational research division.

These officials have held four informal conferences with the members of the Board of Superintendents of New York City schools and with others responsible for major phases of the city's educational service.

THE NEW LIBRARY BUILDING OF ATLANTA UNIVERSITY

ATLANTA UNIVERSITY'S new library, built at a cost of $300,000 under a grant from the General Education Board and designed to serve the students of all the Negro institutions of higher learning in Atlanta, will be dedicated on Saturday, April 30. According to an announcement by President John Hope, the address of dedication will be made by United States Senator Frederic Collin Walcott, of Connecticut. The chief spokesman of the university will be Dr. James Weldon Johnson, Spence Professor of Creative English at Fisk University, who is a graduate of Atlanta University and a member of its governing board.

On the evening preceding the dedication, Friday, April 29, a special convocation will be held in Sisters Chapel, Spelman College, at which spokesmen of the chief educational foundations and religious organizations that have contributed to the advancement of Negro education will respond to the greetings of Dr. Will W. Alexander, president of Dillard University, New Orleans, who will preside. The chief address will be made by Dr. George Barton Cutten, president of Colgate University, Hamilton, New York.

Following the exercises of dedication on Saturday afternoon the university will be host at a tea at Spelman College, and in honor of the visitors a play and concert will be given that evening in Sisters Chapel.

The new library which is the first of a series of buildings to be erected to house the university is regarded as one of the finest libraries in the South. Designed by James Gamble Rogers, of New York City, it conforms to the most modern ideas in library structure and is in keeping with the Georgian Colonial architecture of the university group. Reading rooms in the library will accommodate 400 students. On the book stacks will be space for 118,000 volumes.

The library stands on a plot of land lying

between the campuses of Morehouse College for Men and Spelman College for Women, which since 1929 have been affiliated with Atlanta University. Under the terms of the grant the library will be available to the students not only of Atlanta University and Spelman and Morehouse Colleges, but will be accessible as well to the students of the other Negro institutions in Atlanta, which may enter into cooperative arrangements with the university for its use. These institutions include Morris Brown College, Clark University and Gammon Theological Seminary.

Miss Charlotte Templeton, formerly librarian at Greenville, South Carolina, and prior to that secretary of the Georgia State Library Commission, is librarian of Atlanta University. Under her direction the book collections of the university and of Morehouse and Spelman Colleges are being brought together in the new library. When the new structure is open there will be available for use about 40,000 volumes.

INSTALLATION OF THE PRESIDENT OF WASHINGTON AND JEFFERSON COLLEGE

DR. RALPH COOPER HUTCHISON was installed as president of Washington and Jefferson College at Washington, Pennsylvania, on April 2. Dr. Hutchison is the ninth to hold the position since Jefferson College, Canonsburg and Washington College were consolidated in 1865.

The inaugural address was given this morning by Dr. Ray Lyman Wilbur, president of Leland Stanford University and Secretary of the Interior in President Hoover's Cabinet, and the university's welcome was extended to him by Dean E. M. Weyer, acting president since Dr. S. S. Baker's resignation a year ago.

At noon in the George Washington Hotel a formal luncheon was served for the guests and those associated with the college and the inaugural ceremonies. Mr. Marcus W. Acheson, Jr., of Pittsburgh, presided at the luncheon and speeches were made by former President Dr. S. S. Baker, of Pittsburgh; President Thomas S. Baker, of the Carnegie Institute of Technology; Dean Arthur A. Hauck, of Lafayette College, of which Dr. Hutchison is a graduate; Provost Josiah H. Penniman, of the University of Pennsylvania; Dr. J. H. MacCracken, associate director of the American Council on Education, and Dr. James N. Rule, Secretary of Education of Pennsylvania, an alumnus of the college.

The formal inaugural ceremonies were preceded by the academic procession from "Old Main" around a city block to the gymnasium. Representatives of 140 colleges and universities, including thirty-five college presidents were among those who participated in this procession.

Judge James I. Brownson, of the Washington County Court of Common Pleas and president of the college board of trustees, presided at the installation and the invocation was offered by the Reverend W. Scott Bowman, moderator of the Synod of Pennsylvania of the Presbyterian Church.

Addresses of greeting were extended by Mr. William B. Beeson, Jr., of Uniontown, for the undergraduates; Dr. J. Claude McGregor, for the faculty; Dr. John L. Lowes, of Harvard University, for the alumni, and by Secretary Wilbur for "The Colleges of the United States."

Judge Brownson administered the oath to Dr. Hutchison; the inaugural prayer was said by Dr. J. Ross Stevenson, president of Princeton Theological Seminary, and the benediction was pronounced by Dr. James A. Kelso, president of Western Theological Seminary, Pittsburgh.

EDUCATIONAL NOTES AND NEWS

THE honorary doctorate of laws was conferred on March 23 by the University of California on Dr. William Wallace Campbell, formerly director of Lick Observatory and from 1923 to 1930 president of the university.

Two paintings in oil were presented to Sir Robert Alexander Falconer, president of the University of Toronto, in recognition of his services to education, at the recent meeting in Toronto of the Ontario Educational Association. The presentation was made by Dr. J. H. Putnam, retiring president of the association.

DR. DICE ROBINS ANDERSON was installed as president of Wesleyan College, Macon, Georgia, on April 8. Bishop W. N. Ainsworth presided and Dr. W. P. Few, president of Duke University, gave the principal address.

THE King of Italy has conferred upon Dr. George J. Ryan, president of the Board of Education of New York City, the rank of Officer in the Order of the Crown of Italy. The honor was bestowed on Dr. Ryan on recommendation of Premier Mussolini and was tendered in recognition of his services to education.

WEBSTER UNIVERSITY at Atlanta, Georgia, conferred on March 15 the degree of doctor of pedagogy on Mr. W. Lee Gilmore, supervising principal of the Oakmont, Pennsylvania, schools.

DR. HAROLD RUGG, professor of education at Teachers College, Columbia University, on his way to the Orient where he plans to spend eight months, was given a luncheon by the State Teachers College of San Francisco on January 27. Over two hundred people were present.

AT the annual meeting of the National Association of State Directors of Teacher Preparation and Certification held during the meeting of the Department of Superintendence at Washington, D. C., Mr. Henry Klonower, director of the teacher bureau of the department of public instruction, Pennsylvania, was elected president for the year 1932–33.

OFFICERS of the New England Classical Association, elected at the recent Worcester, Massachusetts, meeting, are: Professor Harry M. Hubbell, of Yale University, *president;* Miss Mary Adele Allen, Holyoke, *vice-president;* Professor Monroe N. Wetmore, Williams College, *secretary* and *treasurer;* Miss Mary E. Bartlett, Manchester, New Hampshire; Professor Thomas Means, Bowdoin College; Miss Helen F. Hill, Lowell, and William D. Goodwin, Pittsfield, *executive committee.*

MR. E. M. WILLIAMS, for thirteen years president of the Cleveland School Board, has resigned. He is succeeded by Mr. Alfred M. Benesch.

RABBI LOUIS D. GROSS and Dr. Philip A. Brennan, of Brooklyn, New York, have been appointed members of the Board of Higher Education of New York City by Mayor Walker. Dr. Gross succeeds Mr. Ralph Jonas, who resigned from the board, and Dr. Brennan takes the place of the late Arthur Somers.

MR. HARRY P. CHARLESWORTH has become a member in the corporation of the Polytechnic Institute of Brooklyn, New York. Mr. Charlesworth is vice-president of the Bell Telephone Laboratories and has been named as a candidate for the next president of the American Institute of Electrical Engineers. He is a graduate of the Massachusetts Institute of Technology.

MR. CHARLES SCHMIDT, inspector general of the French National Archives, Paris, will be exchange professor at Harvard University during the first half of the academic year 1932–33. Dr. Paul Joseph Sachs, professor of fine arts and associate director of the Fogg Art Museum, will be exchange professor in France for the second half of the year.

DR. J. W. NORMAN, dean of the College of Education of the University of Florida, has been appointed director of the summer school of the university for 1932.

MISS ISABEL WHITE, of Boston, has been elected president of Sage House, the dormitory which houses freshmen and juniors at Cornell University.

MR. JOHN F. FRIESE, of the department of industrial education of the University of Wisconsin, has been appointed associate professor of industrial education at Pennsylvania State College. He succeeds Mr. M. M. Walter, who has been appointed director of the bureau of rehabilitation, State Department of Labor and Industry, Harrisburg.

AT the end of the current academic year Dr. Henry Franklin Cutler will retire from the principalship of the Mount Hermon School for Boys, near East Northfield, Massachusetts, after serving for forty-two years.

MR. DONALD M. CRESSWELL, director of the department of public education and editor of publications for Pennsylvania State College during the past twelve years, has been appointed as editor of publications in the Pennsylvania State Department of Public Instruction.

DR. C. L. HUGHES, associate director of student teaching and assistant professor of education at the University of California, has been elected a member of the research committee of the supervisors of student teaching, a section of the American Association of Teachers Colleges, for a five-year term beginning this year.

GRANTS of the Social Science Research Council include $25,000 to Dr. Charles A. Beard for a study of "National Interest"; $45,000 for a study of the social, economic, political and educational conditions in the Southern States to be directed by Professor Howard W. Odum, of the University of North Carolina, and $5,000 to Professor Wilson Gee, of the University of Virginia, who will direct an inquiry to promote effective corporate organizations among the colleges of the South. Both of the Southern studies will be conducted through the Southern Regional Committee of the council, of which Professor B. B. Kendrick, of the North Carolina College for Women, Greensboro, is chairman.

DR. ALEXANDER DUNLOP LINDSAY, master of Balliol College, University of Oxford, will give the second series of Hewett Lectures at Harvard University during the second half-year. These lectures were established upon a bequest of the late Professor Waterman Thomas Hewett, of Cornell University, and are given at intervals of three or four years. They are administered by the president of the faculty of Andover Theological Seminary, the dean of the Episcopal Theological School, Cambridge, and the president of Union Theological Seminary, New York City, as trustees. The general subject of the present series is "Christianity and Economics." The lectures will be given at eight o'clock at the Episcopal Theological School, Cambridge, and will be open to the public.

AN anonymous gift of money has been made to be used for a James Sullivan lecture to be given in February, 1933, at the New York State College for Teachers at Albany. The lecture will be on a subject relating to the history of books, manuscripts, painting or illustrations and will be in recognition of the interest of the late Dr. Sullivan in those subjects and in the library school. Dr. Sullivan was for fifteen years connected with the State Education Department. It is proposed that the fund be used for an annual lecture at the college on or about his birthday on February 13.

THE REV. FRANCIS J. MCSHANE, formerly president of Villanova College, has died in Philadelphia. He was eighty-six years old. He founded the Augustinian College for Students of the Augustinian Order in Washington in 1918 and has held the offices of president, vice-president and professor at Villanova College, Villanova, Pa., at various times.

DR. ALBERT PERRY BRIGHAM, professor emeritus of geology at Colgate University, died on April 1 in his seventy-seventh year.

LAURA J. WYLIE, professor emeritus of English at Vassar College, died on April 2, at the age of seventy-eight years.

THE death is announced at the age of eighty-five years of William Shepard Crouse, formerly superintendent of Caroline County Schools, Maryland.

WILLIAM H. BARRY, for forty years principal of several schools in Paterson, New Jersey, died on March 28. He was eighty-four years old.

WILLIAM COLGATE, who died on March 7, at the age of ninety-one years, left more than $1,000,000 to charitable organizations. Specific bequests included $150,000 to the Connecticut Junior Republic of Litchfield and $25,000 to the Wolcott and Litchfield Circulating Library. Thirty per cent. of the residue goes to Colgate University.

THE endowment of Cornell College, Mount Vernon, Iowa, has been increased by $308,379 during the last fiscal year, according to an announcement made by President H. J. Burgstahler. Should $20,000 more be raised the debt of $193,175 of five years ago will be entirely wiped out.

THE General Education Board of New York has given $30,000 to the University of Richmond, Virginia, to be used in completion of a group of science buildings. Gifts from the board to the university now amount to $750,000.

APPROXIMATELY $5,000 has been contributed by alumni of Northwestern University to the fund for the relief of more than 200 students who may be obliged to leave the university unless immediate aid is given them. The campaign is being conducted by the foundation and the Northwestern University Club of Chicago.

All available scholarships and loan funds of the university having been exhausted, a special plea is being made to alumni to keep the needy students in school. A fund of $21,000 must be raised at once to meet the needs of these 200 students.

PRESIDENT HOOVER approved on March 31 a bill recently passed by Congress (S. 1590), granting certain public lands to the State of New Mexico for the use and benefit of the Eastern New Mexico Normal School, and for other purposes.

DEAN CASWELL ELLIS, of Cleveland College, has announced that unless it proves possible to obtain by subscription the sum of $180,000, the institution will be forced to close. Mr. Newton D. Baker has made an appeal for subscriptions.

THE daily newspapers report that professors and other faculty members at Long Island University have received monthly salary checks made out for half—and in some cases less than half—the customary amount. With each check was enclosed a notice that the rest due the recipient would be temporarily delayed. Trustees and officers of the institution explained that in recent months many of the students had been unable to meet fully their obligations in the way of payment of tuition and other fees, and that the university had been carrying these students. It was indicated that the sums still due to faculty members would be paid as soon as possible.

THE Attorney General of Illinois, Oscar E. Carlstrom, has ruled that property used exclusively for religious purposes or for school and religious purposes is exempt from taxation. If the property is leased or otherwise used with a view to profit, the exemption is lost. The question arose in connection with the purchase by a religious denomination of several thousand acres of land in Jersey County. Buildings are being erected on the land to be used for the education of students who are affiliated with the denomination.

ATTORNEY GENERAL BENNETT transmitted to the New York State Education Department on March 29 his opinion that the moratorium on state salary increases, recently enacted by the legislature, did not apply to public school teachers. "Chapter 50 of the laws of 1932 suspends temporarily any increase in salary or wages of officers or employees in the state service," he wrote. "This, in our opinion, does not apply to public school teachers. Teachers are employed and their salaries fixed according to law by local boards of education and local school district authorities. The state contributes toward their salaries but does not hire or discharge teachers." The moratorium measure, introduced by the Republican majority after Governor Roosevelt submitted his budget, was intended to save $967,000 in automatic salary increases.

AN Associated Press dispatch reports that the New Mexico Board of Finance by resolution has voted to place New Mexico's educational charitable, penal and reformatory institutions on a semi-cash basis effective on July 1. The order means that on July 1 and after these institutions will receive from the state treasurer only a proportion of actual monies received by the state from taxes in relation to the monies authorized for them in legislative appropriations. The action was taken in view of an impending deficit on June 30 in the state general fund, with due regard to uncertainty of tax collections, and in lieu of a previous proposal that state funds be withdrawn from these institutions during the remainder of the present fiscal year. The resolution adopted instructs the secretary of the board of finance to forward copies of the resolution at once to the heads of the various institutions in order that they may look to conservation of their balances during the remainder of the present year and regulate their expenses in such a manner that they will be able to meet the new system on July 1.

ACCORDING to a cablegram to *The Christian Science Monitor,* the rector of the University of Belgrade, the vice-rector and the deans of all the faculties resigned on March 29 as a protest against the clause in the Finance Act allowing the Minister of Education to dismiss university professors, thus destroying the autonomy of the institution. The resignations have been accepted. The act in question is aimed against anti-government professors. On the following day an academic council consisting of all the regular professors unanimously voted not to accept the resignations of the previous day. The council thus supports the campaign against abrogation of the autonomy of the university by the present Parliament. The Yugoslav Government on the ground of economy recently decided to empower the minister of education to reduce the number of professors. This is said to mean that the government in future may remove any professor with whom it is displeased.

THE Northwestern University Foundation and the Northwestern University Club of Chicago on March 12 started a campaign to raise funds among the alumni and friends of the university for approximately two hundred Northwestern students who may be obliged to leave school unless immediate aid is given them. The first contribution was made by Melvin A. Traylor, president of the First National Bank and a member of the university's board of trustees. The university has already used up all available scholarships and loan funds, it was pointed out by Harry L. Wells, president of the foundation. Professors, in some instances, are paying for the tuition and expenses of students of unusual promise. "Every effort has been made to furnish aid, but the load has been altogether too heavy. Some of the 200 who need help at once to remain in school have come from well-to-do families that have suffered financial reverses; others have been earning their way and can not now get work to enable them to carry on." The number of contributors to the Northwestern University Foundation last year was increased from 4,403 to 5,417, a gain of 23 per cent. The total amount contributed was $35,562 against $35,674 in 1930, a decrease of only 1/3 of one per cent. The average gift in 1931 was $6.56 as against $8.29 in 1930. The money contributed will be used for salaries of members of the faculty, research projects, scholarships and additions to the libraries of the various schools. In the five campaigns which the foundation has fostered since its founding six years ago, a total amount of $165,000 from 8,000 alumni has been received. The goal for 1932 has been set at $50,000, which is equivalent to the annual income of a million dollar endowment.

SENIOR high school students in the states of Minnesota and Wisconsin are to be given an opportunity of winning a university scholarship. This offer is open to both boys and girls graduating during the current year. The award will be $2,000 in cash, payable in four annual installments. The sponsors of the scholarship are the Federal Hardware and Implement Mutuals, a group of insurance companies consisting of the Retail Hardware Mutual Fire Insurance Company, Minneapolis; the Hardware Dealers Mutual Fire Insurance Company, Stevens Point, Wisconsin, and the Minnesota Implement Mutual Fire Insurance Company, Owatonna, Minnesota. The scholarship will be awarded to the student who writes, in the opinion of the judges, the best essay on the subject "Mutual Fire Insurance—its History, Development and Future." Material will be given to students gratis to assist them in writing their essay. Reference will also be made to library books and magazines where additional material may be obtained.

IN a proclamation Dr. Frank P. Graves, New York State commissioner of education, has designated April 22, April 29 and May 6 as the days to be observed as Arbor Day in various sections of the state. April 8 was designated for the observance of Bird Day. The Arbor Day proclamation of Commissioner Graves follows: "Each year the schools of the state observe the annual festival of the trees which we call Arbor Day. They plant trees and shrubs, beautify school grounds and in general encourage a love of all living things. This year the observance has an added significance. Our nation is commemorating the two hundredth anniversary of the birth of George Washington and it has been suggested that one form of observance be the planting of millions of trees as living monuments to the Father of our Country. It is fitting that we should do this. George Washington loved trees and was himself a planter of trees, recognizing their economic value and deeply appreciating their beauty. We shall do well to emulate his example. Thus we shall learn the value of conservation and have our hearts touched by the wonders and beauty about us. Especially in these days are these lessons essential. From intimate contact with nature we shall know what things are good and true and be more appreciative of our many blessings."

School publications which are members of the Columbia Scholastic Press Association on March 12 received awards of bronze medals from the Sigma Delta Chi, national journalistic fraternity, at the association's eighth annual convention at Columbia University. The story, "Snowball Battle Results in Arrest of Five Students," won the medal for the best news article which was awarded to the *Chronicle* of Pasadena Junior College, Pasadena, California. *The Chatterbox* of George Washington High School, Danville, Virginia, won the medal for the best editorial with its discussion, "The Council and the Schools." The medal for the best feature story went to the *Argentian* of Argentine, Kansas, for its story, "Five People Needed to Operate Marionettes and Shadow Show." First award in the contest for handset magazines, which consisted of honorable mention, went to the *Public School Review*, published by the teachers of the Berlin, New Hampshire, public schools. Other awards in this group were to *Co-operator*, published by the School of Industrial Arts, Mt. Vernon, New York; *Junior Citizen*, published by the *Connecticut Junior Republic*, Litchfield; *The Village Crier*, published by the boys and girls of the Children's Village, Dobbs Ferry, New York; *The Vocational Messenger*, published by the Industrial High School, Albany, New York, and *The Voice*, published by the Browning School, Tenafly, New Jersey.

DISCUSSION

A PLEA FOR MORE EXPERIMENTAL WORK BY COLLEGE DEPARTMENTS OF MODERN FOREIGN LANGUAGES

From 1924 to 1927 great advances were made in a scientific study of the problems of modern foreign language teaching as a result of the interest stimulated by the leaders of the Modern Foreign Language Study. One might reasonably have expected that this interest would continue, but recent progress leaves something to be desired, particularly on the part of larger universities.

In the Coleman Report, which synthesized the findings of the Study, some 123 problems are suggested which need more attention than was possible for the workers of the Study to give them. It was hoped that institutions of higher learning would give them consideration in the assignment of theses and dissertations as well as make them subjects for investigation within college departments. As this hope does not seem to be materializing, this communication is a plea for the early initiation of such projects.

The attention of teachers of these languages since the publication of the Coleman Report seems to have been directed toward the discussion of its recommendation for an increased amount of reading and the attainment of the reading objective, now universally recognized as the paramount aim of modern language teaching, by a somewhat different method of approach than that to which we have been accustomed. This discussion was inevitable and necessary in order that all points of view might be presented.

A careful reading of such discussion fails to reveal, however, the presence of a scientific approach to the solution of the problem. Those who favor the reading approach do present a limited amount of evidence in support of their hypothesis; those opposed base their argument on opinion without apparently having taken the trouble to give the new method a trial. Professor Cheydleur, of the University of Wisconsin, has reported the only recent controlled experiment designed to find out by actual experience whether or not the reading approach is superior to the older methods. There is a great need for more experiments of this sort if we are ever to know the relative merits of different methods.

It might be remarked in passing that the University of Wisconsin is assuming a position of marked leadership in the matter of experimentation in the modern language field. Professor Cheydleur has recently reported the results of experiments dealing with the teaching and testing of functional and formal grammar and also a study of placement examinations. An interesting departure from ordinary college procedure is seen at Wisconsin in a recent change in requirements which permits students to be excused from further study in the subject if suitable examinations are passed. This procedure is also reported as part of the new plan at the University of Chicago and as adopted recently at the University of North Dakota. It was reported in the *New York Times* last summer that Professor C. M. Purin, of the Extension Division of the University of Wisconsin, was about to begin some experiments in teaching German by an oral method introduced at Columbia University this summer in Italian by Professor Guarnieri. The Service Bureau for teachers of German at the University of Wisconsin, carried on by Miss Stella Hinz, should also be noted. This university is certainly doing its share to advance progress in modern language teaching.

Ohio State University, too, is carrying on certain experiments, particularly in the effect of oral and aural activities on scholastic achievement. A phonetics laboratory was instituted there about 1925, and from time to time reports concerning the work done have appeared.

Experimental work in the construction of new texts to be used in the reading approach on the secondary-school level is being carried on at the University of Iowa by Professor Helen M. Eddy. This is a much-needed work if the new method is to receive a fair trial. A number of cities have adopted its principles but tools have hitherto been lacking. Few experiments have been reported to show whether or not its adoption is really justified. A curious situation exists in New York which shows the vital need of a knowledge of all the facts. New York City has issued a syllabus incorporating the principles of the reading method, but the new New York State syllabus will have none of it and advocates more traditional methods. A great service would be rendered the modern language cause if one large city would adopt a controlled experimental program for a period of, say, three or five years, teaching equated groups of pupils by each method.

During the last decade we have become accustomed to look to the University of Chicago for leadership in two fields, the high school and the junior college. In the former Professor Bovée has reported interesting and instructive experiments. In the latter the names of Professor Bond in French, Professor Hagboldt in German, and Professors Ransmeier and Castillo are known to all teachers in these fields. Quite independently of the now famous work of Michael West in Bengal, this group of men developed a reading approach to the study of modern languages which accorded more nearly with the announced purposes of the languages as liberal arts subjects than probably any other courses offered in American colleges. The courses, as this group developed them, provided for an acquaintance with a foreign tongue—the reason presumably why the languages are considered an integral part of an arts curriculum—as well as for an introductory training for those who would continue their study. Of late, however, little has been heard from these men.

One wonders what will become of this experimental group under the new plan at Chicago. From the published announcements of the reorganization there would seem to be no place for such a group. Yet its disappearance, assuming as great productivity as in the past, would be a severe blow to modern language teaching. College teachers of the languages, with a liking for and experience in experimental methods, are all too rare. It is to be sincerely hoped that some arrangement can be worked out so that this group can continue its work. It is particularly needed now when so few others are working on the new and much debated methods of teaching.

A few individuals report isolated experiments in modern language teaching. Prominent among them are W. V. Kaulfers, of the Long Beach, California, Junior College, in the prognosis of foreign language success, Professor Colley Sparkman, of the Mississippi State Teachers' College, in reading, Professors Luella C. and Sidney L. Pressey, of Ohio State University, and Professor H. R. Huse, of the University of North Carolina, in the psychology of modern language teaching. With the impetus given by the Modern Foreign Language Study it would seem there should be more.

Perhaps the energy expended during an intensive drive such as that of the study leaves us too fatigued to undertake new work at once. Perhaps the lack of the guidance of a central committee is felt—it is always easier to carry out a task assigned or suggested by another than to initiate a study ourselves. Whatever the reason may be for the recent lack of important investigations, it would seem that more institutions of higher learning should plan a definite attack on certain definite problems. Could not the National Federation of Modern Language Teachers or the American Associations of Teachers of French, German and Spanish take steps to continue the American and Canadian Committees on Modern Foreign Languages or appoint new committees to head up a continuing investigation of the problems of modern language teaching?

ROBERT D. COLE

UNIVERSITY OF NORTH DAKOTA

PROFESSORS AND POLITICS IN ARKANSAS

AN item in SCHOOL AND SOCIETY for March 26, 1932, gives the impression that the board of trustees of the University of Arkansas recently took an action forbidding active participation in politics by members of the university staff in the interest of the governor of the state, who is chairman of the board of trustees of the university, and who was alleged in the article to be a candidate for U. S. Senator. The impression created is wholly erroneous. The governor has not announced himself as a candidate and it is not known whether he will do so.

The resolution in question, before being discussed by the board of trustees, was submitted to a number of the most prominent members of the university faculty, including the president of the local chapter of the Association of American University Professors, and strongly endorsed by all of them. It merely seeks to prevent what might be termed pernicious partisan activity on the part of members of the university staff. It applies not only to the forthcoming campaign, but to all campaigns. In no wise does it seek to prevent the free expression of opinions on public matters by university professors.

J. C. FUTRALL,
President

UNIVERSITY OF ARKANSAS

SELF GOVERNMENT

APPOINTING pupils to act as proctors in maintaining order during teachers' absence is not teaching "self government," although Principal Gustave A. Feingold, of Bulkeley High School, Hartford, seems to have mistaken that plan for the real plan.[1]

First, the spirit of cooperation, willingness to assume responsibility must be aroused and then the proctors must be elected by the students and power to inflict penalties (under teacher guidance) must be given and most of the troubles listed in Dr. Feingold's letter will disappear.

He says, "Pupils are sent to school primarily to study and to be instructed in matters which require the guidance and advice of professionally trained people." We do not agree, and call Dr. Feingold's attention to SCHOOL AND SOCIETY's list[2] of more than thirty chief educators of the country who state the first aim of public school education in our democracy (as also laid down by the fathers of our country) is character education for citizenship.

RICHARD WELLING,
Chairman, National Self Government Committee, Inc.

SPECIAL CORRESPONDENCE

THE PRESENT CONDITION OF EDUCATION IN ECUADOR

ONE of the things which mainly characterize present civilization is an interest, more or less pronounced according to the country, in intensifying, extending and improving popular education. Ecuador also, though small in area and with a limited number of inhabitants, has acquired the conception that education is something fundamental and now holds this problem as one of those that most deeply concern the nation and the people in general.

This inquietude, if it does not signify a full realization of ideals and proposals, is at least a splendid augury of cultural betterment. From the time of the conquest, slowly but surely, the different movements of progress suited to this machine age have taken decisive and advancing steps in the field of education.

Certainly Ecuador has not solved all its educational problems nor has any other country on earth. Nevertheless, I can say without hesita-

[1] SCHOOL AND SOCIETY, January 30, 1932.

[2] Dec. 5, 1931; Feb. 6, 1932.

tion that no theory, no system, no idea, no practice relating to education is foreign to it. Not all the teachers devote themselves to renewing their philosophy of education by giving it solid foundations based on science, psychology and sociology or by becoming acquainted with and trying out the new pedagogical experiments conceived and realized in other countries by exceptional teachers. But nevertheless the work of Dewey, Decroly, Patri, Kerchensteiner, etc., is well known, and in like manner the "progressive schools," "l'ecole nouvelle" or the "arbeitschule," have with us their partisans, admirers and propagandists. Ecuador has therefore accepted the movement for improving the school. With the purpose of transforming the school in its essence and in its methods Ecuador belongs to the International Bureau of Education and was one of the first countries to join it. It now maintains a representative in Geneva and is planning the organization of a modern school of pedagogical experimentation in accord with the ideas of Professor Adolph Ferriere, assistant director of the bureau, who not long since, on the invitation of the Government, visited Ecuador and delivered lectures on the new education in the principal Ecuadorean cities. Along the same line, mention should be made of the National Congress of Primary and Normal Education called by the Minister of Education and at whose sessions, held in the latter part of May, 1930, the reorganization of the Ecuadorean school system was considered, as well as the foundation that should be laid on which to raise the new education, and in a special way the orientation that should be given the Ecuadorean school, within our possibilities, in order to put into practice the principles of the activity school. In like manner some small schools have begun trying with success the Dalton Plan, the Decroly system, etc.

Unequivocal proof of the special attention that is being given to education in Ecuador is that wise provision of Article 169 of the political constitution of the republic, by virtue of which, each year, the allotments to the education branch will be augmented until at the close of five years they will reach 20 per cent. of the general revenues of the nation.

Also, inspired by that noble proposal, the National Assembly of 1928–29, in organizing the branches of the government and establishing functional representation in the senate of the republic, allotted four representatives to the teachers in the different grades of schools.

The constitution of the republic in Article 151, No. 21, defining the guarantees and rights which the Ecuadorean nation recognizes, sets forth the postulates which serve as a basis for our system of education and which may be understood by reading the following transcription of the pertinent portion of the article indicated:

> The Ecuadorean Nation guarantees: Liberty of education, of instruction and of speech.
>
> Instruction is free, without other restrictions than those fixed in the laws; but public instruction and that paid for by the municipalities is essentially secular and lay.
>
> Primary instruction and that in arts and crafts, of a public character, is gratuitous and, in consequence, no fees whatever may be charged. Moreover, the former is obligatory, without prejudice to the right of parents to give their children such instruction as they consider proper.
>
> Neither the Nation nor the municipalities may subvention or aid in any manner directly or indirectly any schools other than the public and the municipal.
>
> Private instruction may be given only in accord with the laws and regulations of that branch and under official supervision.

In implanting laicism in instruction, the legislators desired to guard the child from all kinds of sectarian influences, recognizing its right to accept any religion whatever or to hold to none. In establishing the obligation and the gratuity of primary instruction they have recognized the duty of the nation to give to all its members a minimum of education and their right to receive it.

On the basis of these principles, in essence identical with those which were contained in the former constitution (1906–07), the liberal revolution triumphant at that time formulated the organic law of public instruction, which, from the general revision of 1912 to our time, has undergone a partial but substantial modification. Since 1925 there have been many attempts to change it radically and many official commissions have formulated drafts of a law of education, the last one of which the national congress now has under consideration. The purpose of the new law is to construct a rational system of education which will assure to every Ecuadorean a full and harmonious development of all his capacities and his personality and aiming at social cooperation as well.

Regulations and general courses of study for the different branches of instruction, issued by the minister of education, and special regulations and courses for each province complete the body of Ecuadorean school legislation.

The direction and general responsibility for education belong to the Ministry of Education, made up of special divisions and departments to attend to the different branches of instruction.

Adjunct to the ministry and assisting it in the task of supervising education and fixing certain general norms, there existed until 1925 a Superior Council of Public Instruction, a body with little homogeneity, which lacked certain technical elements and which, like the School Councils of Primary Instruction, had to be suppressed because of its inefficiency. In its place technical divisions were created such as that of primary and normal education and that of physical education, now also suppressed, though it may be only temporarily.

In each province there is a director of studies, who administers all the primary schools in his territorial jurisdiction. In the *colegios* (schools mainly of secondary grade) there is a rector, a vice-rector, an administrative council and a general council of teachers. In the universities, a rector, a vice-rector, the university council and the full university assembly.

Ecuador, not much favored by nature, does not aspire to be a world power, rich and mighty; but it may aim at the goal of becoming some day the best educated country. Such at least is the most profound and enthusiastic hope of the author of these lines.

Emilio Uzcátegui[1]

QUOTATIONS

SAVE HOWARD UNIVERSITY

Education suffers unjust discrimination in the Interior Department appropriations bill now before the Senate. Whether this injustice is deliberate or unintentional is unimportant at this late day. The wrong should be corrected quickly.

Howard University in Washington, one of the few real institutions for higher learning of the Negro in the United States, is the chief victim. Rapid progress has been made by this university in recent years. Howard has won high rating from the national educational organizations and boards, and has the confidence of federal authorities from President Hoover and Secretary of the Interior Wilbur on down.

The pending Senate bill reduces the Howard appropriation to $675,000 for next year, compared with the first budget estimate of $1,942,000 and the current figure of $1,560,000.

In times of depression and federal deficit appropriations must be cut. But the federal outlays for social services and education should be cut least because they already are so pitifully small. At least they should not be asked to take more than their proportionate share of the slash.

This rule has been violated in the case of Howard. The cut in the entire Interior Department appropriations bill in the Senate is only three per cent., while the Howard cut is fifty-eight per cent.

This is not economy. It is close to murder. No institution operating on a shoestring can take a blow like that and survive as an effective school.

We appeal to the Senate to save Howard University.—*The New York World-Telegram.*

PAY FOR CHICAGO'S TEACHERS

Of all the sad snarls into which the skeins of municipal planning and good government have been knotted, the tax tangle in Chicago ranks

[1] Senator, representing primary and normal instruction, former director general of education. According to the new constitution of Ecuador the senate is composed of one senator from each province, of one "senator for the guidance and defense of the indigenous race" and in addition 15 senators of functional representation named by the different groups of institutions existing in the country, such as the press, agriculture, commerce, education, etc.—Editor.

with the worst. And especially as it concerns the payment of school teachers. In nearly a twelvemonth, these faithful warders of to-morrow's citizens have received only ten weeks' pay for their services; none the less, they have been daily at their posts, bravely carrying on.

A recent study of the situation, undertaken by the Chicago Principals' Club, shows these teachers in debt on loans $7,000,000, with $6,600,000 more outstanding on other bills. In addition, some 3,175 teachers, about half those questioned in the study, have a large number of persons dependent upon them.

Some days ago, New York teachers made a splendid overture to aid their Chicago colleagues. They have proposed the establishment of a loan fund from which to meet the needs of those feeling the greatest pinch.

That the situation is grave, no one disputes. When any city, a home of culture and progress, permits thousands of individuals, daily concerned with the advancement of that very culture and progress, to bear the burden of municipal incompetency, avarice and mistaken planning, thought everywhere is challenged. On what, one begins to ask oneself, can a city pride itself if not on its integrity, its moral and ethical culture, its enlightened thinking? Can any city, great or small, allow vicious indifference to such a state of affairs to suggest the thought that those who serve best fare worst?

But there is a right solution even to this problem, and there are evidences that Chicago is awaking to its true responsibility. Certainly, it possesses the courage, intelligence and energy to bring it to a speedy conclusion. And what a splendid thing it will be to see this proper provision for teachers take its place next year with all those other worthy achievements that will be heralded in Chicago's Century of Progress Exposition!—*The Christian Science Monitor.*

THE TEACHER AND POLITICS

A PART of the public has recently been very much interested in the fact that the teachers of North Carolina are showing some interest in the candidates for office, and have shown a tendency to decry the teacher going into politics. There has been some criticism of the association for what was termed the organization's efforts in urging teachers to enter the political field.

Nothing has been farther from the minds of the responsible leaders of the teaching profession than hurling the teachers' association into politics. They realize that the association is a professional and not a political organization. It is not now and never has been the intention or the desire of the officials of the association to put the organization into politics. Its officers, however, have urged teachers to vote—and what is more important to vote only after they have secured information about the stand of the various candidates on the school question. That is merely an effort to see that this large group of people cast an intelligent vote. If urging people to vote and vote with some degree of independence after they have secured information that will enable them to vote intelligently—then the association is urging the teachers to enter politics. And no one connected with the association has any apology to make for such action. It will be continued.

It may be said in this connection that the primaries are five months off. There is no objective in tying up to any candidate or set of candidates just now. The school question is going to be the most important issue before the public during the next few years, and the candidate who expects support of those interested in schools should have some decided opinions about the basis of support and adequacy of support.—*The North Carolina Teacher.*

REPORTS

SUGGESTED ECONOMIES IN SCHOOL ADMINISTRATION

To all public school officials in Pennsylvania there has recently gone a communication from Superintendent James N. Rule, of the Department of Public Instruction, suggesting economies in school administration to meet the financial emergency. Superintendent Rule begins as follows:

The 1932–33 school budget is now demanding attention. Sound budgetary procedure is an all-important factor affecting economy and efficiency in school financing. Where drastic reductions must be made, great care should be exercised so that there will be the least possible curtailment of educational advantages. Hasty and ill-considered reductions in school budgets may do harm to the education of children which can never be overcome. It should be remembered that the boys and girls who are now in school are entitled to this opportunity to secure their education. Whatever is eliminated for them at this time may be lost forever.

Pointing out that "no list of possible economies can be suggested which may be applied satisfactorily to all school systems," Superintendent Rule emphasizes the need in each individual situation for "both expert professional knowledge and common sense." Those responsible for the financial administration of the public schools should keep in mind, he writes, that "while every effort must be made to balance budgets, nevertheless the following general principles are of vital importance as controls:

(1) The elimination of teachers or the increasing of the number of pupils per teacher in general only serves to aggravate the existing unemployment situation.

(2) The unnecessary reduction of salaries only adds to the reduced consuming power of the local community.

(3) Wherever the resources of the local community makes it possible, needed major repairs to existing buildings and the construction of needed new buildings should be undertaken in order to relieve the unemployment situation, and to secure for the district the advantage of existing favorable prices.

(4) "Education is the goose that lays the golden eggs of prosperity." Census experts inform us that our population will soon become relatively static. This means that business men must depend in general for the expansion of their business not upon more customers but upon better customers. Education, through the program now being developed in the public schools, especially in such subjects as art, music, health education, science, literature, citizenship and all the fine and practical arts, refines and creates new economic wants and demands. It is this that makes the wheels of industry go round. From a business point of view we have not reached a condition of overproduction in education.

(5) We spend annually probably not less than six billion dollars in insurance premiums for protection against fire, death, disease and accidents. Education provides at a relatively low cost social insurance essentially not only to the development of the Commonwealth and Nation, but also to its safety and happiness. Education can be depended upon to make its full contribution to the development of a stabilized prosperity for all.

The following suggestions are worthy of careful consideration in balancing the school budget:

(1) *General Control:* Reduce expenses of general control by reducing excessive fees paid collectors of school taxes, and by eliminating fees of school board treasurers. The treasurer of a school district may be any corporation duly qualified and legally authorized to transact a fiduciary business in the Commonwealth. In many school districts such corporations serve as school district treasurers without charge.

(2) *Operation Cost:* Reduce the cost of operation of schools by carefully checking the amount of fuel used, by using lower priced fuel where feasible, by limiting supplies and janitorial service so far as possible, and by rigid economy in the use of light and power.

(3) *Capital Outlay:* Reduce cost of projected new buildings and equipment by obtaining information relative to economical types of buildings, arrangement and size of rooms, heating, lighting, ventilation, *et cetera.* The School Buildings Division of the Department of Public Instruction will gladly render service to school boards desiring reliable information relative to economies in school building.

(4) *Debt Service:* Reduce the cost of debt service by issuing serial bonds. A report from the Department of Internal Affairs indicates that in a school district floating a $75,000 bond issue by issuing a serial type of bond rather than the sinking fund type, the net saving to the district amounted to $24,000. Another school district floating a $250,000 bond issue found that by issuing a serial rather than a sinking fund type of bond, $79,000 would be saved.

(5) *Instruction:* Reduce high school costs by eliminating small classes through combinations and alternations wherever possible, by omitting elective subjects chosen by small groups, by offering elective subjects in alternate years where the number electing a subject is not large enough to justify offering the subject every year, by fuller use of

the school plant by means of overlapping shifts, and in general by increasing the pupil-teacher ratio where practicable.

(6) *Transportation of Pupils:* Reduce the cost of transportation of pupils by keeping the contract price commensurate with the service rendered and the lower costs now prevalent.

(7) *Teachers' Salaries:* There is one irreducible minimum for effective education. This one basic requirement is competent teaching. Such service can be expected only from men and women of broad training and high personal qualities. Such people are everywhere and always in demand. If the schools can not compete with other agencies to secure this type of teacher, the most important single element of educational efficiency is lost. Retrenchment in teachers' salaries tends ultimately to retain the poorer teachers and to drive the better teachers into other careers. At the same time, desirable candidates for teacher training institutions may be discouraged by the economic unattractiveness of the field.

EDUCATIONAL RESEARCH AND STATISTICS

IS THE AMERICAN COLLEGE IN DANGER?

CONSIDERABLE anxiety has recently been manifested by those responsible for the colleges of liberal arts as to what the future is to bring. It has been felt, with justice, that any permanent harm done these institutions by depressed and changing economic conditions would mean a serious loss to American education. However, much of the discussion has been based upon a sentimental or emotional view-point, and a certain hysteria has been manifest in a few instances as income from investments and tuition fees decreased.

Loss of income from rents and investments has of course not been confined to arts colleges alone. Great universities as well as small colleges have had to face suspension of interest payments on endowment, but there is a general feeling that the small college has been hardest hit by loss of students. The well-known attendance tabulations of Dean Walters of Swarthmore show that even the existing depression has not entirely stopped the increase in student numbers (reckoned for all types of institutions), though it has slowed it down materially. Naturally, however, many smaller colleges have lost revenue in an alarming manner and, being in some cases less firmly established, they are in rather serious difficulties.

It is doubtful whether forced publicity, radio advertising, etc., of however urgent a character, will serve to reverse the process of economic law. If the arts college is a worthy institution (and most of us are convinced that it is worthy), it will survive temporary depression *as an institution.* The fact that some insecurely established or unfavorably located colleges may succumb does not prove that America rejects the arts college. It might therefore be better to concentrate on individual first-aid measures for the worthy institutions in difficulties rather than to waste resources in popularizing the arts college idea for a nation already convinced of its merit.

To sum up this line of reasoning the writer maintains that the college of liberal arts, as such, is not a dying nor even a failing institution, though some of its representatives are in serious trouble. That stern law, the survival of the fittest, is operative here as elsewhere, but the American college is an amazingly vital creature, and probably most of the sufferers will eventually pull through.

When one realizes what a fertile mother the arts college has been, one can not help admiring her many contributions to the field of knowledge and particularly to the field of applied knowledge. Wherever a pure science was stirred to life by the application of its principles to practical daily experience, a new son went forth, leaving alma mater strangely strengthened rather than weakened by the process of birth. Thus, mathematics and physics emerged as engineering; economics as business training; psychology as education; and even in the older professions the natural sciences underlay medicine as the social and political sciences underlay law. Each son established his own home, and so we have to-day schools of engineering, business, education, etc., but the standing and resources of the college of arts are thereby advanced rather than diminished. Nowadays these children, somewhat ungrateful, are encroaching on the parental field by the undertaking of pure research, but, notwithstanding this, the college of arts goes on its way undiminished in prestige or in numbers.

The arts college has never been a paying institution. It has always needed substantial endowments to maintain it, just as the professional schools have done. Chancellor Brown, of New York University, in his Report for 1930–31, says of University College:

> The college, which has been a consistent producer of deficits after the manner of its kind, has now brought its income up to the level of its expenditures. How long this unusual condition can prevail, is a question. It has been brought about as an emergency revenue measure, through an increase of enrolment beyond the natural capacity of the plant. Fortunately, the study, lecture and lounge facilities provided by a special floor in the new gymnasium will stave off the more imminent needs of the enlarged student body for the present.

Unfortunately, most colleges, located as they are in smaller communities, have not been able to adopt increased attendance as an emergency revenue measure. For that reason, perhaps, among others, they have been less willing to exclude from their curricula all courses which have an applied or vocational flavor, as Mr. Flexner would have them do. President McCracken of Vassar strikes a true note when he says:[1]

> What utter nonsense to say that these colleges are free from vocational courses! And why should they be? Why should not the bachelor's degree include certain specific applications and techniques? The notion that theory and principle must never be accompanied with technique and practice, that literature and history must not approach the present age, that art practice does not compare in value with art history and criticism, is at war with the entire trend of modern education. A fair and discriminating association of theory and practice, with an approach toward application in upper college years, is sound common sense.

What, then, are the factors which ensure to a college prosperity in good times and strength to withstand depression in bad times? Is it favorable location in large communities, abundant endowment, prudent investment, established position due to long existence and an honorable record, loyalty of alumni, willingness to adapt the curriculum to modern conditions, administrative efficiency, faculty distinction—is it to the influence or lack of these factors or of others even less capable of definition that we owe the spectacle of some colleges succeeding and others failing during the last critical five years?

The writer does not believe that the figures which follow are by any means sufficient to answer these queries. His compilations are entirely of a formal nature and throw no light on the less ponderable but perhaps more important reactions of the human mind as it affects college progress. Perhaps the greatest value in the accompanying tabulation is the picture which it gives of what has actually taken place in the attendance at a considerable number of American colleges during the past five years. It would be futile to try to draw too many conclusions from such insufficient data.

The 87 colleges included in this study were all chosen from the list used by Dean Raymond Walters in his reports on college attendance in SCHOOL AND SOCIETY. An effort was made to select from this list all, or nearly all, of those institutions which approximated the status of the independent arts college, *i.e.*, they must be not associated with a large university and must have the college of liberal arts as their central and chief endeavor. Naturally, it was not possible nor desirable to exclude certain institutions which had professorships or departments somewhat at variance with the pure arts college type, as, for example, in applied economics, education, etc. Such cases, when chosen, were believed, however, to be predominantly colleges rather than professional schools.

As an initial procedure the figures for attendance given by Dean Walters for each institution for the years 1926–27 and 1930–31, together with percentage of gain or loss, were sent to the respective presidents of 94 institutions, with a request for possible corrections and for permission for publication in the contemplated study. The five-year period from 1926–27 to 1930–31 was chosen because it is of most recent

[1] "Flexner and the Woman's College," *Journal of Higher Education*, October, 1931.

significance and covers times both of inflation and depression. The present year 1931–32 was not included, partly because it is economically so extremely abnormal, and partly because complete attendance figures were not available at the time of the request. Eighty-five institutions returned the information desired and expressed willingness that it be used publicly. Nine institutions failed to respond. For these the figures of Dean Walters have been used in the tabular compilation, but they have not been identified by name. Only one institution definitely refused both information and permission to publish. Of the 85 colleges answering favorably, seven have been excluded from the list, either by reason of the complexity of their organization or because final definite information had not yet been received at the time of tabulation. As a result, the list here given contains 87 institutions. Among them are:

Agnes Scott College; Alfred University; Allegheny College; Amherst College; Beloit College; Bowdoin College; Bryn Mawr College; Carleton College; Carthage College; Centre College of Kentucky; Clark University; Coe College; Colby College; Colgate University; College of St. Theresa; College of William and Mary; The College of Wooster; Connecticut College for Women; Dartmouth College; Davidson College; Denison University; DePauw University; Dickinson College; Doane College; Earlham College; Elmira College; Franklin College of Indiana; Franklin and Marshall College; Goucher College; Grinnell College; Hamilton College; Hamline University; Haverford College; Hobart College; Hunter College of the City of New York; Illinois College; Illinois Wesleyan University; Illinois Woman's College; Knox College; Lafayette College; Lake Erie College; Lake Forest College; Lawrence College; Macalester College; Marietta College; Middlebury College; Milwaukee-Downer College; The Monmouth College; Mount Holyoke College; Muhlenberg College; North Central College; Oberlin College; Ohio Wesleyan University; Otterbein College; Park College; Pomona College; Radcliffe College; Ripon College; Simpson College; Smith College; Sweet Briar College; Trinity College (Hartford, Conn.); Trinity College (Washington, D. C.); Vassar College; Washburn College; Washington and Jefferson College; Washington and Lee University; Wellesley College; Wells College; Wesleyan University; The Western College for Women; Westminster College (New Wilmington, Pa.); Wheaton College (Norton, Mass.); Whitman College; William Jewell College; Williams College; Wilson College; Wittenberg College.

The following table is arranged, not alphabetically, but in descending order of percentage of gain, as indicated in the final column:

TABLE I

THE SECOND COLUMN GIVES THE TYPE OF INSTITUTION; M = MEN, W = WOMEN, C = COEDUCATIONAL. THE THIRD COLUMN GIVES THE POPULATION OF THE COMMUNITY IN WHICH THE INSTITUTION IS SITUATED. THE LAST COLUMN GIVES THE PERCENTAGE OF GAIN OR LOSS IN ATTENDANCE

	T	Population	Attendance '26–'27	Attendance '30–'31	Per Cent. of Gain or Loss
1	W[1]	6,930,446	3,142	4,614	+46.8
2	M	164,073	227	325	+43.0
3	C[1]	3,778	1,003	1,416	+41.1
4	M	6,729	291	386	+32.6
5	M	16,053	259	330	+27.4
6	W	17,747	332	418	+26.0
7	C	6,554	321	396	+23.4
8	M	59,949	595	730	+22.7
9	M	1,700	838	1,009	+20.4
10	C	638	419	492	+17.4
11	M	3,060	260	300	+15.4
12	C	4,153	807	918	+13.0
13	W	20,850	299	339	+13.0
14	W[2]	389	242	270	+11.6
15	C	1,238,048	618	682	+10.4
16	C	271,606	424	456	+ 7.5
17	W	29,640	529	567	+ 7.2
18	C	28,830	625	667	+ 6.7
19	W	3,060	437	460	+ 5.3
20	W	486,869	366	384	+ 4.9
21	W[3]	13,788	426	443	+ 4.0
22	W	113,643	849	881	+ 3.8
23	M	3,900	774	802	+ 3.6
24	M	6,144	544	561	+ 3.1
25	M[2]	3,043	2,253	2,323	+ 3.1
26	C	12,596	536	552	+ 2.9
27	C	639	475	488	+ 2.7
28	W	102	454	466	+ 2.6
29	C	271,606	488	499	+ 2.3
30	W	47,397	582	595	+ 2.2
31	W	6,773	1,001	1,023	+ 2.2
32	C	2,003	629	640	+ 1.7
33	C	2,865	236	240	+ 1.7
34	C	25,267	717	728	+ 1.5
35	M	3,752	903	915	+ 1.3
36	W[2]	40,288	1,144	1,157	+ 1.1
37	C	15,976	559	564	+ 1.0
38	C	16,698	600	603	+ 0.5

TABLE I—(*Continued*)

	T	Population	Attendance '26–'27	Attendance '30–'31	Per Cent. of Gain or Loss
39	C	10,742	896	894	– 0.2
40	C	34,938	643	641	– 0.3
41	W	578,249	380	379	– 0.3
42	M	1,445	635	631	– 0.6
43	M[2]	1,475	457	454	– 0.7
44	C	23,611	486	482	– 0.8
45	W	2,588	395	391	– 1.0
46	C	17,747	394	389	– 1.3
47	C	5,118	472	466	– 1.3
48	W[2]	11,439	1,588	1,550	– 1.9
49	C	8,675	1,860	1,821	– 2.1
50	M	92,563	463	453	– 2.2
51	C	68,743	964	935	– 3.0
52	C	1,467	856	829	– 3.2
53	C[2]	24,554	604	584	– 3.3
54	W[3]	24,381	2,067	1,986	– 3.9
55	C	195,311	327	314	– 4.0
56	C[2]	4,292	1,720	1,652	– 4.0
57	M[2]	5,888	702	672	– 4.3
58	M[2]	34,468	1,050	1,002	– 4.6
59	W	85,864	393	375	– 4.6
60	C	14,285	352	333	– 5.4
61	C	8,666	481	454	– 5.6
62	C	64,120	709	666	– 6.1
63	C	57,527	432	405	– 6.2
64	C	56,097	881	822	– 6.7
65	C	2,719	847	781	– 7.8
66	C	2,240	287	264	– 8.0
67	W	40,661	822	756	– 8.0
68	C	30,930	749	687	– 8.3
69	C	4,613	1,572	1,435	– 8.7
70	C	907	457	416	– 9.0
71	M	24,545	498	452	– 9.2
72	W	10,944	201	182	– 9.5
73	C[2]	15,454	679	612	– 10.0
74	C	5,682	342	305	– 10.8
75	C	4,949	755	673	– 10.9
76	C	3,984	418	372	– 11.0
77	C[4]	2,737	510	450	– 11.7
78	C	3,516	518	442	– 14.7
79	C	3,488	953	805	– 15.5
80	M	10,355	452	381	– 15.7
81	W	804,874	1,046	878	– 16.1
82	C	32,493	507	425	– 16.2
83	W[5]	13,276	538	450	– 16.4
84	M	498	284	237	– 16.6
85	W	15,197	327	263	– 19.6
86	C	16,428	420	324	– 22.9
87	C	2,897	492	354	– 28.0
		Totals	59,085	60,163	+ 1.8

[1] Institutions 1 and 3 are publicly controlled. All others are under private control.

[2] Limits student numbers.

[3] Limits resident students.

[4] Decrease in dormitory facilities.

[5] Changes in entrance procedure and requirements.

It is immediately apparent that the total attendance for the 87 institutions shows a slight increase (1,078 students) for 1930–31 over 1926–27. It must be noted, however, that if the first institution (Hunter College) be eliminated, the remaining 86 colleges show a total loss of 394 students instead of a gain. Generally speaking, then, it may be said that attendance for the group has neither greatly increased nor diminished during the five-year period.

Of the total list, 38 colleges show a gain and 49 show a loss. This must, however, be interpreted in the light of the fact that 4 institutions showing gain and 10 showing loss have been exercising some sort of limitation of numbers. Taken by type, 13 women's colleges show gain and 10 show loss; 10 men's colleges show gain and 8 show loss; but only 15 coeducational institutions show gain, while 31 show loss. Numerically also, the coeducational college is the only type showing a loss of students for the whole list:

	Men	Women	Co-ed.
1926–27	11,485	17,560	30,040
1930–31	11,963	18,827	29,373
Gain or Loss	+ 478	+ 1,267	– 667

It is noticeable that size of college, when considered alone, does not seem to be an important factor. Of the 38 institutions showing gain, 17 (or 44.7 per cent.) had less than 500 students in 1926–27, while of the 49 showing loss, 22 (or 44.9 per cent.) were under the 500 mark.

It is evident that large local population in the college community plays some rôle in maintaining attendance. This is most noticeable in the large increase shown by Hunter College, which ranks first in percentage of gain. Naturally, also, the fact that Hunter is a public institution must be taken into consideration. In fact, the only other publicly controlled institution on the list (the College of William and Mary), ranks third in gain, though in a small community. However, only 3 of the 49 colleges showing loss are in cities of more than 100,000 population, while of the 38 colleges showing gain, 7 are in cities of more than 100,000 population. Perhaps this tendency is best illustrated by comparing the population in the cities containing the 23 highest institutions and the 23 lowest in point of attendance gain or loss. In the upper

23, there are 6 cities with over 100,000 people, 7 cities with over 50,000, and 9 cities with over 25,000. But in the lower 23 there is only one city with more than 100,000 inhabitants, only one over 50,000, and only 4 over 25,000.

From the foregoing it may be gathered that the coeducational institution and the institution in the smaller community have been somewhat harder hit than the others. This is borne out by an examination of the population of those communities in which the 31 coeducational institutions with decreasing attendance are located. Such a study shows that 16 of these cities have less than 10,000 population, 26 have less than 50,000 and only one city exceeds 100,000 inhabitants. On the other hand, of the 15 cities containing coeducational institutions with increasing attendance, 7 cities have less than 10,000 population, 12 have less than 50,000 and 3 exceed 100,000 inhabitants. This picture is further strengthened when we note that of the 15 lowest coeducational colleges, only 4 are located in cities of more than 10,000 people, the largest city in the group having only 32,493 inhabitants.

While these figures throw some light upon the situation it would be dangerous to draw too definite conclusions from them, since many local factors doubtless influence every case. Generally speaking, the picture presented shows nothing startling and rather confirms beliefs already commonly held. It is evident that the colleges, as a body, have suffered no serious loss. There is evidently some tendency for growth on the part of the institutions in larger cities at the expense of those in the lesser communities.

The men's colleges have done a little more than hold their own. The women's colleges apparently have gained most, but this is a false conclusion, as may be seen when we eliminate the first institution (Hunter) from the list, for then the remaining 22 women's colleges show a total loss of 105 students instead of a gain of 1,267. However, these figures are so insignificant as to be practically negligible, and we are justified in believing that the women's colleges, too, are weathering the storm without important loss in total attendance.

With the coeducational colleges the situation is somewhat different. While the total loss for the 43 institutions is small (667), there has evidently been considerable shifting of student population. This seems to have been, in part at least, toward the larger cities. It would not be fair, however, on the basis of present information, to decide that this is the only factor which plays a part. One thing, however, is evident —namely, that the small coeducational college in the small community has suffered more than any other type. To prove this, only a glance at the last 20 institutions on the list is necessary. But it would be wrong to believe that occasional decreases in attendance are symptomatic of failure or decay. They are the inevitable concomitant of hard times, and, as has recently been shown, there is a lag of from one to two years between economic changes and the manifestation of their influence on college attendance.[2] If one believes at all in the future of the Nation, one must believe in the eventual recovery of the colleges.

PARKE R. KOLBE
THE POLYTECHNIC INSTITUTE OF BROOKLYN

NEW BOOKS IN EDUCATION

ASSOCIATION OF AMERICAN UNIVERSITIES: *Journal of Proceedings and Addresses of the 33rd Annual Conference Held at the University of North Carolina, 1931.* Pp. 154. University of Chicago Press. $1.00.

BEACH, WALTER G. *Social Aims in a Changing World.* Pp. ix + 165. Stanford University Press. $1.75.

Buying Guide for Elementary School Libraries: Based on the Titles Selected for the University of Michigan Elementary School Library. Pp. viii + 93. University of Michigan Press.

DEPARTMENT OF SUPERINTENDENCE, TENTH YEARBOOK: *Character Education.* Pp. 535. National Education Association.

EMERSON, HENRY P., IDA C. BENDER and BLANCHE J. THOMPSON. *Modern English.* Book I: Pp. 249. Illustrated. $.60.
Book II: Pp. xxi + 342. Illustrated. $.64.
Book III: Pp. xvi + 406. Illustrated. $.68. Macmillan.

HUBBARD, ALICE and ADELINE BABBITT. *The Golden Flute: An Anthology of Poetry for Young Children.* Pp. xi + 320. John Day. $3.00.

JOHNSTON, HAROLD W. *The Private Life of the Romans.* Revised by Mary Johnston. Pp. 430. 326 figures. Scott, Foresman. $2.24.

NICHOLS, TALMAGE. *Woodworking Manual for Students.* Pp. 79. 54 figures. Manual Arts Press. $1.00.

PATCH, EDITH M. and HARRISON E. HOWE. *Hunting.* Pp. viii + 161. Illustrated. $.80. *Outdoor Visits.* Pp. xi + 212. Illustrated. $.84. Macmillan.

2 "The Relation of College Enrolment to Economic Depression," *Bulletin* of the American Association of Collegiate Registrars, New Series, Vol. 7, No. 2, January, 1932.

SCHOOL AND SOCIETY

EDITED BY J. McKEEN CATTELL

WITH WHICH IS COMBINED THE

EDUCATIONAL REVIEW

EDITED BY WILLIAM McANDREW

Volume 35 | Saturday, April 16, 1932 | Number 903

THE UNKNOWNS IN HIGHER EDUCATION[1]

By Dr. SAMUEL PAUL CAPEN

CHANCELLOR OF THE UNIVERSITY OF BUFFALO

The American university is being reformed. The educational profession does not need to be reminded of this fact. The fact is indeed so patent that every intelligent layman is aware of it. The layman knows also why the university is being reformed. So do we. To recapitulate the reasons on an occasion like the present would be a waste of time.

But I do not think the layman knows *how* the university is being reformed—except as he may be instructed concerning the new plans of his own alma mater through reading its official literature. I do not think he knows what obstacles must be overcome before the reform which both laymen and educators desire can be consummated. I am not even sure that we of the profession have yet faced the full implications of the vast and comprehensive movement in which we are now so obviously caught up. If I am right in doubting whether either the profession or the laity have sensed the true character of the movement, then the discussion of certain of its phases is appropriate at a conference that celebrates the acquisition of new instruments for the scientific study of education by this institution which has so frequently led the way in educational reform.

Let me first call your attention to a few contrasts. University reform is no new thing in America. It has been going on spasmodically for a long time, quite recognizably over a period of sixty years at least. Beginning with the promulgation of the elective system and the development of the graduate school—practically simultaneous phenomena—recurrent waves of reform have swept over us. There have been brief intervals between the waves during which the academic community could catch its breath and plant its feet to resist the next onset. Sometimes in these intervals the undertow pulled us back a little, which made it all the more difficult to withstand the next following wave.

This figure of speech suggests that the reforms of the last two generations did not arise spontaneously out of the university community itself. And that is the case. Every one of them which might be described as structural was somebody's reform. Each is associated with the name of an individual. Eliot and Gilman and Harper, for example, Angell and Van Hise, White and Wilson. These men, and not the faculties over which they presided nor the boards that controlled their respective institutions, were the authors and

[1] Address given at the Conference on Higher Education held on the occasion of the opening of the Graduate Education Building of the University of Chicago on March 15, 1932.

directors of the considerable reforms that remolded and enlarged the universities of their day.

Who is the author of the reform in the midst of which the universities now find themselves? There is no single author. There is no one spokesman even. There is no gospel according to Smith or Jones, however diligently Smith or Jones may be proclaiming one and asserting proprietary rights therein. Ours is a mass movement, of which there are leaders, to be sure, but no generalissimo.

The earlier reforms contrast with the present movement in another way. They came singly and decently spaced. Each was aimed at the improvement of a single important aspect of university education. It might be admission requirements, or the college curriculum, or the method of teaching medicine, or the extension of the service of the university to the state. Those directly concerned with the change in question might be filled with enthusiasm or with dread. But meanwhile the main current of the university's life flowed serenely on, a very placid stream. And that was not strange, because our generalissimos could not be expected to promote more than one disturbing idea at a time. But now everything is in flux: relations of secondary school and college; purpose and method and organization of the college; standards and content of graduate instruction; range and type of professional education; objectives, processes, philosophy, all of it.

In a still more significant fashion the attitude of the university community, leaders and all the others, toward the reform which is proceeding under their hands differs from that of the past. The earlier reforms were not the product of doubt, seldom even of disconcerting facts purposely or accidentally discovered. They were the product of certainty, one might almost say the product of a revelation. A prophet clothed in a duly authenticated mantle, speaking from a seat of authority, declared what should be done. Neither he nor those who heard and obeyed, nor yet those who listened and resisted, entertained the slightest doubt as to the essential excellence of the institution which it was proposed to improve. The institution needed, said the prophet, just this specific to cure its single ailment; just this and no other. His opponents protested that it had no ailment and needed no specific. On neither side was there anything but certainty. Both sides knew. Does any one now know? A few, perhaps. The line of the ancient prophets is not quite extinct. But the contemporary revelations fall on deaf ears. We are not convinced. The certainties have been so many times disproved.

This, the most thoroughgoing of all the reforms that have affected our universities, finds us for the first time in our history facing—I hope courageously if not always intelligently facing—a bewildering array of unknowns. They outnumber the certainties altogether.

Of what are we sure? Of one thing, research. That is definite; its ends are clear, its effects are beneficent. We may not always know how to do it. But finding out how to do it is one of the ingredients of research itself and causes no one concern, except the person who has to find out.

Every other educational activity that the university conducts is groping its way. Sometimes the objectives are plain; often not even the objectives have been satisfactorily determined. If this seems an extreme statement, review in your minds a few of the major enterprises of the university as they are already affected by the rising tide of reform.

Take the college. Who should be admitted? Are we sure of that? On what basis should students be accepted? How long should the course be, two or three or the traditional four years? If the consensus of opinion favors the latter alternative, as at present it appears to, should the college be divided in the middle? If so, what should be the difference in content and method between the two parts? Are honors courses and tutorial conferences more or less effective than lectures and discussion groups in leading young people to increase their knowledge and cultivate intellectual independence? Is an examination just a record, and if so a record of what? Or is it a device to spur the indolent, expose the inept and encourage the able? What kind or kinds of examinations accomplish one or another of these purposes best? Should the curriculum be definitely organized in the interest of general education as the faculty conceives it; or should the curriculum be practically abolished to enable the student to follow his bent? How much and what sort of guidance do students need? What kind of product in terms of human attitudes and capacities should the college try to turn out? In other words, what is the objective of the college?

Although this list of questions may sound formidable, I need not point out that it covers only a few of the issues with which the college is engaged. Each progressive institution has its own answer to most of the questions. The answers exhibit an almost biological variation. Some of us swear by our answers. But if the answers were based on proved results there would not be so many of them. There would then emerge a group of constants, of certainties. Of these there are perhaps already a few, but they are minor and peripheral. No, we must admit that the college, its social and educational purpose, its relations to other units of the system, and all its chief concerns belong in the category of the unknowns.

What is the objective of the graduate school; or does it have several? The graduate school, one does not need to recall, was the child of the German university; of the Faculty of Philosophy. Although brought up among strangers of an alien race, its foster parents were at infinite pains to see that nothing but its native idiom was spoken in its presence and that it was thoroughly imbued with the customs and traditions of its family. It long ago came to man's estate and took out citizenship papers. But the naturalization was political, not psychological. The family trade, which it has practiced much as its parents did, is a fine and useful occupation. But in some respects the old world techniques have never quite fitted the new environment. As long as the trade was a luxury trade, that did not much matter. The market has grown, however. It seems to demand adaptations which this conscientious but inflexible foreign craftsman finds it difficult to make.

I ought not to push the parable too far, or it will break down. The point I would suggest is doubtless clear. What is the social function of the graduate school, now and in the years just ahead? There are views of all sorts on this matter. Some of the most arresting and persuasive of them have originated in the university which is our host. Experimental attempts to translate some of the views into practice are visible here and there on the educational map. But in volume and variety of experiment the college is still a long way ahead of the graduate school. On the whole, it seems fair to say that the graduate school does not yet know what is the matter with it, or whether anything is. But this happy state of innocence can not long persist. The college is bound to infect it with its own peculiar disease, that is, the disease of knowing too much to be comfortable and not enough to be certain.

Professional education has in the past been singularly well supplied with revelations. To legal education there was early vouchsafed the revelation of Langdell. Turner and Rogers and Schneider form an apostolic succession of lawgivers in engineering education. In medical education there have been many revelations, but most recently the joint revelation of Flexner and the American Medical Association. In the education of teachers we have had—but I had better not go into that in this presence.

These potent pronouncements, plus the watchful guardianship of the professions, have kept professional schools on the given course with only minor deviations. For the most part they appear not to have been greatly troubled with misgivings—until just now. Now, however, the professional schools find themselves facing a society that has changed, professions on which new responsibilities are placed, and a rapidly increasing body of scientific and technical knowledge. To cope with these, the old formulas do not suffice. What should the new formulas be? There is no sector of the university, not even the college, in which this question is being raised more insistently.

Examples of the current uncertainties might be drawn from almost any of the fields of professional education. But since the medical school has been more keenly self-critical and more disposed to experiment than other professional schools, its case may serve for the purpose of this discussion to illustrate the nature of the perplexities by which all professional schools are confronted.

The domain of medicine is uncompassable. No human mind can acquire and retain more than a small fraction of what is already known about it. With what, then, should the brief preparation of the practitioner principally deal? Should it be chiefly an introduction to fundamental principles and methods and sources; or should it be chiefly specific with reference to facts and techniques of immediate practical utility? Neither element can be omitted. Which should preponderate and what should the proportions be? The practice of a profession demands more than scientific knowledge. A profession is also an art. What is the rôle of the school in teaching the art of medicine? Clinical teaching is in part concerned with inculcating the art of medicine. How should it be done; who should do it; and should clinical teachers be a monastic order kept pure and unsullied from the world? What relation of school and hospital is at once economical and effective? The prevalence of human disorders changes with the development of scientific controls. Old plagues and epidemics pass. The horrors of smallpox and typhoid fever give place to the creeping blight of degenerative maladies and mental ailments. Should the teaching of the school immediately respond to and perhaps forestall the new incidence of disease? Should it likewise forecast the altered social demands on the profession, and so remake the profession in advance?

In a word, is it the function of the university in higher vocational education to man society's service stations with tinkers who can patch things up and make them run again somehow in the same old way, or to be the conscious architect of a finer society? However emphatically you and I may believe that the obligation of the university lies in the latter direction, the professional schools, with a few notable exceptions, have been committed to the tinker theory. How to change their total polarization, with all the infinite involvement of detail, that is the question. And let no one think that the answer is plain.

One large activity of the university is not directly or primarily educational. I refer to administration. Administration may be a necessary evil, but it is at any rate necessary; and it consumes much energy and money. There are included in it not only such gross material affairs as the care of dollars and plant and records, but also all sorts of intricate relationships among boards and officers and staffs and students; likewise powers and spheres of influence and controls. Although there is so much of it, we really know very little about administration. Consider a few of its simpler aspects.

What should a president do, for instance, and what should he not under any circumstances try to do? Or a dean? Professors are known to have rather positive opinions on these matters, some of which the forces of nature tend at the moment to defeat. The opinions of boards of trustees are often not exactly the same. Charters and legislative acts also enter into the situation. Presidents and deans may, and generally do, have opinions that differ from those of both of the other parties at interest. No one, I think, would maintain that the existing divergence of opinion is either wholesome or necessary.

There is perfect certainty about the protection of the university's money through well-tested procedures of disbursement and recording. But for what objects and in what proportion should a university's money be spent? The outlay for instruction ranges all the way from twenty-odd per cent. to approximately seventy per cent. of the total expenditures of universities. The amount a university can spend for instruction is conditioned chiefly by the cost of maintaining the plant. Very well, how many and what kinds of buildings does a university need, your university, my university or any other? There are those who complain that American universities spend too much on buildings and equipment. Faculties complain bitterly of the overshadowing importance of buildings in the eyes of boards and donors. But the complaint is directed at a general situation. It is seldom translated into a self-denying ordinance when a building for one's own department is in prospect. Is there any but an arbitrary relationship between the size of a university, the character of its constituent units and its resources on the one hand, and buildings on the other?

I might continue almost indefinitely to catalogue the unknowns. But it is unnecessary to go on. If any of my hearers have gathered that I am offering an indictment of American higher education, I should like to correct the impression. This is not an indictment, it is a testimonial. Why are there so many unknowns to-day? Because, paradoxical as it may sound, we know more. We know more about human beings, about their infinite variations, their motives and their capacities. We know a great deal more about nature and about society; and most important of all, we know more ways of finding out things than our fathers ever dreamed of. The current reform of the university is the result of this enlargement of knowledge. And out of our deepening insight comes increasing awareness of the unknowns. That dogmatic assurance has given place to doubts and self-questionings and willingness to experiment is a sign of health rather than of disease.

But universities, modern universities, are in part maintained to locate the unknown, to attack it and gradually to conquer it. Every mystery, every undetermined action of men in the mass now or in the past, every blind undirected fumbling of individuals or groups or social institutions, is a challenge to the university. "Something lost behind the ranges!" The urge to find it is the mainspring of our institutional life.

Now that we have become aware that education itself, especially on its higher levels, is a mysterious process, carried on in the interest of imperfectly defined social objectives by devices largely empirical, the attitude of the university toward its own operations is of necessity changed. University education comes within the purview of our scientific curiosity. More than that, the reduction of the number of the unknowns must take rank among our primary concerns. It is, indeed, of absolutely crucial importance. For what shall it profit us if we gain the whole world and lose our own souls?

Notwithstanding the spread of experimentation and the very considerable number of investigations already made or projected, I do not think universities have yet grasped the magnitude of the task ahead of them. It can not be accomplished in a year or two. The solution of each problem will disclose others, as yet unperceived. The task is, in fact, interminable; unless the universities should sink back into self-satisfied stagnation. And of course we can never reach certainty with regard to many of the issues I have touched upon in this paper. Some of them must remain in the realm of statesmanship—which I take to be the realm in which policies are formed on the basis of a few facts and a good deal of common sense. But many more facts than we have ever been provided with can be assembled. Fundamental investigations of human beings and of pertinent social phenomena can be made. Educational results can be studied by scientific instruments already at hand. Controls can be set up to guide and to measure experiment.

The stronger universities now possess agencies qualified to do these things—and generally they do not use them. Insofar as institutions are conscious of the need to steer reform by investigation, educational investigation, they commonly turn the job over to committees composed of laymen. For that is what mathematicians and classicists and historians are when it comes to educational research. Faculties vote on schemes for the improvement of instruction which involve the subtle intricacies of the learning process and the obscure springs of human motivation without consulting those who have devoted their lives to the study of these matters. Curricula are still constructed on the familiar principle of political log-rolling. Superficial reviews of data easily accessible to the uninitiated form the basis for determining policies in graduate and professional education that are of the most far-reaching social import. And when a really ambitious study of some phase of higher education is undertaken perhaps a chemist or a physicist is chosen to direct it.

I think this is unintelligent. If a university should select an economist to head an archeological expedition, meanwhile keeping its archeologist at home in the university museum, that would represent a comparable situation. No university would do anything so silly.

The prejudice against departments of education is ancient, and very honorable. It is one of the most characteristic stigmata of our profession. If one fails to share it he feels slightly apologetic, and in any event he is at pains to conceal his solecism. Perhaps there has been ground for this prejudice in the past. The educationists have not always been either learned or discreet. Some of their activities have been trivial. Some that were not trivial have seemed so to the critically inclined observer, just as some of the activities of biologists seemed trivial before biology became respectable. But the academic community should be the first to remember that the creation of a new scientific discipline is a slow undertaking. There are many by-paths that have to be inspected before they are seen to be by-paths and are closed to further traffic. The time has come when the science of education can stand on its achievements and fear no honest assessment. If, in these later years of its adolescence, it were not unduly modest, it might point out, both what it has contributed to the recasting of elementary and secondary education, and also how far it alone is responsible for furnishing the instruments by which the university makes the few reliable measurements that are now made of the personnel and the product of higher institutions.

There is no escaping the conclusion that university reform can not proceed at a rate commensurate with the university's needs and the needs of society without enlisting much more extensively the aid of departments of education. I will go further. University reform will be checked and occasionally frustrated, unless a new subspecies of educationists is bred and nurtured. The field of higher education demands and deserves its own votaries. It is unnecessary to remind this company that the University of Chicago was one of the first institutions to recognize this demand and to begin to supply it.

To some of us this celebration has a dual significance. It crowns with a visible symbol a lifelong service to educational science of unparalleled resourcefulness, integrity and courage. It recognizes an influence exercised nation-wide in conformity with the finest traditions of our craft. But it is also an augury. It foreshadows a just appreciation by universities generally of the scientific study of education as a university enterprise. It is altogether appropriate that that appreciation should be signalized here, and by means of this magnificent new establishment. The university world is by long habit accustomed to look to the University of Chicago for realistic appraisal of each new educational situation as it arises, for bold exploration and experiment and for equally bold defiance of tradition, whenever tradition is proved to be outworn.

COORDINATION OF EFFORT IN THE FIELD OF HIGHER EDUCATION[1]

By Dr. GEO. A. WORKS

PROFESSOR OF EDUCATION, DEAN OF STUDENTS AND UNIVERSITY EXAMINER, UNIVERSITY OF CHICAGO

The careful student of the growth of higher education in this country can not help but be impressed by the lack of balance, when measured in terms of the needs, that characterizes this development. The reference is to interinstitutional relationships and programs rather than to the internal growth of the individual institutions. We have been lavish in the establishment of higher institutions and liberal in the financing of their programs, once they were established. The present financial conditions serve to accentuate some of the difficulties flowing from this haphazard development. One need not be classified as a confirmed pessimist if he expresses doubts regarding the return of the "whoopee era" in higher education. In view of this situation, it behooves all who are interested in what higher education may mean in the way of individual and social progress to give consideration to the ways and means by which the funds available may be spent to bring the maximum returns.

Undoubtedly, there are many things that we shall ultimately learn which may contribute to that end. The purpose of this discussion is to present briefly two phases of the problem which have had some attention but should have much more consideration than they have thus far received, especially from educators. These two phases relate to: (1) The possibility of the development of a greater measure of coordination of effort on the part of tax-supported institutions of higher learning than now obtains in most of the states. (2) The desirability of a greater measure of cooperation among institutions of higher learn-

[1] Address given at the Conference on Higher Education, held on the occasion of the opening of the Graduate Education Building of the University of Chicago on March 15, 1932.

ing regardless of state boundaries and of sources of support.

Neither subject is new. The facts bearing on them have been assembled at this time with the idea that the present financial conditions may result in their being given more serious attention than they were given when funds were plentiful.

The possibility of developing a unitary program of tax-supported higher education is a live subject in several states at the present moment. It is, during the current year, under consideration, in a more or less serious fashion, in California, Georgia, South Carolina, North Carolina, and Mississippi. It has had attention in several other states recently. The statements which follow are from the reports of surveys made in recent years and will serve as a basis for some constructive suggestions.

This preceding résumé of the points of conflict between the university and the agricultural college, together with the commission's recommendations concerning each field of friction, serves to introduce and to emphasize the need for some thoroughgoing method of coordinating the higher education carried on by the State of Utah. The commission has examined the facts in so far as it could find them; it has sought the opinions of officers of both institutions, of the boards of both institutions, of outside disinterested citizens, and of special interests organized for the purpose of securing one or another object. It is clear that the presidents, the boards, the student bodies, the graduates and the former students of the university and of the agricultural college have taken sides in a controversy which is wasteful of both money and energy.[2]

Institutions have been established without a clear formulation of the State's policy and governing boards have been multiplied correspondingly. Naturally these boards soon develop deep interests in the institutions over which they have control and make appeals to the Legislature for support. The result is that the demands for the support of higher education become seemingly excessive and the State hesitates to meet them. In fact, sometimes the State can not meet them.[3]

One of the outstanding features of the growth of higher education in the State is that it has occurred without any definite plan on the part of the State. There are too many State institutions for present demands and some of them are unfortunately located. . . . The time is at hand when the State should take stock of its provision for higher education and adopt a clear policy for the future. By this means waste can be prevented and progress can be economically promoted. It is a task which will require sound judgment, clear vision, and a firm hand.[4]

Undoubtedly the situation that caused the most concern in the State and which was most influential in securing the passage of the law creating the department of higher education was that of the relations between the university and the Oregon State College. During 20 years hundreds of pages of "briefs" had been submitted at various times to the State board of higher curricula by the university and by the State college, each in defense of its own claims and in refutation of the claims of the other. It is not necessary to charge either institution with bad faith in order to account for the conflict of interest which has so largely characterized the relationship of these two great educational centers in the past. Institutional pride and ambition and their less praiseworthy sister, institutional jealousy, dominate these briefs in many cases to the neglect of the interests of the State and of the individual students.[5]

Wasteful rivalries now prevail among the three state colleges for white students. Each is eager to secure a larger physical equipment and a more impressive enrollment. There is much needless duplication of work.[6]

Ample evidence is furnished by these statements that many states have not found a satisfactory solution to the problem growing out of their efforts to provide higher education adequate for their needs. In some states, if those who sponsored the creation of new institutions had gone forward in their efforts with the deliberate intention of creating educational chaos, their ambitions could hardly have been more fully realized than they

[2] "Survey of Education in Utah," p. 262, 1926.

[3] "Texas Educational Survey Report," pp. 40–41, 1925.

[4] "Public Education in Oklahoma," p. 132, 1922.

[5] "Survey of Public Higher Education in Oregon," p. 45, 1931.

[6] "Public Education in Mississippi," p. 214, 1925.

are under present conditions. But, of course, there was no such intention. In fact, the contrary was true in some states which now find themselves unable with their present administrative organization to develop a unitary program of higher education. Two examples may suffice.

Article VII, Section 13, of the Constitution of Texas, contains the following statement: "The Agricultural and Mechanical College of Texas, established by an act of the legislature, passed April 17, 1871, located in the County of Brazos, is hereby made and constituted a branch of the University of Texas."

A few years ago the programs of the university and the agricultural college were being developed quite independently of each other and not in the spirit indicated by the portion of the constitution just read.

In Alabama provision was made for the establishment of a state university in the Constitution that was adopted in 1819. Alabama Polytechnic Institution, the land-grant institution, is independent of the university, yet one finds these words in Section 10 of the Constitution of 1868:

The General Assembly shall as soon as possible provide for the establishment of an Agricultural College and shall appropriate federal lands for this purpose and may make the same a branch of the University of Alabama for instruction in agriculture and mechanic arts and the natural sciences in connection therewith and place the same under the supervision of the board of regents.

Still later, when the Alabama Technical Institute and College for Women was established, the way was left clear to make it a branch of an already existing institution. But again no attempt was made to move in the direction of a coordinated state program. Further examples might be cited to show that the original sponsors of state institutions of higher learning did not contemplate that each institution should develop independently of the others.

Instead of having a unitary program of higher education that is responsive to the needs of the state and that meets those needs with the maximum degree of effectiveness, many states find that they have several—even more in some instances—colleges and universities, each a rival for financial favor at the hands of the legislature. In the face of these demands, the ordinary legislature is helpless when it comes to taking intelligent action. It lacks factual bases for the determination of policies and for reconciling the claims of the rivals. At best, it can only compromise with competing demands instead of formulating a program based on the available resources and the needs for higher education of the state.

To these conditions, a number of factors have contributed. Legislatures in the past were too free and easy in the establishment of new institutions of higher learning. Too frequently, their establishment was a matter of legislative log rolling, with the result that sometimes a legislature attempting to establish an institution of higher learning emerged from its activities—I won't say deliberations—not with one new institution but with two or more. Half a century ago, when the state appropriation for the maintenance of a state university or college did not amount to more than the local appropriation for a village high school does at present, this was not a serious matter. However, the experience of the last half century has taught us a great deal about the cost of maintaining good institutions of higher learning, and we have also learned that poor institutions are very costly. We can not afford them.

Not uncommonly, the location of a new school was determined by the amount of land, or money, or both that could be obtained from the community. Schools were sold to the highest bidder. A community, once having contributed to the establishment of a school, is naturally desirous of seeing the institution prosper, since the return of its contributions is conditioned by this growth. A state institution of higher learning, once established in a community, is subject to constant pressure for expansion, not in the light of state needs but in terms of local ambitions.

The entire responsibility for these ill-advised ventures in higher education can not be shouldered on legislatures and the commercial interest of local communities. Faculties and administrators have in many instances been guilty. The arguments that have been framed by educators to justify the introduction of new curricula and courses are numerous when, in reality, the actuating motive was the presence of the same work in another tax-supported institution in the same state. Too frequently the result is that programs of higher education lack the adjustment to the needs that the taxpayer has a right to expect. In some instances, it would be more accurate not to speak of a state's program of higher education, but rather, of its programs, that have been developed in terms of institutional ambitions instead of in the light of the state needs. The following statement from a study of higher education in Texas presents a picture that is too frequently accurate.

> Attention has already been called to the fact that the presidents of the various institutions feel impelled to appear before the legislative committees, requesting appropriations for their respective institutions. Each president makes his own appeal. There is no consolidation of effort, no unification of policy, and no consistent program for the State presented to the Legislature. A dynamic and forceful politician at the head of some one of the higher institutions of learning may be able to secure far more money for his institution than it should have in view of the needs of other institutions. A man who is an educational leader, who looks well after the internal organization, management, and administration of his college, who spends his hours on the campus devoting himself diligently to the welfare of his institution, may find that his devotion to campus affairs, and his neglect of political affairs, has resulted in a loss in appropriation. This should not happen. Steps should be taken to prevent it.[7]

These conditions have not been presented to provide the setting for a perfect solution. The methods used in the several states to meet the problems that have been under discussion are varied. However, it is doubtful if the final solution has been found. The answer, in all probability, is not to be found in any single form of organization, but rather in the adaptation of the method to the governmental, economic, and geographical conditions of the state under consideration.

However, the following general suggestions are deemed appropriate:

(1) Those who are engaged in educational work as administrators and teachers should take a more active interest in attempting to cope with the problems involved in the development of unitary programs of state supported higher education. Most of the movements that look toward this end have their inception in and support from lay groups rather than with educators—as a body educators are too apathetic in the presence of this problem. They have a greater degree of responsibility for attempting to meet the issues involved in the solution of this problem than they have thus far manifested.

(2) The questions involved are not simply educational in nature. Political institutions of the state are involved. In the solution of these problems the services of the political scientist should be used. The resources available and the methods best adapted to reaching them are problems calling for the knowledge of the economist. The relationship of the support of higher institutions of learning to the state budgetary organization needs careful study. No one will deny the advisability of giving to those responsible for the administration of institutions of higher education, the control of the expenditure of the funds within the scope of the legislation that made them available. Interference by an outside budgetary organization should not be permitted. However, the legislature must have the right to protect the state in the amount of the financial obligations that may be incurred against its resources. On the basis of these facts, it will be necessary to devise means

[7] "Texas Educational Survey Report," pp. 44–45, 1925.

whereby the budgetary system may be used and at the same time the control of the funds be retained in the hands of those who are professionally competent.

To meet these questions and to answer them satisfactorily will call for closer cooperation among the educators, political scientists, and economists than we have thus far had in the study of our educational problems at any level.

The second phase of the subject of this paper has to do with the cooperation among institutions of higher learning without reference to state boundaries and sources of support. Cooperation has been used to describe the relationship that might be developed as contrasted with coordination when the institutions are within a state and drawing their support from public sources.

Various problems are involved in this aspect of the subject. In one instance they may be concerned with the number of institutions that have been developed in a given area for doing essentially the same types of work. There are in New England seven agricultural experiment stations—Connecticut has two—supported by funds from the federal government and state sources. A man from Mars who approached the question of providing for the needs of agricultural research in this region in the most effective and economical manner would certainly not propose that this region, which agriculturally is not greater than one state in the Middle West, should provide itself with six entirely independent and one semi-independent instituion for meeting these research needs.

A study of forest education as it has been developed in this country is just being completed. It reveals the existence of too many four-year programs of forest education. An extreme case is found in New York State, where in two separate state-supported institutions, only fifty miles apart, not only four-year programs for professional training in forestry but programs of graduate work as well have been developed. The tendency has been to permit institutional ambitions, rather than social needs, determine the development of forest schools.

In the development of graduate and research facilities, we should have closer interinstitutional relationships than now obtain. The extent to which duplication exists of laboratory facilities in the sciences, and the library facilities in the humanities and social sciences, is wasteful in the extreme.

If there is to be the maximum development of research in this country, there must be a more complete definition on the part of institutions, of the type of research they propose to undertake. These limitations should be established in the interests of scholarship. Some fields of research are so specialized that only a limited number of centers are needed. In some fields of knowledge the printed resources are too limited to provide adequately for more than one or two centers. These conditions demand the type of cooperation from faculties, administrators, and trustees that will make for the maximum opportunity for scholarship. Institutions will have to make a choice between mediocrity of work in a wide range of subjects, and a relatively high type of research in a limited number of fields.

President James R. Angell has made the following statement bearing on this problem:

> At no point in the present administration of research interests in educational institutions is there perhaps more need for searching analysis of present practices than in the methods, or lack of methods, whereby particular lines of research are undertaken. Almost every great university is put in the position of attempting to foster all the major fields of research and an unlimited number of accessory ones. Local pride has repeatedly led to the effort to develop forms of research which may be intrinsically of minor consequence and altogether anomalous in the regions where they

are undertaken. State institutions are constantly subjected to pressure of this character, leading to the formation of new departments, some of which have no substantial justification beyond the gratification of the ambition of some energetic professor or some small group whose interests will be theoretically promoted in this way. There exists at present no adequate device by which an indefinite continuation of these conditions may be avoided. Indeed, it is but quite recently that there has grown up any considerable body of opinion recognizing the wastefulness of the present practices. It is of course a matter of the utmost delicacy, and one calling for great breadth of knowledge and great sanity of judgment, to attempt in any fashion to allocate responsibility for particular kinds of research. At the very outset one is met with the contention that any such artificial distribution of functions would operate seriously to cripple individual initiative. And yet the contrary consideration is quite as urgent. To equip every university in the country to carry on research in agriculture, in forestry, in all the branches of engineering, and for that matter, in all the physical, chemical, and biological sciences, would obviously be wasteful of equipment and physical resources, and all but impossible of execution in the matter of personnel. Certain rough lines of division are in point of fact at present operative. Some institutions by mere virtue of the fact that they secured an early occupancy of a field have developed to a considerable degree of advancement research work in special directions which might perhaps have been more advantageously developed elsewhere. But meantime, being in possession of the property, it would be ill-advised to attempt to dispossess them. In any event while it is futile, and were it not futile it would be unwise, to attempt any arbitrary and coercive methods in the solution of this general problem, it is not too much to hope that by intelligent voluntary cooperation something may be done to safeguard the situation against an indefinite continuation of the present condition.[8]

A statement made by Dean Guy S. Ford, of the Graduate School of the University of Minnesota, gives a view of the situation from the angle of library resources.

The matter of competing in single purchases as between libraries that should be cooperating is significant of a more expensive competition into which we may be led by imitation or the zeal of departments. I hesitate to name the Universities whose libraries—irrespective of their faculties—furnish ''unrivaled facilities for studying western history''; the list of these ''strong in the pamphlet and other source material of the French Revolution'' is equally extensive. The next decade will see us bidding and building against each other for South American and oriental history, politics, and literature—not a selected country or period or phase—but all South American and the whole Orient. All the middle western and perhaps the eastern Universities may have to check influences within and without that would want to make them the greatest centers for the study of the history, literature, and institutions of all the countries which have contributed large numbers of immigrants to the tax-paying population of their section. All this means spreading out—horizontal distribution of funds—mediocre results at greatly enhanced expenditure. . . .[9]

Is it too much to hope that educational institutions will cooperate in the improvement of teaching and research? Is it not time to declare a moratorium on expansion and to devote our energies to the improvement of the quality of work we are doing in our institutions of higher learning? The need for these changes is especially pressing in the case of certain forms of professional education and in many of the forms of specialized graduate instruction and research. To bring these changes about is an obligation that rests on the educator, whether he works in the tax-supported or the endowed institution. In the last analysis, the resources that maintain these institutions are taken from society, and society has a right to expect for its contribution the maximum return. This it can not hope to get unless constructive steps are taken among the institutions of higher learning to develop a greater measure of coordination and cooperation.

[8] ''The Organization of Research,'' Journal of Proceedings and Addresses of the Twenty-first Annual Conference of the Association of American Universities, p. 29, 1919.

[9] ''The Library and the Graduate School,'' Journal of Proceedings and Addresses of the Fifteenth Annual Conference of the Association of American Universities, pp. 43–44, 1913.

EDUCATIONAL EVENTS

EDUCATIONAL CONDITIONS IN SHANGHAI

A COMMUNICATION dated March 2 has been received by the Secretary General of the League of Nations from Mr. W. W. Yen on behalf of the Chinese delegation. Mr. Yen transmits the following letter from Dr. Tsai Yuan-pei, the president of the Academia Sinica of the Chinese Government at Nanking.

In their present campaign of aggression against China, the Japanese military by their indiscriminate bombardment of Shanghai have particularly aimed at the wholesale destruction of China's educational and cultural establishments. Up to date, such organs which have been razed to the ground, include the well-known Commercial Press, China's premier publishing concern, which has been bringing out 70 per cent. of the country's text-books for the past two decades, together with its priceless public library; the well-known National Chinan University; Tung-chi University; Chi-chi University and the Medical College of the Central University. Wherever the arms of Japanese militarism reach, China's educational and cultural organs collapse under their wanton aerial and artillery bombardment.

Wilful destruction of educational and cultural organs is prohibited even in time of war, and while the Tokyo Government have, on the one hand, openly declared that Japan is not waging war against China, on the other hand, their military have deliberately destroyed even what, international law has definitely decreed, shall be preserved.

It is to be hoped that the intellectual leaders of the world will feel constrained to publicly condemn such barbarity of the Japanese military in destroying China's educational and cultural organs and also to devise means for the prevention of any such further action on the part of Japan.

VOCATIONAL TRAINING IN HAWAII

VOCATIONAL training in Hawaii has become so popular that the schools can not take care of all applicants, according to a statement given by James R. Coxen, regional agent for the Federal Board for Vocational Education, to a representative of the *U. S. Daily* on March 29 upon his return from an inspection trip to the islands.

Both the industrial and the agricultural training is based upon the economic conditions of each locality and instruction of immediate practical value is given.

Some vocational schools in Hawaii differ from those in the United States in that they are separate from the regular academic schools and teach nothing but vocational subjects, and the courses are not given for any special period of time.

Mr. Coxen stated that a very high grade of work is done in the vocational schools in the Hawaiian Islands. In the trade and industrial schools, for instance, pupils are admitted on trial and those who do not measure up to the school standards are weeded out in the course of a month or six weeks and advised to try some other field of work.

Boys in the trade and industrial classes are given training in auto mechanics, machine shop work, carpentry, electrical work and welding, while girls receive training in cafeteria work, dressmaking, weaving and similar crafts. Pupils attend school for seven hours a day.

Classroom work is supplemented with practical work. Instead of being compelled to attend classes for a set period of time, pupils are permitted to register for courses at any time, the period devoted to school work depending entirely upon the ability of the pupil. The only requirement is that those who enter the schools be at least fifteen years of age.

The success of vocational education in the Islands depends largely upon what is done in agriculture, which is the dominant industry in Hawaii.

That the students get practical training in the vocational agriculture schools is attested by the fact that as a part of their practice work they take over the production of sugar cane, coffee or pineapples on the plantations in the community. A contract is made with the plantation officials whereby boys from the vocational schools are made responsible, under the supervision of the vocational teacher, for the production of the crop raised on these plantations.

In addition to getting practical training, these boys are paid for their work on the plantations on the basis of a certain sum per ton of product raised. Sugar cane projects for which students are made responsible often amount to $25,000 or $30,000 in value.

Home economics courses in the Hawaiian vocational schools emphasize instruction in family budgeting and financing.

Child care is also taught. Many schools have practice cottages, built on the scale of the homes from which the girls come, where babies are brought for the girls to care for as a part of their practical training.

THE SCHOOL OF JOURNALISM OF COLUMBIA UNIVERSITY

ADOPTION of a new educational policy embracing higher standards of admission and training is announced by the School of Journalism of Columbia University. The changes, sanctioned by both the university council and the university trustees, will take effect on July 1, when the school will have completed twenty years of academic service.

More exact professional instruction through wider use of New York City as a laboratory for reporting and editing, and through courses of study adapted to the news of the day, is planned. These courses will be more closely related to the current practices and requirements of the newspaper profession.

Broader general education will be accomplished by a freer utilization of university classes and scholarship, students being either required or advised to pursue courses in other departments, including such fields as constitutional law, international relations, public finance, contemporary American politics, the business of journalism, economic problems of the post-war period, social legislation, history of science, economic geography, contemporary dramatic literature, religion, typography and recent history of the United States.

Candidates for admission must have completed three years of work in an approved college or university, and must undergo inquiry into their general intelligence, moral character and fitness for the work of the school. The course of study, leading to the degree of bachelor of science, will be limited to two years. At present the school confers the degrees of bachelor of literature and master of science. The graduate course for which the degree of master of science is awarded will be discontinued.

The courses will be organized on a time basis. Eight hours of work a day for five days a week during the academic year will be demanded. The point system will be abolished, and student work will be appraised solely on the basis of "passed or failed."

SURVEY OF SCHOOL FINANCE PROBLEMS

THE National Survey of School Finance is now working on six important studies in state school finance, according to a statement issued by Dr. Wm. John Cooper, U. S. Commissioner of Education.

These studies, detailed plans for which have been approved by the Board of Consultants of the survey, include:

1. The study of the educational effects of certain major economy measures which promise a saving of expenditure without injury to educational programs.
2. The basic facts needed for state legislatures in the distribution of state aid in such a way as to relieve critical points of financial stress now endangering education.
3. The formulation of more adequate standards which may be readily used to determine reasonable costs of supporting schools in various sizes of communities.
4. Further study of the proper tax base to be used in determining the amount of aid to which districts of varying wealth are entitled.
5. Summarization of recent findings of various tax commissions and tax experts in their bearing on the problem of financing education.
6. The development of the best possible standards for the reorganization of rural school districts in such a way as to improve educational opportunities and eliminate unnecessary expenditures.

Immediate investigation of these problems is expected to make available within a few months, to groups interested in bringing about adaptations in their financial systems next year, first-hand information on state school finance and rural reorganization. Studies of economies made possible within limitations of budgets for the next fiscal year will also be made.

A list of possible topics to be investigated by students in school administration and finance is being prepared by the research staff of the National Survey of School Finance, and will be made available, in the near future, to research agencies in the various states. This plan to stimulate a large amount of research in the field of school finance was endorsed by the board of consultants of the survey and groups of representatives of various universities, state departments of education and state teachers colleges.

THE NEWLY-ELECTED PRESIDENT OF AMHERST COLLEGE

Mr. Stanley King, formerly a business leader of Boston and for many years a prominent figure in state and national public affairs, has been elected president of Amherst College, according to an announcement made by Mr. George A. Plimpton, president of the board of trustees. Mr. King, who becomes, at forty-nine years of age, the eleventh head of the college, succeeds Dr. Arthur Stanley Pease, who resigned recently to accept a professorship at Harvard University.

Mr. King, who was born on May 11, 1883, at Troy, N. Y., is a son of Judge Henry Amasa King, of the Massachusetts Superior Court, a graduate of Amherst in the class of '73. Stanley King was graduated from Amherst in 1903. Afterwards he entered Harvard Law School and was admitted to the bar of Massachusetts in 1906. From then until 1917 he was associated with the W. H. McElwain Company, of Boston, living abroad from 1914 to 1916, and resuming his connection with the firm in 1920, becoming in 1921 eastern manager of the International Shoe Company. He retired from business in 1927, and since then has devoted himself to the interests of Amherst and to other public endeavors. He is chairman of the state commission on stabilization of employment.

For many years Mr. King has been associated actively with the affairs of Amherst. From 1915 to 1918 he was a member of the organization committee of the alumni council, of the council itself and of its executive committee. In 1920 he acted as vice-chairman of the centennial gift committee, which raised $3,000,000 for the college. In 1921 he was elected an alumni trustee and last June he was elected to the permanent board of trustees. Recently he has been chairman of the board's executive committee.

Felicitations to the trustees upon their choice of Mr. King to be head of Amherst have been received in messages from former Secretary of War Baker, former President Pease, Mr. Frederick S. Fales, president of the Standard Oil Company of New York, and president of the Society of Alumni of Amherst College; Dr. Frederick J. E. Woodbridge, Johnsonian professor of philosophy at Columbia University, New York; Dr. Ernest Martin Hopkins, president of Dartmouth College; Mr. Walter Lippmann, special contributor to the *New York Herald Tribune;* Mr. Alfred E. Stearns, principal of Phillips Academy, Andover, and alumni trustee of Amherst, and Dr. Karl T. Compton, president of the Massachusetts Institute of Technology.

THE RESIGNATION OF THE PRESIDENT OF THE MASSACHUSETTS STATE COLLEGE

Dr. Roscoe W. Thatcher, because of ill health, has tendered his resignation as president of the Massachusetts State College.

A statement issued by the trustees says the resignation "was accepted with deep regret, to be effective on September 1," and the "board immediately extended to the retiring president an appointment as research professor at the Massachusetts Experiment Station, Amherst, said appointment to be effective early in 1933, after Dr. Thatcher has had an opportunity for several months' rest and vacation." Dr. Thatcher has been president of the college since 1928. The salary is $7,500. In his letter of resignation Dr. Thatcher said:

It is with very great regret, and only after long and careful consideration, that I have come to the conclusion that I must tender to you my resignation as president of the college.

Two factors have been deciding ones in leading me to this conclusion. Both of these are, however, the result of my own ill health. As you know, I am now under the physical handicap of an apparently irremediable high pulse pressure. This is aggravated by mental and nervous strain, and both my own experience and the advice of physicians indicate that I must keep as free as possible from this if I am to avoid grave risk of serious consequences.

My first and most serious consideration is the welfare of the college. I am convinced that this college is now entering upon the most important era in its history. Ex-President Butterfield has told me that, during his administration, it was his plan to build up the faculty and physical plant of the college to an extent which would provide adequate facilities for a student body of 1,000 persons.

This enrolment of students has now been reached and passed, and it may be said truthfully that the facilities of the institution for resident teaching are now being used to their maximum efficiency. The recent additions of the Memorial and Physical Education Buildings have provided well for the social and physical welfare of our present student body.

My immediate predecessor, Dr. Edward M. Lewis, in his letter of resignation expressed it as his belief that the "immediate problems of the Massachusetts Agricultural College are primarily those of definition, adjustment and organization." I think that it can be said truthfully that these problems have been worked out during the past five years to such an extent that the college is now "ready to go" upon a program of service to the Commonwealth which is limited only by the amount of funds which the state will be able and willing to provide for its support.

To meet the opportunities which are thus before it, the college needs vigorous and constructive leadership from its president, such as it is impossible for me to give if I am to follow the imperative admonitions of physicians that I must refrain from severe nervous strain and too vigorous physical efforts.

The second aspect of the situation is the personal one. For many years it has been my hope and plan to retire from active administrative work early enough in life so that I might engage again in some form of research work in agricultural chemistry as an avocation for the remaining years of my life. My tentative plans have called for such retirement after about ten years in my present administrative position. But it is now evident that it is highly improbable that I will be able again to engage in productive research work if I continue much longer my present administrative service, with its inevitable unfavorable effect upon my health. It seems to me, therefore, to be only fair to myself and to those who are dependent upon me to discontinue this type of effort before I am incapacitated by it for other productive work.

APPROPRIATIONS FOR THE UNITED STATES OFFICE OF EDUCATION

ACCORDING to information sent us by Mr. S. D. Shankland, executive secretary of the Department of Superintendence of the National Education Association, the Bureau of the Budget allowed $549,600 for the Office of Education. The House cut this item 11 per cent. The Senate Committee on Appropriations has further cut it to $360,000, which is a reduction of 34 per cent. from the original estimate. Detailed figures are as follows:

	Budget	*House*	*Senate*
Salaries	$285,600	$280,000	$250,000
General Expenses	29,000	25,000	20,000
Teacher Training	70,000	70,000	50,000
School Finance	100,000	50,000	Nothing
Printing	65,000	62,000	40,000
Total	$549,600	$487,000	$360,000

If this reduction is made, eleven specialists must be dropped from the staff of the Office of Education and salaries of others reduced. It will render impossible the printing of a considerable portion of the results of the nation-wide investigation of teacher training which is almost complete; thus results for which money has already been expended will be unavailable. The investigation of school finance, already under way and for the initiation of which money has already been spent, will be abandoned, at a time when there is wide-spread imperative need for facts on financing education.

Dr. J. W. Crabtree, secretary of the National Education Association, has sent out a statement which reads:

Unless the leaders in education prevent it, Congress will seriously cripple the Office of Education, placing it back to where it was when Commissioner Tigert decided to leave the commissionership for another position. The inclosed, which is a copy of a letter sent out to a number of the members of the Department of Superintendence, explains the situation.

Why should education be hit harder than any other bureau or division in the government? We may yet save the day. The bill is now before the Conference Committee. This committee will make its recommendations back to both Houses in a very short time.

It occurs to me that life members and officers would like to lend a hand, hence I am writing to a few hundred. A wire to your favorite congressman or senator urging him to use his influence with the Conference Committee for at least the amount the House recommended, will reach Washington in time to help. This is a critical day for the Office of Education.

EDUCATIONAL NOTES AND NEWS

Dr. William J. Davidson, for the past ten years president of the Illinois Wesleyan University, has tendered his resignation, to take effect on September 1. The trustees of the university, who refused to entertain a similar action on the part of Dr. Davidson a year ago, have regretfully voted compliance with his present resignation.

At the installation of Dr. Dice Robins Anderson as president of Wesleyan College at Macon, Georgia, on April 8, Bishop W. N. Ainsworth, of the Methodist Episcopal Church, South, chairman of the board of trustees of Wesleyan College and a former president of the institution, presided. The principal speaker was Dr. W. P. Few, president of Duke University and Trinity College. Dr. David Allan Robertson, president of Goucher College, spoke in behalf of other colleges for women. Other speakers at the ceremonies and the luncheon which followed it included Chancellor Charles M. Snelling, of the University of Georgia; Mrs. C. C. Hinton, president of the National Wesleyan Alumnae Association; Dr. Walter Hullihen, president of the University of Delaware, and Dr. Harvey W. Cox, president of Emory University, of Atlanta. Dr. Anderson, who was president of Randolph-Macon Woman's College at Lynchburg, Virginia, eleven years, succeeds Dr. W. F. Quillian as president of Wesleyan College. Dr. Quillian now is general secretary of the general board of the Methodist Episcopal Church, South.

Dr. William H. Welch, who recently retired from the professorship of the history of medicine at the Johns Hopkins University, where he had previously been for thirty-two years professor of pathology and later for nine years director of the School of Hygiene and Public Health, celebrated his eighty-second birthday on April 8. As usual he was given a dinner by his colleagues in Baltimore.

Dr. Alexander G. Ruthven, president of the University of Michigan, was the honor guest at a luncheon given on April 8 at the Bankers Club, New York, by Mr. Henry Wollman, lawyer and graduate of the University of Michigan. The guests included Dr. Frederick B. Robinson, president of the College of the City of New York; Dr. James M. Kieran, president of Hunter College; Dr. James C. Egbert, dean of the School of Business, Columbia University; Dr. Marshall S. Brown, dean of the faculties, New York University; Dr. John H. Finley, of *The New York Times,* and Mr. Henry Morgenthau.

Dr. Thomas Woody, professor of the history of education at the University of Pennsylvania, was the guest of honor at the April meeting of the Educational Society of Baltimore.

To commemorate Margaret E. Tuger's fifty years of teaching, forty of them in Herkimer, New York, the South Side School of that city has been renamed the Tuger School.

The Jugoslav decoration of St. Sava in recognition of outstanding educational achievements has been awarded to the following members of the faculty of Georgetown University: The Rev. Dr. William Coleman Nevils, president; the Right Reverend James Hugh Ryan, rector; Professors James Brown Scott and Thomas H. Healy.

Dr. David E. Faville, dean of the School of Business Administration at the University of Oregon, has sent his formal resignation to Dr. Arnold Bennett Hall, president of the university, in order to accept an appointment as associate professor of marketing at Stanford University. Dean Faville will remain at Eugene until next fall.

Dr. J. H. Inman, head of the department of education at Simpson College, has been appointed to the research staff of the National Survey of School Finance, conducted by the Department of the Interior.

Dr. Samuel C. Kohs, who resigned recently as executive head of the Brooklyn Federation of Jewish Charities, which position he had held since 1928, has accepted the position of head of the department of social technology in the Graduate School for Jewish Social Work.

At the request of a Citizens Committee of Fifteen of Fresno, California, Dr. Walter Crosby Eells, of the School of Education of

Stanford University, has been engaged to make a salary and cost study of the city school system.

Four Yale graduates have been nominated by the Alumni Board of Yale University for the office of alumni fellow of the Yale Corporation to fill the vacancy which will be created in June by the expiration of the term of Mr. Edwin M. Herr, of New York City. The candidates are as follows: John Loomer Hall, of Boston, Mass.; Reeve Schley, of New York City; Elton Parks, of New York City, and Edward Larned Ryerson, Jr., of Chicago.

Dr. Henry Neumann, leader of the Brooklyn, New York, Society for Ethical Culture, will be a member of the summer session faculty at the University of California. He will offer a course in the principles of education.

Miss Lucy E. Allen, dean of the Thayer Academy, South Braintree, Massachusetts, has been selected to head the mathematics and science departments of the girl's division of the Overseas Educational Institute, which will conduct an eleven weeks summer session in Europe this year.

Professor A. A. Cock, head of the department of education and philosophy at University College, Southampton, will be visiting professor at the General Theological Seminary, New York City, for four months from October, 1932, until February, 1933.

Dr. Alfred Sturtevant, of the California Institute of Technology, will lecture on genetics and experimental zoology at the University of Birmingham during the autumn term; at the University of Leeds during the second term, and at Armstrong College, University of Durham, Newcastle, during the third term. Dr. Sturtevant is one of two lecturers appointed by the Carnegie Endowment for International Peace to be visiting members of staff in residence at the British newer universities for the academic year 1932–33.

Dr. Ellery C. Stowell, head of the department of international law at the American University, Washington, D. C., has been invited to lecture at The Hague this year on "The Law of Intervention."

Professor Paul Knaplund, of the University of Wisconsin, will give courses on imperial modern English history at the summer session of the University of Michigan; Professor Edgar Holmes McNeal, of the Ohio State University, will teach courses in medieval history.

The speakers at a recent meeting in the Metropolitan Museum of Art, New York, included Dr. Frederick P. Keppel, president of the Carnegie Corporation; Professor A. Leroy Jones, director of admissions, Columbia University; Mr. Robert W. Higbie, a regent of the University of the State of New York; Mr. Frederick A. Whiting, president of the American Federation of Arts; Miss Ruth A. Folger, recent president of the art section of the New York State Teachers, Eastern District; Mr. Forest Grant, director of art in the New York City public schools, and others.

At the eighteenth annual Conference of Massachusetts Superintendents of Schools, to be held at the State Teachers College, Bridgewater, on April 20, the speakers include Dr. Paul Mort, Teachers College, Columbia University; Dr. William G. Carr, director of the research division of the National Education Association, and Mr. Henry C. Long, commissioner of corporation and taxation of Massachusetts. The Commissioner of Education of Massachusetts, Dr. Payson Smith, will preside.

Dr. Charles Henry Rammelkamp, president of Illinois College, died on April 5, at the age of fifty-eight years.

Commencement exercises at Cumberland University will be held from May 22 to 25. The baccalaureate sermon will be preached by Dr. Monroe G. Everett, Presbyterian pastor at the University of Pennsylvania. The Honorable James V. Allred, attorney general of Texas, will deliver the class address to law graduates. Dr. Archie M. Palmer, associate secretary of the Association of American Colleges, will deliver the commencement address.

An International Conference on Secondary Education will be held in London from July 19 to 23, under the auspices of the International Federation of Associations of Secondary Teachers. At a similar conference in Paris last year forty countries were represented. Entertainment is being arranged for the delegates and trips will be planned to near-by centers of interest, including Oxford, Cambridge, Eton and Winchester.

A SEMINAR in Social Science Research in Paris, under the auspices of the University of Paris, will be held from June 15 to July 31. This seminar, designed to guide and aid students and traveling fellows in the utilization of research facilities in Paris and its environs, is under the direction of Professor William Jaffé, of Northwestern University. Each member of the seminar will be expected to work on a special problem of his own choosing and to present reports which will be criticized from the point of view of form, content, methodology and theoretical implications. Careful attention will be given to the individual problems of each research worker. The proceedings will be in English. The seminar is open only to graduate students having a reading knowledge of French, and bears three semester-hours of credit, applicable toward graduate degrees at Northwestern University and subject to usual conditions governing the transfer of credits to other institutions.

THE annual spring conference of elementary school principals will be held at the State Teachers College at Buffalo on April 22 and 23. The conference is sponsored by Mr. Chester A. Pugsley, professor of elementary school administration, in cooperation with the New York State Association of Elementary School Principals.

THE annual Conference of Principals of Junior and Senior High Schools and the annual meeting of Deans of Girls will be held from April 26 to 28 at the State Teachers College at Framingham, Massachusetts. Mr. Frank P. Morse, supervisor of secondary education of the State Board of Education, will preside. The speakers will include the following: Dr. Clyde M. Hill, professor of secondary education and chairman of the department of education, Yale; Miss Marquis Robb, teacher, Brookline High School; Mr. Thornton Jenkins, principal, Malden High School; Mr. Daniel P. A. Willard, teacher, Newton High School; Maurice R. Ridley, professor, Balliol College, Oxford; Francis T. Spaulding, associate professor of education, Harvard University; Herbert C. Parsons, executive secretary of the Massachusetts child labor committee; Richard D. Allen, assistant superintendent of schools, Providence.

A CHAPTER of Phi Beta Kappa was installed at the University of Arkansas on April 4. Dr. Clark S. Northup, of Cornell University, national president of the order, presided at the installation. President John C. Futrall, of the university, was elected first president of the chapter. In the evening there was a dinner for some forty people, including the members to whom the charter was granted, the newly elected members and visitors. On the morning of April 5, at a general convocation in the university auditorium, public exercises were held at which Dr. Northup presented the charter, and a Phi Beta Kappa oration was delivered by Dr. John Clark Jordan, dean of the Graduate School of the university.

THE united chapters of Phi Beta Kappa announced recently the formation of an association in Hawaii among the sixty-three members living in Honolulu and elsewhere in the territory. They include the honorary president of the association, Mr. Walter F. Frear, who drafted the present Constitution of the Territory, of which he was chief justice for seven years and governor during three terms: Mr. Wallace R. Farrington, former governor, known also as an editor, and Dr. G. A. Johnstone Ross, the British preacher, who taught for fourteen years at Union Theological Seminary, and Frank E. Midkiff, head of the Kamehameha schools.

THE city council of Seattle, Washington, has passed an ordinance accepting the Fuller gift of $250,000 for the erection of a public art museum building. The city assigns a site in Volunteer Park and undertakes to provide water, light, heat, electric power and janitor and custodian service and to keep the building in repair, but makes no direct financial grant to the museum. Control of the museum and all property rights in the building and collections remain vested in the board of trustees of the Art Institute of Seattle, a self-perpetuating body. Five city officials—the mayor, the comptroller, and the presidents of the city council, the park board and the school board—will be members of the board. The ordinance provides that the building shall be completed within eighteen months from January 11, 1932.

DR. ALBERT R. MANN, provost of Cornell University, reported that the university will have a deficit of approximately $250,000 this year. It is feared that a reduction in salaries may be necessary, this much-to-be-regretted possibility to be applied only as a last resort in view of effort to bring salaries to their present level. Salaries at Cornell are still markedly lower than those in many other institutions in Cornell's class. In order to avoid the threatened deficit, additional savings or increased incomes, including the unrestricted contributions through the Cornell Council of approximately $250,000, are required. At least one third of this now appears assured. The major financial task for the current year is to secure this amount of added income less such savings as can be effected.

THE necessity for dropping 125 more teachers from the public schools of Syracuse, N. Y., effective on June 30, has been announced by Dr. G. Carl Alverson, superintendent. "Insufficient funds in the budget to continue them in service" was given as the reason. This will bring to 205 the total number of teachers removed from the payrolls.

ACCORDING to the London *Times,* the Spanish Minister of Education has decided to transform the Jesuit College of Deusto, near Bilboa, into a law university if sufficient pupils are forthcoming. For this purpose a matriculation list has been opened. The former pupils of the Jesuits, up to the present, show an inclination to pursue their studies in independent schools in makeshift premises rather than enter the establishments opened by the government in former Jesuit colleges. Thus at Indauchu, where, recently, some 300 boys went out with the lay teachers in charge, only two boys returned to the government's classes 48 hours later. Similar stories come from Valencia and Barcelona.

THE Executive Council of the British National Institute for the Blind has issued its annual report which gives a full account of the work and activities of the institute with many illustrations. The output of braille books and periodicals was on the whole greater than for many years, and no less than 27,136 bound volumes were produced. The production of manuscript works and text-books in braille for blind students has been continued by a band of volunteer writers, and this library now numbers 7,000 volumes. The income of the institute has been maintained, but the future naturally gives cause for anxiety. The British "Wireless for the Blind" fund provided 13,000 wireless sets to date, and it is hoped that a further 7,000 sets will soon be distributed, thus equipping with sets the estimated 20,000 blind persons without means of obtaining them.

A SPECIAL sub-committee appointed after a private conference on cinema films held over a year ago and presided over by the Bishop of Kingston, has presented the following conclusions to the Public Morality Council: "That the film censor be invited to publish a classified list of subjects of films with some indication of the nature of the films, and that efforts also be made to issue an unofficial list of films for the information of religious and educational organizations throughout the country desiring the same. That an immediate effort be made to arrange for a conference between the film censor and recognized representatives of religion and education on the subject of theme and tendency of certain films exhibited in this country. That the strongest expressions of support be extended to the Home Secretary in proposals to bring the licensing authorities into closer touch with the film censor and as regards steps to coordinate and develop the powers of local authorities in their control of cinema theaters by the appointment of a standing committee or in any other way deemed expedient and effective.

"THE Year Book of Education, 1932," has been published in London. The name, according to the *Times,* is not fully descriptive of the book, which is not so much a work of reference as a series of articles, some seventy in all, explaining educational policy and tendencies in all branches and in all parts of the world. Lord Eustace Percy is the editor-in-chief, and also a substantial contributor, and he has gathered round him an exceptionally brilliant body of experts. All the articles are signed, except those written or inspired by officials, and the whole thus carries great weight and authority, without being in any sense an official publication. Rather more than half the 1,000 pages are concerned with education in Great Britain; these are followed by summaries of the position in the Dominions and some Crown Colonies, and finally a series of descriptive essays on the systems prevailing in the principal foreign countries.

According to the *British Medical Journal* the medical and dental treatment of school children under the arrangements made by the London County Council for the year commencing April 1, 1932, includes provision for 42,150 eye cases, 21,380 ear, nose and throat cases, 488 ringworm cases, 78,210 cases of minor ailments and 147,070 dental cases. This is a slight increase upon the number authorized for the present year, but the total expenditure (£116,189) is about £1,000 lower. It is reported that there is a gradual elimination of ringworm cases amongst the school population, justifying a further decrease in the annual provision under this head. The scheme under which children suspected of being rheumatic or requiring observation for rheumatism are dealt with at certain hospitals and treatment centers continues to be greatly appreciated by parents. Under the scheme for next year, arrangements have been made for cases to be dealt with at seven hospitals and eight centers, where the council's assistant medical officers will attend. There are at present ten special ear centers where ionization treatment of children suffering from discharging ears is carried out. Provision has been made for two additional centers. The standard charge made by the council to parents in respect of medical and dental treatment is two shillings a case, and for minor ailments one shilling. All children operated upon for tonsils and adenoids are now retained in the various centers as in-patients, and the cost to the council averages 17s. per case, but the parents have hitherto been asked only to pay two shillings; it is now proposed that their contribution shall be raised to five shillings.

DISCUSSION

BENJAMIN PEIRCE AT HARVARD

In my list of 1932 centennial dates in the history of education[1] occurred the statement that in 1832 "Benjamin Peirce became professor of mathematics and natural philosophy at Harvard, marking an epoch in the history of mathematics teaching at Harvard and in the United States."

My authority for this statement was the recognized historian of mathematics, Florian Cajori, who in his "Teaching and History of Mathematics in the United States", 1890, (p. 133) says:

> The year 1932 marks an epoch in the history of mathematical teaching at Harvard. It was then that Benjamin Peirce became professor of mathematics and natural philosophy.

My attention has just been called to the fact that this statement is in error. An earlier as well as more authoritative statement is found in the "History of Harvard University," written by President Josiah Quincy and published in 1860. In Vol. II, (p. 381) the following statement occurs:

> In May, 1833, the Corporation, with the assent of the Overseers, established a University Professorship of Mathematics and Natural Philosophy, to take the Superintendence of all the instruction to Undergraduates, in the various branches of pure Mathematics, to be conducted by hearing and criticizing recitations, or by oral communications or public lectures, as the Corporation might direct. Benjamin Peirce was then elected University Professor on this foundation and has since fulfilled the duties of the office.

Very interesting characterizations of this distinguished and influential mathematician written by President Emeritus C. W. Eliot, President A. Lawrence Lowell, Professor Emeritus W. E. Byerly, Chancellor Arnold B. Chace, and Professor R. C. Archibald may be found in the *American Mathematical Monthly* for January, 1925. Thus President Lowell says:

> Looking back over the space of fifty years since I entered Harvard College, Benjamin Peirce still impresses me as having the most massive intellect with which I have ever come into close contact, and as being the most profoundly inspiring teacher that I ever had.

[1] School and Society, January 16, 1932, pp. 91–92.

The error made in the date of the beginning of the career of this outstanding educator should not go uncorrected.

WALTER CROSBY EELLS
SCHOOL OF EDUCATION,
STANFORD UNIVERSITY

THE GREAT TRADITION

IN the issue of SCHOOL AND SOCIETY dated March 5, 1932, a reviewer of Mr. Albert Jay Nock's excellent discussion of "The Theory of Education in the United States" asks "why this great perspective, in the days when The Great Tradition was in full swing, failed to get the world quit of serfdom and slavery, plagues of black death, scourges of famine, burnings for heresy, imprisonment for finding that the earth moved. When in the history of man the largest number were reading Greek and Latin, was civilization the most advanced and progress most promoted? The lectures need footnotes citing the blessings existent when The Great Tradition was in flower. Too many readers of this doubting generation have been told that The Great Tradition bakes no bread, cures no diseases, unlocks no secrets of physics or chemistry, or of the attainment of the good life by the majority."

Granted that "plagues of black death" have been largely banished of late, and that "burnings for heresy" are no longer the rule, one may perhaps ask whether The Great Tradition was not still alive when "slavery and serfdom" were abolished from most of the world, and whether the period of The Great Independence has been able to abolish it from the rest, and whether imprisonment and fines for finding new truths or expressing new political opinions is different in kind or only in degree from "burning for heresy" and "imprisonment for finding that the earth moved." Why, since men have been freed from the terrible effects of blind obedience to classical training, does a large portion of the population of the world continue in danger of starvation? Why does the liberated and enlightened economist of the modern day know little more about establishing credit in times of financial crisis than the Emperor Tiberius in the first century? Why has the scourge of war not been banished from the earth? When men no longer read the classics in great numbers, do they spend their time wholly in the betterment of mankind, or do some of them discover new poisonous gases and new explosives for military uses; others, new ways of mechanizing life and taking out both the joy and the interest? If these questions seem unfair to your writer, he must remember that they merely apply to his point of view the criteria of judgment with which he himself evaluates The Great Tradition, which, in the last analysis, has granted eternal joy to those who can understand, a boon to humanity which would be, after all, of considerable weight, even if it were the only one.

Moreover, one may be permitted to question the reviewer's use of such words as "civilization" and "progress." What does he mean by them? Apparently it is "the attainment of the good life by the majority" which he implies by these terms, and these lead one to wonder what "the good life" may be. *De gustibus*—

GEORGE MCCRACKEN
GRADUATE COLLEGE,
PRINCETON UNIVERSITY

SPECIAL CORRESPONDENCE

A COLLEGE DEPARTMENT OF BIOGRAPHY

WHEN Mr. Ambrose W. Vernon, in 1919, founded a department of biography at Carleton College, it was a novelty in the academic world. Since that date, interest in Mr. Vernon's experiment has become wide-spread. Dartmouth College founded a department in 1924, again with Mr. Vernon at its head. Wittenberg College established a third in 1928. Individual courses in biography are to-day to be found in the curricula of other schools, though they may be listed under traditional departmental names. Yet, despite the substantial growth of interest in biography, it is still a comparative alien in the halls of learning, occasionally the victim of ridicule. Its aims deserve to be better known.

Biography is only one of several names which might have been chosen for the new academic venture. Mr. Vernon had in mind, at one time, the title "psychography"—a word with which readers of Mr. Gamaliel Bradford are familiar. "Biography," however, is really accurate enough. Indeed, a naïve conception of the title will come nearest to the truth. Biography studies men and women—great men, representative men, if you will—but men as individuals. With the aid of biographies as such, of letters or other literary memorials, it attempts to study the man behind his bulwarks. It is not interested primarily in dates or events, nor in the tittle-tattle of gossip. Its aim, in a word, is not history, but the characters behind history, their attitude toward the every-day problems of moral strife, their wisdom or their folly. It is a pity that the word "moralist" in English, unlike its French equivalent, has gathered about itself an unhappy connotation of piety, for the teacher of biography is precisely a moralist, one who explores human nature. He may or may not dream of writing text-books on psychology, ethics or religion; he is at any rate dealing freshly with the realities behind all these, or indeed behind all abstractions that seek out the heart of man's mystery.

Clearly, the subject-matter of biography is no novelty. It is not a new department of knowledge, as are aeronautics and television. It is not a new *Wissenschaft,* with its *Prolegomena* and *Handbücher,* with its specialized jealousies and hatred of rivals. A graduate school might not know quite what to do with it. Luther or Cromwell or Tolstoy have not been compelled to wait for a department of biography to be discovered. Nor does biography aim at a mere technique. It is not a division of rhetoric, dreaming of a generation of biographers. It does not even make a fetish of biographies as such, nor of text-books on the art of biography, however much it may result in a student's familiarity with Boswell or Lockhart or the newest fashions in cynical analysis of the Victorians.

The novelty of biography consists, perhaps, in being no new department of knowledge at all, but in a return to the study of man himself, in whom, when all is said and done, all departments of knowledge find both their rise and their fall. In the present day of hair-split specialties, it is a puzzle to think what an entomologist and an expert on medieval verbs can say to each other, even at a dinner party, unless it be by way of gossip of the stock exchange. Yet a bond of union on a higher level than newspaper gossip does exist between the two. We are most alike in those very things which we hide from one another's view. As Emerson says, "We condescend to meet." We ought to be made to unlock those secret chambers of mind and heart in which every son of Adam really lives, in which he curses or prays, wins or loses his "civil war of the cave." Unlock these chambers, and scientist and theologian, statesman and rebel can talk to each other—especially in that serene world of biography, where the fever of life is over and where the weary are at rest.

Biography, then, viewed academically, is at least one attempt to counteract the Balkanization of the modern college curriculum which has gone far to dehumanize the educational world. Every science, be it ever so technical, has of course originally made its peace with human needs, has arisen, as the new German philosophy of Heidegger has it, from *Sorge,* from "mother care." But as a science or an academic discipline grows old, it becomes autonomous; it fashions for itself its own ends. And man, the concrete man of flesh and blood, is left academically uncared for. Even the humanities, in their struggle to retain a place in the sun, have largely surrendered themselves to rivaling the natural sciences in their own field, instead of trying the apparently humbler but possibly more successful course of remaining themselves. History is to-day a social science. Theology is threatening to become one. The authority in religion of all its prophets, even of the words of Jesus, is endangered by doctrinaire relativity. Psychology, especially of the behavioristic kind, has renounced the birthright of its name and has ceased to speak of a "soul." Even the study of literature, if Mr. Irving Babbitt is right, has gone far toward surrendering to its ancient enemy. Research into the obscurities of literary history, not the attempt to relate the past to modern life, is frequently its aim. There is a danger, in a word, that all our scientific and pseudo-scientific disciplines are going to forget what an individual man looks like. No one, in fact, has a right to quarrel with any of these disciplines, not even with behavioristic psychology, for being honestly themselves. They have placed priceless tools into the hands even of the humanist. But one has the right to quarrel with the assumption that to study the individual man from within has become useless. As we, each of us, live our little lives, we know very well that "character," "soul" and "free-will" are still realities of experience quite beyond the soundings of the latest "Book of Knowledge." Certainly, in an undergraduate curriculum, which does not pretend to the omniscience of the gradute school, a fresh study of men and women, freed from the necessity to fit them into scholastic systems, ought to find a place. Biography tries to do precisely that. And I am inclined to think that it can win the respect of its more sophisticated academic sisters, despite its apparent naïveté, and despite the fact that liberal culture, which Mr. Irving Babbitt calls "assimilative and reflective scholarship," is bound to appear a trifle foolish in a day when scholarship is frequently in the hands of the statistician.

Biography, accordingly, differentiates itself from its academic neighbors not so much in subject-matter as in pedagogic method and in its desired end. History, for example, is not, and perhaps can not be, interested in throwing light on the mysteries of personality. It must be impersonal, dealing with tendencies and movements. It is, furthermore, the servant of chronology. It disjoins men and times. Figures of the past are made to know their place; they become shadows thrown against a rich background. Now, surely, such historical discipline is indispensable in all humane studies. Nevertheless, it calls for a supplement. The individual can still claim his rights over against society and historical determinism. A professor of biography, to be sure, does not spend his days in scholastic defense of the "great man" theory of history. He may never mention the problem of free-will in a single lecture. Yet biographical study, by the very nature of things, is likely to act as a wholesome check on deterministic dogmatism. The study of an individual soul from the inside reveals five-act dramas of character no less important than Austerlitz and Cannae. "All theory," says Samuel Johnson, "is against the freedom of the will; all experience is for it." Human experience, the creative adventures of an individual soul, is precisely biography's stock in trade. Biography, furthermore, can supplement history by bringing men and women out of their isolation, by making them shake hands across the chasms of time, by reenacting the discovery of the Renaissance that the ancients were men akin to ourselves.

A distinction between biography and the study of literature is also worth noting. It is the student of literature who has frequently launched against a biographical point of view the sharpest attacks. And justly so, no doubt, if esthetic enjoyment is taken to be the sole end of art. In disparaging the biographical approach to literature, the latter is itself combatting the particular form of historicism which is for it the most dangerous. There is no reason why an ode of Keats should not be freed from its biographical environment and tasted for its own sake. Yet it may be well to insist that esthetic categories can become tyrannical also. Voltaire can be studied piecemeal in courses in the drama, in prose fiction, in philosophy, in the art of letter writing, but he can also be studied as a man, distilling his wisdom or his folly into a multitude of forms, not all of them even esthetically important. The student of biography, too, would like to apply an esthetic norm to biographical literature and deal only with classics, such as Boswell or Plutarch. It is sad to think that the goddess of dullness herself seems to have brooded over whole shelves of memoirs of our forefathers. The surprising fact is that interest in biographical reading has maintained itself, despite such an evident handicap. The reason is, plainly, that a purely esthetic standard is not the only one to apply even to literature. One may read to enjoy; one may also read to become wise. Positive students of life in literature, for whom truth is above all important, have been fond of biographical writing. "Biography," says Samuel Johnson, "is, of the various kinds of narrative writing, that which is most eagerly read and most easily applied to the purposes of life. . . . . . Books without the knowledge of life are useless; for what should books teach but the art of living." The moralist, the student of concrete human life, does not force the literary remains of the past through too fine an esthetic sieve. A Robert E. Lee, though he is probably mentioned in no history of literature, may prove as interesting to him, in his comparative study of character, as do Emerson or Whitman. Furthermore, the student of biography may suggest that whenever imaginative creation of life tends to look at human nature wrongly, either by sentimentalizing life and thus explaining away its harsh actuality, or by running to the opposite extreme, exemplified by current fiction, giving us merely the cynic's view of man devoid of intimations of immortality, biography can be the corrective. It, too, can veer from the truth, and present a distorted picture, but with far less impunity.

Biography, then, is an academic novelty; but its novelty turns out to be a return, I believe, to some of the forgotten ideals of liberal education. Just how liberal culture can be defined, I do not know. It does seem a bit curious that the education of our grandfathers, consisting of a reading of ancient texts, should have produced something which we with all our increased efficiency view with at least a modicum of envy. Did its value consist in the ancient texts? In part, no doubt, it did. Fifth-century Athens can still offer unrivalled riches to any student of the past. But it can hardly have been merely the avalanche of modern knowledge which destroyed even the classics. It may have been in part a disease which is endangering modern humane studies as well. One characteristic certainly of the liberal education of a century ago was its apparent naïveté. It dealt freshly with life. Those old Greeks and Romans were studied as if they meant something. Historical relativity had not swamped the reading of Homer or Plato. Students read ancient authors as fundamentalists still read their Bible. Chapter and verse could be quoted as though they were applicable here and now. The wisdom of the ages had not yet been accounted for and thus shut up in vacuum. Just as art for art's sake had not yet devitalized poetry, facts for fact's sake had not emasculated the humanities.

Now fundamentalism has become, of course, impossible in the humanities as in religion. No one in his senses desires its return, nor a disdaining of the marvelous instruments which the modern scientific disciplines have placed in our hands. But any teacher of biography can testify that he is rediscovering some of the secrets of liberal education. By focusing his attention upon individual human lives, by exploring the mysteries of personality, he touches something unchanging in human experience, a one amidst the many. Relativity need not destroy the value of the past nor drown it in a whirl of progress. Plutarch is, in all essentials, our contemporary as much as Gamaliel Bradford. Plutarch's heroes are individualized. No formula of sociology reduces them to a common level. Yet by reason of this very fact, because they are viewed from within and not as abstractions from without, the hungry generations have not destroyed their kinship with us. And an educational discipline which occupies itself thus with a study of human personality is in the nature of things again a moral education, even though the teacher may despise a moralizing classroom lecture quite as much as the most cynical of his colleagues. It is directly applicable to contemporary life. It may even point the way to a rediscovery in religion of those values which our text-books on sociology, our mechanized view of man seem to have crowded out of the picture. "A man is greater than a town," says Emerson. "What shall a man give in exchange for his own soul?" says Jesus. If religion be anthropomorphic, let it be anthropomorphic, but wisely so, and utilizing the one royal treasure of experience of which the past can boast—that long march of the undying spirits of our race, each one a lone figure in his battle with the gods, yet in his very uniqueness most like unto ourselves.

T. O. WEDEL

CARLETON COLLEGE

QUOTATIONS

THE EDUCATIONAL CRISIS IN SPAIN

THE dissolution of the Jesuit order and the consequent departure of its members from Spain has caused an educational crisis. In the early months of the republic, when the decree of separation of church and state was issued, the government, realizing the crisis that would follow if the Jesuits closed their schools, warned them that they must not abandon their work. Even after the adoption, in December, of the new constitution, it was believed that the government would bide its time so that it might have an opportunity to organize on its own account the educational work being done by the order. But after the holidays there came a drive on the part of the more extreme anti-clericals for immediate action, and as a result the Jesuits' work in their twenty-five colleges and other educational or scientific centers was disrupted.

The colleges and other schools have been taken over by the various state educational authorities, but their efforts to carry on have for the present been futile. For one thing a majority of the former students refuse to attend the reorganized classes. At Bilbao only two students were on hand for the resumption of work.

But what is more serious is that the government finds itself without personnel, organization or equipment to continue the work. In the matter of equipment it is charged that the Jesuits destroyed or removed it. This correspondent can report that what actually happened is that, as long ago as May, the Jesuits removed their most valuable equipment, books, art objects and other personal property, feeling themselves within their rights. They carried on successfully with a minimum of equipment. It was this minimum of equipment which was handed over to the state.

There is still another reason why educational work finds itself upset and that is the specialized character of some of the Jesuit activities. The order, finding its labors in the field of more general education restricted by law, turned to specialized scientific instruction and research. As a result it established three scientific centers which acquired fame all over Europe. These were the Chemical Institute at Barcelona, the observatory of the Ebro at Tortosa near Barcelona, and the Engineering Institute of Madrid. There was also their observatory of lesser significance at Granada. The engineering institute was removed to Liége, in Belgium, some months ago at the invitation of the Belgian Government.

The director of the Ebro Observatory, the most important in Spain, Father Luis Rodés, has decided to exile himself from his fellow-Jesuits by staying at his post. He refused offers from five observatories in other parts of Europe so that he might continue his work. A few days after he had successfully refused to deliver the observatory over to the government, the International Union of Astronomy named him as its member to represent Spain on its commission to study the relation between solar and terrestrial phenomena.

The case of Father Rodés is unique, for he seems to have bluffed the government. The observatory, like most of the property occupied by the Jesuits, was not owned by them but by independent corporations or foundations. In the face of this fact, the government undertook to confiscate it. Father Rodés stood his ground, however, and the government, for the time being, is in the position of having backed down. It had no man to replace Father Rodés and it could not risk a discontinuance of his work.

In the past the government has subsidized the observatory to the extent of 25,000 pesetas (about $2,000) a year. In return the observatory supplied a complete daily meteorological report. "If the government attempted to provide the same service it would cost it at least eight times as much as the subsidy it gives us," said Father Rodés.

The Barcelona Chemical Institute, now closed, had not even a near rival in Spain and had, like the observatory, acquired Europe-wide fame. Its founder and director, Father Eduardo Vitoria, is the author of books on chemistry which are quoted in scientific circles almost everywhere. The institute gave a three-year course in higher chemistry. In contrast with the 400 hours of chemistry study required in a state university during a similar period, the institute exacted 1,000 hours in which no other subject was studied. Its students were required to be either college graduates or men already professionally devoted to work in chemical, electrical or engineering fields. Industrial corporations frequently sent members of their staffs to take courses, and since the advent of the republic a number of ex-army officers became students in order to prepare for civil professions.

The state did not allow the institute to give a

diploma, but in Spain its certificates were accepted at face value by employers in preference to the diploma of a university student, and they were also recognized by the universities of France.

This correspondent, in trying to understand the resentment against the Jesuits, finds it springs from extravagant rumors and fears which seem grounded on the suspicion that they exercised too much influence in high places. Perhaps the case of the Chemical Institute certificates may help to explain how this suspicion formed. In addition, however, there is no denying that in a country like Spain the Jesuits number members of the best families among their alumni. A fact about the Jesuits is that they are capable of inspiring an extraordinary loyalty. Naturally, therefore, they exercise an influence upon their alumni in later life, and consequently also upon that part of their alumni who may be occupying high business, professional or even political positions.—Lawrence A. Fernsworth, special correspondent in Barcelona of *The New York Times.*

REPORTS

A SURVEY OF EDUCATION IN BOLIVIA

A survey of education in Bolivia was made in 1931 by a technical commission appointed by the executive authority acting under an authorization of the national congress. The report of the commission and its recommendations are embodied in an *Informe* presented by its chairman, Dr. George Rouma, to the national government. The commission gave most of its attention to the primary schools and the two normal schools for training primary teachers.

The total number of primary schools in 1931, according to the report, was 646, with an enrolment of 49,732 pupils, distributed as follows: 52 national schools in the capitals of the 8 provinces, with 12,651 pupils; 43 private schools in the capitals, 6,177 pupils; 70 municipal schools in the capitals, 10,141; and 481 national schools in the provinces, 20,763. The primary school course is 6 years. Considering 7 to be the normal age for the first year, the commission found that in the national schools 35 per cent. of the boys were from 1 to 3 years over age; 11 per cent., from 3 to 6 years. In the second year of the course, 35 per cent. and in the third and fourth years, from 30 per cent. to 50 per cent. were retarded more than 2 years; while in the fifth and sixth years, two thirds of the boys were two, three and four years older than the normal age. Retardation among the girls was greater than among the boys. While some small part of this is due to mental abnormality, the commission feels that it is mainly accounted for by irregular and indifferent attendance. The average of absence is 24 per cent.; in some localities it is as high as 40 per cent.

The schools for secondary education, 10 national *colegios,* attended mostly by boys, and 6 *liceos* for girls, enrolled 3,363 pupils, of which 905 were girls. This course is also six years in duration; its completion is marked by the degree of *bachiller en humanidades.* The commission found that the enrolment in the third year of the course was less than half the number in the first year and that about one fourth the pupils that enter the secondary schools finally reach the sixth year. On these data it bases a recommendation that two more years of general training be added to the primary school course to take care of these children that desire more than the six years of the primary school but do not intend or are unable to complete the secondary school.

The two primary normal schools at Sucre, one for men and one for women, enrolled 165 students, 94 of them women. The course is four years, but *bachilleres* are allowed to enter its third year, and those that have completed the fourth or fifth year of the *colegio* or *liceo* may enter its second year, and reductions in the term of study are made for other reasons, such as experience. These reductions the commission condemns and recommends that no student be graduated who has not completed the full four-year course.

In the administration of the school system the commission found two parallel organizations: The National Council of Education, which by law held all the powers of initiative, organization and direction of national primary, secondary, normal and special education; and the Ministry of Instruction, which controlled physical education and that of the indigenous races and presented the annual budget for education and defended it before the national congress.

In the plan of administrative organization offered by the survey commission, physical education and that for the indigenous races are united with the general education system, and all are placed under a direction general of education which shall have full responsibility for the administration, normal conduct and progress of instruction. The National Council of Education is retained in the nature of an advisory body without administrative authority. The Ministry of Public Instruction, as the national office, will act largely on the plans placed before it by the Direction General.

Among other recommendations of the commission are: Reestablish the kindergartens which were closed because of the financial stringency; secure for the two normal schools the services of a specialist in child and experimental psychology; revise the secondary school programs; create a rural normal school; promote the creation of practical vocational schools to suit the needs of the country; and favor the opening of private schools that will offer at least a minimum program of studies fixed by the Direction General and will accept inspection by national authorities.

J. F. ABEL

OFFICE OF EDUCATION,
DEPARTMENT OF THE INTERIOR

SOCIETIES AND MEETINGS

THE ATLANTIC CITY CONVENTION

THE accumulated resources of three quarters of a century stand back of the National Education Association as it prepares to hold its seventieth annual convention at Atlantic City, from June 26 to July 1. During this most fruitful period of American democracy the professional associations of teachers in community, state and nation have enabled our educational institutions increasingly to meet the needs of a rapidly changing world. Annual conventions for the discussion of important problems have been an important factor in improved professional service.

In only five of the seventy-five years of its existence has the National Education Association, on account of war or epidemic, failed to hold its annual meeting. The organization will celebrate its diamond jubilee with a program worthy of the high position it has earned through at least five generations of educational leadership. Very appropriately President Florence Hale has chosen for the convention theme "Looking Forward in Education."

The Sunday evening general session is being built around the topic, "Looking Ahead in Moral and Spiritual Relationships." Well-known religious leaders will discuss the effect of current economic and social tendencies upon the age-old reverence in which men hold the high ideals of religion. The school has ever been a stabilizer of human behavior, and an important factor in preserving those modes of conduct by which men achieve the greatest good for the greatest number. The recent critical tests to which these long-established principles of action have been put make their consideration of paramount interest to all who are concerned with shaping to-morrow's world.

The second general session will be devoted to the subject of "Education, Crime, and Social Progress." Opinions differ as to whether or not crime is increasing in the United States. Students of criminology see a change in the types of crimes committed. Penologists are studying the relation of education to crime. Educators are developing new curricula and new methods of teaching ideals of sound character. Representatives of these three fields will discuss the school's part in the prevention of crime.

"School, Society and the Business World," a topic which greatly interested the thousands of teachers who attended the Los Angeles meeting last summer, will be the theme of addresses by outstanding leaders of business and education who will appear on the Monday evening program.

The Tuesday program will begin with a discussion of "Plans to Meet the Present Emergency in Education." This session will be of vital interest to every teacher. The schools have been successfully defended against the attacks made upon them in many communities. In some states and cities the efficiency of the school systems is still threatened. Miss Hale plans a consideration of the crisis which will result in placing behind every teacher and every community the combined efforts of local, state and national associations in the profession's greatest struggle to maintain the standing of American educational opportunity.

That educational associations not only plan to hold the line for the schools, but also to improve their services, is a significant indication of the confidence and determination of the American teacher. Two sessions on Tuesday will be devoted to "Methods in the Modern School and Modern Trends in Education." President Hale plans to present new movements in administration, organization and instruction in a vivid way. Teachers will hear these new trends analyzed and evaluated, and in some cases will see them demonstrated.

Since research and experimentation point the way in many of the innovations in education, the Wednesday morning session will be devoted to "Research and Educational Planning." Prominent specialists in research will summarize the contributions of their field to progress already achieved, and also discuss the direction in which projects now being carried out promise to lead educational practice. A second Wednesday morning session will be devoted to "Preparation of Pupils for Life and Work." Such aspects of pupil preparation as parental education, vocational education and adult education will be discussed.

On Wednesday evening, Atlantic City teachers and students will present a George Washington Bi-centennial pageant. Pageants are a speciality of the Atlantic City schools. The schools use the convention auditorium for these annual projects. Partly because of this superior opportunity for rehearsals and presentations, the teachers and pupils of the city have won nation-wide recognition for their artistic and colorful pageants.

The Thursday sessions include a special program for "Teachers Professional Organizations." It is designed to help city and county superintendents and association officers in making plans for institutes and conventions. Among other topics for the final day are "Methods of Grouping School Classes," "Radio in Education" and "International Relations."

The assembly of delegates will hear some of the best numbers of the convention program as well as devote time to conducting the business of the association.

A unique feature of the convention program which President Hale plans is the presentation of both sides of some important controversial subjects. Well-known exponents of theory and practice, who disagree fundamentally in their conclusions will be invited to defend them before the convention sessions.

The success of the meeting will be greatly aided by the splendid convention facilities of Atlantic City. The auditorium is the largest of its kind in the world. Its design and equipment are the culmination of many years of experience in producing the best accommodations for large gatherings. The hotels are located conveniently with reference to the auditorium. Hotel rates have recently been much reduced. Excellent living quarters, suitable for every purse and taste, are easily obtained. Guests enjoy the use of the famous boardwalk where they meet their friends as they come and go.

The playground and relaxation opportunities at Atlantic City are unexcelled. At reasonable rates conventioners may enjoy bathing, swimming, yachting and other sports.

Because of the great size of the convention meeting place, the exhibits of books, apparatus and other school supplies will be effectively displayed. Those who wish to keep the material equipment of teaching equal to the needs, at an economical price, will derive much help from the exhibits of those who lead the way in the production of many of the tools of teaching.

Following the convention, some teachers will remain in the well-known sea resort to complete their vacation. Some will travel to other playgrounds along the coast or in the mountains, or will enjoy the education afforded by visiting places rich in associations with the early history of the nation. Plans for additional travel beyond the convention city or for detours on the way are encouraged by railroad rates. Conventioners will have privilege of the usual low convention fares to and from Atlantic City—rates which will be extended for round trips beyond the convention destination. Hundreds of teachers will travel to Atlantic City by automobile on the scores of well-paved highways which pass through interesting scenic and historic territory *en route*. Many teachers are planning to continue the professional inspiration gained at the convention in summer study at one of the many eastern schools within short distance from Atlantic City. Not for many years have National Education Association summer convention plans so combined the opportunities of play, professional inspiration and academic study with economy of money and time.

BELMONT FARLEY

EDUCATIONAL RESEARCH AND STATISTICS

NEGRO HOLDERS OF THE PH.D. DEGREE

INTEREST in the degree of doctor of philosophy or some other symbolism of corresponding, technical training is rapidly increasing with the ever-increasing demand for teaching quality in our colleges and universities for Negroes. The Negro college authorities have accepted the Ph.D. degree as an almost infallible guide and standard for measuring the fitness of professors for the institutions, and so acute has been the passion that apparently our college heads are either not cognizant of, or they are indifferent to, the insistent demands of certain educational leaders that the Ph.D. degree be subjected to rigid examination to determine the validity of its requirements for college teaching. Notwithstanding, to one who has just casually kept apace with the progress of Negro education, with all its concomitant handicaps, it must seem remarkable and startling to note the progress the colored man has made in the educational enterprise of winning doctoral degrees.

The purpose of this article is to present some significant and perhaps interesting facts relative to holders of the Ph.D. and equivalent doctoral degrees. It is hoped that the results of the study will show the pressing need of teachers of a very high order at a time when some educators in this field are greatly worried over the problems of oversupply of professional workers for the schools.

I

SOURCE OF INFORMATION AND METHOD USED

The writer secured from the Negro Year Book, published at Tuskegee Institute, a list of names of colored men reputed to have won the Ph.D. *in cursu*. This list was supplement by data taken from the *Crisis Magazine*, newspaper reports and "Who's Who in Colored America, 1928–29." The final list was then verified by letters directed to officers of the universities in question, and from these latter data the study making possible this article has been based.

II

FINDINGS AND RESULTS OF STUDY

Sixty (60) names of colored men and women who have attained the doctor of philosophy degree or its corresponding equivalent were found. This list was a result of a scaling down of an originally compiled list of sixty-eight (68). Newspapers and even college catalogues are not often very reliable sources of information for giving exact data on matters of this kind. Letters and transcripts from the universities show some discrepancies in all the secondary sources used in this study. Of the sixty holders of the doctoral degrees in question eight are women. Some members of the list have deceased. Data giving the accurate number are not available. At least three are known to be dead. There are also no data indicating accurately the field of service in which such persons are engaged. We know with certainty that forty-seven are (or were) in educational work of some kind, including three college or university presidents and three principals of elementary and high schools. One is an assistant professor of pathology at the University of Chicago; another is a very outstanding journalist, writer and social leader; still another is a senior educationalist in the Office of Education in charge of research in the education of Negroes. The Bureau of Juvenile Research in Chicago has one on its staff. Massachusetts School of Technology is reported as having another on its staff as research associate in chemical engineering. Three others are engaged in research, writing, journalism, welfare and religious work. One (a woman) is an eminent lawyer and three others are physicians.

INSTITUTIONS REPRESENTED

The simple tabulation below gives the institutions that awarded the sixty doctorates to colored men and women.

TABLE I

UNIVERSITIES REPRESENTED BY HOLDERS OF THE PH.D. AND OTHER EQUIVALENT DEGREES

Institution	Number
University of Chicago	13
University of Pennsylvania	9
Yale University	5
Harvard University	4
Columbia University	4
Boston University	2
Northwestern University	2
University of Illinois	2
Clark University (Mass.)	2
Cornell University	2
New York University	2

The Ohio State University, the University of Cincinnati, the University of London (England) the University of Jena (Germany), the University of Michigan, Radcliffe College, La Sorbonne (Paris), the Massachusetts Institute of Technology, the University of Heidelberg (Germany), the University of Southern California, Middlebury College, the University of Syracuse, Illinois Wesleyan University and the University of Wisconsin are institutions that awarded one each. Twenty-six colleges and universities are here represented. Four foreign universities are included in the aggregation.

If it is a fact that Northern universities in the main are superior to Southern universities and the latter will continue to keep Negroes from their schools of higher learning, then by a subtle twist of fate Negroes of superior ability will receive advanced training superior to the whites in the South who elect to do their graduate work in that section. Thirty-six or a little over 58 per cent. of the doctorates are from five outstanding universities. Twenty-one per cent. was contributed by the University of Chicago.

III

Noteworthy and interesting is a study of the academic fields in which these degrees were won. The following table is designed to shed some light on this aspect of the problem.

TABLE II

ACADEMIC FIELD-GROUPS REPRESENTED BY HOLDERS OF THE PH.D. AND EQUIVALENT DEGREES

Field-Group	Number
(1) Social and political sciences	15
(2) Biological sciences	7
(3) Physical sciences and mathematics	9
(4) Education	7
(5) Philosophy and psychology	2
(6) Ancient languages	4
(7) English and modern languages	10
(8) Religion	2
No field reported	4

Tables of specific fields have been omitted by reason of the usual limitation of space to an article of this character. The data in Group 1 show two with graduate majors in sociology, two in economics, three in history, one in anthropology and seven in two or three allied fields within the social science group. Group 2 contains two in biology, two in physiology, one in zoology, one in anatomy and one in pharmacology. Five degrees in chemistry, two in physics and two in mathematics are included in Group 3. In Group 4 one degree each was won in the field of teacher education and higher education, one in the principles of education, one each in the field of elementary education and school administration and one in educational psychology. Group 5 includes one degree in pure psychology and one in philosophy. There are two in Latin and Greek, one in general linguistics and one in Semitic languages, included in Group 6. Group 7 contains three degrees in English, four in German, two in one or two of the Romance language group and one in "modern languages." Both of the degrees in Group 8 are in Old Testament history and literature.

Among these doctoral degrees appears a doctor of science (Sc.D.) and Doctor of Modern Languages, from Massachusetts Institute of Technology and Middlebury College, respectively. There is, of course, a possibility that a few holders of the degree may not have reported the fact, but it is very highly improbable, since the honor is not only socially valuable, but financially a very great asset.

IV

During the year 1927–28 a study[1] was made of the relation of the Ph.D. to the Negro. That study showed that 39 Negroes received doctorates from fifteen American and foreign universities. The leading fields of major specialization were the social sciences and natural sciences, with nine and eight, respectively. English and modern languages had five to their credit, while the field of professional education registered two. The present study indicates remarkable progress within this short period. There are in 1931 at least sixty doctorates awarded by twenty-five American and foreign universities. The leading fields of major specialization are natural sciences and social sciences, with fifteen and sixteen, respectively. English and modern languages have doubled their record during the four years, while the field of professional education also had an increase of 100 per cent. There has been a gradual spreading out from the narrow range of fields of specialization and choice of universities, which in the writer's opinion, is educationally desirable and racially beneficial.

The first Ph.D. degree was granted in 1863 by Yale University. During the earlier years the awarding of the Ph.D. to a Negro was an exceptionally rare practice, for very few members of the race frequented the universities in quest of the coveted degree. Due mainly to the pressure of the standardizing agencies, an increasingly large number of colored men and women have been seeking these academic honors. Philanthropic foundations, such as the General Education Board and the Rosenwald Fund, have made large contribution to the advancement of the race to this educational level. It is significant that, during the year 1931 at commencements and convocations, ten Negroes received the degree, which is far larger than the number of any previous year.

General Conclusions

It is to be expected with some certainty that the passion for the doctoral degrees will be greatly intensified by virtue of the ardent desire of Negro colleges and universities to become fully accredited institutions. No Negro higher institutions, so far as the knowledge of the present writer is accurate, have been rated by the Association of American Universities. Howard University, in Washington, D. C., Lincoln University, in Pennsylvania, Morgan College, in Maryland, West Virginia State College, Fisk University, in Tennessee, and Talladega College, in Alabama, are the six institutions out of over seventy that are ranked in Class A by regional agencies. To maintain the ratings of these schools and provide for the ratings of others will make imperative a substantially large number of colored men and women on the instructional staffs with the training of the Ph.D. or the corresponding technical equivalent. Atlanta University has become a "Flexnerian" university in small degree, and is devoted exclusively to graduate work. Howard, Lincoln and Fisk are doing some work of graduate level. The new Dillard University in New Orleans may enter this new field. The legislature of West Virginia has authorized the establishment of a university at the West Virginia State College, and recently the Texas legislature has appropriated $24,000 for the next biennium for graduate study at Prairie View State College.

With the increasing difficulty to secure and maintain the services of first-class white men, the demand for high-grade colored teachers and research workers, is pressing, immediate and imperative, and unless the generosity of foundations continues, Negro higher education will lag further behind the American college and university. The salaries provided for high-class professors of this intellectual level are woefully low in the main. If salaries are not raised substantially, presidents will be declaiming in defense to the teachers devoid of the degree, "We pay you poorly because you are inefficient." The teachers in defensive restrain will retort, "We are inefficient because we are poorly paid."

Harry W. Greene
West Virginia State College

[1] Harry W. Greene, "The Ph.D. and the Negro," *Opportunity*, New York, September, 1928.

NEW BOOKS IN EDUCATION

Boje, Andreas, Ernest J. Borup and Holger Rützebeck, Editors. *Education in Denmark.* Pp. 290. Oxford University Press. $2.50.

Crawford, Albert B. and Stuart H. Clement. *The Choice of an Occupation.* Pp. ix + 495. Yale University Press.

Gentles, Harry W. and George H. Betts. *Habits for Safety.* Pp. 228. Illustrated. Bobbs-Merrill.

O'Hara, Elizabeth F. *Taming the Wild Grasses.* Pp. viii + 69. Illustrated by Kate Seredy. Macmillan. $.60.

SCHOOL AND SOCIETY

EDITED BY J. McKEEN CATTELL

WITH WHICH IS COMBINED THE

EDUCATIONAL REVIEW

EDITED BY WILLIAM McANDREW

Volume 35 — Saturday, April 23, 1932 — Number 904

THE CRUX OF THE TEACHING PROGNOSIS PROBLEM

By Professor M. E. HAGGERTY

UNIVERSITY OF MINNESOTA

In recent years students of education have sought a means of predicting the probable teaching success of students in training. From Boyce to Brown there have been more than a score of investigations bearing upon this matter. It must be admitted that the total result of these studies is disappointing. Apparently we are still far away from any adequate technique of foretelling the degree to which a college graduate will succeed in teaching, or if, in fact, he will succeed at all. The examination of a long list of published researches in this field leaves one with a sense of futility as to further investigations projected along the lines of those already reported. Even the legerdemain of statistical analysis seems not to promise a great deal.

The writer ventures the opinion that these studies have failed because they have overlooked the essential element in the teaching situation, and that further experimentation should develop a new procedure. If this view is correct, the overlooked essential element is the matter of teacher-pupil relationship, which is something quite distinct from teacher status now measurable in a variety of ways.

Let us illustrate in the matter of scholarship. To what degree does subject-matter mastery contribute to successsful teaching? To put it differently, how much scholarship, as measured by college marks or standard tests, is essential to teaching skill? The view here ventured for consideration holds that the question as stated can not well be answered by experimental methods, since two of the factors essential to a study of the situation are not given. The first omitted item is the scholarship of the pupils to be taught; this item is important because it is necessary to a determination of the third, which is the crux of the whole matter. This third and crucial item may be described as the relationship between the scholarship of the teacher and the scholarship of the pupil. It is this relationship which should be studied rather than the status in scholarship of the teacher or that of the pupil.

Since this crucial factor has been so completely ignored by students of the problem it is worth while to clarify it diagrammatically. In the figure the first vertical line (T) is assumed to represent a scholarship scale for the teacher; St is the point on the scholarship scale which represents the status of the teacher when measured by any of the usual methods of evaluating

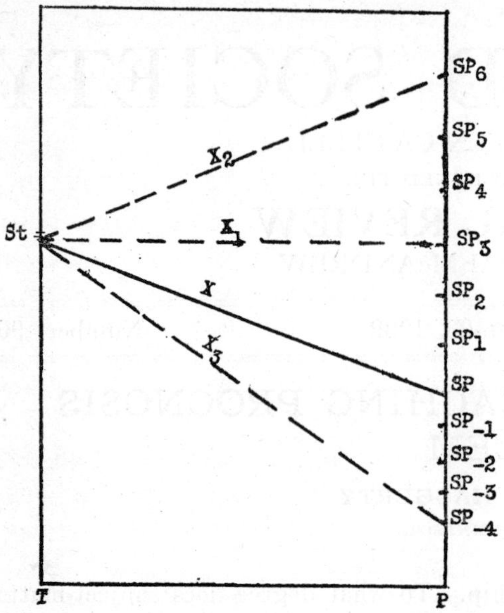

scholarship; the second vertical (P) is a similar scale for the pupil; and SP represents the scholarship status of the pupil.

The diagonal line X pictures the relationship between the scholarship of the teacher and that of the pupil, a relationship which obviously may be stated in a mathematical as well as a diagrammatic way. The angle of this X may now be thought of as representing the most desirable relationship between the two individuals in the matter of scholarship. The teacher knows more and just enough more than the pupil to provide for the most effective teaching situation. It is the situation which we should like to think prevails in all our schools.

Now let us consider what happens when the point on either of the two vertical scales shifts. First let us shift the point on the pupil scale upwards to SP_1, SP_2, SP_3, SP_4, SP_5, etc. If X represents the optimum situation, then each upward shift represents a less desirable condition. The teaching problem is certainly complicated at SP_3, where the pupil's knowledge equals that of the teacher and becomes hopeless as the shift proceeds upward. Likewise if X represents the optimum relationship, then any shift downward in pupil status represents a less desirable situation and becomes similarly hopeless at SP_{-4}, where the pupil's status is so greatly below that of the teacher that the latter has little appreciation of the pupil's difficulties in learning.

If we think of the several points along the vertical P as so many different pupils then this picture represents a condition not greatly unlike that prevailing in many classes where the teacher's scholarship is correct for the pupil located at SP but less satisfactory for those located at points above and below this optimum status.

Now the variation in the adequacy of the teacher's scholarship for the several points on scale P occurs without any change in its location on Scale T and suggests why a measure of scholarship in the teacher can not possibly be a satisfactory predictive measure of teaching success.

It may be pointed out that the use of this factor of teacher-pupil relationship does not lie outside the possibilities of experimental study, even though it has not thus far been employed. The use of the same standard examinations on pupils and teachers alike would seem to be a beginning in the matter. The essential factor to seek is a technique for expressing the relationship in objective terms so that it may be utilized in further experimentation. The discovery of such a satisfactory technique is in itself a preliminary experimental problem.

Scholarship has been used thus far in this discussion because of its accepted importance in teaching competence and also because it has been so widely employed, though disappointingly, in previous studies. The fundamental theory this paper would exploit covers much more than scholarship. Consider the matter of ability as measured by the current verbal intelligence examinations. Over a long period of time we have collected data on students at the University of Minnesota who are preparing to be teachers. Combining these data it becomes perfectly clear that the several curricula select quite different levels of mental competence. Thus, on the Miller Mental Ability Test, Form A, the prospective teachers of trade and industrial subjects all fall below the median score of the entire group of senior students, whereas 84 per cent. of mathematics majors rise above this median. The history group divides about this same point of reference, 36 per cent. being above and 64 per cent. being below. The honor point averages attaching to the marks of history and mathematics majors do not differ greatly, indicating that the determinable differences in intelligence have little influence upon the ability of the two groups of students to achieve satisfactory marks. The obvious inference, and one worthy of further experimental analysis, is that it requires a higher level of verbal intelligence of the type measured by this test to master the mathematics curriculum than is demanded by the history requirement.

Inadequate data exist for carrying this finding over to the lower schools but a number of studies would seem to support it. One of the most recent of these may be cited as typical of others. Fehr[1] reports results of the Otis Self Administering test on 134 high school seniors. These seniors were grouped according to the election of a subject two or more years. He found the following results for intelligence quotients and failures:

Latin	I.Q., 117.3, failures 30 per cent.;
Mathematics	I.Q., 117.8, failures 29 per cent.;
History	I.Q., 106.8, failures 9 per cent.

He concludes: "The brighter students are taking mathematics and Latin, getting lower grades, failing three times as often, and rating lower than less capable students electing history."

[1] Fehr, Howard F., "Intelligence As a Factor in Promotion," *Junior-Senior High School Clearing House*, 5: 528–531, May, 1931.

Then we might assume that in the high-school mathematics classes there is necessarily a higher level of intellectual activity than takes place in history classes. Certainly this argument would not be difficult to maintain as between mathematics and music, or mathematics and art. These results would seem to lend support to the argument of this paper. Teachers of history having lower intelligence levels than those in mathematics may be equally successful because the intellectual activity present in history learning is appreciably lower than that required in the learning of mathematics. Competence in mathematics probably makes a greater demand upon the type of intellect measured by currently used intelligence tests than does any other field of knowledge exploited in the schools.

The thesis advanced earlier in this discussion would thus explain why two teachers of very different intellectual gifts may be equally successful if the subjects they teach follow the same differential level of intellectual requirement. The problem of the amount of intellect necessary to good teaching is thus seen to be conditioned by the subject to be taught. The question is not that of the absolute intellectual equipment of the teacher; it is again a matter of relationship between the levels of intellect required. One may not possess the necessary intellect to succeed in teaching higher algebra and yet suffer no handicaps while dealing with the relatively simple materials used with subnormal children.

Further, let us consider all those qualities variously grouped under the term temperament, personality, etc. The basic question concerning any one of them is not that of any absolute amount possessed by a teacher. It is again one of relationship between a teacher and a pupil. Take the commonly recognized trait of dominance. Some self-assertion, aggressiveness, dominance is undoubtedly necessary in a teacher. How much is most effective is conditioned quite as definitely by the status of related traits in the pupils as it is by the absolute amount possessed by the teacher. Our diagram is quite as applicable here as it is in the matter of scholarship. Let X represent the optimum. Then all the other X's picture less satisfactory situations. Where the situation suggested by X_3 prevails, the pupils will be cowed by an over-dominant personality, but in X_2 the pupils, not the teacher, control the situation.

The considerations here advanced suggest why the methods of individual psychology have so far failed to give us a technique for predicting teaching success, and further why they probably will continue to fall short. The problem whose resolution we seek is not in essence a problem of individual psychology at all. It is a problem of social psychology and requires a different experimental approach from that which individual psychology employs.

Students of this problem have frequently sought refuge from their failure to find high correlations in the conclusion that the measures used are unreliable. Those who render judgment upon teaching success have been described as incompetent to judge good teaching or the instruments of judgment have been termed unreliable. There is little doubt that to a degree this common explanation has validity. But the more serious difficulty lies in the fact that thus far we have focused our inquiries inadequately. Until we bring our methods to bear upon the relational problems involved we shall not come to the heart of the matter of predicting success. We must derive an adequate social psychology on the experimental level to supplement the admirable advance which recent years have shown in the development of individual diagnosis.

Those aspects of this problem which we have sought to render definite in this discussion are recondite only to experimentalists. The practical school administrator is no stranger to them. He knows that the Phi Beta Kappa graduate can not be guaranteed to be a successful teacher. He knows also that Miss A, who fails to teach well in the eighth grade because of lack of adequate scholarship, may be an excellent teacher in grade three. He knows that Miss B, who can not manage the boys in the upper grades, may experience no similar difficulties in the kindergarten, and that Miss C, who imparts the boredom of her task to her fifth grade pupils, comes to life in the senior high school. In fact, a large part of his administrative skill with a teaching corps derives from his intuitive perception of possible effective teacher-pupil and subject-matter adjustments. In experimental work we need to seize this common-sense understanding, to refine it, and to bring it within the scope of our measuring devices so that we may use it for predictive purposes.

The implications of this discussion go somewhat deeper than may at first appear, even though its evident bearings upon experimental study would be sufficient warrant for exploiting the theory now. The more general implications concern the distribution of teaching ability among the human family. It is now commonly believed that learning capacity is a characteristic of all human beings if not indeed of all animal matter. While we may not assume an equally wide distribution of all those human traits which are aggregated under the term teaching ability, it is obviously false logic to erect any dichotomy of the human race into those who can and those who can not teach. All normal human beings direct the learning of others. Mothers teach their babies, little children teach other children, corporals teach recruits, foremen teach workers, policemen teach motorists, statesmen teach their constituencies, professors teach students, and morons on the playground and elsewhere seek out those whom they can lead and influence. The social relationship which we describe by the term teaching may not be as universal as the characteristic of learning, but it certainly is not the attribute solely of that million of the population whom we designate as teachers.

Thus, it appears that if we could derive a measuring technique for the teaching relationship, we would have something much more widely useful than a mere predictive measure of teaching success.

EUROPE FOR RETIRED TEACHERS?

By Professor ISABELLE BRONK

SWARTHMORE COLLEGE

Before the advent of the different teachers' pensions systems with all their accompanying benefits, a successful college professor or teacher in a school could "carry on," unless incapacitated by physical disabilities, until the end of his or her days upon this mundane sphere. Or, if a pecuniary competence had been amassed, he—or she—could gather the robes of respectable elderliness about him —or her—and depart quietly from scholastic circles, with thoughts fixed joyfully upon uninterrupted leisure or upon dwelling in an atmosphere better attuned to preparation for the life beyond the grave than was the one just abandoned. Now, at a certain point in the professor's or school teacher's career, his or her age is blazoned forth to the world, and public announcement is thereby made that the period of natural activity on the part of this particular individual is supposed from this time to cease, and that henceforth he or she is to enjoy only the occupations and pleasures compatible with senility.

If old age has not yet descended in force upon the person designated above, if the red corpuscles are still racing through the blood with considerable speed, this person is loath to sink back in total inactivity upon the sustaining couch of more or less softness which has been provided for him or her by a charitable millionaire, or by cooperation between himself or herself and some educational institution or a paternal city government. The prospect of unlimited time for musing over the mistakes made in the pedagogical career just closed does not seem a cheerful one. Retrospection and reminiscence may be pleasant avocations, but they are unsatisfactory vocations. Hand or head must have some absorbing interest, for lack of interests, it has been noticed, kills "the retired" more quickly than does a plenitude of interests. Channels must certainly be provided for energies not yet extinguished.

Sometimes such channels are near at hand; sometimes they must be created. Statistics setting forth the various ways in which incumbents of teachers' annuity systems enliven their enforced surcease from toil have not yet been compiled. For, in general, it is supposed that when pedagogues arrive at the incumbent stage they are past caring for anything but the ease of slippers and a place near the fireside. By good rights they should be in this condition, but they do not always "run true to form," and the fact is that we find many of them participating actively in life in secretarial positions with learned bodies, on the lecture platforms, gamboling at Florida seashore resorts, imparting instruction to the heathen in foreign missionary fields, on the staffs of papers or magazines, etc.

Often at the parting of the ways the question arises, shall any future stage of activity and usefulness be as in the past, or shall it be located far from the scenes of previous toil and previous interests? If the former, there will be constant painful reminders—of privileges for serving no longer to be had, of a past significance which exists no more, of the good old times and the good old faces. Then, too, a certain mark has been set upon the brows of these recipients of annuities, and no amount of vitality and activity on their part can eradicate it. They are labeled "old," and old they must remain in the estimation of the community. This community may be a peculiarly youthful one, in which case still another argument is presented for taking up one's residence elsewhere, in a place where there are more of one's own-age kindred. There, too, it is reasoned, the fresh environment and fresh opportunities may act with rejuvenating effect upon a face rather the worse for wear, and, as a consequence, it may not be suspected that the owner of the face is one who has been laid upon the shelf.

A chance sabbatical year or pleasant vacation days have often rendered some foreign land dear to the professor's or school teacher's heart. So, in trying to decide upon a new place of residence, the thoughts turn fondly to this distant country, brought nearer, perhaps, by the ties of professional interests and consequent sympathetic understanding. Europe it is that has oftenest been the foreign workshop or picnic-ground. If the speciality has been the language and literature of some European country, or any other subject connected with the civilization of that country, there is naturally a special pull to that part of the earth. At any rate, in Europe greater material ease is to be had, there is more beauty to nourish the artistic sense, there, in short, can be found a more finished civilization. So Europe can wisely be chosen for the scene of one's late operations. Thus reasons the unincumbered pensioner, who in the majority of cases is a woman, as it was in the case of the writer. And because France was the country in which she was most interested, she decided that to France she would go. There she would sink her roots into the French soil, wind the tendrils of her heart around French institutions, and bring forth the fruits of new achievements.

And is it so easy after a certain period for any one to submerge in a different soil from the soil in which they have been embedded the roots of one's being? It may not be too late for transplantation, especially if the new environment is enriched with the fertilizing elements of hospitality and friendliness. And in the case of the European born who have been connected with American educational institutions in the capacity of instructors, a return to the countries of their birth after retirement does not seem very unnatural. But if one's roots have been embedded in the old soil long enough to have become a part of it, long enough to have had an influence upon the surrounding atmosphere, these roots do not sink very quickly into the new soil. In the case of the writer, her family had been in America so long that on both her father's and mother's side she could count back nine generations. Those of the first generation had fled to America for the greater privileges to be enjoyed in that land, and here was she, flying back to the old world with that selfsame object in view. So at first her slumbers used to be disturbed by visions of the *Mayflower* ancestor; of the colonial forefathers and especially foremothers, their severe countenances turned, not towards the path of ease and dalliance, but towards the thornier road of plain and hard duty; and of grandparents more or less distantly removed, all laboring in the upbuilding of a new civilization. She and hers had had no hand in the making of this older civilization. And the strains of the "*Marseillaise,*" sent forth from tuneful, vigorous throats, still produce within her fewer thrills than the "Star Spangled Banner," feebly hummed by a small gathering, not many of whom are sufficiently familiar with the words to get beyond the second stanza, nor in possession of sufficient musical ability to be able to touch the top note. If it is possible for any one to possess more than one fraction of this earth's surface, well and good, she feels, if a part be located in a foreign country. But one must be most impersonal by nature, or else have attained the spiritual heights reached by Schiller and look upon all mankind as brethren and all the earth as one's fatherland, to have one's only possession of a patch of earth in any country but one's own. For this older soil has been tilled by the hands of another race, it has received the seeds of other hopes and its own particular blessing.

As for loving the institutions in the country of a late adoption, some of these institutions will never seem anything but foreign. How, for instance, is an American ever to feel at home among the festivals celebrating the three hundred and sixty-five saints of the French calendar, born and bred as he or she has been to connote nothing more sacred with national holidays than the heroic effort to attain truthfulness on the part of young George Washington? And when even those Americans trained in the saintly lore of the Roman Catholic church are not always sympathetic if they arrive in Paris for a short sojourn during the month of August and find shops and museums taking a three days' or even seven days' repose in honor of the Virgin Mary? Then the school and university system never grows quite familiar, nor the significance of the academic degrees, even when translated into approximate American equivalence. The social life of the ordinary American church can be badly missed, especially if one has come from a small town. There is nothing like it in the native European churches and, in a great city, acquaintance-making with the members of a transplanted American church is almost like acquaintance-making with the members of a procession. But no change in daily habits must be allowed to upset one's mental or spiritual poise, the frequent lowness of temperature in living-rooms must not lower the tone of one's disposition. Nor can the mental habit of comparing customs abroad with those in one's native land be encouraged very strongly. One's irritation at reading in the foreign press silly news or erroneous reports from the home land must be put down. And, above all, one must learn not to suffer from the ignorance of visiting compatriots, but to view the older ones of these with compassion, the younger ones with hopefulness.

Unless one becomes a member of the "American colony," one of the things with which it is necessary for the late settler on foreign shores to dispense is the gossip of the home town. Not that there is a dearth of gossip in any inhabited part of this earth's surface, but for this particular individual it must largely be restricted to the microcosm of the family or the macrocosm furnished by a hotel world. The cozy exposé of actions in lives known to us as well as the open pages of a book must be foregone.

About the children one meets in the streets or parks of a foreign land there is no suggestion of relationship to those known in days agone, no flash of the eye or peculiar turn of the head that instantly suggests some branch of their family tree, no feature of the gait that reveals a well-known parent. Delicious little specimens of humanity they are, all of them, but they are the offspring of fathers and mothers unknown to us, and who, in these days of kidnapping, are suspicious of friendly overtures to their children. And we love these winsome little beings, because they are winsome and little, not because they are anything more to us than children in the abstract.

There are so many factors which render the transplanting of the soul, when one has gone a long way through life, far more difficult than the transporting of the body!

And how about the rejuvenating effects of another country? In the home land, the faces and forms of one's contemporaries record one's own age; in countries as abundantly supplied with mirrors as some of the countries in Europe no other and more personal reminders of the passing years are necessary. So a person suffers no delusion regarding the rejuvenating effects experienced physically from a change of climate. Time, it is observed, does not turn backward in its flight through any latitude or longitude. Still, with the casting off of old responsibilities there may come a straightening of the form; a semblance of a dash may be perceived in the new stride which accompanies the new way of living; new fire in the eye, that now rests constantly on new people and new scenes. And these outward manifestations may be the indication of a mental revival.

If one is to spend his final years in another land than that which gave him birth, he can thank his progenitors if they have bequeathed him a predilection for foreign tongues, a taste for history and a certain amount of adaptability. He can be grateful to his own memory, when he is an American, if it is possible for him to recall the Indian tales he heard or read in his youth, his grandfather's stories of backwoodsmen's encounters with bears and wolves, the trials of the early American settlers, the political fights and freaks of American history. For all these interest this foreign environment more even than Poe's mysterious tales or Kipling's jungle stories, and thereby bring to the teller the prestige which attaches itself to those who scatter enjoyment over life's pathway.

"The fruits of new achievements" in another land have been mentioned. New achievements on the part of old performers are usually a continuation or outgrowth of former endeavors, or they may be the result of what has for years been lying dormant in the blood or heart, awaiting an opportunity for expression. So a retired professor or school teacher may find contentment by continuing his researches in laboratory, observatory or library. Or, like the lawyer or steel magnate who has passed a certain milestone in life, he may stake his happiness upon playing a certain number of holes in golf, bringing out a book which will prove a good seller, or taking an active part in some philanthropic or religious movement for the uplift of the race. The laboratories and observatories in Europe are not always free to all, any more than they are in America. Nor might they seem like home ground to former American teachers of the subjects they represent. For physical apparatus, material surroundings, change with the country and with the times. Great free public libraries are, however, a European as well as American growth, and the delights as well as trials of library research are known to every professor. But if the desire is to produce something original, happy then are "the retired" who will make their laboratory or observatory of the great tide of humanity, for nowhere does this flow more freely than in Europe, nowhere does it present more familiar as well as unfamiliar aspects to the beholder. And it is oftenest retired workers in the fields of language, literature, fine arts or some of the social sciences who do this.

That their observatories and their laboratories are more portable is not, however, the only advantage that the members of the last-mentioned class have over retired scientists. Another advantage is that interest in their subjects is less transitory, less shifting. In 1907, just after the death of the great professor and scientist, Berthelot, Emile Faguet, of the French Academy, writing about him to *le Gaulois,* suggested that, although he had invented alone three or four different sciences, any one of which would have been sufficient to immortalize a man, although his existence had been crowded full of honors and all kinds of happiness, one thing had been lacking in his life—worldly fame, the popularity of salons, *la gloire amusante.* Of all glories, added M. Faguet, this is the most pungent, the most penetrating, the one that is most like a caress. Berthelot never had it, because he was unfortunate enough not to have been born in his own epoch, *suo secolo,* as the Latins used to say, and his epoch was the eighteenth century. Then it was not Shakespeare or Milton, it was Newton who was the god of the hour. Science was the fashion. Yes, man's material and passing achievements, as expressed scientifically, hold the world agape at times, but it is his essential characteristics, the general history of our race in its spiritual struggle upward and onward, which maintain a steady interest through the centuries. The exploits of Lindbergh awaken our wonder; but it is Lindbergh the man in his various manifestations who holds our continuous interest and sustains our admiration.

Now the question arises, in what manner are the aspects presented by the European human tide, with the feelings and ideas which they engender, to be utilized by the ancient onlooker? In the speech of these great surging throngs, even an ancient linguist's ears can become cognizant of new sounds and forms, from which he can deduce new principles with their exceptions. Even the ancient philosopher's eyes can detect startlingly modern modes of conduct, which arrest his attention. And the old lover of the fine arts finds as strongly here as in his youthful years the inspiration for his head and hand. But can a general literary form be given to these aspects with the suggested ideas and feelings? The dreams of youth are past, and with long experience in the world of fact, not fancy, has come a tendency to regard life from the prosaic rather than the poetic side. Poetry might seem impossible, even the prose-formed poetry of the day. Still, there may be lurking in the depths of a retired teacher's being well-springs of feeling, which have been awaiting only the encouragement of leisure and new surroundings to spring to the surface. Their waters may not be so effervescent and stimulating as those from freshly formed although shallower pools, but they may contain elements of a healing power, derived from a deep knowledge of humanity and its needs. Such feeling can possibly find for itself some sober poetic form.

Realistic prose would, however, seem a more natural and logical kind of literary expression for those who have passed the *soixantaine.* And they might even take up novel-writing, if inspired by an environment where this form of composition is rather general. But there would first be a pause and doubtful wonderment. For years "the retired" have been laboring to instil into the young principles of decency, discretion and lofty idealism. Shall they at this late day launch their bark upon the popular current? Shall they begin now to study the effect of the sexual impulse upon all-impulsive humanity, or the psychology of the depraved youth of the world, when their interest has been so largely with the normal, the regenerate and the pure-minded? But there is another course open. If the bald continental realism is repellent, even as an instrument to impart great moral lessons, one can bring to these old shores our Anglo-Saxon limitations in the treatment of nature, human and otherwise, our greater delicacy in the language with which all this is presented. And by so doing one will be aiding in the efforts here on the continent of a group that is striving for the elimination from the novel of all that could appear to any one indecent.

Then there are the short sketch—the shorter the better, if it is to be at all didactic—and the essay, to the writing of which the years of careful observation and well-regulated thought, which are supposed to constitute the teacher's life, should lead naturally.

These are mere suggestions as to the manner in which members of a certain class of "the unemployed" can busy themselves. The efforts this class might thus be putting forth may seem puerile to those who are still rejoicing "like the strong man to run a race." It might even be pointed out that the latter part of teachers' lives should be spent, as were usually the latter years of fashionable women in the seventeenth century, solely in good works and in repentance for the sins committed earlier. The "good works" will not be wanting on the part of those who have for years been laboring for the good of others, and in Europe, as in America, not having taken out letters of citizenship does not mean being shut out of opportunities for useful service. Tears of repentance can not wash away the sins of a teacher's career, the most flagrant of which are incompetence and insincerity. Nor do vain tears ever lead to tranquillity of spirit. And this should be the gift of the gods to retired teachers. This class is increasing in numbers with the increase of educational institutions and annuity endowments. Increasing, too, in length is the span of years which separates all members of "the profession" from the beginning of their careers. If they do not fall along the way, one day they, too, will be admitted to the class of the would-be employed. So let them not jeer at the ambitions of the latter to justify their existence and to render it pleasurable, but rather rejoice that this earth's surface is large enough to afford the ex-teacher more than one point of approach to a happy and useful old age.

EDUCATIONAL EVENTS

SUMMER COURSES IN EUROPE

ADVANCED holiday courses in Europe open to foreign students have been listed by the League of Nations Institute of Intellectual Cooperation, and are reported to the *Christian Science Monitor* by its Paris correspondent. The booklet containing the list describes 135 different courses to be held during 1932 in 17 different countries and 82 different cities.

The subjects in which instruction is to be given are the following: Languages, literature, history and civilization, philosophy and religion, education and psychology, law, politics, economics, sociology, international law, international relations, geography, commerce, science, fine arts, technology, history of art, music, physical training, gymnastics, dances, folk-dancing and eurythmics.

In France, courses are to be given at Bagnères-de-Bigorre (under the auspices of the University of Toulouse), Besançon, Biarritz (under the auspices of the University of Bordeaux), Bordeaux, Boulogne-sur-Mer, Calais, and Dunkirk (these three under supervision of the University of Lille), Caen, Clermont-Ferrand, Dijon, Fontainebleau (at the American School of Fine Arts and Conservatory of Music), Grenoble, Liéfra (near Fontette), Nancy, Paris, Saint-Jean-de-Luz (under direction of the University of Bordeaux), Saint-Servan, near Saint-Malo (auspices of the University of Rennes), Strasbourg, and Tours (under the University of Poitiers).

Courses in Germany are to be offered at Berlin, Bonn, Clausthal-Zellerfeld, Cologne, Frankfürt-on-the-Oder, Freiburg (Breisgau), Giessen, Hamburg, Heidelburg, Iéna, Kiel, Marburg-on-the-Lahn, Munich and Munster.

In Great Britain, courses are offered at Abbotsholme, Derbyshire (under auspices of the University College of Nottingham), Bristol, Cambridge, Exeter, Harlech (in cooperation with the University of Wales Extension Board), Llandrindod Wells, London, Oxford and Seascale.

In Italy, courses are offered at Fienza, Florence, Peruggia, Pisa, Ravenna, Rome, Siena, Varese and Venice.

In Switzerland, special instruction is being provided at Berne, Bourg-Saint-Pierre (under the Botanical Institute of the University of Geneva), Geneva, Lausanne and Neufchatel.

In other countries the principal centers where holiday courses have been arranged are as follows: in Austria, at Graz, Salsburg and Vienna, in Belgium, at Ghent; in Czechoslovakia, at Prague; in Denmark, at Copenhagen and Elsinore; in Hungary, at Debrecen; in Yugoslavia, at Belgrade, Ragusa (Dubrovnik) and Zagreb; in the Netherlands, at Leyden and The Hague; in Poland, at Cracow and Warsaw; in Portugal, at Coimbra; in Roumania, at Monastirea Neamtului; in Spain, at Barcelona, Burgos, Granada, Jaca, Madrid, Panplona, San Sebastian and Santander; in Sweden, at Lund.

This list of courses has been published in English, French and German. The English edition is obtainable from the World Peace Foundation, Boston, Mass., or from Humphrey Milford, Oxford University Press, London. The French edition can be obtained from the Librairie Vuibert, Paris, and the German edition from Alfred Lorentz, Leipzig.

THE EMPLOYMENT OF MARRIED WOMEN AS TEACHERS

THE results are given below of a study recently completed by the National Education Association, as announced in the last issue of the *News Letter* of the Women's Bureau of the Department of Labor.

In 1930–31 the National Education Association obtained from school authorities in nearly 1,500 cities a statement of the general policy of each school system with respect to the employment of married women as new teachers and the retention of single women teachers who marry. Of the cities reporting, in all population groups, about 77 per cent. do not employ married women as new teachers. The figures vary from 69 per cent. in cities over 100,000 to 80 per cent. in cities of 10,000 to 30,000 in population. No definite relationship is apparent between the size of cities and their practice on this point.

Only 37 per cent. of all cities reporting permit single women teachers to continue teaching after marriage, and a number of these permit it only in the case of teachers who have been elected for permanent service. More than one half of the remaining 63 per cent. require women teachers to resign at once if they marry, while nearly as many require their resignation at the close of the school year. In a mere handful of cities the rules make it optional with the school board in each case as to whether the teacher may continue or is required to resign.

As to the legal aspects of the question, apparently no state has passed any legislation with respect to married women as teachers. In at least six states and the District of Columbia, decisions on the question have been handed down by the courts, the child state school official, or the state board of education.

Two authorities conclude from these analyses of these decisions that in these states marriage is not in itself a valid cause for dismissing a teacher who is under contract or who is teaching under a tenure law which permits dismissal only for specified causes. It is, of course, unsafe to assume that similar decisions would be made in the other states if cases of this kind should come up for adjudication.

The most recent decision on the subject was handed down on December 21, 1931, by the Maryland State Board of Education in response to an appeal from Wicomico County. The board ruled that a woman teacher in the public schools of Maryland can not be dismissed because she marries.

It also stated that a clause in a teacher's contract reading, "If a female teacher marries in any school year she will be expected to resign at the close of the school year," is in plain conflict with the state tenure law. This law provides no basis for discrimination on account of sex or marital status.

SENIORS GRADUATING FROM WISCONSIN HIGH SCHOOLS

THE University of Wisconsin has announced that 14,569 seniors who this year will graduate from the public and private high schools of Wisconsin have signified their intention of seeking higher education either at the University of Wisconsin or at various colleges, normal schools or trade schools in various parts of the state.

This is shown by answers given by Wisconsin high-school seniors recently to the fourth annual questionnaire and psychological test sent out to them by the bureau of guidance and records at the university. These questionnaires and tests are sponsored each year by the committee on cooperation for Wisconsin secondary schools and colleges.

The questionnaires and tests were sent to 23,242 seniors in 438 public high schools and 29 private high schools in the state, and of this total, 14,569 or slightly less than 63.7 per cent. of all the seniors graduating from Wisconsin high schools this year signified their intention of continuing their work.

10,292 students explained that they hoped to go to colleges or universities, while 4,277 answered that they were going to enter various teacher-training schools in the state. County normal schools attracted 1,181 of this latter group; business colleges, 1,791; technical and trade schools, 405; music and art schools, 195; while 705 made known their intentions of entering nurses training work.

Of the grand total, 1,169 seniors asserted they were going to out-of-state schools, while 2,807 did not specify what kinds of colleges or teachers' colleges they would enter.

Scarcity of jobs has brought the seniors to the realization that college training is needed in present day competition, according to Frank O. Holt, registrar of the university and director of the bureau of guidance and records.

The testing program gives valuable information to both the high schools and to the colleges involved, Mr. Holt said. This information and the scholastic record of the student makes it possible for the school authorities to advise graduates intelligently on the advisability of going on to college and of the type of institution to enter.

The rapid growth of enrolment in Wisconsin schools is indicated by the increasing number of high-school seniors to which the questionnaires and tests have been sent. In 1929, when this procedure was inaugurated, they were sent to 16,590 seniors; in 1930, to 16,966 seniors; in 1931, to 20,000 seniors, and this year to 23,242.

THE CLOSING OF SUMMER SCHOOLS

THE closing of a large number of summer schools on account of economic conditions bars thousands of students and unemployed from further education, according to an oral statement made by E. M. Foster, chief of the Division of Statistics at the United States Office of Education, to a representative of the *U. S. Daily.*

Summer school enrolment this year will fall far below that of previous years in spite of the movement to keep more young people in school. The reason for this is due to the "view of many administrators of education that summer-school work and night-school work are frills which, during a time of retrenchment financially, can be dispensed with."

Mr. Foster called attention to the following statistics on summer school enrolments:

Since 1922 summer school enrolments have steadily increased. In 1922 there were 280,507 enrolled. The number had increased to 492,638 by 1930. The cost of upkeep in 1922 was $1,152,981 compared with $4,043,433 in 1930.

Between 1922 and 1930 the number of supervisors, principals and teachers increased 48.3 per cent. In 1930 there were 14,481 supervisors, principals and teachers.

Summer-school applicants in a number of city systems are now limited to seniors who, depending upon their summer work, would otherwise not be eligible for graduation and entry into college at the opening of the fall sessions. This means that students below the senior rank are barred from summer courses.

The financial straits into which most of the

states and municipalities have fallen have compelled an adjustment in their educational expenses. The elimination of summer schools, unfortunately at a time when so many unemployed could take advantage of them, is one method of meeting curtailed school budgets.

THE PREPARATION OF TEACHERS AT SYRACUSE UNIVERSITY

THE Teachers College of Syracuse University is now making public for the first time an outline of its program of reorganization which will lead it in the near future to become an upper division college and graduate school offering five years' training for the profession of teaching. During the past two years, since the coming of Dr. Harry S. Ganders from the University of Cincinnati to be dean of the college, the development has been steady in the direction of this goal. Teachers College has been brought into closer cooperation with the other colleges of the university, so that students planning to teach in special fields might have not only the professional training of Teachers College but the technical training offered by such schools as agriculture, home economics, business administration, etc.

According to a statement issued by Dean Ganders, the preparation of teachers is already a cooperative enterprise between the Teachers College and the other colleges and schools of Syracuse University. A broad cultural foundation being essential to sound professional training, two years of liberal arts work is already essential to entrance into Teachers College. Tests showing a high-grade of scholarship ability and character must be satisfactorily passed before this step can be taken by any student.

Freshmen entering in the fall of 1932 who desire teacher training will be required to enroll in the College of Liberal Arts for the "General Pre-Teaching Curriculum" and during the freshman year to advise with the deans of the College of Liberal Arts and of Teachers College in planning their further preparation.

Prospective teachers of academic subjects and also of physical education, industrial arts, vocational education, teacher-librarians and nursing will hereafter enroll for the first two years in appropriate "Pre-Education Curricula" in the College of Liberal Arts. Prospective teachers of commercial subjects, public-school music, public-school art, home economics and agriculture will continue to enroll in appropriate curricula in the Colleges of Business Administration, Fine Arts, Home Economics or Agriculture.

During the transition period in addition to the five-year recommended plan and the four-year program, consideration will be given to the applications of a limited number of students, who may, on the approval of the director of admissions and the deans of Liberal Arts and Teachers Colleges, be admitted to a combination program leading to the bachelor of arts degree upon conditions in each case, mutually agreed upon by the deans concerned. Such program will be subject to the same regulations for entrance and the same requirements as the other combination courses.

CONVENTION OF HIGH-SCHOOL STUDENT COUNCIL PRESIDENTS

STUDENT council presidents from the high schools of the United States will meet in Atlantic City during the convention of the National Association for the purpose of forwarding the activities of the National Association of Student Government Officers. The following five objectives were adopted at the first meeting held in Los Angeles, California, July 3, 1931:

To establish a medium for the exchanging of ideas relative to student activities of both extra and regular curriculum. The first objective is to be the key-note of the association in that a magazine is to be edited and distributed to the high schools holding membership in the organization.

To organize the high schools into a closer relationship for the purpose of becoming acquainted with the activities and progress of other schools. The second objective is to be carried out through the organizing of student council presidents into conference, or district groups within the state, and the forming of state associations.

To acquaint leading educators with the activities of youth and to secure any information from the students that the administration might desire. In this manner educators will have the perspective of the students in their activities of extra and regular curriculum.

The moulding of closer relationship between the

students and the administration. Education must look to the future for progress and to inform the students of the financial and administrative problems that confront educational institutions.

To work toward international good-will by international correspondence and the exchanging of information and ideas. Student correspondence between nations will be made possible through the cooperation of the World League of International Education Associations, San Francisco, California.

The program for the meeting will consist of talks by Warren E. Schuell, president; Dr. Willis A. Sutton, sponsor; E. H. McCune, superintendent of schools, Sapulpa, Oklahoma; John Moffett, Olney High School, Philadelphia, and round-table discussions of problems in student councils. The activities of the association will be begun through the appointment of the following committees with duties as proposed:

Literature committee, to distribute any writings of the association to the members; *membership committee,* to secure and record the membership; *convention committee,* to formulate convention plans for annual meetings; *program committee,* to assist the president and the board of governors in arranging a program for the convention; *high school organizing committee,* to assist by suggestions those high schools desiring to form a student council; *publication committee,* to assist in editing a magazine on student council problems; *international correspondence committee,* to conduct a bureau of correspondence between students.

Any accredited secondary school is eligible for membership in the association, and representatives to the convention should be an incoming president and the past-president, or junior and senior representatives from the council.

The convention in Atlantic City is to be held Tuesday afternoon, July 28. Representatives attending the convention, and those persons interested in the activities of the association may secure further information by writing Warren E. Schuell, president, Sapulpa High School, Sapulpa, Oklahoma.

Warren E. Schuell,
Founder and first president of the National Association of Student Government Officers

SHAKESPEARE LIBRARIES

The Folger Shakespeare Library in Washington, erected by the late Henry Clay Folger, president of the Standard Oil Company of New York, and bequeathed by him to the trustees of Amherst College, will be dedicated on April 23, the birthday of Shakespeare.

The keys to the library will be presented by Mrs. Folger and will be accepted by Mr. George A. Plimpton, president of the Amherst trustees. The dedicatory address will be delivered by Dr. Joseph Quincy Adams, supervisor of research at the Library of Congress. The ceremonies will be followed by an inspection of the library, which is situated on Capitol Hill across from the Library of Congress and houses the collection of Shakespeariana of the donor, regarded as the most extensive and rare in this country if not in the world.

Especially rich in early editions, it includes writings by and concerning Shakespeare, and other material associated with him and his times to the number of more than 100,000 articles and pieces. The building erected at a cost of $2,000,000 is provided with an endowment of $10,000,000.

The library covers a city block and is built of Georgia marble. Outwardly it conforms in architectural designs to the public buildings of the capital. The interior, however, is in Elizabethan style, and includes a theater of Shakespeare's time.

On the same day will take place the formal dedication of the Horace Howard Furness Memorial of the University of Pennsylvania, which contains a priceless collection of Shakespearean and Elizabethan dramatic literature. It contains about 12,000 volumes, 8,000 of which are strictly Shakespearean. Other dramatists are represented in nearly 1,500 other works and the rest of the library is made up of books of a more general character.

The collection was bequeathed to the university with a fund for its maintenance as a memorial to his father by Dr. Horace Howard Furness, Jr., also a recognized Shakespearean scholar, who died two years ago.

The dedication exercises, starting at 3:50 o'clock, are in charge of President Thomas B. Gates, who, with Provost Josiah H. Penniman and Dr. Felix E. Schelling, professor of history and English literature, will speak.

THE FIFTY-FOURTH ANNUAL CONFERENCE OF THE AMERICAN LIBRARY ASSOCIATION

More than 1,500 representatives of libraries will gather in New Orleans for the fifty-fourth annual conference of the American Library Association, which meets from April 25 to 30. Miss Josephine Adams Rathbone, president of the association, will preside at the general sessions, and the conference will be opened on Monday evening, April 25, with the presidential address, of which the subject will be "Creative Librarianship."

Mr. Edwin R. Embree, president of the Rosenwald Fund, will speak on "Cultural Problems and Prospects in the South" before the second general session on Tuesday morning, April 26, and Frederick H. Koch, professor of dramatic literature at the University of North Carolina, will describe "Making a Regional Drama" at the same meeting. Mr. Koch is the originator of community drama through cooperative authorship.

President Frank P. Graham, of the University of North Carolina, will speak on "The Public Library in American Life" before the third general session on Tuesday evening, April 26, at which Lieutenant-Colonel J. M. Mitchell, secretary of the Carnegie United Kingdom Trust, will speak on "The Library Movement in Great Britain." "A Historian Looks at a Changing World" is the subject upon which Mr. Hendrik Van Loon, author of "The Story of Mankind," will address the fourth general session Saturday afternoon, April 30.

Count Rene d'Harnoncourt, artist and illustrator of children's books, who has recently published a volume of "Mexicana," illustrating life and customs of modern Mexico, will speak before a meeting of the section for library work with children on the subject "Your Neighbor—Mexico." "Enlisting the Parents' Interest in Children's Reading" will be discussed at the same meeting by Mary Frances Cox, of the Carnegie Library of Atlanta, and Marian A. Webb, of the Fort Wayne Public Library, will speak on "The Value of a Community Survey of Children's Reading." Vera Winifred Schott, of the Wichita City Library, will have as her subject "The Children's Department and the Children's Theater."

At this meeting, which is scheduled for Wednesday, April 27, the John Newbery Medal award for the year's most distinguished contribution to children's literature will be announced. It is expected that the author of this year's prize-winning book will attend the conference to receive the award in person.

Teachers as well as librarians will be welcomed at the open meetings of the school libraries section. A symposium on current practice in training of part-time librarians will be held by the school library training round table on Tuesday afternoon, April 26. Librarians of teachers colleges and special educational collections will hold a round table for the discussion of library standards in teacher-training institutions on Thursday morning, April 28, at which Mr. G. W. Rosenlof, of the Nebraska state department of education, and Mr. Jackson E. Towne, librarian of the State College of East Lansing, Michigan, will be the speakers.

"The High-school Library in the Changing World" will be the subject of a paper by Mrs. Mae Parkinson Webb before a round table of junior-senior high-school librarians on Friday morning, April 29. A discussion of problems of budgets, classroom libraries and teacher use of the school library will follow.

Children and books, however the contact is made, will be discussed at a joint meeting, Friday afternoon, April 29, with the section for library work with children. Mr. Lesley Newton, of the Lakewood, Ohio, Public Library, will speak on "The Changing School Curriculum and the Library." "To-day's Children" will be the subject for an address by Mr. Ralph E. Boothby, of the Metairie Country Day School, New Orleans; Oscar H. McPherson, of the Lawrenceville School, will address the group on "School-Boy Readers—Gentle and Otherwise," and Mrs. Frances Clarke Sayers, formerly assistant of the American Library Association Board on the Library and Adult Education will describe "The World that Does not Change."

Elementary school service will be the topic for a meeting of the school libraries section Saturday morning, April 30. Mr. B. Lamar

Johnson, formerly of the U. S. Office of Education, will speak on "The Library Project of the National Survey of Secondary Education." "The School Library and the Unusual Child—Retarded or Gifted" will be the subject of an address by Olive O. Powers, of the Greenfield Elementary School, Pittsburgh.

Edith A. Lathrop, of the U. S. Office of Education, will speak on "Elementary School Library Service as it is and should be," and Dr. Doak S. Campbell, associate director, division of surveys and field studies of the George Peabody College will speak on "Standards for the Training of School Librarians."

EDUCATIONAL NOTES AND NEWS

Dr. Robert C. Clothier, who took office as president of Rutgers University early in March, will be installed at a formal ceremony at commencement on June 11.

Mr. Douglas Huntley Gordon, at the time of his election a lawyer of Baltimore and member of the Maryland Legislature, will be formally installed as president of St. John's College, Annapolis, Maryland, on April 30. Dr. Joseph S. Ames, president of the Johns Hopkins University; Dr. William H. Welch, director emeritus of the Institute of the History of Medicine, and Rear-Admiral Thomas C. Hart, superintendent of the U. S. Naval Academy, will be present.

The reported resignation of Dr. Elmer Ellsworth Brown, as chancellor of New York University, has been officially denied by the university authorities.

Mrs. Herbert Hoover will receive the honorary degree of doctor of letters and humanities from the College of Wooster next month when she goes to Wooster to witness a pageant depicting 125 years of progress of the town where her great-grandfather was a pioneer.

A portrait of Miss Lucetta Daniell, welfare director of Teachers College, Columbia University, who is retiring after forty-one years service as teacher and administrator, has been presented to the college by her colleagues. The painting, the work of Mr. H. E. Ogden Campbell, will be hung in the Grace Dodge room.

The Walter Burns Saunders Medal, awarded each year to the nurse who has rendered the most praiseworthy service to the profession, was presented on April 12 to Miss Annie Warburton Goodrich, dean of the Yale University School of Nursing. The medal was awarded during the conventions of the American Nurses' Association, the National League of Nursing Education and the National Organization for Public Health Nursing, at which two thousand delegates were in attendance.

Dr. Earle R. Hedrick, professor of mathematics and chairman of the department of mathematics at the University of California at Los Angeles, has been named by the French government an "Officier d'Académie" "for services rendered to the cause of culture and science."

In recognition of his services to Hungarian literature, Professor Watson Kirkconnell, of Winnipeg, has been given an honorary fellowship by the Petofi Society of Budapest.

Mr. Francis S. Hutchins, a member of the faculty of Yale-in-China since 1925, who has returned to the United States, was welcomed by the trustees of Yale-in-China at a dinner in his honor on April 15, at which President Angell presided. Mr. Hutchins, a graduate of Oberlin College in 1925, is the son of President William J. Hutchins, of Berea College, and a brother of President Robert M. Hutchins, of the University of Chicago.

Dr. Charles R. Watson, president of Cairo University, Egypt, was the guest of honor on April 5 at a tea given in his honor by Dean Henry H. Meyer, of Boston University School of Religious Education and Social Service, and Mrs. Meyer. Dr. Watson spoke in the chapel and also before the School of Theology on "Education in Egypt."

Mr. Patrick T. Campbell, superintendent of the Boston public schools, was given a dinner and reception at Perkins Hall, Boston, on April 7, by the Boston League of Women Voters, in cooperation with the Women's Educational and Industrial Union.

The appointment of four visiting professors

to Columbia University for 1932–1933 has been announced. They are: Dr. Jan J. L. Duyvendak, professor of Chinese in the University of Leyden; Dr. Herbert J. C. Grierson, professor of rhetoric and English composition in the University of Edinburgh; Dr. Fritz Strich, professor of the history of German literature in the University of Berne; M. Georges Ascoli, Victor Hugo professor of French literature at the Sorbonne. Professor Grierson will direct courses throughout the academic year. Professors Duyvendak, Strich and Ascoli will serve during the spring session.

PROFESSOR J. W. HARVEY, at present professor of philosophy at Armstrong College, Newcastle-on-Tyne, England, has been appointed at the University of Leeds to the chair of philosophy, in succession to Professor C. M. Gillespie, who retires at the end of the present session.

CLIFFORD S. BRAGDON, who has been acting superintendent of schools in New Rochelle, New York, since the death of Dr. Albert Leonard, has been elected unanimously by the Board of Education as superintendent of schools to succeed Dr. Leonard. This action was taken at the meeting of the board held on April 5.

DR. T. M. SIMPSON, head of the department of mathematics of the University of Florida, was recently elected president of the Southeastern Section of the Mathematical Association of America. His associate Dr. F. W. Kokomoor was appointed one of a committee of five southern college professors to make a study of the teaching of mathematics in high schools.

OFFICERS elected at the annual meeting of the Massachusetts State Home Economics Association were Dorothea Beach, Bradford, *president;* Edna Skinner, Amherst, *vice-president;* Mary McAuliffe, Worcester, *second vice-president;* Annie D. Scott, Haverhill, *secretary;* Sarah Thames, Boston, *treasurer;* Mrs. Annette Herr, Amherst, *councilor;* Mrs. Gladys B. Jones, Boston, *alternate councilor;* Mrs. Mary Molloy, Mrs. R. R. Hasker, Mildred Collins, *directors.*

MR. FRANK L. POLK, New York, formerly under-secretary of state, was elected president of the New York Public Library at a meeting of the board of trustees on April 13. Mr. Polk, who has been secretary and second vice-president of the board, succeeds the late Lewis Cass Ledyard, who died on January 27. Mr. Wilson M. Powell was chosen secretary of the library's board and Mr. Lewis Cass Ledyard, Jr., son of the former president, was elected a trustee.

DR. RUPERT EMERSON, assistant professor of government and tutor in the division of history, government and economics at Harvard University, has been granted leave of absence for the next academic year so that he may carry on research work under a grant from the Bureau of International Research.

DR. CHARLES E. SPEARMAN, of the University of London, delivered the principal address at the annual meeting of the Kentucky chapter of Phi Beta Kappa. His subject was "The Abilities of Man."

DR. HAMILTON HOLT, president of Rollins College, formerly editor of *The Independent,* has spoken during the past week at the following secondary schools in Greater Boston: Rivers School, Brookline; Milton Academy, Milton; Country Day School, Newton; May School and Lee School; Beaver Country Day School, Chestnut Hill.

DR. ROSS A. BAKER, secretary of the Division of Chemical Education of the American Chemical Society and professor of chemistry in the College of the City of New York, addressed the Eastern New York Section of the American Chemical Society at its meeting in Troy on April 16. The subject of the address was "Chemical Education."

DR. CHARLES E. MERRIAM, head of the department of political science of the University of Chicago, will speak on "Primaries and the Machinery of Their Operation," on the combined program of the Voters' Service and the Committee on Civic Education by Radio on April 26. These programs, broadcast every Tuesday evening from 8:00 to 8:30 P. M., are sponsored by the National League of Women Voters and the National Advisory Council on Radio in Education. They are heard over the WJZ network of the National Broadcasting Company.

MISS JULIA LATHROP, first director of the

Child Welfare Bureau of the Federal Department of Labor, died on April 15 at the age of seventy-four years. When she was appointed director of the new bureau by President Taft in 1912 she was the first woman to be head of a federal bureau. Prior to this appointment she had been an influential member of the Illinois State Board of Charities. In that position she had been instrumental in obtaining the passage of laws for the abolition of child labor, for juvenile courts, factory inspection, control of tenement house conditions and improved management of state and county charitable institutions.

DR. PAUL WHITFIELD HORN, president of the Texas Technological College since its establishment in 1925, died on April 13 at the age of sixty-one years.

THE REV. DR. G. D. GOSSARD, president of Lebanon Valley College, died on April 16 at the age of sixty-three years.

DR. JAMES ROOD ROBERTSON, since 1908 head of the department of history and political economy at Berea College, Kentucky, died on April 15 at the age of sixty-eight years.

DR. RALPH MONROE EATON, assistant professor of philosophy at Harvard University and at Radcliffe College, committed suicide on April 14 as a result of a nervous breakdown.

THE REVEREND J. O'REGAN, dean of men and athletic director of St. Louis University, died on April 11 at the age of forty-four years. Father O'Regan's appointment as athletic director in St. Louis University broke a long-standing custom. Previously athletics at the school had been directed by laymen. He also taught theology and philosophy at the university.

THE REV. DR. C. J. S. BETHUNE, for fourteen years professor of entomology at Ontario Agricultural College, Guelph, and previously head master of Trinity College School for thirty years, died on April 18 in his ninety-fourth year.

SIR PATRICK GEDDES, director of Scots College, Montpellier, France, died on April 17 at the age of seventy-eight years. Professor Geddes was distinguished as a biologist and was well known for his work in education and as a sociologist, philosopher and playwright. He had held teaching positions in London, Aberdeen, St. Andrews and Edinburgh universities. The Hebrew University Building in Jerusalem was designed by Sir Patrick.

THE annual meeting of the trustees of Science Service will be held in Washington on Thursday, April 28. On the preceding day there will be a round-table conference and a dinner to consider how Science Service may further its purpose of making science better known and appreciated by the general public and contribute its share in advancing modern civilization. Those who will take part in the conference include President Karl T. Compton, Massachusetts Institute of Technology; Dr. Edwin G. Conklin, Princeton University; Dr. Simon Flexner, Rockefeller Institute for Medical Research; Dr. Frank B. Jewett, Bell Telephone Laboratories; Mr. A. H. Kirchhofer, Buffalo *Evening News;* Dr. John C. Merriam, Carnegie Institution of Washington; Dr. A. A. Noyes, California Institute of Technology; Mr. Robert P. Scripps, Scripps-Howard Newspapers, and Dr. E. B. Wilson, Harvard University School of Public Health. Speakers at the dinner will be Dr. John H. Finley, *The New York Times;* Dr. Robert A. Millikan, California Institute of Technology, and Dr. H. G. Moulton, Brookings Institution.

DISCUSSION

PROSELYTING PUBLICITY AND THE PROFESSIONALIZATION OF TEACHING

CRITICISM of teachers and teaching is not rare, nor is it likely that it ever has been since formal education first began. An honest critical attitude toward public education and those responsible for its promotion is desirable. A definite need for this exists. However, there is a persistent effort on the part of various life insurance companies, book publishing concerns and private business colleges to draw men and women from teaching into some other calling through the use of questionable publicity. In soliciting for salesmen or students they employ advertising methods which tend to undermine the respect which teachers themselves have for their calling.

Illustrations of what may be termed proselyting publicity, gathered by the writer during the past six years, indicate that many concerns canvass the ranks of school teachers, principals and superintendents to persuade them by criticism of their calling to desert it for other fields of activity. Excerpts from such proselyting publicity follow.

One company has addressed teachers and principals, saying:

> Have you not felt the desire to leave an elective salaried position that gives scanty remuneration for your labor and little promise for the future, and engage in some calling that offers unlimited opportunity and a promise of competence, at least, for old age? No other business or profession to-day offers greater opportunities to men of character, culture, energy and industry, than the life insurance field.

Another insurance company suggests that "to most men education serves as a stepping stone," and on that basis has developed an argument for leaving education to engage in life insurance salesmanship.

Part-time work devoted to the sale of insurance policies is suggested by another company, which supplies the following information:

> Those engaged in educational work are especially fitted for the life insurance business, and many of our most successful representatives were once engaged in school work. Starting out on a part-time basis, soliciting after school and in the evening, these workers found that their life insurance work was more profitable than teaching and eventually gave it their full time. . . If you can not see your way clear to give your full time to the work to begin with, we shall be glad to have you hold a part-time contract. . . .

A former school superintendent, turned sales promotion manager for an insurance company, wrote to teachers and school executives in his state saying:

> The teaching profession, although a noble profession, has no real future, then why not, now, make plans to go into a line of work that has a real future. As a friend of education you must also be a friend of Life Insurance. A great number of teachers . . . have graduated from the high calling into the service of the ——— Insurance Co., a service much more remunerative and second only to the ministry of the gospel in the good done to humanity.

Some publishing as well as some life insurance companies employ statements similar to the foregoing to persuade men and women now engaged in teaching to desert it. Although the results may be insignificant as measured by the number of teachers who turn salesmen, such tactics are undesirable psychologically. Persistent negative publicity of this sort inevitably serves to undermine faith in the occupation of teaching and respect for it as a worthy career.

The most serious indictment is deservedly brought against various business colleges which trample underfoot unmercifully education as a life work, in their efforts to recruit students from among those engaged in teaching. One illustration of such proselyting publicity, by no means extreme in its class, follows:

> The teaching profession is a noble one, but the opportunities it offers do not seem to satisfy the ambitious. If you intend to make teaching your life work and to advance in the profession, you must have university or college training and even your Master's degree. To accomplish that takes time and the majority of young people feel that life is too short, especially when better results can be obtained in the business world after a few months' special training and preparation.
>
> Many young women who taught school for a term or two and then took up commercial work are now earning fabulous salaries and living in an atmosphere of culture and refinement. They are finding opportunities for developing their individuality and latent power that could never have been brought about in the class room. And then they have the satisfaction of knowing that advancement is sure to come to them as soon as they merit it. The daily grind that you find in the school room does not fall to their lot.

Thus boldly are the opportunities in education minimized and those of the commercial field misrepresented and over-emphasized. From such publicity the reader may gather that one who is satisfied with teaching as a life work is lacking in ambition; that the amount of time and training required to reach the heights in the profession are unreasonable; that life is too short to do so in view of greater returns for less time and effort in other fields; that fabulous salaries are earned in business as compared with teaching; that business positions enable individuals to live in "an atmosphere of culture and refinement" which presumably is denied to teachers; that teaching does not permit one to develop one's individuality nor "latent power" (whatever that is); that merit is not certain to be rewarded in teaching, whereas in business it always is; and, finally, whereas figuratively the path of the business woman is strewn with roses, the public school teacher is rapidly being beaten down by "the daily grind that you find in the school room."

The present surplus of teachers can not be advanced as a valid reason why proselyting publicity of this kind should be encouraged. There never will be an oversupply of efficient teachers and the obstacles met in the professionalization of teaching are already too great for us to disregard any one of them. Until teaching as an occupation attains a status of such high excellence that it becomes impervious to the aspersions now cast upon it in the daily press and in the humor columns of current periodicals, misrepresentations concerning teachers and their work must be combatted.

It is to be noted that although teaching is referred to as a profession, in a technical sense it has not yet attained professional standing. This should be a matter of concern to teachers, for they can play an important part in combatting the factors which hinder the attainment of professional status. Then, too, our national commissioner of education, William John Cooper, has said: "The poor standing of the teaching profession in social esteem has been largely due to the teachers themselves. It can be corrected only by a change in the attitude of those of us who enter it. So long as we do not respect our own calling others will not respect it."

In the judgment of the writer, insofar as a calling lacks social esteem, to that degree will its members tend to be weaned from its service and competent individuals discouraged from entering it. Because proselyting publicity such as has been illustrated tends to undermine respect for education as a life work, to exaggerate its shortcomings, to obscure its compensations, and to mislead those engaged in public-school work concerning the opportunities or lack of them in other fields of endeavor, those engaged in school work should be warned of its influence, and counter-publicity should be undertaken to combat it to the end that the further professionalization of teaching may thereby be promoted. Every person now engaged in education may contribute something to that end if he will.

I. O. FRISWOLD

COLLEGE OF EDUCATION,
UNIVERSITY OF MINNESOTA

A BASIS FOR APPRAISING TEACHERS UNIONS

IN the *Educational Review* section of your issue of February 6 I find a long editorial by Mr. William McAndrew on "Appraising Radical Teachers' Unions." The editorial appears to have been suggested by an editorial entitled "The Social Policy of the American Federation of Teachers," by the late Professor M. V. O'Shea, which was printed in the December, 1931, issue of "The Nation's Schools."

Editor McAndrew says, "What the professor (O'Shea) criticizes is the absence of professional ideals: promise of high grade devotion to educational and social service, not stressing the intention to cooperate in raising the standards of teaching. 'Other professions,' says Professor O'Shea, 'put more emphasis on ethical and professional attainments than they do upon the rights of members.'" Mr. McAndrew continues with his own views: "The impression is often created that teachers are more keen for themselves than for their cause. If the public were convinced that teachers desire and intend to make themselves as necessary for the welfare of society as are physicians and sanitary engineers, the establishment of good salaries, tenure and pension would be easier."

The first quotation was meant to apply to the American Federation of Teachers. A careless reader might think that the succeeding quotation also referred to the teachers of the same organization, but it is obvious that it applies to teachers in general. So do the additional three columns written by Mr. McAndrew. Thus his editorial heading, "Appraising Radical Teachers Unions," is misleading. The editor attempts no real appraisal of teachers unions. By indirection he adds to an indictment which others have drafted.

The union movement among teachers has developed independently of the conception which is held by old-line educators that teachers should preserve the attitude of guaranteeing their loyalty to the standards of "educational and social service" that were approved by these educators. Indeed, with such a beginning there might have been assurance that the Pollyanna type of teacher would not be the one to develop as a by-product of the movement. Union teachers soon began to realize that certain social forces of economic and political origin were operating to press the schools into line for the maintenance of the *status quo,* and the children into the matrix of conformity. Union teachers also found that when issues of freedom in teaching arose, the old-line educators tended to take the side of the oppressors, regardless of the importance of freedom as an educational prerequisite.

We have found that such a reactionary influence as that exerted by the unnatural "Daughters" of our late Revolution has made headway in conventional educational circles in dictating the conduct of teachers deemed by them to be proper. To them we owe the movement to require public-school teachers to take oaths of loyalty. This non-professional dictation we condemn unqualifiedly, as we do the petty dictation of country school trustees who order the length of women teachers' skirts. We also condemn the New York State Legislature when it passes a bill that provides for the dismissal of teachers who for five consecutive years fail to register and vote, as if teachers were wards of the state. The teachers unions stand practically alone among teachers organizations in opposition to these impositions which tend to discredit the status of teachers in communities.

The Fifteenth Annual Report of the American Federation of Teachers, and its earlier reports, contain a great deal of material which explains why our members have come to be occupied with other thoughts than those of conformity, or with reproducing such patterns of behavior as are upheld by those who have already lived. For example, I find in our last report, and in earlier reports, the following ideas among our recommendations. They are here stated in comprehensive form:

1. We urge the general adoption of the program of providing for a thorough examination of the physical health of school children, as well as their mental health.

2. The classroom must be freed from such unnatural restraints and exterior compulsions as are transformed into inner compulsions.

3. Efforts must be made by public school systems to advance by experimentation. Experimental schools established within public school systems may be the means by which teachers and school officials may learn how to improve public education and make it effective.

4. Teachers must become better qualified for their work through the study of social problems, social institutions and social movements. Public education itself in relation to other social institutions should be comprehended by all teachers who expect to prepare children for intelligent citizenship. High academic qualifications for teachers must be supplemented by an understanding of the forces that bear on human living.

5. We believe that freedom in teaching is a condition absolutely necessary to good teaching on the part of teachers and effective educational growth on the part of children. We believe social adjustment and progress and character training are not possible except when learners are free to inquire into reality.

6. We believe that those social forces which represent special privilege in human society constitute the most serious obstacles to progress through public education.

These extracts may show in brief how our thoughts have drawn away from the contemplation of codes of professional conduct, and such, to the consideration of ideas of fundamental social and educational bearing. We are not contemptuous of the old-time amenities in teacher behavior, but we believe that in the large the acts of looking and hoping for official approval of conduct have the effect of continuing the ties to the old educational order, and in turn tend to maintain the social *status quo.* In other words, we believe that teachers should be helped to grow out of the primary and dependent grade of experience, where close association with undeveloped minds in the school and outside may tend to keep them, into the realm of rank and file adult experience in common with other workers. We believe that working and thinking as adults about their experience in terms of the general social welfare will tend to develop among teachers a new leadership which public education sadly needs. Moreover, we may well expect to derive better teachers as the solid qualities of intelligence and understanding emerge.

We think it is more than accidental that many teachers are already thinking ahead in terms of a considerable reconstruction of public education as a major feature of a better social order.

Henry R. Linville,
President of the American Federation of Teachers

As for me, not guilty! I had no notion of "adding to an indictment that others have drafted." I haven't seen it. The six bits of creed presented seem to me, all but the fifth, to be the beliefs of a growing number of school superintendents. Such officers, having, themselves, so very little of the freedom here mentioned, do quite generally eulogize it in general, and squelch it when it leads into the approval of liberties which a large number of school supporters regard as immoral or as disruptive of such organized effort as seems necessary to get school work done. It looks to me as though the risk of alienating public opinion through unusual claims made by the more polemic members of teachers organizations, disastrous as it sometimes is, is more than balanced by the corrective effect on school bosses of having some considerable party watching their step. I don't know of any one who has a heavier load of traditional reputation for conceit to live down than the schoolmaster. For associations objecting to his doing all the thinking, he may well give thanks.

William McAndrew

SPECIAL CORRESPONDENCE

ELEMENTARY AND VOCATIONAL EDUCATION IN BELGIUM

The International Bureau of Education, Geneva, reports to School and Society that much interest centers around the organization of public instruction in Belgium, especially in connection with elementary and vocational education. In December, 1931, Mr. Tobie Jonckheere, professor at the University of Brussels, issued a pamphlet entitled "L'Enseignement en Belgique," from which the following particulars have been taken.

Compulsory education (from 6 to 14 years) was introduced by the law of 1914 which obliges heads of families to give their children suitable elementary instruction, by sending them to a public or private school or by teaching them at home. Heads of families must see that their children attend school regularly, *i.e.,* they must not be absent for more than three half days per month without legitimate reason. The law imposes fines and imprisonment on parents guilty of neglect or ill-will in this respect.

There are three categories of elementary schools: Communal schools, recognized schools and recognizable schools. (1) The law specifies that there shall be in each commune at least one communal school in suitable premises. The communal school is organized by the commune and placed under the immediate control of the local authority, which defines its rules and regulations, its syllabus of work, nominates its teachers, fixes their salaries and provides for the school's upkeep. This is the public or official school. (2) Communes may recognize schools which satisfy given conditions and allow their work to be inspected. These conditions are as follows: The school must be established in suitable premises; the teaching staff must be of Belgian nationality and must possess teaching diplomas; the syllabus must include those subjects specified by the law; the school must submit to State inspection. By the act of recognition, the payment of the teachers' salaries falls to the charge of public services. (3) The recognizable schools are those private institutions which conform to the legal conditions necessary for recognition, but which have not been recognized by the commune; meanwhile they are subject to a certain amount of governmental control in exchange for grants from state funds. Both recognized and recognizable schools are unofficial.

There is equal pay for men and women teachers. Elementary education is always free, but this freedom from payment does not necessarily imply that all the pupils are indiscriminately provided with school equipment. According to the law, elementary education includes, besides the customary branches of study and moral and religious teaching, needlework, housewifery and domestic economy for girls and, in the rural districts, the rudiments of agriculture and horticulture for both boys and girls. Ministers of various religious bodies are invited to give instruction in religion and moral education or to arrange for such instruction to be given, under their supervision by the teacher himself, if he so consents, or by some other person approved by the communal council. Children, whose parents object in writing, may be exempt from this instruction.

The elementary school, which formerly covered six years of study, by the law of 1914 should cover eight years. These are divided into 4 grades, each of 2 years. The usual subjects are studied in the first three grades. In the 4th or continuation grade—preparatory to technical and vocational training—the usual subjects are supplemented by certain others with a practical tendency. This fourth grade, the final stage of the elementary school, does not in any way encroach on the field of technical and vocational instruction properly speaking, which is a specialization. The organization of the fourth grade has met with great difficulties, especially in the rural districts: in 1927, nearly 50 per cent of the elementary schools were without this grade.

In the communal, recognized and recognizable elementary schools, the children's mother tongue is, in all the grades, the language of instruction But in the application of this regulation, certain compromises are authorized, according to the needs of the schools, in Brussels and its suburbs and in the frontier communes where several languages are spoken. The teaching of a second language is optional, and in no case is it begun until the third grade. The state undertakes the inspection of communal, recognized and recognizable schools (180 district inspectors, 30 elementary inspectors, 2 general inspectors). Women may be employed as inspectors. The inspectorial staff is chosen from among men and women teachers with ten years' experience who have successfully passed a state examination. Special schools or classes exist for backward or subnormal children. For educable abnormal children, compulsory schooling may be extended until they are 16 years old. Those requiring medical care are placed in school-farms of a medico-pedagogical character. There are two public institutions, for deaf and dumb and for blind children.

Technical training is the logical complement of the 4-grade elementary schooling. It is represented by industrial and vocational training organized by the provinces, communes or by private individuals. There is no industrial or vocational training required by law. The vocational school is frequented by young people wishing to learn a certain trade thoroughly; instruction in the trade and its special processes is given, theory being combined with practical work in order to avoid empiricism at the end of the apprenticeship which is detrimental to the training of a good artisan. The vocational schools usually cover a period of three or four years' study, beginning at the age of 14 years. Much the same conditions apply to the vocational training of young girls in vocational schools, domestic vocational schools and domestic training schools. The essential elements of the 4-grade elementary education are revised; apprenticeship to feminine trades is given with a practical bias.

The industrial school is specially concerned with the preparation of foremen and subordinates in industry and commerce. It offers a more complete course than the vocational school and is intended for those who, carrying on their work, do not possess all the necessary theoretical knowledge (general and special) for the complete understanding of their trade, knowledge which the factory can not give them. In 1911, a model institution, the University of Labour, was created at Charleroi, and the town of Brussels contemplates at this moment building a University of Arts and Crafts. Vocational training is rapidly developing. Since 1925, the Institute of Higher Studies, at Brussels, has held courses for the training of vocational advisers.

QUOTATIONS

SALARY PROSPECTS IN ENGLAND

ON March 11 a mass meeting of teachers, representing for the most part the National Union of Teachers, met in the Central Hall, Westminster, to pass a resolution asking the government to remove the statutory 10 per cent. reduction in salary, and on the same day the president of the Board of Education received a deputation from the National Union of Teachers which asked for a review of the same reduction in the near future. The outstanding fact of the whole question is that the National Government, when it felt compelled to reduce the salaries in all schools in receipt of grants, definitely stated that the reduction was to meet the emergency and was not intended to be a permanent reduction. The National Union of Teachers by their action is keeping the interim nature of the reduction before the eyes of the government and the country. No doubt Sir Donald Maclean informed the deputation that the emergency is by no means over. To use a surgical parallel, the operation is over but the patient has to go through the even more painful process of recovery at the hands of both doctors and nurses. The case of the teachers is exceptional, and salaries must come under review as soon as possible. The hardness of the case is admitted on all sides, and it is only right and proper that Mr. Angus Roberts, the president of the union, is fully justified in pressing for some indication of the period when some relief will be expected.

At the same time it is not right to declare that the teachers are "the Cinderella of the Professions." They are united, they are represented by as powerful a Union as any profession possesses, their views have the widest publicity. The Church, the Civil and Defence Services, the Legal and Medical Professions all have been very hardly pressed by the effects of the Economy Act of 1931. The Teaching Profession, at any rate, know the limits of their loss and know that it is only a temporary loss. In the case of some other professions there is the possibility of unlimited and permanent loss, while in the case of the larger taxpayers there is the fear, almost amounting to certainty, that a long continuance of a very high income tax will imperil the profits on which the teachers, in an indirect sense, depend. We are a nation of shopkeepers, and it is the first duty of the nation to keep the shop profitable. We are running the shop at a loss to-day, and it has been only possible to carry on at all by the use of capital and new taxation which in many cases means the use of hardly won capital. In all the circumstances the best policy for the teachers is to press for a gradual withdrawal of the salary reduction. It is no use talking about the "consequences" of a refusal to withdraw the ten per cent. reduction. As Mr. Mander very rightly said at the mass meeting, "Englishmen of all classes resent any suggestion which even by implication can be construed as a threat." It is wiser to remember that the Burnham Committees will meet again in the autumn to discuss the whole question and not merely the present reduction.—*The London Times Educational Supplement.*

SCHOOL ATTENDANCE

THERE has been a considerable increase in the average daily register of the city day schools taken as a whole—larger than in any other year since 1923–1924. But, as Superintendent O'Shea's report shows, this is due, not to a growing child-population but to the longer period of school attendance by pupils advancing from the lower classes. The general increase is almost entirely because of the greater numbers in the classes of the last two years of the elementary school and in the junior and high-school grades. For the first six years the numbers are practically stationary. Indications of the decreasing birth rate and of the present kindergarten census are that there will soon be a decline in the entering classes.

Though the superintendent suggests no causes for the longer attendance, it is probable that the depression has had something to do with it. Many pupils who might have found work in a more active period are no doubt taking advantage of school opportunities at present. The recent report of the Child Labor Committee states that there are probably a million minors in the United States at work who should be in school, while adult breadwinners are desperately in need of the jobs which these children hold. This can not be true to any large extent in New York. That an increased number who might legally go to work remain in school is a beneficial by-product of adversity. Boys and girls will come the better prepared into their mature years.

The problem of providing for the increasing numbers in the schools would be comparatively simple if only the population had not so high a degree of mobility. Through shifting of families Manhattan has lost nearly 90,000 pupils in the last seven years, while three other boroughs have been making an almost identical gain. This means that some buildings are left partly if not wholly vacant while provision has to be made for the migrants. There is also moving about within a borough. All this has made it difficult wholly to eliminate short-time in the elementary schools, though it would have been done, it is stated, had the population remained stationary.

There is the further factor of retardation. Though the percentage of promotion has "climbed steadily" for several years, there should be made such an adjustment in the kinds of work and the classification of pupils as to obviate this factor of expense to the public and of loss to the pupil.—*The New York Times.*

REPORTS

JOHN SIMON GUGGENHEIM MEMORIAL FELLOWSHIPS, 1932

On behalf of the trustees of the John Simon Guggenheim Memorial Foundation, Henry Allen Moe, secretary, has announced the annual awards of the Foundation's fellowships, established by former U. S. Senator and Mrs. Simon Guggenheim to assist scholars and artists, without restriction of field, to carry on original research and creative work under the freest possible conditions. The Foundation is a memorial to a son of Senator and Mrs. Guggenheim and has a capital fund of $4,500,000 donated by them.

Fifty-seven fellowships have been awarded by the Foundation for 1932–33. Of these, forty-two have been granted to scholars and artists from the United States, and fifteen to scholars from Latin America. On the list of fellows from Latin America are four from Argentina, five from Mexico, three from Chile, two from Cuba and one from Porto Rico, all of whom will carry on their studies in the United States. Ten fellows from the United States will work in various countries of Latin America and the others will go to Europe. More than fifteen hundred persons competed for Guggenheim fellowships this year.

The fellowships announced bring the total number of persons assisted since the Foundation was established in 1925 to 417. The grants are made to young scholars and artists who have done distinguished, original work, and are available to assist research in any field of knowledge or creative work in any of the fine arts. The fellowships are open to men and women, whether married or unmarried, of every race and creed, on equal terms. Fellowships are awarded usually for one year, but in special cases are granted for longer or shorter terms. The normal stipend is stated to be $2,500, for a period of twelve months.

The list of fellows now announced contains the names of nine American artists, six poets and novelists, three composers of music, and the names of several other creative workers in other branches of the fine arts.

The trustees of the Foundation, in addition to the founders, Senator and Mrs. Guggenheim, are Francis H. Brownell, Carroll A. Wilson, Charles D. Hilles, Roger W. Straus and Charles Earl, all of New York City. The offices of the Foundation are at 551 Fifth Avenue, New York City, New York, in charge of the secretary, Henry Allen Moe. Otto L. Myers is the treasurer.

The Committee of Selection included President Frank Aydelotte, of Swarthmore College; Dr. Isaiah Bowman, director of the American Geographical Society; Professor Lafayette B. Mendel, of Yale University; Dean Marjorie Nicolson of Smith College, and Professor Edwin

Bidwell Wilson, of the Harvard University School of Public Health.

The Committee of Selection were advised, with reference to applications in the Fine Arts, by an art jury consisting of James Earle Fraser, sculptor, Eugene Speicher and Gifford Beal, painters, of New York City.

With reference to applications from creative writers, the committee were advised by Governor Wilbur L. Cross, of Connecticut, former dean of the Graduate School of Yale University; Dr. Henry Seidel, Canby, editor of the *Saturday Review of Literature,* and Miss Harriet Monroe, editor of *Poetry: A Magazine of Verse,* published in Chicago.

Among the fellows from the United States are the following writers, who plan to do the work indicated:

Mr. Lewis Mumford: The completion of a book on "Form," by the addition of material obtained at first-hand in Europe. Mr. Mumford is the author of "The Story of Utopias," 1922; "Sticks and Stones," 1924; "The Golden Day," 1927; "Herman Melville," 1929; "The Brown Decades," 1931.

Mrs. Evelyn Scott: The completion of a novel. Mrs. Scott is the author of "Precipitation" (a volume of poetry), 1920; "The Narrow House" (novel), 1921; "Narcissus" (novel), 1922; "Escapade" (autobiography), 1923; "The Golden Door" (novel), 1924; "Migrations" (novel), 1927; "Ideals" (five novelettes), 1927; "The Wave" (novel), 1929; "Winter Alone" (a volume of poetry), 1930; "A Calendar of Sin" (2-volume novel), 1931. She is also the author of two children's books "In the Endless Sands" and "Witch Perkins," and of a play "Love," produced by the Provincetown Players in New York City, 1921.

Mr. Louis Adamic: The writing of a novel. Mr. Adamic is the author of the following books: "Dynamite: The Story of Class Violence in America," 1931; "Laughter in the Jungle," an autobiographical narrative, to be published in the Spring of 1932; "Robinson Jeffers—A Portrait," 1929; and of many articles in magazines.

Mr. H. L. Davis, of Bainbridge Island, Washington: The writing of a historical-dramatic poem. Mr. Davis' poetry has been published in *Poetry, The Miscellany, The Frontier* and the *American Mercury.* Poems by Mr. Davis are included in the following anthologies: "The New Poetry," edited by Harriet Monroe and Jessie Henderson; "La Nouvelle poesie Americaine," edited by Eugene Jolas; the Braithwaite Anthology, Best Poems of 1929. He was awarded the Levinson prize of *Poetry: A Magazine of Verse,* 1919.

Mr. George Dillon, of Chicago: Creative writing in poetry. Mr. Dillon is the author of two volumes of poems: "Boy in the Wind," and "The Flowering Stone." His poems have been reprinted in many anthologies, including the following: "Modern American Poetry" and "British and American Poetry," edited by Louis Untermeyer; "Our Singing Strength," edited by Alfred Kreymborg; "The New Poetry," edited by Harriet Monroe and Jessie Henderson; "The Anthology of Magazine Verse," edited by Stanley Braithwaite; and "La Nouvelle poesie Americaine," edited by Eugene Jolas. He was awarded the Young Poet's Prize of *Poetry: A Magazine of Verse* in 1925; and in 1931 received the first poetry prize of the Chicago Foundation for Literature.

Mrs. Caroline Gordon Tate, of Clarksville, Tennessee: The writing of a novel. Mrs. Tate is the author of "Penhally" (a novel), 1931, and of short stories. She is the wife of Allen Tate, poet and critic, who was awarded a Guggenheim fellowship in 1928.

Miss Martha Graham has been awarded a fellowship to assist her in making studies of the native dances of Mexico and Yucatan.

Miss Graham was a student of Ruth St. Denis, and she was a member of the Denishawn company from 1919 to 1925. Since that time Miss Graham's appearances have been devoted to the presentation of creative and experimental works of the dance. She was selected by Leopold Stokowski, conductor of the Philadelphia Symphony Orchestra, and by Nikolai Sokoloff, conductor of the Cleveland Symphony Orchestra, to create the leading roles in Strauss' "Ein Heldenleben," Stravinsky's "Le Sacre du Printemps" and Loeffler's "Pagan Poem" for the presentation of these works by the Philadelphia and Cleveland Orchestras.

Painters who have received fellowships are the following:

Mr. Andrew M. Dasburg, of Santa Fe, New Mexico.

Mr. Ernest Fiene, of New York City.

Mr. Peter Blume, of Gaylordsville, Connecticut.

Mr. Peppino Mangravite, head, Art Department, Ethical Culture Schools, New York.

Sculptors on the list of awards are:

Mr. John B. Flannagan, of New York City.

Mr. Antonio Salemme, of New York City.

Mr. Mitchell Fields, of New York City.

Mr. Benjamin Greenstein, of New York City.

Mr. Howard Norton Cook, lithographer and etcher, of Granville, Massachusetts, has been awarded a fellowship to enable him to engage in creative work in etching, wood engraving and lithography in Mexico.

The following-named fellows will go to various countries of Latin America for the work indicated:

Mr. J. Frank Dobie, associate professor of English, University of Texas: The collection of tales told by Mexicans in northern Mexico, and the preparation of a book that will reflect the character and history both of these people and their country. Professor Dobie is the author of the following books: "A Vaquero of the Brush Country"; "Colorado's Children," and "On the Open Range." He is also the editor of the publications of the Texas Folklore Society.

Dr. Isaac Goldberg, author, Roxbury, Massachusetts: The preparation of a history of the modern literature of Spanish and Portuguese America. Dr. Goldberg, who is a lecturer at Harvard University, is the author of the following books in the field of the work he plans to do as a fellow: "Studies in Spanish-American Literature," and "Brazilian Literature." He is also the author of "Havelock Ellis"; "The Story of Gilbert and Sullivan, or the 'Compleat' Savoyard"; "The Fine Art of Living"; "Tin Pan Alley: A Chronicle of the American Popular Music Racket"; "George Gershwin: A Study in American Music"; "The Man, Mencken: A Biographical and Critical Survey," and "The Drama of Transition."

Dr. Frank Tannenbaum, economist, Washington, D. C.: Studies of agricultural problems of Peru. Dr. Tannenbaum is the author of the following books: "The Mexican Agrarian Revolution"; "The Labor Movement"; "Darker Phases of the South"; "Wall Shadows," and of part of the report of The Porto Rican Survey of the Brookings Institution, 1930.

Dr. Arturo Torres-Rioseco, associate professor of Latin-American literature, University of California: A study of the Spanish-American novel with regard to its historical development, its psychological expression and its sociological influences.

Dr. Ivan Murray Johnston, research associate, Arnold Arboretum, Jamaica Plain, Massachusetts: A study and analysis of the distribution of the numerous plants of temperate, semiarid parts of South America which reappear or have their closest relatives in similar areas of North America.

For the past ten years Dr. Johnston has been assembling data concerning a problem in the dispersal of plants in the two continents of the Western Hemisphere. There exist a large number of identical or immediately related plant species which occur in the Western United States and then reappear in far distant areas of South America. As these plants are chiefly those from temperate climates, many of them from very dry habitats, the problem of how they migrated across the equator and became separated by wet tropical forests is a complex one. On that problem Dr. Johnston, during his fellowship, intends to work.

Mr. Karl Patterson Schmidt, a curator of the Field Museum of Natural History, Chicago, will prepare a systematic account of the amphibians and reptiles of Upper Central America, and make studies of type material in European museums. Mr. Schmidt is the author of numerous scientific papers on the reptiles and amphibians of the Americas.

Mr. Owen Lattimore, author of "High Tartary," "The Desert Road to Turkestan," and "Manchuria, Cradle of Conflict," will continue his studies and explorations in high Asia, preparatory to the writing of a work on "The Frontiers of Inner Asia."

Fellowships were granted to three composers of music:

Mr. George Antheil, of Trenton, New Jersey. Mr. Antheil is the author (music and libretto) of an opera entitled "Transatlantic" produced at the State Opera House in Frankfort a-M, Germany, in 1930. He has recently completed the score of an opera, "Helen Retires," to John Erskine's libretto.

Mr. Adolph Weiss, of New York City.

Mr. Mark Wessel, of Bronson, Michigan.

Grants for research in historical fields are the following:

Rev. Dom Anselm Strittmatter, O.S.B., instructor in religion, Trinity College, Washington, D. C. Studies in the history of Christian life and thought. Dom Strittmatter, who is a Benedictine monk, will, in particular during his fellowship year, devote himself to the preparation of an edition of a manuscript written about 800 A. D., which is the oldest euchology of the Byzantine Rite known to be extant.

Dr. Fulmer Mood, instructor in history, Harvard University: Studies in the literature of Anglo-American promotion and expansion. Dr. Mood's work is concerned with the history of American Colonial ideas. The materials which he proposes to use consist of the tracts, treatises, broadsides, advertisements and general propaganda which, published between 1578 and 1660, attracted the capital of the English mercantile leaders, and won the physical support of the English immigrants, thus resulting in the settlement of the Atlantic seaboard of North America.

Dr. Earl Morse Wilbur, president, Pacific Unitarian School for the Ministry, Berkeley, California: Study in European libraries and archives of materials for a comprehensive history of the Socinian-Unitarian movement, as a movement toward freedom, reason and tolerance in religion.

Professor Levi Arnold Post, associate professor of Greek, Haverford College, Haverford, Pennsylvania: A study of the text tradition of Plato's Laws; research chiefly in the Library of the Vatican.

Mr. William Henry Chamberlin, Moscow correspondent, *Christian Science Monitor,* will write a history of the Russian revolution from the downfall of tsarism in March, 1917, to the adoption of the new economic policy in March, 1921. Mr. Chamberlin is the author of a book entitled "Soviet Russia: a Living Record and a History," 1930, and "The Soviet Planned Economic Order," 1931.

Literary studies will be carried on by the following named fellows:

Mr. Howard Mumford Jones, professor of English, University of Michigan: To write a life of Thomas Moore with a view to exhibiting him as an author representative of "Regency" taste in literature, and showing the currents of thought found in his work; research in England and Ireland.

Dr. Norman Lewis Torrey, assistant professor of French, Yale University: Studies of the philosophy of Voltaire, in preparation for the writing of a biography of his mind from a literary standpoint; research in the Public Library at Leningrad.

Dr. Edwin Hermann Zeydel, professor of German, University of Cincinnati: Researches into the life and works of Ludwig Tieck (1773–1853), the German Romantic poet and critic, with a view to writing a critical biography of him set off against the background of his age.

In the biological sciences the following studies will be carried on:

Dr. Hermann Joseph Muller, professor of zoology, University of Texas: Investigation of problems concerning the mechanism of mutation and evolution, and the nature of the gene. Dr. Muller proposes to enter into a series of conferences with various European geneticists on the subject of the hereditary material of living organisms and the methods by which it becomes changed in the causation of organic evolution. Dr. Muller's researches have established that the hereditary materials, known as "genes" may readily be caused to undergo sudden heritable variations, or "gene mutations," by means of the application of high-energy radiation, such as X-rays. For this work he was awarded, in 1927, a $1,000 prize of the American Association for the Advancement of Science.

Dr. Samuel Gelfan, assistant professor of physiology and pharmacology, University of Alberta: Investigations of the nature of the sub-maximal contractions of the single muscle fiber, chiefly with Professor E. D. Adrian, Cambridge University, England. Dr. Gelfan has made important discoveries concerning the functioning of muscles. He is a citizen of the United States who has been teaching at the University of Alberta since 1930.

Dr. Herbert Orion Calvery, assistant professor of physiological chemistry, University of Michigan: Studies of embryonic protein metabolism, in certain European laboratories.

Dr. Filmer S. C. Northrop, associate professor of philosophy, Yale University, author of "Science and First Principles," proposes to review and evaluate current conceptions of the nature of mathematics and formal logic, and in the light of these findings and contemporary knowledge from physics of the existence of order in the physical world, to determine the status of form in nature.

For work in the physical sciences, the following fellowships have been awarded:

Dr. Francis Arthur Jenkins, associate professor of physics, University of California: Studies in the measurement and interpretation of intensities in band spectra, chiefly in the Physical Laboratory of the University of Utrecht.

Dr. Robert S. Mulliken, associate professor of physics, University of Chicago: Studies abroad of problems connected with the subject of the formation and dissociation of molecules and the assignment of quantum numbers for electrons in molecules.

Dr. William Theodore Richards, assistant professor of chemistry, Princeton University: Studies in the application to surface phenomena of the methods of statistics and quantum mechanics; research in certain European laboratories.

Dr. Oliver Reynolds Wulf, physical chemist, U. S. Department of Agriculture, Washington, D. C.: An experimental and theoretical study of the relation between the structure of the electronic states of the nitrogen molecule and the ability of this molecule to interact with other simple molecular species such as oxygen and hydrogen atoms; and a spectrographic study of a possible source of the green auroral line of oxygen in the light of the night sky; in certain European laboratories.

The following named scholars from Argentina, Chile, Cuba, Porto Rico and Mexico have been appointed to Latin-American exchange fellowships of the Foundation:

FELLOWS FROM ARGENTINA

Sr. Tomás Leandro Marini, chief of the division of fisheries and pisciculture of the Argentine Department of Agriculture: Studies in the fields of marine biology, oceanography and pisciculture in the United States.

Sr. Angel Guido, civil engineer and architect, professor of the history of architecture in the Universidad Nacional del Litoral, Rosario: Studies in the fields of architecture and city planning in the United States.

Sr. Nicanor Alurralde, civil engineer, Argentine State railway engineer: Studies of problems of railway engineering in the United States.

Sr. Julio Fingerit, author, inspector of secondary, normal and special schools of the Ministry of Public Instruction: Studies of contemporary literature of the United States.

FROM CHILE

Sr. Fernando Devilat Rocca, professor in the department of architecture of the Catholic University of Chile, and architect to the Board of Public Charities of Chile: Studies of the architecture of hospitals, and the organization of hospital services in the United States.

Srta. Aida Laso Correa, professor of civil government in the Academy of Fine Arts of the University of Chile, and in the Teachers' Lyceum of Santiago: Studies in the organization of educational guidance and students' welfare in certain universities of the United States.

Dr. Manuel Elgueta Guérin, first assistant of the genetics division; Experimental Station of the National Society of Agriculture of Chile: Studies in theoretical genetics and in the application of genetics to the improvement of plants, at the University of California.

FROM CUBA

Dr. Carlos Guillermo Aguayo, assistant professor of biology and zoology, University of Havana: Taxonomic studies in the fields of malacology and entomology, at Harvard University.

Dr. Herminio Portell Vilá, instructor in Cuban history, University of Havana: Studies in the historical relationship between Cuba and the United States, in particular the question of annexation, in the Library of Congress and the Archives of the State Department.

FROM PORTO RICO

Mr. José A. B. Nolla, former assistant plant pathologist of the Porto Rico Insular Experiment Station: Continuation of studies on the inheritance of disease resistance in tobacco, at the University of Wisconsin and University of California.

FROM MEXICO

Professor Moisés Sáenz, educator, Mexico City: Study of indigenous groups in the southwestern part of the United States with especial reference to educational problems and procedures as part of a larger study of the problem of cultural incorporation of the Indian in the Americas. Professor Sáenz is one of the best known leaders of what has been termed the "educational renaissance" in Mexico.

Dr. Donato G. Alarcón, practicing physician, Tampico, Mexico: Studies of the clinical practice and treatment of tuberculosis and of the methods of procedure in anti-tuberculosis public health campaigns, in the United States.

Ing. Francisco G. Mootezuma, civil engineer, Mexico City: Studies of the theory and practice of water supply engineering with especial reference to the disposition of sewage.

Sr. Enrique Beltrán, biologist, Mexico City: Studies in marine biology with especial reference to the Gulf of Mexico, in the United States.

Dr. Juan Farill y Solares, practicing physician, Mexico City: Study of the clinical theory and practice of orthopaedics with especial reference to the non-surgical treatment of deformities in children.

The Committee of Selection in Argentina consisted of Dr. Alfredo Colmo, president of the Argentine-North American Cultural Institute; Dr. Carlos M. Mayer, lawyer, president of the Argentine Telephone Company; Dr. Alejandro E. Bunge, professor of economics in the University of Buenos Aires; Dr. Pedro Chutro, professor of clinical surgery in the College of Medicine of the University of Buenos Aires, and Dr.

Angel Gallardo, ex-minister of foreign affairs, and ex-ambassador to Italy of the Argentine Republic. The secretary of the Committee of Selection in Argentina is Dr. Enrique Gil, a lawyer of Buenos Aires.

The Committee of Selection in Chile consisted of Señor Don Manuel Foster Recabarren, professor of international law in the Catholic University of Chile, ex-minister of war; Ing. Ramon Salas Edwards, professor of mathematics both in the University of Chile and the Catholic University of Chile, Señor Don Carlos Vildósola, editor of the newspaper *El Mecurio* of Santiago; Dr. Lucas Sierra, professor of clinical surgery in the University of Chile; Señor Don Guillermo Subercaseaux Perez, head of the statistical department of the Central Bank of Chile, professor of political economy in the University of Chile; Dr. W. C. Culbertson, ambassador of the United States in Chile. Mr. Manuel G. Hidalgo, a Chilean engineer, is secretary of the Committee of Selection in Chile.

The Committee of Selection in Mexico consisted of Ing. Javier Sánchez Mejorada, president of the National Railways of Mexico; Arq. Carlos Contreras, head of the department of national planning in the ministry of communications and public works; Lic. Fernando González Roa, commissioner for Mexico on the special Mexican-American claims commission; Dr. Roberto Medellin, head of the Central Laboratory, department of public health; Lic. Luis Cabrera, lawyer and one-time Minister of Public Finance for Mexico. Dr. Eyler N. Simpson is secretary of the Committee of Selection in Mexico.

The Committee of Selection for the fellowships for Cuba and Porto Rico consisted of President Frank Aydelotte, of Swarthmore College; Dr. Harry T. Collings, professor of commerce, Wharton School, University of Pennsylvania; Dr. Elmer Drew Merrill, director of the New York Botanical Garden, and Dr. Richard P. Strong, professor of tropical medicine in the Harvard University School of Medicine.

EDUCATIONAL RESEARCH AND STATISTICS

EXTRA-CURRICULAR ACTIVITIES OF COLLEGE STUDENTS

Some years ago the writer made a detailed study of extra-curricular activities at the University of Minnesota.[1] Later he made a survey of extra-curricular activities at Wittenberg College, Springfield, Ohio. In this article a comparison will be made between the activities at these two institutions.

This comparative study of extra-curricular activities is based on the extra-curricular life of 7,130 students at the University of Minnesota in 1924–25 and 962 students at Wittenberg College, in 1927–28. Questionnaires were filled out by 65 per cent. of the university students and by 95.8 per cent. of the Wittenberg College students. A detailed study was made of the 300 campus organizations at the University of Minnesota and of the 80 campus organizations at Wittenberg College.[2]

Since 1887 a total of 533 organizations had come into existence at the University of Minnesota, and 233, or 44.1 per cent., of them, had ceased to function, while at Wittenberg College 177 organizations had developed since 1891, and of this number 97, or 54.8 per cent., had become defunct. These organizations can be divided into three groups, as follows: Those that are purely local, as musical organizations, literary societies, publications and miscellaneous clubs; those that are local but receive faculty support, as oratory, debate, dramatics, departmental clubs, athletics and military organizations; and those that are supported by national organizations or are a part of the college or university organization, as fraternities, sororities, honor societies, religious organizations and student government. The percentage

[1] O. Myking Mehus, "Extra-Curricular Activities at the University of Minnesota," *Journal of Educational Sociology*, Vol. i, pp. 545–552, May, 1928.

F. Stuart Chapin and O. Myking Mehus, "Extra-Curricular Activities at the University of Minnesota," Minneapolis, The University of Minnesota Press, 1929. ix + 140 pp.

[2] For a complete summary of this study see article by Dean J. V. Breitwieser on "Extra-Curricular Activities of College Students" in "The School of Education Record of the University of North Dakota," Vol. xvii, pp. 73–94, December, 1931.

of organizations that ceased to function in each of the three groups is nearly the same at each institution. They are as follows: First group, University of Minnesota, 70.6 per cent.; Wittenberg College, 77.6 per cent.; second groups, University of Minnesota, 43.5 per cent.; Wittenberg College, 47.9 per cent.; third group, University of Minnesota, 23.8 per cent,; and Wittenberg College, 20.0 per cent.

At the University of Minnesota the students have student self-government to a greater extent than do the students at Wittenberg College. The All-University Council is the congress of all the students at the university. In addition to this there are student councils for each of the colleges and student commissions for each of the classes. Another all-university organization is the Minnesota Union, which is a men's organization which sponsors a clubhouse for men. Analagous to this in many respects is the Women's Self-Government Association. It does not have its own club house, however. The two organizations at Wittenberg College that most resemble the above-named organizations are the Boost Wittenberg Association and the Women's League. These are connecting links between the whole student body and the university or college administration.

The point system has been adopted at the University of Minnesota by the All-University Council. Its purpose is to prevent over-zealous students from holding more offices than is consistent with good scholastic standing. The rules for the women are enforced by the Women's Self-Government Association, while the rules for the men are enforced by the All-University Council.

There are seven student publications on the University of Minnesota campus and three at Wittenberg College. The University of Minnesota has a Board in Control of Student Publications that elects the managing editor and business manager of each of the major publications, while at Wittenberg College they are elected by the staff members.

Oratory, debate and dramatics are strong in both institutions and are closely connected with the regular class work in these fields. There are ten literary societies at the University of Minnesota and only one at Wittenberg College. The musical organizations at each institution are coming more and more under the control of the music faculties, and academic credit is being given for the work done. In other words, oratory, debate, dramatics and music are gradually losing their extra-curricular standing and are becoming more and more a part of the regular curriculum.

There are 24 departmental clubs at the University of Minnesota and five at Wittenberg College. The function of these clubs is the same at each institution—namely, to bring together students and faculty in a less formal atmosphere than is found in the average classroom and to make them better acquainted through social intercourse.

The religious side of the students' life at the University of Minnesota is given stimulus through 17 organizations supported by churches near the campus. Four of these organizations are found on the Wittenberg campus. The religious life is emphasized in certain required courses in religion at Wittenberg College, which can not be given in a state university. Hence the extra-curricular religious organizations play a very important rôle in the religious life of the University of Minnesota students.

Athletics loom large in the life of the students at both institutions. There are 14 athletic organizations and 20 kinds of sports at the university, while there are 2 athletic organizations and 10 different sports at Wittenberg College. At each institution football is the main sport, with basketball second. Each is fully equipped with a stadium and a field house for all forms of athletics at a cost of $750,000 at the university and $100,000 at Wittenberg College. The field house at the university was completed in 1928 and cost $600,000, while the new gymnasium completed at Wittenberg College in 1930 cost $400,000.

There are 36 academic fraternities and 31 professional fraternities at the university and 8 academic fraternities at Wittenberg College. There are 21 academic sororities and 8 professional sororities at the university and 8 academic sororities at Wittenberg College. There are 40 honorary and semi-honorary societies at the university and 12 such organizations at Wittenberg College (8 of them are called professional fraternities, but they are in reality semi-honorary groups). The average membership in the academic fraternities and sororities at each institution is between 30 and 35. The deferred rushing rule is enforced for fraternities at the university. This means that no student can be pledged to a fraternity until after his second term in residence at the university. There is no such rule at Wittenberg College. There is an Inter-Fraternity Council and a Pan-Hellenic Council at each institution. These are organizations whose memberships are made up of representatives from fraternities and sororities, respectively.

At the University of Minnesota the fraternity initiation fee ranges from $50.00 to $100.00. The average dues are about $3.00 a month. Board costs about $1.00 a day and room at a fraternity house about $10.00 a month. Four parties are held each year, of which one is a formal party. The formal party costs each member about $10.00, while the informal parties cost about $4.00 for each member. At Wittenberg College the initiation fees range from $35.00 to $90.00. Pledge dues run from one dollar to three dollars a month, while actives' dues run from $3.00 to $6.00 a month. Room rent varies from $2.50 to $3.50 a week, while board varies from $5.00 to $7.00 a week. Each fraternity is entitled to eight dances during the college year—one formal dance, one semi-formal and six "drop-ins" or informal dances given at the chapter house. On an average semi-formal dances cost $150, while the formal dances cost more. The custom of giving favors at dances is forbidden at Wittenberg College.

It costs a girl at the University of Minnesota $150 more to belong to a sorority than not to belong. The initiation fee ranges from $35.00 to $60.00. Board costs $1.00 a day and room $10.00 a month. Dress, however, is an important item of expense of a sorority girl. Every sorority is allowed two functions each quarter, but only one of these is formal. At Wittenberg College sorority expenses for members living in sorority houses vary from $35.00 to $46.00 per month. The expenses for a non-resident member range from $3.00 to $9.00 per month. This is exclusive of dances and other social functions. The cost of the dances ranges from $30.00 to $125.00. The initiation fee varies from $15.00 to $60.00.

The above figures seem to indicate that the initiation fees for both fraternities and sororities are slightly higher at the university than at Wittenberg College. Living expenses at fraternity or sorority houses are about the same at each institution, while formal and informal parties seem to cost more at the university than at Wittenberg College.

Any fraternity at the university that fails to maintain a "C" average will be placed on probation. If sufficient improvement is not shown at the end of the year, the administration will refer the matter to the national chapter of the delinquent organization. The scholarship rule pertaining to sororities provides that no chapter shall initiate any girl (freshman or upper classman) until she has received an average of "C" in all her work for the entire quarter at the university immediately preceding initiation. At Wittenberg College a student must have an average grade of "C" for the semester preceding his initiation before he can become a member of a fraternity or sorority.

The honorary and semi-honorary societies play an important rôle in each institution in stimulating students to do superior class work. In many cases it seems that a student has reached the height of his ambition when he is privileged to wear the emblem of certain honorary fraternities.

There are 29 extra-curricular organizations at the University of Minnesota and nine at Wittenberg College that can not be classified under any of the above groups and therefore they are classified as "miscellaneous." Most of these are societies that are purely social in their nature.

O. Myking Mehus

Northwest Missouri
State Teachers College

NEW BOOKS IN EDUCATION

Adams, Sir John. *The Teacher's Many Parts.* Pp. 351. Ivan Deach, Los Angeles.

Cattell, J. McKeen. *Leaders in Education: A Biographical Directory.* Pp. vi + 1037. The Science Press. $10.00.

La Révision des Manuels Scolaires. Pp. xvi + 224. Société des Nations Institut International de Coopération Intellectuelle, Paris.

Monroe, Marion. *Children Who Can Not Read.* Pp. xvi + 205. 47 figures. University of Chicago Press. $2.50.

O'Hara, Elizabeth F. *From Hunters to Herdsmen.* Pp. viii + 67. Illustrated by Kate Seredy. Macmillan. $.60.

Theisen, W. W. and Sterling A. Leonard. *Real Life Stories: Open Spaces.* Pp. xii + 378. Illustrated by E. A. Furman. Macmillan. $.84.

SCHOOL AND SOCIETY

EDITED BY J. McKEEN CATTELL

WITH WHICH IS COMBINED THE

EDUCATIONAL REVIEW

EDITED BY WILLIAM McANDREW

Volume 35 — SATURDAY, APRIL 30, 1932 — Number 905

TEACHER-TRAINING AND THE LIBERAL COLLEGE[1]

By Dr. THOMAS ELIOT BENNER

PROFESSOR OF EDUCATION AND DEAN OF THE COLLEGE OF EDUCATION OF THE UNIVERSITY OF ILLINOIS

FROM its earliest history, the American liberal college has been a teacher-training institution. It is a teacher-training institution to-day,—*the* teacher-training institution, as far as the preparation of high-school teachers is concerned. The only important exceptions are the independent teachers colleges whose development during recent years has been so extraordinarily rapid.

It is hard to understand why throughout its life the liberal college has so consistently declined to face frankly the importance of this function or to make adjustments to it. In general, those adjustments which have taken place have been made under protest and are due to pressure from state departments of education or accrediting agencies and from the competition of the teachers colleges. It must be confessed, in defense of the liberal college, that the changes which have been imposed have not always been statesmanlike.

In the universities, it has become the custom to refer to the college of education as the teacher-training organization, in spite of the fact that only about one fifth of the prospective high-school teacher's total program is taken within the college, while four fifths, in the case of the majority of students, are commonly taken in the college of liberal arts, according to the data which are being gathered for the National Survey of the Education of Teachers, now in progress. This usage has tended to prevent recognition in the universities that the most serious problems of teacher-training for the secondary schools of the United States are problems growing out of deficiencies in the programs of liberal arts colleges.

In the training of a prospective high-school teacher three objectives must be kept carefully in mind. The first of these may be identified by the unsatisfactory phrase, "general culture." It is what President Glenn Frank had in mind when in an address in this city two days ago he spoke of "socializing the student." The second objective may be described as specialization, which President Frank in the same address characterized as "scholarizing the student." The third objective and the only one at all adequately within the control of the college or department of education may be characterized as professional.

In referring to "general culture" as the

[1] Address given at the Conference on Teacher Training, held on the occasion of the opening of the Graduate Education Building of the University of Chicago, on March 14, 1932.

first objective, it is recognized that the term is so vague as to be almost meaningless. Even in this group it would be almost impossible to secure agreement as to what the words imply. In spite of that fact, it may be said that "general culture" is one of the principal ends sought in the program of secondary education, including that continuation of secondary education which occurs on the college level.

Some years ago an Eastern college for women considered the desirability of admitting home economics to its curriculum. The faculty were in general agreement that no subjects should be offered which were not in keeping with the nature of a liberal college. They accordingly agreed that home economics should not be admitted unless it could justify itself on the ground of cultural value, their theory being that a liberal college is an institution solely interested in the development of cultural values among its students.

The use of the phrase "cultural value" was satisfactory until attempts were made to apply it to the problem in hand. It was then found that there was no agreement as to the interpretation of these words. For weeks the committee worked faithfully on the problem of devising a definition which would be satisfactory, and after many hours of reading and discussion finally discovered in Aristotle the suggestion of an interpretation of the phrase which was acceptable to the group. As a result of their deliberations, they proposed to the faculty that a subject might be rated for cultural value in terms of its "saturation point for theory." Ditch digging, they pointed out, has a low saturation point for theory and, therefore, a low cultural value. Chemistry, on the other hand, with its high saturation point for theory would be rated as of high cultural value. On this basis, it is clear that much closer agreement could be reached as to the placing of the several subjects commonly found in a home economics department on a scale of cultural values.

It is to be doubted whether this definition of general culture would be satisfactory to most of those who have been giving consideration to this problem in recent years. They would find in it a tendency to confuse culture with what may be called discipline; and the things connoted by the two words can scarcely be said to be the same.

Perhaps a better description of the general atmosphere suggested by the phrase, "general culture," is to be found in President Frank's "socialization." Others have called it "social intelligence." A crude but slightly more elaborate definition is the following: "An understanding of the nature of the more important problems which have confronted man and mankind, of the attempts which have been made to find solutions, of the ways in which these solutions have succeeded or failed and the principal reasons for these successes and failures, plus an understanding of the points at which the individual may hope to make his contribution to the discovery of better solutions."

If such a definition of general culture as an objective in teacher-training be accepted as indicating one of the important qualifications of the secondary school teacher, at once a number of corollaries appear. The first of these is that the development of this socialized individual calls for a different type of program in the secondary school and in the liberal college than is usually found in these institutions. It becomes almost an impertinence to mention this commonplace within the walls of the University of Chicago, where the question is receiving such outstanding consideration.

Perhaps one of the obstacles to the ready acceptance of the types of programs implied in this fundamental objective of a liberal education grows out of the fact that there has been an instinctive recognition by college faculty members that its successful attainment does not require as high an intelligence level in the student as is necessary for his "scholarization." Hence, there has been a tendency in liberal colleges to regard any concessions in this direction as undesirable in view of the fact that they result in the setting up of programs which are "soft." Courses directed toward this end are thought of as not meeting college standards, not because they do not offer enough to occupy the interest and capacity of the ablest student to the limits of his abilities, but because the student of more limited abilities does not so conspicuously fail to profit by them that he can be lightheartedly thrust into outer darkness as can so easily be done in the case of the usual college offering.

Perhaps there may be agreement from this group that this offers no excuse for the failure of the liberal college to provide for socialization. The University of Chicago has recognized the situation and provided for tests intended to determine which members of the group who have had access to the benefits of the program of socialization have also the additional qualifications which make them promising candidates for the process of "scholarization." The program under discussion at the University of Minnesota has in mind the same problem.

A second corollary of the general culture objective in teacher-training is that there must be a faculty group in the liberal college selected specifically with this end in view. After selection, the qualities desired must be encouraged and developed by suitable recognition in the form of promotions in salary and rank.

This consideration suggests, in turn, a third corollary: The liberal college, or at least that portion of the liberal college which has as its primary objective the advancement of general culture, must be organized in such a form as to give appropriate independence from those other branches of the college or university whose primary interest is in "scholarization." The failure of the American liberal college to adapt itself to the almost desperate needs of the twentieth century may be attributed in no small degree to an administrative set-up under which each faculty member belongs to a department whose head is primarily interested in scholarship and who, therefore, tends to rate all members of his department in terms of the degree of their devotion to specialization. The research point of view which is so vital to both college and university has been permitted to control not only in the areas appropriate to it but also in those areas in which it should be the servant and not the master.

In brief, the first of the three suggested objectives of teacher-training, general culture, though a vital part of the preparation of a good high-school teacher, is at the present time being attained only accidentally, if at all, in the vast majority of teacher-training institutions in this country. The task is the task of the American liberal college. Except in the independent teachers colleges it can not be solved unless the American liberal college faces its failures in this respect frankly; and even in the teachers colleges it can not be done till accrediting agencies cease their efforts to force these institutions into the traditional liberal college pattern.

The second objective in teacher-training for the high-school level has been identified as specialization, or "scholarization." In one of his reports as dean of the graduate school of Columbia University, Professor Woodridge pointed out that in the earlier stages of the program of higher education interest is focused primarily on the question, "What changes can this program effect in the student?" These changes, it has been suggested, should aim to give him a background of general culture. At a later stage, he continues, the emphasis may be better expressed by the question, "How successfully can this student adjust himself to the demands of a field of learning?"

The transition from the first emphasis to the second takes place presumably within the period traditionally occupied by the four-year liberal college. Ideally, there should be no sharp break. On the lower levels, at least, there will certainly be courses which point toward specialization but which still contain a large measure of the general culture objective.

It will serve, nevertheless, to define what is meant here by specialization if it be called that part of the liberal college program which concerns itself with the success of the student in conforming to the demands of the field or fields of knowledge to which he chooses to devote the greater part of his attention. The prospective teacher of high-school English, for example, must not only have a background of general culture but must also have specialized training in the field which he is to teach. In other words, he must have submitted to a respectable part of the discipline imposed by that area of knowledge.

It will be conceded perhaps that the liberal college has been more successful in the performance of its teacher-training function in this area than in the general culture area. Yet the fact remains that woeful deficiencies still exist.

Preliminary reports of the data collected by the National Survey of the Education of Teachers indicate that among 57 colleges and universities, selected as representing better practices, there were to be found in the major subjects of prospective teachers of English only two courses taken by as many as 20 per cent. of the group. These were the required freshman composition and rhetoric, taken by 91.2 per cent., and a course in English literature, taken by 66.7 per cent. Next in frequency came a course in American literature, taken by 17.5 per cent.

Here, certainly, is no evidence of agreement among liberal colleges as to what constitutes the nature of that specialization, or "scholarization," which is the appropriate equipment of the prospective teacher of high-school English. The special training of such teachers is sufficiently like the training which will best serve as a foundation for graduate study to suggest that the liberal college, despite its domination by the graduate school point of view, is not even making its proper contribution to the very group in whose special interests it is now conducted.

Greater agreement seems to exist as to what constitutes the core of specialization in the physical sciences, mathematics, Latin and Greek than in the social studies and the biological sciences. This is peculiarly unfortunate. If it be agreed that it is of vital importance that the American high school in the revision of its program move in the direction of greater socialization, certainly one measure of the effectiveness of the training of prospective high-school teachers is the extent to which they have been prepared to participate in movements away from excessive formalization and subject-matter isolation toward reinterpretations of the traditional subjects in terms of great human problems which clamor for attention in the world of to-day. How can it be hoped that this need will be met until the social studies and the biological sciences define more successfully what should constitute undergraduate specialization in these fields and cooperate in programs making it possible?

At a great state university in the Middle West which has been conducting a testing program in the high schools of the state, it was found recently that high-school students scored higher on history tests built around the courses offered in the secondary schools than did history majors in the university in their senior year. In an effort to discover some of the possible reasons for this, a check-up was made in another Mid-western state unversity of the nature of the programs of students about to graduate whose majors were in the field of history. This check-up, based on a systematic sampling of the group, revealed that the programs of these samples contained only four courses which were taken by at least 50 per cent. of the group. These consisted of an introductory course in the history of the United States continuing through two semesters, taken by 80 per cent. of the group; an introductory course in modern European history, continuing for two semesters, taken by 70 per cent. of the group; a course in the teaching of history, taken for one semester by 70 per cent. of the group; and a course in English history to 1700, continuing for one semester, taken by 50 per cent. of the group. The programs of ten of these students contained a total of 40 different semester courses in history, of which the four already mentioned, totaling six semesters, represent all which were taken by as much as 50 per cent.

Only two semesters of instruction in United States history were found to be common to the programs of as much as 50 per cent. of this group. These consisted of a first semester of an introductory course in the history of the United States, taken by 90 per cent., and the second semester of the same course, taken by 80 per cent. The median number of semester courses in United States history taken by this group of prospective history teachers in the secondary schools was three.

These data suggest in the case of the training of prospective teachers of history serious failure to define objectives, in the case at least of the liberal colleges of the universities in question. Preliminary data from the National Survey of the Education of Teachers would indicate that this situation does not differ largely from that to be found among the rank and file of American liberal colleges.

Here, then, is a suggestion that the second of the objectives under discussion, that of specialization, is not being satisfactorily attained by the American liberal college. From this it follows that at this point also the quality of the secondary school teachers trained in these institutions is suffering.

A further examination of the data would reveal rather clearly that this deficiency goes even further and offers complete explanation of the inability of the vast majority of American secondary school teachers to participate effectively in bringing about the long-recognized and badly needed modifications of the traditional program of secondary education. The nature of the specialized training which has been given is neither such as to make these teachers sufficiently competent in the traditional subject-matter fields nor such as to give them the breadth of outlook necessary, if the barriers between some of these related fields are to be broken down in the interests of the socialization of the secondary school program.

This deficiency of the teacher-training program is one which must be met by the liberal college. However great the interest of the university college of education in an improvement of the situation, it can at best do nothing more than help to stimulate consideration of the problem by the liberal arts faculty.

As to the third objective of the teacher-training program, that of "professionalization," there will be made here only one or two generalizations concerning relationships to the two preceding aspects of teacher-training which have already been discussed. Preliminary data from the National Survey of the Education of Teachers indicate that in 57 colleges and universities selected as representing better practices, the median number of semester credits prescribed in education is 25.5. The range is from 18 to 34 semester hours. The question may be properly asked whether this does not perhaps represent a greater proportion of the four-year undergraduate program than is needed for accomplishing that degree of professionalization which may be considered a reasonable objective.

In view of the acute problems which have been presented growing out of the failure of the liberal college successfully to accomplish the two objectives in its charge—general culture and specialization—could not the university college of education better attain the ends to which it is dedicated by redefining and further concentrating its undergraduate professional offering and devoting its attention much more energetically to stimulating the development of a liberal college program more conscientiously and more intelligently focused on the "socialization" and "scholarization" of its students?

The liberal college is greatly disturbed by the inroads being made on its enrolment by the growing number of teachers colleges throughout the country. It has reason to be afraid. In the teachers college is found the opportunity to focus attention on the three objectives which have been presented here. A faculty can be selected with these objectives definitely in mind. The promotion of individual faculty members in both salary and rank can be based on the success with which they contribute to the cooperative program aimed at the attainment of these objectives. In such an institution, it should be possible more effectively to attain not merely the objective of professionalization but also the objectives of general culture and of specialization than in most of the liberal colleges as they are now organized and oriented.

The teachers colleges are too new and too handicapped by traditions of an earlier period and by the exactions of standardizing agencies which have sought to make them over in the image of the decadent liberal college to make it reasonable to expect that they should yet have attained a satisfactory level of efficiency in these respects. If they do not make the mistake of taking over the typical university graduate school and permitting it to dominate the undergraduate program, as has been the case in the university colleges, it is not too rash to predict, however, that within the next ten years the outstanding institutions of liberal education in the United States may be teachers colleges.

Unity of control and unity of objective are the features which suggest the reasonableness of this prediction. The same unity of control and of objective must in some way be secured for the teacher-training program in the university. It is not to be hoped that this will come about by placing this program under the entire direction of the university college of education. It must come about by placing it under the direction of the university liberal college. This implies the gradual reeducation and the gradual liberation of that college for the performance of the services which are the primary reasons for its existence.

When the day shall have arrived that the liberal college in this country is successfully focusing its attention on the development of a background of general culture for its student body and the erection upon this foundation of a program of well-considered specialization for those competent to avail themselves of its facilities, the faculty in education will find the problem of developing a professional point of view greatly simplified and the present excuses for maintaining a separate undergraduate college of education no longer in existence. The most pressing problems of teacher-training for the high-school level in the United States at the present time are problems of the reorganization of the American liberal college.

INVENTION AND THE MAP

By Professor H. G. GOOD
OHIO STATE UNIVERSITY

As a painting reflects the ideals, feelings and technical skill of its period, so a map reveals the knowledge, intelligence and mechanical ability of its date. And maps are also documents as well as historical remains. Besides reflecting the general intelligence of their periods they furnish concrete information about the changes on the earth's surface made by man and by nature. An old map of a city being placed in comparison with newer ones will show changes in the population area; how early given streets were laid out; what fortifications existed and countless other details. From both of these standpoints, as remains and as documents, the history of maps and of map-making is a rich but uncultivated field. There are indeed many histories of maps, of globes and of the art used in their construction, but they have nearly all been written by collectors, antiquarians and bibliographers, not by historians. Old maps are rare and curious and our rather idle curiosity has gotten the better of more serious scholarly and practical interests. Turning for a moment to school-maps, the Germans have paid some attention to the history of these, but perhaps there is not even in German a study which tries to see the history of the map as an example and an index of the increasing powers and the diversified techniques of the school. The school can accomplish or even attempt only those aims for which it has the equipment, and as the equipment develops, the possibility at least of a new and more versatile school emerges. This equipment consists far less of buildings than of books, including dictionaries of which previous articles have spoken,[1] of laboratories, of shops, of paintings and of all kinds of instructional material. This material under the control of personalities and ideas has created the school as we know it. The map as a portion of the equipment which has transformed the bare and barren school of an older time to the rich school of to-day is the theme of the present article.

Maps, like so many other things of permanent importance, had their beginnings in prehistorical times. (So Freeman thought he saw the germ of the English Parliament in the folkmoots of the forests of Germany. Or is it only that the search for origins is a necessary fact in our mental history and the concept of origin a Kantian category?) Almost all primitive peoples make maps; each regards its own position and area as the center of the earth's surface; and these ancient drawings very often are attempts to grasp the known and the imagined world as a whole—another interesting fact in our mental history. On this side, geography with its maps is like the other sciences, an offshoot from philosophy. On the other side of its two-fold stem, the map has descended from the bit by bit observations of ancient travelers, warriors and sailors. These map-makers, unlike the former, cared little about the whole and the remote, but wished to plot the material things of every day, reef and rock, harbor and road. We may label the former of these approaches to a picturing of the earth the cosmographical, and the latter, the exploratory; both are necessary but not until modern times were they united in the making of accurate maps, correct in their own details and in their relations to the rest of the world.

There are examples of earth-drawings among the remains of the Egyptians and

[1] For the previous articles in the series, see SCHOOL AND SOCIETY, 33: 815–818, June 20, 1931; and 34: 492–496, October 10, 1931.

the Babylonians,[2] some mural, some on clay-tablets and some on papyrus. The Babylonians developed a sexagesimal notation, the use of the gnomon and other scientific devices; and these were adopted by the Greeks and their Alexandrian successors, including Ptolemy; but for us of the West the history of maps begins with the Greeks. Homer's world was still a shield-like disc encircled by the mighty, ever-flowing river of ocean; and although he was thus ignorant of true geographical ideas, yet a recent writer guesses that the author of the Odyssey borrowed his information from a periplus or sailors' manual.[3]

By the sixth century ideas were changing. Pythagoras used rational arguments to establish the doctrine of a spherical earth and Aristotle scientific ones, including the circular shadow on the moon and the new constellations seen by travelers to southern lands. Eratosthenes calculated the length of a meridian arc, and his result was only about one sixteenth in error; but Posidonius meddled with his determination, decreasing the degree by one third. And this error, adopted by Ptolemy and later ages, so diminished the calculated size of the earth that the discovery of America by Columbus was made possible and actual.

Ptolemy's work as it related to map-making was that of applying astronomy to geography, using stellar observations to fix points on the earth's surface. If he did not himself draw maps, maps using his results and showing meridians and parallels were drawn. Ptolemy's "Geographia" and his "Almagest" were taken up by the Arabs, and "discovered" by Europe in the fifteenth century; in 1410, when the first Latin translation of the "Almagest" appeared, and in 1475 when it was first printed; and in 1460 when the first Latin version of the "Geographia" was printed. Later editions were supplied with sets of maps generally innocent of new observations and perpetuating the original errors.

We have been dealing so far with the work of scholars, however traditional much of it may have been; but before the era of the great discoveries which preceded and followed that of Columbus, there was another line of activity, the exploratory, which eventually came to influence map-making. The ancient world was without the compass, and ancient travelers and sailors were without the instruments or the skill necessary to take astronomical observations. What they could do and did was to compile itineraries and sailing directions or periploi. Herodotus, for example, discarded the circular disc theory, but he did not bother overmuch to substitute any other. He started from Halicarnassus in 464 B. C. to roam about the world of Egypt and Libya, back across the Nile into Palestine, down into Mesopotamia and perhaps India, north to the Caspian and Black Seas regions and through Thrace into Greece. Having returned he proceeded to describe what he had seen, and in this way became not only the "Father of History" but a geographer also. The greater part of the concrete information of the scientific Greek geographers, Eratosthenes, Marinus of Tyre, Ptolemy and others was taken from itineraries and voyages, although Ptolemy only, of all the ancient writers, it is said, alludes to seamen's charts. These, though they may have existed in numbers, have all

[2] For an early Babylonian earth-diagram see an article in the *American Anthropologist*, Vol. 26 (N. S.), 160–174, 1924. For the history of the map the reader may consult the writings of J. K. Wright, Sir H. G. Fordham, Edward Luther Stevenson and W. E. Johnson's "Mathematical Geography" (American Book Company, 1907) which has a chapter on "Map Projections," a subject on which there are several excellent little books. See also H. N. Dickson, "Maps: How they are made." (London, G. W. Bacon and Company, 1912).

[3] Victor Bérard, "Did Homer Live," London, J. M. Dent, 1931. I have not seen the book. My remark above is based upon a recent review in the London *Nation* (Aug. 15, 1931).

been lost; but several itineraries and periploi remain.

A periplus is an ancient description of a coast-line with its harbors, reefs, winds and currents. One of these mentioned by Herodotus is that of Scylax, which describes the entire circuit of the Mediterranean. "I shall begin," says the compiler, "at the Pillars of Hercules in Europe, and shall continue to the Pillars of Hercules in Libya, and to the land of the great Ethiopians." He goes on, giving distances, harbors, trading stations, locations where drinking water may be obtained, rocks and shoals and other sailors' information. Almost the whole Mediterranean coast is described in this way. Distances are usually given in sailing periods, one day's sail or a day and a night and so forth, but also frequently in stadia. Other Greek periploi have been preserved, the latest dating from the fourth or fifth Christian century. After a gap of six or seven hundred years this type of practical seaman's literature was reborn—if it had actually been extinct—in the Italian portolans. The oldest existing portolan was written in the eleventh century, and several examples have survived. They follow the general lines of the periploi but give more details.

Accompanying the portolans were the portolan charts, of which more than five hundred have been preserved. They are closely related to the revival of commerce and the introduction of the compass. They show the coast lines drawn with fidelity, have a network of compass lines, are oriented with the north at the top, are drawn roughly to scale though not always to the same scale in all parts of a chart and give place-names in great profusion. They are very much more accurate for the coast regions which they cover than the contemporary maps based upon Ptolemy.

The Romans we have omitted because they not only made no advance in map-drawing but retrogressed. The maps of the Middle Ages, "cloister maps," might also be omitted, except that they show a curious reversion to the cosmographic attitude of Homeric and pre-Homeric times. They are interesting as indications of the state of geographical ignorance at the time. Perhaps the encyclopedic and traditional character of the Medieval learning—and the loss of learning—could not be shown better than by these remains.

With the advance of discovery the major errors of Ptolemy were corrected partly through the influence of the portolan charts, more radically by the new findings of the great discoverers. At the same time printing and copper-plate engraving (1460) made possible a new technique in map production. America is first shown upon maps in the early sixteenth century, the Contarini map of 1506, the Waldsee-Müller map of 1507. Waldsee-Müller was one of the most skilful map-makers of the time and prepared a globe the map for which was printed on gores. Globes, both terrestrial and celestial, whence the old educational phrase, "instruction in the use of the globes," came in at this time, although the ancient world also had constructed a few globes. Conrad Celtes used globes (1501) to illustrate his lectures at the University of Vienna. When in the sixteenth century maps began to accumulate, Ortelius in 1570 issued the first general atlas of modern Europe and called it the Theatrum Orbis Terrarum, a theater being a display. Gerhard Kraemer or Mercator, the friend of Ortelius, built up a collection of maps which was issued under the title Atlas. Other titles for maps and collections of maps used in that period are: Speculum, Prospect, Tabula, Type, Geographia, Cosmographia, Chorographia and Charta. Most of these picturesque titles have been eliminated, and only three terms, Map, Atlas and Chart, for a sea-map, retained.

By the invention and improvement of instruments and methods for observing, measuring and engraving modern maps have been greatly developed. This included on the one hand such mathematical work as the development of new projections and on the other the use of aerial photography which was effectively applied during the war. Modern equipment has made possible the accurate determination of location, distance, orientation, direction, elevation and other factors. Together with the general development of geography and of science at large, it has led almost in our generation to the project of an international map of the world, the *Carte du Monde au Millionieme.* Originating in the Congress at Berne in 1891, it has by successive steps become a world undertaking. When compiled on its uniform scale of one millionth of nature, it will enable schools to do away with some of the misunderstandings which arise from the use of maps drawn to many different scales.

Immediately upon the rise of modern geography in the sixteenth century educational writers began to insist upon its educational value, but it required several centuries for the subject to separate itself from its medieval matrix, geometry, and to attain an independent life of its own. The humanists considered it useful chiefly for the understanding of classical writers, and by them authors were recommended because they were filled with curious information, singular adventures or interesting descriptions of out-of-the-way places. So great a man as Erasmus, for example, had no inkling of the meaning of a science of geography and, of course, no appreciation of its educational value as science. Vives did a little better and was conscious of "the recent discoveries in the East and West from the Navigation of our people." Social realism had its vogue in the sixteenth century, and geography is mentioned as a proper study for gentlemen and the globes are considered necessary equipment by writers of that school. Elyot shows some appreciation of geography as a science in process of becoming exact. Locke makes much of a formal use of map and globe, but has no hint of an appeal to nature. It was the mathematical aspects of geography that Locke most stressed. If he appealed to the sense of sight he directed the pupils' eyes only to maps and globes and not to things. The *Heimat-Kunde* he did not envisage. That was left for Rousseau, Salzmann and the nineteenth century.

There were very few elementary textbooks in geography until well into the eighteenth century, and those were poorly supplied with maps—or not at all. The early geography texts, European and American, were of the encyclopedic type, an inheritance from the medieval compendia. Jedidiah Morse prepared his "Geography Made Easy" in 1783, and six years later his "American Universal Geography," which in some editions reached fifteen hundred pages. These and the other books of this period, unaffected by the rising "natural method," all have the same encyclopedic, useful-information, question-and-answer character, rag-bags of historical-statistical details, the Germans call them. The reader may consult the report of the subcommittee conducting the annual examination of the grammar schools of Boston in 1845 for an illustration of the formal geography teaching in the schools of a large city at the late date indicated.[4] Doubtless similar practises still persist. Books and maps are better to-day, but they may still be unintelligently used.

Meanwhile a new conception of elementary geography based upon *Heimat-Kunde* and map-making was developing. Rous-

[4] O. W. Caldwell and S. A. Courtis, "Then and Now in Education, 1843–1923." Yonkers, N. Y., World Book Co., 1924. See pp. 185–190, 255–259 and the index.

seau may at this point as at so many others have been anticipated, faintly by the Franckean school and the Englishman, Hezekiah Woodward, and clearly although not completely by Comenius, who would have children in the "Mother School" learn and see what a field is, what a mountain, forest, river. Rousseau is explicit on the subject—and enthusiastic! Addressing his imaginary tutor of an imaginary pupil on a subject that yet existed only in the author's mind, he says:

"You wish to teach this child geography and you provide him with globes, spheres and maps. What elaborate preparation! What is the use of all these symbols; why not begin by showing him the real thing so that he may at least know what you are talking about?" And they are set to watch the setting and the rising sun while Rousseau launches into a criticism of the school-use of the armillary sphere! The pupil's "geography will begin" according to him with "the town he lives in and his father's country house, then the places between them, the rivers near them, and then the sun's aspect and how to find one's way by its aid. . . . Let him make his own map, a very simple map, at first containing only two places; others may be added from time to time, as he may be able to estimate their distances and position. You see at once what a good start we have given him by making his eye his compass."[5]

Rousseau improved the analytic approach of Comenius by adding synthesis, by having the pupil study a region instead of individual items merely, by using orientation, direction and scale, by the setting of problems, and by using the conventional symbols in binding all these into an image. His immediate followers introduced these ideas into the school. Pestalozzi actually had his pupils make relief models from direct observation, although usually his geography lessons were formal in the extreme. Salzmann opened his school in 1784 and Karl Ritter, his first pupil, later the great geographer, was brought up on the principles of Rousseau. Ritter had intended to become the head master of a boys' school. Pestalozzi urged him to write an elementary geography, and long after his visit to Yverdon, Ritter wrote: "Pestalozzi knew less geography than a child in one of our primary schools, yet it was from him that I gained my chief knowledge of this science; for it was in listening to him that I first conceived the idea of the natural method."[6] Herder declared for home geography, the use of problems, illustrations and maps and the linking of geography and history. Geography and history he considered "twin sisters"—so they are, but it has been said that they need not be regarded as Siamese twins—who together teach the most useful philosophy in the world, namely, the philosophy of civilization; and Dr. Arnold saw in geography the meeting-place of history and natural science.

Gradually elementary geography developed a series of steps which may be listed somewhat as follows: *Heimat-Kunde,* with the making of plans and maps and preparation for the use of maps; physical geography in relation to plants, animals and human life and society; map-reading and map-drawing; the solution of simple problems which may lead to an understanding of factors and processes and their application to practical life. Oscar V. Peschel urged teachers to dispense with books, depending wholly upon nature and the map from which the pupils were to draw all the essential geographical knowledge. This, he said, is the method truly Socratic. It would require a good deal of travel, more than most children may command.

Thus after many centuries of work along many lines, by speculation, travel, exploration, exact measurement and surveys; by the creation of new projections; by means of printing, engraving, lithographing, coloring; by aerial photography; by the

[5] "Emile," Everyman edition, pp. 131–134.

[6] R. H. Quick, "Educational Reformers," pp. 347–8. New York, D. Appleton and Company, 1924.

development of an elaborate symbolism such as hachures, contour lines and so on; by the general progress of the sciences, the map in many kinds and for many purposes has been made available to schools. Further, the making from nature of plans and maps in the school has been made possible. Teachers have learned the use of map-making and map-reading in a scientific manner as central activities in the study of geography. By these inventions the range of school activities has been extended and the achievement of new effects has been rendered feasible; the map is a sixth sense or better a longer arm and more skilful hand; its invention has helped to make the school what it is to-day. Yet unintelligent practise continues in many places after a century and a half of scientific progress in geography, in psychology and in education, scientific progress which shows that the formal learning of boundaries, places, products and definitions is dull and intellectually sterile.

EDUCATIONAL EVENTS

WESTERN AUSTRALIAN UNIVERSITY

THE London *Times* reports that the University of Western Australia, youngest of the Australian universities, officially moved into its new quarters on their riverside site near Perth on April 13. A stately block of buildings, including the Great Hall, Senate Chamber, administrative suite, undergraduates' club rooms, and library, will be opened. Hitherto the university has been housed in what were little more than asbestos and timber shanties.

The correspondent of the *Times* writes "as the university is state-endowed, its students have, during its short life, had the privilege of attending courses free of the payment of fees. For a long time the intention had been that a new home of learning should be raised on a site set apart by the state on the banks of the Swan, but successive promises of funds from state premiers resulted in the erection of nothing but one science building. A few years ago, a windfall of nearly £600,000 came the way of the university, in the form of a bequest from the late Dr. Winthrop Hackett, a general benefactor of the state. This money enabled immediate work to be begun on the new buildings and the university's first college, which is already in use. The premises have been built by Mr. Rodney Alsopp, a Melbourne architect, in a style best described as Mediterranean, but containing also Florentine, Gothic and general Renaissance elements. The buildings are in coarse sandstone and fine Donnybrook sandstone, with small but attractive window-space. The roofs are of red Cordovan tiles. Detail, in conformity with modern taste, is slight, but colonnades of cloisters, a campanile on the Italian pattern (containing a clock which is said to be one of the largest in the southern hemisphere), and the graceful lines of the centrally-placed Senate Chamber, lend to the three-sided block dignity and harmony. The ceiling of the Great Hall has been decorated with motifs from Australian aboriginal design.

"The grounds surrounding the Great Hall extend for hundreds of acres, and are laid out in playing fields. In one part there will in future years be a Temple of Nature, formed of trees taken from the various Commonwealth States and planted in the form of a cathedral, with pines forming the columns and piers. Here it is hoped to hold services and give musical and dramatic performances."

The opening ceremony is to be performed by a member of Sir Winthrop Hackett's family.

EDUCATION IN PORTO RICO

The New York Sun gives the following details in regard to educational methods in Porto Rico taken from the last report of Governor Theodore Roosevelt.

Each school in Porto Rico is built on a small farm from five to fifteen acres in size, which is cultivated by the boys under the direction of a farmer. The crops raised are such as are profitable in the surrounding country. One third of the proceeds goes to the boys; two thirds is either sold for school funds or used in the school lunchrooms. Each boy is also encouraged to have at his home a small truck garden. These gardens are inspected by the school authorities and prizes are awarded, useful prizes, such as pigs, chickens or rabbits.

Barbering, carpentry and cobbling are included in the school training for boys. Useful articles such as chairs, tables, beds and washboards are produced in the manual training shops and nearly all school furniture is made by school children. One very comfortable house in which everything—building and furniture—was made by the children recently at a cost of approximately $250.

Girls are instructed in the home economies which are adapted to the conditions in which they live. They are taught sewing and embroidery and to prepare and serve the school lunches.

Throughout the island there has been a minimum of social contact and communication due to the extreme poverty and inaccessibility of many rural districts. For this reason school workers try to bring about more social contacts and a better understanding of practical problems by adults. Social workers of Porto Rican rural schools visit families and explain basic principles of health, sanitation and diet. In several districts three social workers have been put in charge of milk stations where they supervise the feeding of babies and children of preschool age.

There is an organized effort to make the schools social centers. Fairs and dances are held in them and exhibits of the vegetables raised in the school gardens and handiwork of the children. Adults also hear lectures in the schools on questions ranging from health to market conditions. They see moving picture films occasionally.

Education by radio is developing in Porto Rico. It is planned eventually to have a receiving set in every school and to arrange both educational and recreational programs so as to draw the vast majority of the local population to the schools.

THE VALUATION OF SCHOOL PROPERTY IN THE UNITED STATES

School property in the United States represents a total value of $6,211,327,040, according to a statement issued by the Federal Office of Education. This is the value of all property used for public elementary and secondary schools in 1930.

Between 1928 and 1930, the valuation increased from $5,486,938,599, or approximately $725,000,000. Other statistics disclose an increase in expenditure for the public elementary and secondary schools from $2,184,336,638 in 1928 to $2,320,776,036 in 1930.

The value of school property per pupil enrolled varies from $407 in New York to $72 in Georgia. States, such as New York and California, expended approximately five times as much per pupil as such states as Georgia and Mississippi. For the United States, the value of school property per pupil enrolled was $242 while expenditure per pupil enrolled in the public elementary and secondary schools was $90.38.

In 1930, 82.9 per cent. of the pupils attended school daily. Actual enrolment in the public elementary and secondary schools was 25,678,015, while those in average daily attendance numbered 21,264,886.

Public school property for elementary and secondary schools exceeds $100,000,000 in 16 American states. New York valuation is $871,000,000; Pennsylvania, $512,000,000; Illinois, $441,000,000, and California, $427,000,000. The valuation in Ohio is $409,000,000; in Michigan, $338,000,000; in New Jersey, $292,000,000, and in Massachusetts, $243,000,000. The valuation in Texas is $206,000,000, while in Connecticut, Indiana, Iowa, Minnesota, North Carolina and Wisconsin it ranges above $100,000,000.

Expenditures per pupil vary from $26.18 by Georgia to $168.81 by New York. The District of Columbia expends $156.44 per pupil, Nevada, $152.71, and New Jersey, $148.52.

Six states expend more than $100,000,000 annually on public elementary and secondary education while one, New York, spends more than $360,000,000. The states which spend more than $100,000,000 are: California, $148,000,000; Illinois, $154,000,000; Michigan, $119.000,000; New Jersey, $117,000,000; Ohio, $145,000,000, and Pennsylvania, $184,000,000.

THE SUMMER SCHOOL FOR WORKERS AT THE UNIVERSITY OF WISCONSIN

With the approval of a $2,400 budget fund for salaries and expenses approved by the regents of the University of Wisconsin at a recent meeting, preliminary plans for the 1932 summer school for workers in industry are being made. Miss Alice Shoemaker is the executive secretary of the school.

The school convenes at the same time that the university summer session opens. Started as an experiment seven years ago under the direction of Professor Don D. Lescohier, it rapidly proved a success. The school is designed to give workers in industry an insight into the world of education and its relation to industry.

Many of the students who annually enroll did not finish work in the grammar school, and only a few continued their work beyond the first year or two of high school. The school's classes are held in such subjects as English, economics, public speaking and physical education, with much attention given to discussion and group action. Open forums are held in the evenings and a student publication of compositions is put out each year during the course.

Last year 46 students were enrolled, representing 12 Wisconsin and several out-of-state cities. The students studied the political, economic, educational, social and recreational aspects of twelve Wisconsin communities as one of their projects during the course. The school also sponsored an economic conference last summer at which the subject of state and national planning was discussed from all angles.

HANDICAPPED CHILDREN

THE report on handicapped children by the White House Conference on Child Health and Protection states that there are in the United States 3,000,000 children with impaired hearing, 18,000 totally deaf; 1,000,000 with defective speech; 1,000,000 with weak or damaged hearts; 450,000 mentally retarded; 300,000 crippled; 14,000 wholly blind, and 50,000 partially blind.

The conference recommends that for every child who is blind, deaf, crippled or otherwise physically handicapped and for the child who is mentally handicapped, such measures be taken as will early discover and diagnose his handicap, provide care and treatment and so train him that he may become an asset to society rather than a liability. Expenses of these services should be borne publicly where they can not be privately met.

Of the 14,000 blind children 6,000 are being educated in public or private schools; of the 50,000 partially seeing children who should be in sight-saving classes, only one tenth are enrolled in such classes. Fewer than 20,000 deaf children out of 3,000,000 with impaired hearing in various degrees are enrolled in schools and classes for the deaf.

There are 1,000,000 school children between the ages of 5 and 18 years who are so defective in speech that they require remedial treatment and training, but only 60,000 are receiving it. One hundred thousand of the 300,000 crippled children need special attention, and of these about 12,000 are enrolled in institutions and schools.

The 1,000,000 school children who have weak or damaged hearts include 375,000 with serious heart disease, and they require special education adapted to their capabilities. Enrolled in elementary school grades are 450,000 pupils who are mentally retarded to a degree requiring special education to make the most of their possibilities, but fewer than 60,000 of these are enrolled in special classes.

The need for education of the handicapped is said to be shown further by the 500,000 individuals found in prisons, hospitals for mental diseases, almshouses and institutions for feebleminded, 70,000 persons every year admitted for the first time to hospitals for the mentally diseased and 300,000 persons every year committed to prison. These are largely the driftwood, according to the report, which has not been detected in the schoolrooms and wisely trained.

EDUCATION AND THE RADIO IN EDUCATION

THE seventh annual meeting of the American Association for Adult Education, and the second annual assembly of the National Advisory Council on Radio in Education, will be held during the week of May 16 at the Hotel Statler, Buffalo, New York. The meetings of the American Association for Adult Education will begin on Monday, May 16, and will continue through Wednesday, May 18, closing with an evening session held jointly with the Radio Council. The meetings of the council will continue through Friday, May 20.

The American Association for Adult Education will depart from previous custom in the presentation of its program. Instead of general lectures, followed by a number of round-table discussions, five of the sessions will be devoted to a single round-table each. Although the entire convention attendance will be invited to participate in the round tables, responsibility for leadership will rest upon a chairman and a "panel" of twelve individuals chosen in advance of the meeting. The chairman will outline the subject to be considered at the opening of each session, it will then be discussed by the members of the panel in the hearing of the general audience, and at the conclusion of this part of the program the audience will be given an opportunity to enter the discussion.

Subjects to be considered at the round-table meetings are social education, education for culture, education for citizenship and occupational education. The round table for Wednesday morning will take the form of a special demonstration of educational and guidance service for the unemployed, as exemplified in the program of the Employment Stabilization Institute of the University of Minnesota.

Among those taking part in these discussions are James E. Russell, Felix Warburg, John Erskine, Everett Dean Martin, Robert S. Lynd, Frederick P. Keppel and Harry A. Overstreet.

There will be one general session on Tuesday evening at which a number of addresses dealing with adult education in general will be given.

Following the joint meeting with the association on Wednesday evening, the council will devote the Thursday morning and afternoon sessions to reports from the committees responsible for the radio programs on psychology, economics, vocational guidance, labor and civics now being broadcast. The committee chairmen will discuss problems involved in devising and broadcasting various types of educational programs. The chairman of the Committee on Engineering Developments will report on the latest scientific developments in radio. Experienced librarians will suggest ways and means through which the public library may cooperate with the broadcaster offering educational programs.

The topic for the evening session will be "Broadcasting into the Schools." Miss Florence Hale, president of the National Education Association, is in charge of this meeting, and Dr. William John Cooper, U. S. Commissioner of Education, will preside.

The Friday morning session will include addresses on "The Broadcasting Station as a Community Enterprise," and "The Ultimate Control of Radio." "What the Radio can do for the Farmer and the Rural Community," "Broadcasting Abroad" and "Development of Radio Legislation" will be discussed during the afternoon session. The evening meeting will be devoted to the consideration of radio advertising from the standpoint of the broadcaster, the advertiser and the general public.

Others who will address the sessions include Cline M. Koon, U. S. Office of Education; Lyman Bryson, of the California Association for Adult Education; Senator Arthur Capper; Walton Hale Hamilton, of the Yale University Law School; William Hard, political correspondent; Carroll Dunn, director of research, Crosley, Inc., and Harold Lafount, Federal Radio Commissioner.

THE CASE OF THE EDITOR OF THE COLUMBIA SPECTATOR

On the advice of John Godfrey Saxe, counsel for Columbia University, Mr. Reed Harris, editor of the *Columbia Spectator,* was reinstated as a student of Columbia University on April 20 and immediately thereafter withdrew. Professor McKnight, who has been acting as dean in the absence of Dean Herbert E. Hawkes, issued the following statement: that Reed Harris has been reinstated as a student in Columbia College and has tendered his resignation, which has been accepted.

Dean McKnight further stated that the university authorities fully sustained Dean Hawkes in the action which he had taken as to Reed Harris and that Reed Harris's case did not come within the principle of free speech and freedom of the press, and that as to free speech and freedom of the press it is and has always been the university's policy not to discipline a student for the exercise of any rights guaranteed to him by the Federal or State Constitution.

Reed Harris voluntarily submitted to Dean Hawkes an apology in form satisfactory to the dean for Harris's letter of April 1, which precipitated the disciplinary action.

Roger N. Baldwin, director of the Civil Liberties Union, which has taken up the legal case against Columbia University, has issued the following statement:

Columbia University's reinstatement of Reed Harris, student editor, is a plain confession of error, despite its face-saving conditions. It acknowledges the overwhelming public condemnation of the expulsion of a student merely for criticizing the conduct of university affairs. Further, it states in plain terms the university's adherence to the principle of free speech and free press for students. That at least is clear gain, despite the self-conscious denial that this issue was involved.

The university's statement sustaining Dean Hawkes's expulsion of Harris when at the same time Harris is reinstated leaves us a little breathless. But face-saving does not contribute to consistency.

The university's action may be construed not only as a confession of error but as unwillingness to have the issue threshed out in the courts. While previous court decisions did not encourage hope of success, the university obviously would be embarrassed to have Harris's charges sifted in public. Nor could President Butler have relished going on the stand as a witness to explain how he applies his professed liberalism to the Harris case.

THE AMERICAN PHILOSOPHICAL SOCIETY

At the annual meeting of the American Philosophical Society, held in Philadelphia on April 21, 22 and 23, the following members were elected:

Dr. Edward Goodrich Acheson, chemist, St. Petersburg, Florida, formerly president of the Electrochemical Society.

Dr. Edward Cooke Armstrong, professor of French, Princeton University.

M. Gilbert Chinard, Department of French Literature, the Johns Hopkins University.

Dr. Ralph Erskine Cleland, professor of biology, Goucher College.

Dr. Arthur J. Dempster, professor of physics, University of Chicago.

Dr. Arnold Dresden, professor of mathematics, Swarthmore College.

Dr. Herbert Fox, professor of comparative pathology, University of Pennsylvania.

Dr. Edwin Francis Gay, professor of economic history, Harvard University.

Dr. George Lincoln Hendrickson, professor of Greek and Latin literature, Yale University.

Dr. Edwin Walter Kemmerer, professor of international finance, Princeton University.

Dr. Thomas William Lamont, New York.

Dr. Arthur Oncken Lovejoy, professor of philosophy, the Johns Hopkins University.

Dr. Elmer Drew Merrill, director of the New York Botanical Garden.

Dr. John Raymond Murlin, professor of physiology and director of the department of vital economics, University of Rochester Medical School.

Dr. Charles P. Olivier, professor of astronomy and director of the Flower Observatory, University of Pennsylvania.

Dr. Ernest Minor Patterson, professor of economics, Wharton School of Finance and Commerce, University of Pennsylvania.

Dr. Henry A. Sanders, professor of Latin, University of Michigan.

Dr. Jacob Richard Schramm, editor-in-chief of *Biological Abstracts*.

Dr. Charles P. Smyth, associate professor of chemistry, Princeton University.

Dr. Edward Lee Thorndike, professor of psychology and director of the division of psychology, Institute of Educational Research, Teachers College, Columbia University.

Dr. Richard Chace Tolman, professor of mathematical physics, California Institute of Technology.

Dr. Henry Van Peters Wilson, Kenan professor of zoology, University of North Carolina.

Dr. Sewall Wright, professor of zoology, University of Chicago.

Foreign members elected were:

Ramon y Cajal, Madrid.

Dr. William H. Collins, Canada.

Professor David Hilbert, Göttingen.

M. Emmanuel de Margerie, Paris.

Dr. Ivan Pavlov, Leningrad.

Mr. Roland S. Morris, formerly United States Ambassador to Japan, and member of the Philadelphia bar, was elected president. He succeeds Dr. Henry Norris Russell, professor of astronomy at Princeton University. Dr. James H. Breasted, of the University of Chicago; Dr. Elihu Thomson, of Lynn, Massachusetts, and Dr. Edwin G. Conklin, of Princeton University, vice-presidents; Dr. Arthur W. Goodspeed, of the University of Pennsylvania, and Dr. John A. Miller, of Swarthmore College, secretaries;

Mr. Eli Kirk Price, of Philadelphia, treasurer, and Dr. Albert P. Brubaker, curator, were reelected. Dr. Cyrus Adler, Dr. Henry H. Donaldson, Dr. Herbert S. Jennings, Mr. William L. Phelps and Dr. Heber D. Curtis were elected members of the council.

EDUCATIONAL NOTES AND NEWS

THE one hundred and fiftieth anniversary of the birth of Friedrich Froebel, founder of the kindergarten, occurred on April 21.

DR. ALFRED FRANKLIN HUGHES, for four years president of Hamline University, tendered his resignation to the board of trustees of that institution on April 7. In 1916 Dr. Hughes assumed the presidency of Evansville College and held that office until 1927, when he was elected to the presidency of Hamline University. Dr. Henry Leslie Osborn, dean of the faculty, has become acting president.

DR. E. GUY CUTSHALL, president of the Iliff School of Theology at Denver, Colorado, has been elected by the trustees of Nebraska Wesleyan University to succeed Dr. Isaac Butler Schreckengast as chancellor, the appointment to take effect on September 1. Upon his retirement Dr. Schreckengast, who has been elected chancellor emeritus, will assume the chair of Biblical literature.

DR. ROBERT N. MONTGOMERY, of Tarkio College, Missouri, to the presidency of which he was elected two years ago, will succeed his father, the late J. Knox Montgomery, as president of Muskingum College, New Concord, Ohio.

MR. J. RAYMOND ENGLE, chairman of the board of trustees, has been named acting president of Lebanon Valley College, succeeding the late Dr. George D. Gossard. Mr. Engle, who has served as chairman of the board for several years, will become president at the close of the June term.

DR. JOHN WYCKOFF, secretary of the New York University and Bellevue Hospital Medical College since 1916, has been appointed dean. He is to take office immediately. Dr. Currier McEwen, associate in medicine at the Hospital of the Rockefeller Institute for Medical Research, has been appointed assistant dean, effective on July 1. Dr. Wyckoff succeeds Dr. Samuel A. Brown. In the acceptance of Dr. Brown's resignation the council adopted a minute in appreciation of his services to the college for sixteen years as dean. Dr. Brown has been at New York University for nearly forty-two years as student, teacher and administrator.

DR. JACOB GOULD SCHURMAN, formerly president of Cornell University and later ambassador to Germany, addressed the Chicago alumni of the university at a dinner given in his honor on April 13.

DR. WILLIAM F. BLACKMAN, formerly president of Rollins College, at Winter Park, Florida, has been elected president emeritus by the board of trustees of that institution. He became president in 1902 and served for thirteen years, retiring at that time on account of ill health.

DR. ERNEST HERMANN, director of the Sargent School of Physical Education of Boston University, was elected a fellow of the American Physical Education Association at a recent meeting in Philadelphia in recognition "of distinguished service rendered our profession."

DR. HANS KURATH, of the Ohio State University, has been appointed professor of German at Brown University for the academic year 1932–33.

DR. HENRY CREMER, head of the School of Education of Rider College, Trenton, New Jersey, will be visiting professor of educational psychology during the summer session of the University of Porto Rico.

UNDER a special grant from the Carnegie Corporation, Mr. George E. Downing, of Harvard University, has been appointed assistant professor of art at Brown University for the academic year 1932–33. Mr. Downing's course is entitled "An Art Survey of European Culture."

PROFESSOR GEORGE F. BATEMAN has been placed in charge of the Schools of Engineering of Cooper Union with the title of acting dean.

Professor Bateman replaces Dean Francis M. Hartmann, who died recently after thirty years' service on the engineering faculty. Assistant Professor Norman L. Towle has been given charge of the department of electrical engineering, with the rank of full professor.

At Wesleyan University, Dr. John W. Spaeth has been advanced to a full professorship in the classics and Dr. P. A. Reynolds has been promoted to an assistant professorship in philosophy.

Dr. Edmund B. Delabarre, who has been professor of psychology at Brown University since 1896, will retire at the end of the academic year.

Professor Ambrose W. Vernon, head of the department of biography at Dartmouth College since 1924, has presented his resignation to the Board of Trustees.

Professor Pitman B. Potter, of the department of political science at the University of Wisconsin for the last twelve years, will resign at the end of the academic year to carry out research work at Geneva, Switzerland, on international relations, with particular emphasis on the League of Nations.

Mr. Arthur D. Arnold, principal of the Passaic, New Jersey, High School, has been elected superintendent of schools for a period of two years to succeed Dr. Fred S. Shepherd. The salary has been placed at $7,000 a year.

Mr. W. E. Sheffer, superintendent of the schools of Manhattan, Kansas, has arranged with the Manhattan Board of Education for a year's leave of absence and will spend the year at Teachers College, Columbia University, doing work leading to a doctor's degree. During Mr. Sheffer's absence Principal F. V. Bergman, of Manhattan High School, will serve as acting superintendent.

Mr. Clyde A. Erwin has been elected president of the North Carolina State Education Association; Mr. H. P. Harding has been elected vice-president.

Dr. H. A. Brown, formerly president of the Oshkosh State Teachers College and now president of Illinois State Normal University, at Normal, was elected president of the American Association of Teachers Colleges, at the recent annual meeting in Washington.

Miss Mildred Lincoln, visiting lecturer in guidance and personnel at Teachers College, Columbia University, has been elected president of the National Vocational Guidance Association for the ensuing year.

Mr. C. W. Pugsley, president of South Dakota State College, has accepted an invitation from the U. S. Commissioner of Education, Dr. W. J. Cooper, to serve as one of the advisers from South Dakota to the research staff of the National Survey of School Finance.

Dr. Emil L. Larson, associate professor of education in the University of Arizona, has recently been appointed by the State Board of Education to direct the work of revising the course of study for the elementary schools of the state. The State Board has designated three of its members—Dr. C. O. Case, state superintendent of schools; Superintendent C. K. Davis, Miami, and Superintendent D. M. Hibner, Ray—as a curriculum committee to cooperate with Dr. Larson.

Dr. Walter V. Bingham, director of the Personnel Research Federation of New York, will administer individual and group tests to help students to estimate their natural characteristics and abilities, in an experiment in vocational or collegiate guidance for boys which will take place from August 13 to 17 at the Engineering Camp of the Stevens Institute of Technology in northern New Jersey.

Dr. George H. Chase, John E. Hudson professor of archeology and dean of the Graduate School of Arts and Sciences at Harvard University, has been appointed a trustee of the Boston Museum of Fine Arts to represent the university.

Dr. Frank Pierrepont Graves, president of the University of the State of New York and New York State Commissioner of Education, will deliver on May 30 the commencement address at Goucher College. His subject will be "The Obligations of a College Education."

Mr. Joseph L. Wheeler, librarian of the Enoch Pratt Free Library, discussed "Books, Brains, Bricks and Boys" at a recent meeting of the Baltimore Polytechnic Parent-Teacher Association.

Mr. Hobart M. Corning, superintendent of schools, Colorado Springs, will conduct a "Practicum" at the summer school of the University of Denver. It is to be confined to school principals and assistants, and superintendents and their assistants, and will take up problems such as school building, relation of teacher and pupil, planning of diagnostic and remedial programs and economies in school administration.

At the annual conference of the Westchester County, New York, Teachers Association the speakers included Dean John W. Withers, of New York University; Dr. Harry Elmer Barnes, of New York City, and Chancellor Charles W. Flint, of Syracuse University. The following officers were elected: Mr. H. Claude Hardy, associate superintendent of schools, White Plains, *president;* Mr. O. E. Huddle, Briarcliff, *vice-president;* Miss Ethel Wood, Thornwood, *secretary,* and Charles E. Benedict, Tarrytown, *treasurer.*

Dr. Carl Leo Mees, president emeritus of the Rose Polytechnic Institute, died on April 20, at the age of seventy-nine years. Dr. Mees was professor of physics in the Rose Polytechnic Institute from 1887, becoming president in 1895 and retiring in 1919.

Dr. Roland Thaxter, emeritus professor of cryptogamic botany at Harvard University, and honorary curator of the Farlow Herbarium, died on April 22 in his seventy-fourth year.

The death is announced of Charles Ford Langworthy, chief of the Bureau of Home Economics in the U. S. Department of Agriculture. Dr. Langworthy was sixty-four years old.

Mr. John Ashhurst, librarian of the Free Library of Philadelphia for the past sixteen years, died on April 22 at the age of sixty-six years. Mr. Ashhurst was engaged for many years in circulating literature among the blind and was a director of the Pennsylvania Home Teaching Society and the Circulating Library for the Blind.

Dr. William E. A. Slaght, professor of psychology and philosophy at Cornell College, died on March 27, at the age of fifty-seven years.

Dr. J. C. Glashan, formerly inspector of public schools at Ottawa, died on March 14, at the age of eighty-eight years.

At the general meeting of the American Philosophical Society, Philadelphia, on April 21, 22 and 23, Dr. Paul Van Dyke, professor of modern European history at Princeton University, spoke on "The Human Washington."

The twentieth convention of the American Association of College Registrars opened on April 19 at the Stevens Hotel, Chicago. Professor E. J. Moulton, dean of the graduate school of Northwestern University, gave the address of welcome. Among those who spoke at the morning session were Professor I. L. Kandel, Columbia University; Dr. W. S. Learned, Carnegie Foundation for the Advancement of Teaching; Professor H. H. Armsby, Missouri School of Mines, and R. M. West, University of Minnesota. The afternoon session was devoted to sectional meetings. At the banquet on April 20 Professor George A. Works, dean of students and university examiner, spoke on the reorganization of the University of Chicago, and Dr. Joseph T. Singewald, Jr., professor of economic geology at the Johns Hopkins University, gave an illustrated lecture entitled "From Capetown to Cairo by Automobile."

The Massachusetts Teachers Federation, made up of 183 teachers' associations throughout the state with a membership of about 20,000, held its annual meeting of delegates at the Boston Chamber of Commerce Building on April 18. The business meeting was followed by a luncheon at which the speakers included Mr. Edward R. Clarke, president of the federation; Dr. Kenneth C. M. Sills, president of Bowdoin College; Dr. Payson Smith, state commissioner of education; Miss Anna C. M. Tillinghast, commissioner of immigration at Boston, and Dr. Albert E. Winship, editor of *The Journal of Education.*

The Association for Childhood Education will meet in Washington for its thirty-ninth convention from May 4 to 7. The Convention Committee is working out a program which it is believed will surpass the programs of the past in interest and educational value, on which will be speakers of nation-wide reputation. There will be an educational exhibit and ample opportunity will be offered to visit class-rooms in all sections of the city in both public and private schools, and arrangements will be made to follow up these observations by discussion.

Indiana State Teachers College, Terre Haute, Indiana, will be host for the second annual Teacher-Training Conference, on May sixth and seventh. Dr. Shelton Phelps, dean of the Graduate School of George Peabody College for Teachers at Nashville, Tennessee, will be the conference speaker. Dr. Phelps will speak at three general sessions on Friday afternoon and evening, and on Saturday morning. In addition, there will be a general session on Friday morning devoted to "A General Survey of Home Economics Conditions as Seen by the Itinerant Teacher," and a general session on Saturday morning at which the movie, "America's Teachers at Work," which was made at the Los Angeles meeting of the National Education Association, will be shown. Group sessions will be held on Friday morning, Friday afternoon and Saturday morning. The departments which will have meetings are commerce, education, English, home economics, industrial arts, Latin, physical education, Romance languages, science and social studies.

The nineteenth annual Conference on Educational Measurements was held at Indiana University on Friday and Saturday, April 22 and 23, 1932. In accordance with the custom of the last eight years the School of Education arranged for a Conference on Elementary Supervision in conjunction with the Measurements Conference.

We are informed by the National Education Association that, at the request of American friends, Dr. Max Zimpel, who spoke at the Minneapolis Convention, is arranging a hiking trip beginning on July 15 in Frankfurt, Germany, and leading from there through the Rhone Mountains to the Thuringian Forest to Weimar and from there through the Harz Mountains to the valleys of the Ruhr and the Rhine. This is in keeping with the "Goethe-Jahr," which is being celebrated in Germany during 1932. Those wishing further information may address Dr. Max Zimpel, Rektor der Hufnagel-Mittelschule, Idsteinerstrasse 47, Frankfurt, a-M., Germany.

Mrs. Prescott Lawrence has given $10,000 to Harvard University to establish the Prescott Lawrence Memorial Fund in memory of her husband on the fiftieth anniversary of his graduation from Harvard College.

A bequest of $100,000 to the trustees of Yale University is made in the will of Margaret S. Bedell, of Catskill, New York. This bequest is in memory of her brother, the late Bradbury Bedell. Miss Bedell also bequeathed $5,000 to the University of Pennsylvania and $15,000 to the Society for Ethical Culture of New York.

Through a bequest from the late Colonel Austen Colgate, Colgate University is enabled to provide eighteen competitive scholarships for men who graduate in the upper one fifth of their secondary-school classes and who are eligible for admission. One quarter of the total scholarship is awarded each year after it is won, providing the student maintains a standing in the upper one fifth of his class. The university is offering for the first time for the coming year six teaching fellowships of the value of $1,200 each for graduates who will work toward the master's degree for a period of two years.

The Virginia Legislature has accepted the offer of Judge John Barton Payne, president of the American Red Cross and a native Virginian, of a gift of $100,000 for the erection of a museum to house art works owned by the state. Judge Payne's offer is contingent on the raising of an additional $100,000 for the museum. In accepting the offer the legislature provided that in case no other suitable site was offered the museum is to be erected on the Soldiers Home property in Richmond. The governor and the art commission are authorized to accept the donation of a site, to receive contributions toward the additional $100,000, and to proceed with the erection of the museum when the necessary funds are in hand.

The Division of Publications of the National Education Association is sponsoring the second national high-school paper editorial project as a means of promoting the interpretation of education and the schools to students and the public. Editors of all high-school publications printing editorials are invited to submit some of the best editorials of the year on subjects relating to education and the schools.

Limitation of freshman enrolment to 300, seventy-five of whom are to be girls, and a total enrolment in the four-year degree courses of not more than 850, has been announced for next year by the Massachusetts State College. Mr. Robert D. Hawley, secretary, stated that on recommendation of a special committee named by President Thatcher to study the enrolment problem, the board of trustees had adopted the restrictions in view of the large number of applications for entrance in the four-year course and the impossibility, under existing appropriations, of accepting all qualified applicants. The limitation of girls was attributed to lack of suitable housing facilities. Enrolment for the four main classes last year was 756, an increase of 20 per cent., and indications are that the quota of 850 students for next year will be filled. This will mean an increase of 35 per cent. in two years.

Museum News reports that a new museum building constructed of concrete and designed to be proof against earthquakes has been erected at Corinth, Greece. It was designed by W. S. Thompson, of New York, and paid for with a $50,000 gift of an anonymous American donor. It contains reading, reception and map rooms in addition to the space for exhibits, which are to be made up of material excavated by the American School for Classical Studies at Old Corinth. The new building takes the place of a smaller one damaged by earthquake in 1928. It will be operated by the Government of Greece.

DISCUSSION

SHALL WE TAX COLLEGE PROPERTY?

IN the early years of the nation any kind of education was at a premium. There were few men of great wealth and fewer still who would use their wealth to support schools. To encourage education, each state, as it entered the union, made provisions to exempt from taxation a part, or all, of the property of charitable institutions. Frequently schools and colleges received contracts which in later years proved more or less disadvantageous to the local communities as new situations arose. The early institutions called on the local communities for little or no service. Oil lamps were used for artificial lighting, wells on the campus supplied the water, and sanitary sewerage systems received little or no attention. To-day, the community which expects to retain a thriving school must look well to its pavements, its water and sewerage systems, milk supplies and dozens of other expensive services.

Institutional expenses have soared to new high levels, as have community expenses. Although endowments have piled up, it seems that there is yet a dearth of funds. Presidents and boards of trustees spend lavishly on fine buildings, stadia and athletic fields, yet they plead inability to pay taxes on them. The business of a college, or university, according to the late Charles W. Eliot, is to spend all it can get on the educative process. Mr. Henry Pritchett, of the Carnegie Foundation, recently warned college presidents that if colleges continue to professionalize their sports and entertainments, they may expect to be called on to help share the burden of government.

To-day, we find a current of thought which takes issue with the doctrine of local tax exemptions on property of higher institutions of learning. This feeling, coming largely from business, has been intensified by the practice of these schools investing a large share of their endowment funds in property which competes with property held by business men. There are a number of cases where schools operate hotels, restaurants, pharmacies, groceries, farms, apartments and office buildings, as well as water works, laundries and small factories. Many states have enacted laws to tax such businesses, while others have been content to place the tax burden on the remaining property of the community. A few states have passed strict provisions to remedy this injustice, only to have them set aside by the judgments of courts, or interpreted in a manner to nullify their intentions.

The practice of some states of exempting the investment properties of schools has wrought havoc in local communities. For instance, about the middle of the nineteenth century the state of Tennessee gave the University of the South a charter which permitted it to possess a thousand acres of land free from taxes, both local and state. The university in due course of time erected on a part of this land classrooms, administration buildings, dormitories and other necessary edifices for the operation of an institution of learning, and divided the remainder of its holdings into lots upon which it either erected, or permitted others to erect, dwellings, business houses, hotels, *et cetera,* to the number of 300. These were leased for periods ranging from 1 to 33 years, many carrying renewal options. Suit was entered against the university on the ground that the state constitution did not contemplate such wholesale tax exemptions. The courts held in favor of the school, and the village of Sewanee was left to work out its own salvation. (University of the South *v.* Skidmore, 87 Tenn. 155, 9 S. W. 892.)

Another case at hand is that of Berea College, of Berea, Kentucky. This college has invested a large part of its wealth in local property. It owns many business houses and operates many businesses. It is in the hotel business, the city water business, the city light business, the laundry business, and owns and rents a large number of dwellings, as well as thousands of acres of land. The laws of the state of Kentucky exempt such property from taxes as long as the income from same is used for educational purposes. (Commonwealth *v.* Berea College, 149 Ky. 95, 147 S. W. 929.) As a result, a comparatively wealthy village finds it difficult to operate and maintain in an efficient manner its own enterprises, such as public schools, proper fire protection and street paving, without a subsidy from the college.

If such exemptions applied only to localities in which the institutions live, their evil effects would be somewhat limited to persons who receive some compensatory advantages. But they are of a wider range. In Trustees of Kentucky Female Orphan School *v.* City of Louisville (100 Ky. 470, 36 S. W. 921), the school, a private institution, sought relief from paying city taxes on property which it holds in Louisville as an investment. The school is located at Midway, a village some one hundred miles distant from Louisville. In rendering the decision, the highest court of the state said in part: "An exemption of an educational institution from taxation will include property held by it for rent, the income of which is used for the work of the institution, unless there are qualifying words which show, or tend to show, that only property used by the institution, or connected with it, is to be exempted." And this same doctrine was upheld in the Town of New Haven *v.* Trustees Sheffield Scientific School (59 Conn. 163, 22 Atl. 156.), when the court ruled that an exemption from taxation of the property of a college so used for the promotion of science exempts property so invested as to produce an income which is used for the purposes of the college.

The city of Nashville, Tennessee, is the home of eighteen or twenty private institutions of learning of varying grades, some of which possess large local real estate holdings. As such property in that state had been tax exempt, even when it entered into competition with taxed enterprises, the state legislature of 1899 attempted to remedy this weakness of the tax exemption clause by adding a provision that all property belonging to educational and charitable institutions, used in secular business competing with a like business having paid taxes, should be non-tax-exempt. (Acts of Tenn. 1899, p. 1084, Ch. 435, section 2, subsection 2.) But an effort on the part of the city of Nashville to collect taxes from Vanderbilt under the provision resulted in a peculiar interpretation of the law by the highest court in the state. Said the court:

> . . . it is not necessary for the property to be physically used for religious, charitable, or educational purposes, that is to say actually occupied, but that if the income and profits derived from such property are applied exclusively to the purposes aforesaid, the property is entitled to immunity from taxation.

The learned judges who in previous cases had rendered their decisions according to "the intention of the law," now reverted to an unusual type of logic to overcome the intention of the law. The decision further read:

> . . . it is obvious that two things must concur before the property of an educational institution can be taxed: (1) It must be used in secular business; and (2) it must come in competition with a like business that pays taxes to the state.

. . . no owner of property is taxed, or can be taxed, on the mere act of renting out his own property, and hence when an educational institution rents out its own property, it does not come in contact with a like business that pays taxes. . . . renting out corporate property owned by the institution is not the persuit of business, and the property is not taxable because its income is devoted to educational purposes.''

Of course the court overlooked the fact that an individual, or a corporation, is not taxed for renting out his property, but is taxed because he has rentable property.

Previous to the Vanderbilt decision the highest tribunal of the state had rendered in favor of the Methodist Episcopal Church, South, in a similar case. (Methodist Episcopal Church, South *v.* Hinton, County Trustee, 92 Tenn. 188, 21 S. W. 321.) A publishing house in Nashville, incorporated as an arm of the church for the manufacture and distribution of books disseminating knowledge of a religious nature, used its profits for the benefit of superannuated preachers. A part of the volume of business done was derived from what was termed by the defense as secular work—printing secular books, handbills, letter-heads and other job work. The court held that the publishing concern was a charitable and religious institution, devoting its income to charitable causes, and, therefore, exempt from taxes.

Cambridge has a special contract with Harvard University relative to the taxing of the university's property. Without such an agreement Cambridge found it difficult to balance her budget.

Securities held by schools and other charitable institutions are tax exempt in most of the states. Many states, however, do not exempt real property unless such is used for campus and college building purposes. This is a much fairer practice, for it permits the local governmental unit to collect taxes for its proper functions. The tax exemption clause of the Ohio law has been interpreted so that if only a fraction of a building owned by a charitable institution produces an income, the fraction must bear its part of the tax burden. (Cincinnati College *v.* State, 19 Ohio 111.)

Kenyon College (Ohio) constructed a pumping station to supply water for college purposes. In addition to this service, the station supplied water to a few citizens, for which the college received about $200 a year. The court held that the college was justified in installing a water system for its own use, and that such a plant should not be taxed if it supplied only institutional needs, but when the plant was used to supply water to citizens, a proportionate part of the plant was subject to taxation, "so long as it continues to supply water to those other than the college." (Kenyon College *v.* Schnebly, 12 O. C. C. (n. s.) 1, 21 O. C. D. 150.) There are at least a half dozen cases in Ohio decided on this principle.

There are many disadvantages in the practice of exempting from local taxes, college endowment funds invested in real property. It not infrequently pauperizes the many services which the local governments should render, and forces them to accept subventions. These subventions too often make "cat's paws" of the local leaders and thus establish a sort of college oligarchy.

The chief economic disadvantages of such exemptions have been ably set forth in the dissenting opinion in the case of the Trustees of Kentucky Female Orphan School *v.* City of Louisville cited above. According to the dissenting judge:

Such immunity would lead not only to manifold injustices in the manner of placing burdens upon the other property in a community, but would lead corporations conducting such institutions to select, for the purpose of investment, those cities and towns which had the higher tax rates, in order to benefit by the advantages thereby given in competition for tenants. For, just in proportion as the surrounding property is subjected to a greater tax, is a greater bonus given the corporations which own the exempted property, a part of which bonus they can afford to give in the shape of reduction of rent whereby to entice tenants away from the owners of surrounding property. Just in proportion to the increase of the exempted property held by such corporations in a city or town, must the tax rate become higher, and the inducement greater to such corporations to invest their surpluses there. And this leads to further injustice. The tenants of such corporations, induced to become such by a reduction of rent, are thereby enabled to undersell their neighbors, who are compelled to contribute their just proportion toward bearing the burdens of taxation placed upon the property they occupy.

In the case of Dartmouth College an entire township was exempted from "public taxation." A large part of this land was divided into lots and sold. The buyers of the lots built on them, and the town of Wheelock was born. The property holders claimed immunity to local taxation because they had bought exempted land. (Morgan *v.* Cree, 46 Vt. 773, 14 Am. Rep. 640.) The court held that the phrase "public taxes" referred to state taxes and not to local taxes. Had the decision been otherwise the burden of local government would have fallen entirely on personal property. Yet in a similar case in New Orleans, an opposite decision was rendered. (Le Franc *v.* City of New Orleans, 27 La. Ann. 188.)

When a court has once set a precedent in a tax exemption case it is pretty hard to change its view in future cases, even with new laws, as witness the Vanderbilt case in Tennessee. Then, there is always the danger of broadening the meaning the descriptive terms, charitable, religious and educational. The Kentucky court of appeals once held that a gymnastic association was an educational institution. (German Gymnastic Association *v.* City of Louisville, 117 Ky. 958, 80 S. W. 201.)

In Illinois, a Greek letter fraternity, whose members were students of the University of Chicago, owned a large fraternity house. The courts declared the fraternity an educational institution, and its property exempt from taxation. (People *v.* Omega Chapter of Phi Upsilon, 335 Ill. 317, 167 N. E. 16.)

Higher education has been considered a prime obligation of the state. On this basis the states have exempted property actually used by colleges from local and state taxes. This the local district has not resented. But many states have extended the exemption to cover any property owned by colleges the income from which is used to support the work of the colleges. This practice has sometimes brought poverty to local governmental institutions. Justice demands that real property bear its share of local governmental expenses, no matter who owns it, as long as the basis of local taxation is real property. This is true, even if the property is owned by the state. The writer has in mind a case where a wealthy coal operator donated the surface rights of a large tract of land, some 20,000 acres, to a state university. As a result the local government was deprived of the taxes thereon, and the remainder of the property felt the burden keenly.

Jay L. Chambers

Muskingum College,
New Concord, Ohio

STUDENTS IN GRADUATE SCHOOLS

I am moved to comment briefly upon Dr. B. W. Kunkel's article, "The Representation of the College in Graduate and Professional Schools," in the March 12 issue.

If the first step in the compilation of statistics is questionable, then, obviously, the findings are rather futile. The first step in this present compilation is the selection of an arbitrary group of graduate schools. Whether this selection was made up by the author, or taken from some list, its arbitrariness, in view of the nature of the findings, is patent. Students, in general, go to schools, both undergraduate and graduate, in their vicinity. It may be that the graduate school selected is not one that has ever come under the purview of the pundits, but graduate school it may be nevertheless; and we all know that the ambitious young student will get ahead or not get ahead largely upon his own native qualities, regardless of the school of his origin or of his graduate study.

Hence, on the face of things, it follows automatically that, if, for example, in the State of Pennsylvania, only one of its three outstanding graduate schools is selected, then the other two will make a poor showing. Also it follows that those small schools near the chosen graduate school will have an advantage over their fellows, who happen to be near one of the unselected graduate schools, and which, most naturally, send most of their graduates to the nearest graduate school.

Let me select just one other point, because of its apparent significance. The author says, "It is obvious that, as a group, the independent colleges making no attempt to conduct a graduate school do not send as many of their alumni to graduate schools as do the larger institutions with affiliated graduate schools."

Of course not, on the basis of these arbitrarily chosen figures. One can readily reach that conclusion without indulging in sheets of statistics. These small schools have to send their graduates away from home, and they do in large measure, but, unless they are near one of the selected graduate schools, they are out of luck. The "large institutions with affiliated graduate schools" naturally take very many of their own graduates, and, ergo, they lead the parade.

L. P. Sieg,
Dean
The Graduate School,
University of Pittsburgh

SPECIAL CORRESPONDENCE

A SEMINAR ON FAR EASTERN STUDIES AT HARVARD UNIVERSITY

A seminar on Far Eastern studies will be held this summer at Harvard University under the auspices of Harvard-Yenching Institute, the Society for the Promotion of Japanese Studies, and the committees on the Promotion of Chinese Studies and on Japanese Studies of the American Council of Learned Societies.

From this beginning, it is hoped, a widespread movement to improve instruction in this field in American colleges and universities will develop. Failure alike among scholars and the public to understand the Oriental view-point, as illustrated by the Sino-Japanese difficulties, is attributed largely to the inadequate training of American teachers.

The aim of the seminar is to bring together for the six weeks of the summer session of Harvard University a group of trained and mature scholars who, although their major training has been in other fields, find it necessary or desirable to offer instruction in the Far Eastern civilizations, either by teaching courses devoted to them or by introducing into general courses in history, philosophy, and the fine arts, appropriate consideration of the Far Eastern phases of those disciplines.

The group will meet daily, excepting Saturday, for general directed round-table discussion under the leadership of eminent specialists in Far Eastern studies, and in smaller groups for the consideration of specific problems. The discussions will attempt in some measure to provide the necessary background usually lacking when, for instance, a professor of medieval English history endeavors to give a course in Far Eastern history.

They will supplement factual information with consideration of bibliography, tools of research and instruction, criteria for differentiating fact and opinion, status of present-day research in the fundamental problems, organization of Far Eastern studies and repositories of information concerning them, and similar topics.

Arrangements will be made for special instruction in the Chinese and Japanese languages specifically designed to meet the needs of the scholars who attend. Plans are now in progress for special exhibitions at the museums in and near Boston and of private collections of Far Eastern materials.

A considerable number of special lectures, many of which will be held in the evening and will be open to the public, will be offered by authorities in Far Eastern subjects. It is possible, too, that conferences will be held on the promotion of Far Eastern studies, which will bring to Cambridge most of the scholars engaged in those studies at that time in America.

Arthur W. Hummel, chief of the Division of Chinese and Japanese Literature, Library of Congress, Washington, D. C., has been appointed professor of history and director of the seminar. Lucius C. Porter, professor of philosophy in Yenching University and visiting professor at Harvard University, will be professor of philosophy. Langdon Warner, fellow of the Fogg Art Museum for research in Asia and lecturer in the fine arts at Harvard University, will be professor of Oriental art.

There will be an especially designed course in the Chinese and Japanese languages by James F. Ware and Hideo Kishimoto, both of Harvard. Special lectures will be given by many leading scholars, including:

Edward Sapir, Yale University, on linguistics and phonetics; Kojiro Tomita and Ananda K. Coomaraswamy, Boston Museum of Fine Arts, on oriental art; Ryusaku Tsunoda, Columbia University, on Japanese civilization; Roland B. Dixon, Harvard University, on anthropology; George P. Cressey, Syracuse University, on geography; Esson M. Gale, University of California, on early economic history; Lewis Hodous, Hartford Seminary, on Buddhism; G. Nye Steiger, Simmons College; Charles S. Gardner, Newtonville, Massachusetts.

George H. Chase, of the Harvard-Yenching Institute, has been named chairman of the committee of direction of the seminar. Other members are: Fletcher S. Brockman, New York City; Kenneth S. Latourette, Yale University; Mortimer Graves, American Council of Learned Societies, Washington, D. C.

The seminar, though directed by an independent committee, will be an integral part of the summer session of Harvard University, and its members will be entitled to all the privileges of residence. Its size will be restricted so as to assure all the benefits that arise from the concentrated study of particular problems by a small group.

Financial aid for twenty seminar students of $125 each will be provided. Applications for this assistance should be made to the American Council of Learned Societies.

QUOTATIONS

INTERNATIONAL MATERNAL AND CHILD WELFARE

WHILE great difficulty would attend the task of laying down a system of rules for maternal and child care which would be equally valid in all countries, there are certain general principles which hold good everywhere and which can form the basis of a health service without regard to climate or customs of the country. It is on such broad principles that the health organization of the League of Nations has founded its report on maternal welfare and the hygiene of infants and children of pre-school age.[1] The material which forms the report is based on an analysis of the experience obtained in different countries, and on studies made by various members of the committee appointed to carry out this task.

The report is divided into three sections, under the headings of maternal welfare, infant welfare, and the health of the pre-school child, and in each section the special dangers encountered by those persons in the group are discussed before the suggestions for preventive measures are set out. The section on the health of the pre-school child seems to us to be particularly interesting, since in this country little provision is made for the care of the child between 2 and 5 years of age, with the result that children admitted to the infants' departments of elementary schools have been described as "damaged goods." The same lack is apparent in other countries, and indeed in one direction they are even less fortunate than ourselves, since elsewhere school attendance commonly becomes compulsory at the age of 6 instead of 5. Statistics for the pre-school period are generally incomplete. The morbidity is only known from the few infectious diseases which are notifiable, and mortality statistics are often misleading owing to individual variations in certification—deaths following complications of measles, for example, may be certified as due to bronchopneumonia only.

The pre-school period is a particularly critical one for the child, since it is at this time that he is most likely to encounter and contract the acute infectious fevers. The committee notes in its report that mortality in the pre-school age is still, after mortality in the first year, the highest recorded up to the age of 45 or even 50, and this appears to hold for all the countries investigated. Great emphasis is laid on the importance of preventive measures, the most effective of which depend on systematic and regular supervision of the health of the child until he comes under the care of the school doctor. Propaganda and education are necessary to make parents realize the importance of such supervision once the anxious early months of life are successfully accomplished, but the increasing attendance at ante-natal clinics and infant welfare centers is an indication of the results which may be achieved by education of this kind. The writers of the report consider that supervision of the pre-school child should be ex-

[1] Allen and Unwin (League of Nations Publication Department), 40, Museum Street, London, W.C.1. (2s.)

ercised from centers under the same organization as infant welfare centers. No scheme is set out proposing the inclusion of the family doctor as the supervisor of the pre-school child; this seems to us to be an omission worthy of fresh consideration. A reference is made in the final paragraph of the report to the allotment of work and the relations of the social services to the medical profession, but only to the extent of suggesting special inquiries into these relations with a view to utilizing as wisely as possible the human and material resources available. The rôle of the general practitioner in the care of the pre-school child is one which might well be developed at less expense than would be incurred by a wide extension of public health machinery.

The value of day nurseries, nursery schools, and nursery classes is well recognized by the committee, but it feels that the dangers of epidemic infection in such gatherings of children must not be regarded lightly. Where the accommodation is unequal to the demands made upon it—and that is everywhere at the present time—those responsible are warned to resist the temptation to admit a greater number of children than the institution is designed to hold. The committee thinks it desirable that all children should be submitted to anti-diphtheritic vaccination between the ages of 1 and 2, and suggests that free vaccination might usefully be given once a year by all local authorities. The appearance of measles in a day nursery, residential institution, or hospital ward should be followed immediately by inoculation of all the children present with convalescent serum.

The report throughout is informative, and the proposals made are practical and suggestive. The committee lays great stress on the importance of co-ordination between the various public, voluntary and professional interests concerned, to secure economy of effort and to prevent overlapping.—*The British Medical Journal.*

REPORTS

ACTIVITIES OF THE JOINT OFFICE OF THE ASSOCIATION OF AMERICAN COLLEGES AND COUNCIL OF CHURCH BOARDS OF EDUCATION

The time of the twenty-second annual meeting of the Council and the nineteenth annual meeting of the Association is fixed for the week beginning the ninth of January, 1933. The meeting is to be at Atlantic City, with the Chelsea Hotel as headquarters.

The Smaller College Study: One hundred and twenty-seven colleges are now participating in this study being carried on under the direction of Archie M. Palmer. All these colleges enroll less than 700 students.

The study is covering the following areas: (1) Educational policy, (2) organization and administration, (3) personnel, (4) student supply and alumni, (5) instructional facilities and technique, (6) physical plant, (7) financial situation and needs, and (8) such selected areas as student life, religious life, personnel guidance, extra-curriculum activities, enrolment trends and special activities.

Through the use of a series of brief schedules specific data have already been gathered, (1) on the aims and objectives of the college, (2) on the board of control, (3) on the internal administration of the college, (4) on the faculty organization, (5) on the recognition of the worth and services of the college, (6) on the contributions of the college to the community, (7) on the curriculum and instructional facilities, and (8) on the student body. There remains yet to be obtained certain information on the physical plant and on the financial and fiduciary practices.

Special Intensive Studies: In connection with the smaller college study, special intensive studies are being made of various phases of groups of colleges located in different states throughout the Union. This work is being done under the direction of Robert L. Kelly.

Included in these special studies are Piedmont College, Georgia, eight Friends Colleges, eight other colleges located in the same eight states, and about the same number of colleges related to the Church of the Brethren.

Graduate Fellows of the A. A. C.: A special feature of the general and intensive studies referred to above of the small colleges is the participation of a group of candidates for the doctorate registered in various universities—Columbia, New York, Oklahoma, Yale, Geneva, etc. Other graduate schools throughout the country are planning to cooperate with the association in special studies of this sort.

The Music Study: The Carnegie Corporation has made an appropriation of $25,000 to the association to make possible a study of general music courses in the colleges. The director of this study has not yet been announced. The members of the sponsoring committee are: President Ernest H. Wilkins, Oberlin College, *chairman,* Dean H. L. Butler, Syracuse University, Professor G. S. Dickinson, Vassar College, Dr. John Erskine, Juilliard School of Music, Director Howard Hanson, Eastman School of Music, The University of Rochester, Professor Walter E. Hartley, Occidental College, Dean Ernest Hutcheson, Juilliard Graduate School, Dr. W. S. Learned, The Carnegie Foundation for Advancement of Teaching, Professor Douglas Moore, Columbia University, Dean James B. Munn, New York University, President Garfield B. Oxnam, DePauw University, President Robert P. Pell, Converse College, Mr. Myron C. Taylor, United States Steel Corporation, Secretary Burnet C. Tuthill, National Association of Schools of Music, Professor Paul J. Weaver, Cornell University, Professor Karl Young, Yale University, President F. C. Ferry, Hamilton College, *ex officio,* Robert L. Kelly, *ex officio,* Archie M. Palmer, *secretary.*

The Comprehensive Examination Study: Dr. E. S. Jones has just completed a tour of the Northwest and Pacific states in connection with the comprehensive examination study which has now been in process for several months. A special report by Dr. Jones for the first six months is published in the Association *Bulletin* for May. The General Education Board contributed $25,000 for this study.

Architecture and Fine Arts Booklets: As a result of an appropriation by the Carnegie Corporation, Mr. Larson, of the association's Commission on College Architecture and Instruction in the Fine Arts, and Mr. Palmer, the associate secretary, are preparing material for two booklets, one to cover the field of recent architectural construction and the other recent developments in the teaching of the fine arts.

Committee on Classification of Colleges: The committee of the association on the classification of colleges, consisting of Dean Raymond Walters, of Swarthmore College, Chancellor Samuel P. Capen of the University of Buffalo, and Dr. F. J. Kelly, of the U. S. Office of Education, Washington, in conjunction with the headquarters office of the association is now engaged in making a tentative classification of colleges and universities of the United States. This classification is not being made with the view of setting standards but merely for purposes of adequate future compilation of statistical data, and it is expected that when perfected it will be adopted by the U. S. Office of Education and other agencies collecting statistical data regarding the colleges.

Federal Revenue Bill: Protests are coming from the colleges all over the country because of the suggested changes in the new Federal Revenue Bill which it is believed will work an unusual hardship upon colleges and other charitable objectives. The opinion is expressed by high legal authority that under the new bill recently passed by the House, a residuary charitable bequest would be subject to the payment of the inheritance taxes of the entire estate, which would of course largely reduce the bequest to the assured. Proposed Section 807 is an attempt to reinsert the bunglesome amendment of 1924, repealed in 1926, and if for no other reason taxpayers and their counsel are entitled to be relieved of the useless expenditure of valued time in attempting to work out algebraic formulas in taxation.

Architectural Advisory Service: The association office now has an extensive layout of plans and costs of recently constructed college buildings. Not only is this service being used by the college officials, but also through contacts which have been made by Mr. Larson, architects are consulting the association's files when contemplating new buildings.

Financial and Fiduciary Service to the Colleges: Dr. A. W. Anthony, the chairman of the association's Commission on Permanent and Trust Funds, will direct a financial and fiduciary service with special reference to the needs of colleges. The plan is as follows:

(1) The chairman of the commission will maintain an office at headquarters, *i.e.*, 111 Fifth Avenue, New York, and, with stenographic assistance there, will undertake to answer every form of inquiry relating to financial and fiduciary matters, by at least making known sources of information among specialists of every kind, if the information is not at hand in the office. The chairman will be in this office at stated intervals.

(2) A forward-looking program for each college should be encouraged, based upon and following up, the reports of 63 colleges, reported in the *Bulletin* of November, 1930, pp. 367–418. This means efforts to have every college plan its program in advance.

(3) Reports from institutions which have stood the stress of the financial depression well should be assembled and published (with permission of the institution in each case). These reports should illustrate conditions such as: (a) Increase of income from investments—the kinds of securities held; (b) Practical maintenance of income; (c) Increase of tuition, offsetting loss of income; (d) Increase of gifts, offsetting loss of income; (e) Balancing the budget by economies in administration; (f) Increment of capital by judicious exchange of investments; (g) Outstanding experiences with Trust Companies as managers of funds; (h) Conspicuous instances of gains by reason of reduced costs, *e.g.*, in building.

(4) The publication of these statements and the exchange of ideas involved will easily develop into a continuing forum of discussion and stimulation.

(5) Material would be assembled for presentation at the annual meeting showing important features in the whole field.

Council Committees: The College Committee of the Council, under the chairmanship of Dr. W. F. Quillian, General Secretary of the General Board of Christian Education, Methodist Episcopal Church, South, and the University Committee, under the chairmanship of Dr. George R. Baker, Associate Secretary of the Board of Education of the Northern Baptist Convention, are projecting especially comprehensive programs of work. The University Secretary, Mr. Leach, has submitted reports of recent visits to the Universities of Iowa, Illinois, Missouri, and Kansas State College, where the constituent Boards have successful work.

Compensations of the Depression: Some of the compensations mentioned below were suggested by members of the executive committee of the association and some others by member college presidents who have written in from different sections of the country.

(1) There is a distinctly greater intellectual interest being shown by students with less attention to the side shows on the college campus.

(2) Colleges generally, and especially those which are located in or near large centers of population, are having a larger enrolment of day students than heretofore. In not a few cases colleges, from whose immediate field a good many students have usually gone to other institutions, particularly in the East, are also having an increased enrolment.

(3) There is a tendency on the part of many colleges—because of and under the excuse of present conditions—to cut out a good many of the frills and to reduce their curriculum offerings to the more necessary and more cultural subjects. Colleges are discovering that they can proceed with their educational program without loss of effectiveness and indeed frequently with great gain, with fewer departments, fewer courses, fewer small classes and less expenditure for administration. In the effort to concentrate work upon the educational program the increased intellectual interest of the students is being capitalized and students are profiting accordingly as they are thrown more upon their own initiative and are allowed to develop their own resourcefulness. All colleges are watching their expenditures more closely than usual and are finding that it is quite possible to cut down their budgets to a considerable extent without loss of educational effectiveness.

(4) Colleges depending largely upon tuition for their resources find themselves in better relative condition financially than those colleges whose income has usually been drawn very largely from invested funds.

(5) While some colleges are reporting reductions in the number of the staff the result may eventually mean better salaries for those who remain connected with the institution.

(6) An increase in the number of applicants for admission for next year, as compared with the situation at this time a year ago, is reported from numerous sections of the country.

(7) A greater proportion of the students both in college and applying for admission for next year indicate the need of financial assistance, all of which points in the direction of greater appreciation of the services which the colleges render.

(8) Extraordinary efforts are being exerted by

alumni groups, students, faculties and others to provide funds for students who are in dire straits because of economic situation. The time is opportune for appeals for scholarship and loan aid for worthy students.

(9) There is an unexpected optimism on the part of college administrators and their friends. They have not lost faith in their institutions or in their work. The following sample comment illustrates the stuff of which college presidents are made: "The economic conditions in our state are extremely bad. We have had in succession in the last four years a most destructive flood, a great drought, bank failures and the depression. This leaves the purchasing power in our state very low. The college itself, however, is getting along quite well."

ROBERT L. KELLY

SOCIETIES AND MEETINGS

THE NATIONAL COUNCIL OF TEACHERS OF MATHEMATICS

THE thirteenth annual meeting of The National Council of Teachers of Mathematics was held at the Hotel Raleigh, Washington, D. C. The following papers were presented: "Curriculum Adjustments," by Mr. William C. Myers, Washington, D. C.; "A Comparative Study of the Teaching of Mathematics in the United States and Germany," by Professor William D. Reeve, New York City; "Improving America's Mathematics," by Mr. Harry C. Barber, Exeter, New Hampshire; "What do We Owe to the Brighter Pupil," by Miss Beulah I. Shoesmith, Chicago, Illinois; "Regents' and College Entrance Board Examinations in Mathematics," by Professor W. S. Schlauch, New York City; "What Mathematics Means to the World," by Professor E. R. Hedrick, University of California at Los Angeles. All of the above papers will appear in forthcoming issues of *The Mathematics Teacher*.

Three new standing committees were established: (1) Committee on Individual Differences; (2) Committee on Geometry; (3) Committee on Policy, which is to formulate a body of *first principles* that should govern the teaching of secondary mathematics. The Committee on Cooperation with Official Examining Boards was continued for another year as well as the Committee on Handbook in Mathematics.

The results of the annual election are as follows: *President*—Mr. William Betz, specialist in mathematics, Rochester, New York; *Second Vice-President*—Mary A. Potter, supervisor of mathematics, Racine, Wisconsin; *Directors*—Mrs. Elsie P. Johnson, High School, Oak Park, Illinois; Mr. John P. Everett, State Teachers College, Kalamazoo, Michigan; Mr. Raleigh Schorling, University of Michigan, Ann Arbor, Michigan.

The National Council of Teachers of Mathematics, which had a very modest beginning in Cleveland, Ohio, in February, 1920, when approximately seventy-five charter members created the organization, has now grown to a membership of nearly six thousand, representing every state in the union and many foreign countries.

EDWIN W. SCHREIBER,
Secretary

STATE TEACHERS COLLEGE,
MACOMB, ILLINOIS

EDUCATIONAL RESEARCH AND STATISTICS

CHANGE AND CONSTANCY IN GROUP TEST I.Q.S

THE teachers and administrators who use mental ages and intelligence quotients obtained from group tests of general mental ability are often disturbed because large differences appear where two or more tests are given to the same pupil. These differences occur not only when the testing is done at widely different times, but also when the interval is as short as a month or a week. The study which this paper reports was undertaken with the object of discovering something about the nature, extent and significance of the group test I.Q. changes under ordinary school conditions.

The 154 children used as subjects for this study were those who in 1931–32 were regular seventh grade pupils at Reading, Massachusetts. They had all been in Reading schools from the third grade on, and most of them had spent all

TABLE I

I.Q. CHANGES OF 154 PUPILS IN THREE GROUP TESTS

	Change in I.Q. Points									N
	0	1–4	5–9	10–14	15–19	20–24	25–29	30–34	35	
Gains		54	53	25	17	6	1	2	1	159
Losses		57	71	60	24	6	1	0	1	220
Total changes	11	111	124	85	41	12	2	2	2	390

their school lives in this system. Group intelligence tests had been given to these children when they were in the third, fourth, and sixth grades. The tests used in these grades were Otis Primary, National A, and Terman A, respectively, and all tests were given and scored by one of the writers (Wadleigh). Because of absences at the time of testing and the acceleration of some superior pupils, not all of the 154 subjects had taken three tests.

For the study of the I.Q. change, all possible differences between the various I.Q.'s of each pupil were computed. If the child had taken only two tests there was, of course, only one difference. When three tests had been taken, however, there were available three differences; namely, the differences between the first and second, the first and third, and the second and third I.Q.'s. In all, 390 I.Q. differences were obtained from the tests of the 154 pupils.

In Table I are presented distributions of the changes in I.Q. Only 11 cases showed absolutely no difference; while there were 159 gains and 220 losses on the later tests. The percentage of changes of 10 points or more was 36.9, and 31.3 per cent. changed less than 5 points.

The medians and quartiles of the distributions are shown in Table II. The gains and losses are apparently about equal in average amount, in spite of a considerable difference in number. The main interest of the reader will lie in the total changes summarized in the last line of the table. The median 7.29 means that approximately half the changes were less than 7 points, and slightly more than half the changes were greater than this amount. A quarter of the differences were insignificant, being not over 4 points, but the highest twenty-five per cent. were very substantial, since they amounted to 13 points or more.

At this point the reader will naturally ask the question, how do these group test changes compare with the changes in the more reliable individual intelligence tests?

TABLE II

MEDIANS AND QUARTILES OF THE I.Q. CHANGES

	Q1	Md	Q3	N
Gains	3.94	7.41	14.45	159
Losses	4.86	7.32	13.08	220
Total	4.12	7.29	12.74	390

Some years ago Rugg and Colloton presented a valuable study in which they summarized a number of important investigations on I.Q. constancy.[1] The average variations in Stanford Binet I.Q.'s reported in this paper ranged from 4.5 to 7.7 points, with a median of the averages amounting to just over 6 points. These early findings have been confirmed by later investigators. Lincoln, in 1922, reported a median change in one group of 5.25 points, with an upper quartile of 11.5 points.[2] Wentworth, in 1926, found a median change of 5 points, and 20.0 per cent. of her variations were 10 points or more in magnitude.[3] Altogether it seems fair to state that the median I.Q. changes on repeated Stanford Binet tests average about 5 or 6 points, and that 20 or 25 per cent. of the changes are greater than 10 points.

If the above statement is true, it will be seen that the group test results at Reading compare very favorably with the results of the individual

[1] H. Rugg and C. Colloton, "Constancy of the Stanford-Binet I.Q. as Shown by Retests," *Journal of Educational Psychology*, Vol. XII, No. 6, September, 1921, p. 315–322.

[2] E. A. Lincoln, "The Constancy of Intelligence Quotients," *Journal of Educational Psychology*, Vol. XIII, No. 8, November, 1922, p. 384–395.

[3] M. M. Wentworth, "Individual Difference in the Intelligence of School Children," Harvard University Press, p. 27, 1926.

tests. The median group test change is only a point or two greater than the average individual test change, and about the same discrepancy is found in the upper quartiles. It is to be noted, however, that there are more large changes—those above 10 points—in the group than in the individual results.

Those teachers and administrators who use the intelligence quotients generally employ them to determine the classification of the pupil in one of several groups, usually designated as feeble-minded, dull, inferior, average, superior and very superior. When the 390 group I.Q. changes were distributed to show what variations they would make in the classification of the pupils into groups as noted above, it was found that in 206 cases, or 52.8 per cent., there was no change in classification. In 67 cases, or 15.9 per cent., there was a gain of one step or group in the later classification. In 92 cases, or 23.2 per cent., there was a loss of one step or group. It is interesting to note that 38 of the losses in classification were drops from very superior to superior, and that another 46 losses were drops from superior to average.

There are some instances, of course, when a large I.Q. change does not indicate a change in the pupils' classification. A change from 140 to 155, for example, or the reverse, is not significant because the pupil is still classed as a very superior child and is treated accordingly. With this in mind, the 144 changes (36.9 per cent.) of 10 points or more were examined individually to see what effect they had on classification. In 36 cases there was no change, which indicates that only three quarters of the large changes were really significant from the practical point of view.

Another thing to be held in mind is the fact that the wise teacher or administrator does not do anything to, with, or for the child on the basis of the I.Q. alone. Results of achievement tests, teachers' marks and judgments, school history, health status, and all other pertinent factors must be taken into consideration in diagnosis and prescription.[4] Sometimes the I.Q. is the least important factor in the case.

[4] E. A. Lincoln and V. L. Wadleigh, "Ability Grouping at Reading, Massachusetts," SCHOOL AND SOCIETY, Vol. XXXI, No. 805, May 31, 1930, p. 746–748.

It is also to be remembered that as a child moves on through school and is tested from time to time, it will be increasingly easier to estimate his true I.Q. from the accumulating evidence. It may be true that some children are actually inconstant and highly variable in their general ability, but for the majority this is not so, and by the time they are ready for junior high school it is probable that 85 to 90 per cent. can be rated very accurately.

One other fact is of much importance in the interpretation of the present study. Three different group tests were used in getting the intelligence quotients of these 154 children. It has been the experience of workers with tests that there are sometimes constant differences of considerable magnitude between the results of different group tests which are given to the same children under practically identical conditions. If this factor was at work in the present case, the real changes are somewhat less than the results would indicate.

On the whole, the implications of this study are very encouraging. It seems possible to obtain, with due care, group test I.Q.'s which are fairly consistent. Nevertheless, it is very clear, as has been pointed out many times before, that a single I.Q. obtained early in the child's school career, can not be used to indicate his ability throughout his later years. Even though it is known that seventy per cent. of the first I.Q.'s will not change substantially, there is no way of knowing which seventy of any hundred are correctly measured, and which thirty will later turn out to be very different. It is only by a program of repeated testing and careful record-keeping that dependable data may be obtained for use in educational guidance.

EDWARD A. LINCOLN
HARVARD UNIVERSITY
VERNA L. WADLEIGH,
Director of School Research
READING, MASSACHUSETTS

NEW BOOKS IN EDUCATION

EATON, THEODORE H. *College Teaching: Its Rationale.* Pp. xi + 264. Wiley. $2.50.

KULP, DANIEL H., II. *Educational Sociology.* Pp. xvi + 591. 17 figures. Longmans, Green. $3.50.

LANDMAN, J. H. *Human Sterilization.* Pp. xviii + 341. Macmillan. $4.00.

McGUCKEN, WILLIAM. *The Jesuits and Education.* Pp. xxv + 352. Illustrated. Bruce. $4.00.

SCHOOL AND SOCIETY

EDITED BY J. McKEEN CATTELL

WITH WHICH IS COMBINED THE

EDUCATIONAL REVIEW

EDITED BY WILLIAM McANDREW

Volume 35 SATURDAY, MAY 7, 1932 Number 906

AFTER LITERACY—WHAT?

By Professor WILLIAM S. GRAY

THE UNIVERSITY OF CHICAGO

THE purpose of this article is to discuss briefly the educational opportunities that should be provided for adults who have just attained literacy and who desire to continue their education.

By literacy, as the term is used in this discussion, is meant that level of achievement in the language arts which enables adults to read and understand simple newspaper accounts and various types of printed materials of similar difficulty, to carry on personal correspondence and to participate in other simple activities requiring ability to read and write. In attaining this level of literacy adults pass through three distinct stages of progress based largely on achievement in reading, in the case of native-born illiterates, and in the use of oral English and achievement in reading in the case of foreign-born illiterates. These stages have been described in the "Manual for Teachers of Adult Illiterates," prepared for the National Advisory Committee on Illiteracy.

Literacy, however, is not an end in itself and should not be required apart from other types of mental and social growth. It is rather an accompaniment of the general educational progress of the individual. Hence, the instruction given while literacy is being attained should provide "helpful information relating to personal and civic problems; it should acquaint adult illiterates in so far as necessary with essential duties of citizens and cultivate pride in good citizenship. It should stimulate their minds and enrich their experiences as much as time and facilities will permit. It should reveal wider opportunities and desirable forms of pleasure and recreation." It should also cultivate keen interests and strong motives that will stimulate adults to continue their education after literacy has been attained. With this type of training as a background, what is the nature of the educational opportunities that should be provided for adults who have made little or no progress beyond the level of functioning literacy?

An analysis of the opportunities now provided in schools and classes for adults reveals two distinct types of curriculums. One type includes a wide range of courses which have been planned to meet the needs of special groups, such as those who wish to naturalize, those who are preparing for service in a specific vocational field, and those who wish to satify a special avocational interest. Such courses are very essential and must be included in any adequate program of adult education. The offerings must of necessity vary in different communities according to local demands. The second type of curriculum includes courses in reading, writing, spelling, English, literature, history, geography, civics and arithmetic. In theory, at least, these courses are given in response to common needs of adults of limited education and are assumed to enrich their experiences, to increase their personal and civic efficiency, to broaden their interests, and to extend their opportunities for enjoyment and recreation. Any training that actually achieves these aims is essential both to personal advancement and to industrial, political and civic progress, and should constitute the core of the curriculum provided for those who have just attained functioning literacy.

Unfortunately, however, much of the training given to adults of limited education is open to two significant criticisms. The first is that it often gives chief emphasis to the development of habits and skills involved in the tool subjects. In fact, instruction in many centers is limited to courses in English, arithmetic, spelling, handwriting and reading. That some provision should be made for training in these subjects can not be denied. The error lies in organizing instruction primarily in terms of the tool subjects rather than providing appropriate emphasis upon them as a subordinate part of an enriched curriculum.

The second criticism relates to the fact that most of the informational subjects provided, such as history, geography, civics and literature, utilize the content usually taught to elementary-school pupils rather than present materials based on adult needs in contemporary life. As a rule, they provide information and cultivate appreciation in only a few of the fields of primary importance to adults. Furthermore, they are taught as isolated compartments of knowledge with little or no relation to each other or to daily life. They also fail frequently to provide the breadth of vision, to develop the variety of interests, and to cultivate the various types of enjoyment and appreciation that are essential in developing intelligent, useful, happy citizens. Such criticisms should be followed by constructive suggestions.

The chief function of the educational opportunities provided for those who have attained literacy is to give a modest, yet comprehensive, understanding and appreciation of the elements of life that touch most closely their needs and activities. As pointed out by Bobbitt, the age of attaining one's literacy doesn't materially affect his fundamental needs. "The things that are most important to adults are the same whether they learn to read at six, sixteen, or thirty. The largest problem is to find and make accessible suitable materials, things thoroughly concrete, yet adapted to the level of the mature mind; things that provide for abundant experience, yet always from fresh and interesting angles; and an abundance of concreteness out of which the generalized understanding can grow."

The content of a desirable curriculum can be determined most satisfactorily only through a series of research studies. A preliminary analysis, however, has resulted in the identification of at least six fields in which appropriate instruction should be provided. The first is an informing, stimulating course in the field of the social studies. Among other things it should contribute the following: (a) illuminating information about the city, state and nation, including a simple, narrative account of the historical development of the United States and some of its most important geographic facts and relationships; (b) vital acquaintance with the social, civic, and religious institutions which affect the individual and an understanding of the outstanding features of modern community life; (c) clear realization of the elemental duties and obligations of citizens, including an understanding of important principles and ideals that should characterize life in a democracy; (d) consideration of simple business, industrial and economic relations, including the relation of employer and employee; (e) understanding and appreciation of the more personal types of social institutions, such as the family, the club, and the library. These and many other items should be presented in an integrated view of social relations and conditions.

A second important field relates to the sciences, both biological and physical. The material presented should be very elementary but should give some understanding of the principles that determine natural growth and physical phenomena of everyday life, also the simple processes that underlie our mechanical age. It should explain the contributions of science to convenient, happy living, as exemplified by the radio, telephone, gas engine, manufacturing instruments, etc. It should also cultivate hobbies in this field, such as photography, study of birds, flowers, trees and stars, radio construction and gardening. There is a wealth of informing, inspiring, information in the science field which should be made available for all adults of limited education.

A third field is represented by the appreciational arts and the avocational aspects of life. There is special need in this age of routine work and shortened hours of labor of introducing adults to those fields of experience which contribute hearty enjoyment and provide for the wholesome use of leisure time, such as music, literature, drama, pictures, and sculpture, etc. It is not enough for adults of meager education merely to learn of such possibilities of enjoyment and enrichment; opportunities must be provided for actual participation in them. This may be achieved in various ways, such as presenting programs in which good artists participate, taking classes to exhibit halls and museums, and organizing clubs of various types among the students, such as those devoted to literature, drama, and the graphic arts. The chief goal of all these activities is to enrich the lives of adults, to open up numerous possibilities of hearty enjoyment in various recreational fields, and to initiate interests that will persist throughout life. Judging from current courses for adults, much is done along these lines for those who have already had considerable schooling. Far too little, however, is being done for those of meager education.

The fourth field includes health, first aid, hygiene, sanitation, life saving, home nursing and other problems suggested by the term "health education." There is a wealth of information along these lines that should be provided for students in adult classes. It is equally important that right attitudes toward health matters be cultivated and, insofar as possible, right habits established. Furthermore, students should be instructed concerning various health agencies and the kinds of help that can be secured from them. Insofar as possible, adult students should be taken to the clinics in the community and learn through concrete experience of the valuable service rendered.

The fifth field includes the fundamentals in the language arts and arithmetic, insofar as training is needed in them. As a rule, English, spelling, handwriting, guidance in reading, and the basic processes in arithmetic have absorbed most of the time of students of meager education. Carefully planned instruction along these lines should be provided in a definite period, but it should be limited to its due proportion of the student's time and energy. In this connection intensive studies are needed to determine the types of training of greatest value and the methods by which that training can be provided most effectively.

A sixth possible field considers the differentiated needs of men and women. Instruction with respect to home making, marketing, sewing, labor-saving devices, and efficiency in daily routine, should be provided more or less widely for women, particularly married women. Vocational guidance is equally important for men and unmarried women. Since these types of training are differentiated to a greater or less extent for different groups it may be unwise to include them in a core curriculum. They should at least parallel the basic instruction, if they are not included as an integral part of it.

The discussion thus far has emphasized the need of an expanded and enriched curriculum for adults who have recently attained literacy and for others of very meager education. If such a curriculum is provided, steps are necessary at once to develop the types of instructional materials that are needed. The six fields referred to were mentioned merely to indicate the general lines along which an expanded curriculum might be developed. A deliberate study of the needs of adults who have recently attained literacy would doubtless reveal other major fields that require emphasis and might suggest a radically different basis of organization. For example, the Division of University Extension, Massachusetts Department of Education, has recently announced the following series of courses for adults in so-called "intermediate classes": every-day economics, every-day science, every-day civics, English structure, literature and arithmetic. Whatever sequence of courses may ultimately be adopted, there is little question concerning the need of instruction that gives to adults an understanding and appreciation of the various phases of life with which they have or should have vital contacts.

Two plans for developing new curriculum materials might be adopted. The first provides that adult education leaders organize themselves into a curriculum committee for the purpose first of studying the needs of adults of meager education and of determining the major fields of instruction that should be provided. As soon as this has been done the committee should be divided into a series of subcommittees, each of which should be responsible for developing an outline and ultimately the actual materials of instruction in a specific field. An advantage that attaches to this plan is that adult education leaders are probably more intimately acquainted with the needs of adults of limited education than any other group that might be selected. Two limitations of the plan are that most adult education workers already have very crowded schedules and that many of them lack an intimate acquaintance with some of the new materials in specialized fields which should be included in the courses that are organized.

The second suggestion provides that adult education workers make independent studies of the needs of adults in local communities to determine the major fields in which instruction should be provided. While this work is going forward, steps should be taken to secure funds for use in the development and refinement of instructional materials that could be used throughout the nation. As a first step in carrying out this plan, conferences of representative adult leaders should be held to crystallize thinking and to formulate a general plan of procedure. Objective studies should then be made, the results of which would refine judgments concerning the character of the materials needed. As a third step, cooperation should be secured from specialists in different subject-matter fields who could assist in preparing the materials in form for classroom use. The foregoing proposal has many obvious advantages. Its chief limitation attaches to the fact that funds for such purposes are difficult to secure. The need is so urgent, however, for improved curriculums for adults of limited education that vigorous effort should be made to secure them.

Equally as important as the enriched content that has been proposed is the form in which the new materials of instruction are prepared. In this connection, two facts should be kept clearly in mind. The first is that only a limited proportion of those who need instruction will attend classes. Consequently, the material that is developed should be prepared in attractive form for use by adults in the home or in the library, as well as by those who attend school. It should be so simply and clearly written that it can be read and interpreted independently by those who have just attained literacy. Unfortunately, there is very little reading material available today for such adults. Consequently, the habits that are cultivated as adults learn to read soon disintegrate through disuse. If the proposal which has been made were carried out a series of attractive booklets, full of informing content could be provided which would enable literate adults to continue their education independently. The fact can not be over-emphasized that the preparation merely of teachers' guides or outlines will fail to serve the needs of a large proportion of the adults who would gladly read if appropriate reading materials were available.

It is essential also that the materials published should be prepared in a graded series with respect to difficulty. As far as can be determined at present, they should correspond roughly in difficulty, with respect to the mechanics of reading, to books prepared for use in the fourth, the fifth, and the sixth grades. An investigation which is now nearing completion aims to define objectively several levels of difficulty appropriate for adults at different stages of advancement between mere ability to read and mature reading habits.

In conclusion, the following summary statements may be made: The educational opportunities provided at the present time for adults who have just attained literacy give large emphasis to the tool subjects and to traditional types of curriculum material. They are not based upon a fundamental analysis of the needs of adults. A preliminary study of the problem shows clearly that materials which extend and enrich the experiences of adults, awaken new interests, and open up new opportunities for hearty enjoyment might be provided in at least six important fields. There is urgent need of cooperative studies to determine the common needs of adults of limited education and to specify in detail the types of instructional materials which will prove most helpful. There is equally urgent need of steps which will result in the preparation of simply written and carefully graded materials, with respect to difficulty, that can be used in adult classes, or read independently in the library or at home.

SOME REMARKS ON EDUCATION

By Professor A. S. PEARSE

DUKE UNIVERSITY

MAN is remarkable among animals for his education. He passes through a long adolescent period during which he has the care, example and tutelage of adults. His intricate brain and his time-binding civilization give him powers and opportunities such as no other animal enjoys. He was rightly named *Homo sapiens* by Linnaeus.

Modern education serves various functions and stands for various ideals. It preserves the learning of the past in libraries and in the minds of scholars. It attempts continually to encourage the discovery of new facts and the formulation of new theories—to foster research. The usual function of education, the field in which teachers and students spend most of their effort, is in giving and acquiring training. An educated man is trained for living. He knows social customs and procedures; how to behave like others and how to think like others. He knows how to make a living through more or less knowledge of social and economic conditions and is equipped with special knowledge and training in his particular field of endeavor. He may also be able to think, but this is usually the last thing that a man gets from formal education or from human educational institutions. Thinking is hard work. It tries nerves and spirits. Most people avoid thinking by keeping busy with work or amusement. It is human nature to dislike to think.

There are three generally recognized means for formal education in the world to-day—home, church, and public and private schools. Instruction in the home is unfortunately falling more and more into neglect. Parents shed responsibility on the church and school. This saves them from thinking. Fathers are too busy and mothers are often occupied with matters which preclude routine, daily attention to children. A child early gets most of his ideals and standards for the conduct of every-day life from his parents. The responsibility for such training should not be avoided. Parents can usually give it better than any one else. No one else has the same degree of interest in having a child become a decent, successful member of society.

Instruction by the agents of churches is usually narrow and partisan. Creed is its primary purpose. It is sometimes little but propaganda. In most communities, however, young people get a considerable portion of their ideals and ethical standards from the church. The church teacher is at his best when he recognizes that he is the servant of society more than the mouthpiece of God. If he is wise, loving, and responsible, his teachings are good. If he is bigoted, narrow, jealous and partisan, his teachings are bad.

Teachers in public schools are as a rule not exceptional personalities. They are average, or less. Society recognizes this by paying them poorly and thus putting them in their proper places among its other average members. This appears to be justified at present but is in some respects regrettable. It would be a fine thing if teachers were the wisest and most capable persons in each community. This will be hard to bring about because it is doubtful if teachers will ever think enough. The ablest members of society are usually not teachers. The average society does not want its teachers to think. A pedagogue who tries to be original and to attain new heights often loses his job because the community in which he works thinks he is a radical and dislikes his departures from the average. Nature (and its favored child, society) fears and resents any departure from the average. Most members of average communities look upon the school as a means for training children to be like themselves. Teachers are naturally average on account of public sentiment, their own inertia, and their quite human inclination to avoid thinking and keep themselves busy with routine. They are always limited by their training and knowledge. They are therefore quite naturally afraid to discuss or to allow students to discuss things about which they know little or nothing. Thus school education must always be limited by public sentiment, school equipment, the horizon of the teacher, and other factors.

Public schools serve the mass of society more directly than private schools. The latter are in some cases retreats for weaklings but in others furnish exceptional opportunities for gifted youths. They have more individuality than public schools. State universities in the United States are overcrowded, their professors overworked, and their students inadequately served. Private colleges and universities are more and more limiting numbers and therefore, on the whole, are better institutions for instruction and the accomplishment of research. Educational institutions are conservative. Every school must have a more or less standardized curriculum. This is largely a matter of expediency. It makes transfers from one school to another easier, it permits teachers to know what to know at the proper time and they can therefore do more systematic work. It enables executives to hold up standards by making all cover ground in allotted time and give training which prepares for standard examinations. Such systems are quite efficient, but of course will never permit anything but standardized mediocrity.

There can be no single ideal for education. An educational institution must give polish and culture, teach young people how to earn a living, and train professional scholars. There is a growing tendency to separate trade and technical schools from those which foster "culture" and scholarly pursuits. Society becomes more and more specialized. There is greater division of labor each year. A member must accept a lowly social position or prepare through long years for a specialty. High schools in small towns are obliged to train together boys and girls for artisanship, business, entrance into technical schools and universities. Large cities are segregating youths into various types of schools.

There are two great defects in modern educational systems:—(1) Practically all effort is devoted to the acquisition of knowledge and practice, or training for being a member of society. Every student learns in great detail how to be average, but he is actually impeded if he attempts to learn to think. John Does are encouraged, but it is increasingly difficult to produce a Darwin or a Pasteur. Human society is growing ripe and perfect. (2) Education is too slow. It takes too long for a youth to become educated. A hundred years hence, if present systems continue, each person must in early youth embark on a career as a specialist. He or his parents must decide that he is to prepare to be an engineer, a lawyer, or what not and teachers must begin to hasten him through a long training which he can not hope to complete before he has reached middle life. Either that or educational systems must evolve into something which better fits environment. Education is very conservative, but there seems to be no doubt that it must change. The schools must compress their learning or in some way enable students to make more rapid progress. Perhaps this means cutting out some dead wood, pruning faddy growths, or changing the whole nature of the organization. The time seems ripe for an educational congress which would represent a great variety of interests and which might consider for months or years how to modify present educational systems so that youths can gain training and ability in less time.

What does an educated man have? There is a deal of ill-feeling and misunderstanding about this. Self-made men enjoy pointing a scornful finger at the incompetent educated fool. College graduates themselves are often surprised to find that they have little ability to succeed in society. Comic papers perennially find material for their pages in the learned, absent-minded, impractical professor. Education does nothing but offer opportunity. It does not make good or bad, incompetent or competent men. Each man, educated or uneducated, by struggling continually and thus increasing his potentialities or by loafing and thus allowing his abilities to dwindle, must make or break himself. In education a man finds a golden opportunity to increase his ability to go out in society and make a living—quicker, more surely, and better. For example, a certain young man of good ability finished four years of training in an engineering college and accepted a job as a section hand on a railroad. A year later he was a section boss; in three years a roadmaster; in ten years, a superintendent; and after twenty-four years, general manager of the railroad. Without his education this man would probably have become a section boss after five years and perhaps a roadmaster after twenty-four years. Education gives opportunity to acquire those vague qualities, culture and polish—greater appreciation of the things esteemed highest and best in life; appreciation of social contacts, literature, art, music, science and religion. Yet many college graduates spend most of their leisure in gambling, drunkenness and sexual adventures. Education does not make a man cultured or vulgar. He must make himself. "Illiteracy is always a bad thing, but literacy may be an evil thing. Reading the wrong books may make a man worse than an ignoramus. Learning writing may qualify him for forgery and learning arithmetic for swindling. . . . The main object of education in a democracy is not to teach the students how to vote right, but to train him how to think right. Under any form of government, in an autocracy no less than in a democracy, the real power lies in the people, and it is their individual every-day conduct, guided by their personal beliefs, that determines whether the nation shall advance, stagnate or retrograde." (Slosson.) An educational system must stand for elevating things, but it can not be expected to elevate every personality that comes in contact with it. Education should give training for life, polish, culture and increased ability, but it must have potential ability to influence and be supported by earnest effort on the part of the recipient in order to be effective.

Everything that a man acquires brings additional cares and responsibilities—"Blessed is nothing." An educated man has more responsibility to and for society than an uneducated one. Education is not a magic charm which makes a dull, shiftless beggar into a supercilious noble who treads on slaves of ignorance. Rather is it for a strengthening potion which permits a man to carry heavier burdens for himself and for his fellow men. An educated man should be more thoughtful, more enlightened, more liberal, more tolerant, more capable and more helpful than his less fortunate fellow. He should be a leader—by merit, not by favor.

EDUCATIONAL EVENTS

THE INTERNATIONAL SOCIETY FOR COMMERCIAL EDUCATION

The fifth triennial congress of the International Society for Commercial Education will be held in London in the last week of July. The congress has not before been held in England.

On April 27 Mr. H. Ramsbotham, M.P., Parliamentary Secretary to the Board of Education, will address the Royal Society of Arts on "Education for Commerce," and on June 21 Sir Francis Goodenough, the chairman of the administrative committee of the International Congress, will give his presidential address to the Association for Education in Industry and Commerce. As a preparation for the International Congress there will be an economic course, open to students from all countries, at the London School of Economics from July 14 to July 21.

The International Congress will be attended by delegates from many Continental countries, the United States, Egypt, Canada, Persia, India and a large number of delegates from commercial and educational organizations in Britain. The congress has the support of the Lord Chancellor, the present and past presidents of the Board of Education, the president of the Board of Trade, and the heads of the universities, the leading municipalities, and the Dominions and Colonies. The delegates will be welcomed on July 25 by the Lord Mayor of London, and the opening general session will be addressed by the President of the Board of Education, the president of the International Society for Commercial Education (M. Charles E. Boissevain, of Holland), and the president of the congress (Sir David Milne-Watson). The Prince of Wales will make an address at the closing session on July 29. The program will include sessions dealing with the following subjects:

Methods of giving students an interest in foreign countries and an understanding of their peoples.

Methods of imparting a knowledge of merchandise to students.

Training in methods of salesmanship.

The training of responsible business administrators.

The teaching of foreign languages—scope, method, and importance.

Women in business.

Recruitment for commerce; preliminary training of (*a*) higher personnel; (*b*) clerical and other routine workers; vocational guidance and selection; psychological tests, etc.

Training for office work.

Retail trade—methods of training boys and girls for employment in retail distribution.

Mechanical aids for teaching commercial subjects—the cinema, the gramophone, the radio, etc.

Commercial teachers—the supply and training of commercial teachers; methods of keeping teachers in contact with commercial practice.

The development of commercial education since the war.

The session dealing with "Women in Business"—a subject specially recommended by the American branch of the International Society—will be presided over by the Duchess of Atholl, M.P. Mr. H. Ramsbotham, M.P., will preside over and address the session dealing with "The Training of Responsible Business Administrators."

The congress will be entertained by the government hospitality committee at a reception at Stafford House on July 25 and by the Lord Mayor, Aldermen, and Corporation of London at a conversazione at Guildhall on July 26.

APPROPRIATIONS OF THE GENERAL EDUCATION BOARD

Appropriations of $9,162,722, including $5,-139,485 for Negroes, and $3,647,621 for whites, were made by the General Education Board in the fiscal year ended on June 30, 1931, according to the report of that institution for 1930–1931.

The extent to which the General Education Board has increased its bond holdings is shown by the report which lists the total investments at $77,472,832, including $34,154,605 in bonds, an increase of $7,556,149, and $43,318,227 in stocks.

Since the General Education Board was founded in 1902 by Mr. John D. Rockefeller, it has made total appropriations of $221,778,087, of which $123,213,819 was appropriated from principal and $98,564,268 from income.

The total appropriations since the foundation of the General Education Board represent $185,-122,940 for white and $30,898,419 for Negroes. Of the total amount appropriated for white institutions $164,075,183 has been paid, and of the total appropriations for Negro institutions $21,617,448 has been paid. A total amount of $190,922,411 has been paid out of the appropriations granted in the lifetime of the institution.

The General Education Board has increased its bond investments from approximately 28 per cent. of its total investments in 1929, to 38 per cent. in 1930 and 44 per cent. in 1931. The largest single bond holding is $3,500,000 of the United States Fourth Liberty 4¼s maturing from 1933 to 1938.

The General Education Board reported income of $4,251,783 received in the year ended on June 30, 1931, which together with undisbursed income on hand as of that date of $13,-032,232, and refunds on account of payments made in previous years of $5,890, brought the total amount available for disbursement up to $17,289,906.

REDUCTION IN COURSES AT HARVARD UNIVERSITY

THE governing boards of the university have voted "to approve and adopt the recommendation of the Faculty of Arts and Sciences that, beginning with the year 1932–33, the number of courses required for the degree of A.B. or S.B. be reduced to fifteen, in addition to prescribed English, for all candidates who graduate in not less than four years in fields having general examinations."

According to the *Harvard Graduates Magazine*, this change was proposed by the Faculty Committee on Instruction, as set forth by Professor A. C. Hanford, dean of Harvard College, in his report to the president of the university. The new rule will give undergraduates additional time for tutorial work in their fields of concentration during the junior and senior years.

The committee recommended also that in all courses above those of elementary grade there should ordinarily be not more than one hour examination in a half-year and that, wherever possible, seniors who are candidates for honors should be altogether free from examinations. The final decision on hour examinations rests with each department but it is understood that all are following the general recommendations. Each will make its own minor adjustments.

The Committee on Instruction states that "the present requirements of sixteen courses plus English A were established long before the tutorial system and general examinations were superimposed upon them. There is no question that tutorial work for honor candidates and for all other serious-minded students adds a burden equivalent to at least one full course per year."

In discussing hour examinations, the report goes on to say that the committee is strongly of the opinion that for the best interests of both course instruction and tutorial work there should be a material reduction in the number of hour examinations for all upper-classmen, and special relief for honors candidates in their senior year.

The desire of the committee to provide more time for tutorial work is made clear by the stipulation that the new ruling in regard to the number of courses is intended only for candidates who graduate in not less than four years. It is one more step in the growth of tutorial instruction and the Harvard plan of a four-year course leading to a general examination. The decision not to reduce the number of courses in which the candidate must attain grades of C or higher will, it is believed, maintain course work at its present level. Candidates for a degree who graduate in not less than four years in a field having general examinations, whose requirements are fifteen courses, must attain grades of C or higher in at least eleven courses. Candidates whose requirements include also English A, making a total of sixteen courses, must attain grades of C or higher in at least eleven and one half courses.

THE EXPERIMENTAL COLLEGE OF THE UNIVERSITY OF WISCONSIN

BEFORE any further educational experimentation projects are inaugurated at the University of Wisconsin, a representative committee of the faculty is to make a thorough study of changes in educational procedures and teaching methods now under way not only in other colleges and universities but also in the state university as well.

This was the course taken by the faculty of the college of letters and science recently when that body adopted three resolutions, two of which referred to recommendations for further educational experimentation to the special committee created by the faculty some time ago.

The resolutions adopted were:

1. That the recommendations contained in the Bleyer report, providing for a new experimental unit for freshmen and sophomore instruction with an initial size of 200 freshmen, and with a "50–50" curriculum consisting in part of an integrated study of one or more communities, societies or civilizations, shall be referred to the special committee.

2. That an amendment to the Bleyer report, proposed by the advisers of the Experimental College, providing for a new unit of 100 freshmen with a "75–25" curriculum, consisting of an integrated course of study which would make up three fourths of the student's work, also be referred to the committee.

3. That the committee should follow a definite

form of objectives in its study of educational changes in the freshman and sophomore years of American universities and colleges, and that such changes as have already or are now being put into effect at the University of Wisconsin shall be included in the study. This resolution, which contained a long list of objectives which the committee should consider in its study, was submitted to the faculty by President Glenn Frank.

The recommendations of the Bleyer report had been submitted to the faculty of the college several weeks ago but action on them was postponed until further consideration could be given to them. This report, made by a committee of which Dr. Willard G. Bleyer was chairman, refused to endorse the original recommendations of the Experimental College advisers. These recommendations provided for four educational units in the university, for both men and women, and with or without dormitory arrangements for the different units.

THE SEMI-CENTENNIAL OF THE BERKELEY, CALIFORNIA, HIGH SCHOOL

CEREMONIES to celebrate the semi-centennial of the Berkeley High School will be held as part of the commencement exercises on June 2.

Student speakers, as is customary at high-school commencements, will speak on "The Early History of the High School, 1882–1900"; "The Growth of Berkeley High School, 1900–1932"; "Academic and Art Courses"; "Commercial and Industrial Courses"; "Physical and Social Activities," and "The Relation of Berkeley High School to the Community." The occasion will also mark the close of twenty years of service by C. L. Biedenbach as principal.

In May, 1880, a special committee of the Board of Education, appointed at a previous meeting to investigate the advisability of establishing a high school, recommended "that a High School class be formed at the beginning of the next school year to be under the care of a grammar principal." In December, 1880, the committee on classification reported that there were seven "scholars" pursuing high school studies, five at the Kellogg School, which was located on the south side of Center Street between Oxford and Shattuck, and two in the San Pablo Avenue School, and recommended that these classes be united.

In 1882 the high school was organized in the Kellogg building, a complete course of study was adopted, the high school was graded so as to allow students to prepare for the state university, and W. W. Anderson was appointed principal.

Berkeley High School was accredited by the University of California in 1884, the first school in the state to be so accredited. It has remained on the accredited list continuously since that date.

The first graduate of the school, and the only member of the class of 1883, was John C. Dormin, who is still a resident of Berkeley. The total number of graduates of the present school year including members of the December and June classes is approximately 712.

Henry Veghte served as principal from 1884 until 1890 when S. D. Waterman was elected to the position, which he filled until 1899 when he was elected superintendent. M. C. James, now deputy superintendent of schools, was high school principal from 1899 until 1910, and G. N. Brink served from 1910 to 1912.

In 1910 with the organization of the Berkeley junior high schools, the Berkeley High School became a three-year school embracing the tenth, eleventh and twelfth years. The total enrolment of the school in 1896 was 270 and in 1917 over one thousand. The present enrolment is about 2,800.

THE COMMITTEE ON HEALTH OF THE NEW YORK PRINCIPALS ASSOCIATION

THE Committee on Health of the New York Principals Association plans a series of meetings to make known to principals, assistants to principals, grade teachers, teachers of health education, and parents, the work of the committee and to spread further the ideals of health education.

A general session will be held at 9:30 on the morning of May 21, at the Waldorf-Astoria Hotel, New York City, during which very brief accounts of the White House Conference and of the Committee on Health will be given. This will be followed by a series of group meetings conducted by the chairmen of the sub-committees. Specialists in each branch of health work will address these groups. All phases of health education of interest to the supervisor, to the teacher, and to the parent will be discussed. The tentative list of group conferences follows:

Mental Hygiene—Arthur Bowie
Parent Cooperation—I. Victor Burger
The School Plant and Child Welfare—Mamie Fay
Health Day—Ella Gross
Safety—Regina C. M. Burke
Cooperation with the Department of Health, Medical Associations and other agencies—Jacob M. Ross
Health Counselors—Mary A. Hallinan
The Health of the Young Child—Alice V. McCormick
Teacher Health—John J. Loftus
Playgrounds and Recreation—Simon Hirsdansky
Teacher Training—Mesmin Arenwald
Health Teaching in the Elementary School—Minnie Obermeier
Administrative Problems—Shirley Friedman

At 12:30 every one will be given an opportunity to go to all the sub-committee rooms to see the charts and to receive the mimeographed reports the Sub-Committees have prepared. Much valuable mimeographed and printed material will be distributed. All will meet at a luncheon to begin at about one o'clock when there will be five or six short talks on the various phases of health education. Among the speakers will be Dr. Ray Lyman Wilbur, Secretary of the Interior, Washington, D. C., Dr. Shirley W. Wynne, Health Commissioner of the City of New York, and Commissioner Edward P. Mulrooney, of the Police Department of the City of New York.

It has been found necessary to limit the attendance at the symposiums to those who buy tickets for the luncheon.

SCIENCE SERVICE CONFERENCE

THERE were held in Washington on April 27, the day preceding the annual meeting of the trustees of Science Service, a conference and a dinner to discuss the plans and work of the service. Science Service was established eleven years ago with an endowment of the value of $500,000 by the late E. W. Scripps, head of the Scripps-Howard chain of newspapers. The object of the service is the dissemination of scientific information to as wide a public as possible and to emphasize the place of science in modern life. The questions considered at the conference were how these objects can be accomplished most effectively and to consider among other matters how far the scope of the service should include the social and economic sciences.

At the conference in the afternoon Dr. J. McKeen Cattell, president of Science Service, presided, and short addresses were made by a number of scientific men and newspaper editors. These included: Dr. Simon Flexner, Rockefeller Institute for Medical Research; Dr. C. G. Abbot, secretary of the Smithsonian Institution; Dr. Karl T. Compton, president of the Massachusetts Institute of Technology; Dr. John C. Merriam, Carnegie Institution of Washington; Dr. F. P. Keppel, Carnegie Corporation; Robert P. Scripps, Scripps-Howard Newspapers; Dr. F. G. Benedict, Carnegie Institution of Washington; Dr. F. G. Cottrell, Washington; Dr. Knight Dunlap, the Johns Hopkins University; Dr. Paul R. Heyl, U. S. Bureau of Standards; Dr. F. B. Jewett, Bell Telephone Laboratories; Dr. A. E. Kennelly, Harvard University; A. H. Kirchhofer, *Buffalo Evening News;* Dr. A. A. Noyes, California Institute of Technology; Dr. C. R. Stockard, Cornell University Medical College; Dr. W. F. G. Swann, Bartol Research Foundation of the Franklin Institute; Dr. E. B. Wilson, Harvard School of Public Health, and Dr. William H. Howell, the Johns Hopkins University.

At the dinner in the evening Dr. William H. Welch, of the Johns Hopkins University, presided and addresses were made by Dr. Robert A. Millikan, of the California Institute of Technology; Dr. Harold G. Moulton, of the Brookings Institution, and Dr. John H. Finley, of *The New York Times.*

At the meeting of the members, followed by the meeting of the trustees, officers and five trustees were elected, the complete board being as follows:

Research Council (*Vice-president and Chairman of Executive Committee*).

Representatives of the National Research Council: Vernon Kellogg, National Research Council; C. G. Abbot, Smithsonian Institution; Harrison E. Howe, Industrial and Engineering Chemistry.

Representatives of the Scripps Estate: R. P. Scripps, Scripps-Howard Newspapers, Ohio; Thomas L. Sidlo, Cleveland, Ohio; H. L. Smithton, Scripps-Howard Newspapers (*Treasurer*).

Representatives of the Journalistic Profession: Marlen E. Pew, Editor, *Editor and Publisher*, New York City; John H. Finley, *New York Times*, New York City; Mark Sullivan, Washington, D. C.

THE ADULT EDUCATION ASSOCIATION AND THE RADIO COUNCIL

EDUCATIONAL and vocational guidance service for the unemployed, broadcasting into the schools and radio advertising are among the topics scheduled for discussion at the annual meetings of the American Association for Adult Education and the National Advisory Council on Radio in Education, to be held in Buffalo, New York, at the Hotel Statler, during the week of May 16.

The meetings of the association will begin on Monday, May 16, and will continue through Wednesday, May 18. The sessions of the council start on the evening of May 18 and continue through May 20.

Special emphasis will be placed upon adult education for the unemployed, at the meeting of the American Association for Adult Education. The Employment Stabilization Institute of the University of Minnesota will give a demonstration of the aptitude and interest tests being given unemployed adults, in an effort to determine whether such tests, coupled with a program of adult education and vocational rehabilitation, can make a contribution toward the elimination of existing unemployment or toward the prevention of future unemployment. Social education, education for culture, education for citizenship and occupational education will also be discussed.

Among those who will address the sessions are Dean James E. Russell, Felix Warburg, John Erskine, Everett Dean Martin, Robert S. Lynd, Frederick P. Keppel and Harry A. Overstreet.

Broadcasting into the schools, the broadcasting station as a community enterprise, development of radio legislation, and what the radio can do for the farmer and the rural community, will be considered at the meetings of the National Advisory Council on Radio in Education. One session will be devoted to the consideration of radio advertising from the standpoint of the broadcaster, the advertiser, and the general public.

The committees in charge of the radio programs on psychology, economics, vocational guidance and civics now being broadcast will report. The chairman of the Committee on Engineering Developments will give the latest scientific developments in radio. Experienced librarians will suggest ways and means through which the public library may cooperate with the broadcaster offering educational programs.

Speakers on the council's program include Florence Hale, president of the National Education Association; William John Cooper, United States Commissioner of Education; Cline M. Koon, U. S. Office of Education; Senator Arthur Capper; Harold Lafount, federal radio commissioner; William Hard, political correspondent; Walton Hale Hamilton, of the Yale University Law School, and Lyman Bryson, of the California Association for Adult Education.

EDUCATIONAL NOTES AND NEWS

MR. CHARLES N. SHAVER, superintendent of schools at Huntsville, Texas, has been appointed by Governor Ross S. Sterling State Superintendent of Public Instruction to succeed the late S. M. N. Marrs, who died recently. The appointment is for the remainder of the current year.

THE Georgia Education Association at its recent annual meeting in Macon gave Dr. Lawton B. Evans a dinner in honor of his fiftieth anniversary as superintendent of public schools of Augusta, Georgia. It is believed that Superintendent Evans's record of fifty years as superintendent of the Augusta schools is not exceeded by any other living superintendent.

THE degree of doctor of letters was conferred upon Superintendent James N. Rule on the occasion of the Founders Day exercises on April

15, celebrating the fifty-sixth anniversary of the establishment of Juniata College. Dr. Rule made the principal address, speaking on "The Depression and the Schools of To-morrow." Dr. Robert L. Kelly, executive secretary of the Association of American Colleges, brought greetings on this occasion and made an address the following day at the Educational Conference on "The Renaissance of the American College."

Professor A. V. Williams Jackson, Columbia University, was elected a fellow of the American Institute for Persian Art and Archeology at the recent annual meeting of the institute, at its new headquarters at 724 Fifth Avenue, New York City. Dr. Jackson has served as honorary president of the institute since its incorporation in 1920. Mr. Franklin Mott Gunther was reelected *president;* Professor John Shapley, of the University of Chicago, *vice-president,* and Myron Bement Smith, *secretary.* Mr. E. Vail Stebbins was made *treasurer* and Mr. Herbert E. Winlock, recently appointed director of the Metropolitan Museum of Art, was elected to the board of trustees, as were also Messrs. Philip Hofer, Louis Cartier, Henry Field, Mrs. Samuel Barlow, E. Vail Stebbins and Dr. Stephen P. Duggan.

Professor Alice H. Bushee, chairman of the department of Spanish at Wellesley College, has been elected to membership in the Spanish Academy of Science and Art at Cadiz, Spain, in recognition of her contributions to Spanish American scholarship and education.

At the recent Washington convocation of Delta Kappa Pi, Miss Jane Addams, Dr. J. McKeen Cattell and Dr. Truman Lee Kelley were elected to membership in the Laureate Chapter.

Mr. Douglas Huntley Gordon was formally inaugurated as the fourteenth president of St. John's College, Annapolis, Maryland, on April 30. Governor Albert C. Ritchie and Dr. Ernest M. Hopkins, president of Dartmouth College, were the principal speakers. Over a hundred delegates from other colleges and universities attended the ceremonies.

Officers elected at the New Orleans meeting of the American Library Association are: Harry Miller Lydenberg, assistant director of the New York Public Library, *president;* Miss Julia Ideson, librarian of the Houston, Texas, Public Library, *first vice-president;* Joseph L. Wheeler, librarian of the Enoch Pratt Free Library, of Baltimore, *second vice-president;* Matthew S. Dudgeon, librarian of the Milwaukee Public Library, *treasurer,* and John O'Leary and Eugene M. Stevens, of Chicago, *trustees* of the endowment fund. Members of the executive board elected were Miss Lillian H. Smith, chief of the boys' and girls' division of the Toronto Public Library, and Dr. Malcolm G. Wyer, librarian of the Denver Public Library.

At the tenth meeting of the Association of Colleges and Universities of the Pacific Southwest held on April 18, the following officers were elected: *President,* Dr. Rufus B. von KleinSmid, University of Southern California; *vice-presidents,* Dr. W. B. Munro, California Institute of Technology, and Dr. Arthur G. Coons, Occidental College; *secretary-treasurer,* Professor Charles T. Fitts, Pomona College; *executive committee,* Dr. W. S. Hertzog, California Christian College; Dean Marvin L. Darsie, University of California at Los Angeles; Professor H. E. Marsh, University of Redlands; Dr. H. W. Frantz, La Verne College, and Dr. Herbert E. Harris, Whittier College.

Dr. Augustus G. Pohlman, research professor of anatomy at the St. Louis University School of Medicine, has been appointed dean of the School of Medicine at the University of South Dakota.

Palmer H. Graham, chairman of the department of mathematics at the Washington Square College of New York University, has been appointed assistant dean of the college.

Dr. Albert J. Farmer, of the University of Grenoble, France, will return to Brown University in September for a second year as visiting professor of French. Other appointments in the department of Romance languages are Robert H. Williams, assistant professor of Spanish, and Edmund L. Loughnan, assistant professor of French.

Dr. Homer F. Carey, professor of law at the University of Michigan, has accepted a similar position at Northwestern University.

At Harvard University Jacob Pieter Den Hartog, graduate of the Technical University of

Delft, Holland, will be assistant professor of applied mechanics. Henry Melvin Hart, Jr., secretary to Associate Justice Louis Brandeis, of the United States Supreme Court, and a graduate of Harvard Law School, will become assistant professor of legal history. Wassily Leontief, a research associate with the National Bureau of Economic Research, will become an instructor in economics.

Mr. Frank G. McCormick has been promoted to be director of the department of physical education and athletics at the University of Minnesota. He will assume office on July 1 when the resignation of Mr. Crisler becomes effective.

Appointment of Raphael Johnson Shortlidge to succeed Dr. Murray Peabody Brush, who recently resigned as head master of the Jacob Tome Institute, Port Deposit, Maryland, was announced on April 30. Dr. Brush has become head master of the California Preparatory School for Boys at Covina.

W. Harry King, of Mitchell, South Dakota, recently appointed a member of the Federal Board for Vocational Education representing the interests of agriculture, assumed the duties of his office on April 20. His appointment was made to fill the vacancy on the board created by the recent death of Claude M. Henry.

Harry T. Collings, of the Wharton School of Finance and Commerce of the University of Pennsylvania, was on April 28 appointed chairman of the delegation which will represent the United States Government at the triennial congress of the International Society for Commercial Education in London on July 25. Other delegates are: William L. Cooper, commercial attache, London; Dr. John R. Gregg, New York; Dr. Thomas H. Healy, Georgetown University; W. H. Leffingwell, New York; Dr. Everett W. Lord, Boston University; Dr. Leverett S. Lyon, Brookings Institution, Washington; Miss Imogene Pilcher, Lincoln High School, Cleveland; Dr. Henry B. Rathbone, New York University; Miss Eleanor Skimin, Northern High School, Detroit; Dr. John A. Stevenson, Philadelphia; Dr. Harold J. Stonier, American Institute of Banking, New York.

Dr. Robert A. Millikan, director of the Norman Bridge Laboratory and chairman of the council of the California Institute of Technology, who has been attending the annual meeting of the National Academy of Sciences of which he is foreign secretary, and Dr. Ray Lyman Wilbur, Secretary of the Interior, with leave of absence from the presidency of Stanford University, were guests of President Hoover at his first week end this year at the Rapidan camp.

Dr. Henry Fairfield Osborn, president of the American Museum of Natural History, has returned to New York on the *Berengaria,* after a 27,000 mile trip on the motorship *Polaris.* He visited the South Sea Islands, Fiji Islands, Java, Sumatra, Saigon, Siam, Singapore, Ceylon and Cairo.

Dr. Francis T. Spaulding, associate professor in the graduate school of education of Harvard University, has been given leave of absence for the second half of the year 1933–34.

While on a recent visit to Minneapolis at the invitation of the Employment Stabilization Research Institute, Dr. W. V. Bingham gave on April 15 a public lecture on industrial psychology at the University of Minnesota, and addressed an audience of faculty members on the experiment in vocational counseling of preparatory school boys carried out last August at the engineering camp of Stevens Institute of Technology. Dr. Bingham also lectured at Northwestern University and at the State University of Iowa, and conferred with investigators in Rochester, New York, Chicago, Beloit, Ames, Cincinnati and Washington.

Dr. M. M. Chambers, now on temporary appointment as chairman of the department of the social sciences at the Teachers College of Kansas City, will teach in the department of school administration at the Ohio State University during the summer quarter.

Dr. F. C. Borgeson, professor of elementary education at New York University, will teach at the summer session of the School of Education of the University of Southern California at Los Angeles.

Dr. J. E. W. Wallin, head of the department of psychology and mental hygiene in the now defunct Atlantic University, has received a grant-in-aid from the Social Science Research

Council for the preparation for publication of an accumulation of original data that he has gathered from his graduate and undergraduate students in several universities on minor mental, social and educational maladjustments in normal people.

DR. W. J. MILLER, professor of geology and chairman of the department of the University of California at Los Angeles, delivered the annual faculty research lecture on May 2. The lecture was on "Magmatic Intrusion."

DR. BESS GOODYKOONTZ, assistant U. S. commissioner of education, and Mrs. Marion R. Mack, member of the New York City Board of Higher Education, spoke at a meeting of the New York City branch of the National Council of Administrative Women in Education, which was held on May 5.

DR. JOHN LIVINGSTON LOWES, Francis Lee Higginson professor of English literature at Harvard University, will deliver the Graduate School convocation address at Brown University on June 18.

KING VICTOR EMMANUEL of Italy granted on April 29 a pardon to the Belgian professor, Leo Joseph Moulin, who was sentenced last September 2 to two years' imprisonment for anti-Fascist propaganda.

THE fifteenth annual meeting of the American Council on Education is being held in the Brookings Institution, Washington, on May 6 and 7. The annual report of the director will be submitted by Dr. C. Riborg Mann. According to the preliminary program the principal subject of discussion is "Who and What Determine the Major Educational Policies of Professional Education in the United States." Dr. Ray Lyman Wilbur, Secretary of the Interior, opens the discussion for medicine, and Mr. James Grafton Rogers, Assistant Secretary of State, the discussion for law. President W. E. Wickenden, of the Case School of Applied Science, planned to discuss the subject from the standpoint of engineering schools, and Dean Luther A. Weigle, of Yale University, from the standpoint of theology. Discussions include what standards should be set for admission to the practise of law and medicine, and who should determine how many lawyers or doctors the country needs. On Saturday morning, Dr. John C. Merriam, president of the Carnegie Institution of Washington, and Professor John J. Coss, director of the Summer School at Columbia University, will discuss "Education for Leisure" and Dr. Albert B. Meredith, formerly superintendent of public instruction of the State of Connecticut, now professor of education at New York University, "State Policies with Reference to Teacher Preparation."

THE Institute for Administrative Officers of Institutions of Higher Education will meet on July 13, 14 and 15 at the University of Chicago. Among the principal speakers will be Dr. Ernest H. Wilkins, president of Oberlin College; Dr. H. E. Hawkes, dean of Columbia College; Dr. J. B. Johnston, dean of the College of Science, Literature and the Arts at the University of Minnesota, and Dr. Charles Judd, dean of the School of Education at the University of Chicago.

THE conference which Dr. William John Cooper, U. S. Commissioner of Education, in cooperation with commissioners of education in Maine, New Hampshire, Vermont, Massachusetts, Rhode Island and Connecticut, called on homemaking education was held at Massachusetts State College, Amherst, on May 2 and 3. Among the speakers were: Florence Hale, president of the National Education Association; The Honorable Joseph B. Ely, Governor of Massachusetts; Bertram E. Packard, commissioner of education in Maine; Walter E. Ranger, commissioner of education, Rhode Island; James N. Pringle, commissioner of education, New Hampshire; Payson Smith, commissioner of education in Massachusetts; Ernest W. Butterfield, commissioner of education, Connecticut; Francis L. Bailey, commissioner of education, Vermont; Roscoe W. Thatcher, president of the Massachusetts State College, who is host to the conference, and Commissioner Cooper.

THE New England Association of College Educators held its annual meeting at Bates College on April 22, with Professor R. A. F. McDonald, of Bates College, president of the association, in the chair. The topic for discussion was "The Place of the Liberal Arts Colleges in Preparing Teachers for New England Secondary Schools." Professor J. L. O'Gorman, of Holy Cross College, was elected president for the coming year. The annual meeting will be held next year at Holy Cross College. Professor B. Holmes Wallace, of the University of Vermont, was reelected secretary.

Temple University has announced the membership of the committee which will take charge of its eighth annual conference on secondary education this year: William Bristow, Harrisburg; Wallace Savage, principal, Upper Darby High School; Ruth Wanger, South Philadelphia High School; Ira Kraybill, principal, Cheltenham High School; John P. Lozo, principal, Reading High School; Frank R. Morey, supervising principal, Swarthmore; Parke Schoch, associate superintendent, Philadelphia; Olive Hart, principal, Girls High School, Philadelphia; Elton E. Stone, principal, Easton High School; Arthur M. Seybold, head master, Oak Lane Country Day School; Dean Walk, Teachers College; Derwood G. Tew, Camden, N. J.; Charles Miller, superintendent, Lansdowne, *chairman;* Jos. S. Butterweck, Teachers College, Temple University.

The sixth annual Iowa State Conference on Child Development and Parent Education will convene at Iowa City, Iowa, on June 21, 22 and 23, under the auspices of the Iowa State Council for Child Study and Parent Education. The Iowa Child Welfare Research Station, the Extension Divisions of Iowa State College and the State University of Iowa, and the Iowa State Teachers College will cooperate in the meetings.

A reduction of $257,381 in the 1932–33 budget of Northwestern University was approved on April 27 by the university's board of trustees. The reduction was effected without cutting salaries. The total budget for the year 1932–33, as approved by the trustees, is $4,401,482, as against $4,658,864 for the present year. An anticipated deficit of $78,992 was authorized, but it is expected by the board that this sum will be made up during the year.

DISCUSSION

THE UNIVERSITIES AND DEMOCRACY

To one who takes but a casual glance at what has happened and is happening in Russia, Austria, Germany, Spain, China, India and Mexico, it must be evident that the great countries of the world are moving in the direction of some form of government that will give to the workers more power, and a larger share in the products of industry. The United States can not escape the influence of these world movements.

If one will go to almost any library, the librarian will tell you that the books on Russia are out all the time, and have to be spoken for long in advance. The number of articles on some phase of the developments there is myriad. Many professors are going there to study conditions. The tourist trade is developing rapidly. Amtorg announces that 74 new hotels are now being completed for the tourist trade of next summer.

The world movement, of which the Russian development is but one phase, is not coming from the universities but from the workers themselves. Universities have been known to dismiss professors for very mild socialistic expressions.

When changes of this sort are in the air, they usually come in revolutions, as they did in France at the end of the eighteenth century, as they did in Russia two decades ago. Such revolutions in the past have been violent, bloody and unreasonable. They have destroyed immense treasures of wealth, art and religion. The universities at present are doing little to guide this growing sentiment among the people. Their only contact is through their extension and home study courses.

It is not certain that they can do much; but if democracy rather than communism is to prevail, civilization must in some way provide its workers with a living wage, insurance against accidents, sickness and unemployment and a reasonable security in old age. It must restrain within reasonable limits the wasteful and undirected competition of the present, and it must learn to put competent people in office and hold them responsible for their actions.

This training should come from the universities. Our present brand of patriotism consists largely in prejudice against all other countries and throwing up your hat, and putting out the flag on the Fourth of July. We need a patriotism of a different sort—one that does not consist of national animosities or even of a willingness to serve in time of war primarily, but rather of a willingness to serve in time of peace, that demands competence and honesty in public officials, the suppression of the criminal and the enforcement of law.

The great opportunity that the universities have to mould the future, that seems to be coming on, is through their extension and home study courses, but at present they have few contacts with the labor unions, and the courses being offered are not along the lines in which these groups are thinking.

HENRY S. CURTIS
HOME STUDY DEPARTMENT,
COLUMBIA UNIVERSITY

FACTORS ASSOCIATED WITH POOR READING ABILITY OF ADULTS

THE writer has been carrying on remedial work with poor readers in college during the past four years, and at the present time is conducting a remedial class for a group of poor readers at a western college. Like others who are interested and working in this field, the writer has endeavored to keep up on all of the research studies that have been reported in the educational journals. The purpose of this article is (1) to exchange with others who are working along similar lines the experience and findings of the writer, and (2) to suggest possible approaches to further researches in the field.

In examining the case histories of more than 100 college students who have come to the writer for assistance in reading during the past four years, some interesting and, perhaps, significant facts are revealed. In order to be of maximum benefit to these students it has been necessary in each case to get certain items of information concerning the early training and experience of each individual. While it is true that each student presents a different case from every other student, nevertheless, certain factors appear more frequently than would be accounted for by chance. Some of these are listed below; the order of the items has no significance:

(1) Little or no recreational reading as a child. In some cases this was due to lack of reading material; while in others to lack of interest, or failure on the part of parents to encourage the reading habit, were contributing factors.

(2) Lack of interest in reading when young.

(3) Lack of reading material in the home.

(4) Attended a rural school (usually one-room) during the first three grades.

(5) Attended two or more elementary schools.

(6) Small vocabulary (reading, writing and speaking).

(7) Slow mentally. Some research on this point prompts the writer to question the reliability of the mental ratings obtained by the poor reader on most mental tests which involve reading comprehension.

As soon as time permits, it is the hope of the writer to further investigate the various factors suggested in this report. In the meantime he will anticipate the reactions of others who are working in this most interesting and valuable phase of education.

F. W. PARR
Professor of Secondary Education
OREGON STATE COLLEGE,
CORVALLIS, OREGON

A UNIT OF INSTRUCTION ON VAN DYKE'S "FISHERMAN'S LUCK"

Purposes:

(1) To enjoy the experience of reading the essay
(2) To share this enjoyment with a social group
(3) To enjoy vicariously the experience of fishing
(4) To share this enjoyment with a social group
(5) To create something which shall express these satisfactions

Aims:

(1) To learn about trout-fishing
(2) To learn about other kinds of fishing
(3) To learn about the value of fish as food
(4) To learn about the economic importance of fish

(5) To learn the place of fish in secular and religious history

(6) To learn the effect of fish and fishing upon language

(7) To learn to manipulate fish—living, dead, and cooked.

Objectives:

(1) Vocational; opportunities and needs in fishing; is it a blind alley vocation?

(2) Wise Use of Leisure: what wise men have fished?

(3) Health: food value of fish; vitamins in cod-liver oil.

(4) Home Making: preparation and cooking of fish.

(5) Social-civic: Fisheries in colonial days; in the Revolution; in connection with arbitration. How we always won.

(6) Religious and ethical: Jonah; miraculous draught of fishes; the fish as a religious symbol; keeping Lent. Kindness to fish.

Big Objective:

To realize the place of fish in the modern world.

Goal:

The fish-centered school.

ACTIVITIES (leading to further activity)

Unit I. (fusion with science) Make and care for an aquarium.

Unit II. (fusion with home economics) Prepare and serve: Creamed codfish—boiled salmon—fish chowder.

Unit III. (fusion with commercial education) Study the mail-order ads. of Frank E. Davis, and make better ones.

Unit IV. (fusion with language) Make a list of such expressions as "poor fish," "gudgeon" (*obs.*), "sucker."

Unit V. (fusion with library work) Cut out all the pictures of fish from books in the library, and paste them in a notebook.

Unit VI. (fusion with handwork) Make a seine of all the string in all your homes (creative group-project for the entire class through the term).

Unit VII. (fusion with composition) Write a letter to Dr. Van Dyke, presenting to him the seine, scrap-books, chowder, aquarium, etc., and inviting him to address the school.

ALLAN ABBOTT

TEACHERS COLLEGE,
COLUMBIA UNIVERSITY

SPECIAL CORRESPONDENCE

THE AMERICAN COLLEGE OF SOFIA IN RELATION TO THE BULGARIAN STATE EDUCATIONAL SYSTEM

IN Bulgaria all children are required to attend school for seven years. As a matter of fact, in a large number of smaller villages only four years of schooling is provided. The elementary school consists of two divisions, first, the primary school with a course of study covering four years, and second, the progymnasium with a course of study covering three years, making a total of seven years. The school age begins at seven. This elementary system, therefore, corresponds in general to the grammar school in the United States. Normally, children complete the progymnasium in their fifteenth year. Following the progymnasium is the gymnasium, with a course of study five years in length. Admission to the gymnasium is by examination. There are gymnasia in all the larger towns but not in the villages. In general, the work of the primary schools and the progymnasia is good. Many new school buildings have been built all over Bulgaria during the last ten years. The work of the gymnasium suffers from lack of laboratory and library facilities and also from the fact that the classes are much too large. Normally, classes contain from thirty-five to fifty students. On completion of the gymnasium courses, students are admitted to matura examinations. The students who succeed in passing the matura examinations are eligible for admission to the University of Sofia.

In addition to the state schools there are a number of private schools of both primary and gymnasium grades. These are mainly foreign schools, as French, German and Italian. There are also private schools conducted by the Jewish, Armenian and other minority groups in

Bulgaria. These private schools are all organized in conformity with the national school system.

The University of Sofia

At the head of the state educational system stands the University of Sofia. It has seven faculties, or departments. These are law, medicine, theology, social sciences, mathematics and physics, biological sciences, and philology. Theoretically, all students who have successfully completed the gymnasium course are eligible for admission to the university, but most departments of the university strictly limit admission to the applicants having the highest scholastic record. Some departments accept only a certain number of applicants selected on a basis of scholarship. The courses of study in the university are strictly professional. The diploma is ordinarily obtained on the completion of four years of specialized study. The average age of admission to the university is about twenty. Probably not more than 40 per cent. of the students admitted complete the course of study and secure a diploma. In general, the work of the university is good although it suffers from lack of teaching equipment.

The Department of Education

The department of education is of the same rank as other governmental departments, and the Minister of Education has a seat in the cabinet. The department is organized with a chief secretary as the executive officer, and with under-secretaries for each of a number of divisions, such as the division for higher schools, for progymnasia, for primary schools, etc. Each division has inspectors who regularly visit all schools in the country. There is a division charged with the preparation of courses of study and the preparation or selection of text-books. No school in the country can secure recognition for its work unless it has secured the authorization of the department of education. In general, the department of education exercises careful and severe control over the work of all schools. All teachers in the national schools are appointed by the department of education. Each school district throughout the country has a local school committee which cooperates with the department of education in maintaining the local school.

The American College

The American College is regularly recognized by the department of education and carries on its work in close cooperation with the national school system. Relations with the department of education are most cordial. The Minister of Education and all officials in the department regularly show the greatest consideration for the work of the college. During the past five years the college has secured much valuable assistance from the department. The college is given entire freedom to develop its courses of study and all other work on condition that it fulfils the requirements of the general school laws. These requirements do not lay any particular burden upon the college. All higher schools are required to teach the Bulgarian language, Bulgarian history and Bulgarian geography. These must be taught in the Bulgarian language by a Bulgarian citizen. Since the college would teach these subjects in any case, this requirement is not burdensome. All other subjects are left to the discretion of the college administration with the general requirement that the amount and quality of the work done must not be less than the minimum required in the state gymnasia. Since the courses of study in the college are much higher than similar courses in the gymnasia, this requirement also is not a burden. The state requires that all teachers in institutions of gymnasium rank or higher shall be graduates of some university, the minimum requirement being the diploma of the University of Sofia. This diploma is approximately equivalent to the degree of Master of Arts from an American university. Close control is exercised over teachers who are Bulgarian citizens, but foreign teachers are not required to submit their diplomas to the department of education. The department does not interfere in any way with the employment of teachers, although it is ready to help find teachers if requested to do so. Some of the best Bulgarian teachers in the college have been secured through the department of education. The department has the right to inspect all schools. The department appoints a representative to be present at the final or matura examinations. All students on the completion of the course of study are required to take matura examinations. The representative of the department of education signs the diplomas along with the President of the college. The signature of this representative gives the diploma validity in Bulgaria and thus gives the graduates of the college all the rights and privileges accorded to graduates of state institutions.

ADMISSION

Students are admitted to the first preparatory class, directly from the state progymnasia. Except in rare cases, students are admitted only into the first preparatory class. If an applicant is not a graduate of a progymnasium, he must take special examinations given in the progymnasia in order to qualify as having preparation equivalent to that given in the progymnasia. The same course of study is given in all progymnasia in the country. Therefore, all students admitted to the college have had the same previous training. The average age of admission to the first preparatory class is fourteen years and six months, with very little variation. Applications are accepted only from students in the upper half of their class in the progymnasium. All applicants are also required to take a special examination for admittance into the college. As the number of applicants during the past five years has regularly been much greater than the number of places available, it has been possible to secure a group of students representing the best graduates of the progymnasia.

CURRICULUM

The course of study is six years in length, comprising two preparatory classes, and four college classes designated as freshman, sophomore, junior and senior. About 20 per cent. of the students admitted are unable to complete their work in six years. These must either drop out or spend seven years in the college. The course of study is so arranged that students who are unable to continue in the college may drop out and reenter the national school system at the end of the first or second preparatory year. In this way, most of the weaker students who have gained admission are able to transfer back into the national system without loss of time.

FINAL EXAMINATIONS AND STANDING

As indicated above, on the completion of the college course all applicants for the diploma must take final or matura examinations. These examinations are in six subjects and are both written and oral. They are severe, including a written examination of four hours in each subject, and an oral examination of half an hour in each subject. The oral examination is given by a committee of three or more teachers. The diploma of the college is given in conformity with the Bulgarian school law. The diploma admits the holder to the University of Sofia and to all universities of Europe. During the past five years, no graduate of the college has failed to secure admission to any European university. A graduate of the college secures no additional recognition in the university for work done above that required in the gymnasia in the country. The reason for this is the fact that the college gives no professional courses. This year there are sixty-five graduates of the college enrolled in the professional schools of the University of Sofia, and almost as many more in foreign universities. Practically all boys who graduate from the college expect to pursue higher professional studies. The majority of the girls graduating do not expect to continue their studies, although some graduates continue in the university. Such ordinarily become teachers, lawyers, doctors, pharmacists and dentists.

Thus, the work of the college is coordinated with the work of the national school system, both by the requirements for admission and for graduation. All students come into the college from the national progymnasia in their fifteenth year and graduate from the college in their twenty-first year, qualified to continue their studies in any professional school in Bulgaria or in Europe. It is the policy of the college administration to organize the work in such a way that students may derive the benefits of the training offered without being separated in any way from the life of their country. Hence, in addition to keeping the scholastic work of the college in harmony with the state system and promoting the closest cooperation with the department of education, other contacts are constantly sought, such as lectures by leading men and women, participation in sports, etc. Also, the professors in the college contribute articles to Bulgarian periodicals and in other ways take part in the public life of the country. The Bulgarian teachers in the college are regularly members of the state teachers organizations and take part in their conferences. In these various ways, the college has come to be regarded in Bulgaria as an indigenous rather than as a foreign institution.

FLOYD H. BLACK,
President

NEAR EAST COLLEGE ASSN.,
NEW YORK, N. Y.
FEBRUARY, 1932

QUOTATIONS

FROM THE SEAT OF THE SCORNER

As Diogenes once sought an honest man, so Abraham Flexner seeks an honest-to-goodness university; and in America he finds not one. The Johns Hopkins began right, but could not stay on the straight and narrow path. When Gilman's leadership had been withdrawn, it fell away. Harvard had possibilities, though Eliot was rather Gilman's follower than quite the leader Harvard men have taken him to be; but Harvard wastes its talents now on business schools and college houses. Columbia is but a vast collection of unsatisfactory, semi-academic units, offending most of all in Teachers College and the cheap, commercialized instruction of a correspondence school. This country has no university deserving of the name. Dr. Flexner himself is starting one—the Institute of Advanced Studies, to be developed, somewhere in New Jersey, as a company of scholars with a few disciples, the scholars very eminent and amply paid, the students far beyond the need of credits or degrees, and all concerned exclusively with scholarship. In Dr. Flexner's recent book on universities, and now in an *Atlantic Monthly* article, he states his views in cutting phrases that dismiss our present universities as false, enfeebled, or estranged from grace. The Business School receives the brunt of the attack, so far as Harvard is concerned; for business, dubbed by our commencement phrase "The oldest of the arts and the youngest of the professions," is neither, but an occupation merely, whose major aim is money-getting; and a school that trains its students for an occupation so devoid of social worth, so little intellectual, should never have been made a part of Harvard University.

If Dr. Flexner had confined himself to a protest against the university teaching of business in the spirit of mere competitive money-grabbing, Harvard men would generally have lent him an attentive ear, including most graduates of the Business School and its entire staff. The Harvard School is a Graduate School of Business *Administration* (Dr. Flexner marks the word for scorn) for the very reason that the school intends its graduates to manage business enterprises with general social ends in view. Business needs administration for the common good; left undirected, it remains a cut-throat struggle; and the task of raising it above that level is a difficult and deeply intellectual undertaking. This, we are persuaded, is the basic theory of the Harvard Business School. If so, Flexnerian castigations will not greatly damp its ardor.

But scorn of business does not tell the tale of Dr. Flexner's condemnation of our universities. They should not train for anything; their sole and ample task is comprehension. A university should study problems; but vocational schools, wherein practitioners prepare for labors in an actual world, in courts, or schools, or hospitals, or churches, should not have a part in university development. Dr. Flexner does not actually say that a university medical school should graduate no doctors fit to practise; but on medicine and law his views are not entirely consistent with his views on business and those other petty occupations on which the various graduate schools at Harvard squander their attention.

It is hard to state without some irony a doctrine that is both self-righteous and, at bottom, based on something very like perversity of understanding. No one denies that universities should concern themselves mightily and continuously with research; no one would have them devote themselves to matters trivial or superficial, or to mere routine, in any occupation; nor to training for vocations that are socially inconsequential or shallow intellectually. But no university need forfeit its title because it has, besides a graduate school for pure research, vocational schools that train practitioners for many of the great professions. Vocational schools should never overwhelm the liberal departments, and they should themselves be centers of research. If Dr. Flexner had but warned of the dangers here, without insisting that vocational schools are only money changers in the temple, to be driven forth with whips, we might have thanked him with no irony. Thanks are due to him still, and his attacks, for all their caustic quality, will do the universities a service. His own undertaking deserves to succeed and will have the good wishes of every one who values liberal studies carried to their uttermost. But who can take his general doctrine as a serious guide for university administration?—*Harvard Alumni Bulletin.*

THE EXPERIMENTAL SCHOOL IN NEW YORK CITY

IT is difficult to understand the attitude which has been taken by Dr. William J. O'Shea, superintendent of schools, in reference to continuing the experimental program which has been in operation in Public School 41, Manhattan.

When the Public Education Association announced that it could no longer finance this program—one of the outstanding educational activities of the city—parents of the children who were in the experimental classes rallied to the support of the project. They appointed a committee and solicited financial pledges. These pledges soon assured a fund of more than $8,000, whereupon the parents requested the Board of Superintendents to reopen the matter in order to give consideration to the possibility of continuing the cooperation of the school authorities if the entire budget could be assured. A hearing was held, following which it was announced that the Board of Superintendents had decided not to authorize continuance of the program, on the ground that "the appraisal of the work so far conducted would not justify the board to rescind its former decisions to discontinue the experiment at the end of June, 1932." This statement was made in the face of the fact that the question of the appraisal of the work had not been raised at the hearing and of the further fact that, in his reply to the letter from Mr. Howard W. Nudd, director of the Public Education Association, informing him that the association could not continue the work because of lack of funds, Superintendent O'Shea said nothing about "appraisal," but based the decision to discontinue the experiment upon the inability of the school system to supply the additional funds needed.

The statement is the more strange in that the Evaluating Committee, which last September "earnestly" recommended "that the experimental program at Public School 41 be continued for another year and that such further evaluation be made as may be necessary for more conclusive findings," is engaged in making a second appraisal and has issued no report. Mr. Nudd pertinently asks whose appraisal was accepted and what its bases are. These are proper questions. To snuff out the experimental work which has been going on at Public School 41 without giving specific and cogent reasons for the action would be to show a deficient sense of responsibility. Instead of rebuffing the parents who have dug into their pockets and persuaded others to do likewise in order that the experiment may continue, the Board of Superintendents ought to welcome their offer of support and be grateful for the existence of such generous and public-spirited citizens.—*New York Evening Post.*

THE CENTENNIAL OF LAFAYETTE COLLEGE

LAFAYETTE'S BENEFACTORS

THE years will be rolled back during the week of May 16 at Lafayette College when the institution celebrates the one hundredth anniversary of its opening with a centennial conference on "The French Backgrounds of American Civilization" and a great pageant which will depict dramatic episodes in the life of the Marquis de Lafayette and the outstanding events in the history of the college.

It was in September, 1824, that General Lafayette—last hero of a glorious age—came to the United States for his triumphal visit. He was the guest of the nation, and for more than a year "the way of his journey was like the trail of a comet—a line of coaches, escorts of horsemen, torches by night, bonfires on hilltops, speeches, handshakings, cheers." It was the gallant figure of Lafayette which was in the minds of that group of public-spirited citizens of Easton, Pennsylvania, who gathered in White's Hotel on the northeast corner of the Public

Square on the evening of December 27, 1824. For several months there had been a growing conviction that by reason of its location and attributes, Easton should become the site of a college. And on that evening, when the assemblage voted "that it is expedient to establish at this place an institution of learning" there was coupled with it a resolution "that as a testimony of respect for the talents, virtues and signal services of General Lafayette in the great cause of freedom, the said institution be named Lafayette College."

On March 9, 1826, the petition of the Easton inhabitants, which had been presented to the Senate and House of Representatives of Pennsylvania, was passed and a charter granted. Nearly six years elapsed before the college trustees witnessed the actual beginnings of instruction in the new institution. The Reverend George Junkin accepted the first presidency of the college in February. A farm and buildings comprising sixty acres of land south of the Lehigh River, directly opposite the borough of Easton, was leased for two years by the trustees. In March President Junkin, assisted by a number of prospective students of the college, began the work of fitting the farm buildings for college use. And then on the morning of May 9, 1832, forty-three students reported at the institution and regular instruction commenced.

One of the greatest crises in the history of Lafayette occurred during the Civil War. The late Professor W. B. Owen writes: "War, always bad, was particularly bad for Lafayette at that time, for it was one in a series of discouraging strokes. The income of the college was rapidly falling off, the president had resigned, the faculty dwindled away because of the inability of the authorities to pay their salaries; the students, what few there were, scattered, many of them to the army, and in 1863, the year that General Lee invaded Pennsylvania, there were no commencement exercises at all.

"It became a serious question whether the college should go on. In this crisis, a few of the professors—Professor Coffin, Professor March, Dr. Coleman, and Dr. Eckard—volunteered to keep the doors open, and keep the classes going for another year, satisfied with whatever might be forthcoming in the way of salary."

It was at this critical period that Dr. William C. Cattell became an important factor in the destinies of the college. Formerly a member of the faculty, he agreed to accept the presidency of the college, with a full realization of the prolonged struggles with adversity which had marked the administration of his predecessors. With a freshman class of six, which was later increased to ten, the new college year under President Cattell opened in September, 1864. The income of the college was about $3,200 a year. The college was heavily in debt. It was necessary to raise $30,000 within the year or the board of trustees would be forced "to consider, not the propriety, but the necessity of suspending operations."

The year 1864 was a fateful one. The life of the institution hung by a slender thread. With the senior members of the faculty continuing their endeavors with but slight hope that they would receive a salary, President Cattell undertook the work of procuring the "prodigious sum of $30,000." When eleven of the twelve months had elapsed President Cattell had been able to raise only $10,000.

On an eventful Sabbath in September, 1865, it chanced that the pulpit of the Presbyterian Church of Hazleton, Pennsylvania, was occupied for the day by President Cattell. Among the regular attendants of the church was Ario Pardee, prosperous self-made man of business. The services concluded, President Cattell accompanied Mr. Pardee to his home, remaining there over night as a guest. On the following morning President Cattell and his host walked in the spacious grounds surrounding the Pardee home. The story of Lafayette came pouring from the president's lips. Mr. Pardee knew of Lafayette College only vaguely, for he had been in Easton but once or twice in his life. After he had listened attentively to the president's tale of the long-continued and heroic struggle of the institution to carry on its work, Mr. Pardee turned to President Cattell and said:

"Yes, I see. I thought you had come to Hazleton to preach but you came here to ask me for money to carry on a college. Well, I would really like to know how much you expected to get from a plain business man like me."

At this critical moment President Cattell did not lack courage. "Mr. Pardee," he said, as the "plain business man" looked straight in the face of the audacious college president, "I trust you will give us twenty thousand dollars. But I realize that this is a great sum of money even for a rich man like you to give, and you know nothing of our great work and our great need, except what I have told you to-day. Come to Easton! Look over the whole ground for yourself; talk with the professors at their homes—and then decide."

"No," said Mr. Pardee unhesitatingly, "I understand it all now as well as if I were in Easton. I will give you the twenty thousand dollars now."

The subsequent benefactions of Mr. Pardee for Lafayette are well known. Within a year he had become a trustee of the college, and shortly thereafter he gave $100,000 to endow the Pardee Scientific Course. In 1868 he bestowed another $30,000 on the college and in 1871 he provided a quarter of a million dollars for a building and equipment for the scientific course which he had established.

At the rededication of Pardee Hall in 1880, replacing the building which had burned to the ground, Governor Hoyt, of Pennsylvania, said: "Lafayette is certainly having its full share of days, many of them red-letter days. They have a courageous philosophy here, born of a cheerful kind of adversity, a chastening kind of prosperity, a sort of jugglery with bricks and brick-dust. Only a few short months ago the sightly structure disappeared; now this graceful one fills the heavens. Pardee Hall is a new pledge that it will so equip the college that their worst work of to-morrow will equal the best work of yesterday."

Truly, Lafayette College has had its share of red-letter days—days which glow the more vividly when contrasted with the black and gloomy days of the early years. There was the red-letter day when Mr. Fred Morgan Kirby provided funds exceeding half a million dollars for the beautiful building to house the work of the college of civil rights, government and law, which he had previously established with a generous endowment in 1920; there was the never-to-be-forgotten day in 1928 when Mr. John Markle, of New York, thrilled the college with the gift of $500,000 for a magnificent new Mining Engineering Hall, and then added another $400,000 for its endowment on the day the hall was dedicated.

Other days are no less vivid in the calendar of the college; the day in 1907 when an endowment fund of $500,000 was completed in celebration of the seventy-fifth anniversary; the day of loyalty in 1920 when the million dollar endowment fund was oversubscribed by fifty thousand dollars; the eventful day in 1924 when Mr. John D. Larkin, of Buffalo, endowed the chemistry department with a gift of $200,000 increased to $250,000 in 1925 by his children; the triumphal day when the citizens of Easton and Phillipsburg completed the fund of $200,000 for the dormitory, Easton Hall; the splendid day in the history of Lafayette when the athletic committee of the board of trustees, with the aid of the board, a few friends and numerous alumni, raised a fund of $400,000 for the athletic field and a new stadium.

Finally, Lafayette cherishes the thought of other memorable days; the day when John Welles Hollenback completed the fifty-fifth year of generous and devoted service as a trustee of the college; the auspicious day when Dr. Ethelbert D. Warfield assumed the presidency of Lafayette and for twenty years the college forged forward under his loyal and vigorous leadership; and the significant day when Dr. John H. MacCracken was inaugurated as president and under his inspiring leadership the college began a new era of academic and material progress.

In 1927 Dr. William Mather Lewis was called from the presidency of George Washington University to become president of Lafayette. The five years of his administration have been conspicuously marked with educational and material advancement by the college. The John Markle Mining Engineering Hall, considered one of the best equipped buildings for the teaching of mining engineering in the country, was dedicated in 1929, while the beautiful Kirby Hall of Civil Rights with its generous endowment from Fred Morgan Kirby was dedicated in the spring of 1930. The Gates Memorial Dormitory was formally opened in the spring of 1931. In such ways has Lafayette progressed materially in the past five years. These years have also witnessed higher standards of scholarship, cultural additions in the form of more numerous lectures by prominent authorities, recitals and other kinds of artistic expression, and in general a bettering of the students' morale, intellectual interests and personnel.

Thus it is fitting that in May Lafayette College should celebrate this century of growth and service with a geat pageant which will depict in the first place dramatic episodes in the life of the Marquis de Lafayette, and secondly, the outstanding events in the history of the college. Another aspect of the celebration will be the conference on "The French Backgrounds of American Civilization," which will convene on the campus on May 17 and 18. Already a large number of scholars, educators, statesmen and men prominent in public life from both France and the United States have accepted invitations to attend. The celebration in May will fittingly close Lafayette's first century of growth and educational service.

Thomas P. Robinson

THE AMERICAN COLLEGE[1]

When Lafayette College opened its doors seventy-five years ago, Harvard College had ten professors and 216 students; Columbia College, six professors and 125 students. Harvard was then 196 years old, Columbia sixty-eight years old. To-day Lafayette has twenty-three professors and 411 students. Should Lafayette grow as Harvard and Columbia have grown, then when our grandchildren and great-grandchildren gather to celebrate the hundred and fiftieth anniversary, they would find here five hundred professors and ten thousand students. The alumni would be invited to contribute toward an additional endowment of twenty million dollars.

The days to be, even more than the times of the past, are for us a book with seven seals. None knows what things lie on the knees of the gods; it is more than we can do to re-collect what has been strewn from their hands. But we at least believe that the American college was an important factor in the higher life of our country during the nineteenth century, and that the part of Lafayette, in the days of its adversity and in the days of its prosperity, has been no mean one.

[1] Address at the celebration of the seventy-fifth anniversary of the founding of Lafayette College.

The citizens of Easton who met at White's Hotel on December 27, 1824, and resolved to establish an institution of learning in their beautiful village had foresight and courage. They were men of patriotism, naming the institution Lafayette College in recognition of "the signal service of General Lafayette in the great cause of freedom," and resolving that military engineering and tactics should be taught, because, as they said, "a freeman's arm can best defend a freeman's home." In the annual report of the trustees following the death of Lafayette, they said:

> We record an event unparalleled in the annals of the world's history, of one man's death arraying in the habiliments of mourning, all the friends of freedom on the globe. . . . Let ours be the sacred duty of imitating his illustrious example and holding it up for admiration to the wondering gaze of the dear youth of this institution, which bears his venerable name.

There were difficulties to overcome, but in 1832 George Junkin, a true leader of men, was elected president and three professors were called. Two of them were in mathematics and the sciences, one of whom, Samuel P. Gross, became a great surgeon of the last century. The traditional curriculum of Latin, Greek and mathematics was, however, adopted, and in its simplest form. The first half-year was devoted to the first book of Euclid; the third half-year to the fourth, fifth and sixth books. More than a year was given to Horace. There is in retrospect a curious incongruity between the gentle epicureanism of the Odes, and the lives of these young men, who had morning prayers at five o'clock and drank coffee for breakfast because milk was too expensive.

At the instance of President Junkin manual labor was substituted for military training. The early reports lay stress on the importance of the movement—how it assured the health of the students, gave them honorable independence and broke down class distinctions and class jealousies. The plan failed; to the misfortune of the college it may be. The existence of an agricultural department and of a mechanical department then and there is not without interest for the history of our educational system.

Another plan that failed was the course for

teachers established at the beginning and seven years before the first normal schools of Massachusetts. In their second annual report the trustees wrote:

> As to elevating the standard of common school instruction, we propose to effect it by training teachers to that business as a profession. . . . Incompetent teachers very frequently receive inadequate support; and the inadequacy of the support secures and perpetuates the incompetency of the teachers. . . . Let teachers be well educated, that is, let them be taught thoroughly the branches which they will be called upon to teach, and, which is the principal thing, the art of *communicating* instruction and *governing* a school; and let their services be secured permanently in that business, by adequate pay.

In still another direction the founders of Lafayette notably anticipated educational development, namely, in advocating the study of English and modern languages. By the terms of the charter—one of its two definite provisions—a professorship of German was to be established. In their original memorial to the legislature, the founders said that it is to be regretted that students commonly limit their attention to the dead languages. They pointed to the ease with which the romance languages can be acquired after Latin, and said that German and Anglo-Saxon ought long since to have been made a part of education. They add:

> But the language most neglected in our seminaries of learning is the English. It is, we think, one of the follies of the learned to expend time and toil and money in minute investigation of the languages of other times and other people, at the expense of omitting the equally curious and more useful investigation of their own.

While these ideas do not seem to have affected the early curriculum, they are a prevision of the most important contribution made to education by Lafayette under the leadership of Professor March, the great teacher, the great scholar and the great man, who just fifty years ago became professor of the English language and comparative philology, and introduced into our colleges the scientific study of English and Anglo-Saxon.

The Cambridge College, transplanted to the new Cambridge in 1636, and later to Virginia, Connecticut, New Jersey, Pennsylvania and New York, brought hither its organization and its curriculum; and these have been slowly and partially adapted to an industrial democracy. The curriculum and culture of the English College were esoteric. The church of the semi-reformation and the dead languages were in nominal control, but they touched lightly the young gentlemen destined to manage their feudal estates and to extend the British empire. The aristocratic English college of church and state with its classical curriculum was transplanted to scenes not excessively caricatured in Martin Chuzzlewit or by Mrs. Trollope, yet not alien to men such as Franklin or Jefferson, not lacking tendencies such as those expressed by Emerson or Whitman. The new colleges, following closely on the footsteps of the pioneers, were naïve, not crude; simple and narrow, but not Philistine; lacking in perspective, but rich in ideals.

The American college has performed a great service. The statistics which show that college graduates are more likely than others to succeed in certain professions are not in themselves significant. One might as well argue for compressed feet, because Chinese women who follow the practice are more likely than others to marry mandarins. The ablest and most energetic men have gone to college, and the college has been the normal gateway to certain careers. It was, however, a gain to bring together many of the more promising young men and to give them such training and culture as might be. The college was the natural threshold to the church, to law and to medicine, so long as adequate professional schools were lacking. But when to these professional schools others in engineering, education, journalism and business have been added, it is not obvious how the old college of liberal arts will maintain its place. Technical studies should begin in the high school and liberal studies should be continued in the professional school. The college must adjust itself to these conditions.

Nothing in our educational history, indeed nothing in our whole civilization, is more hopeful than the increase of public high schools from 2,500 in 1890 to more than 8,000 to-day; of the students from 200,000 to more than 700,000. Nothing is more scandalous than the circumstance that 75 per cent. of the boys who enter the high school are driven away by its futility and feminization. The obsolescent culture of the college imposes itself on the high-school curriculum, even though of twelve boys who enter the high school only one proceeds to the college. The high school should and must primarily give training for the life work of the student, but with this should be united sympathetic appreciation of what is best in the past and present of the world, and the impulse to improve and create. We shall have 10,000 centers for training, culture and research, as soon as we produce educational leaders to man them. And the high school will educate its students so far as is possible without specialization beyond the capacity of the community in which it is placed.

Students who complete the work of the high school at the age of eighteen can not to advantage spend the four subsequent years in a country club, where what time can be spared from athletics and social enjoyments may be given to studies that are irrelevant to their work in life. Such a system may be proper for a hereditary aristocracy of wealth, but it no longer obtains even in Great Britain. The newer universities are primarily professional schools, and Oxford and Cambridge are continually moving in this direction. The colleges of Oxford and Cambridge have on the whole maintained high standards of thinking and living, and many leaders have gone forth from their gates. But Oxford and Cambridge are great universities, not as the result of their curriculum or their monastic life, but because the English are a great race. Besides it is not now the "poll" course, but the highly specialized honor courses which attract the best men. We may hope that our educational system will ultimately set standards for other nations, but we must first learn from the experience of England, France and Germany.

Nearly all our colleges have been founded and fostered by religious denominations. Our common schools have been supported by taxation, and sectarian influences have been carefully excluded, whereas our institutions of higher learning have been dependent on private charity for which denominational zeal appears to have been requisite. Another circumstance accounting for this somewhat anomalous condition is the fact that the colleges were largely training-schools for the gospel ministry, the only profession that usually required an academic course. Of the first 277 alumni of Lafayette 112 became clergymen.

Lafayette was established under Presbyterian influences, but by the act of incorporation the college was strictly undenominational, and the governor of the state was empowered to appoint visitors, whose reports should be laid before the legislature. In 1833 the legislature made an appropriation of $4,000, and $2,000 a year for four years. Financial need rather than religious devotion led Lafayette to place itself under the care of the synod of Philadelphia in 1854. But it is not certain that this step led to increased support. The entire income of the college in 1862 was $3,240. When in 1866 an urgent appeal was made by the synod to the churches for funds to erect a chapel, the sum of $360.21 was collected. In the same year Lehigh University—whose funds now amount to two and a half million dollars—was established. It was at this time that the states west of Pennsylvania were awakening to the need of supporting higher education, and it was in 1862 that the federal government established the land-grant colleges of agricultural and mechanic arts, which now have an income from the nation and the states of ten million dollars.

If the resources of Lafayette and Lehigh could have been united, and if the state of Pennsylvania had learned the wisdom of doing for higher education what the central and western states have done, we might have had here one of the great universities of the world. Nor need religious or even denominational training have been neglected, for each sect might have established and supported its own college. It is not necessary that each of the thirty-four colleges of Pennsylvania should become a great university, but seven million people could well afford to devote annually a million dollars to each of seven universities, placed say at Philadelphia, Pittsburgh, Easton, Harrisburg, Williamsport, Johnstown and Erie.

A school or a college is self-supporting in the sense that the individual profits more than his education costs; a university is self-supporting in this sense and in addition it is economically the most profitable investment that a people can make. A million dollars spent on the highest education and on research add more than a million dollars to the actual wealth of the country. And if this research is not supported by public funds, it will not be undertaken, for its main benefit is not to the individual, but to the whole people. In a way we are consuming the capital of our country—the natural fertility of the soil, the forests, the coal and iron. Coal is mined in Pennsylvania to the annual value of $200,000,000. We are indeed thriftless if the value of the coal is not reinvested, on the one hand, in foundries, railways, and other material and ephemeral uses, and, on the other hand, in education and research, which are the most permanent of all investments. There are but few fathers who will leave their children less educated than themselves, and research and discovery are endowment policies whose dividends never cease.

But while we need great universities, we need equally high schools, colleges and technical schools. Mere size is entirely unimportant. If the spirit of scholarship and research can be maintained in small institutions, several of them may be more useful than one amorphous university. There is a certain psychological limit of size, beyond which organization becomes increasingly difficult. Perhaps twenty-five professors and three hundred students may be taken as the maximum of efficiency. The faculty in such an institution forms a homogeneous body competent to guide the policy of the institution and to select their successors. Each professor is responsible for the whole and to the whole. He can be the friend of the students whom he teaches, and each student is an integral part of the institution.

Such a college should have buildings and grounds of the value of about a million dollars and an income of at least $100,000. The parks, libraries, museums, art galleries, theaters and lecture halls are not for the professors and students only but for the whole community. The work of the professors and instructors is not only the teaching of the students, but perhaps half of it, more or less, in accord with the ability and interests of the individual, should be for the advancement and diffusion of knowledge, for leadership in all that concerns the higher life of the community.

A college of this character can not cover equally the whole field of knowledge; it should be eminent in some direction. This might be civil engineering. In this case the best possible training would be given to professional engineers, not only expert knowledge and facility in their trade, but broad culture and the impulse to investigate, the tendency to treat conventions lightly, the power to break new paths and advance along them. Students frequenting this college might use civil engineering as a basis for law, medicine, architecture, business or any work in life, a new combination of interests leading to new advances and new professions. Or a college might be eminent in the teaching and investigation of the English language, as Lafayette has been, and this would be the center of its work and its influence. There would be half a dozen great investigators and teachers cooperating in all movements to maintain and improve our language, its grammar and dictionaries, the methods of spelling and printing, studying and making accessible to study its origins, its classics and its contemporary tendencies. Young investigators would gather here, and the students from the start would base their training, their culture and their research on mastery of the English language, it being the basis in after life for work in literature, scholarship, journalism, teaching, the church, or any other profession whatever.

Lafayette is both a school of technology and a college of liberal arts. It has this year 225 students of engineering and 176 students in the arts courses. The future of the work in engineering appears to be more definite and assured than the classical and general courses, due not to any deficiencies in these courses, but to the general tendencies of our civilization. Lafayette may become a great university; it now ranks midway among the hundred leading institutions of the country, and we need at least so many universities. Its situation, as well as its history, gives promise to which no limit need be set. But a man can not by taking thought add one cubit unto his stature, nor would it necessarily be desirable to do so if he could. Loyalty to Lafayette depends on what it was and is, not on what it is not. And it is one of the glories of the American college that it so completely conquers the affection of its students and alumni. Like Job, a man may find new flocks and a new wife and new children; but he can not choose a new college. The associations and memories of the unreturning past are awakened as we come to these festivals—whether as prodigal sons or as wise men bringing gifts—and the renewed piety enables each of us to go back to bear with better courage his share of the Atlantean load.

J. McKeen Cattell

EDUCATIONAL RESEARCH AND STATISTIC

WHO PRODUCES STUDENT PERSONNEL LITERATURE?

During the past decade an ever-increasing amount of attention has been given to student personnel problems in American colleges and universities. Fifteen years ago the word "personnel" had just been introduced into the English language. Although the concept underlying the word had had its share of attention from the earliest days of American higher education, when the army returned from France, the personnel point of view pushed forward vigorously. Since that time an astounding number of books and articles have been written upon both industrial and student problems.

The present writer is devoting the major part of his attention to student personnel research, and to assist him in his work, he has recently collected an extensive bibliography of 4,902 titles. All these titles have been read and analyzed. The most important 2,183 of them, carefully indexed and annotated, have been brought together in a volume entitled "The Personnel Bibliographical Index," published by the Bureau of Educational Research of Ohio State University on May 1 of this year.

As a by-product of this bibliography, the author has been interested in discovering which universities are most productive of student personnel research and in producing books and articles upon personnel problems. His investigation has turned up the fact that sixty-eight individuals, representing twenty-nine colleges and universities and three outside research organizations, have produced 541 of the books and articles included in "The Personnel Bibliographical Index," or almost 25 per cent. of the total.

In Table I are listed the names of these sixty-eight individuals together with their institutional affiliations and the number of articles or books each has included in the index.

TABLE I

Summary of Contributors to the Personnel Bibliographical Index and their Individual Number of Contributions

Sixteen Contributions:
- John B. Johnston, University of Minnesota
- Edward S. Jones, University of Buffalo
- Harry D. Kitson, Columbia University
- Raymond Walters, Swarthmore College

Fifteen Contributions:
- Herbert E. Hawkes, Columbia University

Twelve Contributions:
- Thomas A. Clark, University of Illinois
- L. L. Thurstone, University of Chicago
- Herbert A. Toops, Ohio State University

Eleven Contributions:
- Donald A. Laird, Colgate University
- H. H. Remmers, Purdue University
- George D. Stoddard, State University of Iowa

Ten Contributions:
- Arthur W. Kornhauser, University of Chicago
- William M. Proctor, Stanford University
- Edward L. Thorndike, Columbia University

Nine Contributions:
- Walter V. Bingham, Personnel Research Federation
- Walter Crosby Eells, Stanford University
- Douglas H. Fryer, New York University
- Adam Leroy Jones, Columbia University
- Donald G. Paterson, University of Minnesota
- Carl E. Seashore, State University of Iowa
- Ruth Strang, Columbia University
- Sarah M. Sturtevant, Columbia University
- Charles F. Thwing, Western Reserve University
- Morris S. Viteles, University of Pennsylvania

Eight Contributions:
- Stephen Colvin, Brown University
- W. H. Cowley, Ohio State University
- L. B. Hopkins, Wabash College
- Clarence C. Little, University of Michigan
- Ernest H. Wilkins, Oberlin College

Seven Contributions:
- William F. Book, Indiana University
- Albert B. Crawford, Yale University
- Lonzo Jones, State University of Iowa
- Andrew H. MacPhail, Brown University
- Grace E. Manson, Northwestern University

Mark A. May, Yale University
James B. Miner, University of Kentucky
John Sundwall, University of Michigan

Six Contributions:

Robert A. Brotemarkle, University of Pennsylvania
C. C. Crawford, University of Southern California
H. S. Diehl, University of Minnesota
Esther Allen Gaw, Ohio State University
L. D. Hartson, Oberlin College
William S. Hoffman, Penn State College
A. Lawrence Lowell, Harvard University
Max McConn, Lehigh University
Alexander Meiklejohn, University of Wisconsin
Iva L. Peters, Syracuse University
Luella C. Pressey, Ohio State University
Agnes L. Rogers, Goucher College
Giles M. Ruch, State University of Iowa
Edward K. Strong, Jr., Stanford University
Guy M. Whipple, National Society for the Study of Education
Ben D. Wood, Columbia University

Five Contributions:

J. Howard Beard, University of Illinois
H. E. Burtt, Ohio State University
Nicholas M. Butler, Columbia University
F. Stuart Chapin, University of Minnesota
George A. Coe, Columbia University
M. E. Haggerty, University of Minnesota
Arthur J. Jones, University of Pennsylvania
Leonard V. Koos, University of Chicago
T. A. Langlie, Wesleyan University
Charles W. Odell, University of Illinois
Howard J. Savage, Carnegie Foundation
John M. Stalnaker, University of Chicago
Harry E. Stone, West Virginia University
Percival M. Symonds, Columbia University
George F. Zook, University of Akron

The data in Table I have been summarized in another fashion to produce Table II which gives an analysis of the number of contributions from the eleven institutions which have had two or more contributors to the index.

That personnel administration in American colleges and universities is becoming yearly a more important consideration is attested to by the fact that almost every month a new personnel unit of some sort or other is reported in this college or that university. Nicholas Murray Butler, of Columbia University, devoted several pages of his annual report for the year 1930–1931 to personnel considerations, and President Daniel L. Marsh in his annual report for the same period recorded the establishment of three new personnel units, a placement service, a student health service, and a student counselling service at Boston University. Harvard University announces the appointment of a dean of freshmen and of twelve associates of freshmen to council with Harvard freshmen. Harvard has followed with this appointment similar appointments at Dartmouth, Yale, Ohio State University, and several other institutions.

TABLE II

SUMMARY OF CONTRIBUTORS AND CONTRIBUTIONS BY INSTITUTIONS

	Number of Contributors	Number of Contributions
Columbia University	10	89
University of Minnesota	5	41
Ohio State University	5	37
State University of Iowa	4	33
University of Chicago	4	32
Stanford University	3	25
University of Illinois	3	22
University of Pennsylvania	3	20
Brown University	2	15
University of Michigan	2	15
Oberlin College	2	14
Yale University	2	14
Totals	45	357

The University of Chicago has also within the past year made new additions to its personnel program and has reorganized its entire set-up under the direction of a new officer with the title of Dean of Students. This position is held by George F. Works, former president of Connecticut Agricultural College, who is responsible, under this new plan, for all student-university relations aside from formal instruction. A similar reorganization has since been announced at the University of Oregon.

These examples are illustrative of the expansion of the personnel point of view and the development of personnel units throughout the colleges of the country. Since the movement is so comparatively new, the data brought together in the tables submitted as part of this article will more than likely point university administrators to the individuals who during the past decade have made the investigations upon which the present personnel movement is predicated.

W. H. COWLEY,
Assistant Professor of Psychology
BUREAU OF EDUCATIONAL RESEARCH,
OHIO STATE UNIVERSITY

ON RESEMBLANCE BETWEEN MOTHER-DAUGHTER AND SISTER-SISTER PAIRS

A GOOD many studies have been made showing correlations between academic grades made by various members of the family, fathers and sons, siblings, twins, cousins and others. But the mother and daughter relationship in that particular has been relatively neglected.

R. R. Willoughby[1] reports correlations on a series of 11 tests, selected from various standardized tests, such as the Army Alpha, given to about 100 pairs of mothers and daughters. His median correlation is .28. H. E. Jones[2] reports a mother-daughter correlation of .557 on intelligence tests.

The data for this study were obtained from the records of two colleges for women. The alumnae officers of these schools kindly furnished names of former students whose daughters are, or have been, in attendance, and their grades were secured from the registrars. In some cases the grades of the mothers are those of academy rather than college rank, but since the teaching in the academy was done largely by college faculty members, it is reasonable to assume that the standards were comparable. However, the often observed fact was very noticeable in both colleges, namely, that grading used to be far less strict than it is now. This makes the mothers seem "brighter" than their daughters—or more industrious—and in either case might help to account for the glamor of "the good old days." The median average grade for the mothers in school A was 88, and for the daughters 82; in school B the medians were, respectively, 92 and 79.

The groups are regrettably small, but a very few more college generations will remedy that condition. However, the findings on these two colleges are very consistent, and indicate that there is only a slight tendency for daughters to resemble their mothers in academic ability. For school A a correlation of .287 was found, and for school B one of .257. It may be mentioned, though this paper is not dealing with men's grades, that Schuster and Elderton[3] found a very similar correlation, .31, between the grades of father and son, Oxford honor men.

The question then arose as to how pairs of sisters attending colleges for women would compare in resemblance with sisters attending other types of schools, so correlations were computed for groups of sisters from the two institutions. These figures were too inconsistent to permit of any generalizations, being .645 for school A, and .410 for school B. However, it is usual to find a good bit of range in correlations between siblings. In an earlier study the writer[4] found one of .53 between pairs of sisters attending a state university.

TABLE I

MOTHER-DAUGHTER AND SISTER-SISTER CORRELATIONS

	College A			College B		
	N	r	P.E.	N	r	P.E.
Mother-daughter ...	58	.287	.082	54	.257	.086
Sister-sister	122	.646	.035	76	.410	.065

As a very minor by-product of the study, the correlation was calculated for a group of 8 pairs of twins, all but one pair identical, in College A. This was found to be .92, about what one would anticipate from other studies.

If a logical conclusion may be drawn from a first study in the field it would seem to be that there is considerably less resemblance between the academic ability of mothers and daughters than between that of sisters.

EMILY S. DEXTER
AGNES SCOTT COLLEGE,
DECATUR, GEORGIA

NEW BOOKS IN EDUCATION

CAVENAGH, F. A., Editor. *Herbert Spencer on Education.* Pp. xxxii + 233. Macmillan. $2.00.

EHRENFELD, LOUIS. *The Story of Common Things.* Pp. v + 203. Illustrated by Joe Richards. Minton, Balch. $2.50.

JOYAL, ARNOLD E. *Factors Relating to the Establishment and Maintenance of Junior Colleges, with Special Reference to California.* Pp. vii + 92. University of California Press.

STANHOPE, ROY W. *The Teaching of Chemistry in the Secondary Schools of New South Wales.* Pp. 74. Melbourne University Press.

[1] Twenty-seventh Yearbook, Nat. Soc. Stud. Educ., 1928, Part I, 55–59.

[2] *Ibid.*, 61–72.

[3] D. Starch, "Educational Psychology," 1927, p. 93.

[4] *Ibid.*, p. 94.

EDUCATIONAL REVIEW

Edited by WILLIAM McANDREW

EDITORIAL COMMENT

NOW YOU'RE TALKING

'Rah for the National Radio Advisory Council! 'Rah for the American Political Science Association! 'Rah for the University of Chicago Press! These three are putting on the air the most needful messages of our times: broadcasts on you and your government. John Finley, Thomas Reed, William Bennett Munro, Charles Merriam, Stuart Chase, Charles Beard, Arthur Holcombe, Arthur Knock, Julian Mason, Ruth Morgan, Virgil Jordan, Edward Sait, William Hard, John Dewey, and other economists, historians and journalists every Tuesday at five o'clock Pacific time, six, Mountain time, seven, Central time, and eight, Eastern time, from April 5 to July 5, discuss national economy, foreign policy, domestic problems, political parties, national conventions and related topics. They speak on the theory that you are in duty bound to revive the fundamental conviction of the makers of the nation that each and every one of you must participate in your common government. This is a call to a plain civic duty to save the republic from your manipulating spoilsmen. Here is a patriotic campaign by educators who have no axes to grind, no hobbies to ride, no prejudices to air —a group with as unbiased an adherence to actual science as can be found in the country.

Isn't this something you have been wanting in your high-school service? Isn't it a thing to push, giving your children a mimeographed or printed notice to take home that the score of broadcasting stations may furnish the one to reach the homes of your constituency? You can get the program free by enclosing a stamp to Levering Tyson, 60 East Forty-second Street, New York. Furthermore, by sending $1.50 to the University of Chicago Press, 5750 Ellis Avenue, Chicago, you can get for your high-school classes printed reproductions of all these timely messages. Here is a curriculum up to the minute in the one line that no one can show to be otherwise than the very core of public-school service as conceived by those who made our schools an agency of government.

WHY TEACHERS DON'T TRAIN CITIZENS

A subscriber, who is an officer of the National Self-government Committee, N. Y., writes, "In trying to get the public schools to perform the main duty for which they were set up—training successive generations to maintain honest, efficient government—how are we going to answer the objections raised in his article, 'Democracy in Education?' by E. L. B. Curtis, in School and Society, March 26?"

The Curtis article discredits the assumption that the ideals and habits necessary for good government in a republic are common to public-school teachers. Training schools neglect emphasis upon the need of such ideals and habits; administration by superintendents, school boards and supervisors is against training in democracy. Even the teachers' own organizations, says reporter Curtis, are not self-governing but are steered by those higher up. There are schools and systems that are exceptional, but they are in the minority.

How are we to reply to the Curtis objections? We don't have to. The answers are patent to every one who reads the facts as stated in the article itself.

Centuries of custom and official direction made the teacher a hired man employed to do what had been done before. Monarchies suppressed teachers who assumed to turn the minds of youth toward any suggestion that affairs might be better if different. When, coincident with agitation for an American Constitution and with the adoption of it, the statesmen invited by Franklin undertook the formulation of policies for education in a republic, they pleaded for the overthrow of teaching's timidity and resistance to change: our new political venture, they said, is an experiment. It must not be permitted to harden. Times will change, civilization will progress. Our laws, our ideas, our constitutions must not be worshipped but must be kept mobile for adapting to new situations. Our teachers must be equipped to see new needs and to contrive new satisfactions. Jefferson's plan of government of the University of Virginia by the whole faculty contemplated that those teachers would of necessity be kept alive in governmental thinking. Kirkpatrick's "Academic Organization and Control" (SCHOOL AND SOCIETY, March 5) is a book upon American schools' and colleges' tragic loss of the share of teachers in the formation and change of educational policies.

One derives from the Curtis survey a belief that American public-school teachers have little of experience in managing even the professional societies supported by their own money, and are quite indifferent to the fact. If you observe the business sessions of our associations you will see how true this is. The apathy of the ordinary citizen to the management of our common civic affairs is notorious. We teachers may be as careless as the average run of men.

SUPERINTENDENTIAL BACKBONE

What can change this?

More vigorous exposures like the Curtis one. More protests by independent teachers' organizations which will use psychology enough to avoid disgusting the general public by noisy spilling of the beans.

But, most of all, the intelligent supervisory officer who will throw away the babyish love of power and prominence, and who will recognize that every teaching staff can be coaxed more and more to take up vital matters to discuss and decide.

A man who will take half an hour a day to sit down and ask one teacher after another how we can really train boy and girl graduates who will be the sort of active, watchful, community citizens the pioneers of public education expected is sure to develop a civic-minded staff. He soon finds ideas and ideals sprouting and growing. They develop into practice. Practice, watched and appraised, changes and improves.

Given a realization of the mess we are in and a sense of the reason why schools are financed by the community and not by the parents; given the conviction that your paramount duty is an efficient, honest, self-governing nation, you can soon put one school or college or system in the way of doing what it was established to do. Ten men could have saved Sodom.

To stiffen your backbone read some more of the words of American worthies here continued.

AMERICAN SCHOOLMAN'S BREVIARY

THESE words are to be read in the morning what time you set out to take up the labor of the day; and in the evening when you query, how much nearer am I to that for which I was admitted to The Order of the Sons of Nathan Hale, one life, one duty, one reward?

69. OUR VOTERS IGNORANT. The people, when they do vote do so on inconsequential grounds: the religious faiths of the contestants, the social graces of the candidates and their families, their views on non governmental questions, the cut of their clothes, and other items interesting and irrelevant. PROF. RAYMOND MOLEY, N. Y. Herald Tribune. June 6, 1931.

70. INSIPID CIVIC TRAINING. The schools are still teaching the sort of insipid history and civics that tend to encourage neglect of political duties. With each passing year the people are called on for more money to teach citizenship. Each year has recorded an increasing percentage of the school product which does not even go to the polls. HEINRICH BUCHHOLZ. "Fads and Fallacies," 1931.

71. FUTILE HIGH-SCHOOL INSTRUCTION. Why is public money wasted on high-school algebra, a non-functional and nearly valueless subject for 90 per cent. of all boys and 99 per cent. of all girls? Modern language teaching is a travesty on good education. History, as taught, is a very slight aid to citizenship or culture. The present potential society is neglected. PROF. DAVID SNEDDEN. "School Educations." 1930.

72. DEMOCRACY AT LOWEST EBB. There was never a time in America when the system of boss-rule was so complete and widespread as now. ALBERT BUSHNELL HART, N. Y. Times Current History. Nov., 1930.

73. STRESSING THE WRONG THINGS. Our schools are magnifying individualism. It is stressed in recitation, grading, and marking. There can be no democracy unless the emphasis is changed and put on general welfare. SUPT.

M. C. CLARKE, Sioux City, at National Education Convention. 1927.

74. MUST PUT AMERICAN FAITH INTO PRACTICE. From the time of Jefferson the people have accepted the doctrine that our schools are the most effective instruments we have for the maintenance of free government. It remains for the teachers to put them into practice more responsively. HENRY SUZZALLO. Intro. to "Evolution of a Democratic School System." 1918.

75. ALGEBRA MORE THAN CITIZENSHIP. According to surveys by the United States Bureau of Education more high-school pupils study algebra than are enrolled in classes of civics, United States history, or economics. Listed in the order of the number of pupils studying a subject, American history stands 8th; civics, 13th; economics, 28th; sociology, 32nd. CARL A. JENSEN. "Secondary Education." 1928. But the number of high-school students enrolled in civil government decreased from 21 per cent. of all high-school pupils in 1900 to 6 per cent. in 1928. Adding the pupils registered in civics, there are but 19 per cent. of the high-school pupils taking both or either subject. One per cent. are studying "Problems of Democracy." FRANK M. PHILLIPS, U. S. Bureau of Education Chief of Statistics. "Statistical Summary of Education." 1928.

76. NO HELP FROM COLLEGES. No liberal arts college seems to be interested in the future of public education for the masses. The college is busy developing its students largely for the purpose of enjoying life, particularly leisure time, to the fullest. These colleges warp the high schools out of proper service by requiring the salt pork and rye bread of algebra, dry-as-dust ancient history and Latin—subjects that prepare for nothing in the world but college. GEORGE W. FRAZIER. "Responsibilities of Higher Institutions." 1931.

77. DISAPPOINTMENT WITH COLLEGE. Much of the discouragement with the American college is due to its attempt to apply old-world social ideas. It is obligated to serve and improve American society. American concern over its failures is a serious matter. "Higher Education in America." TWENTY-FOUR PRESIDENTS AND PROFESSORS.

78. CIVICS TEACHING NOT YET IN HIGH REGARD. In the 478 page volume of Trusler's "Essentials of School Law," 1927, no mention is made of any of the statutes requiring the teaching of citizenship although there are mentioned laws affecting drawing, music, base ball, cosmetics and khaki uniforms. Author TRUSLER, who is dean of a university law school, does not include civic teaching among the "essentials."

79. MORE SCHOOLS, MORE CRIME. Schools were made part of the American governmental machine so as to get people to think, to improve our political affairs. The proponents of school taxes said we would save more than the cost by reducing crime, courts, and jails. "More schools, less policemen," promised Horace Mann. Now we have more of both. Education has not developed a sense of duty. SHELDON DAVIS. "Teacher Relationships." 1931.

80. WESTCHESTER JURY INDICTS SCHOOLS FOR NEGLECT. Our schools pay little or no attention to how to live or how to govern. They afford only weak or inadequate instruction in American principles of government, no practical teaching in living or morality. The pupils are not made conscious of their relation to society, of the rights of others, respect for law and order, or obedience to proper authority. Crime is rapidly increasing, especially among the young. We have reached a stage of the highest criminality of the nation, higher than any other people. "PRESENTMENT OF WESTCHESTER COUNTY N. Y. GRAND JURY." Nov., 1930.

81. SCHOOLS REASONABLY SUCCESSFUL—YET THEY ARE NOT. In the same column, one under the other, appear these two items of news. United States Commissioner of Education, WILLIAM JOHN COOPER, telegraphs a greeting to the International Foreign Students' Conference at Storm King. "Our schools have been reasonably successful in making our people conscious of the responsibilities they have as citizens of the community, citizens

of the state and citizens of the Federal Union." Under it is this: ERNEST MARTIN HOPKINS, President, told a group of 2,200 Dartmouth undergraduates yesterday that the forces of disruption are gaining momentum steadily. It is time for college students to learn to accept responsibility. College men have the vital defect of unwillingness to accept it. They do not lack capacity; they lack the will. N. Y. Herald-Tribune. Sept. 18, 1931.

82. WE MUST DEFINE OUR FAILURES. I suggest among the major lines of attack that we define the respects in which our schools have failed to meet the problems of the time; that we catalog the inadequacies in our society, taking for study those things in which our leading thinkers are in agreement, that we hunt for the factors responsible for these deficiencies and the possibilities of offsetting or eliminating them through education. Such studies are merely begun. The inability of many of our citizens to cooperate in the public good is a serious civic deficiency. The social studies must be completely overhauled. We must teach economics, political science, psychology, and sociology. We must have more moral and ethical instruction. WILLIAM JOHN COOPER, U. S. Commissioner of Education. "Education for a New America," 1929.

83. EDUCATION FAILS TO STUDY POLITICS. It is obvious that the crisis through which we are now passing is the result of our own folly and incompetence. We must concede that education has signally failed. Americans may with justice inquire what has education done all these years if it has been unable to prevent our present situation? The remedy for our ills requires more study of human problems. ROBERT HUTCHINS, Pres. University of Chicago. N. Y. Times. June 30, 1931.

84. MORTGAGED TO THE PAST. Poverty, misery, and unemployment stalk in the midst of plenty. The bedtime story of many of the captains of industry who have mired in the clay they have produced sends mankind after disappearing rainbows. Government is at the cross roads. Government by expedient rather than by principle is the order of the day. Substitutes for intelligence have been over-emphasized in education. It can not claim to have taught the graduates of yesterday what they now need to know about economics. An education mortgaged to the past serves no useful purpose. Outside are hunger, want and distress. The challenge is peremptory and ominous. LOTUS COFFMAN, Pres. U. of Minn. Commencement address at University of Michigan. June 2, 1931.

SOME OF THE BEST BOOKS

YEAR-BOOK EXTRAORDINARY[1]

THE tenth year-book of the national association of school superintendents will be a long time unsurpassed as an example of industry, intelligence, loyalty and service. Nine generous collaborators appear as the responsible authors: Denver Threlkeld, Washington Backus, Chicago Freeman, Birmingham Glenn, Detroit Rankin, Baltimore Weglein, Omaha Belle Ryan, and Columbia Counts and Watson. They express praise and gratitude for you thousands of school men and women who answered the questions they sent out through the department's division of research. They commend Mrs. John Norton and Sherwood Shankland of the permanent staff for care, industry and speed in getting out the book.

Until you have read it, take my word for it that here is the most reasonable, helpful, unprejudiced and useful work on schools and character that has appeared in print.

It would not be hard to prove that the authors have undertaken the most difficult of the tasks attempted by the makers of the department's year-books, of which this is the tenth.

I remember my first National Association meeting, forty-four years ago. One superintendent, summing up the speeches of the San Francisco convention, declared the one great want in the public schools is more productive attention to moral instruction, character build-

[1] Commission, "Character Education." Department of Superintendence, National Education Association, Washington, D. C. 536 pp. $2.00.

ing. Two of the brilliant speeches on the occasion were on that moral need. One of the orators, afterwards, went to jail for stealing school moneys. The other, accused in three cities of immorality with women of the teaching corps, suicided himself out of this world by means of a gulp of poison. Year after year the program-makers get the teaching of morals before the conventions. Resolutions repeat that it is the most important work the schools should do. Church, press, statisticians report more vice and crime each year and our infamous superiority in this over the other nations of the world. The authoritative plans for training character have broken down. The honest teacher recognizes the present duty and confesses he doesn't know how to perform it. He and his fellows in curriculum-making and in conventions can find relief only in hiding the head deeper in new-type examinations, project method and perfection of teaching the unconsequential subjects that are lodged in the course.

Wavering Theories

Into this sort of atmosphere these nine contributors enter on their brave adventure. We are not going to extend the old fight between moral theorists, they say. For a foundation we have the accepted belief that the schools are established and supported to train for right living, for the sake of society. They are the most gigantic organized force for this that exists in the world. The school program, serving all people alike, is for general welfare.

On this social theory rather than on a pious project of helping each to save his own soul the development of character as a function of the school is worked out in a notable survey and appraisal of seventeen concepts of moral purposes of education as gathered from the thousands of syllabuses, plans and beliefs of school workers. The appraisal is, I think you will conclude, unsurpassed by any study the Department of Superintendence has sponsored. The most of the moral schemes outlined in the schools are only aids for this or that situation. Counting checks on the score cards does not create a sufficient objective. How will this do? The objective of character education should be the creation or discovery of a way of living which conserves and produces as many values as possible for as many persons as possible for as long a time as possible. Character education is the facilitation of this way of life.

Agreement on this is not difficult. The trouble, remarks this commission, comes from diversity of views as to ways of realizing the objective. Scientific evidence is lacking to base conclusions on results of teaching. But an examination of each issue in detail shows that the case is not so bad as you might think. This is a field in which there is much ignorance of such scientific evidence as does exist. There is a set against following such evidence and a tendency to dogmatize our moral philosophy. Our political theories, our business maxims are derived from traditions twenty-five centuries old, dating from the days of Plato. A vicious assumption has been that each generation should live in accordance with ideas governing the lives of its fathers. We are living in the first period of human history for which this assumption is false. Authoritarianism is dead.

Various forces have produced a situation which is bringing many cries of alarm. Youth is abandoning the severe sex prohibitions of the past. The sanctity of marriage is challenged. The dogmas of the church lose their power. The traditional purposes of living fail to satisfy. Religion is threatened with confusion and uncertainty. The church speaks with a faltering voice.

Our society looks for the integration of knowledge, aspiration and human purpose which will take into account the findings of science, the theory of evolution, the advance of technology, the growing powers of laboring classes, as well as the influence of great spiritual leaders.

These authors have prepared for you valuations of the character contributions of home, community, industry, the church, property, press, motion pictures, radio, automobile, democracy, sport, lodges, science, literature, art. The school is the only agency that is under the conscious direction of society. Any general improvement society desires for itself will have to come through the school. Therefore the school's central function should be critical and evaluative. This is not the school's present service. Its methods will have to be changed. If the school's teachings are not directed toward the improvement of society they will not bear fruit.

What are the methods and procedures which tend to produce the most values for the most persons for the longest time possible, that is, to develop character?

Three hundred seventy-five rich pages proceed to discuss the question.

Drives, sets, ideals, traits, precepts, habits, maxims, reflection, codes, are given opportunity for defense by their attorneys and are stripped of their pretensions. A hundred pages are devoted to what research has attempted and secured in the field of moral education. Sex education has a chapter. Class-room procedure, school administration, counselling, home influence cooperating agencies, tests, measurements and other problems are discussed.

The time and energy put into this cooperative service by its self-sacrificing workers, the broad outlook of it, its selection of things valuable to teachers on the daily job, make this book a superb accomplishment.

There is a good deal of cynicism loose these days. As an antidote to it and a tonic for your own mental health you may profitably spend a few minutes daily perusing this year-book and realizing the remarkable old-fashioned adherence to duty its authors have maintained in the hard work of serving you.

ADVENTURESOME CITIZENSHIP

THE Lady from Louisiana[2] had no intent, you may be sure, to write a romance. Yet her accounts of remarkable awakenings to neighborliness up and down the state exhale a warmth of story-book atmosphere and move to happy endings. Mary Mims, founder of folk schools in Louisiana, has seen her patriotic project of community cooperation grow to more than three hundred local organizations studying markets, buying seed and equipment, selling produce through their own committees, building community houses, planting flower gardens in the front yards, turning vacant lots into town parks, landscaping school grounds, enlisting the children in general welfare work, promoting neighborhood dances, dramatics, orchestras and choral unions, managing fairs, learning economic farming, refining home life and toning up the state. Mrs. Georgia Williams Moritz is cited as collaborator in preparing the book. Dean Charles Pipkin, of the Graduate School of the State University, comes into it, along with the State Library Commission, the Farm Bureau, the State Board of Health and other organizations. The sketches of drab and dreary back country settlements losing their boys and girls to the cities where they are worse off than at home, the portraits of the ever-present pessimists, the most unhappy in an unhappy land, and the best arguers that the town is too dead ever to live again, the accounts of pitiful handfuls of respondents to the call for the first meetings, the absurd obstinacy of the lady organizer who doesn't know she is defeated, the gradual shedding of husks of isolation, suspicion and laziness until an orchestra and a chorus are drawing thousands together, fill the book with the jolliest kind of stories. There are scores of bright histories of the awakening of this or that rural section. There are programs of the monthly entertainments, the actual games, songs, ceremonies, and debates, from which you may select what you want in similar services for your own neighbors.

In the midst of these, Miss Mary gives a spirited account of the trip of a Louisiana committee to rural Denmark and leaves you with a strengthened conviction that the American country problem, if handled in frank imitation of the Danish successes, will certainly move toward the hope of the song writer who hailed Columbia.

Here is a book by a woman who has met every reason why a thing can not be done and now details the methods by which the neighborly spirit has been awakened. "We do not organize clubs. There are no dues or roll-calls. No one is asked to become a member. Every man, woman and child of every age belongs. The only way to escape the responsibilities of citizenship is to move out of the community."

How they start, how they get objectives stated at the very beginning, how they reduce them at first to those known to be most easily workable, how they get the school children to see that in return for the school tax levied on the

[2] Mary Mims, "The Awakening Community." The Macmillan Company, New York. 273 pp. $2.00.

whole community, not on their parents alone, the children must in plain honesty be paying back to the community, now, while the getting is good, how the neighborly cooperation is the breeder of a more perfect union in the whole nation and a forerunner of international peace and understanding—these and a wealth of worth-while ideas pertinent to our present untoward circumstances are modestly and convincingly set forth.

I would now wish to be a community organizer with Mary Mims as my boss.

MANUALS FOR SOCIAL SERVICE[3]

THREE more decidedly practical volumes putting into convenient form the offerings of the nation's experts at the last White House Conference on Child Welfare have been issued in attractive form by the Century Company.

"Nursery Education" is devoted to the undeveloped asset represented in sixteen millions of children under six years of age. What institutions are devoted to serving part of this multitude, what they are doing, what your locality should do, are treated by more than a score of well-known authorities.

The "Special Education" volume considers the crippled, the blind, the poor-sighted, the deaf and hard of hearing, defective in speech, mentally retarded, problem children and the gifted.

"Public-Health Organization" records a change of the social concept so as to include in the welfare problem the promotion of mental and physical health as well as cure of disease. Determination to demonstrate what is being done and what can be accomplished give each volume a gratifying, practical tone.

ECONOMY DRIVING OUT ART

ONE beautiful November day, five years ago, I had hard luck in Winfield, Kansas. It is such a pretty town with handsome buildings, wide streets, with strips of grass and flowering shrubs down the middle, the food served there is so delicious, brought in by such handsome young women in spotless white, the Kansan who entertained me with pioneer adventures was such an interesting talker, that I neglected to rehearse a talk I was engaged to deliver that night. Though I had a superior audience and a lovely introduction by young McConnell, the school superintendent, I lost my grip on those good people in front of me by fumbling with my notes. I tried hard to rally them, but I made only a 70 per cent. score or worse.

That young McConnell, before I turned in, set out to console me. He lied like a gentleman. He picked out one or two not so bad points I had made. He fanned them into what seemed like a cheerful glow and left me wanting to sing an old vaudeville song: "Just a word of consolation sometimes heals a broken heart." Isn't it silly that an old duffer of sixty-four winters would appreciate being pulled out of a slough in which he ought to flounder until punished well for going before an audience when he is not letter-perfect in his piece?

I recall that McConnell, in other matters, was disturbed over the high-school trend in America. The cultivation of selfishness by our athletics, dramatics, dances and multitudinous clubs; the fatuity of our abstract mathematics, our classical culture, our blind teaching of languages, seemed to be bothering him. He thought that an attack directly upon the valueless studies was the most difficult and least effective move we could make. It would meet the opposition of so-called best people who won't think into the situation. There is the obstacle of intrenched college professors and high-school teachers who had spent time and money on the traditional subjects. The more effective way is to push studies that will take up the time, that are more easy to defend, and that will crowd the futility exercises out.

I was struck by McConnell's selection of art as one of the needs and one of the cures of school. The superintendents of my generation knew nothing of music and art and were so foolish as to say so aloud, with a suspicion of boasting. Art, insisted McConnell, that evening, is friendly to life. Form, color, combination of masses are convincing. Art insinuates itself securely into human affairs. Once begin to feel it and you never go back. You can't keep it

3 White House Conference, "Nursery Education." 187 pp. $2.00; "Special Education, The Handicapped and the Gifted." 604 pp. $4.00; "Public Health Organization." 150 pp. $3.00. The Century Company, New York.

out of school. Economy may stampede a school board to throw it out. They pick on the newer things first. That's absurd. In danger, the children should be thought of first; they are the newest. "We can't afford to try to make artists of our children," is the old stuff the frightened school boards fall back on. Bunk! We are much more concerned about what art does to boys and girls than we are about what boys and girls do to art or with it.

YOUNGER SUPERINTENDENTS AND ART

I thought then, and I think now, that McConnell is typical of the young generation of school superintendents who bid fair, if the public wakes up to their value, to give us a system of schools more immune from the increasing discontent than most of them are now. For McConnell insisted on hammering into my head that he must hold, as closely as the public and the school boards will let him, every teacher to the conscious purpose of producing good citizens who will habitually devote a fair portion of their strength to general welfare instead of following the usual American chase for personal wealth, fame and power. My boys and girls, he said, must support just, capable, efficient and honest politics in Winfield, Kansas, the United States and among the nations. General welfare is an inevitable motive, conscious or unconscious, in art. The creator of beauty has to share it with others. It is an inexhaustible *cruse*. Among the latest members of the school family of studies it must be strengthened to hold its own with mathematics and language, for it is as old and respectable as they.

ART APPRECIATION

This memory of a profitable conversation with a bright young chap in Kansas is revived by receipt of a beautiful book by two entertaining and widely observant New York women[4] who have been studying and trying out ventures in making art function in an American public-school program.

Whether one in a thousand of us will design a cathedral, produce a great painting, or make a living from posters, we are all consumers of art and bound to be. In each is the desire, hidden or expressed, to enjoy beauty. That this high pleasure is increased by contact and thought is undeniable. Let's see how it can be heightened and refined.

Through fascinating pages brightened with new pictures and old masters the two experienced guides develop and illustrate design, dress, architecture, painting, sculpture, prints, community problems, home making, lettering, posters, industrial arts and gardening. The biographies of great artists are remarkably well done. Every chapter has a set of study projects skilfully contrived to make the student see, think, appreciate and enjoy. Here is a book embodying the principles of education that have become accepted in other lines of school procedure. I imagine that in case your art teacher were called away for a spell you might take this volume as a guide and hold his classes well until he returned.

FOUR BOSWELLS

Speaking of art and its growing grip on the schools, do you give your high-school library the benefit of *The Art Digest?* This journal, appearing twenty times a year, with four Boswells as main sponsors, has marched to the front of art journalism through able news reporting, vivacious writing and generous use of pictures. The debates it carries, in which the apostles of different schools set forth their beliefs, the readability of all its matter, the universality of its grasp, the general sprightliness of it, explain why it has forged to the front. Its calendars of exhibits everywhere—Del Monte, Atlanta, Kirksville, Elmira, Dayton, New York, some place or other near you—pages of programs, are alone worth the yearly subscription, $3.00, payable at 116 East 59th St., New York.

ART FOR EVERY ONE

NOR do we forget *Everyday Art,* the colorful periodical which goes free to art directors and full-time art teachers who ask Cyrus Knouff, of Sandusky, to send it to them. Others get it for $1.00 a year. It is a radiant and generous collection of articles by school people and by artists, a summary of news and projects, a provider of patterns and work of teachers and

[4] M. Rose Collins, Olive L. Riley, "Art Appreciation for Junior and Senior High Schools." Harcourt, Brace and Company, New York. 334 pp. $1.80.

pupils, showing designs, posters, paintings and sketches in black-and-white and color.

WELCOME GRANT SHOWERMAN

We readers of the *Educational Review* of more than thirty years ago when Grant Showerman, a brilliant youngster, was shooting common-sense shafts tipped with a new wit into the school follies of the day, reach gladly for any offering he puts upon the counter.

"Rome and the Romans"[5] is Scholar Showerman's latest prize winner. Not merely a textbook, it is a survey and interpretation addressed to all readers that they may know the people whose character and institutions are at the foundations of our modern culture. Teachers of the classics will hail it with delight. Others of us have come to regard the study of Latin as a serious impediment. It is among the things that keep schools from their duty of attempting a whole-hearted preparation of Americans to take hold of the pressing economic and political problems confronting a citizenry never trained to think public-mindedly. We of the anti-Latin party should give this book a hearty welcome for that it will give in one sixteenth of the time, and a hundred times better, the meaning and significance of the Roman influence that is being gleaned from the mulling over three Latin authors who are pressed down upon our high-school youth—with parents' consent and approval.

Showerman, I think, could make Choctaw life fascinating. This book is a lively visit with boxers, emperors, sailors, soldiers, orators, lawyers, gladiators, road builders, cooks, teachers, physicians, bankers, farmers, actors, writers, architects, all sorts. It is as engaging as any news-film I ever saw.

The morals of our own day, writes our author, are those of ancient Rome. The classic ideals passed into the Christian code, into modern law, into the education of the ruling classes, and into the fiber of human character through the centuries. Roman society was composed of classes with fixed and definite limits. It mattered whether you were born on one side of the line or the other, both as to your rights and as to the esteem you might hope to gain. In spite of every attempt at change, ancient ideals of blood and character persisted and had their effect in notable men and times. Pius and Aurelius, a hundred and fifty years after the establishment of the empire, were upholding the Roman type. The last of the emperors, Romulus Augustulus, harks back to founders' days. The most bitter of Roman prejudices, our author reminds us, were against the foreigner and the Christians.

We, ourselves, are a hundred and fifty years old as a nation. Our prerevolutionary tendency to caste and blood and hatred of strangers is good old Roman virtue, isn't it? Let our Gracchi learn Roman ways. Old Rome is the best place in which to study the rights of the rich.

The Roman Failure

Dr. Showerman's survey of the status of Roman children is one of the many new lines on which he departs from the traditional study of classic life. The Roman baby was laid at the father's feet to accept or reject. He could sell the child into slavery if he wished or put it to death. The influence of this right on loyalty, obedience and discipline was the foundation of Rome's power and greatness. But even in the days of the republic there was a weakening in character of both men and women, and an increase of the immorality that clusters about slavery. Wealth brought the means of defying opinion and law. The game of politics was much the same there as here—building fences, bribing voters, pulling wires. Coincident with the growing jealousy and hatred to Carthage began the typical Roman sport, the gladiatorial combats. They became the emperor's great resource in keeping the people from breaking down his rule. Dr. Showerman takes you to a matinee in the Colosseum and gives you a series of bloody thrills. These spectacles, he says, had the element of sportsmanship and they were very useful to the candidates for political advancement. The man who financed the better show got the more votes. A bodyguard of gladiators, ready to beat up or assassinate your rivals, was as useful in Rome as in Chicago.

Dr. Showerman knows how to paint, whether

[5] Grant Showerman, "Rome and the Romans." The Macmillan Company, New York. 643 pp. $2.40.

it be the charming scenes in a Roman villa or the vulgar upstarts gambling not from purses but from chests, husbands renting out their wives, gluttons eating and drinking to their ruin, broken citizens accepting the dole, sons of venerable families degrading with every meanness the names they bear, noble women charitable and brave, honest men viewing their times with shame.

To me, a startling quality of Classicist Showerman's book is the honesty of it. The writers of texts for my school-room study in 1878 left me with a feeling that an era all glorious was that of Roman history. Grandeur got into the language of my Latin teacher when he related the deeds of the brave days of old. Now comes our long-admired Showerman with his two hundred pictures and his moving descriptions and I get no one-sided view. To you his survey may bring, as, for all I know, it may bring to Dr. Showerman, a revived admiration for the Romans and their triumphs. To me it is a reminder of what chains the Romans clamped upon civilization. They worshipped wealth and despised science. They failed to nurture seeds of genius in common men. They brutalized art, corrupted statesmanship, neglected intelligent commerce, left the most dangerous part of Europe unannexed to their system, had no vision of a future and, as it seems to me, saddled habits and ideas upon us which are still clogs preventing an otherwise better destiny. I'd like to take this Showerman masterpiece and use it for teaching civilization's failure and world calamity called Rome.

SAMPLES OF CLASSIC MASTERPIECES

THE monotony of sticking to a single author for a whole semester is undeniable. Professor Avery[6] finds that the collections of Latin poetry offered in several universities have been so profitable that a miscellany of interesting prose is desired by many of his colleagues. But no single text was available. He brings out a book of eighty-five complete extracts, biographical, historical, literary and social, drawing from Seneca, Sallust, Petronius—sixteen authors in all. He gives, in English, a sketch of each author and adds notes for lighting obscurities that might bewilder the amateur Latinist.

ESTABLISHING TRUTH

A HIGHLY profitable book for college classes, and for persons who have to persuade and convince, is Professor Fritz's work on argument.[7] He starts with an analysis of the means of finding truth and of transmitting or producing belief in it. He gives an illuminating chapter on appraising the audience, then considers the determining of a proposition, the analysis of it, making the brief, composing and delivering the speech. Debate, refutation, group discussions, delivery, are treated in helpful detail illustrated by modern instances and copious selections from eminent speakers.

SPEECH WAS MADE TO OPEN MAN TO MAN

COLGATE PROFESSOR SMITH[8] converts me, and I'll venture will persuade you, also, from a prejudice against extemporaneous speaking. We have thought it a wasteful use of speakers' and hearers' time. Before you are through with him you will consider the short impromptu a prime exercise in thought, order, emphasis, courage and good manners. Over and again he returns to the audience as the main consideration. These people out in front take the conceit out of you; they help you do your best. I can't remember any better advice than his that you seek to touch the deeper springs of interest that lie beneath the transient mood of the group seated before you. These basic interests grow out of man's necessities and desires: the protection of life and health, acquisition of the means of happy living, sympathy for humankind, family, friends, school, country and race. All these are slumbering beneath the varied thoughts behind those faces that are turned toward you. These people are expectant of benefit; they want you to succeed; they are a very present help in trouble. A compact audience gets much more out of a speech than a scattered one. A contact of elbows makes a

[6] Maurice W. Avery, "Latin Prose Literature. Cato to Suetonius." Little, Brown and Company, Boston. 400 pp. $2.40.

[7] Charles A. Fritz, "The Method of Argument." Prentice Hall, Inc., New York. 395 pp. $2.50.

[8] Elmer William Smith, "Extemporaneous Speaking." Prentice Hall, Inc., 70 Fifth Avenue, New York. 402 pp. $1.60.

live electric circuit. A wide gap in front of the speaker is a chilling depressor.

I'd like to take from Dr. Smith's book all that he says on this point, print it and mail it to every one responsible for educational meetings. "Will those in the rear please come forward" is a remainder of the lack of professional interest among teachers and a confession of lack of foresight from the planners of the meeting. Even so great an orator as Henry Ward Beecher admitted that he could not speak unless his hearers were crowded around him. "I don't mind," he said, "any amount of space behind you, but if you have it in front of me or allow it between yourselves I shall not waste myself on indifference so manifest."

William Evans, teachers' superintendent of Columbia County, Pennsylvania, has offset this sort of discourtesy shown to speakers. He uses the cleverest strategy yet. He follows teacher-nature by favoring the back seats. He packs the auditors in solid mass extending forward from the rear wall. He puts his speakers smack against the front row of listeners, on the level.

Henry West says that Schuylkill County teachers are the dread of speakers. Planted back in a dimly-lit moving-picture theater, most of them equipped with books and magazines to pass the time away, these individually well-mannered men and women, he says, have a mass rudeness that brings from many an invited speaker refusal ever to come again.

I have read a "Study of Institutes" which carries these self-evident truths for directors.

Your mass meetings are unwieldy. Abandon the theaters. Take an ordinary-size church and a near-by school auditorium.

Stop reprimanding and scolding the audiences.

Start with music.

Put on two speakers at forty-five minutes each, alternating at the two meetings, running until 10 o'clock.

Follow these by round tables on special subjects in class-rooms, programs made by teachers, of teachers, for teachers.

Afternoon: two o'clock to three, another period to four, all small meetings in many rooms.

Solid work in the daytime; concerts, etc., at the evening sessions.

Unless state superintendents take a hand in reforming institutes and put them to conformity with psychology, mental hygiene and common sense, they are leaving unguarded an opening through which some muck-raking magazine writer will come to make a lot of trouble.

Where did I leave Professor Smith? He was voicing convictions on the notable rôle a rightly managed audience plays in getting a worth-while address. The sympathetic speaker gets the sympathetic audience. Between them they develop a warmth of mutual appreciation and understanding that sends each homeward in a glow of satisfaction.

Smith's book is full of homely truths like these:

If you get to be known as an "I man" people do not want to hear you talk.

Successful extemporaneous speakers have made many preparations that were not used.

Even a social party or dinner deserves your forethought on topics suitable for conversation.

In controversy the man of breeding comments on the arguments and not on his opponents.

Understatement is stronger than the bold truth, for the listener restates the case in his own mind more powerfully than you have done and comes more surely to where you want him.

Whether in his short chapters on demands, practice, outlining, thinking, emotion, preparation, ending, different varieties, audiences, parliamentary usage, essentials of success, or in his timely review of the remarkable national oratorical contest on the Constitution now an assured country-wide event, or in his pointed exercises for practice and power, Professor Smith is free of the shallowness and padding too common in treatises on this subject. His high purpose is evident all through. His practice is up to his persuasive preaching. He has made a class-A book.

RETURN OF THE MUSE[9]

POETRY! Although we can not define it we can talk about it. We can thus increase our enjoyment of it. That enjoyment is a noble pursuit. Come, let us reason together. This

[9] Andrew Smithberger, Camille McCole, "On Poetry." Doubleday, Doran and Company, Garden City, New York. 191 pp. $1.00.

is the spirit of the Smithberger-McCole enjoyable discourse on form, words, rhythm, meter, rhyme, kinds, stanzas, sonnets, European styles, free verse, figures, some poets and some critics. It will refresh the English teacher, tired by the slowness of the children of the machine age, to awaken to beauty of "jewels five words long that on the stretched forefinger of time sparkle forever."

LITERATURE RESCUED

Reading Edmund Broadus's book[10] is like listening to Professor Ypsilanti Louis McLouth, who had such an agreeable voice and so companionable an instinct that an afternoon walk with him was an inspiration leading to many hours' enjoyment browsing in the normal-school library. Dr. Broadus's adventure is a discourse on English literature. He is a traveler telling of the journeys you may take where "sweet birds all the summer sing and dream of their glad melody." He is not a man of dates or labored analysis. Literature, as he presents it, is an alluring fulfilment of a universal desire. What he enjoys and reproduces from Beowulf to Masefield is, by the catholicity of his taste, the sort of sustenance you find yourself liking also. Without tedium his scholarship illuminates by friendly talk, reviving historical and social backgrounds, moods and movements of letters and drawing you to great works of genius. The Macmillans have offered him in a splendid volume, bright with colored reproductions of priceless manuscripts, fascinating maps and done in the perfection of the printer's art.

OLD ENGLISH ATMOSPHERE

The Laidlaws continue their output of historical stories. The last one[11] I have read is a picture of life in old England at the time when a Virginia colonist returned thither with progressive new-world ideas that got him into many an adventure and brought him happily through.

FRANCE IN FRENCH

For a snappy book in elementary French try Hills and Dondo's[12] flowing account of the geography, the politics, the schools and the personalities of our engaging European neighbors. The authors traverse the history of the nation and beautify the book with pictures. To keep the student from reading ahead too rapidly there are questions for them to answer *par des phrases complets.*

NOTABLE MOVE AHEAD

You will enjoy acquaintance with Professor Tiegs.[13] He makes a highly technical subject not only clear and simple but pleasantly instructive. He would reduce the bewilderment and the over-confidence brought about by the test waves that have swept upon education. How to proceed in solving class-room problems is what he tells. At least half of American teachers still use the essay type of test and think they believe in it. From samples taken, Dr. Tiegs guesses that a quarter of the teachers in the nation have no conception of the development of tests and measures during the last ten years. Nor do they realize the value of modern tests to the teaching profession. This distresses the progressive Dr. Tiegs. I suppose it ought to distress me and every American, but just between ourselves, to find only twenty-five per cent. of teachers indifferent to this important means of putting their business on a notably more respectable basis is so much better a showing than could have been made when we older fellows began supervising that it seems to me a sign of such progress as to indicate our continuing movement ahead. I have the lists of teachers I worked with in 1890, in 1900, in 1910, nice people, good-natured, companionable folks. Not one per cent. of them ever manifested in those days any real interest in a scientific approach to teaching. It honestly bored them. The applause at educational meetings, when some master of sarcasm paid disrespects to Dr. Cattell, Dr. Thorndike or Dr. Rice, was hearty and sustained. Within five years I have

10 Edmund Kemper Broadus, "The Story of English Literature." The Macmillan Company, New York. 634 pp. $1.96.

11 May Winne, "The Masked Rider." Laidlaw Brothers, Chicago. 256 pp. $1.50.

12 E. C. Hills, Mathurian Dondo, "La France, son histoire, sa Civilization." D. C. Heath and Company, Boston. 290 pp. $1.32.

13 Ernest W. Tiegs, "Tests and Measurements for Teachers." Houghton Mifflin Company, Boston. 470 pp. $2.40.

seen, in that same Brooklyn, audiences of teachers attending to discussions of best ways to measure. I have noted as deep an interest as a roomful of physicians show for a demonstration of a method in medicine. Dr. Tiegs' book, itself, is an evidence of the remarkable growth of the professional spirit. His treatises upon the nature and function of measurement, the old and new, type tests, standardization, diagnosis, ability grouping, appraisal of teaching efficiency, objectives, organization, research and improvement would not be published, would it, if there were not belief in someone's practical head that there is a large demand for this good stiff brace to teaching? Tiegs lays down his plans with reasonableness and caution, gives arguments for and against certain recommendations, orders his propositions in attractive sequence, and treats his teacher reader with dignity, confidence and respect.

HOW LIBERAL IS THE LIBERAL ARTS COLLEGE?

The University of Michigan in Ann Arbor is eight miles from the Michigan State Teachers College in Ypsilanti. When I was a student in each institution the assumption in each place was that the cultural scholastic atmosphere of the university was superior. I thought then and I believe now that this is nonsense. Dr. Margaret Kiely[14] has subjected this snobbery to careful measurement. Her study is calm, circumstantial and full of sidelights of penetrating illumination. New Hampshire had need of data like this research's in 1928, Pennsylvania should profit by it now. We may still hold this truth to be self-evident, that all men, etc.—and women—insofar as their rights to teach are concerned, are not to be pushed down or up on traditional assertion.

THE SCIENCE AND ART OF MAKING ONE'S SELF

A pioneer in the introduction of personality study into training for business, President Theobald gives himself away in his book.[15] It is a forceful collection of the fatherly advice the genial educator has given to a long procession of youngsters wanting to succeed. It would be readable without it, but the assortment of experiences of Armours, Babsons, Bradstreets, Vails and the hundred others gives a variety and authority that make palatable food for you and your young people if you add the book to your school library. "You can be a warrior or a whittler," concludes Counselor Theobald. "It depends on what you do to your own mind. You can wait for a romance or a tragedy to lure or jolt you into action. So, you are a whittler. But make no mistake about this, it is your mind, your own, and no one is entitled to be the boss of it but you. There isn't any respectable theory of life other than that you can make your mind bring you to a very much better position than you are now in."

That's the way to talk in these days of absurd conclusions about I.Q.'s and their settlement of one's destiny. The history of progress, its discredited Grants, Beechers, Sewards, Roosevelts, doing big things with their so-called second-rate talents, furnishes plenty of exceptions. Aren't you an exception to a general rule? Aren't we all? Give me Walter Dill Scott's studies. I want to be reminded that statistical research establishes the worth of will, loyalty and honesty over brains. Give me Theobald; he puts the spice into this doctrine.

GUIDANCE TO WORK

A hundred fifty cities, state departments of labor, social and employment agencies, helped Anne Davis and Edith Campbell, experienced placement advisers, make the vocational manual of the White House Conference.[16] The logical and convenient arrangement Editor Campbell has given the book, its complete and handy index, make it indispensable for the school superintendent's office. It defines terms, surveys practice, discloses conditions to be met and guides suggestions by means of a clear statement of principles. Curriculum desirabilities, individual study, psychological tests, counseling, follow-up, waste and improvements needed are covered in detail.

[14] Margaret Kiely, "Comparisons of Students of Teachers College and Students of Liberal Arts Colleges." Bureau of Publications, Teachers College, New York. 147 pp. $1.50.

[15] J. J. Theobald, "Personalysis." Prentice Hall, Inc., 70 Fifth Avenue, New York. 222 pp. $2.60.

[16] M. Edith Campbell and Consultants, "Vocational Guidance." The Century Company, New York. 385 pp. $3.00.

AND NOW THE PARENT

DRAWING upon students and researchers like Sidonie Gruenberg, Ruth Andrus, Helen Atwater, Jessie Charters, Herbert Stolz and others; utilizing the experiences of the Child-Study Association of America, the National Congress of Parents and Teachers, federal and state boards of health and departments of education, university clinics, nursery schools and allied agencies, the White House Conference's big book[17] on parent education comes with a dedication to the great adventure of marriage and child-rearing. In the last ten years, the editor tells us, organized provision for training parents has advanced more than in the whole of previous history of mankind.

What this training now is has been surveyed by the compilers with much labor. What it can and ought to be is outlined by experienced and practical contributors. Methods and usages are described as they exist in the more successful centers. Radio service, lectures, experience meetings, counseling, clinics, training of leaders, mistakes, extension and broadening of objectives, come in for helpful consideration. Here is a chronicle of a changing world and a guide for getting the next generation to find a worthwhile place in it.

AN HOUR ON HEALTH

A MASTER of plain talk, Dr. Fishbein, of Chicago, editor of *The Journal of the American Medical Association,* appears in the reading-hour series of the Lippincott Company[18] dispensing elixirs of life and beauty. "How long will you live?" he asks, and answers. Fads and fallacies, what we have found out and what we haven't, what care keeps our precious machines running smoothly, why you should or shouldn't play golf, and a wealth of facts about medicine in this changing world will give you, I venture, more solid benefit in an hour than you have had in a long time.

TOO MANY TEACHERS

WITH an abundance of diagrams Dr. Overn, professor of education, University of North Dakota, summarizes his detailed study of the ten-year supply and demand as found in teaching positions in Minnesota.[19] This careful analysis of situations common to all parts of the country is, as Minnesota Dean Haggerty says in his introduction to the book, something due to give a jolt to the inconsiderate continuance of unrestricted output of would-be teachers by the training institutions. Managers of other vocational courses are generally avoiding preparation of workers for occupations oversupplied with applicants. The injustice of letting thousands spend time in normal schools only to enter an unsuccessful scramble does not stop with the harm done to the applicants. It is not only flooding the country with distressed seekers for positions who are willing to work for half pay. Pressed by taxpayers, school boards are debilitating the school service by underpaid teaching. Study, improvement of skill, advancement of instruction, are impossible with teachers who believe themselves giving more than they are paid. We can not escape, says Dean Haggerty, the fact that a surplus of unemployed teachers lowers wages, degrades the quality of teaching and upsets tenure. We are likely to see in our calling the establishment of a control of preparation and entrance similar to that exercised by the typographical union and the medical fraternity. Educators are slow to sense the meaning of oversupply. The loss of what professional status education has, the degradation of teaching, confront us.

This, coming from the head of a university school engaged in furnishing teachers, is serious counsel. From 1910 to 1928 the number of students in teachers colleges rose from 113,685 to 512,247. Oversupply began before the economic débâcle of 1929.

Such information as is tabulated by Dr. Overn gives state authorities a basis for an intelligent program for the education of teachers. The absence of such facts has led to floundering among guesses and has prevented telling would-be teachers the plain truth. Overn has gone farther in this needful investigation than any previous inquirer.

17 Louise Stanley and Collaborators, "Parent Education." The Century Company, New York. 354 pp. $2.50.

18 Morris Fishbein, M.D., "Health." J. B. Lippincott Company, Philadelphia. 158 pp. $1.00.

19 Alfred Victor Overn, "Indices of Supply and Demand in Teaching." University of Minnesota Press. 253 pp. $2.50.

SCHOOL AND SOCIETY

EDITED BY J. McKEEN CATTELL

WITH WHICH IS COMBINED THE

EDUCATIONAL REVIEW

EDITED BY WILLIAM McANDREW

Volume 35 SATURDAY, MAY 14, 1932 Number 907

EDUCATION FOR A CHANGING SOCIAL WORLD[1]

By Professor DAVID SNEDDEN

TEACHERS COLLEGE, COLUMBIA UNIVERSITY

ALL well-informed Americans are aware that very significant changes are taking place in our own societies as well as in those of other regions. We are not well agreed as to how momentous or how critical for the future well-being of ourselves and our children these changes are likely to prove. But more than any earlier people in history we are convinced of the desirability and practicability of at least affecting, if not controlling, many of these changes in the interests of human well-being—by more science or better social machinery, by legislation or education, as the conditions warrant.

And for purposes of to-night's discussion, it is important to note that one very important social change of our times, and especially characteristic of Americans, is that of regarding our educational systems themselves as agencies which can and should move and readjust with the times.

In order to avoid triteness and repeating what are platitudes for this audience, it is my intention to select for discussion here what seem to me certain relevant findings of my sociological studies as to which widely varying opinions are properly to be held because of our insufficient scientific knowledge. It is hoped that some of these topics will incite to further thinking, as presented under five heads:

(a) The need of very discriminating thinking about social changes. (b) Recognition of the enormous potentialities of America's greatly expanded educational facilities. (c) Certain needed shiftings of our educational purposes and objectives. (d) Certain needed shiftings of our educational means and methods. (e) And certain probable shiftings of our emphases on school personnel. It is proposed in the following paragraphs to give fairly dogmatic expressions to the writer's present convictions on these points.

I. THE NEED FOR DISCRIMINATIVE THINKING ABOUT SOCIAL CHANGES

Economic depressions and wars, the headlines of our newspapers, the urgent messages of our magazine contributors and some few of the new mechanisms of communication and of power distribution are all undoubtedly intensifying a variety of crowd-minded, heavily emotionalized reactions amongst modern peoples which greatly disturb both their senses of perspective and their appreciation of fundamental human values.

[1] Notes of an address to the Department of Superintendence of the National Education Association, February 24.

Young persons and ardent persons and disillusioned persons are especially prone greatly to exaggerate both the substance and the probable consequences of what may well turn out to be minor fluctuations in the collective life of peoples.

In spite of the varied assortment of history studies now offered in our schools and colleges, it seems very doubtful whether most young Americans yet acquire anything like adequate appreciations of how great, even cataclysmic, have been the social changes of past eras—whether we think of the expansions of the Roman Empire, the spread of Christianity, the invasions of the barbarians, the rise of the feudal system and next its collapse, the Hundred Years' Wars, the ruinousness of the Thirty Years' Wars, the effects of the discovery of the New World, the inventions of gunpowder and printing, the French Revolution or the spread of British imperialism.

Like some modern catastrophic events, or some huge marches of particular peoples, or some transforming powers of new inventions, all the foregoing entailed some changes in civilized societies of great import, whilst in many other respects working no momentous changes whatever.

Not a few modern writers of note seem to think that historic civilization is to be swept from its moorings because certain new agencies of destruction have been brought into warfare, or because certain types of production have learned to employ new science and new mechanisms, or because certain venerable religious beliefs or moral standards no longer evoke devoted adherence, or because a few governmental agencies for the collective actions of great numbers seem to become partly paralyzed, or because some of the more articulate of revolting youth become impatient of the achievements of the elders.

These heavily emotionalized disturbances of men and women of good native powers of intelligence and of sensitive altruistic spirits seem frequently to reflect a new type of herd-mindedness and herd panic deriving from several sources. All those of our modern peoples who read newspapers, listen to the radio and frequent libraries have, obviously, increased enormously what may be called the receptivity of their collective or social nervous systems. A slight shock, a momentary disturbance, anywhere in the world is almost instantly transmitted to the sensoriums of millions, already sensitive and raw from countless other shocks which even a century ago would hardly have been perceived at all.

Again, large proportions of the more sensitive spirits of our time, possibly above all those who have shared deeply in the advantages of our secondary and collegiate schools of learning, seem to have fallen victims to "Great Expectations." They seem somehow to have come to believe in visions of painless life, enduring prosperities, wide-spread good-will among men, controls of the adverse conditions of nature and other good things which neither human nature nor outward nature nor deity itself prove to be capable of producing.

Inevitably, disillusionments of many kinds and degrees are certain to overtake these sensitive souls. They have tried hard to escape from old conditions which seemed bad. They have hoped much from pending changes. But they soon learn also to apprehend much from changes which practical men promote and control. They speak often with terror in their voices. Their disappointments, apprehensions and angers are not dissimilar from those exhibited ages ago by men who had hypnotized themselves into believing that the gods would give succor and salvation which it was later found the gods could not or would not give.

If, then, educators are to take drastic action in shifting educational policies and practices, either to adapt them to pending social changes or else to enable the men and women equipped by our educational agencies the better to adapt themselves to such changes and even in degrees to control them towards increase of the goods of life for men, they must very discriminatingly study such changes and rely for advice especially upon the really sane and competent evaluators of such changes. These educators must above all resist present wide-spread dispositions to become either panic-stricken or fascinated by particular types of change or by novel doctrines of what religion or government or industry or even education should do about it all. Perhaps above all they should strive to remain clear-headed and cool-headed in the presence of the numerous subtle propagandistic movements which are everywhere openly or secretly on foot.

Perhaps we need frequently to remind ourselves in these days of intense dynamic enthusiasms among educators that in most of the vital areas of social change it is always difficult, and often impossible, for schools and colleges as such, as well as for the professional personnel conducting their instructional and other educative functions, to originate findings of importance. Schools and colleges, like newspapers, libraries and other sources of endless possible learnings, are primarily agencies of diffusion of findings.

One man can make an invention, write a splendid new book or discover a novel means of social control through research. Then thousands, even under some circumstances, scores of thousands of teachers in schools can make the new discoveries available to millions.

Even in the crucial matter of deciding which among new inventions, interpretations, valuations, explorations and foundations of creeds, every day being made, should be incorporated into the curricula of offerings of our schools, few educators can afford to rely upon their own judgments alone. Here, too, they must often defer to centrally placed specialists, even in the new increasingly critical areas of social or eudemic valuation.

II. America's Splendidly Expanded Material and Personnel Foundations for Educations

Educators, social scientists, political policy makers and others strongly convinced of the possibilities and our collective obligations of making educations serve far more effectively than they do as yet the changing needs of our time, should not fail to appreciate how splendidly our people have in recent years expanded the material and personnel facilities for effective educations.

Upon our public elementary and high schools are now being expended some three billions of dollars of public monies annually. Nearly five million of our ablest-minded youth are voluntarily attending high schools. Our colleges and universities are enrolling something like a million students. Relatively few of public schools are now in session fewer than thirty-two to thirty-six weeks per year. Compulsory full-time school attendance to age fourteen prevails in substantially all states, whilst in many part-time or full-time attendance becomes obligatory to sixteen or beyond. Nowhere else in the world are educational systems staffed by such large proportions of non-teaching officers and other specialists as with us. Nowhere else in the world are so many and varied types of research and other inquiry toward the improvement of education being prosecuted as with us. And certainly in few other countries are public faiths in the socially ameliorative potentialities of school and college educations anywhere nearly as wide-spread and persistent as with us Americans.

At the session of this department held two years ago in Detroit, the general subject for discussion was "Achievements of American Education." Impressive exhibits of achievements were then made—in such areas as buildings, attendance, teacher-training, staffing, equipment.

Unfortunately, we possess as yet but few reliable measures of the final social efficiencies resulting from our gigantic educational achievements in materials supplied and personnel reached. We can, indeed, evaluate literacy as one of the precious end-products of school educations. And educators can hold that in general America is now nearly completely a literate people.

But other end-values—superior moral character, better health, high vocational competencies, fine personal cultures, approvable civic behaviors in conforming to law and order, the civic initiatives of our abler men and women—all these are as yet nearly impossible of appraisal as products of our expanded schools and colleges.

We know, indeed, that the physical health of the American people is steadily improving in certain decisive respects; and there are good reasons for holding that our elementary schools have had an important share in bringing such results to pass.

But as respects criminality and vagrancy and political incompetency and crudeness of culture and moral greed and fickleness of taste and civic rectitude and family morality and popular regard for scientific interpretation, it is obvious that we still fall far below our aspired-after and our education-promised goals. One must wonder that the faiths of Americans in the virtue-producing powers of their schools and colleges still hold so firm as they do. Upon this note we can take up what the present writer believes to be by far the most important specific topic of the present discussion.

III. Shifting Our Educational Objectives with the Changing Social World

The efficient educations of to-morrow, whether conceived as stabilizing and perpetuating valuably functional parts of the social inheritance, or as equipping men and women to adapt themselves to changing needs and conditions in their societies, must more and more find and define their guiding purposes in terms of proven social values, tangible things of worth in the large and small societies now or prospectively functional.

The concrete objectives of our school and college educations—that is, the actual goals of learning, not only qualitatively defined but also quantitatively delimited—must be more and more related to socially valuable purposes; otherwise the chances of miscarriage of effort, of missing the mark, are far too great.

The ostensible purposes of America's secondary and liberal college educations are still far too much of the nebulous and aspirational order. Commonly there exists an unbridged gap of unknown breadth between our sentimentalized expressions of purposes at these school levels and the actual objectives of learnings of algebra or ancient history or written composition or chemistry or home economics or Latin as actually achieved.

Especially are we under obligations to discover and delimit the purposes of our school educations in terms of proven concrete social utilities if we wish such educations to serve and better to serve the changing, the evolving, needs of our dynamic world. Let us take a concrete example from that easiest of all departments of school education in which to define really functional objectives, namely, that of health-conserving educations.

Three generations ago, the dangerous and destructive diseases of these United

States included cholera, yellow fever and typhus fever. If the schools and colleges of that time had undertaken serious responsibilities for health-conserving educations, they would surely have made much use of whatever science, practical art and other means of prevention and cure of those diseases which might be available. To-day, our programs of hygienic education need never mention such ailments except as, for our country, historic curiosities.

A generation ago, the dread children's disease, diphtheria, ran every year through our population like a fire in the undergrowth. Like the infantile paralysis of today, it prowled "as a thief in the night," it struck savagely, it could seldom be prevented and not often cured.

But of its hygiene there was little to teach the rank and file of either children or parents. Science had not yet learned to prevent or cure diphtheria. Teachers could only describe it, deplore it, and pass on.

To-day, what a difference! Modern medicine is equipped to banish diphtheria from our land, along with yellow fever and cholera, so soon as it can have the general cooperation of parents. Even very young children can be authoritatively told things about the prevention and cure of this disease which they can and will remember, even to the extent of changing the hygienic and expert-service-using habits of parents.

And the opportunities of our schools from the lowest to the highest to contribute to really functional educations toward the further personal and social control and improvement of the health of our people multiply as medical science advances. Here, indeed, are we in the midst of social change! Here, truly, we can yearly "off with some of the old" and "on with something new"—provided we educators do not so much claim empty powers of originating as we yield ourselves to the expert guidance of specialists in this field.

If, now, advances in modern medicine and other controls of personal health and community sanitation obviously require that we should frequently readapt our educational objectives in that field, how even more urgent are our obligations to change and improve with the times as respects those educations which are supposed to prepare for effective political citizenship!

It is the present writer's conviction that America's systems of public schools and colleges are weakest in just this division of social needs and values. In part this weakness is due to the absence, perhaps a necessary absence, of a single, simple focusing center for civic education, such centers as are clearly in evidence, for example, in France, Japan, Italy, Russia, and some other patriotically well-oriented peoples. Because of the traditional devotions of our people to the flexibilities and individualisms of democracy; because of America's divisions of sovereignty between state and nation; because of the meager and halting political experience of our teachers; and because, above all, our educational policy has never yet been able to agree upon definitive philosophical foundations for programs of effective educations for wholesome political membership—because of these things, most of our innovations and current practices in the field of civic education have been and still are indeterminate, feeble and, probably, of nearly zero measures of actual functioning, if we except our achievements in educations for literacy. Where in the United States have we even yet set out seriously to train specialist teachers for this supremely important division of educational needs and values?

IV. The Shifting of Educational Means

If we contemplate the reconstructing of educational objectives as necessarily entailed by the new demands of a changing social world, we become, of course, prepared to accept corresponding changes in the means and methods of our educative processes.

But a changing social world calls for even more than that. Efficient systems of education will constantly search for improved methods of achieving long-established values no less than will medicine, engineering or transport.

Take, as an example, that area of common cultural educational values which embraces scientifically discovered knowledges of hundreds of kinds in the physical world about us. It is the writer's opinion that all our courses in natural science, from the first to the twelfth grades, are doing enormous amounts of grandmotherly fussing over topics and items here which were indeed of vital importance to learners two or one or half a century ago, but which are now so much a matter of the omnipresent social heritage that we no more need to teach them in schools than we need teach in schools the family vernaculars or the household moralities of our peoples.

To this critic at any rate, some two thirds of the instructional units set up as concrete means and methods of natural science instructions in the just published thirty-first year book of the National Society for the Study of Education have no more functional significance for school education than the pot-hook methods once used in teaching handwriting, or the "a, b, ab" methods once used in teaching reading.

As another example, take our present-day elementary school courses in the geographical and historical studies. Enthusiastic specialists in both those fields are so constantly enriching them, as elementary school studies, that they have become in effect masses of fruit-cake offerings, certainly calculated to produce chronic indigestion if the intellectual "tummies" of our children are seriously induced to try to assimilate them. And our high-school courses in history with their encyclopedic inclusiveness, their unapperceivable interpretations, are certainly no better—but in that respect they are not greatly worse than most of our other secondary school studies.

Now the objectives set up by the supporters of these studies, especially in the areas of cultural values, are valid and important enough. (The persistent allegations and hopes of history specialists that any except the most recent of histories can be made vitally functional towards realization of genuine civic values are probably fantastic.) But the means employed are too frequently antiquated, out-moded. Much of our present encyclopedic history and geography instruction with its endless recounting of detail is little better than the old verbally memorized subject-matter.

V. Letting Small Children Grow Naturally

There are wide-spread beliefs, some supported by men of superior scientific insight, that not a few of the changing social conditions of the world tend steadily to impose increasing, or at any rate novel, burdens upon the nature-given human machine; that is, the human body, the human nervous system, the human brain. The highly specialized works of the modern world, the large proportions of indoor work, the widely needed subjections of certain types of primitive emotional expression, the increasing solicitudes of men for their futures, the complexities of social adjustments required, at least from those holding responsibilities of leadership—all these, it is contended by many authorities, are steadily increasing the nervous strains which adults must bear, and are leading in extraordinary numbers of cases to premature breakdown.

If these surmises are correct—and they probably are in some degree—one inference of great importance is that children in their early, physically plastic, years should have conserved to them in every practicable way the conditions of optimum nutritional, nervous, emotional and other basic growths.

Civilized societies now generally forbid specialized or routine vocational employment for children even as mature as fourteen. It is here contended that civilized societies must also learn to withhold their children from the artificialities of school environments and persisting regimented controls during the tender years before nine.

We speak often of a "good start in life" for our children. But one of the most precious of all kinds of "good starts" is that of a sound, slowly matured, normally grown physical body, and especially those parts or components of that body which we somewhat differentiate as the nervous systems affecting, and affected by, our more emotionalized and intellectualized experiences.

In some degree, doubtless, all our urban or suburban reared, automobile-driven, radio-entertained, household-guarded, much-cleaned babies and young children are today the victims of over-stimulation, premature ripening, excessive socialization. But if to such artificializations there be added those of the hot-house nursery school, or the socially exciting and experience-congesting kindergarten, or the inevitably regimented primary school, then in all probability we are still further handicapping the affective natures, especially of gifted persons, for the long strains of successive civic, vocational, cultural and other adjustments needed by our changing civilization.

TRENDS IN TEACHER-TRAINING

By Dr. FRANK WEBSTER SMITH
WINTER HAVEN, FLA.

Time and time again, so often it has become a habit, with all the advantages and disadvantages of habit, it has been said or implied that our public schools are the mainstay of the Republic. It is more to the point to indulge a larger habit and say that education is the foundation of organized community life. It is a broader and more significant thought because it comprehends all constructive forces of personal and national development—religious and secular, artistic, ethical and utilitarian, public and private, technical and industrial, realistic and humanistic education, education in the home and in the community. Public-school training is not always or necessarily synonymous with education. At best it assures only partial education. It concerns itself particularly with accumulating information and giving conventional habit-trends. It is elementarily effective in many, but not in all directions. It busies itself too little with thought and imagination, construction and creation, the esthetic and the spiritual, all-round development, wherein lies the strength of a community. The limitations of public-school teaching are becoming keenly felt, and this feeling is quite general. A movement to reduce some of these limitations began long ago. The Department of Superintendence has lately devoted a great deal of time and effort to one field of study in this connection, character education, and made it the subject of its current Year Book. It also made it one of the most prominent topics of its recent Convention.

The key to progress in education and the removal of some of the shortcomings of public-school work lies in improving the personnel of teaching, and by personnel is meant far more than is produced by scholarship or achieved by courses and credits which have ruled judgment too much and too long.

Teacher-training has been more in evidence in recent conventions of the Department of Superintendence than any other topic. At Washington a score of programs, besides two important and far-reaching conferences, were devoted wholly or in part to this subject. At Detroit last year there were quite as many programs of this nature.

The improvement of teacher personnel and so of teaching in all schools, public and private, from kindergarten to high school, and now even to the college, is the business of teacher-training institutions. They are taking it perhaps more seriously than ever before. It is the supreme topic in present-day education. Interest in quantitative enrolment is declining, in qualitative enrolment increasing. Teacher shortage is giving place to surplus. Plans for admitting only students of promising teaching personalities and graduating only superior teachers are occupying close attention. Progress in this direction in the last few years is remarkable, but it is conspicuous at present only in limited areas.

Three ways of improving teacher personnel are in evidence:

(1) By carefully restricting admission to normal schools and teachers colleges to specially qualified candidates giving promise of becoming genuine teachers interested in studying individuals and making themselves constructive forces in organizing and leading groups of young people. This applies to all schools. Nowhere is care in teacher selection more needed than in the higher levels, and nowhere is it more neglected.

Teaching is not a commercial venture. It is not an occupation or vocation merely. It is an absorbing enterprise in which youth is the raw material and men and women of high character ruled by high principles and charged with fine public spirit are the product.

To receive into our teacher-training schools all candidates who have completed a secondary school course or even those of high scholarship in their secondary school work is becoming out of date. To select by academic examinations is more so. Professional examinations are of course out of the question. Scholarship tests have failed conspicuously. Intelligence tests have failed even more completely, as shown conclusively by several recent scientific studies. The best teacher-training schools are now strongly in favor of carrying their study of candidates back into the early reaches of the high school or even into the elementary school, laying special stress on personality—this in whole-souled cooperation with secondary and elementary school faculties. This gives to vocational guidance a special value and furnishes a most enticing field for effort. Nowhere has guidance such vital significance. It gives would-be candidates most fruitful opportunities to study the requirements and implications in teaching, and it brings most productive cooperation in recruiting teaching forces with teaching personalities that will multiply the number of master teachers. One would hardly dare to place the number of such teachers at present as 25 per cent. of our teaching population. One would be rash in saying that two thirds are above the mediocre grade. This adds emphasis to the quest for distinctive teaching personalities.

The study of teaching personalities goes on after entrance into the training school. Unpromising students are eliminated early, and the eliminating process goes on till graduation. In developing a citizenry of high qualities and ideals imperfect methods of selecting candidates for teaching are disastrous. Nothing will do more to improve this citizenry than the multiplying of master teachers who appreciate their work.

The tendency to improve the process of selective admission to normal schools and teachers colleges is very noticeable in recent convention programs. There are notable examples of superior work in this direction both in the Middle West and in the East. But these examples do not represent the general practice. It is passing strange that the record is not stronger.

This initial step in improving teaching is the most important one because it is the key to all the others. Given a higher type of student personnel and teacher-training curricula will function more effectively in improving teaching.

(2) The education of teachers can be enlarged and strengthened in another direction, through richer and more vitalized courses of instruction and especially through broader and better organized practice teaching programs. Improvement in the latter lies in two directions, in enlarged and more varied practice work to aid the student in finding himself and to give data for final placement, and in provision for more effective cooperation between instructional work and practice teaching. Instructors in psychology, school and class administration, English method, history method, and all the rest, should observe their students persistently after they enter their practice work and determine whether their courses of instruction meet the test in the practical work of the classrooms to which these students go for practice, or need to undergo revision to fulfill the demands of actual teaching. More than this, why should not instructional work be developed more concretely in close affiliations with elementary and high school teaching? Nothing will so surely bring improvement in the instructional work of normal school and teachers college as this double affiliation with the practical work of the schools.

In the organization of teacher-training the student's practice teaching may be made more educative, more thought-stimulating, more prolific in opportunities for originality and creative work, than any other element of his course. A month of it will give more professional education than a year of the preceding instructional work. Strangely enough organization of practice teaching in general has lagged far behind its possibilities and practicabilities here. The administration of practice teaching has been a prominent center of interest in some recent programs affiliated with the meetings of the Department of Superintendence, and much constructive work has been done.

The organization of instructional work has often received more thorough attention than the practice program. It has been revised, enlarged and made more responsive to present conditions. The standard two-year course of a decade or two ago no longer rules. We often find the course extended to three years, in many cases to four years, and in at least one notable case to five years. *Pari passu* with these changes there seems to have arisen a tendency in many cases to make teacher-training academic more than professional. It is a question whether degrees and honors, largely academic, have not taken precedence over teaching power. This tendency has already awakened some apprehension. In spite of these defects, however, courses for teachers have been impressively and progressively improved. It remains to give a better balance in the two departments of training and to change the incidence of interest and effort.

It is worth noting here that at least one

experiment in radical reorganization of educational courses has been undertaken in one of our leading universities with a good deal of promise.[1] It will bear watching. If finally successful it will happily pave the way for the affiliations referred to in an earlier paragraph.

In considering the curriculum, both the instructional courses and the practical work, we must not lose sight of the fact that through this twofold education much may be done to develop teaching personalities. In teacher-training, as in other fields of education, the tendency has been to give the major share of attention to equipment rather than to the person to be equipped. It is now in order to reverse the emphasis.

(3) One of the liveliest topics for discussion at present is in what has been called in-service training. This is the third means of improving teaching. The normal school or teachers college graduate at best has been able to touch only briefly and lightly the profession or even the vocation of teaching. He needs to extend the period of initiation. He requires better perspective, finer adaptations, the vitalizing of principles and ideals, comradeship of more experienced teachers. Advice, suggestion and help are as essential now as in preservice training. All of which engenders confidence and power in a profession which is one of the chief agencies in developing virtues and checking vices in current community life.

If a normal school or teachers college administration is in hearty cooperation, as it ought to be, with local school administrations for which it supplies teachers, its assistance is invaluable, first, in the placement of teachers and in revising placements where they have not proved happy ones; second, in improving the work of young teachers through new demonstrations and by conferences and discussions, always in connection with local principals and supervisors; third, by supplying afternoon and Saturday courses for the further education of graduates. The fact that the normal school or teachers college understands these beginning teachers better than any one else lends emphasis to this type of cooperation which distinctly broadens and enlarges supervisory work. The municipal teacher-training schools obviously have a far better opportunity and better facilities for carrying on this constructive work than other schools, but it can be carried on very helpfully, in one degree or another, by all schools. Local jealousies and antagonisms which may occasionally occur under some conditions are unworthy of the profession and will readily yield to a real cooperative spirit. Some of the most interesting discussions in recent meetings have given prominence to this third means of advancing teaching. Persistent work for the improvement of teaching through the three means referred to will bring notable results.

Progress in the education of teachers has been handicapped by a lack of cooperation and affiliation among associations and organizations interested in study and research in this field. Results of this study and research have thus been in a degree lost or obscured. Each organization has pursued its course in greater or less, chiefly greater, isolation, content with discovery and discussion in its own restricted field. There has been no clearing house for gathering, organizing and disseminating results. The latest movement, which appeared for the first time in tangible form at the late Washington meeting, is toward affiliation and cooperation of the various bodies interested in the education of teachers. With hearty cooperation the next decade should witness greater progress in improving teaching than any decade since the one that inaugurated normal school work.

[1] Professor Schorling's cooperative class in the University of Michigan.

EDUCATIONAL EVENTS

A CENTRAL ADVISORY BOARD ON EDUCATION FOR INDIA

The Educational Supplement of the London Times reports that after consultation with the Provincial Governments, the Government of India has decided to resuscitate the Central Advisory Board on Education which was abolished in 1923. The board will be set up "as soon as financial conditions improve."

The announcement of this intention was made by Sir Frank Noyce in a debate in the Legislative Assembly at Delhi on a motion of Dr. Ziauddin Ahmad, formerly pro-vice-chancellor of the Aligarh Moslem University, recommending the appointment of a committee to suggest suitable modifications in the existing system of education in India. The House rejected both the motion and an amendment recommending, instead of a committee, the summoning of a conference of the educational authorities in India.

Sir Frank Noyce gave good reasons for the claim that the present is not an opportune time for appointing a committee or convening a conference. Committees, he said, are very expensive things in themselves, and very large funds are required to implement their recommendations. He quoted the observation of the Finance Member, Sir George Schuster, in reference to the Report of the Central Banking Inquiry Committee, and those of the associated provincial committees. "How much attention has the result of those labors received from the public," asked Sir George Schuster, "just at this time when everybody's mind is turned to big political developments, to the immediate troubles in the country, or to the impending constitutional changes in the near future?"

The *Times* points out that in recent years there have been two education inquiries of great importance—the Sadler Commission and the Hartog Committee, the latter covering all branches of education from all provinces. Further, the Royal Commission on Agriculture devoted a very important chapter of their report to education. The subject is also prominent in the report of the Whitley Commission on Industrial Labor. These several documents provide ample material for thought and action by the educational reformer.

The Hartog Committee according to the *Times* came to the right conclusions in holding that the divorce of the Government of India from education since the establishment of the Montagu-Chelmsford Reform has been unfortunate, and that steps should be taken to consider anew the relation of the Central Government with this subject.

The committee suggested that this relation should be that of a center of educational information and a means of coordinating the educational experiences of the different provinces. The report proposed the revival in a somewhat different form of the Bureau of Education, and the reestablishment of the Central Advisory Board. That board consisted of the Educational Commissioner with the Government of India, who was chairman; an expert from the United Kingdom when required; two vice-chancellors of universities in India, one of whom was a whole-time officer; two principals of privately managed colleges; four provincial directors of public instruction, and four non-official members specially interested in education.

Sir Frank Noyce was able to announce that most of the provincial administrations recognized the need for reestablishing the advisory board, which will be in a position to advise provincial governments on all matters of policy, administration, studies, examination and spending of public funds referred to it by the provinces.

ACCESSIONS TO THE LIBRARY OF CONGRESS

ACCORDING to a report of the chief assistant librarian, the collection of printed books and pamphlets, comprising over 4,200,000 volumes in the Library of Congress is now the largest in the western hemisphere and the second in the world and is increasing at the rate of 1,000,000 every six years.

The main collections are strongest in bibliography, history, political and social sciences, public law and legislation, the fine arts, American local history, biography and genealogy. Through the Smithsonian Institution extensive files of the scientific transactions and proceedings of foreign learned societies are received. Under the operation of the copyright law has been built up (chiefly since 1870) the most complete collection in existence of the products of the American press.

Through the international exchange service are now received annually about 36,000 volumes of the publications of foreign governments.

The special book collections include the library of Thomas Jefferson; the Peter Force collection of Americana, 60,000 books and pamphlets; the Toner collection of medicine and American local history, presented by Dr. Joseph M. Toner in 1882; the Yudin collection, 80,000 volumes chiefly in the Russian language, particularly valuable for the history of Russia, Siberia and Alaska, acquired in 1907; the Japanese collection, 12,350 volumes, purchased in 1907 with many later accessions; Huitfeldt-Kaas collection of Scandinavian literature, 5,000 volumes; the Weber collection of Sanskrit literature, 4,000 volumes; The Hoes pamphlets relating to the Spanish-American War; the Chinese collection of 142,000 volumes (fascicules) acquired for the most part since 1906.

The collection of John Boyd Thacher, bequeathed to the library by Mrs. Thacher in 1927, is especially noteworthy; European incunabula, 840 titles (929 volumes) printed before the year 1501; works relating to Columbus, and the discovery of America; the French Revolution, 1,581 printed volumes; "Outlines of the French Revolution told in autographs" (a collection of letters and other manuscripts); and autographs and other documents of crowned heads and other European personages, 1,300 pieces.

The Vollbehr collection of 3,000 incunabula, including one of three extant perfect vellum copies of the Gutenberg 42-line Bible, acquired by purchase in 1930 at a cost of $1,500,000, brought the total collection of incunabula up to 4,545 titles, placing the Library of Congress among the first dozen of the world's principal owners of fifteenth-century books.

The library is also purchasing great works of the masters of science in the early fifteenth to eighteenth centuries, forming the foundation in the history of science studies.

THE ELEMENTARY PUBLIC SCHOOL POPULATION OF NEW YORK CITY

According to an article in *The New York Times,* for thirty years following the establishment in New York City of the consolidated, city-wide educational system, registration and average daily attendance showed substantial increases every year. The attendance figures nearly trebled during that period. Later statistics establish the fact that the elementary school population forecast by dwindling figures some time ago, has not only ceased to grow but may be expected to decline further in the future.

The growth of the system may be gauged by the increase of the average daily enrolment from 350,000 pupils in the elementary schools during the first school year of the consolidated city—1898–1899—to an estimated 712,000 for the current semester.

The latter figure represents a decrease of several thousand from last year's total. The first serious check to the growth of the elementary school population occurred in 1929 when the decrease amounted to nearly five per cent. compared with the previous year's total, although the board included the growing junior high schools in the computation.

The decrease in the elementary schools is more than offset by the considerable increases in high-school register and attendance. But the elementary schools form a better index of permanent growth since their student body is more than three times as large as that of the secondary schools. Furthermore, the elementary schools also constitute the basic reservoir of the secondary schools and should the percentage of primary school graduates entering high school become stationary, the actual numbers of new secondary students would also reflect the decline in primary school population. For the time being, the number of elementary school graduates going to high school is on the increase, due particularly to the economic crisis and prevailing unemployment.

The reasons for the decline in elementary school attendance are a dropping birth rate and immigration restrictions. A graphic picture of the amazing growth of school population between 1906 and 1930 may be obtained from the figures published by the statistical division of the board.

The total elementary and junior high-school

population was 492,906 pupils in 1906. Until 1917 and 1918, when a temporary decrease occurred, the figure swelled by many thousands every year. The same situation prevailed from 1918 to 1925, when the total was 300,000 in excess of the 1906 figure. A small decrease was registered in 1926, but by 1928 the total attendance in elementary and junior high schools had risen to 810,000 pupils.

More impressive is the growth of the high-school attendance, from about 20,000 students in 1906 to the present figure of 210,000 students.

FACULTY APPOINTMENTS AT BENNINGTON COLLEGE

PRESIDENT ROBERT D. LEIGH, of Bennington College, which is to open in September with eighty students, twelve of whom have been accepted for admission from Greater Boston, has announced, according to *The Boston Evening Transcript,* the appointment of some of the faculty and staff for next year.

The faculty now appointed are making plans for the curriculum which it is planned to be adapted to suit the interests and needs of the individual student, the fine arts being a major branch. The appointees are listed below:

Kurt Schindler, formerly director of the Schola Cantorum in New York City, to be director of music.

Julian H. de Gray, graduate of Columbia, who recently gave his first New York concert after studying in Paris and in London under Tobias Matthay, to be teacher of piano and composition.

Edwin Avery Park, formerly on the faculty of Yale and of Princeton, to be director of art.

Mrs. Dorothy Canfield Fisher, author and educator, to give individual instruction in creative writing.

Jane Ogborn, now completing graduate work at the Yale School of Drama under George P. Baker, to be director of the drama.

Paul H. Garrett, graduate of Wabash and Ph.D. of Columbia, to teach physics and mathematics.

Wilmoth Osborne, M.D., formerly medical adviser to women at University of Oregon and at present Commonwealth Fellow at Yale University in Student Mental Hygiene, to be director of health.

Ann Louise Steger, graduate of University of Chicago, Ph.B. from Cornell, to teach biology.

Mr. and Mrs. Lewis Webster Jones, Mr. Jones with a Ph.D. from Brookings College, Mrs. Jones a graduate of the London School of Economics, both to teach in the social studies group.

Miss Gladys Stephens, now hostess and manager of the Bryn Mawr Club of New York City, to direct the dining halls and residences.

Miss Martha Hill, a former member of Martha Graham's dance recital group and now in charge of dancing at New York University, will direct the instruction in dancing at Bennington while keeping her connection with New York University.

J. Fitch King, associate professor of chemistry at Williams and a Ph.D. from the Johns Hopkins University, will teach chemistry on a part-time basis during the first year.

The administrative staff consists of Mrs. Mabel Barbee-Lee, director of admissions; Mrs. Gladys Y. Leslie, librarian; Miss Myra H. Jones, comptroller, and Frederic H. Kent, treasurer.

THE BUDGET OF CORNELL UNIVERSITY

As a result of deliberations of the Board of Trustees, according to an announcement made by President Farrand, Cornell University will operate on a practically balanced budget for the academic year beginning on July 1 and ending on June 30, 1933.

The expenditures approved for the endowed colleges at Ithaca for next year, amounting to $2,720,661, exceed estimated income by less than one per cent.

Owing to savings and economies effected throughout the entire university, the budget was approved by the trustees without the necessity of resorting to salary reductions. Cornell thus follows the practice of other large eastern universities where salaries have survived the drastic programs of retrenchment. Faculty salaries at Cornell are regarded as below the competitive scale of comparable institutions.

This result is hailed as a major financial achievement by the university authorities. It involved the closest scrutiny of every item of income and expense, and was made possible by the thorough cooperation of the entire university. Speaking for the board, President Farrand stated that "The trustees are appreciative of the cordial and painstaking cooperation of all departments of the university in effecting every possible economy and saving for the ensuing year. It was this that made it possible to adopt the budget without resorting to salary reductions."

Among the economies listed for next year are the following: large reductions in departmental operating expenses, leaving vacant temporarily certain positions left open by retirement, resignation or leave of absence; reorganization of schedules in certain departments, and the redistribution of the teaching load in others.

The income of the university, which has been conservatively forecast for next year, includes a continuance of alumni support through the Cornellian Council, the alumni fund-raising agency, which it is expected will provide this year about $100,000 in small gifts for emergency needs.

INVESTIGATION OF COLLEGE TEACHING BY THE AMERICAN ASSOCIATION OF UNIVERSITY PROFESSORS

A NATION-WIDE survey of the current practise and standards of teaching in the colleges and universities of the United States has been formally launched under the direction of the American Association of University Professors, according to an announcement released from the national office. This investigation, made possible by the grant of $20,000 by the Carnegie Foundation for the Advancement of Teaching and the Carnegie Corporation, will aim to discover and evaluate the present quality of academic instruction and to recommend standards and methods for its improvement.

Among the definite problems focussed for study are the following:

Is there evidence that courses in education contribute to the making of a better college teacher?

How much emphasis should be placed on background and general culture in the training of college teachers?

How important is it that college teachers know something about the major problems of higher education? How can such knowledge be obtained?

How can methods used in the selection and enlistment of teachers be improved?

Under what conditions, if any, can student and alumni rating of teachers be successfully employed?

How can recognition of good teaching be increased?

The committee in charge of the work consists of Professor W. B. Munro, California Institute of Technology, *chairman;* Professor F. K. Richtmyer, Cornell University, *vice-chairman;* Professor Fernandus Payne, Indiana University, *secretary,* and Professors C. H. Judd, University of Chicago, A. L. Bondurant, University of Mississippi, Alzada Comstock, Mount Holyoke College, Hardin Craig, Leland Stanford University, and George Boas, the Johns Hopkins University.

An assisting advisory committee includes President E. H. Wilkins, Oberlin College; President W. E. Wickenden, Case School, Cleveland; Chancellor S. P. Capen, University of Buffalo; Professor Paul Monroe, Teachers College, Columbia University; President J. R. Angell, Yale University; Dr. Kathryn McHale, American Association of University Women; President L. D. Coffman, University of Minnesota, and Dr. H. W. Tyler, general secretary of the association.

At a recent meeting, the council of the association received a report from the field director of the survey, Professor H. L. Dodge, of the University of Oklahoma, who is giving full time for several months to the study of teaching conditions in many institutions. His preliminary conferences with representative professors and administrators at the Universities of Chicago, Minnesota and Iowa and the Ohio State University, and at the meeting of the Association of American Colleges in Cincinnati have served to assemble the best informed current views concerning the problems, aims and expected results of the survey. Professor Dodge is now making a tour of representative institutions in the East, to be followed by similar visits through the West. Elaborate plans have been effected to enlist the cooperation of the institutional chapters of the association, numbering nearly two hundred. The results of the survey will be published as a supplement to the monthly *Bulletin* of the association.

SOCIAL SCIENCE RESEARCH LABORATORY AT THE COLLEGE OF THE CITY OF NEW YORK

THE Social Science Research Laboratory of the College of the City of New York has been in operation experimentally for about two years, and its success from the point of view of a score of cooperating social and civic agencies, as well as that of the students, now assures its permanence.

The laboratory was developed by Professor Samuel Joseph who directs the sociological courses of the college and the practical field work in sociology. So effective has this work become that it has attracted the active interest of leaders in civic and philanthropic undertakings, some of whom have formed an advisory committee to cooperate with Professor Joseph in its direction. The members of this committee are:

Henry Bruere, president, Bowery Savings Bank.

Howard S. Cullman, commissioner, Port of New York Authority.

John H. Finley, associate editor, *The New York Times*.

Jane M. Hoey, assistant director, Welfare Council of New York City.

Darwin R. James, president, New York State Board of Housing.

George W. Kirchwey, lecturer, New York School of Social Work.

Solomon Lowenstein, executive director, Federation of Jewish Philanthropic Societies.

Harry L. Lurie, director, Bureau of Jewish Social Research.

Robert M. MacIver, executive officer, Department of Social Science, Columbia University.

Frances Perkins, industrial commissioner, New York State Department of Labor.

Aaron Rabinowitz, member, New York State Board of Housing.

Victor F. Ridder, president, New York State Board of Social Welfare.

Dudley D. Sicher, president, New York State Conference of Social Work.

Mrs. Arthur Hayes Sulzberger.

Working under the supervision of experts in various fields of social service, public health and government, 161 students at the College of the City of New York have been carrying on 73 research projects. The volunteer service of these students and their technical advisers has made it possible for many of the agencies cooperating with the college to undertake research studies which, though they have been badly needed, would otherwise have gone undone; it has at the same time given the student worker in this new type of laboratory an appreciation of what he will face when he leaves college such as is impossible to secure from lectures and books alone.

THE CENTENNIAL CELEBRATION OF LAFAYETTE COLLEGE

THE Lafayette College Centennial Celebration will be held from May 17 to 21. The formal opening of the centennial celebration will take place on Tuesday morning, May 17, with convocation ceremonies in the Colton Memorial Chapel. This will be preceded by an academic procession made up of guests of the college, delegates to the conference, representatives of other colleges, trustees, faculty and alumni. At noon a luncheon will be given in the Alumni Memorial Gymnasium in honor of the French guests. The first session of the conference will convene on Tuesday afternoon, following which there will be a reception for the conference delegates and representatives of other colleges. The second and third sessions will take place on Wednesday morning and afternoon, May 18.

The principal address will be made at 11 o'clock on May 17 by Dr. Stephen P. Duggan, director of the Institute of International Education, New York. He will speak on "French Influence on American Education."

Among the speakers at various sessions of the conference on The French Backgrounds of American Civilization are Professor Charles Cestre, University of Paris; Jacques Greber, architect, Paris; Dr. John H. Finley, *The New York Times;* Professor Dixon Ryan Fox, Columbia University; Professor Albert Bushnell Hart, Cambridge; William Francklyn Paris, editor of the Legion d'Honneur.

The celebration will consist of two principal parts. On May 17 and 18 a conference on "The French Backgrounds of American Civilization" will be held. The second part of the celebration will consist of a pageant staged in the stadium on the evenings of May 17, 18 and 20. It will necessitate 1,000 participants, and will reproduce in nine episodes the dramatic incidents in the life of the Marquis de Lafayette. The latter part will depict the history of the college.

Another feature of the centennial celebration will be a Lafayette historical exhibit which will consist of two main divisions. The first will be made up of souvenirs of General Lafayette, and the second of various pictures and other memorabilia relating to Lafayette College.

EDUCATIONAL NOTES AND NEWS

The faculty of Princeton University has presented to Dr. John Grier Hibben, retiring president, a resolution expressing the "lively sense of loss which they will suffer by the termination of his official association with them." The resolution, engrossed and illuminated, was signed by each member of the faculty. The resolution passed by the faculty reads in part: "From the first Dr. Hibben chose to be *primus inter pares,* taking the faculty into his confidence, entrusting to it a full measure of responsibility, steadily safeguarding its privileges and dignity. To this policy, consistently maintained, and to the personal character of the president, the university owes its extraordinary unity of spirit."

Resignation of Professor James C. Egbert as dean of the School of Business of Columbia University is announced by President Butler. Dr. Roswell Cheney McCrea, Hepburn professor of economics, has been appointed to succeed him. Professor Egbert, who has been administrative head of the School of Business since it was established in 1916, has been in the service of the university for forty-nine years. He will retain the post of director of university extension, which he has held since 1910.

Dr. Vierling Kersey, California State Superintendent of Public Instruction, has withdrawn his tentative acceptance of the position of superintendent of schools at Long Beach. The *Pasadena Post,* as quoted in the *Los Angeles School Journal,* writes: "Mr. Kersey's real reason for remaining in the state superintendency is his belief that his resignation would play into the hands of a political group which is intent on dominating the schools of California and especially the state teachers' colleges. To circumvent this plan, he is willing to sacrifice $5,000 a year, to spend half of his time away from his family, and—most of all—to fight."

Dr. Dana Gardner Munro, U. S. Minister to Haiti, has been appointed professor of Latin-American history and affairs in the School of Public and International Affairs of Princeton University.

Dr. Charles Louis Kuhn, curator of the Germanic Museum, Harvard University, and instructor in fine arts, will be exchange professor to the Western colleges, Beloit, Carleton and Pomona, for the first half of 1932–33. Dr. Philip Putnam Chase, lecturer on history, will be exchange professor at Colorado, Grinnell and Knox during the second half of the same academic year.

Dr. Kurt Koffka, director of the Smith College research laboratory in experimental and educational psychology, has accepted an invitation to join a Russian scientific expedition to study isolated peoples in remote parts of the country, by the State Institute of Psychology at Moscow, which includes for the first time a foreigner in the personnel of one of its expeditions. Dr. Koffka will lecture on his experiments at Smith College at Moscow and at Charkov.

Dr. Y. R. Chao, who was recently appointed director of the Chinese Educational Mission, has arrived in the United States to take up work in connection with this position.

The Rev. Hugh Latimer Elderdice, for thirty-five years president of the Westminster Theological Seminary, has resigned and has been made president emeritus. He has accepted the chair of practical theology at the seminary. The Rev. Fred Holloway has been named to succeed him.

Dr. Charles Edwin Friley has been elected dean of the Division of Industrial Science at the Iowa State College to succeed the late S. W. Beyer. Dr. Friley goes to Iowa from the Texas State College, at which institution he was dean of the College of Arts and Sciences.

Dr. A. N. Vernon, Eastman fellow specializing in the psychology of music at the University of Iowa, has been appointed to fill the vacancy in the department of psychology at Cornell College caused by the death of Professor W. E. A. Slaght.

Dr. Charles H. Keene, professor of hygiene and director of the department of hygiene and physical education at the University of Buffalo, has been appointed director of the summer courses in physical education at Harvard University.

DR. W. A. FREEMAN, professor of health administration at the Johns Hopkins University, has joined the faculty of the recently organized summer school for public health workers at the University of Kentucky.

DR. ROBERT CEDRIC BINKLEY, acting professor of history at Western Reserve University, will be visiting lecturer at Harvard University during the next academic year.

DR. LEE WILSON DODD, professor in the department of literature at Sarah Lawrence College, has been appointed to the Frank B. Weeks visiting professorship at Wesleyan University.

DR. ELISABETH BENTLEY has assumed the position of dean of women at Intermountain Union College. She succeeds Miss Gertrude Boyd Crane, who recently resigned because of ill health. Dr. Bentley had previously served as dean of women at Simpson College and at Baker University.

DR. JAMES J. DECK, for thirty-one years professor of modern languages at the West Virginia Wesleyan College, has resigned.

ALFRED RIGLING, librarian of Franklin Institute, was elected chairman of the Special Libraries Council of Philadelphia at a recent meeting of that organization.

PROFESSOR WILLIAM M. SMITH, professor of mathematics and registrar of Lafayette College, has recently been appointed by the Association of Liberal Arts Colleges of Pennsylvania a member of their committee on mathematics.

ROBERT W. KESLER, of Bala, Pennsylvania, and Edward P. Scherer, of Philadelphia, have been awarded Zilph Hayes Palmer scholarships of $2,500 each, given annually (for study and travel abroad) to two members of the senior class of Princeton University.

DR. FELIX FRANKFURTER, professor of administrative law at the Harvard University Law School, has been granted leave of absence for the second half of the next academic year.

PROFESSOR MICHAEL I. PUPIN, of Columbia University, was recently tendered a testimonial dinner by friends at the Faculty Club, in honor of his having been made an honorary member last summer of the Royal Institution of London.

THE degree of honorary doctor of medicine has been conferred by the University of Amsterdam on Dr. Harvey Cushing, Moseley professor of surgery in the Harvard Medical School and surgeon-in-chief of the Peter Bent Brigham Hospital. Dr. Cushing plans to relinquish his work at the school and the hospital at the end of the academic year.

DR. HENRY C. LANCASTER, professor of French literature and chairman of the Romance languages department of the Johns Hopkins University, has been made a chevalier of the French Legion of Honor on May 7.

THE Theodore William Richards Gold Medal was presented to Dr. Arthur Amos Noyes, director of the Gates Chemical Laboratory of the California Institute of Technology, at a meeting of the Northeastern Section of the American Chemical Society in Boston on May 4. The program included a survey of the work of Professor Arthur A. Noyes by Professor Arthur B. Lamb, of Harvard University, president-elect of the American Chemical Society. Professor Lyman C. Newell, of Boston University, gave the history of the medal. William P. Ryan made the presentation and after accepting the medal Professor Noyes spoke on "Education for Chemical Research."

MRS. SIDONIE MATSNER GRUENBERG, director of the Child Study Association of America, was awarded the annual medal for "outstanding work in parent education," by *The Parents' Magazine* at the eleventh annual dinner of the United Parents' Association of New York City. Professor Patty Smith Hill, of Teachers College, Columbia University, made the formal presentation. Mrs. Henry S. Pascal, president of the association, presided.

MRS. LAURA A. ARMER, author of "Waterless Mountain," the story of a Navajo Indian boy, has been awarded the Newbery Medal for the most distinguished contribution to children's literature of 1931 by the section for library work with children of the American Library Association. The award was presented to Mrs. Armer by Miss Emma Lee, chairman of the section, at a meeting held in connection with the fifty-fourth annual conference of the American Library Association in New Orleans.

DR. GEORGE D. STRAYER, professor of education at Teachers College, Columbia University, will address the twenty-seventh annual conference of the National Child Labor Committee on May 27. His subject will be: "The Maintenance of School Services during the Period of Economic Depression."

DR. CHARLES H. JUDD, dean of the College of Education of the University of Chicago, will deliver a series of ten lectures during the fourth annual state education conference at the University of Alabama. The conference will open on June 13, in connection with the summer school.

PROFESSOR JAMES W. TOUMEY, a member of the faculty of the School of Forestry at Yale University since it was established in 1900, and formerly dean of the school, died suddenly on May 6, at the age of sixty-eight years.

THE REVEREND DAVID ALLEN REED, founder of Springfield College and for many years its president, died on April 28 at the age of eighty-one years.

THE death is announced of Dr. E. C. Hills at the age of sixty-five years, for the past ten years professor in the department of Romance languages at the University of California.

DR. ELLEN CHURCHILL SEMPLE died on May 8. She was sixty-nine years old. She was a professor of anthropogeography at Clark University.

MISS EDITH DEBORAH DIXON, for the last three and a half years extension service specialist in child training and parental education at the New Jersey College of Agriculture and Experiment Station, died on May 5, at the age of fifty-five years.

DR. JAMES BREBNER, for forty years registrar at the University of Toronto, died on May 5, at the age of seventy-three years.

SIR ERNEST GRAY, formerly member of Parliament and president of the National Union of Teachers of Great Britain, died on May 7, at the age of seventy-six years.

THE American Association for Adult Education will hold its seventh annual meeting at Buffalo from May 16 to 18, with headquarters at the Hotel Statler.

A SERIES of eight conferences on secondary education will be held at Teachers College, Columbia University, during the first week of summer session, July 5–9 inclusive. Participating in the conferences will be William John Cooper, United States Commissioner of Education; Professor Leonard V. Koos and Professor Arthur K. Loomis, of the University of Chicago; Professor Francis T. Spaulding, of Harvard University; Professor Emery N. Ferriss, of Cornell University, and Dr. Richard D. Allen, assistant superintendent of schools at Providence, Rhode Island, and fourteen members of the staff of Teachers College, will report on phases of the recently completed national survey of secondary education. These conferences will be open without fee to all who are interested to attend.

FELLOWSHIPS and scholarships for graduate study in library science have been awarded to ten librarians from the United States, and three from Canada, according to an announcement from the American Library Association in Chicago. Acting under a grant from the Carnegie Corporation, the Committee on Fellowships and Scholarships, of which Harrison W. Craver, Engineering Societies Library, New York, is chairman, has made the awards to enable persons who have shown promise of contributing to the advancement of the library profession to pursue a year of special study or research in library problems. Two of the awards are renewals granted to present holders of stipends to enable them to complete their studies. Ninety-one candidates were considered and the following appointments for 1932–33 were made: Colman J. Farrell, librarian of St. Benedict's College; J. Harris Gable, student of the Department of Library Science, University of Michigan; Peyton Hurt, research assistant, Brookings Institution; Harry F. Koch, student, School of Library Science, Columbia University; Margaret I. Lee, director of school libraries, Hudson, N. Y.; Evelyn Steel Little, student, Department of Library Science, University of Michigan; Helen Martin, assistant professor of library science, Western Reserve University; John R. Russell, classifier, New York Public Library; Miriam Snow, instructor, Library School, George Peabody College for Teachers;

Lee Wachtel, student, Graduate Library School, University of Chicago; Helen B. Armstrong, assistant of Toronto Public Library; Mary Duncan Carter, assistant director, McGill University Library School, Quebec; Jessie F. Montgomery, librarian, Department of Extension, University of Alberta, Canada. Named as alternates are Jeannette J. Murphy, librarian, St. Mary's College, and Louis Shores, librarian of Fisk University.

The University of Paris will receive outright bequests and deferred legacies valued at over $250,000, according to the will of the late Mrs. Harriet Hale Wooley. The sum of $90,000 will be divided among other educational and scientific institutions.

According to the commissioner of education, Bertram E. Packard, municipal appropriations of Maine towns and cities, made in most cases at annual meetings in March, indicate that approximately half the public school teachers in the state will have to submit to reductions in salaries. About 7,000 teachers are employed and the average rate of reduction will be 6 or 7 per cent.

A plan for averting salary reductions in the Boston school department by having all teachers and employees turn back a proportion of their salaries next year to the department treasury was outlined by Joseph J. Hurley, former chairman of the school committee, before the Boston Sub-Masters Club at the annual dinner of the organization at the Boston City Club on April 28. He said that reduction of expenditures other than salaries in the department had been found inadequate. John F. Brodhead, assistant superintendent of schools, in discussing economy steps, said that the Boston schools will open on September 12 for the 1932–33 season, instead of the normal date, September 8. Other speakers included Chairman William A. Reilly, of the school committee; William B. Snow, assistant superintendent of schools; Joseph F. Gould, director of evening schools, and James E. Dolan, president of the club.

The election of women to the board of trustees of Rutgers University was made possible for the first time since the founding of the university in 1766, under an amendment to the charter filed on April 20 with the Secretary of State at Trenton. The amendment, which calls for an increase in the number of trustees and opens several vacancies, was adopted by the board a few weeks ago. Dr. Robert C. Clothier, president of the university, said that the amendment had been adopted to provide representation by women on the board for the New Jersey College for Women, which is a part of Rutgers University. He said that five women probably would be made members of the board at a meeting in June, and that they would be selected from prominent women throughout the state.

DISCUSSION

THE ADVISER'S PART IN THE PERSONNEL PROGRAM

No two persons are born alike but each differs from the other in individual endowments, one being suited for one thing and another for another, and all things will be provided in superior quality and with greatest ease, when each man works at a single occupation, in accordance with his natural gifts.—*Plato.*

A properly descriptive title for this article would be too long. In order to save the time of readers the purpose of the present discussion is defined in the first paragraph. It is: to consider the division of functions in the liberal arts college between the personnel office and the individual faculty member serving as adviser to one or more students on problems related to the choice of and preparation for a life work.

The faculty-student committee on vocational guidance at one of our New England liberal arts colleges recently sent a questionnaire to several alumni asking what courses they would recommend to undergraduates who anticipate entering the occupations in which these alumni are now engaged. A modified form of this questionnaire was also sent to the faculty, whereupon righteous indignation descended violently upon the committee. The contention of the faculty was that such a consideration of vocational objectives would defeat the purpose of the liberal arts college. They anticipated, of course, that the alumni would recommend the selection of courses closely related to the anticipated occupation, and perhaps that they would even suggest the introduction of training courses.

The situation was not without its amusing aspects, for the returns from the alumni questionnaire indicated that the graduates of this institution, at least, were overwhelmingly in favor of a broad cultural background. They recommended strongly that the undergraduate secure his liberal education while in college and add to it professional training either in the graduate school or in specialized study after obtaining a position.

The opposition to vocational guidance which is found in some liberal arts colleges is perhaps due more than anything else to the failure to distinguish between it and vocational education. Vocational guidance aims to help a student choose his career; vocational education seeks to train him for it after he has made the choice. Vocational guidance precedes vocational education just as the liberal arts college precedes the professional school. To make the liberal arts college an institution for vocational education would defeat the very purpose of vocational guidance, inasmuch as it would take from the student his present opportunity to spend four years tasting a great variety of activities and sampling many fields of knowledge, as a result of which he should be better able intelligently to choose a career.

The popular conception of vocational guidance is naïve. The average layman believes it to be a mysterious process by which a vocational counselor, aided by some psychological stethoscope, diagnoses the capacities and limitations of an individual and then tells him what occupation he should enter. Nothing could be further from the truth. It is, of course, to be hoped that some day such a process may be possible, but with our present tools no one would even attempt to do it, except some of the charlatans who read character at sight.

Vocational guidance to-day aims rather to provide the student with reliable information about the occupations in which he is interested in order that he may make a more intelligent decision than would otherwise be possible. Beyond this no sane counselor or personnel director will attempt to go, although he will, of course, recommend to the student due consideration of his own capacities and limitations so far as he may be aware of them.

The first reaction of the faculty member appointed as an adviser may be to wonder why the personnel department does not do its own job instead of asking him to do it. Justification for this point of view may, of course, be found in the lack of preparation for such work on the part of the average instructor, who may have had no study of psychology beyond an introductory course in college, no knowledge of occupations beyond the few he may have experienced, and who may never even have heard of the "technique of the interview." Despite these obvious limitations there is a place in the personnel program for the faculty adviser. No matter how adequately organized and staffed the department of personnel may be there will always be some students in college who prefer to discuss their individual problems with favorite professors. There will always be some men on the faculty who, without even trying, win the confidence of students whom no one else can reach. Such instructors have an obligation to their students if not to the administration. They are advisers in fact, even if they have not been officially designated. Their contact with the general personnel program of the institution comes when they feel the need of more complete or more accurate information about occupations or when they wish to see cumulative records which the personnel office has assembled on each student. The first duty of the adviser, then, is to interview those students who would rather talk with him than with any one else and to help these students secure the information which will enable them intelligently to progress toward the solution of their problems.

The second function of such advisers is comparatively simple. It consists merely of referring to the personnel department advisees whom they feel can be more adequately served by the director of personnel. In such cases, of course, the adviser should inform the department of any significant facts which have a bearing upon the case, provided these facts have not been given the adviser in confidence.

A third function of the adviser is to route to

the personnel department any occupational information which may come to his attention, particularly about occupations related to the field in which he is a specialist. He should be a consultant for the department on questions related to these occupations and he should permit other advisers to send to him students who may have a major interest in the fields about which he is informed, provided, of course, that this privielge is not abused to the point of interfering with his major job as an instructor.

Finally, on those occasions when there comes to his attention the accomplishment of some student which reveals significant ability on the part of the student, the adviser should be conscientious about notifying the personnel department in order that this information may be added to the student's permanent record and thus become available to other advisers who may be seeking to help the student in question.

It is, of course, understood that every adviser should be free in every case to give the advice which he thinks is needed. If he believes that a broad cultural background is more important than immediate specialization, he should by all means give the student this advice and should not be criticized for so doing. The student also should be free to consult as many instructors as he may wish and finally to act upon his own best judgment. No faculty member should be expected to counsel students upon any problem in a field where the adviser feels himself to be incompetent. Professors of English and physics can not be expected at the same time to be competent psychiatrists and physicians. When service of this kind is needed a consulting specialist should be called in. There is, however, a moral and professional obligation upon every adviser, indeed upon every member of the faculty, to do all that he honestly can to aid any student who seeks his advice.

One may summarize most of the above suggestions in the statement that the adviser is expected to do nothing except what the best teacher has always done. The personnel program merely introduces an added service bureau for the collection of data on occupations and on individuals, which enable the adviser to do his old job better and with less effort.

ROBERT HOPPOCK
NATIONAL VOCATIONAL
GUIDANCE ASSOCIATION

DEPRESSION AND CLASS-SIZE

PROFESSOR CARTER ALEXANDER warns young persons who are aspiring to become educators that large classes must be met (SCHOOL AND SOCIETY, March 12, 1932). While it appears that classes of fifty each are quite as well taught as those of fifteen, as yet no research has revealed whether teachers of six or seven classes of fifty each retain health, vigor and inspiration as long as those who handle three classes of these high numbers. The effect of large pupil load on the amount of sick leave has not been made public.

A teacher at Lincoln, Nebraska, has secured publication of the following statement (*Lincoln State Journal,* March 24, 1932): "It is not a happy circumstance for the unemployed teacher to watch the more fortunate one trying to do the work of two while he stands idly by with folded hands hoping eventually to take his or her place if fortune so dictates."

"Delinquent Girl—Sixteen" relates in a leading magazine (*Harper's,* April, 1932) how she arrived at her present state of uselessness and crime. No teacher in the large city, where classes are huge, was aware that this child was getting nothing out of school.

The debate between R. S. Jewett and Dr. W. H. Pillsbury (SCHOOL AND SOCIETY, March 19, 1932) shows clearly the failure of teachers' organizations to comprehend economic conditions at the present time. Thousands of people are willing to teach because pay is certain and forthcoming when due. Earnings of engineers, lawyers and doctors are frequently difficult to collect even where practice is available. A few professional people earn high incomes but the majority envy the teachers.

Laboring people who have saved and slaved with low earnings to provide homes for old age, which are being taken from them by high taxes, can not comprehend why human beings with steady jobs can not provide decently for old age. Teachers who are successful argue: "Good teachers are very difficult to find. Such persons should be very well paid and must be treated with great consideration." But unemployed college graduates who have trained for teaching are demanding jobs and many of them can teach very well if they are given a fair chance with classes which are moderate in size.

If large classes continue to exist it is because executives and organized teachers consider that high salaries are more important than the child who needs individual attention. They also regard high remuneration for a few to be of more consequence than great numbers of unemployed teachers who will eventually break down tenure laws. At present teachers' organizations should put emphasis on tenure rather than on salaries or pensions. Study of the sacrifices made by labor unions for unemployed fellow workers might be highly profitable to teachers' organizations.

CAROLINE BENGTSON

HASTINGS, NEBRASKA

SPECIAL CORRESPONDENCE

THE SUMMER QUARTER OF THE UNIVERSITY OF CHICAGO

SIX hundred and five courses to be offered by the University of Chicago during the coming summer quarter are listed in the most recent "announcements" issued by the university. The offering embraces work for undergraduates and graduate students in the university's four upper divisions and for professional students in seven schools, a complete and varied program equal in all respects to the university's schedule for other quarters of the academic year.

The faculty for the 1932 summer quarter will number 352, of whom 142 are full professors and 129 are associate or assistant professors. A modification of the university's policy this year has increased the proportion of regular members of the university staff who will continue teaching throughout the summer and has reduced the number of visiting faculty members to 25.

The policy of compacting the summer quarter work into ten weeks, which was inaugurated last year for the convenience of teachers who wish to study during the summer, will be continued this year. The first term will begin June 20 and close July 22, and the second term will open July 25 and close August 26. Each term is credited toward a university degree as a minor, those registering for one term only being privileged to complete the major through the university's home-study department.

A total of 4,957 different students registered for either or both terms of the summer quarter last year, 3,273 having graduate status, 1,234 being undergraduates and 450 unclassified.

The School of Education headed by Dean Charles H. Judd, as usual, leads in the number of courses offered. Fifteen full professors, all of them members of the regular university faculty, and twenty-three staff members of lower rank, will offer a total of sixty courses. The work is divided into nine subdivisions: Introductory courses; the school in the social order; educational psychology; educational administration; curriculum, methods and supervision; statistics and measurement; higher education; secondary education; and elementary education. The work of the school is housed largely in the new Graduate Education building, erected at a cost of $600,000, which was formally opened March 14 and 15.

Two conferences will supplement the academic work in education during the quarter, the seventh annual conference of administrative officers of institutions of higher education, to be held July 13, 14 and 15, and the conference of public-school administrative officers to be held July 18 and 22.

Three visitors will supplement the law faculty, Robert L. Henry, judge of the Mixed Court, Alexandria, Egypt; Sigvald Nielson, of Stanford University and Roger J. Traynor, of the University of California. The Divinity School, which is headed by Dean Shailer Mathews, will offer 49 courses. The staff of 33 members, including 17 full professors, will include Edmund S. Conklin, professor of psychology at the University of Oregon; Leslie Blanchard, executive secretary, National Student Council, Y. M. C. A.; Richard H. Edwards, executive director, National Council on Religion in Higher Education; W. Hubert Greaves, professor of public speaking, Yale University; and

Justin W. Nixon, pastor, Brick Presbyterian Church, Rochester, N. Y. A pastors' institute will be held August 1–10.

Carlton B. Joeckel, professor of library science at the University of Michigan, and Francis L. D. Goodrich, librarian of the College of the City of New York, will be members of the Graduate Library School faculty during the summer quarter. The School of Commerce and Administration will offer 21 courses and the School of Social Service Administration 27 courses, these offerings being supplemented by a large number of courses in closely related fields administered through other departments.

Of the four upper divisions, the Biological Sciences, which includes fourteen departments and the University Medical School, under the direction of Dean Frank R. Lillie, will offer 163 courses. The staff of 109 includes as visitors Katherine J. Densford, professor and director of the School of Nursing, the University of Minnesota; Harriet Frost, director of the Department of Instruction, the Visiting Nurse Society of Philadelphia; and Heinrich Siedentopf, Privat-dozent, Universitäts-Frauenklinik, Leipzig.

One hundred and seven courses will be offered through the eleven departments in the Humanities Division which is headed by Dean Gordon J. Laing. The staff of 52 faculty members will include as visitors under the Frederick Ives Carpenter fund, Kemp Malone, professor of English at Johns Hopkins University, and Baldwin Maxwell, chairman of the department of English, State University of Iowa. Carl F. Tauesch, associate professor of business ethics in the Harvard Graduate School of Business Administration, will offer a course in the department of philosophy.

The Physical Sciences Division, embracing seven departments, will have a staff of forty-three and will offer 93 courses. Visitors include Wilhelm Blaschke, professor of mathematics, University of Hamburg; Gerrit Bol, Privat-dozent in mathematics, University of Hamburg; and Aristide von Grosse, in chemistry. Dr. Henry G. Gale is dean of the division.

The Social Sciences Division, under Dean Beardsley Ruml, will include 61 staff members, 35 of whom are included in other divisions or schools, and will offer 63 courses. Dr. Ralph Linton, of the University of Wisconsin, will be a visiting professor of anthropology.

A program of nearly one hundred public lectures will be offered in addition to the regular courses. The university also provides an extensive program of social and recreational events. Physical facilities added during the current year include a series of residence halls providing unusual living accommodations for 400 men; the new Graduate Education building; and the new Museum of the Oriental Institute.

QUOTATIONS

CHILD HEALTH DAY

IN few, if any, periods in our national medical history has more concerted effort been directed toward child welfare in its varied aspects. Every phase of the child's life is receiving scientific investigation and attention. Specialists have developed in every field of infantile and juvenile activity. Numerous organizations have been created to study the status of the health and well-being of the children of the United States and its possessions, to report what is being done, and to recommend what ought to be done and how to do it.

This is admittedly a large task, and it has been relegated for the most part to experts who serve without compensation and make their efforts a "labor of love." In a recent address, Dr. Ray Lyman Wilbur said that there are 45,000,000 growing children in this country. They represent more different racial strains than make up the body of any other nation. They have widely different backgrounds. To get a composite picture of this complex American child, to find out how he rates, physically, mentally and morally, what our rapidly changing civilization is doing to make or mar him, to determine where our social, educational and governmental machinery is at fault in training him to his utmost capacities, and where it may be strengthened, is a challenging task.

The scientific studies of the child have been

published in many medical periodicals and in many special publications which reach parents and teachers in the public schools. May first, which has been set aside by presidential proclamation as Child Health Day, should serve to keep awake the great interest in the problems and possibilities of child welfare and to help promote those movements, including public health measures, that will serve to attain the objectives of their sponsors. Fact finding is not enough. There must be concerted effort to put well known prophylactic procedures into effect, so that prepared minds in wholesome bodies will be the characteristics of the rising generation.

The demands of childhood are not limited to the field of medical service, including growth and development, prenatal management and maternal care. The child is involved in public health problems such as communicable disease control, in the technical aspects of education and training, and in those complicated details that relate to the physically, socially and mentally handicapped. It has been remarked that every child is now our child, because so many artificial conditions have been injected into our industrial civilization that the old normal relationships of mother and child, child and family, family and neighborhood, have been changed.

An illustration of the immediate opportunities for more forceful medical leadership is apparent in the results of a recent study. A cross-section survey of the country has shown the extent to which preventive medical procedures are reaching children under 6 years of age.[1] In this group only 22 per cent. are vaccinated against smallpox in the urban areas and only 7 per cent. in rural areas. When we realize, says the writer, the peculiar susceptibility to smallpox of children under 6 and that for the last ten years we have had a yearly average of 55,000 cases of smallpox, we can not fail to grasp the truth of this conclusion. What is true of smallpox is true also of diphtheria. We have available procedures which if universally applied would eliminate both of these diseases within relatively few years. Lack of progress in health conservation not infrequently is due to the unfortunate tendency to neglect well established and proved methods. That is why the Child Health Day proclamation properly brings the perennial reminder of "the fundamental necessity of unremitting effort for the protection and development of the health of the nation's children."—*The Journal of the American Medical Association.*

[1] *United States Daily*, section II, Washington, D. C., April 6, 1931, "Foreword."

THE CHILDREN'S BUREAU

Just twenty years ago President Taft signed the Borah bill, creating the Children's Bureau of the Department of Labor. To-day false economy threatens its usefulness.

This bureau stands high among all government bureaus in possession of efficiency, integrity and sympathy. It was born of storm and stress. Lillian D. Wald, of Henry St. Settlement, first urged its creation in 1906. It finally came to being in 1912.

The Children's Bureau has helped more than 12,000,000 mothers to save and raise their little ones; administered wisely an infancy-maternity welfare law; opposed child exploitation; saved thousands of mothers' and babies' lives.

To-day its ministrations are more than ever needed. But the Senate committee originally voted a slash of $100,000, or 25 per cent., from its meagre budget of $395,000—compared with the general cut of 10 per cent. ordered by the Senate.

Out of a $4,000,000,000 federal budget it would seem that sufficient economies could be made without crippling this friend of friendless children.—*The World-Telegram.*

REPORTS

STATE SUPPORTED HIGHER EDUCATION IN MISSISSIPPI

The committee on university and colleges at the 1931 convention of the Mississippi Education Association presented its report, Part I, which listed and discussed twenty major recommendations.[1] The association voted unani-

[1] Final report of the committee on university and colleges to the Mississippi Education Association, Jackson, Mississippi, April 28, 1932.

mously: (1) to approve the report; (2) to authorize such changes as in the judgment of the committee might seem necessary; (3) to direct the committee to prepare and recommend to the legislature of 1932 in the name of the association a law as Part II of the report which would embody these recommendations.

We have performed these duties. No sufficient reason was presented or seen for changing the recommendations, and, although at times where was considerable clamor for certain changes, we refused to be swerved from continuing to offer the recommendations approved by the Mississippi Education Association.

Under competent legal advice, a law was prepared embodying these recommendations and a copy furnished to every member of the legislature.

Naturally the legislature did not accept the proposed law *in toto,* but made four or five important changes, some of which we did not approve and tried to prevent. Yet, it should be kept in mind that the responsibility for law-making was the legislature's, not ours. Having made and urged upon it these recommendations, our responsibility ceased. However, the fact that a reorganization law which embodied most of the committee recommendations was passed and passed unanimously by both the House and the Senate as the first major project of the new administration shows how deeply impressed the people of the state and the lawmakers were by the soundness of the recommendations.

A brief survey of the recommendations compared with the law as passed serves to indicate just which ones were approved, directly or by implication:

1. Recommended that the state-supported higher educational institutions be under the control of a board of trustees, separate from other state educational institutions.

Approved.

2. Recommended that the state-supported higher educational institutions be under the unified control of one board of trustees.

Approved.

3. Recommended that the board of trustees of the state-supported higher educational institutions be made up of a lay body; *i.e.,* that its membership be selected from the citizenship at large, irrespective of occupational or other special affiliation.

Approved.

4. Recommended that there be no *ex-officio* member of the board of trustees.

The law provides that the governor shall be an *ex-officio* member of the board of trustees.

5 and 6. Recommended that the board of trustees shall consist of ten members (with one extra for the university). That the ten members be appointed from the state at large (with one member for the university from DeSoto County).

The law provides that the board of trustees shall consist of eleven members, one being the governor and another being the citizen of DeSoto County, the trustee for the LaBauve Fund for the university, the regular members representing the three supreme court districts.

7. Recommended that the terms of the trustees shall be overlapping and of sufficient length to reduce the possibility of political interference and lead to continuity of policy: two for two years; two for four years; two for six years; two for eight years; two for ten years, and all regular terms thereafter shall be for ten years.

The law embodies the overlapping principle but makes the length of a regular term twelve years; provides further that the appointed members shall be: three for four years; three for eight years and three for twelve years, and that terms thereafter shall be for twelve years.

8. Recommended that eight members of the board of trustees be appointed in the beginning by the State Board of Education: two for two years; two for four years; two for six years; two for eight years, and that the governor, by and with the consent of the Senate, appoint two for ten years.

The law provides that the governor, by and with the consent of the Senate, appoint the entire board: three for four years; three for eight years; three for twelve years, and every four years the extra member for the university.

9. Recommended that the governor each two years shall appoint two members for ten years to fill regular vacancies and expressly specified that no governor during any administration shall appoint more than four regular members and the extra member for the university.

The law provides that each succeeding governor shall appoint during the administration three members to fill regular vacancies and that no governor shall appoint more than three regular members.

10. Recommended that a member to fill an irregular vacancy be appointed by the State Board of Education.

The law provides an irregular vacancy be filled

by appointment by the governor from recommendation of two names by the State Board of Education.

11. Recommended that a per diem of $10 for not more than twelve days per year, plus traveling and hotel expenses, incident to meetings of the board, be paid.

Approved.

12. Recommended that members of the board of trustees shall not be removed during their term of office except on proved charges, etc.

Approved.

13. Recommended that a member be ineligible for reappointment after a regular term.

Approved.

14. Recommended that the power to regulate non-state-supported higher educational institutions be not extended to the board of trustees.

Approved by implication.

15. Recommended that responsibility for capital outlay expenditures (bond issues) for state-supported higher educational institutions be placed in the hands of the board of trustees rather than specially created commissions.

Approved in the law, but could be set aside by any legislature. This ought to be the subject of a constitutional amendment.

16. Recommended that the functions of the board of trustees shall be policy-making, that is, legislative and judicial, and that the functions of the administrative heads be executive.

Approved. The law definitely commits the board to electing the faculty personnel only upon recommendation of the administrative heads of the institutions.

17. Recommended that the legislature do not hamper the board of trustees by trying to regulate with petty legal limitations matters of internal policy, and that appropriations for all schools be made in a lump sum.

Approved. It is evidently the intent of the legislature to follow this recommendation. We note with satisfaction the proposal to make appropriations for all institutions in a lump sum, to be allocated by the board to the several institutions.

18. Recommended that the board be required to have two regular meetings and as many special meetings as necessary.

Approved.

19. Recommended that a majority of the members have the power to call the board into special meeting upon ten days' notice.

Approved.

20. Recommended that the board of trustees employ a full-time, non-member secretary, a well qualified professional educational research worker, and maintain an office with adequate clerical help.

Approved.

Our work is done. The Mississippi Education Association has fought another good fight for the youth of Mississippi. Yet we can not bring to a close this final report without bespeaking for the new board of trustees and for our state-supported higher educational institutions the sympathetic understanding and support of all patriotic Mississippians.

THE COMMITTEE ON UNIVERSITY AND COLLEGES

MRS. W. D. COOK
MRS. R. S. RALSTON
O. H. SWAYZE
W. B. JONES
C. J. DARBY
JOSEPH E. GIBSON, *Chairman.*

EDUCATIONAL RESEARCH AND STATISTICS

WHAT CAN BE DONE REGARDING UNFOUNDED BELIEFS?

IN some of our previous publications we have reported the extent of belief and influence of certain common superstitions and other unfounded beliefs.[1] The investigations reported in those papers were made in order to provide a basis for specific factual instruction regarding some of the unsupported but widely prevalent ideas. Units of subject-matter that are already being used in school subjects of study have been examined to determine which ones of the unfounded beliefs are logically related to the factual elements of these units. Then, certain units have been rewritten so as to include both the factual elements and relevant experiences, that are commonly used in these

1 "Students' Attitudes Regarding Unfounded Beliefs," Otis W. Caldwell and Gerhard E. Lundeen, reprinted from *Science Education* for May, 1931. "A Study of Unfounded Beliefs Among High-School Seniors," Gerhard E. Lundeen and Otis W. Caldwell, reprinted from *Journal of Education Research* for November, 1930. "Are Students Influenced by Unfounded Beliefs," Otis W. Caldwell and Gerhard E. Lundeen. Paper read before section on Education, American Association for the Advancement of Science, New Orleans, December, 1931.

units, and also those which relate to the unfounded beliefs. Through the use of this reorganization it was hoped to give direct and effective instruction which would include the facts about unfounded beliefs, as well as the facts usually included in the units which were selected for this series of experiements. Thus, the pupils were not made especially conscious of efforts bearing upon unfounded beliefs, but the teaching efforts and materials were directed toward effective learning of the factual elements and meanings of the whole unit.

The unit of instruction discussed in this paper was prepared for use in general science of the junior high school. This unit considers: (1) some of the work accomplished by the human body; (2) some aspects of the care of the body, and (3) includes certain related attitudes or unfounded beliefs which sometimes prevail. The special purpose of this experimental unit was to determine whether desired attitudes may be developed by direct and specific instruction regarding common ideas that have little or no basis in fact.

Reading material for the study of each problem was provided either in the typed manuscript that was supplied or by citations specifically made to general science text-books. The texts used were: Caldwell and Curtis, "Introduction to Science"; Pieper and Beauchamp, "Everyday Problems in Science"; Webb and Didcoct, "Early Steps in Science"; and Wood and Carpenter, "Our Environment: How We Use and Control It." Any one of the texts cited or any other standard text in general science might be used as the accompanying reading material for this unit. The supplementary material was supplied in order to provide a well-rounded and reasonably complete presentation of the whole unit, since different text-books vary somewhat in their treatment of a unit. Discussions of common erroneous ideas were regularly incorporated as parts of subject-matter of the unit. Factual knowledge was presented in regard to these ideas, valid reasons for belief or disbelief were given, and teaching tests were included for these beliefs as for the other elements of the unit. Suggestions regarding instruction were supplied. Test forms and instructions for their use were sent to each cooperating teacher.

Sixteen teachers assisted by teaching the unit to eighth and ninth grade pupils in their general science classes during the spring of 1931. Nine hundred pupils received this instruction, representing 26 classes in 10 different high schools. The schools cooperating were located in different states of the Union—two in California, two in Indiana and one in each of the following states, Minnesota, Michigan, Ohio, Pennsylvania, Connecticut and Illinois. The records of 61 pupils were incomplete, possibly due to their absence at the time of one or more of the tests, thus preventing their responses from being usable. The responses of 839 pupils (455 boys and 384 girls) who had received instruction on the unit and had taken all the required tests were used in checking up the results of the work.

The instructors who cooperated in teaching the unit were asked to submit reports giving information in regard to their method of presentation, length and number of class periods used, whether the subject-matter was a duplication of previous subject-matter presented to these pupils during the year and other information. All the sixteen teachers sent these reports. In checking up the reports it was found that the methods of instruction varied considerably. Some teachers used definite daily assignments which were followed by class discussions, the more capable pupils being given additional work from time to time. Other teachers used individualized instruction, each pupil proceeding at his own rate, and additional assignments were given to those pupils who were able to complete the unit in less time than the average pupil. Various methods of teaching, sometimes in combination with those mentioned above, were used by some of the teachers. The average time spent in teaching the unit was 16.8 full hours. Twelve of the sixteen teachers reported that the subject-matter used in the unit was not a duplication of subject-matter previously studied during the year. The other four said that some of the topics had been discussed previously in one connection or another.

Tests were given which dealt with the important ideas presented in the unit. A True-False Test (Form A) was given as a preliminary test before instruction on the unit. After instruction was completed, two tests were given, the Multiple-Choice Test (Form B) and then the True-False Test (Form A). This True-False Test was the same as was given before instruction on the unit.

The achievements made by the pupils during the period of instruction may be measured by comparing the scores made in the preliminary and final tests.[2] Detailed records of individual classes are not presented in this report. It was found, however, that some classes made higher scores on the preliminary tests than did others, and, also, higher scores on the final tests. The difference in the achievement scores between classes may be due to a variety of factors, such as, methods of study and instruction, accuracy of instruction, differences in classes and time allotted to work on the unit.

The primary object of this investigation was to secure objective data which would indicate whether knowledge and attitudes, in regard to unfounded beliefs, may be changed by special instruction. The test items II, 13, 35, 37, 38, 40, 42, 43, 45, 47, 48 and 50 listed in Table III deal with erroneous ideas which were incorporated into the unit and which were presented as a regular part of the study of the subject-matter. A summary of the scores made by pupils of all classes in the different schools on the 12 items involving unfounded beliefs is presented in Table I. The mean score on the 12

TABLE I

SCORES MADE ON THE ITEMS INVOLVING UNFOUNDED BELIEFS IN THE PRELIMINARY AND FINAL TESTS (MAXIMUM SCORE IS 12)

	Preliminary True-False[3]	Final True-False	Difference	Per cent. Gain
Mean	6.06	10.05	3.99	33.3
S.D.	4.35	3.03		
V	71.80	30.10		
Cases	839.0	839.0		

[2] Scores were determined by subtracting the number of wrong answers from the number of correct answers.

[3] The correlation between the scores made on the True-False Test before and after instruction is .321 ± .02.

items in the True-False Test before instruction is 6.06 (approximately 50 per cent). After instruction the mean score on the same test is 10.05 (approximately 84 per cent). The difference between the mean scores before and after instruction is 3.99. This achievement score (3.99) divided by the maximum score (12) shows an average gain of 33.3 per cent. This achievement demonstrates the effectiveness of instruction in regard to the 12 unfounded beliefs.

The difference between the sigmas (S.D.) of the mean scores in the preliminary and final tests does not indicate the complete change in variability, since the means are unequal (Table I). In order to compare the relative variability of the scores about their respective means, it is necessary to compare the coefficient of variation (V) of each test which considers both the average score and the variability. The coefficient of variation in the preliminary test is 71.8, and 30.1 in the final test. That is, the scores in the final test are 42 per cent. as variable as the scores in the preliminary test. The scores cluster more closely around the mean (10.05) in the final test than they do around the mean (6.06) in the preliminary test. This shows that instruction has resulted not only in distinct increase in the mean score but that the performance of the group as a whole has been distinctly improved.

One hundred thirty-six of the 839 pupils made perfect scores in regard to the 12 unfounded beliefs in the preliminary test while 463 made perfect scores on these items on the final test. One hundred eighty-three pupils made zero scores on the same 12 items in the preliminary test and 29 pupils made zero scores on these 12 items on the final test. There were 104 pupils who made perfect scores in both tests on these 12 items. These individuals evidently desired and possessed rational attitudes in regard to these misconceptions before this period of special instruction. Twenty-one pupils made zero scores in both tests. This may possibly indicate that some of these 21 pupils were absent during part or all of the period of instruction; or that instruction was ineffective in changing them regarding these unfounded beliefs; or that unknown factors may have been operative. Sixty-eight pupils who scored zero in the preliminary test made perfect scores in the final test. This strikingly interesting change in scores of these 68, while doubtless due in part to the direct knowledge results of specific instruction may also be due to changes in general attitudes which the instruction may have produced.

The records from almost all the 839 pupils as revealed by their responses before and after instruction are valid evidences that instruction did produce more reasonable attitudes in regard to these 12 beliefs that have little or no scientific foundation.

Table II presents the mean scores of the whole group on all the 50 items of the True-False Test before and after instruction. It must be kept in mind that the 12 unfounded beliefs are included in the 50 items. The mean score of 24.71 (approximately 50 per cent.) shows that the pupils already possessed much information regarding the items included in the test previous to the instruction that was given on this unit. In the final test the mean score is 35.91 (approximately 72 per cent.). The achievement score is 11.20 (difference between the two means) which is an average gain of approximately 22.4 per cent. at the close of the period of instruction.

TABLE II

Scores Made in the Preliminary and Final Tests (Maximum Score is 50)

	Preliminary True-False[4]	Final True-False	Difference	Per cent. Gain
Mean	24.71	35.91	11.20	22.4
S.D.	9.09	7.72		
V.	36.8	21.5		
Cases	839.0	839.0		

The Multiple-Choice Test which involved exactly the same items as did the True-False Test was, also, given after instruction on the unit. The chief purpose of giving this additional test was to have a check on the True-False Test. The mean score on the Multiple-Choice Test is 40.42 ± 5.56. The correlation between the two final tests is $.77 \pm .009$. This is a fairly high correlation when we consider that we are dealing with different types of tests, and it indicates that they measure approximately the same phases of knowledge.

[4] The correlation between the preliminary and the final True-False Tests is $.54 \pm .16$. The correlation between the scores made on the odd and even items of the initial test is $.76 \pm .009$.

Table III presents the summary of the pupils' responses to each of the 50 items of the True-False Test previous to and following instruction. The amount of change of attitude in regard to each of the 12 unfounded beliefs may be approximated by the change in the responses that the pupils recorded in regard to these beliefs in the final test.

The number and per cent. of correct responses to the whole list of 50 items that the pupils recorded in the preliminary tests are high in regard to many of them. The possibility for improvement in regard to their knowledge and attitudes was not great in many cases since so many of the pupils already possess the desired attitudes to a considerable degree. This fact in no sense lessens the importance of specific instruction, but rather shows that instruction may improve good qualities that are already somewhat developed regarding the list of items included in this experiment. It should be recalled that an increase in a possession that is already good is most significant from an educational point of view.

The final test shows a gain for all items, excepting items 14, 27, 30 and 33. These items show a loss in the final test. A reading of these four items in the table indicates that the reason for this loss may be found in the ambiguity of the test items themselves; or possibly there was lack of clarity of the subject-matter in the unit as it dealt with these ideas.

Conclusion

(1) The mean achievement score or gain in desirable responses in regard to the 12 unfounded beliefs following the instruction was 33.3 per cent.

(2) The number of perfect scores in regard to the 12 unfounded beliefs in the final test was 463, which is more than 55 per cent. of all the pupils concerned.

(3) Judging from the responses that the pupils recorded to the 12 items in the preliminary and in the final tests a change of attitude in regard to the unfounded beliefs included in this study may be produced by direct and specific instruction.

TABLE III

NUMBER AND PER CENT. OF CORRECT RESPONSES TO EACH ITEM OF THE TRUE-FALSE TEST BEFORE AND AFTER INSTRUCTION. THE MAXIMUM NUMBER OF CORRECT RESPONSES IS 839[5]

Items	No. of correct responses				Per cent. of correct responses			
	Pre-test	Final test	Gain	Loss	Pre-test	Final test	Gain	Loss
1. Bacteria are simple one-celled animals	291	616	325		34.7	73.4	38.7	
2. Most dependent organisms are beneficial or harmless	497	687	190		59.2	81.8	22.6	
3. The true cause of communicable disease was discovered by Pasteur	574	642	68		68.4	76.5	8.1	
4. Communicable diseases are caused by improper food	531	670	139		63.3	79.9	16.5	
5. Diphtheria is a communicable disease	724	797	73		86.3	95.0	8.7	
6. Toxins are produced in the body by disease germs	467	662	195		55.7	79.0	23.2	
7. A person may become immune to smallpox by vaccination	745	816	71		88.8	97.3	8.5	
8. The body opposes communicable diseases by producing more blood	496	576	80		59.1	68.7	9.5	
9. When sick a person should consult his family physician	820	826	6		97.7	98.5	0.7	
10. Tuberculosis is a disease which may be cured by fresh air, sunshine, rest and wholesome food	806	832	26		96.1	99.2	3.0	
*11. Any disease can be produced by thinking too much about it	669	698	29		79.7	83.2	3.5	
12. Typhoid fever may be spread by water	789	819	30		94.0	97.6	3.6	
*13. A disease is produced as a direct punishment for some particular wrong-doing	776	820	44		92.4	97.7	5.2	
14. An adult human needs food for energy	808	807		1	96.3	96.2		0.1
15. Cooking gives all foods an improved taste	442	573	131		52.7	68.3	15.6	
16. Proteins supply the body chiefly with materials for tissue repair	658	711	53		78.4	84.8	6.3	
17. Carbohydrates and fats supply the body largely with materials for repairing old tissue	459	589	130		54.7	70.2	15.5	
18. Vitamins prevent diseases like scurvy, beriberi and rickets	670	805	135		79.9	96.0	16.1	
19. Vitamins are essential in the diet	779	819	40		92.9	97.6	4.8	
20. Milk is pasteurized to kill dangerous disease germs	822	833	11		98.0	99.3	1.3	
21. The value of pasteurization was discovered by Edison	817	828	11		97.4	98.7	1.3	

[5] It must be kept in mind that the numbers in these columns refer to the correct responses and not to the individual pupils' scores.

TABLE III—(*Continued*)

Items	No. of correct responses				Per cent. of correct responses			
	Pre-test	Final test	Gain	Loss	Pre-test	Final test	Gain	Loss
22. Milk is the most essential food for a child	827	833	6		98.6	99.3	0.7	
23. Some typical protein foods are cheese, lean meat and beans	557	750	193		66.4	89.4	23.0	
24. The necessary food elements that the body needs are best secured by eating large amounts of meat	809	814	5		96.4	97.0	0.6	
25. Foods may be preserved at a low temperature	660	742	82		78.7	88.4	9.8	
26. One condition favorable for the growth of bacteria is moisture	714	774	60		85.1	92.3	7.2	
27. The process by which a food is changed to a soluble and liquid form is called absorption	440	404		36	52.4	48.2		4.3
28. Starch is in part at least changed to sugar in the mouth	564	744	180		67.2	88.7	21.5	
29. The process by which the digested food is transferred through the walls of the alimentary canal into the blood is called circulation	447	466	19		53.3	55.5	2.3	
30. The union of the carbon of the food with the air is called oxidation	314	167		147	37.4	19.9		17.5
31. It is in the stomach that the entrance of food into the blood is chiefly accomplished	379	477	98		45.2	56.9	11.7	
32. The exchange of gases in the lungs and in the cells of the body is called respiration	570	710	140		67.9	84.6	16.7	
33. The oxidation of food in the body takes place in the lungs	595	483		112	70.9	57.6		13.4
34. One function of the circulation of the blood is to bring oxygen and digested food to all parts of the body	689	808	119		82.1	96.3	14.2	
*35. Red hair is a sign of a violent temper	722	817	95		86.1	97.4	11.3	
36. Intelligence is the capacity for learning, and for proper action	762	804	42		90.8	95.8	5.0	
*37. Brains and beauty are rarely found in one person	608	747	139		72.5	89.0	16.6	
*38. An accurate estimate of an individual's intelligence may be made upon the basis of his facial appearance	638	773	135		76.0	92.1	16.1	
39. The most important function of the muscular system is to provide body movements	767	814	47		91.4	97.0	5.6	
*40. Among pupils of equal age, the most intelligent are on the average physically smaller than those of less intelligence	609	708	99		72.6	84.4	11.8	

TABLE III—(*Concluded*)

Items	No. of correct responses				Per cent. of correct responses			
	Pre-test	Final test	Gain	Loss	Pre-test	Final test	Gain	Loss
41. The work of the various organs of the body is controlled and governed by the nervous system	683	784	101		81.4	93.5	12.0	
*42. A high forehead indicates superior intelligence	574	774	200		68.4	92.3	23.8	
*43. Long slender hands indicate an artistic nature	522	796	274		62.2	94.9	32.7	
44. Intelligence is best determined by mental tests	703	811	108		83.8	96.7	12.9	
*45. The ability to look directly at another person while talking with him is a reliable method of judging a person's honesty	359	740	381		42.8	88.2	45.4	
46. The higher mental processes such as learning, thinking and reasoning take place in the frontal areas of the "large brain"	523	746	223		62.3	88.9	26.6	
*47. A reliable estimation of a person's character may be secured from the features of his face	487	717	230		58.1	85.5	27.4	
*48. Brunettes are more trustworthy than blondes	701	810	109		83.6	96.6	13.0	
49. The mind, that is, the ability to observe, to think and to remember, is very intimately associated with the nervous system	663	734	71		79.0	87.5	8.5	
*50. A heavy square jaw is an indication of unusual will-power	568	780	212		67.7	93.0	25.3	

(4) The achievement rating as measured by the tests on all of the 50 items including the 12 unfounded beliefs was 22.4 per cent.

(5) The majority of the teachers (12 of the 16) who assisted in the experimental try-out of this unit stated that the subject-matter of the unit was not a duplication of previous subject-matter taught during the year in their general science classes. The mean score in the preliminary test was high, being approximately 50 per cent. of the 50 items. The evidences seem to indicate that the subject-matter included in the unit was in part a review of work accomplished in other school subjects or in science instruction during previous years. The cumulative results of such instruction, however, are regarded as highly desirable.

(6) The cooperative experiments with this unit have provided evidences by means of which to improve the clarity both of statement of problems and subject-matter discussions.

Otis W. Caldwell
Gerhard E. Lundeen

Institute of School Experimentation, Teachers College, Columbia University

NEW BOOKS IN EDUCATION

Chapman, John J. *New Horizons in American Life.* Pp. 51. Columbia University Press. $1.50.

Cobb, Ernest. *One Foot on the Ground: A Plea for Common Sense in Education.* Pp. 248. Putnam's. $2.00.

Gardner, Helen. *Understanding the Arts.* Pp. 336. Illustrated. Harcourt, Brace. $1.96.

Seibert, Louise C. *A Series of Experiments on the Learning of French Vocabulary.* Pp. 105. Johns Hopkins Press.

SCHOOL AND SOCIETY

EDITED BY J. McKEEN CATTELL

WITH WHICH IS COMBINED THE

EDUCATIONAL REVIEW

EDITED BY WILLIAM McANDREW

Volume 35 SATURDAY, MAY 21, 1932 Number 908

CREATIVE LIBRARIANSHIP[1]

By JOSEPHINE ADAMS RATHBONE

SCHOOL OF LIBRARY SCIENCE, PRATT INSTITUTE, BROOKLYN, NEW YORK

BEFORE entering on my main theme, I wish to say a few words about the American Library Association and upon the presidency thereof as the office appears after a term's incumbency.

Would that every critic, nay, every member, of the association might be privileged to serve as its president. Though a member of the organization continuously for nearly 40 years, never until this past year have I comprehended the association in all its aspects, in all its activities. Never before have I, nor should I otherwise have, read the Proceedings from cover to cover, the annual reports of its headquarters staff, its boards and its committees from the first to the last page. To the president comes the opportunity of attending the meetings of its principal boards and committees, of listening to their discussions, understanding their problems and realizing how much time, thought and hard work each one is giving to the affairs of the association. And, above all, never before did I spend a week at headquarters, sitting with each officer and studying the work of each department in turn, and but for this term of office never should I have had this enlightening experience. For until you do all these things at least once you can not understand and appreciate as a whole the work the A. L. A. is doing or trying to do. Therefore, since it is probable that, besides the office force, only the president will do these things, I wish the doing of them, and especially the visit to headquarters, might be made part of the duty of each president, and I strongly recommend that an appropriation be made each year for the president to visit Chicago for a week when there is no meeting going on, but at a time when the staff is pursuing the even, though strenuous, tenor of its usual tasks. For as I conceive it, one of the most important functions of the president is to interpret the organization to its members. We are now so large that only a very small percentage of our 15,000 members can see and realize for themselves the magnitude, the variety, the importance of what goes on at headquarters; its far-reaching influence, the extent to which people of all sorts, from college presidents to labor unionists, turn to it for information and advice; the extent to which people not only in North America but in South America, not only in Europe but in Asia and Africa and Oceanica as well, write to it for help in solving library problems, in setting up library service or in selecting books for libraries, and if the

[1] Address of the president of the American Library Association, New Orleans, April 25.

president has not a realizing sense of all this, he can not perform his mission of interpreting the working organization to the rank and file with enthusiasm and conviction.

This work of interpreting the organization to its members is, as I said, one of the most important functions pertaining to the office of the presidency. It is useless to expect people to read long reports or papers or proceedings; you know, each one of you, that that is true of yourselves, perhaps not invariably true for all reports, all papers, all proceedings (indeed, one member told me that he never listened to a presidential address but that he always read it), but we have each of us, I am sure, had the experience of saying to ourselves, "I am glad to get the Proceedings and some day I am going to read it all through." But does that day always arrive? I fear not. But while few of its members read all the material, and some read very little of the material issued by the organization, and not all of us who read comprehend the bearing of what we read and therefore sometimes get quite erroneous impressions, the president of the A. L. A. can command a respectful hearing (for a reasonable length of time at least) and words spoken with understanding and conviction will get across, will promote better understanding, and will bring the association home to the members. Because the president was convinced that the association needed to be explained and interpreted to its members she has this year tried to accept every invitation to speak that has come her way and has talked quite simply and frankly about the A. L. A., its organization, its aims and its accomplishments before state associations, local clubs, staff meetings and other gatherings. From the response she has met and the comments she has heard, she has been greatly encouraged and feels that the effort was well worth while. But the experience also deepened her conviction that to many of its members the national association is a far-off entity; they fail to realize that it is theirs, that it exists for the promotion of their interests, for the solution of their problems; that the officers are their representatives, that the headquarters' staff are their employees, that all are working to advance librarianship, and that whatever advances librarianship benefits each library and every librarian.

The word librarianship brings me to the main subject of this discourse, which I have called "Creative Librarianship." However widely opinions differ as to just how this thing we call librarianship should be classed, as a profession, a craft, a service, an art or a science, we are all agreed that it is essentially that calling which collects and organizes books and other printed matter for the use and benefit of mankind and which brings together the reader and the printed word in a vital relationship. Librarians may have other relations to books, but those other relations are side lines, incidental to, not essential parts of, librarianship. Perhaps you remember a paper that was read at a library meeting in the South two or three years ago and subsequently published, reproaching librarianship for not having contributed to the development of a great imaginative literature, and citing the late Frances Newman as the only author of originality and creative power that librarianship has produced. That would be a reproach indeed if authorship were our business, but I submit that it is not, and the series of "Library Authors" the *Library Journal* has been running this past year or two, perhaps by way of answer to that critic, convinces me not at all. Librarianship did not produce Frances Newman any more than pharmacy did Keats or medicine Brett Young. Of course some librarians have written books, a book may happen to any one in the course of a lifetime, but the writing of books is no part of a librarian's job. It is doubtful if he is a better librarian for having done so, except as anything that enlarges our experience tends to make us better librarians, and he may be a less effective one if his book distracts him from the efficient performance of his real task. In any case it is simply irrelevant.

Nor is it essential that a librarian be a bibliographer, though some great bibliographers have also been librarians and some librarians have also been bibliographical scholars. But while librarians must know bibliography, and organized librarianship must produce bibliographies to meet its needs, and must be skilled in their use, a librarian may function with entire success without having himself ever compiled a bibliography or written a treatise upon it. Similarly, what is called productive scholarship, that research that contributes some modicum to the store of knowledge, is not necessarily part of a librarian's job. He must be familiar with the methods and materials of research that he may aid it, but the actual carrying on of research itself, except in the case of the specialist, is no essential part of librarianship.

In all this talk of librarian authors, in the attempt to remove from our calling the stigma of failing to produce poets, novelists, historians, productive scholars, research specialists, let us not lose sight of the real essence of our job, which is to know books and to understand the book needs of people. It is up to us, collectively at least, to know books of all sorts, to know book values, to be familiar with the literature of all important subjects (so that we not only know what books are of permanent value, but those which have become superseded, and those which are superficial or misleading); to know the different kinds of books contained in different classes, the different points of view they present, and to know source materials, the raw stuff of books, and that for the widest possible range of subjects. We have coped with this part of our job with fair success.

Attention has been concentrated on the book for the past thirty years, principles of book selection have been worked out and codified, courses in book selection based on these principles are taught in all our institutions for library training, scores of tools for the evaluation and aids for the selection of books have been compiled, our resources in serial literature, in special collections of all sorts have been enumerated and appraised. We have also given much attention during the latter part of the same period to the personnel of the profession, those by whom our libraries are collected, organized and administered. We have investigated and accredited our training agencies, have formulated schemes of service, have set up systems of certification, all looking to the improvement of the service rendered by our libraries. And now signs are not lacking to indicate that we are beginning to realize that a knowledge of books and tools is not enough, but that in order to select books and to use them wisely we must know more about people than we do, not only people collectively or in groups, but as individuals. We must know about the reading tastes, capacities, needs and habits of individual readers on all levels of the social structure.

That this is a move in the right direction, that the world expects of us a knowledge of reading tastes and interests, is shown by the chapter on the "Library as Market" in the Cheney "Report on the Book Industry." In order to find out the value of libraries to the trade the question was asked of public libraries, "What have you found the most effective method of studying the reading habits of your community?" Replies from 200 libraries indicate that 40 used personal contact, 35 studied circulation figures, 31 studied requests and 31 reported observation through books borrowed, 5 followed study club programs and 4 reported contact with local organizations, while 67 admitted that they do not study reading habits at all. Cheney's comment, "How many of these methods could be accurately designated as a study of reading habits and reading interests, how many are adequate as a sound basis for serving the whole community?" is perhaps deservedly ironic and should serve to arouse us to a realization that the time has come for us to develop an organized body of information about the human needs we exist to direct and to meet.

This does not mean of course that the 67 libraries who reported no specific study of reading habits, or the others whose methods seemed to Cheney so inadequate, have not adapted their choice of books to the needs of their public empirically with some fair measure of success, just as there were well-selected, well-balanced collections of books before the principles of book selection were formulated and taught in library schools. And up to very recent times no one, not even psychologists, have known much about reading interests; indeed, one eminent psychologist assured an inquiring readers' adviser that if she came back in twenty years he might be able to answer her questions. So it is hardly a reproach to us that we do not know more than we do, we have only just gotten to the point where we are in a position to study this aspect of our problem at all. It is only since the new emphasis on adult education, during the last decade, with the consequent appointment of readers' advisers and the establishment of a readers' advisory service, that libraries have been able to make systematic investigation into and to record the reading tastes, interests and habits of individual readers. When readers' advisers have had time to collect and study these records, to compare their experiences as they are doing, they will be able to work out conclusions founded on a considerable body of data. Then shall we have a basis for the formulation of effective methods of adapting book selection to reading habits. Some of the best brains of the profession are now at work on this problem. Psychologists and students of pedagogy are also investigating in this field, and we can doubtless use some of their findings, possibly adapt some of their techniques, but the problem is our problem, and to be of use to us the data, the methods and the conclusions should be our own.

With the whole range of book knowledge and reading interests as our field we have creative possibilities before us vast enough to employ all our intelligence and all our energies for lifetimes to come. Why not recognize this and set up our own standards instead of adopting those of other professions?

Instead of urging assistants in public libraries (college libraries may find themselves so tied up with the prevailing academic standards that they must perforce adopt them), instead I say of urging assistants in public libraries to spend their all too scanty leisure accumulating credits by taking college courses that have no direct bearing upon their work as librarians, courses that will not make them better able to select books, to advise readers, to assist scholars, why should we not urge them to read more and to study the reading of others? Why should we not study the reading habits of our own assistants, have them report from time to time on the books they have read and on their experiences in recommending these books to others; give them opportunity to read the more important of the recent books, have staff libraries, as some are now doing, or staff copies of the stimulating, horizon-widening books that will help them keep abreast of the time and that will enable them in turn to stimulate and guide the reading public to the selection of worth-while books? We may make our educational requirements for entrance into library work as high as is needed, but why should not advancement depend, not on the acquirement of higher degrees, but upon the quality and quantity of reading done, upon increased book-knowledge, upon the value of reference or readers' advisory service rendered, upon the successful administration of a branch or department, in a word, upon growth in librarianship based upon standards appropriate to librarianship, not upon the obtaining of degrees which are based upon academic or pedagogic standards. Let us realize also that work in a library is educative in itself. Given a good background, a basic technical training, a taste for reading, an inquiring mind and an interest in people, the qualities that make for successful work with readers, as knowledge of books, imagination, sympathy and understanding of human nature and human needs, can better be developed by work in the circulation or reference departments or children's rooms of a good library under the stimulus of a broad-minded inspiring chief than they can be in college classrooms, and it is also true that the acquisition of a higher degree is no evidence of their possession. We should also realize that this work of fitting the book to the reader, child, youth or adult is truly creative, though the results are not concrete and can not be appraised by the canons of art or measured by the instruments of science.

Let us not make the mistake that the educational world has been criticized for making, that of judging and rewarding teachers in secondary schools or colleges not by their teaching but by their degrees and by their contributions to so-called productive scholarship, with the result that the teachers' best energies are too frequently expended not in the classroom but on their own studies, while the students who should look to them for stimulus and for inspiration too often leave school or college unsatisfied.

In addition to knowing books, selecting them wisely and using them productively, a librarian has the opportunity of creating within the library an atmosphere favorable to the finest and best use of that collection, of developing an organization of staff members capable of interpreting and adapting the library to its public. If you think that is not a creative job of the highest order, remember what the late Henry E. Legler did with the Chicago Public Library by breathing into it his own spirit of enlightened and devoted service. Mr. Legler was only incidentally an author or a bibliographer, but he was one who loved books and his fellow men, and he recreated a library that became a living force in the community.

Librarians can not only create a library, make opportunities for intensive as well as extensive book service, inspire a staff to render the best possible book service by knowing books and understanding people, but they must have a comprehensive view of social trends and movements, that they may ally themselves and their libraries with all the constructive forces in the community that are helping to build a better world than the one we now live in.

Those engineers and economists who have vision, who see paths out of our present difficulties, seem agreed that this is no mere cyclical depression, but the end of an epoch —the era of production—and that prosperity, even our civilization itself, depends on ways being found to bring about a wider and more equable distribution of purchasing power among all the people, and that among the methods to reach this end are the breaking up of the huge unwieldy inhuman combinations into lesser units, not concentrated in large cities, but scattered over the country in smaller communities, where living conditions are better, rent and food cheaper, and also in the wider distribution of employment by means of far shorter hours of labor. It is hardly necessary to point out to a library audience what these two factors, the development of smaller industrial centers throughout the country and greatly increased leisure, mean to the libraries of the country in the way of enlarged opportunities for usefulness. Of the libraries' part in providing thinking Americans with the best and mostly timely literature on economic and social subjects much has been said during the past six months, and much has been done by librarians in cooperation with other book agencies to put this material into the hands of the reading public.

Of the need for educating the public to a realization of the social value of the library both as a purveyor of ideas and as an element in keeping up morale much has also been said, and something has been done to bring before the budget-makers this aspect of the situation.

There is another angle from which I wish to consider our part in the remaking of the common life. A very suggestive book, "The Twilight of the American Mind," appeared just before the end of the late jazz age and deserved far more attention than it received. In it Professor Walter Pitkin pointed out that we were educating for the higher executive positions in industrial life a vastly greater number of young people than industry with its tendency toward consolidation of organization is going to require or find place for. We are also educating more lawyers, more doctors, and now it seems more librarians than we need or than there are places for in the several professions. What is to become of these young people? How are they to get that satisfaction that comes from the exercise of their trained minds, their constructive abilities? For unless these are employed the ensuing discontent will express itself in social revolt, in destructive rather than in constructive activities. They will probably have to seek employment along the lower levels of industrial life, but when it is possible to make a living by working a few hours a day even at a mechanical task contentment may be achieved if there be time and opportunity for a cultural or creative life during one's leisure hours.

So there must be outlets provided for the energies of our educated youth, opportunities for creative activities in every community, a change of emphasis, perhaps of direction, so that the ideals that are held up shall be those of an inner development; so that success shall not mean the accumulation of money, but the attainment of the good life in which each man and woman has the leisure and the opportunity for the development of his innate tastes and aptitudes. There should be more chance everywhere not only to hear but to take part in the production of good music, there should be choruses and orchestras in every community, there should be more participation in the production of plays and pageants, more folk dancing, more widely diffused skill in the use of the pencil and brush, more knowledge of natural science, more activity in the crafts, so that in each community beautiful pottery or rugs, or handwoven fabrics may be produced, gardens cultivated, experiments made in horticulture, in breeding, more study of birds, of plants, of soils, so that each member of a family shall be interested in raising or producing something that shall contribute to the beauty, the comfort or the interest of the home and to the enrichment of his own life. Fortunately, there are already organized forces at work to stimulate and encourage activities along many of these lines.

In the forwarding of these manifold interests the library can and must play a most important part; it may be a center from which shall radiate not only information but quickening impulses, dynamic forces, spiritual influences. An example of this was brought to my attention recently. There came a few years ago to a rather drab little manufacturing town a librarian who was a flower lover. She planted flowers in the front yard of the library and in the back. When a club leader came to ask advice on a program for the season she suggested gardens and bought and borrowed a collection of alluring garden books for their use. Next spring there was vigorous planting in many neglected yards. A little later a garden club was started, prizes were offered, and within three years the whole aspect of that shabby little town was changed and an absorbing interest brought into the common life.

Such opportunities lie all around us. Many of you are now taking part actively in the development of such local interests. One library is leading in the little theater movement, another is lending framed pictures as well as books, another is conducting discussion clubs. Recently at the Boston Public Library there was held an exhibition of beautiful pottery which was made by the members of a club started at one of the branches. We must each of us open our eyes to the needs of the times. Let us have vision and conceive of our job not only as one of detail or techniques, of research or of academic standing, but creatively as one of the greatest potential forces making for a more interesting as well as a more equably ordered world.

THE NEW ORLEANS MEETING OF THE AMERICAN LIBRARY ASSOCIATION

"ALL our historic American shibboleths about equality of opportunity are tested as to their sincerity, not on the Fourth of July, but when we come to make the budget of a community or a commonwealth," Frank P. Graham, president of the University of North Carolina, told those attending the fifty-fourth annual conference of the American Library Association in New Orleans, from April 25 to 30.

"A deep cut in the library budget can cut deep into the social returns of a democracy to those who do the work of the world. The schools and libraries are the chief resources with which we will restore and advance the good things of the common life. To tear down is a wasteful way to save. Let us save at every point, tighten our belts all along the budgetary line, but let us have no hysterical runs on the schools and libraries.

"Let us not surrender to depression, defeatism and despair, but rather create our way out by the long-run building up of the capacities and powers of the people. We must continue to invest in the intellectual and spiritual resources of youth."

Other speakers at the conference were: Edwin R. Embree, president of the Julius Rosenwald Fund; Frederick H. Koch, professor of dramatic literature at the University of North Carolina; Lieutenant Colonel John Malcolm Mitchell, secretary of the Carnegie United Kingdom Trust, Dunfermline, Scotland; Josephine Adams Rathbone, president of the American Library Association, 1931–32; and Hendrik W. Van Loon, author.

The negotiation of a contract for annuities and pensions for members of the American Library Association was approved by the council of the association. Harold F. Brigham, chairman of the committee on annuities and pensions, presented the retirement plan, which is to be underwritten by one insurance company and will enable any library to provide retiring annuities for its employees on a contributory basis (library and librarians sharing the cost) and any librarian to obtain through his library a retiring annuity on an employee-pay-all basis. Adequate protection after retirement is the goal for which the committee is working. The contributory contract is the ultimate objective. It is anticipated that the plan will be in operation within the next six months.

The establishment of an information and advisory service for college libraries at American

Library Association headquarters in Chicago was recommended in a report made by the college library advisory board, Donald B. Gilchrist, chairman, and presented by Charles Harvey Brown. The recommendation provided for a full-time secretary, who would give assistance in such matters as buildings, staff, books and collections, instruction in the use of the library, student reading, bibliographical aids to research, college administration and finance. The council formally approved the plan outlined. It also made the following statement:

Librarians and library authorities are urged by the American Library Association to meet sympathetically the demands of appropriating bodies for the utmost efficiency and economy in all public activities. At the same time they should stand unflinchingly for the maintenance of those library services which help to sustain morale and to increase understanding of the many difficult problems now confronting the American people.

This country has millions of unemployed men and women whose spirit is threatened by idleness and deadly discouragement. For many of them the library is one of the most essential agencies for combatting these tendencies.

The library should make every effort to have the details of its budgets and activities thoroughly and intelligently studied and understood.

Librarians should continue to seek new and better ways of doing the necessary work at the least possible cost. Notable progress in this direction has been made.

Library salaries should be commensurate with those of other educational professions.

Regardless of the size of the book fund, some investment should be made from month to month in the best of the new books on current problems. In this time of stress when clear thinking on public questions is essential, the function of the library as an agency for the diffusion of ideas should not be curtailed.

When millions of men and women, old and young, are attempting to equip themselves to get or to hold jobs, the library should not be allowed to decrease its effective service in technical, business, and other vocational fields. When these and other millions are in greatest need of finding in free library service the only recreation they can afford and one of the few opportunities for renewing their faith in organized society, the library should not fail to meet its obligations to the community.

In the matter of salary scales, the council took this attitude:

Salary standards in the library profession are among the lowest of all professions and have been for many years;

The breaking down of present standards will inevitably mean a serious lowering of the character of library service and have a disastrous result on the morale of the profession;

Therefore be it *Resolved,* That library trustees, librarians, and directors of library schools be urged to do all in their power to maintain salary scales commensurate with similar professions;

And, that the American Library Association through its *Bulletin* and in other ways make available to its members all possible information that will be useful in presenting facts to tax-levying and appropriating bodies, bearing on this all important matter.

Principles for school and public library development adopted at a pre-conference meeting called by the library extension board and the school libraries committee of the association also received council approval. They were as follows:

(1) An adequate library program includes both free public and school library service for all the people.

(2) This program to be adequate must recognize and ultimately attain accepted standards of service in each of the above fields.

(3) Administrative centralization is desirable whether it be for public library service only, for school library service only, or for a combination of both.

(4) In instances of combined school and public library administration, the cost of maintaining centralized service should be provided from school and public library funds in proportion to the service given in each field.

(5) It has been demonstrated that adequate library service to both communities and schools in rural areas can be given economically and effectively by means of a centralized administration from a county or larger region library, when properly financed and adequately administered by a trained personnel. This demonstrated success points toward the more general adoption of the plan.

The council indorsed the following resolution adopted at the pre-conference meeting already mentioned:

Whereas, it has been the experience of county governmental, educational and social agencies that their work is often retarded by such conditions as: restricted area, sparse population, topographical features, and inadequate financial resources, and

Whereas, to further the success of agencies so handicapped there is needed a political unit large enough to provide adequate tax support at a smaller per capita cost, and,

Whereas, the library profession in its effort to extend free library service to rural communities on the basis of the county as a unit has been similarly handicapped and retarded and,

Whereas, it is the consensus of this conference that in general a larger political unit will make possible a more economical and more effective rural library service, therefore,

Be it resolved:

(1) That this conference go on record as indorsing the principle of consolidation of counties where these conditions exist.

(2) That it recommend to library agencies the collection and dissemination of available literature on this subject for the purpose of informing governmental officials and the public.

(3) That this group recommend to the council of the American Library Association that it subscribe to the principle of the consolidation of counties where conditions warrant and that the association cooperate with other interested agencies for the furthering of this purpose.

A third resolution on school library development, passed by the pre-conference group, embodied principles for establishment of school library service in communities where public library service is not yet developed. It declared that:

An adequate library program includes both free public and school library service for all the people.

It is recognized that many individual schools and many school systems in communities where adequate public library service does not now exist are faced with the problem of developing a library service to meet the immediate needs of the changing curriculum and the standards of the accrediting associations.

It is recognized that professional personnel is essential to successful administration of any library service and that the school librarian in such communities has a dual responsibility: that of rendering efficient service to the school, and the responsibility and opportunity of encouraging the ultimate establishment of public library service.

It is the desire of those attending this conference to cooperate in every way with school authorities in developing library service that shall meet the present needs of the schools, but which shall look toward the ultimate goal of adequate library service for the whole community.

A follow-up conference at a later date with representatives of the Association of Colleges and Secondary Schools of the Southern States and others interested in southern library development was recommended to the library extension board and the school libraries committee at the conclusion of the pre-conference meeting.

On recommendation of Sydney B. Mitchell, chairman of the preliminary committee on research, studies, surveys and special projects, the council approved the creation of an advisory board for the study of special projects. Duties of the board will be to make recommendations to the executive board of the association on proposals for research, studies, surveys and special projects and to consider with other organizations proposals of mutual interest which come within the new board's province.

Carleton B. Joeckel presented recommendations, from the committee on supply and demand of the Association of American Library Schools to the council of the American Library Association, which dealt with the oversupply of trained librarians and the consequent need of reduction in the size of library school classes "through a more rigid scrutiny of applicants, as to both scholarship and personality."

Officers elected for 1932–33 were: *President,* Harry Miller Lydenberg, Public Library, New York City; *first vice-president,* Julia Ideson, Public Library, Houston, Texas; *second vice-president,* Joseph L. Wheeler, Enoch Pratt Free Library, Baltimore, Maryland; *treasurer,* Matthew S. Dudgeon, Public Library, Milwaukee, Wisconsin; *trustees of endowment funds,* John W. O'Leary, Central Republic Bank and Trust Company, Chicago, and Eugene M. Stevens, Federal Reserve Bank, Chicago; *members of the executive board,* Lillian H. Smith, Public Library, Toronto, Ontario, Canada, and Malcolm Glenn Wyer, Public Library, Denver, Colorado.

EDUCATIONAL EVENTS

PUBLIC SUPERVISION OF PRIVATE SCHOOLS IN ENGLAND

THE report has been issued of the departmental committee set up by Sir Charles Trevelyan, when president of the British Board of Education in the labor government, "to survey the present position of the Board of Education and the local education authorities in relation to schools not in receipt of grants from public funds, and to consider what legislative or other changes were desirable for the purpose of securing that the children attending such schools should receive an adequate education under suitable conditions." Mr. J. Chuter Ede was chairman of the committee.

The main conclusions and recommendations of the committee, as printed in the London *Times*, are:

There are many excellent private schools, and the majority are above serious reproach. On the other hand, a small proportion are so defective that they are harmful to the mental and physical welfare of their pupils. A larger proportion are seriously weak and inefficient.

The existing powers of the local education authorities and the board of education are cumbersome and ineffective. A remedy should be sought through a scheme of public supervision. Supervision should be based on inspection; with certain exceptions, all private schools should be inspected. Inspection should be of a liberal type and should cover both the instruction and the premises, including the residential accommodation in boarding schools.

The scheme should include power to compel the closure of schools which fail to comply with certain minimum requirements. In general, the question whether a school complies with these requirements should be determinable ultimately by a court of law. The statutory minimum requirement as to education should be efficient instruction in reading, writing and arithmetic of a scope and standard suited to the children's age and capacity. It should be a legal obligation on the proprietor of a school to provide such instruction for children of school age attending his school.

The minimum requirement as to premises should be prescribed by the board of education in statutory regulations framed *ad hoc* in respect of private schools. A high standard should not be required. The general aim of the regulations should be to secure what is essential for health and decency and to prohibit anything that might be harmful or dangerous.

No requirements should be made regarding the qualifications of teachers in private schools.

The proprietor of a private school, subject to inspection under the proposals of the report, should have a right of choice between inspection by the local education authority and inspection by the board of education.

All private schools liable to inspection under the proposals of the report should be inspected. Inspection should be periodical, but no fixed interval should be prescribed; the inspecting authority should have the right to inspect the school at any reasonable time without notice.

Regular medical inspection of children in private schools should be encouraged in every possible way, but no statutory obligation should be placed on proprietors of private schools to provide such inspection.

The last chapter of the report makes suggestions for a scheme of supervision which, the committee considers, would safeguard freedom, avoid irritation and economize cost.

COMMITTEES OF THE NATIONAL SURVEY OF SCHOOL FINANCE

WILLIAM JOHN COOPER, U. S. Commissioner of Education, has announced that committees composed of leading citizens in each state have been named to work with the National Survey of School Finance. These committees were nominated by state superintendents and commissioners of education, and include state legislators and officials, school officials, university professors and other prominent citizens.

Problems of financing the schools have brought demands for information which can throw light on special questions confronting each state. For this reason it has been deemed advisable by the survey's board of consultants, authorities in finance, education and research, to invite participation by state "contact" groups.

Leaders selected in each state will be informed of the progress and advance findings of the nation-wide study of school expenditure, and will be asked for advice from time to time by the national survey research staff. Each state committee will meet with Commissioner of Education Cooper, director of the survey, or Dr. Paul R. Mort, associate director.

Federal funds for this survey are provided until July. Funds from private auspices will support continuation of the work. It is expected that study on the major project of state aid to schools will be far enough advanced to permit state committees to work with state legislatures next session.

The names of committeemen appointed to date for each state are available on request to Commissioner of Education, William John Cooper, Office of Education, Washington, D. C.

THE KELLETT FELLOWSHIPS

Columbia College has been the recipient of a fund from the will of the late Euretta J. Kellett for the support of fellowships, to be known as the Euretta J. Kellett Fellowships, in Oxford and Cambridge, England, for the study of the humanities. In this connection the humanities include all subjects of study except the natural and experimental sciences. The funds are adequate for the support of one candidate each year in each of the two great English universities.

Dean Hawkes has returned from a visit to Oxford and Cambridge Universities where he made arrangements for the administration of these fellowships providing for the acceptance by Clare College, Cambridge, and Oriel College, Oxford, of one Kellett Fellow each year with the understanding that the tenure of the fellowship shall be for two years.

Clare and Oriel Colleges were founded in the same year, 1326, and have enjoyed continuous and honorable existence ever since. According to tradition the poet Chaucer was connected with Clare. The names of Lord Bryce and Cardinal Newman are among those connected with Oriel.

It is anticipated that one Kellett Fellow will be appointed each year at Clare and at Oriel, making four English fellows in residence at these colleges simultaneously. The first candidate to be accepted by Clare College in Cambridge is Mr. David N. Jones of the present senior class. Mr. Jones is reported to be not only a student of very high standing but is also chairman of the Student Board and one of the leading tennis players in the United States.

No nominations for the Kellett Fellowship at Oxford will be made until next year.

AN EXPERIMENTAL SCHOOL

The experimental school, hitherto supported by the Public Education Association as part of Public School No. 1, New York City, which has been discontinued by the city board of education on account of lack of funds and disinclination of the board to use funds derived from private sources, will be carried on by the staff.

In announcing its plans to open its own school with the same program, it is stated that the new school will strive to approximate, as nearly as possible, a public school situation, in order that, in addition to caring for the children of the neighborhood whose parents wish a progressive school, it may also serve as a demonstration school.

The new school will be used by New York University and the Cooperative School for Student Teachers of the Bureau of Educational Experiments for the training of students and will be open to public school teachers as a demonstration center. There will be four or five classes of thirty children each, including 6 to 10-year-old children.

The group in charge plans to keep expenses within the range of public school budgets and to pay public school salaries. A small budget will be raised and a tuition of $125 a year for each pupil will be charged. The group hopes that some scholarships will be contributed.

Miss Elisabeth Irwin who has been in charge of the work heretofore for the Public Education Association will be the director of the new school. The advisers are:

Ruth Andrus, State Department of Education.
Professor John Dewey, Columbia University.
William E. Grady, Associate Superintendent of Schools.
Leta Hollingworth, Teachers College.
William Heard Kilpatrick, Teachers College.
Paul Klapper, Dean of the School of Education, City College.
Edouard C. Lindeman, New York School of Social Work.
Howard W. Nudd, director, Public Education Association.
Dr. Bruce B. Robinson, director, Department of Child Guidance, Board of Education, Newark.
John W. Withers, Dean of the School of Education, New York University.

QUALIFYING EXAMINATIONS IN THE COLLEGE OF EDUCATION AT THE UNIVERSITY OF MINNESOTA

OVER 400 students, all the juniors of the College of Education at the University of Minnesota, will be examined this month in an attempt to measure the degree of their preparation for assuming charge as student teachers of classes in their respective teaching majors. The examination, which requires eight hours in all, is composed of four parts of two hours each, as follows:

(1a) An examination in such content of the candidate's major teaching field as is commonly taught in elementary and secondary schools.

(1b) An additional examination in the major teaching field covering such material as may constitute a more complete and thorough mastery of the field, over and above that commonly taught in the lower schools—in other words the margin of scholarship.

(2) A comprehensive examination in education covering one of the two fields as indicated below.

(a) Educational psychology, secondary education and techniques of high-school teaching.

(b) Educational psychology, the elementary school, techniques of elementary school teaching.

(3) An examination in written English.

Examinations in the twenty-six teaching major fields were constructed by committees composed of members of the department giving instruction in the major field and of those in charge of student teaching. These committees, appointed by Dean M. E. Haggerty, at whose instance the committee on examinations of the College of Education undertook the project, have for the greater part evidenced a keen interest in the project and in the construction of the examinations.

The degree to which the examinations prepared by members of the various departments were objective in nature is indicative of the trend in that direction among the instructional staff in all colleges of the university. While in general the examinations were such as called for writing, in a number of instances other types of performance tests have been devised. Among these are a pronunciation test in modern languages, a public speaking test by the department of speech education, and performance tests in art, industrial arts and physical education.

The purposes of these examinations, as stated in the formulation of the program adopted by the faculty of the College of Education in January are as follows:

(1) To stimulate a more careful, thorough and permanent preparation in the major teaching field and in the fundamental professional knowledge.

(2) To furnish a basis for disqualifying or diverting by advisory means from student teaching, students of inadequate preparation.

(3) To determine to what extent it is possible by such examination, in connection with other criteria, to predict successful performance as a teacher.

The examination will be repeated during the freshman week of the fall quarter for all newly entering seniors in the college.

Corollary to the plan of examining students over the three principal fields of professional preparation—psychology of learning and the learner, the educational institution and methods of teaching—an integrated nine-hour course covering the three fields is to be instituted, beginning in the fall of 1932.

ADMISSION TO THE MASSACHUSETTS INSTITUTE OF TECHNOLOGY

AN alternative method of admission to the Massachusetts Institute of Technology has been announced for students from accredited preparatory and high schools. These changes include admission without examination of students who have been in the upper fifth of their class for the last two years of school, and acceptance of the New York State Regents examinations with high standing.

In announcing this alternative method of admission, Professor James L. Tryon, director of admissions, said:

> The institute has always maintained that the thorough training in English, history, languages, mathematics and science given in the better class of high and preparatory schools is the best preparation for its courses. A recent study of the records obtained in the institute by men

trained in such schools shows that the majority of those who rank in the upper fifth of their classes have done exceedingly well in their studies.

In order to give recognition to such systematic and thorough preparation, technology will try the experiment of admitting without examinations those applicants who submit satisfactory evidence of having completed their fundamental training with high standing. Beginning in September, 1933, a limited number of students without examinations will be admitted.

The institute desires to encourage those students whose qualities of character and intellect indicate their adaptability to an academic environment and who show promise of development into useful and forceful citizens.

In addition to maintaining a standing within the upper fifth of his class for the last two years of his preparatory work, the student seeking admission without examinations must have completed the program of subjects required by the institute. It will also be necessary to present letters of recommendation from the principal and from two persons who are not relatives vouching for personal qualifications and ability.

In accepting the New York State Regents examinations, a record of 80 per cent. will be required. Students will be admitted, as in the past, by their own examinations given at the institute, which are held in September, or by the College Entrance Examination Board examinations, held in June.

THE SUMMER-SCHOOL PROGRAM OF TEACHERS COLLEGE, SYRACUSE UNIVERSITY

The Summer-School Program of Teachers College, Syracuse University, has recently been announced by Dr. Harry S. Ganders, dean of the school.

The individual instruction technique, as employed in the much-observed Bronxville School System, will be demonstrated by men and women familiar with this method. Others will teach and demonstrate according to the "activity program," which seeks to develop the student by encouraging his participation in varied activities. The "mastery formula," under which the student must learn a given amount of material regardless of time will be studied and discussed.

The Progressive Education Institute will return to Syracuse for the second successive year. Burton P. Fowler, president of the Progressive Education Association and head master of Tower Hill School at Wilmington, Delaware, and a large number of teachers in service who participated in the institute last summer are expected to attend.

The Syracuse public school system is cooperating with Teachers College by turning over for use as a demonstration school for six weeks a modern, well-equipped building near the campus. Children will enroll in all grades from kindergarten to junior high school. Here carefully selected teachers from many of the country's best schools will demonstrate theories which have been expounded in the classrooms. Not only will summer-school students have an opportunity to observe, but they will also be allowed to teach actual classes under expert supervision. Thus, children in learning situations will be the central core of the Teachers College program.

The resident staff, in addition to Dean Ganders, includes Dr. Albert S. Hurst, Dr. William T. Melchior, Dr. Harry P. Smith, Dr. Orlie M. Clem, Dr. Helene W. Hartley, Dr. John N. Washburne and Ralph F. Strebel. Visiting lecturers will be Clifford L. Brownell, associate professor of education, Teachers College, Columbia University; Dr. Henry C. Morrison, professor of education of University of Chicago; Dr. Frederick Rand Rogers, dean of student health and physical education, Boston University, and Carleton W. Washburne, superintendent of schools, Winnetka, Ill.

Seventeen distinct programs of study for school teachers will be incorporated in the program. The first session, in which most of the education work will be concentrated, will start on July 5 and end on August 16. Credits earned can be applied either toward the baccalaureate, master or doctorate degrees. A recent ruling of the Syracuse University Graduate Council makes possible the granting of a doctor's degree in Teachers College.

A HIGHER EDUCATION CONFERENCE AT NEW YORK UNIVERSITY

New York University, through Chancellor Elmer Ellsworth Brown, has announced that a conference of universities has been called to meet in New York in November for a discussion of the obligation of universities to the social order.

Six hundred institutions of higher learning and associated institutions have been invited to send representatives to the convention at the Waldorf-Astoria Hotel, November 15, 16 and 17. Invitations to the conference carried the following message:

A part of the world is charging the universities with responsibility for the present situation. It is said that the success of these institutions in the cultivation of physical science is reflected in an industrial development in which production is dangerously out of adjustment with distribution and consumption; that society can now produce more than society knows how to use; that a new development of the social sciences is needed, comparable with that of the physical sciences, and capable of assuring a new balance of the physical and the spiritual in human affairs.

A discussion of this problem at New York University has been followed by consultation with representatives of other institutions. It has been agreed on all hands that a conference of universities for the consideration of questions such as these might clarify the views and purposes of our institutions of higher education, and point the ways in which they may more fruitfully serve the coming age. The economic, governmental, moral and international aspects of university leadership will be separately considered.

At New York University, an historic sentiment has entered into this proposal. One hundred years ago, the fathers of this university invited the leading Americans of that day, in education and public affairs, to meet in convention in the City of New York for a discussion of the question, What does our country now require in the way of higher education? The published proceedings of that convention are read with interest in these days.

The questions now before us are certainly as weighty as those of a century ago, and as wide in their interest for the body politic and academic. In view of these considerations, New York University has undertaken to sponsor a second conference, not unlike that of a hundred years ago, making it a part of this university's centennial celebration. The questions proposed are, however, of no private interpretation. Accordingly, New York University has sought, and has been happy to receive, the active participation of leaders of other universities and related institutions in the shaping of plans and programs for this conference.

EDUCATIONAL NOTES AND NEWS

At a Founder's Day banquet on May 6 Purdue University paid tribute to the ten years administration of President Edward C. Elliott. Four hundred citizens and the governor of the state were in attendance. An oil painting of Dr. Elliott by Robert W. Grafton, of Michigan City, was unveiled by James W. Noel, an alumni trustee. Dr. William Oxley Thompson, president emeritus of the Ohio State University, was the principal speaker. Other speakers were: David E. Ross, president of the board of trustees; C. R. Clauer, president of the student council, and President Elliott.

As part of the ceremonies for the opening of an exhibit of portraits of eminent Frenchmen at the University of California M. Meric de Bellefon, French consul-general in San Francisco, conferred upon President Robert Gordon Sproul the title of Chevalier of the Legion of Honor, by the authority of the Government of France. In conferring the title, Consul-General de Bellefon stated that President Sproul has been selected as a member of the legion because of his eminent position as head of one of the world's largest universities, because of the work of its department of French, and because of the personal interest which the president has taken in that department.

Dr. Edward E. Allen, director emeritus of the Perkins Institution for the Blind, at Watertown, Massachusetts, was recently awarded a gold medal by the National Institute of Social Science for "his work in promoting the education of the blind through the Pennsylvania Institute at Overbrook as well as at the Perkins Institution." The presentation was made by Dr. John H. Finley, of *The New York Times,* at the annual dinner of the society on May 12.

At a luncheon on May 14 given to Dr. John Grier Hibben, president of Princeton University, it was announced that $19,000 had been contributed by the alumni to a loan fund for deserving undergraduates established in honor of Dr. Hibben.

Dr. Nicholas Murray Butler, president of Columbia University, has been elected a foreign member of the Hungarian Academy of Sciences.

Mrs. Herbert Hoover, granddaughter of one of its founders, was the guest of honor of the city of Wooster, Ohio, on the occasion of the celebration of its one hundred and twenty-fifth anniversary on May 14. The program included the presentation to Mrs. Hoover of the honorary degree of doctor of letters of humanity from Wooster College.

The degree of D.Litt., *honoris causa,* was conferred on May 17 by the University of Oxford on Dr. G. L. Kittredge, professor of English literature at Harvard University.

Mrs. Alice Hargreaves, original "Alice" of Lewis Carroll's "Alice in Wonderland," received the honorary degree of doctor of letters from Columbia on May 2. Mrs. Hargreaves is eighty years of age.

William E. Mott, retiring director of the College of Engineering of the Carnegie Institute of Technology, Pittsburgh, was the guest of honor at a dinner recently given by Dr. Thomas S. Baker, president of the institute.

Superintendent F. L. Smart, of Davenport, Iowa, was honored by one hundred and sixty teachers of the county at a banquet given recently in recognition of the completion of fifty years of service in the teaching profession. Mr. Smart has been for the past twenty-five years in Davenport, going there from Dubuque in 1906. He was given a life membership in the National Education Association in appreciation of his service.

Dr. Joseph H. Wade, retiring district superintendent of schools and first president of the New York Academy of Public Education, was honor guest at a dinner given by the academy on May 12 in the Tower Room of City College in celebration of the twentieth anniversary of its founding. Dr. Wade has been connected with the school system since 1885 as a teacher, principal and supervisor. Speakers who paid tribute to Dr. Wade for his leadership in the educational system included Superintendent of Schools William J. O'Shea and Professor Albert Shiels, charter members of the association; Dr. William L. Ettinger, superintendent of schools emeritus; Miss Olive M. Jones, former president of the National Education Association, and Dr. William L. Felter, principal of Girls High School, all past presidents of the organization; Dr. Joseph Taylor and Dr. J. R. Mott.

The medal awarded annually by the *Parents' Magazine* to the author of the most useful book of the year for parents has been awarded for 1931 to Miss Grace Langdon, of the Kindergarten Department of Teachers College, Columbia University, for her book "Home Guidance for Young Children," published by John Day Company of New York. Miss Langdon has taught in the department for seven years, and for the past two years has divided her time between the Child Development Institute and this department.

Joseph M. Cumming, newly elected president of the Mechanics Institute in San Francisco, will fill the vacancy on the Board of Regents of the University of California, caused by the recent death of Dr. Arthur W. Scott.

At the annual meeting of the Boston branch of the American Association of University Women held at the Massachusetts Institute of Technology, Miss Margaret McGill was again elected president. Mrs. B. Alden Thresher is to be the new vice-president, and Mrs. Marshall Dolton will serve as assistant treasurer. Mrs. William R. Bell, Mrs. F. Alexander Magoun and Miss Beatrice S. Woodman will each serve another term as recording secretary, corresponding secretary and treasurer, respectively. Miss Janette Jones was elected chairman of the international relations and foreign students committee, taking the place of Dr. Fannie Fern Andrews.

Professor Elmer D. Mitchell, director of intramural sports at the University of Michigan, was at the recent convention in Philadelphia of the American Physical Education Association reelected secretary-treasurer and was given a vote of appreciation for his activities in the cause of American physical education.

Mr. O. W. Haisley, of Ann Arbor, Michigan, has been elected president of the Michigan Education Association for the next year.

MISS LOUISE DOHRMAN, of the University of Cincinnati, was elected president of the National Student Council at the recent meeting in Minneapolis.

THE following promotions in the Harvard faculties, to take effect at the beginning of the academic year 1932–1933, have been announced: Sheldon Glueck from assistant professor of criminology to professor of criminology in the Law School; Sam Bass Warner from assistant professor of penal legislation and administration to professor of law; Edward Ballantine from assistant professor of music to associate professor of music; Carl Joachim Friedrich from assistant professor of government to associate professor of government; Ralph Hartley Wetmore from assistant professor of botany to associate professor of botany; Henry Edward Bent from instructor in chemistry to assistant professor of chemistry; Harry Rowe Mimno from instructor in physics to assistant professor of physics; Morgan Upton from instructor in general physiology to assistant professor of general physiology; Robert Hugo Woodworth from instructor in botany to assistant professor of botany.

CHANGES in the faculty of Cornell University for the coming year include: Lieutenant Colonel John J. Fulmer appointed professor of military science and tactics to succeed Colonel Joseph W. Beacham, transferred; Dr. Karl M. Dallenbach, who has been teaching at Columbia University, returns as professor of psychology; Dr. C. C. Murdock promoted from assistant professor to professor of physics. Faculty members retiring this June are: Professor L. M. Dennis, head of the department of chemistry; C. A. Martin, professor of architecture, and Nathaniel Schmidt, professor of Semitic languages and literatures and Oriental history.

BLAKE R. VAN LEER, assistant secretary of the American Engineering Council, has been appointed dean of engineering at the University of Florida. The late John R. Benton was dean of the school from 1909 until his death in January, 1930. In the interim Dr. P. L. Reed, head of the department of civil engineering, has served as acting dean.

DR. CARNEY LANDIS, research associate in psychology at the New York State Psychiatric Institute Hospital, has been appointed assistant professor of psychology at Columbia University.

DR. HERMANN COOPER has been formally appointed director of State College Education in the New York State Education Department. He has held provisional appointment in the department since last September. Before going to Albany Dr. Cooper was principal of the State Normal School at Fredonia for two years.

FRANK RUSSELL PAGE has been elected superintendent of schools at Sharon, Massachusetts. He was graduated from Harvard in the class of 1896 and received graduate degrees from the Harvard Graduate School of Education and Teachers College, Columbia University. Mr. Page was formerly superintendent of schools in Watertown and was recently head master of Utica Country Day School and Great Neck Preparatory School.

O. E. DUFF, of Columbus, Ohio, has been elected principal of the high school at South Amherst, to succeed E. E. Keller.

DR. WEBSTER STOVER has been elected head master of Perkiomen School, Pennsburg, Pennsylvania, succeeding the late Dr. Oscar S. Kriebel, founder of the boys' preparatory school. Dr. Stover is a graduate of Ursinus College, Union Theological Seminary and Columbia University. He received the degree of doctor of philosophy from Columbia University in the field of educational administration. Dr. Stover is the author of the book: "Alumni Stimulation by the American College President." He has taught at the College of William and Mary, Ursinus College and Bates College Summer School.

ANNOUNCEMENT has been made that Charles W. Bradlee, formerly head master of the Country Day School of Kansas City, Missouri, has accepted the head mastership of the Pebble Hill School, a country day school for boys of Syracuse, New York, and vicinity.

HENRY VINCENT HUBBARD, Charles Dyer Norton professor of regional planning at Harvard University, has been appointed by President Hoover a member of the National Capital Park and Planning Commission for six years. Frederick A. Delano, president of the Harvard Alumni Association, is chairman of the commission, Charles W. Eliot, Jr., grandson of the late President Eliot of Harvard, is executive city planner.

Governor Franklin D. Roosevelt, of New York, has accepted an invitation to give the commencement address at Oglethorpe University, Atlanta.

Shelby M. Harrison, general director of the Russell Sage Foundation, will be the speaker at the seventy-fourth annual commencement of Northwestern University on June 13. The Rev. Paul Wolfe, pastor of the First Presbyterian Church in Evanston, will deliver the baccalaureate address on the preceding day.

Professor Cyril Bailey, of the University of Oxford, gave the annual public address of Phi Beta Kappa at the University of California on May 12 on "Meaning in the Arts."

Professor Harry T. Collings, of the University of Pennsylvania, will lecture at the Universities of Berlin, Heidelberg and Hamburg in July on "Die Handelspolitik der Vereinigten Staaten" and in English on "The Psychology of the American People." Professor Collings is also to be a delegate of the United States to the third International Congress on Commercial Education in London, July 25–29, where he will give a paper on the "Graduate Study of Business in the United States."

The fourth of five awards of funds provided by the Rockefeller Foundation for a year's visit by an American university professor to the Keio Gijuku University of Tokyo, Japan, has been granted to Dr. Winterton C. Curtis, who has for thirty-one years been a member of the faculty of the University of Missouri. As a visiting professor Dr. Curtis will maintain an office in the Keio School of Medicine, in a building erected by the Rockefeller Foundation. He will give instruction in the School of Medicine and in addition will carry on research work.

Dr. David P. Barrows, professor of political science at the University of California, has sailed for Germany. He plans to spend much of his time in Berlin and to travel throughout Germany to familiarize himself with the political and economic situation there.

Dr. Felix Frankfurter, professor of administrative law at Harvard University, will be on leave of absence from the Harvard Law School the second half of the next academic year.

Dr. Ernest Martin Hopkins, president of Dartmouth College, has sailed for a short visit to Europe.

Leave of absence for study abroad for the academic year 1932–33 has been granted by New York University to Harold Holme, assistant professor of history; Bruce W. McCullough, associate professor of English; Walter A. Schneider and Carel W. Van Der Merne, associate professors of physics.

Dr. Hastings H. Hart, consultant in the Russell Sage Foundation's department of delinquency and penology and a penologist who had done much for prison reform, died on May 9 at the age of eighty years He was a brother of Dr. Albert Bushnell Hart, professor emeritus of government at Harvard University.

Dr. Charles Carroll Marden, Ford professor of Spanish at Princeton University and president of the Modern Languages Association of America, died on May 11 at the age of sixty-four years.

Dr. Avard L. Bishop, professor of business administration in the Sheffield Scientific School of Yale University since 1918, died on May 8. He was fifty-seven years old.

Harriet E. Porritt, assistant principal of Public School 141, Long Island City, died on May 13. Miss Porritt was prominent in the movement that eventually brought about the establishment of the present pension system for teachers. She was elected a member of the retirement board when the system was begun in 1917.

Professor Erasmo Braga, adviser on education to the Brazilian government, died on May 11 in Rio de Janeiro. Professor Braga was chancellor of the Federation of Evangelical Schools of Brazil and professor in the Union Theological Seminary of the Protestant Churches of Brazil. He had just finished a survey of religious and educational conditions in Brazil, now being published by the World Dominion Press in London.

THE University of Louisville, in cooperation with the Juilliard Foundation, will open a School of Music next September. This will be a standard school offering a four-year curriculum leading to the degree of bachelor of music, and will be in addition to the other schools now comprising the university: the College of Liberal Arts, the School of Medicine, the School of Law, the School of Dentistry and the Speed Scientific School of Engineering. Mr. Jacques Jolas, of the Juilliard Foundation, will be acting director for the first year. This project is to be undertaken in view of the closing of the Louisville Conservatory of Music in February, 1932. The school will be housed in the same quarters as those formerly occupied by the conservatory.

THE Rockefeller Foundation has given $85,000 to the University of Cincinnati for the development of a program for training instructors in public administration.

MRS. HARRIETT HALE WOOLLEY has made the University of Paris a gift of $50,000 for the upkeep of rooms in the American Dormitory, which Dr. Gage had erected in the University City, Boulevard Jourdan. The right to occupy these rooms will be reserved to the beneficiaries of the scholarships established by Mrs. Woolley.

THE League of Nations Non-Partisan Association and Smith College receive in equal shares the residuary estate of Miss Alice Miller Dike, which appraised at $122,202 net.

ANNOUNCEMENT has been cabled by the Carnegie Foundation for International Peace in New York of a donation of $27,000 to assist in rebuilding the University of the Witwatersrand at Johannesburg, part of which was destroyed by fire four months ago. The public of Johannesburg is subscribing $500,000 toward the project.

THE salaries of teachers in Cleveland, Ohio, have been reduced from $6\frac{3}{4}$ per cent. on smaller, to 15 per cent. on higher salaries.

FOUR recommendations which have as their purpose the abolition of university inspection and accrediting of those public high schools in the State of Wisconsin, now inspected by the State Department of Public Instruction, were adopted recently by the faculty of the University of Wisconsin. Although the recommendations provide that the university accept for accrediting purposes the list of high schools approved by the state department, the university will issue a list made up of the independent public high schools and private high schools not inspected by the department. Because the educational interests of the university and the public high schools coincide at so many points, the recommendations also provide that the university maintain its policy of keeping up contacts with the public high schools of the state. They also make provision for the inspection and accrediting of private high schools in Wisconsin, upon the application of such schools and on the understanding that the bare cost of inspection will be borne in such schools.

DISCUSSION

SHALL THE STUDENTS PAY?

IN times of financial stringency that gospel which advocates making the college student pay a larger part of the cost of his college course has a peculiar potency of appeal. At this particular time institutions of higher learning may feel strongly the persuasive power of this doctrine. It may be unusually difficult to balance the budget. Income may be restricted. Financial campaigns are harder and less productive of results. In seeking appropriations from legislatures, publicly supported institutions may meet competing demands of elementary and secondary schools in which most citizens complete their formal education. Retrenchments in public expenditures loom ominous in the face of probable decreases in public revenue. Economy measures are the mode.

Under such conditions, the proposal to vote higher fixed charges to college students may hold a certain allurement entirely aside from any question as to the social validity of the principle involved. The policy of charging students higher fees and tuitions may offer a course of least resistance in the face of financial deficits.

Alternative ways out of a financial stringency offer formidable difficulties. It is not easy to economize wisely and expeditiously. Apparent wastes commonly may be due to such factors as inadequate budgetary and accounting procedure, unbusinesslike administration of supplementary activities, over-staffing, padded offerings, inefficient scheduling, overlapping of administrative functions and duplications of function by adjacent institutions under the same control. Yet to demonstrate acceptably the degree of any such wastes and to remove them satisfactorily is likely to be a difficult and oftentimes a time-consuming task.

It should be remarked parenthetically, in mentioning the difficulties of wise economy, that a recognition of constructive efforts in this direction is not to be left out of the picture. The persistent force of continuous self-survey programs, the efforts of a watchful administration and the thoughtful study of research contributions do much in many cases to assure efficient utilization of the institution's resources. In general, however, it is perhaps fair to say that development in this direction lags behind the needs.

It is possible now, as it was in the days of Horace Mann and Henry Barnard, to find various apparent theoretical justifications for a further departure from the cherished tradition of free higher education. Do not some students spend more on the annual prom than the amount of fees and tuitions for the year? Does it not appear that free, public higher education is in some measure a gratuity made possible oftentimes by the partial confiscation of one man's property to educate another man's child? Do not the findings of some investigators strongly suggest, or indeed seem almost to prove, that the college education adds enough to a person's wealth-getting or income-earning power to make the education a good commercial investment? If society profits financially when a person secures a college education, does not the educated man profit more? Should not the needs of the masses for formal education be cared for by public support of free elementary and secondary education before the needs of publicly supported colleges and universities receive such support? Have not moderate increases in tuitions and fees of colleges and universities been characteristically accompanied by some increase in enrolments? Does not the amount of tuitions and fees in many institutions seem inconsequential and small? Will not charging a fee cause the student to appreciate more the value of what he gets, teach lessons of loyalty, responsibility and the like? Are not increasing tuitions and fees a sign of the times? Is it possible to justify public support of selective education? Is it not possible to ask the students to pay the current operating costs of the institution and yet to guarantee financial democracy in higher education by wise administration of liberal student aid funds? In the main, is it not true that the person who is of truly college caliber will get his college education regardless of financial handicaps and provincialism of outlook accompanying family poverty? And so on, might be multiplied the number of such questions which have been raised and are being raised. The early faith which, after a grim, strenuous battle, eventuated in the establishment of colleges or universities virtually free to the student is again receiving critical scrutiny.

In view of these various forces, it may be understood, if not pardoned, when sometimes historic faiths in the social values potential in higher education glimmer a bit. Money spent by the public in the fiscal support of higher education may come to be viewed as a cost, or even as a gratuity, rather than as an investment likely to bear rich returns, spiritual and financial, both to the body politic and the individuals educated.

The indispensable contribution to society that educated leadership may make in the fields of industry, politics or professional service may be undervalued, or valued only in terms of immediate, personal, financial profits. Possibly the more obvious, direct and immediate rewards to the college trained individual, representing as they do the apparent "cash-in value" of his education, unduly obscure oftentimes the less tangible and the indirect, albeit indispensable, contribution to the public weal which his service is. We can all too lightly reckon with the imperative necessity to the state of utilizing to the full its human resources through the process of diffusing opportunity for self-realization through an education of that quality which in truth serves to deepen human sympathies and to broaden social consciousness. The platitude that civilization is a race between catastrophe and education may be a live principle worthy of our serious meditation at the present juncture. The historic American ideal of democratic education wrought out through a century of struggle may not wisely be put aside. Educational opportunity as properly a class privilege or prerogative of the rich is anathema to one who cherishes the democratic ideal.

For the most part, contemporary zeal for increasing fixed charges to students stops short of avowedly restricting educational opportunities according to the pocketbook of the child or of the parent. The implications of any such position would appear ugly when projected against the background of American traditions of education.

As yet, the way of maintaining and increasing the economic democratization of education, while at the same time increasing costs to students, is scarcely clear. Problems of securing student aid funds and, more particularly, of administering such funds acceptably, involve recognized difficulties of the first magnitude. Student aid programs may do irreparable damage to beneficiaries. No form of student aid appears to be free from certain serious criticisms. However indispensable programs of student aid may be, the key to the problem of preserving democracy appears not to reside solely in such programs. Guarding against over reliance in this path out of difficulty may merit consideration today.

Recent research seems in a fair way to puncture any sweeping generalization that contemporary higher education has a high "cash-in value." Particularly is there room for doubt regarding the "cash-in value" of the liberal arts education which is being provided to undergraduates. Education beyond a certain point seems to reduce money getting efficiency.

The price, or scarcity value, of any commodity or service is a function of the complex variables, demand and supply. Market conditions of the day might cause certain types of education to have extremely small or extremely high "cash-in value." An uneducated demand might put a higher cash value on contraband liquor, for example, than on the service of persons educated to serve as teachers or social workers. Public demand is not always compatible with conceived social needs. If a function of higher education is to raise standards of conduct, and to improve progressively public demands, it is a dubious procedure to evaluate the educational activity in terms of the standards which are in need of modification. From the view-point of those who hold in high esteem the non-pecuniary values sought in higher education, an attempt to evaluate higher education, especially liberal arts education, by the criterion of market price is futile and dangerous. In the final analysis that theory of fiscal support of colleges and universities, which takes its point of departure with the assumption that investment in a higher education is properly and primarily a commercially profitable investment to the individual educated, would seem to lead logically to an evaluation of educational programs largely by cash-in or market price standards of the day.

Up to the present time it appears possible to build at least quite as good a case for a program of fiscal support of higher education based on the principle of allocating costs to non-student sources as for any of the very recent proposals to make the student pay. Irrespective of the developments that may come in the prevailing theory of fiscal support it appears reasonable to urge that resources be utilized fully through the elimination of wastes. Raising fees and tuitions to meet fixed needs that exist in some measure because of avoidable wastes appears intolerable as a policy. Also, it is fair to ask that a clear distinction be maintained between the goals immediately acceptable in view of any exigencies due to present material limitations, and the goals which are socially defensible as ultimate objectives in fiscal support. Temporary or emergency measures must be distinguished from permanent policies. The ideal of progressive modification must persistently manifest itself in action. Probably, too, it is wise to reckon with the potency of a financial stringency to challenge fundamental social concepts. Administrators need courage to guard against any subtle attractions of a convenient theory merely because it seems convenient. It is dangerous, in other words, to rationalize. Administrators and others concerned must accept full responsibility for making higher education of a quality to merit confidence in its basic social values.

R. W. Ogan
Muskingum College

CRITICAL COMMENTS ON THE PROGRAM FOR TEACHING SCIENCE IN THE YEARBOOK OF THE SOCIETY FOR THE STUDY OF EDUCATION

The Thirty-first Yearbook passes on to the science teacher positive statements as to how he is to revise curricular offerings in science. It is to be regretted that the authors did not catch the idea that the language can not be too simple nor the illustrations too numerous for the reader who is not an expert in educational theory.

If the committee could have taken time enough to have made an index, they might have avoided making contradictions on the value of observation and the transfer of training. On page (5) it would appear that "Nature study, with emphasis on observation, . . . is obsolete"; and yet on pages (143, 144, 176, 179) they do "not deny the importance of identification and observation." They tell you forcefully that observation for disciplinary values is old fashioned. Why they are not equally anxious to emphasize that observation for interest and for richness of experience is legitimate is difficult to see. In their strenuous effort to deny the theories of G. Stanley Hall they have become inaccurate. His theories have not been "entirely discredited." They have been changed. If Hall went to one extreme, the committee has gone to the opposite extreme.

The same tenor of sharp criticism has been extended in a sweeping accusation that the majority of the workers in the nature study field are making claims that are obsolete. For example: On page (148) the authors say that "Some have contended that no illustrative material should be used except that which is in the natural environment of the school." What the nature enthusiast has in mind is that one should ordinarily select the common objects of the environment as opposed to the curios from foreign lands that once held all too prominent a part. That is not different from what the committee has in mind on page (175) when it says that "Illustrative materials will be selected from those available in each community."

The book is more critical than appreciative of the nature study movement. It would seem that there are more than charitable reasons for recognizing the past. A chapter on the foundations which lead to newly stated premises would make the contribution more scientific and thereby more effective. The only reference to esthetic appreciation implies that it is "manifestly extravagant" (page 15). Notwithstanding, the primary objective of many an "educated layman" in nature study is the enjoyment of nature which is akin to the appreciation of literature, music and art.

The third criterion, viz: "Certain objectives that are selected for elementary science should conform to those facts, principles, generalizations and hypotheses of science that are essential to the interpretation of the natural phenomena that commonly challenge children" page (141) is surely no improvement upon what Mrs. Comstock said over twenty years ago: "Nature-study is, despite all discussions and perversions, a study of nature; it consists of simple, truthful observations that may, like beads on a string, finally be threaded upon the understanding and thus held together as a logical and harmonious whole."

As Palmer points out, *much* of the content of the book is based on unreliable basic studies. Furthermore, many of the findings from tests simply corroborate self-evident truths. Corbally concludes, for example, page (87), that "The determining factor is the teacher, not the method or device." Mrs. Comstock said: "Some teachers may give a live lesson from a stuffed specimen, and other teachers may stuff their pupils with facts about a live specimen; of the two, the former is preferable." In the case of Mrs. Comstock it was opinion just as in the case of the committee it is opinion that general biology should come in the tenth year. Mrs. Comstock's premise, however, was much more self-evident.

There are many other places in which the committee might be more scientific in material. Take the case of the "Illustrative Material by Grades," which begins on page (170). Almost every statement needs revision.

The only place that the committee mentions camps is on page (155). Here they state that "The claim that a teacher of these subjects must be both a naturalist and a scientist is unwarranted. The extravagant demands that have sometimes been listed for teachers of nature study are probably due to confusion of the duties of 'nature guides' in summer camps and those of teachers of science." It is surprising that this Yearbook Committee would think that a naturalist is not a scientist. It is to be regretted that the tenor of this book tends to separate nature study from so-called elementary science. Not many schoolmen would concede that the teacher should be any less prepared than the nature guide in camp. This is rather of an astonishing statement to come from Teachers College, Columbia University, when that institution is now planning a camp training course in connection with Professer Alexander's "New College."

William G. Vinal
Western Reserve University

QUOTATIONS

ART SCHOOLS IN INDUSTRY

The exhibition in London of the Royal Academy of Arts, which was opened to the public this week, is but one of the many activities of that institution which was founded in 1768. Sir William Llewellyn, the president of the Royal Academy, in his speech at the annual banquet on April 30 declared that, though the exhibition ranked high in public estimation, the main functions of the academy are the education of students free of any expense to themselves and the awarding of traveling scholarships and premiums; the maintenance of a high standard of technique unaffected by fashion; the improvement of the taste of the general public; and the administration of many trust funds for educational and charitable purposes.

He drew attention to the fact that one of the trustees of the late Lord Leverhulme had recently given a most valuable addition to their scholarship funds by which students of promise, educated in their schools, might be assisted over that most difficult period which came between completing their studies and establishing themselves as professional artists.

Lastly, the president said that the legacies of highest value that were left to posterity are works of art of many kinds. They are the monuments of what was truly great in a nation's history. Therefore he begged all responsible bodies, the government, corporations, municipalities, colleges, schools, and all enlightened persons to encourage a knowledge of art and its practice, for by so doing they were contributing to the welfare and advancement of the whole nation.

These extracts from a notable speech at once bring the Royal Academy of Arts into touch with education as a whole, and perhaps especially in the region where art and industry meet.

What are English educationists doing in the region of art? A great deal in almost every sphere from the little rural primary schools to the academy itself. Direct state intervention is to be seen in the Royal College of Art, providing an advanced training in the practice of drawing and painting, engraving, sculpture, architecture, design for decorative arts and industries and certain handicrafts. Royal exhibitions, national scholarships and free studentships tenable at the college are awarded annually on the results of the Board of Education's examinations in art. No fewer than 141 awards in art were made in 1930 to the Royal College, while twenty awards were made at other art schools. These provincial art schools are of singular importance, since there are no fewer than 7,000 full-time and 51,000 part-time students in attendance. The students are caught young in many cases. An instance is the Central School at Plymouth, where full-time courses of instruction are provided for children who have shown marked artistic ability in connection with a senior department of a primary school. In various leading art schools, as at Lancaster, Liverpool and Sunderland, industrial art courses have been introduced, with the most gratifying results. Sir William Llewellyn said, in his academy speech, that many authorities agreed with him that it was through art that many industries would rise to their old prosperity and power and that artists were among the nation's most essential workers. There is undoubtedly a growing appreciation of that fact. The latest report of the board of education declares that there is "a gratifying and considerable increase in the interest and assistance given to art schools by employers," especially among the painting, decorating and printing firms. The exhibition held in Manchester in November, 1930, of designs for printed and woven textile fabrics by students in art and technical schools in the cotton area of Lancashire and Cheshire was a notable instance of cooperation between the art schools and industry, and the report of the board notes with pride that it was undertaken at the suggestion of two of H. M. Inspectors. Prince George's plea for the cooperation of art and industry comes at a very timely moment.

The growth of art education is to some extent shown by the subjects and results of art examinations held in 1929 and 1930 in the report of the Board of Education. In 1929 there were 990 candidates and 573 passes; in 1930 there were 1,149 candidates and 678 passes. The subjects were drawing, painting, modeling, pictorial design and industrial design. The standard of the examination is high and only eight of the candidates "passed with distinction." That is all to the good, and in fact real distinction in art work, the distinction that amounts to genius, could not be expected except in a small percentage of the candidates, rather more than one per cent. in 1930. The number of students in the art schools from which the candidates are drawn is (for the whole country) 5,145 full-time students and 51,909 part-time students. The distribution of these students is a matter of interest. There are 1,393 full-time students in the rural districts, 2,896 in the county boroughs, and 856 in the County of London. There are 17,232, 28,123 and 6,544 part-time students in the same areas. These figures do not include the junior departments in art schools, which give instruction to about 2,000 pupils in drawing and artistic handicraft and general education. Of these pupils 181 are in London, 1,284 in the county boroughs, and 497 in the rural districts. If these figures are included, some 60,000 pupils in England and Wales are attending specific art classes. All over the country, and not merely in the larger towns, is the cult of art pursued, and a very large number of the pupils are under eighteen years of age. In addition to these features of national art it has to be remembered that drawing and elementary art are included in the curriculum of all primary schools, and in the report of the Consultative Committee on the Primary School issued last year great stress is laid on the importance and significance of this instruction. The spontaneous impulses of these children under the age of eleven "will help to form a foundation for a more conscious appreciation of the great achievements in fine and applied art." Everything turns on "the influence and personality of the teacher" and "the character of the child's environment." The sense of beauty will be instilled while the child plays a definite part in producing things of beauty. The report on the education of the adolescent dwells on the teaching of drawing and applied art to older children and on the importance to the whole community of the improvement of taste to which Sir William Llewellyn referred last week as one of the goals of the Royal Academy. Efforts are being made, therefore, in our whole educational system to make art a function of national life, and the results of those efforts are not negligible even to-day and must become more and more effective as art and industry join hands to make the common things of life things of beauty.—*The Educational Supplement of the London Times.*

BOOKS AND LITERATURE

The Democratic Philosophy of Education. By H. H. HORNE, Ph.D. With a frontispiece of John Dewey from the Epstein bust. The Macmillan Company, XVII, 547 pp, 1932.

How frequently it has happened in the history of civilization and human culture that the meaning and intent of a master-mind, of a great teacher, have been misunderstood, misinterpreted or misapplied by his disciples. Confucius, Aristotle, Mohammed, Luther, Rousseau, Spencer, Darwin, scores and hundreds of masters in more immediately recent years have all suffered at the hands of their devoted or fanatical followers. It is always interesting to speculate as to what Christianity would be to-day if St. Paul had not taken it upon himself to interpret and apply the teachings of the Master. Was the democracy of Socrates actually what the disciple, Plato, so convincingly set forth? Would Pestalozzi and Froebel give the stamp of their approval to all the "activity programs" nominated by disciples as at least implicit in their philosophies?

Among modern masters in the field of thought probably no one has suffered more acutely and yet more uncomplainingly from the influence of over-zealous disciples than has Dr. John Dewey. Only to read or to hear the master and then to misinterpret him has been to misunderstand and unwarrantably to advocate and apply. The high degree to which the doctrine of interest, for example, has been misunderstood and incorrectly applied is exceeded only by the extreme and wholesale misapplication made by Dr. Dewey's disciples of his *Democracy and Education.* The fine tolerance of Dr. Dewey toward this situation is no doubt occasioned largely by his own recognition of the fact that responsibility for the misunderstanding is largely his, due to the difficult style in which the book is written.

Because this text has proven to so many earnest students "a confusing wilderness of stimulating ideas," and because another master holds certain views not wholly in accord with those of Dr. Dewey, a novel method has recently been employed by Dr. H. H. Horne, of New York University, in an effort to clarify and state anew the democratic philosophy of education. The method employed is to attempt, chapter by chapter, an "Exposition" of Dr. Dewey's discussions in his "Democracy and Education" and by avoiding the stylistic difficulties of Dr. Dewey to state clearly—not to interpret—his ideas. This paraphrase is followed by "Comments," in which Dr. Horne points out the incompleteness, or the discrepancies, or the contradictions, of Dr. Dewey's position while suggesting the fuller and richer meanings possible in the basic concepts. The new book is in no sense an effort to discredit Dr. Dewey or to minimize his influence but rather to make clear what has been confusing, the better to assist arrival at truth and also to present a more hopeful philosophy of democracy in education. To this effort Dr. Dewey gave his generous approval and consent, an attitude of mind less likely to be found among some of his disciples. Whatever of contention may be found in Dr. Horne's book grows out of the differences in fundamental philosophies between him and Dr. Dewey, not out of any spirit of animosity or wish to be hyper-critical. Both masters are seeking and both desire only the truth and each visions truth in the light of individual experience and reason.

In the "Preface" (p. xiii) it is pointed out by Dr. Horne that in his opinion the style of Dr. Dewey is difficult because of: "the use of familiar words with unfamiliar meanings; the use of words with pregnant meanings; the use of long, involved and highly concentrated sentences; the development of different important ideas in the same paragraph; and not making it clear when he is stating the views of others and when his own." It is further guessed that the wealth of associations in Dr. Dewey's mind rush together in such profusion as to result in confusion when he attempts to write these associations down; further, it is guessed that Dr. Dewey does not write from an outline and makes few revisions of what is once written; and finally, it would seem that Dr. Dewey assumes a too nearly accurate and too wide knowledge of history on the part of his readers and which future followers of his educational theories will possess to an increasingly smaller and smaller degree. With these postulates and assumptions in mind Dr. Horne attempts, in the sections designated "Exposition" within each chapter, to overcome these difficulties and to state accurately and concisely what Dr. Dewey had attempted to say in "Democracy and Education."

The sections designated "Comments" are very largely presentations of the extended implications to education which the philosophy of idealism offers beyond what the philosophy of pragmatism suggests. It is the position of Dr. Horne, clearly evident throughout his book, not that pragmatism is an unsound philosophy upon which to build an educational program but that it is an incomplete and insufficient philosophy; that it is one-sided, giving too much emphasis to method in the educative process and too little emphasis to content. This insufficiency and disproportionate emphasis, it is Dr. Horne's position, can be corrected through conserving the proper values of pragmatism and adding thereto the values which idealism has to offer. In other words, Dr. Horne would not discard the meanings of pragmatism for education but he would interpret these meanings in the light of a philosophy which finds in the nature of man ideals as well as activities. To Dr. Horne pragmatism applied to education results, in performance, activity, behavior, centering the process around dynamics; idealism applied to education relates and directs these acts, these behaviors, centering the process around an organism which operates from, for, and to a purpose.

Whether or not Dr. Horne has been successful in preparing clearer statements of Dr. Dewey's ideas than Dr. Dewey himself did is not a question for one person to answer, each reader will have to decide that for himself—having both volumes in hand to study and to compare. The case for idealism as an improvement upon pragmatism appears to be well but not completely stated—for completeness of statement one needs to go to Dr. Horne's book "Idealism in Education." From beginning to end, however, the book sustains the interest of a reader and raises many questions without by any means settling them with finality, the style of writing rising at times almost to what might be termed literary.

It is very probable that opinions of the book will depend largely upon the philosophy of life held by the readers. While the volume is mechanically well constructed and typographically satisfactory with an excellent index, it is heavy to hold and more or less forbidding externally. That it proposes to question the authority of a beloved master and that it seriously questions the sufficiency and finality of science and experimentalism as an explanation of life may rouse prejudices and inhibit the impulses to discriminating thought. On the other hand if one has honestly attempted to understand Dr. Dewey and has found him difficult—not to say impossible at times—then one will welcome this penetrating and lucid commentary volume. Besides this, if one has arrived at a certain understanding of Dr. Dewey and his philosophy and has felt a dissatisfaction, a cold and unimpassioned response, a lack of spiritual warmth, then one will eagerly read, ponder, and consider how Dr. Horne's treatment forces one to realize that "Life is more than meat and the body than raiment," and to realize that, if "Education is life," then it must take on all and not only some of life's characteristics. In any case the book if thoughtfully read and studied is bound to be provocative of discussion, stimulative to thought.

L. A. Williams

University of California,
Berkeley, California

REPORTS

AWARDS FROM THE MILTON FUND OF HARVARD UNIVERSITY

Announcement was made on February 29 of twenty-seven awards to officers of instruction or administration in the university, in accordance with the provisions of the Milton Fund for Research. Grants from the fund are made for not more than two years, and the special committee which considers the applications feels that regular annual grants to the same applicant should be avoided as this tends to limit the freedom of the funds and to prevent the extension of aid to other worthy applicants. The sum of $42,650 for the coming year (1932–33) has been awarded in grants of varying amounts. Harvard received the legacy, yielding an annual income of about $50,000 in the spring of 1924.

After the death of his wife the bulk of the estate of the late William F. Milton, '58, was to go to Harvard University for the building of a university library, or if the university had a suitable library building, to defray the expenses of any special investigation of a medical, geographical, historical or scientific nature. It was further stated that such investigation should be "in the interests of or for promoting the physical and material welfare and prosperity of the human race, or to assist in the discovery and perfecting of any special means of alleviating or curing human disease, or to investigate and determine the value or importance of any discovery or invention, or for any other special or temporary object of the nature above stated."

A committee was appointed at Harvard, consisting of Frank B. Jewett, electrical engineer, of New York, chairman; Professor William M. Wheeler, and Professor W. S. Ferguson, of Harvard University, to advise the President and Fellows of Harvard College (the corporation) in making a selection among the investigations proposed by any member of the instructing, scientific, or administrative staff of the university. Requests for aid in such research were received by the committee this year up to January 10.

According to the recommendations of the committee, grants from the Milton Fund for next year have been awarded to the following persons for the objects specified:

Wilbur Cortez Abbott, Francis Lee Higginson Professor of History; to aid in the preparation of a Parliamentary History of the Reign of Charles II, instead of the preparation of a volume on the French Revolution as designated in the grant for 1931–32.

Bancroft Beatley, Associate Professor of Education; to enable him to extend the study of pupil achievements in the junior high schools made some years ago to the same pupils, many of whom will be seniors in high schools in 1932–33.

Percy Williams Bridgman, Hollis Professor of Mathematics and Natural Philosophy; to enable him to extend his high pressure measurements to high temperatures and to low temperatures.

Charles Franklin Brooks, Professor of Meteorology; to enable him to complete the work on the "Handbuch der Klimatologie" which was originally undertaken by Professor R. deC. Ward under aid from the Milton Fund but which was not completed at the time of his death; to enable him to observe the atmospheric changes caused by the solar eclipse on August 31, 1932.

Frank Morton Carpenter, Associate in Entomology; to enable him to collect carboniferous and permian insects in Kansas, Colorado, Oklahoma and Pennsylvania.

Hubert Lyman Clark, Associate Professor of Zoology; to assist him in his studies on the history of the Australian continent by enabling him to acquire a knowledge of marine fauna.

Stanley Cobb, Bullard Professor of Neuropathology; to enable him to have a number of Greek and Latin treatises on epilepsy translated.

Carleton Stevens Coon, Associate in Anthropology; to permit him to complete his revision of Ripley's "Races of Europe."

Joseph Augustine Cushman, Lecturer on Micropaleontology; to assist him in his comparison and correlation of Cretaceous Foraminifera of North America with those of Europe.

Walter Fenno Dearborn, Professor of Education; to enable him to complete the construction of a stereoscopic optometer and to continue an investigation of the asymmetry of retinal images in school children having difficulty in learning to read.

Merritt Lyndon Fernald, Fisher Professor of Natural History; to enable him to employ competent artistic help to make the illustrations for a book on the "Edible Wild Plants of Eastern North America."

Willard James Fisher, Lecturer on Astronomy, Harlow Shapley, Paine Professor of Practical Astronomy, Ernest Julius Öpik, Lecturer on Astrophysics; to assist a scientific expedition to Arizona for the study of meteors.

Edwin Francis Gay, Professor of Economic History; to enable him to prepare a volume on the Industrial Revolution, primarily in England.

Russell Gibson, Assistant Professor of Economic Geology; to assist in a field investigation of regional geology, glaciation, igneous geology and mineral deposits in northwestern Montana.

Edward Pendleton Herring, Instructor in Government; to enable him to investigate the relations between certain private interests and federal administrative authorities in Washington.

Oliver Dimon Kellogg, Professor of Mathematics; to enable him to write a handbook of potential theory.

Lewis Don Leet, Instructor in Geology, to enable him to continue his study of the elastic constants of rocks by measuring the velocity of transmission of vibrations from dynamite blasts.

Marston Morse, Professor of Mathematics; to continue his work in preparing for publication his American Mathematical Colloquium Lectures on calculus of variations.

Ralph Barton Perry, Edgar Pierce Professor of Philosophy; to enable him to record the thought and character of William James, as revealed in unpublished correspondence, notes and marginalia.

Robert Henry Pfeiffer, Assistant Professor of Semitic Languages and/or David Gordon Lyon, Hancock Professor of Hebrew and Other Oriental Languages, Emeritus; to modify previous grants to Professor Lyon to include the preparation of the archeological report of the Harvard excavations at Nuzi and to record Professor Pfeiffer as associated with Professor Lyon in the management of the available balances of the grants.

Gregory Pincus, Assistant Professor of General

Physiology; to enable him to continue and extend his investigation of the nature of the development of the temperature-regulating mechanism in mice.

Carroll Cornelius Pratt, Assistant Professor of Psychology, Edwin Garrigues Boring, Professor of Psychology; to enable them to purchase audio-oscillators and related electrical equipment to aid in the study of the psychology and psychophysiology of tonal hearing.

Oscar Knefler Rice, Instructor in Chemistry; to enable him to obtain technical assistance for his experiments to throw light on the mechanism of energy exchange between activated and unactivated molecules in unimolecular gas reactions.

Francis Bowes Sayre, Professor of Law; to assist a follow-up study of the ex-inmates of Concord reformatory ten years after their discharge.

Henry Maurice Sheffer, Associate Professor of Philosophy; to enable him to secure clerical assistance on the book "Notational Relativity."

Frank William Taussig, Henry Lee Professor of Economics; to supplement grants previously made to investigate the social stratum from which American business leaders spring, whether success is due to nature or nurture, to inborn traits or to propitious environment.

Jeffries Wyman, Jr., Assistant Professor of Zoology; to enable him to continue work in progress on the electrical properties and behavior of amino acids, polypeptides, and proteins, as revealed by their dielectric behavior.

From the fund established under the bequest of the late Joseph H. Clark, '57, awards have been made to the following persons:

Arthur Burkhard, Assistant Professor of German, Charles Louis Kuhn, Instructor in Fine Arts; to enable them to prepare a catalog of German drawings and paintings in America.

Archibald Thompson Davison, Professor of Choral Music; to assist him in his work connected with a dictionary of choral composers and a bibliography as a background for the study of the history of choral music.

Allan Evans, Instructor in History; to enable him to prepare a glossary of Medieval Italian terms of coinage and to complete the edition of Pegolotti's "Merchants' Manual."

Gerald Sandford Graham, Instructor in History; to enable him to study in Canada and England the British Trade Policy in its relation to Canada up to the final abandonment of the Trade and Navigation System.

Wilbur Kitchener Jordan, Instructor in History; to enable him to study in England the development of religious toleration in England from the beginning of the English Reformation to 1689.

Kirsopp Lake, Winn Professor of Ecclesiastical History, Robert Pierpont Blake, Professor of History; to aid in the photographic work on the excavation of Samaria, editing New Testament and early Christian texts, and the preparation for publication of complete dated Greek manuscripts.

André Morize, Professor of French Literature; to enable him to bring up to date a bibliography of modern French literature.

Gaines Post, Instructor in History; to aid a study of the origins of the corporation of the University of Paris in its relations with the Papacy and with the history of the theory of corporations from 1175 to 1235.

Whitney Wells, Instructor in English; to enable him to make a biographical study abroad of early sixteenth-century poets.

Morley Jeffers Williams, Assistant Professor of Landscape Architecture; to enable him to continue his study of American landscape design from 1750 to 1850 as illustrated by the estates in Maryland and Virginia.

EDUCATIONAL RESEARCH AND STATISTICS

SCHOLASTIC APTITUDE AND FRESHMAN ACHIEVEMENT

IN the spring of 1929 the colleges and universities within the State of Wisconsin initiated a comprehensive testing program that began with the testing of every senior in the high schools in Wisconsin. On April 17, 1929, the Ohio State University Psychological Test, Form 13 or 14, was given to 16,619 seniors in 434 public high schools and 14 private high schools within the state. The tests were scored in the various colleges in Wisconsin and then sent to the University of Wisconsin where the scoring was checked, the results tabulated, and various research studies undertaken. This study, directed by Dr. V. A. C. Henmon, scientific director of the Bureau of Guidance and Records, aims to investigate the value of the Ohio State Psychological Test, as given in 1929, as an instrument of prediction of freshman achievement at the University of Wisconsin.

The data with which this study deals consist of:

(1) The results of the Ohio State University

Psychological Test given to 16,619 seniors in 448 high schools in Wisconsin on April 17, 1929, and expressed in raw scores and percentile ranks.

(2) The rank in the high school class of the members of the freshman class at the University of Wisconsin, 1929–30, expressed in percentile ranks.

(3) The achievement of the freshman class at the University of Wisconsin, 1929–30, as shown by grade point averages and percentile ranks. The grading scale is as follows:

Grade	Grade Point per Credit
A	3
B	2
C	1
D	0
E (Condition)	$-\frac{1}{2}$
F (Failure)	-1

A student's average is determined by dividing his grade points by his credits.

To determine the presence of selectivity in the freshman class, the scores made in the test by all the high school seniors and the scores of those who matriculated as freshmen at the University of Wisconsin were tabulated. To add significance to the tabulation, the scores of all the high school seniors who, in April, 1929, indicated the intention of entering some college in the following September, and the scores of those seniors who entered colleges other than the University of Wisconsin were also tabulated. Table I demonstrates the distribution of test scores by deciles and quartiles made by the individuals in each group, and also shows the tendency toward selectivity.

TABLE I

THE SELECTIVE INFLUENCE OF COLLEGES AND UNIVERSITIES

Distribution by Deciles and Quartiles

Percentile Rank	Number Who Intend To Enter College	Number Who Enter Some College	Number Who Enter U. of Wis.	Number Who Complete 1st Semester
91–100	1,150	659	507	475
81– 90	972	475	306	288
71– 80	893	397	235	235
61– 70	802	367	216	216
51– 60	692	277	160	150
41– 50	698	318	141	123
31– 40	656	268	125	123
21– 30	553	203	82	82
11– 20	559	230	80	73
1– 10	429	174	65	60
Total	7,404	3,368	1,906	1,825
Q^3	84	86.7	90.8	
Median	61	66.4	74.2	
Q^1	36	38.9	48.8	
S. D.	37.06	40.77	37.66	

The selective influence of colleges and universities in relation to scholastic success as measured by the Ohio Psychological Test is summarized on the following table:

TABLE II

THE SELECTIVE INFLUENCE OF COLLEGES AND UNIVERSITIES

	Number	Median
High school seniors in Wisconsin	16,600	50
High school seniors who declared an intention of going to college	7,404	61
High school seniors who entered some college in September, 1929	3,249	67
1929 high school graduates who entered University of Wisconsin in September, 1929	821	75
Freshmen at the University of Wisconsin, 1929	1,906	74
Freshmen who completed the first semester, 1929, with regular schedules	1,825	74

It is evident from the above tables that there was a selective influence at work in determining which high school graduates were to become freshmen at the University of Wisconsin and at other institutions of collegiate rank. The median of the group who intended to enter college is more than ten points above the median of all high school seniors; likewise, the median of the group that actually did enter some college in September, 1929, is six points above the median of the group who merely intended to enter college, and the median of the freshman class at the University of Wisconsin is equivalent to Q^3 of the entire high school senior group, or twenty-five points above the median of the high-school seniors.

However, it is equally obvious from Table I that the selective influence at work is not a very rigorous one. As there were 1660 high school seniors in each decile group, it will be seen on this table that practically one fourth of the lowest decile intended to enter college while less than three fourths of the highest decile had such an intention. Furthermore, it is evident that less than one half of the individuals in the highest decile actually did enter some college or university while one fourth of those in the lowest two deciles enrolled in a college or university.

To further determine the scholastic caliber of the freshman class, the rank in high school class, converted into percentiles ranks, was tabulated. The rank in high school class could be obtained for only 968 of the 1906 freshmen. Table III shows the distribution.

Completely satisfactory conclusions may not be drawn from these data, as only slightly over 50 per cent. of the freshmen are here represented. However, it is significant that while there is a tendency for the freshmen to be drawn from the upper half of the high school class, this tendency can not be considered a rigorous factor of selection—277 of the group of 968, or 28 per cent., were from the lower half of their high school classes and 100 freshmen, or over 10 per cent. of the groups of 968, were from the lowest quartile of their high school classes.

TABLE III

PERCENTILE RANK IN HIGH SCHOOL CLASS
1929 Freshmen, University of Wisconsin

Percentile rank	Number
96–100	80
91–95	89
86–90	89
81–85	77
76–80	67
71–75	64
66–70	62
61–65	57
56–60	57
51–55	49
46–50	43
41–45	29
36–40	41
31–35	34
26–30	30
21–25	29
16–20	22
11–15	18
6–10	21
1–5	10

The relation between the Ohio Psychological Test results and freshman achievement was first calculated by correlating the psychological test percentiles, based on the scores of the 16,619 high school seniors, and the grade point percentiles of the 1825 freshmen who completed the first semester's work at the University of Wisconsin with regular schedules of study. This number does not include students in the Experimental College or freshmen with reduced schedules. The following results were obtained:

	Psychological test percentile	First semester grade percentile
Median	74	50
S. D.	26.5	37.06
P. E.	17.87	25
Q^3	91.87	75
Q^1	56.13	25

Coefficient of correlation $= +.36$

The coefficient of correlation of .36 shows that a positive relation exists between the psychological percentile and the first semester's grades, but it is obvious that this correlation is too low to be of value in forecasting scholastic success from aptitude as measured by the test.

The percentile ranks used in the correlation above were based on all 16,619 high school seniors for the psychological test percentiles and on only the 1825 University freshmen for the first semester grade percentile ranks. It has been shown that the freshman group was selective as compared to the high school seniors. Because the two groups were really not comparable, new percentile ranks were calculated for the test rankings, based on only the test scores of the selective group of college freshmen. Raw scores in the test were available for only 1774 of the 1825 freshmen. The revised percentiles of these 1774 freshmen were then correlated with the grade percentiles, and the following results were obtained:

	Psychological test percentile	First semester grade percentile
Median	57.5	53.55
S. D.	27.75	28.75
P. E.	18.71	19.39
Q^3	76.21	72.94
Q^1	38.71	34.16

Coefficient of correlation = +.48

This correlation is considerably higher than that found when the psychological test percentiles based on the entire high school senior group were used.

The relation between scholastic aptitude as shown by the test results and scholastic aptitude as demonstrated by the position in high school class was determined by correlating the psychological test percentiles and the percentiles ranking in the high school class. The following results were found:

	Psychological test percentile	High school class percentiles
Median	77.5	67.5
S. D.	26.3	24.75
P. E.	17.74	16.69
Q^3	95.2	84.2
Q^1	59.8	50.8

Coefficient of correlation = +.508

To settle the question of whether a different correlation might be found if raw score instead of percentile ranks were used, the raw scores in the psychological test and the grade point averages for 1774 freshmen were correlated. A correlation of .48 was found to exist between the raw scores and grade point averages. This indicates that for this particular group the percentile score, in spite of its seeming lack of fine discrimination between differences in raw score, is as accurate for correlation purposes as the raw scores themselves.

In order to determine the relation between the scores in the psychological test and the first year's work, the raw scores made on the test and the grade point average for the year were correlated. The correlation was figured for the 1452 freshmen who completed the year, 1929–30, with regular schedules of study and for whom raw scores in the psychological test were available. The following results were obtained:

	Psychological test scores	Grade point average of freshman year
Median	195.5	1.3
S. D.	43.9	.65
P. E.	29.6	.44
Q^3	225.1	1.74
Q^1	165.9	.86

Coefficient of correlation = +.43

The question of how high a correlation could be expected between a semester's grades in the freshman year and another criterion was answered by correlating the first semester averages with the averages in the second semester of 1520 freshmen. The following results were obtained:

	First semester grade point averages	Second semester grade point averages
Median	1.3	1.3
S. D.	.68	.71
P. E.	.46	.48
Q^3	1.8	1.78
Q^1	.6	.6

Coefficient of correlation = +.73

It is obvious that no single instrument could predict scholastic success better than scholastic success itself, that is, that no single test could predict, for example, the second semester's grades more accurately than the grades of the first semester will predict them. The correlation of +773 is, therefore, the highest correlation that could be expected between the 1929–30 freshman grades at the University of Wisconsin and any other single criterion.

Consideration of the various correlations listed above introduced the question of whether it would be possible to weight the high school ranking and the psychological test score in such a way as to predict with these two rankings the probable achievement of an individual in the 1929–30 freshman class. The following data were used in the derivation of such a prediction formula:

1 = Grade point percentile
2 = High school percentile rank
3 = Psychological test percentile rank

$r_{12} = +.484$	S. D.$_{\cdot 1}$ = 5.72	Median$_1$ = 52.74
$r_{13} = +.48$	S. D.$_{\cdot 2}$ = 5.26	Median$_2$ = 66.36
$r_{23} = +.508$	S. D.$_{\cdot 3}$ = 4.95	Median$_3$ = 75.2

$r_{12,3} = +.32$
$r_{13,2} = +.314$
$r_{23,1} = +.364$

A prediction formula was derived from these data, based on the regression equation:

$$X_1 = b_{12.3}X_2 + b_{13,2}X_3 + K$$

By substituting the data in the score form of the above equation the following prediction formula was obtained:

$$X_1 = .353X_2 + .367X_3 + 1.72$$

in which X_1 is the predicted grade point percentile for an individual, X_2 his high school class percentile rank, and X_3 his psychological test percentile rank.

Using this formula, grade point percentiles were predicted for 300 students selected at random from the freshman class. The predicted grade point percentiles were then correlated with the actual grade point percentile ranks of the 300 students at the end of the semester. Following are the results:

	Actual grade point percentile rank	Predicted grade point percentile rank
Median	47.5	47.5
S. D.	25.5	16.15
P. E.	17.2	10.89
Q^3	64.7	58.39
Q^1	30.3	36.61

Coefficient of correlation = +.626

An analysis of the predicted and the actual first semester grade percentiles reveals more significantly the value of the prediction formula. The minimum satisfactory average for a freshman may be said to be the point below which he would incur scholastic probation and above which he would be free from probation. The 40th percentile may be regarded as this point for the first semester of 1929–30. Exactly 119 of the freshmen considered in the above correlation fell below this satisfactory average. Of this number, 81, or 67 per cent., had a predicted average of below the 40th percentile. Of the 300 freshmen, 134 were actually below the median grade point percentile and of this number 75 per cent. were below the predicted median grade point percentile. Only 5 students from the upper quartile of the predicted grade point percentile fell below the median of actual grade points earned. The prediction formula thus points out the poor students with an accuracy beyond the prognostic value that might be expected from the correlation coefficient of .626. The discrepancy between the actual and the predicted averages is apparently found in the cases of students with a high potential capacity but with other shortcomings which detract from the quality of their college work, and in the cases of the students with mediocre talent but of efficient study habits and a keen motivation which raise their achievement higher than their capacity would, under normal conditions, predict.

From this study of scholastic aptitude and the college achievement of the 1929–30 freshman class at the University of Wisconsin the following conclusions may be drawn:

(1) The freshman class at the University of Wisconsin in 1929–30 was a selective group according to the scores in the Ohio State University psychological test. The median of the freshman class was twenty-five points above the median of the 1929 seniors in the high schools of Wisconsin. However, the selective factor was not highly rigorous for less than one half of the individuals in the highest decile of high school seniors entered the university, while one fourth of those in the lowest two deciles enrolled in a college or university.

(2) The freshman class was a selective group according to the rank in high school class of the students. Seventy-two per cent. of the

freshmen, for whom the high school rank in class was available, were from the upper half of their high school classes. The selective factor is not highly rigorous here either, however, for over 10 per cent. of the group were from the lowest quartile of their high school classes.

(3) The coefficient of correlation between the psychological test percentile ranks based on the scores of the 16,619 high school seniors, and the first semester grade point percentiles of 1825 freshmen was .36. When the psychological test percentiles were recalculated and based on the test scores of only those individuals who entered college, the correlation was raised to .48. The coefficient of correlation between the raw scores in the test and the grade point averages, not converted into percentiles, was also .48. This indicates that the percentile rank is as accurate a measure as the unconverted, raw scores, if the percentiles are calculated on comparable groups. There is a loss of accuracy when the psychological test percentiles are based on the 16,619 scores and the grade point percentiles are based on the smaller, more selective group of college freshmen.

(4) The coefficient of correlation between the psychological test percentiles and the high school rank in class percentiles was .508. Since the correlation between psychological test ratings and composite standings of pupils usually lies between .40 and .60, this coefficient is typical.

(5) The coefficient of correlation between the first and the second semester grade point averages was .73. This represents the highest possible correlation between a semester's standings of the 1929–30 freshmen and any other single criterion.

(6) The coefficient of correlation between the psychological test scores and the year's average is .43. This may be lower than the correlation in which only a single semester's grades were considered because a number of poor students with low psychological test scores were dropped from the University at the end of the first semester. Between achievement and the test scores for these students there would have been a very high correlation. Eliminating them from the group who completed the entire first year tended to pull down the correlation.

(7) The prediction formula derived from the correlations between psychological test scores, high school rank in class, and the first semester grade point averages, predicted 300 averages that had a correlation of .626 with the actual averages obtained by the students.

(8) From an analysis of the predicted and the actual grade averages it is apparent that the prediction formula has its highest accuracy and probably its greatest usefulness in pointing out those students who are poor college risks. Sixty-seven per cent. of the students who actually did unsatisfactory work received a predicted average that was unsatisfactory. Seventy-five per cent of the students who actually fell below the median grade point percentile were also below the predicted grade point percentile.

The score in the Ohio State University psychological test and the high school rank in class used together in a prediction formula, would, therefore, predict with significantly high accuracy, failure in college. Failure is predicted more accurately than success because an individual with a real lack of scholastic ability usually does not make up for this lack with any other characteristics that will enable him to do successful college work. On the other hand, many individuals with outstanding aptitude fail because of lack of study or motivation to measure up to their capacity.

RUTH K. BYRNS
UNIVERSITY OF WISCONSIN

NEW BOOKS IN EDUCATION

ANDERSON, EARL W. and RICHARD R. FOSTER. *Teacher Supply and Demand in Ohio, 1929–1930.* Pp. xii + 170. Ohio State University.

BOGOSLOVSKY, CHRISTINA S. VON H. *The Educational Crisis in Sweden.* Pp. xiv + 301. Columbia University Press. $3.50.

A Program of Art Education for Connecticut. Pp. 122. Illustrated. Connecticut State Board of Education.

DODGE, HARRISON H. *Mount Vernon: Its Owner and its Story.* Pp. 232. Illustrated. Lippincott. $2.50.

HAYES, CARLTON J., THOMAS M. PARKER and JOHN W. WAYLAND. *World History.* Pp. xviii + 912. Illustrated. Macmillan. $2.20.

WHIPPLE, GUY M., Editor. *The Thirty-first Yearbook of the National Society for the Study of Education.* Part I. *A Program for Teaching Science.* Pp. xii + 370. Part II. *Changes and Experiments in Liberal-Arts Education.* Pp. ix + 310. Public School Publishing Company.

SCHOOL AND SOCIETY

EDITED BY J. McKEEN CATTELL

WITH WHICH IS COMBINED THE

EDUCATIONAL REVIEW

EDITED BY WILLIAM McANDREW

Volume 35 | SATURDAY, MAY 28, 1932 | Number 909

MARK HOPKINS ON A LOG

By Professor CYLDE M. HILL and ANNA L. BLAIR

YALE UNIVERSITY

COLLEGE teaching once meant that scholarly persons could find excitement and adventure to their taste in the study and the classroom, but teachers are no longer permitted to pursue a tranquil course of academic seclusion. They are engaged in a tremendous undertaking which subjects itself to the appraisal, the admiration or the attack of large and varied groups, comprising students and trustees, endowment-campaign orators and fundamentalist legislators, editorial writers and graduate research workers. Out of the confusion of conflicting opinion and irreconcilable detail emerges the fact that the college and its faculty matter a great deal to educators and observers who write and read and hear the opinions so freely and sometimes so shrewdly delivered.

No college can legitimately exist for any reason other than teaching. In its final analysis the college stands or falls by the effectiveness of its teaching unit or by the lack of it. Where there is good teaching there is a good college, even though the hearts of far-flung alumni are saddened by the radio announcements every Saturday of the football season. An inadequate library can not stifle the vigorous performance of the faculty, nor can drafty corridors nor dingy classrooms. A high percentage of Ph.D.'s after faculty names in the catalogue often looks amazingly attractive to an administration; but the existence of not a single college is justified on such pride if it stops with pleased contemplation of brilliant research and does not investigate classroom execution. The liveliness of popular concern is warrantable, therefore, if it lifts standards in the selection of teachers and in conditions contributing to impressive instruction.

Twenty or thirty years ago the attitude toward teaching was contemptuous more than anything else. Bernard Shaw's epigram, "Those who can, do; those who can not, teach," cleverly expressed for the bourgeois what they felt was the correct way to view a man unaccountably choosing to enter the teaching field. But there is a visible alteration nowadays when a schoolmaster may expect as many luncheon-club preferments as his brother who entered medicine or theology or jurisprudence. He may be found here on book-club editorial boards and there in high political places. The advancement is recent, but it is less notable for its recency than for its significance. The credit belongs to a steadily increasing number of people who have devoted themselves to a thorough study of the whole problem of education. The results of this study have influenced teaching and opinions of it for several reasons. In the first place, a substantial body of information is now at the teacher's disposal. This information has lent security to the instructor, and the security has bred the self-respect which is the invariable product of confidence. Besides this, the study has made its invaluable contribution by integrating the members of the profession and the effect has been so impressive that numerous erstwhile scoffers are keeping a civil tongue in their heads, if not actually deferring to the new aristocracy.

Many are not deferring, however, nor even maintaining silence. Especially is discontent outspokenly urged with regard to advanced degrees. When a speaker of national importance declares that "the best teaching in America is in the primary grades, the next best probably in the high schools, and the poorest in the college," and when the discussion from the floor seems to agree with the speaker and to direct responsibility toward the Ph.D.'s on our faculties, the time has arrived to evaluate the situation as justly as may be done. But it is notoriously difficult and manifestly inaccurate to compare the relative effectiveness of different levels of instruction, nor can such a comparison be made a satisfactory basis for constructive criticism. All along the line there are pedants and charlatans and hucksters making a living in both elementary schools and colleges. People must take the risk of sending their infant and adolescent children to classrooms presided over by clumsy or erratic pedagogues. But in the very next room there may be one whose ability and genius are as quick for good as the other influences are for dullness and danger. No one can say with justice that the evil or the good is at the beginning or the end of school life. The real reason is rather with the charge that college teaching is not so good as it should be. If it is not producing the results that may be reasonably expected—a thoughtful attention to life situations and a skilled participation in them—then some, at least, of the discontent is justified and the demand for improvement is in order. What is to be the nature of this improvement, to what degree it is to be insisted upon, how its effectiveness is to be measured and made permanent, the critics themselves are not as yet agreed. While the curriculum and the extra-curriculum, social conditions and entrance requirements, equipment and administration all become intermittently the target in the daily papers and popular magazines, on lecture platforms and in educational conclaves, for students, cartoonists, laymen and educationists, it is the college teacher and the instruction that he gives which receive the most persistent arraignment.

It is fair to conclude that such outspoken criticism in the college field still prevails because there it has not yet met squarely the forces which have, to some extent at least, successfully countered it elsewhere—professional self-respect born of scientific professional knowledge, and professional integration among the teachers themselves. Can it be that better results might come if college instructors could or would yield their historic position of emphasizing subject-matter to the total exclusion of the means of presentation? Is it possible that it would improve matters not to ignore so utterly the values in other subjects and their relations to special fields and to the all-round development of the student? Uncompromising refusal to consider technique has eclipsed the value of courses to many a student who has taken notes industriously and returned them scrupulously in examinations, without once having realized a single connection between himself and the subject. Perhaps the courses in the theory of methods, in practice and in curriculum devised for elementary and secondary teachers, urged by their superintendents to spend their summers in resorts boasting a normal school, having borne more fruit than their academic critics have thought to find. At any rate from 60 to 80 per cent. of the holders of the Ph.D. degree from American graduate schools enter the profession of college teaching; it seems, then, not unreasonable to inquire what besides academic training is needed, if college teaching is to be made more effective. Perhaps the dull among the learned might find nourishment for their souls and refreshment for their courses if trustees suggested an occasional sojourn in some graduate school of education. Such measures would be humiliating and unpopular, and it is easily possible to place too much emphasis on mere devices and skills. The best teacher probably has a feeling for procedure and a certainty for kindling a class to a fine enthusiasm as natural as the color of his hair. He can defend his subject and his technique at any time. He knows that blustering talk about "faculty psychology" and "discipline of the mind" is simply ignorant or hypocritical or both. Nevertheless, until college teaching is based upon professional ability and at least some preparation in professional techniques rather than upon individual inspiration or more or less successful research, it can never be satisfactorily adjusted in our system of education, nor can there be any standards of excellence operating to enhance success or to eliminate incompetence.

It is true that the college teacher is at times the victim of circumstance, due to traditions or to a faulty administration. When employment and promotion depend upon research, often totally unproductive as far as his classroom is concerned; when his salary must be supplemented by earnings from other sources which have divided his time and his ability; when, a specialist in one field, he is compelled by an administrative exigency to teach in another, it is illogical to expect a high grade of instruction. But difficult to defend is the teacher who is ignorant of problems of method and of student psychology, as is also he who ignores such problems and, absorbed in his own special field, fails to interpret its significance in relation to the objectives of education as a whole. Though equipment and administration may help or hinder, they can never make a bad teacher good nor render a good teacher entirely ineffective. It is rather in the hands of college teachers themselves where lies the success or the failure of college instruction. Such success is at present far too sporadic, though by no means rare.

Regardless of the causes contributing to the prevalence of poor teaching at the college level, the need of the hour is improvement. Entrenched as he is behind long years of venerable precedent, secure in the strength of academic scholarship, the college teacher is but tardily having his performance subjected to the critical analysis which is already beginning to give to teaching from the kindergarten through the secondary school some semblance of scientific accuracy. The Pennsylvania study of secondary school and college coordination is a forerunner of other investigations sure to follow in the near future and an indication of the attitude of the public and the profession toward the real problems in this particular field, where the immediately urgent need is that accurate instruments be created, that reliable data be assembled and that scientific studies be made. Now there is little but a storm of negative criticism which bewilders the college teacher without pointing a way out of the classical tradition which was formerly all that his public demanded. What, then, does society now expect of him? Is it possible, in the absence of scientific investigations, to analyze the work of great teachers (for there have been many such); or is it practicable to study his functions to the end of determining the qualifications necessary to accomplish them efficiently? By what standards shall he evaluate his equipment and his performance?

So much sentimentality has been emitted about the Ideal Teacher that even to mention the phrase suggests the shallow eulogies of professional inspirationalists. One who brings intelligence to bear on the conception feels with Emerson that the ideal teacher who is a scholar is, as a matter of course, Man Thinking. But "character," continues Emerson, "is higher than intellect, and a great soul will be strong to live as well as to think. . . . Let the grandeur of justice shine in his affairs and the beauty of affection cheer his roof." This virility in living, this passion for justice and beauty and affection posits in the ideal teacher permanent intellectual curiisity and a sturdy interest in those whom he teaches. He has too much imagination to exaggerate the importance of his own field of labor, but his enthusiasm for it is honest and he has no regrets for the choice he made. He is disturbed when he can not develop the potentialities of his students, and uneasy when they merely learn his subject without learning to like it. He has a soul as well as a head; he is a man as well as a teacher; he is as far as possible the incarnation of the truth he espouses.

Before colleges were invented or learning specialized, a homely little man in Athens demonstrated what could be done by intelligence and power of personality alone. Socrates needed no building, no equipment, no library, yet the self-control and self-knowledge which he exemplified and propagated, the theory that vice is essentially ignorance and that no man wills to be evil, survive as the most dynamic principles in modern social reforms. His cunningly devised questions which drew his companions out sometimes resulted in confusion and contradiction for his disciples, but Socrates led them eventually to the truth. Always he recognized the importance of personality and that its integrity is the very heart of the teaching relation. One wonders what he would say if asked to head up the philosophy department of a great modern university. Would he repeat the remark that he made when he strolled through the bazaars of a fair, "So many things there are that I do not need."?

Unfortunately the approach to a consideration of another great teacher is obscured for realistic appreciation in a mist of doctrine and tenet. If one will lay aside temporarily his religious conviction or agnosticism, and will read the narrative of Jesus' teaching as it is developed in the Synoptic Gospels in the same way in which he reads any other book, he will discover at least four outstanding marks of good teaching that place Jesus in the position of the greatest teacher who ever lived. The first of these distinctions is that he was concrete, that he explained by metaphor and parable all his principles of life here and hereafter. Talking mainly to a group of simple country people, he reminded them of husbandmen and vineyards, shepherds and sheep, sowers and seed, yokes for oxen, lost coins and unexpected and hungry visitors. Fencing with Pharisees and lawyers, he illustrated with kings and marriage banquets, the superscriptions of coins, cups and plates and whitewashed tombs. There is an interesting sentence in Plato's "Republic" where Socrates notes that the "soul is radiant with intelligence when resting upon that on which truth and being shine." Jesus says simply, "I am the light of the world," but the thought is the same. He was quick to utilize the poetic suggestibility of doors, of life-giving water, of salt, of leaven, of a single pearl of great price. Some of his expressions betray a pungent irony, an implication of humor—figs from thistles and grapes of thorns, filtering the gnat and swallowing the camel, praying on street corners and giving alms with a flourish of trumpets. Aristotle announced that there is a universal pleasure in imitation, in recognizing the familiar, and it is partly this pleasure in illustrations of common and every-day things that made large multitudes follow Jesus.

From primary to graduate school an apt illustration secures attention. Jesus never degenerated into a tale-teller for the sake of the tale. The illustration drove home the point and revealed the truth, but the thinking was done by the person to whom the illustration was disclosed. The rich young ruler went sorrowfully away because he had less courage than imagination; nothing was wrong with his thought processes; he had simply been too unhappily conditioned by ease to accept the terms of the conclusion Jesus forced him to make concerning his neighbor. For the first time in her degraded life a Samaritan woman thought of the life of the spirit rather than the life of the flesh. A learned authority, Nicodemus, came to have signs and wonders explained, and went away with a whole new conception of life and light.

By being concrete and by stimulating individual thinking, Jesus was able to lead people to clear, clean-cut, essential conclusions. Unorganized group discussion is not an unmixed good. Peter reminds his Lord a little too eagerly that the disciples left their homes to follow him. Jesus instantly replies that no one has made sacrifices who will not be rewarded both on earth and in the life to come. Finally, the good social motivation of Jesus' teaching rounds off his pedagogical excellence. He began not where he left off but where the situation warranted it. He taught not subject-matter alone. He was primarily interested in teaching men. If his teaching was unsystematic, it was alive and its record exists yet in the hearts of men.

To a more modern age belongs another great teacher. As Socrates and Jesus were interested in men and women and little children so was Pestalozzi, the Swiss, with whom we have the satisfaction of enjoying a more direct contact than with his great predecessors. "Leonard and Gertrude" and "How Gertrude Teaches Her Children" are products of the last century and a half. In them we see his educational theories advanced concerning the progress of consciousness from observation, thence to speech and harmonious development of various skills and powers. The best type of the modern school with its emphasis on investigation and experimentation, its enthusiasms for the practical and the concrete is the lineal descendant of Pestalozzi's pedagogical ideal.

Hosts of others there have been, sung and unsung, who have raised the standards of their individual excellence, and of these the college has had its share of Arnolds and Hopkinses and Kilpatricks, who challenge the emulation of earnest teachers of other lands and other times. Their success, like that of the supreme masters, reveals specific and essential techniques, which they acquired and developed through long application and practice. Especially now, with the widely increased intellectual and social range among college students, does the question of teaching techniques become important. On the other hand stands the increased specialization among scholars themselves. The further the instructor ventures into the mazes of specialized knowledge, the more he needs the compass of a scientific technique to keep him in sane instructional paths. Without them scholarship alone becomes in the classroom sterile pedantry; enthusiasm obliterates the true perspective; and college teaching remains a fair target for criticism.

The task itself has changed. With the vastly increased scope of knowledge, the function of the teacher has been shifted from that of mere instruction, which, whether the most educative or not, was yet a possible interpretation of his work when complete mastery of human knowledge lay within the reach of the individual mind. The situation demands a skilful selection of subject-matter and its clear organization with reference to relative emphases as well as to its interrelations with other fields of knowledge and contributions to life itself. If the student is not to waste precious time in searching out of the general mass a few facts relevant to the problem he has in hand, then the teacher must take definite steps to prevent it. Nor can the student perceive for himself the relative importance of facts; to make these clear is also the teacher's function. A scholarly enthusiasm and mastery the teacher must have, but he must be able to maintain an objective attitude towards his subject, as only a segment of desirable knowledge; towards his students as his true objectives; and towards his teaching, as a scientific process and not inspired guesswork.

Skilful instruction demands such selection and organization, but it demands more. In college, too, the successful teacher begins with the known and proceeds to the unknown. He takes into deliberate account the undergraduate point of view, which is no longer that of a receptive and unassertive disciple. He takes into account, also, the capacity and attainments of the individual student. The crowded colleges of to-day, with their heterogeneous student bodies, present teaching problems increasingly akin to those of elementary schools which have long wrestled with the instructional problems created by great individual differences among their pupils. The materials selected and organized for any college course will differ from year to year, from class to class, and it may be from student to student. Nor does the effective teacher instruct too much. He does not try primarily to save the student the trouble of looking up anything that can be told him, but rather tells just enough to whet his appetite for more. This intellectual cocktail means, above all things, that the presentation must be interesting. Unless the student learns to like the subject, he is not likely to pursue it further than the day of the examination. Getting the student to want to know is an art in itself but it is an art that can be cultivated.

It goes without saying that such teaching necessitates daily and thorough preparation, for such a teacher recognizes the fact that every teaching situation presents new elements and the old elements in new combinations. Nor will any one method of instruction be equally effective in all of them. The lecture, the text-book, the laboratory, the group discussion, all contribute to the broadest success. Fads or the superficial unpopularity of an effective technique will not be allowed to obscure the real issues of instruction. At present, the rediscovered value of self-expression to the learning process has augmented the popularity of the discussion method. Here the rôle of the teacher is important and difficult, demanding the nicest balance of perceptions and skills. He must, himself, be an adept in clear expression, but must not, himself, dominate the discussion. He must be able tenaciously to hold to the main objective, while encouraging and stimulating universal participation. He must evaluate accurately and justly the contributions made, and yet must give full recognition to the personality of each student and respect to his opinion.

The prevailing situation makes impossible the assumption that college students possess proper study methods and habits. Without caviling about who is responsible for this state of things (if indeed anybody is), the present responsibility for directive criticism and specific suggestion must be assumed by the college teacher, who can do this most effectively only if he is familiar with what science is teaching us about the learning process. When the direction of learning is regarded as the primary function of the teacher, the recitation, the quiz and even grades lose much of their usual supreme importance. The problem becomes not how many mistakes were made, but how and why they were made; how they can be prevented rather than how they can be corrected. The assignment assumes a new significance. Through it the study habits of students are moulded and faulty methods can be revised. Clear and definite, well proportioned throughout the course so that cramming is neither necessary nor profitable, regulated within the time allotted to the subject in the curriculum, and having a definite objective of which the student as well as the instructor is conscious, the assignment can be a powerful instructional instrument. But the teacher who conceives it as such will never assign "twenty pages in advance."

Nor will he be content to assume the effectiveness of his instruction or of his students' study without objective evidence to that effect. If, in the college field he must still, for the most part, devise his own instruments for measurement, he can learn much about measuring from the progress that has been made elsewhere in this field. Whether he will or not, the times demand of him some more concrete evidence of his achievement than is furnished by his own subjective evaluation in terms of per cents. and credit hours. These he should be eager to secure, however, not because a critical public demands them, but because a just measure of achievement is essential to progress and because it is an integral part of the teaching process, instead of being merely a convenient basis for scholastic punishments and awards.

All these excellences, the selection and organization of subject-matter, skilful instruction, study guidance and measurement, may be frustrated by a lack of skill in the management of a classroom. Details, not insignificant because they are small, may consume a vast amount of time and many a well-planned piece of work has been rendered futile because the instructor ignored their power for harm in his classroom routine. If it be true that the elementary teacher has sometimes been overtrained in devices for facilitating classroom procedures, the college teacher ignores them at his peril.

It can not be overemphasized that the function of the college educator is broader than instruction. For that reason his relations with his students are direct, personal and tactful. He is, to be sure, interested in his subject but even more interested in making it contribute to the self-realization of his students. To that end sarcasm and dogmatism are alike ruled out by the simplest laws of salesmanship, as well as by those of courtesy. For the teacher is a salesman; he desires to convince the student that he needs just the help this study can render. He sincerely wants the student to like the subject, and he knows full well that students usually associate the teacher and the subject taught so that to like the one is to like the other. It is not, then, with him a desire for personal popularity which causes him to seek to make his relations with students pleasant, but a professional desire to make more effective all his instructional procedures by bringing to their support the hearty good-will of the class. He is, therefore, easily accessible to his students. When they have reason to consult him privately they find a friend in a man who is self-reliant and self-confident, without being egotistic or conceited; his personality is observable but not obtrusive; distinct but not oppressive. He is a gentleman with a cordial manner and a careful appearance, without idiosyncrasies which repel. In other words, they find, as nearly as may be, an embodiment of the truth they are being taught; a concrete example of the kind of a man he is trying to make out of the raw material in his classroom. He knows a good teacher must *be* before he can *do;* must first learn the way of life before he can lead others into it. He deems it justly due his profession, then, that his private life be above reproach.

The modern educational scheme makes other demands upon the teacher who aspires to professional success. In other times the great teacher, equipped by nature and experience, was a law unto himself. All knowledge was his field and his students looked to him alone for guidance and instruction. To-day that is no longer true. The college teacher is a coworker with his fellows in a common task. There is rapidly developing a code of professional ethics, a common stock of professional experience and an increasing fund of reliable scientific data bearing upon his tasks, available in a literature of considerable scope. Much is still to be accomplished by the profession itself as to standards for admittance and for accomplishment, but the college teacher who aspires to ultimate success acknowledges a responsibility to his group and avails himself of the common stock of experience, opinion and reliable data for the continual improvement of his own performance. Such a professional attitude immediately demands open-mindedness, constant alertness for new and better ideas, and the courage and energy necessary to put a good idea to the test. He devotes a reasonable amount of time to research for the sake of the freshness, the "toning up" of his system such endeavor will give and, incidentally, may contribute to the general knowledge in the field. The key to his success is a constant effort to improve the methods of his own teaching by thoughtful experimentation. Having become familiar with subject-matter, methods, student psychology and the objectives of college teaching, a wide-awake teacher tries to think of improvements he can put to the test to increase his own effectiveness. A plan he has thus worked out for himself will have advantages, other things being equal, over the ideas he reads in the last issue of an educational journal. However, he must be constantly on the alert to keep informed as to recent developments. He does not allow his own experimentation to supplant general reading in the field.

The importance of a good teaching personality and native capacity is not to be under estimated, but the adage of Mark Hopkins on the log has long been used to justify a laissez-faire attitude toward college teaching, as if there were a mysterious, occult quality, neither to be acquired nor developed, which determines the success of the college teacher. It was this attitude that brought about the anomalous situation which prevailed in our educational scheme until the last few years. When a teacher-training policy was inaugurated in this country and normal schools began to be founded, their function was long concerned solely with rural and elementary teachers; academies and high schools were to be taught by teachers prepared in colleges or in the academies themselves. It was as if instructional problems and teaching techniques had no place on the secondary level. Strange as that seems now, it has remained for the last twenty-five years to consider seriously the application of teacher training to college faculties. It is still as if the laws of learning and theories of instruction, for some mysterious reason, ceased to function at the portal of the college. Far too long college students were left to educate themselves in some fashion, while college teachers engaged in technical research and read them scholarly lectures, considering their duty done if examination papers were marked and not too high. Only now is vigorous criticism beginning to bear fruit in the increasing number of books and articles that are appearing in the field. The future still holds the secret of what the college will be when its principles are as closely anlayzed and its products can be as systematically measured as can be those of the elementary and secondary schools. Undoubtedly the day will come when the candidate for college teaching will be as well prepared by thorough training in the techniques of his profession as is now the physician or the lawyer for his. Meanwhile, however, the college teacher himself need not await that day to set about the development of higher standards of equipment and instruction. Great teachers offer him more than inspiration; they reward analysis, as does also the task that faces him in his own classroom. Such analyses always reveal the fact that the qualities which characterize good teaching and which the work demands can be attained and developed.

Mark Hopkins on a log? Yes, but just because he *was* Mark Hopkins he had studied that boy before him, skilled to use every bit of knowledge he could acquire of budding attitudes and uncertain mental processes. He was the lad's friend, winning his confidence and awakening his ardent enthusiasm, himself an example well worthy of emulation. He exerted himself to the utmost, not to instruct, but to guide and nourish and develop a growing ability to think. To accomplish his purpose in that young life he counted no effort too great and he would have hailed with delight help from any source.

A LAYMAN LISTENS TO MUSICIANS—AND TO MUSIC[1]

By Professor THOMAS H. BRIGGS

TEACHERS COLLEGE, COLUMBIA UNIVERSITY

I VERY vividly remember the thrill that I had, years ago, when for the first time I heard a high-school orchestra—at Richmond, Indiana, under Mr. Earhart. Its selections of good music and its performance not only gave me keen pleasure, but they presaged the coming of a new era, an era in which we no longer hang our heads as a non-musical nation. The rapid development of music-loving and of skilled and semi-skilled performance is one of the three or four most significant features of modern education. I have never ceased to thrill with pride and with hope. I congratulate you, and I hang over your heads the laurel of distinct and eminent achievement in contributing a means of pure joy, especially at a time when a nation needs surcease from its sorrows.

You have invited me, an unskilled layman, not to speak this morning on the techniques of your craft but to bring you a point of view that may direct your efforts to even more significant achievements. How, you ask, does it seem to a layman

[1] An address delivered before the silver anniversary of the National Supervisors of Music at Cleveland, April 8, 1932.

that music functions in a community? Wherein does it fail? And what should be its future course? I shall not waste your time in citing occasional lapses of incompetent teachers from the high standards that are generally upheld or in expressing the strong inclinations to murder when a conductor of group singing for pleasure interrupts his choir to give directions which his own neglect has failed to provide before the beginning. Participating in group singing I sometimes wonder when trivial selections are proposed by the conductor if you do not lack faith in your improvement of taste in the past generation. If we love good music, why should we not be permitted and encouraged to produce it? One of my pleasantest memories is of singing the classics with a group of men, no one of whom had a good voice or any unusual skill.

I have only praise for your efforts to teach children and youth to perform on some instrument. More than anything else I regret that I am skilled only on the radio, the victrola, and the Duo-Art piano. Despite your very general opinion to the contrary, however, I am increasingly convinced that there is a no inconsiderable fraction of people who are not so blessed by nature that they can ever by a reasonable effort learn to sing or to play an instrument with pleasure to others or to themselves. To paraphrase Bernard Shaw, hell is full of this kind of musical amateurs. Of course all who are so blessed should be taught, that they may have this inexhaustible fountain of pleasure. Some are like Alcestis. "She was not an artist like Admetus. There was poetry in her, because poetry comes unconsciously out of deep feeling, but there was no artistic eloquence."[2] But all of both groups can and do enjoy music. It is regarding this phase of your work that I wish to speak this morning. As I talk with my many musical friends I seem to detect a distinct tendency to deprecate the teaching of appreciation without performance. As one of the inarticulate I regret this beyond measure. Sometimes I suspect that the attitude of yours is a result quite as much of a failure to achieve success in teaching appreciation as of enthusiasm for performance, in which you of course have skills to share.

[2] Gilbert Murray, "Introduction to Alcestis."

Six years ago, at your Detroit meeting, I argued that appreciation is of three distinct kinds, the proper blending of which affords the highest and most perfect kind. The first is sensuous, the joy in sweet sounds, harmony, melody, and rhythm. To a great extent this type of appreciation is naïve: even an infant is soothed or excited by music; primitive man responds to it; and none is ever so highly educated as to depart entirely from its influence. It can, of course, be increased and refined by enriching experiences and by wise direction. One can be taught to perceive a purer tone, to detect subtler harmonies and rhythms, and joyously to follow more intricate patterns of melody.

The second, to which you tend to give the major emphasis, is intellectual. Appreciation of technique is not naïve; it has to be learned. Technique concerns the means of producing effects, and those means change from nation to nation and from age to age. Because man has an intellect he enjoys knowing how effects are produced, distinguishing the timbre of the English horn from that of the clarinet, perceiving the announcement and the development of themes, or following the intricacies of a fugue. When combined with the other two types of appreciation, or even with sensuous joys of sound, this leads to high pleasure, the intellect supporting the emotions to a most satisfying result. But in your knowledge, and in the exercise of your intellectual appreciation, I am inclined to think that you often run so far ahead of the mass of people that you are no longer leaders. You tend to become impatient with those of us who are ignorant, who have merely sipped instead of drinking deep at the Pierian spring. You tend to forget that there are other types of appreciation, each, I think, more possible and more important to the great majority of those who listen.

Let me make clear before proceeding that I place high this intellectual type of appreciation, that I envy you your knowledge of it, that I constantly strive to share it. Let me make clear, also, that I would not have you cease your efforts to impart this means of a high pleasure to others. What I am trying to emphasize is that it is only one of three means to appreciation, that its achievement is possible to only a limited extent to the great majority of those whom you teach in the schools and on whose approval the very existence of your vocation depends. I would call your attention, too, to the phenomenon that sometimes appears in your teaching, a substitution of understanding of the means for enjoyment of the product.

Lest you think me unjustifiably critical, let me quote from one of your standard books:

> The whole first theme of César Franck's "Symphony in D Minor" is presented canonically—the announcement in the trombones, tuba and basses being answered, a half measure later, by trumpets and cornets. The rest of the recapitulation, with necessary modulations and slight expansion, corresponds closely to the first portion. The coda, beginning after the same echo-effects heard at the close of the exposition, is founded on one of the counterpoints of the first subject. . . . Gathering headway it leads to an imposing assertion *fff*, in canon form, of the main motto which concludes, with a widely spaced chord, in the brilliant orchestral key of D major.

A footnote explains that it is brilliant by reason of the fact that the four principal tones in D major are produced by the open strings on the violin.

I submit that this is interesting description of the technical details used to attain an effect, interesting to those who fortunately have the knowledge to understand it. But when the book continues, page after page, with only this type of comment I fear that the effects which César Franck intended are forgotten; I am sure they are not conveyed to the amateur who seeks to increase his pleasure by appreciating, with the means at his command, the noble symphony. One would as well substitute for appreciation of a poem comment on assonance, alliteration, rhyme, tropes, and stanza form. All such details are meaningful only after other appreciation has been achieved.

The third kind of appreciation is based on the connotation of music. Every stimulus to man is both denotative and connotative. A word, like "mother" denotes an immediate female ancestor; it connotes or calls on one to contribute any number of the tender associations that experience has stored up. The chief reason why Whistler's portrait of his mother is a vastly superior work of art to his Carlyle is not that the former is painted with greater technical skill, but that it calls up in every normal beholder scores of tender associations that simply do not exist for the Scottish sage. Music is peculiarly able to evoke from memory pleasurable associations of experience, and in encouraging them we are adding tremendously to the joys that music can bring.

This type of appreciation, which I think you are too much inclined to neglect or to deprecate as being a pleasant relative but not a member of the immediate family of Euterpe, is second only to appreciation of the sensuous in its universality and in its general exercise. Its encouragement would make the intellectual appreciation of technical details more desired by the amateur, who after keen enjoyment of his own kind could more easily be led to desire to understand.

My conception of the creation of any art is that a sensitive person experiences beauty of one kind or another and then, desiring to share it with others, uses the medium at his command to arouse in others emotions similar to those that have suffused him. Seldom, if ever, does he merely reproduce. He makes records in his notebook of the significant features of his experience; through meditation he assimilates them; and after he has understood their significance he presents them, transmuted by his personality, to stimulate others. Appreciation, then, is going backward over this path. One begins by responding to the stimulus, whether it be of sound, or form, or color, by recreating an experience and mood similar to that of the original composer. I say "similar" and not "the same," for the personality and the experience always cause the response to be different. "Art is a tryst" between two souls who love beauty. Chopin may have been inspired, when composing his "Marche Funebre," by the plight of Poland. Recreating, we think nothing of that unfortunate country, but we envisage a wholly harmonious phenomenon—a funeral of some person of large dignity, held in magnificent gloom, with a resulting mood that must be all but identical with the original. It would be impossible to imagine the glittering march of the military, or even the touching procession at the requiem of some one intimately dear.

Because music is a tryst, each sensitive and imaginative listener will create for himself a similar mood with a similar but never an identical setting. In the second act of Tristan, when Isolde listens for the decrescent hunting horn of her liege lord, a solo clarinet traces an ascending melody of subdued chromatic tenderness through the vague and glamorous haze of orchestral tone, and we stand in the magic of a summer night in an Old World garden. The details we paint for ourselves, but the general picture and the mood Wagner unmistakably creates for us. More than this, the music evokes for us not only Isolde's garden, but every garden over which night and esctasy have breathed enchantment. In the slow movement of Debussy's Iberia the oboe sings its brooding song above an accompaniment of muted cellos and violas, and there rises in our imaginations a picture of still another night—an amorous, enchanted night, a sultry, Castilian night, heavily perfumed and languid. From this indefinite common each listener makes his definite particular. It is not by accident that when Melisande, standing with Pelleas beside the timeless fountain of the blind, looks into its strange still waters and exclaims, "Oh, l'eau est claire" the music calls up for us those silent, liquid, and mysterious depths. It is not by accident that Rachmaninof, in his "Isle of the Dead," creates a picture as well as a mood, or that MacDowell, in his "Wandering Iceberg," by softly sonorous chords in slow-paced movement, calls up varied memories or equally varied imaginings of frozen and glittering splendor.

When music makes me respond by contributing out of my repertoire of experience and by the active exercise of my imagination I can not be persuaded that the composer did not intend this kind of pleasurable appreciation, that it is negligible, or that it is inferior to the colder intellectual understanding of technique. Music that makes us picture and associate lovely memories with harmonious sounds is sometimes by the intellectuals deprecated as "program music." This type may be as crude as in the "Hunt in the Black Forest," with its hokum of hoof beats, dog yelping, and vocal yells; or it may be as elevated as in the symphonies known as

"The Eroica," "The Pathetique," and "The Pastoral," or in the tone poem "L'Apres-Midi d'un Faune." Beethoven surely made it respectable. It is not wise to forget that of the consumers of music, on whom you depend for the success of your craft, there are more on the level of the Hunt than have attained to the heights that you revere. It is only by beginning with the former that they can be led to climb to the latter.

Fundamental to understanding appreciation, and to teaching it, is the fact that it is and of necessity must be individual. As Faust says, "Man sees what in his bosom lurks."

> A small song the lyrist sings:
> A muted phrase; tinted wings;
> Faint perfume; pale blossomings.
>
> This is all the verses are—
> Unless one finds in them the far
> Reflection of his own star.[3]

We have a significant illustration in Beethoven's "Seventh," which has been variously interpreted, from Berlioz to Isadora Duncan. Wagner heard in it the apotheosis of the dance; to Schumann it was a village marriage ceremony; George Grove viewed it as a romantic symphony; Alberti reads into it the joy of Germany released from the French yoke. A knightly festival, the Moors in Spain, a cathedral procession, a battle of giants returning to the feasts of victory are only a few of the pictures conjured by the work. One tends to become impatient with interpretations differing from his own. But every listener has the right—nay, it is his duty—to interpret honestly according to his own experiences, his own imagination. The listeners' imagination cooperates with the suggestions conveyed by the composer: the result is art. When a piece of music is ineffective the cause is likely to be a lack of rich experience or a failure to exercise the imagination enough to make the necessary appropriate contributions.

There are many evidences that composers and artists, as well as listeners, seek this type of appreciation, that they consider their works connotative—to draw out all sorts of cooperative responses that add to enjoyment. If they did not feel so, we should have for titles only "Opus No. 7" or "Fugue in B Flat." "Dreams," "Memories," "Le Son du Cor s'afflige vers les Bois," "The Spinning Song," "Le Papillion," "The Flying Dutchman," and a thousand other titles give evidence of an appeal to something other than technical harmony. Even when titles are not given by the composer, as in "Lieder ohne Worte" and in Schumann's "Carnival," music lovers have come generally to call the numbers "Consolation," "Meditation," and the like. The intimate alliance of music with words in songs of all kinds and with both words and action, as in the opera, further support the thesis that there is a natural tendency to supplement pure melody and harmony.

Perhaps in all this I am carrying coals to Newcastle. But as I listen to musicians —and to music, I do not think so. This layman appreciates your highly successful work, and he would like to have you do even more than he thinks you are doing to encourage the listener's responses to connotative sonal appeals. He would have you consistently recognize that the contributions from experience and from imagination are common, important and pleasurable, that they furnish a type of appreciation essentially basic for the structures of understanding, production and creation. He would have you more consistently encourage the expression of individual interpretations, the comparison of them with others, and the synthesizing of interpretative details to the appreciation of larger wholes. Many youth without training interpret and enjoy only small units.

[3] Monroe Heath, "The Singers."

They see the sun, the cloud,
But not the spring.

They need help in learning to put small units together so that they acquire a mansion of beauty. He would have you respect individual interpretations, even when they are not respectable. One grows by developing cells, not by violently replacing them.

I am greatly honored by your invitation to address you. I am even more honored that you have listened so patiently to what I have had to say. If you do not agree with the emphasis that I have given, may I beg that you will justify your generosity in inviting a layman to address you by giving his argument the benefit of your reflective judgment, generously excusing the deficiencies and supplying from the wealth of your knowledge what is needed.

In conclusion may I not state in bare outline what it seems to me music does for mankind?

Music
takes us out of our far too routine selves,
dispels disagreeable moods,
furnishes a catharsis for passion,
induces new sensations and pleasurable moods,
reveals unexperienced or unimagined beauty,
ennobles us by the endowment of rich experiences of sensitive and sensible souls,
integrates us with others of similar sensitiveness,
expresses in beautiful form what we inarticulate folk have vaguely felt,
interprets sensations that have been perceived, but not understood,
composes beauty in ways satisfying to an orderly mind,
sets up dissatisfactions with the ugly or the merely commonplace,
substitutes yearnings for loveliness, not merely of tone but of all forms of purity and beauty,
incites to expression through various media,
stimulates inventive thought,
prepares for and excites a desire for more and higher experiences of a similar kind.

All those things, perhaps others still, music does for some people and may, in varying degrees, do for all. They are so important, so magnificently important, that those of you who serve the high mistress may respect yourselves as apostles of no mean rank. I congratulate you, and I envy you your opportunities to lead myriads of youth into the realms of felicity.

EDUCATIONAL EVENTS

EDUCATION UNDER THE LONDON COUNTY COUNCIL

At a recent meeting of the London County Council, under the presidency of Mr. Angus Scott, the chairman, estimates amounting to £12,776,710 for education were considered. In response to the urgent request of the government, estimates were reduced from £14,327,639 last year. Of the total of £12,776,710, the ratepayers have to find £7,781,305. The balance comes from government grants.

Captain Edward Cobb, chairman of the Education Committee, in introducing the estimates, said, according to a report in the London *Times,* that they had been framed under considerable difficulty owing to the national crisis and the economy order. Instead of receiving a 50 per cent. grant from the Exchequer a lesser sum would be allocated, based on a formula which was unintelligible except to mathematicians. On the basis of last year's estimates London would lose grants this year amounting to £1,325,000. By stringent economies the committee had reduced estimates by £1,550,929. That, however, did not altogether compensate for the loss of grant. The gross estimated expenditure was reduced by £1,550,929, the Exchequer grant was reduced by £1,907,935, and the additional burden would be £345,481. He felt it necessary to point out the narrow margin in which they had to work; of estimates last year of over £14,000,000, salaries and pensions accounted for over £10,000,000, and debt charges and rates over £1,000,000, leaving a balance of under £3,000,000. Their saving of £600,000 was equal to 20 per cent.

The total capital estimates were £190,000, which compared with an estimate of £700,000 last year and an expenditure of £400,000. Included in this was provision for a new playing field and the extension of an existing secondary school, so that even in these difficult times the council was making provision for the future.

There was, under the new scheme, an alteration in the proportion between rates and taxes. In 1931–32 the rates found 52 per cent. of the expenditure and the taxes 44 per cent. In the coming year the ratepayer would bear 61 per cent. and the taxpayer 35 per cent. The effect of government economy, therefore, had been to transfer some expenditure from the taxpayer to the ratepayer. The committee had combed every branch and made economies wherever possible, but it was necessary to warn the council that some savings could not be repeated.

Referring to the lot of the teachers, and admitting that most of the economies had been made at the expense of the staff, Captain Cobb said that not one teacher had lost his employment and his reduction had been limited to 10 per cent. He believed that it would be a mistake to reduce further, for an underpaid and dissatisfied staff was false economy.

A FLOATING UNIVERSITY

A "FLOATING UNIVERSITY," which will have a student body of approximately 600 and will travel more than 35,000 miles around the world in eight months, is being planned for next autumn. The movement is said to be supported by a large group of men and women prominent in social, educational and business circles.

A transatlantic liner, equipped with lecture rooms, study hall, science laboratories, library, auditorium and gymnasium, will be chartered and will serve as "home and campus" during the two semesters that the students are at sea or in foreign ports. Present plans call for a visit to forty-three countries and sixty-one ports.

Announcement of the plans was made by Mrs. Stanley P. Woodard. She is heading a small group of men and women who are planning the "university" as a means of "broadening the outlook of American university men and women by giving them, along with their regular college work, a first-hand knowledge of foreign peoples and conditions."

Dr. James E. Lough, formerly professor of psychology and dean of Extramural Divisions of New York University, who headed a similar educational trip in 1920, is a member of the board of governors.

Dr. Lough is reported to have said that a faculty of fifty-five professors and instructors, most of whom will be on sabbatical leave from colleges and universities both here and abroad, will be assembled. The hope is that the idea can be worked out so that the university will be continued for at least five years and perhaps as a permanent institution.

The students will be selected on the basis of character and scholastic standing with a quota assigned to each state, proportioned to the number of students resident in the state. A special effort will be made to have the student body represent "the best in American college life." Patrons and patronesses are being chosen in every state to aid in making selections.

The quota allotment outlined at present provides for 60 students from Pacific Coast States, 85 from the Western States, 115 from the Middle West, 95 from the South, 105 from New York and the Middle Atlantic States and 100 from New England.

The ship has not yet been selected, but the tour is scheduled to begin in October. A chancellor "prominent in educational life" will be in charge of the university. The board of directors, besides Dr. Lough, will include Thomas G. Cook, Charles K. Cooper, John L. Merrill, Dr. Charles F. Thwing and Dr. S. P. Woodard.

THE FOURTH SCOUT NATURALIST EXPEDITION TO YOSEMITE NATIONAL PARK

Two months with a government geological party in the High Sierra country of Yosemite National Park is the main feature of the program for the Fourth Scout Naturalist Expedition to the national parks.

Eleven Eagle Scouts, each chosen by tests conducted by his council, will make up the expedition which will assist Mr. François E. Matthes, of the United States Geological Survey, in an important survey of the region north of the Tuolumne River in Yosemite Park. Mr. Matthes, a well-known geologist, has conducted scientific investigations in Yosemite for several years. He is the author of numerous articles and books on the geology of Yosemite National Park. The study proposed will involve observations on the present rate of shrinkage of the glaciers in the High Sierra and facts indicating any marked changes that have taken place in the extent of the glaciers within the last thousand years.

The scouts will join Mr. Matthes in Yosemite on June 15, to remain until August 9. Prior to that, they will make a two weeks' trip through the southwest and visit the Grand Canyon, Bryce Canyon and Zion National Parks. In each of these three parks, the resident park naturalist will take the boys on geologic trips into the canyons. They will hike across the Grand Canyon by way of the Bright Angel Trail and make an excursion into the Painted Desert.

During the field work in Yosemite, the party will camp in Little Yosemite Valley, at Merced Lake, Lake Tenaya, Glen Aulin, Pate Valley, Tiltill Valley, Matterhorn Canyon, Tuolumne Meadows, and many other famous beauty spots of the park. The trails followed will lead to some of the most interesting areas in the park, including the Grand Canyon of the Tuolumne, Waterwheel Falls, and Tuolumne and Forsythe passes. The boys will have a chance to test their skill in some of the finest fishing streams in the world.

Each scout chosen for this expedition must be at least 15 years old and have attained the rank of Eagle by June of this year. In addition to having an unquestioned scout and health record, he must have a general knowledge of natural history, be able to speak at public meetings, and to write. Boys who have accompanied previous scout naturalist expeditions have received many invitations to lecture and write about their experiences. They must be experienced in camping, cooking and woodsmanship, and carry complete equipment for knapsacking expeditions, including bedding and personal cooking utensils. They will have entire charge of a pack train of 15 burros.

The naturalist expeditions to the parks are organized each year by Ansel F. Hall, senior park naturalist and chief forester of the National Park Service. Although organized and financed privately, these expeditions have the official approval and cooperation of the Park Service.

THE SUMMER SESSION OF THE UNIVERSITY OF CINCINNATI

THE University of Cincinnati is developing several exceptional features for its summer session of 1932. Professor John Dewey, of Columbia University, is the visiting intersession lecturer for its period from June 6 to June 18. Intersession students spend all their time upon intensive work involving two lectures and conferences daily. Dr. Dewey's special lectures will be directed to the philosophy of education, with special reference to progressive education. Dr. Dewey succeeds, as intersession lecturer, Professor Lewis M. Terman, of the 1931 session, earlier lecturers having been Professor E. L. Thorndike, Professor William H. Kilpatrick and others.

A laboratory school, organized on the principles of progressive education, opens immediately following the close of Dr. Dewey's institute. Demonstration classes are organized from the kindergarten throughout the elementary school period, taught by visiting specialists selected because of their creative work in classroom procedure. A number of basic theory courses are made to exemplify the practices as set forth in the demonstration teaching program.

The laboratory school, together with a number of added special features, is scheduled for the first regular term from June 18 to July 26. This is followed by a second regular term from July 26 to August 27.

As the original center for training work in the field of sight conservation, the university is conducting sight conservation training courses again this summer, these involving a special demonstration class laboratory of partially sighted children and extensive clinical work presented in cooperation with the College of Medicine of the University.

Regular and visiting professors are presenting many instructional opportunities in all the major fields of liberal arts, education, fine and applied arts, commerce and engineering and physical education.

The summer session is under the directorship of Dr. Louis A. Pechstein, dean of the Teachers College of the University of Cincinnati.

AMERICAN HOME ECONOMICS ASSOCIATION

The twenty-fifth annual meeting of the American Home Economics Association will be held in Atlanta, Georgia, June 20 to 25, 1932. Headquarters will be at the Atlanta-Biltmore Hotel. The central theme of the program will be "Revaluations in Home Economics."

The president of the association, Miss Frances L. Swain, supervisor of home economics in the Chicago public schools, will open the first general session on Tuesday evening, at which President O. C. Carmichael, of Alabama College, will speak on "Home Economics in Higher Education," and Dr. Willis A. Sutton, superintendent of schools in Atlanta, on "The Place of Home Economics in the Educational System."

Miss Mary Anderson, of the Women's Bureau, U. S. Department of Labor, Dr. John Lovejoy Elliott, of the Hudson Guild, New York City, and Dr. Paul H. Nystrom, of Columbia University, will be the speakers at the other public meeting on Thursday evening. They plan to bring out social and economic aspects of the home and the family.

Dr. John M. Gries, director of the President's Conference on Home Building and Home Ownership; F. B. Bomberger, of the Federal Farm Board; Professor Ralph P. Bridgman, of Columbia University, and Professor John E. Anderson, of the University of Minnesota, are others whose presence on the program shows the close connection between home economics and outstanding questions of the day.

Special group meetings will provide for the interests of the various divisions of the association, such as those dealing with family relationships and economics, the house, nutrition and clothing. Other sessions will consider the problems of home-economics teachers, extension and research workers, business women and practical homemakers.

Monday, June 20, will be devoted to a conference on home economics in education by radio at which representatives of government agencies, school and college radio programs and commercial concerns will take part in the discussion. There will also be informal talks by Armstrong Perry, of the National Committee on Radio; Cline M. Koon, of the U. S. Office of Education; Mrs. Marian S. Carter, of the Columbia Broadcasting System, and Morse Salisbury, of the U. S. Department of Agriculture.

There will be the usual business sessions of the association and its council, the annual banquet on Friday evening, luncheons and dinners for special groups, trips to schools, hospitals and other places of professional interest, besides various excursions to show the visitors the attractions of Atlanta and its environs. An unusual feature will be the Wednesday evening performance of "Heaven Bound," the "modern miracle play," by the choir of the Big Bethel African Methodist Church of Atlanta.

CONFERENCES ON SECONDARY EDUCATION

There will be a Conference on Secondary Education at Teachers College, Columbia University from July 5 to 9. This conference will be addressed by authorities in the secondary school field. To it are invited junior and senior high school principals, teachers, professors of education, and other interested persons.

The program is as follows:

Tuesday Evening, 8:00 P. M., July 5.

Professor Thomas H. Briggs, Teachers College, Columbia University, "A Vision of Secondary Education." Dean William F. Russell, Teachers College, Columbia University, "As Goes Secondary Education, so Goes the Nation."

Wednesday Afternoon, 3:00 P. M., July 6.

Professor Grayson N. Kefauver, Teachers College, Columbia University, "The Organization of Secondary Education: a report from the National Survey." Dean Emeritus James E. Russell, Teachers College, Columbia University, "Vocational Education; its Relation to Secondary Education."

Wednesday Evening, 8:00 P. M., July 6.

Professor E. L. Thorndike, Teachers College, Columbia University, "Secondary School Students and Subjects." Professor Maxie N. Woodring, Teachers College, Columbia University, "The Widening Margin; the Teacher's Increasing Responsibility."

Thursday Afternoon, 3:00 P. M., July 7.

Mr. Richard Allen, assistant superintendent, Providence, R. I., "The Program of Guidance in Secondary Schools." Professor Percival M. Symonds, Teachers College, Columbia University, "Diagnosing the Personality of Youth."

Thursday Evening, 8:00 P. M., July 7.

Professor George S. Counts, Teachers College, Columbia University, "Secondary Education and the Social Problem." Professor E. K. Fretwell, subject to be announced.

Friday Afternoon, 3:00 P. M., July 8. Reports from the National Survey.

Professor A. K. Loomis, the University of Chicago, "Recent Trends in the Curricula of Secondary Schools." Professor Emery N. Ferriss, Cornell University, "Certain Major Problems of Rural Secondary Education."

Friday Evening, 8:00 P. M., July 8. Reports from the National Survey.

Professor Francis T. Spaulding, Harvard University, "The Reorganized Secondary School." Professor Leonard V. Koos, the University of Chicago, "The American Secondary School."

Saturday Evening, July 9. Place and time to be announced.

Speakers: Dean Herbert E. Hawkes, Columbia University; Professor Rexford G. Tugwell, Columbia University, and The Honorable William J. Cooper, United States Commissioner of Education.

THE ADMINISTRATION OF PRINCETON UNIVERSITY

EDWARD D. DUFFIELD, a life trustee of Princeton University and president of the Prudential Insurance Company of America, has been named acting president of Princeton University. Pending the appointment of a permanent successor to Dr. John Grier Hibben, who announced several months ago his desire to retire from the university with which he has been associated as professor and president for forty-one years. Mr. Duffield will administer the affairs of the university by a special administrative arrangement and in cooperation with Dr. Luther Pfahler Eisenhart, professor of mathematics and dean of the faculty.

Under this arrangement Mr. Duffield will continue his connection with the Prudential Insurance Company, making periodic visits to Princeton during his occupancy of the office of acting president. In the periods of his absence from the university, and in accordance with the university by-laws which provide that whenever the president of the university is absent the dean of the faculty shall perform his duties, Dean Eisenhart will be head of the university.

Dr. Hibben, who celebrated his seventy-first birthday this spring, intended to remain at Princeton until the completion of the present term. Mr. Duffield will come to the university immediately to familiarize himself with the administrative duties.

Dr. Hibben, commenting on the action taken by the board of trustees, said:

> The arrangement of the board for the administration of the university meets with my very hearty approval. I have been closely associated with Mr. Duffield and Dean Eisenhart for many years and I am confident that in their hands the university will be wisely and faithfully administered.
>
> As a life trustee Mr. Duffield has taken an active part in all of the deliberations and decisions of the board, commanding always the respect and confidence of his colleagues. He has had an extensive knowledge and an intensive interest in all Princeton affairs through his contact with the most important committees of the board, including finance, curriculum and administrative committees, and particularly through his chairmanship of the committee on undergraduate life.
>
> The whole scholastic machinery of the university has been under the immediate direction and guidance of Dean Eisenhart, and he is well equipped by knowledge and experience to continue his labors in this field. There has come to him also a wide knowledge of all phases of university life through his membership on many committees of the faculty.

Dean Eisenhart was a member of the original faculty committee which formulated the Princeton "upper-class plan of study," and has been dean since 1925.

EDUCATIONAL NOTES AND NEWS

DR. PAUL MONROE, director of the International Institute of Teachers College, Columbia University, and president of the World Federation of Education Associations, has been appointed president of Robert College and of Constantinople Woman's College, the two American educational institutions at Istanbul, Turkey. Dr. Monroe will serve as joint executive of the two schools, maintaining relations with the Turkish authorities and directing the educational policies.

Dr. Mirza Issa Khan Sadiq, who took his degree at Teachers College, Columbia University, in 1931, has been appointed president of the State Teachers College in Teheran, Persia. He began his new work in April. The whole educational system of Persia is being examined by Dr. Sadiq with a view to bettering the schools of that country.

Dr. Howard Rufus Omwake, formerly dean of Franklin and Marshall College, was installed on April 18 as president of Catawba College, a coeducational institution operated under the auspices of the Reformed Church in the United States at Salisbury, North Carolina. Dr. Charles E. Schaeffer, of Philadelphia, president of the general synod of the church, delivered an address outlining the qualifications and duties of the head of a college. In his inaugural address, President Omwake pointed out that education is at present overorganized, overstandardized and overmechanized. He advocated extensive use of the research method in college teaching, with a view to the development of independent thinking. At the seventy-ninth commencement, which was held from May 21 to 24, the Rev. Dr. Theodore F. Herman, of the Theological Seminary, at Lancaster, Pa., preached the baccalaureate sermon. Dr. Holland Holton, professor of education in Duke University, delivered the commencement address. The senior class presented Barrie's play, "The Admirable Crichton."

According to press reports James T. Jardine, of Corvallis, Oregon, is being considered for the presidency of the Massachusetts State College at Amherst to succeed Dr. Roscoe W. Thatcher, who recently resigned. Mr. Jardine was director of the Oregon Agricultural Experiment Stations from 1920 to 1924, which position he again filled after serving as inspector of the secretary's office in the U. S. Department of Agriculture in Washington and as inspector of the Agricultural Experiment Station in Alaska.

Dr. Andrew M. Soule has been reelected president of the State Agricultural College, Georgia.

Dr. Charles E. Hamilton, for the past seventeen years president of Cazenovia Seminary, New York, has been reelected by the board of trustees for a four-year term.

Professor Alfred Vivian, after completing thirty years of service in the cause of agriculture in Ohio, is resigning as dean of the College of Agriculture of Ohio State University.

Dr. Henry E. Sigerist, director of the Institute of the History of Medicine at the University of Leipzig, will succeed Dr. William H. Welch as professor of the history of medicine at the Johns Hopkins University. Dr. Welch, whose eighty-second birthday was celebrated on April 8, has become professor emeritus.

Mrs. Mary M. Fitz-Gerald, deputy superintendent of San Francisco schools since 1925, recently retired after many years of service. She began teaching in the old Mission Grammar School and later became vice-principal of the San Francisco Normal School.

Silas Gaiser, immediate past president of the Montana Education Association and superintendent of schools at Sidney, has accepted the superintendency of the Freewater and Milton, Oregon, consolidated schools.

George M. Harris, superintendent at Hardin, Montana, is resigning at the end of the year to devote his time to the National Bonds, Inc., Billings, as secretary. He has held this position nominally for the past three years. Mr. Harris has been engaged for twenty years in teaching, eleven of them being spent in Hardin as high-school principal and superintendent.

Superintendent Charles A. Powers, of Holdrege, has been elected secretary of the State Education Association of Nebraska to succeed E. M. Hosman, who recently accepted a position at the Municipal University at Omaha.

Mrs. Dorothy Canfield Fisher, Arlington, Vermont, was elected president of the American Association for Adult Education at its recent annual meeting. She succeeds Felix M. Warburg, New York. New vice-presidents chosen include Dr. William Allan Neilson, president of Smith College, and Dr. Charles A. Beard.

Superintendent J. E. Mathis, of Macon, Georgia, has been elected president of the Georgia State Education Association.

Dr. John Van Antwerp MacMurray, director of the Walter Hines Page School of International Relations at the Johns Hopkins University, and Mrs. MacMurray, will leave Baltimore for Russia on June 15.

An investigation of the problems and policies of present-day religious instruction in the educational systems of Europe, recommended by the Administrative Board of Social and Religious Work at Columbia University, will be undertaken by Chaplain Raymond C. Knox, who will sail for Great Britain shortly after commencement. Dr. Knox will remain abroad at least a year, investigating religious trends in universities of England, Scotland, Norway, Sweden, Germany, France, Switzerland, Spain and Italy. His present duties at the university will be assumed for 1932–33 by Assistant Chaplain Wendell Phillips.

A portrait of Dean G. Carl Huber by Gari Melchers was presented to the University of Michigan at ceremonies on the afternoon of May 16, with President Ruthven, Dr. Frederick Novy and Dr. Huber as the speakers. The painting was made possible by funds raised by associates and former students of Dr. Huber.

Dr. George L. Kittredge, Gurney professor of English literature at Harvard University, was entertained at luncheon by the Pilgrim Society of London on May 10.

Dean Henry M. Bates, of the University of Michigan Law School, has been honored by receiving the annual trust fund award of the California Bar Association, granted for the purpose of bringing some well-known figure in the legal world to address the annual convention of California lawyers. Previous to the convention in September, Dean Bates will address law alumni of Michigan in Washington, Oregon and California.

The degree of doctor of letters will be conferred on the occasion of the eighty-seventh commencement exercises of Knox College, Galesburg, Illinois, on Miss Louise Fitch, dean of women at Cornell University, and on Miss Caroline Palmer, a worker in religious education among young people.

Dr. Albert Bushnell Hart, Eaton professor of the science of government, emeritus, at Harvard University, presided at the George Washington Bicentennial meeting of the American Historical Association, held at the Library of Congress in Washington on May 7.

Dr. W. O. Thompson, president emeritus of the Ohio State University, will speak to the graduating classes at Utah State Agricultural College, the University of Idaho, Washington State College, the Northern Montana College at Havre and the Eastern Montana Normal School.

Brigadier General William Barclay Parsons, chairman of the board of trustees of Columbia University since 1917, who was also a trustee of the New York Public Library and of the Carnegie Institution of Washington, died on May 10, at the age of seventy-three years. General Parsons was a member of the engineering staff in charge of the construction of the Panama Canal and was the builder of the Cape Cod Canal.

The death at the age of seventy-six years is announced of Dr. Arthur W. Scott, president of the Mechanics Institute and for twenty-two years principal of the Girls High School, San Francisco.

Professor Arthur Leslie Wheeler, chairman of the department of classics at Princeton University since 1926, died on May 22, at the age of sixty years.

Dr. Albert Augustus Stanley, composer and musical director emeritus of the School of Music of the University of Michigan, died on May 19. He would have been eighty-one years old on May 25.

The sixth Conference of the International Federation of University Women is to be held in Edinburgh from July 27 to August 4. It is twelve years since this triennial conference has been held in the United Kingdom. The federation was founded in 1919, and its chief aim is the promotion of international good will.

The annual meeting of the Association of American Colleges will be held at Atlantic City, on January 12 and 13, 1933, with headquarters at the Hotel Chelsea.

Commissioners of education, or their representatives, from all the New England States were the guests of Dr. Ernest W. Butterfield, commissioner of education of Connecticut, at a conference at Hartford, Connecticut, on May 17. Following an inspection of school buildings an informal conference was held in the quarters of the State Board of Education. Among those who attended were Commissioner Bertram Packard, Maine; Commissioner James N. Pringle, New Hampshire; Commissioner F. L. Bailey, Vermont; First Assistant Commissioner Robert O. Small, Massachusetts; Commissioner Walter E. Ranger and Lucius Whipple, of Rhode Island.

MRS. JACOB H. SCHIFF has donated $250,000 to the Boy Scouts of America for the establishment of a training school for Scout leaders in memory of her son, Mortimer L. Schiff, a charter member of the National Council and elected its president a few weeks before his death last June. The gift was announced at a dinner of the organization at the Waldorf-Astoria attended by 500 delegates. The late Mr. Schiff bequeathed $100,000 to the scouts in his will. The provisions of the gift specify that $150,000 may be used to buy a suitable site and for the construction of buildings to be used as a training school and also for demonstrations of scouting. The remaining $100,000 is to be set aside as a maintenance fund.

BY the will of the late Mrs. Frances R. Briggs, New York University receives $100,000. $25,000 is left to Alfred University and $10,000 to the Child Educational Foundation. There are numerous other minor bequests.

THE Institute for Research in Social Science of the University of North Carolina, of which Dr. Howard W. Odum is director, has received from the Rockefeller Foundation an additional three-year grant of $30,000 a year, to start with the beginning of the next fiscal year, July 1. The university has also been awarded another three-year grant of $5,000 a year to assist full-ranking professors of the university in the promotion of scientific research.

THE National University of Mexico received from the Ministry of Finance on May 1 1,000,000 pesos (about $330,000 at present rates) for the construction and equipment of primary schools in the Federal District. About thirty schools will be erected. Most of them will be built in Mexico City, but some will be placed outside the city, in communities which make financial contributions.

AN Associated Press dispatch from Sofia, Bulgaria, reports that in a drastic effort to balance the budget, the government has ordered dismissal of the twenty professors, twelve honorary professors and thirty-eight assistant professors who form the theological faculty of the University of Sofia.

ACCORDING to *The New York Times,* teachers in the schools and universities in Hankow, China, are on strike because their salaries have not been paid for more than four months. Under the previous régime the educational institutions were supported with municipal funds, but last year the Nanking Government ordered that provincial taxation must support all schools. The reason assigned for not paying the teachers is that new provincial taxes which were supposed to replace former levies are producing only a very small revenue. These substitute taxes included rental taxes and large business assessments based upon working capital, and the people have flatly refused to pay them. At the suggestion of a majority of the parents the primary schools only were reopened on a temporary basis, the parents themselves paying special tuition fees. This arrangement can not last long because a vast majority of the families are too poor and because the teachers say they will again close the primary schools if all arrears in pay are not made up very soon. The teachers of the grade schools and universities refuse to resume work under the tuition fee plan until after the Provincial Government has paid them at least 25 per cent. of their overdue salaries, and a measure is now being discussed to raise the necessary money by a new "special tax" on opium.

The Christian Science Monitor reports that women teachers in England and Wales have decided to press for salaries equal to those paid to men teachers. The present scales of salaries are so framed as to give to women teachers approximately 80 per cent. of the salaries payable to men. These scales are binding for another year or so, and are due to terminate in March, 1933. Before that date the joint committee of teachers and education authorities responsible for teachers' salaries, the Burnham Committee, will undertake the task of formulating new scales. The reasons for the demand are that men and women teachers have the same qualifications and teach children up to the same standard of attainments under identical conditions. The demand for equal pay will stimulate the movement for allowances for dependents. Miss Eleanor Rathbone, member of Parliament, is pressing this policy, so that when equal pay is granted, married men with children will receive additional grants toward the additional legal and moral responsibilities which they have to shoulder. Already the London School of Economics has granted equal pay to the women and men on its staff, together with substantial allowances to married men for each child receiving education, under the age of 23. Besides the Association of Assistant Mistresses in Secondary Schools, the great organization of teachers in elementary schools, the National Union of Teachers, is also committed to equal pay for men and women; and this organization will endeavor, as one of the constituent bodies of the Burnham Committee, to bring about the achievement of that policy.

THE annual report of the Committee of University College, London, for the year ending in February, 1932, states that the number of students on the books of the college last session was 3,225. The income of the establishment account amounted to £224,278, £76,851 being provided by fees, £38,012 by income from endowments, £98,268 by the recurrent grant from the court of the university and the balance by sundry grants and donations. A further extension of the college site has been effected by the acquisition of a portion of the property immediately south of the college, known as Upper Gower-mews. It includes buildings with a floor space of more than 100,000 square feet, fitted for adaptation to the use of scientific departments. The department of zoology and comparative anatomy will, with the aid of a special grant of £30,000 made for the purpose by the court of the university, be rehoused and reequipped as speedily as possible in one section of these buildings. In close association with this, a munificent appropriation has been made by the Rockefeller Foundation of New York, amounting to £88,000, for the development of research in the department of zoology and comparative anatomy.

THE *Journal* of the American Medical Association reports that the Department of University Health, Yale University, made 5,322 routine examinations of students during the academic year 1930–1931, as compared with 5,221 the previous year, according to the annual report of its director, Dr. James C. Greenway. There were 30,973 consultations as compared with 27,710 the preceding year. For the first time all the health supervision is now carried on under one roof except hospital care, orthopedic examination of freshmen and care of medical students. There were 757 admissions to the infirmary with a total number of 2,477 infirmary days, an average stay of 3.3 days as contrasted with 3.1 the preceding year. The increase was due to a threatened epidemic of influenza. This was the first year that the division of student mental hygiene had functioned in close and continuous association with the department. Out of 209 new patients who sought the division, 71 were voluntary; 46 became patients at the time of the routine health service contact, while an additional 17 were referred either by other patients or by friends. These figures indicate that out of 209 patients 134, or 64 per cent., came to the division as the result of direct contact between the division and the student, no other referring agency coming in between. In the freshman class, 568 men were assigned to the corrective group; of these, 66 were excused. No deaths occurred in the student body during the college year reported.

DISCUSSION

THE GLORY OF THE SELF-MADE MAN

AT the beginning of every academic year prospective students of the state colleges and universities throughout the country who hope to work their way through school are being warned against enrolling unless they have sufficient funds to tide them over emergencies of unemployment. Difficulty in finding work during the past year has forced many students to withdraw from school. Perhaps this year's withdrawals will exceed those of previous years by a goodly number, or they may be fewer than those of the preceding year because of President Hoover's student employment plan. Time, however, will soon reveal the actuality.

The story is not alone that of state-supported institutions; it applies without doubt, to privately supported colleges and universities as well. Increased enrolment has flooded the colleges with more employment-seeking students than there are jobs available. The inevitable result is that many would-be students, some worthy, some not, are denied the educational opportunities they seek.

Intelligent men and women are aware of the fact that the working student has been made the subject of over-sentimentalization. It has become a part of the great American tradition to pay homage to the self-made man—the boy who rises to the top despite numerous handicaps. He is pursued for interviews, he is praised, he is revered and he is cheered. And that is all that is ever done for him. His admirers will tell you that he will get more out of college than the boy who lives on the family pay-check, and if you suggest to them that they lighten his burden of work. they will tell you that such a course would rob the boy of a great educational advantage. So the working student works perhaps all night, sleeps half of the day, goes to classes the other half, and with a dead-tired brain studies in between. Think of the glory that is his!

All honor, indeed, to the ambitious student who has complete confidence in his ability and who, with unconquerable will power and unyielding determination, brushes aside every obstacle and wins for himself a place in society (which he so earnestly desires and so rightfully deserves) by working his way through the university. He probably is more serious in purpose than many of his fellow-students, but does that mean that he is getting all that he should or all that he deserves out of his university career? Alas, no!

However, it should not be implied that every working student is serious minded or even deserving of a college education. Many, like numerous non-workers, would do better by never going to college. If relieved from the task of bread-winning, they would probably spend the time elsewhere than in the pursuit of learning. But the boy who has a purpose (and there are many in this category) and who wants to learn, knows there is nothing but hokum in the glorification of the self-made man.

The only way to learn is by the single-hearted pursuit of learning. The working student may be better able to appreciate what opportunity he has, he may make the most of the time at his disposal, but can he serve two masters at once and do a good job for both? It is possible for the working student to have a singleness of purpose? No. His extra endeavor, in spite of its logical sobering influence, robs him of the full benefits of a university course. Should attendance at classes and preparation of assignments be thought of as real education? Does he not need some leisure time in which to read more than the assignment, to digest what has been read, to meditate, to weigh important questions, and to play?

The admiring citizens could do more for the deserving student by making it unnecessary for him to divide his attention between seeking physical sustenance and mental development than by honoring his determination.

President Hoover's student employment plan (though not new to many college and university administrative bodies) is a healthy sign of the approaching dawn of a new educational era in America, but it will not make the task of the working student any easier. He will continue earning his bread and butter at the expense of his education.

Perhaps an educational system patterned after that of Czecho-Slovakia, which subsidizes worthy students who need financial support, may solve the problem. Czecho-Slovakia has a universal income tax system which makes available to the educational authorities information concerning the economic status of each family. Fees and scholarships are regulated on the basis of the family's financial standing. Without any ado, the student in the junior college or in the University finds his fees already determined. If his family is poor, he is supported by the state and is left free to devote himself to the task of getting an education—a task that demands more time and energy than one can ever give to it.

This is part of an ideal of secondary education for all. It applies to all students in the secondary schools and universities. It does not have any relation to mass education. The strenuous educational program in the secondary schools means that only the worthy can survive the junior colleges, and only the worthy are subsidized, therefore, where support is necessary.

Education for all is no less an ideal in America than it is in Czecho-Slovakia. America is proportionately far wealthier than this progressive European state. Yet, where Czecho-Slovakia proceeds to make its ideal more than a topic of boast, America chooses to throw all her youth into the educational melting-pot and let them get along as best they can. Under such circumstances subsidization would take on gigantic aspects. Yet educational subsidies might be of more ultimate good to the nation than ship subsidies and similar forms of paternalism.

The present American attitude of penuriousness toward the colleges and universities precludes any likelihood of the adoption of student subsidy programs. The "Everybody Welcome" and "Bigger and Bigger" manias are largely responsible for this. Surely there is no reason why the goats should be sent along with the sheep. But has there ever been a time when the citizenry showed itself not only willing but desirous of assuming such a burden? Oh, no. The glory would fall away, and the sawdust "self-made man" tradition would die if the working student wearied of his job; and, besides, it is so much more pleasant to talk of the sterling qualities of the man than to give him the assistance these qualities merit.

CHRIST LOUKAS

SYRACUSE UNIVERSITY

THE OTHER SIDE

UNQUESTIONABLY our teaching of history has been too chauvinistic. In too many cases the pupil hears only one side of an international or sectional controversy. How many teachers of American history present the British side of the causes of the Revolutionary War, or the Tory side of the Loyalists in that struggle, or the Mexican view-point of our struggle with her, or the Confederate reasons for the Civil War? The philosophy of modern education is to teach pupils to weigh evidence and draw conclusions based on adequate data. Can pupils form proper conclusions if they hear only the plaintiff?

We have read six text-books of history which are written from the British point of view, and used in the public schools of Canada. We have been studying American history several years. We have taught it in elementary and high schools, and we believe that the English and Canadians are fairer in their histories than we Americans are.

Some years ago a British ambassador to America said: "Englishmen now recognize that in the Revolution you were fighting their battles." Green, the great English historian, said: "The shame of the darkest hour of England's history lies wholly at his (George III) door. . . . I rejoice that America has resisted." —*Pitt.*

We shall now quote from "A New History of Great Britain and Canada," by W. Stewart Wallace. "British army officers, like Braddock, were at small pains to conceal their contempt for even colonials like George Washington." In speaking of the Fenian troubles Wallace says: "But with these episodes the government of the United States had no connection." "Among them (the American patriots) towers preeminent the figure of Washington, whose clear sincerity, dauntless courage, and self-sacrificing devotion to his country command the reverence of friend and foe alike."—*Roberts,* in *"A History of Canada."* Surely no American could pay a greater tribute to the immortal Washington. "The war, made possible by the selfish stupidity of Parliament."—*Roberts.* In the Western Canada Series (of history texts for public schools) George Washington is referred to as wise and moderate.

The Tories or Loyalists have usually been subject to obloquy, but after we read pages 64 to 73 of "A New History of Great Britain and

Canada," by Wallace, we find that thousands of them endured untold hardships for conscience' sake. Teachers of American history should read "An United Empire Loyalist" in a delightful little book, "With Sword and Trowel." The "other side" of the Tories will also be found in "A New History of Great Britain and Canada" and in chapter xv of "A History of Canada" by Roberts.

American children are taught that after the Revolutionary War the British refused to give up some of the western forts. A British historian says that these forts were held because we Americans failed to fulfil our treaty obligations toward the loyalists.

It is especially incumbent upon every fair-minded teacher of American history to study the "other side" before teaching anything about the causes of the War of 1812. The writer was taught that this war was caused by the impressment of American sailors into the British Navy. So far so good. This is the truth, but it is not the whole truth. The British claim that their sailors were deserting to American ships. "American captains had acquired a habit of seducing the British man-of-war's men from their duty by the offer of higher wages and easier discipline. Angered by this conduct, the British government ordered its captains to seize any deserters found on American ships, and to search all ships suspected of harbouring deserters." A British historian claims that the real purpose of the War of 1812 was to broaden the borders of the Union by annexing Canada. Americans who had lately crossed the border in search of better lands wished nothing better than annexation. They became so objectionable that Brock was compelled to dissolve the legislature of Upper Canada and proclaim martial law. In the later stages of the war there were in the American army two battalions of Canadian Volunteers; and at least one member of the legislature of Upper Canada died fighting for the Stars and Stripes. If the War of 1812 was caused by the British attacks on American commerce, why were the maritime interests, that is to say, New England, openly hostile to the war? And why was the war started after the British orders-in-council were repealed? And why was the war declared against England when 389 American ships had been seized by English ships and French seizures of American ships totaled 558? Why did the treaty of peace ending the war say nothing about impressment?

We are also taught that the English stirred up the Northwest Indians against the Americans. Mr. Louis M. Hacker, a graduate of Columbia University, writing in the November, 1931, *American Mercury,* says, "What unrest there existed among the Indians was due to the vicious official policy of the American government." Mr. Hacker also says that we Americans were jealous of English supremacy in the fur trade, and that this supremacy was achieved because the English paid fairly for their pelts while we Americans swindled the Indians.

History seems to support the British contention that the War of 1812 was fought for the purpose of annexing Canada. Calhoun predicted that our forces would have Canada in four weeks. Another young American patriot declared with enthusiasm: "The northern provinces of Britain are to us great and valuable objects.—To me, sir, it appears that the author of Nature has marked our limits in the south by the Gulf of Mexico and on the north by the regions of eternal frost." John Randolph said: "Sir, if you go to war it will not be for the protection of, or defence of your maritime rights.—Agrarian cupidity, not maritime rights, urges the war. Ever since the report of the committee on foreign relations came into the House, we have heard but one word—Canada! Canada! Canada!" Every teacher and student of the War of 1812 should read Mr. Hacker's article, "Mr. Madison's War" in the November, 1931, *American Mercury.*

The writer is a natural-born American. His forebears have lived in America for several generations. He holds no brief for England or any other foreign nation. His only motive in preparing this article is to be fair and to see the "other side." American teachers and American children should hear the defendant as well as the plaintiff. When teaching about our foreign wars, wouldn't it be fine to have some of the students represent the "other side" and have access to books written from our antagonist's view-point? Let us have the evidence from both sides and then weigh, sift and evaluate.

Teachers can make a good beginning by reading such books as: "A History of Canada," by Roberts, " A New History of Great Britain and Canada," "With Sword and Trowel" and "A First Book of Canadian History," all by Wallace. It is easy for American schools to secure these books.

Albert Earley
Department of Public Instruction,
Georgetown, Delaware

SPECIAL CORRESPONDENCE

THE SUMMER QUARTER OF STANFORD UNIVERSITY

Following the trend of recent years in the summer quarter of Stanford University, the session this year, June 23 to September 3, provides an especially wide variety of subjects for advanced and graduate students, while provision for undergraduates, including those who begin their university work at this time, has been extended, according to the announcement of Professor Eliot G. Mears, director, who has just completed arrangements for the summer.

For a number of years there has been increasing emphasis on the work of graduate students at Stanford and this has been reflected in the summer quarter and even accentuated by the fact that so large a proportion of the students at that time are engaged in specialized work in particular fields. At the same time an increasing number of regular Stanford students continue their work through the summer in order to shorten the period required for obtaining their degrees. The number of these regular students this year, it is thought, may be even larger than ordinarily on account of the difficulty of obtaining "summer jobs" with income to help to pay expenses in the following quarter.

It is problematical, in Director Mears's opinion, whether the Olympic Games at Los Angeles during the summer, along with the exceptionally large number of national conventions that will be held in California and low transportation rates, will operate to increase or decrease attendance at the Stanford summer quarter. Stanford has always had a considerable number of summer students attracted by the fact that the upper Santa Clara valley, in which the university is situated, has a cool summer climate, and that San Francisco and many other points of interest are within easy distance by automobile, train or auto stage. Trips for parties are organized to the historic Monterey peninsula, the redwood country, the top of Mt. Hamilton, with its great telescope, and other near-by localities.

Two track and field events of national interest will take place in the immediate vicinity of Stanford, the I. C. A. A. A. A. track and field meet at the University of California, July 1 and 2, and the final try-outs for candidates for the American Olympic Games team, which will be held in the Stanford stadium, July 14 and 15.

The summer quarter at Stanford is of the same length and on precisely the same academic plane as the other three quarters, but at the same time the somewhat different character of its student body and the opportunity to bring in a large number of scholars from other American and European universities to the summer quarter faculty gives the summer term a noticeably different complexion from that of the others.

The School of Education and the School of Law make definite changes in their arrangements for the summer quarter. The School of Education on account of the large number of teachers who attend during the summer and who must return to their schools before the end of the regular session abbreviates the session to an eight-week term, with classes held more frequently than the normal and limiting the number of courses that may be taken. Practically the entire faculty of the School of Education is on duty in the summer and is supplemented by about an equal number of visiting educators. This summer especial attention is being paid to courses of value to college educators and administrators.

The Law School arranges its summer work, with classes meeting twice a day, into two halves, the first ending July 30, enabling students to obtain complete courses in either half if they can not attend the full quarter. It draws a larger number of practicing lawyers who take this opportunity to develop their knowledge in advanced law courses. It also provides courses for those beginning their law studies, so arranged that they can be matched into the regular curriculum of the other quarters, enabling students studying for degrees to save time.

E. W. S.

THE SCHOOL OF EDUCATION OF THE UNIVERSITY OF PITTSBURGH

BEGINNING in September, 1932, the School of Education of the University of Pittsburgh will be organized as an upper division, professional school, admitting students from a pre-education curriculum in the college, at the end of the sophomore year. Announcement concerning this plan was made recently through the offices of the dean, following approval by the Board of Trustees.

Admission to the School of Education will be based upon a number of criteria, some of which have not been definitely determined. As these criteria will not have to be applied until September, 1934, the faculty will have plenty of time for experimentation.

Tentative bases for the admission of students to the school from the pre-education curriculum have been indicated by a committee of the faculty charged with the details of the plan. These are: (1) Better than average in scholarship, (2) a superior rating in the subject of a student's major interest, (3) a physical examination, (4) demonstrated ability in a try-out course, (5) intelligence, aptitude and English tests, (6) personal interview.

Students now registered in the School of Education will be permitted to continue and will be graduated under the regulations existing prior to the adoption of the new plan. Freshmen, entering in September, 1932, who desire to prepare for the teaching profession will be registered in the college in a specially designated pre-education curriculum.

The pre-education curriculum, which will be administered with the advice of the faculty of the School of Education, will be in conformity with the general plan of teacher preparation, but will enable a student, who fails to satisfy admission requirements to the School of Education by the end of the sophomore year, to continue to pursue study in the College of Liberal Arts and perhaps to receive a degree from that school.

Students registered in the college, who heretofore have been permitted to remain in the college while preparing themselves for certification to teach, will be required to apply for admission to the School of Education exactly on the same basis as will those registered in the pre-education curriculum.

According to Acting Dean L. P. Sieg, the plan of deferred admission to the School of Education is not intended to decrease the number of teachers, but to make possible better teachers.

"It is the desire of the faculty and administrative officers of the School of Education of the University of Pittsburgh," said Dr. Sieg, "to turn out as a teacher an individual who is not only well prepared, but who also has those qualities of personality and character that should go into the making of a good teacher. If all the students who are admitted to the pre-education curriculum in the college attain the standards set up for admission to the School of Education, they will all be admitted. Our goal is better preparation, not elimination. Every student has a right to a certain type of instruction; our desire is to try to determine the place into which a student will fit best."

The present curriculum will be revised so that the professional education courses may be given in the School of Education during the last two years. In addition to pursuing the necessary courses in education, students will continue study in the academic subjects to round out the requirements of a sound program.

Only one professional education course will be scheduled for students in the pre-education curriculum. This will come during the second semester of the sophomore year and will be in the nature of a demonstration or try-out course. It is planned to register students in small sections and give them an opportunity to show before the group their ability in organization and presentation of material; to demonstrate their "teaching personality," and to show their voice, mannerisms and other characteristics as they address the class. With the exception of this try-out course, the first two years of study will be entirely of an academic character. The same number of hours will be required for graduation as under the former plan.

QUOTATIONS

THE DECLINE IN THE PRESTIGE OF THE TEACHER

THOSE of us who went to college not later than the last decade of the nineteenth century remember many of our teachers with respect and affection. They were generally gentlemen familiar with the amenities of life and they were students of mellow and generous scholarship. Narrow specialists had just begun to enter the ranks of the teachers but the respected teacher was, as a rule, the all-round scholar. The professor of history knew a good deal of philosophy: the professor of philosophy knew much of literature: the professor of literature was no stranger to economics. With the unprecedented growth of colleges and universities, new types of administrators of ability became necessary. But in most cases the glory of the institution was still the inspiring teacher who roused in young men and women an abiding desire to engage in intellectual pursuits.

At the turn of the century the activity so beloved of Abraham Flexner was exalted to primacy in our institutions of higher education—research. A growing number of narrow specialists in all branches of scholarship were thrust upon the world, thoroughly grounded in a knowledge of their special fields, slightly familiar with cognate fields, generally ignorant of the facts and movements of more remote fields. Society was provided with excellent scholars in physics and chemistry, woefully ignorant of the social implications of the discoveries that were made in their fields of work, and with scholars in economics and politics too often unaware of these discoveries themselves. The scholar of a previous day who had touched life and its forces at many points, was eclipsed.

The label which seemed to give assurance that the owner possessed research ability was the degree of doctor of philosophy. It gave entrance to college teaching. Practically no position was obtainable without it. Personality, even teaching experience, could not compete with it. The degree gradually became commercialized so that the graduate schools of our universities were crowded with young men and women whose primary purpose was not excellence in research but the obtaining of the doctor's degree as the necessary step in securing a position as a college teacher. Once in such a position, promotion came not as the result of inspiring teaching but of being "productive." Productive of what? Of men or even of students? No! Of books, monographs, theses. For that, dullness in teaching was often tolerated.

Nor was this all. With the passage of time institutions of higher education became more and more crowded with students. New departments were created. Deans, directors and administrators of all kinds were needed. Where were they to be found? Among the teaching staff. The most successful teachers were induced to leave their teaching to accept administrative positions because those positions brought advancement in rank and pay. Inspiring teaching *per se* became less and less the path to preferment within the college. Outside the college it received little recognition. The great foundations were ready at all times to help the proved research scholar but an inspiring teacher, they asserted, did not fall "within the domain of our activities."

Research is an absolute essential to the advancement of knowledge and one can only rejoice that the research scholar can now be relieved of other work in order to devote himself solely to investigation in his chosen field. Moreover, research is a necessary part of the teaching process. The two can not be wholly divorced and the teacher who does not engage in any research is in danger of becoming rusty in his subject and of losing the power of wisely guiding his students in their work. But it is nevertheless true that no vocation has received such lip service as that of the teacher. Orators at commencement and authors of educational volumes emphasize his preeminence. He is referred to as the very core of the school or college. It is to him that we look to inspire the students with fine ideals of life and to stimulate in them an admiration for things intellectual. His reward, however, is to be in the consciousness of work well done. One is reminded of Milton, the most praised and least read of our poets.

In France, except under unusual circumstances, a man can not become a university professor unless he has taught at least two years in a lycée. He must also have his doctorat d'état, which is conferred after years of careful investigation in his field. The two vital factors in effective college and university teaching, skill in research and ability to teach, are combined in him and give the inspiring teacher promise of promotion. A similar situation exists in Germany. To have studied under Oncken, Rickert, Friedländer, Planck or Strygowski meant primarily to have listened to an inspiring teacher. The changed economic situation which has prevailed there since the war has made the life of the teacher difficult indeed but the admiration which has always been extended to him when he has been recognized as an inspiration to his students, survives in full force.—STEPHEN P. DUGGAN, in the *News Bulletin of the Institute of International Education.*

SOCIETIES AND MEETINGS

THE CONFERENCE ON HIGHER EDUCATION AT THE UNIVERSITY OF KENTUCKY

UNDER the joint auspices of the U. S. Office of Education and the University of Kentucky, a conference on educational research in the college field was held at the university on May 7.

President Frank L. McVey, of the University of Kentucky, presided at the two general sessions. Dr. Fred J. Kelly, chief of the Division of Colleges and Professional Schools of the U. S. Office of Education, was present and added much to the worth-whileness of the occasion by his address on the status of research in higher education and by his participation in the discussions. Professor Herbert A. Toops, of the Ohio State University, presented in a clear and interesting way the cooperative intelligence testing and the guidance and research program of the Ohio colleges and secondary schools. This was especially valuable to the Kentucky college men for the reason that they, through the Association of Kentucky Colleges, have entered upon a similar program Professor J. E. Winter, of the West Virginia University, also made an important contribution to the success of the conference by his report of his research on the effect on scholarship of training in how to study.

In addition to the papers of the out-of-state visitors reports on research were made by Professor E. J. Asher, of the University of Kentucky, on the use of tests at the University of Kentucky for sectioning of classes and advising of students; by Dean W. B. Hughes, of Asbury College, on the relation between occupations of parents and student scholarship; by Professor C. C. Ross, of the University of Kentucky, on the influence on the student's achievement of a knowledge of his progress; by Mr. John McQuitty, assistant registrar at the University of Florida, on the scholarship of students transferring to the University of Kentucky compared with their previous records and with their fellow students; by Professor L. P. Jones, of the Western Kentucky State Teachers' College, on large and small classes; and by Miss Alice Keys, of the University of Kentucky, on the relation of student load to scholarship, intelligence and outside activities.

During the noon hour a conference was held under the direction of Professor Jesse E. Adams, of the University of Kentucky, chairman of the State Associations' Committee on Educational Research in the College Field. Valuable suggestions emerged from this for the guidance of the committee. At six o'clock a dinner was given for the visiting speakers, at which time the discussions were continued.

Throughout the program opportunity was given for questions and discussions, the attempt being made to keep before the conference matters of validity of techniques and significance of the results attained. The conference was noteworthy because of this emphasis on the application of research and scientific ideals to the problems of higher education. It was felt that such a meeting would result in the improvement of the techniques of those already engaged in such research and would lead to the active, interested participation in such an attack on educational problems by other teachers not connected with departments or colleges of education.

About one hundred and twenty-five attended the conference, and almost every college and university of the state was represented.

PAUL P. BOYD

UNIVERSITY OF KENTUCKY

SPECIAL ARTICLES

WHAT IS THE PER CAPITA COST OF EDUCATING TEACHERS IN THE TEACHER-TRAINING INSTITUTIONS OF THE UNITED STATES?

THE emergence of teacher-training institutions has been rather sudden as the history of educational institutions in Europe, Asia and America goes. As separate and distinct institutions, set apart specifically for the training of teachers, such schools have not been in existence more than one hundred years. But the recent development of the four-year-curriculum type of degree-granting institutions for the training of teachers, known as the teachers college, has been phenomenal and has a brief history extending no farther back than the world war. Although teachers colleges are having phenomenal growth, they have scarcely found a place for themselves in the hierarchy of higher institutions of learning.

This sudden development and the rather false conceptions of teacher-training in our early normal schools have led some to think of the training obtained in teachers colleges as of a mushroom type of growth and therefore of cheap and inferior kind. Without doubt it is financially cheap, but not necessarily of an inferior quality. Its cheapness will become evident by a study of the following tables.

There have been several studies within the last half-dozen years to determine the cost of education of teachers in professional schools set aside solely for teacher-training purposes. The most recent of these studies is that of Dr. Herman J. Magee in a doctorial dissertation (No. 489) which was printed by the Bureau of Publications of Teachers College, Columbia University, in the late autumn of 1931, entitled "Unit Costs of Salaries in Teachers Colleges and Normal Schools." Dr. Hamilton, in 1925, also contributed to the determination of student costs in his dissertation, "The Fiscal Support of State Teachers Colleges." In addition to these two important studies, the Bureau of Education, Washington, D. C., and the Research Division of the National Education Association have increased our knowledge of the subject. But Dr. Magee has developed a rather elaborate technique for per capita cost determination and his contribution is the most thorough and important.

TABLE I
PER CAPITA COST BASED ON GENERAL RUNNING EXPENSE

Dollars	
0– 50	0
51– 100	1
101– 150	7
151– 200	16
201– 250	21
251– 300	28
301– 350	22
351– 400	15
401– 450	3
451– 500	7
501– 550	0
551– 600	1
601– 650	1
651– 700	0
701– 750	1
751– 800	1
801– 850	1
851– 900	0
901– 950	0
951–1000	0
1001–1050	0
1051–1100	1
Total	126

Mean—$303.00

TABLE II
PER CAPITA COST BASED ON CAPITAL OUTLAY

Dollars	
0– 200	3
201– 400	5
401– 600	7
601– 800	18
801–1000	18
1001–1200	12
1201–1400	10
1401–1600	15
1601–1800	8
1801–2000	8
2001–2200	7
2201–2400	2
2401–2600	1
2601–2800	0
2801–3000	1
3001–3200	2
3201–3400	1
3401–3600	2
3601–3800	0
3801–4000	0
4001–4200	1
4201–4400	1
4401–4600	0
Total	122

Mean—$1,321

TABLE III
PER CAPITA COST BASED ON SALARIES

Dollars	
0– 50	1
51–100	7
101–150	24
151–200	36
201–250	32
251–300	17
301–350	4
351–400	0
401–450	1
451–500	0
501–550	1
551–600	1
601–650	0
701–750	0
751–800	0
801–850	0
851–900	0
901–950	1
Total	125

Mean—$203.00

TABLE IV
PER CENT. TUITION IS OF TOTAL MONEY SPENT

Per cent.	
0– 5	32
6– 10	24
11– 15	19
16– 20	17
21– 25	16
26– 30	4
31– 35	3
36– 40	2
41– 45	2
46– 50	0
51– 55	0
56– 60	0
61– 65	0
66– 70	0
71– 75	0
76– 80	1
81– 85	1
86– 90	0
91– 95	1
96–100	1
Total	123

Mean—16 per cent.

In this study a blank was sent to each member institution of the American Association of Teachers Colleges to secure data on the per capita outlay of educating teachers in teachers colleges, to determine the percentage of this per capita cost which goes to salaries, and also to determine the percentage which is paid for by students' tuition and fees, etc.

The tables are so numerous and lengthy that we are not including many of them in this article. However, summarizing them, we find the average winter enrolment in institutions to be 776; the average summer enrolment to be 890.62 (the average length of the summer terms being 9.15 weeks). On the average, it was found, each state spends $262,112.45 as a capital investment in teacher training.

TABLE V
TOTAL ENROLMENT ON BASIS OF NINE MONTHS (36 WEEKS)

0– 200	3
201– 400	17
401– 600	25
601– 800	18
801–1000	12
1001–1200	13
1201–1400	13
1401–1600	7
1601–1800	4
1801–2000	4
2001–2200	2
2201–2400	1
2401–2600	3
2601–2800	2
2801–3000	1
3001–3200	2
3201–3400	0
Total	127

Mean—1007

TABLE VI
PER CENT. SALARY IS OF TOTAL RUNNING EXPENSE

Per cent.	
30– 35	0
36– 40	2
41– 45	5
46– 50	4
51– 55	10
56– 60	10
61– 65	12
66– 70	15
71– 75	27
76– 80	21
81– 85	8
86– 90	7
91– 95	3
96–100	0
Total	124

Mean—60.07 per cent.

CONCLUSIONS

Data in some of the above tables were correlated in order to see: (1) whether there was any relationship existing between the size of the enrolment and the per capita cost; and (2) whether there was any relationship existing between the capital investment which the state is making per student and the size of the enrolment. The correlation between the per capita cost based on general running expense and the size of the enrolment gave a negative correlation –.307 (P.E. .055). This, interpreted, indicates that as the enrolment increases, there is a slight tendency toward a lower per capita cost; since, however, the correlation is so small, it is not significant and we are justified in saying that there is little, if any, relationship between the size of the student body and the per capita cost.

Table II, when correlated with the enrolment, gave a negative correlation of .296 (P.E. .056). This means that there is a tendency toward a lower per capita capital investment as the enrolment increases; but since this correlation is small it is also of little or no significance.

Another bit of supporting evidence to these correlations is that obtained when the money received for running expense was correlated with the enrolment. This gave a Pearson r of plus .7265 (P.E. .03). This confirms the above statement that there is no necessary relation between the per capita cost and the enrolment, which may be explained by saying that as the enrolment increases, the running expense increases. We may say, therefore, that the number of students in the school has little to do with the actual cost per student. Roughly speaking, then, a college of two hundred enrolment would cost little, if any, more per capita than a school of two thousand enrolment. If, indeed, there should be a slight difference, one may well argue that smaller groups of students get better attention through closer supervision.

While the task assigned in this report does not concern the per capita cost of university students, it is thought proper to list data from studies concerning unit costs in universities. The following facts are taken from certain tables in Chapter 2 of Hamilton's study "Fiscal Support of State Teachers Colleges":

The median per capita cost in teachers colleges, exclusive of capital outlay, for the decade 1913–1923, increased from a median per capita of $162.50 in 1913–1914 to a median per capita cost of $239.59 in 1922–1923. During the same period for universities and agricultural colleges, it showed a median cost of $412.50. The table on page 750 will present the matter in more concise form:

The low cost of education of teachers as compared with unit costs in universities is probably due at least to two factors:

(1) The hostility to the movement of establishing teachers colleges with degree-granting

Universities	Cost per student 1922–1923
Illinois	$506.01
Minnesota	625.13
Washington	232.77
Colorado	383.01
Kansas	351.14
Iowa	399.55
Michigan	525.19
West Virginia	578.28
Missouri	285.04
Agricultural Colleges	
Colorado	$491.22
Kansas	657.46
Iowa	....
Michigan	764.98
Massachusetts	1,267.20
Median	$525.00

privileges. This hostility often shows itself among some of the older and traditionally accepted liberal arts colleges and universities. These have had a great pull on the purse strings of legislative bodies and wealthy donors who have contributed to the support of the older established institutions. This preference has probably been based upon the tendency to the traditional types of liberal arts education which has always held that a knowledge of content is sufficient preparation for teaching, at the same time often belittling the importance of professional training for teaching. Wealthy donors to cultural education and legislators have doubtless reflected this attitude of mind which places a higher value on the knowledge of the classics than it does upon professional training.

(2) The low cost in teachers colleges, for the last ten years at least, is probably due to the fact that those responsible for the organization and development of teachers colleges have had more thorough training in educational administration and finance and have in many cases been able to apply a strict economy both in organization and in the expenditure of money when developing teacher-training work around a professional ideal.

It seems quite evident when all the facts are in that in our American society teachers colleges are ugly ducklings when financial support and general prejudices of the work these institutions do are considered.

To state our conclusions more specifically:

(1) There is no significant relationship between the size of the school and the student per capita cost.

(2) Granting faculties equal in training, it is considerably cheaper for the state to maintain teachers colleges than universities

(3) According to Magee's study of unit cost of salaries in teachers colleges, there is a direct relationship between student cost and number of curricula offered.

BIBLIOGRAPHY

In addition to data obtained from the blanks sent out specifically for this study, the following bibliography has been consulted:

"Unit Costs of Higher Education," American Council on Education, Macmillan Company, 1924 and 1925.

"Statistics of Universities, Colleges and Professional Schools: 1927–28," U. S. Dept. of Interior, Office of Education Bulletin No. 38, 1929.

"Publicly Supported Higher Education, 1929," State Survey Commission, State of Missouri.

"Statistics of Teachers Colleges and Normal Schools, 1927–28," U. S. Dept. of Interior, Bureau of Education Bulletin No. 14.

"Statistical Circular No. 9," Department of Interior, Bureau of Education, July, 1927.

"Biennial Survey of Education, 1926–1928," U. S. Dept. of Interior, Bulletin No. 16, 1930.

A. O. BOWDEN,
President

NEW MEXICO STATE TEACHERS COLLEGE

NEW BOOKS IN EDUCATION

HARDING, T. SWANN. *The Joy of Ignorance.* Pp. 369. Godwin. $3.00.

HAUCK, ARTHUR A. *Some Educational Factors Affecting the Relations between Canada and the United States.* Pp. 100. Author.

SALMON, DAVID, editor. *The Practical Parts of Lancaster's Improvements and Bell's Experiment.* Pp. li + 112. Cambridge University Press, Macmillan. $2.00.

UNITED STATES OFFICE OF EDUCATION. *Report of the Youngstown School Survey.* Pp. 230. Youngstown (Ohio) Chamber of Commerce. $2.00.

WILKINS, ERNEST H. *The College and Society.* Pp. xi + 173. Century. $1.75.

WOOD, BEN D. and FRANK N. FREEMAN. *An Experimental Study of the Educational Influences of the Typewriter in the Elementary School Classroom.* Pp. ix + 214. Illustrated. Macmillan. $2.00.

SCHOOL AND SOCIETY
EDITED BY J. McKEEN CATTELL
WITH WHICH IS COMBINED THE
EDUCATIONAL REVIEW
EDITED BY WILLIAM McANDREW

Volume 35 SATURDAY, JUNE 4, 1932 Number 910

THE LIBERAL ARTS COLLEGE AND THE TECHNIQUE OF BUSINESS AND PROFESSIONAL LIFE

By Dr. J. EDGAR PARK
PRESIDENT OF WHEATON COLLEGE, NORTON, MASSACHUSETTS

THE human organism is a very complicated machine. The modern automobile is a recently created simplicity compared with the intricate mechanism which goes to make up the average specimen of the human race.

There is also this difference. It is perfectly clear what an automobile was made for. It is rather hard to figure out why the average member of the human race was manufactured. Yet we keep on being made. And in spite of our naïve modernity there are very few of us who can claim that we exist because two people arranged to bring us into being for a clearly defined purpose. We all of us have occurred either accidentally or as by-products, or at the best because two people were so pleased with themselves that they thought it would be "cute" to have us in their home to call their own. However we got here and with what idea or lack of idea we were conceived, most of us would admit that we are more or less here. And being most of us past the "cute" stage we are left to discover what we are here for.

Simply to exist, make a living, and produce or care for other productions of our careless race, does not seem to be a satisfactory reason for continuing to exist. The end of the machine is a healthy life with as few knocks and grinds and squeaks as possible spent in producing the definite thing for which the machine was made. Its existence is justified when the goods expected fall into the hopper end of the machine. This is easy because as far as we know its insides are all outsides. It has no inner life. It is simply an outside for some one else's inside to use. A human being, on the contrary, whose life is summed up in the fact that he is used by some one else to produce certain material goods or results is a failure. An efficient human machine is simply a stop gap till some one can take half a day off to invent a real machine to take his place. Human life is judged by its fruits but not by the market value of its fruits.

Now life has become so specialized and mechanized that if you do not become somebody before you are moulded and slipped into the machine as a cog-wheel, the chances are you will never be anything but a cog-wheel. The qualities needed for commercial or professional success are not in themselves the ingredients of a satisfactory life.

Mere work, in spite of all the praise which has been lavished upon it, is an opiate only, unless it can be viewed objectively and humorously as a means to further ends.

Few people are quite sure what the end of human life really is. I seem to have some faint impression of the general idea underlying the experiment of which we are a part—when for instance out for a walk in the woods with a friendly dog, or gradually getting to understand one of Botticelli's pictures, or listening to Bach, or reading Chaucer or Goethe, or after a real evening of companionship with friends. At such times I am inclined to think that the end of the human machine is to grow, continually enlarging the inner temple of the mind. Be this as it may—it is generally true that if you do not start doing this when you are young, your insides set and you become finished into a machine.

Now the qualities which go to make a successful machine—regularity, accuracy, dependability, uniformity, do not do anything to improve the machine but only help to keep it going and wear it out.

Every one admits these days that the social machine of which we are a part needs improvement. The mere shooting out into the machine of more cog-wheels to take the place of those worn out will do nothing much to change the operation and intent of the machine.

The commercial, professional, social and political worlds need for their direction other qualities than these which produce at present material success in them.

Young people must be caught before they are wholly occupied in gaining material success, their attention must be diverted from the mere task of making a living, they must be given a glimpse of the fun of achieving humanity for themselves if the social organism is to be improved by them.

Such defects as narrowness of perception, the one-track mind which is such an obstacle to real progress must be cured by absorption in abstract scientific and mathematical problems which demand that one see not merely with snap vision but all around the problem on its many sides. They should gain the power of becoming at home in regions strange to them, of finding themselves by innate common sense where they have no map, through experience gained in cognate fields. Such aptitude as comes to one who has submitted to examinations not in courses but in subjects.

They must have learned by which end to pick up a new problem with hope of its ultimate solution. They must gain some dim idea of what they are really after in life, and develop if possible something of creative imagination on the foundation of ordered fact.

The aim of the liberal arts college is to bring young people into touch with the best and happiest moments of the best and happiest minds, and so stimulate them to the enlargement of their own minds and hearts, to provide incitement to thinking which is the difficult process of inner enlargement of being, to introduce them to study loved for its own sake.

Such people are better prepared than others to master the technique of a business or a profession. A love for Euripides and admiration for Aristophanes will save the politician from much claptrap and from endeavoring to repeat endlessly the mistakes of the past. A knowledge of the life of the great women of the Renaissance in Italy will prevent the teacher from thinking meanly of the capabilities of women. Some understanding of Rembrandt is of the utmost importance to the commercial photographer, and a passion for the English literature or music of the eighteenth century will give form and distinction to any business one can mention.

Medicine, law, teaching—all the professions need people who are not merely trained but educated. A well-trained person can do what was in the book, and an educated person can act wisely when faced with a new problem not yet in any book. A well-trained person can perform operation x on object y. The educated person recognizes that the operation is more than x and the object than y, and can catch the logical chain of deduction at a point just before it becomes absurd.

All the trades and professions want capably trained people—but they also want them to be, if possible, people before they are trained, people of that intangible something called taste, people, if possible, with originality and who know what to do with a new idea when they get one, people who can get on with other people unlike themselves—objective minds who are able to detach themselves from a problem and get to the heart of it because seeing it unclouded by presuppositions or prejudices.

There is the question whether vocational training can not be made as cultural as what is called liberal arts education.

The answer seems to be that vocational training must almost of a necessity be mechanical and narrowly specific, and that the attention does become centered upon the money value of what is being learned. Classes in "bedside manner" or surgery for medical students, or in typewriting and secretarial science for stenographers are devoted to developing skill for making a living. The liberal arts education tries to develop skill in living.

Individuals such as Justice Holmes or Justice Cardozo were real people before they became lawyers. We have met many others who were simply lawyers. They got the "dope" in law school and go on reproducing what was taught them there.

Perhaps it is in business and the medical profession that we see most clearly the need for a background of love for science or literature or art or economics or history, in order that the man or woman may live a satisfactory life in a chosen profession. Men like Dr. Osler in the medical profession, men like Mr. Balfour or Mr. Asquith in politics, men like John D. Rockefeller, Jr., in business, have a breadth of vision and make an impress on their times which is largely due to the fact that they are more than specialists with one trick—their interests are liberal and sane.

All this requires that people in their youth should gain a heightened consciousness of things such as the study of art gives, and intensification of experience, a prophetic glimpse or two of meaning.

The liberal arts colleges are supposed to send into life people who have developed in some such ways, and who are thereby better fitted to catch the knack of a business or profession. They have not been entirely successful in doing so. This has been partly because they have had to have money on which to operate and have therefore had to cater to a certain extent to the idle rich. They have not dared to open their doors only to young people seriously interested in culture and learning. They have tolerated large groups of young people who use them as country clubs.

One result of this has been that students tend to look upon college as a place where a certain grade in classes gives them the right to enjoy otherwise their extended week-ends, and if possible make their week-ends meet.

Instead of concentrating on the things of the spirit—their only concentration has been on the grade necessary (for arbitrary reasons) if they are to stay on. The college has set an artificial standard and they take artificial means of meeting that standard.

Be physically present at a certain number of classes, cram up before exams on notes mostly borrowed—get a grade—forget the stuff—this has been too largely the program of study.

The liberal arts college has in the last few years taken preliminary steps to right itself and get back to its last. The College Entrance Examination Board examinations are, at least in the most progressive colleges both for men and women, weeding out the unfit, and are producing a college body more capable intellectually of appreciating the scholarly opportunity of college life.

The general examination, which is in a subject and not in courses, is encouraging really devoted study in college and is turning the attention of the student away from bookkeeping in grades back to interest in developing and enlarging the inner capacities of the mind and heart.

"Work for honors," which has made a propitious start with the better students at college, will soon be the only kind of work of all students. Gradually it will come to be that preparatory schools will impart general information and place in the students' hands the tools of study, while colleges will devote themselves to the real task of giving the student an opportunity to gain thorough knowledge and perhaps wisdom in a chosen field. For a thorough knowledge of one field is more cultural than a general, spotty "Ask me another!" knowledge over many fields.

The other reason for the comparative failure of the liberal arts college to turn over to the businesses and professions really original, alert, broadminded, cultured, capable young people is the dearth of real teachers. A kind of pseudo-scientific method by the use of which an uninspired teacher can find compensatory consolation in the presence of real scientists—this has in America done much to spoil the teaching of the liberal arts.

Archeology and philology, facts to be gathered or memorized rather than understood, these take the place of such teaching of art and literature as flourishes in the universities of the old world. The uselessness and dryness of some of the subjects taught in the liberal arts college has led many of them to feel that they would be better teaching vocational subjects. If a woman is going to spend her life managing a cafeteria or a husband, why not teach her how to do things at college instead of letting her waste all her time over the Medici family or the art of Shakespeare? Most liberal arts colleges have capitulated as far as the profession of teaching is concerned and do offer courses in teaching—but this is due rather to legal necessity than to inner conviction.

The historic position of the liberal arts college has been that the best way to teach persons how to teach a subject in the best way is to teach them that subject in the best way. And the liberal arts college follows its own teaching in this matter, for it prefers to engage on its faculty those who know the subject rather than those who only know how to teach the subject. This, however, is a very controversial subject and there are many sides to it. The liberal arts college does not belittle the work of teachers' colleges in research and experiment on the art of teaching, but it is still inclined to hold that the best way to learn how to teach a subject and a person is through a study of the subject and of people, and most of all by learning oneself how to learn as one ought to do at college. It might be prepared to defend the precarious thesis that the power of teaching a pupil a subject is a by-product of understanding people and subjects, plus a little experience in trying to teach.

As to other vocational courses the liberal arts college holds with the experience of the Civil Service in the British Empire. It has taken year by year the most brilliant students of the British universities, those schooled in the classics or sciences or mathematics or history, and has turned them loose in their posts in British colonies to pick up there the particular technique of their job. The attempt being made in some quarters to-day to teach everything which our forefathers felt was best picked up in experience by intelligent educated people is of doubtful validity. Oratorical critics of our system of liberal education held forth on the folly of turning young men and women loose in the world without giving them courses on "The Art of Accepting, Rejecting or Choosing a Life Partner," or "The Best Methods of Spending Leisure Time," or "Clubs and Societies to Keep Out of," or "The Care by Husbands of the Oil Burner in Stove and Furnace." The liberal arts college goes on teaching Homer and Shakespeare and the history of the French Revolution and zoology and economics and logic and the art of the Italian Renaissance—and hoping that people who have learned taste and discrimination in these fields may not be entirely at a loss to pick out their way in the world of the home or office or school. This is the relation between the liberal arts college and the technique of business and professional life. To help professional and technical schools the liberal arts college should send them people whose minds, hearts and imaginations have been awakened, who have learned how to think. Men are born as blind as kittens; the liberal arts college attempts to open their eyes before the technical school attempts to aid them in earning a living by teaching them tricks.

EDUCATIONAL EVENTS

UNIVERSITY EXPENDITURE IN GREAT BRITAIN

THE total income of those universities and university colleges in Great Britain which receive Treasury grants was £5,830,936 during the academic year 1930–31, according to the annual report of the University Grants Committee, which was recently issued and has been summarized in the London *Times*. Of this sum £2,113,856, or 36.3 per cent., was from Parliamentary grants, and £1,825,084, or 31.3 per cent., from fees.

The total for England was £4,620,779, of which London University received £1,607,149, Oxford and Cambridge, £1,053,477; Scotland, £863,389, and Wales, £346,768. The expenditure for the year was £5,694,723. Departmental maintenance, which includes salaries, accounted for £3,672,961.

With the increased resources at the disposal of all the universities and colleges has come, according to the *Times*, a great improvement in their financial stability. Whereas in 1929–30 out of the university institutions concerned three balanced their revenue accounts, 21 showed deficits, and 28 showed surpluses, for the academic year 1930–31, four balanced their accounts, 10 showed deficits, and 40 showed surpluses. Moreover, of the 10 deficits, amounting in the aggregate to no more than £11,403, only two were at all serious, and the committee has good reason for hoping that they will not be repeated. Only a minority of the institutions are wholly free from debt, but there has been a substantial decrease in the accumulation of deficits on revenue account.

The decision of the government, subject to the over-riding necessities of national finance, to make no reduction in the recurrent grants to universities has been a source of profound encouragement to the universities on moral no less than material grounds, for it can fairly be claimed as a sign of faith in the value of their work and in their capacity to make an indispensable contribution to national recovery. The universities have lost no time in reviewing their position with the utmost thoroughness and care, and have taken active steps to secure all such economies as are possible without impairing their effectiveness as centers of advanced education and research.

THE INCREASE OF RECREATION FACILITIES

AN increase in the use of public recreation facilities since 1929 is revealed in the year-book of the National Recreation Association which has just been published. In 1,010 cities and towns in the United States and Canada, out-of-door playground attendance rose 17 per cent. in 1930 and 1931. At in-door recreation centers, participation in dramatics, music, athletics, craft activities and educational classes increased 63 per cent. and in separate recreation buildings such as community houses, 70 per cent.

Last year's attendance of adults and children

at out-of-door playgrounds reached an estimated total of 271,000,000 and participation at indoor centers 75,000,000. Much of the increased attendance both in-doors and out-of-doors reflects the presence of unemployed men and women, and of children from homes where income has been reduced. The figures indicate that the recreation movement has responded to the challenge presented by the large amount of leisure time resulting from wide-spread unemployment.

This increased service was given by recreation directors with fewer areas and centers than in 1929. The total separate play areas, numbering 13,324, were somewhat fewer than in 1929, while the in-door recreation centers reported open last year were 12 per cent. fewer.

The average cost to communities each time an individual used a playground, swimming pool, bathing beach or in-door center was less than 5 cents. The total cost of municipal recreation was 1 per cent. of all local governmental cost.

Twenty-seven cities voted bond issues for recreation purposes in 1931 as against 41 in 1930 and 37 in 1929. Many of the 1931 issues were devoted to giving the unemployed work in clearing or improving land for athletic or other recreational uses.

While the total number of separate play areas was slightly less than in 1929, certain facilities within these areas were more numerous. Baseball diamonds numbered 4,396 in 1931 as against 4,024 in 1929; bathing beaches, 470 in 1931 as against 409 in 1929; tennis courts, 8,804 in 1931 as against 7,960 in 1929; and swimming pools, 1,093 in 1931 as against 1,010 in 1929.

DECREASE IN THE NUMBER OF CHILDREN

Approach of an era of decreasing population in the United States is indicated by decline in the number of children under 5 years of age and a considerable increase in the proportion of the population in the older age groups during the last census period of 1920–30. An analysis of the population trends in age composition and in specific birth rates, by P. K. Whelpton, of the Scripps Foundation for Research in Population Problems, in the May issue of *The American Journal of Sociology,* carries also the prediction that the census of 1940 will show additional indication of declining population.

Dr. Whelpton points out that the 1930 census was the first in the United States to show fewer children below 5 years than in the age groups 5–9, 10–14, or 15–19. Likewise, the 1930 census was the first to show fewer children below 5 years than the preceding census.

"There were about 10 per cent. fewer births in 1930 and 1931 than in 1925 and 1926, which makes it practically certain that in 1940 there will be fewer children 5–9 than 10–14," the population expert says. "And unless the decline in births which has been going on almost without a break since 1921 is soon checked, the 1940 census will show fewer children 0–4 than 5–9. The 10–14 age period is sure to be smaller than the period 15–19 in 1940, since in 1930 there were fewer children 0–4 than 5–9, hence each age period would be smaller than the one above it up to 15–19."

While the population under 5 was declining, the older age period became larger, and, in general, the older the age period, the greater was the rate of increase. The number of persons between 5–9 was 10.6 per cent. larger than in 1920, but the number 75 years of age and older went up 30.2 per cent. This is a situation, Dr. Whelpton says, which has held true for several decades and is likely to be intensified in the next few decades. The foreign-born population shows a decrease not only in the 0–4 age period, but in all groups up to and including 30–34, the main cause for the decrease in the foreign-born being the smaller immigration since 1914.

Large movement off the farm during the decade brought the farm population from 31,400,000 to 30,100,000 in spite of a large rural excess of births over deaths, relatively more young adults than elders going to the cities. There also was a greater decline in birth rates for specific age groups in agricultural than industrial regions.

"School facilities and teaching staffs will be affected by this age shift. In some parts of the country the number of children under school age was much higher in 1930 than in 1920—in Detroit, Los Angeles, Hammond and White Plains, for example. Here, the problem of how to build schools and hire teachers fast enough may continue for some time, since there will be more children entering school from 1931 to 1936 than there were from 1921 to 1926.

"A more common situation, however, will be that of Boston, Chicago, Bay City and most of the farming areas of the United States where the number of children below school age is declining. These places will soon be able to abandon certain obsolete buildings or ease crowded conditions, and to weed out some of the less able teachers.

"A complicating factor in some cities, however, is that while there may be fewer children to enter school now than ten years ago, they are quite differently distributed within the city boundaries. New York furnishes a striking example, children under 5 in Manhattan decreasing 45.8 per cent. from 1920 to 1930, while in the Bronx they increased 35.2 per cent."

AN OPPORTUNITY FOR STUDYING INTERNATIONAL RELATIONS

PROGRAMS are now completed for the three Institutes of International Relations to be conducted during ten or twelve days of June by the American Friends Service Committee, in Haverford and Wellesley Colleges, and Northwestern University. All these will offer opportunities for the study of world relationships and related problems. In each case, eight or ten courses of college grade will be offered, some continuing throughout the entire period, the program being so arranged that each student may attend all the classes.

European international relations before the war, and international organization afterward will be discussed; and the economic, political, moral and ethical implications of war and peace. There will be courses on the effects of present-day economic facts and tendencies on world peace and on the issues in the Far East. The history and problems of disarmament in this country and abroad will be presented. Finally, the effective use of the information and ideas gained will be taught in courses on creating peace attitudes in schools, summer conferences and local groups.

Among those presenting these courses will be Sidney B. Fay, of Harvard University; Pitman B. Potter, of the University of Wisconsin; the Rev. Leyton Richards, of Birmingham, England; Harry D. Gideonse, of the University of Chicago, an expert in international economics; Devere Allen, assistant editor of *The Nation;* Kirby Page, editor of *The World Tomorrow;* Grover Clark, consultant on Far Eastern affairs; James W. Garner, of University of Illinois, and writer on international law; Will Carson Ryan, Jr., director of education, Indian Affairs.

A feature of all the institutes will be the series of nine or ten evening lectures, open to the public without charge, which will be given by men such as Bishop Francis J. McConnell, Norman Thomas, W. E. Burghardt Du Bois, Hamilton Holt, Glenn Frank, James G. McDonald, and Yusuke Tsurumi.

The Institute at Haverford College will be held from June 13 to 25; at Wellesley College, Wellesley, Mass., from June 23 to July 2; at Northwestern University, from June 20 to July 2. The general schedule throughout for all will be: classes in the morning; recreation in the afternoon; lectures in the evening. The charge to regularly enrolled students will be only $35 for the entire period, for room, board and tuition (at Northwestern this does not include breakfast). For further information, write to the American Friends Service Committee, 20 South Twelfth Street, Philadelphia, Pa.

THE PRESIDENCY OF DEFIANCE COLLEGE

THE difficulties at Defiance College, Ohio, have led to the retirement of the president, Dr. W. Vernon Lytle. His letter of resignation, sent to the board of trustees on May 24, reads as follows:

> When I came to Defiance a year ago the endowment of the institution was represented to me as amounting to slightly less than half a million dollars with an indebtedness of approximately $105,000. I set about constructing a program that would be educationally sound and financially possible from the standpoint of our resources. By a reduction of the budget and a slight reorganization within the faculty I made possible a number of economies. The statement of profit and loss which I have just presented to you reveals full well the financial success of this year's program as compared with that of the previous administration for a number of years. So far this year we show a profit sufficient to carry the college through

all but two months of the college year. A slight deficit might be encountered, but with a united front this slight deficit could be raised and a balanced budget for the year made possible. This achievement is quite remarkable in the light of recent financial reverses in operation. The result is all the more remarkable in the light of a very unresponsive and, at times, antagonistic attitude on the part of some members of the board of trustees, faculty, students, alumni and townspeople, who have been misled by vicious propaganda scattered by disgruntled faculty members and students whose conduct was such as to call forth severe disciplinary measures in order to develop for the college a reputation for wholesomeness of living conditions and high moral standards.

However, in spite of the remarkable financial showing this year, the effect of mounting financial deficits in the past must be recognized. I consider the present status of the college, financially and educationally, to be critical. The endowment memorials were practically wiped out when I came here. The financial statement presented when I was called to Defiance was found to be far from correct. The annuities, upon which many innocent parties depend for a living, they having entrusted their funds to the college, have been endangered. I, personally, will not consent to a program which would result in a complete loss of income for these annuity investors. I am not able to reconcile myself to the procedure of the past which resulted in endowment memorials being used for current expenses and thus depleted.

This procedure, I have recently discovered, has been carried to such an extent that the situation is critical. Not only is the financial condition critical, but the reputation of the college, educationally and as a custodian of endowment funds and annuities, is called into question.

Under the circumstances, I do not wish to continue my connection with the institution for the three-year period for which you called me to attempt to reestablish the college. I, therefore, present to you my resignation to take effect June 30, 1932.

CITATIONS FOR DISTINGUISHED TEACHING AT THE UNIVERSITY OF CHICAGO

Ten faculty members in the new college division of the University of Chicago were honored on May 25 with a special citation for "distinguished teaching contributions" by Dr. Chauncey S. Boucher, dean of the college.

The selection follows President Hutchins' policy, announced in 1930, of recognizing unusual teaching ability in the same way that unusual research productivity has been recognized at the graduate level. The citations are:

Gerald E. Bentley, assistant professor of English, prepared excellent syllabi for two introductory courses in the study of the drama and in the study of Shakespeare, and has distinguished himself by the excellence of his instruction.

Otto F. Bond, associate professor of Romance Languages in the college and chairman of modern languages in the college, and Peter Hagboldt, associate professor of German in the college, have attracted attention to the University of Chicago throughout the country by the development of remarkably successful methods in elementary language instruction.

Merle C. Coulter, professor of botany and adviser to premedical students in the college, has served as chairman of the group who prepared and are now revising the syllabus for the new introductory course in the biological sciences, and has been responsible for the administration of this excellent and stimulating course.

Harry D. Gideonse, associate professor of economics, is a brilliant teacher and has served as chairman of the two groups responsible for the content and administration of the first- and second-year general courses in the social sciences.

Mary B. Gilson, instructor in economics, and Eugene Staley, assistant professor of economics, as discussion group leaders and in their individual conferences with students in the introductory general course in the social sciences have inspired and effectively trained many students.

Harvey B. Lemon, professor of physics, has been untiring and faithful in an immense amount of work connected with designing and administering the introductory general course in the physical sciences and the special museum set-up in cooperation with the Museum of Science and Industry.

Norman F. MacLean, instructor in English, as a leader of discussion groups and in his personal conferences with students in the introductory general courses in the humanities, has proven himself one of the most effective teachers in the college.

Louis Wirth, assistant professor of sociology, has been invaluable in the organization and administration of the first- and second-year general courses in the social sciences.

The first citations for excellence in undergraduate teaching were made two years ago to

Professors J Harlan Bretz, Merle C. Coulter, William D. Hutchinson, Jerome G. Kerwin and Einar Joranson.

MEMORIAL TO CHARLES BRANTLEY AYCOCK

EDUCATION, as well as a distinguished man, was honored at a ceremony in the United States Capitol, on Friday, May 20, when a bronze statue of Charles Brantley Aycock, educational governor of North Carolina, was placed in the Hall of Fame.

Governor Aycock's administration was marked by never ceasing efforts to promote a state-wide public school system in North Carolina. His influence extended far beyond the confines of his own state, and was felt throughout the entire south. He did for North Carolina and the South what Horace Mann and Henry Barnard did for New England. Governor Aycock died with the word "education" on his lips, during an address he was making at a convention of educators in Birmingham, Alabama, April 4, 1912.

Underneath his statue in the Hall of Fame, these words are embossed on a bronze plate:

> *Equal*, that is the word! On that word I plant myself and my party—the equal right of every child born on earth to have the opportunity "to burgeon out all that is within him."—CHARLES B. AYCOCK.

The dedication ceremony was carried out with Governor Max Gardner presiding. Addresses were made by the Honorable Josephus Daniels, former Secretary of the Navy, the Honorable Lindsay Warren, congressman from North Carolina, and Dr. J. Y. Joyner, formerly state superintendent of public instruction in North Carolina.

During the administration of Governor Aycock and for many years before and after his administration, Dr. Joyner was a close personal friend of the educational governor, and himself made a great contribution to the development of the public-school system of his state. Dr. Joyner was president of the National Education Association in 1909–10. In 1910 Mrs. Ella Flagg Young, superintendent of schools, Chicago, was elected president. She was the first woman to hold this office, and her election was hailed as an important step in the democratization of the National Education Association.

Dr. Joyner read letters of tribute to former Governor Aycock from the National Education Association and the United States Office of Education. He presented on behalf of these two organizations a wreath of flowers, the first to lie at the foot of the new statue.

EDUCATIONAL NOTES AND NEWS

DR. ROBERT C. CLOTHIER will be installed as the fourteenth president of Rutgers University on commencement day, June 11. Governor A. Harry Moore will preside. Dr. William I. Chamberlain, of New York City, will give the invocation, and Dr. William H. S. Demarest, president of Rutgers from 1905 to 1925 and now president of the New Brunswick Theological Seminary, will give the historical address. Dr. Philip M. Brett, of New York, acting president prior to the selection of Dr. Clothier, will speak for the university, and Supreme Court Justice Clarence E. Case, of Somerville, will administer the oath of office.

DR. SAMUEL P. CAPEN, ninth chancellor of the University of Buffalo, will be the guest of honor at a dinner on June 13, to be given jointly by the university alumni and the council of the university "as a special manifestation of the community's deep appreciation for his undivided and singularly loyal service to the university." The speaker on the occasion will be Dr. Henry Suzzallo, president of the Carnegie Foundation for the Advancement of Teaching and former president of the University of Washington.

AMONG those receiving honorary degrees at the convocation of McGill University on May 26 were Dr. John H. Finley, of *The New York Times,* and Dr. Alfred North Whitehead, professor of philosophy at Harvard University. Dr. Finley delivered the convocation address.

AT the commencement exercises of Fordham College on June 8, the degree of doctor of letters will be conferred on the Right Reverend

Edward A. Pace, vice-rector and dean of the School of Philosophy of the Catholic University, Washington, and on Dr. Joseph J. Reilly, professor of English at Hunter College.

Dr. Ernest Hatch Wilkins, president of Oberlin College, is chairman of a committee appointed by the Association of American Colleges to make a study of music and liberal arts colleges. For this purpose the association has received a grant of $25,000 from the Carnegie Corporation.

Dr. John Grier Hibben, who is retiring from the presidency of Princeton University, will sail for England in the middle of July. Dr. Hibben plans to spend five months in Europe.

President Hoover was reelected honorary president of the Boys Clubs of America, at the annual convention at Atlantic City. Elected as honorary vice-presidents were: Thomas Chew, Fall River, Massachusetts; Cyrus H. K. Curtis, Philadelphia; Senator James J. Davis, Washington; Chief Justice Charles E. Hughes, and Samuel Insull, Chicago.

Officers elected by the National Association of Public School Officials in convention at Los Angeles during the last week in May are: W. E. Record, Los Angeles, *president;* Joseph Miller, New York, *vice-president;* John S. Mount, Trenton, New Jersey, *secretary,* and Henry W. Huston, Trenton, New Jersey, *treasurer.*

Melville Dozier, for many years a member of the Los Angeles school system as teacher, assistant superintendent and board member, celebrated his eighty-sixth birthday on May 29.

H. S. Upjohn, formerly superintendent of Los Angeles County Schools, has accepted the position of city superintendent of schools of Long Beach. Mr. Upjohn has recently returned from a trip abroad. It will be remembered that Dr. Vierling Kersey, state superintendent of public instruction, had accepted the superintendency at Long Beach, but decided to retain the state superintendency in the interest of the California schools.

George C. Jensen, assistant superintendent of schools of Sacramento, California, has been appointed principal of the Sacramento High School.

Harvey B. Heath has been elected superintendent of schools of the first supervisory district of Delaware County, New York, to fill the vacancy caused by the death of Superintendent Charles F. Ferry. Mr. Heath was formerly superintendent of schools of the first supervisory district of Broome County.

Victor O. Skyberg, superintendent of the Minnesota School for the Deaf, has been appointed to succeed Dr. Isaac B. Gardner as principal of the New York Institution for the Instruction of the Deaf and Dumb. Dr. Gardner resigned recently because of ill health.

Maurice G. Osborne has been appointed assistant in the finance division of the New York State Department of Education. Since October, 1930, Mr. Osborne has been an inspector in the attendance division of the department. Before going to Albany he was principal of the Lyon Mountain High School for four years.

We learn from *Museum News* that C. H. Collins Baker, keeper of the National Gallery in London, has accepted a position on the research staff of the Henry E. Huntington Library and Art Gallery. He will be in charge of research in the history of art. His resignation from the National Gallery will take effect the end of September and somewhat later he will establish a permanent residence in California.

Dr. Frederick C. Eiselen, for the past eight years president of Garrett Biblical Institute, Chicago, has been elected corresponding secretary of the Board of Education of the Methodist Episcopal Church by the quadrennial conference. He succeeds Dr. William S. Bovard, who has been corresponding secretary since 1924.

Professor Grayson N. Kefauver, of Teachers College, Columbia University, has been granted leave of absence for the school year 1932–33, including the summer session of 1933. During this time he will serve as visiting professor at Stanford University.

Dr. Robert L. Kelly, executive secretary of the Association of American Colleges and executive secretary of the Council of Church Boards of Education, made the address on Education Night, May 30, at the General Assembly of the United Presbyterian Church, Beaver,

Pennsylvania. Dr. Kelly is to deliver commencement addresses at the following institutions: Wofford College, Spartanburg, South Carolina; Davis and Elkins College, Elkins, West Virginia; Lafayette College and Heidelberg College. He will also speak at Bates College, Lewiston, Maine, on June 13.

DR. ROBERT MCELROY, professor of American history at the University of Oxford, will deliver the commencement address at New York University.

DR. RALPH BARTON PERRY, professor of philosophy at Harvard, will be the commencement speaker at Smith College on June 20.

JAMES A. FARRELL, who recently retired as president of the U. S. Steel Corporation, will deliver the address at the sixtieth annual commencement of the Stevens Institute of Technology at Hoboken, New Jersey.

PROFESSOR ELBERT K. FRETWELL, of Teachers College, Columbia University, will lecture at the North Texas State Teachers College, Denton, from June 14 to 17, in a special course on education arranged by Dean W. J. McConnell. From June 20 to 30 he will teach in the Colorado State Teachers College at Greeley.

A PORTRAIT of Dr. Samuel F. Mordecai, dean of the Duke University law school from its establishment in 1904 until his death in 1927, will be unveiled at commencement on June 7, and presented to the university as a gift of his former students. Judge J. P. Frizzelle, of Snow Hill, president of Duke law alumni, will make the presentation.

TRIBUTE was paid to the memory of Gertrude Howes in the official dedication of the new playground bearing her name on Winthrop Street, Roxbury, Massachusetts, on May 25. Miss Howes was for many years a Boston public school teacher and devoted the last years of her life to community interests. She was the founder of the Field and Forest Club. James L. Tryon, director of admissions at the Massachusetts Institute of Technology, gave the main address.

DR. OLIN FRANK WILSON, founder of Converse College at Spartanburg, South Carolina, died on May 24, at the age of sixty-nine years.

THE death is announced of Professor Martha Van Rensselaer, one of the two directors of the New York State College of Home Economics at Cornell University.

DR. EDWARD RYNEARSON, director of vocational education in the public schools of Pittsburgh, died on May 25 in Mercy Hospital, three weeks after he suffered a heart attack in his office. He was sixty-five years old and had been connected with the Pittsburgh school system for thirty-six years.

THE centennial celebration of Gettysburg College opened on May 26. Dr. James R. Angell, president of Yale University, delivered the centennial address and Dr. John H. Finley, of New York, made the commencement address. Dr. Frederick H. Knubel, president of the United Lutheran Church in America, preached the baccalaureate sermon.

PRESIDENT JAMES R. ANGELL delivered the principal speech at the recent formal opening of Homewood House, at the Johns Hopkins University, with Dr. Joseph S. Ames, president of the university, presiding at the exercises. The house, the residence of the son of Charles Carroll, of Carrollton, has become the property of the university and stands on the campus. Its restoration was directed by Dr. R. T. H. Halsey, professor of colonial art at St. John's College, Annapolis. Funds for the restoration and refurnishing were given by Mr. and Mrs. Francis P. Garvan, of New York.

AT the meeting of the American Association for the Advancement of Science to be held at Syracuse University from June 20 to 25, the sections of education and psychology plan to hold sessions. There will be a number of meetings devoted to discussions of general education problems. Among the speakers are Dr. Edward L. Thorndike, Dr. J. G. Needham and Dr. E. R. Hedrick. Dr. Thorndike will deliver a general evening lecture using the title "The Psychology of Capital."

THE Philadelphia School of Design for Women, the oldest industrial art school in the United States, will receive the income from a $3,000,000 trust fund left by Mr. Joseph Moore, Jr. The will provides that the estate should be used to endow a Philadelphia institution for the education of women in the arts, sciences and industry, empowering the trustees with the selection of the institution. The name of the school will be retained, but it will be merged with a new foundation which will be called the Moore Institute of Art, Science and Industry.

Twenty-five thousand dollars has been appropriated from the Laura Spelman fund to the University of Cincinnati for research and training of men in municipal work. Eighty-five thousand dollars had been contributed previously by the Rockefeller Foundation.

Chase S. Osborn, formerly governor of Michigan, has given Harbor Island to Tulane University as a summer camp for students and a resting place for faculty members. It is expected to prove of value to the university as a base for biological and other scientific studies. Harbor Island is unique. It is a thousand-acre knoll, rising from the blue waters of Potaganissing Bay just off the coast of Drummond Island, in Chippewa County, Michigan. The island derives its name from a land-locked harbor, several acres in extent, contained completely within two curved arms of the south shore.

The Rockefeller Foundation has offered to appropriate a sum not exceeding $2,300,000 in order that it may contribute up to three fifths of the total cost as estimated by the Bodleian Commission of extending the Bodleian Library, together with an additional 10 per cent. of the estimated cost of construction to meet any rise in prices not foreseen by the commission, on condition that the university shall have received before December 31, 1936, a total amount of £377,720 in cash or collectible pledges.

The Cleveland School Board has appropriated $100,000 for the School of Education of Western Reserve University, a decrease of $22,000. It is reported that this is the first step in gradual withdrawal of support from the school.

The appropriation for publishing *The Chicago Schools Journal* was so cut in the 1932 budget of the Chicago Board of Education that only three issues can be published during the current year. The January issue has appeared; the present issue is dated for February, March, April, May, and June; the one issue appearing before January 1, 1933, will be dated for September, October, November and December.

Salaries of the faculty and staff of the University of North Carolina were cut 20 per cent. in the pay checks distributed for the month of April. A like cut will also apply on June 1, and on July 1 the reduction may go up or down, depending upon the collection of university accounts outstanding. This 20 per cent. salary cut for the last three months of the fiscal year 1931–32 is made necessary by the decrease in state appropriations to the university for the last six months of the year 1931–32. The cut is in addition to the 10 per cent. cut that became effective at the beginning of the present fiscal year, making the faculty salaries for the last three months of the year slightly over 70 per cent. of the amount received for the corresponding three months of last year. The original state appropriation to the university for 1931–32 was $721,000. The reductions effected so far amount to $195,500, giving the university a total from the state for 1931–32 of $525,500.

Library schools at the University of Oklahoma and Kansas State Teachers College have been fully accredited by the Board of Education for Librarianship of the American Library Association, and those at the University of North Carolina, Louisiana State University and the University of Denver have been provisionally accredited. The school at the North Carolina College for Women has been reclassified as a senior undergraduate library school for the training of school librarians. Safeguarding of library service at this time was urged in the following resolution passed by the National Congress of Parents and Teachers at Minneapolis, May 20: "We believe that the essential services of existing libraries must be safeguarded in this period when people are turning to books as never before; and that library opportunity must be extended to rural people through the establishment of county libraries." A similar resolution has been passed by the Illinois Congress of Parents and Teachers.

The State Pension Survey Commission, Trenton, New Jersey, on February 19 made public its recommendations to the Legislature for reducing the volume and cost of state care of dependent children in New Jersey. The recommendations were set forth in a statement by the commission as follows: (1) Limit the number of dependent children transferred from local to state supervision by establishing specific requirements of direction of the State Board of Children's eligibility for state care. (2) Place under the Guardians all investigations of the need and eligibility of dependent children for state supervision. (3) Require review by the county adjuster of a child's eligibility for county relief under the settlement provisions of the poor law, before the cost of such relief can become a charge against county funds. (4) Make the plan of relief grants and supervisory care the same for all dependent children resident with mothers or relatives. (5) Develop as rapidly as possible the administrative program the State Board of Children's Guardians already has under way for decentralizing state care of dependent children through the establishment of district or county offices.

CONSIDERABLE progress is being made on the National Survey of School Finance which was authorized by Congress in February, 1931, and upon which work was begun last July. On September 14, a tentative outline of procedure in the form of a comprehensive list of pertinent problems confronting school patrons and taxpayers was submitted by the associate director, Dr. Paul R. Mort, to a board of seventeen expert consultants for criticism and approval. This board will meet from time to time as occasion demands to evaluate and criticize major problems of procedure. In addition, the present plans call for regional conferences in as many states as time will permit, as part of the first year's program. At these meetings, the associate director hopes to learn at first hand what problems of school finance are considered of most importance in the various sections of the country. Dr. Mort recently returned from a series of these regional conferences in Minnesota, North Dakota, Montana and Idaho. He reports that the meetings were attended by representatives from state departments of finance and education, state granges, state teachers associations, farmers organizations, state universities and by professors of education, taxation and government, school board members and other prominent citizens. Those present at the meetings evidenced a keen interest in the study and the specific questions under discussion. Reorganization of rural school areas to effect economies without reducing educational efficiency, the establishment of the proper relationship between state and locality in the financing of schools, the extent of state responsibility for secondary and higher education, and the problem of keeping the people in the various states in touch with the national study were emphasized as financial problems of immediate importance.

ACCORDING to the London *Times* the effect of the present economic situation on the employment of university graduates is reflected in the report of the Oxford Committee for Appointments, which was recently published. It is reported that there was a heavy fall in the number of government vacancies, and that business and general vacancies were thirty-six per cent. less than they were two years ago. There was a serious reduction of recruitment by firms which took men regularly from the university. Education, which remained unaffected in 1930, last year began to feel the effect of the prevailing conditions, and the vacancies were short of the 1930 total by approximately 25 per cent. There was a specially heavy decrease in the case of preparatory schools. The names on the committee's books of men seeking appointments have doubled since 1929. "The committee feel that, had it not been for the efforts made to increase their connections in industry and business during the last five years, the present depression would have had more serious effects. It is satisfactory that in a difficult year it has been possible to maintain the number of educational appointments at last year's level."

A WIRELESS message to *The New York Times* reports that conferences are in progress between the university and Polytechnic School of Breslau looking toward consolidation of the two institutions. If this comes about Germany will have its first university with a department of engineering. In a joint statement the rectors of the two institutions say "the combination may yield greater scientific and cultural good without added financial tax on the state, and close cooperation between pure and applied science would effect mutual fertilization. In view of the desperate plight of the fatherland it is also desirable to create on its threatened eastern border a cultural bulwark of special size and strength. Incorporating the Technological Institute as a faculty of engineering sciences in the greater organism would fashion a real university."

DISCUSSION

AN EXPERIMENT TO DETERMINE THE RELATIVE RÔLES OF HEREDITY AND ENVIRONMENT IN HUMAN BEHAVIOR

It is an absurd situation that so important a question as the relative rôle of heredity and environment in human behavior should still find social scientists so far apart. This is mainly because there has been no well-controlled experiment such as to be clearly convincing to those with an interfering bias one way or the other.

Such an experiment would be as follows: Select not less than one hundred infants born within a week or two of the same date in hospital, whose mothers would contribute to the experiment in consideration of a contract to educate and care for them through 18 years of age under conditions that are as ideal as reasonably can be and with promise of college education for highest 10 per cent and payment of the obstetrical and hospital costs of the mother. At 18 they would be returned to the parents. Such a method of gathering material would doubtless give a large range of racial composition although a more restricted range of economic and social status than would be desirable. As full a study of the ancestors, as well as uncles, aunts, brothers, sisters and cousins as they would permit, should be made. By using hospital babies the only conditioning circumstances would be known and under control. All the data as to the identification of each child should be kept completely from the custodians and testers, who are to carry out the care and testing of the children. Children would be identified by foot prints and an assumed name only. The experiment consists of keeping these children in a *scrupulously similar* environment, except as their own activities and responses tend to produce a differential response. Separate records should be made of their developmental progress by systematic tests carried on at intervals. This experiment should continue until the subjects are 18 years of age. The final test before discharge should be particularly thorough.

Two things ought to be observed: (1) The extent to which variation arises in this identical environment, and (2) the extent to which these differences can be correlated with what is known of the relatives of each child.

If this experiment was carried out it would excite an unusual public interest and become a classic in the literature of sociology and physiology. I doubt if any bit of scientific investigation would arouse such wide-spread interest. In fact, this would be so true that it would probably be wise to have it conducted on an island to avoid visitors and possible escapes.

This proposed investigation should be submitted to the National Social Research Council for their approval or any modification and the personnel to conduct it be chosen by them, so as to escape any imputation of bias on the part of those who organize it. The advisory board, of course, would include a geneticist such as Sewall Wright, of the University of Chicago, an expert on child psychology, such as Arnold Gesell, of Yale University, a psychometrist, such as Professor McCall, of Columbia, and experts on child care and education.

ROSWELL H. JOHNSON

PITTSBURGH, PA.

CHOOSING COLLEGE ENTRANTS

There is still considerable room for improvement in the methods through which students are admitted to college. Continued experiments with scholastic aptitude tests, steady revision of the uniform examinations for college entrance and constant complaint from college teachers on the student material sent them testify to the sharp need for a more intelligent system of choosing those on whom the opportunity for higher education shall be conferred.

The suggestion in this brief paper is that colleges, particular about the type of student they get, borrow a leaf from the manual of industry and commerce and admit students only on personal interview and individual investigation. No business firm of any standing would think of accepting an applicant for a responsible position until the applicant had been met and interviewed personally. Is there any good reason why a college should be any less thorough in picking its students?

It isn't logical to maintain to-day that every student aspiring to college is entitled to the opportunity for higher education. Existing facilities are too limited. Until there comes a time when there is room in college for every high-school graduate and ample provision for teaching a wide variety of subjects to a group of widely varying intelligence and ability, there must, of necessity, be some sifting process whereby the relatively limited accommodations in colleges and universities are accorded directly to those best fitted to make the most of higher educational advantages. Efficiency demands this. American colleges have already paid all too dearly for failure to establish a rigid system of selecting our college population.

Present practices along this line leave room for the suspicion that many colleges regard a place on their enrolment more lightly than the business man does a place on his payroll. Higher education gives the impression of regarding its work as less important than that of business and industry. The business man is careful because he wants to be certain, within the limit of his power to ascertain, that the one he takes into his business will be productive and dependable. A college can not afford to be less eager that its students will produce.

A machinery for selecting college entrants personally could easily be set up. Take, for example, any college admitting, let us say, five hundred students annually. Consider that these students are to be taken from the entire United States. For these five hundred places in the freshman class there would possibly be twenty-five hundred applicants. A staff of fifteen traveling representatives, perhaps less, could handle this problem nicely.

Suppose these examiners were to be distributed in fifteen localities throughout the country. Let them work forty weeks out of the year. Averaging five interviews a week, each examiner could handle two hundred applicants annually. Fifteen workers would have full opportunity for a thorough, personal examination of at least three thousand applicants.

The cost of such an organization would not be prohibitive. Indeed, it is doubtful if this cost would compare in dollars and cents alone with the heavy cost involved in college failures and the admission of wrong students to college. Certainly the toll of disappointment and wasted years would be happily reduced.

The advantages of such a plan seem obvious. For one thing, it would eliminate considerable unfairness and hypocrisy. The unfairness referred to is that of judging a student's ability to capitalize college advantages on the basis of brief, inconclusive examinations in subject matter or a certificate marking that varies greatly in different schools. The hypocrisy alleged above is of that forgivable, unwitting variety found in the stretch-a-point-in-the-student's-favor reports that principals and headmasters must be inclined to submit in behalf of certain students who desire admission to college. An astute examiner should learn more of a student's college potentialities in one day spent with the student's record and personality than could be told in a ream of principals' letters or dozens of "college board" examinations.

Let the examiner spend a couple of hours talking with the applicant's principal and in a personal inspection of the student's grades. Spend as much time as possible with the applicant personally and some time too in talking with the parents. If this could be done, subject-matter examinations would become supplementary and secondary. Which is as it should be, for the material which comes through the college gate in September is human material and should be treated in its selection as something more than a shipment of algebraic relationships and Latin conjugations.

The problem of education is a human problem and should be treated throughout with the human relationship. Indeed, it is a reflection on education if colleges allow a condition under which business, supposedly inhuman and cold, acts more on the personal basis and places more emphasis on personality than higher education does.

William E. Slater
Minneapolis, Minn.

GRADUATES OF UNION COLLEGE IN GRADUATE SCHOOLS

Would you be kind enough to allow a little space in your valued periodical to correct a false impression conveyed in an article by Professor B. W. Kunkel in your issue of March 12?

In his tables showing the representation of colleges in graduate schools, he makes it appear that Union College has only 49 men in such schools, or 6 per cent. of its undergraduate enrolment. He entirely overlooks the fact that Union College is a part of Union University, which includes the Albany Medical School (a class A institution) and the Albany Law School.

In the year 1930–31 there were 66 Union College graduates in the Albany Medical School and 44 in the Albany Law School, neither of which institutions was included in Professor Kunkel's list. If these 110 men are added to the 49, it will be seen that Union College had in that year 159 of its graduates in reputable graduate schools, or 19.5 per cent. instead of 6 per cent.

President Frank Parker Day joins me in the hope that it will be possible to rectify these figures, so that Union will not be classified among the colleges whose graduates do not continue their work in more advanced institutions.

Harold A. Larrabee

REPORTS

COMMONWEALTH FUND FELLOWS

Twenty-five British students have been awarded Commonwealth Fund fellowships for study in American colleges and universities and for travel in the United States during the next two years. These men and women, chosen from 231 applicants by a committee of which the Prince of Wales is honorary chairman, form the eighth such group to come to this country under a plan initiated by Edward S. Harkness, president of the Commonwealth Fund, to promote understanding between Great Britain and the United States. They bring the total number of fellows, past and present, to 207.

Three of the new appointees are service fellows—men holding technical positions under some government in the British Empire. Christiaan J. Jaubert, of the Department of Agriculture of the Union of South Africa, will work on the biological control of insect pests at the Riverside Experiment Station of the University of California. David William Dodwell, of the Indian Civil Service, will do research at Columbia in financial and economic problems which are of present importance to India, such as the organization of banking, questions of currency and exchange, and tariff systems. William M. McNeill, of the Forest Department of Ceylon, will investigate plant geography, forest engineering and exploitation, and the marketing of forest products, at Yale.

The remaining appointees are graduate students who will study a variety of subjects in preparation for professional or business careers in Great Britain or other parts of the British Empire. Grouped by the American institutions where they will study, they are as follows:

University of California: William A. MacFarlane, from Balliol College, Oxford, to study chemistry; Jean M. Stewart, from Newnham College, Cambridge, to study literature.

University of Chicago: Kenneth E. Boulding, from New College, Oxford, to study economics; Robert M. Shone, from the University of Liverpool, to study economics; Charles R. Spencer, from Magdalen College, Oxford, to study education.

Clark University: George Tatham, from the University of Liverpool and University College, London, to study geography.

Columbia University: Arthur Smithies, from the University of Tasmania and Magdalen College, Oxford, to study economics.

Harvard University: Kingsley C. Dunham, from Hatfield College, Durham, to study geology; Denis Winston, from the University of Liverpool, to study architecture.

University of Illinois: John H. Chesters, from the University of Sheffield, to study physics.

Johns Hopkins University: Margot E. Metcalfe, from the University College of Wales, Aberystwyth, to study zoology; W. Charles Price, from the University College of Swansea, Wales, to study physics.

Massachusetts Institute of Technology: David N. Truscott, from the Imperial College of Science and Technology, London, to study engineering.

University of Michigan: George W. C. Allan,

from the University of Glasgow, to study engineering; Angus S. Roy, from the University of St. Andrews, to study physics.

University of North Carolina: John H. Kirk, from Natal University College, Durban and King's College and Christ's College, Cambridge, to study economics.

Princeton University: James Pace, from the University of Liverpool, to study chemistry.

Rockefeller Institute: Emil T. Stiller, from the University of Glasgow and the University of St. Andrews, to study chemistry.

Stanford University: Norman E. G. Hill, from University College, London, to study engineering.

Union Theological Seminary: Alexander M. Honeyman, from the University of St. Andrews and Edinburgh University, to study Biblical literature.

Yale University: Alfred A. Cooke, from Jesus College, Cambridge, to study literature; A. Gifford Hooper, from the University of Leeds, to study literature.

Under the plan which has been followed since the first awards in 1925, each fellow spends one full year at the university to which he is assigned, devotes the summer vacation to travel, usually by motor car, returns to his university for a second academic year, and then goes home. Appointees are under obligation to return to the British Empire on completion of their work here. Many of them take teaching positions in British universities where their knowledge of America is passed on to younger men and women.

During the past year three returned fellows have published books: W. R. Crocker, who studied at Stanford, a monograph on "The Japanese Population Problem"; Sean O'Faolain, Harvard, a book of short stories, "Midsummer Night's Madness"; and Eric R. Linklater, Cornell, a study of "Ben Jonson and King James."

Appointments to the Commonwealth Fund fellowships are made by a British committee of award, of which the active head is Sir Walter Buchanan-Riddell, chairman of the university grants committee. The committee makes its selection by personal interview after candidates are endorsed by their own colleges. The fund maintains headquarters in London for the use of this committee and as a center where returned fellows can keep in touch with American newspapers and magazines.

FINANCIAL CONDITIONS OF NEW ENGLAND UNIVERSITIES AND COLLEGES

The Boston Evening Transcript addressed recently a questionnaire to university and college presidents of New England in regard to the financial condition of the institutions. In a recent issue it prints the letters received in reply, and gives in addition the following condensed statement of their contents:

Amherst: No deficit expected. Budget for next year same as this. Income from investments decreased no more than 3 per cent. Additions to endowment fund have offset considerable part of this small shrinkage.

Bates: Loss of income from invested funds between $3,000 and $5,000. Increase of $40,000 in income from students (tuition up $50; sixty more students). No salary cuts or staff reductions. Financial condition best ever.

Boston College: Deferred payment and installment paying has affected about 20 per cent. of tuitions. Extensive loss as residuary legatee. No salary reductions. Faculty will not be reduced. Number of students receiving financial aid has increased 100 per cent.

Boston University: Made reduction of 3 per cent. in general budget this year. Salaries down 5 per cent. for last three fourths of year. No deficit expected. No members of staff laid off.

Bowdoin: Anticipates deficit of about 5 per cent. Income from invested funds off about 8 per cent. Will not add new members to staff. May reduce budget next year. Hopes there will be no salary reduction.

Clark: No staff reductions. No salary cuts.

Colby: Does not anticipate deficit. Income from invested funds to show shrinkage of about $6,000. No loss of income from student fees. No reduction in staff or in salary schedule expected.

Connecticut Agricultural: No anticipation of appropriation changes during coming academic year.

Connecticut College: Income down less than $10,000. To balance small drop in income from investments by adding five to ten students. Not cutting salaries; not dropping members of staff; not failing to replace those resigning. To cut budget.

Dartmouth: Budget deficit of $237,500 will probably be reduced by $135,000 raised by alumni fund. Not cutting salaries; not cutting staffs; not failing to replace those resigning. No additional appointments.

Emerson: No faculty reduction. No salary cuts.

For first time, larger enrolment second semester than first. Total number of students for year slightly smaller. Entering class larger than last year.

Harvard: Rate of interest for funds in general investments 4.8 per cent. next year, as against 5.25 per cent. this year. This will mean decrease in income from endowment of $450,000. No deficit expected in any department. No decrease in enrolment expected. No general reduction of salaries contemplated.

Massachusetts State: No salary cuts or staff reductions. Cutting out all new projects; summer session discontinued; reducing expenditures for consumable supplies, replacements, repairs.

M. I. T.: Operating deficit for year of about $33,000—1 per cent. of operating budget. Has not decreased staff or made cuts in salary. Expects operating income next year will be reduced 10 per cent. Will not be able to reappoint some members of staff. Uniform reduction in salaries may be necessary.

Mount Holyoke: Income somewhat reduced. Slight shrinkage of income from investments. Only small deficit expected. Not cutting salaries. Not reducing staff.

New Hampshire: Salary increases halted. Financial policy of trustees not to be changed greatly next academic year.

Northeastern: Loans, scholarships, deferred agreements increased. Balanced budget expected. No salary cuts. No reduction in staff. Entire program carried on.

Radcliffe: Suffering 2.7 per cent. reduction in income. College full; lower enrolment in graduate school. Only nominal deficit, if any. No staff reduction contemplated. Endeavoring to raise emergency funds for fellowships, scholarships, loans.

Rhode Island State: Appropriation up 8 per cent. No proposal of salary cuts. No increases contemplated. To add ten instructors to staff next year. Enrolment up this year from 647 to 813.

Simmons: Enrolment increased. Drop in income from securities very small. No difficulty in meeting expenses. Will not dismiss instructors or reduce salaries. Will grant usual salary increases. Deficit in dormitory account.

Smith: Loss of investment income of about 7 per cent. Student income slightly decreased. Not cutting salaries or staff; making necessary new appointments. Does not anticipate deficit.

Trinity: Income from endowment showed increase of ½ of 1 per cent. Increase of 20 per cent. in student body. No salary cuts; no staff reductions; no budget reductions.

Tufts: Will finish the year "in black." Will not reduce staff or cut salaries. College in rather a favorable situation financially. Relatively small losses of income from investments.

Wellesley: Hopes to get through year without deficit. Income has dropped $45,000 to date. Not cutting salaries; not giving customary increases. Not reducing staff substantially; making only a few new appointments.

Wesleyan: Salary increases of $25,000 to be made during 1932. No appointments will terminate. Faculty will be largest in history. Enrolment higher than ever. Fifty thousand dollars in scholarships and loans. Larger gifts for current income than in any recent year. Small decrease in budget expected.

Wheaton: Income from invested funds has shrunk slightly. Rather gained than lost in enrolment. Heavy demand for scholarship aid. No increases or reductions in salaries.

Williams: Probable decrease in income from investments of from 6 to 7 per cent. Budget reduced; hopes to avoid deficit. Salaries uncut; sabbatical leaves postponed; some vacant positions unfilled.

Worcester Tech.: No deficit anticipated. Increase in receipts from tuition fees compensated for loss in income from investments. Added $4,000 to reserve during last academic year. Not cutting salaries or reducing staff.

Yale: Ten per cent. reduction in budget for next year proposed to offset anticipated $500,000 deficit this year. Places of twenty-two instructors will not be filled; 300 per cent. increase in number of students seeking financial aid.

EDUCATIONAL RESEARCH AND STATISTICS

THE UNDERGRADUATE POINT OF VIEW ON STUDENT PARTICIPATION

STUDENT self-government in colleges and universities has become an ever-widening field for speculative discussion. Some students of higher education have been wondering just how genuine student participation is. There is also a question as to whether present-day American university undergraduates feel any share in administrative responsibility.

In order to discover something more definite

about this feeling in Rutgers University, the writers submitted some direct questions to the student body and then tabulated the results. From a student body of 1,278, responses were secured from 802 men, by having the questions answered during sessions of the university chapel devoted to this purpose. The questions sought to sound out the group on such matters as the extent of undergraduate confidence in student council and other governing media, the effectiveness (in the opinion of the students) of the college newspaper, and the desire, if any, of the students for direct participation in such matters as curricular requirements, athletic policy, regulations governing class attendance and probation, the regulation of undergraduate social functions and compulsory chapel.

Evidently students change their minds, as time goes on, as to the effectiveness of some of the agencies set up to give them participation. For example, their response to the first question suggested a constant decline from the freshman to senior year in their regard for the efficacy of student council. When asked, "Is it your opinion that the will of Student Council is given consideration by administrative authorities?" four fifths of the freshmen replied in the affirmative, but the numbers dwindled until barely half of the seniors answered in the same vein.

Student Council received another test in question number three. "Would you petition Student Council if you wished to effect an administrative change?"

	Yes	Per cent.	No.	Per cent.
Fresh.	210	73.9	74	26.1
Soph.	110	71.4	44	28.6
Jr.	72	56.7	55	43.3
Sr.	83	62.	51	38.
	475	68.	224	32.

This tabulation evidences the marked break between the underclass and upperclass years, with the noticeable feature that the senior year displays an upward swing above the severe drop from sophomore to junior. Since the freshmen, with two months at Rutgers (at the time of interrogation), and the sophomores, with an additional year, show so little difference and are again quite distinctly grouped apart from the upperclassmen, the writers conclude that the freshman year gives little insight into the actual workings of the student-government relationship.

The Targum, the campus semi-weekly newspaper, ranks high in the estimation of the undergraduates, because in response to the question, "Would you enlist the aid of *The Targum* in an editorial campaign to effect an administrative change?" the newspaper received more favorable replies than did Student Council in the preceding query.

Although *The Targum* has more efficacy as a reform agent in the opinion of the students, they feel that student council is far and away the best of their representative organizations for most purposes. This was shown when the men were asked to check which of the following groups they considered the best medium of student participation:

Student Council
Association of Campus Activities
Interfraternity Council
Student Business Activities Committee
Board of Managers
Student Members, Council on Athletics
Committee of Twelve

Student council was the selection of 420 undergraduates, and the Interfraternity Council, of 102. The other bodies were far in the ruck.

In listing which of the above would have most weight in proposing a change in (a) curriculum and (b) chapel regulations, the same two organizations led in the same order by counts of 460 to 61 and 427 to 65. As might be expected, when the question was applied to altering the athletic eligibility rules, the Council on Athletics received the most checks, with 304 to 156 for Student Council.

The majority of the respondents do not believe "that the Interfraternity Council would be given absolute freedom in drawing up a set of rushing rules," as the tabulation indicates. Interesting in the replies is the similarity of opinion of the freshman and senior classes, a change from the upperclass-underclass differ-

	Yes	Per cent.	No	Per cent.
Fresh.	100	37.5	167	62.5
Soph.	74	52.4	67	47.6
Jr.	58	49.1	60	50.9
Sr.	48	38.4	77	61.6
	280	**43.**	**371**	**57.**

ences. Inasmuch as the freshmen are the class primarily affected by the rules and the seniors, the men who aided in the formulation of the code, their opinion may be considered as that of the undergraduate groups most familiar with the situation.

The reader's attention is called to the striking percentages listed under number twelve, "Do you as a student feel that you have ever had a share in determining a Rutgers administrative policy?"

	Yes	Per cent.	No	Per cent.
Soph.	12	8.0	138	92.
Jrs.	18	14.0	110	86.
Srs.	18	13.8	112	86.2
	48	**11.8**	**360**	**88.2**

Discounting the freshmen, who had been in Rutgers less than two months and whose opportunity to share was exceedingly minimal, only forty-eight of 408 students, 11.8 per cent., felt that they had shared. Despite this opinion, 306 of 418 members of the three upper classes had bothered to vote for Student Council members last spring. The almost identical judgment of the junior and senior classes, who had greater opportunity by virtue of mmbership in governing groups and longer attendance, suggests an accurate reflection of student participation.

In the tabulation by colleges the writers noted a marked difference, in most cases, between the opinions of the college of agriculture students and those in the other four divisions. This may suggest that the faculty and administration of that college are more sympathetic toward their undergraduates than the other groups, and consequently affect affirmatively the student judgment of the administration.

After probing the students' opinion of what they have or do, a test was made of what they would like to do. Six queries were carried under question thirteen:

Do you favor student participation to the extent of *direct initiative and referendum* in such matters as:

Curricula
Number of class cuts
Policy of the athletic organization
Probation rulings
Regulation of social functions of undergraduate groups
Compulsory chapel?

The results show little inclination to be concerned about curricula or class cuts, but a generally strong desire to share in the determination of the athletic policy. Apparently, the students want little to do with the question of scholastic probation, and the seniors least of all. But when such personal matters as regulation of social functions and attendance at compulsory chapel are in question, almost 90 per cent., desire direct action. In other words undergraduates as a group care much less about technical factors of college than they do concerning the regulation of their personal liberty.

In addition to the keynote of the preceding paragraph, the writers conclude that the effect of the freshman year is practically negligible in regard to the matter of student participation, and that sympathetic faculty treatment mellows the student view-point of the entire field of student participation.

Ernest E. McMahon
C. R. Foster, Jr.
Rutgers University

NEW BOOKS IN EDUCATION

McCloy, Charles H. *The Measurement of Athletic Power*. Pp. xiv + 178. Barnes. $3.00.

Marique, Pierre J. *History of Christian Education*. Vol. III. Pp. xiii + 286. Illustrated. Fordham University Press.

Ogburn, William F., Editor. *Social Changes in 1931*. Pp. v + 855–997. University of Chicago Press. $1.00.

Shambaugh, Mary E. *Folk Festivals*. Pp. xi + 154. 59 illustrations. Barnes. $3.00.

Sixty-fifth Annual Report of the State Board of Education, Showing Condition of the Public Schools of Maryland for the Year Ending July 31, 1931. Pp. 351. Illustrated. Department of Education of the State of Maryland.

Washburne, Carleton. *Remakers of Mankind*. Pp. 339. John Day. $3.00.

EDUCATIONAL REVIEW

Edited by WILLIAM McANDREW

EDITORIAL COMMENT

SAVING THE SCHOOLS FROM THE RETRENCHERS

Any one listening to the counsel exchanged during Minnesota's "Schoolmen's Week" might well broadcast the most of it to the rest of the country. For the nineteenth year the state university called in the educational managers from St. Vincent to Sumner, Laverne to Grand Portage and all between. There were bronzed schoolmen from the Lake of the Woods, from the iron country, from the prairies, from the sources of the Mississippi and from cities proud of their urbanity. The few guest speakers from out of the state did their duty in the matter of exhorting to "breadth of view," but the aid the schoolmen carried home was chiefly what every state is hungering for just now, help to keep a hysteria of economy from shattering the schools.

Quite properly the superintendents had a tax expert guest as speaker. He is the chairman of the research committee of the Minnesota Taxpayers Association. For an hour this clear-headed analyst expounded by means of graphic charts the large proportion of public funds that go to pay for schooling. There were no intimations from the man of mathematical mazes that the state is getting more than its money's worth from the schools. The masters listened with keen appreciation. One after another rose to compliment and thank the expositor for his clearness and skill. Beyond any doubt that audience appreciated the time and trouble bestowed upon them. I began to fear that there was to be a repetition of the old-time servility of schoolmen's meetings when we used to sit before eminent collegiate committees of entrance requirements and swallow like good little boys their absurd prescriptions for running our schools. But after, like gentlemen, the Minnesotans had thanked their guest, the men of the sky-blue water, the Gophers, as they call themselves, rose, one after another, and, in the best of good nature, pumped more than figures and statistics into the discussion.

"With all this," said one, "our friend may also keep the Taxpayers Association reminded that the best known bulwark against more depression is the maintenance of the highest degree of efficiency in the schools. The history of every country demonstrates what good schools do for prosperity. France and Spain are about the same size. In natural resources Spain has probably the better of the two. France has for many years maintained a good system of education. Spain has had almost none. Result? The wealth of France per capita is amazingly many times more than that of Spain. So is this true of Holland as compared with Italy. Brave little Denmark was starving to death. She organized a plan of universal schooling. She stands, to-day, an example of marvelous prosperity. Compare United States and Canada with our southern neighbor, Mexico. Why has that Spanish-American country, rich with the minerals, the petroleum, the soil, which generous Mother Nature has bestowed upon her, remained in poverty, while we, no more plentifully endowed, are so much better off? Schools, Brother, schools. I know you will keep reminding the Taxpayers Association of facts like this."

From one after another of the rural and urban schoolmen who took the floor I gathered from nine plain speakers these morsels to chew.

Minnesota Maxims

"Here are two towns ten miles apart, Bankton and Carter. Bankton boosts its schools. It chooses teachers with care and makes it worth their while to stay. Its retail business increases. Store windows are more attractive. Its newspaper gets more readers; its banks, more deposits; its homes are better painted; its yards are handsomer. Families move in, more homes are built. Poor Carter, with a tightwad school-board, is sapping the root of prosperity. Its more intelligent families have moved to Bankton because of better schools. Empty stores, fly-specked goods, cobwebs in the windows, litter in the streets are Carter's marks. This sort of thing is inevitable whenever a short-sighted policy cuts into schooling."

"My honorable board concluded it had to cut down salaries twenty per cent. We have lost from our twelve teachers three of our best and filled their places with inexperienced girls. Parents are complaining. We're cutting prosperity's throat."

"We are with the Taxpayers Association in favoring every real economy in our schools. We are for consolidation of all the adjacent 12 pupil schools, but the money we save should go to pay for better teaching. We have never had good enough, because we have never been given the money to buy it."

"You are not going to get anywhere by cutting teachers' pay. These are your own daughters. They live here. They spend here. All that they earn goes into Minnesota communities."

"What you should tell your Taxpayers Association is to campaign to stop the birth of children." (Laughter and applause.)

"Make no mistake about this. If a bridge falls down you can get along with a flatboat ferry for a time. If the roads wear out you can ride more slowly for a season. But you can't put off the education of the children. They are growing rapidly out of the educable age. Damage done now is irreparable loss to the community."

"The demand for lower salaries is made by those whose children have graduated. We must show that it is still true, as Adam Smith proved a hundred and fifty years ago, that 'wages are the encouragement of industry.' You can't get work out of thoroughbreds if you cut down their oats. You can't run your car on watered gasoline."

Teaching and Joy-Riding

"The country is suffering after its joy-ride. But the teachers had none of the post-war prosperity. Prices went up away beyond their wages. They are worse off now than they were in 1913."

"Tell the respected taxpayers what we are saving them by organized service. The regular rate of tutoring, if a parent had to hire it himself, is $2.00 an hour per child. That is $10.00 a day per child, $200.00 per day for the twenty our teachers care for—in the majority of cases they teach many more—that is $1,000. a week, $4,000. a month, $40,000.00 a year for each teacher. Then ask the taxpayers to see how many teachers are getting $40,000. a year. Why, man, we are the biggest money-savers you have."

Lighting the Home Fires

All through the week this theme of depression and education kept creeping into the speeches and discussions.

There were frequent exhortations to the participants that they organize for enlightenment as soon as they get home. "Get teachers and citizens into classes and retail the points you have gathered at these meetings. Organize your drives as you did the campaigns to sell Liberty bonds. Train your people to converse on the crisis. Keep a tally sheet for every worker. Whom will you see? When? Whom have you seen? What did he say? Get your key persons in your district. Don't whine nor complain. Say you enjoy teaching their children and serving this community. Saying so often enough will get you to believing you are of that sort."

Coffman Counsel

A climax in this line was the address of Lotus Coffman, president of the state university.

"Our Democracy," he said, "is faced as never before in your lifetime with the necessity of outlining and pursuing programs for the present and far into the future. No patched-up arrangement will do."

Needs can not be defined in terms of mere statistics. Education is investment. You must remind your people that they desire that the common life of their community and of the state shall go on and at a high level. They have been wise and courageous in daring to build a democracy in which the training of youth does not fluctuate up and down with the stock market. It may be necessary that adjustments be made. They should be in terms of educational reorganization rather than in terms of destructive retrenchment. You can and should redistrict, consolidate certain agencies and abandon others. You will so improve the service. But a move for retrenchment based on attacks on educational institutions is too full of prejudice and too lacking in foresight. Retrenchment must not mean poor teachers, restricted programs, shortened terms, poor equipment and lowered salaries. For it is too plain that this means cheap teaching, cheap citizens, less buying, less production, more pauperism and crime.

CAPITALIZE THE CRISIS

This crisis demands the making of a constructive, orderly and well-integrated educational program for the state.

It is an issue as great and an opportunity as genuine as you schoolmasters ever faced. The issue is: Shall we surrender to the depression our spiritual vision, our intellectual outlook, and our social hopes for the country, or shall we hold fast with grim determination to plan a better day? If we neglect our duty our educational system will follow wayward and uncertain business cycles.

With commendable tenacity since pioneer days we have held that the life of the nation turns upon the education of its citizens. The facts have justified this belief.

Curtailments of education will dry up the sources of community strength and future wealth.

We are still spending billions for nonessentials and luxuries.

We pay more for the operation of automobiles than we do for food, clothing or shelter.

In balancing the budget we must not cripple those agencies that are essential to economic welfare. No state can expect a revival of finances by underfeeding the forces of growth and idealism. Budget-making in depression is a test of what we really believe in.

And the children keep coming. There is no shortage of youth. More and better training is needed by each succeeding generation, for the abundant opportunities of an unoccupied continent disappear. Only by better trained intelligence can the new complexities be met. The expansion of education has come through the demands of the people themselves. Show them what they have. Ask that their fostering care be not hastily withdrawn. Make clear the situation of the educational workers. For twenty years they have been living on deflated incomes, struggling to advance learning. They have been willing to devote themselves to social progress. They took the vows of a self-denying profession for the benefit of youth and of humanity.

It is of the highest importance that the American people reassert their faith in fundamental matters at this time. In curtailing budgets we must not lose our democracy. Economic distress has led to dictatorships, communism and encroachments by special interests in other parts of the world to the impairment of the ideals of democracy. We are not without signs that some of these forces are stalking boldly in America.

Here the chief joy of the poor man is the opportunity the schools afford his children. Equality and excellence as well as economy must be safeguarded.

Dr. Coffman's presentations gave the schoolmen the ammunition they want for defense at home. They asked for a copy of his address and proposed to mimeograph it and supply every member with a transcript.

"We can do better than that," said he, "I'll print it."

Accordingly, by this time, each has a twenty page pamphlet as supplement to the counsel and direction all are giving their home folks to ward off a great disaster.

BREACHES IN THE BREASTWORKS

Are you not thinking of some other aspects to which you should direct the attention of your school workers at this time?

It scarcely seems probable that there is any notion among your citizens that the equipment and efficiency of their fire-prevention service should be reduced.

The safeguarding of water supply and health measures of the town will not be permitted to lapse.

But there is a considerable and growing fault-finding with schools as not being as alive as they should be to the kind of service they should be rendering to the community. This magazine has been presenting, once a month, the views of eminently respectable people that too much of the school's offering is of antiquated matter that is of less use to the country's present needs than other training would be. The lower grades have cleaned house of a great deal of such antiques—useless spelling tables, unused arithmetic complexities, and so forth. But the doubts assembled by Briggs. Rugg, Allen, Bode, Russell, Eldridge, Frazier, Munro, Snedden, Dewey, Kilpatrick and Prosser, to name only a dozen out of a counted two hundred well-known critics, are that the teachers of the higher grades are spending time on mulling over subjects that the majority of taxpayers can not see the value of. President Frazier contends that the college-entrance boards are the main obstacle against getting rid of these "dry husks of past learnings." There is the additional fact that a considerable number of your teachers have spent much time to make their living by these subjects. The weak, unproved contention that these things put an edge upon the mind, enabling it to cut away our economic and political evils, gets nowhere with your every-day citizen or with the newspaper editors who direct his thinking. The isolation and selfishness of American high schools is still a fatal weakness in thousands of them. "We must reorganize our education," said President Coffman just now, "to meet the changing conditions." These conditions are of a bewildered citizenry not trained to cooperative solution of community problems.

Doesn't it seem that now is the time to end this isolation of schools from direct community service and to put them into such evident welfare work that the whole town must see it?

"What have you done this week for Fairhaven?" is the question asked each Friday by the teachers in Charles Prior's Massachusetts town. "Clean up, paint up!" the Chicago high-school boys and girls are saying—and doing. If anything is likely to wind a community's affections around its schools it is to see that these youngsters, whose education is costing more than any other tax-paid project, are doing good things now in return, at the actual time they are receiving their largesses. "You boys," says Henry Wollman, attorney, addressing the New York High School of Commerce," are actually hired by the city as much as the street-sweepers are. Now, what are you doing for the city now? Roosevelt's address to the Ithaca students was in the same tenor. If you had worked this thing out on this line in the past, you would not be so near to danger as you are. There are few signs of this dissatisfaction dying out. The future support of education depends on a demonstration of direct aid to community life rendered by your school.

This leads up to some more quotations from men who have thought out the whole theory of education in a democracy. Here are some views of those who at the beginning of the Republic conceived the plan of taxing the whole people for the training of the children of those who in the older days themselves paid the cost. The change of responsibility followed a new philosophy. The promise was made by the revolution. Fulfilment rests on you.

CHOICE BOOKS

GETTING ACQUAINTED WITH DEMOCRACY

"Don't guess; base your answers on facts," says Dr. Capen,[1] beginning a workbook on government, its nature, forms and functions.

Bless me, what a revolution will come when the schools of the country have delivered an electorate who will thus answer the problems presented by the ballot!

This book merges history, politics, economics and law as they are integrated in the life of the nation. There are plans for debate on unsettled questions; there are objections and approvals of our democracy as it now is; there are discussions of party policies; there are civil service, World Court and League of Nations. The boy or girl who comes through these exercises will possess, done by his own hand, a treatise on what the Union is and what it ought to be. The plan is the result of the trials of an experienced high-school teacher.

[1] Louise Irving Capen, "Workbook in Local, State and National Government." American Book Company, New York. 246 pp. 60 cents.

WHY SCHOOLS LACK EDUCATIONAL SIGNIFICANCE

"A classic of educational doctrine," must be your estimate of the report of the American Historical Association's commission on social studies.[2] Charles Beard, Hoosier, New Yorker, world citizen, historian, whither-mankinder, has drafted it. Krey, Ballou, Bowman, Counts, Day, Newlon, Horn, Comstock, Craven, Ford, Hayes, Johnson, Marshall, Merriam and Steiner are the other barons of this Magna Charta. They have been concentrating on it for seven years, working specifically on this report since 1929. They have gathered opinion from teachers, boiled it down, framed conclusions, criticized their own work, reached agreement and entrusted it to Expert Beard to clothe in fitting language. He has given it a dignity and poise suggestive of the best political classics of our history.

"Our own age and the past," says Chairman Krey in his preface to the charter, "have been drawn upon in this effort to open for teachers and for men and women in every walk of life the prospect of an understanding of the world to-day and of the forces with which youth must reckon in shaping the world of to-morrow."

We are convinced, say these students of our situation, that our educational program needs readjustment. Educators are not unconcerned. Our curricula have been characterized by investigators as being a chaos.

This charter considers the disturbing fact that political questions are highly controversial but the schools can not ignore them. Almost regularly our government is shaken by scandalous revelations and involved in bitter conflicts. On every hand dissatisfaction is found with our present industrial order. Yet these questions are excluded from the text-books. In some communities, supposed to be enlightened, teachers are forbidden to discuss Russia without denouncing her. According to the testimony of members of this commission on the social studies, teachers of history in one of our states do not dare to have it known they have books on Russia in their possession. School boards have specific rules forbidding the presence of controversial matters in school exercises. Superintendent Maxwell ordered the discontinuance of essays on woman suffrage when that question was rife. The school board of Washington disciplined a woman teacher who permitted a class in civics to investigate Bolshevism.

What are School Essentials

But pupils from the seventh grade up are keen to gain information upon these matters. Nor is it possible for school boards to escape the necessity of dealing with live issues.

What are they? They are the very essentials of the aim of civic instruction, chiefly for which American schools were made the agency of a democratic state. The public school is supported by taxation chiefly for strengthening democratic institutions, for making clear their workings, for pointing out defects generally agreed upon, for providing more effective leadership, for illuminating every possible corner of the political scene, for promoting habits of criticism among the electorate. This has not been done and can not be by the majority of the prevailing lessons in the schools, or by reciting creeds or repeating ceremonial formulas, even in the presence of the flag. You have to make direct studies of the actual pressures operating in politics and government and of the concrete issues behind the verbalism of partisan oratory. Amazing to say, this is the very thing forbidden by school boards and administrators and is also the preponderating activity which the original promoters of schools at public expense prescribed.

If schools do not participate in creative political enterprise it will continue to go on without them and keep them deprived of significance in the educative process.

On page 79 is a tabular summary of American goals. It is so simplified that it is impossible to condense for this brief review the industrial, educational, political, recreational, sanitary and esthetic needs of the communal life.

Plain-spoken, but by no means despairing, is the charter's survey of the obstacles in the way of a reasonable school program—the static school boards, the timid teachers, the superintendents with ears to ground, the money invested in existing texts, and all the excuses real and visionary that keep us away from the great adventure.

It is a judicious presentation. Its urge is not unduly emotional but comes from a remarkable assembling of elemental facts of axiomatic quality.

[2] Charles A. Beard, "A Charter for the Social Sciences in the Schools." Charles Scribner's Sons, New York. 122 pp. $1.25.

This work is a notable triumph, worth the 1932 prize. Bravo, Committeemen! Bravo, Beard!

WHAT'S THE MATTER WITH HIGH SCHOOL?

If University-of-California Smith entitled his book[3] as I do my review of it, you negative-minded people would assume it to be a list of ailments. A moralist may well weep over the number of words like "villain," "wench," "asylum" and "politics," that have lost their good names. Once I heard an election crowd in Quebec cry, "What's the matter wit' Laurier?" and answer themselves, "He's planty well."

This survey of secondary education, remarkable for its breadth and vision, finds good matter and monumental stupidities. Smith's measuring sticks are straight and definite. He convinces you they are the criteria that must be used. No doctrines of educational authorities, no college-entrance boards, no high-hat classical investigation is too sacred to escape his calm, keen appraisal. After the author has brought you up to 1890 by one of the clearest extant narratives of the history of near-modern education, you are launched into a series of chapters that will put you into unescapable critical reflection. If ever a multitude of facts were digested you have them thus conditioned here. Professor Smith must have refined his outline over and again; for the pieces of his composition fit into one another like the inlaying of a master craftsman. I hesitate to quote parts lest I make a jumble. The theme cementing the book together is the fact that the democracy that was planned in 1787 must determine what public schools shall do. In spite of the demands of the thinkers who expounded the theory of education for a nation of self-governors, high schools soon lost their legitimate aim and, up to 1890, at least, served mostly as a college-preparatory agency which was democratic in name only. Nominally, high school is open to all children of secondary-school age. In practice it administers to little more than one half of those who need it. Its curriculum is closed to much that is of vital interest in contemporary life. We are still, in too much of our program, allied with the secondary-school usage of other countries, where this grade of educational service is selective and aristocratic. They aim at the training of socially and intellectually élite. Even abroad, this exclusive policy is on the defensive. It is in a desperate struggle to maintain the schools as they were.

Our high-school workers are, on one hand, the formalists clinging to a given scheme, maintainers of an exploded theory of mental discipline believed obtainable from algebra, language and standard courses. Their hope is to force minds into beaten paths. They fit for only a static world order (or college). They do not prepare for a dynamic, changing civilization nor for active participation in a modern democracy. They have given us generations with no foundation or ability to think on economic and political problems.

On the other hand, there are coming to the front educators who give little heed to disciplinary studies. They admit no ready-made adult régime for which youth must be prepared. Instead, they conceive that the future must be moulded and shaped on new lines. By intelligence and will a world of understandings, knowledge and wisdom must be built.

An Antiquated Aim

"Active, dynamic citizenship" recurs often in these pages. It must integrate the secondary school. A democracy can not rise above the level of its constituents. Self-government depends on self-determining citizens. The new high-school curriculum-maker selects the traits and characteristics which constitute the indispensable as well as desirable equipment of the good citizen. Then he selects and organizes the activities and experiences through which these may be realized. Such exercises make the daily, weekly and six- or four-year program of a legitimate American high school. Where is an institution thus ordered? The planners in 1787 made curriculums of that sort. But they were statesmen with their eyes on preserving and perfecting a democracy. The scholastic curriculum retainers failed to grasp the revolution. They continued to imitate the plans devised by scholars for scholars. Democracy, politics, self-government, community welfare, even after the legislatures have been induced to put the cost

[3] William A. Smith, "Secondary Education in the United States." The Macmillan Company, New York. 429 pp. $2.50.

of the schooling also on people who had no children, gained no entrance by a revolution of school aims. The most famous high-school document of modern times, the celebrated Report of The Committee of Ten, was a defense of scholarly subjects as subjects, a plan for a more satisfactory preparation of a few favored youth for college.

You see running through this Smith book the the vein of protest such as marks the work of Snedden, Cox, Kilpatrick, Watson, Bagley, Dewey, Briggs, Russell and Harold Clark, during the last three years. They are making publishers afraid of offerings that accept such defenses of high-school procedure as the high-school people are wont to offer. I saw a masterly written manuscript yesterday that had been rejected by three houses already because "it is good for 1925 but not for now," "too complacent," "old stuff."

The modern high school, argues our Smith, must be a miniature democracy. Every pupil must get plenty of practice in cooperative government. Experimentation in this line must be encouraged. Pupil representatives, loyal to the general good, must be elected; self-seeking school politicians, curbed. The high school must be a veritable civic laboratory. The program of pupil participation in school government must be sequentially planned and carefully articulated at successive levels through the junior and senior high-school period. The absolute teacher government does inestimable harm. The social studies curriculum should grow out of this pupil civic experience. It is easier to administer each separately. It is easier to go on than to change. If the high schools were to organize on the basis of serving the community, much that is now taught would at once be seen to be obsolete. The general report of the classical investigation is a conspicuous example of using what is as an argument for what ought to be. It was an attempt to get better teaching of Latin, but it side-stepped the question whether Latin should be taught at all.

These considerations, selected by me here and there from the book, show its trend. They do not do justice to the prevailing tone of its constructive measures. In its treatment of characteristics of pupils, curriculum construction and practices, extra-curricular trends and needs, examinations, promotions, ability groupings, prevention of failure, and so on, it is an inspiring guide for the administration of both junior and senior high schools. This craftwise Smith, "with force of fervent heat, the hardest yron soone doth mollify, that with his artful sledge he can it beat, and fashion it to what he list apply."

READING THE THOUGHT OF THINKING SOULS

To lure from cheap reading to what Stuart Sherman called the large language of the gods, the high style of heroes of the great days before the flood, requires art in the selection of the substitutes offered. Rainey and Johnston's collection[4] is made up of pieces with a verve and tang, making the call to duty a more important motive than commonly conceived by the despairing English teacher. The Abbé Dimnet is not the only cultivated observer who calls our American readers depraved by pep, punch, razz, jazz, the daily paper and the quick-selling magazine.

Here are 142 compositions arranged as expositions, arguments, addresses, descriptions, narrations, letters, biographies, essays and short stories. Under each classification the specimens are further classified by designated qualities to facilitate finding when the rhetoric instructor is in a particular field. The authors employed vary from John Henry Newman to O. Henry. Here are Huxley, Lamb, Schopenhauer, Emerson, Darwin, Dickens, Scott, Ruskin, Thoreau, Stevenson, Galsworthy, Poe, Lincoln, Woodrow Wilson, Broun, Morley, Wister, Benet, Stefansson, Ingersoll, Elihu Root, Page, Conrad, Upton Sinclair, Alexander Woollcott, Carlyle, Irving, William Allen White, *The Christian Science Monitor* and *Time*. The selected writers are concerned with matters varying from Maude Adams, American politicians and taxi drivers to education, liberty and the destiny of man.

The book is a boon to English teachers in high school and college. It is planned as ac-

[4] Andrew Robert Rainey, Winifred Johnston, "Readings in English Prose." Doubleday, Doran and Company, Garden City, New York. 651 pp. $2.00.

companiment to the university freshman course in rhetoric with or without formal text-book.

The authors consider it a manual for training in techniques and for appreciative reading. They introduce each group of compositions by means of short evaluating suggestions. I have not seen a more enlivening course of reading.

SCHOOLMASTERY EXTRAORDINARY

If I have gone too far in telling the compilers of "The Principal and His Community"[5] that you are enthusiastic and grateful for this notable Eleventh Yearbook of the nation's schoolmasters, the fault is yours for not warning me. I find it tremendously stimulating. These people are certainly aware that the depression threatens some coldness of the people, other than parents, toward education and that the public-school principal is in the position that puts the duty on him to keep the community's affection warm. The editors begin by telling you that the principal is the social engineer of his district and that the non-school forces must be utilized. William John Cooper and Frank Cody have been allowed to say a few good words for a starter; some social-aid workers are sprinkled here and there, but the richness and practicality of the book lie in the contributions of the experienced men and women in command of schools, north, south, east, west and in our territorial possessions.

The damage of complaining and negative letters to parents, the delicate handling of excellent missionaries who rush to school with their cherished moral campaigns, the clever advertisers, the wicked newspaper editors, the splendid support of parent cooperating clubs, visiting teachers, direct community service by schools, every large social welfare interest aided by schools, and some which ought to be, are covered by workers who impress you as full of definite, practiced information. A copious index makes this collection into a manual, a guide for new principals, a tonic corrective for old ones.

[5] Earl Lang, Aaron Kline, Isabel Tucker, Helen Shove and 71 contributors, ''The Principal and His Community. Eleventh Yearbook.'' Department of Elementary-School Principals. National Education Association, 1201 16th St., Washington, D. C. 621 pp. $2.00.

ELEVEN THOUSAND EDUCATORS EPITOMIZED[6]

Once the table companions of Alexander the Great were discussing musical instruments. What is the most pleasing musical sound, that of the flute, or of the lyre, or of what? Some one said, "Let's ask the Big Chief." As Alexander came in the question was put to him. He answered, "The sweetest sound in all the world is the voice of him who sings my praises." The praise in Dr. Cattell's encyclopedic book of worthies is in its title: "Leaders in Education." All the rest is plain facts. Frank Cody is not credited with his smile, nor is Edwin Broome called the handsomest schoolman in America; nor Charles Glenn, Willis Sutton or Norman Crozier cited for perfection of manners. They and the 11,000 other tenders of the light are all biographed in this plain style: **"Potter, Supt. Milton C(hase)**, Administration Building, Public Schools, Milwaukee, Wis. Otsego, Mich, Nov. 5, 73. Ph.B, Albion, 95; Ph.M, Chicago, 05; Litt.D, Denver, 15; M.Pd, Mich. State Nor. Col, 15. Teacher, Springport, Mich, 95–96; prin, elementary sch, Oak Park, Ill, 96–98; high sch, Superior, Wis, 98–03; *supt. schools,* Idaho Springs, Colo, 03–07, Pueblo, 07–12; St. Paul, Minn, 12–14; *Milwaukee, Wis, 14–* Lecturer, Wisconsin and Colo. State Nor. Col, 16–19. Pres, state board education, Colo, 10. N.E.A. (director, 14–15); Dept. Supt. (pres, 32); Colo. Ed. Ass. (pres, 11–12); Wis. Teachers Ass. (pres, 16–17). School administration; English treatises and text-books." Fifty-nine years in fifteen lines.

The editor is a scientist and thereby objective. The early dictionaries, he says, contained comments as well as definitions. Thus Dr. Johnson, after defining "pension," says, "it is generally understood to mean pay given to a state hireling for treason to his country." Webster, after defining "sauce," remarked, "cranberries make the best sauce." No such appraisement will be found in this book. The sketches, like the definitions in the modern dictionary, are intended to be strictly objective, giving only information that relates to the educational career.

At the beginning of each entry is the full

[6] J. McKeen Cattell, ''Leaders in Education. A Biographical Directory.'' The Science Press, New York. 1037 pp. $10.00.

name with title and the mail address. The part of the name ordinarily omitted is in parentheses in accordance with the method introduced by the editor in his "American Men of Science" in 1906. There then follow the place and date of birth with the educational institutions attended and the degrees awarded, with the dates. Positions held are given in some detail, the present position being in italics. Honorary, temporary and minor positions are then recorded, followed by membership in educational societies. The sketch concludes with a brief statement of the character of activities and publications. The abbreviations are intended to be self-explanatory.

Honor Rolls Before

Twenty-six years ago, after Dr. Cattell had been in control of the weekly journal, *Science*, for ten years, he published the first edition of "American Men of Science" containing about 4,000 brief biographies. The fifth edition, due next January, will carry 20,000 sketches, a five-fold increase of scientific work in America in these twenty-six years. A principal object of the work is the maintenance of a common interest and spirit of cooperation among writers in science by enabling them to become better acquainted with one another and one another's work. School and Society was established, and this directory, "Leaders in Education," is now published to further the same ends among workers in education. The directory, like the journal, is concerned with the whole field from the pre-nursery school to the educational service for the oldest learners. It includes those working in libraries, museums, social agencies and other activities outside the standardized schools and colleges. It covers the United States and Canada. The editor hopes it will in a modest way emphasize and promote the unity of education. The omissions, if you note any, are due to failure or delay by some who were asked to reply. A second edition can be more complete. Most of the women have divulged their birth date; some of the men have not.

The constant worker on the long task of collecting and arranging the data was the experienced manager, Mrs. E. E. Ross.

Are you familiar with earlier efforts of this sort? Twenty-five years ago Albert E. Winship compiled a few short biographies of the several hundred schoolmen he admired and printed them in alphabetical portions in his *Journal of Education*. Eleven years ago William H. Allen brought out his "Who's Who and Why in After-War Education," a pioneer effort to start fact-based, specific, impersonal, unprejudiced, growing, freshly repleted forward steps for and in education." The questionnaire used to collect these data frightened some of the modest men. "What forward steps have you taken since 1917, widely helpful in defining the objects of education and helping the public see them?" This was the main question, followed by 25 specific suggestions as to what such steps ought to be. Ettinger, superintendent of New York City schools, got off with one word and three letters. Columbia Butler's alleged "forward steps" were fourteen red-hot sneers at the education of the time. Charles Hubbard Judd got one line; John Dewey, two; the superintendent of Fennimore, Wisconsin, 43. The list ran over 2,000 entries. I note 29 Smiths in the Allen book. Dr. Cattell has 127, six of them being Johns. Allen has a dozen Joneses; Cattell, 58; Allen's Browns, 14; Cattell's, 48. I do like research, or advertising, whichever it is I am here doing.

Our Migratory Scholars

Are you addicted to uses of alphabetized matter other than looking for something you already have in your mind? If not, you have missed much of the joys of the educated man. Justice Thomas Churchill, sometime president of the New York City Board of Education; the late Justice Gaynor, once mayor of the metropolis, both brilliant conversationalists and rich in expressive words, used to read the dictionary as Bridget O'Reilly reads the list of those present at the Van Bluster ball—for the sheer joy of it.

Take your "Leaders in Education." After you have felt the thrill of seeing your own name in bold print or have withstood the pang of finding it left out, start anywhere. Read and ponder:

How many schoolmen grow up with their town and stay by it?

How many towns have the plain sense to keep

an educator after he has learned his art at the expense of the community?

How does the permanence of a schoolman compare with that of a factory foreman?

What would you advocate to avoid this waste?

Leonard Ayres' rating of the states according to his criteria for efficient educational service was a noteworthy piece of research. The distress of faculty committees at finding fresh investigations to be made by their candidates for a degree of doctor of philosophy could be lessened in at least one instance if they set some one to comparing cities on the holding power exercised over their superintendents of schools. The president of the Norwalk board of education, praising its superintendent, said they knew that they must lose him as other cities would pay him more. When you come to think of it, isn't this a most absurd idea, to confess, as a matter of course, that a school manager is too good for Norwalk?

Through page after page I read the amazing itineraries of the professors and superintendents. Sample: "Teacher, rural schools, Cass County, Nebraska, 06–08; prin. high school, Bloomfield, 08–09; supervisor demonstration high school, University of Nebraska, 09–10; supt. schools, Plainview, 10–11; asst. prof. education, University of Wisconsin, 11–13; assoc. prof, University of Kentucky, 13–14, head of agr. exp. sta, 14–17; research specialist marketing, Washington Col, 19–21; bur. agr. econ, U. S. Dept. Agr, 21–22; engaged in business, Wash, 22–23; prof. econ, Westminster, Pa, 23–24; agr. ed. and agr. econ, University of New Mexico, 24–28; U. S. Census, 29–32." Most of the biographies are like that. What first-hand geography these unmossy rolling stones might teach!

But when I go back to Ypsilanti, it seems to me that my old gentlemen and ladies who are living in the original family homestead are the lucky ones. They know where the old photographs and souvenirs are that they bring out to gladden the memory of happy days. We schoolmasters can't find anything. Some driver of a moving van stole the family Bible. The stuffing of grandfather's chair has been ripped out by the rocker packed next to it. Successive breaking of ties between a schoolmaster and his neighbors is fatal to the friendliness which education needs. I'd sooner be Levi Douglas Wines (page 1012). There's the boy! Born 1852, Ann Arbor, teacher mathematics, Ann Arbor High School since 1879. Member park board Ann Arbor, treasurer musical society and choral union, president Michigan Schoolmasters Club.

Dear old "L.D.," welcoming to his classes the boys and girls whose fathers and mothers he taught; L.D., discovering the same kinks in the youngsters' heads one or the other of the parents had had twenty-five years before. Imagine the invitations to birthday parties and weddings! Fancy having within walking distance of you a family of a thousand foster children who "liked geometry" because they liked you! And imagine the delight of having a clientele so strong you can, without a tremor, tell a board member who gets bothersome he's crazy!

But, as to 10,000 of these alphabetized torch-bearers, they are "far from the fair land that gave them their birth." Dr. Johan Arnd Aasgaard, who is the Abou Ben Adhem of the list, is exceptional. Born in Albert Lea, Minnesota, his teaching has been in Wisconsin, in Colorado and is now in Minneapolis. Professor William Zuker, last on the noble roll, sees the light in a Kansas town, works in Colorado, Des Moines, and now labors in Dubuque.

If the distances these 11,000 men and women are from their birthplaces were added together it would make a journey well toward Betelguese, if any one cares to go thither.

Fading Names and Persisting

Are you curious to know how the names of famous educators of former times are represented among present leaders? There is no Luther; but a Milton guides the high school in St. Joseph, Michigan. Rabelais, Montaigne and Rousseau are missing; but Bacon lives and moves in Forty Fort, New Haven, Evanston, Kalamazoo, Annapolis and Hanover. Sturm is absent, but a Sturmer is dean of Philadelphia College. Our own pioneer Franklin could find seven of his name on the roll; Jefferson, only one, teaching geography in the Michigan State Normal College in Ypsilanti. Of Horace Mann's tribe there are ten; of Barnard's, four, William T. Harris' name-children are 23 in all; Mary Lyon's, 8; Emma Willard's, 6. Eight notables are rubbing off the smear of Ichabod

Crane; an equal number are the professional sons and daughters of Schoolmaster Nathan Hale. There is no Harvard; one Yale.

You'll find no end of research material in this book if you will give yourself the pleasure of using it.

Do you care to investigate how to become a college president?

Be born in Vermont, attend college in Michigan, take postgraduate courses in Harvard, Halle and Berlin, teach in Minnesota and Chicago, get to be a dean somewhere, and the presidency of Yale is yours.

Or, start your life in Salem, Indiana; attend the normal school and the state university, teach in your own state, become professor of education in the University of Illinois, the same in the University of Minnesota for five years. When you reach the age of 45 your own board will make you president.

Degrees After Sun-up

Another study worth your spare moments might consider the awarding of honorary degrees. This fat volume offers abundant suggestion that the donors give you these when you need them least. It is like the issue of railroad passes. When you are an humble impecunious member of a railroad staff and wish you could, on your short vacation, go back home to see your mother, no connecting railway will give you anything. But after you have risen to be president and are drawing a salary large enough to cover *de luxe* travel, all the transportation companies send you annual passes without your asking. You may observe a similar procedure by observing in this volume the dates of the conferring of academic degrees. You may study hard and succeed as superintendent of Stonebridge schools, working better and more energetically than ninety-nine hundredths of the higher-ups who are getting a new degree every year. No one gives you one when it would be of use to you. When the turn of fortune puts you on the roof of a famous institution, the collegiate world comes running with gew-gaws that are of no use to you—ladders you no longer need.

Decline of Shame

Another study the book might suggest to you is whether the old reproach that no schoolmaster wants his son to be one still holds true. Frederick Luther Gamage (p. 338) ought to remember the canvass John Buchanan made of the New York Schoolmasters' Association in 1894, getting a unanimous statement that none of us went into teaching with intent to stay and none of us wanted our children to come in. But a little while ago this Gamage, after forty-eight years' enjoyment, told me of his delight that his son, doing well in business, had concluded that teaching is the most satisfactory of pursuits. The James and William Russells (pp. 807, 808), the Angells (p. 25), the McMurrys (p. 611); the Holmeses, Stanley and William, are a few of the cases of interfamilial imitation and gladness in following father's footsteps.

And will some one who counts the amazing number of widely placed educators who have been transplanted from Maine investigate the reasons?

I could say a deal more of this book but forbear for fear you might think I was persuading you to buy a copy.

It is a monument of industry and skilled labor, a most important utility for the schoolman's library.

Eleven thousand short and simple annals of the poor.

LURE OF THE SHIP[7]

I REMEMBER attending a school entertainment in Arizona and hearing a boy recite, "The sea! the sea! the open sea! The blue, the fresh, the ever free! Without a mark, without a bound, it runneth the earth's wide regions round."

"He must be a New Englander," I said.

"No," answered the teacher, "he was born here and his folks were raised in Missouri."

Frank Whitney once called my attention to the prevalence of marine pictures on the walls all through Montana. At Great Falls, in that state, a man had a square-rigged ship big enough to carry eight people and with hardly room to turn around in the river. He had to install a motor.

Toy ships are sold in New Mexico and South Dakota.

There seems to be some salt water in the blood of us all.

[7] Ellison Hawks, "The Romance of the Merchant Ship." Thomas Y. Crowell Company, New York. 319 pp. $3.00.

Your youngsters will revel in Ellison Hawks' magnificent book, "The Romance of the Merchant Ship." He is the editor of *The Meccano Magazine,* which is a favorite with boys. He starts with the floating log, covers the ships of the ancients, of the explorers, of the clipper period and uses fascinating pictures. The coming of steam, liners of to-day, the companies and owners, engines and motors, cargoes, tankers, refrigerators, tugs, ice-breakers, dredges, whalers, building, launching, navigating, and much beside, are described with enthusiasm. It will be a favorite in your school library.

THE SCHOOL BOARD GRILLED

WHEN Louis Benezet was a Hoosier schoolmaster one of his lines of research was on the reading done by board members. He couldn't find educational matter present except in the amounts which, too small to measure, are given by chemical analysts the designation, *"traces."* Even these, Benezet could not discover in relation to his own reports as superintendent addressing the board. George Grill, Ohio schoolmaster, has written a book[8] particularly for school boards. If anything can lure them into the habit of reading about education in other than the local newspapers, George's effort ought to do it. For he starts with the things the board meets at every session: Minutes. How will you number and index them? How will you save time wasted over them? How correct them? What philosophy does the secretary need? Mr. Grill asks and answers these and many other questions. Acting on the well-established principle that corporate bodies speak through their minutes, this experienced schoolman is careful to reproduce forms of resolutions and contracts, types of action and recording, so explicit that in cases of disputes the minutes will leave little chance for doubt as to what the board intended and did. With this purpose the book covers actions relating to teachers, pupils, janitor, engineers, finance, bonds, real estate, building construction, maintenance, supplies and text-books.

An appalling amount of valuable time is wasted by school boards, says the author. The large questions of educational policies are crowded out.

It will pay you to requisition for the school library as many copies as you have board members and to ask the librarian to issue a copy to each trustee. They will find that the superintendent, who appears as "A. L. Wright" throughout the book, is a model of respectful attitude.

8 George W. Grill, ''The Minutes of a Board of Education.'' Bruce Publishing Company, Milwaukee. 215 pp. $3.15.

A NEW LINCOLN[9]

EMANUEL HERTZ, tireless collector of Lincoln manuscripts, papers, clippings and all, finds periods of the president's life hitherto unaccounted for among the documents published in the standard editions of Lincoln's works. Collectors have hidden choice papers for years. A mass of such treasure was burned in the Chicago fire. From new material that he has obtained by a study of catalogues of dealers in autographs, from Russian archives, from hundreds of hitherto undiscovered sources, Dr. Hertz goes through thirty-five hundred new documents, messages, notes of speeches, and so forth, and prints 460 pages of intimate Lincoln material—letters to wife, to friends, to complaining constituents and to congratulators, memoranda on legal actions, notes of speeches, a rich collection of authentic phases of a kaleidoscopic life.

In fifty-two brilliant chapters the indefatigable author imparts his enthusiasm, affection and worship for the great war president. The themes are such as only a richly equipped biographer could handle: Lincoln, the Lawyer; Lincoln, the Legislator; Lincoln, the Diplomat; Lincoln, the Politician; Lincoln, the Statesman; Lincoln, the Friend; Lincoln, the Military Man; Lincoln, the Literary Artist; Lincoln, the Ridiculed; Lincoln, the Seer, and so on. This plan of writing reverses a common type of Lincoln biography in which a history of the slavery struggle overshadows the personality of the hero. Dr. Hertz's work is a series of vivid word-pictures of the man which are done with abundant warmth and spirit. The reproductions of paintings, photographs, engravings and cartoons of Lincoln portraits are marvelous in amount and interest. Nicholas Murray Butler has an introduction to the volumes, commending Dr. Hertz's years of patient industry and his loving enthusiasm for the martyr president.

9 Emanuel Hertz, ''Abraham Lincoln. A New Portrait.'' Horace Liveright, Inc., New York. 1006 pp. 2 vols. $10.00.

SCHOOL AND SOCIETY

EDITED BY J. McKEEN CATTELL

WITH WHICH IS COMBINED THE

EDUCATIONAL REVIEW

EDITED BY WILLIAM McANDREW

Volume 35 SATURDAY, JUNE 11, 1932 Number 911

THE WEST POINT SYSTEM OF EDUCATION

By Lieutenant-Colonel C. L. HALL

U. S. MILITARY ACADEMY, WEST POINT, N. Y.

FROM time to time, and more especially after a war, the United States Military Academy receives a great deal of unfavorable criticism. Not much of this criticism is based on analysis either of the West Point course or of the character of the student body. Usually the critic judges from his personal experience with graduates with whom he has been thrown in contact. He has no means of determining if the men he served with are typical. He also usually fails to examine his own mental conditions at the moment of the incident of which he complains.

In war, the army is enormously expanded. Officers are placed in positions of responsibility for which they have not had progressive training. They are required to deal with subordinates of an intellectual and social position entirely different from that which they are accustomed to find in the lower grades of the army. Moreover, the expansion is so sudden that some total misfits are sure to be found in high places, at the beginning of a war, at any rate. If the medical profession were expanded so rapidly that every interne were suddenly expected to perform major operations, or the legal profession so that every law clerk had important cases in the Supreme Court, there would be sad tales from intelligent laymen suddenly conscripted as anesthetists or as junior law partners.

In the nature of things, therefore, relations between permanent and temporary officers in war are sometimes strained. During the late war, this strain was evident in all armies. The post-war English and French memoirs are full of echoes of pride hurt by regular army tactlessness, of promotion held up by regular army distrust of able reserve officer subordinates, and of brains shocked by regular army lack of intellectual breadth. None of the authors, however, deem it necessary to put the blame on Sandhurst or on St. Cyr. The writer's personal experience, in fact, was that the most acid criticisms of regular officers to be heard anywhere during the late war were those by French reserve medical officers about the French regular army medical personnel. There was no school available here upon which to put the blame.

In spite of the universal existence of strain in regular reserve relations, some American critics have seen fit to put the whole blame therefor on certain alleged errors of West Point. Such action is clearly unfair. Imagine what a case could be made against Harvard if thousands of graduates of other institutions had been compulsorily employed for two years under Harvard alumni younger than themselves, and all the grudges induced had been summarized without analysis. The university's logicians would have had no difficulty in proving the unfairness of the resultant criticism.

West Point has also been blessed with much praise. Part of this comes from men who were lucky in war in the kind of graduate they served under. Part of it is based on the large number of graduates among successful military leaders. In view of the Military Academy's predominant place in the production of army officers, this doesn't prove so much. The most really flattering criticism is by foreign officers who have compared West Point with their own military schools, but very little of this is printed; and what does get printed seldom reaches the American public.

Informed criticism has been rare, because few domestic critics have made an internal study of the institution; and those who have done so have generally lacked knowledge both of American colleges and of the capabilities of college training. The academy is itself partly to blame. Those powerful engines of information, the press and the news film, play up the spectacular part of cadet life; parades, reviews and athletics. Seldom is a prominent visitor escorted to a classroom or to a professor's office, and there photographed. Yet these two places are much more important than the parade ground. What makes the graduate is what and how the cadet studies.

The curriculum is West Point. It is the classroom which decides whether a cadet shall graduate. His rank in classes determines his initial seniority on graduation, his freedom in choosing his first branch of the service, and his promotion for many years after graduation. His hours in a recitation room are the most intensive in his life, and the ones best remembered. Eight hours a day five days a week, and four hours on the sixth day, are spent either in a classroom, or in his own room. This room he can not leave during study hours, and no one else can enter it. All the extra-curricular activities, taken together, including practical military training, do not bulk as large in his life. Men have gotten through West Point who could barely ride, whose appearance and deportment were just passable, whose athletic prowess was nil, who made no friends; but no one ever beat the curriculum. Those who tried to do so did not graduate.

The curriculum was originally designed to produce educated military engineers in a country totally devoid alike of other military schools and of other engineering schools. That design may be said to have been altered in the course of time. To some slight extent new subjects not of a technical character have crowded out technical ones. To a much larger extent the country's ideas of an engineering school have expanded, so that what seemed higher engineering instruction in 1802 now seems elementary. Purely military instruction in the classroom occupies a very small portion of the cadet's time during the first three years. It consumes nearly half his time in the last year, but the major military subject (ordnance and gunnery) is scientific in character.

The course is based on mathematics. After two years of pure mathematics, a cadet spends a year on applied mathematics and natural science. During the final year he studies engineering (civil, mechanical and military), and the military but highly scientific subject of ordnance and gunnery. Coincident with this four years' scientific course, a cadet studies English, French, Spanish, history, economics and law. There are some minor subjects like drill regulations, hygiene and elements of surveying; and a very good practical course in topographic and mechanical drawing.

Except in drawing, instruction is primarily by recitations based on text-books. Towards the conclusion of each half year, there are a number of written tests in review of the course. Cadets who are below a certain proficiency on these tests are required to take a written examination. Deficiency in the examination and in the course results in a cadet's discharge.

The method of instruction has nothing novel about it, being a good deal like that used in the secondary schools. But, in order to ensure that every cadet recites every day in every subject, the classes (called sections) are small, containing usually about twelve men. This division into sections is followed in large courses in most colleges, though seldom are the sections so small. But at West Point cadets are placed in sections according to proficiency. Thus the members of the first section in mathematics all have a standing in that subject for the half year to date higher than that of any other member of the class. Every two weeks, there are transfers. Cadets whose marks have fallen below those of the high members of the section just below them are transferred down, and the cadets who have beaten them are transferred up.

The intellectual competition is thus continuous. At the commencement of the first year cadets are arranged in sections alphabetically. At the end of about five weeks, they are rearranged into sections on the basis of their work to date. When a new course is taken up, arrangement is according to the most comparable course already taken. Thus the initial arrangement in Spanish is according to final merit in French.

The method of instruction and the character of the course undoubtedly do part, at any rate, of what they set out to do. They ensure that every cadet studies every day, and that there is a fair and equable basis of arranging a class in scholastic merit upon its graduation. These two objectives are, however, hardly ends in themselves. The real points of criticism are what they are in every institution of learning—the method of instruction, the character of the faculty and the subjects studied.

The dialectic method of instruction tends to become a system of continuous oral tests, in which the student learns what he can from the text, and explains what he has learned to the instructor, who must give every one who recites a mark. The instructor may thus become more of an examiner than a teacher. But a more serious difficulty is the local deification of the text-book. The cadet is indeed trained to think on his feet, to display what knowledge he has in his answers and to expound in an orderly manner. But, in the nature of things, he can not be encouraged to question the accuracy of the statements in the text; still less to question their philosophy.

One obvious result of a highly competitive system without electives is that the cadets at the top in any subject do not feel it profitable to broaden their acquaintance with that subject at the expense of accuracy of knowledge of minor details. In some courses, the first section pursues an advanced course. Normally, their marks in this course would be below the higher cadets in the second section taking the less advanced course. Hence they sometimes are given a bonus so that the bottom man in the first section will continue to rank the top man in the second. Otherwise a high-stand cadet might lose by pursuing an advanced course. Such an arrangement can only be fairly made at the very end of a course; and then affects a comparatively small number of men. An interest in any subject which would unduly diminish the time spent on some other would, from a mark standpoint, probably cease to pay.

The most unusual feature of the Military Academy is the faculty. As in most colleges, the subjects studied are parcelled out into departments, each with a professor at its head. The heads of the non-military departments are permanently appointed and remain at West Point until they retire for age. Every one else in the faculty is an army officer serving a tour, normally of four years, and expecting to go back to the army at its conclusion. This "every one" includes the superintendent (or president), the commandant of cadets (or combination of professor of tactics and dean of discipline) and all the assistant professors and instructors. The permanent professors hold rank as colonels or lieutenant colonels in the army, and are usually themselves graduates of West Point. But as about the only army officers in the world, except perhaps British royal princes, whose future careers are independent alike of their own efforts and of the opinions of their military superiors, the permanent professors occupy a very peculiar situation.

The system is attacked by educators on the ground that no permanent advance can be made with a shifting teaching body. Military men usually base their criticisms on the fact that the permanent tenure of the professors makes them immune to any kind of suggestions. Both criticisms have some point to them.

It is not true that instructors are ignorant. They are practically all graduates who, when cadets, had high class rank in the subject they are to teach. Thus they start with as much knowledge as teaching fellows in the average college. All have served as lieutenants in the army for three or four years, and hence have had some experience in handling men. Most of them have served abroad. The officers of the technical corps (Engineers, Ordnance and Signal Corps) have practically all had post-graduate courses in civil educational institutions. Instructors are encouraged to use their annual vacations at summer schools, where their tuition is paid by the government. Instructors in modern languages often spend their summers abroad. It is fair to say that the average West Point instructor in his fourth year knows as much of his subject as the average college instructor of similar standing. But he gets no further. After four years he goes back to the army. A few men serve a second tour in their middle thirties as assistant professors. Generally, though, the instruction is by younger men of necessarily limited experience.

Some professional educators are horrified by this arrangement. They forget that there are no ossified instructors, of a type often seen in college towns, in contact with cadets. Over the college instructor of any seniority, who is not regarded as good enough to give graduate instruction, the West Point instructor has, in dealing with cadets, a physical and psychological advantage difficult to overestimate. Compared with the hypothetical civilian educator willing to spend his life in giving undergraduate instruction at a military institution, he has an even greater advantage.

The permanent professors, since they correspond in tenure and duty to their civilian colleagues, are less criticized by the educational world. They are the subject, however, of much discussion by their comrades in the army. Little complaint is usually made at the time of a professor's appointment. Almost invariably the new man has been a highly successful instructor and assistant professor, and has extended his knowledge sufficiently so that he knows enough of his subject to handle his job. Generally, he starts with a great burst of energy; and a sensible improvement is made in his text-books and course of instruction. Under the military system, he has an almost free hand in his department. This does not mean that he has complete personal independence, for he must wear uniform, secure leave of absence in order to absent himself from West Point, and otherwise follow military routine. But in his department he is supreme. He is separated by a great gulf in age and rank from his instructors, and this gulf increases with time. He has no graduate students to force him to work; and no electives with which to measure his appeal to the student body. His economic and military status are alike fixed. If he should claim that his knowledge of his subject was complete, universal and exclusive, no one would deny the claim in his presence. After a while, no matter how good he was once, he tends to become set.

Many army officers would like to see most of the professors detailed from the army. This scheme, however, also has disadvantages. It takes a new professor a good deal more than four years to accomplish maximum results. A first class officer would hardly be willing to abandon his military career for eight or ten years, and then go back to the army so far behind in his profession. Finally, temporary professors, sitting together as an academic board, would necessarily lose that freedom of action in selecting deficient cadets for discharge and in arranging the curriculum, which have maintained West Point standards against the enormous political pressure always brought upon those who live on public funds. The disadvantage of the professor's independence can not be removed without destroying its very real advantages.

It is often said that the subjects studied at the Military Academy lack cultural features. It may well be that a text-book knowledge of general history, secured in one year, is a poor foundation for military scholarship. Many think that a man who has studied neither philosophy nor psychology can hardly claim to be educated at all. The sun, however, rises and sets only a limited number of times in four years. If Napoleon (and nearly every other military scholar) is right in asserting that mathematics is the proper foundation of a military education, the time for cultural subjects is strictly limited. Great improvements have been, and are being, made in the West Point cultural courses, but their development to true university standards is impossible, unless the course is increased in length or its basic mathematical foundation is eliminated. Engineering schools have been subjected to similar attacks, without any one pointing out a solution which did not require an extension of their four-year course.

It has been sometimes said of the highly rigid curriculum that it saps initiative. This statement is not true. Most of the mathematical and scientific recitations are based on problems. Nothing pleases an instructor more, nor secures a better mark, than a truly original solution to such a problem. Originality of ideas in the non-mathematical courses is equally welcomed. An acute and retentive memory, divorced from mathematical aptitude and willingness to think, gets a cadet nowhere. Initiative is one thing which West Point prides itself on developing.

But the academy does discourage one quality much sought in modern education, namely, intellectual skepticism, using that word without any reference to religion. Initiative is welcomed, as it was in pre-war Germany military instruction, but it must be within the scope of the field of knowledge determined by higher authority. A questioning of the bases of this knowledge is certainly discouraged. The reasons for such an attitude in a military training school are clear enough to a soldier; even if they are not so clear to an educator.

The major extra-curricular activity, and the only one needing special consideration, is the military organization. Practical military training, interior discipline and life out of the classroom generally are all based on this organization. The barrack life of the cadet, though following army titles and drill regulations, does not really correspond to any sort of life to be met with in the army. The system was designed as a means of converting the English public school organization of prefects and forms into a military hierarchy, without altering the public-school ideas of discipline, courage and honor. Like all successful systems it uses both negative and positive means. Negatively, a cadet reported for any breach of discipline receives demerits. These demerits adversely affecting his class standing. Enough of them in any month bring some form of military punishment.

Positively, the most soldierly cadets can look forward to being corporals during their third year and officers or sergeants during their fourth year. The higher cadet officers wear particularly gorgeous chevrons, and exercise very conspicuous functions at military ceremonies. The highest officer of all, the first captain, occupies a position much more conspicuous and sought after than that of the captain of the football team, or of the class president.

The system requires that cadets be placed on an equal economic status, and this is accomplished by depriving them of money. No one knows what a cadet's economic status is, except by the appearance of his parents' car on a Sunday afternoon. No one cares.

The system can claim great success in the inculcation of standards of honor. A cadet can go almost anywhere by saying "all right" to the sentinel, or cadet in charge of quarters, or other cadet on duty. This "all right" has a definite meaning, namely, that his conduct at the time does not violate regulations, and will not violate them until his return. It is thus a sort of parole. The temptation to break that parole by a youth surfeited with monasticism is great. Yet violations are very, very few. When discovered by other cadets they are invariably reported, so that the offending cadet can be eliminated. The honor system in the classroom works with absolute perfection. Instructors can safely leave a classroom where recitations are being prepared on the blackboard, and return assured that no one has received a bit of information improperly. Honor, though not a curricular subject, is in fact the subject best taught at West Point, and the one of which its graduates are most proud.

Going back to the curriculum proper, the method of instruction, faculty and character of the course are all three adversely affected by the purely undergraduate spirit. Naturally the taxpayer's money can not be spent to provide graduate courses in mathematics and applied science merely to stimulate a faculty. But the army itself has an elaborate system of graduate schools, in which the average officer spends from three to five years of his commissioned service as a student officer. The system culminates in the War College, where the students are nearly all over forty years of age. Owing to the physical limitations of land at West Point, and to political insistence that federal expenditures be distributed and not concentrated, this system of schools has almost no effect on the Military Academy. If the older professors had contemporaries in the War College faculty with whom to argue, if the younger instructors did part-time work as student officers in graduate schools, if the cadets more often heard military lectures from the army's best teachers, the effect would be very great indeed. This idea must be regarded—for the present, at least—as a dream.

Since colleges are not an end in themselves, but a means of producing something, it is necessary, in weighing a college, to assay its product. This product may be defined as a presumably educated youth in his twenties. The college is judged by this youth, as he appears at the time; and by the life he leads after he graduates. In a publicly supported training school, it is primarily necessary that the graduate be prepared to fulfill his public functions. From that standpoint, West Point does well. Its alumni are superior second lieutenants, and a reasonable number of them are competent generals in later life. Some may lack breadth in dealing with certain non-military questions; but no basic training can overcome the effects of a subsequent environment. Narrow well-educated men are found in all alumni bodies.

Secondly, the product of the West Point system of training may be considered from a general, instead of a purely military, standpoint. Many graduates have entered civil life. A surprisingly large number have been successful. Incidentally the high-stand men have usually been more successful than the low-stand ones. An examination of the careers of former cadets successful in civil life will show that they have nearly always gained their reputation by service as executives trusted for willingness to work at any task assigned them, by discipline, by good habits and physique and by high standards of honor. These are exactly the qualities with which West Point consciously tries to indoctrinate its student body. Usually the successful graduate admits his indebtedness to his alma mater.

But of course a true educator makes a different set of demands on any institution of learning. By him, the college is expected to produce men capable of adding to the store of human learning. He also expects a college to teach a man how to enjoy the use of his intellect, as distinct from his wits. Educators differ greatly as to the extent to which the modern college meets these demands. But West Point does not pretend to meet them at all. It can not do so without entirely changing itself. The compulsory, competitive, dialectic course will not produce intellectual skeptics with an educated taste for some particular branch of knowledge. And no reform is possible. For an army officered by men with a "show me" attitude towards the dictates of higher authority can not be relied on to win battles. It may be asserted, however, that West Point does produce a larger proportion of graduates indoctrinated with its own qualities of zeal, subordination and honor than the average American college produces of bachelors of arts who are either potential scholars, or men of any very marked degree of intellectual curiosity.

EDUCATIONAL EVENTS

INTERNATIONAL CONFERENCE OF UNIVERSITY WOMEN

THE sixth conference of the International Federation of University Women is to be held this year at Edinburgh from July 27 to August 4. It is 12 years, according to the London *Times,* since this triennial conference has been held in the United Kingdom, and British university women are making eager preparations to welcome their colleagues from all over the world. The federation, which was first started in 1919, now has a membership of 36 national federations of university women, comprising about 50,000 individual members.

The ways in which the International Federation encourages international understanding are many and varied. A large number of clubhouses have been established in different countries, chief among which are Reid Hall in Paris, carried on by the American Association, and Crosby Hall in London. Individual traveling members are given letters of introduction, and receive many offers of hospitality when abroad.

Another part of the work of the International Federation is the granting of research scholarships, some of which are given by individual national federations, and some by a central fellowship fund. Since 1919 fifty fellowships have been awarded, and for many of these a condition of tenure is that the fellow shall carry on her work in some foreign country.

A number of exchanges between secondary school teachers of different countries have been effected, notably between England and America and Australia, and America and Germany. This very valuable work is now being extended to members of other professions, such as librarians and lecturers.

In addition to these activities the International Federation makes a special effort to cooperate as widely as possible with other international organizations, and in particular a standing committee is in constant touch with the Committee for Intellectual Cooperation of the League of Nations. The president is Professor Winifred Cullis.

The program of the conference includes consideration of a report on the work accomplished in favor of disarmament, and meetings and lectures on such subjects as: "Training and Prospects in Department Stores," and "Is the Secondary School Child Over-worked?" The special subject for discussion is "Does a University Education Fit the Modern Woman for Life in General?" Some of the meetings are open to the public, and among those who have accepted invitations to speak are the Duchess of Atholl, Miss Amy Johnson and Dr. Harriette Chick. There will be a civic reception by the Lord Provost, a dinner with Scottish music and dancing, a number of excursions, several musical programs, and a party at the Zoological Gardens, given by the Edinburgh Association.

NEW HIGHER EDUCATION REPORT BLANKS FOR THE OFFICE OF EDUCATION

The U. S. Office of Education is preparing a new set of report blanks for collegiate and professional schools, to be used in connection with the Biennial Survey of Education, 1930–1932. The blanks are to be issued in two parts: one for personnel data and the other for finances.

The personnel blank for universities, colleges and professional schools, and that for teachers colleges and normal schools are in many respects similar to those used in 1930, but some extraneous material has been omitted and some rearrangement and rephrasing of the questions has been done in order to make the data more comparable as between the different types of schools.

A special blank has been prepared for reporting the personnel of junior colleges. This blank takes into consideration some of the peculiar functional characteristics of the junior college by asking for information of value to junior-college people and omitting much which is not applicable to this type of institution. Comparability of the general data as between the junior college and other types of college has also been kept in mind.

All institutions of higher education, universities, colleges, professional schools of all sorts (including teachers colleges and normal schools) and junior colleges, both public and private, will be asked to report their finances on a uniform blank, which embodies many of the principles adopted by the National Committee on Standard Reports for Institutions of Higher Education. Five groups of funds are set up, as follows:

I. *Educational and General,* including receipts classified by source and expenditures for administration and general control, resident instruction, research, extension, libraries and operation and maintenance of the physical plant;

II. *Auxiliary Enterprises and Activities,* including receipts and expenditures for dormitories and dining halls, athletics, student health service, college bookstore, student unions and the like;

III. *Other Non-Educational Purposes,* including operations of a fiscal character, such as income from investments for scholarships and fellowships, annuities, donations to be used directly for scholarships, as well as expenditures for scholarships, annuities, debt service, financial campaigns and the like;

IV. *Capital Outlay,* including receipts and expenditures for increase or expansion of the physical plant, and

V. *Receipts for Increase of Permanent Funds,* such as student aid funds, annuity funds and endowment, restricted and general.

There are also the usual items in the inventory, grouped under land and buildings, equipment and funds.

HENRY G. BADGER

WASHINGTON, D. C.

APPEAL TO THE FEDERAL GOVERNMENT BY CHICAGO TEACHERS

AN appeal to the federal government for temporary relief by the Chicago school teachers, whose salaries have been unpaid for five months, was made on June 4 before a subcommittee of the Senate Manufacturers Committee, considering relief legislation.

According to a report in the *U. S. Daily,* the attention of the committee was called also to relief needs generally in the city of Chicago by Senators Glenn (Republican) and Lewis (Democrat) of Illinois. Both emphasized that relief to the schools should come through the state, which in turn would secure aid from the federal government, rather than the assistance being given direct to the schools from federal sources.

Charles B. Stillman, president of the Joint Conference of Teachers and Principals, Chicago, presented the request of the group, pointing out that the situation has developed in Chicago to such an extent that it has "grave national implication." He explained that among the causes for lack of payment of teachers there is the delay occasioned in the collection of taxes. About $20,000,000 in back pay is due and about $25,000,000 will be needed temporarily to carry on until city funds are made available.

Irving A. Wilson, president of the Principals' Club, Chicago, is reported to have said that the credit of the Chicago Board of Education has completely collapsed. A survey showed the loss by teachers of homes, lapse of life insurance policies on the part of many, with large amounts due for rent, food, and for doctors and dentists bills. He said: "We have reached the breaking point, it is impossible for the Chicago school situation to go on as it is without some relief. We apply to you because we believe education is fundamental to the preservation of the ideals of this nation. The federal government can not afford to let 500,000 boys and girls remain on the streets of the second largest city in the nation, and we are certain that that is imminent unless some relief comes and comes immediately."

Senator Glenn called attention especially to the general needs in Chicago, presenting a telegram received by himself and Senator Lewis from a Chicago committee, including the Mayor, pointing out that funds are exhausted and relief stations have been ordered to close June 4.

Agnes Clohesy, president of the Elementary Teachers Union, Chicago, testified that the general relief conditions in Chicago were affecting the homes of teachers directly and that the failure of payment to those members of the family who were teaching made the condition doubly acute.

The telegram to Senators Glenn and Lewis, under date of June 3, signed by Anthony J. Cermak, mayor, and others of Chicago, follows:

For many months the Illinois emergency relief commission has been taking care of 111,000 families or about 600,000 of the destitute. The $10,500,000 fund contributed by the citizens and the $12,500,000 additional, being the proceeds of State of Illinois notes, in all $23,000,000, are exhausted. Accordingly, the relief stations in Chicago have been notified by the Illinois emergency relief commission that all available funds having been exhausted, the stations must close to-morrow night.

The undersigned representing the business interests in Chicago are meeting in an effort to raise sufficient funds to temporarily prevent this catastrophe until federal aid can be made possible. We respectfully request that you make every effort to bring about the immediate passage of legislation authorizing the Reconstruction Finance Corporation to make advances to states for relief purposes, as a separate emergency measure. The money thus advanced to be secured by pledge of the state authorizing such advances to be deducted from federal aid thereafter made to the several states for highway purposes.

LABOR INSTITUTE AT THE UNIVERSITY OF MICHIGAN

THE unemployment problem will undergo a critical examination by labor leaders and university economists and sociologists at the first University of Michigan Labor Institute to be held from June 20 to 23. Lectures and open discussions by experts on both the practical and academic aspects of the stabilization of employment and the relation of the press to labor problems are planned. Dr. Charles A. Fisher, assistant director of the University Extension Division, which, with the University Department of Economics and the Michigan Federation of Labor, is sponsoring the institute.

In view of the fact that unemployment is the overshadowing economic problem of the day, the Labor Institute was called to put at the service of those most affected the modern knowledge of the science of economics through the university's faculty and facilities. A frank discussion of the extent, causes and remedies of the situation is planned, without offering special explanations, viewpoints or panaceas. Interchange of ideas and information between the fields of labor and education is the fundamental object of the institute.

Morning meetings will be given to addresses on phases of the problem and discussion from the floor; afternoons will be given to free group discussion of the morning's subject; while the evening will be given to lectures by authorities on labor or economics. At the first meeting on Monday evening at the Michigan Union, President Alexander G. Ruthven will welcome the visitors and John P. Frey, secretary-treasurer of the metal trades department of the American Federation of Labor, will speak on, "The Causes of Unemployment." At the second session, "What Unemployment Does to Us," will be told by Arthur Evans Wood, professor of sociology of the University of Michigan, and Professor J. A. Estey, of Purdue University. At the third session Wesley W. Maurer, instructor in journalism, will discuss, "The Press in Labor Controversies"; at the fourth, Professors Max Handman and Morris A. Copeland, of the department of economics, will speak on "The Causes of Unemployment"; at the fifth, Spencer Millers, Jr., secretary of the Workers' Education Bureau of America, will talk on "Some Aspects of Unemployment," and at the sixth and final session, Professor William Haber, of the Michigan State College, and John P. Frey will describe "What can be Done about Unemployment."

THE SUMMER SESSION OF THE UNIVERSITY OF WISCONSIN

ELEVEN states are represented by the twenty-five visiting lecturers who are to be brought to the University of Wisconsin this summer to teach in the summer school classes. Dr. Scott H. Goodnight is dean of the summer session.

The visiting lecturers come from educational institutions in Illinois, Pennsylvania, New York, Michigan, Minnesota, Connecticut, Ohio, Washington, Oregon and Missouri, as well as from Wisconsin.

Included among the new courses to be taught this year is one entitled "Choral Verse Speaking," to be given by Virginia Sanderson, of the Teachers College of Columbia University. Students taking this course of study will attempt to improve their speech through the recitation of verse in chorus.

Others on the faculty this summer are: Mrs. Mildred E. Berry, Rockford College, "Introduction to Phonetics" and "The Teaching of Speech"; Carrie Rasmussen, Madison, "Creative Dramatics for Children"; Carl B. Cass, University of Pittsburgh, "Elements of Acting and Dramatic Expression"; Francis L. Bacon, Evanston, Ill., "Principles of Secondary Education" and "High School Administration"; "Operation of the School"; Harry J. Baker, Detroit Schools, "Psychology of Exceptional Children"; Prudence Cutright, Minneapolis, Minn., "Foundations of Methods" and "Supervision of Elementary School Subjects"; Leonard R. Evans, Sheboygan, "Advanced Problems in Part-time Education"; Regina Groves, Madison vocational schools, "Teaching Commercial Subjects in the Part-time Schools"; Kai Jensen, Connecticut Agricultural College, "Child Psychology" and "Psychology of Individual Differences and the Measure of Intelligence"; Margaret Johnston, Madison, "Advanced Course in the Teaching of Home Economics"; Delia E. Kibbe, Madison, "Investigations in the Teaching of Reading"; Delbert Oberteuffer, state supervisor of physical education, Ohio, "Supervision and Administration of School Health" and "Principles of Physical Education and Problems of Organization"; Francis C. Rosecrance, Milwaukee schools, "Principles of Vocational and Educational Guidance"; Clifford W. Stone, State College of Washington, "Educational Tests" and "Elementary School Curriculum"; Harry C. Thayer, Wisconsin Board of Vocational Education, "Teaching Shop Subjects in the Part-time School"; Richard T. Thill, Lawrence College, "Legal Aspects of School Administration" and "Principles of Educational Administration"; Mrs. Jennie McMullen, Madison, "Advanced Course in the Teaching of English in the Part-time School"; Roy R. Van Duzee, West Allis, "Advanced Problems in the Supervision of Industrial Education"; Guy F. Wells, New York Teacher Training College, "History of American Education" and "History of Secondary Education"; Alma M. Ganz, Madison, "Methods of Teaching Home Economics in the Part-time School"; Jane B. Welling, College of Detroit, "Appreciation of Art in Everyday Life" and "Art Curriculum Construction"; William Chandler, Marquette University, "Technique of Basketball"; Ernestine Troemel, University of Oregon, "Technique of Swimming for Women" and "Elementary and Advanced Clogging"; Cannon Hearne, University of Missouri, "Organization and Planning of Extension Work."

CONSOLIDATION OF THE STATE EDUCATIONAL INSTITUTIONS OF NORTH CAROLINA

IT will be remembered that the legislature of the State of North Carolina in 1931 consolidated the State University of North Carolina, the State College and the North Carolina College for Women. It provided that instead of a separate board of trustees for each institution a single board of one hundred members should be constituted. It also provided that a commission of twelve members should, with the Governor of the State, submit a report as to details of consolidation to the new board by July 1, 1932. It was made mandatory upon the commission that it employ experts in the field of higher education to make a study of consolidation and to assist the commission "with regard to form, extent, procedure, and details of unified guidance and control."

Complying with this procedure the commission, six of whose members were appointed by Governor Gardner and the other six by the presidents of the three institutions, employed Dr. George A. Works, professor of higher education at the University of Chicago, to take charge of the survey, with the cooperation of Dr. Frank L. McVey, president of the University of Kentucky, and Dr. G. S. Ford, dean of the Graduate School of the University of Minnesota. Specialists and the fields which they investigated, were:

> Extension, Morse A. Cartwright, executive secretary of the Adult Education Association; Business Administration, Dean R. E. Stevenson, of the School of Business Administration of the University of Minnesota; Education for Women, Dr. C. Mildred Thompson, dean of Vassar College; Engineering Education, President W. E. Wickenden, of the Case School of Applied Science; Training of Teachers, Dr. Charles H. Judd, director, and Dr. W. S. Gray, dean of the School of Education of the University of Chicago.

The board of critics and counsellors who considered the findings of the staff of specialists in their general aspects was composed of:

> President Lotus D. Coffman, of the University of Minnesota, a member of the survey commissions of Texas, Kansas and New Jersey; President E. C. Elliott, of Purdue University, formerly chancellor of the University of Montana; Dr. F. J. Kelly, expert in higher education, U. S. Office of Education, and formerly president of the University of Idaho; Dr. Henry Suzzallo, president of the Carnegie Foundation for the Advancement of Teaching, a member of the California Survey Commission, and a former president of the University of Washington, and President George F. Zook, of the University of Akron, formerly specialist in higher education of the U. S. Office of Education.

Several months have been required to complete the surveys and all phases of the life of the three institutions have been subjected to the closest investigation.

PROMOTIONS AT THE OHIO STATE UNIVERSITY

FIFTY-SEVEN promotions on the teaching staff of the Ohio State University are provided in the budget for 1932–33. Contrary to the custom in normal years, the general promotions did not carry increases in pay.

Completing the current biennium, the budget brings the total reduction in the university payroll from state appropriations to $480,488 less than was received from state funds in the previous biennium. This has been accomplished by eliminating about 100 positions of all kinds and by reductions in salaries ranging from 5 to 10 per cent., starting at $3,000. The salary reduction was made last summer.

The reductions in personnel were made by doing away with some assistantships, by abolishing part of the university's personal program with individual students such as special study courses, by not filling vacancies in some departments, by increasing the size of some classes, and by curtailment of off-campus services rendered to Ohio industries and organizations.

Sixteen faculty members were raised to full professorial rank, 18 were elevated from assistant professorships to associate professorships, 18 from instructorships to assistant professorships, and four others were made instructors. Margaret Reilly, acting superintendent of University Hospital, was made superintendent. The changes which are effective on July 1 are as follows:

Full professors: Jesse E. Day and Wesley G. France, chemistry; Lewis H. Tiffany, botany; Harlan H. Hatcher, English; Edmund H. Spieker, geology; Theodore N. Beckman, business organization; Ralph W. Tyler, educational research; Joseph A. Leeder, music; Harold B. Alberty, H. Gordon Hullfish and Laura Zirbes, principles of education; Rollo C. Baker and Ralph A. Knouff, anatomy; Walter R. Hobbs, veterinary medicine; L. H. Grinstead, business research, and Dick P. Snyder, dentistry.

Associate professors: Leighton G. Foster, C. G. McBride, C. E. Lively and C. R. Arnold, rural economics; Wallace R. Brode, chemistry; Robert O. Roseler, German; Arthur H. Noyes, history; L. Edwin Smart, economics; Edward V. O'Rourke, mine engineering; John W. Means, surgery; P. J. Reel, gynecology; W. N. Taylor, genito-urinary surgery; R. E. Rebrassier and J. N. Shoemaker, veterinary medicine; Paul A. Barry and Marion O. French, military science; Harlan G. Metcalf, physical education, and Viva B. Boothe, business research.

Assistant professors: Glenn W. Blaydes, botany; W. C. Fernelius, chemistry; Walter Gausewitz, German; Henry H. Simms, history; Robert V. Zumstein, Jerome B. Green, Marion L. Pool and Harold P. Knauss, physics; N. Gilbert Riddle, business organization; Will Rannells and Hoyt L. Sherman, fine arts; Josephine MacLatchy, educational research; Charles G. Duncombe and Joseph Koffolt, chemical engineering; Oscar J. Marshall and Arthur G. Wyatt, civil engineering; John F. Byrne and K. Y. Tang, electrical engineering, and Howard Brunsman, business research.

Instructors: Mary K. Helz, pathology; Lloyd A. Cook, sociology; Erwin Zepp, fine arts, and Marie K. Mason, phonetics. Wallace D. Hooper, research assistant in the bureau of business research, was made research associate.

HONORS CONFERRED BY COLUMBIA UNIVERSITY

AT the commencement exercises of Columbia University the honorary degree of doctor of laws was conferred on Albert Henry Wiggin, chairman of the board of the Chase National Bank; on Thomas William Lamont, partner in the firm of J. P. Morgan and Company; the degree of doctor of letters on Edwin Hatfield Anderson, director of the New York Public Library; on Robert Frost, poet; on Walter Lippmann, journalist, and on Dr. George Norlin, president of the University of Colorado; the degree of doctor of science on Dugald Caleb Jackson, professor of electric power production and distribution in the Massachusetts Institute of Technology, and the degree of doctor of music on Channing Lefebvre, organist and choirmaster of Trinity Church. Owing to the illness of Dr. Anderson the degree was conferred on him *in absentia*.

Ten medals were awarded to alumni. The presentations were made by President Nicholas Murray Butler with citations as follows:

EDWIN CORNELIUS BROOME, superintendent of schools at Philadelphia, Ph.D., 1902—Guiding and directing with skill and high purpose the public school system of the great city of Philadelphia.

CLARENCE HERBERT COOK, teacher in the Columbia Grammar School; student in Columbia College from 1875 to 1877—Laden with the gratitude of an army of youth who have turned to him for instruction and guidance through a full half century.

LEON FRASER, Alternate to the President, Bank for International Settlements; A.B., 1909; A.M., 1912; B.Litt., 1913; Ph.D., 1915—Deservedly holding an influential position in the world of international finance; second in command at the Bank for International Settlements at Basle.

JOHN KINSEY GORE, actuary and vice-president of the Prudential Insurance Company; A.B., 1883; A.M., 1886—A scholarly and highly successful administrator of the great business of life insurance in this land.

CLAYTON HAMILTON, playwright and dramatic

critic; A.M., 1901—Author, editor and dramatic critic of exceptional insight and skill; member of the National Institute of Arts and Letters.

JOSEPH GREGOIRE DE ROULHAC HAMILTON, Kenan Professor of History and Government in the University of North Carolina; Ph.D., 1906—Accomplished scholar and teacher of history, as well as author of distinction and high record.

EMIL JOSEPH, member of the bar, Cleveland, Ohio; A.B., 1879; LL.B., 1881—Devoted son of Columbia; foremost in all good works in the community of whose life he is a recognized leader.

CHARLES RIBORG MANN, director of the American Council on Education; chairman of President's Advisory Committee on Federal Relations to Education; A.B., 1890; A.M., 1891—Broad-minded and untiring student and administrator of education and of public policies in relation thereto.

RICHARD CUNNINGHAM PATTERSON, JR., commissioner of correction of the City of New York; E.M., 1912—Using his university training and his business experience in the service of the unfortunate and the misguided with exceptional success and large human feeling.

WILLIAM BOGERT WALKER, clergyman; A.B., 1865—Graduated from old Columbia College sixty-seven years ago with highest honors and at the top of his class; laden with affection for the rich fruits of a well-spent life in the service of God and man.

EDUCATIONAL NOTES AND NEWS

DR. KARL T. WAUGH, formerly dean of the college of letters, arts and sciences and professor of psychology at the University of Southern California, was formally installed as nineteenth president of Dickinson College, Carlisle, Pennsylvania, on June 3. Bishop Ernest G. Richardson, of the Philadelphia area of the Methodist Episcopal Church, delivered the charge of induction. Dr. Walter Spahr, president of the board of trustees, presided.

HOMER WOODHULL DAVIS was appointed president of Athens College, Greece, at the annual meeting of the trustees. Mr. Davis was made head of the English department of the college when it was formed in 1925, became principal of the preparatory department two years later and has been acting president since 1930. Prior to his association with Athens College Mr. Davis was an instructor in English at Robert College, Constantinople, and an assistant professor at Constantinople Women's College. The organization of Athens College, one of the group of six American colleges in the Near East, consists of a Greek board of directors in Athens and an American board of trustees in the United States, the members of which are Professor Edward Capps, Dr. Stephen P. Duggan, Dr. John H. Finley, George D. Graves, Charles P. Howland, Harold C. Jaquith, Ery Kehaya, William G. Mather and Dr. Kenneth C. M. Sills.

DR. ENDICOTT PEABODY observed his seventy-fifth birthday on May 30. He at the same time completed his fiftieth year as head master of Groton School.

THE honorary degree of doctor of science was conferred upon Dr. Karl T. Compton, president of the Massachusetts Institute of Technology, at the thirty-third commencement at Clarkson College, Potsdam, New York. Dr. Compton was the commencement speaker.

LAFAYETTE COLLEGE has conferred the honorary degree of doctor of science on Dr. Thomas S. Baker, president of the Carnegie Institute of Technology.

OKLAHOMA CITY UNIVERSITY conferred at commencement the degree of doctor of education on Cecil K. Reiff, superintendent of the public schools in Oklahoma City, and the degree of doctor of religious education on Leonidas Franklin Sensabaugh, for Sunday School work in the Methodist Episcopal Church, South.

THE honorary doctorate of laws will be conferred on Dr. Edward D. Roberts, superintendent of the Cincinnati schools, by Wooster College at the commencement exercises on June 13.

THE Roosevelt medal for distinguished service has been awarded to Dr. Robert A. Millikan and will be presented to him at a dinner to be given on the seventy-fourth anniversary of President Roosevelt's birth on October 27. Heretofore since the establishment of the medal in 1923 three awards have been made annually. In a statement announcing the single award this year Dr. James B. Garfield, president of the

Roosevelt Memorial Association, said: "Dr. Millikan combines in a striking degree the qualities of a scientist, an administrator, a teacher, a philosopher and a public servant. He has been conspicuous in the movement of scientific speculation away from the materialistic and mechanistic theories of the nineteenth century toward spiritual conceptions in harmony with the aspirations of religion."

A FEATURE of the Birmingham-Southern College annual commencement was the presentation to the college by the senior class of a portrait of President Guy E. Snavely, by Alfred S. Bairnsfather. The baccalaureate sermon was preached by Bishop William N. Ainsworth, and the baccalaureate address was delivered by President Snavely. The degree of doctor of the humanities was conferred upon Miss Rosa V. Strickland, principal of Powell School, Birmingham, and upon Comer M. Woodward, dean and professor of sociology at Emory University. Curtis B. Haley, assistant book editor of the Southern Methodist Church, Nashville, was awarded the degree of doctor of letters.

AN informal reception and tea was given on June 9 at the Herman Ridder Junior High School by the principals and teachers of Districts 19 and 20, New York City, in honor of District Superintendent Joseph H. Wade, who will retire from the school system at the close of the term.

DR. ABRAHAM FLEXNER, of the Institute of Advanced Study, Newark, New Jersey, has been elected president of the board of trustees of Howard University.

DR. GEORGE C. KYTE, of the University of California, was recently elected president of the California Educational Research Association, Northern Section.

DR. WILLIAM B. MUNRO, professor of history and government at the California Institute of Technology, has been elected a vice-president of the Association of Colleges and Universities of the Pacific Southwest.

PROFESSOR LEON B. RICHARDSON, of the department of chemistry of Dartmouth College, has succeeded Professor W. S. Messer as president of the college chapter of the American Association of University Professors.

MISS JANE L. JONES, dean of women at St. Lawrence University, was elected president of the New York division of the American Association of University Women at the closing session of the Ithaca meeting on May 28. Other officers elected were: *Vice-presidents,* Mrs. Emerson Fite, of Poughkeepsie, first; Mrs. John Taylor, of Schenectady, second, and Mrs. Homer C. Thompson, of Ithaca, third; *Secretary and treasurer,* Miss Louise Reynolds, of Canton.

PROFESSOR L. M. DENNIS, head of the department of chemistry, Cornell University, will become professor emeritus at the close of the academic year in June. He became instructor at Cornell in 1887 and head of the department in 1903.

DR. GIUSEPPE A. BORGESE, of the University of Milan, will be visiting professor of comparative literature at Smith College on the William Allan Neilson Foundation next year. The foundation was established five years ago in honor of President Neilson. It has hitherto been devoted to psychological research under Dr. Kurt Koffka, who will spend the coming year in Russia. It has now been decided to make the tenure for one year, the chair to be held by representatives of various departments.

DR. FREDERIC LOGAN PAXSON, of the University of Wisconsin, has been appointed as the first Byrne Professor of United States History at the University of California. The Margaret Byrne Professorship was established this year as a result of a bequest by James William Byrne.

DR. LOUISE H. GREGORY, associate professor of zoology at Barnard College, Columbia University, has been appointed to the newly established position of associate dean of the college.

SHIRLEY ERNEST FIELD, instructor in mathematics at the University of Michigan since 1920, will join the faculty of the new Junior College in Ironwood. In addition to teaching, Mr. Field has been for ten years one of the university's inspectors of high schools.

DR. GEORGE M. WILEY, New York assistant state commissioner of education, will be on the staff of the forty-first summer session at Cornell University.

DR. MARY J. MCCORMICK, head of the department of sociology at the College of Mt. St. Joseph-on-the-Ohio, Cincinnati, has been appointed guest professor of social sciences in the Marquette University summer session of 1932.

S. C. ROBERTS, of Washington State College, for many years in charge of the training of industrial arts teachers, will retire from his position at the end of the summer session. He will be succeeded by U. G. Whiffen, who at the present time holds a similar position at the Northwest Missouri Teachers College at Maryville.

DR. R. T. H. HALSEY has resigned after serving as resident member of the board of visitors and governors of St. John's College, Annapolis, for four years and as a professor of Colonial art for two years. He is the fourth member of the faculty to leave St. John's this year. Two months ago Dean Robert E. Bacon announced that he would not return next year, and owing, it is said, to a series of disagreements with the board and the president he left the college without completing the school year. Leonard Arnaud, for five years a member of the French department, handed his resignation to the board soon after. Clarence W. Stryker, for twenty-five years a professor in the history department, will leave St. John's after completion of the present term.

DR. FRANK W. BALLOU, superintendent of the public schools of Washington, D. C., has been re-elected for a three-year term by the Board of Education. Dr. Ballou will lecture this summer on public school administration at Yale University.

PERCY DAVIS, city superintendent of Santa Ana, California, has been elected superintendent of the Santa Monica schools, to succeed E. T. Martin, who resigned recently.

PAUL W. GORDON, a member of the staff of the Institute for Government Research, has been appointed director of education for Alaska. He has had experience in educational work in the American School of Japan in Tokyo and at Fisk University. During the war Mr. Gordon was a member of the Friends Relief Work in France, and later spent a summer among the Osage Indians under the Friends Home Mission Board.

MR. EDWARD W. MARCELLUS has been appointed national director of the American Junior Red Cross, effective on July 1. The directorship has been open for more than a year, following the resignation of Dr. H. L. Wilson because of ill health. Mr. Walter S. Gard has been serving as acting director. Mr. Marcellus has occupied positions in the educational field ranging from class-room teacher to superintendent of schools, and was for three years a member of the faculty of Northwestern University.

PROFESSOR JOHN K. NORTON, of Teachers College, Columbia University, has been appointed an adviser on the research staff of the National Survey of School Finance.

AMONG Americans who will attend the meeting of the International Congress of Mathematicians to be held in Zurich, are Dr. David Eugene Smith, professor emeritus of mathematics at Teachers College, Columbia University, and Dr. W. A. Hurwitz, professor of mathematics at Cornell University.

DR. JOHN H. FINLEY, of the editorial department of *The New York Times*, addressed the graduating class of Gettysburg College, Pennsylvania, on May 30 and gave the commencement address at Swarthmore College on June 6.

PRESIDENT M. G. NEALE, of the University of Idaho, delivered the address at the fourteenth annual commencement of Gooding College, Wesleyan, Idaho, on May 23.

DR. THOMAS NIXON CARVER, professor of political economy at Harvard University, gave the commencement address at Iowa Wesleyan College on June 6.

THE death is announced of Charles W. Townsend, city superintendent of schools, Santa Clara, California. Mr. Townsend had been connected with the Santa Clara system for twenty years and had served as superintendent for the past twelve years.

GEORGE W. CROZIER, first superintendent of Inglewood, California, schools, has died after serving for twenty years. The Inglewood intermediate school is named in his honor.

A PLAN to establish a memorial to Dr. Albert Leonard, late superintendent of public schools in New Rochelle, New York, has been approved. The memorial will take the form of a scholarship fund, the income from which will be used as an annual award to the most deserving student graduating from the senior high school.

THE thirty-eighth summer meeting of the American Mathematical Society, together with the sixteenth colloquium of the society, will be held at the University of California at Los Angeles, beginning on Tuesday, August 30. Dr. Earle R. Hedrick, past president of the society, is chairman of the committee on arrangements for the meeting. There has been planned a series of five colloquium lectures by Professor J. F. Ritt, of Columbia University. Professor D. N. Lehmer, of the University of California; Professor Tibor Rado, of the Ohio State University, will deliver addresses; Professor Lehmer's subject being, "The Continued Fraction Representing Cubic and Higher Irrationalities," and Professor Rado speaking on "Recent Work in the Problem of Plateau." Accommodations for members and their guests have been provided on the campus of the university. Provision has also been made for an excursion on Thursday afternoon for a visit to Mount Wilson Observatory, and to the various colleges and universities in Los Angeles and near-by cities.

MR. JAMES A. MOYER, Massachusetts state director of University Extension, has announced that the colleges and universities at Boston are offering avocational and commercial courses free of charge, to which more than 1,200 unemployed men and women have responded eagerly. The program represents a cooperative effort under the auspices of the State Emergency Committee on Unemployment between its education committee, of which Mr. Moyer is chairman, and the colleges and universities, including Harvard University, the Massachusetts Institute of Technology, Boston University, Radcliffe College, Wellesley College, Boston Museum of Fine Arts and others. There is no operating expense, as the instruction is given by volunteer teachers appointed by the faculties of the cooperating colleges and universities. Their offerings consist of twenty-two condensed afternoon courses in general subjects designed to be both of interest and of help. Any man or woman of high-school education who has the time available is eligible. A registration fee of 25 cents admits to as many as five courses.

DISCUSSION

IS ABILITY GROUPING FALLACIOUS?

WITHIN the past few months current educational literature has contained a number of articles which have attacked the principle of ability grouping. One article appearing in the March 26 issue of SCHOOL AND SOCIETY, entitled "The Fallacy of Ability Grouping," and written by Mr. Laurence B. Brink, is, I think, fairly typical of quite a number that have appeared recently. Mr. Brink says that "the system of ability grouping breaks down on five counts," which he lists as follows:

"(1) The groups can not, except in a very large school, be organized with statistical validity.
(2) Administrative difficulties still further interfere with effective grouping.
(3) The bases of classification are not satisfactory.
(4) Teaching procedures can be better adapted to individual needs by a different method.
(5) Whatever advantages homogeneous grouping may have for the learner are more than counterbalanced by inevitable losses."

Let us take up each of the categories of objections and see what value should be attached to them.

Mr. Brink's first category of objections is given the caption of "Statistical Invalidity." He is alarmed by the fact that if sigma distances from the mid-point be laid off on the base line of a total distribution that fits the normal frequency curve, a sigma distance on the base near the mid-point would include a much larger per cent. of the total distribution than a sigma distance further removed from the center of distribution. Putting it more simply, if we should organize three classes or sections of equal size from a group of 120 pupils, there would be a wider range of ability among the best and poorest classes than among the pupils of the middle section. This is true and so obvious that it needs hardly to be stated. Granted that the range of abilities within the three groups of equal size is not the same, is this a potent argument against the principle of ability grouping? Though the range of abilities for either the upper or lower group is greater than for the middle group, in no case is the range of abilities as great as if no attempt at ability grouping had been made.

Mr. Brink's second category of objections has to do with "Administrative Difficulties." That ability grouping entails a certain amount of administrative difficulty can hardly be denied. But is it not true also that the best results in any line of activity are seldom gained by following the line of least resistance? If ability grouping is a desirable plan of school organization the best educators will not refuse to use it even though certain difficulties involved have to be met.

Mr. Brink's third category of objections concerns itself with the use of mental tests as criteria for segregating school pupils into groups according to ability. He says that tests are unsatisfactory because they are not infallible. Any one who will accept no educational plan or device except an infallible one is justified in objecting to the use of mental tests for ability grouping or for any other purpose for that matter because we have objective proof, verified from many angles, that mental tests are not infallible. There is, however, abundant evidence to show that a good intelligence test is one of the best criteria to be used in ability grouping and if grouping must be done upon short acquaintance an intelligence test is the best single criterion at our disposal. Moreover, the results of intelligence tests almost always afford invaluable supplementary data to knowledge gained in other ways through long acquaintance. Suppose we grant that intelligence tests are not adequate criteria. That is not legitimate reason why we should condemn the principle of ability grouping. Let us use some additional criteria that are more adequate. Many school systems practice the principle of ability grouping and use the mental test as only one of a number of criteria that are employed. The idea of gaining information from as many sources as possible and using all the data as criteria for ability grouping is the idea that has commended itself most favorably to the practical schoolman. Mr. Brink's only objection to such practice is that "the gathering and evaluation of such data are *almost* impossible." Such an objection is not new. It is as old as scientific progress, not only in education but elsewhere as well. No worth-while undertaking has ever been begun to which some did not respond by saying that it was an impossible undertaking. Mr. Brink is to be commended for qualifying his statement with the word "almost." This little word puts a window in the age-old phrase through which there shines sufficient light to enable the real pathfinders in education to continue their progress.

Another type of objection which Mr. Brink raises against the practice of ability grouping is that it is accompanied by "Inadequate Curriculum Adjustment." He says that ability grouping "is merely a gesture unless the course of study is so modified as to provide for the difference thus recognized." There are those who offer what appear to be valid reasons for refusing to accept this statement as it stands. To these objections we will return presently. But for the time being let us accept Mr. Brink's contention as valid. Objection may then be raised to the application of the principle contained in the statement. Mr. Brink assumes that the only modification of the course of study adequate to meet the needs of three different groups segregated on the basis of ability is three courses of study entirely different, both qualitatively and quantitatively. Mr. Brink then adds, "Such a trilogy of courses I have yet to find." There is no need, however, for amazement at this last statement. We might even go further and state that Mr. Brink is not likely to find such a trilogy in the future unless he constructs it himself. No one else perhaps believes that such a trilogy would be advisable. Most educators believe that there should be elements of difference in the curricula of groups differing in ability and this does not conflict with the belief that a great share of educational elements should be common to all of them. The substitute curriculum adjustment which Mr. Brink offers can readily be accepted by those who believe in and practice ability grouping. As a matter of fact the substitute curriculum adjustment which he offers turns out to be not so much a substitute for our present practice in curriculum adjustment as it is for a purely imaginary type of adjustment which he says does not exist and which, according to most educators, ought not to exist.

Now let us return to the statement that unless there is a marked difference in the curriculum, ability grouping becomes a mere gesture. There are those who believe that different objectives may set up for, and different methods used with, the same curriculum. I am of the opinion that the need for different methods for groups of different ability is greater than the need for different curricula. Closely related to the matter of methods is that of objectives. The objectives of teaching arithmetic to those who will stop short of algebra might legitimately differ from the objectives of teaching arithmetic to those who might be expected to complete one or more courses in algebra.

Under "Positive Disadvantages of Homogeneous Grouping," Mr. Brink says that his greatest objection to homogeneous grouping is that it is "unnatural" to the point of being "vicious." "It sets up a situation not to be found in the world outside of school." This can hardly be accepted as true. During the world war the army applied the principle of ability grouping of the new recruits entering the service and it also made use of mental tests almost entirely as the basis for grouping. Even here the principle was not new, even though the methods were a bit so. It is difficult to imagine a sound principle upon which our present-day schemes of educational guidance, vocational guidance and vocational selection could be based if not on the principle of ability grouping. As a matter of fact in what phase of life is the principle of selection not being applied? Wherever the principle of selection is found, it means that there is an attempt at ability grouping. Mr. Brink contends that after school days are over "a youth must compete not against those of his own ability group, but against an unselected population." Is it not true that the only successful competition which can be legitimately expected of an individual is competition with members of his own ability group? Is a lawyer worthy to be counted a success if he can do as well as one taken at random from an "unselected population"? Is a school superintendent doing as well as legitimately can be expected of him if he directs the destinies of his school system in as successful a fashion as one who has been chosen by lot from an "unselected population"? Many such questions as these may be raised and to raise them is to answer them. The weight of what evidence we have on the subject points to the conclusion that the optimal intellectual level for the different vocations varies greatly. Society is most likely to be served best, and the individual is most apt to be contented, if he finds his way into a vocation, and into a type of life generally, where the optimal level of intelligence most nearly corresponds to his own. It is true that one must generally live in a community where the people are fairly heterogeneous, but who can doubt that the abilities of various communities differ markedly and that different groups in the same community are very dissimilar.

All the currents of life tend toward ability grouping. The recent attempts in the school in this direction have introduced no new principle. They represent an endeavor to do a bit more purposefully and possibly a bit more scientifically that which life has ordained as at least wise, if not inevitable.

Those who object to ability grouping must assume that a heterogeneous group is more effectively taught than a homogeneous one. If such an assumption be true, then another one follows naturally, namely, that the more heterogeneous, the better. If the latter assumption be true, then we should expect to obtain maximum results by teaching idiots and geniuses in the same class.

T. M. CARTER

ALBION, MICHIGAN

HOW FAR IS MODERN EDUCATION MODERN?

MORE than twenty centuries ago classic philosophers were discussing educational problems, many of which are still far in advance of modern practice. For example, as early as 550 B. C. Pythagoras would receive only students of ability and character into his school at Crotona.

Plato more than three centuries before the Christian era planned for the specific care of children from birth to the age of three years. Thereafter for four years they were to have a definitely planned program for training in sports. This work was to be supervised by a nurse and over-supervised by guardians of the law. Plato believed that the early training of children influenced their adult behavior.

Aristotle, a pupil of Plato and the greatest thinker of his age, if not of all time, planned that the first five years of childhood should not be cumbered with labor or study, but should be utilized for a rich play life, which, he says, should not be vulgar, or tiring or riotous. "The directors of education should be careful what tales or stories the children hear, for the sports of children are designed to prepare the way for the business of later life. . . .

"The Directors of Education should take care that children are left as little as possible with slaves. Even at this early age, all that is mean and low should be banished from their sight and hearing. Indeed there is nothing which the legislature should be more careful to drive away than indecency of speech, for the light utterance of shameful words is akin to shameful actions. And since we do not allow improper language, clearly we should banish pictures or tales which are indecent. Youth should be kept strangers to all that is bad."

Quintilian, a Roman educator of the first century, believed that as soon as a son was born the father should conceive for him the best possible hopes, as he would then grow more solicitous about his improvement from the very beginning. He should also select a nurse with the greatest possible care as to morals and grammatical speech, for it is the words of the nurse that the child will hear first and try to imitate. We are by nature most tenacious of what we imbibe in our infant years, therefore let the child not become accustomed to phraseology which must be unlearned.

Plutarch, contemporary with Quintilian, said: "To speak generally, what we want to say about the arts and sciences is also true of moral excellence. For its perfect development these things must meet together, natural ability and training and practice. For natural ability without training is blind, and training without natural ability is defective, and practice without both natural ability and training is imperfect. For just as in farming, the first requisite is good soil, next a good farmer, next good seed, so also here the soil corresponds to the natural ability, the training to the farmer and the seed to the precepts and instruction."

Plutarch, speaking of the pre-school child, continues: "Infancy is supple and easily molded. What children learn sinks deeply into their souls while they are young and tender, whereas everything hard is softened only with difficulty. Just as seals are impressed on soft wax, so instruction leaves its permanent mark on the minds of those still young. The divine Plato seems to me to give excellent advice to nurses not to tell their children any kind of fables, that their souls may not in the very dawn of existence be full of folly and corruption. Phocylides, the poet, also seems to give excellent advice when he says, 'we must teach good habits while the pupil is still a boy.'"

Dr. Thorndike declares that as long as we use our best minds to clothe and feed us and our least competent to teach us, we can not hope to progress. Plutarch voiced a similar idea when he said, "good slaves are made farmers, or sailors, or merchants, or stewards, or money lenders; but if they find a winebibber, a greedy and utterly useless slave, to him parents commit the charge of their sons."

These few quotations are convincing proof that the Greek and Roman leaders of thought had definite ideas on the importance of training carefully the preschool child with some attention to individual differences. Further research in their educational philosophy reveals studies on health, diet, motivation of subject-matter, classification on the basis of mental ability, preparation for leisure and other topics which carry headlines in our current educational magazines. To be sure they had small, if any, notion of the application of their ideas in a world such as we know to-day. But they have, nevertheless, added to the rich social inheritance of this generation.

He who would be skilled in modern pedagogy or educational prophecy will find it interesting to sit at the feet of the masters, classic and medieval, as well as modern, and will find there a justification for including history of education in the course for the professional training of teachers.

CANDIS NELSON

SEATTLE PACIFIC COLLEGE

SPECIAL CORRESPONDENCE

SOME PHASES OF DEVELOPMENT OF THE CZECHOSLOVAK EDUCATIONAL SYSTEM

CZECHOSLOVAKIA has a famous and long-established background for her present development of education. The Charles University, founded in 1348, was the first university north of the Alps and east of France. The country produced the great educational reformer, John Amos Comenius. Thus it is not surprising that Bohemia, Moravia and Silesia had in the old Austro-Hungarian Monarchy the lowest number of illiterates, *viz.*, scarcely 3 per cent.

As it is a peculiarity of Czechoslovakia that it divides its schools according to the language in which instruction is given, we must notice that it was only at the end of the eighteenth century that the Latin was replaced by German, and in the Hungarian section (present Slovakia) by the Magyar language. The mother tongue, which is a form of Slavic, began to be used very slowly at the end of the same century.

The formation of Czechoslovakia placed an enormous burden on the state as far as education was concerned. Slovakia and Carpathian Russia, having been notoriously neglected by the pre-war masters, still had a great number of illiterates, and the schools, with very few exceptions, were Hungarian. Consequently the conditions in these two sections of Czechoslovakia are not normal and this is reflected in the statistical tables quoted below, as, for example, in the number of pupils in primary grades in Carpathian Russia. It is cheering to note that this number is growing most rapidly.

The statesmen of Czechoslovakia have been quite determined in supporting the demands of modern education on their country. In 1922 an eight-year compulsory school attendance law was passed; the previous requirement was but six years in Slovakia and Carpathian Russia; in addition, boys and girls over fourteen years who do not receive education in other schools must attend continuation schools for at least two years. The whole system of public instruction was unified, the standards raised and the administration simplified. All schools were placed under the direct supervision of the ministry of education with the exception of agricultural and military schools. Several new methods in teaching have been introduced. One of the most unusual provisions is that the parents can file a request that their children shall not be taught religion.

According to the most recent statistics, the picture of the development of Czechoslovak education is as follows:[1]

Schools	1921–22		1927–28		1929	
	Schools	Pupils	Schools	Pupils	Schools	Pupils
Elementary	16,690	2,249,531	17,913	1,834,106	18,425	1,878,612
Continuation	1,595	140,006	2,850	201,553	2,913	202,803
Professional	579	85,991	709	95,306	722	97,866
Secondary	370	100,807	353	95,541	354	90,853
Higher institutions	16	29,272	17	29,642	16	30,272
Total	19,250	2,605,607	21,842	2,256,148	22,430	2,300,406

It is evident that the number of educational institutions is steadily increasing, while the number of pupils reached the high-water mark in 1921–22. The subsequent decrease is explained by the low birth-rate during the war; the war generation is now attending the schools and is numerically weaker. The loss is felt especially in the secondary and primary grades, and less so in the continuation schools. The grammar schools attendance is slowly increasing.

While in 1921–22 the pupils formed about one fifth of the whole Czechoslovak population, in 1927–28 the rate was about one sixth. On

[1] Based on the periodical statistical reports of the ''Státní Úřad Statistický'' (State Statistical Institute), Prague, and especially its publication series II, No. 11, *Školy v Republice Československé* (*The Schools in the Czechoslovak Republic*), Prague, 1929.

the average this period had, we might say, about 20,000 schools, which averages about one school for less than seven square kilometers and about 690 inhabitants; or to be more exact, in 1921–22, one school served 712.9 inhabitants, and in 1927–28, 661.1, the estimated population being 13,722,892 in 1921–22 and 14,438,971 in 1927–28.

It is also interesting to note the development of each province, which is as follows:

	Schools	
	1921–22	1927–28
Bohemia	9,330	10,532
Moravia and Silesia	5,318	6,028
Carpathian Russia	664	894

	Pupils	
	1921–22	1927–28
Bohemia	1,308,985	1,063,009
Moravia and Silesia	687,908	598,851
Carpathian Russia	99,944	102,227

The increase is especially noticeable in the case of Carpathian Russia, though the growth is also evident in Slovakia if the statistics are examined for each year.

In view of the fact that Czechoslovakia is not without its problem of minorities, it is to be noted that in 1928 the pupils were distributed as follows: Czechoslovaks, 1,507,180 (66.8 per cent.); Russians, Carpathian Russians, Ukrainians, 79,067 (3.5 per cent.); Germans 496,426 (22 per cent.); Hungarians 119,046 (5.3 per cent.); Poles 16,893 (0.7 per cent.); Jews 33,449 (1.5 per cent.); and other nationalities 4,087 (0.2 per cent.). If we attack the problem from the view-point of how much opportunity of getting instruction in each minority language the Czechoslovak school system offers to each nationality, we must conclude that the proportion seems to be more than fair: 1,486,583 pupils of Czechoslovak nationality were instructed in institutions, which were exclusively Czechoslovak, the proportion being 97.6 per cent.; 66,835 Carpathian Russians, Russians and Ukrainians in Russian schools, *viz.,* 84.5 per cent.; 474,502 Germans in German schools, *viz.,* 95.6 per cent.; 97,632 Hungarians, in Hungarian schools, *viz.,* 82 per cent.; and 14,156 Poles in Polish schools, *viz.,* 83.8 per cent.

Not content with these favorable figures, the Czechoslovak educational system is undergoing a period of transition. A revision of the admission requirements into the secondary schools has provoked heated discussions in the academic circles of Czechoslovakia. Due to it and also to the increasing desire of the Czechoslovak people to find professional employment, the secondary schools, not to speak of the universities, are overcrowded. The economic crisis is especially felt by the graduates of the higher institutions. One third of the last year's graduates have been unable to find employment. The law of supply and demand is now markedly decreasing the income level of this "educated proletariat"—as they are called by the press of their country. The men of over thirty years of age and with academic degrees have greatest difficulties in finding a position, as there are younger ones willing to work for lesser wages. The appreciation of the value of the higher education is losing ground. However, the writer feels that the whole difficulty does not lie so much in the fact that so many people are being educated in Czechoslovakia as in the attitude of all the classes of that country that every graduate of the secondary and higher education is entitled to secure a "white collar" position, or, even better, a civil service position.

This aspiration is reflected in the following facts. For every 125 inhabitants there is one pupil in a secondary school. According to the investigation of 1922 the pupils came from the following classes: 15.8 per cent. from farmers' families, 15.1 per cent. from industrial families, 26.2 per cent. from commerce and trade, 32.8 per cent. from state employees, 10.1 per cent. from free professions. The socially lowest classes contributed 19.5 per cent. of the whole number. As the greatest proportion came from the state employees, it may be assumed that it leads to the propagation of the same class and the overcrowding of the positions that the state can offer.

In addition, the male graduates are met with the increasingly keener competition from women. It was not until 1890 that the Czech women petitioned the Vienna Parliament for permission to study at the universities. In 1899 only ten women were admitted to the higher institutions of learning in Austria. Miss Zd. Barborová, who received her doctorate in June, 1901, in Prague, had the distinction of being the first woman to get that degree in Czechoslovakia, creating quite a sensation throughout the country by virtue of the fact. All newspapers ran her picture on the front page. In 1930 there were nearly 4,000 university girls divided among the four Czechoslovak universities, not including certain women studying for engineering, architecture, agricultural posts, etc. It is interesting to note that among the medical students far the greater part enter the dental department and that the students of philosophy devote themselves mostly to journalism, the teaching professions, library and secretarial work. With the growing number of the women students, the question of their employment in suitable occupations is also becoming of first importance.

One of the most important influences exercised on the development of Czechoslovak education is that of America. James and Dewey, Baldwin and Hall were known even before the war, but Thorndike's influence is now most apparent. The tendency towards internationalism especially is a very strong one. This is evident from the teaching and knowledge of foreign languages in all grades, and the emphasis placed on teaching of peace ideas and ideals. The teachers are instructed to approach their subjects from this point of view. For example, the following subjects are given attention in the eighth school year: national culture, the League of Nations, civilization of mankind, equality of races and nationalities, international arbitration tribunals, international treaties and guarantees, war and peace, pacifism, religion and religious toleration. In 1926 the ministry of education decreed the so-called "half hour of peace talk," which is given on certain important dates of the year and especially on March 28, which is the anniversary of the birth of Jan Amos Comenius. The idea behind this instruction is that Comenius was not only a great nationalist but also a great internationalist, who was convinced that humanity can be led to the insurance of universal peace only upon the basis of the general education and enlightenment of all nations. The speaker on these occasions has complete freedom to choose his subject, but it is suggested that he is to refer to the peace efforts made during the various past stages of the history of the Czech people.

These efforts on behalf of peace are connected with the instruction in foreign languages. In the higher elementary grades the teaching of foreign tongues is partly compulsory and partly voluntary. German is taught that way and in some schools French and English are offered. The last figures teach us that in 1930–1931 the courses in German were required in 299 higher elementary schools; 1,347 such schools offered selective courses to the total number of 148,308 pupils; two schools taught compulsorily Russian to 2,696 pupils; 97 pupils selected the Hungarian language in one school, while 44,982 pupils had to take Czechoslovak in 67 schools and selected it in 404 institutions; 24,172 were learning the rudiments of the French language and 611 were spending their time on English. In primary schools a certain amount of attention was also paid to foreign languages: 976 schools had compulsory and 834 schools had selective courses for 146,054 pupils in Czechoslovak; the German language was required in three grammar schools and offered also in 1,726 schools, for 111,685 pupils; 186 schools required compulsory courses in the Ruthenian language and one school made the subject selective.

JOSEPH S. ROUCEK
CENTENARY JUNIOR COLLEGE,
HACKETTSTOWN, N. J.

QUOTATIONS

THE NEW DEPARTMENT OF SECONDARY EDUCATION

PERHAPS one of the most important steps taken at the Los Angeles meeting of the National Education Association was the final vote of the delegate assembly favoring a Department of Secondary Education, a department for high-school teachers only. For thirty-eight years, that is, from 1886 to 1924, such a department had existed. During the period of the world war and immediately thereafter, other subjects than secondary education commanded attention. In these later post-war years, secondary education has again taken a commanding position. Secondary schools have multiplied many times, and the number of earnest men and women engaged in secondary work has increased correspondingly. New types of secondary-school courses and new models of secondary-school buildings have been developed. Wholly new departures have been made in the preparation of secondary-school text-books. New methods, new aims, and a new spirit have vitalized secondary work in the United States, all of which makes for world leadership in precollege, or better still, pre-adult training. Under such conditions the reawakening of the Department of Secondary Education was to be expected.

Immediate action was brought about through hundreds of petitions from all states in the Union, brought together through the agency of the High-School Teachers Association of New York City, and forwarded to the governing bodies of the National Education Association. An interim organization, the National Secondary Education Association, held crowded meetings at Columbus, Ohio, in July, 1931, discussed the pressing problems of secondary education, and made plans and elected officers for the year to follow. That organization met again in Los Angeles in 1932.

The history of the re-establishment of the once-important department is of no great moment; the future work of the department is all-important. In the first place, the department, national in scope, is made up of earnest teachers from all sections of the United States, banded together to do constructive work, not for salaries, pensions, tenure of office, or other similar matters, but for courses of study, methods of organization and teaching, and for the general vitalization of all secondary work in accordance with practical needs and desires.

For years teachers in secondary schools were content to confine themselves to the pages of specific text-books, thinking more about special studies than about pupils, courses of study, or the broader purposes of education. In recent years a great change has taken place. Such organizations as the National Council of Teachers of English have become national in work and literally world-wide in influence, lifting teachers away from their desks and limited books and leading them to plan for work as part of a whole course of training. That change has taken place along the entire line of secondary-school work. A kind of democracy has entered secondary education, marking a revolt against the long endured tyranny of college-entrance examinations.

The results of this new independence of the secondary-school teacher are already apparent in every state. Under the influence of teacher suggestion and control, courses of study have been entirely revised. Those who were close to the daily lives of individual pupils saw clearly that the over-classical demands of college-entrance examinations could not elicit the best work or the best life-development. More practical demands were substituted, with an immediate advance on the part of secondary schools. New courses of study were organized to meet special needs, and these new courses were followed at once by the development of new types of schools. As a natural accompaniment new types of text-books, closely related to daily life and ordinary needs, were written. A few years ago nearly all the text-books used in secondary schools were written by college professors or at least by superintendents and principals. To-day great organizations of teachers plan the courses of study, and secondary-school teachers write many of the text-books.

With this new democracy of the secondary school, there has come a new pedagogy, not founded upon classical precept but upon the natures of American boys and girls. Put side by side two somewhat similar text-books, one published in 1900 and the other published recently, and the different attitude toward the pupil and pupil-interest is at once apparent. To-day's secondary-school books are those that are close to reality.

In the second place, the Department of Secondary Education consists of teachers who wish to consider seriously all the associated problems that concern secondary education, problems relating to social and industrial life, to politics and government, to social service and national ideals. "The American high school is the people's university," says a modern adage. The American high school is also the people's inspiration toward civic consciousness.

The spontaneous development of numerous secondary organizations, with their great influence and power, such as the High-School Teachers Association of New York City, and of other large cities, representing one type, and the National Council of Teachers of English, representing another, shows the irresistible force behind the movement for democratizing all secondary schools.

The National Education Association has gained new power by welcoming into its membership as a department, a clearing house for all branches of secondary education, and especially for all the numerous organizations of secondary-school teachers in all parts of the United States.

The work of the new department will lead to sweeping changes in the present secondary schools, making stronger relationships between junior and senior high schools, and between senior high schools and junior and senior colleges; changing the courses of study by casting out what is kept by mere tradition and by introducing or expanding what is really vital; relating all the work of secondary schools far more closely than ever before to social conditions and civic needs, thus leading to a more effective coping with lawlessness and crime, and to nobler conceptions of national duty and honor. At the same time the position of the secondary teacher will be elevated to higher respect.

Fortunate indeed are those who will take part in the meetings of the Department of Secondary Education at Atlantic City in June, for they, like the patriots of the early days of the United States, will stand at the beginning of a road that will lead to greater happiness, greater usefulness, and greater benefit to the American people.—*Frederick Houk Law, in the Journal of the National Education Association.*

REPORTS

FAR WESTERN SUMMER SCHOOLS

Mr. E. M. Foster, Chief of the Division of Statistics of the United States Bureau of Education is quoted in School and Society, April 23, 1932, to the effect that (1) the closing of a large number of summer schools will bar thousands of students and unemployed from further education, and (2) the summer school enrolment this year will fall far behind that of previous years in spite of the movement to keep more young people in school. This challenging forecast is of extreme interest to all directors or deans in charge of these summer programs.

How far these general observations are applicable to the Far Western section of the United States, in the light of recent records, is the subject of this brief article. Conditions here are probably not typical of other American regions, yet the trends disclosed are significant and suggestive.

Due consideration, however, should be given to such special geographical features as location many hundred miles away from the nation's center of population—a factor which is balanced somewhat by the heavy summer travel, the area of each one of the western states, the unusual influence of state-supported universities and colleges, and the few private universities and colleges of even moderate size. The area of the eleven western states consists of 1,177,000 square miles with a population of nearly 12,000,000, compared to New England with 62,000 square miles with a population of somewhat over 8,000,000; the population per square mile amounts to 10 for the Far West contrasted with 132 for New England and 41 for continental United States. Thus the geographical background of this western empire is clearly distinctive.

A questionnaire was sent out from Stanford University, in March, 1932, to a selected list of leading universities and colleges, including teachers colleges and normal schools, based upon the latest Educational Directory issued by the United States Department of the Interior. Inquiries were sent to 12 universities and colleges on the Pacific Coast, and to 13 in the Rocky Mountain district; replies were received from all except one university in Utah (with a recorded registration on 461 in 1930). To these returns are added those of Stanford University. Inquiries were sent to 13 teachers colleges and normal schools on the Coast and to 6 in Arizona, Colorado, Idaho, and New Mexico; replies were received from all but two on the Coast (however, incomplete data from other sources included) and from all but one in the Interior (data procured elsewhere disclose an attendance of 148 in 1928 and 197 in 1930). The returns from the questionnaire are unusually complete but not always comparable. The validity of limiting our analysis to a relatively few institutions of higher learning is shown by the situation in California, where the 14 thus selected account for 80–85 per cent. of the total summer session enrolments for California colleges and universities, as reported by the State Department of Education.

Are these summer schools being closed in large numbers? The answer is no. Based upon those in existence two years ago, one Colorado college ceased its summer session in 1930, and one (in Oregon) plans to abandon this year. Neither college has had as many as 200 students in any summer of record. There is no evidence that the leading western summer schools are materially curtailing their activities in 1932.

Directors of summer work seem to anticipate a probable decline in registration this year in comparison with 1931, but hunch rather than concrete information is their guide. The writer can do little more than indicate decided trends derived from the statistics for the period 1926–1931, for this year more than ever before the intangibles are exceedingly difficult to gauge. We in the West are at a loss to determine satisfactorily either the actual or the relative importance of the major factors of unemployment, smaller individual savings, and the Olympic Games.

The enrolment statistics give no portent of decline; if anything, they show an opposite tendency. Contributory information for the American collegiate (not summer) registration is reported by Dean Raymond Walters of Swarthmore, in SCHOOL AND SOCIETY, December 12, 1932, as a gain this year over last year of six tenths of one per cent. Summer school figures for the 43 western educational institutions totaled 39,253 in 1926, 42,121 in 1929, 41,923 in 1930, and 43,998 in 1931. While the rate of increase has slowed down in recent years, since 1929 unquestionably due to the depressed economic situation, nevertheless there were more students registered in 1931 than in either of the preceding years. On the other hand, there is a fairly wide-spread feeling on the part of the summer directors that a general decrease in the number of students is to be expected this summer in line with the changing educational and dire economic trends.

The Dean of Summer Sessions of one of the largest Coast universities, commenting on the situation in his particular institution, writes:

> You will notice, of course, the marked decline in attendance since 1928. My own thought is that this decline is due rather to the competition of the State Teachers Colleges than to the financial depression. These colleges offer a wide range of courses with a low tuition fee ($15.00), and their summer attendance has been increasing, while ours has been falling. The decline in out-of-state visitors since 1929 is no doubt due, in part at least, to the financial depression.

It is of more than passing interest to learn to what extent these observations are of wide application. Let us consider now the universities and colleges, other than the teachers colleges and normal schools, in the States of California, Oregon and Washington, and those in the Rocky Mountain region. The statistics follow:

UNIVERSITIES AND COLLEGES

	1926	1929	1930	1931
California (7)	14,258	15,494	14,032	13,847
Oregon (3)	1,838	2,268	2,488	2,682
Washington (3)	3,186	3,743	4,031	4,825
	19,282	21,505	20,551	21,354
Interior (12)*	8,343	8,709	9,449	10,372
	27,625	30,214	30,000	31,726

* One less in 1931.

From the foregoing table, it is apparent that (a) the attendance was 9 per cent. greater in 1929 than in 1926, (b) attendance was nearly the same in 1929 and 1930 but 5 per cent. greater in 1931 than in the preceding two years,

(c) contrasting 1931 with 1929, the striking geographical changes are a loss of 11 per cent. for California, and gains of 19 per cent. for the Rocky Mountain states, 46 per cent. for Oregon, and 51 per cent. for Washington. These averages, however, are to be taken as averages, notably in the case of the 7 California institutions which exhibit the following weird changes from 1929 to 1931: +120 per cent., +29 per cent., +12 per cent., +8 per cent., −19 per cent., −22 per cent., and −33 per cent.

The teachers colleges and normal schools report the following enrolment:

TEACHERS COLLEGES AND NORMAL SCHOOLS

	1926	1929	1930	1931
California (7)	3,721	4,390	4,388	4,420
Oregon (3)[1]	1,172	1,444	1,329	1,242
Washington (3)	2,370	2,332	2,336	2,391
	7,263	8,156	8,053	8,053
Other states (5)	4,363	3,751	3,794	4,219
	11,626	11,907	11,847	12,272

[1] One less in 1926.

Based on the foregoing table, one discovers that (a) teachers colleges and normal schools have been having an exceedingly slow growth from 1926 on, (b) the California teachers colleges had an identical figure for 1930 and 1931, (c) total enrolment for 1930 was somewhat less than in 1929, (d) enrolment in 1931 was 3 per cent. greater than in 1929, and (e) gains have been chiefly in the interior states, the loss in Oregon. The Eastern Oregon Normal School at Ashland did not open until 1929. The enrolment in Montana, Arizona, and New Mexico has increased greatly, while that in Idaho has declined during the past three years.

The conclusion, therefore, is that, during 1929–31, the universities and colleges in Oregon, Washington and the Rocky Mountain states have grown much more rapidly than the teachers colleges and normal schools, while the reverse is true in California. The aggregate rate of increase for the former group is nearly twice that of the institutions devoted almost exclusively to teacher training. This result runs counter to the commonly reported belief.

The direct effect of tuition upon registration is difficult to measure. No one can question the importance of the relationship. A tabulation of tuition fees justifies the assumption that usually these fees in teachers colleges and normal schools are less than those in liberal arts universities and colleges under state control, and that private institutions ask the highest tuition. Comparing the registration in the liberal arts institutions under public and private control, respectively, on the Pacific Coast, four public universities showed gains and two showed losses, four private institutions showed gains, one a loss, one unchanged. Carrying this comparison to the Rockies, two of the 10 public universities suffered small losses in 1931 compared with 1929, one private college ceased to function in 1931 after a large percentage drop in the preceding year, and the only private university recorded a gain of 40 per cent. However, the institutions are too few in number and the data too contradictory to warrant any generalization regarding the influence of tuition *per se*. It is somewhat surprising that the evidence is not more clear-cut.

The geographical distribution of students is a significant feature of educational statistics. To illustrate, since the smallest of the eleven western states is larger than the combined states of New York, New Jersey and Massachusetts, and the largest is roughly two and a half times as great, transportation fares alone constitute a large item for residents as well as non-residents. The State of New York, with an area only one twenty-fifth as extensive as the Far West, has actually a larger population. The fact that a person comes from outside the state, therefore, means much more than in the case of the smaller Eastern states. One would look, therefore, for an unusually small percentage of outside students in the Far West. The results however do not bear out this prediction, for not only is the percentage of non-residents increasing in the majority of liberal universities and colleges, but also the percentage itself is striking.

Comparing 1931 with 1926, the percentage of non-residents has increased from 40 per cent. to 53 per cent. for Colorado Agricultural College, 15 per cent. to 28 per cent. for the University of Southern California, 13 per cent. to

22 per cent. for the University of Arizona, and 4 per cent. to 10 per cent. for the University of New Mexico. The highest percentages of non-residents are found at University of Colorado 76 per cent., Colorado Agricultural College 53 per cent., Oregon Agricultural College 35 per cent., Stanford University and the University of Washington 30 per cent., University of Southern California 28 per cent., University of California (Berkeley) 25 per cent., University of California (Los Angeles) 23 per cent., University of Arizona and University of Nevada 22 per cent., University of Denver 20 per cent., and University of Oregon 19 per cent. Only four universities and colleges have less than 10 per cent. from other states. However, in the case of teachers colleges, naturally the vast majority of students are residents; in one teachers college in California, 69 per cent. of the students come from one county. On the other hand, noteworthy exceptions are San Diego Teachers College, New Mexico State Teachers College (Silver City), and Colorado State Teachers College (Greeley), where 25 per cent. to 30 per cent. of the students reside outside of the state.

The "graduates" in a teachers college or normal school are not to be classed with the "graduates" in liberal universities and colleges, for the reason that in the former case this term is commonly applied to holders of a teacher's certificate, in the latter instance to holders of a baccalaureate degree. As reported by one of the teachers colleges in the Northwest:

> Some explanation may be necessary regarding the term ''graduate students.'' Until September last year, our school offered the two-year course for elementary teachers. Students having completed this course and returning for more work are regarded as graduate students. The number of graduate students given on the form we are sending includes all third year and fourth year students, and any college graduates—of whom there were thirteen last summer.

In teachers colleges and normal schools the number of teacher-certificate graduates is increasing, but few of their students are college graduates. Teachers colleges in California do not offer graduate courses, therefore the liberal universities and colleges in California and elsewhere are in a favored position because of the notable trend towards summer registration by holders of the bachelor's degree.

In spite of the fact that the Far West affords a great summer playground, the most conclusive result of the Stanford questionnaire is the unmistakable finding that summer work is becoming less of a vacation and more of an opportunity for serious study. The rapidly growing enrolment of graduate students furnishes ample proof. While the data are not complete, it is noteworthy that there is no instance of a smaller percentage of graduates in 1929 than in 1926, or in 1931 than in 1926. In practically every case the percentage was considerably higher in 1931 than in 1929; for example, the increase at Stanford University was from 56 per cent. to 60 per cent., Claremont Colleges 36 per cent. to 47 per cent., University of Idaho 32 per cent. to 45 per cent., Oregon State Agricultural College 20 per cent. to 40 per cent., University of Colorado 23 per cent. to 30 per cent., University of Utah 18 per cent. to 24 per cent., and College of the Pacific 5 per cent. to 17 per cent. Only one institution on the Coast reported less than 15 per cent. graduates, similarly for only four in the Interior including two which offer no graduate instruction. According to the information furnished by directors of summer schools, the percentage of graduates to non-graduates in 1931 was as follows: Stanford University 60 per cent., Washington State College 49 per cent., University of California (Berkeley) 48 per cent., Claremont Colleges 47 per cent., University of Southern California 45 per cent., Colorado Agricultural College and the Oregon State Agricultural College 40 per cent., University of California (Los Angeles) 34 per cent., College of the Pacific 33 per cent., the University of Colorado 30 per cent., and the University of Oregon 26 per cent. The aggregate graduate representation in the western universities and colleges has been as follows: 1926, 24 per cent.; 1927, 29 per cent.; 1928, 33 per cent.; 1929, 34 per cent.; 1930, 35 per cent.; 1931, 39 per cent.

The prospective attendance this year in Far Western summer schools remains a matter of considerable conjecture. The two prime factors seem to be (1) the precise value placed upon further study and credits by both employed and unemployed teachers, and (2) the ability to finance the extra study. Teachers continue to make up the largest group of students. Without question, the Pacific states are requiring higher and higher credentials for teaching positions. New state regulations for teachers are immediately reflected in summer enrolment. Sometimes the urge is a stated requirement, sometimes it takes the form of a strong recommendation by a school authority. These two excerpts from recent letters are pertinent:

It was interesting to me to note that last summer our percentage of graduate students was quite large, and that there has been a rapid increase in the number of graduate students attending our summer session. This was due in considerable part to the new standards of certification which went into effect September 1, 1931.

We plan the curriculum entirely for our Idaho teachers and superintendents. We have a large percentage of the superintendents of the state here during the summer. At the present rate it will be only a short time until nearly every superintendent in the State of Idaho will have been a student at the University of Idaho either in the summer or winter sessions. The growth of the summer session has been almost entirely in the graduate work.

One of the largest universities in California raises certain queries with special reference to their local situation.

We are somewhat puzzled what to anticipate both in the number of students and the type of work that will be needed in our forthcoming summer session. The unknown factors are: (a) the influence of the National Education Association on last year's enrolment; (b) the effect of the general economic situation; (c) the Olympic Games in Los Angeles in 1932, and (d) the effect of a recommendation of the City Superintendent's Office that all holders of Special Credentials (approximately 2,500 in number) secure the General Secondary Credential at the earliest date possible.

I would hazard the guess that the statements attributed to Mr. Foster, of the United States Bureau of Education, are more applicable to the weaker than the stronger summer schools, furthermore, that the influences cited are not likely to be felt in such pronounced form on the western frontier as in the United States as a whole. In matters affecting registration, everywhere the bases for pessimism are more readily discernible than the offsetting factors on the other side of the picture. It should not be overlooked, moreover, that the foregoing quantitative statistics have not been subjected here to quality tests, for example, attendance may be for the duration of a month without credit or a full term conforming to the standards of the regular academic year. There are still educational institutions which, rightly or wrongly, appear to lay chief emphasis upon scenic and social attractions. Nevertheless, I believe that the directors and deans of western schools would be practically unanimous in declaring that the motivating force in the summer session program has now become that of serious purpose rather than educational recreation.

Eliot Grinnell Mears,
Director, Summer Quarter
Stanford University

EDUCATIONAL RESEARCH AND STATISTICS

A TEST IN EDUCATIONAL MEASUREMENTS

In view of the amount of attention given to the field of educational measurements and to instruction therein within the past twenty or twenty-five years, it is rather surprising that so little has been done by way of constructing standardized and commercially available tests in this field. At first thought, one would expect that workers in educational measurements, who supposedly advocate the construction of tests and scales in all subjects, would have made this subject one of the first in which standardized tests were available. Probably the chief reason why this was not done was that, because of the newness of the field, the content of courses offered therein was quite variable from institution to institution, and even from instructor to instructor within the same institution. Although this situation still exists to a considerable degree, the diversity in courses bearing the same, or approximately the same, names is less than was formerly the case, and there seems to be available a sufficient body of material common to a large enough fraction of the beginning courses in the field to justify the preparation and publication of a test thereon.

In view of this fact, and his interest in the field, the writer has undertaken the construction of a test[1] designed to fulfil the function implied in the last sentence of the preceding paragraph. In other words, it is intended to cover the more common and more essential items included in beginning general courses in measurements. Such courses, in most institutions, give some attention to both standardized and informal tests, to both achievement and intelligence tests, and to testing on both the elementary and secondary school levels. Their prime purpose is to provide a broad general foundation of knowledge in the field, that will serve as a basis for future more specialized and advanced courses, and at the same time assist the many individuals who do not take further courses in the testing they will actually do in their teaching. The test was constructed with a three-hour semester course particularly in mind, but was intended to contain enough material usually included in shorter courses that it may appropriately be used therein, and also some items usually included in more advanced courses, provided they are not too specialized, so that it will serve to some degree to measure the outcomes of these courses also.

The test in its final form is the outgrowth of several years of testing by the writer in his own introductory course in the field. During this time, he accumulated a fairly large number of short answer elements of several types, with student responses thereto. When he began definitely to formulate the test, he was able to select from these elements many, which, on the basis of the results obtained in actual class use, appeared to be satisfactory for the purpose they were intended to serve. The preliminary forms of the tests were thus constructed with the addition of a few new elements, and in the light of content studies which will be referred to in describing the several sub-tests. After these preliminary forms had been tried out in the writer's classes, they were revised, given further try-outs in his classes and also in those of another institution, then printed, tried out in several other institutions and finally put into the present form. The students who participated in the various try-outs included those in from one to six classes each from five universities, one college and one normal college, in addition to the writer's own institution. About three hundred students took each form of the test at the last try-out, whereas on previous occasions more than that number had taken each form. In all cases, the students tested were just completing courses in the subject. In some instances these were term courses, and in others semester courses. The number of meetings varied from two to five per week. At least two of the classes tested were largely composed of students who had had previous work in the subject.

The test, as finally printed, consists of two forms, 1 and 2, each of which contains four subtests, as follows:

Sub-test I.	Multiple-answer statements on educational measurement in general.
Sub-test II.	Matching exercises on prominent workers in the measurement movement.
Sub-test III.	True-false exercises on available supplies of tests in various fields.
Sub-test IV.	True-false exercises on educational measurement in general.

Sub-test I consists of thirty-nine elements, one of which is used as a sample, covering the general field of educational measurements. There are five suggested answers for each element. Most of the statements are of the nature of definitions, explanations or statements of functions. The last five or six deal, however, with the dates of outstanding events in the history of the educational measurement movement. The items included were chosen as a result of a study of all general text-books in the field of either elementary or high-school testing or both that were published within the last four or five years before the preparation of the test. A number of those that occurred most frequently and seemed to be most fundamental are included in both forms of the test. In such cases, however, the two test elements, one in each form, that deal with the same item are not identical,

[1] The test referred to above is published by the Public School Publishing Company under the title of "Standard Achievement Test on Educational Measurements."

but differ in that the form of the statement is changed. Usually it is reversed, so that an expression that appears in the body of the statement in one form is given as the correct one of the suggested answers in the other form, and *vice versa.*

Sub-test II in each form contains a list of sixteen workers in the field of educational measurement and another of thirteen statements of the contributions made by these workers. As a sample one of the statements is matched with one of the names, thus leaving fifteen and twelve, respectively, to be matched. A tabulation was made of all persons mentioned in all books that may properly be classed as belonging in the field of educational measurements that had appeared within somewhat more than three years before the time of preparation. The twenty-six persons at the head of the list were determined by averaging ranks based upon the number of different books in which each was mentioned and upon the total number of times each person was mentioned in all the books.[2] This list of twenty-six was then divided at random into two of thirteen each. To each list of thirteen there were added the names of three workers in the field who were not included among the first twenty-six but did not fall far below these in frequency. These three names are the extra ones for which no statements of contributions are given and are inserted merely to prevent too easy guessing of the last two or three of the list by a person taking the test who knows all or most of the others. The statements of contributions mention books in the field and important tests or series of tests of which the persons named are the authors, subjects or other fields of testing in which they have worked, and a few other miscellaneous items. For example, in Form 1 the name used as a sample is that of Thorndike and his contributions are stated as follows: "Intelligence, drawing and handwriting scales; general stimulation of movement; first book in field." In inserting this portion of the test the writer recognizes the fact that in many elementary courses little attention is given to the names of workers in educational measurements. He believes, however, that this condition is not a desirable one and that more emphasis should be placed upon this phase of knowledge. The chief reason for this belief is that any one who is unfamiliar with the chief contributions of the leading workers in any field can not read understandingly much of the literature therein, nor is he sufficiently well informed of what has been done to do intelligent creative work himself.

Sub-test III is probably the least valuable portion of the test. It contains, in each form, the names of twenty school subjects or other fields of testing and instructs those taking the test to indicate whether the supply of tests in each should be described as good or poor. The subjects named include those commonly taught in elementary and high schools and the other fields those of interest to educators. Subjects and fields in which it is quite doubtful whether the supply of tests should be called good or poor are not included. As to the value of such information, the writer believes that all administrators and supervisors should be in possession of knowledge of this sort for their general fields and likewise that all teachers in non-departmentalized elementary schools should have this information for that level. The chief limitation of the test is that the correct answers to a part of the elements will undoubtedly change in the course of time as some of the fields in which the supplies are now poor are taken care of in more satisfactory fashion. However, it is unlikely that within a period of two or three years there will be many changes that should be made in the list of correct answers. During the time that has elapsed since the test was put in approximately final form, which has been about a year, not enough new tests of high merit have appeared in any of the fields in which the supply was poor to cause a single change in the correct answers.

Sub-test IV contains thirty true-false statements dealing with general information of the same type as that with which Sub-test I is concerned. In the case of this sub-test also a number of the more important and more common items are dealt with in differently constructed statements in the two forms of the test. The

[2] For a fuller account of this study of persons mentioned in books on educational measurements, see: C. W. Odell, "Who Have Contributed Most to the Educational Measurement Movement?" School and Society, 29: 751–54, June 8, 1929. The list given herein was revised for use in the test.

decision as to whether to test knowledge of an item in this part or in Sub-test I was based in part upon which form of exercise, multiple-answer or true-false, seemed best suited to the item in question, and in part was a matter of chance.

The test is prepared as an eight-page pamphlet, of which the first page contains both the instructions to examiners and those to students. These are relatively short, as is likewise true of the particular directions at the beginning of each of the four sub-tests. A score sheet is provided, which, in addition to the directions for scoring, contains answers so spaced that by proper folding they may be brought immediately alongside the students' answers. In Sub-tests I and II, the scores are the numbers of elements correctly marked, whereas in III and IV they are the numbers right minus the numbers wrong. The highest possible score is thus equal to the number of elements, which is one hundred, not including the two used as samples. A teachers' manual is also provided. It contains much the same material as is found in this article with, however, a few additional points.

In this, as in almost all other tests, the problem of determining validity is a difficult one. In very few cases are there satisfactory criteria with which to compare scores upon tests to determine how well they measure what they are intended to measure. This test is no exception to the rule. The writer endeavored to insure curricular validity by means of the procedures stated above that served as guides in the choice of content and of test elements to measure knowledge of this content. The only figures so far available as to validity are coefficients of correlation or validity between scores on the test and on a traditional examination and a series of ten short objective tests prepared by the writer. The coefficients obtained are given in Table I. The two sets of coefficients given in the table are the average coefficients for the two forms with the indicated criteria for two groups of students.

TABLE I

COEFFICIENTS OF VALIDITY

Test scores with traditional examination covering the same material	.44	.48
Test scores with series of ten short objective tests given throughout the course	.57	.63
Test scores with total points on traditional examination plus series of short tests	.60	.65

Most of the students to whom the test was given after it had been printed took both Form 1 and Form 2, thus rendering reliability data available. The highest coefficient of reliability between the two forms for any group was .89. The average reliability coefficient was approximately .72. If both forms of the test are employed to yield a single score, the coefficient of reliability of such scores, estimated by means of the Spearman-Brown formula, is .84. Inasmuch as most of the classes tested were relatively homogeneous and restricted in spread, the average coefficient of reliability which is given is somewhat lower than would be those obtained if the scores of the students in all the classes were thrown into two correlation tables, one for those who took Form 1 first and then Form 2, and another for those who took them in the reverse order. Other data on reliability in addition to the coefficients are given in Table II.

TABLE II

DATA ON RELIABILITY

	r	N	S.D.	$P.E._{est.}$	$P.E._{meas.}$	$\frac{P.E._{meas.}}{M}$	$\frac{P.E._{meas.}}{S.D.}$
One form	.72	260	10.2	4.8	3.6	.09	.35
Both forms	.84	260	18.9	6.9	5.1	.06	.27

The standard deviations and other measures given in the table are similar to the coefficients of correlation in that they are the averages for single class groups. The probable error of estimate is the probable error involved in estimating a score on one form from an actually obtained score on the other, whereas the probable error of measurement is that involved in estimating a true score from an actually obtained score. The ratios of the latter to the mean and to the standard deviation are probably the best bases of measuring reliability for comparable purposes. From the figures appearing in the first row, it is evident that a single form of the test does not furnish highly reliable individual scores but may well be used for group measurement. This is partly, at least, due to the fact that although the amount of working time allowed is thirty-five minutes, this is purposely made long enough that time is not an important factor, and therefore the test might well be given as a timed test within thirty or even twenty-five minutes. The use of both forms furnishes more satisfactory individual scores. Moreover, the final revision, made after the data given above were collected, probably served to increase the reliability of the test somewhat.

The only norms available at present are for the group of students who took the printed forms of the tests before the final slight revision. The percentile norms for these almost six hundred students are given in Table III.

TABLE III

TENTATIVE PERCENTILE NORMS

Percentile	10	20	25	30	40	50	60	70	75	80	90
Score	28	32	33	34	37	40	44	48	51	54	63

They should be regarded as tentative rather than final. These are average results upon the two forms. On the whole, Form 1 was between two and three points easier than Form 2, but it is believed that this difference has been corrected by shifting a few of the most difficult items from Form 2 to Form 1 and, in turn, a few of the easiest ones on Form 1 to Form 2. Therefore, for the revision now available there should be no material difference in difficulty.

As has already been stated, the total group of students who took the test included classes that devoted various amounts of time to the course and that were composed of students of varying degrees of maturity and preparation. It appears that on the whole whether or not students are just completing a two-semester-hour or a three-semester-hour course makes a difference of ten or twelve points in their scores. Therefore, for those completing only a two-semester-hour course five or six points should be subtracted from each of the percentile norms given above, and for those completing a three-semester-hour course, five or six points should be added to each. Moreover, it appears that in the case of classes of students who have had very little work in education previous to their course in measurements and who are largely underclassmen as contrasted with those who have had several previous courses in education and are chiefly seniors, there is a difference of about the same amount as that stated in the case of two and three hour courses.

Scores were also tabulated for the four subtests separately. The medians and first and third quartiles of these distributions are to be found in Table IV.

TABLE IV

TENTATIVE NORMS FOR SEPARATE SUB-TESTS

Sub-test	I	II	III	IV
Third quartile	25	4	11	12
Median	23	2	8	8
First quartile	19	1	6	5

As was mentioned near the beginning of this article, the content of educational measurements courses is far from being as settled as is that of many subjects. It can not, therefore, be reasonably expected that this or any other test in this field will continue to be as satisfactory as it was when first constructed for so long a period of time as are most tests in many other subjects. New terms and concepts will come into use and new persons into prominence. On the other hand, some terms and some workers are receding from their present places of importance. Points of view and of emphasis are changing with relative rapidity and in at least a few instances what have been considered determined facts are being found not to be so. It is to be expected, therefore, that the present test will serve merely as the beginning of standardized tests in educational measurements, and that other workers, and perhaps the present writer also, will continue activity along this line and provide new tests better adapted to the purposes they should serve, and of increasing value.

C. W. ODELL

UNIVERSITY OF ILLINOIS

NEW BOOKS IN EDUCATION

TURNER, CLAIR E. *Principles of Health Education.* Pp. 326. Heath. $2.00.

WEINBERG, LOUIS. *America in the Machine Age.* Pp. 352. Heath. $1.00.

SCHOOL AND SOCIETY

EDITED BY J. McKEEN CATTELL

WITH WHICH IS COMBINED THE

EDUCATIONAL REVIEW

EDITED BY WILLIAM McANDREW

Volume 35 SATURDAY, JUNE 18, 1932 Number 912

THE CONTRIBUTION OF STATISTICAL METHOD TO EDUCATION

By Dr. HARL R. DOUGLASS

PROFESSOR OF EDUCATIONAL ADMINISTRATION, COLLEGE OF EDUCATION, UNIVERSITY OF MINNESOTA

AN author of a volume on testing in education published several years ago opened his treatise with the following apt quotation from Plato: "If a man can not measure and another who can not measure say to him that he is four cubits high, how can he but believe him?"

If a man can not measure, and another who can not or will not say to him that the project method, or the Dalton plan, or the mastery plan, is the only royal road to learning, and say it to him in flawless, forceful rhetoric, beautifully written or interestingly spoken, how can he but believe? If he is told that the study of geometry has intrinsically peculiar values for improving the power of reasoning, that adolescence marks the beginning of reason, that the study of foreign languages and of mathematics make outstanding contributions to scholastic success in college, that homogeneous grouping develops inferiority or superiority complexes, that the two-year junior college is superior to the four-year type, or that any one of a thousand other things may or may not be true, and if these statements are made in the proper language, with an appropriate stage setting of authority and personality, and with the weaknesses in logic carefully glossed over, he is helpless. If he refuses to be convinced, he is thought to be negativistic, unprogressive or lacking in ability to understand. But if he can measure and reduce his problem to precise quantitative terms, he may then avoid the dilemma.

The organization and administration of schools, the materials and methods of instruction and the supervision and improvement of teaching have traditionally been the legitimate playground for those who enjoy freedom of speculative inquiry and who avoid the rigors and restrictions of quantitative, exact and tedious experimental methods of investigation. If I were to review the meanderings of educational thinking in the past, stopping here and there with outstanding leaders and their methods of inquiry, I am certain that you would recognize the fairness of an assertion that educational thinking has been unfortunately and severely hampered by the lack of objective and quantitative terms and methods. Plato, in his "Republic," outlines and advocates a fantastic curriculum, a type of homogeneous grouping, the nucleus of a methodology, all based upon a psychology that he was forced largely to invent.

Later Quintilian in Rome, Vittorina de

Feltre at Mantua, Sturm at Strassburg, and a succession of early modern authorities left us in documentary form their observations about education, its objectives, materials and methods. Among the latter group may be mentioned Comenius, Rousseau, Pestalozzi, Locke, Herbart, Froebel and Spencer. One should not regard lightly the stimulus which these men gave to educational thinking. That the wheels of educational progress were kept turning, albeit with much lost motion, up until the present century has been largely due to their contributions. With keen intellects and the intuition of genius they have furnished a leadership which has been most useful.

Yet, they have labored under serious handicaps and limitations. The body of facts about learners and learning and about the relative efficacy of various methods and means of organization, administration, supervision and teaching has been a pitifully inadequate nucleus, heavily diluted with assumptions and premises which were apparent, but not true or accurate. However gifted the earlier thinkers may have been in intellectual endowment and training, they were not privileged to start with a large body of known facts as premises or raw material for the exercise of their talents nor to employ refined techniques and instruments which have since been made available.

The nature of their problems magnified and intensified their difficulties. The human mind is not a simple subject or object of study. The problems are too difficult, the datum of the study of learning too intangible and complicated to respond to crude and subjective study even by genius. It is not odd that the development of the sciences of rocks, stars, heat, mechanics, chemicals, plants and flesh have flowered earlier and to a greater extent than has that of psychology and education.

The study of education is further complicated by the lack of uniformity among its items of data. Children do not present uniform capacities for learning, standard interests in the materials of learning, or equally keen desires for knowledge. They do not all respond to educational situations in the same manner. At times it seems that no two respond in like manner, but behave as certain chemicals in a demonstration exercise sometimes used in the teaching of chemistry. In this exercise each of the test-tubes in a rack is partly filled with a different substance. From a beaker a fluid is poured, some into each of the test-tubes. In no two test-tubes are the resulting precipitates of the same color; but in one, brown; in another, black; in another, yellow, and so on; the nature of the precipitate being as much determined by the contents of the test-tubes as by that of the beaker.

One can not hope, therefore, to develop a scientific basis of learning upon data gathered concerning one or a small number of individuals. The study of education is a study of numbers of individuals. It is a study of groups rather than a study of individuals.

It is necessary to describe groups as groups. As numbers increase, it becomes impossible for one to hold in mind the data concerning each of the individuals composing the group. A practical means of summary becomes essential to clear thinking. While, in a general way, groups may be described in such non-numerical terms as bright or tall or having progressed satisfactorily, such expressions are hardly adequate for precise description. To begin with they are not objective, but in all likelihood depend upon the reporter for meaning as well as accuracy. They are also crude. They lack the fineness necessary to careful research. Comparisons may be made only with disappointing reservations. They are awkward and cumbersome. Just as in algebra it is very economical to represent some more or less complex idea as the number of kilowatts of electricity per hour by a symbol such as x or y, and, as it is sometimes quite desirable in order to simplify algebraic manipulation to designate an expression such as $\frac{ab - cd}{2ab}$ by a single letter, *c* or *k* or *t*, so in the description of groups it is necessary to devise simple and exact terms and concepts which free our mental energies for other tasks. When we calculate the arithmetical mean of a group we have a measure of the magnitude of the group and a measure of its central tendency expressed in exact terms, free from human bias or idiosyncrasies.

In describing a group, we need, also, to note and to express precisely the variability of the individuals. To say that they vary widely, or that some are much larger than others, is a rough generalization reasonably suitable for some conversational purposes but definitely inadequate and relatively crude when compared to a precise statement, such as the difference between the upper and lower quartile is 6 or that the standard deviation is 8, or even that the range is 13. Several other and less commonly used means of describing groups may be employed to add definiteness to description and to thinking. Among these are percentiles, coefficients of variation, average deviations and graphical methods. Of the latter the frequency polygon, the histograph and the percentile graph more particularly have been of valuable service.

Ordinarily, we are not so much concerned with the particular group, except as it furnishes the basis for conclusions which may be safely made concerning much larger groups, *e.g.*, all children in general or all of a given range in age or grade. Usually the value of a research study lies in the fact that it enables us to arrive at some generalization which is at least to some degree applicable to groups much larger than those employed in the investigation.

When, either in statistical studies or in non-statistical thinking, our inferences derived from small groups are applied to relatively unlimited groups, we are subject to the possibilities of several types of errors in reasoning. Among these are errors of measurement and of sampling. For example, among the first 10 names drawn at random from a file of 1,000 school pupils, the names of 7 boys may be drawn. To infer that 700 of the 1,000 pupils are boys is attended by some risk, although there may be no particular reason to suspect that the 10 names drawn do not constitute a representative sample of the entire file any more than to suspect that one pint of a liquid is not a good sample of the hogshead of it. We may draw a similar sample of 10 names and discover that but 4 of these pupils are boys. The discrepancy is material. We attribute it to chance.

Limited samples composed of individual cases or units not entirely homogeneous are always subject to chance errors of that sort. We may be satisfied beyond all reasonable doubt that a tossed coin should fall heads exactly one half of the time. Yet we hardly demand, if we toss it seven times, that it stand on edge once in order that the expected proportion of heads to tails may obtain. In fact, we will not guarantee that, if we pitch it an even number of times, a 50–50 performance will result—though we can be sure that as the number of tosses increases, the proportions will approach 50 per cent. heads and 50 per cent. tails.

Through the contributions of Gauss, Emcke, Quetelet, Galton, Pearson, Sheppard, Yule, Spearman, Filon, Kelley and others, statistical techniques are now available which enable us to estimate the probability that the mean, the standard deviation, the coefficient of correlation or any measure of a limited sample lies within any specified deviation from the corresponding measure for an unlimited number of cases. If one knows the mean and the standard deviation of a reasonably normal distribution of a known number of cases, one may accurately and quickly calculate the probable or standard error of the mean. By means of a table prepared by thoughtful and competent individuals, one may also estimate the probability, barring the operation of other than chance errors, that the mean of the cases actually studied lies within any given distance from the mean of the unlimited group, or that it lies beyond a certain distance from the "true" mean, and consequently the probability that the true mean is greater or less by a given amount than the obtained mean. For example, if the mean weight of a representative group of 170 ninth-grade boys with I.Q's of over 135 is 260 kilograms and the standard deviation is 26 kilograms, one may within a minute or two be reasonably sure that there is approximately one chance in a thousand that the mean weight of an unlimited group, of which the group studied is a random sample, is greater than 266 or less than 254 kilograms.

Practical problems of education in a large proportion of instances involve comparisons of two or more groups. Of great importance among these are the studies to determine which of two or more methods or of two or more units of materials of instruction will result in the greatest contributions to certain objectives of education. The use of the method of controlled experiment has been, in a number of other sciences, perhaps the most useful of all methods of research. The discovery of the causes of malaria, typhoid, cholera and other infectious diseases, and consequently our present degree of control of these plagues, has been effected by the method of controlled experiment—the method of the single variable. The concept of the spontaneous origin of life in the decay of organic matter was forever destroyed by the simple procedure of holding constant all variable save that of permitting insects to deposit their eggs in the decayed matter under observation. The greatest contributions of Pasteur to bacteriology were arrived at by this procedure. In his study which enabled him to conclude that bacteria, not dust or other causes, produced mold, he not only employed the method to satisfy himself, but when his critics claimed that the microorganisms left in the filter by liquids exposed to dust were the products of the filter which was itself an organic substance, he confounded them by the simple expedient of employing instead a filter of mineral asbestos.

We have been slow to turn to the controlled experiment in the study of problems of education. De Feltre in the fifteenth century and Ratke in the sixteenth attempted to test their theories of education by putting them into practice in the classroom. Basedow in the eighteenth century put certain phases of the theories of Comenius and Rousseau to actual test in his Philanthropinium at Dessau. Pestalozzi, a few decades later, put his educational theories into practice at schools at Stanz, Burgdorf and Yverdon. Herbart a half century later established a practice and experimental school in connection with his pedagogical seminary at Königsberg. In the latter half of the nineteenth century, the training school at the Oswego Normal School, the experimental school of Francis W. Parker at the Cook County Normal School at Chicago, and still more notably the laboratory school established by John Dewey at the University of Chicago in 1896 are examples of attempts to test educational theories. That the investigations conducted at these schools contributed little of permanent scientific value to education may be directly attributed to the lack of adequate means of measurement and the lack of statistical methods to refine and objectify the interpretation of results of their experiments.

Statistical method enables us not only to describe groups in exact numerical terms and to compare two or more groups in such terms but also guides us in determining what confidence we should place in the differences or similarities noted between groups. We may know the probability that, as far as chance errors are concerned, the differences obtained between limited groups deviate by given amounts from the true difference. By "true difference" I refer to the difference that exists between unlimited groups of which the limited groups are random samples. If, for example, we discover that 1,000 twelve-year-old girls weigh more than 1,000 twelve-year-old boys, and that the difference in their mean weight is 6.8 kilograms, we are not able to say that this is the exact difference between the mean weight of all boys and girls of whom our groups are true samples, but we may know what are the chances in one hundred or one thousand that the obtained difference lies within one, or four, or any given number of kilograms of the true difference. There are available similar formulae which assist us in arriving at some logical conclusion as to the confidence which we may attach to differences obtained in controlled experiments.

These formulae will not, however, as is sometimes supposed, enable us to make any allowance for a difference between the experimental situation and situations to which we may wish to apply the general principles arrived at from the experiment. With different subject-matter or even in schools in which conditions are different in matters associated with the experimental variables, the principles may apply only approximately and possibly not at all.

One of the great problems of the study of education is to ascertain what things occur concomitantly and the degree to which they do so. Such knowledge is prerequisite to prediction. We need to know what things to do with teaching success, not only that we may predict the success of individual teachers but that, as far as possible, we may prepare successful teachers. We desire to know what goes with success in learning in thousands of types of situations.

If we attempt to keep in mind the data needed in the study of such problems, we find we are not equal to the task. If, for a relatively large number of individual cases, we attempt to hold in mind the concomitant variation in two or more variables, let us say, Latin marks and intelligence quotient, we quickly become confused. When we arrive at conclusions, we have no exact means of expressing the degree of relationship. If several of us examine the records of a hundred or so high-school pupils in an effort to ascertain the degree of correlation between Latin marks and intelligence quotients, it is unlikely that we will agree as to the closeness of relation. Should we do so, we will still be unable to express our conclusion as to the degree of correlation in precise or objective terms except as we resort to some standard device.

In the linear equation, $y = ax + b$, the relationship between y and x is fixed. Any change in x produces a definite and known change in y. The correlation is 100 per cent. The concomitance of change is invariable. But it is apparent that the relationships we wish to study in education are not so simple. Success in teaching may tend to go with training, and school marks to go with intelligence scores, but not invariably and not in any fixed proportion in each case. Correlation is known to exist between many pairs of functions or events of practical interest in education but in few is the correlation perfect. We have need, therefore, of a measure to enable us to evaluate, to conceive of, and to express varying degrees of relationship far more precisely than one may do in non-quantitative terms and statistical method has served that need.

Pearson, Yule, Spearman, Thorndike, and others have made successive important contributions to the further development of the theory and techniques of correlation. Not only may we express degrees of "going together-ness" in exact and quantitative terms ranging from .00 to 1.00, that is, from no correlation to complete relationship as may be expressed in our algebraic equation, but we may now evaluate the significance of any given numerical statement of the degree of correlation for the purposes of estimating one variable from another. For example, we may estimate the usefulness of a correlation as great as that indicated by a coefficient of .50 for classifying pupils in homogeneous groups. By adoption of reasonable assumptions we may know what are the probabilities that each child is being placed in the proper group or that he is placed one group or two groups removed from that in which he belongs. By means of the correlation coefficient we may develop a "regression equation" which will enable us to estimate, let us say for example, college mark from high-school mark, or any variable from one or more others, if there is known to be close correlation between the two variables. If no errors other than chance errors of sampling and measurement have affected our calculations, we are able by means of simple formulae to know the probability that our estimates are within a given deviation from truly accurate estimates.

It is quite uniformly recognized that unless the means of measuring the variables involved in a correlation problem are quite reliable, the resulting coefficients are almost certain to be too small. It is easy to think of situations in which one is not so much interested in the correlation that exists between such things as scores, or marks, which are known to be of imperfect reliability, as in the correlation that would obtain, were the scores derived from completely reliable tests. We may, for example, wish to know to what extent the ability to read is conditioned by size of vocabulary. Unfortunately, one is not permitted to have absolutely reliable measures of ability to read or of size of vocabulary. We do have available, however, a method of correcting for lack of reliability a coefficient of correlation based upon such measures of these variables as we may have to work with, or as it is more frequently called "correcting for attenuation." The use of this device yields a valuable approximation of what the correlation between perfectly reliable scores would be.

In many instances the nature of the problem or of the available data precludes the legitimate use of the conventional product-moment formula for measuring correlation. In the case of the study of the relationship between salary and experience, one degree or type of correlation is usually found to exist through a limited range of experience and other degrees or types of relationship through other sections of the range. The dependence of salary upon experience may not be that represented by a straight line but by a broken line or a curve. Statistical method has developed a technique for that type of situation in the form of the correlation ratio and correlation "eta."

In many instances the available data in one variable may be expressed in but two categories though the variable may actually be one which if expressed in sufficiently fine categories would give evidence of being distributed after the fashion of the normal frequency. An example of this type of situation is the problem of calculating the degree of correlation between intelligence test scores and the occurrence or non-occurrence of graduation from high school. The latter variable which by nature may be expressed in a number of graduated categories such as having finished the 8th grade, or the 10th grade, or a year in college, in some situations may be found to be known as of only one or the other of two categories, namely, the failure to complete a given grade in school. Statistical method, through the technique of "bi-serial r," has enabled us to measure, describe, and express relationships from data in this form which would otherwise be quite difficult to interpret.

It often happens also that data with respect to both variables are expressed only in two categories, for example, having graduated from high school and having one or both parents who attended high school. Here, if both variables may be assumed to be in reality normal in distribution, but expressed only in two categories in the data available, we may utilize that means of measuring and expressing the correlation which has come to be called "tetrachoric r."

In some situations the two variables may not be expressed in quantitative terms. Such would be the case if our variables were the answer "yes" or "no" to two such questions as "male or female———" and "Do you belong to the National Education Association?" or if the variables were "having attended a normal school," and "both parents having been native born."

In other investigations though the body of data may be classified in any one of several categories it may not even be properly thought of at all as being of relative magnitude as in the case of the "occupation of father" and "vocational decision" of son. Researchers in the field of mathematics and statistical method have furnished relatively simple tools for measuring relationship in these types of situations, though I fear that not all research workers in education realize that these aids are available or appreciate their relative simplicity. The avenues of study opened by these instruments and aids to clear thinking are numerous.

Problems without number exist in education, in which it is desired to get at causal relations or to determine the influence of one variable upon another without the interference or cooperation of other variables. There seems to be positive correlation between economic or social status on the one hand and success and persistence in school on the other. Success or persistence in school may be thought of only with difficulty as wielding much influence on economic or social status. Economic status may reasonably be thought of as influencing success in school, perhaps indirectly, but nevertheless definitely.

It is, however, quite possible that both variables are influenced concomitantly by one or more variables other than the two under consideration, in this case by intelligence. The development of the techniques of partial correlations has enabled us to think much more clearly and to approach more closely reliable answers to such questions than we are able to do either by non-numerical reasoning or by the use of zero-order (simple two-variable) coefficients of correlation. Of course one must not place too much confidence in the fact alone that two things are correlated as a basis for concluding that one is the cause of the other. The fact that in certain states the percentage of illiteracy is unusually high and the percentage of students studying Latin is also large may hardly be assumed to constitute proof that either is the cause of the other.[1] The fact of correlation itself

[1] See Quintus H. Flaccus II, "Latin and the Statistical Method," SCHOOL AND SOCIETY, Vol. XXI, p. 51 (January 10, 1925), for a clever "reductio ad absurdum."

is ordinarily not enough to establish the nature of the causal relations. Supplementary facts or principles must be called in to assist in ascertaining what is the cause and what is the effect.

The improvement in clear thinking that may be effected by use of the technique of partial correlations is well illustrated in the study of the relation of certain variables to college marks made by Professor Mark May at Syracuse University. When Professor May calculated the coefficient of correlation between college marks and hours spent in study he was astonished to discover that it was but .32. However, when intelligence was held constant, the correlation between time spent in study and college marks was found to be .71! The explanation lay in the negative correlation between intelligence and hours spent in study. Bright students studied less and yet made higher marks. Less able students studied more and made lower marks.

The contribution of partial correlation to clear thinking may also be seen in a study which I completed recently. The coefficient of correlation between the amount of foreign language taken in high school and average college marks was found to be approximately .20. When intelligence was held constant, the resulting coefficient of partial correlation was only slightly greater than zero.

It is obvious that one should be able to predict more accurately from two or more correlated variables than from one alone. We should be able to improve the forecast of performance, let us say, of school marks, persistence in school, teaching success, or juvenile delinquency, by combining two or more variables in the optimum manner. We may predict school marks from intelligence test scores and from previous marks in school with greater accuracy than with either intelligence test scores or previous school marks alone. In a study of the relation of certain factors to academic success in college, to which I previously referred, I obtained a coefficient of correlation of .45 between the American Council of Education psychological test scores and the average mark in the first two years of college and a coefficient of .56 between average college mark. When high-school mark and psychological test score were combined with the optimum weighting, a coefficient of .63 between the two and average college mark was found.

We may know the proper weighting which should be attached to each of the prognostic variables, and our predictions will be made more accurately than if the various predictive variables are equally weighted. Multiple correlation techniques not only make it possible for us to know by what combination of variables we may predict most accurately and what the inclusion of each additional variable adds to reduce the error of forecast, but to know the probability of the accuracy of the predictions made, and furthermore to determine what weights should be attached to each variable if we are to make our estimates with least possible error.

I have time merely to mention certain other types of contributions which statistical method has made to education. The present stage of development of standard tests was made possible by the development of statistical method. Psychological tests remained on a relatively low level of usefulness for practical school purposes until statistical method developed and opened up possibilities previously undreamed of. The controlled experiment is basically a statistical problem.

All safe and effective programs of guidance have their very roots in statistical methods. Nothing could be further from the truth than the statement made occasionally by individuals, who little realize that such a statement marks its author as disgracefully innocent of any adequate understanding of what he is saying, that statistical method is serving to divert attention away from the individual and in the direction of numbers. As a matter of fact, it is only through the statistical study of groups that one is enabled to render effective service to the individual. Educational guidance, vocational guidance, homogeneous grouping, classification of pupils, carried on without a basis in sound premises built up from careful study involving sufficient cases to insure reliability and validity of the premises, is, in practical analysis, a pretense which borders upon quackery.

It seems to me that within the last quarter century we have been crossing the threshold in education which separates the domain of rough, crude, subjective methods from that of careful and reliable methods of educational research. We have been accumulating an assortment of valuable instruments for research in education which promise to do for education, at least in some degree, what the microscope did for natural science, the telescope for astronomy, and the development of the calculus and advanced mathematics did for physics and astronomy. Until these instruments were made available for natural science, the development of knowledge in this field was necessarily restricted and retarded. Adequate and precise observations could not be made. The area which could be charted on the basis of objective data was limited and the necessity of resorting to speculation was soon reached. Descriptions of the stars and other heavenly bodies were limited only by the fertility of imagination. Superstitions about the causes and means of prevention and cure of disease could not be separated from scientific facts. We had no way of knowing the facts. David Starr Jordan used to say that there never was a time when the people knew the answer to so many scientific questions as in the 13th century, but unfortunately, so few of them were correct.

I have no patience for those leaders in education who speak disparagingly of the usefulness of statistical methods either in research or in the practical field work in education. I can not understand their position nor fathom their motives. Perhaps I should go no further than to say that teachers, administrators, and other students of education should be very hesitant to commit themselves to a leadership which threatens to return the study of education to speculation and to prostitute educational practice to a succession of passing fads, the values of which have not been subjected to any objective investigation. At best I can bring myself to believe that these individuals are not careful to distinguish between the proportion of misapplications of and abuses of statistical methods which may be expected to be permanent and the proportion which may be regarded as merely a symptom of temporary professional indigestion in the pioneer years in which statistical methods are slowly becoming a part of professional equipment.

I have no fear that the use of statistical method will not continue to contribute to the development of a body of scientific facts, principles, and methods for education. I am afraid, however, that much harm will result from the misleading and inaccurate criticisms of statistical methods by those who are prone to rationalize, who love to comfort the unhappy, or who nourish a strong craving for being in the daily news. Too often, I fear, that most of those who read or hear these criticisms are not sufficiently well grounded in statistical methods to evaluate their merits and that they rely somewhat too heavily upon the competence and the disinterestedness of their informers.

Under any circumstances, statistical methods should not be thought of as being other than exact logic dealing with data which have been expressed in exact and precise terms and expressed for the sake of clarity by means of symbols. Statistical treatment of basic data can do but little to improve its validity, but careful statistical treatment will conserve what validity and reliability the data may possess. Any but careful statistical treatment will operate only further to multiply the sources and increase the magnitude of errors. Quantitative data unworthy of statistical treatment may not by any manner of logic be thought of as suitable for any sort of interpretation. Reasoning by statistical method is essentially subject only to those errors also characteristic of non-statistical thinking and is free from a host of possible errors which may result from the inability of the human mind to comprehend and keep constant during prolonged thinking, complex data and situations expressed in non-numerical and subjective terms.

EDUCATIONAL EVENTS

BROADCASTING ABROAD

A REPORT has been issued by the National Advisory Committee on Radio in Education entitled "Broadcasting Abroad" which gives information with respect to the average amount of time devoted to educational programs of fifteen European countries as follows:

Music and musical entertainments, 44.3 per cent.; literature, 5.4 per cent.; talks, 10.5 per cent.; criticism and news, 12.7 per cent.; religious transmissions, 3.65 per cent.; miscellaneous, 25.1 per cent.

The report states that in Europe, as elsewhere, the possibility of broadcasting as a medium of information for the listening masses was realized in the first days, and "talks" were given a place alongside musical transmissions. To-day however the courses of talks are arranged, not as a subsidiary activity of a program director, but by educational authorities or under the advice of a council of experts.

In an ever-growing group of countries educational broadcasting is being extended into the school hours of the afternoon, and the highest authorities in the land are talking to students on subjects intimately related to their school curriculum. This of course entails close collaboration with the educational authorities. In Great Britain this collaboration has been assured by the creation of consultative committees, consisting of representatives of all the interested departments of educational activity.

In the case of adult education emphasis is being laid upon the importance of giving the listener a more positive part than has been the case hitherto. The practice is growing of forming listening "groups" who meet in public libraries or educational institutes, and, under the direction of a trained leader, follow up the educational broadcasts with debates, etc. In other countries the listeners are encouraged to visit the museums, art galleries, etc., and examine personally the exhibits in the light of the information that has been broadcast.

INTERNATIONAL SUMMER SCHOOLS

ACCORDING to a correspondent of the London *Times,* it is hoped to put in force this summer an arrangement for effecting exchanges of students between England and Germany under competent guardianship and management.

It is proposed that young people of both sexes shall participate in the plan. They will, however, be separately grouped. The arrangements at present tentatively agreed with the German authorities are as follows: English students will spend two or four weeks during the period July 24 to August 20 in either a hostel in Berlin or with selected families in Hamburg. Each morning will be devoted to general study, music or physical education in the company of German students and under the supervision of expert German teachers. The afternoon will be left free for recreation, and the day will conclude with debates, dramatic performances, etc., always shared with the young German hosts. The total cost for a fortnight will be about £7 and for a month £12. The numbers of English students for whom arrangements can be made are: In Berlin, 20 boys and 20 girls; in Hamburg, 20 boys. With each party of 20 there will be two English masters or mistresses.

German students from Berlin and Hamburg will visit England during the same period that the English students are in Germany, English students being detailed to act as their hosts or companions. It is hoped that those English students who perform this service this year will be able to go to Germany next year, if the success of the scheme warrants its continuance. Similar educational and recreational arrangements will be made for the German students in England. Accommodation will be provided at Whitelands College, Putney, and at Ramhurst Manor, near Tonbridge. At Whitelands there will be 20 Berlin girls and 20 Hamburg girls with German and English mistresses and 40 English girls acting as hostesses. At Ramhurst Manor 20 German boys from Berlin will be accommodated with 20 English boys to act as their companions, the whole party being supervised by German and English masters. For English students who wish to act as companions to the German students in England the cost for the month is estimated at about £7.

DECLINE IN THE SALE OF TEXT-BOOKS

FACTS brought out in an interview of a representative of the *U. S. Daily* with Dr. William J. Cooper, U. S. Commissioner of Education, and Mr. E. M. Foster, chief of the Division of Statistics of the Office of Education, are reported as follows:

The net sales of text-books sold by 42 leading publishers dropped from $22,977,001 during the six months' period between July and December, 1930, to $19,487,457 for the corresponding period in 1931. If sales from January to July, 1932, which have not been tabulated, show the same drop, the total decrease for the year will probably amount to $7,000,000.

Dr. Cooper said that "school systems are storing up future trouble for themselves by refusing to replace dilapidated books when they should be replaced."

"At present," he continued, "text-books and similar supplies amount to but 3 per cent. of the average school budget. Administrators who think they can introduce a saving by not purchasing as needs arise, but instead try to get along with ragged, torn and sloppy books, will ultimately face a serious replacement bill involving very large expenditures."

In commenting on the significance of the decline in sales, Mr. Foster said:

"An adequate and up-to-date set of text-books should be a part of the equipment of every school, whether the books are owned by the school board or by the pupils. Books are part of the tools with which the students learn. To let this equipment depreciate either in quality, condition or amount is to postpone a cost to a future time which is justly chargeable to the current year. Every effort should be made," Mr. Foster added, "to maintain a high standard of text-book equipment."

The following additional information was supplied by Mr. Foster.

Every month between July and December showed a decline in text-book sales. There was a 12.8 per cent. drop in July, an 18.5 per cent. drop in August, and approximately a 10 per cent. drop in September. The decrease in October was 14 per cent., in November 25 per cent., and December approximately 22 per cent.

Sales in July declined from $3,415,784 in 1930 to $2,977,460 in 1931; in August from $6,195,131 to $5,046,360; in September from $6,920,877 to $6,230,138; in October from $3,345,053 to $2,871,608; in November from $1,736,907 to $1,297,720, and in December from $1,363,249 to $1,064,189.

College text-book sales remained practically what they were in 1930.

Twenty-four publishers reported both the number of books sold and the net value of the sales. The decrease for the six months in 1931 over the same period in 1930 was approximately 13 per cent. both for number of books and value for this group of companies.

These firms sold during the period in 1931 a total of 14,254,857 text-books compared with 16,455,498 in 1930. The value of net sales for these companies declined from $10,866,360 to $9,452,127 during the period.

THE MUSEUMS OF THE UNITED STATES

MUSEUMS, for years large city luxuries, are rapidly becoming the educational need of every community in the United States, according to Laurence V. Coleman, director of the American Association of Museums, reporting to the Office of Education for the Biennial Survey of Education in the United States.

There are now 1,400 museums in the United States, most of which are regarded as important and necessary sources of education. Every two weeks, during the period 1928 to 1930, on an average, a new museum was founded in the United States. Growing public interest in archeology and history, scientific progress and geographical discovery during the last several years has resulted in decided museum development.

The trend in modern times is distinctly away from museums embracing more than one field. There is much discussion of decentralization, and subjects are replacing objects as museum exhibits. Museums of to-day are not only found in houses or buildings, but also in trails through woods and fields, "paths of learning." Some city museums have been moved to search local parks for natural features that can be explained on the spot, and the same influence on history is evident in the new Colonial National Park Monument and the George Washington Birthplace National Monument.

Park historians are being employed to teach history education in a classroom built by nature. During the past decade 13 trail-side museums have been established, including the Wayside Museum at Coolidge, New Mexico, and those in the Glacier National Park and Yellowstone National Park systems.

America's museums range from merest beginnings in rooms to large establishments with buildings and extensive educational and technical activities. Some have exhibits and nothing more. Others are almost disembodied services using temporary displays. Historical houses, themselves exhibits, are the homes of many passive museums.

The majority of museums recently established are devoted to art, science and history. The study shows, however, that there has been a total neglect of art in state and national appropriations for recently established museums. State support is largely directed toward museums which deal with science, and national support is largely given to out-of-door museums. Small town museums favor history; large cities give art the first place. The total capital outlay for public museum buildings during the last ten years in the United States is estimated at $103,181,000.

Thousands of school classes now visit museums, and workable methods of meeting the needs of pupils are being developed. A revolution in museum practice is the exhibition of subjects rather than objects. In 1929 the new Buffalo Museum of Science opened with chapters of natural history, expounded in the following succession: Physics, astronomy, geology, biology, botany, invertebrate zoology, vertebrate zoology, evolution, heredity, geography and concepts of each science.

Another forward step of public interest was that of the Pennsylvania Museum of Art in deciding that art exhibits should be divided into two parts, one for the public with exhibits giving a survey of the arts, and the other for the student consisting of a systematic file of objects for reference.

Forty of fifty recently established museums have been in communities with fewer than 100,000 population. New small community museums have been established in Dearborn, Michigan, New London, Connecticut, Montgomery, Alabama, Phoenix, Arizona, Doylestown, Pennsylvania, Hagerstown, Maryland, Covington, Kentucky, White Plains, New York, Anniston, Alabama, Wheeling, West Virginia, and Dalton, Massachusetts. Most decided museum development in recent years has been in the states of Maine, New York, Pennsylvania, New Jersey, Ohio, Indiana, Illinois, Wisconsin, Michigan, and the Pacific Coast States.

COMPULSORY LEAVE OF ABSENCE FOR DISABLED TEACHERS

A BY-LAW amendment empowering the New York City Board of Superintendents to compel city teachers who become disabled to take leave of absence without pay for a year or less was adopted by the Board of Education at a recent meeting.

The reason for the new policy was explained in the following report to the school board:

> The additional form of leave of absence without application will provide for certain cases where a teacher is temporarily incapacitated to make application for leave or where teacher unreasonably delays making such application.
>
> This provision will, in certain cases, obviate the necessity of suspension and charges where it may seem reasonable to allow a teacher an extension of absence without pay to give opportunity to recover from a mental or physical condition. Since the teacher has the option of terminating the

leave upon resumption of service, this provision does not deprive the teacher of the right to render service.

The by-law, as amended, has been submitted to Assistant Corporation Counsel Mayer and has been approved by him.

Under the by-laws as they stood prior to the amendment, teachers had the right to apply for leave of absence without pay for study, restoration of health or other satisfactory reason, but the school heads had no authority to grant leave unless applied for.

The amendment retains a teacher's right to apply for leave. Following is the text of the new section:

> The Board of Superintendents may grant leaves of absence without pay and without application to members of the teaching and supervising staff whose absence may be necessitated by physical or mental disability, and such leaves shall be terminable at a definite date within one year or terminable at the option of the absentee at an earlier date upon resumption of service.

It was pointed out that disabled teachers who exercise their right to terminate a leave granted without their application will still be subject to suspension and charges if the school heads feel that they are not sufficiently well to continue in service.

INSTITUTE FOR ADVANCED LINGUISTS AT THE COLLEGE OF THE CITY OF NEW YORK

A LANGUAGE institute, at which both advanced students and beginners may study under distinguished scholars, is to be held at the College of the City of New York this summer.

The opening of the institute will mark the crystalization of aims which Dr. Frederick B. Robinson, president of the college, has entertained for many years—to make the College of the City of New York the center for language study in America.

"New York is a city best adapted for such studies," Dr. Robinson said in announcing the program of the institute. "Here we can most easily bring together in the summer the ablest American and European scholars. New York offers special attractions for advanced students and for high school and college teachers, since almost every living language and dialect can be studied here. Many have their newspapers or other periodicals published here, and one can follow the news of the day in Arabic or modern Greek.

"The college library is at the disposal of members of the institute and may be supplemented from other great libraries of the city; the faculty of the college will also be glad to cooperate with the institute."

The language institute will continue the work of the linguistic institute of the Linguistic Society of America. The latter was established in 1928, for the purpose of enabling distinguished scholars to lead a six weeks' conference to stimulate students to research and lay before them the latest discoveries in the field of language. It was held at Yale University for two summers and at the College of the City of New York during 1930 and 1931. When it became known that the society would not be able to continue the work this summer, Dr. Robinson decided to carry it on under the auspices of the college.

The institute will be in session from June 30 to August 11; classes will meet five days a week; two college credits will be given for the work.

Dr. Charles Upson Clark, director of the institute, was on the faculty of Yale University for fifteen years and then became director of the School of Classical Studies at the American Academy in Rome, where he served from 1916 to 1919.

RESIGNATION OF THE DEAN OF LONG ISLAND UNIVERSITY

DEAN GEORGE R. HARDIE, of Long Island University, tendered his resignation on June 11 to the Board of Trustees. They announced they had accepted it and had also granted his request for immediate leave of absence until his resignation became effective on August 31.

Tristram W. Metcalfe was appointed temporary head of the university. He also will serve as acting comptroller and assistant secretary of the board of trustees.

Mr. Metcalfe has been associated with the university for several years in the department of education. He formerly was a member of the Yonkers Board of Education and has edited educational columns in various newspapers for many years.

The resignation of Dean Hardie followed formal charges by members of the faculty sent to the Department of Education at Albany. The faculty members asked his removal on the ground that he had mismanaged the affairs of the institution. The student body supported the faculty.

Long Island University was founded five years ago, when Mr. Jonas, acting chairman of the board, contributed $500,000 as the initial endowment. Dean Hardie had been head of the institution since it was founded. Although some 1,400 students attended the university during the scholastic year which ended on June 13, of whom all except thirty are reported to have paid $300 tuition each, the faculty members have received no pay for two months. More than $50,000 is due them.

The professors and instructors expressed confidence that the financial difficulties would be adjusted under a competent administration. "We are confident that money matters and everything else will be cleared up to the satisfaction of all," said Professor Theodore W. Gibson, who occupies the chair of mathematics. It has been conceded, however, that it may take several years to balance the budget.

Dean Hardie's letter of resignation to Mr. Jonas read:

> Numerous difficulties confront the trustees of Long Island University in connection with various problems which require an immediate solution. I can not now, after five years of strenuous and diligent effort devoted to the furtherance of the interests of Long Island University, be unmindful of my obligations to its board of trustees.
>
> My conception of my duty to the university and to the trustees leads me to the conclusion that it is for the best interests of all for me to tender my resignation as dean of the College of Arts and Sciences at Long Island University, to be effective August 31, 1932, which is the end of the present fiscal year. I do so tender my resignation.
>
> In order to further relieve you and the trustees from any embarrassment in carrying out any plans that you may have for the future, I further request a leave of absence from now until August 31, to be effective immediately.

The statement also said the trustees had received every assurance from the faculty and from the students of their full cooperation in the development of the institution.

THE NATIONAL SURVEY OF SECONDARY EDUCATION

ONE hundred and fifty leaders in education attended a dinner given on June 9 at the Cosmos Club, Washington, D. C., by the National Education Association to mark the completion of the National Survey of Secondary Education directed during the last three years by the Federal Office of Education. Members of Congress, representatives of twenty or more educational institutions and organizations, staff members, officials, and friends of the Federal Office of Education and the National Education Association were in attendance at the dinner. Dr. J. B. Edmonson, of the University of Michigan, a member of the survey consultant committee, served as toastmaster.

Dr. Leonard V. Koos, of the University of Chicago, associate director in active charge of the nation-wide study of high-school problems and progress summarized high points of the survey "findings" based on returns from more than 200,000 inquiry forms answered by principals, teachers, pupils, parents and employers, and on visits by survey staff members to approximately 550 different high schools in practically every state.

Dr. Koos reported enrolment increases from 4 per cent. of high-school age boys and girls in 1890 to more than 50 per cent. to-day—a secondary school enrolment never before equalled in this or any other country. "Increasing proportions of children from what are termed the lower economic levels are being given opportunities of education at the secondary level."

Curriculum changes "have been away from foreign language and mathematics (college entrance subjects) and toward social subjects and physical education." "Non-academic subjects, including fine arts and practical arts have shown decided increase. In many schools non-academic subjects are now said to claim from a third to two fifths of all the pupil's time.

"Unit assignments are serviceable in providing for individual difference," said Dr. Koos, adding, however, that many practices in use under different classifications were found to deviate widely from their originally described characteristics and many were found to be essentially identical in practice.

Other findings of significance are: Increase in trade schools, fewer technical and commercial high schools, development of continuation, evening and summer schools; greater use of correspondence courses; greater flexibility in requirements for admission to college and universities, increasing opportunity for Negro secondary education in the Southern States.

"How essential it is for those responsible for the schools in one state to have made known to them the nature and direction of progress in the schools of other states," Dr. Koos said. "This is the service of the National Survey of Secondary Education. By examining its reports those at work in any community or state in schools at the secondary level will be able to note the progress and trends at that level in all states and sections and will in consequence be able to give more comprehensive and systematic consideration to the next steps to be taken in improving their own practices."

Other speakers were: U. S. Representative Burton L. French, of Idaho; Dr. William John Cooper, U. S. Commissioner of Education and director of the survey; Miss Florence M. Hale, president of the National Education Association, and J. W. Crabtree, secretary of the National Education Association. Guests from Congress, in addition to Representative Burton, were Mrs. Edith Nourse Rogers, representative of Massachusetts; Representative L. Russell Ellzey, of Mississippi; Representative Paul J. Kvale, of Minnesota, and Representative J. W. Summers, of Washington.

Dr. Koos announced that the various projects of the survey would be reported in 28 monographs which are now being prepared for the printer.

W. D. B.

EDUCATIONAL NOTES AND NEWS

DR. ELMER ELLSWORTH BROWN, chancellor of New York University, has notified the council of the university that he intends to resign as administrative head as soon as a successor shall be secured. His retirement closes twenty-one years of administration as the seventh chancellor of the university. Dr. Brown was United States Commissioner of Education from 1906 to 1911, and previously professor of education in the Universities of Michigan and California.

DR. PARKE R. KOLBE, president of the Polytechnic Institute of Brooklyn, has been elected president of Drexel Institute, Philadelphia, to succeed the late Dr. Kenneth G. Matheson. Before going to Brooklyn in 1925, Dr. Kolbe served twelve years as president of the University of Akron.

THE REVEREND A. H. POETKER, S.J., acting president of the University of Detroit since February, has been appointed president for a six-year term.

CHARLES H. WESLEY, professor of history at Howard University, Washington, D. C., has been elected president of Wilberforce University. He succeeds Gilbert H. Jones, who has been president for eight years.

DR. WILLIAM A. BOYLAN will be installed as the first president of Brooklyn College at the institution's first commencement on June 21. Though Dr. Boylan has acted as president of the college since May, 1930, the formal installation was postponed to coincide with the institution's first commencement, two years after the establishment by the board of higher education of Brooklyn College as the third independent center of public higher education in New York City. Dr. Boylan will be inducted by Dr. Arthur M. Howe, chairman of the administrative committee for Brooklyn College of the board of higher education. Mark Eisner, chairman of the board of higher education, will preside.

AMONG the degrees conferred by Boston University were the doctorate of laws on Dr. Lemuel H. Murlin, president of the university from 1911 to 1925, and the doctorate of science on Dr. Karl T. Compton, president of the Massachusetts Institute of Technology.

COLBY COLLEGE conferred at its graduating exercises the L.H.D. on Florence M. Hale, of Augusta, Maine, state agent of rural education and president of the National Education Association, and the doctorate of laws on Dr.

John H. Finley, of the editorial department of *The New York Times*.

DR. CLARENCE COOK LITTLE, formerly president of the University of Maine, received the honorary degree of doctor of literature from the university at the recent graduation exercises.

THE doctorate of laws was conferred at the sixty-ninth annual commencement of Bates College on Dr. John Hope, president of Atlanta University, and the degree of L.H.D. on Dr. Robert L. Kelly, executive secretary of the Council of Church Boards of Education and of the Association of American Colleges.

COLGATE UNIVERSITY conferred the degree of LL.D. on Stanley King, president-elect of Amherst College, at its annual commencement exercises on June 13. Dr. King delivered the commencement address.

THE University of Pittsburgh and Duquesne University, Pittsburgh, on the same day, June 8, conferred on Dr. James N. Rule, Pennsylvania state superintendent of public instruction, honorary degrees of doctor of laws.

AT the recent sixtieth annual alumni reunion of Lehigh University a testimonial dinner was tendered to Dr. Charles Russ Richards on the occasion of the completion of his tenth year as president of the university. Eugene G. Grace, president of the trustees, presided.

DR. CYRUS ADLER, president of the Jewish Theological Seminary of America, received a testimonial of appreciation for his thirty years of service to the seminary at the commencement exercises of the institution on June 5. He was presented with a bound volume containing a letter of greeting with more than five hundred signatures.

A PORTRAIT of Dr. Frank W. Taussig, Henry Lee professor of economics at Harvard University, painted by William James, has been presented to the university by Professor Taussig's friends.

PROFESSOR GEORGE MCLEAN HARPER, Woodrow Wilson professor of literature at Princeton University since the establishment of the chair by Mr. Edward W. Bok in 1926, will retire this month after forty-three years as a member of the faculty.

DR. EDWIN POST, oldest member of the DePauw University faculty in point of service, head of the department of Latin for fifty-three years, has tendered his resignation.

ULYSSES GRANT WHEELER, who is now seventy years old, has retired from the superintendency of the schools of Newton, Massachusetts.

DR. BENJAMIN P. THOMAS, of the Johns Hopkins University and for several years associate professor of history at Birmingham-Southern College, has resigned to become president of the Abraham Lincoln Foundation, Springfield, Illinois. His successor at the college is Professor Joseph T. Ecker, formerly assistant professor of history at the College of William and Mary.

DR. JOHN GRIER HIBBEN, retiring president of Princeton University, and Dr. Dean Lewis, surgeon-in-chief at the Johns Hopkins Hospital and president-elect of the American Medical Association, have been elected members of the board of regents of Mercersburg Academy, Pennsylvania.

SAMUEL INSULL has resigned as trustee of Northwestern University and Dr. Charles Mayo, of Rochester, Minnesota, has been elected in his place.

PROFESSOR RAYMOND D. HAVENS, professor of English at the Johns Hopkins University, has been appointed chairman of the committee of the American Association of University Professors to investigate the removal of Dr. Orlie M. Clem, professor of secondary education at Teachers College, Syracuse University.

AN Associated Press dispatch reports that G. Fred Pearson, chairman of the Dalhousie University board of governors for five years, recently tendered his resignation because the board refused to act on his recommendation for an investigation of the administration of President Carleton W. Stanley. President Stanley went to Halifax from McGill University, where he had been assistant to the principal. He was installed as president of Dalhousie, October 9, 1931, succeeding Dr. A. Stanley Mackenzie.

DR. THOMAS WALLING, director of education at Newcastle, England, has been appointed director of education at Sheffield, subject to the approval of the city council.

DR. CLARENCE A. BARBOUR, president of Brown University, arrived in San Francisco on June 8 from the Far East. He has been engaged in making a survey for the Laymen's Foreign Mission Enquiry and the Institute of Social and Religious Research in New York.

THE commencement address at Pennsylvania State College on June 6 was delivered by Dr. John H. MacCracken, associate director of the American Council on Education, Washington, D. C., on "Purpose and Plan."

DR. WILLIAM ALLAN NEILSON, president of Smith College, was the speaker at the commencement exercises of Springfield College, formerly the International Young Men's Christian Association College of Trinity Methodist Episcopal Church.

DR. FREDERICK B. ROBINSON, president of the College of the City of New York, delivered the address to the graduates of the Newark College of Engineering on June 10.

DR. JAMES L. MCCONAUGHY, president of Wesleyan University, gave the commencement address at Upsala College, East Orange, New Jersey, and at the Horace Mann School for Boys of Teachers College, Columbia University.

PROFESSOR FRANK VOGEL, professor emeritus of modern languages at the Massachusetts Institute of Technology, died on June 9. He was sixty-nine years old. Dr. Vogel had served on the faculty for forty-four years.

THE death is announced of Miss Lucy Hale Tapley, president emeritus of Spelman College, Atlanta, Georgia, a member of the faculty for thirty-seven years.

DR. WILLIAM JOHN COOPER, U. S. Commissioner of Education, has been appointed by the State Department to represent the United States at the Fourteenth International Congress of Secondary Education which will be held in London from July 18 to 23. The agenda for the congress includes the following subjects: (1) Out-of-school activities and their place in secondary school organization. (2) The professional training of the secondary teacher. (Preliminary discussion preparatory to the 1933 Congress.) (3) Report on improvements which have taken place during the school year 1931–32 in secondary-school buildings and equipment from the points of view of teaching, esthetics and hygiene. (4) The relations between the International Federation of Associations of Secondary Teachers and other international associations. Commissioner Cooper will also attend the Sixth World's Conference of the New Education Fellowship at Nice, France, from July 29 to August 12. W. W. Vaughn, president of the organizing committee of the congress, extends through Commissioner Cooper an invitation to teachers of secondary schools in the United States to participate in the sessions.

THE First International Congress on the Teaching of History will take place under the presidency of Professor Altamira, of the University of Madrid, who is one of the judges at the International Court of Justice at The Hague, from June 30 to July 2, at The Hague. The main topics for discussion will be: (1) the history of civilization adapted to primary and secondary schools; (2) national history and universal history, and the relation of history to geography; (3) school manuals primary and secondary; (4) removals from manuals of sentiments and expressions that imply international prejudice and misunderstanding; (5) artistic, literary and school-journey aids in the instruction of juniors. This conference is the outcome of a special study of history teaching for world unity initiated by the International Congress of Moral Education at its meeting in Geneva in 1922. At this meeting Professor Francesco Orestano, of Rome, proposed that the best historical authorities should be invited to pursue this enterprise collectively, and in 1930, at the fifth international congress at the Sorbonne, Paris, the plan was put forward of a conference entirely devoted to this theme.

THE sixteenth session of the International Labor Conference has adopted a new draft convention on the protection of children which, in conjunction with the conventions of 1919, 1920 and 1921, will prohibit the employment of children under fourteen years of age in any undertaking whatever.

A SPECIAL citizens' committee of fifty-three members has been appointed at Baltimore to welcome delegates to the tenth annual convention of the American Hellenic Educational Progressive Association, which meets from August 28 to September 4. Governor Ritchie and Mayor Jackson will be honorary chairmen, and Friend L. Wells has been designated as chairman. More than 5,000 visitors are expected to attend the convention.

EDUCATIONAL officials of institutions of learning throughout the nation are invited to gather at the University of Wisconsin for five days this summer to tackle problems of school administration and teaching. The university will be host to the officials at the first Institute for Superintendents and Principals to be held from July 18 to 22, inclusive. Sponsored by the School of Education, the institute is planned for city and county superintendents, supervising principals, elementary and secondary school principals, supervisors, directors of research, directors of guidance, and all others interested in administering public schools. The programs will consist of a series of round-table discussions, led by nearly 20 educational authorities. Among those from the university who will lead in the discussions are Professors J. G. Fowlkes, T. L. Torgerson, A. S. Barr, M. H. Willing, Max C. Otto, C. J. Anderson, H. H. Ryan, Calla A. Guyles, Curtis Merriman and C. E. Young, Frank O. Holt, director of the bureau of guidance, Professor A. H. Edgerton, Dean Harry Glicksman and John L. Bergstresser, assistant director of the bureau of guidance and records, are also on the program. Professors A. S. Barr, F. L. Clapp and J. G. Fowlkes, chairman of the institute committee, are in charge of the arrangements.

TEACHERS are invited to inquire concerning the Commonwealth College Summer Session and Camp to be held on the school site in the Ozark woods at Mena, Arkansas. Commonwealth College is a school training young people interested in the labor movement, but in the summer welcomes workers, students and professional people as visitors. Most visitors follow the college tradition and work cooperatively 15 hours a week at community tasks on the 320-acre "farm-campus." Such working guests pay $25 a month for room, board, laundry service and educational features. Others pay $50. Discussion circles will be held on the labor movement, world news and present-day problems. There will be swimming, hiking, dancing, tennis and a labor theater. Length of stay is optional. The director is Lucien Koch, formerly instructor at the Experimental College of the University of Wisconsin.

JULIAN MITCHELL announced on June 8 that a loan of $3,400,000 has been obtained from the Reconstruction Corporation through the South Carolina State Bank, of which he is president, to enable the State of South Carolina to pay its school teachers.

WASHINGTON COLLEGE, Chestertown, Maryland, celebrated the one hundred and fiftieth anniversary of its founding as well as the two hundredth anniversary of George Washington's birth on June 4. An elaborate pageant commemorated the connection of the first President with what is said to be the eleventh oldest institution of higher learning in the United States.

THE Lewis Memorial Liberal Arts Hall, Rosary College, River Forest, Illinois, was formally dedicated on Wednesday, June 1, by Chancellor George Cardinal Mundelein. The hall has been erected at a cost of four hundred fifty thousand dollars, of which one hundred fifty thousand dollars was given by Mr. and Mrs. William Harold Lewis, Chicago, in memory of their mothers.

THE newest unit in the Muskegon public schools system, the Angell Elementary School, was formally dedicated on April 6. The new building is named in honor of Dr. James B. Angell, president of the University of Michigan from 1871 to 1909. Webster H. Pearce, state superintendent of public instruction, was the principal speaker on the program. Dr. John VanderLaan officially presented the building as president of the Muskegon Board of Education.

FRANK A. VANDERLIP, former president of the National City Bank, New York, on June 7 presented the Scarborough School with a deed to the school building and property. The gift was announced at the commencement exercises, when diplomas were awarded to twenty-five students. In his address Mr. Vanderlip said: "This gift is in recognition of the untiring efforts of Dr. F. Dean McClusky and his staff and in appreciation of their success in building the school so that not only is it self-sustaining, not only in this year of depression has it had its most successful year, but the school and its graduates have established a reputation for scholarship and scholastic achievement of the highest order."

A MODERN school in actual operation, attended by 550 school children, will be one of the exhibits at the World's Fair in Chicago next year. The six-grade elementary school will overlook Lake Michigan and will contain every modern type of equipment. It is being constructed by the Chicago Board of Education. The building will be of two stories without basement, and of steel and masonry construction. It will include modern facilities, such as library, handicraft room, auditorium, gymnasium, kindergarten play room, kindergarten project room, bathroom, lunch room, administration suite for principal and clerk and equipment for doctor, dentist, visiting teacher and psychologist. The classrooms will be, to some extent, flexible in size, based on teaching situations; large rooms, 62 feet by 22 feet for audience lessons; regular classrooms, 32 feet by 22 feet, for recitations; pupil work rooms, 22 feet by 11 feet, for small groups, and pupil work rooms, 16 feet by 11 feet, for individual study. This layout has been built around a definite plan of instruction which is in operation experimentally in Chicago.

A GROUP of students said to be Communists seized the National University, Santiago, Chile, on June 10 and printed on the university printing press manifestos demanding the right to participate in Chile's new Socialist government. It is stated that the students were headed by Elias Lafferte, president of the Chilean branch of the Moscow Communist party. They demanded the government furnish them with suitable headquarters, suggesting either the Municipal Theater or the aristocratic club De la Union. The revolutionary junta ignored these demands and generally treated the students with amused toleration, but there were indications that stern measures would follow unless they got out of the university.

A WIRELESS message to *The New York Times*, dated from Havana, reports that the University of Havana, which was closed by a Presidential decree on July 1, 1931, because of anti-administration activities of the students, was restored to the normal status on June 10 by another decree of President Machado which puts all professors in a position to claim back salaries. The decree follows a Supreme Court decision of April 26 declaring the closing of the university to have been unconstitutional. Plans are being made, it was reported, to open the university in September, but some doubt is expressed as to the attitude that may be assumed by the students, who are among President Machado's bitterest enemies. It is estimated that some 150 students are prisoners at the Isle of Pines Penitentiary on charges of terroristic and anti-administration activities. So far only six or eight have been brought to trial.

DISCUSSION

THE OLDEST EXTANT MATHEMATICS

PROFESSOR O. NEUGEBAUER, Göttingen, Germany, recently published an article describing parts of an ancient Babylonian text in which quadratic equations are solved by a method exhibiting a knowledge of a modern formula for the solution of such equations.[1] It is especially interesting to note that the two possible roots seem to have been considered when both of them are positive, while in all the extant partial solutions by the ancient Greeks only one such root is noted, although some mathematical historians believe that the Greek mathematicians knew that certain quadratic equations actually have two distinct positive roots. Professor O. Neugebauer regards this text as the oldest of the known mathematical texts, with the exception of such as are very fragmentary or relate only to tables.

He directs attention to the fact that contrary to the commonly accepted view this mathematics of the ancient Babylonians does not exhibit any dependence on astronomical or commercial questions but is pure mathematics in the modern sense of this term and seems to have been culti-

[1] Quellen und Studien zur Geschichte der Mathematik, Astronomy und Physik, Studien, vol. 2 (1932), p. 15.

vated for its own sake. He admits, however, that it is still an unsettled question whether the greater part of the ancient Babylonian mathematics is of this type and that new excavations may at any time throw additional light on this question. He is convinced that the ancient Babylonian mathematics is on a much higher level than that of the ancient Egyptians, which is also contrary to the view expressed by various other writers, including Professor W. W. Struve, who recently translated the Moscow Mathematical Papyrus. In both cases an active early period seems to have been followed by a period of decadence extending through more than a thousand years.

What is perhaps of greatest interest in connection with the article under consideration is the announcement of a plan to publish a considerable amount of additional material relating to ancient algebra. It is well known that the ancient Greeks emphasized geometric methods and that Euclid's Elements begin with geometry. On the contrary, the ancient Babylonian mathematical literature seems to be especially rich along algebraic lines and the history of algebra has already been profoundly affected by translations of ancient Babylonian texts published during the last four or five years. It is important to note that the oldest extant mathematical text under consideration is at least on as high a level as any of the later ones which have become known and hence it is questionable whether the period of greatest Babylonian mathematical activity has yet been reached.

This Babylonian mathematical text, as well as the others which are known, is not dated, but its language seems to imply that it was written during the first Babylonian dynasty and to be from one to two hundred years older than any of these others. In the golden period of Greek mathematics such a period of time is important because it exhibits decided advances, but on account of the stationary character of the ancient Babylonian mathematics the exact dates of the various texts are less important. The greatest weakness of this mathematics from the modern point of view is the lack of proofs and explicit postulates. The existence of general methods has to be inferred from the solution of special problems. Whether these methods were actually understood by them in the modern sense of this term is still doubtful, but the facts that they used such methods and seem to have been interested in pure mathematics are important not only for the student of the history of mathematics but also for students of ancient civilizations.

G. A. MILLER

"SNAP" COURSES IN EDUCATION

THERE has been considerable argument in teacher-training institutions over the relative difficulty or easiness of courses taken in the different departments. Faculty members in the old established divisions like mathematics, science, history and language very frequently express themselves as feeling that students do not find the work at all hard in fields outside the academic departments, and that in the education subjects, especially, any one can "get by" with superior grades.

The departments of education in colleges where teachers are being trained have come up for special criticism from other departments, most probably because the education fields are rather new in origin, and like most new things they have been subject to much suspicion. Eventually they will be taken into the fold and given their proper position among the cluster of college offerings.

In an attempt to discover what divisions really seemed to offer the student the most scholastic difficulty, the authors of this paper make a brief study based upon the grades issued to 100 students selected at random from the registrar's books. Of these 100 students, 50 of them had taken what was called a one-year course and the other 50 had taken the two-year course.

A uniform procedure was followed in every case and the grades issued were translated into honor points, using the following equivalents: A equals 3 honor points per credit hour; B equals 2 honor points; C gives 1 honor point; and D gives one half.

It was decided to study the grades issued in three divisions: (1) Education, including the methods, introductory courses, psychology, observation, etc.; (2) academic, including mathematics, history, sociology, economics, languages, sciences, etc.; and (3) special subjects, including music, art, manual training, physical education, etc.

Every case was studied straight through, that is, the number of honor points earned in education, in academic and in special subjects was counted out carefully for each of the 100 persons, so that in the end the comparison would be made between the grades issued in the three divisions on the same student, and one would not be comparing marks issued in education to one student with marks given in academic subjects to some other student.

Table I gives the summary of the tabulations made in terms of average honor points:

TABLE I

AVERAGE HONOR POINTS

Division	Av. H.P. per credit hour 1 yr. cases	Av. H.P. per credit hour 2 yr. cases	Av. H.P. per credit hour combined cases
Education ...	1.61	1.74	1.67
Academic ...	1.68	1.76	1.72
Special	1.72	2.02	1.88

A study of the above table indicates at a glance that students were able to earn the highest grades in the special subjects, next highest in the academic and lowest grades in education. Although the difference is not great between education and the academic fields, nevertheless, it would seem to indicate that the same students who were able to average a B—in science, history, mathematics, etc.—earned slightly less than that in their education courses.

It would seem that statistics such as these would tend to cause instructors in the respective fields to hold other departments in much higher esteem than might have been the case in several instances.

The table indicates also that students taking the two-year course profited by their second year of training and experience and earned substantially higher marks on the average. Many factors might account for this increased average on the part of two-year students, such as a better knowledge of how to study and make use of time, a better understanding of what various instructors require, further experience and equipment as a background, etc. However, in the case of education *versus* the other divisions again, it indicates that professors of the professional subjects continue to grade lower than the other departments.

The results of a study of this kind might not be altogether reliable because one can not take into account the elements of interest and native ability on the part of the student. Also the education subjects are almost always required, whereas the student elects his academic subjects for the most part. That condition might have a tendency to cause the student to have a better attitude toward his academic work than toward the professional. Yet in a teacher-training institution by his very presence the student has chosen teaching as a career and he should welcome any training in education that prepares him for his chosen task. Attitudes probably do not enter in to predetermine scholastic progress so much as one might think.

SOME CONCLUSIONS

(1) Education courses are not "snap" courses.

(2) In a study of 100 students they earned highest marks in special subjects, next highest in academic subjects and lowest in education.

(3) Students earned higher averages in all three divisions by taking the second year of work.

(4) The results of the study should cause faculty members to have more mutual respect for various departments.

W. W. LUDEMAN
J. R. MCANELLY
SOUTHERN STATE NORMAL SCHOOL,
SPRINGFIELD, S. D.

THE PUPIL LOOKS AT THE TEACHER

IN this age of educational evolution many articles are written setting forth the innumerable deficiencies of our pupils, but seldom does one appear suggesting that something might be wrong with the teacher. It is the purpose of this article to give the pupils a chance to answer some of the charges placed against them.

Many pupils claim the teachers do not make the lessons interesting enough to appeal to them, and they naturally do not try very hard. Following are quotations of pupil comments:

Biology is one of the deadest subjects that ever was originated.

I don't like to pick up the insides of insects and carve my initials on worms.

It's too complicated and has too many hard names.

I don't like the study of animals.

The words are too big and not definite enough.

The teacher does not explain fully the things she tells us.

Chemistry is hard.

Chemistry is a dry subject.

French doesn't agree with me. I think I was passed on my effort.

The teacher makes the subject too hard.

The problems are not understood by the class.

The teacher created no interest in the work, whatever.

I didn't pay any attention.

A few pupils accused teachers of wasting time, as follows:

The teacher was away from the class most of the time.

My teacher talks too much.

So much class time is taken up in marking graphs.

The teacher spent too much time with the other class.

The teacher was out of the room most of the time.

Many pupils charged teachers with unfairness, as is shown by the following:

Tests were based on library work and I can't go to the library.

The teacher based her tests on her lectures and not on the book.

Tests were given without notice.

The teacher played favorites.

The teacher allowed copying.

I was marked down for helping the boy next to me.

The teacher doesn't call on the poorer students enough.

Teacher marks unfairly, especially the girls.

My teacher is too one-sided.

I failed because I forgot to bring a note for being absent one day.

I raised my hand, but she wouldn't call on me.

The teacher changes her mind too much.

The teacher didn't give enough work to judge the marks by.

Our teacher requires us to remember too many details.

Teacher showed partiality.

The teacher marked unfairly.

Teacher depends too much on homework; class period is useless if homework is not done.

I missed some of the teacher's dictation.

I couldn't read the teacher's figures on the blackboard.

I received the same average as another pupil, who received a higher mark.

I erased once.

I couldn't stay after school and type.

Teacher gave us too much library work to do in the required time.

I went after school to make up my work, because she said she would only stay half an hour, but she kept me two hours and a half, so I decided not to make it up.

I failed on only one test and the teacher wouldn't let me make it up.

The teacher didn't give enough tests or oral work to grade us high.

Teacher is very unfair. I am not called on when my hand is raised, but am called on when I am not prepared.

The teacher marks so hard, but I love English in spite of her.

The teacher forces us to remember trivial details, causing us to forget the most important things in the lesson.

I had to slight home study for recitation in order to get all the outside reading done at the library.

I do not know how to study a language; have not the hook of it.

Several pupils accused the teachers of disliking them, some giving no reasons, and others the following:

I made the teacher mad, and she flunked me.

My teacher does not like sororities.

My teacher doesn't like the way I act.

The teacher likes pets, and I don't like to be a teacher's pet, as it is very unfair to other pupils.

Teacher doesn't like the way I play ball.

The teacher doesn't like me; she is influenced by her prejudices.

My teacher doesn't like me or anyone sitting around me, and does all he can to be hateful to us.

A few pupils accused teachers of being too strict, as follows:

Every time we move the teacher takes down our names.

Because there was not perfect quietness in the room we were marked down.

The teacher criticizes too much.

Teacher marks too hard.

You get marked down for the least little thing you do.

The teacher is too hard on pupils just beginning.

My accuracy was one point too low.

Teacher is the worst I ever came across, when she couldn't have me suspended, she had the truant officer sent to my house.

Sarcasm on the part of the teacher was charged in the following quotations:

The teacher is so sarcastic, I am fraid to say anything. She can make you feel like two cents with one word and one cent with two.

I had the worst teacher I ever had, always making sarcastic remarks, and always trying to put the blame on me for something I did not do.

The teacher makes a perfect fool of other pupils causing me to dislike her. You can't work well under a teacher you don't like.

The standards of some teachers were thought too high, according to the following quotations:

My teacher expects too much of me.

Our teacher doesn't give any excellent marks.

The tests were too hard.

Too much outside reading was required.

A few teachers lacked sympathy, according to the following quotations:

The teacher didn't understand me.

Some of my compositions were too funny for the teacher's sense of humor.

I'm too curious and can't help asking the girls around me about their dates and such.

The teacher said my girl friend sat too close to me.

Some teachers are so inconsiderate and aggravating, they just get your goat; no wonder children hate school.

Our teacher is new to the game and treats us like babies. She just tries to show off her authority.

It seems that the teacher did not understand me. She thought I was crazy and perhaps she was right.

I am too thrilled by who sits beside me and I get all flustrated.

Administrative weaknesses are blamed for some poor work of pupils in the following quotations:

I have had five different Math teachers in six semesters, and this time I failed.

I did not have enough algebra before I took this up.

The room was too hot.

I am in a class that is always noisy and I can't think very well.

I failed in Physics because I have had no Math.

The teacher uses scientific methods of medians and there are pupils in the class better than I am, so my mark is always low.

I have taken this same History three times, and am tired of studying the same thing over.

Did not have a text-book from which to study.

The clerk in charge of the Book Room didn't like my doing home work in Office Training period.

I am class secretary. I can't fix the roll and take part in the class.

I fooled around, but almost got an A.

I didn't work.

I loafed around too much.

My first teacher didn't know anything about typing or how to teach it.

My first teacher required accuracy but not speed, my second teacher required speed but not accuracy, and now I have my first teacher again.

I am in Z group and have no inspiration to study.

I always save my Spanish for the last thing every night, and by that time I am too sleepy to study it very much.

A few pupils blamed their poor work on teachers' peculiarities or distractions, which kept them from giving more attention to their studies. Following are the charges:

The teacher gave me such a pain with the way he talked.

The teacher makes so many funny faces when she talks, I forget all about shorthand and watch her face.

My teacher is so good looking I can't keep my eyes off him.

My teacher's actions distract my attention.

I had a fossil of a teacher, who had funny ways.

That beautiful face, I can always see it in my dreams spitting off French.

The teacher didn't know we were looking in our books on tests in the grammar books, so we didn't have to study; and in the reading books I didn't know the words and phrases.

I didn't get along with the teacher.

The teacher kept interrupting us in typing.

My teacher is so cute I can't concentrate on my work.

The teacher does not like me, largely I talk and laugh at something funny, and she does not see the joke.

This is a new teacher and her first class. She marks hard and everything must be done exactly her way.

Besides a few pupils who thought they had been treated fairly, the following are the only complimentary remarks found among over six hundred responses:

I have a very interesting teacher.

My teacher is one of the most interesting ones in school and really makes you like History.

For the first time in my life I really like History, though I hate to admit it.

C. C. Guilford

Eastern High School,
Washington, D. C.

SPECIAL CORRESPONDENCE

AN APPLICATION OF THE PROJECT PROCEDURE TO SWIMMING

If the project procedure is defined as an educational experience in problem solving, initiated by the student and carried out to the point of acceptable skill in its most natural setting, then swimming may be considered as an activity which may become an ideal project.

It is the purpose of this paper to show that swimming may be conceived and learned according to project principles involving the fundamental essentials of self-activity, reflective thinking, concrete achievement and favorable emotional set. The illustrations of an experiment in teaching swimming as a project are taken from actual practice in the swimming classes of the Women's Physical Education Department at the University of Washington.

Learning to swim is a skill in which people engage from the age of three to sixty-five or older, so it is not an elementary nor secondary school nor college subject. Because it is a natural and popular activity, a skill that all may learn and most people are anxious to learn because of the fun, the exercise, and the element of life preservation it has, it would seem to be more of a project type of subject than many others. Swimming is an activity that students at the University of Washington may elect, so that classes are composed of those who have elected to learn swimming, either for the first time or to improve the ability they have. So there is almost no question of arousing interest. The interest is there, particularly if the class is an elementary swimming class. Another element making swimming classes more or less ideal for project method is the size. They are small enough for the instructor to know each student rather quickly, which means knowing the starting ability, the fears and the ambitions of each. Each group is classified as to ability, so the students are working with individuals approximately in the same state of learning as they are. So the project method does perhaps more or less ideally fit this situation, and because of the necessity for thinking, planning and problem solving, it is perhaps, when possible, one of the best methods to be used in physical education. All too frequently, we are criticized for working with our feet more than our head in this field. That criticism used to be more justifiable than now. In the days of drill and passive exercise, of mere movement without thought, there was more muscle work than brain work. Now, when physical activity means a thinking activity, a combination of mental and physical work, the criticism is not warranted.

The part the instructor plays is always important in any teaching situation if marginal responses and concomitant learnings are going to be what we want them to be. The sooner student instructors learn that there is more to teaching than knowing the subject and giving it to the student, the better her chances are for becoming a real instructor. Students can not be treated as machines ready to be filled with oil so they will run. They are people looking for attitudes and opinions and principles and ideals to live by—and they must have opportuinties for expressing themselves. Self-expression possibly is one of the greatest self-developers making for growth in the individual. Expressing oneself, if the environment is desirable, means a shaping and hardening and rounding of the individual that in the end will help toward the best character development. Also then, because the project method of instruction means a purposing, a carrying out of an inner urge, a self-expressive act, it is valuable in swimming as in many other learning situations.

The instructor's part in teaching swimming by the project method is important. Her part is more the assisting, guiding and advising type of leadership. At first there will need to be some instruction, but not a great deal. In swimming, as in many other things, the technique the student learns by progressive self-experimentation is the technique that may prove most useful. Not that all learning should be trial and error. A minimum amount of that is desirable, but this amount is needed in order to make thinking more reflective and more worth while in other more complex techniques. Learning that raising the head or raising the arms out of water in a certain way while floating on the back will make one sink under water may be unpleasant when first tried in shallow water, but that knowledge will be of infinite help when swimming and floating in deep water. Students must know at all times what their own ability is in order that growth may take place as quickly as possible. It is most important, if learning is to be thorough, for students to be able to analyze their own skills. If in swimming the width of the pool on the side the head goes under water every other stroke, a problem arises. Why does it happen? Here is the opportunity for reflective thinking—for real thinking—recognizing a problem, defining it, searching for solution, trying a solution, noting the results. Working out the problem in this way, the student is engaged in thoughtful self-activity. Her foundation in the subject is more substantial. She will profit from the experience many times over.

All is not smooth sailing in this learning process—even if it is a hearty, purposeful act, and there are many sources from which to obtain the information desired. Often with students learning to swim for the first time there is a conflict. No matter what method is used this will always be a problem for the instructor to deal with. Many students are afraid of the water because they have been conditioned by fearing parents or recently have had unhappy experiences. So many times they are anxious to know how to handle themselves in deep water, but this urge is thwarted by their fear of what might happen. Students often forget their fears in their joy in finding that it is possible and even easy to acquire ability in swimming. However, they will many times work successfully and satisfyingly until a situation arises in which their fear blocks the way. A girl may know two strokes and be able to tread water—knowledge sufficient to enable her to handle herself well in deep water—and yet she is afraid to venture forth even though she has acquired her ability through whole-hearted, purposeful, thoughtful self-activity. The instructor then must guide and assist and encourage and understand, in order for the student to continue her purposeful activity.

After the first few meetings of the class, students begin to show individual differences, and from then on taking care of the class is practically a problem of guiding only. Step by step each student is working toward greater ability, working out her own problem with suggestions from the instructor and help and criticism and approval and disapproval at the right times. When students are purposing this way, following a strong inner urge, teaching is most interesting. Each student develops her ability as she wishes to with a few goals in the distance. There is voluntary extra work before class, after class, and days when the class doesn't meet. There is much observation of other swimmers better or worse than themselves. There is much fun and play and many friendly competitions. Sometimes the purpose is less strong, often because of discouragement—the particular technique is too difficult. Some practice with the instructor suggesting or with a student suggesting remedies the situation. Along with learning particular skills comes a need for acquiring certain attitudes about swimming when fatigued, about the effect of exercise, about assisting fatigued swimmers and about helping each other.

Some instructors may feel it is difficult to follow a course of study for swimming if the project principle is followed. It is never possible to allow students to follow their urges utterly, wherever they go. They do not know where they are going themselves, so that one or two goals set up as an end for twelve weeks of work are a help to them as well as the instructor, merely showing which path to follow, which purposes to follow. In learning to swim the goal is almost evident without being named—ability to handle oneself in deep water. In intermediate swimming one or two objectives enable the student to know just where to direct her activity. If the class is too varied in ability for one goal to be set, grading on improvement in ability will be just as satisfactory and many times fairer in the end to the student.

Certain questions might be used to test the results of this method of teaching. For instance: Have the students learned to handle themselves better in the water? Have they passed well the few basic tests set up as goals for other classes of like ability? Have they acquired attitudes that may transfer in part to other situations in life? Has the activity produced a concrete, satisfying result? Will this new activity lead on to bigger activities? Have the right habits of thinking been developed? Do the students have the habit of reflective thinking when practicing swimming? Has there been a close alliance between the subject and the real interests and needs of the individual at all times? In other words, has the project method of teaching carried out the aims and objectives of a swimming course?

In this instance the method proved very satisfactory, and better results were achieved than in some of the more formally taught classes. As to ability achievement, for example, the students passed more difficult tests and learned a greater variety of skills than the students of other classes of the same starting ability.

It would seem, then, that the project method may have a definite place in the field of swimming instruction—it is a valuable, educative process encouraging mental as well as physical activity and resulting in increased growth and development.

HARRIET F. GLOVER
DEPARTMENT OF PHYSICAL EDUCATION,
UNIVERSITY OF WASHINGTON

QUOTATIONS

FRONTING THE BOSPORUS

APPOINTMENT of Dr. Paul Monroe as president of the two American colleges—Robert College and the Constantinople Woman's College—at Istanbul marks the beginning of a new chapter in the life of those two institutions. They stand but a little way apart looking across the Bosporus from Europe into Asia. The heroic labors of their pioneers, Cyrus Hamlin, George Washburn, Caleb Gates and Miss Mary Mills Patrick, established them where the old Greek trading post of Byzantium "reared its head" above all the cities of the East under the name of Constantinople. The old Roman road along which one has pictured the primitive shepherds with their flocks, the daring Greek peddlers and the clanking Roman legions passing has been multiplied into converging railroads and plane routes, but all lead into the capital under a new name which is the gateway to Asia Minor and also the southern water-gate to the Black Sea.

Dr. Monroe brings to this position an experience that is exceptional. It is doubtful if any one else has so wide and thorough-going an acquaintance with educational institutions and methods throughout the world. Detailed surveys have been made under his personal direction in the Philippine Islands, Puerto Rico and Iraq, and first-hand studies and observations in the Far East and the Near East. For years he has been director of the International Institute of Teachers College and has also been a teacher at Columbia University and Barnard. The West in giving him to the Near East is making what might well be called a Constantinian contribution in the field of education.

These institutions of which he becomes the single head are but two of the six American educational centers included in the Near East College Association group, the others being the American University at Beirut, the International College at Smyrna, the American College of Sofia and Athens College in Greece. There are a dozen more institutions of like origin. They are called "American" because they were originated in America, have been more or less under the direction and control of American boards of directors, with more or less American support. They have varying courses and disciplines, from Egypt to Persia. The purpose of all may be defined in the statement of the aims of one: to afford to the young people of the country in which it is located a thorough literary, scientific and practical education that will develop high character and fit them for duties of citizenship in their own country.

The two colleges in Istanbul have the most difficult problems, and it is therefore of first importance that a man of such high qualifications should be selected to go forward in cooperation with the young republic in these its formative years.—*The New York Times.*

CHANCELLOR BROWN'S RETIREMENT

BY character and accomplishment Dr. Elmer Ellsworth Brown has made a deep impression on this city in his twenty years as chancellor of New York University. There can be nothing but regret that "advancing years" impel him to announce his withdrawal from his important office as soon as the university shall have found a new chancellor. If Dr. Brown feels the weight of his seventy years he carries it to admiration. At the New York University commencement last week he was the same strong, wise, alert and gracious chancellor whom thousands of students have held and hold in personal affection.

It was under Dr. Brown's leadership that New York University became the great urban university that it is to-day. Preserving faithfully the democratic ideal of the founders, he built an immense structure on a firm foundation, always with the purpose that "the best knowledge should be applied to whatever mankind is engaged upon." He has exhibited constantly the twofold ability, essential to his task, of educator and administrator. He has worked upon a grand, yet not grandiose, scale, always the sound yet forward thinker, never the visionary.

His place will be hard to fill. A man who can run the complicated machinery of a vast university and keep the heart of it all beating strong and sure must be an educator of rare parts. Dr. Brown notably among college heads has been able "to see life steadily and see it whole." For the influence of his career at New York University this community has every reason to be grateful.—*New York Herald-Tribune.*

COORDINATION OF SCHOOL AND COLLEGE WORK

PLANS OF THE PROGRESSIVE EDUCATION ASSOCIATION

To a large number of colleges and universities throughout the country letters proposing "a fresh scrutiny of the procedure that affects the mutual relations between schools and colleges" have been sent by Wilford M. Aikin, chairman of the commission on the relation of school and college of the Progressive Education Association. The letters invite these higher institutions to share in a study begun about two years ago by the commission, which is being carried on through funds provided by the Carnegie Corporation of New York.

The outcome of the study is a plan by which a small number of schools, both public and private, will follow curricula and methods developed upon a new educational basis, with the understanding that colleges will accept selected students from these schools without regard to the course and unit requirements now generally in force and without further examination. The experimental period proposed is for five years, beginning with the autumn of 1936.

Preliminary work in introducing the purpose and scope of the enterprise was taken during recent months, February to April, in small, informal regional conferences attended by officers of representative colleges and universities. These were held as follows: At the University of Chicago, February 6; at Columbia University, February 27; at the University of Pennsylvania, March 5; at Radcliffe College, April 15; at Harvard University, April 16. "Groups will be called together in other centers if the need arises." The college representatives received the proposals, according to Chairman Aikin's letter, "in a friendly and sympathetic spirit, and almost all of them indicated that the plans will receive approval in whole or in large part when formally submitted to the colleges." Assurance is given that "every phase of the program, including the selection of the participating schools, will have the immediate and close supervision of a directing committee."

A full statement of the plan is given in the contribution by Chairman Aikin.

RAYMOND WALTERS

A PROPOSAL FOR BETTER COORDINATION OF SCHOOL AND COLLEGE WORK

STUDENTS of education in America know that the elementary school has changed fundamentally in organization, curriculum and procedure within the last decade, and that profound changes are taking place in our universities and colleges. But similar reconstruction in the secondary schools is difficult, if not impossible, under present conditions. Recognizing the need of improvement in secondary education, and realizing that any significant change involves the cooperation of the colleges, the Progressive Education Association appointed, almost two years ago, a commission on the relation of school and college. Last December, a generous grant of funds for the work was provided by the Carnegie Corporation of New York.

MEMBERS OF THE COMMISSION

Mr. Wilford M. Aikin, director, John Burroughs School, *chairman*.

Professor Walter Raymond Agard, University of Wisconsin.

Mr. Willard Beatty, superintendent of schools, Bronxville, N. Y.

Mr. Bruce Bliven, editor, *The New Republic*.

Dean C. S. Boucher, University of Chicago.

Mr. A. J. Burton, principal, East High School, Des Moines, Iowa.

Miss Flora J. Cooke, director, Francis Parker School.

Mr. Harold Ferguson, principal, Montclair High School.

Mr. Burton P. Fowler, director, Tower Hill School.

Dr. Josephine Gleason, Vassar College.

Dr. Thomas Hopkins, curriculum research specialist, Lincoln School.

Dr. Leonard V. Koos, University of Chicago.

Dr. W. S. Learned, The Carnegie Foundation.

President Robert D. Leigh, Bennington College.

Dr. John A. Lester, The Hill School.

Dean Max McConn, Lehigh University.

Mr. Clyde R. Miller, Teachers College, New York.

Dr. Jesse Newlon, director, The Lincoln School.

Dr. W. Carson Ryan, Swarthmore College.

Dr. Harold Rugg, Teachers College, Columbia University.

Miss Ann Shumaker, editor, *Progressive Education*.

Dr. Eugene R. Smith, director, Beaver Country Day School.

Mr. Perry Dunlap Smith, director, North Shore Country Day School.

Miss Katharine Taylor, director, Shady Hill School.

Dr. Vivian Thayer, Ethical Culture School.

Professor Goodwin Watson, Teachers College, Columbia University.

President Raymond Walters, University of Cincinnati.

Dr. Ben D. Wood, collegiate education research, Columbia University.

The commission desires to bring about such changes in the relation of school and college as will permit sound experimental study of secondary education. It is concerned with all students, but especially with those who plan to go to college, and it seeks to establish conditions under which schools may develop more fully in all students a strong sense of individual and social responsibility. The commission wishes, also, to make it possible for schools and colleges to help each student shape his course so that it will be best fitted to his needs, and so that his work will have meaning and significance for him.

PLAN FOR COOPERATION

The following plan is presented for approval:

A. A small number of schools, probably not more than twenty, will be chosen to carry on experiments in secondary education appropriate to the purpose of this plan. The number is limited so as not to be unwieldy for experimental purposes. There will be included public and private schools each with funds, faculty personnel and interest, parental support and administrative leadership adequate to the task. Only schools of highest character and excellence and established reputation will be admitted to this group. These schools will enter into an admissions arrangement (described below) with colleges for an experimental period of five years beginning with the autumn of 1936.

Note: As this arrangement permits the schools to change their curricula in the fall of 1933, candidates for admission to college in 1936 will have had three years' experience under the reconstructed curriculum before leaving the preparatory school.

B. A directing committee has been appointed to supervise all aspects of the plan, including the practical coordination between schools and colleges and the securing of effective educational procedure. The membership of the committee, which represents the various types of colleges and schools sharing in the study, follows:

Mr. Willard Beatty, superintendent of schools, Bronxville, N. Y.

Professor Boyd H. Bode, Ohio State University.

Professor Carl C. Brigham, Princeton University.

Mr. Burton P. Fowler, director, Tower Hill School.

Mr. Will French, associate superintendent of schools, Tulsa, Okla.

Dean Herbert E. Hawkes, Columbia University.

Dean John B. Johnston, University of Minnesota.

Dr. John A. Lester, Hill School.

Dean Max McConn, Lehigh University.

Dr. Jesse Newlon, director, Lincoln School.

President Marian E. Park, Bryn Mawr College.

Dr. Eugene R. Smith, director, Beaver Country Day School.

Mr. Wilford M. Aikin, director, John Burroughs School.

As the work develops, the functions of this committee, in its relations to the schools and colleges involved, will become increasingly clear. At the present time it is plain that its responsibilities will include:

1. Selection of the schools to share in the experiment.

2. Examination of plans of work and proposed curricula submitted by the schools.

3. Approval, rejection or revision, in collaboration with the school, of plans submitted.

4. Working with each school in the systematic study and development of its work as it proceeds and obtaining full and adequate reports from time to time.

5. Determining the degree of uniformity necessary or desirable in the work of the schools sharing in the plan.

6. Bringing the schools and colleges into close cooperation in guiding each student's work. As soon as a pupil has indicated his choice of a college, it is hoped that representatives of the college will work with the school in studying and counselling the candidate, and that the school will work with the college after the student begins his college career.

7. Suggesting such modifications in college regulations and procedure for the students entering during the five year period under the new arrangement as will conserve the fundamental educational values of the experiment.

8. Systematic observation of these students during college and as many years thereafter as seems wise, with the idea of evaluating the work of the schools participating in this study.

SELECTION OF STUDENTS

Admission to college for the experimental period will be based upon the following criteria:

A. Recommendation from the principal of the cooperating secondary school to the effect that the graduating student (a) is possessed of the requisite general intelligence to carry on college work creditably; (b) has well-defined serious interests and purposes; (c) has demonstrated ability to work successfully in one or more fields of study in which the college offers instruction.

B. A carefully recorded history of the student's school life and of his activities and interests, including results of various types of examinations and other evidence of the quality and quantity of the candidate's work, also scores on scholastic aptitude, achievement and other diagnostic tests given by the schools during the secondary school course.

It is intended that the tests used will be of such character that the results submitted to the colleges will give a more adequate and complete picture of the candidate than is given by methods now in use. A special committee on records is now at work endeavoring to determine:

1. What information the college needs for wise selection and guidance of students.

2. How that information can best be secured.

3. In what form it should be recorded and presented in the colleges.

The cooperating colleges will not be obliged to admit under this agreement all such students as meet the new requirements. However, during the experimental period and from the limited group of cooperating schools, the colleges agree to accept students under this plan without regard to the course and unit requirements now generally in force for all students, and without further examination. The colleges, for this period, agree also that students applying for admission under the new requirements will be considered without discrimination in comparison with students applying from other schools where present requirements are in effect.

Underlying Ideas

The educational emphasis in this plan is based upon a conviction that the secondary schools must become more effective in helping young people to develop the insight, the powers and the self-direction necessary for resourceful and constructive living. We wish to work toward a type of secondary education which will be flexible, responsive to changing needs and clearly based upon an understanding of young people as well as an understanding of the qualities needed in adult life.

We are trying to develop students who regard education as an enduring quest for meanings rather than credit accumulation; who desire to investigate, to follow the leadings of a subject, to explore new fields of thought; knowing how to budget time, to read well, to use sources of knowledge effective and who are experienced in fulfilling obligations which come with membership in the school or college community.

To this end we should like to provide, more fully than the present organization of secondary education permits, for changes such as are indicated under the following headings:

A. *Greater mastery in learning:*

Acquisition of such techniques as reading with speed and comprehension, observing accurately, organizing and summarizing information; ability to work with many kinds of materials; capacity to see facts in their relationships; ability to state ideas clearly; techniques essential as a foundation for later advanced study.

B. *More continuity of learning:*

The elimination, wherever advisable, of limited, brief assignments and courses; a more coherent development of fields of study; provision for more consecutive pursuit of a particular subject through several years; encouragement (including the devising of ways and means and the allowance of sufficient time in the school schedule) of the desire to investigate; development of the power and impetus to pursue a subject beyond the school requirement, and stimulation of the desire to put ideas to use.

There should be less emphasis on subjects and more on continuous, unified sequence of subject-matter, planned on a four-year or six-year basis. English is the only course that at present even approximates this aim. Continuous courses in the sciences and social sciences would take the place of such fragments of subject-matter as chemistry or modern European history. Chemistry has its biological, geological or astronomical implications that should not be overlooked if the whole of science is to have significance. Similarly, such cultures as those of South America and Asia should have a place in history courses, for comparative study, as well as those of Europe and the United States. Mathematics and foreign languages also would be reorganized in a manner to enable the pupil to get a ''long'' view of these fields of subject-matter.

C. *Release of creative energies:*

Through experience and training in various arts, including both practice and appreciation (example—painting, modeling, writing, drama, music); through the encouragement, in all work, of independent, individual thinking and of fresh combining of thought; through providing opportunities, with guidance, for young people to exercise their desire to do something ''on their own'' (example—tinkering, inventing, constructing, special pursuits in reading, instrumental music).

D. *Clearer understanding of the problems of our civilization, and the development of a sense of social responsibility:*

Through including, in the curriculum, studies bearing upon specific problems of American civilization and that of the modern world, and the outstanding individual and collective efforts to solve these problems; through using every opportunity to help students to realize the interdependence and inter-relationships of human lives; through helping students to develop social responsibility, in feeling and in practice as well as in appreciation of the issues involved, by means of such activities as participation in school community life with concern for the general welfare, discussion groups on social and economic problems, field trips to study industrial processes, housing conditions, or the machinery of government; a model league of nations, or assembly programs which require, as do all the foregoing activities, much reading and investigation in the broad fields of social relationships.

E. *Revision of curriculum materials and their organization:*

Besides the changes in curriculum materials to be inferred from the above-mentioned changes in practice, such other experiments as: reorganizing the sequence of material in different fields of knowledge, for secondary education (example—mathematics, science, history, languages); unifying the subjects of study and removing some of the boundaries now existing between closely related fields (example—history in its relation to the facts of economics, geography, literature and fine arts); addition of new materials from fields of knowledge not hitherto included in typical secondary school curricula (example—certain materials from the fields of economics, anthropology, geology).

F. *Guidance of students:*

The function of guidance in education needs much greater study and emphasis. While it is important that the student should have as much independence and responsibility as he can use wisely, counsel of the best sort should be available when he needs it. Some one should know him well and be able and ready to examine his problems with him and to help him solve them. He should be helped to see his career through school and college as a developing experience, with each phase in a definite relationship toward the whole. Under the directing committee, plans will be worked out to achieve this purpose. The program will include: more thorough study of the needs of individuals, with corresponding adjustment of the school program to their needs; record-keeping for later analysis; more intelligent preparation of the student for the use of the opportunities provided by the colleges.

G. *Teaching:*

It is evident that the changes in secondary education suggested in this memorandum can not occur without teaching of a very high quality. This would be true of any experimental work. We fully recognize the scarcity of teachers who are qualified in background, in training and in personality for this type of work. There are, however, some teachers now at work who could successfully carry through the suggested program. Some of these are already studying its possibilities. Others will be discovered as the work is begun.

Schools, colleges and universities that are undertaking the training of teachers will be interested in helping select the most promising candidates and in training them in the best possible ways for this work. We fully realize that the discovery and training of better teachers must go hand in hand with wise experimentation, and that experiments must move slowly enough to keep within the limits of available good teaching.

WILFORD M. AIKIN

EDUCATIONAL RESEARCH AND STATISTICS

THE GERMAN PRIMARY SCHOOL CENSUS[1]

THE German school census is taken every five years and the preliminary figures for the 1931–1932 census school year, taken on May 15, 1931, have just been made public. Only public primary schools are included in these census figures, but it may be mentioned that such public primary schools constitute 99.4 per cent. of all the primary schools in Germany and number as pupils 91.6 per cent. of all the youth in the obligatory school age.

PUPILS

The number of pupils in German public primary schools amounted to 7,590,000 in the school year 1931–1932, as against 6,660,000 pupils in 1926–1927, which represents an increase of fourteen per cent. This increase may be compared to the decrease of 25 per cent. registered in the period between the school years 1921–1922 and 1926–1927; the latter decrease being accounted for mainly by the heavy decline in births during the world war.

With the dropping out of the youth born in the world war period, the number of pupils in German primary schools began to increase and this increase will probably continue until 1935 is reached, during which year the remaining pupils who were born during the war period will have left the schools. From that period on, the number of pupils will doubtless commence to decrease steadily because of the general decline in the German birth rate which began in 1923.

[1] Consular report from Vice Consul C. T. Zawadzki, Berlin, submitted through the Office of Education, Department of the Interior. Also see "Wirtschaft und Statistik," 1st volume of March, 1932.

The following table illustrates this clearly:

Year	Beginning pupils	Obligatory pupils	Finishing pupils
1925	669,000	7,643,000	1,272,000
1926	1,286,000	7,653,000	1,265,000
1927	1,253,000	7,632,000	1,263,000
1928	1,210,000	7,596,000	1,231,000
1929	1,117,000	7,545,000	1,153,000
1930	1,061,000	7,847,000	754,000
1931	1,116,000	8,283,000	667,000
1932	1,087,000	8,752,000	606,000
1933	1,036,000	9,114,000	661,000
1934	1,011,000	8,841,000	1,271,000
1935	1,021,000	8,611,000	1,238,000

The German population at present in the obligatory school age is not much greater than the number of pupils registered in the primary schools, since a part of this population is entered in other than public schools, in middle schools, and in the higher institutions of learning.

The following table shows the number of pupils in the primary schools in Germany during the last three census periods, and in the more important states of Germany.

	1921–1922	1926–1927	1931–1932
Prussia	5,470,000	4,176,000	4,681,000
Bavaria	1,045,000	761,000	937,000
Saxony	720,000	507,000	568,000
Wurttemberg	362,000	255,000	296,000
Baden	361,000	262,000	301,000
Thuringia	242,000	173,000	207,000
Germany	8,894,000	6,662,000	7,589,000

The number of pupils in Germany per 10,000 persons increased from 1,056 in the school year 1926–1927, to 1,174 in the school year 1931–1932.

TEACHERS

The number of main official teachers on the public primary schools of Germany in 1931–1932, which amounted to 187,704, increased very slightly (0.05 per cent.) as compared to five years ago. This negligible increase, at a time when the number of pupils increased steadily, is accounted for by the attempted reduction in the staff of teachers. From the school year 1921–1922 to the school year 1926–1927, the decrease in the number of teachers did not correspond to the decrease in the number of pupils, since the number of schools and school classes, which would form the basis of any such decrease, could not be diminished correspondingly.

The tendency to reduce the number of teachers may be noticed from the number of pupils per teacher. In 1926–1927 there were 35.7 pupils per teacher in Germany, while in 1931–1932 the number of pupils per teacher rose to 40.4. The following table shows the distribution of teachers in the various states of Germany:

State	1921–22	1926–27	1931–32	Pupils per teacher
Prussia	116,765	112,384	115,410	40.6
Bavaria	24,034	23,447	20,739	45.1
Saxony	16,673	15,752	15,622	36.4
Wurttemberg	7,636	7,214	7,618	38.9
Baden	7,581	6,782	6,818	44.2
Thuringia	5,369	4,817	4,796	43.1
Germany	195,946	186,853	187,704	40.4

Only the figures for all of Germany and the most important states are given in the above table, but the same trend may be noticed in the smaller states. The smallest number of pupils per teacher in 1931–1932 was registered in the city-states of Hamburg, Bremen, and Leubeck, and in the city of Berlin (30 or less per teacher), while the highest number of pupils per teacher may be found in Bavaria, Baden, Upper Silesia, Lower Silesia, East Prussia, Rhine Province, etc. Upper Silesia, with 47 pupils per teacher, records the highest number.

NEW BOOKS IN EDUCATION

HITCHCOCK, CHARLES H., *Translator. The Oresteia of Aeschylus.* Pp. xi + 145. Bruce Humphries. $2.50.

KEILHACKER, MARTIN. *Der Ideale Lehrer. Nach der Auffassung der Schüler.* Pp. viii + 156. Herder, Freiburg.

MARTIN, GEORGE HENRY. *Essentials of Education.* Pp. 217. Badger. $2.50.

REEVES, FLOYD W. and others. *The Liberal Arts College.* Pp. xxxv + 715. 50 figures. University of Chicago Press. $4.50.

Report of the Superintendent of Schools of the City of New York, 1930–1931. Pp. xi + 922. Board of Education, City of New York.

SCHOOL AND SOCIETY

EDITED BY J. McKEEN CATTELL

WITH WHICH IS COMBINED THE

EDUCATIONAL REVIEW

EDITED BY WILLIAM McANDREW

Volume 35 SATURDAY, JUNE 25, 1932 Number 913

THE RENAISSANCE OF THE AMERICAN COLLEGE

THE CENTENNIAL COMMENCEMENT ADDRESS AT LAFAYETTE COLLEGE, MAY, 1932

By Dr. ROBERT L. KELLY

EXECUTIVE SECRETARY OF THE ASSOCIATION OF AMERICAN COLLEGES

THE American college has been called a seventeenth century dream come true. The college has been three centuries in the making; the dream is coming true. On the structural side the college has maintained its unity; it is now as it always has been, whether detached or embedded at the heart of a university, a four-year administrative unit. The exceptions are so rare as to prove the rule. On the functional side the college has gone through many minor and two major transformations. As a magnet it draws to itself highly selected material. It has a way of electrifying some of this material, of transforming some of its potentialities into kinetic energy. Through all the years the spirit, the temper, the outlook of the college has persisted, and it has become, despite its origin at Oxford and Cambridge, distinctively an American creation. It typifies the American spirit at its best.

To attain its unique status, to become the symbol of the American genius, it has survived two major operations. Twice, under the knife as it were, it has struggled forth out of its low-vaulted past into a newness of life.

When Lafayette College was ushered into the family of American colleges a hundred years ago, the Oxford and Cambridge model had not seriously been challenged. The colonial college ideals and methods furnished the plans and specifications for college construction for well over two centuries. This college, like all others of the time, was organized after the colonial pattern. Lafayette could not immediately lift herself by her own boot straps out of her own social and academic environment, although she soon showed signs of discontent with the traditional program. To-day a relatively small group of colleges, of which Lafayette is one, are thrice born colleges. Lafayette was first born into the dispensation of law. Her second birth was into the dispensation of liberty. Her third birth, the consummation of which she has not altogether realized perhaps, is into the dispensation of liberty under law.

Of course not many colleges, it may be not any college, has come entirely through either dispensation into the next and left all its shell behind it. The college social personality is not different in this respect from the individual human personality. There are colleges still dominated by law, and glorying in the power of discipline.

There are others chiefly characterized by liberty, proud of their academic insurgency. A few are pushing, forward as they think, into a third area of academic achievement, attempting to hold fast to the good in the past but lured by the prospect of something better in the future. Perhaps most colleges are content to live and breathe and have their being in an atmosphere compounded with a mixture more or less indiscriminate of many academic ingredients. At least the objectives and methods of few colleges have been clearly stated.

In the first period of college development the administration made the laws. They were handed down and passed on, as if from Mt. Sinai, often with considerable thunder and lightning. The law-makers or codifiers were also the law enforcers. If the origin of the laws was something like the Ten Commandments, the laws themselves were not equally destined to withstand the storms of time. As we read them now, they are as funny as the laws of Congress. If only they had popular currency they would vie with Will Rogers and the *Congressional Record* as unfailing sources of American humor. The curriculum was as static as the laws. No one dared raise the question as to what knowledge was of most worth. There was a certain body of knowledge foreordained to constitute the course of study. And let it be said, in all justice, it was and is yet a remarkable body of knowledge. It required a good deal of toughness of fiber on the part of the student who mastered it. The program of study was centered in the subject-matter. The attainment of specific types of knowledge was the goal of a college education. Such, briefly, was the reign of law.

In the second era of college development this uniform and rigid curriculum was pulverized. This signifies that the method was a forcible one. It was. Charles W. Eliot was the leader of the attack and he had a fight on his hands from first to last. He had two weapons of warfare. He had a sword in each hand: first, scientific subject-matter and method; second, the elective system. Thus was the era of liberty attained for the American student. It was called the "new education." The program became student centered. The motive power, theoretically at least, was student interest. The free elective became the shibboleth of the new education. Some still think that our second estate was worse than our first. The elective system overreached itself, as unlicensed freedom always does, and the new era, the third dispensation, began to be proclaimed.

The third era, in which we now find ourselves, is the era of liberty under law, if the old terminology is maintained. It is sometimes called progressive education. In the language of our own day, it is the era of individual initiative guided by the group. The individual student is a dynamic unit in the guiding group. But the student, any more than studies, is not everything! The individual student is still in command. He is still master of his own spirit. But he must needs make his conquests in the world of persons. The colleges are attempting in a day of social controls to steer their course between the Scylla of rampant individualism and the Charybdis of the mass mind. The program is neither subject centered nor object centered. It is subject-object centered. The modern college is as Einsteinian as Einstein himself. If Einstein has his "time-space" as a single concept, so the progressive college to-day has its two foci, each inherently necessary for the generation of the academic curve. The student is at one focus, the teacher at the other. Life and growth come through electrical contact. And they are but units in a large group-fellowship of teachers and students. Teachers and students are the ultimate particles of electrical mass, of electrical charge, of radiant energy, of momentum, of the new academic atom.

In terms of subject-matter the third era is characterized by the newly born social sciences, as the second was by the physical and biological sciences. The nomenclature of the natural sciences may be carried over into the social science realm, for the achievements of this era are obtained through the constructive processes of synthesis—a synthesis of the arts, the humanities, the sciences into a unified life. This is the ideal of liberal education to-day. On the side of method, for the shibboleth, "the free elective," has been substituted "synthesis." Perhaps all the king's horses and all the king's men can not put Humpty Dumpty back again. The college student either working alone or with the aid of the group must put Humpty Dumpty back. We must see the world as nearly whole as possible.

This third movement has reached such proportions during the past decade or two that it may be called the renaissance of the American college. It attempts to guarantee safety in the college for student interest, provided that interest shows signs of permanency and is supported by demonstrated student capacity; it stands for trust in discipline, freedom in thought, cooperation in action, boldness in experimentation, and encourages the free play of the creative impulse. Its desideratum in our best colleges is the abundant life. This of course is the mark toward which some colleges are pressing forward. No college as yet claims fully to have attained. Some of the terms in which this attainment is attempted in the group of colleges which have entered upon this crusade, are:

The clearing up of the twilight zone between the secondary school and the college in the interest of intelligent guidance in continuity of studies.

The recognition of the two essential functions of the college—exploration in the lower division and concentration in the upper division.

Special advisory systems for freshmen, frequently accompanied by segregation in designated dormitories.

Especial provision for wholesome living conditions for all students, in relatively small groups.

A thorough-going program of personnel service and prevocational guidance in the interest of every student.

The tutorial or preceptorial system, modified according to needs of the institution.

The comprehensive examination, sometimes in conjunction with special work for honors, in addition to or as a partial substitute for, the present unsatisfactory term examinations.

Special reading periods for students and in general the magnifying of the libraries along with the laboratories as centers of the intellectual life.

The inclusion of religion, under wholesome and adequate guidance, as a necessary and component part of a college education.

The most complete approach possible to individual instruction coupled with incursions into group thinking and action.

The encouragement of appreciation and performance as the necessary steps of creative culture.

The synthesis of the arts, the sciences, the humanities into a unified life process.

Finally, the development of a sense of responsibility among faculties and students for both minor and major social tendencies within and without the college.

In other words, this newly born college seeks to place emphasis upon the whole rather than the part, reality rather than appearance, good rather than goods, truth rather than trade, values rather than prices, insight rather than statistics, beauty rather than decoration, human beings rather than automatons. The chief college relationships must be life relationships, not merely preparation for life relationships.

One may speak now only of one phase of this program—the responsibility of the college man for social trends. The American college can not point with the greatest pride to its record in this respect. We are still far behind many of our European neighbors.

We must all have been thrilled some weeks ago at the effect on the French people of the appearance of the new French grammar. After three hundred years of hesitation and delay and three years of arduous labor on the part of a group of venturesome intellectuals, this grammar appeared. Its appearance pushed the doubts and dangers of the depression off the front pages of the newspapers. Of what moment are debts and reprisals and reparations in the presence of an authoritative grammar? One's first patriotic duty is to be grammatical. A French statesman, it is said, will wildly applaud the diction of a speech, the purport of which is entirely repugnant to him. "Absolute drivel, but what beautiful French." Perhaps the American college graduate has not quite reached this standard of appreciation. We can not quite say, with reference to grammar, "Lafayette, we are here!"

The announcement was recently made that a new editor had been chosen for the *Manchester Guardian*. This newspaper probably leads all its contemporaries in all lands in the appropriateness and purity of its English diction. The new editor is an Oxford man, as have been most or all of his predecessors, a man with a liberal education. The incident brings to mind afresh the multitude of Oxford and Cambridge men who have during the centuries largely determined the destinies of the British empire, and have brought into being and are now heroically bearing the heavy burdens of the English commonwealth.

The engineers of Germany became impressed with the fact that most of the positions of power and prestige in their country were held by members of the legal profession. They proceeded to reconstruct the programs of study of their schools of engineering. They placed more emphasis upon the liberal studies—less upon the technical; they planned rather for education than for training. Already, they report, their revised programs are helping to produce a type of engineer better suited to social leadership, who is winning his part of the emoluments of place.

Word is brought back to us by expert American authorities that the worse the times get in Europe, the more the average man reads. Europe will emerge from the present emergency more liberal and more cultured.

It can scarcely be claimed that our cultural opportunities and our social responsibilities enter so deeply, as some of these illustrations indicate, into our lives either as students or as men of affairs. The reported success of Lafayette's Alumni College is certainly very reassuring in this respect. In general, we may still strive for a more highly tempered mind, for greater and more lasting enthusiasm for art and literature and public service. Some American colleges have an honorable name because of the distinguished achievements of their alumni in these fields. In not a few of these instances, however, their most brilliant records were made by the graduates of rather remote vintage.

Of course, the paradox involved is apparent, of urging in one breath that college graduates should strive to use good English, and in the next that they should enter the hurly-burly of American politics. Must not the politician use a language that is understood, if he is to secure votes? How far, you may ask, will good English go in our great metropolitan centers, or for that matter in the corn belt? In an illuminating account of a campaign for the

United States senatorial nomination in a state west of the Fathers of Waters, the present dignified senator refers to his opponent as "the chicken-stew candidate," and this would-be statesman rather neatly announces as his campaign slogan, "Chicken-stew *versus* the same old boloney." But this is not my problem; it is the problem of the new college graduate.

One thing is certain: the stage is being set elaborately in the thrice-born college. The social sciences bulk larger and larger in the curriculum earnings. Our students are delving into history, international law, economics, sociology, politics, education, religion. When President Eliot was carrying on his vigorous conflict in behalf of the laboratory method within the college, he once said: "The student of natural science scrutinizes, touches, weighs, measures, analyzes, dissects and watches things." I am inclined to emphasize "things"; President Eliot did not do so, perhaps. He took things for granted for his purpose. He spoke as a chemist and he was dealing with things. Likewise it may be said the social sciences also "scrutinize, touch, weigh, measure, analyze, dissect and watch"—persons and groups—and they do something besides. They synthesize.

The social sciences are contributing immeasurably to the present movement in behalf of interdepartmentalization, intercommunity action and action intercollegiate, interstate, interparliamentary, interracial, international. In addition to the curriculum offerings, scores of colleges foster lectures and discussions on various phases of contemporary affairs. There are the international exchanges both of students and teachers, the international relations clubs, the cosmopolitan clubs, the model assemblies of the League of Nations, the institutes of politics, of public affairs, of statesmanship and the schools of international affairs, foreign service, international relations. Taken together, these represent a remarkable awareness of social relationships, especially of the wider type.

The problem of the student of social science is not to win prestige in the modern college—his problem is to justify the prestige he has, to give a good account of his stewardship in the post-college years. The social sciences postulate the human spirit as the basis of their work. Their problem involves the question—How to formulate the industrial, social, economic and political and religious problems of this generation that mankind may be better served; how to discover, and if possible guide the irresistible energies of human behavior.

Never have such questions come to college graduates with greater potency and urgency than at this moment. The feudal barons were not practical politicians by profession, perhaps, but a crisis arose when good citizenship demanded that they wrest the Magna Charta from King John. They met the emergency gloriously. Fourteen years ago, in another crisis, Uncle Sam found himself in an emergency and he called on the colleges. "They donned the khaki—585 of them—and undertook to find and deliver the 100,000 needed candidates for officers' training camps." Now, we face a still greater crisis. It is as wide as humanity. We are challenged to mobilize "for a struggle to establish dynamic peace." Past experience furnishes no plans, no specifications, no maps, no charts. It is a fight, as has been said, that can not be won by machines nor money nor technical skill alone. The call is for men of social and moral insight and intelligence. There must not only be insight and intelligence but the will to distinguish between one's personal welfare and the welfare of his fellow men. It is a fight for the life of a civilization. There must be a new social order that will stand.

Evidently it must be founded upon a rock. An American university president wrote a few days ago—"Apparently human affairs have broken loose from human control." The "Gloomy Dean" of England declares, "We are witnessing the suicide of a social order and our descendants will marvel at our madness." But even Dean Inge, with clearer mind, points the possible way out. "We judge our generation mainly by its surface currents. There may be in progress a storage of beneficent forces we can not see."

I undertake to say that this storage of benevolent forces is found in education and religion if harnessed to life. The president of a sister university of great renown, himself just come forth from the stern area of big business to serve his university without compensation, was making his maiden speech before the Association of American Colleges. His subject was "Intercollegiate Athletics." His profound insight into reality is indicated in this remarkable declaration:

> In my opinion, when two million parents of American youth entrust to us one million of their sons and daughters, they are placing upon us a very grave responsibility. We are, for four years, to occupy the place of the father of these boys and girls. I do not believe that their real parents in turning over this grave trust say to us: "Take our sons and our daughters. Give them an education which will consist of the amassing of a certain body of worldly knowledge and an ability to think. We hold you to no accountability for their spiritual welfare." I do not believe that. I believe that this side of the training of the student is definitely a part of our responsibility. Further than that, I believe that at the present time some of us are doing very little about it. I do not believe that we can leave this task to the churches or other agencies off the campus, no matter how earnest and sincere their work may be. It is definitely a part of the task that we should directly undertake in training the student for life, and I, for one, propose that the university over which I have the honor to preside should look toward some constructive steps in the direction of this opportunity for improving the work we are attempting to do.

So faith takes the place of despair. The American people always pin their faith to the men and women who stand upon an educational and religious foundation. These citizens must not be counted among the slackers. This is the challenge to robust American youth. Whether the divine call comes to you in the field of politics, economics, ethics, domestic life, education, religion, I offer you the challenge of our one-time educational, now political, colleague, the governor of Connecticut:

> The opportunity is already in the hands of our muscular young citizens to take the initiative, to make up their minds what our democracy needs, and to use all their educational equipment and organizing powers to get it. From my brief experience in state government, I have learned one thing that our democracy needs to-day above all others. It is the energy of intelligent, aggressive and well-trained young men and women in practical efforts for the public welfare. For their own full and vigorous development as much as for that of the country, I have no hesitation in saying to those who can stand a cold plunge: Come on in—the water's fine.

MOOSEHEART—A SOCIO-PEDAGOGICAL EXPERIMENT

By Dr. RUDOLPH M. BINDER

PROFESSOR EMERITUS OF SOCIOLOGY, NEW YORK UNIVERSITY

WHAT kind of education may be achieved when the pupils are under control for twenty-four hours of the day for the years from babyhood to graduation from high school? That question presents itself inevitably to every visitor to Mooseheart who has the opportunity to spend at least a few days there and to observe the daily life of this small community.

Controlled experiments in the different

sciences are well known, and equally well known are the excellent results which have in the vast majority of cases been produced. Educators have frequently expressed the wish that they might be able to employ controlled experiments in their work, but they have rarely been able to realize their hope. Even in the boarding schools where the pupils are under supervision day and night, this control is not complete because the pupils are given short and long vacations during which other than school factors exert their powerful influence. Length of stay is moreover purely voluntary and may be terminated almost any time.

At Mooseheart all the different factors assuring full control not only exist but are exercised over a period of years extending in many cases from infancy to adulthood. This community provides, consequently, a rare if not unique opportunity for the study of educational principles and theories.

What is Mooseheart? In the simplest terms it is an institution which provides both home and school for orphans or half-orphans of deceased members of the Loyal Order of Moose. It is located about forty miles west of Chicago on a tract of land covering about twelve hundred acres, of which the greater part is used for farming purposes. There are about two hundred buildings near one end of the land, none of which is very large because the tendency is to keep the units small so as to preserve the home atmosphere. The farm provides all the milk and most of the vegetables for the community of about seventeen hundred people, of whom fourteen hundred are orphans. The buildings are scattered over some forty acres and each is surrounded by spacious lawns, trees and shrubbery. The conditions for good health are thus favorable.

The idea of Mooseheart originated with James J. Davis, at present United States Senator from Pennsylvania, and was realized in an embryonic way in 1913, when a few children first occupied the old farm house. The idea and the place have grown and Mooseheart offers now one of the most attractive sights to the visitor and an experiment in community-living to the sociologist and the educator. It attempts to meet all the requirements necessary to produce as far as its resources permit full-orbed men and women. The achievement of that end demands a new type of education.

Every person possesses two kinds of capacities—those which are common to all men, and those which are peculiar to the individual. In the first class we have life in the family, in the state (or citizenship), and in the circle of our friends and acquaintances (or companionship). In the second class we have some sort of special talent which, owing to our uniqueness, every individual possesses to a greater or lesser degree; also some secondary talent for appreciation of the beautiful and the spiritual. The development of our common abilities makes us valuable members of society, that of our special qualities gives value and satisfaction to our lives. Ultimately the real center of life for every individual consists in those intangible valuations which he makes on the basis of activities which he is best able to perform by virtue of his natural equipment; our so-called social activities form only the larger or smaller peripherics of our lives. A rounded-out education means that both our social and our individual capacities are developed.

How does Mooseheart measure up to this standard? It was there from the beginning as the motto, "The School That Trains for Life," indicates. The ideal was somewhat inchoate, as beginnings generally are; it has been clarified in the nineteen years which have passed and is now fairly clear, although not fully, because new developments demand the constant reshaping of that ideal. Life in the community and instruction in the schools are increasingly integrated, so that it is hard to tell where one begins and the other ends. As a matter of fact, no such distinction is made—life there is school, and school is life. This integration is made possible because Mooseheart is a community whose only products are children who are brought there sometimes as tiny babies and sometimes at the age of adolescence, but most frequently between these extremes. All through the different stages, though, the ideal of fitting the children for useful membership in society and for enabling them to make high-grade individual valuations, is the guide and inspiration of the officials.

Normal functioning of any kind is impossible without good health. Mooseheart, consequently, places the greatest possible emphasis on the maintenance and preservation of physical health. The excellent milk from its own farm forms the basis of food for the younger children, each of whom is allotted one quart per day, and in part for the older children who get a pint each. On this basis four types of menus are built: first, for babies under two years of age; second, for children from two to six; third, from six to eight; fourth, from eight and over. Individual needs are carefully taken into account, but a return to the normal menu of the respective age group is made as soon as practicable. Careful and regular health inspections of every child are held at least twice a year and any incipient disease is attended to at once. Every scientific medical preventive is insisted upon and each child must submit to the various tests for preventing diseases. The result is a remarkably small morbidity rate and the smallest mortality rate known anywhere.

These careful provisions for physical health are supplemented by provisions for psychical health. A laboratory for child research has been established under a competent psychologist and psychiatrist. Preceding admission, every child is carefully examined and subnormal children are barred. Frequent examinations keep the psychologist posted as to the progress made by each child and, if necessary, readjustments are made. The social and educational programs are built up on this fairly accurate knowledge of the physical and mental condition of the children from nursery school to high school.

The objectives in the nursery school or "baby village" are to develop desirable physical and mental habits and normal emotional attitudes, to provide an environment in which wholesome social contacts may be made and social adjustments and adaptations to group life achieved, and, finally, to develop a wholesome respect on the part of each child for the rights of others and proper reactions to authority. The program for attaining these objectives consists of all types of manipulations and construction within the mental range of the group, various forms of play, story telling, dramatization of simple situations, singing, games calling for alternate leadership, periods of lively activity and periods of inactivity and silence. Variations in activities are planned not merely to avoid fatigue but chiefly for the purpose of giving as near as possible every child an opportunity to develop leadership. Integrated education for the development of social activities and for individual initiative begins thus as soon as a child enters Mooseheart; and this principle is made the central feature of all activities in this community.

The kindergarten develops the ideas of the nursery school further, appropriate to the more advanced age of the children. The Mooseheart kindergarten has at least one great advantage over those of most private and public schools. It always has a fairly large nucleus of children advanced from the nursery school. These furnish the leaders and make the attainment of kindergarten aims—*viz.*, the acquisition of definite social habits and a feeling for social order by arranging activities in such a way that children get opportunities for learning to live together and sharing willingly—much easier. The program of activities does not vary much from that of other kindergartens, except in two respects: the classes are kept small so that each child receives individual attention, and periodic tests are made by the psychologist to ascertain what progress each child is making, so that activities may be assigned according to his or her capacity. These children have, moreover, the advantage of the "great out-doors" in their nature studies.

The first two grades and the lower third of the elementary school are looked upon as mere extensions of the kindergarten at Mooseheart. The reason for this procedure consists in the fact that the children are still immature and need training chiefly in habit formation. The great stress on habit formation is necessary, because Mooseheart is both a school and a home, and there is no divided authority as there is in the case of public-school children whose habits are formed chiefly in the family while the more formal teaching is done in the school. Teaching is, consequently, done principally by various forms of activity as has been advocated by the most advanced educators. In order to attain this object, criteria, which are evaluated from time to time as new needs arise, are set up. These include among others the following: The interests of the children at a given time; the social value of the activity; the possibility of the activities engaged in for satisfying the children's need in subject-matter and growth in desirable skills, habits, and attitudes; the significance of several types of endeavor being included in one activity; and the richness of emotional satisfaction and of mental growth from any activity engaged in. The expectation that the children build up a rich and varied experience and acquire habits which lead to a well-poised and integrated personality, seems to be justified by the results. Every visitor is impressed by the cheerful, courteous behavior of these children—an impression which is strengthened by a fairly long stay at Mooseheart. Needless to say that the more formal arts of language through oral and written expression and arithmetic are likewise acquired. On the basis of frequent psychological and physical examinations special programs are arranged for those children who show greater or less creative talents in music, art, rhythms, dramatics, or along any other lines.

The upper third, fourth, fifth and sixth grades follow similar grades in other schools with two exceptions—the greatest possible stress throughout is placed on integrated activities since any formal teaching is never left suspended in the air but is always applied in the lives of the pupils; they are likewise made increasingly aware that they are the community and that the welfare and happiness of all depend on the proper social attitudes of each.

The seventh and eighth grade are, as a junior high, linked up more definitely with the high school. It is a try-out period from the vocational point of view. Every boy spends part of the afternoons of twelve weeks in each of eight try-out vocational courses, and every girl a half-year in each of four group courses. The pupils have thus abundant opportunities to test their abilities and predilections in various occupations. Aided by their instructors, they finally reach a decision which usually stands and only a few changes are needed later. The regular academic school work is done principally in the morning.

The high school is not only the apex but the crown and glory of the Mooseheart plan. It brings to a focus all the different principles for which the system stands.

One special feature of the plan is to have every boy and girl go through high school.

In the average community approximately twenty-five per cent. of the grammar school graduates pass through high school; the other seventy-five per cent. either do not enter high school at all or drop out before graduation. The expectation at Mooseheart is that a full one hundred per cent. of the lower schools should graduate from high school. This expectation is necessarily limited by the mental capacity of some boys and girls. In a community like Mooseheart, with children coming from every state of the Union and chiefly from the working classes, there is a small number, just as there is in every community, whose mental capacity is too limited for regular high-school work. But instead of dropping them, they are required to continue and are given courses especially adapted to their caliber; in addition they are given extra work in the trade they have chosen so that they are fully equipped to take it up when they leave, not earlier than the completion of their eighteenth year—the lower age limit at which any boy or girl may leave. They are then well equipped for their work, since they have not merely acquired manual skill but the scientific principles of their activity, and are thus in a better position to attain advancement than the mechanic who has acquired his skill merely by rule of thumb. These boys and girls receive the vocational diploma; their number is small.

The expectation is, though, that every boy and girl should receive a high-school education plus a thorough training in a trade. Since most of the children come from families in moderate circumstances and have few prospects of going to college, the curriculum is arranged with the object that the graduates should be able to make their living as soon as they leave, and Mooseheart maintains an employment agency for this purpose.

This necessity imposes certain limitations upon the curriculum. The frills are cut out, Latin is not taught, and the courses, following what in other high schools is called the "general course," are made to bear on vocational training as far as expedient without interfering with the purely scientific aspect of the work.

In addition to the "general course" more than forty trades and occupations, nearly equally divided between boys and girls, are taught. The mornings and early afternoons are devoted to regular school work, the later afternoons to work in the shops. In addition, three months of the last two summers are entirely devoted to work in the shops under regular conditions prevailing in commercial shops and factories. The object is not merely to produce small imitations of products, but commercially valuable articles. Many thousands of dollars worth of goods are actually sold to outsiders, and many more thousands to other departments at Mooseheart. Some activities have actually produced small profits. Just how serious the work is may be illustrated by three cases. The older girls have charge of the cafeteria, many of the beautiful ornaments on the campus have been produced in the art-cement shop, and boys have supplanted outside workingmen whose wages amounted to $22,000 a year.

To encourage close application and independence, small wages are paid, ranging from fifteen to twenty-five cents an hour. The students in the junior and senior classes are required to provide their clothes out of these earnings and to deposit not less than fifty dollars in the Mooseheart bank before they are allowed to graduate.

This strenuous program seems to exclude any leisure and playful activities. The contrary is true. There are any number of clubs, associations, etc., for amusement, for instance, four football teams, several baseball teams, swimming teams, and other forms of athletics for both boys and girls. The younger children have their Boy Scouts, Campfire Girls, Traffic Squad,

Junior Safety Patrol, Junior Student Council, Girls Auxiliary, etc. There are several bands, string orchestras, dramatic societies, singing societies, debating and art clubs. Every day there are two broadcasts from the Mooseheart radio station, and the more talented students have an opportunity to display their skill. The visitor staying in the "Child City" at first gets the impression as if he were living in a place arranged for pleasure, so numerous and multifarious are the activities of a playful character. As he stays longer, he realizes that very much serious work is done. The successful combination of work and play is due to the economizing of time, and this depends on the fact that the children are under wise supervision for twenty-four hours of the day from babyhood to adulthood.

What are the results of this carefully regulated school-home life? The only way to judge is, of course, by the products of Mooseheart. The children are, unlike those in many other institutions, very happy, as children are apt to be when well and healthy. They have every opportunity for wholesome play and for the development of individual talents, and ultimately nothing else will furnish a higher and more permanent satisfaction.

Judging by more objective criteria, we find that the high-school diploma of Mooseheart is acepted for college entrance by the North Central Association of Secondary Schools and Colleges. On an average, sixteen per cent. of the graduates actually go to college and are self-supporting owing to their thorough mastery of a trade. The high moral character of the graduates is indicated by the absence of any legal procedure for crimes or misdemeanors against any of them.

The graduates have made fair progress financially. A questionnaire was sent out to the 402 young men and women who graduated from 1919 to 1929, and was answered by 312 or 78 per cent.—a very good response. Their average age was twenty-two. Only five per cent., were unemployed during the present industrial depression. Earnings ranged from $15.00 to $100.00 per week, with a median of $36.00 a week, for boys, and $10.00 to $50.00 with a median of $25.00 per week for girls. That compares not unfavorably with the earnings of college graduates with a similar number of years out of college. A fair number of Mooseheart boys has reached responsible positions in industry, a smaller number is teaching in high schools, and a few of the older boys have attained assistant principalships.

While these results are good, they are likely to be better in the future, since the authorities of Mooseheart do not consider their system as in any way perfect; they are alert, experiment all the time, and are willing to adopt and adapt the latest advances in education.

EDUCATIONAL EVENTS

INCREASE IN EDUCATIONAL EXPENDITURE IN ENGLAND AND WALES

LORD EUSTACE PERCY, from 1924 to 1929 president of the British Board of Education, has written a letter to the London *Times* in regard to increased educational expenditure.

According to Lord Eustace a comparison of the actual expenditure in England and Wales for the year 1913–14 with the estimates for 1932–33, shows that the expenditure of the local authorities has increased from £30,000,000 to £76,750,000. The expenditure on higher education has increased from £4,400,000 to £16,280,000, and on elementary education from £25,600,000 to £60,470,000.

The following detailed analysis of expenditure on elementary education is given:

(1) Loan charges have increased from £3,000,000 to £4,300,000, not perhaps an unreasonable in-

crease in view of the springing up of new centers of population since the war.

(2) Medical services and schools for defective children have increased from about £850,000 to about £4,000,000. This, for the most part, represents the creation of a new service of medical inspection and treatment, which is a health rather than an educational service, and is administered by the Board of Education only on behalf of the Ministry of Health.

(3) Local administration and the running expenses of elementary schools have increased from about £5,250,000 to about £12,750,000. From this apparent increase of £7,500,000 should be deducted some allowance for an increase of rates and taxes on school buildings (obviously purely an accounting item); but the real increase can not be less than £6,500,000, of which only £2,750,000 could be justified by the change in the price level. This is probably the item of expenditure which is most difficult to justify, but it is a highly miscellaneous item, on which further information would be desirable.

(4) The salaries of teachers have increased from £16,416,000 to £38,925,000 (*i.e.*, even after the recent cuts). Up to 1931 the number of head and class teachers had increased by only 217, attendance at elementary schools having fallen by rather more than 400,000; but there had been an increase of 17,089 in the number of certificated teachers and a decrease of 16,872 in the number of uncertificated and supplementary teachers. On the other hand there had been a decrease in head teacherships of about 2,000. But the enormous increase in the salary bill is, of course, mainly due to the higher scales of salary. Perhaps the fairest way to state the whole problem of teaching costs is to say that the educational administrator must provide teachers for about 150,000 classes in elementary schools. At present the cost of teaching a class, including handicraft instruction and supervision by the headmaster, is about £255. The question to be decided is whether this is a reasonable cost.

(5) We are spending £350,000 on providing meals for school children. The pre-war expenditure is not ascertainable.

RUSSIAN EDUCATIONAL EXHIBIT IN NEW YORK

The World-Telegram reports that the first comprehensive exhibit in the United States of the education of children in Soviet Russia was opened in New York City on June 16 at the American Russian Institute. It will be open daily except Sunday until June 30.

More than 1,000 items illustrate phases of education of children from 5 to 16 in the seven-year schools, corresponding to elementary schools here.

The predominantly industrial character of education in the Soviet is illustrated even in the children's art work, which pictures factories, trains.

On display are a school wall newspaper, a collection of decorative design, water-colors and crayon drawings, note-books of students.

Text-books dealing with every subject taught in the schools, all of which bear on the building of a socialistic state, are shown. The text-books are in many languages; the Soviet does not attempt to compel all children to learn Russian, but allows each of its divisions to teach in its own language, hoping thereby to develop local pride and to permit the unhampered growth of all its peoples.

Science books are based on the needs of the Five-year Plan. One book, for schools in Azerbeidjan, is called "How Little Al became an Edison" and has a picture of the American inventor on the cover.

All children receive industrial training. They work part time as apprentices in factories and on collective farms and have definite social responsibilities to fulfil. More than 100 photographs of children at their school work are exhibited at the institute.

Among the books used for English language reading are works by Jack London, A. Williams, Seton Thompson, O. Henry and Michael Gold. O. Henry is used for elementary work in reading. There are translations of books by Rudyard Kipling and Victor Hugo.

THE RELIEF OF NEEDY CHILDREN IN NEW YORK CITY

New York City's teaching staff and other Board of Education employees have contributed $2,000,000 for the relief of needy school children, according to an estimate given in a report made public by Frederick D. Chambers, auditor of the School Board and treasurer of the School Relief Fund.

Last month, the report showed that the teachers contributed $256,752 from their April checks. This was a decrease from the $264,173 contributed from the March salaries.

The average daily expenditures from the fund

increased from $846 in October to $4,971 in May. The report shows more than a quarter of a million dollars spent for shoes, another quarter of a million for food supplies and nearly $100,000 for clothing.

At the close of business on May 27, $1,591,088 had been made available to the fund since it started its current season last fall. Of this sum $1,484,226 had been contributed by the teachers and other employees, $1,335 was interest on bank balances, $2,691 was in lump sum contributions, $10,031 was receipts from two foot-ball games and $92,803 was carried over from the fund for the last academic year.

Including $350,000 which has been set aside thus far to continue relief work during the coming summer vacation, $1,588,297 has been spent to provide food, clothing and other necessities for needy children and their families, leaving the fund with an unencumbered balance of $2,791. In addition, the district superintendents and the Bureau of Attendance had a balance of $7,279 ready for use on May 27.

THE FIRST COMMENCEMENT OF YESHIVA COLLEGE

AMONG the hundreds of commencements throughout the United States this spring the exercises of Yeshiva College, a small institution in New York City, held on June 16 had an exceptional educational interest. This interest was attested by the presence on the platform of delegates representing leading eastern colleges and universities and by the addresses of U. S. Commissioner of Education, William John Cooper; Associate Commissioner Herman Cooper, of the New York State Education Department; Dr. John H. Finley, of the *New York Times;* President Frederick B. Robinson, of the College of the City of New York, and others.

The explanation was that the nineteen young men who received the bachelor of arts degree were the first graduates of "the only college of liberal arts and sciences under Jewish auspices in this land." Yeshiva College was founded four years ago as a college granting the degrees of bachelor of arts and bachelor of science, organized at the same time as an integral part of the Rabbi Isaac Elchanan Theological Seminary. As stated by President Bernard Revel in his address to the graduates, Yeshiva College "has set itself the task of training a select group of young men who combine zeal for knowledge with a large ability for learning, to attain intellectual and spiritual integrity; it endeavors to recognize the aptitude of its individual students and to help create the conditions for their growth and development."

The aim of Yeshiva was further expressed by Dean S. R. Safir as "to afford a harmonious union of culture and spirituality, to provide Jewish youth with a college education that will meet the standard of the highest educational institutions in America, but which will be coordinated and closely bound with the spirit and the tenets of Judaism."

The present student body includes young men from seventeen states and Canada. Of the caliber of these undergraduates Dr. Henry E. Garrett, of Columbia University, stated after administering psychological tests that "the Yeshiva student is able to do effectively much more work than the ordinary college student because, as our tests show, he is highly intelligent." Professor Charles F. Horne, of the College of the City of New York, who is an associated faculty member at Yeshiva, said "I have never met youths more able, more alive, more eager to improve and develop themselves."

On the side of scholarship Yeshiva College is making a contribution in the publication, begun last September, of a quarterly journal *Scripta Mathematics,* devoted to the philosophy, history and expository treatment of mathematics. Dr. Jekuthiel Ginsburg is editor, and the associate editors are Drs. Raymond Clare Archibald, Cassius Jackson Keyser, Louis Charles Karpinski, Gino Loria, Lao Genevra Simons and David Eugene Smith.—R. W.

1932 SUMMER OFFERINGS IN HIGHER EDUCATION

REPERCUSSIONS of the present financial situation, which have been felt in higher educational institutions this year, have had their inevitable effect upon many curriculum programs. The efforts that have been made during the past decade to develop, through courses dealing with problems of college administration and college teaching, opportunities for the in-service professional improvement of college administrators and faculty members, have suffered a serious setback. This is particularly true in the case of the 1932 summer session offerings. A number of institutions have been forced, in line with retrenchment programs, to sacrifice their work in this field; some are deferring it entirely during the present emergency, while others are finding it financially desirable to offer only those courses most likely to enroll the largest number of students. On the other hand, several universities are this summer for the first time projecting professional courses on higher education and, as in previous years, a number of institutions are continuing the comprehensive programs they have developed.

The more comprehensive programs are to be found at the Universities of Chicago, Kentucky, Michigan and Southern California; at New York, Ohio State and Stanford Universities; at George Peabody College for Teachers, and at Teachers College of Columbia University. Basic or general courses on the organization and administration of the American college and university, as well as specific problems of instruction and the professional duties of the various administrative officers will be offered this summer at these institutions. General courses will also be given at the Universities of Illinois, Minnesota, Pittsburgh, West Virginia and Wyoming; at Duke University, and at Iowa State College.

While problems of student personnel and guidance are included in the general courses on administration, specific professional courses in this growing area of work will be offered at the Universities of Chicago, Michigan, Southern California and Wyoming; at New York, Ohio State, Pittsburgh and Syracuse Universities; at George Peabody College, and at Teachers College of Columbia University. At the last named institution a series of lectures and discussions on special problems in student housing will be conducted as a conference extending from July 18 to 29.

Interest in courses concerned with the junior-college movement has been growing steadily, and such course offerings and the registrations in them this summer will in all probability exceed those of previous years. Courses dealing specifically with the junior college are being offered at the Universities of California, Chicago, Nebraska and Southern California; at Northwestern, Ohio State, and Stanford Universities; at George Peabody College, and at Teachers College of Columbia University. Problems related to the junior college, both as an administrative unit and as a movement in higher education, are also included in the basic or general courses in college administration and college teaching offered at several of these institutions and at the Universities of Illinois, Michigan, Minnesota and Wyoming, and at New York and West Virginia Universities.

Courses dealing with the organization and administration of teacher training institutions will be given this summer at the Universities of Chicago and Minnesota; at George Washington, New York and the Ohio State Universities; and at Colorado State Teachers College, George Peabody College and Teachers College of Columbia University. In an intersession term running from June 6 to July 1 two courses are now being given at New York University on "Current Problems in Teachers-College and Normal-School Education"; these will be followed in the summer session by a series of related courses dealing with the functions, organization, administration and curriculum problems of teacher-training institutions. Executives, supervisors and instructors in teachers colleges and normal schools will have the opportunity at Teachers College of Columbia University to take a special full year course on "Organization and Supervision of Student Teaching" conducted over a period extending from July 1 to September 16.

There will be several important conferences held in conjunction with these summer programs on higher education. The fourth Institute for Administrative Officers of Institutions of Higher Education will be held at the University of Chicago from July 13 to 15, with a program centering around the theme, "Provisions for the Individual in College Education." A special conference on professionalized subject-matter will be held at New York University from June 28 to July 1. The second annual Conference for College and University Business Officers will be held on the campus of the Ohio State University during the summer quarter; technical problems dealing with the financial administration of higher education will be studied intensively during the three days the conference will be in session.

The demands made upon our colleges and universities, especially since the world war, for an enlarged and more effective service have stimulated a wide-spread professional interest in problems of higher education. These summer courses are concrete evidences of that interest and of the decided movement on the part of those engaged in college teaching and college administration to seek guidance and improvement in their chosen work. Through them positive efforts are being made to "educate the educators."

Archie M. Palmer,
Associate Secretary of the Association of American Colleges

THE ATLANTIC CITY MEETING OF THE NATIONAL EDUCATION ASSOCIATION

The seventieth annual convention of the National Education Association will open in Atlantic City, Saturday evening, June 25. A statement in regard to the preliminary program was printed in the issue of School and Society for April 16, 1932, but further details can now be given. Features of the opening program are an address by the historian, Hendrik Willem Van Loon, author of "The Story of Mankind"; and the keynote address of the convention delivered by Henry Lester Smith, dean of the School of education of the University of Indiana.

An artistic combination of music and addresses characterizes the vesper service which will be held Sunday afternoon in the great ballroom of the Atlantic City Auditorium. The principal address will be delivered by Reverend Edwin Holt Hughes, who was elected bishop of the Methodist Episcopal Church, Washington, D. C., at the quadrennial convention of the general conference recently held in Atlantic City.

At the Sunday night session, Reverend Ralph W. Sockman, author and radio pastor of the Madison Avenue M. E. Church, New York City, will discuss "Character Education of To-morrow." President Clifton D. Gray, of Bates College, will speak on "Living For the Ages."

The Monday morning session will be devoted to the theme: Education, Crime and Social Progress. Lewis E. Lawes, warden of Sing Sing Prison, Ossining, New York, will discuss the "Prevention of Crime through Education." Cora Wilson Stewart, director, National Illiteracy Crusade, Washington, D. C., will show how illiteracy is an important factor for consideration in the crime situation. Albert E. Winship, editor of *The Journal of Education,* Boston, will speak on "America's New Opportunity and Responsibility." Ernest W. Butterfield, state commissioner of education, Hartford, Connecticut, will define the place of education in the solution of social problems.

A high peak of the convention will be reached Monday night at the general sessions when President Florence Hale will deliver the presidential address on the subject, "Firm Foundations." Aaron Sapiro, noted New York attorney, has selected for his topic on this program, "Is Education the Jonah of the Industrial Crisis?" William J. Bogan, superintendent of schools, Chicago, will place before the teachers some important plans for meeting the emergency in education.

Not for many years has an annual convention offered such a variety of program features. The Tuesday night general session will be devoted to an unusual use of the radio in bringing in part of a presentation from New York, while the remainder is given on the auditorium stage. This number will be given by Seth Parker and members of his well-known cast engaged in popularizing many of the old fashioned New England virtues and ideals. President Florence Hale, in connection with this program, will illustrate a regular number of the "Our American Schools" series which she has directed throughout the winter months from the headquarters building of the National Education Association in Washington. The Tuesday night program will close with an address by Mrs. Edith Nourse Rogers, member of Congress from Massachusetts, who will emphasize education for economic independence in an address entitled, "The Most for Your Money."

Convention sessions are pointed toward the critical period through which education and all other public services are passing. They will be designed to help educators to return to their positions best prepared to maintain the services of the schools at their present standard. Educational leaders from Kentucky, Virginia,

Iowa, California, Wisconsin and Illinois will tell the conventioners how the schools of their states are meeting the emergency in education. Miss Bess Goodykoontz, assistant U. S. Commissioner of Education, will represent that office on this program.

The convention city is the world's playground, and teachers and local citizens are making available to teachers the amusements and recreations which the city affords. Hotel rates have been specially reduced for the convention and because of the economy of attendance and the proximity of Atlantic City to large population centers, a great number of delegates and members is expected.

Belmont Farley

EDUCATIONAL NOTES AND NEWS

Members of the the faculty of Bowdoin College on June 17 tendered an informal dinner to President Kenneth C. M. Sills on his completion of fifteen years of administration as active head of the college. Some forty-five members of the teaching staff were present at the dinner, which was held in the Moulton Union. Professor Wilmot B. Mitchell, senior member of the active faculty, served as presiding officer, and presented the President and Mrs. Sills with a silver bowl.

A portrait painting of Dr. Ernest Carroll Moore, vice-president and provost of the University of California at Los Angeles, has been presented to the university by three hundred art students and members of the art faculty. The presentation was made at a formal meeting in the exhibition hall of the Art Department by Miss Laura Frances Andreson, an art student. Regent Edward A. Dickson accepted the gift on the part of the university. The painting is the work of Edouard A. Vysekal, lecturer in fine arts, who has worked for nearly two years on the portrait.

A portrait of Dr. Arthur Stanley Pease, retiring president of Amherst College, was presented to the college at the annual alumni dinner on June 18.

A portrait of Dr. J. McKeen Cattell has been presented to him by colleagues and former students. The painting is by Leopold Seyffert, N.A. The committee in charge consisted of Professor A. T. Poffenberger, of Columbia University; Professor S. I. Franz, of the University of California at Los Angeles, and Dr. Frederick P. Keppel, of the Carnegie Corporation.

Dr. Joseph S. Taylor, for twenty-five years a district superintendent of schools, New York City, now retired, received at the recent commencement of the Dalton School, New York, a medal for outstanding service to the institution. Dr. Taylor is a member of the board of trustees of the school. He received a similar medal at the commencement of New York University on June 8, "to honor one who through good deeds has served Alma Mater." Dr. Taylor holds the degree of Pd.D. and Ph.D. from New York University, and his son, Deems Taylor, the composer of "The King's Henchman" and "Peter Ibbetson," also has from the same institution the degrees of A.B. and of doctor of music.

Lehigh University recently conferred the honorary degree of doctor of laws upon Raymond Walters, a graduate of Lehigh in the class of 1907, who since 1921 has been dean of Swarthmore College and a member of the staff of School and Society. Dr. Walters is president-elect of the University of Cincinnati.

Chancellor Frederick M. Hunter, of the University of Denver, has received the honorary degree of LL.D. from the University of Colorado in recognition of his educational activities and as a "friendly gesture."

Dr. Harvey N. Davis, president of the Stevens Institute of Technology, gave the commencement address at Haverford College. On this occasion the honorary degree of doctor of laws was conferred on Louis Round Wilson, librarian of the University of North Carolina, and Dr. H. H. Goddard, psychologist of the Ohio State University.

At the sixty-second annual commencement exercises of the University of New Hampshire the degree of doctor of laws was conferred on

Miss Grace Abbott, chief of the Children's Bureau of the United States Department of Labor.

THE doctorate of laws has been conferred by Boston College on Dennis A. Dooley, dean of the Boston College Law School, and on Joseph H. Beale, assistant dean of the Harvard Law School.

ALFRED UNIVERSITY conferred at commencement on June 14 honorary degrees as follows: doctor of laws, Dr. John Cayce Morrison, assistant commissioner of elementary education of the New York State Department of Education; doctor of pedagogy, Jay William Crofoot, principal of Grace High School in China, and Edgar G. Lantman, executive secretary of the State Teachers Retirement System; doctor of music, Percy Fullinwider, director of the violin department of the Lawrence (Wisconsin) Conservatory of Music; doctor of science, Joseph Charles Park, director of the Industrial Teachers Training State Normal School. Dr. Morrison gave the oration, his subject being "Liberal Education in Elementary Schools."

HELEN KELLER has sailed for Europe to receive the degree of LL.D. at Glasgow University. Her first public appearance in London will be on Monday, July 4, when she will attend a complimentary luncheon at the headquarters of the National Institute for the Blind in Great Portland Street, and open the institute's new school for blind masseurs.

THE Henry Russel Award of the University of Michigan for 1932 has been made to Dr. William Leake Ayres, assistant professor of mathematics. Each year a member of the faculty is selected to deliver the Russel lecture and at the time the lecture is presented a younger member of the faculty, of the rank of assistant professor or instructor, is cited for the Russel Award.

As a part of the commencement activities of Colgate University, the alumni held in the Huntington Gymnasium on June 11 a dinner in honor of fifteen members of the university faculty whose terms of service aggregate 537 years. The guests of honor, with their subjects and years of service at the university, were as follows: Joseph Frank McGregory, chemistry, 49 years; William Henry Crawshaw, literature, 45 years; William Franklin Langworthy, botany, 42 years; Robert Webber Moore, German, 42 years; Elmer William Smith, English, 41 years; Wayland Morgan Chester, biology, 37 years; Frank Lucius Shepardson, Greek, 36 years; Clement Dexter Child, physics, 34 years; Frank Carman Ewart, Romance languages, 33 years; Roy Burnett Smith, chemistry, 33 years; Ellery Channing Huntington, physical education, 32 years; Arthur Whipple Smith, mathematics, 30 years; Albert Burns Stewart, mathematics, 29 years; Harold Orville Whitnall, geology, 28 years; William Mangam Lawrence, Christian ethics, 26 years. The speakers at the dinner included James C. Colgate, president of the board of trustees; Dr. George B. Cutten, president of the university, and Professor William Henry Crawshaw.

THE *Journal* of the National Education Association for June prints portraits of presidents of Teachers Colleges who have been elected during the last year. These are: W. E. Lessenger, Detroit, Michigan; H. C. Gossard, Las Vegas, New Mexico; M. A. Beeson, Edmond, Oklahoma; Albert Lindsay Rowland, Shippensburg, Pennsylvania; Forrest R. Polk, Oshkosh, Wisconsin; J. D. Hill, Superior, Wisconsin.

DR. JOHN DEWEY will be visiting professor of education at the Johns Hopkins University during the first term of the academic year, and Dr. Isaac L. Kandel during the second term.

BERNARD FAY, professor of American civilization at the Collège de France, has been appointed visiting professor of French studies at the University of Buffalo for the first semester of the coming academic year. The professorship, of which he is the first occupant, was established through a gift of the late Mrs. Joseph T. Jones, of Buffalo.

DR. CARROLL D. CHAMPLIN, of the Pennsylvania State College, will exchange positions with Dr. J. J. Osuna, of the University of Puerto Rico, during the first semester of next year. Dr. Champlin will offer courses in educational psychology and the history of education.

PROFESSOR FRANK H. RISTINE succeeds Professor Edward Fitch as dean of Hamilton College, Clinton, New York, and Wallace B. Johnson succeeds Professor Samuel J. Saunders as registrar.

MR. HAROLD P. THOMAS, director of research at Springfield, Massachusetts, has resigned in order to accept the directorship of the department of education at Lehigh University.

DR. RHYS CARPENTER, director of the American School of Classical Studies at Athens, has resigned this position and has returned to the United States.

AFTER thirty-seven years as head of the music department of Vassar College, Professor George Coleman Gow has retired. Although his retirement was announced last year, he remained to see the dedication of Belle Skinner Hall of Music. A large bas-relief of Professor Gow was unveiled in the hall on June 9.

N. HENRY BLACK, assistant professor of education and successively instructor of mathematics, who was lately appointed director of the summer school of Harvard University, has been made assistant professor of physics.

SUPERINTENDENT C. C. RUSSELL, of New Haven, Connecticut, has been reelected for a five-year term.

DR. ROBERT CHESTER ROBERTS, head of the department of chemistry, has been elected president of the Colgate chapter of the American Association of University Professors. Carl W. Munshower, assistant professor of mathematics, was elected secretary.

DR. EARLE B. BABCOCK, associate director of the European center of the Carnegie Endowment for International Peace at Paris, will be the American representative this year on the League of Nations Committee on Intellectual Cooperation, substituting for Dr. R. A. Millikan. The plenary sessions of the committee will open at Geneva on July 18.

PROFESSOR WILLIAM A. BROWN, JR., and Carel Jan Smit, of the department of economics of Brown University, have undertaken with a grant from the Rockefeller Foundation a study which aims at a reinterpretation of the international gold standard in the light of its history.

JOS. F. WRIGHT, director of radio station WILL, University of Illinois, has replaced R. C. Higgy as a member of the National Committee on Education by Radio. Mr. Wright was recently elected president of the Association of College and University Broadcasting Stations, and as such represents that organization on the committee. Mr. Higgy has been a member of the committee since it was organized in 1930.

THE next biennial conference of the World Federation of Education Associations will be held in Dublin.

The Pennsylvania School Journal reports that in calling the next meeting of the Pennsylvania Education Congress for next November 9 and 10 at Harrisburg, State Superintendent Rule announces that it will be largely a forum session with a view to obtaining opinions from leading schoolmen and laymen alike on just what should be done in the future development of education in the commonwealth. The program will revolve around plans for the 1933 General Assembly, with special reference to the problems of school finance and the proposed larger unit organization throughout the state. There will be a predominance of informal discussions rather than set speeches by educators from outside the state. General sessions will be conducted on the forum plan in an effort to obtain viewpoints on educational problems as they exist in various parts of the state. To add to the effectiveness of the program prominent laymen will be called in so as to obtain for the congress the best informed lay opinions in the immediate future of education. The congress is an official gathering called by the superintendent of public instruction and made up of all county and district superintendents and presidents of the state teachers colleges, with invitations to all independent colleges and private schools for voluntary participation.

THE Public Congress for Childhood Education will be held from October 1 to 5 in Berlin-Schöneberger Rathaus under the auspices of the Bund Entschiedener Schulreformer. The purpose of the congress is to call to the attention of individuals, the family and public corporations their responsibility in regard to the education of children. General information concerning the meeting may be obtained from Professor Paul Oestreich, Berlin-Friedenau, Menzelstrasse 1, Germany.

THE National University Extension Association has admitted to membership the University of Denver after an investigation of the latter's extension activities.

BEGINNING with the new term students attending evening courses in the engineering school of Cooper Union, New York City, will be able to obtain regular college degrees. Under an arrangement with the New York State Board of Education at Albany a six-year evening course will be accepted as the equivalent of the regular four-year day course.

AN Associated Press dispatch reports that President Hoover on June 11 signed a measure long under consideration, designed to remove juvenile offenders against federal laws from the United States courts and into the juvenile courts of their home communities. Proposed by the Wickersham commission many months ago, and carrying the endorsement of social workers throughout the country, the act will remove juvenile treatment from the federal courts entirely, except where local courts refuse to accept the cases. In signing the measure in the presence of Mr. William D. Mitchell, Attorney-General, who indorsed it, the President said: "This measure is an important step forward in that it sets an example through its recognition by the Federal Government of the principle that even the relatively small number of juveniles in the federal system be handled on a modern scientific basis. It is also a recognition by the Federal Government of the juvenile court as the proper place for the handling of the cases of all juveniles and is an acceptance of the principle that juvenile offenders are the product of and the responsibility of their home communities."

SEVEN members of the Culver family have relinquished ownership of Culver Military Academy to make it the trust of a permanent foundation, according to an announcement made by Bertram B. Culver, son of the founder and one of the owners. All the buildings, property and funds of the academy, valued at about $6,000,000, have been placed in trust for the foundation. Mr. Culver, who is president of the board of trustees, made the announcement at the school's thirty-eighth commencement exercises. Among the scheduled speakers at the commencement were Dr. Robert M. Hutchins, president of the University of Chicago; Admiral Hugh Rodman, former commander of the Pacific fleet, and Albert R. Erskine, chairman of the board of the Studebaker Corporation. Henry Harrison Culver, a St. Louis stove manufacturer, founded the school in 1894, but he died when it was only a few years old. His son, Edwin Raymond Culver, was at its head until his death in 1930. The members of the family who have relinquished ownership are Mr. and Mrs. Bertram B. Culver, Bertram B. Culver, Jr., Mrs. Edwin R. Culver, Edwin R. Culver, Jr., and Henry Harrison Culver, of St. Louis, and Gene Gordon Culver, of Philadelphia.

THE development during recent years of interest in commercial education has led a group of English teachers to organize a summer school specially for teachers engaged in the commercial departments of central or secondary schools, and for those who aspire to secure such appointments. The course now being organized will be held at Wadham College, University of Oxford, for 12 days beginning on July 25. Intensive study and practice will be undertaken each morning session in shorthand, bookkeeping and typewriting, together with an introduction to modern language study and to commerce. Students may select from these the subjects which they particularly wish to study; and all students will attend the seminar on method, to be held each afternoon as an integral part of the course. No previous knowledge of the various subjects will be assumed. Teachers of well-known experience in commercial education have been appointed to take the subject-courses. Professor J. J. Findlay, who has been associated with language learning and with commercial education during the last few years, will act as director of studies and chairman of the committee. Applications for the prospectus, which gives full information regarding the summer school, should be addressed to the Honorable Assistant Secretary, Mr. C. F. Charie, Kern House, Kingsway, London.

REDUCTIONS in the salary budget of the University of Michigan, ranging from 6 to 10 per cent., with a few cases amounting to 26 per cent., were announced by the Board of Regents at their monthly meeting on May 27. University scholarships for senior students in the professional schools and for American Indian students were announced at the meeting also. A blanket slash in salaries such as has occurred in some institutions was discarded as uneconomic, and a system of individual reductions was followed after investigation in order to adjust all salaries on an equitable basis, said Regent R. Perry Shorts in a press statement. In balancing the budget every activity and position was fully studied to determine where expenses could be decreased with least permanent damage to the institution. After eliminating certain positions and adjusting teaching loads a general reduction of all salaries, amounting to from 6 per cent. on the lower salaried employees to 10 per cent. on the higher salaried staff, was made, with some individual reductions as high as 26.8 per cent. The result is a total reduction of the salary budget amounting to approximately 8 per cent., exclusive of the University Hospital. State appropriations for the university were cut about 15 per cent. for 1932–33, but income from fees, endowments and other sources made the operating budget only about 11 per cent. less than before.

SPECIAL education for the more than 13,600 mentally retarded school children in California is recommended by the Committee on Mental Hygiene which recently completed its state-wide survey, according to the Children's Bureau of the U. S. Department of Labor. California had in its public schools more than 13,600 mentally retarded children at the time of a recent mental-hygiene survey. More than 5,700 of these had intelligence quotients below 70 and might be considered feeble-minded. Of 38 school systems specially investigated during the survey, 26 provided special classes for the training of retarded children. The committee appointed by the State Department of Social Welfare to direct the survey recommended that every school system having more than ten children whose low intelligence makes them classroom problems, should appoint a specially trained teacher for the group, the state to give financial aid when the community resources are insufficient for the purpose. It also recommended the establishment of school clinics, vocational guidance work and the employment of visiting teachers.

THE deposit of funds of a school board in the trust department of a trust company which has been unable to obtain the required depository bond would be illegal in Pennsylvania, according to an opinion by Deputy Attorney General Harris C. Arnold addressed to W. M. Denison, deputy state superintendent of public instruction. Under an act of 1929, trust companies are permitted to use in their business trust funds awaiting investment or distribution, provided certain securities are set aside to protect the funds so employed. This act, however, applies only to the administration of funds held by trust companies in fiduciary capacities and has nothing to do with deposits. If a school board should enter into an agreement whereby a trust company would be created a trustee for the administration of school funds, so as to bring the money within the terms of the 1929 act, the school board would be surrendering control of its funds, which it could not lawfully do.

DISCUSSION

TEACHER TRAINING PRIMARILY A STATE FUNCTION

IN an article entitled "Teacher Training for Large Cities," which appeared in SCHOOL AND SOCIETY, September 19, 1931, the author deplores the fact that so many teacher-training institutions are located in rural districts and in small cities, and so few in large cities. The present writer concedes that the argument there presented was very true in many respects, but believes that there were certain fallacies that should be pointed out.

The author has very properly emphasized the fact that teacher training has been more definitely accepted as a state function than has any other form of higher education except agriculture. His statement that state authorities acted unwisely in allocating teacher-training institutions by omitting so many large cities which include so large a percentage of a state's population and which pay so large a share of the bills of the state, is valid. However, when the argument is carried to the point of recommending the abandonment of state control and the substitution of city control, the present writer finds himself in total disagreement. Educational science and history have established in the United States the wisdom of state control as against local control of education, and the teacher-training institutions very properly constitute a division of the state's educational system. The fact that the states have failed at times to give sufficient consideration to large cities and have taken the theory of geographical distribution of teacher-training institutions too literally does not invalidate the principle of state control, nor does it in the writer's judgment invalidate the entire plan of distribution. The essential principle in this plan is sound and should not be minimized or discarded, but retained and interpreted broadly, instead of strictly and literally. The state should, where possible, locate some teacher-training institutions in some of the larger cities of the state. It would not, however, be possible to include all the large cities in most states, because their great number forbids. Even if possible it would not be desirable. Neither is it necessary nor desirable entirely to omit smaller cities.

A state plan, giving due consideration to rural as well as city units, should, therefore, take precedence over all other relating matters. The rural units should have a smaller number of these institutions because they include a minor portion of the state's population. But much of the argument against these rural training institutions is not valid. Granting the truth of the claim that the intelligence rating of the students of the state teachers colleges is lower than that of students of city teachers colleges, and assuming, therefore, that the city product should be chosen because of its better quality, nevertheless, in accordance with our principles of democracy, the rural population deserves a proportionate place in the program.

A better way to attack this problem is by setting up a selective principle which would eliminate the unfit and the undesirable students, irrespective of residence.

By setting up high standards for teachers and by applying our better methods of selection, based upon such data as high-school records, teacher estimates, intelligence and subject tests, state teacher-training institutions could secure a sufficient number of good students fitted by native ability, interest and character to become excellent teachers. The argument that the better students reside in the large cities and that they would not be interested in attending teacher-training institutions unless it were located in their city, is not convincing. If students become as much interested in the teaching profession as they do in law, medicine and other professions, they will find ways of attending the state school wherever located. Obversely many students of city teacher-training institutions have no genuine interest in teaching. The reasons for attending these institutions are frankly stated by such students as the low cost of training and its direct pathway to economic competency. These reasons are not good and sufficient, and in effect they operate in direct opposition to our principles of vocational guidance, to our basic principles of democratic education and to the standards of the profession.

It seems clear, then, that city teacher-training institutions would defeat in a large measure the purpose for which they are created, by enticing into them students without proper natural aptitudes and full appreciation of the duties and responsibilities of the profession.

Our philosophy of education, above all things, purports to build up large group consciousness, as free as possible from local bias and prejudice. The inbreeding which would inevitably result from the city teacher-training system would surely defeat in some measure this great objective. Its effect would be slow, subversive and subtle. New ideas, new slants and new blood are indispensable to the healthy growth and best development of thought and of life activities. To reduce the evil effects of inbreeding, some cities deliberately plan to draw in from other school systems a certain number of teachers each year, even when scores of graduates of their own city normals are on the waiting list clamoring for appointment. This policy obtains, notwithstanding their claim of greater efficiency in training and the higher rating of their institutional product. The good effects lie presumably in the added stimulation of intellectual and professional interest resulting from the inclusion of these outside people. Similarly, it may reasonably be assumed that a better group of students of the state institutions would be found, because the state set-up would facilitate the operation of the selective principle.

The political feature of the city teacher-training system alone is bad enough to damage greatly the best plans and programs of education, the best interests of the people of the city, and ultimately the best interests of the state and nation. The writer is thoroughly convinced that city residence, political connections, and the prospect of an easy way to the city payroll are the determining factors in the minds of a vast number of students. Where the set-up is such as is usually true of city teacher-training institutions, and such that graduation from these institutions means automatic appointment to a permanent teaching position in these city school systems, these institutions are inclined to take on a commercial atmosphere, which submerges the atmosphere of idealism which should suffuse the entire student body. Failing in the idealistic objective, these institutions in this respect fail to function at the proper level, and hence fail to render a most vital and indispensable service. The extent to which the city institution thus crippled suffers will vary, but any lowering of standards in this respect would have far-reaching results of such a nature and character as largely to defeat the best purposes of the entire school system.

Summarizing, then, the principle of state control of teacher-training institutions under state boards that are carefully selected with reference to intellectual and personal qualifications, is far better than complete control by local or city governments. Just as local, rural and village school boards are being eliminated and county boards representing larger areas are replacing them, and local power of certification of teachers has been withdrawn in favor of state control, likewise, in recognition of the vital underlying principle of our democracy, *viz.*, the greatest good of the largest number, local units should not be permitted to set up independently their own standards and to operate accordingly without state supervision and control. In the interest of larger intellectual development of broad sympathetic understanding, of the diminution and elimination of bias, prejudice, sectionalism and localism, a program which calls for the modification and perfection of the state's plan of administering teacher-training institutions is the proper course to pursue instead of the relinquishment of state authority to city control.

J. A. WILLIAMS

FULLERTON, CALIFORNIA

THE PROBLEM AND VALUE OF COLLATERAL READING

THE problem of collateral reading is as old as teaching itself. How it can be done and how to get it done has vexed teachers in every department of school activity. This paper will not show how to get it done, but will reveal one method of how it has been done by one teacher over a period of two years, and some of the probable values accrued to the students thereby.

First, a simple method was set up and followed. In each history class a minimum requirement of 150 pages of reading each week was required for each student. At the end of the week each one had to turn in a bibliography card, on which was stated the author, book and number of pages read in each book. Also, each student had to hand in notes in the form of short quotations taken from the readings. The note had to be properly headed; it had to be one specific idea, or complete thought; and at the bottom of the card the name of the author, book and exact page from which the quotation was selected had to be cited. On Mondays the teacher took a few minutes at the beginning of the recitation to comment on the notes, ask questions about the books read, and receive general criticism (good and bad) from the students about their readings.

Publicity was given to the relative readings of the class on a bulletin board posted in the history room. Each student had a number, and in his column each week was posted the number of pages he had read. At the end of the quarter the total number of pages for each one was posted. On this same board the test grades of the students were recorded from time to time. Thus every student knew all the time just how he ranked with the rest of the class as to readings and as to test grades. This helped produce a spirit of competition in the class.

Records have been kept over a period of two years. During that time there were 38 classes above the freshman level and 6 first-year college classes which were checked. In these classes were 934 upper classmen and 228 freshmen, a total of 1,164 students. Of this number 9 per cent. made A; 42 per cent B; 38 per cent. C; 7 per cent. D; and 4 per cent. F. The average rankings in the freshman class alone were a little below these. The freshman percentage of A's and B's was smaller; the percentage of C's and D's was larger; and the F group was the same.

The value of collateral reading might have been shown in the relative number of high grades, and then again the teacher might be entirely responsible. So we can only attempt to evaluate these grades with reference to collateral reading by a comparison of the grades with the readings. With the fact in mind that students were required to read only 150 pages a week over an average period of ten weeks (the first and closing weeks of the quarters were not counted) the following tables were worked out. In making the tables the following terms are used: "Barely" means 1,500 pages, more or less; "one third" beyond means 2,000 pages more or less; "two thirds" means 2,500 pages more or less; and "twice" means 3,000 pages or above.

READINGS OF THE F GROUP

Barely, or below	90 per cent.
One third	10 " "

READINGS OF THE D GROUP

Barely	62 per cent.
One third	18 " "
Two thirds	20 " "

READINGS OF THE C GROUP

Barely	45 per cent.
One third beyond	23 " "
Two thirds beyond	20 " "
Twice	12 " "

READINGS OF THE B GROUP

Barely	20 per cent.
One third beyond	25 " "
Two thirds beyond	25 " "
Twice	30 " "

READINGS OF THE A GROUP

Barely	8 per cent.
One third beyond	6 " "
Two thirds beyond	24 " "
Twice	62 " "

An interpretation of these tables shows some interesting facts. Those who were consistently high in their readings fell in the A or B groups on their final grades. In the A group were a few scanty readers, but 86 per cent. of those who made A had done much more reading than was required. In the B group 55 per cent. had done more reading than was required. In the C group 32 per cent. had read more than was required, and the other 68 per cent. had stayed around the minimum. In the D group 62 per cent. had barely met requirements. The F group showed that 90 per cent. had read 1,500 pages or less. Consistently steady readers made consistently high grades on their tests and final examinations, while those who did very little reading generally averaged low grades on both tests and final examinations.

While the writer lays no claim to scientific conclusions on these data, there are some things that seem evident from this study, and they are herewith presented for what they are worth.

(1) A definite plan for handling the reading problem should be worked out in as simple a form as possible. If the competitive scheme can be used it will help create interest.

(2) The reading requirements should not be so high that students can not find time to do them, but they should require a definite amount of work each day or week.

(3) Class discussion of readings and notes will help create interest and cause students to read more widely and more carefully than they otherwise would.

(4) The consistent and wide reader is the more dependable student, and will not only make better grades, but will contribute more to the good of the class as a whole.

(5) If the teacher himself is thoroughly acquainted with the books used for collateral reading he can cite them, occasionally relate a story about them or their authors, and direct students to them for specific information. This adds to the interest of the students and shows them the value of studying more than one book in a course.

(6) Outside reading enlivens the course; it does away with rote recitation and brings into the class bits of information which help the

students to add to grasp the important details.

(7) There is no "dead class" which has a "live" instructor before it. A teacher dies (from the shoulders up) when he ceases to saturate his mind with a thorough knowledge of his subjects and the material written about them.

Z. T. JOHNSON

STATE TEACHERS COLLEGE,
HATTIESBURG, MISSISSIPPI

SPECIAL CORRESPONDENCE

EDUCATION OF THE JEWISH AND ARAB POPULATION IN PALESTINE[1]

EDUCATION in Palestine can conveniently be divided into two systems, that of the Jewish and the Arab population respectively, since the two have developed along totally different lines. That of the Jews is largely in the hands of the Education Department of the Zionist Executive, which undertook the task of organizing a uniform system of Hebrew education, which would be available for all Jewish children in Palestine, and which aimed at establishing a new Hebrew culture, uniting the old heritage of the East with the scientific achievements of the West. Of the 307 Jewish schools at present in Palestine, at least 207, with an attendance of over 28,000 pupils, are managed by the Zionist Department of Education. Hebrew is the language of instruction. Compulsory school attendance for Jews was established without any pressure from the State and boys and girls receive equal attention, about 53 per cent. of the pupils in the Zionist Executive's schools being girls. Even in the smallest villages elementary schools are established; kindergartens are a prominent feature, much attention being given to the physical well-being of the young pupils. Meals are supplied in nearly all of them and modern methods introduced. There are seven professional and technical schools; these include the agricultural training school for boys at Mikveh Israel, another for girls at Nahalal, the handicrafts school of the *Alliance Israélite* at Jerusalem, and the school of Arts and Crafts (Bezalel) at Jerusalem. There are also institutes for the teaching of music and commercial subjects. At the summit of the system is the Hebrew University, the foundation stone of which was laid in 1924; it has Arts and Science faculties, and devotes a good deal of time to research work.

[1] The educational systems in Palestine are described by the author in "The Holy Land under Mandate."

Arab education has had quite a different history. Under the Ottoman government the educational system was of a very elementary nature and Christian education was conducted entirely by private religious bodies or individuals. The Arabs were not allowed to use their own language in schools, Turkish being the only official tongue. Consequently hardly anyone was acquainted to any extent with the history or literature of the Arabic language. During the war an attempt was made to introduce a better type of school, but it was not until the British occupation that the work of educational reconstruction was really begun. Schools which had previously existed were re-opened and new ones established, and since these government schools were nearly all attended by Arabs, Arabic became the medium of instruction. A much more adequate system of education was planned and carried out. In 1919 the military administration voted 53,000 Egyptian pounds for the education budget. During this year 52 village grants-in-aid schools were opened, as well as new schools in nearly all the towns. The following year, the newly-appointed director of education under the civil administration, which was set up on July 1, 1920, drew up a program for the opening of 75 new schools per year for four years, which would, it was thought, give every child in Palestine an opportunity of attending school. Arrangements were also made for peripatetic teachers to visit the Bedouin tribes in outlying districts, and provisions were made for better qualified teachers. It was about this time, too, that courses of secondary education were instituted. Among a section of the Moslem population there was a certain prejudice against the education of women, but in the larger centers there is now an increasing demand for girls' schools and especially for instruction in hygiene and domestic science. In 1924–25 a revised elementary school syllabus was put into operation, providing in the larger centers for an eight-year course, the first two years of which were to be spent in kindergarten classes. Among the subjects taught figure the following: Arabic language, arithmetic, geometry, history, geography, nature study, hygiene, elementary science, English language, drawing, handwork, religion both Moslem and Christian, and physical training. Government education in Palestine is not confined to elementary instruction, provision being made for secondary classes in boys' schools in most of the towns. There is at present no government day school providing a secondary education for girls. The Women's Elementary Training College, and the Government Arab College, formerly the Men's Training College, train teachers for work in the schools, but the supply of available teachers is not equal to the demand, and untrained elementary teachers still have to be appointed temporarily to fill emergency vacancies. Special attention is given to technical and agricultural education, but here again lack of competent instructors has seriously handicapped the work. In recent years an interesting line of development has taken place in the matter of educational conferences which now play an important rôle. Besides the government schools there are numerous educational institutions conducted under Moslem authority, the chief of these being the kindergartens, elementary schools, secondary classes or schools and the theological seminary controlled by the Supreme Moslem Council. Many of the villages have shown a marked enthusiasm for education, and have raised very considerable sums of money for the erection of new school buildings, the repair of existing ones and for other educational requirements.

FANNIE FERN ANDREWS

QUOTATIONS

THE ANNUAL REPORT OF THE PRESIDENT OF YALE UNIVERSITY

THE annual report of Dr. James Rowland Angell reviews the progress made by Yale University during the ten years of his administration. The following summary has been given out by the secretary's office:

Among the outstanding developments were the payment of more nearly adequate salaries to the faculty, and the creation of a retiring allowance fund for Yale's teachers; the adoption of a group insurance plan for all faculty members and other employees; great additions to scholarship, fellowship and loan funds; the launching of the new residential college plan; the establishment of the School of Nursing and the Institute of Human Relations; the creation of the Department of Drama in the School of the Fine Arts; the erection of many new buildings, and the establishment of greatly needed professorial chairs. Many of these developments were made possible by special gifts. Others, such as the retiring allowance fund and the group insurance plan, together with enlarged scholarship aid and reduced income from investments, will result in a deficit of over $500,000 in the university's budget for this year.

In 1920–21 student enrolment at Yale was 3,820; in 1930–31 it was 5,914. If the university had not definitely limited its enrolment early in the decade these attendance figures would doubtless have doubled or trebled. The university has definitely adopted the policy of taking only as many students as it can teach effectively, and selects these from the many applicants as carefully as possible.

As a result of this procedure, carried into effect in the case of the undergraduate group by the careful and experienced chairman of the Board of Admissions and his colleagues, we not only have a very high average quality in our student body, but we have almost wholly eliminated the familiar college problem of the essentially incompetent. Students who fail after entrance do so by reason of laziness, distraction of outside affairs, or ill health and financial troubles. The improvement in undergraduate scholarship, while not reflected with entire accuracy by marks, is in many respects most reliably indicated in this manner. It is therefore interesting to observe that the average rating of our students has steadily and definitely risen throughout the decade, and twice in that period students in Yale College have broken all existing Yale records for excellence in scholarly achievement.

President Angell refers to Yale College's program of increased emphasis upon independent achievement, which includes honors work and the reading periods. There can be no question that both the depth and the breadth of scholarly interest among the students of the college has notably increased, and for this result all concerned are to be genuinely congratulated.

The development which has thus been going on has given occasion, like the parallel development in the severity of entrance standards and the seriousness of the work in the other undergraduate divisions, for abundant expression among Yale alumni of the radically divergent views which are current among them, as among the graduates of other American colleges. Dr. Angell continues:

There are not a few who still conceive the college as properly a kind of glorified country club, where young men of decent lineage and some pretense to education may live pleasantly for four years in an atmosphere not too heavily laden with the odor of books, with sport and the amenities of social life as the issues of most consequence. Over against this view, entertained in perhaps its most violent form by occasional well-to-do parents whose sons either can not, or will not, meet any but the most infantile tests and standards, stands the steady onward movement of all the leading educational institutions toward an honest emphasis on serious intellectual achievement and the qualities it breeds, as constituting the predominant justification for the existence of the college as an institution. The other qualities which may attach to it, or flow from it, are altogether secondary, valuable as many of them doubtless are. No one, for example, who has observed carefully and free of bias can doubt the values which inhere in athletic sports. But equally no such observer can question that too often the conduct of college sport has been open to the severest criticism, both as to its ideals and its practices.

The more serious of the abuses which had crept in are undoubtedly on the way to complete elimination, and in many institutions—Yale among them—the general tone of the sports program in its entirety is excellent. But whatever the prejudices involved in the country club conception, Yale at least is headed directly away from that ideal toward one in which solid intellectual endeavor at a high level is unequivocally requisite. Persons who are seeking a more relaxed and languid intellectual opportunity must look for it elsewhere. Nor does this for a moment mean that Yale is stressing merely the interests of the supposedly pale intellectual. Robust all-round personality is fortunately in no essential particular hostile to solid intellectual attainment.

I think it will be the opinion of later historians of Yale that in this decade no more striking advance has been made than that in the professional schools and the Graduate School. In part, this may be attributed to the fact that there was at this point more room for drastic improvement and certainly more flexible conditions in tradition and practice. In general, I believe this to be true. But, on the other hand, the situation is quite as genuinely due to the presence of a remarkable group of leaders in these divisions of the university, backed by faculties which, as their personnel was strengthened with able men, became increasingly ambitious for the promotion of the very highest and finest educational standards.

I feel sure that no American university has ever seen the status of an entire group of professional and advanced schools move forward so rapidly and so successfully to recognized leadership as have those at Yale in this decade now closed. The personnel has in most of the schools been greatly strengthened, and the educational procedures have, in many instances, been substantially revolutionized and in all instances materially improved.

Furthermore, this process of advancement has had as one of its important features a drastic limitation of the student body at many points, with the ensuing ability to select the very ablest candidates for admission—not simply the students qualified to meet the tests for entrance, but the very best of these. Five of these schools require the bachelor's degree from a reputable institution for admission. One requires two years of college work, and the remaining two restrict their degrees to students who have accomplished at least the equivalent of a college course. Throughout the entire group of professional schools, there has been a steady tendency to assimilate their scholarly standards to the highest requirements of the graduate schools; in other words, to train not merely men fit to take their places in the ranks of the professions, as these are now prosecuted in American life, but also men whose education will give them the richest possible contact with the whole historic and social background of contemporary life, and with a real understanding of the meaning of sound scholarship and the technique of creative work and of fundamental research. This trend which can, and should, go much further has brought about a unification of outlook and program (best exemplified in the Institute of Human Relations) which has been of inestimable value in creating a real university spirit, a real sense of the university as the vital center of their activities.

While this process of integration and development has been going forward in the professional schools of the university, a similar process, as between the undergraduate interests and the professional interests, has also developed in increasing measure wherever it was really practicable. Many undergraduates pursue studies in the School of the Fine Arts and in the School of Music where they receive preliminary training in one or other of the arts which later they plan to take up professionally. Through the collections assembled in the university galleries they are put in touch with the critically important contributions of the arts to the development of culture. Advanced undergraduates are also given instruction by members of the Graduate School faculty, when qualifications render this practicable and advantageous.

Not a few of our students are thus drawn into the academic profession and under particularly favorable conditions. I need not add further illustrations of the same trends. Suffice it to say that all these tendencies operate to give considerable numbers of our undergraduate students a much more vital sense than formerly of the range of the university's activities and the essential solidarity of these interests as part of the total educational program upon which the university is engaged.

REPORTS

POSTPONEMENT OF QUALIFICATION TESTS OF THE COLLEGE ENTRANCE EXAMINATION BOARD

THE proposal for qualification tests to be conducted by the College Entrance Examination Board will not be undertaken next year, according to a report recently made by Professor Carl Brigham, of Princeton University, associate secretary of the board. Professor Brigham states frankly that "we have had almost no response to our memorandum from the colleges," and further that "the number of candidates now provisionally promised is not sufficient to warrant the launching of the program in 1933." He estimates that approximately 1,300 candidates might be available if the proposed series of tests were offered next year but says that this "is too small a number to guarantee the solution of the technical difficulties. The scheme will not be set up unless it is technically sound."

As has already been set forth in SCHOOL AND SOCIETY, the proposed qualification tests would be taken by candidates for college in the middle of their last year in secondary school, the fields being English, mathematics and the modern foreign languages.

Protests were made against the plan at the meeting last spring of the Classical Association of New England because no provision was included for reading tests in Latin. The reply of Dr. Brigham, in his report, is that "we do not propose a permanent injunction against giving tests in Latin; we merely say that as we are setting up the program in the beginning we can not include this type of measurement for certain reasons."

The fundamental point is then emphasized by Dr. Brigham that the qualification tests would not duplicate the purpose of the examinations now given by the board or by the Educational Records Bureau, that "we are not proposing to give examinations in school subjects." He continues:

The board now has definitions of requirements covering its June examinations in forty or more school subjects or subdivisions of them. And, similarly, the examinations of the Educational Records Bureau are in specific school subjects. But in preparing the qualification tests, we are not compelled to write an examination within a definite requirement. These tests are more or less generalized examinations which are experimentally evolved. The verbal test will find out how well a candidate can read, but beyond that it does not trespass. We do not care whether he has learned to read by studying English or Latin or history, and we do not regard this ability as a necessary function of any particular classroom experience. We do not tell him to read any particular books or any particular body of literature.

The qualification tests will cover generalized fields. Instead of measuring a candidate's proficiency in physical geography, or Cicero or chemistry, or any other specific school subjects, these tests propose to describe several more or less independent characteristics of the individual. One proposed test will assign the candidate a position on a scale which locates him with respect to other individuals in his skill in reading his own vernacular and in his range of vocabulary. We test his efficacy as a social communicant. Another test will estimate his proficiency in a vernacular other than the one to which he was born. These reading tests in the modern foreign languages will closely resemble the tests in his own vernacular. Another test will describe his facility in using numbers and symbols for general numbers according to the rules of elementary algebra, and to perform those elementary symbolic manipulations necessary to future work in mathematics and science. Still another proposal is that of testing the candidate's efficiency in spatial thinking or in mental experimentation with spatial schemata.

Dr. Brigham concludes his report by stressing the purpose to "proceed in the future with experiment and controlled observation. We would justify all our procedures in the universe of repeated observation and fact."

EDUCATIONAL RESEARCH AND STATISTICS

CRITERIA FOR DETERMINING EQUALITY OF GROUPS[1]

THE most reliable method man has yet invented for securing decisive information in regard to the effect of any cause is controlled experimentation. I am sure all in this group include the "Law of the Single Variable" as one article in their scientific creeds. We are agreed that in any finite situation an effect may, with certainty, be ascribed to a given factor as cause only when the effect of every other factor has been held constant.

The general mode of procedure in educational experimentation under the law of the single variable is to select two groups of subjects, matching them by pairs so that for every individual in one group there is a corresponding individual in the other group exactly like him, as near as may be. The two groups are thus (supposedly) made equal. Certainly they have the same mean and the same standard deviation in all the traits for which they have been matched. If now conditions in one group are held constant (control group) and in the other group all the factors save one are also held constant (experimental group), any difference observed in the second group is considered to be caused by the variation in the single factor.

My thesis to-day is that such procedure in education does not yield reliable information; that, in dealing with all situations involving biologic growth, further precautions are necessary. It should go without saying that I have no quarrel with the law of the single variable; that is absolute. My contention is that matching on the basis of scores in single tests, as ordinarily carried on, is not an adequate method of rendering two groups equal. I shall propose new criteria both for equating groups and for proving that the equated groups are equal.

For instance, Mrs. Garnette Watters,[2] supervisor of English in the elementary schools of Hamtramck, Michigan, has recently devised a series of unusual practice tests for beginning grades in spelling. They include not only practice in spelling, but practice in reading, writing and composition as well, and are unique among practice tests in that they also provide for creative activity on the part of the children and aim to develop in the children pur-

[1] A paper read before the American Educational Research Association, Section A, Techniques of Research, at Washington, on February 20, 1932.

[2] I am very greatly indebted to Mrs. Watters, not only for permission to use the data in this paper, but for assistance in preparing the data for publication.

poses and methods of attack upon spelling problems.

Naturally, the question arises, "How effective are these new devices for teaching spelling?" Accordingly, a control experiment was set up involving 25 teachers and approximately 1,500 children in grades high first, low second, and high second. A special test of thirty-three words, based on those in the practice tests, was devised and used with a test of general power in spelling throughout the semester from September to February, two trials of the test being given early in October, two in November, one in December, and one in January—six tests in all.[3] Records of essential data were kept on cards by individuals, making it possible to combine and recombine the data in a variety of ways.

This report is not at all concerned with the effect of the practice tests, but with the technique of equating groups. The determination of the efficiency of the practice tests will not be complete until the end of another semester for measurement. But the fact that the children were measured repeatedly makes it possible to determine how nearly alike any groups remain.

From September to December all children were taught by ordinary mass instruction methods. In other words, for Tests 1, 2, 3, and 4, there were only such differences between classes and children as ordinarily are found in schools. Differences in score were caused by differences in ability in the teachers or by differences in the natures and nurture of the children. In November the classes were matched on the basis of class medians and divided into three approximately equal groups. The control group continued the mass instruction method; one of the experimental groups began

TABLE I

DIAGRAM OF PROGRESS OF THE EXPERIMENT

Test No.	1, 2	3	4	5	6
Type of work:					
Control	Mass	Mass	Mass	Mass	Mass instruction
Experimental ...	Mass	Mass	Mass	Practice	Practice tests

[3] The actual dates of the various tests were: Test 1, Oct. 6; Test 2, Oct. 7; Test 3, Nov. 2; Test 4, Nov. 30; Test 5, Dec. 21; Test 6, Jan. 27.

using the practice tests.[4] Test 5, therefore, was given after one month of special work and Test 6 after two months.

For the purpose of this paper, the boys and girls in the experimental groups of the high second grade were matched individually with boys and girls of the control group on the basis of score in Test 1. The scores in all subsequent tests were then determined (Table II).

TABLE II

COMPARISONS OF MEDIAN SCORES FOR NUMBER OF WORDS SPELLED CORRECTLY, EXPERIMENTAL AND CONTROL GROUPS, HIGH SECOND GRADE, INDIVIDUALS BEING PAIRED ON ACHIEVEMENT IN FIRST TEST

Groups (Girls and boys)	Tests 1	2	3	4	5	6	Final power test
Control (N = 49)	14.3	14.0	19.5	23.2	26.2	29.8	6.7
Experimental (N = 49)	14.3	15.0	17.9	22.8	24.2	27.7	7.5
Differences ...	0.0	−1.0	+1.6	+.4	+2.0	+2.1	−.8
Median deviations of medians C.	1.1	1.1	.9	.8	.6	.4	.3
Ex.	1.1	1.0	.9	.8	.6	.6	.6

In no tests were there significant differences in the central tendencies of the group. The control group exceeds the experimental in all tests save one, and then in the final power test, the experimental group has slightly higher scores.

These results are typical of the usual control experiment in education. Careful experimental comparisons of large and small classes, of seven- and eight-months school-year, of the use of flash cards in beginning reading, of the effect of intelligence on handwriting, etc., show similar conflicting differences which, however, are seldom statistically significant. The results of most of our educational experimentation to date have been negative.

The writer of this paper believes he knows the explanation. His work the last few years with the growth curve proves conclusively to him, at any rate, that the unsatisfactory charac-

[4] The other experimental group used still another method. No reference to the scores of this group will be made.

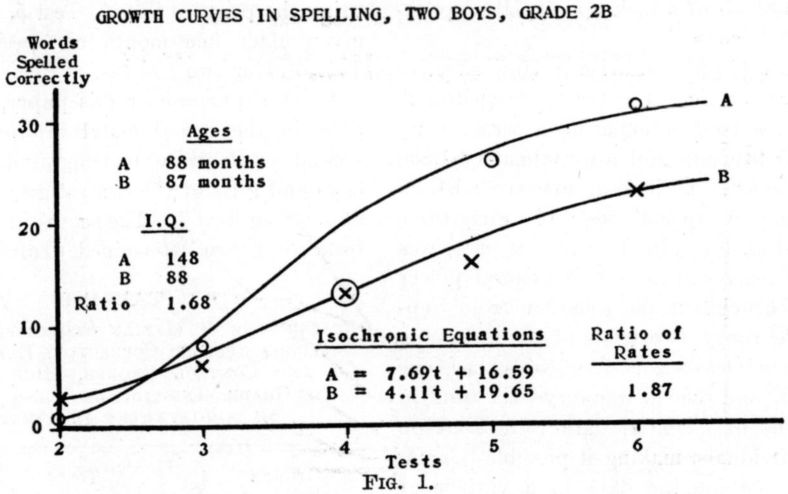

FIG. 1.

ter of the results of our experimental work is caused by our failure to recognize the effect of significant factors which always operate to distort the effects being measured.

For instance, consider the growth curves of two boys in the 2B grade (Fig. 1). Boy A was 88 months old and had an I.Q. of 148. Boy B was 87 months old and had an I.Q. of 88. But Boy A scores in Tests 1 and 2, given October 6 and 7, were but 2 and 1 respectively, while Boy B who, in terms of his I.Q. ought to have made much lower scores, actually spelled 5 and 3 words correctly on the two tests.[5]

Taking the scores[6] in the series of tests as a whole and fitting isochronic growth curves to them, we obtain the two equations:

$$A = 7.68\ t + 16.59$$
$$B = 4.11\ t + 19.65$$

In these equations the first constant in each case is the rate of growth and the second represents the degree of development at the beginning of the growth cycle. The interpretation is that for some cause, which may be either in heredity or in environment, Boy A was further developed at the outset than Boy B. Consequently, he made a score of 3 which, in comparison with Boy B's 1, is a large difference. In any scheme of matching based on scores in a single test, the validity of the match may in similar fashion be undermined by the fact that a single score does not take account of differences in starting points, or in other factors that may be operating. To insure reliability in making equal groups, matching must be based on achievement *and* growth.

For instance, note the scores in Test 4, Fig. 1. Boy A and Boy B made identically the same score—"13"—although at this time the actual development of B was 7 words higher than A's. The explanation is that the low score was caused by a fluctuation in effort.[7] Such variations average out in a group, but if on this test these two boys had been matched as equal in achievement, the match would have been invalidated by the effect of the uncontrolled and unrecognizable "effort" factor.

The best way to appreciate how complex is the process of growth, as it occurs in our classrooms, is to select a group of children as nearly alike as possible and trace their individual progress (Fig. 2). The curves in the figure represent the growth curves of seven boys, in the same grade, of the same age (within eight months). The differences in the curves tell a vivid story of the dispersion caused in sup-

5 The scores made by the boys were as follows:

Test:	1	2	3	4	5	6
Boy A	2	1	8	13	26	31
Boy B	5	3	6	13	16	23

6 See "Maturation Units for the Measurement of Growth," SCHOOL AND SOCIETY, xxx, November 16, 1929.

7 See Courtis, S. A., "Why Children Succeed," pp. 124–139.

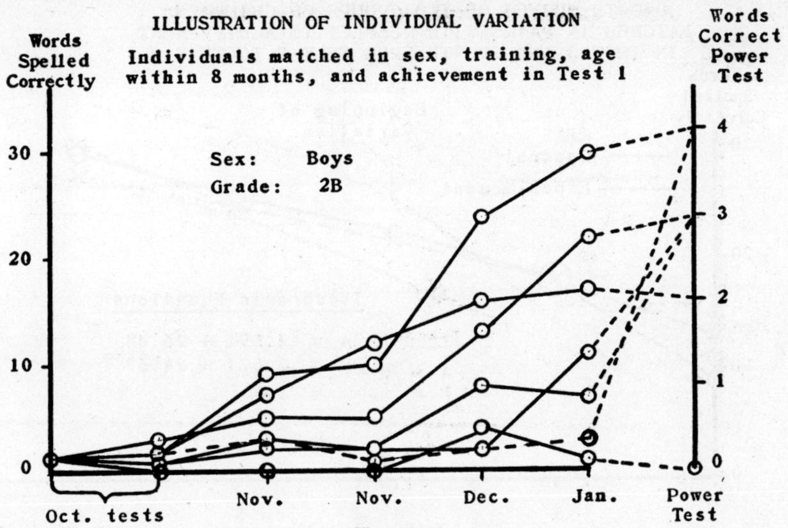

FIG. 2.

posedly equal individuals by starting points and other special factors.

To illustrate the effect of the use of both achievement and growth as criteria, two equal groups were made, matching on achievement in Test 3 and change in score between Test 3 and Test 4, as nearly as might be.

TABLE III

COMPARISONS OF MEDIAN SCORES FOR NUMBER OF WORDS SPELLED CORRECTLY, EXPERIMENTAL AND CONTROL GROUPS, HIGH SECOND GRADE, INDIVIDUALS BEING PAIRED ON ACHIEVEMENT IN TEST 3 AND CHANGE FROM TEST 3 TO TEST 4

Groups (Girls and boys)	Tests 1	2	3	4	5	6	Final power test
Control (N = 34)	9.0	11.0	18.0	22.5	25.5	29.5	5.9
Experimental (N = 34)	13.0	14.0	18.0	22.0	25.0	30.0	6.8
Differences	–4.0	–3.0	0.0	+.5	+.5	–.5	–.9
Median deviations of medians C.	1.1	1.1	1.1	.9	.9	.6	.3
Median deviations of medians Ex.	1.3	1.1	1.1	.8	.7	.6	.6

The two groups could not be matched exactly on change from Test 3 to Test 4. The attempt to match resulted, not in two equal groups, but in groups having different starting points and different rates of growth (Fig. 3).

The isochronic equations for the two curves were determined. The scores in each test computed by these equations were as follows:

	Test 2	Test 3	Test 4	Test 5	Test 6
Control					
Computed results from Equation A	11.0	17.6	22.5	26.4	28.9
Actual results	11.0	18.0	22.5	25.5	29.5
Differences	0.0	–.4	0.0	+.9	–.6
Experimental					
Computed results from Equation B	13.4	18	22.0	25.1	27.5
Actual results	14.0	18	22.0	25.0	30.0
Differences	–.6	0	0	+.1	–2.5

As differences of .5 of a word represent mere chance variation, the fit of the two curves is good except for Test 6. Unfortunately, it is hard to keep the human element out of experimental situations, and one teacher was found offering her children ice-cream cones if they would beat a certain score. Fortunately, she was not teaching in this grade, but, in all grades, there was some tendency for the rate of growth during the experimental period to increase over those of the earlier period. However, if the

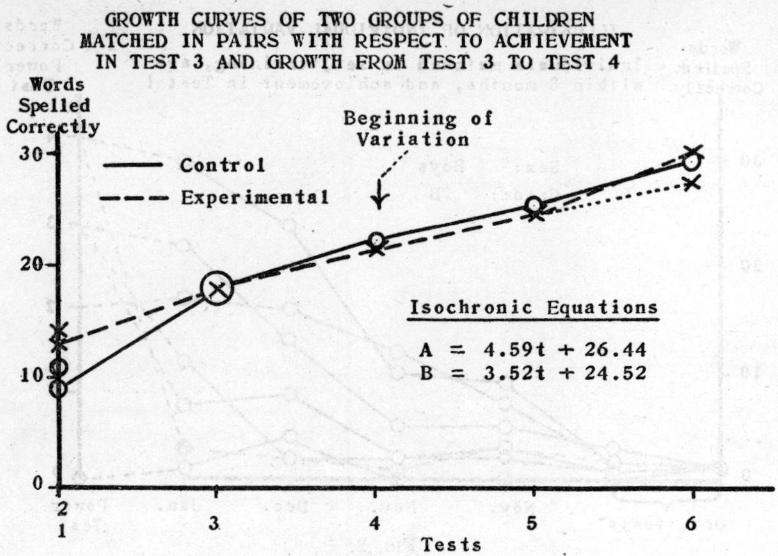

FIG. 3.

isochronic rate of growth during the period 5–6 is compared with the average rate of growth for the earlier periods, the results are: for the experimental group, 9.13 ÷ 3.52 = 2.6, and for the control group 6.13 ÷ 4.59 = 1.3. In other words, on the basis of these results the experimental group grew twice as rapidly as the control group during the last month of the experiment. They also made a higher score in the final power test.

Ideally, one should have sufficient information about each individual taking part in a control experiment to match pairs on the constants of their growth curves. Then, the only factors causing variations would be chance factors. In the absence of such ideal knowledge, however, it seems to me the use of four criteria will materially increase the certainty of results.

A. Give a series of tests separated by intervals sufficient to permit a real growth in all subjects. At least three such tests should be given.
B. Match pairs on achievement in Test 2 and growth from Test 2 to Test 3.
C. Predict the scores that will be made on Test 4 in both groups. Deviations of actual scores from predictions measure the validity of the matching. Compare groups by distributions of individual growths. If predictions and scores do not agree, rematch the two groups, and again predict.
D. As soon as the groups are proved equal by criterion C, introduce the experimental factor into the experimental group. Predict growth of control group.

If now the control group makes the predicted score, the difference between experimental and control scores may safely be ascribed to the experimental factor. The variation of the actual from the predicted scores for the control group becomes a measuring stick for determining how much dependence may be placed on the differences between the experimental and control groups.

Needless to say, I personally believe a fifth criterion essential. All scores should be made comparable by being expressed in maturation units before matching and tabulations. Under such conditions, scores would be truly comparable, intercorrelations would rise, and prophecy could be based upon the results with assurance.

S. A. COURTIS

UNIVERSITY OF MICHIGAN

NEW BOOKS IN EDUCATION

LASHLEY, K. S., Editor. *Studies in the Dynamics of Behavior.* Pp. xiv + 323. Illustrated. University of Chicago Press. $5.00.

Leisure Reading for Grades Seven, Eight and Nine. Pp. 132. Illustrated. Prepared by the Committee on Leisure Reading of the National Council of Teachers of English, Chicago.

THORNDIKE, EDWARD L. *The Fundamentals of Learning.* Pp. xvii + 638. 16 figures. Teachers College, Columbia University. $6.50.